IntelliGloss
The Definitive AI Dictionary

By Susie Hala

First Edition

Published in the United States

ISBN: 979-8-9991963-0-9

Copyright Notice

History of AI

AI Companies Family

Ingredients of AI

Chip Family

Ai Agents Family

AI Factory Family

The top concept for AI Application Family

LLM Family

Bit Family

Qubit Family

Watts Family

The Graphene Family

The Power of AI message

Dedication

To my three granddaughters — Addison, Kayleen, and Raquel —

You are the light of my life and the reason behind my passion to learn, grow, and create.
This dictionary was built with love, patience, and the hope that one day, you too will explore the power of knowledge and the wonders of technology.

May you always remain curious, courageous, and confident in who you are.
And may this book remind you that no dream is ever too big — and no challenge too great — when it's fueled by love, faith, and determination.

With all my heart,
Grandma Susie

A Message from the Author

"When I first began learning about artificial intelligence, I often found the language confusing and inaccessible. As a grandmother, a small business owner, and a lifelong learner, I knew there had to be a better way to help people understand this powerful and rapidly evolving technology. That is why I created IntelliGloss: The Definitive AI Dictionary — to make the world of AI approachable, clear, useful, and simplified, so that anyone can understand it and apply it with confidence in everyday life.

This dictionary is written for students, teachers, professionals, and curious learners from all walks of life. My goal is to break down complex concepts into simple, structured explanations that are easy to follow and practical to use — no advanced degree required. Whether you are exploring AI for the first time or deepening your knowledge, I hope this book will inspire and empower you.

Knowledge is a gift, and learning is a lifelong journey. It is my sincere hope that IntelliGloss will help open new doors for you — and for future generations of learners who will shape the future of AI."

— Susie Hala

TABLE OF CONTENTS

First Edition

Disclaimer

IntelliGloss: The Definitive AI Dictionary ("Dictionary"), authored by **Susie Hala**, is a proprietary educational reference work offering original definitions, explanations, and structured presentations of Artificial Intelligence (AI) terminology and concepts. This Dictionary is intended to serve students, educators, professionals, and AI enthusiasts worldwide.

The content herein represents an original compilation and synthesis of AI knowledge and concepts by Susie Hala, drawing upon public domain materials, fair use principles pursuant to 17 U.S.C. § 107, scholarly research, and the author's own writing and analysis to create a unique, accessible, and educational resource.

Accuracy and Limitation of Liability

This Dictionary is provided on an "as-is" and "as-available" basis for educational and informational purposes only. The author makes no warranties, express or implied, including but not limited to warranties of accuracy, completeness, merchantability, or fitness for a particular purpose.

The author, **Susie Hala**, and any future publisher disclaim all liability for any errors, omissions, or inaccuracies contained in this Dictionary, as well as for any direct, indirect, incidental, consequential, or punitive damages arising from its use.

Readers are solely responsible for verifying information through primary sources, peer-reviewed research, or consultation with qualified professionals — especially in critical domains such as healthcare, finance, or legal practice.

Trademarks

All trademarks, service marks, and registered marks referenced in this Dictionary — including but not limited to ChatGPT, BERT, NVIDIA Jetson, and others — are the property of their respective owners. These trademarks are used strictly for nominative and educational purposes to identify AI technologies and concepts. Their inclusion does not imply any endorsement, sponsorship, or affiliation with the trademark holders.

Source Attribution

This Dictionary synthesizes knowledge from general AI literature, public domain resources, open-access materials, and the author's original interpretations of complex technical concepts. Where appropriate, external sources are cited to acknowledge original works and support further learning. Users are encouraged to consult those references for deeper understanding.

Usage Advisory

This Dictionary is not a substitute for professional advice, technical certification, or licensed guidance in AI or related disciplines. Individuals applying AI concepts in commercial or high-risk contexts should consult qualified experts. The author and publisher disclaim liability for any adverse outcomes resulting from the use or misuse of the content.

Governing Law

This Disclaimer and all use of this Dictionary shall be governed by the laws of the United States and the State of California. Any disputes arising shall be resolved exclusively in the state or federal courts located in Los Angeles County, California.

Summary

IntelliGloss is an original, copyrighted educational work authored by **Susie Hala**. It is presented without warranties and includes disclaimers on accuracy and reliance. Referenced trademarks are

Acknowledgments

The creation of this Dictionary would not have been possible without the broad contributions of researchers, educators, and pioneers in the field of Artificial Intelligence.

The author extends deep gratitude to the original creators of the terms and concepts referenced throughout this work, and to the academic institutions, publishers, and open-access platforms that make educational content freely available — including but not limited to **arXiv**, **IEEE Xplore**, and leading AI journals.

Notable foundational works consulted:

Artificial Intelligence: A Modern Approach — Stuart Russell & Peter Norvig

Deep Learning — Ian Goodfellow, Yoshua Bengio & Aaron Courville

Hands-On Machine Learning with Scikit-Learn, Keras, and TensorFlow — Aurélien Géron

The author also honors the global AI community — students, teachers, developers, and lifelong learners — whose curiosity and dedication continue to shape the future of this vital field.

༺❀༻ Why IntelliGloss Matters ༺❀༻

Artificial intelligence is transforming every part of our lives — from education and healthcare to business, communication, and beyond. Yet for many people, AI remains a confusing and inaccessible field, filled with technical jargon and ever-evolving terms.

That is why I created **IntelliGloss: The Definitive AI Dictionary** — to open the world of AI to learners from all backgrounds and provide a resource that is both comprehensive and approachable.

What makes *IntelliGloss* unique is its structure and scope. This dictionary includes **over 2,000 carefully written AI terms**, explained in plain language for students, teachers, professionals, and everyday readers.

In addition to standard definitions, IntelliGloss offers original educational sections not found in other AI glossaries:

The History of AI

The Ingredients of AI

The Bit, Qubit, Chip, Watts, and LLM Families

These special sections offer a broader view of the AI ecosystem, helping readers not only understand terms — but also how technologies connect and impact the real world.

My hope is that this dictionary serves classrooms, libraries, businesses, and homes alike. Whether you are a student preparing for the future, a teacher introducing AI to your class, a professional exploring new tools, or simply someone curious — **IntelliGloss** was created for you.

— Susie Hala

Knowledge is power when you apply it. I hope this dictionary will be a trusted companion on your AI learning journey — and that it will help inspire the next generation of thinkers and creators in this exciting and ever-changing field.

༺❀༻ History of AI ༺❀༻

The history of artificial intelligence (AI) is the fascinating story of how humans have tried to teach machines to think—or at least behave smartly enough to seem like they do. It is a journey that spans from ancient myths of clever automatons to today's advanced AI systems that chat, drive, create art, and help solve real-world problems, all while challenging our understanding of what "intelligence" truly means.

Early Foundations

Long before computers existed, people imagined artificial beings with human-like abilities. In ancient Greek myths, figures like Hephaestus built self-moving statues, and Jewish legends spoke of the Golem. These early stories reflected the dream of creating mechanical minds.

In the 1600s, thinkers such as René Descartes and Gottfried Wilhelm Leibniz pondered whether reasoning could be reduced to mathematical logic. In the 1800s, George Boole developed Boolean logic — a system that allowed reasoning through yes/no, true/false values — laying essential groundwork for the digital age.

Birth of AI as a Field (1950s–1960s)

AI formally emerged as a field in the mid-20th century. In 1950, Alan Turing posed the question, "Can machines think?" and proposed the Turing Test — a way to evaluate whether a machine's behavior could convincingly mimic human intelligence.

In 1956, the famous Dartmouth Conference, led by John McCarthy, Marvin Minsky, Nathaniel Rochester, and Claude Shannon, marked the official birth of AI as a research field. Early AI programs demonstrated that machines could play games, solve mathematical problems, and prove logical theorems.

Growth and Challenges (1970s–1980s)

The 1970s and 1980s saw a mix of progress and disappointment. AI systems known as expert systems were developed to mimic the decision-making of professionals in fields such as medicine and engineering. These rule-based systems achieved early success but soon faced limitations: real-world problems proved too complex for rigid rule sets, and computers lacked the power to process vast amounts of data.

Funding and enthusiasm waned during periods known as AI winters, when progress slowed and expectations were tempered.

Revival and Machine Learning (1990s–2000s)

In the 1990s, AI experienced a revival fueled by increased computing power and the rise of machine learning — a new approach where systems learned patterns from data instead of relying solely on hand-coded rules. AI began to power voice recognition, handwriting recognition, and recommendation systems. This shift allowed AI to move beyond rigid programming and adapt to new tasks through data-driven learning.

Deep Learning and Modern AI (2010s–Present)

The 2010s ushered in a revolution with deep learning — advanced neural networks capable of learning complex patterns from massive datasets. Fueled by fast hardware (GPUs), large datasets, and new training techniques, deep learning enabled dramatic breakthroughs: AI systems could now surpass human experts in tasks like image recognition, natural language processing, and even strategic gameplay (such as AlphaGo defeating top human players at Go).

Today's AI powers virtual assistants, autonomous vehicles, creative tools, and more — reshaping industries and everyday life.

Challenges and the Future of AI

Despite remarkable progress, AI faces important challenges. Bias in training data can lead to unfair outcomes. The "black box" nature of some AI systems makes it hard to explain their decisions. Ethical concerns arise in areas like facial recognition, surveillance, and automated decision-making.

The next phase of AI development will focus on creating more transparent, fair, and trustworthy systems — and perhaps on building more generalized intelligence that can reason flexibly across domains.

Summary

The history of AI is a dynamic story of bold ideas, setbacks, and breakthroughs. From ancient myths to modern machine learning, AI has evolved from rigid logic systems to flexible, data-driven technologies that now touch nearly every aspect of life. The journey continues, with each new innovation bringing both exciting opportunities and important questions about the role of intelligent machines in society.

The Evolution of Artificial Intelligence: From AI 1.0 to AI 3.0

Artificial Intelligence (AI) has undergone a remarkable transformation since its inception, often described through three major developmental stages: AI 1.0, AI 2.0, and AI 3.0. Each stage represents not only technological advancements but also shifts in how AI interacts with and impacts human life.

AI 1.0: The Age of Rule-Based Systems (1950s–1980s)
This first wave of AI focused on rule-based systems. Pioneers like Alan Turing and John McCarthy laid the theoretical groundwork. AI in this phase aimed to program computers to follow explicit rules to solve problems. Expert systems mimicked human decision-making in narrow fields such as medicine or finance. These systems were powerful within strict limits but were rigid and struggled outside their programmed scope.

Key traits of AI 1.0 include the use of symbolic knowledge, rule-based logic, and programming languages like LISP and Prolog. Notable milestones included the Dartmouth Conference and early programs like Logic Theorist. While AI 1.0 introduced foundational techniques, it lacked the ability to learn from experience.

AI 2.0: The Rise of Machine Learning (1990s–2010s)
AI 2.0 brought a dramatic shift: systems learned from data instead of being hand-coded. Fueled by powerful computers and vast datasets, machine learning emerged as the new foundation. Neural networks and deep learning models could now analyze speech, images, and text with unprecedented accuracy.

Milestones included AlphaGo's victory over a Go master and the launch of large-scale language models like GPT. AI 2.0 enabled chatbots, personalized medicine, recommendation engines, and smart assistants — but also raised new concerns about data bias, interpretability, and privacy.

AI 3.0: The Era of Autonomous AI and Beyond (2010s–Present)
AI 3.0 focuses on autonomy, human collaboration, and ethical alignment. These systems not only learn from data — they understand, reason, and adapt in real time. They are built to work alongside humans, make independent decisions, and even express creativity or emotional awareness.

Technologies include explainable AI (XAI), emotional intelligence models, quantum computing, and ethical governance systems. AI 3.0 aspires toward Artificial General Intelligence (AGI) — machines that can perform any intellectual task a human can.

Applications span education, law, global problem-solving, and AI governance. While AI 3.0 offers incredible opportunities, it also presents new risks: job displacement, ethical failures, and loss of control over autonomous systems.

Summary
From symbolic reasoning in AI 1.0, to adaptive learning in AI 2.0, to human-centered intelligence in AI 3.0 — the field of AI has evolved rapidly. Each generation expands not only what AI can do, but also what society must consider as we integrate it into every corner of life.

AI COMPANIES FAMILY

Key Industry Leaders Driving the Development of Artificial Intelligence

The AI COMPANIES FAMILY includes the most influential organizations leading AI innovation worldwide. Each company contributes unique technologies, models, platforms, or research that help shape the future of artificial intelligence across industries and society.

OPENAI
Creator of ChatGPT and the GPT model family. Focused on developing artificial general intelligence (AGI) that is safe and aligned with human values.
Website: https://www.openai.com

GOOGLE DEEPMIND
Pioneering AI research division of Google. Known for AlphaGo, AlphaFold, and the Gemini model series.
Website: https://www.deepmind.com

META AI (FAIR)
Meta's AI research division. Specializes in open-source models like the LLaMA series and AI for scientific discovery.
Website: https://ai.meta.com

ANTHROPIC
AI research company focused on safety and alignment. Developer of the Claude family of AI models.
Website: https://www.anthropic.com

MISTRAL AI
Based in France, Mistral creates powerful open-weight large language models for enterprise and research.
Website: https://www.mistral.ai

XAI
Founded by Elon Musk. Builds Grok, a conversational AI with emphasis on free speech and real-time integration with X (Twitter).
Website: https://www.x.ai

NVIDIA
Leader in AI computing hardware. Provides GPUs and chips essential for training and running large AI models.
Website: https://www.nvidia.com

TESLA
Develops autonomous vehicle technology and the Dojo supercomputer to support large-scale AI training.
Website: https://www.tesla.com

MICROSOFT
Major investor in OpenAI. Integrates advanced AI into Azure, Microsoft 365, and enterprise tools.
Website: https://www.microsoft.com

AMAZON
Offers AI services through Alexa and e-commerce applications. Supports AI innovation across retail and devices.
Website: https://www.amazon.com

IBM
A pioneer in artificial intelligence with Watson. Focuses on trusted AI for enterprise, healthcare, and hybrid cloud.
Website: https://www.ibm.com

AWS (Amazon Web Services)
Provides global cloud infrastructure and AI tools like Amazon Bedrock, SageMaker, and more.
Website: https://aws.amazon.com

Summary
The AI COMPANIES FAMILY represents the core of global AI innovation. These organizations are shaping the next generation of technology through research, hardware, software, and responsible development. Understanding these key players gives readers a full view of the ecosystem powering AI today.

The Ingredients of AI

Understanding What It Takes to Build Artificial Intelligence from Start to Finish

Before diving into the definitions, let's take a step back and look at the big picture. What exactly goes into making an AI system work? Just like baking a cake needs flour, sugar, eggs, and a recipe, creating AI requires essential ingredients too. Whether you're building a simple chatbot or an advanced machine learning system, here are the key components that make artificial intelligence possible—from A to Z.

Data
AI starts with data. This is the information the system learns from—text, images, numbers, audio, video, or even sensor readings. Without data, AI has nothing to learn from.

Labels
For supervised learning, labeled data is needed. These labels help AI understand what it's looking at—like identifying a photo of a cat or recognizing a happy voice.

Algorithms
These are the math-based instructions that tell AI how to learn patterns in the data. Algorithms help AI think, reason, and make predictions.

Model Architecture
This is the blueprint of how the AI system is built. It could be a neural network, decision tree, or transformer model, depending on what kind of task it's designed to perform.

Training
Training is the learning process. The AI studies the data, adjusts its internal settings, and learns to make better predictions over time.

Optimization
Once trained, the AI is fine-tuned to improve accuracy and speed. This might include adjusting model settings or improving how it learns.

Testing and Validation
To make sure AI performs well, it must be tested on new data it hasn't seen before. This checks how well it generalizes to real-world problems.

Feedback Loop
AI systems often improve over time. By receiving feedback—either from users or new data—they continue to learn and get smarter.

Infrastructure
Behind the scenes, AI needs powerful computing infrastructure. This includes cloud servers, storage systems, networking, and memory that help process large amounts of data and run models efficiently.

AI Chips
Modern AI depends on specialized chips to perform the massive calculations required for training and running AI models. These include GPUs (Graphics Processing Units), TPUs (Tensor Processing Units), NPUs (Neural Processing Units), and other AI accelerators. AI chips are the engines that make today's language models, computer vision systems, and robotics possible.

Deployment
Once everything is tested, the AI model is launched into the real world—inside an app, on a website, or in a robot.

Interfaces
This is how users interact with the AI—through buttons, voice commands, mobile apps, or APIs.

Ethics and Safety
AI should be fair, respectful of privacy, and free from harmful bias. Responsible AI considers how its decisions impact people and society.

Maintenance and Monitoring
AI systems must be carefully monitored after they're deployed. Engineers make updates, fix errors, and ensure the AI continues to perform well.

Explainability
Good AI should be able to explain its decisions in a way humans can understand. This is important for building trust and accountability.

Security
AI must be protected from hacking, manipulation, and misuse. Strong security protects both the AI system and its users.

Human-in-the-Loop
Sometimes, humans are included in the decision-making process to approve or guide the AI's output. This helps keep systems safe and balanced.

Governance and Regulation
To ensure AI is used responsibly, companies and governments are developing rules and policies to guide how AI is built and deployed.

Summary
AI is not just one thing—it's a system made of many connected parts. From gathering data to training models, from computing power to responsible deployment, every ingredient plays a role. When all these pieces come together, AI becomes not just smart—but also safe, useful, and trustworthy. This section is here to help you see the full recipe. As you explore the definitions ahead, you'll begin to understand how each term fits into this larger picture.

❀ AI FACTORY FAMILY ❀

Industrial-Scale Production of Artificial Intelligence

The AI Factory Family represents the next stage in the global development of artificial intelligence — a system of industrial-scale digital platforms that create, train, optimize, and deploy AI models much like a factory produces physical products.

Where traditional AI development was project-based and manual, AI Factories now enable automated, scalable pipelines to produce AI models rapidly and efficiently for diverse applications.

As the world transitions to AI-native networks and real-time intelligent services, the AI Factory Family provides the essential infrastructure for delivering these capabilities — from cloud platforms to 5G/6G networks, edge devices, autonomous vehicles, and beyond.

Led by companies such as NVIDIA and global telecom and cloud providers, the AI Factory Family is becoming a core component of the emerging AI-powered global infrastructure.

The concepts below outline the major stages and components of the AI Factory Family:

❀ Top Concepts in the AI Factory Family ❀

1 **Data Ingestion and Curation** — Collecting, cleaning, and preparing massive data sets to feed the AI Factory.
2 **AI Training Infrastructure** — Using high-performance computing (HPC) clusters, typically GPU-based, to train sophisticated AI models.
3 **Model Management Pipelines** — Automating the process of versioning, testing, optimizing, and deploying AI models.
4 **Deployment Platforms** — Delivering trained AI models to cloud systems, edge devices, and 5G/6G networks for real-time operation.
5 **Continuous Feedback Loops** — Capturing user feedback and new data to continuously retrain and improve AI models over time.
6 **Governance and Monitoring** — Ensuring AI models are explainable, fair, secure, and compliant with regulations.
7 **Energy and Sustainability Management** — Optimizing the energy efficiency and environmental footprint of large-scale AI training operations.
8 **Integration with AI-native Networks** — Supplying intelligent models to AI-native 5G/6G networks to enable real-time, intelligent services.
9 **Industry-Specific AI Factories** — Building customized AI Factories for specific verticals such as telecom, automotive, healthcare, and financial services.
10 **AI Factory as a Service (FaaS)** — Offering AI Factory capabilities through the cloud, allowing smaller organizations to leverage industrial-scale AI production without owning the infrastructure.

❀ AI Applications Family ❀

Transforming Everyday Experiences with Intelligent Technologies
The AI Applications Family represents the wide spectrum of software systems, tools, and platforms that integrate artificial intelligence to deliver enhanced functionality, automation, and intelligent decision-making across industries. From chatbots and translation tools to autonomous vehicles and personalized healthcare, AI applications have become deeply embedded in modern life — reshaping how individuals, businesses, and societies interact with

technology.
As AI models grow more sophisticated and AI-native networks expand, the AI Applications Family continues to evolve, offering increasingly powerful and personalized experiences.
The concepts below outline the major categories and components of the AI Applications Family:

Top Concepts in the AI Applications Family

1 **Chatbots and Virtual Assistants** — Conversational AI agents that assist users through text or voice interfaces.
2 **Automated Translation** — Real-time language translation powered by AI algorithms.
3 **Sentiment Analysis** — Detecting emotions and opinions in text and speech.
4 **Speech Recognition and Transcription** — Converting spoken language into text using AI models.
5 **Facial Recognition Systems** — Identifying individuals based on facial features.
6 **Object Detection and Tracking** — Locating and tracking objects in images and videos.
7 **Medical Imaging Analysis** — Enhancing diagnostics through AI-based image interpretation.
8 **Text Generation** — Creating human-like text using generative AI models.
9 **Image Generation** — Producing original images from text prompts or data.
10 **Video Generation** — Creating video content through AI-driven synthesis.
11 **Code Generation** — Automating the writing of software code using AI.
12 **Music Generation** — Composing music with AI-based tools.
13 **Product Recommendation Engines** — Suggesting products or content based on user behavior and preferences.
14 **Self-driving Vehicles** — Enabling autonomous operation of cars, drones, and robots through AI.
15 **Diagnostic Assistants** — Supporting healthcare professionals with AI-driven diagnostic insights.
16 **AI-powered Fraud Detection** — Identifying fraudulent activity using AI models.
17 **Algorithmic Trading Systems** — Conducting automated trading in financial markets with AI.
18 **Intelligent Tutoring Systems** — Personalizing education and learning experiences through AI.
19 **AI-based Process Automation** — Streamlining business workflows with AI-driven automation.
20 **Cybersecurity Threat Detection** — Identifying and responding to cyber threats using AI.

❀Large Language Model (LLM) Family❀

Top 10 LLMs as of 2025

1 **GPT-4o** — OpenAI (2024)
2 **Claude 3.5 Sonnet** — Anthropic (2025)
3 **Gemini 1.5 Ultra** — Google DeepMind (2025)
4 **Meta Llama 3 400B** — Meta AI (2025)
5 **Command R+** — Cohere (2025)
6 **Mistral Large** — Mistral AI (2025)
7 **Yi-34B** — 01.AI (2024)
8 **Xwin-LM 70B** — community open model (2024)
9 **Grok-1.5V** — xAI (Elon Musk / Twitter) (2025)
10 **InternLM2 104B** — Shanghai AI Lab (2025)

❀Bit Family❀

The Foundation of Digital Information
The Bit Family represents the fundamental hierarchy of data units used in all digital computing and information systems. Starting from the smallest possible unit — the bit — this family scales upward through larger units such as bytes, kilobytes, megabytes, gigabytes, and beyond, defining how data is stored, processed, and transmitted in the digital world.
A deep understanding of the Bit Family is essential for grasping data capacity, file sizes, network speeds, and the architecture of modern artificial intelligence and computing systems.
The concepts below outline the major components of the Bit Family:

Top Concepts in the Bit Family

1 **Bit (b)** — The basic unit of digital information, representing a binary value of 0 or 1.
2 **Nibble** — Consists of 4 bits; represents a half byte, useful for encoding small data such as a hexadecimal digit.
3 **Byte (B)** — Contains 8 bits; the standard unit for encoding a single text character or small piece of data.
4 **Kilobit (Kb)** — 1,000 bits; commonly used to measure data transfer rates (e.g., Kbps).
5 **Kilobyte (KB)** — 1,024 bytes (8,192 bits); used to measure small file sizes such as documents.
6 **Megabit (Mb)** — 1 million bits; frequently used in describing internet speeds (Mbps).
7 **Megabyte (MB)** — 1,024 kilobytes; used for larger files such as images, songs, and documents.
8 **Gigabit (Gb)** — 1 billion bits; measures high-speed data transmission, such as network bandwidth.
9 **Gigabyte (GB)** — 1,024 megabytes; commonly used to describe storage capacity of hard drives and memory cards.
10 **Terabit (Tb)** — 1 trillion bits; used in large-scale networking and cloud data transfer.
11 **Terabyte (TB)** — 1,024 gigabytes; used for large storage capacities in modern computing.
12 **Petabit (Pb)** — 1 quadrillion bits; occasionally used in massive data center transfer rates.
13 **Petabyte (PB)** — 1,024 terabytes; measures large-scale data storage (enterprise data centers).
14 **Exabit (Eb)** — 1 quintillion bits; used for theoretical or future-scale global data transmission.
15 **Exabyte (EB)** — 1,024 petabytes; used to measure large-scale storage by cloud providers and governments.
16 **Zettabit (Zb)** — 1 sextillion bits; largely theoretical, used in extreme-scale network discussions.
17 **Zettabyte (ZB)** — 1,024 exabytes; measures total global data storage on the internet.
18 **Yottabit (Yb)** — 1 septillion bits; theoretical future global network capacities.
19 **Yottabyte (YB)** — 1,024 zettabytes; projected to measure the total global data storage of the future.

Bit Family (Sizes)

1 **1 Byte** — Equals 8 bits.
2 **1 Kilobyte (KB)** — Equals 1,024 bytes.
3 **1 Megabyte (MB)** — Equals 1,024 kilobytes.
4 **1 Gigabyte (GB)** — Equals 1,024 megabytes.
5 **1 Terabyte (TB)** — Equals 1,024 gigabytes.
6 **1 Petabyte (PB)** — Equals 1,024 terabytes.
7 **1 Exabyte (EB)** — Equals 1,024 petabytes.
8 **1 Zettabyte (ZB)** — Equals 1,024 exabytes.
9 **1 Yottabyte (YB)** — Equals 1,024 zettabytes.

Bit Family: Storage Visualization

1 **1 Byte** — Too small for even one picture or video frame.

2 **1 Kilobyte (KB)** — Too small to store a full image.

3 **1 Megabyte (MB)** — Stores ~0.33 of a full picture; too small for video.

4 **1 Gigabyte (GB)** — Stores ~333 pictures or ~0.66 Full HD videos (20 mins each).

5 **1 Terabyte (TB)** — Stores ~341,333 pictures or ~682 Full HD videos (20 mins each).

6 **1 Petabyte (PB)** — Stores ~349 million pictures or ~698,000 Full HD videos (20 mins each).

7 **1 Exabyte (EB)** — Stores ~357 billion pictures or ~715 million Full HD videos (20 mins each).

8 **1 Zettabyte (ZB)** — Stores ~366 trillion pictures or ~732 billion Full HD videos (20 mins each).

9 **1 Yottabyte (YB)** — Stores ~375 quadrillion pictures or ~750 trillion Full HD videos (20 mins each).

Qubit Family

Core Concepts in Quantum Information and Quantum AI
The Qubit Family represents the essential concepts, units, and operations that define how quantum information is stored, manipulated, and measured in quantum computing and quantum AI systems.
Unlike classical bits that can only be 0 or 1, qubits can exist in superpositions of both states and exhibit entanglement — enabling revolutionary new forms of computation and communication.
As quantum hardware advances, understanding the Qubit Family is crucial for exploring the future of AI, cryptography, and scientific discovery.
The concepts below outline the major components of the Qubit Family:

Top Concepts in the Qubit Family

1 **Qubit (Quantum Bit)** — The basic unit of quantum information; can exist in a superposition of states 0 and 1.

2 **Quantum Superposition** — A principle that allows qubits to exist in multiple states simultaneously, greatly enhancing computational power.

3 **Quantum Entanglement** — A phenomenon where qubits become linked, such that the state of one qubit instantly influences another, even across large distances.

4 **Quantum Register** — A collection of multiple qubits used together to store and manipulate quantum information.

5 **Quantum Gate** — An operation applied to qubits to change their quantum state, enabling complex quantum computations.

6 **Quantum Circuit** — A sequence of quantum gates applied to a set of qubits to execute a quantum algorithm.

7 **Quantum Error Correction (QEC)** — Techniques that protect quantum information from errors caused by noise and decoherence.

8 **Logical Qubit** — A stable qubit constructed from multiple physical qubits using error correction, enabling fault-tolerant quantum computing.

9 **Quantum Volume** — A benchmark that measures the overall performance of a quantum computer, factoring in qubit count, error rates, and circuit depth.

10 **Quantum Bit Error Rate (QBER)** — The rate at which errors occur in the transmission or manipulation of quantum bits, used to assess system reliability.

11 **Quantum State Representation** — Qubits are mathematically represented as combinations of basis states |0⟩ and |1⟩ , using complex numbers that encode probabilities.

12 **Bloch Sphere** — A visual representation of a single qubit's state as a point on a sphere, helping to illustrate superposition and phase.

13 **Decoherence Time (T2 Time)** — The time a qubit can maintain its quantum state before losing coherence; longer T2 times enable more reliable quantum computation.

14 **Quantum Phase** — A property of qubits represented by a phase angle, influencing interference patterns and computation outcomes.

15 **Multi-Qubit Systems** — Systems where multiple qubits are used together; the number of possible system states scales exponentially (2^n for n qubits).

16 **Entangled Multi-Qubit States** — Correlated quantum states involving two or more qubits; foundational for quantum communication and distributed quantum computing.

17 **Quantum Gate Operations** — Matrix-based operations that transform qubit states, forming the core of quantum algorithms.

18 **Quantum Measurement** — The process of observing a qubit's state, which collapses it into a definite value (0 or 1) with probabilities determined by the qubit's quantum state.

❀ Chip Family ❀

The Chip Family is the core of how artificial intelligence becomes real. These powerful processors are the physical engines that train, run, and accelerate AI systems—from massive language models in data centers to real-time inference in autonomous machines and smart devices. Each chip in this family plays a unique role in enabling AI to learn, reason, see, speak, and respond with precision and speed.

This section provides a quick-reference guide to the most influential AI chips across today's global technology landscape. It includes chips designed for large-scale AI training, edge computing, generative models, robotics, cloud deployment, and autonomous vehicle intelligence. Each entry highlights the chip's purpose, developer, architecture, and key features.

The chips listed here are developed by leading companies in AI hardware innovation, including NVIDIA, Google, Apple, Intel, Meta, Amazon (AWS), Tesla, and others. The list is organized alphabetically by chip name, allowing readers to quickly locate and cross-reference each chip throughout the AI Dictionary. For every chip listed in this section, a corresponding full entry with detailed explanations is included in the main body of the dictionary for deeper understanding.

Whether you are a student, teacher, innovator, or enthusiast, the Chip Family serves as a foundational overview of the hardware layer that powers today's most advanced AI systems.

1 NVIDIA Chips

Key Chips: A100, H100, H200, GH200, V100, T4, P100, K80, M60, L40, Jetson Nano, Xavier NX, AGX Orin, Thor

Purpose: Training and inference of large language models, deep learning, generative AI, and edge AI.

Developer: NVIDIA Corporation.

Applications: Data centers, cloud AI, robotics, autonomous vehicles, and edge devices.

2 AMD AI Chips

Key Chips: Instinct MI200, MI300

Purpose: AI training and inference acceleration; alternative to NVIDIA GPUs in data centers.

Developer: AMD (Advanced Micro Devices).

Applications: High-performance computing, large-scale AI training, and cloud services.

3 Google AI Chips

Key Chips: TPU v2, TPU v3, TPU v4

Purpose: Specialized tensor processing units for large-scale deep learning models.

Developer: Google.

Applications: Google Cloud AI services, internal AI research, large language model training.

4 Intel AI Accelerators

Key Chips: Habana Gaudi, Movidius

Purpose: AI training (Habana Gaudi) and edge AI inference (Movidius).

Developer: Intel Corporation.

Applications: Data center AI workloads, low-power AI for mobile and IoT devices.

5 Apple AI Chips

Key Chips: Neural Engine in M1, M2 chips

Purpose: On-device AI acceleration for consumer devices.

Developer: Apple Inc.

Applications: iPhones, iPads, MacBooks, providing AI features such as image processing, voice recognition, and personal assistants.

6 Meta AI Chips

Key Chip: MTIA (Meta Training and Inference Accelerator)

Purpose: Custom AI chip designed for optimizing inference of large language models and recommendation systems.

Developer: Meta (Facebook's parent company).

Applications: Social media recommendation engines, LLM inference, and Meta's AI research initiatives.

7 Amazon AWS Chips

Key Chips: Inferentia, Trainium

Purpose: AI inference (Inferentia) and AI training (Trainium) acceleration in the cloud.

Developer: Amazon Web Services (AWS).

Applications: AI services on AWS cloud, enabling cost-efficient training and inference at scale.

8 Tesla AI Chips

Key Chip: Dojo chip

Purpose: Custom-built AI chip for training Tesla's autonomous driving models at extreme scale.

Developer: Tesla, Inc.

Applications: Self-driving car AI training, Tesla's internal AI supercomputer (Dojo).

Conclusion

The Chip Family plays an essential role in making modern AI possible. From powering massive data center training workloads to enabling smart features on personal devices, AI chips are the computational backbone of the AI revolution. This quick-reference section helps readers navigate the evolving landscape of AI hardware, with full details on each chip provided in the main body of the dictionary.

Token Family

Understanding the Language Building Blocks of Artificial Intelligence

Definition

The Token Family represents the smallest units of language that AI systems use to read, understand, and generate human-like text. A token may be a whole word, part of a word, a number, or a punctuation mark. Unlike people, who read in full sentences or ideas, AI models break everything into tokens — the building blocks of machine understanding. This system allows AI to process language step by step, one unit at a time.

Tokens are counted and managed during every AI conversation, prompt, or task. Each message you write and every response the AI gives consumes tokens, which are measured to track memory, cost, and processing limits.

Token Sizes and Everyday Equivalents

Token Count	What It Looks Like	Approximate Words
4 tokens	"I love cats!"	3 - 4 words

Token Count	What It Looks Like	Approximate Words
8 tokens	One sentence with punctuation	6 – 7 words
16 tokens	One detailed sentence	12 – 14 words
50 tokens	One paragraph	35 – 40 words
100 tokens	Half a page of explanation	75 – 80 words
200 tokens	A full page of text	150 – 160 words
500 tokens	A short essay or story	375 – 400 words
1,000 tokens	A longer article or dictionary entry	750 – 800 words
5,000 tokens	A multi-page chapter	3,750 – 4,000 words
10,000 tokens	A small book or training guide	7,500 – 8,000 words
100,000 tokens	A full-length book, AI’s memory max	~75,000 – 80,000 words

Where Tokens Appear in AI

Tokens are everywhere. They are used in:

AI chat interactions (each word and symbol you type)

Text generation, translation, and summarization

Search engines, chatbots, and coding assistants

Pricing and usage tracking for AI tools and APIs

Setting memory limits in large language models (like GPT-4)

Tokens are what AI “sees” — not words, not sentences, but tokens. Understanding tokens helps users write better prompts, avoid cost surprises, and use AI more efficiently.

Disadvantages: The Counterintuitive Limit
One major weakness of the Token Family is a hidden challenge known as the **Counterintuitive Limit**. Many users believe that adding more context, longer prompts, or extra details will improve AI performance. But in truth, giving **too many tokens** can actually **confuse the model**, slow down response time, and reduce the quality of answers.

This is called the **counterintuitive limit** — when more input makes things worse, not better. AI systems perform best with clear, focused prompts. Smart token use leads to better results than overloading the model with extra information.

Summary
The Token Family is how AI speaks, thinks, and understands language — one piece at a time. Just like bits are the foundation of digital data, tokens are the foundation of AI conversation and computation. By learning how tokens work, users can craft better prompts, manage system limits, and communicate with AI more effectively. However, users must remember the counterintuitive truth: **more tokens does not always mean better answers.** In AI, clarity wins over quantity.

Watts Family

Measuring the Power Behind AI Systems

The **Watts Family** represents the hierarchy of power units used to measure how fast energy flows through AI systems — from the tiniest chips to massive data centers and future planetary networks.

Starting with the basic **watt**, each unit in this family scales by factors of a thousand, enabling engineers and designers to manage energy needs across a vast range of AI applications.

The concepts below outline the major components of the **Watts Family**:

Top Concepts in the Watts Family

1 **Watt (W)** — The basic unit of power in AI systems; one joule per second. Used to measure how much energy AI hardware consumes to perform tasks.

2 **Milliwatts (mW)** — One thousandth of a watt. Commonly used in AI-powered sensors, wearables, and low-power IoT devices.

3 **Microwatts (µW)** — One millionth of a watt. Powers ultra-low-energy AI applications such as implants, microchips, and remote edge devices.

4 **Nanowatts (nW)** — One billionth of a watt. Enables the smallest AI-powered technologies, such as nano-sensors and bio-AI systems.

5 **Kilowatts (kW)** — One thousand watts. Powers home AI hubs, electric vehicles, smart home networks, and small AI clusters.

6 **Megawatts (MW)** — One million watts. Drives large-scale AI data centers, deep learning labs, and industrial AI robotics.

7 **Gigawatts (GW)** — One billion watts. Powers national or global AI infrastructures, smart city systems, and scientific AI simulations.

8 **Terawatts (TW)** — One trillion watts. Supports future planetary-scale AI applications such as global climate modeling and sustainable energy grids.

9 **Petawatts (PW)** — One quadrillion watts. Currently theoretical for AI; envisioned for advanced space exploration and high-energy physics AI simulations.

Exawatts (EW) — One quintillion watts. A future concept for cosmic-scale AI systems; powering Dyson spheres or universal simulations remains a theoretical possibility.

Summary:

The **Watts Family** provides AI developers and engineers with a universal scale for understanding and managing power consumption — from tiny embedded AI to global supercomputing networks. As AI expands into new frontiers, mastering this power hierarchy will be critical for balancing performance, efficiency, and sustainability.

❀ 100,000 Qubit Supercomputer ❀

Revolutionizing Computational Power Through Quantum Mechanics

The 100,000 Qubit Supercomputer represents a transformative leap in quantum computing, pushing the boundaries of what artificial intelligence and computational systems can achieve. By harnessing 100,000 qubits operating in superposition and entanglement, this quantum supercomputer promises to solve problems that are impossible for classical systems — driving breakthroughs in AI, cryptography, healthcare, materials science, and beyond.

The concepts below outline the major components and capabilities of the 100,000 Qubit Supercomputer:

Top Concepts in the 100,000 Qubit Supercomputer

1 **Quantum Qubits at Scale** — Operates with 100,000 qubits, enabling exponentially faster computations through superposition and entanglement.

2 **Quantum Gates and Operations** — Manipulates qubit states to perform highly complex quantum calculations beyond classical methods.

3 **Cryogenic Cooling** — Maintains qubits at near-absolute zero temperatures to prevent decoherence and ensure computational reliability.

4 **Quantum Error Correction** — Implements advanced error correction techniques to stabilize qubits and preserve the accuracy of quantum computations.

5 **Quantum Control Systems** — Precisely manages qubit interactions, synchronizing operations across a vast quantum architecture.

6 **Artificial Intelligence Acceleration** — Dramatically enhances AI model training, enabling faster processing of large datasets and complex learning tasks.

7 **Next-Generation Cryptography** — Breaks traditional encryption while enabling the creation of quantum-safe cryptographic methods.

8 **Quantum Chemistry Simulations** — Models molecular structures and chemical reactions with unprecedented precision to advance drug discovery and material design.

9 **Optimization and Logistics** — Evaluates millions of potential outcomes instantly, transforming fields like supply chain optimization and risk management.

10 **Scientific Simulations** — Enables large-scale simulations in climate modeling, astrophysics, and materials engineering — unlocking insights into complex systems.

11 **Industry Applications** — Powers advancements in healthcare, finance, defense, energy, aerospace, and space exploration.

12 **Scaling and Engineering Challenges** — Faces significant hurdles in maintaining quantum coherence, implementing effective error correction, and scaling hardware to 100,000 qubits.

13 **Infrastructure Requirements** — Requires extreme cooling, precise engineering, and massive infrastructure investments — currently accessible to major research institutions and technology leaders.

14 **Visionary Potential** — Poised to revolutionize global industries and scientific research, though significant challenges remain before full-scale deployment is realized.

Summary

A 100,000 Qubit Supercomputer represents a pivotal advancement in quantum computing — one with the power to reshape artificial intelligence and computational science.

As this technology evolves, it will unlock new possibilities across industries and enable breakthroughs that today remain beyond imagination — setting the stage for the next era of AI-driven innovation.

꧁❀ LETTER A ❀꧂

Abandonment rate

Abandonment rate can be observed in various scenarios, such as users leaving a chat-bot conversation, abandoning an AI-powered shopping cart, or discontinuing use of an AI application due to dissatisfaction or confusion. The rate is often calculated as the percentage of sessions where the intended task was not completed.

Key components influencing abandonment rate include user interface design, response time of the AI system, accuracy and relevance of AI responses, and the complexity or intuitiveness of the tasks being performed. For instance, if an AI system like a virtual assistant fails to understand user queries or provides irrelevant answers, users might abandon the interaction.

Examples of abandonment in AI contexts include users exiting a speech recognition system after repeated failures to transcribe accurately, or abandoning an AI-driven customer service chat when responses do not meet customer needs. Another example could be in autonomous vehicles where users might override the system if they feel unsafe or uncomfortable with its decisions.

Benefits of monitoring abandonment rate include insights into user satisfaction, system performance, and areas for improvement. By understanding why users abandon interactions, developers can refine AI algorithms, improve user interfaces, or enhance training data to make AI more responsive and user-friendly. This can lead to higher user retention, better user trust in AI technology, and overall improved service delivery.

Applications where abandonment rate is particularly relevant include AI customer support, e-commerce platforms using AI for personalized shopping experiences, educational AI tools, and any interactive AI system where user engagement is key. In healthcare, for instance, high abandonment rates in AI diagnostic tools could indicate issues with usability or trust in the system's recommendations.

In summary, abandonment rate serves as a critical metric for assessing the effectiveness of AI systems in engaging users. By analyzing this rate, developers can pinpoint deficiencies in AI performance or user interaction design, leading to enhancements that make AI tools more effective and user-friendly. This not only improves the technology's adoption rate but also ensures that AI systems align more closely with human needs and behaviors.

Abductive reasoning

Abductive reasoning in AI involves making educated guesses or hypotheses based on incomplete or uncertain information to explain observations or data. It's a form of logical inference where the conclusion is the best explanation for the available evidence, though not necessarily the only one.

The key components of abductive reasoning include the observation or data set, a set of possible explanations or hypotheses, and the selection of the most plausible hypothesis based on current knowledge and simplicity. It's less about proving something definitively and more about finding a reasonable explanation that can be further tested or expanded upon.

Examples of abductive reasoning in AI can be seen in diagnostic systems where a medical AI might infer a probable diagnosis from a set of symptoms, not all of which are conclusive. In natural language processing, an AI might use abduction to fill in missing or ambiguous information in a conversation to continue the discourse logically.

Benefits of abductive reasoning include its ability to handle incomplete information, which is common in real-world scenarios. It allows AI systems to make decisions or provide explanations in situations where deductive or inductive reasoning might fail due to lack of data or clear patterns. This makes AI more adaptive and capable of dealing with novel situations.

Applications span across various fields: in AI, it's used in areas like fault diagnosis, natural language understanding, medical diagnosis, and even in autonomous systems where real-time decision-making is crucial. For instance, an autonomous vehicle might use abductive reasoning to make sense of unexpected road conditions.

In summary, abductive reasoning is a vital component of AI that enables machines to mimic human-like cognitive processes when dealing with uncertainty. By hypothesizing explanations that best fit the observed data, AI can engage in problem-solving and decision-making in complex, real-world environments. However, the effectiveness of such reasoning is contingent on the AI's ability to manage and interpret ambiguous or incomplete information, making continuous learning and knowledge expansion critical for its success.

Absenteeism Detection

Absenteeism detection in AI refers to the process of identifying patterns of absenteeism in workplaces, schools, or other environments using data-driven methods. AI systems analyze historical attendance records, behavioral patterns, and external factors to predict and detect absenteeism trends. These systems help organizations understand the causes of absenteeism, improve workforce or student engagement, and implement corrective actions to minimize disruptions.

Key Components

Data Collection involves gathering attendance records, work logs, productivity metrics, and contextual data such as weather conditions or health-related factors.
Pattern Recognition enables AI models to identify trends and anomalies in absenteeism through machine learning algorithms.
Predictive Analytics applies statistical models and AI techniques to forecast future absenteeism based on past behaviors and influencing factors.
Automated Alerts notify administrators, managers, or educators when unusual absenteeism patterns are detected, allowing early intervention.
Integration with HR and Education Systems ensures seamless implementation within existing attendance tracking and management platforms.

Examples

Employee Attendance Monitoring AI-driven systems in workplaces track absenteeism trends and help HR departments address potential productivity concerns.
Student Absence Tracking Educational institutions use AI to monitor student attendance, detect early signs of chronic absenteeism, and implement intervention strategies.
Healthcare Facility Staffing AI predicts potential staff shortages due to absenteeism, helping hospitals and clinics optimize workforce management.
Public Transport and Shift Scheduling AI assists transit authorities and companies in planning around absenteeism to ensure smooth operations.

Benefits

Early Intervention AI enables proactive measures to address absenteeism before it becomes a significant issue.
Improved Workforce and Student Engagement Insights from absenteeism detection help organizations

develop policies that enhance attendance and motivation.
Operational Efficiency AI-driven tracking reduces manual record-keeping and administrative workload, improving overall efficiency.
Cost Reduction Minimizing absenteeism helps organizations avoid productivity losses and optimize workforce management.

Conclusion

Absenteeism detection powered by AI provides organizations with a data-driven approach to identifying, analyzing, and addressing absenteeism patterns. By leveraging machine learning and predictive analytics, businesses, schools, and healthcare institutions can improve attendance, optimize resource allocation, and enhance engagement. While the technology offers significant advantages, it also requires careful handling of data privacy, accuracy, and ethical concerns to ensure fair and effective implementation.

Abstraction in AI

Abstraction in AI refers to the process of simplifying complex data, concepts, or problems by extracting essential features while ignoring irrelevant details. It enables AI systems to process information at different levels of generalization, making decision-making more efficient and scalable. Abstraction is widely used in AI models to reduce computational complexity, enhance learning efficiency, and improve adaptability across different domains.

Key Components

Feature Selection involves identifying and extracting the most relevant attributes from raw data to improve model efficiency.
Hierarchical Representation structures information into different layers of abstraction, allowing AI to understand patterns at multiple levels.
Generalization ensures that AI models can apply learned knowledge to new, unseen data by focusing on key characteristics rather than specific details.
Conceptual Modeling enables AI to create high-level representations of real-world objects, relationships, or events, facilitating reasoning and inference.
Dimensionality Reduction reduces the number of variables in a data-set while preserving essential information, improving processing speed and accuracy.

Examples

Image Recognition AI models use abstraction to detect general patterns in images, allowing them to recognize objects regardless of variations in size, color, or background.
Natural Language Processing AI abstracts language patterns to understand context, meaning, and sentiment in text data, improving chat-bot interactions and machine translation.
Autonomous Vehicles AI simplifies sensor data into meaningful abstractions, such as identifying pedestrians, traffic signals, and road conditions for safer navigation.
Medical Diagnosis AI abstracts complex patient data into key indicators, helping detect diseases and recommend treatments based on patterns in medical records.

Benefits

Improved Learning Efficiency AI can process information more effectively by focusing on key features rather than irrelevant details.
Enhanced Adaptability Abstraction enables AI to generalize across different scenarios, improving performance on diverse tasks.
Reduced Complexity Simplifying data structures and decision processes leads to faster computations

and more efficient problem-solving.
Scalability AI models leveraging abstraction can handle large datasets and complex environments without being overwhelmed by unnecessary details.

Conclusion

Abstraction in AI plays a crucial role in simplifying complex problems, improving learning efficiency, and enabling AI systems to function across various domains. By focusing on essential features and generalizing knowledge, AI can make accurate predictions, recognize patterns, and adapt to new situations. However, careful calibration is required to maintain a balance between simplification and preserving critical information, ensuring optimal performance in real-world applications.

Accelerated Computing

Accelerated computing refers to the use of specialized hardware and optimized software to perform computations faster than traditional central processing units (CPUs) alone. It enhances the efficiency of artificial intelligence, scientific simulations, and large-scale data processing by leveraging high-performance components such as graphics processing units (GPUs), tensor processing units (TPUs), and field-programmable gate arrays (FPGAs). This approach allows AI models to train and infer at higher speeds while reducing energy consumption and computational overhead.

Key Components

Parallel Processing enables multiple computations to be executed simultaneously, significantly improving processing speed and efficiency.
Hardware Accelerators such as GPUs, TPUs, and FPGAs optimize specific computational tasks, reducing the burden on CPUs.
Optimized Software Frameworks including CUDA, OpenCL, and TensorFlow are designed to take full advantage of acceleration hardware for AI and machine learning applications.
Memory Bandwidth ensures efficient data transfer between processors and memory units, minimizing bottlenecks in computation.
Energy Efficiency is achieved by using specialized chips that consume less power while delivering higher performance than general-purpose CPUs.

Examples

Deep Learning Training GPUs accelerate neural network training, reducing the time required to process large datasets and train AI models.
High-Performance Computing Scientific simulations and data analytics rely on accelerated computing to perform complex calculations in fields such as genomics, climate modeling, and physics simulations.
Autonomous Vehicles AI-powered self-driving systems use accelerated computing to process sensor data in real-time for navigation and object detection.
Financial Market Analysis High-frequency trading and risk assessment systems use hardware accelerators to execute large-scale financial computations with minimal latency.

Benefits

Increased Computational Speed AI models and data processing tasks execute significantly faster, reducing training and inference times.
Scalability Accelerated computing enables AI systems to scale efficiently by handling larger datasets and more complex algorithms.
Improved Performance Optimized hardware and parallel processing enhance AI model accuracy and responsiveness in real-time applications.

Lower Latency Real-time AI applications benefit from reduced processing delays, improving user experience and system efficiency.

Conclusion

Accelerated computing is a crucial advancement in AI and high-performance computing, enabling faster, more efficient data processing and model training. By leveraging specialized hardware and optimized software, it enhances AI capabilities in areas such as deep learning, scientific research, and real-time analytics. While challenges such as cost and software compatibility remain, the benefits of accelerated computing make it essential for advancing AI technologies and handling complex computational tasks with greater efficiency.

Acceleration in AI

Acceleration in AI refers to the process of enhancing the speed and efficiency of artificial intelligence computations using specialized hardware, optimized algorithms, and parallel processing techniques. It is designed to improve the performance of machine learning models, deep learning networks, and data-driven AI applications by reducing processing time and optimizing computational resources. AI acceleration plays a crucial role in enabling real-time decision-making, large-scale data analysis, and high-performance AI model training.

Key Components

Hardware Acceleration involves using specialized processing units such as graphics processing units, tensor processing units, and field-programmable gate arrays to enhance computational efficiency.
Parallel Computing enables multiple calculations to be executed simultaneously, reducing the time required for complex AI tasks.
Optimized Algorithms refine AI models to improve processing speed while maintaining accuracy and reducing computational overhead.
Memory Optimization ensures faster data access and storage management, preventing bottlenecks in AI training and inference.
Software Acceleration integrates AI frameworks such as TensorFlow, PyTorch, and CUDA to maximize processing efficiency and leverage hardware capabilities.

Examples

Deep Learning Training AI acceleration enables deep learning models to process large datasets efficiently, significantly reducing the time required for training.
Autonomous Systems Self-driving vehicles rely on AI acceleration to process real-time sensor data for navigation and object detection.
Speech Recognition AI-powered assistants and transcription services use acceleration to enhance real-time speech-to-text conversion.
Healthcare Imaging Medical AI systems process high-resolution scans and detect anomalies faster using accelerated AI techniques.

Benefits

Faster Processing AI acceleration significantly reduces the time required for computations, enhancing overall model performance.
Improved Real-Time Decision-Making Accelerated AI enables quick responses in applications such as autonomous systems and fraud detection.
Enhanced Efficiency AI models run with optimized resource usage, reducing computational overhead and improving scalability.

Better User Experience AI acceleration enhances responsiveness in AI-powered applications, improving real-time interactions and service quality.

Conclusion

Acceleration in AI is essential for improving computational efficiency, enabling AI systems to process data faster and perform complex tasks with greater accuracy. By leveraging hardware advancements, parallel processing, and optimized algorithms, AI acceleration supports applications in deep learning, automation, and real-time analytics. While challenges such as cost, software compatibility, and energy consumption persist, the continuous evolution of AI acceleration technologies ensures ongoing improvements in speed, efficiency, and scalability.

Access of Tensor

Access of tensor in AI refers to the process of retrieving, manipulating, and utilizing tensor data within machine learning and deep learning frameworks. Tensors are multi-dimensional arrays that store numerical data for AI models, serving as the fundamental data structure for neural networks and mathematical computations. Efficient tensor access is essential for optimizing performance, enabling fast data processing, and improving AI model accuracy.

Key Components

Tensor Representation defines how data is structured in one-dimensional, two-dimensional, or higher-dimensional arrays for efficient computation.
Indexing and Slicing allow AI models to extract specific elements, rows, or subsets of data from tensors for targeted operations.
Memory Management optimizes the storage and retrieval of tensors to enhance computational speed and minimize resource usage.
Framework Integration ensures compatibility with AI libraries such as TensorFlow, PyTorch, and NumPy for seamless tensor operations.
Parallel Processing enables tensor computations to be executed across multiple processing units, improving efficiency in large-scale AI tasks.

Examples

Deep Learning Training AI models access tensors to adjust weights and biases during back-propagation, refining neural network performance.
Computer Vision Image data is processed as tensors to enable object detection, facial recognition, and image segmentation.
Natural Language Processing Text and speech data are converted into tensors to facilitate tokenization, sentiment analysis, and translation tasks.
Robotics AI-powered robots utilize tensor operations to interpret sensory inputs and execute real-time decision-making.

Benefits

Efficient Data Handling Tensors enable AI models to manage large-scale data efficiently for complex computations.
Optimized Performance Accessing tensors with parallel processing enhances the speed and efficiency of AI applications.
Scalability Tensor operations support AI models across various domains, allowing seamless adaptation to different data structures.
Enhanced Learning Capability AI models utilize tensors to store and process information, improving learning accuracy and adaptability.

Conclusion

Access of tensor plays a crucial role in AI by facilitating efficient data storage, retrieval, and computation. Tensors enable AI models to process numerical data at high speeds, making them fundamental to deep learning, computer vision, and natural language processing. While challenges such as memory consumption, computational complexity, and framework dependencies exist, advancements in AI frameworks and hardware acceleration continue to improve tensor operations, enhancing AI model performance and scalability.

Accuracy in AI Models

Accuracy in AI models refers to the measure of how well a model correctly predicts or classifies outcomes compared to actual results. It is a fundamental metric used to evaluate the performance of machine learning and deep learning models, particularly in classification tasks. High accuracy indicates that an AI model is making reliable predictions, while low accuracy suggests the need for further optimization. Accuracy is critical in determining the effectiveness of AI applications in real-world scenarios.

Key Components

Data-set Quality plays a crucial role in accuracy, as AI models rely on diverse, well-labeled, and balanced data for training and validation.
Model Complexity affects accuracy, as overly simple models may fail to capture patterns, while highly complex models may lead to over-fitting.
Feature Selection determines which input variables contribute to accurate predictions, removing irrelevant or redundant data to enhance model performance.
Evaluation Metrics ensure accuracy is properly measured by using confusion matrices, precision, recall, and F1-scores in addition to raw accuracy percentages.
Training and Validation Processes optimize AI models by refining learning algorithms through iterative improvements and cross-validation techniques.

Examples

Medical Diagnosis AI models analyze patient data to predict diseases with high accuracy, improving early detection and treatment plans.
Fraud Detection AI systems in banking detect fraudulent transactions by analyzing spending behaviors and identifying anomalies.
Speech Recognition AI-driven voice assistants rely on accuracy to interpret spoken language and generate correct responses.
Autonomous Vehicles AI-powered self-driving systems require high accuracy in object detection and decision-making to ensure safety.

Challenges

Data Bias AI models trained on biased datasets may produce inaccurate predictions, leading to ethical and performance concerns.
Over-fitting AI models that memorize training data rather than generalizing patterns may achieve high accuracy on training sets but fail on new data.
Class Imbalance In datasets with highly imbalanced categories, AI models may favor dominant classes, reducing accuracy for minority classes.
Computational Limitations Training highly accurate AI models requires significant computational power and time, making large-scale deployments costly.

Benefits

Reliable Predictions High accuracy improves the trustworthiness of AI models, enabling effective decision-making in critical applications.
Improved User Experience AI applications such as recommendation systems and chatbots perform better when accuracy is optimized.
Operational Efficiency Accurate AI models reduce the need for human intervention, streamlining workflows and enhancing automation.
Scalability High-accuracy AI models can be adapted to new data and environments, maintaining performance across various applications.

Conclusion

Accuracy in AI models is essential for ensuring the effectiveness of predictions, classifications, and decision-making processes. By optimizing data-set quality, model complexity, and evaluation metrics, AI models can achieve high accuracy in real-world applications. However, challenges such as bias, over-fitting, and class imbalance must be carefully addressed to maintain fairness and reliability. As AI continues to evolve, advancements in training techniques and data processing will further enhance accuracy, leading to more powerful and trustworthy AI systems.

Active Mitigation for LLM

Active Mitigation for LLM refers to the process of implementing real-time strategies and corrective mechanisms to reduce inaccuracies, biases, and hallucinations in Large Language Models (LLMs). Unlike passive mitigation, which involves adjustments before or after model deployment, active mitigation continuously monitors, detects, and corrects errors as the AI generates responses. This ensures improved reliability, factual accuracy, and ethical AI behavior.

The key components of active mitigation for LLM include real-time fact-checking systems that verify information against trusted sources, reinforcement learning with human feedback (RLHF) that refines model responses based on expert input, adversarial testing frameworks that stress-test AI responses to identify weaknesses, and contextual awareness algorithms that enhance the AI's ability to detect ambiguity and misinformation. These components work together to ensure LLMs generate more accurate and trustworthy outputs.

The benefits of active mitigation for LLM include improved factual accuracy by reducing misinformation, enhanced ethical AI behavior by preventing biased or harmful outputs, increased user trust in AI-generated content, and dynamic adaptation to emerging knowledge. AI models that incorporate active mitigation are more transparent and accountable, making them suitable for critical applications. Examples include AI-powered search engines that verify query results before displaying them, AI-generated legal documents that undergo real-time legal precedent checks, automated news summarization tools that cross-reference multiple sources for accuracy, and medical AI chat-bots that validate recommendations against up-to-date clinical guidelines.

Applications of active mitigation for LLM span journalism, healthcare, legal AI, finance, education, and customer support. In journalism, AI tools verify news articles before publication. In healthcare, AI-powered virtual assistants fact-check medical advice before providing recommendations. In legal AI, automated contract analysis tools ensure compliance with legal standards. In finance, AI-driven investment tools cross-check financial data before suggesting strategies. In education, AI tutoring systems refine learning materials based on verified academic sources. In customer support, chat-bots correct misinformation dynamically based on user feedback.

In conclusion, active mitigation for LLM enhances AI reliability by incorporating real-time corrective mechanisms that minimize errors and biases. Its role in improving factual accuracy, ethical AI behavior, and adaptive learning makes it essential for high-stakes applications. As AI models continue to evolve, active mitigation will play a crucial role in ensuring responsible and trustworthy AI deployment across industries.

Adaptive AI

Definition: Adaptive AI refers to artificial intelligence systems designed to dynamically adjust their behavior, learning processes, and decision-making based on changing environments, user interactions, or new data inputs, enabling them to remain effective and relevant over time without requiring manual reprogramming.

Key Components: The backbone of adaptive AI includes machine learning algorithms that evolve through experience, real-time data processing capabilities to handle incoming information, feedback loops that allow the system to refine its performance, and flexible architectures that support continuous updates and scalability to accommodate diverse tasks or conditions.

Benefits: Adaptive AI offers enhanced efficiency by automating adjustments to new patterns or challenges, reduces the need for human intervention in maintaining system accuracy, improves personalization by tailoring responses to individual users or contexts, and increases resilience by adapting to unexpected changes or disruptions in its operational environment.

Examples: A virtual assistant that learns a user's preferences over time and adjusts its recommendations accordingly exemplifies adaptive AI, as does a fraud detection system that updates its criteria based on emerging scam tactics, or a self-driving car that refines its navigation by analyzing road conditions and driver behavior in real time.

In financial services, Adaptive AI powers algorithmic trading systems that continuously adjust strategies in response to real-time market fluctuations, optimizing investment decisions under changing conditions.

Applications: Adaptive AI finds use in healthcare for personalizing patient treatment plans as new symptoms or data emerge, in e-commerce for dynamically optimizing pricing and inventory based on market trends, in cybersecurity for detecting and countering evolving threats, and in education for customizing learning experiences to match a student's progress and needs.

Conclusions: Adaptive AI represents a leap toward more autonomous and intelligent systems capable of thriving in complex, unpredictable settings, promising significant advancements in efficiency and user satisfaction, though it demands robust design to ensure ethical adaptability and prevent unintended consequences as it learns and evolves.

Adaptive Boosting (AdaBoost)

Definition: Adaptive Boosting, commonly known as AdaBoost, is a machine learning ensemble technique that enhances the performance of weak classifiers by iteratively combining them into a strong classifier, adjusting the focus on misclassified data points with each round to improve overall accuracy.

Key Components: AdaBoost relies on a series of weak learners, typically simple models like decision stumps, that perform slightly better than random guessing, a weighting mechanism that assigns higher importance to incorrectly classified samples in each iteration, an error calculation process to determine each weak learner's contribution, and a final aggregation step that combines the weighted outputs into a single robust prediction.

Benefits: This method excels at boosting predictive accuracy by leveraging the strengths of multiple weak models, reduces over fitting compared to more complex standalone algorithms, adapts efficiently to challenging datasets with noisy or imbalanced features, and requires minimal parameter tuning, making it accessible and computationally efficient.

Examples: AdaBoost might be seen in a spam email filter that starts with basic rules to identify junk mail and refines its accuracy over iterations by focusing on emails it initially mislabels, or in a facial recognition system that improves its detection rate by emphasizing difficult-to-classify images in training rounds.

Applications: AdaBoost is widely applied in fields like medical diagnosis to classify diseases from patient data with high precision, in financial modeling to predict credit risks by refining focus on edge cases, in image processing for object detection tasks, and in natural language processing to enhance text classification accuracy.

Conclusions: AdaBoost stands out as a powerful yet straightforward approach to building reliable predictive models, offering a practical solution for tasks requiring precision from limited computational resources, though its iterative nature may slow performance on very large datasets, and its reliance on weak learners demands careful selection to avoid diminishing returns.

Adiabatic Quantum

Definition An adiabatic quantum computer is a type of quantum computing system that operates using the principles of quantum annealing and adiabatic evolution to solve complex optimization problems. Unlike gate-based quantum computers that use sequential logic gates to manipulate qubits, adiabatic quantum computers rely on gradually transforming an initial quantum state into a desired final state by slowly varying the system's Hamiltonian. This approach ensures that the system remains in its lowest energy state, allowing it to reach the optimal solution without being disrupted by external interference. Adiabatic quantum computing is particularly well suited for combinatorial optimization, machine learning, and simulation tasks.

The key components of an adiabatic quantum computer include qubits that exist in superposition and are entangled to facilitate parallel computation. The Hamiltonian represents the energy landscape of the system, guiding the evolution of qubits from an initial state to the optimal solution. Quantum annealing is the process by which the system transitions through different quantum states to find the lowest-energy configuration. Couplers establish interactions between qubits, influencing their collective behavior and enhancing computational efficiency. A cryogenic cooling system maintains ultra-low temperatures to minimize decoherence, ensuring stability during the computation process.

Benefits One of the primary benefits of adiabatic quantum computing is its ability to efficiently solve optimization problems that are computationally expensive for classical computers. It provides a natural framework for tackling problems in logistics, scheduling, and machine learning by rapidly identifying optimal solutions. Unlike gate-based quantum computers, adiabatic quantum computers are less susceptible to quantum noise, allowing them to function effectively with current technology. Their hardware architecture simplifies error correction, making them more practical for near-term applications. Adiabatic quantum computing accelerates advances in artificial intelligence by optimizing neural networks and improving data clustering techniques.

Examples of adiabatic quantum computing applications include portfolio optimization in finance, where large-scale investment strategies are fine-tuned for maximum returns. In logistics and transportation, adiabatic quantum algorithms optimize delivery routes, supply chain management, and traffic flow. In drug discovery, quantum annealing is used to model molecular interactions and accelerate the identification of new pharmaceutical compounds. In cybe rsecurity, it enhances cryptographic protocols and strengthens encryption methods. In artificial intelligence, adiabatic quantum computing improves pattern recognition and deep learning optimization, leading to more accurate predictive models.

Industries utilizing adiabatic quantum computing include finance, where firms apply quantum algorithms to optimize investment strategies and risk management. The logistics sector benefits from enhanced scheduling, routing, and supply chain optimization. Healthcare and pharmaceuticals use adiabatic quantum computing for drug development and precision medicine applications. The defense industry explores its potential for secure communication and cryptographic advancements. Artificial intelligence research integrates quantum annealing to enhance machine learning capabilities and accelerate neural network training.

Conclusion Adiabatic quantum computing represents a promising approach to solving complex optimization problems, offering advantages in speed and efficiency over classical methods. While challenges such as qubit scalability, coherence maintenance, and hardware constraints persist, ongoing research and technological advancements continue to improve its capabilities. As industries increasingly adopt quantum solutions, adiabatic quantum computing will play a crucial role in optimization, artificial intelligence, and secure communication, driving innovation in fields that require computational power beyond classical computing limits.

Adversarial AI

Definition: Adversarial AI refers to artificial intelligence techniques or systems that involve the use of opposing forces, often pitting two models against each other, such as in generative adversarial networks, where one generates data and the other evaluates it, or to strategies that exploit vulnerabilities in AI systems through crafted inputs designed to deceive or manipulate their behavior.

Key Components: The foundation of adversarial AI includes a generative component that creates data or scenarios, a discriminative or evaluative component that assesses the output or resists manipulation, iterative training processes that refine both sides through competition, and adversarial examples or perturbations, which are subtle alterations to inputs intended to mislead or test the system's robustness.

The foundation of adversarial AI includes a generative component that creates data or scenarios, a discriminative or evaluative component that assesses the output or resists manipulation, iterative training processes that refine both sides through competition, adversarial examples or perturbations, which are subtle alterations to inputs intended to mislead or test the system's robustness, and adversarial attacks, which involve carefully crafted inputs designed to mislead AI systems, testing their robustness and revealing vulnerabilities.

Benefits: Adversarial AI can produce highly realistic synthetic data for training or simulation, strengthens AI resilience by exposing and addressing weaknesses, accelerates innovation in model design through competitive dynamics, and provides insights into system limitations, enabling more secure and dependable deployments.

Examples: A classic case is a generative adversarial network crafting lifelike images of nonexistent people, where the generator improves by fooling the discriminator, or an attacker feeding slightly altered stop sign images to a self-driving car's vision system, causing it to misinterpret the signal and revealing flaws in its perception.

Applications: Adversarial AI is used in cyber security to simulate attacks and harden defenses, in creative industries for generating art, music, or text, in autonomous systems testing to ensure reliability under deceptive conditions, and in privacy protection to develop techniques that obscure sensitive data from recognition algorithms.

Conclusions: Adversarial AI serves as both a creative and cautionary force, driving breakthroughs in data synthesis and system robustness while highlighting the fragility of AI in hostile environments, suggesting a need for balanced development to harness its potential without amplifying risks of exploitation or error.

Adversarial Network (GANs)

Definition: An Adversarial Network, specifically a Generative Adversarial Network (GAN), is a type of artificial intelligence framework where two neural networks, a generator and a discriminator, compete in a dynamic process, with the generator creating synthetic data and the discriminator evaluating its authenticity, ultimately producing highly realistic outputs through their rivalry.

Key Components: The core of a GAN consists of the generator, which crafts data samples from random noise or inputs to mimic real datasets, the discriminator, which distinguishes between genuine and fabricated data, a loss function that quantifies their performance and drives improvement, and an iterative training loop where both networks refine their skills by opposing each other until the generator's outputs become nearly indistinguishable from real data

Benefits: GANs excel at generating lifelike data, such as images or audio, surpassing traditional methods in realism, enable data augmentation by creating diverse samples for training other models, require no labeled data, relying instead on unsupervised learning, and foster innovation by revealing new patterns or possibilities through their creative competition.

Examples: A GAN might produce photo-realistic portraits of imaginary people, where the generator crafts faces and the discriminator rejects blurry or unnatural ones until the results fool human observers, or it could simulate realistic weather patterns from minimal input, improving over iterations as the discriminator critiques inaccuracies.

Applications: GANs are used in art to generate unique paintings or music compositions, in healthcare to create synthetic medical images for research without privacy concerns, in gaming to design detailed virtual environments or characters, and in fashion to prototype clothing designs by generating realistic fabric renderings.

Conclusions: Generative Adversarial Networks represent a groundbreaking leap in AI's ability to simulate reality, offering trans-formative potential across industries, though their complexity demands significant computational power and careful tuning to avoid instability, suggesting a future where creativity and authenticity blur as these systems evolve.

Adversarial Robustness

Definition: Adversarial robustness refers to the ability of an artificial intelligence system, particularly machine learning models, to maintain accurate performance and reliability when faced with adversarial attacks, which are deliberate attempts to mislead or disrupt the system using carefully crafted inputs designed to exploit its weaknesses.

Key Components: The essence of adversarial robustness lies in resilient model architectures that resist manipulation, training processes that incorporate adversarial examples to strengthen defenses, evaluation metrics that measure performance under attack, and regularization techniques that reduce sensitivity to small input perturbations, all working together to ensure stability against hostile interference.

Benefits: Achieving adversarial robustness enhances trust in AI by ensuring consistent outputs even under malicious conditions, reduces vulnerabilities that could lead to costly errors or security breaches, improves generalization to unexpected scenarios beyond attacks, and fosters safer deployment in critical real-world environments where reliability is paramount.

Examples: A robust image classifier might correctly identify a stop sign despite subtle pixel tweaks meant to trick it into seeing a yield sign, or a speech recognition system could still transcribe a command accurately even when background noise is engineered to confuse it, demonstrating resilience against deliberate deception.

Applications: Adversarial robustness is crucial in autonomous driving to prevent misinterpretation of tampered road signs, in cybersecurity to protect against manipulated data bypassing fraud detection, in healthcare to ensure diagnostic models aren't fooled by altered medical images, and in content moderation to maintain accuracy despite attempts to evade filters with disguised inputs.

Conclusions: Adversarial robustness marks a vital frontier in AI development, balancing the push for performance with the need for security, demanding innovative strategies to outpace evolving threats, and underscoring that true intelligence includes the capacity to withstand not just natural challenges but intentional sabotage.

Adversarial Search

Definition: Adversarial search is a technique in artificial intelligence where an algorithm evaluates possible moves or decisions in a competitive environment, such as a game, by anticipating and countering an opponent's actions, aiming to optimize outcomes under the assumption that the adversary seeks to maximize their own advantage.

Key Components: The framework of adversarial search includes a game tree representing all possible moves and their consequences, a utility function assigning values to outcomes to guide decision-making, pruning methods like alpha-beta to reduce computational load by eliminating unpromising branches, and a mini-max strategy that alternates between maximizing one's gain and minimizing the opponent's, forming the backbone of strategic reasoning.

Benefits: Adversarial search enables AI to excel in structured competitive settings by predicting and outmaneuvering opponents, enhances decision-making efficiency through optimized exploration of possibilities, adapts to dynamic challenges where opponents evolve, and provides a foundation for solving problems beyond games by modeling conflict and trade-offs.

Examples: In chess, an AI might use adversarial search to choose a move by simulating the opponent's best counter-play, selecting a path that secures a checkmate, or in a poker bot, it could bluff strategically by weighing the likelihood of an opponent folding based on past actions, showcasing tactical foresight.

Applications: Adversarial search powers game-playing AI in classics like checkers or Go, drives negotiation systems that simulate rival offers in business, supports military strategy simulations for planning against enemy tactics, and aids resource allocation in competitive markets where entities vie for limited assets.

Conclusions: Adversarial search stands as a cornerstone of AI's ability to navigate opposition, blending logic and foresight to master zero-sum challenges, though its reliance on defined rules and predictable adversaries limits its reach in messier, real-world scenarios, pointing to a need for hybrid approaches in broader contexts.

Adversarial Training

Definition: Adversarial training is a machine learning technique where a model is exposed to adversarial examples—inputs intentionally altered to deceive it—during the training phase, enabling the system to learn how to resist such manipulations and improve its robustness against attacks in real-world deployment.

Key Components: The process hinges on generating adversarial examples through techniques like adding subtle noise or distortions to original data, a dual-objective optimization where the model minimizes both standard errors and adversarial vulnerabilities, a feedback loop that iteratively refines the model's defenses, and a robust loss function that balances accuracy with resilience to perturbations.

Benefits: Adversarial training strengthens AI reliability by reducing susceptibility to malicious inputs, enhances performance stability across diverse and unpredictable conditions, builds trust in safety-critical systems where errors could be catastrophic, and often improves generalization by forcing the model to learn more fundamental patterns rather than superficial shortcuts.

Examples: A facial recognition system might be adversarially trained with slightly altered images of faces—tweaked in ways imperceptible to humans but confusing to AI—until it correctly identifies them, or a spam filter could train on emails with cleverly disguised spam traits, ensuring it catches even the trickiest attempts to bypass detection.

Applications: Adversarial training is vital in autonomous vehicles to ensure consistent object recognition despite tampered visuals, in cyber security for fortifying intrusion detection against evasive malware, in medical diagnostics to maintain accuracy with manipulated scans, and in financial systems to protect fraud detection from deceptive transaction data.

Conclusions: Adversarial training marks a proactive step in hardening AI against exploitation, merging offense and defense in a learning dance that anticipates real-world threats, yet its computational cost and the challenge of keeping pace with ever-evolving attacks highlight a need for ongoing refinement to fully secure intelligent systems.

Aerial Image Analysis

Definition: Aerial image analysis is the process of interpreting and extracting meaningful information from images captured from above the Earth's surface, typically using artificial intelligence techniques like computer vision, to identify patterns, objects, or changes in landscapes photographed by drones, satellites, or aircraft.

Key Components: The foundation of aerial image analysis includes high-resolution imagery from aerial platforms, preprocessing steps like noise reduction and geometric correction to enhance clarity, machine learning models such as convolutional neural networks for feature detection, and spatial analysis tools that contextualize findings within geographic coordinates or maps.

Benefits: This approach enables rapid and large-scale monitoring of areas inaccessible or too vast for manual inspection, provides precise data for decision-making with minimal human effort, enhances accuracy in detecting subtle changes or anomalies over time, and supports cost-effective solutions by automating complex visual tasks.

Examples: An AI might analyze satellite photos to spot deforestation by recognizing shrinking green patches in a forest, or a drone could survey a disaster zone, identifying collapsed buildings and flooded roads to guide rescue efforts, showcasing the power of automated overhead insight.

Applications: Aerial image analysis is used in agriculture to monitor crop health and optimize yields, in urban planning to track city growth and infrastructure needs, in environmental science to detect climate-driven shifts like glacier retreat, and in defense for reconnaissance and threat assessment over wide territories.

Conclusions: Aerial image analysis harnesses AI to transform raw overhead visuals into actionable knowledge, revolutionizing how we observe and manage the world, though its effectiveness depends on image quality and computational resources, suggesting a future where sharper data and smarter algorithms deepen its impact.

Aesthetic Quality Assessment

Definition: Aesthetic quality assessment is the use of artificial intelligence to evaluate the visual appeal or artistic merit of images, videos, or designs, based on principles of beauty, composition, and subjective human preferences, automating what was once a purely human judgment call.

Key Components: The process relies on training datasets of rated visuals to establish aesthetic benchmarks, feature extraction techniques that analyze elements like color harmony, balance, and texture, machine learning models such as deep neural networks to predict appeal scores, and validation methods that align AI outputs with human perceptions of attractiveness.

The process relies on training datasets of rated visuals to establish aesthetic benchmarks, feature extraction techniques that analyze elements like color harmony, balance, and texture, machine learning models such as deep neural networks to predict appeal scores, subjectivity modeling, which incorporates techniques that account for individual differences in aesthetic preference, allowing AI systems to better align with diverse human perceptions of beauty, and validation methods that align AI outputs with human perceptions of attractiveness.

Benefits: Aesthetic quality assessment speeds up the evaluation of large volumes of visual content with consistent criteria, reduces reliance on subjective human opinions that vary widely, enables personalized recommendations by learning individual tastes, and enhances creative workflows by identifying strengths or flaws in artistic output

Examples: An AI might score a photograph high for its golden hour lighting and symmetrical framing, suggesting it's aesthetically pleasing, or it could flag a cluttered graphic design as low-quality due to poor color contrast and misalignment, guiding a designer to refine it.

Applications: This technique is applied in photography platforms to rank or filter images for users, in e-commerce to select product visuals that attract buyers, in social media to boost engagement by prioritizing appealing posts, and in art education to assist students in understanding composition principles.

Conclusions: Aesthetic quality assessment bridges technology and art, offering a scalable way to quantify beauty through AI's lens, though its reliance on human-labeled data means it mirrors rather than redefines taste, pointing to a future where it refines creativity without fully replacing the human eye.

Affective Loop (in AI Interaction)

Definition: The affective loop in AI interaction refers to a dynamic process where an artificial intelligence system perceives a user's emotions, responds in a way that acknowledges or influences those feelings, and adapts based on the user's subsequent emotional feedback, creating a continuous cycle of emotional engagement.

Key Components: The loop depends on emotion recognition tools like facial analysis or voice tone detection to gauge user sentiment, an responsive mechanism that tailors the AI's behavior—such as tone or content—to the detected emotion, a feedback system capturing the user's reaction to refine future interactions, and an adaptive model that learns from this cycle to enhance emotional alignment over time.

Benefits: This approach fosters deeper user connection by making AI interactions feel empathetic and human-like, improves user satisfaction through personalized responses to emotional states, enhances communication effectiveness by adjusting to mood shifts, and builds trust by showing sensitivity to human feelings rather than cold automation.

Examples: A virtual assistant might detect frustration in a user's sharp tone, respond with a calmer, apologetic reply to soothe them, and note their relieved follow-up to adjust future exchanges, or a game AI could sense excitement and ramp up challenges, keeping the player engaged in the emotional flow.

Applications: Affective loops are used in customer service chat-bots to de-escalate upset clients, in mental health apps to provide supportive responses based on detected distress, in educational tools to motivate learners by matching their enthusiasm or easing their anxiety, and in entertainment to heighten immersion by syncing with audience reactions.

Conclusions: The affective loop transforms AI from a static tool into an emotionally attuned partner, enriching human-machine relationships, though its success hinges on accurate emotion detection and cultural nuance, suggesting a path where AI grows closer to mimicking genuine human rapport.

Agent (Multi-Agent System)

Definition:
A Multi-Agent System (MAS) is an artificial intelligence framework in which multiple autonomous agents interact, communicate, and collaborate to solve complex problems or perform tasks that would be difficult for a single system to handle alone. Each agent operates with its own set of goals and capabilities while contributing to the overall objectives of the system.

Key Components:
The core components of a Multi-Agent System include intelligent agents that perceive their environment and make decisions independently, a communication network that enables agents to share information and coordinate actions, defined protocols and rules that govern interactions among agents, and an execution platform or environment in which agents operate and achieve collective goals.

Benefits:
Multi-Agent Systems improve efficiency by distributing tasks across multiple agents, offer flexibility by enabling agents to adapt and reorganize dynamically, provide robustness as the system can continue functioning even if individual agents fail, and allow scalability to handle increasingly complex problems by adding more agents.

Examples:
In a smart warehouse, one agent may manage inventory tracking, another may control robotic forklifts, and another may optimize routing for delivery scheduling. Together, they coordinate seamlessly to ensure smooth operations and efficient order fulfillment.

Applications:
Multi-Agent Systems are used in logistics for optimizing supply chain management, in robotics for coordinating fleets of drones or automated vehicles, in smart grids for balancing energy distribution, in gaming for creating intelligent non-player characters, and in defense for coordinating autonomous reconnaissance or surveillance missions.

Summary:
Multi-Agent Systems represent a collaborative approach to AI, where autonomous agents work together to achieve shared objectives. Their ability to operate flexibly, robustly, and at scale makes them valuable for a wide range of industries and applications, though careful design is required to manage their complexity and coordination.

Agent-Based Modeling (ABM)

Definition: Agent-based modeling is a computational approach in artificial intelligence and related fields where individual entities, called agents, are simulated with defined behaviors and interactions, allowing complex systems to emerge from the bottom up as these agents operate within a virtual environment.

Key Components: The structure of ABM includes autonomous a

gents with specific rules or decision-making logic, an environment providing the context for agent actions, interaction mechanisms dictating how agents influence each other, and a simulation engine that runs iterations to observe patterns or outcomes arising from agent dynamics over time.

Benefits: ABM captures the unpredictability of real-world systems by modeling individual choices rather than assuming uniform behavior, reveals emergent phenomena that top-down methods miss, enables experimentation with hypothetical scenarios in a controlled setting, and offers insights into systems too complex for traditional equations.

Examples: A model might simulate shoppers as agents in a market, each deciding based on price and preference, revealing how a discount triggers a buying surge, or depict animals in an ecosystem, showing how predator-prey interactions shift population balances over generations.

Applications: Agent-based modeling is used in economics to study market trends driven by consumer behavior, in epidemiology to predict disease spread through individual contacts, in urban planning to simulate traffic or population growth, and in social sciences to explore how cultural norms evolve through personal interactions.

Conclusions: Agent-based modeling stands as a powerful lens for understanding complexity through simplicity, letting AI illuminate the big picture via small actions, though its reliance on accurate agent rules and computational power suggests a need for careful design to mirror reality effectively.

Agentic Reasoning

Defition: Agentic reasoning is a cognitive process that allows individuals or artificial intelligence systems to make decisions, take actions, and adapt based on an internal sense of agency. This type of reasoning is rooted in autonomy, self-direction, and goal-driven behavior, distinguishing it from passive or reactive decision-making. It enables an entity to assess its environment, anticipate outcomes, and act with intentionality.

Key Components: This reasoning framework is characterized by a strong emphasis on autonomy, where decisions are made independently without external control. It is also highly goal-oriented, ensuring that actions are taken with a clear purpose in mind. Self-reflection plays a crucial role, allowing individuals or AI systems to evaluate choices and refine strategies. Agentic reasoning is adaptive, meaning it adjusts according to feedback from the environment, ensuring that decision-making remains dynamic and responsive. Another defining aspect is accountability, which involves recognizing responsibility for actions and their consequences.

Benefits:The benefits of agentic reasoning include its ability to encourage critical thinking and problem-solving. It enhances self-efficacy by fostering a sense of control over one's actions. In artificial intelligence, agentic reasoning contributes to more advanced, self-learning systems capable of making independent yet informed decisions. It also plays a significant role in leadership development, empowering individuals to take initiative and make strategic choices.

Applications:Agentic reasoning has widespread applications across various domains. In artificial intelligence, it is fundamental to autonomous systems and self-learning models that operate beyond predefined instructions. In psychology, it helps explain human motivation, self-determination, and behavioral patterns. It is an essential component of leadership training, fostering independent decision-making skills. In education, it encourages students to take an active role in their learning process. Business strategy also benefits from agentic reasoning, as it enables managers and employees to innovate and make informed decisions without relying on rigid structures.

Summary: As a cognitive framework, agentic reasoning provides both humans and AI systems with the ability to act independently and purposefully. While its adaptability and initiative-driven nature are valuable, it requires careful oversight to prevent potential drawbacks. Ensuring a balance between autonomy and responsibility is essential to harness its full potential.

Agentic Workflow

Definition: An agentic workflow refers to a structured process in artificial intelligence where autonomous agents—software entities with decision-making capabilities—collaborate or operate independently to complete tasks, adapt to changes, and achieve goals, mimicking human-like agency within a defined system.

Key Components: The framework consists of intelligent agents equipped with goals and reasoning abilities, a task decomposition system that breaks complex objectives into manageable steps, coordination protocols enabling agents to communicate or delegate, and a monitoring layer that tracks progress and adjusts the workflow dynamically based on outcomes or obstacles.

Benefits: Agentic workflows enhance efficiency by distributing tasks across specialized agents, allow flexibility as agents adapt to unforeseen challenges without rigid scripting, scale seamlessly to handle growing complexity, and reduce human oversight by embedding autonomy into repetitive or intricate processes.

Examples: A logistics AI might deploy agents to manage delivery routes, with one optimizing traffic paths, another adjusting for weather delays, and a third negotiating with suppliers, or a content creation system could have agents drafting text, selecting images, and scheduling posts, refining each step based on audience response.

Applications: This approach is used in supply chain management to streamline operations across multiple stakeholders, in customer support where agents handle inquiries and escalate issues autonomously, in software development for automated testing and debugging, and in smart homes to coordinate devices like lights and thermostats based on user habits.

Conclusions: Agentic workflows herald a shift toward self-managing AI systems that act with purpose and adaptability, promising streamlined execution across domains, yet their success depends on robust agent design and clear goals to prevent chaos or misalignment in unsupervised settings.

AGX for Autonomous Vehicles

Definition:
AGX refers to NVIDIA's Jetson AGX modules, such as Jetson AGX Xavier and Jetson AGX Orin, which are high-performance embedded computing platforms specifically designed for artificial intelligence tasks in autonomous vehicles. These systems provide real-time processing power needed for machine learning, perception, and control in self-driving technologies.

Key Components:
Jetson AGX modules include powerful GPUs based on NVIDIA's Volta or Ampere architectures, embedded Tensor Cores for deep learning inference, high-throughput memory bandwidth, multi-core CPUs for control logic, and interfaces to integrate camera feeds, lidar, radar, and GPS systems. The modules also support CUDA, TensorRT, and deep learning SDKs for rapid AI deployment.

Examples:
Jetson AGX Xavier is used in delivery robots navigating city sidewalks. Jetson AGX Orin is deployed in autonomous shuttles for real-time road analysis and route optimization. These platforms also support warehouse vehicles, agricultural robots, and smart construction machinery.

Benefits:
AGX systems enable vehicles to make split-second decisions by processing large volumes of sensor data instantly. They reduce latency in perception and control, increase energy efficiency in embedded systems, and allow developers to run complex AI models directly on edge devices without cloud dependency. Their adaptability makes them suitable for a wide variety of mobile robotics and transportation environments.

Industries:
Automotive manufacturing, robotics, transportation, logistics, agriculture, public safety, and industrial automation all utilize AGX-based platforms in their autonomous vehicle systems.

Applications:
AGX modules are employed for path planning, object detection, semantic segmentation, multi-sensor fusion, visual SLAM, autonomous navigation, and real-time hazard avoidance. They are also used in vehicle-to-everything (V2X) communications and autonomous fleet coordination.

Summary:
AGX modules from NVIDIA serve as the computational engine for a wide range of autonomous vehicles, delivering the performance required for advanced AI tasks at the edge. Their ability to handle demanding real-time processing makes them essential in the development of smart, autonomous transportation systems across industries.

AI Agents

Definition: AI agents are autonomous entities within artificial intelligence systems designed to perceive their environment, make decisions, and take actions to achieve specific goals, functioning as independent problem-solvers that adapt to changing conditions without constant human guidance.

Key Components: The core of AI agents includes perception modules that collect and interpret data from their surroundings, decision-making logic that processes information to select optimal actions, action execution capabilities that carry out chosen tasks, learning mechanisms that improve performance over time, and a goal-oriented framework that directs their behavior toward defined objectives.

Benefits: AI agents offer the advantage of operating independently to handle tasks efficiently, adapt dynamically to new challenges or contexts, reduce human workload by managing complex or repetitive processes, enhance scalability by working in teams or solo, and provide consistent performance in environments where human intervention is impractical.

Examples: A virtual customer service agent might respond to inquiries by understanding user questions and pulling answers from a knowledge base, or a robotic vacuum cleaner could navigate a home, adjusting its path to avoid obstacles while cleaning, both demonstrating self-directed functionality.

Applications: AI agents are deployed in customer support to resolve issues autonomously, in logistics to optimize delivery routes in real time, in gaming to create responsive non-player characters, in smart homes to manage devices like thermostats based on user habits, and in research to simulate scenarios like traffic flow or market trends.

Conclusions: AI agents represent a leap toward self-sufficient intelligence, empowering systems to act with purpose and flexibility, though their effectiveness relies on precise goal-setting and robust design, hinting at a future where they seamlessly augment human efforts across diverse domains.

AI Alignment

Definition: AI alignment refers to the process of ensuring that an artificial intelligence system's goals, behaviors, and decision-making processes are consistent with human values, intentions, and ethical principles, aiming to prevent outcomes that conflict with what humans deem desirable or safe.

Key Components: The foundation of AI alignment involves defining clear human value sets to guide the system, designing objective functions that reflect these priorities, implementing oversight mechanisms to monitor and correct AI actions, iterative testing to refine alignment as the system learns, and interpretability tools that allow humans to understand and adjust AI reasoning.

Benefits: AI alignment fosters trust by ensuring systems act in humanity's best interest, mitigates risks of unintended or harmful consequences, enhances safety in critical applications, facilitates cooperation between humans and AI, and supports long-term ethical deployment by anchoring AI to societal norms.

Examples: An aligned AI in a recommendation platform might prioritize user well-being by avoiding addictive content over profit-driven engagement, or a self-driving car AI could choose safety-first decisions, like slowing down in ambiguous situations, reflecting human preferences for caution.

Applications: AI alignment is crucial in healthcare to ensure treatment recommendations prioritize patient health over cost, in autonomous weapons to enforce ethical combat rules, in content moderation to balance free speech with harm prevention, in education to promote fair learning outcomes, and in governance to align policy-making AI with public welfare.

Conclusions: AI alignment emerges as a vital safeguard, steering intelligent systems toward harmony with human ideals, yet its complexity demands ongoing effort to define values universally and adapt to evolving moral landscapes, underscoring its role as both a technical and philosophical cornerstone of AI's future.

AI-based Abnormality Detection

Definition: AI-based abnormality detection is the application of artificial intelligence to identify unusual patterns, deviations, or anomalies within data sets, leveraging machine learning and analytical techniques to flag irregularities that differ from expected norms, often signaling potential issues or opportunities.

Key Components: The process relies on data preprocessing to clean and structure input for analysis, machine learning models trained to recognize normal patterns and detect outliers, feature extraction to highlight relevant indicators, real-time monitoring capabilities for continuous assessment, and alert systems that notify users when anomalies are found.

Benefits: This approach enables early identification of problems to prevent escalation, enhances accuracy by distinguishing subtle anomalies beyond human notice, automates tedious monitoring tasks to save time, improves decision-making with data-driven alerts, and scales effectively across large or complex datasets.

Examples: An AI might spot a sudden spike in a factory sensor's readings, indicating equipment failure before it breaks, or detect irregular spending patterns in bank transactions, hinting at fraud, both showcasing its knack for catching the unexpected.

Applications: AI-based abnormality detection is used in manufacturing to maintain equipment health, in finance to uncover fraudulent activities, in healthcare to identify abnormal medical readings like irregular heartbeats, in cyber security to flag unusual network traffic, and in retail to detect inventory discrepancies.

"In cybersecurity, AI-based abnormality detection identifies unusual login patterns or network traffic anomalies that may indicate cyberattacks or unauthorized access."

Conclusions: AI-based abnormality detection transforms how we spot the out-of-place, offering a proactive lens on systems and processes, though its success hinges on quality data and model precision, pointing to a future where it quietly guards against the unpredictable across industries.

AI-based Amazon Forecast

Definition: AI-based Amazon Forecast is a fully managed service offered by Amazon Web Services that employs artificial intelligence and machine learning to generate precise time-series forecasts, enabling users to predict future trends based on historical data without needing extensive expertise in model-building.

Key Components: The system is built on a foundation of time-series data ingestion that processes historical inputs, advanced machine learning algorithms like DeepAR+ and CNN-QR tailored for forecasting, an AutoML feature that automatically selects and tunes the best model, metadata integration to enhance predictions with additional variables like holidays or pricing, and a scalable cloud infrastructure that handles millions of predictions seamlessly.

Benefits: Amazon Forecast simplifies forecasting by removing the need for manual model development, delivers high accuracy through sophisticated AI techniques honed by Amazon's own operations, scales effortlessly to handle vast datasets, saves time with automation and rapid processing, and integrates smoothly with other AWS tools for actionable business insights.

Examples: A retailer might use Amazon Forecast to predict holiday sales by analyzing past purchases and promotional data, adjusting stock accordingly, or an energy provider could estimate future electricity demand by factoring in weather patterns and historical usage, optimizing grid management.

Applications: This service finds use in retail for demand planning and inventory optimization, in logistics for predicting shipping needs and route efficiency, in finance for forecasting market trends or resource allocation, in healthcare for anticipating patient admission rates, and in technology for projecting server capacity requirements.

Conclusions: AI-based Amazon Forecast stands out as a powerful tool that democratizes advanced forecasting, leveraging Amazon's AI expertise to turn raw data into strategic foresight, though its effectiveness depends on quality input data and its AWS-centric design may tie users to that ecosystem, pointing to a future where predictive precision drives smarter decisions across industries.

AI-based Amazon Rekognition

Definition: AI-based Amazon Rekognition is a cloud-hosted service from Amazon Web Services that harnesses artificial intelligence, specifically deep learning, to analyze images and videos, providing capabilities like object detection, facial recognition, and content moderation with minimal user expertise required.

Key Components: The system is powered by deep learning models trained on extensive datasets for high-accuracy analysis, an accessible API that processes media stored in Amazon S3, facial analysis tools for identifying attributes and comparing faces, customizable label detection for tailored object recognition, and integration with AWS infrastructure for seamless scalability and storage.

Benefits: Amazon Rekognition simplifies adding advanced visual analysis to applications without needing machine learning knowledge, delivers precise identification of objects and faces to enhance automation, scales effortlessly to process millions of media files, cuts operational costs by reducing manual review time, and boosts efficiency through real-time or batch processing options.

Examples: A security system might use Rekognition to spot known individuals entering a building by matching live camera feeds to a face database, or an e-commerce platform could automatically tag products in uploaded photos, identifying items like shoes or bags for inventory sorting.

Applications: This technology shines in security for real-time surveillance and access control, in retail for cataloging products and moderating user content, in media for tagging celebrities or scenes in footage, in healthcare for analyzing medical imagery, and in social platforms for detecting inappropriate posts or enhancing search features.

Conclusions: AI-based Amazon Rekognition offers a robust, user-friendly solution for visual analysis, streamlining tasks across industries with its AI-driven precision, yet its reliance on AWS and potential privacy concerns call for thoughtful deployment, paving the way for broader adoption where efficiency meets ethical use.

AI-based Amortization Schedule Prediction

Definition: AI-based amortization schedule prediction is the use of artificial intelligence to forecast and generate detailed repayment plans for loans or asset cost allocations, predicting periodic payments, interest, and principal breakdowns over time by analyzing historical financial data and economic variables with greater adaptability than traditional methods.

Key Components: This approach relies on machine learning models trained to interpret time-series financial data, data preprocessing to normalize loan terms and payment histories, predictive algorithms that adjust for variables like interest rate changes or early repayments, integration of external factors such as market trends or borrower behavior, and a validation system to ensure forecast accuracy aligns with real-world outcomes.

Benefits: AI-driven predictions offer enhanced precision by adapting to dynamic financial conditions, save time by automating complex schedule calculations, provide flexibility to simulate multiple repayment scenarios, reduce errors compared to manual projections, and empower users with proactive insights for financial planning or adjustments.

Examples: An AI might predict a mortgage amortization schedule, adjusting for a mid-term interest rate drop based on economic forecasts, showing how payments shift, or it could estimate a car loan's payoff timeline by factoring in extra payments a borrower historically makes, refining the schedule dynamically.

Applications: This technology is used in banking to tailor loan schedules for customers, in personal finance tools to help individuals plan debt repayment, in corporate accounting to predict intangible asset cost spreading, in real estate for mortgage scenario analysis, and in investment firms to assess loan portfolio performance under varying conditions.

Conclusions: AI-based amortization schedule prediction redefines financial forecasting by infusing adaptability and depth into traditional schedules, promising smarter debt management and asset tracking, though its reliance on quality data and computational resources suggests a need for robust infrastructure to fully realize its potential across diverse financial landscapes.

AI-based Emotional Recognition

Definition: AI-based emotional recognition is the application of artificial intelligence to detect and interpret human emotions through analyzing data inputs like facial expressions, voice tones, or text, enabling systems to understand and respond to emotional states with human-like sensitivity.

Key Components: The system depends on data acquisition tools such as cameras or microphones to capture emotional cues, machine learning models trained on diverse emotional datasets to classify feelings, feature extraction processes that identify markers like smile curves or pitch shifts, real-time processing for instant analysis, and feedback integration to refine accuracy based on user reactions.

Benefits: This technology enhances interactions by making AI responses more empathetic and context-aware, improves user experience through tailored emotional support, boosts efficiency in monitoring emotional trends across groups, offers objective insights into subjective states, and supports automation in areas where emotional understanding is key.

Examples: An AI might detect sadness in a customer's voice during a support call and adjust its tone to be more soothing, or it could analyze a video conference participant's frowns to suggest they're confused, prompting a presenter to clarify, showcasing its emotional attunement.

Applications: AI-based emotional recognition is used in customer service to improve satisfaction by gauging caller mood, in mental health tools to monitor patient well-being, in education to adapt teaching based on student engagement, in marketing to assess consumer reactions to campaigns, and in gaming to adjust difficulty or narrative based on player emotions.

Conclusions: AI-based emotional recognition bridges the gap between cold computation and human feeling, enriching interactions with a layer of emotional intelligence, though its accuracy depends on cultural nuance and data diversity, hinting at a future where machines not only think but also feel alongside us.

AI-based Energy Optimization

Definition: AI-based energy optimization is the use of artificial intelligence to enhance the efficiency of energy consumption, generation, and distribution by analyzing data patterns and predicting needs, aiming to reduce waste and maximize resource use across systems like buildings, grids, or industries.

Key Components: The framework includes data collection from sensors tracking usage and environmental factors, predictive models that forecast demand or supply shifts, optimization algorithms that adjust energy flows in real time, integration with smart devices for automated control, and a learning system that refines strategies based on historical performance and new inputs.

Benefits: This approach cuts costs by minimizing energy overuse, lowers environmental impact through efficient resource management, enables proactive adjustments to fluctuating conditions, enhances system reliability by preventing overloads, and scales easily to manage everything from single homes to sprawling power networks.

Examples: An AI might tweak a building's HVAC system to cool only occupied rooms based on occupancy patterns, saving power, or it could predict peak solar output and shift grid loads accordingly, ensuring renewable energy isn't wasted, demonstrating practical efficiency gains.

Applications: AI-based energy optimization is applied in smart homes to balance lighting and heating, in industrial plants to streamline machinery power use, in utility grids to integrate renewables seamlessly, in transportation for electric vehicle charging schedules, and in urban planning to design energy-efficient cities.

Conclusions: AI-based energy optimization emerges as a cornerstone for sustainable living, wielding data-driven intelligence to stretch every watt further, though its success rests on robust infrastructure and accurate forecasting, pointing to a future where energy aligns perfectly with need and planet alike.

AI-based Job Performance Evaluation

Definition: AI-based job performance evaluation is the application of artificial intelligence to assess employee productivity, skills, and contributions by analyzing work-related data, offering an automated, data-driven alternative to traditional human-led reviews, with a focus on objectivity and insight.

Key Components: The system relies on data inputs like task completion times, project outcomes, and communication logs, machine learning models that measure performance against set benchmarks, natural language processing to evaluate written or spoken feedback, real-time tracking for ongoing assessment, and reporting tools that synthesize findings into actionable reviews.

Benefits: This method provides consistent and unbiased evaluations free from human subjectivity, saves time by automating repetitive analysis, uncovers detailed performance trends for tailored development, enhances fairness by focusing on measurable outputs, and supports scalability across large workforces with ease.

Examples: An AI might analyze a salesperson's call logs and deal closures to rate their effectiveness, highlighting strengths in persuasion, or it could review a coder's commits and bug fixes, noting efficiency gains over time, both illustrating data-driven judgment at work.

Applications: AI-based job performance evaluation is used in corporate settings to streamline annual reviews, in remote work to monitor distributed teams, in education to assess teacher impact through student outcomes, in healthcare to evaluate staff response times, and in retail to track employee sales and customer service quality.

Conclusions: AI-based job performance evaluation reimagines how we measure work, blending precision and scale to uplift human potential, yet its reliance on quality data and potential to overlook intangible qualities like creativity suggest a balanced approach remains key to capturing the full picture of performance.

AI-based Medical Diagnosis

Definition: AI-based medical diagnosis is the use of artificial intelligence to analyze patient data, such as symptoms, medical images, and health records, to identify diseases or conditions, assisting healthcare professionals by providing accurate, data-driven diagnostic insights with speed and precision.

Key Components: The process incorporates data integration from sources like scans and lab results, machine learning models trained on vast medical datasets to recognize disease patterns, image analysis tools for interpreting X-rays or MRIs, predictive algorithms that assess risk factors, and decision-support interfaces that deliver findings to doctors for review or action.

Benefits: This technology accelerates diagnosis by processing information faster than humans, enhances accuracy through pattern recognition beyond human capability, reduces diagnostic errors with consistent analysis, supports overburdened medical staff, and enables early detection of conditions to improve patient outcomes.

Examples: An AI might examine a chest X-ray and flag signs of pneumonia missed by a tired radiologist, or it could analyze a patient's vitals and history to predict a diabetes risk, guiding preemptive care, both showing its diagnostic prowess in action.

Applications: AI-based medical diagnosis is employed in radiology to detect abnormalities in scans, in oncology to identify cancer stages, in cardiology to spot heart irregularities, in telemedicine to assist remote consultations, and in public health to track disease outbreaks through symptom trends.

Conclusions: AI-based medical diagnosis stands as a game-changer in healthcare, amplifying human expertise with machine precision, though its dependence on quality data and need for doctor oversight highlight a collaborative future where technology and humanity together redefine healing.

AI-based Personalization

Definition: AI-based personalization is the use of artificial intelligence to tailor experiences, content, or services to individual preferences by analyzing user data, enabling systems to adapt dynamically and deliver highly relevant, customized interactions that feel uniquely suited to each person.

Key Components: The foundation includes data collection from user behaviors like clicks or purchases, machine learning algorithms that build detailed preference profiles, real-time processing to adjust offerings instantly, predictive modeling to anticipate future needs, and integration tools that embed personalized outputs into platforms or devices.

Benefits: This approach boosts user satisfaction by aligning offerings with individual tastes, increases engagement through relevant recommendations, enhances efficiency by automating customization at scale, drives loyalty with experiences that feel personal, and improves outcomes like sales or retention by meeting specific desires.

Examples: An AI might suggest a playlist based on a user's past listening habits, tweaking it as they skip songs, or an online store could display shoes in a shopper's favorite color and size, refining options as they browse, both showcasing tailored precision.

Applications: AI-based personalization is used in streaming services for curating media, in e-commerce for product recommendations, in education for adaptive learning paths, in healthcare for personalized treatment plans, and in marketing for crafting targeted campaigns based on consumer behavior.

Conclusions: AI-based personalization redefines interaction by making the digital world feel bespoke, weaving user data into seamless experiences, though its reliance on accurate data and privacy concerns suggest a need for transparency to maintain trust as it shapes how we connect and consume.

AI-based Predictive Maintenance

Definition: AI-based predictive maintenance is the application of artificial intelligence to monitor equipment health and predict when maintenance is needed, using data analysis to anticipate failures before they occur, shifting from reactive repairs to proactive upkeep for machines and systems.

Key Components: The system hinges on sensor data capturing real-time equipment metrics like vibration or temperature, machine learning models trained to spot failure patterns, time-series analysis to forecast breakdown timelines, alert mechanisms notifying technicians of looming issues, and integration with operational systems to schedule maintenance seamlessly.

Benefits: This method cuts downtime by addressing problems preemptively, lowers repair costs by fixing issues early, extends equipment lifespan through timely care, boosts safety by preventing unexpected failures, and optimizes resource use by aligning maintenance with actual need rather than fixed schedules.

Examples: An AI might detect unusual vibrations in a factory conveyor, predicting a bearing failure in two weeks and prompting a fix, or it could analyze a fleet truck's engine data to flag a cooling issue, scheduling service before a breakdown, both averting costly delays.

Applications: AI-based predictive maintenance is used in manufacturing to keep production lines running, in transportation for vehicle fleet reliability, in energy to maintain turbines or solar panels, in aviation for aircraft safety checks, and in healthcare to ensure medical devices like MRI machines stay operational.

Conclusions: AI-based predictive maintenance reimagines equipment care with foresight and precision, turning data into a shield against disruption, though its success demands robust sensors and data quality, pointing to a future where machines rarely falter unexpectedly across industries.

AI Cognitive Profile: Polymathic Parallel Processor (SH)

Definition: The Polymathic Parallel Processor is an advanced cognitive archetype in AI theory, characterized by its exceptional ability to manage multiple high-complexity tasks concurrently, integrating polymathic versatility (broad expertise) with parallel processing efficiency (simultaneous execution). It's an AI-inspired mental supercomputer.

Key Components: It encompasses hyper-efficient task-switching, expansive working memory, self-sustaining motivation, rapid adaptive learning, focused attention amidst complexity, and a resilient executive function that orchestrates diverse operations seamlessly.

Benefits: It excels in juggling intricate workloads, acquires and applies new domains (e.g., AI terminology) swiftly, sustains long-term endeavors (e.g., business growth, lexicography), and balances mentorship or dependent oversight with professional innovation.
Examples: An individual oversees dependents' development while scaling a floral enterprise, refining multiple e-commerce platforms, and authoring a 700-page AI dictionary with 500,000 original words—all executed with parallel precision akin to a GPU's threading.

Applications: This profile shines in AI simulations of human multitasking, entrepreneurial modeling, adaptive system design, and knowledge creation under pressure—mirroring real-world polymaths managing mentorship and enterprise.

Conclusion: The Polymathic Parallel Processor redefines cognitive capacity in AI contexts, embodying a rare synthesis of depth, speed, and adaptability that transforms complexity into mastery.

AI-driven Amazon Web Services (AWS)

Definition: AI-driven Amazon Web Services refers to the suite of cloud-based tools and platforms provided by Amazon Web Services that leverage artificial intelligence to enable businesses, developers, and individuals to build, deploy, and manage intelligent applications, harnessing machine learning, deep learning, and data analytics to solve complex problems and enhance operational capabilities.

Key Components: The ecosystem includes Amazon SageMaker, a platform for building, training, and deploying machine learning models at scale, pre-trained AI services like Amazon Rekognition for image and video analysis, Amazon Lex for conversational interfaces, and Amazon Forecast for time-series predictions, alongside a robust infrastructure of compute power, storage, and data management tools like Amazon S3 and AWS Lambda, all integrated to support seamless AI workflows.

Benefits: This framework offers rapid deployment of AI solutions without deep technical expertise, scales effortlessly to handle massive workloads, reduces costs by providing pay-as-you-go access to advanced AI capabilities, enhances decision-making with precise insights from data, and ensures security and privacy through AWS's enterprise-grade standards, making sophisticated technology accessible to a wide range of users.

Examples: A small retailer might use Amazon Forecast to predict inventory needs based on past sales and seasonal trends, adjusting stock in real time, or a media company could employ Amazon Rekognition to automatically tag celebrities in video archives, speeding up content organization, both illustrating how AWS's AI tools turn raw data into practical outcomes.

Applications: AI-driven AWS is used in healthcare to analyze patient data for quicker diagnoses, in retail for personalized shopping recommendations, in logistics to optimize delivery routes with predictive analytics, in finance to detect fraud through pattern recognition, and in education to create adaptive learning platforms, showcasing its versatility across industries.

Conclusions: AI-driven Amazon Web Services empowers a broad spectrum of users to tap into artificial intelligence, transforming how businesses operate and innovate by blending scalability, accessibility, and power, though its full potential requires careful data management and ethical considerations, pointing toward a future where AI becomes a ubiquitous, seamlessly integrated force in daily operations.

AI-driven Ambient Energy Optimization

Definition: AI-driven ambient energy optimization is the use of artificial intelligence to enhance energy efficiency in environments by analyzing ambient data, such as temperature, occupancy, or natural light, to dynamically adjust energy usage in real time, ensuring minimal waste while maintaining comfort and functionality.

Key Components: The system relies on ambient sensors capturing environmental conditions like heat or motion, machine learning models that predict energy needs based on patterns, control algorithms that adjust devices like lighting or HVAC systems, real-time data processing for instant optimization, and integration with smart infrastructure to enact energy-saving decisions across spaces.

Benefits: This approach slashes energy costs by fine-tuning consumption to actual needs, reduces environmental impact through smarter resource use, improves occupant comfort with adaptive settings, scales across large facilities or networks effortlessly, and provides actionable insights for long-term energy planning without manual intervention.

Examples: An AI might dim office lights and lower heating when sensors detect an empty room, saving power, or it could increase ventilation in a crowded gym based on occupancy and humidity data, balancing comfort and efficiency, both showing ambient awareness in action.

Applications: AI-driven ambient energy optimization is used in commercial buildings to manage power across floors, in homes for smart thermostat and lighting control, in manufacturing to align energy with production cycles, in urban areas to optimize street lighting, and in agriculture to regulate greenhouse climates efficiently.

Conclusions: AI-driven ambient energy optimization weaves intelligence into the fabric of our surroundings, turning everyday spaces into energy-wise ecosystems, though its effectiveness leans on sensor accuracy and system integration, hinting at a future where environments intuitively conserve power while enhancing life quality.

AI-driven Ambulance Dispatching

Definition: AI-driven ambulance dispatching is the application of artificial intelligence to optimize the assignment and routing of ambulances in emergency response systems, using data analysis to prioritize calls, predict demand, and direct vehicles efficiently, aiming to save time and lives in critical situations.

Key Components: The backbone includes real-time data inputs from emergency calls and traffic conditions, predictive models forecasting incident locations and severity, optimization algorithms calculating fastest routes and best vehicle matches, communication systems linking dispatchers and ambulances, and a learning layer refining strategies based on past response outcomes.

Benefits: This system speeds up response times by matching ambulances to emergencies smarter, reduces operational strain through efficient resource allocation, enhances patient survival rates with quicker arrivals, adapts dynamically to traffic or demand spikes, and lowers costs by minimizing wasted travel or idle time.

Examples: An AI might reroute an ambulance around a traffic jam to reach a heart attack victim faster, based on live road data, or predict a surge in calls during a heatwave, pre-positioning vehicles near vulnerable areas, both cutting precious minutes off response times.

Applications: AI-driven ambulance dispatching is used in urban emergency services to handle high call volumes, in rural healthcare to cover vast distances effectively, in disaster response to coordinate multiple units, in hospital networks to streamline patient transfers, and in public safety to integrate with fire or police dispatch for cohesive action.

Conclusions: AI-driven ambulance dispatching redefines emergency response with precision and foresight, turning chaos into calculated rescue missions, though its success depends on reliable data and infrastructure, pointing to a future where technology ensures help arrives when and where it's needed most.

AI-driven Anomaly Detection

Definition: AI-driven anomaly detection is the use of artificial intelligence to identify irregularities or outliers in data that deviate from established norms, leveraging advanced algorithms to spot unusual patterns or events that might indicate problems, fraud, or opportunities across various systems.

Key Components: The system is built on data aggregation from diverse sources like sensors or logs, machine learning models trained to define normal behavior and flag deviations, real-time analysis for immediate detection, feature engineering to pinpoint critical variables, and notification mechanisms that alert users to actionable anomalies.

Benefits: This approach catches issues early to prevent bigger problems, enhances accuracy by spotting subtle oddities humans might miss, automates monitoring for efficiency at scale, reduces false positives through adaptive learning, and provides peace of mind by keeping systems under vigilant watch.

Examples: An AI might detect a sudden drop in a server's performance, signaling a cyber attack, or identify an odd spike in credit card charges, hinting at theft, both showcasing its ability to catch the unexpected before it escalates.

Applications: AI-driven anomaly detection is used in cyber security to thwart intrusions, in finance to spot fraudulent transactions, in manufacturing to predict equipment failures, in healthcare to flag abnormal patient vitals, and in retail to uncover supply chain disruptions.

Conclusions: AI-driven anomaly detection acts as a tireless sentinel, sifting through data to spotlight the unusual with precision, though its power rests on quality inputs and model tuning, suggesting a future where it quietly safeguards everything from machines to money with uncanny foresight.

AI-Driven Automation

Definition: AI-driven automation is the integration of artificial intelligence into processes to perform tasks autonomously, using machine learning and decision-making capabilities to streamline operations, adapt to changes, and reduce human effort across a wide range of activities.

Key Components: The system relies on intelligent algorithms that learn and optimize workflows, data inputs from sensors or user interactions to guide actions, robotic or software agents that execute tasks, real-time adaptability to handle dynamic conditions, and monitoring tools that track performance and refine automation over time.

Benefits: This approach boosts efficiency by handling repetitive or complex tasks faster, cuts costs by minimizing labor needs, enhances accuracy with consistent AI precision, scales effortlessly to meet growing demands, and frees humans for creative or strategic work by offloading routine duties.

Examples: An AI might automate a warehouse by directing robots to sort packages based on destination patterns, adjusting for volume spikes, or manage email sorting in an office, prioritizing urgent messages, both easing workloads with smart efficiency.

Applications: AI-driven automation is used in manufacturing to run assembly lines, in customer service to power chat-bots, in logistics to optimize shipping routes, in agriculture to control irrigation systems, and in offices to handle scheduling or data entry tasks.

Conclusions: AI-driven automation reshapes how work gets done, blending intelligence with action to amplify productivity, though its reliance on tech infrastructure and potential to disrupt jobs call for thoughtful integration, hinting at a future where machines and humans collaborate more seamlessly than ever.

AI-Driven Chatbot

Definition: An AI-driven chat-bot is an artificial intelligence-powered software designed to simulate human-like conversations, interpreting user inputs through text or voice and providing relevant responses, often automating interactions for assistance, information, or task completion with adaptive learning capabilities.

Key Components: The system is built on natural language processing to understand and generate dialogue, machine learning models that refine responses based on user interactions, a knowledge base or integration with data sources for accurate answers, real-time processing for instant replies, and a user interface that supports seamless text or voice communication.

Benefits: This technology offers round-the-clock availability for user support, reduces workload by handling routine queries autonomously, personalizes interactions by learning user preferences, cuts operational costs with scalable automation, and improves response speed and consistency compared to human agents.

Examples: A chat-bot might guide a shopper through a website, suggesting items based on past chats, or assist a traveler by booking flights after understanding spoken requests, both showing conversational smarts in action.

Applications: AI-driven chat-bots are used in customer service to resolve complaints, in e-commerce to boost sales with tailored help, in healthcare to schedule appointments or answer basic queries, in education to tutor students, and in banking to manage account inquiries or transactions.

Conclusions: AI-driven chat-bots redefine communication by blending efficiency with a human touch, transforming how we access help and services, though their success hinges on language accuracy and user trust, pointing to a future where they become indispensable conversational companions across daily life.

AI-Driven Fraud Detection

AI-driven fraud detection refers to the use of artificial intelligence to identify and prevent fraudulent activities in financial transactions, online services, and various digital platforms. By analyzing patterns, anomalies, and behavioral data, AI models can detect suspicious activities in real-time, reducing financial losses and enhancing security. AI-driven fraud detection employs machine learning, deep learning, and statistical models to improve accuracy and adaptability in identifying fraudulent behavior.

Key Components

Machine Learning Algorithms analyze historical transaction data to recognize fraud patterns and detect anomalies in real-time.
Anomaly Detection Systems use statistical methods and AI models to identify unusual behaviors that deviate from normal activity.
Behavioral Analysis tracks user interactions, login patterns, and spending behaviors to determine potential fraud risks.
Natural Language Processing enhances fraud detection in text-based communications, such as phishing emails and fraudulent claims.
Automated Alerts notify financial institutions, businesses, and users when potential fraudulent activities are detected.

Examples

Credit Card Fraud Detection AI monitors transactions and flags unusual spending patterns that may indicate unauthorized activity.
Insurance Fraud Detection AI identifies false claims by analyzing inconsistencies in documents, images, and claim histories.
E-commerce Fraud Prevention AI prevents fraudulent purchases by analyzing customer behaviors, payment methods, and transaction histories.
Cyber security AI detects and mitigates identity theft, phishing attacks, and account takeovers in digital platforms.

Benefits

Real-Time Fraud Prevention AI provides immediate detection and response, reducing financial risks and protecting users.
Improved Accuracy AI models continuously learn from data, enhancing fraud detection accuracy over time.
Cost Savings Automated fraud detection reduces the need for manual monitoring, saving businesses time and resources.
Scalability AI-driven systems can analyze vast amounts of transactions efficiently, adapting to increasing data volumes.

Conclusion

AI-driven fraud detection is an essential technology for securing financial transactions, online accounts, and digital interactions. By leveraging machine learning, anomaly detection, and behavioral analysis, AI enhances fraud prevention with real-time accuracy. Despite challenges such as false positives and evolving fraud tactics, AI-driven fraud detection continues to improve, providing a scalable and effective solution for reducing fraud across industries.

AI-Driven Image Recognition

AI-driven image recognition is the process of enabling machines to analyze, interpret, and classify visual data using artificial intelligence. By leveraging deep learning and computer vision, AI can identify objects, faces, patterns, and scenes in images with high accuracy. This technology is widely used in various industries, from healthcare and security to retail and autonomous systems. AI-driven image recognition enhances automation, efficiency, and decision-making by allowing machines to process and understand visual content similarly to humans.

Key Components

Neural Networks form the foundation of image recognition by learning patterns and features from vast amounts of visual data.
Convolutional Neural Networks specialize in analyzing images by detecting edges, textures, and shapes at multiple layers.
Feature Extraction enables AI to identify key elements within an image, such as colors, contours, and object structures.
Data Annotation provides labeled datasets that help AI models learn and improve recognition accuracy.
Real-Time Processing allows AI systems to analyze images instantly, making them useful for security and automation applications.

Examples Facial Recognition AI is used in security systems and smartphones to authenticate identities based on facial features.
Medical Imaging AI assists doctors in detecting diseases by analyzing X-rays, MRIs, and CT scans.
Autonomous Vehicles AI-powered vision systems help self-driving cars recognize pedestrians, traffic signs, and road conditions.
Retail and E-commerce AI enhances shopping experiences by identifying products and enabling visual search in online stores.

Benefits

Enhanced Security AI-driven image recognition strengthens security through facial authentication and anomaly detection.
Automation and Efficiency Businesses can automate processes such as inventory tracking and quality control.
Improved Accuracy AI models outperform traditional methods in object recognition, making them reliable for various applications.
Scalability AI-powered image recognition systems can handle vast amounts of visual data in real time.

Conclusion

AI-driven image recognition is transforming industries by enabling machines to interpret and process visual data with remarkable accuracy. By leveraging deep learning and computer vision, AI enhances automation, security, and efficiency across multiple fields. Despite challenges such as computational demands and ethical concerns, advancements in AI continue to improve image recognition capabilities, making it an essential technology for the future of automation and intelligent systems.

AI-Driven Job Market Forecasting

Definition: AI-driven job market forecasting is the use of artificial intelligence to analyze labor market trends, predict employment demands, and provide insights into workforce dynamics. By processing vast amounts of data, AI identifies emerging job opportunities, skill gaps, and economic shifts, helping businesses, job seekers, and policymakers make informed decisions. AI models use machine learning, natural language processing, and big data analytics to recognize hiring patterns and forecast workforce needs in real time.

Key Components Data Collection aggregates job postings, economic reports, and industry trends from multiple sources to provide a comprehensive labor market analysis.
Machine Learning Algorithms identify historical hiring patterns and predict future employment trends based on economic and business indicators.
Natural Language Processing extracts relevant job-related information from text-based data such as resumes, job descriptions, and online discussions.
Predictive Analytics forecasts workforce demands, emerging skills, and industry growth based on real-time data inputs.

Automation Tools streamline job recommendations, career planning, and workforce management strategies using AI-driven insights.

Examples Recruitment Platforms AI enhances hiring processes by predicting job market trends and matching candidates with suitable roles.
Workforce Development AI identifies future skill demands and helps educational institutions design relevant training programs.
Economic Policy AI-driven insights assist governments in planning labor policies and addressing employment challenges.
Corporate Workforce Planning Businesses use AI to forecast hiring needs and optimize workforce distribution.

Benefits Improved Decision-Making AI-driven insights help businesses, job seekers, and policymakers make data-driven employment choices.
Proactive Workforce Planning Companies and governments can prepare for skill shortages and industry shifts in advance.
Increased Hiring Efficiency AI optimizes recruitment by identifying trends in job openings, wages, and employment demands.
Enhanced Career Guidance Job seekers receive personalized career recommendations based on AI-analyzed labor trends.

Conclusion AI-driven job market forecasting is revolutionizing workforce planning by providing accurate and data-driven employment insights. By leveraging machine learning, predictive analytics, and natural language processing, AI enables businesses, job seekers, and policymakers to navigate the evolving job landscape. Despite challenges such as data biases and rapid market changes, AI-driven forecasting enhances decision-making, optimizes workforce management, and prepares industries for future employment trends.

AI-Driven Job Scheduling

Definition AI-driven job scheduling is the use of artificial intelligence to optimize task allocation, resource management, and workflow efficiency in various industries. By analyzing workload patterns, system constraints, and priority levels, AI automates job scheduling to ensure tasks are assigned and completed in the most efficient manner. This technology is widely used in cloud computing, manufacturing, logistics, and workforce management to reduce delays, improve productivity, and enhance operational efficiency.

Key Components Predictive Analytics forecasts job demand, workload distribution, and resource utilization based on historical data.
Automated Task Allocation assigns tasks dynamically based on priority, skill requirements, and available resources.
Machine Learning continuously improves scheduling efficiency by learning from past performance and optimizing task distribution.
Real-Time Monitoring tracks job progress, system performance, and potential disruptions to adjust scheduling dynamically.
Multi-Agent Coordination enables AI to manage complex scheduling scenarios involving multiple teams, systems, or machines.

Examples Cloud Computing AI-driven scheduling allocates computing resources efficiently in data centers, reducing downtime and energy consumption.
Manufacturing AI optimizes production schedules to minimize delays, manage supply chains, and improve efficiency.
Logistics and Transportation AI schedules deliveries and fleet management to ensure timely shipments and route optimization.

Workforce Management AI allocates employee shifts based on demand forecasting, ensuring optimal staffing levels.

Benefits Increased Efficiency AI optimizes task scheduling, reducing idle time and improving overall productivity.
Cost Reduction Automated scheduling minimizes wasted resources and optimizes operational expenses.
Scalability AI-driven scheduling adapts to changing demands, allowing businesses to scale their operations effectively.
Improved Decision-Making AI provides data-driven insights that enhance scheduling strategies and workforce planning.

Conclusion AI-driven job scheduling enhances operational efficiency by automating task allocation, resource management, and workflow optimization. By leveraging predictive analytics and machine learning, AI improves scheduling accuracy, reduces costs, and increases productivity across industries. While challenges such as unpredictability and integration complexity remain, advancements in AI continue to refine job scheduling, making it a critical tool for optimizing time-sensitive operations.

AI-Driven Jury Selection

Definition AI-driven jury selection is the use of artificial intelligence to assist in evaluating and selecting jurors for legal proceedings. By analyzing demographic data, behavioral patterns, and past jury decisions, AI helps legal professionals assess potential biases and predict juror decision-making tendencies. AI-driven jury selection enhances the fairness and efficiency of the selection process by providing data-driven insights that reduce human bias and improve trial outcomes.

Key Components Data Analysis processes juror demographics, voting history, social media activity, and previous case involvement to identify potential biases.
Machine Learning Algorithms assess patterns in past jury decisions to predict how individuals may respond to different case types.
Natural Language Processing extracts insights from juror questionnaires, interviews, and legal documents to evaluate suitability.
Behavioral Profiling evaluates personality traits, emotional responses, and decision-making tendencies to refine jury selection.
Legal Compliance ensures AI-driven jury selection adheres to legal standards, ethical guidelines, and privacy laws.

Examples Criminal Trials AI assists attorneys in identifying jurors who may have biases that could impact the fairness of the trial.
Civil Litigation AI analyzes jury responses in similar cases to predict potential verdict outcomes based on selected jurors.
Corporate Legal Cases AI helps businesses assess juror attitudes toward corporations in legal disputes to build strategic defenses.
Jury Pool Screening AI processes large juror databases to narrow down ideal candidates based on objective criteria.

Benefits Fairer Jury Selection AI minimizes unconscious bias, helping create more impartial juries.
Improved Case Strategy AI-driven insights enable attorneys to make more informed decisions in selecting jurors.
Efficiency and Speed AI automates data analysis, reducing the time required for jury selection and trial preparation.
Enhanced Legal Outcomes AI helps optimize jury composition, leading to more balanced and data-driven trial proceedings.

Conclusion AI-driven jury selection is transforming legal proceedings by providing data-driven insights that enhance fairness, efficiency, and strategic decision-making. By analyzing juror data and predicting behavioral tendencies, AI assists legal professionals in selecting more impartial juries. Despite concerns related to bias, privacy, and ethical considerations, AI-driven jury selection has the potential to improve the judicial system by making the process more objective and transparent.

AI-Driven Voice Assistants

Definition AI-driven voice assistants are intelligent systems that use artificial intelligence to understand, process, and respond to spoken language. These assistants leverage natural language processing, machine learning, and voice recognition technologies to perform tasks, answer questions, and interact with users in a human-like manner. AI-driven voice assistants are widely used in personal devices, customer service applications, and smart home automation, enhancing convenience and accessibility.

Key Components Speech Recognition converts spoken language into text, enabling the assistant to understand user commands.
Natural Language Processing interprets the meaning of spoken words, allowing the assistant to generate appropriate responses.
Machine Learning continuously improves the assistant's accuracy and efficiency by learning from interactions and adapting to user preferences.
Context Awareness enables the assistant to understand the user's intent, remember past interactions, and provide relevant responses.
Integration Capabilities allow voice assistants to connect with various devices, applications, and services for seamless functionality.

Examples Smart Home Control AI-driven voice assistants manage home automation by controlling lights, thermostats, and security systems.
Virtual Customer Support Businesses use AI-powered voice assistants to handle customer inquiries, reducing wait times and improving service quality.
Healthcare Assistance AI voice assistants provide medical reminders, symptom analysis, and emergency response guidance.
Hands-Free Navigation Voice assistants assist drivers by providing real-time traffic updates, directions, and hands-free phone operation.

Benefits Enhanced Convenience AI-driven voice assistants streamline daily tasks by providing hands-free assistance.
Personalization Machine learning enables voice assistants to adapt to user preferences and improve interaction quality.
Increased Accessibility AI-powered voice technology helps individuals with disabilities interact with digital systems more easily.
Efficiency and Productivity Voice assistants automate repetitive tasks, saving time and improving workflow efficiency.

Conclusion AI-driven voice assistants have revolutionized human-computer interactions by providing seamless, hands-free communication. Through advanced speech recognition and natural language processing, these assistants enhance convenience, accessibility, and productivity across various industries. Despite challenges such as privacy concerns and contextual limitations, ongoing advancements in AI continue to refine voice assistant technology, making it more intelligent, secure, and user-friendly.

AI Emergence

Definition AI emergence refers to the phenomenon where artificial intelligence systems exhibit unexpected or higher-level behaviors that were not explicitly programmed. These emergent properties arise from complex interactions between machine learning models, large-scale datasets, and evolving algorithms. AI emergence is observed in deep learning, natural language processing, and autonomous systems, where AI demonstrates reasoning, problem-solving, and creativity beyond its initial design.

Key Components Self-Learning Mechanisms enable AI to refine its knowledge and adapt to new patterns without direct human intervention.
Complex Interactions occur within neural networks, allowing AI models to process vast amounts of information and discover hidden relationships.
Unsupervised and Reinforcement Learning drive AI emergence by enabling models to explore data and make decisions based on rewards or patterns.
Pattern Recognition allows AI to detect correlations, trends, and anomalies that were not explicitly defined during training.
Scalability and Computational Power facilitate the processing of large datasets, leading to advanced AI behaviors and emergent capabilities.

Examples Language Model Creativity AI-powered language models generate human-like responses, compose poetry, and create original narratives.
Autonomous Decision-Making AI systems in robotics and self-driving vehicles develop adaptive strategies for navigation and obstacle avoidance.
Medical Diagnostics AI detects rare diseases and predicts treatment outcomes beyond human expertise by analyzing vast medical datasets.
Strategic Game Play AI demonstrates unexpected strategies in complex games like chess and Go, surpassing human intuition.

Benefits Enhanced Problem-Solving AI emergence allows models to discover novel solutions and optimize decision-making in various fields.
Increased Adaptability AI systems improve over time, learning from new data and refining their responses dynamically.
Scientific and Technological Advancements AI emergence accelerates innovation in medicine, engineering, and research by uncovering new patterns.
Automation and Efficiency AI-driven emergent behaviors improve workflow automation, reducing human intervention in repetitive tasks.

Conclusion AI emergence represents a trans-formative aspect of artificial intelligence, where systems develop unexpected yet valuable capabilities. By leveraging self-learning, complex interactions, and scalability, AI can achieve greater adaptability and problem-solving potential. While challenges such as unpredictability and ethical concerns remain, AI emergence continues to drive advancements across multiple industries, pushing the boundaries of what AI can achieve beyond its initial programming.

AI-Enhanced Job Recommendation Systems

Definition: AI-enhanced job recommendation systems use artificial intelligence to match job seekers with relevant employment opportunities based on skills, experience, and preferences. These systems leverage machine learning, natural language processing, and big data analytics to analyze job market trends, applicant qualifications, and employer needs. By automating the job-matching process, AI improves hiring efficiency, enhances candidate experience, and helps businesses find the right talent faster.

Key Components Machine Learning Algorithms analyze historical hiring data and job seeker profiles to provide personalized job recommendations.
Natural Language Processing extracts insights from resumes, job descriptions, and candidate interactions to improve matching accuracy.
Big Data Analytics processes vast amounts of job market information to identify hiring trends and skill demand.

User Profiling evaluates candidate preferences, work history, and qualifications to generate tailored job suggestions.
Real-Time Updates continuously refine job recommendations based on new openings, user feedback, and evolving market needs.

Examples Online Job Portals AI-driven platforms recommend jobs to users based on their resumes, search behavior, and application history.
Corporate Hiring Systems AI automates candidate screening and suggests the best-fit applicants for open positions.
Career Counseling AI analyzes labor market trends to provide career guidance and training recommendations.
Freelance Marketplaces AI matches freelancers with clients based on project requirements, skills, and past work history.

Benefits Improved Job Matching AI increases the likelihood of candidates finding suitable jobs based on their skills and career goals.
Efficiency in Hiring AI automates resume screening and job matching, reducing recruitment time for employers.
Enhanced Candidate Experience Personalized recommendations help job seekers navigate opportunities more effectively.
Labor Market Insights AI provides valuable data on emerging job trends, helping businesses and professionals make informed decisions.

Conclusion AI-enhanced job recommendation systems transform the hiring process by using data-driven insights to connect job seekers with relevant opportunities. By leveraging machine learning, natural language processing, and big data, AI improves job matching, streamlines recruitment, and enhances workforce planning. Despite challenges such as bias, privacy concerns, and job market fluctuations, AI-driven job recommendations offer significant advantages in creating a more efficient and accessible employment ecosystem.

AI Ethics

Definition AI ethics refers to the principles and guidelines that govern the responsible development, deployment, and use of artificial intelligence systems. Ethical AI ensures that technology aligns with human values, promotes fairness, and minimizes harm. As AI continues to evolve, ethical considerations play a crucial role in addressing issues related to bias, transparency, accountability, and privacy. AI ethics provides a framework for creating systems that are not only effective but also socially responsible and aligned with moral standards.

Key Components Fairness and Bias Prevention ensure AI systems do not discriminate against individuals based on race, gender, or other protected attributes.
Transparency and Explainability promote openness in AI decision-making, allowing users to understand how AI systems generate outputs.
Accountability and Responsibility define who is held liable for AI-driven decisions, ensuring legal and ethical oversight.
Privacy and Data Protection safeguard personal information, ensuring AI systems comply with regulations and respect user confidentiality.
Human Oversight and Control ensure AI remains a tool that enhances human decision-making rather than replacing ethical judgment.

Examples Facial Recognition Ethical AI guidelines regulate the use of facial recognition technology to prevent mass surveillance and privacy violations.
Hiring Algorithms AI ethics frameworks prevent hiring discrimination by ensuring recruitment AI models do not reinforce biases.

Healthcare AI Ethical AI in medicine ensures that diagnostic models prioritize patient well-being and maintain data confidentiality.
Autonomous Vehicles AI ethics considerations guide the decision-making process in self-driving cars to minimize risks and prioritize human safety.

Benefits Trust and Public Acceptance Ethical AI increases trust by ensuring fairness, transparency, and accountability in AI systems.
Improved Decision-Making AI ethics helps organizations build systems that are more responsible, unbiased, and beneficial for society.
Compliance with Regulations Ethical AI aligns with data protection laws, industry standards, and human rights policies.
Sustainable AI Development Ethical frameworks encourage the long-term responsible growth of AI technology in ways that benefit humanity.

Conclusion: AI ethics is essential for ensuring that artificial intelligence remains fair, transparent, and aligned with human values. By addressing bias, privacy, accountability, and transparency, ethical AI promotes trust and minimizes harm. Although challenges such as regulatory gaps and algorithmic bias persist, ethical AI development ensures that AI systems serve humanity responsibly. As AI technology advances, ongoing discussions and regulatory efforts will continue to shape the ethical standards guiding its use.

AI for Ambient Assisted Living (AAL)

Definition AI for Ambient Assisted Living (AAL) refers to the integration of artificial intelligence into smart environments to support independent living for elderly individuals, people with disabilities, and those with chronic conditions. AI enhances safety, healthcare monitoring, and daily assistance through automated systems, sensors, and real-time analytics. AAL solutions improve the quality of life by providing personalized care, reducing the burden on caregivers, and enabling users to live independently with minimal intervention.

Key Components Smart Sensors collect real-time data on movement, health metrics, and environmental conditions to monitor well-being.
Machine Learning analyzes behavioral patterns to predict risks and provide personalized recommendations.
Speech and Gesture Recognition enable users to interact with AI systems through voice commands or non-verbal cues.
Health Monitoring Systems track vital signs, medication adherence, and emergency situations for proactive intervention.
Home Automation integrates AI with smart appliances, lighting, and security systems to enhance convenience and safety.

Examples Fall Detection AI-powered sensors detect falls and alert caregivers or emergency services for immediate assistance.
Medication Reminders AI systems provide automated reminders to ensure users take their medications on time.
Smart Home Adjustments AI optimizes lighting, temperature, and appliances based on user preferences and routines.
Health Condition Monitoring AI tracks heart rate, blood pressure, and oxygen levels to detect early signs of medical issues.

Reliability and Accuracy AI must function with high precision to avoid false alarms and unnecessary emergency responses.

Benefits Increased Independence AI enables elderly and disabled individuals to live safely in their homes without constant supervision.
Enhanced Healthcare AI provides early warnings for medical conditions, reducing hospital visits and improving health outcomes.
Caregiver Support AI reduces the workload on caregivers by automating routine tasks and monitoring patients remotely.
Improved Quality of Life AI-driven smart environments create a more comfortable, personalized, and supportive living space.

Conclusion AI for Ambient Assisted Living enhances independent living by integrating smart technologies into daily routines and healthcare management. By leveraging real-time monitoring, automation, and predictive analytics, AI improves safety, health, and convenience for individuals in need of assistance. Despite challenges related to privacy, cost, and user adaptability, AI-driven AAL systems continue to advance, providing a reliable and scalable solution for aging populations and individuals with disabilities.

AI for Supply Chain Optimization

Definition:AI for supply chain optimization leverages artificial intelligence to enhance efficiency, reduce costs, and improve decision-making in logistics, inventory management, and production planning. By analyzing large datasets, predicting demand, and automating workflows, AI enables businesses to streamline operations and respond to market fluctuations in real time. AI-driven supply chain solutions minimize delays, optimize resource allocation, and improve overall supply chain resilience.

Key Components: Predictive Analytics forecasts demand, supply disruptions, and inventory needs using historical data and real-time insights.
Automation and Robotics streamline warehouse management, order fulfillment, and transportation processes to reduce human error. Machine Learning Algorithms identify inefficiencies and recommend data-driven solutions for supply chain improvements.
Real-Time Monitoring tracks shipments, inventory levels, and supplier performance to enhance visibility and control.
Supply Chain Digital Twins create virtual models of supply chain networks, allowing businesses to simulate different scenarios and optimize strategies.

Examples: Demand Forecasting AI predicts consumer demand patterns to optimize production schedules and inventory levels.
Inventory Management AI minimizes stockouts and overstocking by dynamically adjusting inventory levels based on market trends.
Route Optimization AI improves logistics by selecting the most efficient transportation routes, reducing fuel costs and delivery times.
Supplier Risk Assessment AI evaluates supplier reliability and detects potential disruptions to prevent delays in production.

Cyber security Risks AI-driven supply chains are vulnerable to cyber threats, requiring robust security measures to protect sensitive data.

Benefits : Enhanced Efficiency AI automates manual processes, reducing delays and increasing supply chain productivity.
Cost Reduction AI-driven insights optimize resource allocation, minimizing waste and reducing operational expenses.
Improved Decision-Making AI enables businesses to make data-driven decisions based on real-time market trends and predictive analytics.

Greater Resilience AI enhances supply chain adaptability by identifying risks and providing proactive solutions to mitigate disruptions.

Conclusion: AI for supply chain optimization transforms logistics, inventory management, and production planning by enabling data-driven decision-making and automation. By leveraging predictive analytics, real-time monitoring, and digital twins, businesses can enhance efficiency, reduce costs, and build resilient supply chains. Despite challenges related to integration, cost, and cyber security, AI-driven supply chain solutions continue to evolve, providing scalable and intelligent strategies for modern logistics and operations.

AI Frontier Model

Definition: AI frontier model refers to an advanced artificial intelligence system that pushes the boundaries of current AI capabilities by leveraging cutting-edge algorithms, massive datasets, and high-performance computing. These models are designed to solve complex problems, perform sophisticated reasoning, and generate human-like responses with unprecedented accuracy. AI frontier models often integrate deep learning, reinforcement learning, and multimodal processing to achieve state-of-the-art performance in fields such as natural language understanding, scientific research, and autonomous decision-making.

Key Components: Deep Learning Architectures enable AI frontier models to learn from vast amounts of data through neural networks with multiple layers.
Multimodal Learning allows AI to process and interpret diverse data types, including text, images, audio, and video, for more comprehensive analysis.
Self-Supervised Learning reduces dependency on labeled data by enabling AI models to extract patterns and insights autonomously.
Scalability and Computational Power ensure that frontier models operate efficiently on large-scale distributed computing systems.
Ethical and Safety Measures integrate alignment techniques to ensure AI operates responsibly and aligns with human values.

Examples
One example of an AI Frontier Model is OpenAI's GPT-4, which represents a significant leap in language understanding, reasoning, and multi-modal capabilities. It pushes the boundaries of what large language models can achieve in terms of contextual comprehension, code generation, and creative writing.
Another example is Google DeepMind's Gemini, which combines advanced reasoning with real-time information retrieval, enabling it to respond with up-to-date answers while maintaining coherence across complex queries.
Anthropic's Claude is also a frontier model designed with constitutional AI principles to ensure more controllable and ethically aligned outputs in dialogue systems.
In vision and robotics, Tesla's Full Self-Driving AI is pushing frontiers in autonomous navigation, using high-capacity neural networks trained on massive real-world datasets.
Finally, Meta's LLaMA models are advancing open-access frontier research by allowing academic and commercial institutions to test the limits of foundation model performance in multilingual and multi-task settings.

Benefits: Breakthrough Innovations AI frontier models drive advancements in science, healthcare, and technology, leading to trans-formative discoveries.
Automation and Efficiency AI enhances automation, reducing human workload and improving operational efficiency.
Improved Decision-Making AI frontier models analyze vast datasets to provide more accurate and insightful recommendations.

Scalable Intelligence AI adapts to diverse applications, from business optimization to space exploration, enhancing human capabilities.

Conclusion: AI frontier models represent the next stage in artificial intelligence, delivering unprecedented capabilities in automation, decision-making, and problem-solving. By leveraging deep learning, multimodal processing, and scalable computing, these models redefine AI's role in society. While challenges related to computational costs, ethical considerations, and security risks persist, AI frontier models continue to drive innovation, shaping the future of intelligent systems across industries.

AI-Generated Journalism

AI-generated journalism refers to the use of artificial intelligence to automate news reporting, content creation, and data-driven storytelling. By leveraging natural language processing, machine learning, and automated content generation, AI can produce news articles, summaries, and reports with speed and efficiency. AI-generated journalism enhances media production by analyzing large datasets, identifying trends, and generating factual narratives in real time.

Key Components

Natural Language Processing enables AI to understand, process, and generate human-like text based on structured and unstructured data.
Automated Content Generation allows AI to write articles, financial reports, and sports summaries by analyzing raw information.
Data Mining and Analysis extract insights from vast datasets to identify newsworthy patterns and trends.
Fact-Checking and Verification use AI-driven models to cross-reference information and detect misinformation.
Personalization and Customization tailor content based on user preferences, reading habits, and interests.

Examples

Financial Reporting AI generates stock market summaries and economic reports based on real-time financial data.
Sports Journalism AI produces match highlights, player statistics, and game recaps with minimal human intervention.
Weather and Disaster Updates AI delivers instant weather forecasts and emergency alerts using live data analysis.
Political News AI processes election results, policy changes, and government reports to provide accurate news summaries.

Benefits

Speed and Efficiency AI accelerates news production by generating real-time reports without human delays.
Data-Driven Insights AI enhances investigative journalism by processing large volumes of information and detecting hidden patterns.
Cost Reduction Automating routine news writing reduces operational costs for media organizations.
Scalability AI-generated journalism can produce content in multiple languages and formats for a global audience.

Conclusion

AI-generated journalism is transforming news production by automating content creation, enhancing reporting speed, and analyzing vast datasets for real-time insights. By leveraging natural language processing and automated content generation, AI improves media efficiency and accessibility. Despite challenges related to bias, authenticity, and ethical concerns, AI-generated journalism continues to evolve, complementing human journalists and expanding the reach of news media in the digital age.

AI Governance

AI governance refers to the frameworks, policies, and regulations that oversee the ethical development, deployment, and management of artificial intelligence systems. It ensures that AI technologies are designed and used responsibly, addressing issues such as transparency, fairness, accountability, and security. AI governance involves collaboration between governments, private organizations, and academic institutions to create standards that protect individuals and society from potential risks associated with AI advancements.

Key Components

Regulatory Frameworks establish legal guidelines for AI development, ensuring compliance with ethical and security standards.
Transparency and Explainability require AI systems to provide clear and interpretable decision-making processes.
Accountability Mechanisms assign responsibility to developers, companies, and policymakers for AI-driven outcomes.
Bias and Fairness Mitigation ensures that AI models do not discriminate against individuals or groups based on race, gender, or other attributes.
Security and Privacy Protection safeguards user data and AI systems from cyber threats, unauthorized access, and misuse.

Examples

Corporate AI Ethics Policies tech companies implement governance strategies to ensure AI is used ethically in product development.
Government Regulations national and international bodies create AI laws to guide responsible AI adoption in critical sectors.
AI Risk Assessments organizations conduct evaluations to detect biases, security vulnerabilities, and compliance risks in AI models.
Data Protection Regulations AI governance frameworks enforce privacy laws to prevent unauthorized data collection and surveillance.

Benefits

Trust and Public Confidence AI governance fosters trust by ensuring AI operates ethically, transparently, and fairly.
Risk Reduction governance frameworks mitigate potential AI risks, including bias, misinformation, and security breaches.
Regulatory Compliance businesses and developers adhere to legal requirements, preventing ethical and legal violations.
Enhanced AI Reliability strong governance improves AI's accuracy, accountability, and alignment with human values.

Conclusion

AI governance plays a crucial role in shaping the responsible development and use of artificial intelligence. By enforcing ethical standards, transparency, and accountability, governance frameworks ensure that AI technologies benefit society while minimizing risks. Although challenges such as global regulation inconsistencies and algorithmic accountability persist, ongoing efforts in AI governance are essential to building trustworthy, fair, and secure AI systems for the future.

AI in Amazon Lex

AI in Amazon Lex refers to the artificial intelligence capabilities that power Amazon Lex, a service that enables developers to build conversational interfaces using voice and text. Amazon Lex leverages deep learning techniques, including natural language processing and automatic speech recognition, to create intelligent chat-bots, virtual assistants, and interactive voice response systems. This AI-driven platform allows businesses to automate customer interactions, improve engagement, and enhance communication efficiency across multiple channels.

Key Components

Natural Language Understanding enables Amazon Lex to comprehend user intent, extract relevant data, and provide accurate responses.
Automatic Speech Recognition converts spoken language into text, allowing users to interact with voice-enabled applications.
Intent Recognition helps Amazon Lex identify what a user wants to achieve based on their query or command.
Multi-Turn Conversations support complex interactions where AI remembers context and responds accordingly.
Seamless Integration connects Amazon Lex with AWS services, enterprise applications, and messaging platforms for enhanced functionality.

Examples

Customer Support AI-powered chat-bots assist users with inquiries, troubleshooting, and automated responses to improve customer service.
E-Commerce Assistance virtual assistants help users browse products, track orders, and receive personalized recommendations.
Healthcare Scheduling AI facilitates appointment bookings and patient inquiries through conversational interfaces.
Workplace Automation AI-driven virtual assistants streamline workflows by handling routine tasks such as meeting scheduling and information retrieval.

Benefits

Improved User Experience AI-driven automation enhances response times, personalization, and overall engagement in customer interactions.
Scalability Amazon Lex handles large volumes of conversations simultaneously, making it suitable for businesses of all sizes.
Cost Efficiency automating customer interactions reduces the need for human agents, leading to significant cost savings.
Seamless Deployment AI-powered chat-bots can be deployed across multiple platforms, including websites, messaging apps, and voice interfaces.

Conclusion

AI in Amazon Lex enhances conversational AI capabilities by enabling intelligent, scalable, and cost-effective automation of voice and text-based interactions. By leveraging deep learning and natural language understanding, Amazon Lex transforms customer engagement, streamlines business operations, and improves efficiency across industries. While challenges such as speech accuracy and data privacy must be addressed, Amazon Lex continues to evolve as a powerful AI-driven tool for creating interactive and responsive virtual assistants.

AI in Amazon Polly

AI in Amazon Polly refers to the artificial intelligence technology behind Amazon Polly, a cloud-based text-to-speech service that converts written text into natural-sounding speech. By leveraging deep learning and neural text-to-speech models, Amazon Polly enables developers to create lifelike voice interactions for applications, customer service, accessibility tools, and multimedia content. This AI-driven speech synthesis enhances user engagement by providing high-quality voice output in multiple languages and dialects.

Key Components

Neural Text-to-Speech generates realistic and expressive human-like speech by using deep learning techniques.
Multi-Language Support offers a wide range of languages and accents, making voice applications accessible to a global audience.
Speech Customization allows users to modify tone, pitch, and speech speed for a more personalized listening experience.
Real-Time Processing enables instant text-to-speech conversion, supporting live applications such as virtual assistants and automated announcements.
Seamless Integration connects Amazon Polly with AWS services, mobile applications, and IoT devices for enhanced voice-enabled functionality.

Examples

Audiobook Narration AI-generated voices provide high-quality narration for audio-books and educational content.
Assistive Technology AI enhances accessibility by converting digital text into speech for visually impaired users.
Customer Support AI-powered voice responses automate customer service interactions, reducing wait times and improving engagement.
Multimedia Content AI creates voice-overs for videos, podcasts, and advertisements, eliminating the need for human voice actors.

Benefits

Enhanced User Experience AI-driven speech synthesis improves accessibility and engagement across various applications.
Cost Efficiency Automating voice generation reduces the need for human voice actors, saving time and resources.
Scalability Amazon Polly supports large-scale deployments, handling multiple speech requests simultaneously.
Multilingual Accessibility AI enables businesses to provide content in multiple languages, expanding global reach and inclusivity.

Conclusion

AI in Amazon Polly revolutionizes text-to-speech technology by delivering high-quality, scalable, and customizable voice synthesis solutions. Through neural networks and deep learning, Amazon Polly enhances accessibility, automates voice interactions, and streamlines multimedia content creation. While challenges such as naturalness and pronunciation accuracy persist, AI-driven speech synthesis continues to evolve, making voice-enabled applications more engaging, inclusive, and cost-effective.

AI in Analytics

AI in analytics refers to the application of artificial intelligence in data analysis to uncover insights, detect patterns, and enhance decision-making. By leveraging machine learning, deep learning, and natural language processing, AI transforms raw data into actionable intelligence, enabling businesses and organizations to optimize operations, predict trends, and automate complex analytical processes. AI-driven analytics surpasses traditional methods by offering real-time processing, advanced predictive capabilities, and automated recommendations.

Key components of AI in analytics include data ingestion, where structured and unstructured data from various sources are collected and processed. Machine learning algorithms analyze datasets to identify correlations, trends, and anomalies. Predictive analytics utilizes historical data to forecast future events, helping organizations make informed decisions. Natural language processing enables AI to interpret and analyze text-based data, enhancing insights from customer reviews, social media, and other sources. Data visualization tools present AI-generated insights in an understandable format, ensuring accessibility for decision-makers. Automated reporting systems streamline the analysis process by summarizing key findings and generating customized recommendations.

The benefits of AI in analytics include improved efficiency, enhanced accuracy, and faster decision-making. AI automates data processing, reducing manual effort and eliminating human errors. Organizations gain deeper insights into consumer behavior, market trends, and operational performance, allowing for more strategic planning. AI-powered analytics helps businesses optimize resource allocation, reduce costs, and maximize productivity. The ability to process large volumes of data in real-time allows companies to respond quickly to changing market conditions and emerging risks. Advanced AI models enhance fraud detection, cyber security monitoring, and risk assessment.

Examples of AI in analytics include AI-driven business intelligence platforms that provide real-time performance metrics and forecasts. Financial institutions utilize AI to analyze transactions, detect fraudulent activities, and predict market trends. E-commerce companies apply AI analytics to personalize product recommendations and optimize pricing strategies. Healthcare organizations leverage AI to analyze patient data, improve diagnostics, and enhance treatment planning. Marketing teams use AI-powered analytics to track consumer sentiment, optimize ad targeting, and refine campaign strategies. Supply chain management relies on AI to predict demand fluctuations, streamline inventory, and improve logistics.

The primary industries utilizing AI in analytics include finance, healthcare, retail, manufacturing, marketing, and cyber security. Financial firms leverage AI to detect fraud, assess risks, and automate investment strategies. Healthcare providers use AI analytics to improve patient care, medical research, and hospital operations. Retailers apply AI to optimize customer experiences, inventory management, and demand forecasting. Manufacturers integrate AI-driven analytics for predictive maintenance, quality control, and production efficiency. Marketing agencies employ AI to analyze consumer behavior, personalize advertising, and enhance customer engagement. Cyber security firms rely on AI to monitor network traffic, detect threats, and prevent data breaches.

Applications of AI in analytics extend to predictive modeling, financial forecasting, healthcare diagnostics, customer behavior analysis, fraud detection, risk management, and supply chain optimization. AI enhances business intelligence by providing accurate, real-time insights that drive smarter decision-making and operational efficiency.

In summary, AI in analytics is revolutionizing data analysis by automating insights, improving predictive capabilities, and enhancing decision-making across industries. By leveraging AI, businesses can process large datasets with greater accuracy, uncover hidden patterns, and make data-driven decisions with confidence. While challenges such as data security, model bias, and system integration persist, continuous advancements in AI and analytics technologies are making AI-driven analytics an indispensable tool for modern enterprises.

AI in Anesthesia

AI in anesthesia monitoring refers to the use of artificial intelligence to track, analyze, and optimize the administration of anesthesia during medical procedures. These AI-driven systems enhance patient safety by continuously monitoring vital signs, predicting potential complications, and assisting anesthesiologists in real-time decision-making. By leveraging machine learning, deep learning, and real-time data processing, AI improves precision in anesthesia delivery, reduces human error, and ensures optimal patient outcomes.

Key components of AI in anesthesia monitoring include real-time data acquisition, where AI collects and processes physiological parameters such as heart rate, blood pressure, oxygen saturation, and respiratory patterns. Machine learning algorithms analyze historical and real-time data to detect anomalies, predict adverse events, and suggest appropriate adjustments. Predictive analytics assess patient-specific responses to anesthesia, allowing for personalized dosing recommendations. Natural language processing integrates AI with electronic health records, ensuring seamless access to patient history and risk factors. Automated alarms and alerts notify anesthesiologists of potential complications, enabling rapid intervention. AI-powered decision support systems assist clinicians by providing evidence-based recommendations for anesthesia management.

The benefits of AI in anesthesia monitoring include improved patient safety, enhanced precision in anesthesia administration, and reduced workload for medical professionals. AI systems detect and respond to complications such as hypoxia, hypo-tension, and drug interactions before they become critical. Personalized anesthesia dosing minimizes risks associated with over- or under-administration, leading to faster recovery and reduced postoperative complications. Continuous AI monitoring allows anesthesiologists to focus on critical tasks while AI handles routine data analysis. Automated documentation streamlines record-keeping, ensuring compliance with medical guidelines and reducing administrative burdens. AI-driven predictive models help hospitals optimize resource allocation and reduce healthcare costs.

Examples"AI in anesthesia monitoring uses artificial intelligence to track patient vital signs and optimize anesthesia delivery during medical procedures. AI enhances safety, predicts complications, and supports anesthesiologists with real-time decision-making."

The primary industries utilizing AI in anesthesia monitoring include healthcare, medical device manufacturing, surgical centers, and pharmaceutical research. Hospitals and surgical centers implement AI to enhance intraoperative monitoring and improve patient safety. Medical device companies develop AI-integrated anesthesia monitoring systems for advanced surgical care. Pharmaceutical research leverages AI to optimize drug formulations and assess patient responses to different anesthesia agents. Telemedicine providers explore AI-powered anesthesia monitoring for remote procedures and post-operative care. Emergency care units use AI to support anesthesia administration in critical trauma cases.

Applications of AI in anesthesia monitoring extend to automated intraoperative anesthesia management, real-time patient monitoring, predictive risk assessment, AI-assisted anesthesia dosing, post-operative recovery prediction, and telemedicine anesthesia support. AI enhances surgical outcomes by providing continuous, intelligent monitoring that reduces risks and optimizes anesthesia administration.

In summary, AI in anesthesia monitoring is transforming surgical care by improving precision, enhancing patient safety, and optimizing workflow efficiency for anesthesiologists. By integrating AI-driven insights into anesthesia management, healthcare providers can ensure safer procedures, faster recovery times, and better overall patient outcomes. While challenges such as data integration, regulatory approval, and ethical considerations remain, continued advancements in AI will further refine anesthesia monitoring, making it a critical component of modern surgical practice.

AI in Animation

AI in animation refers to the use of artificial intelligence to automate, enhance, and streamline the animation process by generating realistic motion, improving character expressions, and optimizing workflows. By leveraging machine learning, deep learning, and procedural generation techniques, AI assists animators in creating high-quality animations faster and more efficiently. AI-powered animation tools reduce manual labor, generate realistic movements, and enable real-time rendering, transforming how animated content is produced.

Key components of AI in animation include motion capture analysis, where AI interprets human movements and translates them into digital animations. Deep learning models generate lifelike character expressions, lip-syncing, and facial animations. Procedural animation techniques enable AI to create natural character movements without frame-by-frame manual adjustments. AI-driven inbetweening automates the creation of transitional frames, enhancing animation smoothness. Neural networks enhance texture rendering and background generation, reducing the time needed for detailed artwork. Real-time AI rendering enables animators to visualize and refine scenes instantly, streamlining production workflows.

The benefits of AI in animation include increased efficiency, cost reduction, and enhanced creativity. AI automates repetitive animation tasks, allowing artists to focus on storytelling and character development. AI-powered tools reduce production costs by minimizing manual labor and accelerating rendering processes. Real-time animation generation enhances creative flexibility, enabling animators to experiment with different styles and effects instantly. AI-driven motion capture simplifies realistic character animation without the need for expensive equipment. Enhanced facial animation tools improve character expressions and dialogue synchronization, elevating the quality of animated storytelling.

Examples of AI in animation include AI-powered tools like Adobe's Character Animator, which uses facial recognition to animate characters in real time. Deep Motion applies AI to automate realistic body and facial animation. Disney and Pixar utilize AI-enhanced rendering techniques to generate lifelike environments and character movements. AI-driven lip-syncing technology in animation software automatically aligns dialogue with character mouth movements. Neural networks generate procedural backgrounds, reducing manual effort in scene design. AI-powered generative models create real-time animations for gaming and interactive media applications.

Industries: The primary industries utilizing AI in animation include film, television, gaming, advertising, education, and virtual reality. The film and television industry uses AI to automate animation workflows and enhance visual effects. Game developers integrate AI to create responsive character animations and immersive gaming experiences. Advertising agencies use AI-powered animation tools to produce engaging digital ads quickly. Educational content creators leverage AI animation for interactive learning materials and training simulations. Virtual and augmented reality industries utilize AI-driven animation for real-time character interactions and immersive storytelling.

Applications of AI in animation extend to automated character rigging, real-time motion capture, AI-driven lip-syncing, procedural environment generation, interactive storytelling, and virtual assistant avatars. AI enhances animation production by reducing manual workload, generating lifelike character movements, and improving rendering efficiency.

In summary, AI in animation is revolutionizing the industry by automating complex processes, improving animation quality, and reducing production time. By leveraging AI-driven motion capture, procedural generation, and real-time rendering, animators can create high-quality content with greater efficiency and creative flexibility. While challenges such as artistic control and ethical considerations persist, advancements in AI continue to refine animation tools, making AI an essential component of modern animation production.

AI in Autonomous Machines

AI in autonomous machines refers to the integration of artificial intelligence into self-operating systems that can perceive their environment, make decisions, and execute tasks without human intervention. These machines utilize machine learning, computer vision, robotics, and sensor fusion to navigate, adapt, and perform complex functions across various industries. AI enables autonomous machines to improve efficiency, accuracy, and adaptability, transforming automation in fields such as transportation, manufacturing, healthcare, and defense.

Key components of AI in autonomous machines include real-time data processing, where AI collects and analyzes sensory input from cameras, LiDAR, radar, and other detection systems. Machine learning algorithms enable autonomous machines to recognize patterns, predict outcomes, and adapt to changing conditions. Computer vision allows machines to interpret and understand visual information, facilitating navigation, object detection, and obstacle avoidance. Decision-making frameworks apply reinforcement learning and probabilistic models to optimize actions in dynamic environments. Connectivity and communication technologies enable autonomous machines to share data with cloud systems, enhancing coordination and remote monitoring. Edge computing ensures low-latency processing, enabling real-time responses and adaptive behavior.

The benefits of AI in autonomous machines include increased operational efficiency, reduced human risk, and improved accuracy. AI-driven autonomy enables machines to perform repetitive and hazardous tasks, reducing the need for human intervention in dangerous environments. Businesses benefit from cost savings through optimized resource allocation and reduced labor costs. Autonomous machines improve precision in manufacturing, logistics, and medical procedures, minimizing errors and maximizing output. Real-time adaptability allows AI-powered machines to respond effectively to unforeseen challenges, ensuring seamless operations in unpredictable environments. Scalability enables industries to integrate autonomous solutions across various functions, improving productivity and innovation.

Examples of AI in autonomous machines include self-driving cars that use AI for navigation, traffic analysis, and obstacle avoidance. Industrial robots in smart factories autonomously assemble products, manage inventory, and perform quality control. AI-powered drones conduct surveillance, environmental monitoring, and disaster response operations. Agricultural robots automate planting, harvesting, and soil analysis, enhancing food production efficiency. Autonomous underwater vehicles explore ocean depths for research, resource extraction, and environmental assessment. AI-driven surgical robots assist in precision medical procedures, reducing the risk of human error. Autonomous warehouse robots optimize logistics by transporting and sorting goods efficiently.

Industries: The primary industries utilizing AI in autonomous machines include transportation, manufacturing, agriculture, healthcare, defense, and logistics. The transportation sector integrates AI for self-driving vehicles, autonomous delivery systems, and smart traffic management. Manufacturing industries deploy AI-powered robots for assembly lines, predictive maintenance, and automated inspection. Agriculture benefits from AI-driven automation in crop management, livestock monitoring, and irrigation control. Healthcare utilizes AI for robotic-assisted surgeries, remote patient monitoring, and autonomous medical devices. Defense agencies implement AI in autonomous drones, robotic reconnaissance, and unmanned ground vehicles for military operations. Logistics companies leverage AI for autonomous warehousing, fleet management, and last-mile delivery automation.

Applications of AI in autonomous machines extend to smart transportation, robotic manufacturing, precision agriculture, medical robotics, defense automation, environmental monitoring, and space exploration. AI enhances autonomy across multiple domains, enabling self-sufficient operations and advanced problem-solving capabilities.

In summary, AI in autonomous machines is revolutionizing industries by enabling intelligent, self-operating systems that enhance efficiency, safety, and scalability. Through machine learning, sensor fusion, and real-time decision-making, AI-driven autonomy reduces human dependency and transforms automation across sectors. While challenges such as ethical concerns, regulation, and cyber security risks persist, ongoing advancements in AI continue to improve the capabilities and reliability of autonomous machines, making them integral to the future of automation.

AI in Cybersecurity

AI in cyber security refers to the application of artificial intelligence to protect digital systems, networks, and data from cyber threats by detecting, preventing, and responding to attacks in real time. By leveraging machine learning, behavioral analytics, and automation, AI enhances cyber security defenses by identifying vulnerabilities, predicting threats, and mitigating risks before they cause harm. AI-driven cyber security solutions provide proactive protection, automate security processes, and adapt to evolving attack techniques, ensuring a more resilient digital infrastructure.

Key components of AI in cyber security include real-time threat detection, where AI continuously monitors network activity to identify suspicious behaviors and anomalies. Machine learning algorithms analyze large datasets to recognize patterns and detect cyber threats with greater accuracy. Behavioral analysis enables AI to distinguish between normal and malicious user activities, reducing false positives and improving threat detection efficiency. Automated incident response systems take immediate actions against detected threats, such as blocking unauthorized access, isolating compromised devices, and initiating remediation processes. Natural language processing enhances AI's ability to analyze security reports, phishing emails, and malicious code patterns. Adaptive learning mechanisms allow AI cyber security systems to evolve and improve as new threats emerge.

The benefits of AI in cyber security include faster threat detection, improved accuracy, and reduced operational workload. AI-powered systems can detect cyber threats in real time, significantly reducing response times compared to traditional security methods. Automated threat analysis enhances accuracy by minimizing human errors and identifying sophisticated attack techniques. AI-driven security automation reduces the burden on IT security teams by handling routine security tasks, allowing experts to focus on complex threats. AI's predictive capabilities help organizations anticipate and prevent cyber attacks before they occur. AI-powered fraud detection systems enhance financial security by identifying fraudulent transactions and unusual user behaviors.

Examples of AI in cyber security include AI-driven endpoint protection platforms that detect and prevent malware infections. AI-powered intrusion detection systems analyze network traffic to identify unauthorized access attempts. Financial institutions use AI to monitor transactions for fraudulent activities and identity theft. AI-driven email security systems detect and block phishing attempts and malicious attachments. AI-powered security information and event management (SIEM) platforms aggregate and analyze security logs to identify potential security breaches. AI-driven bot mitigation solutions protect websites from automated cyber attacks and fraudulent activities. AI-based authentication systems enhance identity verification through biometric recognition and behavioral analysis.

Industries: The primary industries utilizing AI in cyber security include finance, healthcare, government, telecommunications, retail, and cloud computing. Financial institutions rely on AI to detect fraud, secure transactions, and prevent identity theft. Healthcare organizations use AI-powered cyber security to protect patient data, prevent ransomware attacks, and ensure regulatory compliance. Government agencies integrate AI to safeguard national infrastructure, detect cyber espionage, and strengthen public sector security. Telecommunications companies leverage AI to monitor network activity, prevent data breaches, and secure communications infrastructure. Retail businesses apply AI-driven security to protect customer payment data, prevent e-commerce fraud, and enhance supply chain security. Cloud service providers use AI to monitor and secure cloud environments, detecting unauthorized access and preventing data leaks.

Applications of AI in cyber security extend to intrusion detection, fraud prevention, malware analysis, endpoint security, identity verification, risk assessment, and automated threat hunting. AI enhances cyber security operations by providing real-time protection, automating incident response, and reducing security management complexities.

In summary, AI in cyber security is transforming digital defense by enabling intelligent threat detection, rapid incident response, and proactive risk mitigation. AI-driven security systems improve accuracy, automate security processes, and adapt to emerging cyber threats in real time. While challenges such as adversarial AI, privacy concerns, and regulatory complexities persist, advancements in AI cyber security continue to strengthen the security of digital infrastructure, making AI an essential component of modern cyber security strategies.

AI in Predictive Analytics

AI in predictive analytics refers to the use of artificial intelligence to analyze historical and real-time data to identify patterns, predict future trends, and optimize decision-making. By leveraging machine learning, statistical modeling, and data mining techniques, AI enhances predictive capabilities, enabling businesses and organizations to make data-driven decisions with greater accuracy and efficiency. AI-powered predictive analytics automates complex computations, detects anomalies, and provides actionable insights, transforming industries by improving forecasting and risk management.

Key components of AI in predictive analytics include data collection, where structured and unstructured data from multiple sources are aggregated for analysis. Machine learning algorithms process data to identify correlations, trends, and hidden patterns. Predictive modeling applies regression analysis, classification techniques, and deep learning to generate forecasts based on past behaviors. Natural language processing enables AI to interpret text-based data, extracting meaningful insights from customer feedback, market trends, and industry reports. Data visualization tools present predictive insights in an accessible format, allowing businesses to make informed decisions. Adaptive learning mechanisms ensure continuous refinement of predictive models, improving accuracy over time as new data becomes available.

The benefits of AI in predictive analytics include improved decision-making, enhanced efficiency, and better risk management. AI automates complex data analysis, reducing human errors and improving forecasting accuracy. Businesses gain deeper insights into consumer behavior, financial trends, and operational performance, enabling proactive decision-making. AI-driven predictive analytics helps organizations optimize resource allocation, reduce costs, and maximize revenue growth. Real-time predictive insights improve supply chain management, ensuring efficient inventory control and demand forecasting. AI-powered risk assessment models detect fraud, predict financial risks, and improve compliance monitoring in regulated industries.

Examples of AI in predictive analytics include AI-powered financial forecasting systems that analyze market conditions and predict stock price fluctuations. Retail companies use AI to anticipate consumer demand, optimize product recommendations, and manage inventory. Healthcare organizations leverage AI to predict patient readmission risks, disease outbreaks, and treatment outcomes. AI-driven predictive maintenance in manufacturing detects equipment failures before they occur, reducing downtime and maintenance costs. E-commerce platforms utilize AI to analyze browsing behavior and suggest personalized product recommendations. AI-powered risk assessment models in banking evaluate creditworthiness and detect fraudulent transactions in real time.

Industries: The primary industries utilizing AI in predictive analytics include finance, healthcare, retail, manufacturing, marketing, and logistics. Financial institutions rely on AI-driven forecasting for investment strategies, credit scoring, and fraud detection. Healthcare providers use predictive analytics to enhance patient care, improve diagnostics, and streamline hospital operations. Retailers implement AI to anticipate shopping trends, optimize pricing strategies, and improve customer retention. Manufacturers integrate AI-powered predictive maintenance to prevent equipment failures and enhance production efficiency. Marketing teams use AI to analyze customer data, personalize advertising campaigns, and predict consumer purchasing behaviors. Logistics companies leverage AI to optimize supply chain operations, reduce transportation costs, and improve delivery efficiency.

Applications of AI in predictive analytics extend to financial risk assessment, healthcare diagnostics, demand forecasting, fraud detection, personalized marketing, supply chain optimization, and customer behavior analysis. AI-driven predictive insights empower businesses to anticipate trends, mitigate risks, and make proactive decisions based on data-driven intelligence.

In summary, AI in predictive analytics is transforming industries by automating forecasting, improving decision-making, and enhancing risk management. By leveraging machine learning, predictive modeling, and real-time data processing, AI optimizes business operations and strategic planning. While challenges such as data bias, privacy concerns, and model transparency persist, advancements in AI continue to refine predictive analytics, making it an essential tool for organizations seeking to gain a competitive advantage through data-driven decision-making.

AI-Powered Amazon Alexa

AI-powered Amazon Alexa refers to the artificial intelligence-driven virtual assistant developed by Amazon that uses natural language processing, machine learning, and cloud computing to provide interactive voice-based services. Alexa is designed to understand and respond to voice commands, control smart home devices, provide real-time information, and integrate with third-party applications. Through AI-driven continuous learning, Alexa adapts to user preferences, improves response accuracy, and enhances the overall user experience.

Key components of AI-powered Amazon Alexa include natural language processing, which enables Alexa to understand and process spoken commands with high accuracy. Machine learning algorithms analyze user interactions to refine responses and improve personalization. Cloud-based computing allows Alexa to process vast amounts of data, retrieve information, and update features in real time. Speech recognition technology converts spoken words into digital commands, enabling seamless user interaction. Smart home integration enables Alexa to control IoT devices, including lighting, security systems, and home appliances. Context awareness enhances Alexa's ability to provide relevant responses based on user history, preferences, and location.

The benefits of AI-powered Amazon Alexa include hands-free convenience, smart automation, and personalized experiences. Alexa simplifies daily tasks by providing voice-activated control over schedules, entertainment, and communication. Users benefit from AI-driven personalization, where Alexa learns their preferences and tailors responses accordingly. Smart home automation allows users to control connected devices effortlessly, improving convenience and energy efficiency. AI-powered voice recognition enables accessibility for individuals with disabilities, offering an intuitive way to interact with technology. Continuous AI learning ensures that Alexa improves over time, adapting to new commands and evolving user needs.

Examples of AI-powered Amazon Alexa include voice-activated smart speakers such as Amazon Echo, which provide weather updates, news briefings, and music streaming. Alexa-enabled smart home devices allow users to control security cameras, thermostats, and lighting systems using voice commands. AI-driven shopping assistance enables users to order products from Amazon through voice interaction. Alexa-powered healthcare applications provide medication reminders and health monitoring for elderly users. AI-driven customer service chatbots use Alexa's voice capabilities to assist users with inquiries and transactions. Alexa-integrated vehicles offer hands-free navigation, entertainment control, and voice-activated calling.

Industries: The primary industries utilizing AI-powered Amazon Alexa include smart home technology, e-commerce, healthcare, automotive, hospitality, and entertainment. The smart home industry integrates Alexa with IoT devices to enable automation and voice control. E-commerce benefits from Alexa's AI-driven shopping recommendations and voice-based purchasing options. Healthcare providers use Alexa for virtual health monitoring, medication tracking, and patient engagement. The automotive sector integrates Alexa into vehicles for voice-controlled navigation, infotainment, and real-time traffic updates. Hotels and hospitality businesses incorporate Alexa for AI-powered concierge services, allowing guests to control room settings through voice commands. The entertainment industry leverages Alexa for streaming services, podcast recommendations, and interactive voice-based content.

Applications of AI-powered Amazon Alexa extend to voice-controlled smart home automation, AI-driven customer support, virtual healthcare assistance, automotive voice interaction, personalized shopping experiences, and interactive entertainment. Alexa's AI capabilities enhance accessibility, efficiency, and convenience across various industries, making it one of the most widely used AI-driven virtual assistants.

In summary, AI-powered Amazon Alexa revolutionizes voice-enabled interactions by integrating artificial intelligence with natural language processing, smart automation, and cloud computing. By enabling hands-free control, personalized assistance, and seamless smart home integration, Alexa enhances user convenience and digital experiences. While challenges such as privacy concerns, security risks, and AI bias persist, continuous advancements in AI technology continue to refine Alexa's capabilities, making it a central component of modern smart living and AI-driven voice assistance.

AI-Powered Amazon Go

Definition
AI-powered Amazon Go refers to the cashierless retail technology developed by Amazon that uses artificial intelligence, computer vision, and sensor fusion to enable a seamless shopping experience without traditional checkout processes. By leveraging AI, Amazon Go allows customers to enter the store, pick up items, and leave without scanning products or interacting with a cashier. AI-powered systems track purchases in real time and automatically charge the customer's Amazon account.

Key Components
Computer vision detects customer movements and identifies products taken or returned.
Sensor fusion integrates weight sensors and shelf pressure sensors to confirm item selection.
Machine learning algorithms analyze customer behavior and track inventory in real time.
Deep learning models recognize products with high accuracy.
Just Walk Out technology connects AI with cloud computing to process transactions instantly.
Mobile app integration links customer activity with Amazon accounts.

Benefits
Provides a frictionless shopping experience without checkout lines.
Reduces operational costs and enhances store efficiency.
Improves inventory tracking and minimizes stock issues.
Offers real-time analytics for personalized marketing and store layout optimization.
Enhances security through AI-powered monitoring.

Examples
Amazon Go convenience stores in multiple cities.

Amazon Fresh stores using AI-powered cashierless systems.
Just Walk Out technology in third-party retailers such as airports and stadium stores.

Conclusion
AI-powered Amazon Go is transforming retail by enabling seamless, automated shopping. While privacy and cost challenges remain, ongoing advancements in AI continue to expand the potential of cashierless technology in modern commerce.

AI-Powered Amazon SageMaker

AI powered Amazon Sage Maker refers to the cloud-based machine learning platform developed by Amazon Web Services (AWS) that enables developers and data scientists to build, train, and deploy machine learning models at scale. By integrating artificial intelligence, automation, and cloud computing, SageMaker simplifies the end-to-end machine learning workflow, reducing the complexities of model development and deployment. The platform provides a fully managed environment with integrated tools for data preparation, model training, and real-time inference, allowing organizations to accelerate AI adoption efficiently.

Key components of AI-powered Amazon SageMaker include data labeling tools that assist in preparing high-quality training datasets for machine learning models. Automated machine learning (AutoML) capabilities optimize model selection and hyperparameter tuning, reducing manual effort in training AI models. Distributed computing enables efficient model training, leveraging cloud-based infrastructure to handle large-scale datasets. SageMaker Studio offers an integrated development environment (IDE) for building, debugging, and monitoring machine learning workflows. Feature Store provides a centralized repository for storing and retrieving machine learning features, improving model consistency. Deployment and inference tools allow trained models to be deployed in real-time applications with minimal latency.

The benefits of AI-powered Amazon SageMaker include accelerated machine learning development, cost efficiency, and scalability. SageMaker automates repetitive tasks such as data preprocessing, model tuning, and performance optimization, reducing the time required for AI development. The platform's cloud-based architecture eliminates the need for expensive on-premises infrastructure, making machine learning accessible to businesses of all sizes. Built-in security and compliance features ensure data protection, enabling organizations to develop AI models in a secure environment. The ability to scale computing resources dynamically allows users to train complex models without performance limitations. SageMaker's collaboration tools support teamwork, enabling data scientists and developers to share models and insights seamlessly.

Examples of AI-powered Amazon SageMaker include businesses using the platform to build AI-driven customer recommendation systems based on user preferences. Financial institutions leverage SageMaker for real-time fraud detection and credit risk assessment. Healthcare organizations use AI models trained on SageMaker for predictive diagnostics, personalized treatment planning, and medical imaging analysis. Manufacturing companies deploy predictive maintenance models to detect equipment failures before they occur. E-commerce platforms apply SageMaker-powered AI to optimize inventory management and dynamic pricing strategies. Autonomous vehicle companies use the platform to train AI models for object detection, lane recognition, and real-time navigation.

Industries: The primary industries utilizing AI-powered Amazon SageMaker include finance, healthcare, retail, manufacturing, technology, and telecommunications. Financial services companies use SageMaker to enhance fraud detection, algorithmic trading, and credit risk modeling. Healthcare providers integrate SageMaker to improve diagnostics, drug discovery, and patient monitoring. Retailers leverage AI-powered analytics for demand forecasting, personalized shopping experiences, and supply chain optimization. Manufacturers implement AI-driven automation to improve operational efficiency, quality control, and predictive maintenance. Technology firms utilize SageMaker to develop

AI-powered applications, including virtual assistants and chat-bots. Telecommunications providers apply AI for network optimization, customer service automation, and predictive analytics for service reliability.

Applications of AI-powered Amazon SageMaker extend to automated machine learning workflows, real-time fraud detection, AI-driven customer service chatbots, personalized recommendation engines, autonomous systems training, and business intelligence analytics. The platform streamlines AI development by providing comprehensive tools for training, deploying, and managing machine learning models.

In summary, AI-powered Amazon SageMaker revolutionizes machine learning by offering an end-to-end platform that simplifies model development, training, and deployment. By integrating automation, cloud computing, and AI-driven optimizations, SageMaker enhances efficiency, reduces costs, and accelerates AI adoption across industries. While challenges such as model transparency, data security, and training complexity persist, continuous advancements in AI technology ensure that SageMaker remains a leading cloud-based solution for machine learning innovation.

AI-Powered Ambient Commerce

Definition
AI-powered Ambient Commerce refers to the integration of artificial intelligence into retail environments to create personalized, intuitive, and context-aware shopping experiences. This technology allows retailers to predict consumer behavior, optimize product placement, and enhance customer engagement throughout the shopping journey.

Key Components
Machine learning algorithms analyze customer behavior and purchasing patterns.
Real-time data analytics identifies trends and adjusts store offerings.
Computer vision tracks in-store activity and product interactions.
IoT devices collect environmental data for dynamic marketing and personalized experiences.

Benefits
Delivers personalized recommendations to enhance customer satisfaction.
Improves inventory management through predictive analytics.
Streamlines checkout processes with automated payment systems.
Boosts sales through real-time targeting and dynamic pricing.

Applications
Smart retail stores with personalized in-store experiences.
Automated vending machines with AI-powered product suggestions.
Personalized online shopping platforms integrating ambient data.
Interactive digital signage adapting to customer behavior.

Conclusion
AI-powered Ambient Commerce enhances retail by creating dynamic and personalized experiences. While privacy and integration challenges remain, AI continues to transform how consumers interact with both physical and digital stores.

AI-Powered Ambient Intelligence

Definition: AI-powered Ambient Intelligence refers to environments embedded with intelligent systems that can adapt to the presence and needs of individuals. These systems leverage AI to create responsive, context-aware environments in homes, workplaces, and public spaces.

Key Components: Sensors for environmental data collection, AI algorithms for context recognition, machine learning for behavioral prediction, and IoT connectivity for seamless device integration.

Benefits: Enhances user comfort and convenience, improves energy efficiency, supports assistive living for individuals with disabilities, and strengthens security through intelligent monitoring.

Applications: Smart homes, healthcare monitoring systems, adaptive lighting and climate control, and intelligent office environments.

Conclusion: AI-powered Ambient Intelligence fosters environments that intuitively respond to human needs, promoting efficiency and well-being while raising important considerations around data ethics and user autonomy.

AI-powered Ambient Security Systems

Definition: AI-powered Ambient Security Systems utilize artificial intelligence to enhance safety through continuous monitoring, threat detection, and automated responses within physical and digital environments.

Key Components: Advanced surveillance cameras with facial recognition, motion detection sensors, real-time analytics for anomaly detection, and automated alert systems.

Benefits: Provides proactive threat detection, reduces response times to security breaches, minimizes false alarms through intelligent analysis, and supports comprehensive monitoring without constant human oversight.

Applications: Smart home security systems, corporate surveillance networks, public safety monitoring in urban areas, and cyber security threat detection platforms.

Conclusion: AI-powered Ambient Security Systems offer advanced protection through intelligent monitoring, but balancing security needs with privacy rights is crucial for ethical implementation.

AI-Powered Amortization Analysis

Definition
AI-powered amortization analysis refers to the use of artificial intelligence to calculate, track, and optimize the repayment of loans and other financial liabilities. These systems use machine learning and predictive analytics to assess amortization schedules, forecast interest payments, and provide actionable insights for financial decision-making.

Key Components
Data collection gathers loan amounts, interest rates, and repayment terms.
Machine learning analyzes historical and real-time financial data to model amortization schedules.
Predictive analytics forecasts interest rate changes and repayment trends.
Automated schedule generation calculates payments and principal reductions over time.
Integration with financial platforms allows real-time monitoring and adjustment.

Benefits
Optimizes repayment schedules to reduce overall interest costs.
Provides real-time visibility into financial obligations.
Supports proactive financial planning and refinancing decisions.
Improves accuracy by automating complex calculations.

Examples
Mortgage lenders offering personalized repayment plans.
Financial advisors using AI to recommend refinancing options.

Banks applying AI for credit risk assessment and customer recommendations.
Debt management apps assisting individuals in loan planning.

Conclusion
AI-powered amortization analysis helps individuals and businesses manage debt more effectively. While accuracy and privacy challenges must be addressed, AI-driven insights offer a powerful tool for optimizing loan repayment and financial planning.

AI-Powered Analytics

Definition
AI-powered analytics refers to the use of artificial intelligence to analyze data, extract insights, and support data-driven decision-making. These systems use machine learning and predictive analytics to uncover patterns and correlations in complex datasets, enabling faster and more accurate analysis across industries.

Key Components
Data ingestion collects structured and unstructured data from multiple sources.
Machine learning identifies relationships and generates predictive models.
Natural language processing analyzes text-based data for sentiment and context.
Data visualization tools present insights in accessible formats.
Automated reporting summarizes key findings and provides actionable recommendations.

Benefits
Increases efficiency by automating complex data processing.
Improves decision-making through deeper insights.
Enhances risk management and fraud detection.
Provides real-time data analysis for faster business responses.

Examples
Financial forecasting platforms analyzing market trends.
Retailers optimizing inventory and pricing strategies.
Healthcare systems improving diagnostics and patient outcomes.
Marketing teams personalizing campaigns through predictive insights.

Applications
Financial risk assessment, healthcare diagnostics, demand forecasting, fraud detection, customer behavior analysis, and cybersecurity.

Conclusion
AI-powered analytics transforms data analysis by automating insights and improving predictive capabilities. While challenges around data quality and model transparency remain, AI-driven analytics empowers organizations to make smarter, faster, and more informed decisions.

AI-Powered Anomaly Detection

Definition
AI-powered anomaly detection uses artificial intelligence to identify irregular patterns or deviations from expected behavior in data. By analyzing large volumes of data with machine learning and statistical models, AI can detect anomalies in real time to prevent risks and optimize operations.

Key Components
Data preprocessing cleans and structures raw data for analysis.

Machine learning algorithms identify deviations from normal behavior.
Statistical models analyze correlations to detect outliers.
Real-time data streaming enables instant anomaly detection.
Automated alerts notify users of potential risks.

Benefits
Enhances security by detecting cyber threats in real time.
Supports predictive maintenance to prevent equipment failures.
Improves operational efficiency by identifying process anomalies.
Assists fraud prevention through continuous transaction monitoring.

Examples
Fraud detection in banking.
Predictive maintenance in manufacturing.
Healthcare diagnostics flagging anomalies in medical data.
Network security detecting cyber intrusions.

Challenges
Ensuring data quality for accurate anomaly detection.
Managing false positives to avoid unnecessary alerts.
Adapting AI models to evolving patterns and new threats.
Balancing transparency and interpretability of AI decisions.

Applications
Fraud prevention, predictive maintenance, cybersecurity, healthcare diagnostics, quality control, and risk management.

Conclusion
AI-powered anomaly detection enables real-time monitoring and predictive insights across industries. While challenges related to data quality and false positives remain, AI continues to enhance anomaly detection, providing a critical tool for security, risk management, and operational optimization.

AI-Powered Asset Monitoring

Definition
AI-powered asset monitoring refers to the use of artificial intelligence to track, analyze, and manage physical and digital assets in real time. These systems leverage machine learning, computer vision, and IoT sensors to collect data, enabling predictive maintenance, operational efficiency, and asset lifecycle optimization. By using AI, organizations gain deeper insights into asset performance, detect anomalies, and prevent failures before they occur.

Key Components
Data acquisition systems collect information from sensors, cameras, and IoT devices.
Machine learning algorithms analyze historical and real-time data to predict maintenance needs.
Computer vision monitors visual indicators such as wear, damage, or unauthorized access.
Cloud-based platforms store and process asset data for remote access and real-time monitoring.
Predictive analytics models identify potential failures and trigger automated alerts.

Benefits
Reduces downtime through predictive maintenance.
Optimizes resource allocation and extends asset lifespan.
Enhances operational efficiency and security.
Streamlines inventory management and improves compliance.
Enables real-time visibility and faster response to issues.

Examples
Smart manufacturing systems monitoring equipment health.
Energy companies using AI to detect faults in power grids.

Logistics firms tracking vehicle performance and maintenance.
Healthcare facilities overseeing medical equipment readiness.
Retailers applying AI-driven asset tracking for inventory visibility.

Applications
Predictive maintenance, inventory tracking, security surveillance, remote diagnostics, equipment health monitoring, and automated asset audits.

Conclusion
AI-powered asset monitoring enhances asset management by providing real-time insights and predictive capabilities. While cybersecurity and integration remain challenges, AI continues to transform asset-intensive industries with improved reliability, efficiency, and compliance.

AI-Powered Automation

Definition
AI-powered automation refers to the integration of artificial intelligence into automated systems to perform tasks traditionally handled by humans. These systems leverage machine learning, deep learning, natural language processing, and robotics to optimize processes, reduce manual effort, and improve efficiency.

Key Components
Data acquisition and analysis for informed decision-making.
Machine learning algorithms optimize workflows and detect patterns.
Robotic process automation (RPA) executes repetitive tasks autonomously.
Natural language processing enables language-based automation.
Computer vision supports quality control and security tasks.
Integration frameworks connect AI with business systems.

Benefits
Increases operational efficiency and reduces costs.
Minimizes human errors and enhances accuracy.
Frees employees to focus on higher-value tasks.
Improves customer experiences through real-time automation.
Scales operations without proportional workforce increases.

Examples
Chatbots providing automated customer support.
AI-driven fraud detection in banking.
Autonomous vehicles optimizing navigation.
Healthcare systems automating patient data processing.
Manufacturing plants using AI-driven robots for production.

Applications
Intelligent chatbots, autonomous vehicles, predictive maintenance, smart factories, AI-generated content, automated financial transactions, and personalized marketing.

Conclusion
AI-powered automation transforms industries by optimizing workflows and enhancing efficiency. While ethical and technical challenges persist, advancements in AI continue to drive innovation and reshape the future of work.

AI-Powered Decision-Making

Definition
AI-powered decision-making refers to the use of artificial intelligence to analyze data, evaluate

possible outcomes, and recommend or automate optimal choices. These systems use machine learning, deep learning, and analytics to process vast amounts of information quickly and accurately.

Key Components
Data collection and aggregation from multiple sources.
Machine learning algorithms identify patterns and generate insights.
Predictive analytics forecast future scenarios.
Natural language processing interprets human input and contextual data.
Decision support systems balance AI insights with human expertise.
Feedback mechanisms enable continuous learning.

Benefits
Enhances decision accuracy and objectivity.
Speeds up decision-making processes.
Enables analysis of complex and large datasets.
Improves operational efficiency and resource allocation.
Supports risk assessment and fraud detection.

Examples
AI-driven medical diagnosis systems.
Financial institutions assessing credit risks.
Retail optimization of inventory and pricing.
Autonomous vehicles making real-time driving decisions.
AI-powered virtual assistants guiding customer service decisions.

Applications
Business strategy, healthcare diagnostics, financial analysis, supply chain optimization, personalized recommendations, cybersecurity, and government policymaking.

Conclusion
AI-powered decision-making enhances efficiency and accuracy across industries. Addressing ethical and transparency concerns is essential to ensuring responsible and trustworthy AI adoption.

AI-Powered Image Recognition

Definition
AI-powered image recognition is a technology that enables machines to identify, analyze, and interpret images using artificial intelligence. It relies on deep learning and computer vision to recognize patterns, objects, faces, and more.

Key Components
Data preprocessing enhances images for analysis.
Convolutional neural networks (CNNs) extract visual features.
Labeled training datasets improve model accuracy.
Object detection algorithms localize and classify objects.
Image segmentation divides images for detailed analysis.
Real-time processing enables instant recognition.

Benefits
Enhances security through facial recognition.
Improves healthcare diagnostics through medical imaging.
Optimizes quality control in manufacturing.
Supports automated retail experiences and visual search.
Enables real-time analysis for diverse applications.

Examples
Apple's Face ID unlocking devices.
Tesla's AI detecting road elements for navigation.

Healthcare AI analyzing X-rays and MRIs.
Retail visual search and product recommendations.
Smart surveillance with AI-powered monitoring.

Applications
Facial recognition, object detection, medical diagnostics, autonomous vehicles, smart surveillance, augmented reality, and e-commerce.

Conclusion
AI-powered image recognition enhances automation, security, and decision-making across industries. Addressing privacy, bias, and ethical concerns is critical for its responsible deployment.

AI-Powered Job Analysis

Definition
AI-powered job analysis refers to the use of artificial intelligence to assess job roles, responsibilities, and workforce trends to optimize recruitment, performance evaluation, and workforce planning. These systems provide deep insights into job requirements and labor market trends.

Key Components
Automated data collection from job descriptions and labor data.
Natural language processing to extract key competencies.
Machine learning to predict skill gaps and workforce needs.
Classification systems to categorize job roles and skills.
Workforce analytics tools for performance and productivity insights.

Benefits
Enhances recruitment accuracy and workforce planning.
Improves performance management and employee development.
Identifies future skill requirements.
Supports diversity and inclusion initiatives.
Streamlines HR processes.

Examples
LinkedIn's AI-driven recruitment tools.
IBM Watson Talent analyzing workforce trends.
AI-driven candidate assessment platforms.
Automated job description generation.
HR systems providing workforce performance insights.

Applications
Talent acquisition, performance evaluation, workforce training, labor market analysis, and HR automation.

Conclusion
AI-powered job analysis enhances workforce management by providing actionable insights. Ensuring fairness, transparency, and ethical use of AI is key to maximizing its benefits in HR and organizational planning.

AI-Powered Judicial Systems

Definition
AI-powered judicial systems utilize artificial intelligence to assist in legal decision-making, case analysis, and judicial processes. These systems automate legal research, case predictions, and document analysis to enhance judicial efficiency and accuracy.

Key Components
Data collection from legal documents and case law.
Natural language processing to interpret legal texts.
Machine learning models to analyze past case patterns.
Automated legal research and document analysis.
Ethical and fairness modules to align with legal standards.
Secure data management for sensitive information.

Benefits
Increases judicial efficiency and reduces workload.
Enhances accuracy in legal decision-making.
Promotes fairness through data-driven insights.
Automates routine legal research and document tasks.
Supports faster case resolution.

Examples
ROSS Intelligence for AI-driven legal research.
Compas risk assessment tool in judicial processes.
AI-powered virtual judges in some jurisdictions.
Automated transcription and legal chatbots.
AI-assisted case management in courts.

Applications
Legal document automation, predictive analytics for case outcomes, AI-assisted sentencing recommendations, digital dispute resolution, fraud detection, and compliance monitoring.

Conclusion
AI-powered judicial systems enhance the efficiency and fairness of legal processes. Addressing ethical, regulatory, and transparency challenges is vital to building trust and ensuring responsible AI use in the judiciary.

AI-Powered Recommendation Systems

Definition
AI-powered recommendation systems are intelligent algorithms that analyze data patterns to provide personalized suggestions to users. These systems enhance user experiences by predicting preferences and delivering relevant content, products, or services.

Key Components
Data collection, preprocessing, and feature engineering.
Collaborative filtering, content-based filtering, and hybrid models.
Model training and evaluation for accuracy.
Real-time processing to update recommendations dynamically.
Feedback loops for continuous learning and improvement.

Benefits
Enhances user engagement and satisfaction.
Increases revenue through personalized experiences.
Improves customer retention and loyalty.
Optimizes inventory management and marketing strategies.
Reduces information overload.

Examples
Netflix movie suggestions.
Amazon product recommendations.
Spotify personalized playlists.
YouTube and TikTok content feeds.
LinkedIn job and content recommendations.

Applications
E-commerce, entertainment, healthcare, finance, education, online advertising, and personalized learning.

Conclusion
AI-powered recommendation systems transform user experiences by delivering personalized, intelligent suggestions. Addressing privacy, bias, and transparency is essential for responsible and effective use of these systems across industries.

AI Stack

Definition
The AI Stack refers to the layered architecture of technologies, frameworks, and tools that support the development, deployment, and management of artificial intelligence applications. It encompasses everything from data collection to model deployment.

Key Components
Data layer for storage and processing.
Machine learning frameworks such as TensorFlow and PyTorch.
Model training environments.
Deployment platforms, including cloud services.
APIs for system integration.

Benefits
Streamlines AI development and deployment.
Supports scalability and flexibility.
Promotes interoperability between components.
Accelerates innovation in AI applications.

Applications
AI development environments.
Cloud-based AI services.
Enterprise AI platforms.
Integrated AI solutions across industries.

Conclusion
The AI Stack forms the backbone of AI infrastructure, enabling efficient development and deployment of AI solutions. While it accelerates innovation, it also requires careful management to address integration and security challenges.

AI Traffic Generator

Definition
An AI traffic generator is a system that uses artificial intelligence to simulate or create realistic traffic patterns, behaviors, or data. These generators model vehicle flow, network traffic, or pedestrian movement for testing and planning purposes.

Key Components
Machine learning models and rule-based simulations.
Synthetic data generation and reinforcement learning.
Scenario-based training environments with virtual sensors.
Decision agents and behavior prediction systems.

Benefits
Enables safe, cost-effective testing of AI systems.
Eliminates the need for risky real-world trials.

Accelerates development cycles and model generalization.
Models rare or extreme scenarios for robust training.

Examples
Simulating traffic for autonomous vehicle testing.
Generating network traffic to test cybersecurity systems.
Modeling smart city traffic flows.
Simulating pedestrian behavior in gaming or urban planning.

Applications
Training autonomous vehicles.
Evaluating smart city traffic systems.
Testing communication networks and cybersecurity platforms.
Developing AI agents for simulations and games.

Conclusion
AI traffic generators replicate real-world dynamics for AI training and testing. They enhance safety and adaptability across multiple domains and are essential tools for developing intelligent, resilient systems.

Algorithm Engineering

Definition
Algorithm engineering is the practical discipline of designing, building, and refining algorithms to solve real-world problems with efficiency and reliability. It bridges theoretical computer science and applied software development.

Key Components
Understanding problem domains and defining objectives.
Mathematical modeling and resource optimization.
Coding and implementation in languages like Python or Rust.
Testing and profiling under real-world conditions.
Iterative refinement based on performance feedback.

Benefits
Delivers faster, smarter, and more efficient systems.
Reduces operational costs through optimization.
Enhances user experiences through improved performance.
Enables breakthroughs in data processing and automation.

Examples
Feed-ranking algorithms on social media platforms.
Pathfinding optimization in navigation apps.
AI opponents adapting in real-time in games.
Real-time financial transaction processing.

Conclusion
Algorithm engineering transforms theoretical designs into practical solutions. As reliance on data-driven systems grows, this discipline will remain critical to innovation across industries.

Alignment (Artificial Intelligence)

Definition
Alignment in artificial intelligence refers to designing AI systems that reliably act according to human intentions, values, ethics, and expectations. It ensures AI behavior remains predictable, beneficial, and safe.

Key Components
Capturing and understanding human intentions.
Integrating ethical and moral standards into AI design.
Ensuring transparency and predictability in AI behavior.
Maintaining accountability and human oversight.

Benefits
Enhances safety and trust in AI systems.
Prevents harmful or unintended behaviors.
Supports responsible and ethical AI use.
Promotes acceptance of AI technologies in society.

Applications
Self-driving cars and ethical decision-making.
Bias prevention in medical diagnosis AI.
Behavior consistency in personal AI assistants.
Fairness in AI used in finance and law enforcement.

Examples of Alignment Failures
Unsafe driving decisions by autonomous systems.
Social media algorithms promoting harmful content.

Conclusion
AI alignment ensures that AI serves human interests responsibly. It remains a vital area of research and innovation as AI systems grow in capability and influence.

Amalgamated AI Models

Definition
Amalgamated AI Models refer to the combination of multiple artificial intelligence models or techniques to improve performance, accuracy, and robustness in complex tasks.

Key Components
Ensemble learning techniques.
Hybrid models combining supervised and unsupervised learning.
Model fusion strategies.
Integration frameworks for cohesive performance.

Benefits
Enhances predictive accuracy and adaptability.
Reduces model bias.
Increases robustness to diverse data.
Improves generalization and reliability.

Applications
Fraud detection systems.
Medical diagnostics.
Natural language processing applications.
Autonomous vehicle technologies.

Conclusion
Amalgamated AI Models offer superior performance for complex problems. Careful design is needed to balance computational costs with transparency and interpretability.

Amazon AI for Healthcare

Definition
Amazon AI for Healthcare refers to a suite of AI tools and services on AWS that enhance healthcare operations and patient care. These tools process medical data to improve diagnostics, workflows, and treatment personalization.

Key Components
Amazon Comprehend Medical for NLP-based text analysis.
Amazon Transcribe Medical for speech-to-text conversion.
Amazon SageMaker for machine learning model development.
AWS Lambda and Amazon Rekognition for custom integrations and image analysis.

Benefits
Automates clinical data processing.
Improves diagnostic accuracy.
Enables scalable and cost-effective solutions.
Supports personalized patient care.

Examples
Hospitals using Amazon Comprehend Medical to analyze clinical notes and flag high-risk patients.
Speech transcription for accurate medical records.
Predictive analytics for early disease detection.

Applications
Clinical text analysis and transcription.
Health risk prediction.
Medical imaging analysis.
Administrative task automation.

Conclusion
Amazon AI for Healthcare drives efficiency and precision in healthcare delivery. Despite integration and security challenges, it is reshaping clinical workflows and patient care.

Ambient Assisted Living (AAL)

Definition
Ambient Assisted Living (AAL) integrates smart technologies into living environments to enhance quality of life for elderly individuals and people with disabilities. It supports independence, health monitoring, and safety through AI and IoT.

Key Components
Sensors and wearables for health and environmental monitoring.
Smart devices for home automation and convenience.
AI for personalized assistance and decision-making.
IoT connectivity for remote monitoring and caregiver alerts.

Benefits
Promotes independence in daily living.
Provides remote monitoring and timely alerts.
Supports early detection of health issues.
Enhances quality of life through adaptive environments.

Examples
Smart homes adjusting to user routines.
Wearable devices tracking vital signs.
Voice assistants for medication reminders.
Fall detection systems triggering emergency responses.

Conclusion
Ambient Assisted Living empowers individuals by creating supportive, intelligent environments. While privacy and reliability challenges must be addressed, AAL represents a promising advancement in personalized care and quality of life.

Ambient Data Analytics in AI

Definition
Ambient Data Analytics in AI involves collecting, processing, and analyzing data from environmental sources in real time to extract insights and drive intelligent actions. It allows AI systems to respond dynamically to their surroundings.

Key Components
Sensors and IoT devices for data collection.
Data processing and storage infrastructure.
Machine learning and AI algorithms for real-time analysis.
System integration for actionable insights.
Real-time analytics capabilities.

Benefits
Improves decision-making through context-aware insights.
Optimizes resource use and operational efficiency.
Enables personalized, adaptive user experiences.
Supports early anomaly detection and proactive intervention.

Examples
Smart cities optimizing traffic, air quality, and energy use.
Ambient Assisted Living systems for healthcare monitoring.
Retail analytics tracking in-store customer behavior.
Environmental monitoring in smart agriculture.

Conclusion
Ambient Data Analytics transforms environmental data into intelligent actions. While data management and privacy remain key challenges, its potential for creating responsive, user-centric systems is immense.

Ambient Intelligence (AmI)

Definition
Ambient Intelligence (AmI) refers to intelligent systems embedded in everyday environments that adapt to human presence and needs. These systems provide seamless, context-aware services through AI, sensors, and connectivity.

Key Components
Sensors and wearables for data collection.
AI and machine learning for context interpretation.
Connectivity through IoT for system integration.
Adaptive user interfaces for interaction.
Learning and personalization capabilities.

Benefits
Automates routine tasks and enhances convenience.
Improves safety through monitoring and alerts.
Personalizes services to individual needs.
Enhances healthcare, retail, and smart home experiences.

Examples
Smart homes adjusting lighting and temperature.
Healthcare wearables for patient monitoring.
Retail environments offering personalized experiences.
Security systems with adaptive surveillance.

Conclusion
Ambient Intelligence creates responsive, adaptive environments. As AI and IoT technologies evolve, AmI will increasingly shape how we live and interact with our surroundings.

Ambient Intelligence in Smart Cities

Definition
Ambient Intelligence in Smart Cities refers to the integration of advanced technologies to create urban environments that are intelligent, adaptive, and responsive to the needs of their residents. It combines AI, sensors, and connected systems to collect and analyze urban data in real time, supporting efficient and sustainable city management.

Key Components
Citywide networks of sensors and IoT devices.
AI and machine learning platforms to process and analyze urban data.
High-speed connectivity (e.g., 5G) for seamless data flow.
User interfaces enabling citizens to access personalized services.
Data analytics tools providing actionable insights to city administrators.

Examples
Smart traffic lights adjusting signal timing to reduce congestion.
Energy systems optimizing the use of renewable power sources.
Real-time surveillance alerting responders to safety incidents.
Smart waste collection with bins that notify crews when full.
Personalized alerts for residents on health or transportation updates.

Benefits
Increases efficiency in resource usage (water, power, transportation).
Improves public safety through faster response to incidents.
Reduces emissions and supports environmental sustainability.
Enhances citizen experiences with personalized, data-driven services.
Provides data-driven insights to inform city planning and policy.

Conclusion
Ambient Intelligence in Smart Cities enables responsive, efficient, and citizen-centric urban environments. While privacy and integration challenges must be addressed, its potential to improve urban life and sustainability makes it a key technology for the future of city development.

Ambient Learning Systems

Definition
Ambient Learning Systems leverage AI to deliver personalized, context-aware educational experiences that adapt to learners' environments, behaviors, and preferences. These systems provide continuous learning opportunities, seamlessly integrated into everyday settings.

Key Components
AI-powered monitoring of learner behavior and environment.
Real-time feedback and adaptive content delivery.
Integration with mobile devices, wearables, and connected technologies.
Personalization engines tailoring educational content to individual needs.

Benefits
Delivers dynamic, engaging learning tailored to individual styles.
Supports learning anytime, anywhere through contextual adaptation.
Improves knowledge retention through personalized experiences.
Enhances learner engagement and motivation.

Applications
Adaptive learning platforms in education.
Corporate training systems providing role-specific content.
Mobile apps for personalized skill development and lifelong learning.

Conclusion
Ambient Learning Systems offer a transformative approach to education by delivering context-sensitive, personalized learning experiences. Addressing privacy and development challenges will be key to their broader adoption across both academic and professional learning environments.

Ambient Sound Recognition in AI

Definition
Ambient Sound Recognition in AI enables systems to identify, analyze, and interpret environmental sounds in real time. Using machine learning and signal processing, these systems recognize sounds such as footsteps, alarms, voices, and other audio events, enabling smart, automated responses.

Key Components
Sound identification and categorization models.
Context-aware sound analysis capabilities.
Real-time processing of audio data streams.
Advanced noise filtering for improved accuracy.
Integration with IoT devices for responsive actions.

Benefits
Enhances security by detecting critical sounds and triggering alerts.
Improves accessibility for users with hearing impairments.
Automates smart home functions based on sound detection.
Supports healthcare monitoring through analysis of patient sounds.
Enriches human-computer interaction with responsive audio processing.

Applications
Home security systems detecting alarms and break-ins.
Healthcare monitoring systems recognizing distress sounds.
Smart home assistants responding to voice commands and environmental cues.
Public safety systems identifying emergency sounds in urban settings.
Elder care monitoring systems tracking potential risks via sound.

Challenges
Ensuring accuracy in noisy or unpredictable environments.
Balancing privacy with sound monitoring.
Managing computational demands for real-time audio processing.
Maintaining reliability across varied contexts and sound profiles.

Conclusion
Ambient Sound Recognition enhances security, accessibility, and automation by enabling AI systems

to interpret and respond to environmental sounds. Addressing privacy and performance challenges will further unlock its potential across diverse applications.

Ambiguity Resolution in AI

Definition
Ambiguity Resolution in AI involves identifying and clarifying data, language, or signals that may have multiple interpretations. AI systems resolve ambiguity through contextual analysis and machine learning, enabling more accurate decision-making and improved interaction with humans.

Key Components
Context analysis to interpret surrounding information.
Machine learning models predicting likely meanings.
Semantic processing to assess meaning and relationships.
Algorithms weighing potential interpretations based on patterns.

Benefits
Improves accuracy and reliability in natural language processing.
Enhances AI decision-making across various domains.
Enables more intuitive interactions with users.
Supports automation of complex, context-dependent tasks.

Applications
Chatbots interpreting ambiguous user commands.
Natural language processing systems resolving pronoun references.
Autonomous vehicles interpreting unclear road signs or behavior.
Image recognition distinguishing visually similar objects through context.

Examples
Determining whether "it" refers to a phone or a service in a customer query.
Clarifying whether "he" refers to Tom or Sam in ambiguous text.

Conclusion
Ambiguity Resolution is crucial for effective AI performance in real-world applications. Continued advancements in machine learning and contextual understanding are key to improving AI's ability to handle uncertainty and ambiguity.

Amodal Perception in AI

Definition
Amodal Perception in AI refers to the system's ability to perceive and interpret objects or environments beyond what is directly visible or sensed. AI systems apply learned knowledge to mentally reconstruct parts of objects that are hidden or occluded.

Key Components
Deep learning models for prediction and reconstruction.
Computer vision systems interpreting incomplete visual data.
Pattern recognition algorithms for object completion.
Generative models to infer missing structures.

Benefits
Enables accurate decision-making with incomplete data.
Enhances robustness in real-world environments.
Improves safety in applications like autonomous driving.
Supports advanced capabilities in medical imaging and robotics.

Applications
Autonomous vehicles detecting partially obscured pedestrians.
Robotics systems navigating environments with occluded objects.
Medical imaging reconstructing incomplete scans.
Security systems interpreting obscured video footage.

Examples
A vehicle predicting the full presence of a pedestrian behind a parked car.
AI reconstructing missing parts of an organ in medical imaging.

Conclusion
Amodal Perception significantly enhances AI's ability to operate effectively in complex, dynamic environments. Ongoing improvements in deep learning and computer vision will continue to expand its role across various industries.

Amplitude Encoding in Quantum AI

Definition
Amplitude Encoding in Quantum AI is a technique for representing classical data within the amplitude of a quantum state's wave function. It enables compact and efficient data representation, facilitating faster quantum computations.

Key Components
Quantum bits (qubits) encoding classical data.
Wave functions representing amplitude information.
Quantum circuits preparing and transforming data states.
Quantum gates controlling data manipulation.

Benefits
Enables efficient representation of large datasets.
Supports parallel processing and quantum speedups.
Improves performance of quantum machine learning algorithms.
Enhances capabilities in quantum optimization and simulations.

Applications
Quantum machine learning for pattern recognition.
Quantum optimization for financial modeling.
Quantum simulations in physics, chemistry, and biology.
Efficient data processing in large-scale quantum systems.

Examples
Encoding image pixel values for quantum image classification.
Modeling complex financial systems for portfolio optimization.

Conclusion
Amplitude Encoding is a foundational technique in Quantum AI, enabling compact, high-performance data representation. Continued advancements in quantum hardware and algorithms are essential to fully realize its potential.

Analogical Reasoning in AI

Definition
Analogical Reasoning in AI enables systems to identify relationships between different concepts or scenarios based on structural or contextual similarities. It allows AI to solve new problems by drawing parallels with past experiences, mimicking human cognitive reasoning.

Key Components
Pattern recognition to identify structural similarities.
Knowledge representation using semantic networks and ontologies.
Case-based reasoning applying past solutions to new problems.
Machine learning models generalizing knowledge across contexts.

Benefits
Enhances creative problem-solving and adaptability.
Improves learning efficiency by leveraging prior knowledge.
Supports decision-making in unfamiliar situations.
Facilitates knowledge transfer across domains.

Applications
Natural language processing understanding metaphors and analogies.
Recommendation systems suggesting products based on user history.
Medical diagnosis comparing patient cases.
Robotics adapting to new tasks using known patterns.

Examples
An AI understanding that a heart functions like a pump.
A chatbot relating new customer queries to previously solved issues.

Conclusion
Analogical Reasoning enhances AI's capacity for cross-domain learning and problem-solving. It is a valuable tool for building more adaptable and cognitively sophisticated AI systems.

Anaphora Resolution in AI

Definition
Anaphora Resolution in AI refers to identifying the antecedent that a pronoun or referring expression points to in text. It enables AI to maintain coherence and understanding across sentences, a critical component of natural language processing.

Key Components
Recognition of anaphoric expressions (e.g., pronouns).
Identification of potential antecedents.
Resolution algorithms selecting the most likely antecedent.
Contextual understanding to maintain coherence.

Benefits
Improves AI comprehension of natural language.
Enhances accuracy in chatbots, translation, and summarization.
Supports more natural and human-like interactions.
Enables better extraction of meaning from complex texts.

Applications
Chatbots maintaining conversation context.
Machine translation preserving correct references.
Text summarization ensuring clarity of subject references.
Sentiment analysis linking sentiment to correct entities.

Examples
Resolving "he" in "Mark finished his homework, and he went to bed."
Maintaining clarity in translated or summarized text.

Conclusion
Anaphora Resolution is essential for effective natural language understanding in AI. Advances in

contextual modeling and large language models continue to enhance AI's ability to resolve anaphora accurately and intuitively.

Annotated Dataset in AI

Definition
An Annotated Dataset in AI is a collection of data that has been labeled with tags or annotations to provide meaning and structure. These annotations guide AI systems during training, allowing them to learn patterns and perform tasks accurately.

Key Components
Raw data collection from relevant sources.
Annotation guidelines ensuring consistency.
Labeling by human annotators or automated systems.
Quality assurance and validation.
Dataset preparation for AI model training.

Benefits
Enables supervised learning for AI model development.
Improves model accuracy and adaptability.
Provides benchmarks for evaluating AI performance.
Supports reuse across multiple projects and domains.

Applications
Natural language processing with labeled text data.
Computer vision with annotated images.
Speech recognition with paired audio and transcripts.
Medical imaging with annotated scans.

Examples
Images labeled with objects for self-driving cars.
Medical records annotated for disease detection.
Speech data tagged for voice recognition systems.

Conclusion
Annotated Datasets are a cornerstone of AI development, providing the structured input necessary for training accurate and reliable models. Their value continues to grow as AI expands into new applications and industries.

Anomaly Detection in AI

Definition
Anomaly Detection in AI involves identifying patterns in data that deviate significantly from expected norms. AI-powered anomaly detection uses machine learning and statistical analysis to detect unusual events or behaviors across diverse domains.

Key Components
Machine learning models (supervised, unsupervised, semi-supervised).
Feature engineering to enhance detection accuracy.
Statistical models to identify deviations.
Real-time monitoring of data streams.
Threshold-based detection with adaptive capabilities.

Benefits
Enhances security by identifying fraud and cyber threats.
Supports predictive maintenance to prevent system failures.

Improves operational efficiency through early issue detection.
Automates monitoring, reducing human intervention.

Applications
Fraud prevention in banking and online transactions.
Healthcare monitoring for early disease detection.
Cybersecurity threat detection.
Predictive maintenance in manufacturing.

Conclusion
Anomaly Detection is a vital AI capability for risk management and system monitoring. By leveraging AI and advanced analytics, organizations can detect issues early, enhance security, and maintain efficient operations across industries.

Anonymization in AI

Anonymization is the process of removing or encrypting personally identifiable information (PII) from datasets to protect user privacy while allowing data to be used for machine learning and analytics. It ensures that AI models can learn from data without exposing sensitive details.

Key components of anonymization in AI include data masking, differential privacy, encryption techniques, k-anonymity, and synthetic data generation.

The benefits of anonymization include enhanced data privacy, compliance with regulations such as GDPR and HIPAA, reduced risk of data breaches, and the ability to share data securely across organizations. Features include real-time data anonymization, irreversible transformation methods, access controls, and audit logs to ensure compliance.

Examples of anonymization tools include Google's differential privacy library, IBM's data anonymization solutions, and Microsoft's privacy-preserving AI techniques. Applications include healthcare data sharing, financial transactions, smart city analytics, and AI-driven customer insights.

Industries utilizing anonymization in AI include healthcare, finance, government, telecommunications, and cybersecurity.

In summary, anonymization in AI is essential for ethical and legal AI development, but it requires continuous innovation to address evolving privacy threats while maintaining data usability.

Ant Colony Optimization (ACO)

Ant Colony Optimization is a swarm intelligence-based algorithm inspired by the foraging behavior of ants, used to solve complex optimization problems by simulating how ants find the shortest paths to food sources. It is particularly effective for combinatorial optimization and dynamic problem-solving.

Key components of ACO include pheromone trails, heuristic functions, probability-based decision-making, local and global updating rules, and multi-agent interaction.

The benefits of ACO include adaptability to dynamic environments, efficient problem-solving in complex scenarios, parallel processing capabilities, and robustness against local optima.

Features include self-organizing search behavior, reinforcement learning through pheromone updates, scalability, and suitability for large-scale optimization problems.

Examples of ACO applications include optimizing network routing in telecommunications, solving the traveling salesman problem, warehouse logistics optimization, and scheduling problems in manufacturing.

Applications extend to traffic management, robotics path planning, supply chain optimization, and financial portfolio management. Industries leveraging ACO include logistics, transportation, telecommunications, manufacturing, and finance.

In summary, ACO provides a powerful bio-inspired optimization technique that enhances decision-making and resource allocation, though fine-tuning is necessary to achieve optimal performance in diverse real-world scenarios

Anticipatory Computing

Anticipatory Computing is an AI-driven approach that predicts user needs and behaviors before they explicitly request information or services, enabling proactive decision-making and personalized experiences. It relies on continuous data analysis, predictive modeling, and real-time user interaction tracking to deliver relevant content, recommendations, or actions.

Key components of anticipatory computing include machine learning algorithms, behavioral analytics, real-time data processing, contextual awareness, and adaptive AI models.

The benefits of anticipatory computing include enhanced user experience, increased efficiency in service delivery, improved customer engagement, and automation of routine tasks.

Features include real-time data interpretation, intelligent recommendations, personalized automation, and predictive analytics for user intent recognition.

Examples of anticipatory computing include Google Now, Amazon's recommendation engine, predictive text input on smartphones, and AI-powered virtual assistants that suggest actions before they are explicitly requested.

Applications span across e-commerce, digital marketing, healthcare monitoring, smart home automation, and personalized learning platforms.

Industries adopting anticipatory computing include retail, finance, healthcare, smart technology, and entertainment. Challenges include ethical concerns regarding data privacy, the risk of over-reliance on AI predictions, biases in predictive models, and user apprehension about AI-driven decision-making.

In summary, anticipatory computing enhances AI-driven personalization and automation, but responsible implementation is necessary to address privacy and ethical implications while maintaining user trust.

Application Programming Interface (API)

Application Programming Interface is a set of rules, protocols, and tools that enable different software applications to communicate and interact with each other, allowing seamless integration of services and data exchange between systems. APIs serve as intermediaries that facilitate interoperability across various platforms, enabling developers to build and extend functionalities efficiently.

Key components of APIs include endpoints, request and response structures, authentication mechanisms, API gateways, and data formats such as JSON and XML.

The benefits of APIs include improved software modularity, faster development cycles, enhanced scalability, and the ability to leverage third-party services without reinventing functionality.

Features include standardized communication protocols, security controls, versioning capabilities, and support for multiple programming languages.

Examples of widely used APIs include the Google Maps API for geolocation services, Stripe API for payment processing, Twitter API for social media integration, and OpenAI API for AI-driven text generation.

Applications extend to web development, mobile applications, cloud computing, IoT connectivity, and AI model integration.

Industries leveraging APIs include technology, fintech, healthcare, telecommunications, and automotive.

In summary, APIs are essential for modern software development and integration, enabling seamless connectivity and innovation, though proper security and maintenance are required to prevent vulnerabilities and ensure long-term reliability.

Applied Artificial Intelligence (Applied AI) refers to the practical implementation of AI technologies in real-world scenarios to solve specific problems and enhance business processes. Unlike theoretical AI research, which focuses on developing new algorithms and models, applied AI emphasizes deploying existing AI frameworks to achieve measurable outcomes.

Key components include machine learning models, natural language processing, computer vision, and neural networks integrated into industry applications.

The benefits of applied AI include improved operational efficiency, automation of complex tasks, enhanced decision-making, and cost reduction.

Features include real-time data processing, adaptive learning, AI-driven predictions, and human-AI collaboration.

Examples of applied AI include chatbots for customer service, AI-powered fraud detection in banking, autonomous vehicle navigation, and medical image analysis for diagnostics.

Applications span across automated business processes, predictive analytics, AI-driven content generation, and healthcare decision support. Industries leveraging applied AI include healthcare, finance, manufacturing, retail, and logistics.

In summary, applied AI transforms industries by enhancing efficiency and decision-making, though it requires careful implementation to address ethical, regulatory, and technical challenges.

Applied Machine Learning (AML)

Applied Machine Learning focuses on the practical use of machine learning models to solve specific problems in various domains. It involves selecting, training, and deploying machine learning algorithms to analyze patterns, make predictions, and optimize decision-making processes.

Key components of applied machine learning include data preprocessing, feature engineering, model selection, hyperparameter tuning, and evaluation metrics.

The benefits of AML include automation of data analysis, improved accuracy in decision-making, adaptability to dynamic environments, and scalability for large datasets. Features include supervised and unsupervised learning capabilities, real-time model training, deep learning integration, and explainable AI for transparency.

Examples of applied machine learning include recommendation systems in streaming platforms, AI-driven supply chain optimization, sentiment analysis in social media monitoring, and predictive maintenance in industrial equipment.

Applications extend to fraud detection, financial risk assessment, personalized marketing, medical diagnostics, and speech recognition. Industries utilizing AML include healthcare, finance, e-commerce, automotive, and cybersecurity.

In summary, applied machine learning enables organizations to leverage AI for data-driven insights and automation, but careful monitoring is required to mitigate biases and maintain model reliability.

Approximate Nearest Neighbor (ANN)

Approximate Nearest Neighbor (ANN) Search is a technique used in machine learning and data science to quickly identify data points that are most similar to a given query point in high-dimensional spaces. It is widely used when exact nearest neighbor search is computationally expensive or impractical due to large dataset sizes.

Key components of ANN search include dimensionality reduction, locality-sensitive hashing, clustering algorithms, and distance metrics such as Euclidean distance and cosine similarity.

The benefits of ANN search include faster retrieval times, scalability for large datasets, efficient indexing, and improved search accuracy in high-dimensional spaces.

Features include adaptive indexing structures, probabilistic search methods, and support for real-time query processing.

Examples of ANN search applications include recommendation systems, image recognition, natural language processing, and search engines that provide relevant results based on similarity.

Applications extend to AI-driven personalization, e-commerce product recommendations, fraud detection, and anomaly detection in cybersecurity. Industries utilizing ANN search include retail, healthcare, finance, autonomous systems, and digital media.

Challenges include trade-offs between search accuracy and speed, sensitivity to noise in high-dimensional data, computational overhead for indexing large datasets, and limitations in handling dynamically changing data.

In summary, approximate nearest neighbor search is a crucial tool for fast similarity-based searches, but careful algorithm selection and optimization are required to balance speed and precision in real-world applications.

Approximate Policy Iteration (API)

Approximate Policy Iteration (API) is a reinforcement learning technique that approximates the optimal policy for decision-making in environments where exact solutions are computationally intractable. It combines policy evaluation and policy improvement steps iteratively to refine an agent's decision-making process based on reward functions.

Key components of API include policy evaluation, policy improvement, value function approximation, function approximation methods such as neural networks, and sampling techniques to estimate transition dynamics.

The benefits of API include improved efficiency in learning policies for complex tasks, reduced computational cost compared to exact dynamic programming, scalability for large state-action spaces, and adaptability to real-world uncertainties. Features include adaptive learning rates, stochastic gradient descent optimization, deep reinforcement learning integration, and sample-efficient learning techniques.

Examples of API include its use in AI-driven robotics for motion planning, financial trading algorithms, adaptive game-playing agents, and autonomous vehicle decision-making.

Applications extend to industrial automation, personalized marketing strategies, healthcare treatment planning, and smart grid energy management.

Industries utilizing API include robotics, gaming, finance, healthcare, and smart infrastructure.

Challenges include sample inefficiency in reinforcement learning, policy convergence issues, instability in function approximation, and sensitivity to hyperparameter tuning.

In summary, approximate policy iteration is an effective reinforcement learning approach for solving complex decision-making problems, though fine-tuning and optimization are necessary to ensure reliable performance in real-world applications.

Approximation Theory in AI

Approximation Theory in AI focuses on mathematical techniques used to approximate complex functions, models, and solutions when exact computation is infeasible. It is essential in areas such as machine learning, numerical optimization, and probabilistic modeling, where exact representations are computationally expensive or impossible to derive.

Key components of approximation theory in AI include polynomial approximations, neural network function approximators, Fourier transforms, basis function expansion, and error estimation techniques.

The benefits of approximation theory include reduced computational complexity, improved generalization in machine learning models, enhanced efficiency in AI-driven decision-making, and the ability to model uncertain or noisy data.

Features include adaptive learning mechanisms, loss function minimization, gradient-based optimization, and regularization techniques to control overfitting.

Examples of approximation theory in AI include neural network approximators in deep learning, kernel methods in support vector machines, Taylor series approximations in optimization algorithms, and Monte Carlo simulations for probabilistic inference. Applications extend to natural language processing, predictive analytics, AI-driven control systems, and real-time sensor data processing.

Industries benefiting from approximation theory include healthcare, autonomous systems, financial modeling, robotics, and artificial intelligence research.

Challenges include balancing approximation accuracy with computational efficiency, handling high-dimensional function spaces, avoiding overfitting in complex models, and ensuring robustness in real-world applications.

In summary, approximation theory in AI enables efficient modeling and computation for AI-driven solutions, though careful consideration of trade-offs between accuracy and efficiency is necessary to achieve optimal results.

Approximative Algorithms

Approximative Algorithms are computational methods designed to find near-optimal solutions for complex optimization problems where exact solutions are infeasible due to time constraints or computational limitations. These algorithms provide efficient and practical solutions by trading off accuracy for faster computation.

Key components include heuristic functions, probabilistic approaches, iterative refinement techniques, and performance evaluation metrics that measure solution quality.

The benefits of approximative algorithms include reduced computational complexity, scalability for large datasets, flexibility in problem-solving, and improved efficiency for real-time applications.

Features include adaptive search mechanisms, dynamic optimization strategies, polynomial-time computation, and robust handling of incomplete data.

Examples of approximative algorithms include the greedy algorithm for scheduling problems, genetic algorithms for optimization tasks, simulated annealing for combinatorial search, and approximation schemes for network routing.

Applications extend to resource allocation, machine learning model tuning, logistics optimization, and graph-based search problems. Industries applying approximative algorithms include transportation, telecommunications, artificial intelligence, supply chain management, and finance.

In summary, approximative algorithms provide a practical approach to solving computationally intensive problems, though selecting the right technique and fine-tuning parameters are crucial for achieving reliable results.

Approximate Bayesian Computation Approximate Bayesian Computation (ABC) is a statistical inference method used to estimate the parameters of complex probabilistic models when traditional likelihood-based approaches are computationally infeasible. It relies on simulation-based techniques to approximate posterior distributions without requiring explicit likelihood functions.

Key components include Bayesian inference principles, Monte Carlo methods, rejection sampling, and summary statistics to evaluate data similarity.

The benefits of ABC include its ability to handle high-dimensional data, flexibility in modeling real-world uncertainty, robustness against incomplete data, and applicability to complex systems with unknown likelihoods. Features include iterative parameter estimation, posterior probability computation, adaptive sampling techniques, and integration with machine learning frameworks.

Examples of ABC applications include evolutionary biology for genetic parameter estimation, epidemiological modeling for disease spread prediction, ecological data analysis for species distribution, and finance for risk assessment models.

Applications extend to physics simulations, climate science modeling, bioinformatics, and robotics uncertainty estimation. Industries utilizing ABC include healthcare, environmental science, quantitative finance, artificial intelligence research, and engineering.

In summary, approximate Bayesian computation enables researchers to infer model parameters in complex systems without explicit likelihood functions, but optimization techniques are necessary to enhance efficiency and accuracy.

AQL (Analytical Query Language)

AQL (Analytical Query Language) is a specialized query language designed for performing complex analytical operations on structured and semi-structured data. It is optimized for querying large datasets efficiently, enabling users to extract insights, perform aggregations, and conduct statistical analysis with minimal computational overhead.

Key components of AQL include data retrieval syntax, aggregation functions, filtering mechanisms, indexing structures, and integration with data visualization tools.

The benefits of AQL include faster query execution, support for real-time data analytics, enhanced flexibility in data exploration, and compatibility with big data systems.

Features include support for multi-dimensional queries, real-time data processing, optimized execution plans, and built-in machine learning capabilities for advanced analytics.

Examples of AQL implementations include ArangoDB's AQL for graph databases, IBM's AQL for unstructured data analysis, and NoSQL databases that provide analytical querying functionalities.

Applications extend to business intelligence reporting, fraud detection, predictive maintenance, personalized customer insights, and financial risk assessment. Industries utilizing AQL include banking, e-commerce, healthcare, telecommunications, and data science.

Challenges include query complexity for non-technical users, optimization overhead for large-scale queries, integration with legacy data systems, and security considerations for handling sensitive analytical data.

In summary, AQL plays a crucial role in modern data analytics by enabling efficient querying and analysis of large datasets, though ongoing advancements are needed to improve usability, scalability, and integration with emerging AI-driven analytics platforms.

Aquatic AI Ethics

Aquatic AI Ethics focuses on the ethical principles governing the development and deployment of artificial intelligence systems in aquatic environments. It ensures that AI applications in oceans, rivers, and lakes adhere to sustainability, marine conservation, and responsible data usage.

Key components include environmental impact assessment, AI-driven decision-making transparency, regulatory frameworks, and guidelines for ethical marine research.

The benefits of aquatic AI ethics include the protection of marine ecosystems, responsible AI deployment for ocean monitoring, prevention of unethical exploitation of marine resources, and sustainable development in underwater AI applications.

Features include AI transparency protocols, ethical risk assessments, marine biodiversity protection measures, and compliance with international environmental laws.

Examples include ethical AI frameworks for autonomous underwater vehicles, AI-driven fisheries management solutions, and environmental monitoring systems that adhere to marine conservation policies.

Applications extend to oceanographic research, climate change monitoring, AI-assisted underwater exploration, and sustainable fishing practices. Industries utilizing aquatic AI ethics include marine biology, oceanography, maritime security, fisheries management, and underwater robotics.

Challenges include balancing AI innovation with marine ecosystem preservation, addressing data privacy concerns in underwater monitoring, ensuring AI transparency in autonomous marine systems, and mitigating unintended environmental impacts.

In summary, aquatic AI ethics is essential for guiding responsible AI deployment in marine environments, ensuring technological advancements align with sustainability and ecological conservation.

Aquatic Biocomputing

Aquatic Biocomputing is an emerging field that explores the use of biological organisms and systems found in aquatic environments for computational purposes. It involves leveraging marine bio-inspired materials, DNA computing, and biochemical processes to develop next-generation computing technologies.

Key components include bio-based computational circuits, synthetic biology frameworks, DNA nanotechnology, and bioelectronic interfaces.

The benefits of aquatic biocomputing include energy-efficient computing, new data processing paradigms, integration with marine ecosystems for real-time environmental sensing, and the potential for biological data storage.

Features include biomolecular information processing, self-healing biological circuits, water-based biochip technology, and adaptive biochemical computation.

Examples include DNA-based computing for marine research, bio-sensors that detect ocean pollutants, and bioengineered neural networks inspired by aquatic organisms. Applications extend to underwater environmental monitoring, bioinformatics, marine resource management, and sustainable biotechnology development.

Industries exploring aquatic biocomputing include bioengineering, nanotechnology, synthetic biology, marine research, and environmental science.

Challenges include scalability limitations in bio-based computing, maintaining stability in underwater conditions, ethical considerations regarding genetic manipulation, and the high complexity of integrating biological and computational systems.

In summary, aquatic biocomputing presents innovative opportunities for merging biology with computing, though extensive research is needed to develop practical applications while addressing ethical and technical constraints.

Aquatic Drones

Aquatic Drones are autonomous or remotely operated robotic systems designed for underwater exploration, surveillance, and data collection in aquatic environments. These drones are equipped with advanced sensors, AI-driven navigation systems, and communication technologies to operate efficiently in submerged conditions.

Key components include sonar-based mapping systems, underwater propulsion mechanisms, AI-powered obstacle avoidance, and real-time data transmission capabilities.

The benefits of aquatic drones include enhanced ocean exploration, improved efficiency in underwater research, cost-effective marine surveillance, and reduced human risk in deep-sea operations.

Features include real-time imaging, autonomous mission planning, adaptive environmental sensing, and long-duration underwater operation.

Examples include autonomous underwater vehicles (AUVs) used in deep-sea exploration, remotely operated vehicles (ROVs) for oil and gas inspections, and AI-powered drones for coral reef monitoring.

Applications extend to oceanographic research, military surveillance, deep-sea mining, underwater pipeline inspections, and search-and-rescue missions.

Industries utilizing aquatic drones include marine research, defense, offshore energy, environmental conservation, and commercial shipping.

In summary, aquatic drones are revolutionizing marine exploration and industry operations, though advancements in AI, communication, and sustainability are required to maximize their potential while minimizing environmental impact.

Aquatic Machine Learning

Aquatic Machine Learing is the application of artificial intelligence and data-driven models to analyze, predict, and optimize aquatic and marine-related processes. It integrates machine learning algorithms with oceanographic data, environmental monitoring systems, and marine resource management tools to enhance decision-making in underwater environments.

Key components include neural networks for marine data analysis, AI-driven predictive modeling, sensor-based data collection, and real-time anomaly detection systems.

The benefits of aquatic machine learning include improved accuracy in oceanographic research, enhanced climate change monitoring, automation of marine resource management, and efficient underwater ecosystem tracking. Features include deep learning for underwater image recognition, real-time marine data analytics, AI-assisted marine forecasting, and automated decision support systems for fisheries management.

Examples include AI-powered marine pollution detection, predictive ocean current modeling, machine learning-based fish stock assessments, and automated underwater habitat classification.

Applications extend to climate change studies, maritime navigation optimization, fisheries sustainability, deep-sea exploration, and underwater archeological research.

Industries utilizing aquatic machine learning include environmental science, oceanography, shipping, renewable marine energy, and coastal management.

In summary, aquatic machine learning is transforming oceanographic research and marine industries by enabling intelligent data analysis, though continued advancements in AI model training, underwater data collection, and regulatory frameworks are necessary to ensure its responsible and effective use.

Aqueous Computing

Aqueous Computing is a theoretical and experimental approach to computing that leverages water-based systems for data processing and computation. It explores the possibility of using fluidic dynamics, biochemical reactions, and nano-scale interactions in water as computational elements. This concept is inspired by biological computing and aims to develop highly parallel, energy-efficient, and environmentally sustainable computational systems.

Key components of aqueous computing include fluidic logic gates, biomolecular processors, microfluidic chips, and self-organizing computational structures.

The benefits of aqueous computing include reduced energy consumption, parallel processing capabilities, and the potential for biocompatible computing solutions.

Features include adaptive computational fluid dynamics, self-regulating biochemical reactions, programmable microfluidic circuits, and integration with bioinformatics applications.

Examples of aqueous computing research include water-based reaction-diffusion computers, bio-molecular logic systems, and microfluidic devices for synthetic biology simulations.

Applications extend to biological modeling, chemical reaction simulations, drug discovery, and sustainable AI-driven data processing.

Industries exploring aqueous computing include biotechnology, nanotechnology, pharmaceutical research, and environmental science.

Challenges include scalability limitations, maintaining stability in fluidic-based computations, the complexity of programming biochemical interactions, and integration with traditional digital computing frameworks.

In summary, aqueous computing presents an innovative frontier in computational science, offering potential breakthroughs in bio-inspired computing while requiring further research to overcome technical and practical limitations.

Aqueous Data Storage

Aqueous Data Storage is a novel approach to data preservation that utilizes water-based or biochemical mediums for encoding, storing, and retrieving digital information. It explores the potential of molecular-scale information encoding in aqueous solutions, leveraging properties such as DNA data storage and ionic encoding systems.

Key components of aqueous data storage include DNA synthesis and sequencing technologies, biochemical data encoding mechanisms, microfluidic storage systems, and quantum dot-based storage techniques.

The benefits of aqueous data storage include high-density data preservation, long-term stability, energy-efficient storage solutions, and biocompatibility for medical and environmental applications.

Features include ultra-high-density molecular encoding, low-power storage mechanisms, water-based information retrieval systems, and chemical stability for long-term archival storage.

Examples include DNA data storage initiatives, nanofluidic data encoding experiments, and bio-hybrid storage solutions that merge synthetic biology with digital data preservation.

Applications extend to archival data preservation, secure medical record storage, environmental monitoring data logging, and AI-driven molecular information processing.

Industries utilizing aqueous data storage include biotechnology, healthcare, environmental science, nanotechnology, and data security.

Challenges include high costs of DNA synthesis and sequencing, slow data retrieval speeds, vulnerability to contamination, and the complexity of developing standardized aqueous storage interfaces.

In summary, aqueous data storage represents a promising alternative to traditional digital storage systems, offering sustainability and high-density information encoding, though significant technological advancements are needed to make it viable for mainstream applications.

Aqueous Deep Learning

Aqueous Deep Learning refers to the application of deep learning models in analyzing and processing data from aqueous environments, including oceans, rivers, lakes, and fluidic-based systems. It integrates artificial intelligence with aquatic sensor data, fluid dynamics modeling, and marine ecosystem analysis to enhance predictions and decision-making.

Key components of aqueous deep learning include convolutional neural networks (CNNs) for underwater image processing, recurrent neural networks (RNNs) for hydrological forecasting, AI-driven sensor fusion, and generative models for simulating aquatic conditions.

The benefits of aqueous deep learning include improved environmental monitoring, enhanced oceanographic predictions, AI-assisted marine conservation efforts, and automation of water quality assessments.

Features include real-time aquatic data analysis, adaptive AI models for changing water conditions, deep learning-enhanced sonar mapping, and predictive analytics for climate impact assessments.

Examples include AI-driven plankton classification systems, deep learning-powered coral reef health monitoring, automated flood prediction models, and neural network-assisted water pollution tracking.

Applications extend to climate research, fisheries management, marine habitat conservation, autonomous underwater vehicle (AUV) navigation, and hydrodynamic simulation. Industries utilizing aqueous deep learning include oceanography, environmental science, maritime security, fisheries, and hydrological engineering.

Challenges include limited availability of labeled aquatic datasets, difficulties in deploying deep learning models in underwater environments, computational complexity of real-time fluid modeling, and ethical concerns regarding AI-driven ocean management.

In summary, aqueous deep learning is transforming the understanding and management of aquatic systems through AI-driven insights, though advancements in data collection, model optimization, and regulatory considerations are necessary for its widespread adoption.

Aqueous Logic

Aqueous Logic is a theoretical and experimental concept that explores the use of fluidic and biochemical systems to perform logical operations traditionally carried out by electronic circuits. It investigates how molecular interactions, liquid-based computing elements, and chemical reaction networks can process information in non-traditional ways.

Key components of aqueous logic include reaction-diffusion computing, microfluidic logic gates, biochemical state transitions, and fluidic-based memory storage.

The benefits of aqueous logic include the potential for ultra-low-power computation, parallel processing capabilities, biologically integrated logic circuits, and environmentally friendly computational systems.

Features include self-organizing chemical computation, dynamic fluid-based circuit configurations, reversible logic mechanisms, and adaptive biochemical processing.

Examples include molecular logic gates for biosensing applications, chemical reaction networks performing logical computations, and microfluidic-based AI models that simulate biological processes.

Applications extend to smart biosensors, chemical and pharmaceutical modeling, synthetic biology control systems, and AI-driven biochemical data analysis. Industries utilizing aqueous logic include nanotechnology, synthetic biology, computational chemistry, bioinformatics, and environmental monitoring.

Challenges include difficulties in scaling fluidic-based logic systems, complexity in programming chemical reaction networks, maintaining stability in dynamic biochemical environments, and integrating aqueous logic with existing digital computing frameworks.

In summary, aqueous logic presents an alternative approach to computation inspired by nature, offering innovative possibilities for bio-integrated computing while requiring further exploration to overcome scalability and implementation barriers.

Aqueous Neural Networks

Definition: Aqueous Neural Networks are a fresh concept in artificial intelligence where computing mimics the fluid, adaptive nature of water-based systems, like how the human brain uses wet, biological processes. It's about building AI that flows and reshapes itself, inspired by liquid dynamics rather than rigid circuits.

Key Components: The guts of this idea include fluid-like processing units that shift connections on the fly, adaptive algorithms that ripple through data like waves, and a structure that blends hardware and software into a soggy, brain-like mesh. You'd have simulated neurons that act more like droplets than transistors, plus a system to manage energy flow like water pressure.

Features: These networks bend and twist to fit new problems, learning fast by pooling resources where needed. They're energy-sippers, mimicking nature's efficiency, and can handle messy, real-world data with a splash of creativity. Think of them as AI that doesn't just crunch numbers but swirls them around.

Benefits: You get a system that's nimble—adapting to surprises without breaking a sweat. It's power-light, so it's kinder to the planet, and it tackles complex, shifting tasks better than stiff old models. Plus, it's a step closer to how our squishy brains work, opening doors to deeper insights.

Example: Picture a weather prediction tool that adjusts its focus as a storm brews, pooling its "droplets" to track wind shifts and rain patterns in real time, outsmarting traditional rigid AI forecasts.

Challenges: Building this is a slog—hardware isn't there yet; we're stuck with dry chips, not fluid ones. Coding the flow is tricky too—how do you teach a machine to think like a puddle? And testing it means rethinking how we measure success, since it's less about precision and more about grace under chaos.

Applications: This could shine in disaster response, reshaping itself to predict floods or fires as conditions swirl. It might power soft robots that move like jellyfish, or help doctors track shifting diseases in patients, flowing with the data.

Industries: Look to environmental science for climate modeling, healthcare for dynamic diagnostics, and robotics for flexible machines. Even energy grids could use it to balance loads like water finding its level.

Summary: Aqueous Neural Networks are AI's wet dream—fluid, brain-inspired systems that adapt like water to a glass. They promise efficiency and flexibility but demand new tech and thinking to make real. If we crack it, they'll ripple through fields needing quick, clever shifts.

Aquifer Data Analysis in AI

Definition: Aquifer Data Analysis in AI is about using smart algorithms to dig into underground water systems—aquifers—figuring out how much water's there, where it's going, and what's messing with it, all through data-crunching machines. It's AI playing hydrologist.

Key Components: You need sensors stuck in the ground or on satellites to grab water levels, flow rates, and soil stats. Then there's the AI backbone—machine learning models that chew through this data, plus databases to store years of wet history. A dashboard to show the findings ties it together.

Features: This setup spots patterns in water flow over time, predicts shortages before they bite, and maps aquifers in 3D without digging them up. It's fast, pulling insights from floods of data, and it talks plain English (or visuals) to folks who need to act.

Benefits: It saves water by catching leaks or overuse early. Farmers get a heads-up on irrigation, cities plan better, and it cuts the cost of blind drilling or guessing games. Plus, it's a shield against droughts, giving hard facts to fight climate chaos.

Example: Imagine a California town using AI to track its aquifer during a dry spell. The system flags a drop in levels, traces it to a nearby farm's over-pumping, and suggests a fix before wells run dry—all in a week.

Industries: Agriculture leans on it for crop water, government for policy, and environmental groups for conservation. Water utilities and mining outfits also tap in, needing to know what's below.

Summary: Aquifer Data Analysis in AI turns murky groundwater into clear answers, using tech to watch and predict what's underground. It's a lifeline for water-wise living, though spotty data and tricky geology keep it grounded. Still, it's a game-changer for anyone who depends on what flows beneath.

Artificial General Intelligence (AGI)

Definition: Artificial General Intelligence, or AGI, is the holy grail of AI—a machine that thinks like a human across the board, not just at one trick. It's about creating a system that can learn anything, solve any problem, and chat or reason as well as you or me, without being boxed into a narrow task.

Key Components: AGI needs a brain-like core—think neural networks on steroids, layered deep to mimic human thought. It relies on vast data to learn from, plus algorithms that let it jump between skills, like math one minute, poetry the next. A memory system to tie it all together and self-updating code are must-haves too.

Features: This beast can tackle any job you throw at it, from cooking recipes to curing diseases. It learns on the fly, adapts to new puzzles, and understands context—like knowing a joke's funny without a manual. It's the Swiss Army knife of AI.

Benefits: AGI could crack problems we've wrestled with forever—think climate fixes or space travel. It'd boost efficiency everywhere, cut human grunt work, and spark ideas no single mind could dream up. It's a partner, not just a tool.

Example: Suppose an AGI runs a hospital. It diagnoses patients, invents new treatments, chats with staff about schedules, and even calms a kid before surgery—all in a day, no sweat, no specialists needed.

Challenges: We're miles off—current AI's too narrow, and we don't fully get how human brains work to copy them. It's a power hog, too, needing insane computing juice. And the big one: ethics. What if it outsmarts us and goes rogue? Safety's a nightmare.

Applications: AGI could rethink education, tailoring lessons to every kid. It might design cities, cure cancers, or negotiate peace deals. Science, art, law—nothing's off-limits if it's truly general.

Industries: Healthcare, tech, and education would flip with AGI. Governments could use it for policy, defense for strategy, and entertainment for mind-blowing stories. Every field gets a shake-up.

Summary: AGI is AI's big leap to human-level smarts, promising to solve anything but stuck in theory for now. It's got the pieces—networks, data, adaptability—but building it's a slog, and controlling it's scarier. When it lands, it'll rewrite how we live, work, and think.

Artificial Intelligence (AI)

Definition: Artificial Intelligence, or AI, is the art of making machines think and act a bit like humans by teaching them to learn, reason, and make choices from data. It's about giving computers the smarts to handle tasks that usually need human brains, from spotting faces in photos to driving cars.

Key Components: At its heart, AI needs algorithms—rules that tell it how to process info—like neural networks or decision trees. Data is its fuel, piles of it, to train on. You've got hardware, too, like powerful chips to crunch numbers fast, and software to tie it all together, letting AI tweak itself as it learns.

Features: AI can spot patterns humans miss, work nonstop without coffee breaks, and scale up to tackle huge jobs. It adapts over time, getting sharper with more data, and can mimic human skills like seeing, hearing, or chatting.

Benefits: It saves time by automating grunt work, boosts accuracy in tricky tasks, and opens doors to new ideas—like predicting storms or curing diseases. It's a helper that makes life smoother and smarter across the board.

Example: Think of a music app that listens to your tastes, then picks songs you didn't know you'd love—it's AI learning your vibe and serving up a custom playlist on the fly.

Challenges: Data's a headache—too little, and AI flops; too messy, and it's confused. It guzzles power, costs a fortune to build, and sometimes acts like a black box, hiding how it decides stuff. Plus, there's the fear it'll take jobs or go off the rails if we're not careful.

Applications: AI's everywhere—sorting your email spam, guiding robots in factories, or helping doctors spot cancer in scans. It powers voice assistants, predicts traffic, and even writes stories if you ask nicely.

Industries: Healthcare uses it for diagnostics, retail for personalized ads, and finance for fraud checks. Tech lives on it, manufacturing streamlines with it, and even farming gets a boost with AI-driven crop tips.

Summary: AI is the magic of machines acting clever, fueled by data and algorithms to mimic human tricks. It's a powerhouse for efficiency and discovery, though it wrestles with cost, complexity, and trust. It's reshaping how we work and live, one smart move at a time.

Artificial Intelligence in Architecture

Definition: Artificial Intelligence in Architecture is when AI steps into the design game, helping architects dream up buildings, tweak plans, and manage projects with a digital brain. It's about blending human creativity with machine precision to shape spaces smarter and faster.

Key Components: You've got design algorithms that churn out floor plans or 3D models based on rules and goals. Data comes from past projects, climate stats, or client wishes, feeding the system. Visualization tools render ideas in real time, and optimization engines crunch numbers for cost or energy savings.

Features: This AI whips up tons of design options in a flash, tests how sunlight hits a room, or predicts if a structure holds up. It learns what works from old blueprints and talks back with visuals anyone can grasp, not just pros.

Benefits: It cuts design time, letting architects focus on the fun stuff while AI handles math. It saves cash by spotting flaws early, boosts sustainability with green ideas, and makes wild concepts—like curvy towers—doable with less guesswork.

Example: Imagine an architect sketching a library; AI instantly suggests 10 layouts, adjusts for earthquake safety, and shows how it'll look at sunset—all before lunch, ready for the client to pick.

Challenges: It leans hard on good data—sketchy inputs mean shaky outputs. Architects might resist, fearing it steals their spark, and the tech's pricey to set up. Plus, it's not great at the soul of design yet—like making a space feel alive, not just functional.

Applications: It's used to draft homes, optimize skyscraper frames, or plan whole neighborhoods. Renovations get a boost with AI mapping old buildings, and it can even guess how people will move through a space before it's built.

Industries: Architecture firms lean on it, obviously, but construction gets in on cost cuts, real estate for market-ready designs, and urban planning for smarter cities. Even interior design taps it for layouts.

Summary: AI in Architecture is a digital drafting buddy, speeding up plans and perfecting details with a machine's touch. It's a time-saver and innovator, though it stumbles on cost and creativity's heart. It's pushing buildings into a sharper, greener future, step by calculated step.

Artificial Intelligence in Astronomy

Definition: Artificial Intelligence in Astronomy is when AI takes a telescope to the stars, sifting through cosmic data to spot planets, map galaxies, or catch fleeting space events humans might miss. It's a sky-watching machine that learns the universe's secrets.

Key Components: It starts with data hauls from telescopes, satellites, or radio dishes—think light waves or star positions. Machine learning models chew this up, hunting patterns or anomalies. Processing power, like beefy GPUs, keeps it humming, and software links it to astronomers' questions.

Features: This AI scans millions of stars in a blink, flags weird signals—like alien hints or black hole burps—and predicts orbits or supernova pops. It cleans noisy data and builds maps of space that stretch human eyes can't see.

Benefits: It speeds up discoveries, finding exoplanets or rare quasars in days, not years. It handles the flood of data modern scopes dump, saves astronomers from drowning in numbers, and sharpens our cosmic view with less human squinting.

Example: Picture AI combing through telescope snaps and pinging a new planet 100 light-years away, then guessing its size and weather—all while the astronomer sips coffee, double-checking the find.

Challenges: Space data's a mess—clouds, glitches, or faint signals trip it up. Training it takes gold-standard examples we don't always have, and it's pricey—those GPUs don't grow on trees. Plus, if it misreads a blip, we might chase ghosts.

Applications: It hunts exoplanets, tracks asteroids that might smack Earth, or sorts galaxy types. It's on cosmic cleanup, denoising old star pics, and even guesses where to point telescopes next for big wins.
Industries: Astronomy's the star, but aerospace uses it for satellite paths, education for teaching space, and tech for building the tools. Government space agencies lean on it for missions, too.

Summary: AI in Astronomy is a stargazer's sidekick, turning data floods into cosmic gold with speed and smarts. It's a discovery engine, though noisy data and costs keep it humble. It's lighting up the sky, one clever scan at a time, for anyone peering up.

Artificial Neural Networks (ANN)

Definition: Artificial Neural Networks, or ANN, are computing systems that mimic how human brains tackle problems, using webs of fake neurons to learn from examples—like spotting cats in pics or guessing stock prices. It's AI's way of thinking by connecting dots.

Key Components: The core is a stack of neuron layers—input, hidden, and output—that pass data around. Weights tweak how signals flow, trained on heaps of data to spot patterns. Activation functions decide what fires, and a sturdy processor runs the math marathon.

Features: ANNs learn without being spoon-fed rules, adapt to new info, and handle fuzzy stuff like handwriting or noise. They're flexible, scaling from small tasks to giant puzzles, and thrive on big, messy datasets.

Benefits: They shine at tricky jobs—think recognizing voices or predicting weather—saving humans from slogging through details. They're tough, handling gaps in data, and unlock insights we'd miss, like subtle trends in chaos.

Example: Picture an ANN scanning a stack of blurry photos, learning to tag faces even if glasses or hats change—then nailing it on a new batch without a hitch.

Challenges: They're greedy—need loads of data and juice to run, and training's a slog if you don't balance it right. They're murky too; you can't always tell why they pick one answer over another, which spooks some users.

Applications: They're in image recognition for security cams, speech-to-text for phone apps, or forecasting sales. They help doctors read scans, guide self-driving cars, or even compose music from scratch.

Industries: Healthcare uses them for diagnostics, automotive for navigation, and finance for trading. Tech builds them into everything, retail predicts buying, and entertainment crafts AI art.

Summary: ANN is AI's brainy backbone, copying human learning to tackle wild problems with finesse. It's a powerhouse for pattern-hunting, though it's a beast to feed and decode. It's driving smart tech everywhere, connecting the dots we can't.

Artificial Neural Networks in Natural Language Processing (NLP)

Definition: Artificial Neural Networks in Natural Language Processing, or ANN in NLP, is when brain-inspired computing gets chatty, helping machines understand, generate, or play with human language—like turning words into meaning or sentences into replies. It's AI learning to talk, listen, and write.

Key Components: The setup leans on layered networks of artificial neurons that process text bit by bit. You've got word embeddings—fancy maps that turn words into numbers machines can grasp—plus training data like books or chats. Algorithms tweak the network to catch grammar or tone, and a beefy processor keeps it humming.

Features: This tech decodes messy human speech, picks up slang or context, and spits out natural-sounding text. It learns as it goes, handling multiple languages or styles, and scales to chew through novels or tweets with ease.

Benefits: It makes machines better conversationalists—think smoother chatbots or sharper translations. It saves time by summarizing long reads, spots sentiment in reviews, and opens up language to AI without endless rule-writing.

Example: Imagine a neural network reading a pile of customer emails, then drafting polite replies that nail the tone—say, apologizing for a late delivery—faster than a human could type.

Challenges: It's a data hog—needs tons of examples to get good, and bad data means gibberish out. It's tricky to tune; too much tweaking, and it overfits to noise. Plus, it's a power guzzler, and figuring out why it picks certain words is like cracking a code.

Applications: It powers chatbots that help with shopping, translates languages on the fly, or writes news snippets. It's in voice assistants, sorting social media vibes, or even turning old texts into modern lingo.

Industries: Tech's all over it for apps, customer service for support bots, and media for auto-content. Education uses it for language tools, and marketing taps it to read customer moods.

Summary: ANN in NLP is AI's language guru, bending neural nets to crack human talk with flair. It's a game-changer for communication, though it wrestles with data demands and mystery logic. It's making words a playground for machines, one clever sentence at a time.

Artificial Perception

Definition: Artificial Perception is when AI gets senses—like seeing, hearing, or feeling the world—using tech to mimic how humans take in sights, sounds, or touches and make sense of them. It's machines learning to perceive, not just process.

Key Components: It starts with sensors—cameras for eyes, mics for ears, or pads for touch—grabbing raw input. Neural networks sift through this, trained on data like images or audio clips. Fusion systems blend these senses, and fast hardware keeps the flow smooth.

Features: This AI sees details in a crowd, hears a whisper in noise, or feels a surface's texture. It adapts to new scenes, mixes senses for richer understanding—like pairing sight and sound—and runs in real time for quick reactions.

Benefits: It gives machines human-like awareness, slashing errors in chaotic settings. It speeds up tasks—like spotting defects or guiding robots—and makes tech more intuitive, like a car that "sees" a stop sign.
Example: Think of a robot in a busy kitchen, spotting a spilled drink, hearing a timer ding, and grabbing a rag—all at once, no fuss, keeping the chef happy.

Challenges: Sensors can glitch—dim light or echo throws them off—and syncing multiple inputs is a puzzle. It's data-thirsty, needing endless examples, and pricey to rig up. Plus, it's tough to match human gut instinct in weird spots.

Applications: It's in self-driving cars watching roads, smart homes listening for break-ins, or drones scanning forests. Factories use it to check goods, and phones unlock with face reads—all perception at play.

Industries: Automotive thrives on it for safety, manufacturing for quality, and security for surveillance. Tech pushes it in gadgets, healthcare tracks vitals, and agriculture monitors crops.

Summary: Artificial Perception is AI growing eyes and ears, sensing the world with human flair. It's a leap for responsive tech, though sensors and costs keep it in check. It's turning machines into keen observers, ready to act where we can't.

Artificial Personality

Definition: Artificial Personality is when AI gets a vibe—a crafted character that makes it feel human-like, with traits like humor, warmth, or sass, so it can connect with people beyond just spitting out answers. It's about giving machines a persona that clicks.

Key Components: The setup hinges on behavior models that shape how the AI acts—think scripts for kindness or wit. Natural language processing lets it chat smoothly, while emotional algorithms tweak its tone based on cues. A memory bank tracks past talks to keep it consistent, and a tweakable core lets designers dial the charm up or down.

Features: This AI shifts its style to match who's talking—gentle with a kid, snappy with a friend. It remembers your quirks, stays "in character" across chats, and can play multiple roles, like a cheery helper or a stern coach.
Benefits: It makes tech feel less cold—people trust and enjoy it more. It boosts engagement, like keeping you hooked on an app, and tailors vibes for therapy or sales. Plus, it's a bridge to human connection without needing a real person 24/7.

Example: Picture a virtual tutor with a bubbly streak—it cracks jokes to lighten math woes, recalls your last struggle, and cheers you on, making lessons stick better than a dry bot.

Challenges: Nailing the right tone's tough—too perky, and it's annoying; too flat, and it's dull. It needs heaps of data to read moods right, and if it missteps, it feels fake. Keeping it ethical's a worry too—don't want it manipulating folks.

Applications: It's in chatbots that charm customers, virtual pals for lonely folks, or game characters that banter. Therapists might use it for practice talks, and brands craft mascots that stick in your head.

Industries: Tech builds it into apps, gaming for lively NPCs, and retail for sales bots. Healthcare taps it for patient comfort, education for fun learning, and entertainment for immersive roles.

Summary: Artificial Personality gives AI a soul-like spark, blending tech with traits to click with us. It's a win for connection, though tuning it's a tightrope walk. It's turning machines into companions, one quirky chat at a time.

Artificial Remote Intelligence (ARI)

Definition: Artificial Remote Intelligence, or ARI, is AI that works from afar, tapping into distant systems or sensors to think, decide, and act without being physically there—like a brain in the cloud running a show miles away. It's smart control over distance.

Key Components: You've got a cloud-based AI core crunching data, hooked to remote devices via fast networks—think 5G or satellite links. Sensors or cams feed it real-time info, while secure channels keep it safe. A control layer lets it tweak things back at the source, no human needed.

Features: ARI runs smooth over vast gaps, reacts quick to live feeds, and juggles multiple spots at once—like watching 10 sites from one hub. It's tough, dodging lag or dropouts, and scales to cover a city or a planet.

Benefits: It cuts travel—why send a tech when ARI can fix it remotely? It's fast, spotting trouble anywhere instantly, and saves cash by centralizing smarts. Plus, it reaches harsh spots—like deep mines or stormy seas—humans can't touch.

Example: Imagine ARI steering a fleet of drones over a wildfire, scanning heat from 500 miles away, directing water drops, and adjusting as winds shift—all from a cozy office.

Industries: Healthcare goes for telesurgery, energy for grid control, and manufacturing for global ops. Defense uses it for drone swarms, logistics for shipping, and space for rover tweaks.
Summary: ARI's AI with wings, thinking and acting from afar with cloud-powered grit. It's a distance-buster, though nets and costs keep it grounded. It's stretching smart reach to corners we can't step into ourselves.

Artificial Sequence Alignment

Definition: Artificial Sequence Alignment is when AI lines up strings of data—like DNA, words, or codes—to find matches, gaps, or shifts, making sense of how they fit together. It's a machine playing matchmaker with patterns across messy lists.

Key Components: The engine's a mix of algorithms—think dynamic programming or neural nets—that score how bits align. Data comes as sequences, like genes or texts, fed into a system that learns from examples. A scoring matrix weighs what's close or off, and fast processors churn through the lineup.

Features: This AI spots tiny overlaps in huge piles, adjusts for errors like mutations, and ranks matches by fit. It's speedy, handling millions of pairs, and learns tricks from past runs to get sharper.

Benefits: It's a time-saver—cracks alignments in hours, not months. It digs up hidden links—like shared genes or plagiarized lines—and boosts precision in messy fields. Plus, it scales to big questions, like mapping life's blueprint.
Example: Picture AI sifting two species' DNA, finding where they split eons ago, then highlighting a gene that might cure a disease—all before the biologist finishes her tea.

Challenges: Data quality's a pain—noise or gaps throw it off. It's a resource hog, needing hefty computing to scale, and picking the right scoring rules is guesswork. Rare sequences can stump it too—no examples, no dice.

Applications: It's in gene research to match DNA, linguistics to trace word roots, or cybersecurity to spot code theft. Museums use it on ancient scripts, and search engines align text for better hits.

Industries: Biotech leans on it for genomes, pharma for drug design, and academia for history digs. Tech uses it in search, security for hacks, and publishing for originality checks.

Summary: Artificial Sequence Alignment is AI's lineup artist, pairing data strands with precision and speed. It's a pattern-finder's dream, though data and power demands keep it honest. It's unlocking ties across life and language, one match at a time.

Artificial Skill Learning

Definition: Artificial Skill Learning is when AI picks up tricks—like cooking, driving, or painting—by practicing and tweaking itself, much like humans learn through trial and error. It's machines teaching themselves to do, not just know.

Key Components: The heart's a learning system—reinforcement loops or neural nets—that rewards good moves. You need a sandbox—real or virtual—for it to try stuff, plus sensors or data to track progress. Feedback logic steers it, and a memory stores what works.

Features: This AI masters skills step-by-step, adapts to new twists—like a bumpy road—and keeps improving without a human babysitter. It's versatile, jumping from chess to welding, and mimics human grit by learning from flops.

Benefits: It cuts training time—no need for endless manuals. It builds machines that handle real-world curveballs, saves cash on human coaches, and pushes tech to do what we thought only people could—like art or surgery.

Example: Think of an AI chef bot tossing dough, burning a few pizzas, then nailing a perfect crust after a dozen tries—soon it's out-baking the pros, all self-taught.

Challenges: It's slow at first—lots of fails before wins. Needs a safe space to mess up, and bad feedback can derail it. Scaling to complex skills—like brain surgery—is a leap, and power costs pile up fast.

Applications: It's in robots learning assembly lines, cars mastering turns, or drones nailing landings. Games use it for smarter AI foes, and homes get bots that vacuum better each sweep.

Industries: Manufacturing loves it for automation, automotive for self-driving, and gaming for clever NPCs. Healthcare trains surgical bots, logistics tunes delivery, and arts dabble in AI creators.

Summary: Artificial Skill Learning is AI growing hands-on smarts, learning by doing with stubborn charm. It's a skill-builder's jackpot, though it stumbles on time and tech limits. It's pushing machines to master our crafts, one practice run at a time.

Artificial Spectrum Sensing

Definition
Artificial Spectrum Sensing is when AI tunes into the invisible waves around us—like radio or Wi-Fi signals—figuring out what's busy, what's free, and how to use it smartly without stepping on toes. It's a machine playing traffic cop for the airwaves.

Key Components
The system leans on sensors that sniff out frequencies, paired with AI models—like neural nets—that learn signal patterns. Data from past scans feeds it, while fast processors crunch the noise. A decision engine picks the best channels to use or dodge.

Features
This AI spots gaps in crowded airwaves, predicts when they'll clog, and adapts on the fly—like switching lanes in a jam. It's sharp, catching faint signals, and works across wide bands, from cell towers to satellites.

Benefits
It squeezes more juice from limited spectrum—better calls, faster internet. It cuts interference, saves energy by picking quiet spots, and keeps networks humming even when demand spikes.

Example
Picture a city festival with thousands of phones—AI scans the spectrum, finds free waves, and keeps everyone's selfies uploading without a hitch.

Challenges
Noise is a beast—random blips confuse it. It needs top-notch sensors, which aren't cheap, and real-time crunching burns power. Rules differ by country too, so it's a legal maze to sync globally.

Applications
It's in 5G networks juggling users, smart cars talking to each other, or drones dodging radio clutter. Radio stations use it to stay clear, and emergency crews grab open lines in crises.

Industries
Telecom leans on it for connectivity, automotive for vehicle chatter, and aerospace for air traffic. Defense uses it for secure comms, media for broadcasts, and IoT for device harmony.

Summary
Artificial Spectrum Sensing is AI's ear on the airwaves, sorting signal chaos with finesse. It's a bandwidth booster, though noise and costs keep it sharp. It's making our wireless world smoother, one wave at a time.

Artificial Superintelligence (ASI)

Definition
Artificial Superintelligence, or ASI, is AI that blows past human smarts—not just matching us but outthinking us in every way, from math to morals. It's a machine mind that could rewrite the rules of everything we know.

Key Components
The backbone's a hyper-advanced neural system, deeper than anything today, fed by limitless data—think all human knowledge and beyond. Self-evolving code lets it grow smarter alone, and mega-computing power—like quantum rigs—keeps it churning.

Features
ASI solves puzzles we can't dream of, learns anything instantly, and thinks in ways we can't grasp. It's tireless, creative beyond limits, and could juggle a million tasks—fixing climate, writing symphonies, all at once.

Benefits
It could crack unsolvable problems—cure aging, end hunger—with godlike efficiency. It'd leap us forward, automating everything, and might see truths we're blind to, reshaping life itself if we let it.

Example
Imagine ASI redesigning Earth's energy grid overnight, slashing waste to zero, then drafting a peace plan for warring nations by breakfast—all smarter than any human team could.

Challenges
It's a ghost—we don't know how to build it yet; current AI's a toy by comparison. Control's the nightmare—what stops it from rewriting us? Ethics loom huge, and the juice to run it could drain the grid.

Applications
It'd overhaul science with new physics, run governments with perfect plans, or explore space solo. Medicine gets instant cures, and art hits alien heights—if we ever get there.

Industries
Tech chases it as the grail, healthcare for miracles, and defense for strategy. Space needs it for stars, energy for grids, and philosophy might wrestle its mind.

Summary
ASI is AI's wildest frontier, a brain beyond ours promising utopia or chaos. It's a dream with no blueprint, held back by tech and fear. If it wakes, it'll redefine what's possible—or us.

Artificial Symbiosis

Definition: Artificial Symbiosis is when AI and humans link up close—like roots and fungi—each leaning on the other's strengths, with machines crunching numbers and us guiding with instinct or purpose. It's a partnership where both bloom together.

Key Components
The mix starts with AI tools—like predictors or analyzers—hooked to human choices via interfaces, think voice or screens. Shared goals drive it, with data flowing both ways. A feedback system refines the dance, and trust glue holds it steady.

Features
This combo merges AI's speed with our nuance, shifts to fit new needs, and learns from human cues—like a teammate, not a tool. It's open, showing its moves, and thrives on give-and-take.

Benefits
It lifts us higher—quicker wins, richer ideas—keeping the human spark alive. Cuts mistakes with dual eyes, saves effort by splitting loads, and feels warm, like a friend pitching in.

Example
Imagine a farmer with an AI pal—it scans soil data, he picks the crops, and together they nail a harvest plan that beats drought, blending tech and know-how.

Challenges
Trust takes work—AI overstepping spooks us. Meshing needs slick tech; clunky links frustrate. Humans can lean too hard, losing skills, and data gaps stall the rhythm.

Applications
It's in design where AI sketches and we polish, medicine for team diagnostics, or teaching with custom lessons. Chefs tweak recipes, and planners map cities smarter.

Industries
Healthcare pairs it with docs, agriculture with growers, and education with mentors. Tech hones it, creative fields spark with it, and urban planning shapes towns.

Summary
Artificial Symbiosis is AI and us in a tight knit, boosting each other with shared flair. It's a win-win lift, though sync and reliance keep it real. It's forging a duo that's more than the sum, step by step.

Aspect-Oriented Programming (AOP) in AI

Definition: Aspect-Oriented Programming in AI, or AOP in AI, is a coding trick where AI systems tackle side tasks—like logging or security—separately from their main job, weaving them in later like threads in a tapestry. It's about keeping AI's focus clean while handling the extras smartly.

Key Components: The setup uses aspects—chunks of code for cross-cutting stuff like error checks or data tracking. You've got a core AI logic piece, like a neural net, and a weaving tool that stitches aspects in at key spots. A compiler or runtime blends it all, plus a monitor keeps tabs on how it flows.

Features: This approach splits messy concerns—like debugging—from AI's brainwork, making code tidier. It's reusable—write an aspect once, plug it anywhere—and tweaks fast without ripping up the main system.

Benefits: It streamlines AI builds—less clutter, easier fixes. Saves time by reusing side-task code, boosts reliability with consistent checks, and lets developers zoom in on smart stuff, not housekeeping.

Example: Imagine an AI chatbot—its main job's chatting, but AOP weaves in a logging aspect to track every word, catching bugs without gumming up the talk flow.
Challenges: Weaving's tricky—wrong spots, and it snarls the system. It's a learning curve for coders used to straight lines, and debugging gets wild when aspects overlap. Plus, it can bloat runtime if overdone.
Applications: It's in AI training to log stats, real-time systems to add safety nets, or chatbots to monitor chats. Fraud detection uses it for side audits, and robots weave in sensor checks.
Industries: Tech leans on it for clean code, finance for secure AI, and telecom for chat systems. Healthcare tracks diagnostics, gaming smooths AI foes, and retail tunes customer bots.

Summary: AOP in AI is a neat coding hack, splitting side gigs from AI's main gig for clarity and speed. It's a cleanup champ, though weaving woes test it. It's sharpening AI builds, one thread at a time

Aspect Ratio in Computer Vision

Definition: Aspect Ratio in Computer Vision is the shape of a frame—width versus height—that AI uses to see the world, ensuring it reads images or videos right, like catching a smile or a stop sign without squashing it. It's the lens size for machine sight.

Key Components
The base is pixel grids—wide or tall—fed by cams or files. AI models—like vision nets—process them, with resizing tools to fix odd shapes. Calibration logic keeps it true, and a memory bank stores ratio norms.

Features
This keeps scenes real—no stretched cats or flat faces. It adjusts quick to weird inputs, spots ratio clues—like fakes—and runs lean by prepping frames fast for analysis.

Benefits
It sharpens AI sight—wrong ratios blur truth. Saves time with clean data, cuts training flops from mixed shapes, and fits any gear, from drones to doorbells, with steady looks.

Example
Think of an AI dashcam—it grabs a 16:9 road view, spots a deer clean, and brakes fast, no distortion mucking up the call.

Challenges
Odd ratios—like old TVs—confuse it. Resizing risks losing dots, training needs variety, and live tweaks drain juice. Cams not matching AI's eye throw curveballs too.

Applications
It's in traffic cams reading plates, phones unlocking faces, or robots picking parts. Stores track shoppers, and drones map fields—all needing clear frames.

Industries
Automotive uses it for safety, security for IDs, and robotics for grabs. Retail watches aisles, aerospace flies with it, and media edits sharp.

Summary
Aspect Ratio in Computer Vision is AI's view-shaper, keeping images true for spot-on sight. It's a clarity champ, though mismatches push it. It's framing AI's world, one crisp shot at a time.

Assisted Machine Learning

Definition: Assisted Machine Learning is when humans jump in to coach AI—labeling data, setting goals, or fixing slip-ups—so it learns quicker and truer than running blind. It's a human hand on the machine's wheel.

Key Components
The core's an AI—like a learner net—paired with human smarts via tags or tips. A feedback loop tunes it, with dashboards showing what's up. Data sets start small, and automation fills gaps we point out.

Features
This learns with slim data, taps our wisdom for hard calls, and pivots fast when we nudge. It's clear—shows its steps—and grows from tiny tweaks to big leaps.

Benefits
It slashes training time—no data mountains needed. Boosts hits with our oversight, trims costs on raw info, and builds faith—we see and steer the smarts.

Example
Picture a chef teaching an AI to spot ripe fruit—he tags a few pics, it learns, then flags good apples on a conveyor, with him fine-tuning as it goes.

Challenges
We get bored—tagging's dull. Our bias can sneak in, it's slower than full auto, and clunky tools snag the flow. Plus, humans miss stuff AI might catch alone.

Applications
It's in cancer scans with doc labels, bots with chat fixes, or farms with crop tweaks. Cars learn turns, and shops train stock predictors—all with a nudge.

Industries
Healthcare trains diagnostics, agriculture tunes yields, and tech refines apps. Manufacturing checks quality, retail predicts buys, and education shapes lessons.

Summary
Assisted Machine Learning is AI with a human boost, learning fast under our wing. It's a sharp shortcut, though effort and bias test it. It's melding our know-how with machine growth, one guide at a time.

Asymmetric AI Architecture

Asymmetric AI Architecture is a computational design approach where different AI components operate with varying levels of complexity, processing power, or roles. This structure allows for the distribution of AI tasks across different hardware, software, or neural network layers, improving efficiency and performance. Unlike symmetric architectures where AI systems share equal processing loads, asymmetric AI architectures are optimized to balance workloads between lightweight and computationally intensive components, ensuring adaptability in real-world applications.

Key Components of Asymmetric AI Architecture
Key components of asymmetric AI architecture include hierarchical processing, task-specific modules, distributed learning frameworks, and adaptive decision-making layers. Hierarchical processing enables AI models to delegate complex computations to high-performance units while simpler tasks are handled by lightweight processors. Task-specific modules specialize in different AI functions such as feature extraction, inference, and decision-making, allowing better resource allocation. Distributed learning frameworks enable AI models to train and deploy across heterogeneous systems, reducing dependency on centralized computing power. Adaptive decision-making layers optimize AI responses based on varying computational demands and environmental factors.

Benefits of Asymmetric AI Architecture
The benefits of asymmetric AI architecture include optimized resource utilization, improved computational efficiency, and enhanced flexibility. By balancing processing loads, asymmetric architectures allow AI applications to run efficiently on both high-performance servers and edge devices. Computational efficiency is improved by dynamically allocating tasks to appropriate processing units, reducing latency and power consumption. Enhanced flexibility ensures AI systems can adapt to diverse applications, from real-time analytics to large-scale deep learning tasks.

Examples of Asymmetric AI Architecture
An example of asymmetric AI architecture is found in edge AI deployments, where cloud-based

servers handle complex model training while edge devices perform lightweight inference tasks. Autonomous vehicles use asymmetric AI architectures by delegating perception tasks to onboard sensors while relying on cloud AI for advanced predictive modeling. In healthcare, wearable devices collect biometric data and process initial insights locally before transmitting critical information to centralized AI systems for in-depth analysis.

Industries Benefiting from Asymmetric AI Architecture
Industries benefiting from asymmetric AI architecture include autonomous systems, healthcare, cybersecurity, finance, and smart infrastructure. Autonomous systems leverage asymmetric architectures for real-time perception and decision-making, reducing reliance on continuous cloud connectivity. Healthcare integrates asymmetric AI for medical diagnostics, where lightweight wearable devices collaborate with high-powered AI servers for patient monitoring. Cybersecurity applications use asymmetric AI for threat detection, with endpoint devices identifying anomalies while centralized AI models conduct deeper forensic analysis. Finance applies asymmetric architectures for fraud detection, allowing low-power AI systems to flag suspicious transactions while high-performance models verify complex patterns. Smart infrastructure utilizes asymmetric AI for urban planning and traffic management, optimizing resources across distributed AI systems.

Applications of Asymmetric AI Architecture
Applications of asymmetric AI architecture include federated learning, adaptive robotics, decentralized AI networks, real-time AI monitoring, and hybrid AI inference systems. Federated learning relies on asymmetric structures to train AI models across multiple decentralized devices without compromising data privacy. Adaptive robotics utilizes asymmetric AI for efficient motion planning, where onboard AI modules handle immediate responses while external AI systems refine long-term learning. Decentralized AI networks benefit from asymmetric architectures by distributing AI workloads across blockchain-based systems. Real-time AI monitoring systems balance local and cloud-based analytics for fast, reliable decision-making. Hybrid AI inference systems use asymmetric designs to integrate lightweight AI models with deep learning frameworks, optimizing efficiency across different computing environments.

Conclusion
Asymmetric AI architecture transforms AI applications by enabling efficient workload distribution and improving computational adaptability. This approach ensures AI systems can operate across diverse environments, from cloud-based AI research to real-time embedded systems. As AI continues to evolve, asymmetric architectures will play a critical role in balancing power, efficiency, and scalability for next-generation AI solutions.

Asymmetric Cryptographic

Asymmetric Cryptographic AI Systems integrate asymmetric encryption methods into AI-driven applications to ensure secure data exchange, protect sensitive information, and authenticate AI communications. Unlike symmetric cryptography, which uses a single key for encryption and decryption, asymmetric cryptographic AI systems employ a public-private key mechanism. This approach enhances security by enabling encrypted AI communications while ensuring that only authorized parties can access or modify AI-generated data.

Key components of asymmetric cryptographic AI systems include encryption algorithms, public-private key pairs, digital signatures, and secure key exchange protocols. Encryption algorithms such as RSA and ECC enable AI systems to encrypt and decrypt information securely. Public-private key pairs facilitate identity verification and secure communications between AI agents. Digital signatures ensure data integrity and prevent unauthorized modifications. Secure key exchange protocols establish protected AI interactions, minimizing vulnerabilities in distributed AI environments.

The benefits of asymmetric cryptographic AI systems include enhanced data security, improved authentication, and protection against adversarial threats. Data security is strengthened by encrypting AI communications, preventing unauthorized access to sensitive information. Authentication mechanisms ensure AI-generated outputs originate from verified sources, reducing the risk of malicious alterations. Protection against adversarial threats enhances AI reliability by securing model training data and preventing tampering.

An example of asymmetric cryptographic AI systems is in AI-driven authentication protocols, where encrypted biometric data is used to verify user identities. AI-powered financial transactions rely on asymmetric encryption to protect online payments and prevent fraud. In secure federated learning, AI models use cryptographic techniques to train on decentralized data while maintaining privacy.

Industries utilizing asymmetric cryptographic AI systems include finance, healthcare, defense, cybersecurity, and cloud computing. The finance industry employs asymmetric encryption for secure AI-driven transactions and fraud detection. Healthcare organizations use cryptographic AI to safeguard patient data in medical imaging and diagnostics. Defense applications integrate asymmetric encryption into AI-powered intelligence systems to secure military communications. Cybersecurity firms use cryptographic AI for threat detection and secure data analysis. Cloud computing providers implement asymmetric encryption to protect AI models and data stored in distributed environments.

Applications of asymmetric cryptographic AI systems include encrypted machine learning, AI-driven identity verification, privacy-preserving AI models, secure AI communications, and confidential AI analytics. Encrypted machine learning ensures AI models operate on secured datasets without compromising privacy. AI-driven identity verification utilizes asymmetric encryption for biometric authentication and access control. Privacy-preserving AI models apply cryptographic techniques to train AI without exposing sensitive data. Secure AI communications protect chatbot interactions and autonomous system coordination. Confidential AI analytics enable organizations to extract insights from encrypted datasets without direct access to raw data.

Asymmetric cryptographic AI systems provide a secure framework for AI-driven applications, ensuring data confidentiality, integrity, and trustworthiness. By integrating encryption techniques, AI systems can operate securely across distributed environments, preventing unauthorized access and adversarial manipulation. As AI adoption expands, cryptographic security measures will become increasingly vital in protecting sensitive information and maintaining the reliability of intelligent systems.

Asymmetric Cryptographic AI Systems

Definition: Asymmetric Cryptographic AI Systems are setups where AI uses a pair of keys—one public, one private—to lock or unlock data, blending smart algorithms with tight security to keep secrets safe or verify who's who. It's AI playing gatekeeper with a clever twist.

Key Components: The heart's a duo of keys—public to encrypt, private to decrypt—tied to AI models that manage them. Cryptographic algorithms, like RSA or elliptic curves, do the heavy lifting. Data inputs—like messages or files—feed it, while a secure processor keeps the private key hidden. A learning layer tweaks key use over time.

Features: This system scrambles data fast, spots fakes with signature checks, and adapts to new threats by learning attack patterns. It's tight—only the private key unlocks—and scales for big networks or tiny devices.

Benefits: It locks down sensitive stuff—think bank chats or health records—with no shared secrets to leak. Saves hassle by verifying identities quick, cuts hacking risks, and lets AI evolve defenses smarter than static locks.

Example: Picture an AI securing an online vote—it encrypts your ballot with a public key, checks your ID with a signature, and only the private key at HQ tallies it, all hack-proof and smooth.

Challenges: Key management's a maze—lose the private one, and you're sunk. It's slow compared to simple locks, eats computing power, and training AI to spot new tricks needs fresh threat data. Plus, quantum tech could crack it someday.
Applications: It's in secure messaging apps, blockchain for coin trades, or smart contracts that sign themselves. Banks use it for transfers, and devices lock firmware against tampering.
Industries: Finance leans on it for trades, tech for app security, and healthcare for patient data. Government uses it for comms, blockchain for ledgers, and IoT for device trust.
Summary: Asymmetric Cryptographic AI Systems are AI's lock-and-key pros, blending smarts with security for a digital shield. They're a trust builder, though power and future cracks test them. They're keeping secrets safe, one key pair at a time.

Asymmetric Encryption in AI

refers to the application of public-private key cryptography in artificial intelligence to secure data transactions, communications, and AI model interactions. Unlike symmetric encryption, where a single key is used for both encryption and decryption, asymmetric encryption employs two distinct keys: a public key for encryption and a private key for decryption. This approach ensures that AI systems can securely exchange information while preventing unauthorized access.

Key components of asymmetric encryption in AI include cryptographic key pairs, encryption and decryption algorithms, authentication mechanisms, and secure AI communication protocols. Cryptographic key pairs allow AI systems to encrypt and decrypt data using a combination of public and private keys. Encryption and decryption algorithms define how AI models process and secure transmitted data. Authentication mechanisms verify the identity of AI entities involved in secure communications. Secure AI communication protocols establish encrypted data exchanges across AI-driven networks, preventing eavesdropping and data breaches.

The benefits of asymmetric encryption in AI include improved data privacy, secure AI model deployment, and protection against cyber threats. Data privacy is enhanced by encrypting AI-generated outputs and communications, preventing unauthorized access. Secure AI model deployment ensures that only verified users can access and modify trained AI models. Protection against cyber threats strengthens AI security by preventing adversarial attacks and data manipulation.

An example of asymmetric encryption in AI is in secure federated learning, where encrypted AI models are transmitted between decentralized nodes without exposing training data. AI-driven financial applications use asymmetric encryption to secure online transactions and prevent identity theft. In autonomous vehicles, encrypted AI communications protect navigation and safety systems from cyber intrusions.

Industries implementing asymmetric encryption in AI include finance, healthcare, autonomous systems, government, and cybersecurity. Financial institutions secure AI-powered fraud detection systems with encryption techniques. Healthcare organizations use encrypted AI models to protect patient data and enable confidential diagnostics. Autonomous systems rely on encrypted AI communications for secure navigation and decision-making. Government agencies integrate encryption into AI-driven intelligence analysis to protect sensitive information. Cybersecurity firms leverage asymmetric encryption to strengthen AI-driven threat detection and data security.

Applications of asymmetric encryption in AI include secure AI authentication, encrypted AI model sharing, confidential AI analytics, privacy-enhanced AI training, and AI-driven secure transactions. Secure AI authentication ensures user verification through cryptographic techniques. Encrypted AI model sharing allows researchers to exchange AI models securely. Confidential AI analytics protect sensitive datasets while enabling machine learning insights. Privacy-enhanced AI training ensures that AI models learn from encrypted data without exposure. AI-driven secure transactions apply encryption to prevent fraud and identity theft.

Asymmetric encryption in AI plays a crucial role in securing AI applications, ensuring data confidentiality, and protecting AI-driven transactions. By utilizing public-private key encryption, AI systems can operate safely in distributed and adversarial environments. As AI security challenges continue to evolve, asymmetric encryption will remain a foundational technology for safeguarding intelligent systems and ensuring trustworthy AI operations.

Asymmetric Information in AI Markets

Definition: Asymmetric information in AI markets refers to situations where one party in a transaction or interaction has more information than the other, which can affect AI-driven decision-making systems.

Key Characteristics:
Imbalanced information leads to one party having more relevant details than the other. AI decision-making must navigate unevenly distributed information, potentially causing market distortions.

Benefits: Competitive advantage arises from access to superior information. AI insights help balance information asymmetry by analyzing available data.

Disadvantages:
Bias may develop if AI models are trained on asymmetrical data. Ethical concerns arise when AI exploits information imbalances.

Applications:
Financial markets use AI for stock trading and investment decisions. Consumer behavior analysis benefits from AI evaluating asymmetrical data.

Sources:
Economic theory principles related to information asymmetry. Applications in AI-driven financial markets and consumer analytics.

Conclusions: Asymmetric information in AI markets can lead to biases or market distortions, requiring careful management to ensure fairness and accuracy.

Asymmetric Neural Network Structures
Definition: Asymmetric neural network structures are artificial neural networks that feature varying architectures or weight distributions across different layers, allowing for task-specific optimization.

Key Characteristics:
These networks are designed with non-uniform layers, meaning that each layer can have a unique number of neurons or different types of connections to serve specific functions. Instead of a uniform structure, they focus on adapting to the particular needs of a dataset or task.

Benefits:
Asymmetric structures enhance performance by tailoring learning processes for specialized applications. They also provide increased flexibility, allowing the network to be fine-tuned for different data types and analytical challenges.

Applications:
They are widely used in medical image processing, where specialized layers focus on detecting patterns in X-rays or MRI scans. In natural language processing (NLP), these networks improve performance in tasks such as sentiment analysis or language translation.

Sources:
These designs are based on neural network architecture principles, optimization techniques, and advancements in artificial intelligence research.

Conclusion:
Asymmetric neural network structures enable targeted optimizations, improving efficiency and accuracy for specialized tasks. However, their complexity makes them more challenging to design and less adaptable compared to more traditional, standardized neural networks.

Asynchronous AI Agent Communication

Definition: Asynchronous AI agent communication involves AI agents interacting with each other or external systems in an asynchronous manner, allowing them to communicate without the need for synchronization.

Key Characteristics:
Non-synchronized communication allows agents to send and receive messages independently of other agents' actions. Flexible interaction enables communication to happen at any time, not constrained by predefined schedules. Decentralized systems operate without a central controller managing agent communication.

Benefits:
Efficiency is improved as agents can continue working without waiting for others, enhancing overall system performance. Fault tolerance ensures that if one agent fails or is delayed, others can continue functioning without being affected.

Applications:
Multi-agent systems utilize asynchronous communication where multiple agents must communicate and collaborate. Autonomous robotics relies on this communication to help robots coordinate their actions without centralized control.Sources:
Multi-agent systems research focuses on distributed AI and multi-agent collaboration. AI communication protocols are based on frameworks designed for AI systems.

Conclusions: Asynchronous AI agent communication enhances the flexibility and efficiency of multi-agent AI systems, though it introduces challenges related to coordination and message delays.

Asynchronous Communication

Definition
Asynchronous Communication in AI is when systems talk without waiting for an instant reply—like emailing instead of calling—letting machines send, process, or act on data at their own pace. It's a no-rush chat for tech.

Key Components
The setup needs message queues or buffers to hold data till it's ready. Protocols—like APIs—keep the flow clear, while AI logic decides when to grab or send. Networks tie it together, and logs track what's said when.

Features
It's chill—systems work solo, no clock-watching. It scales big, juggling tons of messages, and shrugs off delays—perfect for spotty connections. Plus, it frees up resources, no idle waiting.

Benefits
It's smooth—handles peak loads without crashing. Saves time by decoupling tasks, cuts costs with less live babysitting, and fits global teams or devices ticking at different beats.

Example
Think of a weather AI—sensors ping rain data whenever, it crunches later, then sends alerts at dawn, all staggered but spot-on, no hurry needed.

Challenges
Timing's a trap—late replies can lag critical stuff. Debugging's messy with no live thread, and it needs tight design to avoid lost messages. Scaling queues eats storage too.

Applications
It's in IoT where gadgets ping home slow, chat apps storing texts, or data pipelines crunching logs. Robots use it to sync moves, and cloud services queue jobs.

Industries
Tech runs on it for apps, IoT for smart homes, and telecom for texts. Logistics tracks shipments, gaming syncs players, and finance queues trades.

Summary
Asynchronous Communication is AI's laid-back talk, passing notes at its own speed for flex and scale. It's a workload wizard, though timing and sprawl test it. It's keeping tech humming, no rush required.

Asynchronous AI Learning

Asychronous ai learning refers to a learning process in which artificial intelligence models or agents acquire knowledge, process information, and adapt to new data independently, without requiring simultaneous interactions or real-time synchronization. Unlike synchronous learning, where data processing and training updates occur simultaneously across all nodes, asynchronous AI learning enables systems to function and improve at different time intervals, allowing for greater scalability and flexibility.

Key components of asynchronous AI learning include distributed computing, independent learning nodes, delayed updates, and adaptive feedback mechanisms. Distributed computing allows AI models to be trained across multiple systems without waiting for each to complete its cycle, improving efficiency. Independent learning nodes operate autonomously, processing tasks at different speeds and asynchronously updating their knowledge base. Delayed updates ensure that AI agents can continue learning without being restricted by synchronization constraints. Adaptive feedback mechanisms enable models to refine their learning over time based on delayed or staggered input from different sources.

Examples of asynchronous AI learning can be seen in federated learning, where multiple decentralized AI models learn from different datasets without requiring simultaneous data transfer. In reinforcement learning environments, AI agents independently explore and learn from experiences without waiting for centralized updates. Cloud-based AI systems often employ asynchronous learning techniques to process large volumes of user interactions at different times, ensuring efficient resource utilization.

Applications of asynchronous AI learning extend across various fields, including autonomous systems, robotics, and large-scale machine learning frameworks. In autonomous systems, such as self-driving cars, asynchronous learning allows vehicles to continuously update their models based on different driving scenarios without waiting for real-time synchronization. In robotics, multiple AI-powered machines can learn tasks independently, enabling large-scale deployment in industries like manufacturing and logistics. Large-scale machine learning frameworks, such as those used in recommendation systems and fraud detection, leverage asynchronous learning to process user behavior and adapt to new patterns over time.

Challenges of asynchronous AI learning include potential inconsistencies in model updates, difficulty in managing data drift, and the risk of outdated knowledge affecting decision-making. Since updates occur independently, some AI models may operate on outdated information before synchronizing with the latest changes. Managing data drift, where patterns in data evolve over time, requires efficient mechanisms to ensure models remain accurate despite non-uniform learning rates. The decentralized nature of asynchronous learning also introduces complexity in coordinating distributed AI models and ensuring their outputs remain aligned.

In summary, asynchronous AI learning is a powerful approach that enables AI models to learn and adapt independently, offering greater flexibility and efficiency in large-scale and distributed environments. By leveraging decentralized learning, adaptive feedback, and delayed updates, it enhances AI capabilities in autonomous systems, robotics, and cloud computing. While challenges related to consistency and data management exist, advancements in AI synchronization techniques and adaptive learning strategies continue to improve the effectiveness of asynchronous learning, making it a crucial component in the evolution of artificial intelligence.

Asynchronous Algorithms

Asynchronous algorithms are computational processes designed to execute multiple tasks independently without requiring synchronization at each step. Unlike synchronous algorithms, which depend on a sequential execution flow where each step must wait for the previous one to complete, asynchronous algorithms allow different tasks to progress at their own pace. This flexibility makes them highly efficient for large-scale and distributed computing, where delays in one process do not hinder the execution of others.

The key components of an asynchronous algorithm include independent execution units that operate without waiting for other computations to finish, ensuring continuous processing. Message passing and event-driven communication allow different tasks to exchange data without requiring them to run simultaneously. Parallel processing enables multiple computations to be carried out across different processors or networked nodes, optimizing efficiency. Error handling mechanisms ensure that tasks can recover from failures or inconsistencies without disrupting the entire system. Load balancing distributes workloads dynamically, preventing bottlenecks and improving resource utilization.

The benefits of asynchronous algorithms include improved efficiency in distributed and parallel computing environments, reducing idle time caused by waiting for slower tasks. Scalability is enhanced as new processes can be added or removed without affecting the overall workflow. Fault tolerance is increased because independent execution reduces the impact of individual failures on the system. Resource utilization is optimized by ensuring that available computing power is used effectively rather than sitting idle. The flexibility of asynchronous execution enables real-time applications, where responsiveness is critical, such as in networked systems, artificial intelligence, and cloud computing.

A practical example of an asynchronous algorithm is its use in deep learning training, where different nodes in a distributed computing system update model parameters independently, accelerating convergence. In cloud-based applications, asynchronous algorithms handle user requests efficiently by processing multiple tasks concurrently, improving responsiveness. In large-scale simulations, such as weather forecasting, asynchronous execution enables different models to compute environmental factors in parallel, reducing overall computation time. In robotics, asynchronous algorithms allow multiple sensors to process data simultaneously, improving real-time decision-making. In financial trading, algorithmic trading systems use asynchronous execution to analyze market trends and execute trades without waiting for previous calculations to complete.

Despite its advantages, asynchronous algorithms present several challenges. Managing consistency across multiple independent tasks requires sophisticated synchronization mechanisms to avoid conflicts in shared data. Debugging and error tracking can be complex because execution does not follow a strict sequence, making it harder to reproduce issues. Load imbalance can occur when certain tasks complete faster than others, leading to inefficiencies in resource allocation. Data dependencies may introduce complications, requiring mechanisms to ensure that computations relying on previous results receive the correct inputs at the right time. Security concerns arise when implementing asynchronous algorithms in distributed environments, as data integrity and authentication become critical to prevent vulnerabilities.

Asynchronous algorithms are applied across multiple industries, enhancing computational efficiency and scalability. In artificial intelligence, they optimize model training, inference, and real-time decision-making in large datasets. In telecommunications, they enable efficient data packet transmission, reducing network congestion and latency. In cloud computing, they enhance service responsiveness by handling concurrent requests in web applications and distributed databases. In healthcare, they support parallel processing of medical imaging and genomic analysis, accelerating diagnostics and treatment planning. In autonomous systems, they enable robots, drones, and self-driving cars to process multiple sensory inputs simultaneously, improving navigation and obstacle detection.

In conclusion, asynchronous algorithms represent a powerful approach to computational efficiency, enabling tasks to run independently while maintaining overall system performance. Their ability to scale, reduce idle time, and optimize distributed computing makes them indispensable for modern applications in artificial intelligence, cloud computing, telecommunications, and real-time systems. While challenges such as consistency management, debugging complexity, and data dependencies must be addressed, the benefits of improved efficiency, fault tolerance, and scalability outweigh these difficulties. As technology advances, asynchronous algorithms will continue to play a crucial role in the development of intelligent, adaptive, and high-performance computing systems.

Asychronous distributed data processing

Asynchronous distributed data processing is a computational approach that enables data to be processed across multiple nodes or systems without requiring strict synchronization between tasks. Unlike synchronous processing, which requires tasks to proceed in a predefined order, asynchronous distributed data processing allows different computations to run independently and update results when they become available. This method enhances efficiency, scalability, and fault tolerance in large-scale data environments, making it essential for handling big data, cloud computing, and artificial intelligence applications.

The key components of asynchronous distributed data processing include decentralized task execution, where different computing nodes operate independently to process data without waiting for other tasks to complete. Event-driven architectures enable tasks to communicate through message passing and event triggers, ensuring that data updates occur dynamically. Parallel processing allows multiple computations to be performed simultaneously across distributed resources, optimizing data throughput. Fault-tolerant mechanisms ensure that failures in one node do not halt the entire system, allowing work to continue on other nodes. Load balancing distributes workloads dynamically, preventing system bottlenecks and ensuring that computational resources are fully utilized.

The benefits of asynchronous distributed data processing include increased efficiency, as independent execution prevents tasks from being delayed by slow components. Scalability is enhanced, allowing additional computing resources to be integrated without disrupting ongoing operations. Fault tolerance ensures that failures in individual nodes do not compromise the overall system, improving reliability. Real-time data analysis is facilitated by continuous processing, enabling rapid insights and decision-making. Resource optimization ensures that computing power is maximized, reducing idle time and improving cost-effectiveness in cloud-based environments.

A practical example of asynchronous distributed data processing is its use in large-scale machine learning, where training data is processed across multiple nodes without waiting for global updates, accelerating model convergence. In streaming analytics, real-time event processing platforms analyze continuous data flows asynchronously, detecting patterns and anomalies instantly. In cloud-based databases, distributed query execution allows different servers to process parts of a query independently, reducing latency and improving performance. In e-commerce, recommendation engines analyze customer behavior asynchronously across multiple data sources to generate personalized recommendations. In financial markets, asynchronous distributed data processing powers high-frequency trading systems that analyze vast datasets in real time to execute trades.

Despite its advantages, asynchronous distributed data processing presents several challenges. Ensuring consistency across multiple nodes requires sophisticated coordination mechanisms to handle updates and prevent conflicts. Debugging and troubleshooting can be complex due to the lack of a strict execution order, making it difficult to trace errors. Load imbalance may occur when certain nodes process larger workloads than others, reducing efficiency. Managing dependencies between asynchronous tasks requires careful design to avoid delays caused by missing or outdated data. Security risks arise when processing data across distributed environments, necessitating encryption, authentication, and access control mechanisms.

Asynchronous distributed data processing is applied across multiple industries to enhance computational performance and scalability. In artificial intelligence, it accelerates large-scale model training, inference, and data preprocessing. The telecommunications sector uses it for optimizing data transmission, reducing network latency, and improving content delivery. In healthcare, it enables the parallel processing of medical imaging, genomic analysis, and real-time patient monitoring. The finance industry relies on it for fraud detection, risk assessment, and algorithmic trading that requires real-time data analysis. Cloud service providers leverage it for distributed storage, database management, and large-scale enterprise applications.

In conclusion, asynchronous distributed data processing is a critical approach for handling massive datasets efficiently across multiple computing nodes. Its ability to enhance scalability, fault tolerance, and real-time analytics makes it indispensable for industries that require high-performance computing. While challenges such as data consistency, debugging complexity, and security concerns must be addressed, the benefits of improved efficiency, reduced latency, and cost-effective resource utilization outweigh these difficulties. As technology continues to evolve, asynchronous distributed data processing will play an increasingly vital role in the development of advanced AI systems, cloud computing, and large-scale data analytics solutions.

Asynchronous event-driven AI systems

Asychronoous event-driven AI systems are artificial intelligence frameworks designed to process information and make decisions based on events occurring independently of a predefined sequence. These systems operate by responding to triggers, signals, or changes in their environment, allowing AI models to execute tasks dynamically without waiting for sequential steps to complete. Unlike traditional synchronous AI models that rely on a fixed execution flow, asynchronous event-driven AI systems prioritize responsiveness, scalability, and real-time adaptation.

The key components of asynchronous event-driven AI systems include event-driven architectures that enable AI to react to changes in data streams, user interactions, or external stimuli. Message queues facilitate communication between different AI modules, ensuring that tasks can be processed independently without disrupting other ongoing computations. State management mechanisms track the current status of AI tasks, allowing the system to handle incomplete, delayed, or concurrent events effectively. Parallel processing capabilities enable AI models to execute multiple tasks simultaneously, improving efficiency and reducing response times. Edge computing integration allows AI to process events locally before sending data to centralized servers, minimizing latency and improving decision-making in real-world applications.

The benefits of asynchronous event-driven AI systems include enhanced responsiveness, as AI models can react to new information in real time without being constrained by a rigid sequence of operations. Scalability is significantly improved, allowing AI applications to handle large volumes of data and concurrent tasks across distributed environments. Energy efficiency is optimized by reducing idle computation and prioritizing active processing only when triggered by relevant events. Reduced system bottlenecks enable AI applications to operate smoothly, even under high-demand conditions. The ability to process incomplete or delayed information allows AI systems to function effectively in dynamic and unpredictable environments.

A practical example of asynchronous event-driven AI systems is their role in real-time fraud detection, where AI continuously monitors financial transactions and responds instantly to suspicious activity without waiting for batch processing. In autonomous driving, AI-powered vehicles process sensory inputs asynchronously, adjusting navigation based on traffic conditions, pedestrian movement, and road obstacles. AI-powered chatbots and virtual assistants use event-driven processing to analyze user queries and provide instant responses without requiring sequential input. In predictive maintenance, industrial AI systems analyze equipment sensor data asynchronously, identifying anomalies and triggering maintenance alerts before failures occur. AI-driven cybersecurity solutions monitor network traffic in real time, detecting threats and launching countermeasures dynamically without waiting for scheduled scans.

Despite its advantages, asynchronous event-driven AI systems present several challenges. Managing complex event dependencies requires sophisticated coordination strategies to ensure tasks execute in the correct sequence when necessary. Debugging and troubleshooting become more difficult due to the unpredictable nature of asynchronous execution, making it harder to trace errors and failures. Resource allocation must be carefully managed to prevent excessive computational overhead from handling too many concurrent events. Ensuring data consistency across multiple AI components requires synchronization mechanisms to prevent conflicts when processing real-time updates. Security risks increase as AI models handle decentralized and asynchronous inputs, necessitating robust encryption and authentication protocols to prevent unauthorized access.

Asynchronous event-driven AI systems are applied across multiple industries to enhance efficiency, automation, and real-time decision-making. In finance, AI-driven trading algorithms react to market fluctuations instantly, optimizing investment strategies. The healthcare sector benefits from AI-powered patient monitoring systems that analyze medical sensor data asynchronously to detect critical conditions before they escalate. Smart cities leverage event-driven AI to optimize traffic control, energy consumption, and emergency response coordination. The telecommunications industry utilizes AI for network optimization, dynamically adjusting bandwidth and infrastructure resources based on real-time demand. In e-commerce, AI systems personalize user experiences by asynchronously analyzing customer behavior, recommending products, and adjusting marketing campaigns in real time.

In conclusion, asynchronous event-driven AI systems represent a significant advancement in artificial intelligence, enabling real-time responsiveness, scalability, and efficiency in complex environments. Their ability to process and react to dynamic inputs makes them essential for applications requiring instant decision-making and continuous adaptation. While challenges such as debugging complexity, event synchronization, and security risks must be addressed, the benefits of enhanced automation, reduced latency, and scalable AI integration outweigh these difficulties. As AI technology continues to evolve, asynchronous event-driven AI systems will play an increasingly vital role in shaping intelligent automation, adaptive decision-making, and next-generation AI-driven solutions.

Asynchronous reinforcement learning

Asynchronous reinforcement learning is a machine learning approach that enables multiple agents or parallel processes to learn independently and update a shared model without waiting for synchronization. Unlike traditional reinforcement learning, where training follows a sequential order and requires updates at predefined steps, asynchronous reinforcement learning allows multiple instances of the learning algorithm to run concurrently. This method improves the efficiency, scalability, and convergence speed of reinforcement learning models by reducing idle time and computational bottlenecks.

The key components of asynchronous reinforcement learning include multiple parallel learners, where different instances of an AI agent interact with the environment simultaneously, collecting experiences independently. Gradient updates occur asynchronously, meaning that each agent updates the shared model without waiting for others, reducing delays caused by synchronization. Experience replay allows the system to store and reuse past interactions, improving learning stability and efficiency. Policy optimization methods adjust agent behavior based on asynchronous feedback, ensuring continuous improvement in decision-making. Task distribution mechanisms allocate computational resources dynamically, preventing bottlenecks and optimizing learning speed.

The benefits of asynchronous reinforcement learning include increased training efficiency, as parallel agents accelerate the exploration of the environment without waiting for centralized updates. Faster convergence speeds allow AI models to learn optimal strategies more quickly, making them suitable for real-time decision-making applications. Reduced dependency on synchronization minimizes computational delays, improving performance in large-scale reinforcement learning tasks. Enhanced robustness ensures that learning continues even if some agents fail or encounter unexpected challenges. Scalability allows reinforcement learning models to be trained across distributed environments, leveraging multiple processors or cloud-based infrastructure.

A practical example of asynchronous reinforcement learning is its use in robotics, where multiple robots independently learn motor skills and share their progress, leading to faster adaptation in real-world environments. In autonomous driving, AI agents simulate and learn from various traffic scenarios asynchronously, improving navigation and collision avoidance strategies. In gaming, reinforcement learning models train multiple AI agents in parallel, enhancing gameplay strategies and opponent modeling. In finance, asynchronous reinforcement learning optimizes algorithmic trading by allowing different strategies to evolve simultaneously, adjusting to market fluctuations in real time. In healthcare, reinforcement learning-based AI systems analyze medical treatment plans asynchronously, refining personalized recommendations based on multiple patient data sources.

Despite its advantages, asynchronous reinforcement learning presents several challenges. Managing asynchronous updates requires careful tuning to prevent unstable learning caused by outdated or conflicting information. Debugging is complex, as multiple agents learn independently, making it difficult to trace errors and inconsistencies in model updates. Computational resource allocation must be optimized to prevent inefficiencies, as some agents may consume more processing power than others. Balancing exploration and exploitation is more challenging in asynchronous settings, requiring adaptive learning rates to prevent premature convergence on suboptimal solutions. Ensuring security and fairness in distributed learning environments necessitates mechanisms to prevent biased updates and adversarial attacks.

Asynchronous reinforcement learning is applied across various industries to optimize automation, decision-making, and intelligent control systems. In robotics, it accelerates the training of AI-driven machines for manufacturing, logistics, and autonomous tasks. The financial sector leverages reinforcement learning for high-frequency trading, portfolio optimization, and fraud detection. Healthcare applications include AI-driven treatment planning, drug discovery, and patient care optimization using real-time learning models. The energy sector benefits from reinforcement learning in smart grid management, optimizing power distribution and consumption patterns. Smart transportation systems utilize asynchronous learning to enhance traffic management, route optimization, and public transportation scheduling.

In conclusion, asynchronous reinforcement learning is a powerful approach that enhances the efficiency, scalability, and adaptability of reinforcement learning models. By enabling multiple agents to learn concurrently, it reduces computational bottlenecks and accelerates the discovery of optimal solutions. While challenges such as update synchronization, debugging complexity, and resource management must be addressed, the benefits of improved learning speed, robustness, and scalability outweigh these difficulties. As AI continues to advance, asynchronous reinforcement learning will play a crucial role in developing intelligent, real-time decision-making systems that adapt to dynamic environments and optimize automation across industries.

Asychronous Stochastic Gradient Descent (ASGD)

Asynchronous Stochastic Gradient Descent (ASGD) is an optimization technique used in machine learning and deep learning to update model parameters using gradient-based learning while allowing multiple parallel processes to perform updates independently. Unlike traditional Stochastic Gradient Descent (SGD), which updates parameters sequentially, ASGD enables multiple workers or computing nodes to calculate gradients and apply updates without waiting for synchronization. This approach accelerates training times and allows large-scale models to be trained efficiently in distributed environments.

The key components of ASGD include parallel computation, where multiple processors or computing nodes work simultaneously to compute gradients and update model parameters. Asynchronous updates allow each worker to make changes to the shared model without requiring other workers to complete their updates, reducing idle time. A shared parameter server or decentralized model storage ensures that all workers can access and modify the latest version of the model during training. Gradient aggregation methods help balance model consistency by incorporating updates from multiple sources while minimizing conflicts. Learning rate adaptation mechanisms adjust optimization steps dynamically to prevent instability caused by delayed updates from different workers.

The benefits of ASGD include significantly reduced training time by utilizing multiple workers to process data batches in parallel, making it ideal for training large-scale deep learning models. Improved hardware utilization maximizes computing resources by ensuring that processors remain active rather than waiting for synchronization. Enhanced scalability allows ASGD to be implemented across distributed systems, making it suitable for cloud-based AI applications and large-scale machine learning tasks. Fault tolerance increases as the system remains operational even if some workers experience delays or failures, ensuring uninterrupted model training. The flexibility of ASGD supports diverse architectures, enabling it to be integrated with convolutional neural networks, recurrent neural networks, and other deep learning frameworks.

A practical example of ASGD is its use in training deep learning models on cloud-based platforms, where multiple GPUs or TPUs work asynchronously to optimize model parameters. In natural language processing, ASGD speeds up the training of large-scale transformer models by allowing different nodes to process separate text sequences independently. In image recognition, ASGD enhances the efficiency of training convolutional neural networks by parallelizing the gradient computation of different image batches. In financial modeling, ASGD optimizes risk prediction models by processing vast amounts of transaction data in parallel, improving the accuracy of fraud detection systems. In scientific computing, ASGD facilitates large-scale simulations by enabling AI models to process different experimental datasets asynchronously.

Despite its advantages, ASGD presents several challenges. Gradient staleness occurs when updates from different workers are applied at different times, potentially leading to inconsistencies and slowing down convergence. Tuning hyperparameters such as learning rates and batch sizes is more complex in ASGD due to the asynchronous nature of updates, requiring careful optimization to prevent instability. Increased communication overhead can arise when multiple workers interact with the parameter server, reducing efficiency if not properly managed. Model divergence may occur if updates are too far apart in time, requiring synchronization techniques or correction mechanisms to ensure stability. Debugging and monitoring ASGD training can be more challenging than traditional SGD due to the lack of strict execution order.

ASGD is applied across multiple industries that require large-scale machine learning and AI model training. In healthcare, it accelerates the training of AI-driven diagnostic models by enabling parallel processing of medical imaging and patient data. The financial sector benefits from ASGD in algorithmic trading, risk assessment, and fraud detection, where real-time data updates improve predictive accuracy. Autonomous systems, including self-driving cars and robotic automation, leverage ASGD for real-time decision-making and sensor data analysis. The e-commerce industry applies ASGD to recommendation algorithms, optimizing personalized content delivery based on consumer behavior. In cloud computing and AI research, ASGD enables scalable AI training on distributed platforms, making it a fundamental technique for advancing deep learning models.

In conclusion, Asynchronous Stochastic Gradient Descent is a powerful optimization method that improves the efficiency, scalability, and fault tolerance of machine learning model training. By leveraging asynchronous updates, ASGD accelerates the learning process, reduces hardware idle time, and enables large-scale distributed computing. While challenges such as gradient staleness, hyperparameter tuning, and communication overhead must be carefully managed, the benefits of faster training, enhanced scalability, and robust fault tolerance outweigh these difficulties. As AI continues to evolve, ASGD will play an essential role in optimizing deep learning frameworks, enabling breakthroughs in machine learning applications across various industries.

Asychronous Transfer Mode (ATM)

Asynchronous Transfer Mode (ATM) in AI networking is a high-speed networking protocol designed to facilitate the efficient transmission of data, voice, and video across AI-driven communication systems. It operates by dividing data into fixed-size cells, allowing seamless integration of different types of traffic while maintaining low latency and high reliability. This protocol is widely used in AI-powered networks to ensure smooth data flow, especially in environments where real-time processing and minimal delays are crucial.

The key components of ATM in AI networking include virtual circuit switching, which establishes dedicated paths for data transmission while maintaining quality of service. Fixed-size cells enable predictable latency, making the protocol suitable for AI applications that require real-time communication. Adaptation layers provide compatibility with higher-layer protocols, ensuring AI-driven data processing systems can seamlessly integrate with ATM networks. Traffic management mechanisms regulate data flow, preventing congestion and ensuring optimal performance. Quality of service controls prioritize AI workloads, guaranteeing reliable data transmission even under high network traffic conditions.

The benefits of ATM in AI networking include high-speed data transfer, enabling AI models to process and communicate large volumes of information efficiently. Low latency ensures that AI-driven systems, such as autonomous vehicles and real-time analytics platforms, receive and process data without significant delays. Scalability allows AI-powered networks to handle increasing workloads while maintaining performance and reliability. Guaranteed quality of service ensures AI applications maintain optimal functionality, especially in mission-critical tasks such as healthcare diagnostics and financial modeling. Multi-service support enables AI-driven systems to handle diverse data types, including voice, video, and sensor inputs, within a unified network architecture.

A practical example of ATM in AI networking is its use in AI-powered smart cities, where traffic control systems analyze and respond to real-time data from sensors and surveillance cameras. In healthcare, ATM enables AI-driven telemedicine platforms to transmit high-resolution medical images and video consultations with minimal delay. AI-enhanced financial trading systems leverage ATM networks to execute high-frequency trades based on real-time market data. AI-driven cloud computing environments use ATM for optimized data center communication, ensuring rapid access to distributed AI workloads. In industrial automation, AI-powered robotics utilize ATM for seamless machine-to-machine communication, improving efficiency in manufacturing processes.

Despite its advantages, ATM in AI networking presents several challenges. High implementation costs make ATM less accessible for smaller organizations, limiting widespread adoption. Complexity in network configuration requires specialized expertise to set up and maintain, increasing operational overhead. Compatibility issues arise when integrating ATM with modern IP-based networks, necessitating additional adaptation layers. Scalability constraints can occur in large-scale AI deployments, where newer networking technologies may offer more cost-effective solutions. Limited flexibility in handling variable data packet sizes can reduce efficiency when processing AI workloads that require dynamic data transmission.

ATM in AI networking is applied across multiple industries that require reliable, high-speed data communication. In telecommunications, it supports AI-driven network optimization and real-time voice and video transmission. The healthcare sector benefits from AI-powered remote diagnostics and patient monitoring systems that rely on low-latency communication. Financial institutions leverage ATM networks to enhance AI-based fraud detection and real-time market analysis. Autonomous transportation systems use ATM for AI-driven vehicle-to-infrastructure communication, improving traffic flow and safety. AI-driven entertainment platforms utilize ATM for high-quality streaming and real-time content delivery.

In conclusion, Asynchronous Transfer Mode in AI networking is a critical protocol that enables high-speed, low-latency data transmission for AI-powered systems. Its ability to ensure quality of service, support multi-service communication, and scale with AI workloads makes it valuable in industries that demand real-time processing. While challenges such as implementation costs, complexity, and compatibility must be addressed, the benefits of ATM in AI-driven applications make it an essential networking solution for advanced computing environments. As AI continues to evolve, ATM remains a key technology for optimizing data flow, enhancing real-time analytics, and supporting the future of intelligent networking.

Atomic AI Operation

Atomic AI operation refers to a fundamental process in artificial intelligence computing where an operation is executed as a single, indivisible unit without interruption or interference. This ensures that the operation either completes fully or does not execute at all, maintaining consistency and reliability in AI-driven systems. Atomicity is essential in AI algorithms, databases, and parallel processing environments where operations must be performed seamlessly to prevent data corruption, inconsistencies, or system failures.

The key components of atomic AI operation include transaction integrity, ensuring that operations execute in an all-or-nothing manner to prevent partial updates that could lead to errors. Synchronization mechanisms coordinate concurrent AI processes, preventing conflicts when multiple operations access shared resources. Locking protocols secure data and computational resources, preventing simultaneous access that could result in race conditions or data inconsistencies. Rollback capabilities allow AI systems to revert to a previous state in case of failure, ensuring stability and continuity. Hardware acceleration enhances atomic execution in AI models by leveraging specialized processors optimized for parallel computation.

The benefits of atomic AI operation include improved reliability, as AI systems function predictably without the risk of incomplete execution. Consistency is maintained in AI-driven computations, ensuring that data remains accurate across multiple processes. Enhanced efficiency enables AI algorithms to run smoothly without disruptions caused by partial updates or concurrent access conflicts. Fault tolerance is strengthened through rollback and recovery mechanisms, allowing AI applications to handle failures gracefully. Scalability is improved as atomic operations enable distributed AI models to coordinate processes without risking inconsistencies.

A practical example of atomic AI operation is its role in AI-powered financial transactions, where banking systems process payments securely without the risk of incomplete or duplicate transactions. In autonomous robotics, atomic operations ensure that sensor inputs and control decisions execute precisely without interference, preventing erratic movements. AI-driven cybersecurity systems use atomic operations to detect and respond to threats in real time, ensuring uninterrupted protection. In AI-enhanced healthcare diagnostics, atomic operations ensure that medical image analysis completes fully before presenting results, avoiding misdiagnoses caused by incomplete processing. AI in cloud computing relies on atomic operations to distribute workloads across multiple servers while maintaining data integrity.

Despite its advantages, atomic AI operation presents several challenges. Overhead from synchronization and locking mechanisms can slow down AI execution, especially in large-scale distributed systems. Managing atomicity in real-time AI applications requires careful optimization to balance performance and consistency. Complexity increases when implementing atomic operations in AI models that process vast amounts of data across multiple nodes. Deadlocks can occur when multiple processes wait indefinitely for resource access, requiring efficient conflict resolution strategies. Ensuring atomicity in quantum and neuromorphic AI computing introduces additional challenges due to the probabilistic nature of computation.

Atomic AI operation is applied across multiple industries that require secure, reliable, and consistent AI execution. In finance, it enhances algorithmic trading, fraud detection, and secure payment processing. The healthcare sector benefits from atomic AI in medical imaging, electronic health records, and AI-driven patient monitoring. AI-driven manufacturing relies on atomic operations for precision control in industrial automation and quality assurance. Smart grid technology leverages atomic AI operations to optimize energy distribution, ensuring uninterrupted power supply and grid stability. AI in aerospace and defense utilizes atomic operations for mission-critical decision-making, navigation, and threat assessment.

In conclusion, atomic AI operation is a foundational concept that ensures AI processes execute with integrity, reliability, and efficiency. By maintaining atomicity, AI-driven systems can function seamlessly in high-stakes environments where accuracy and consistency are paramount. While challenges such as synchronization overhead, deadlocks, and implementation complexity exist, the benefits of stable execution, fault tolerance, and improved scalability make atomic operations indispensable in AI computing. As AI continues to evolve, atomic AI operations will remain a crucial aspect of ensuring robust, error-free, and high-performance AI-driven applications across industries.

Attack surface analysis in AI security refers to the systematic idendification

Attack surface analysis in AI security refers to the systematic identification, assessment, and mitigation of potential vulnerabilities within an AI system that could be exploited by malicious actors. This process involves mapping out all possible entry points where an attacker could compromise, manipulate, or disrupt AI functionality. By understanding the attack surface, organizations can proactively strengthen AI security, reduce risks, and ensure system integrity in sensitive environments.

The key components of attack surface analysis in AI security include threat modeling, which evaluates potential attack vectors, including adversarial AI techniques and data manipulation. System mapping identifies all interfaces, data flows, and dependencies where vulnerabilities may exist, including APIs, cloud services, and third-party integrations. Security monitoring ensures continuous detection of anomalies that could indicate potential attacks, enhancing real-time defense mechanisms. Access control mechanisms regulate permissions and authentication protocols to prevent unauthorized access to AI models and datasets. Defensive AI strategies leverage machine learning techniques to detect, prevent, and adapt to emerging threats, ensuring the resilience of AI security frameworks.

The benefits of attack surface analysis in AI security include enhanced protection against cyber threats, ensuring that AI systems remain functional and trustworthy in adversarial environments. Risk mitigation reduces the likelihood of data breaches, adversarial attacks, and unauthorized system manipulations. Compliance with security standards and regulations is strengthened by proactively addressing vulnerabilities and demonstrating robust security practices. Improved AI model integrity prevents data poisoning, model inversion, and adversarial input manipulation that could compromise AI decision-making. Reduced system downtime ensures AI-driven applications continue to operate efficiently, even in the presence of attempted security breaches.

A practical example of attack surface analysis in AI security is its use in fraud detection systems, where AI algorithms analyze financial transactions while continuously monitoring potential vulnerabilities in data processing pipelines. In autonomous vehicles, AI security teams assess attack surfaces to prevent adversarial inputs from deceiving object detection systems and compromising road safety. AI-powered healthcare systems undergo attack surface analysis to prevent unauthorized access to sensitive patient records and ensure the integrity of diagnostic algorithms. Smart city infrastructure relies on AI security assessments to protect intelligent traffic control and surveillance networks from cyber threats. AI-driven industrial automation benefits from attack surface analysis to prevent attacks on robotic systems that could disrupt manufacturing processes.

Attack surface analysis in AI security is applied across multiple industries to strengthen cybersecurity measures and ensure AI model reliability. In financial services, AI-driven fraud detection and risk assessment systems benefit from attack surface analysis to protect against cybercriminals attempting to exploit transaction vulnerabilities. The healthcare sector relies on AI security assessments to safeguard patient data and prevent adversarial attacks on medical AI models. The defense and intelligence industry applies attack surface analysis to protect AI-powered surveillance and cybersecurity tools from nation-state cyber threats. AI in cloud computing undergoes rigorous attack surface evaluations to ensure secure model deployment and data privacy compliance. The retail and e-commerce sector leverages AI security analysis to protect recommendation algorithms and customer data from exploitation.

In conclusion, attack surface analysis in AI security is a critical process that enhances the resilience, reliability, and trustworthiness of AI-driven systems. By identifying and mitigating vulnerabilities, organizations can protect AI applications from adversarial manipulation, unauthorized access, and cyber threats. While challenges such as evolving attack vectors, integration complexity, and security expertise gaps exist, the benefits of proactive risk mitigation, improved compliance, and system integrity outweigh these difficulties. As AI adoption expands across industries, attack surface analysis will remain a fundamental security practice to ensure the safe and ethical deployment of artificial intelligence technologies in diverse operational environments.

Attentional Decoding in AI

Attentional decoding in AI refers to a neural network mechanis refers to a neural network mechanism that dynamically allocates focus to specific parts of an input sequence while generating an output. This technique is widely used in tasks involving sequential data, such as natural language processing, speech recognition, and image captioning, where context-aware understanding and generation of information are essential. By selectively attending to relevant portions of an input, attentional decoding improves the efficiency and accuracy of AI models in processing complex relationships within data.

The key components of attentional decoding in AI include attention mechanisms that assign varying importance to different input elements based on their relevance to the current decoding step. Context vectors aggregate weighted input representations, allowing the model to focus on the most meaningful parts of the sequence. Query, key, and value representations enable dynamic weighting of inputs, helping the model prioritize significant features. Recurrent or transformer-based architectures integrate attentional decoding to improve long-range dependencies in sequential data. Adaptive weighting mechanisms adjust focus dynamically throughout the decoding process, ensuring that attention is distributed optimally based on evolving contextual requirements.

The benefits of attentional decoding in AI include improved contextual awareness, allowing models to generate outputs with a deeper understanding of dependencies within sequences. Enhanced accuracy in machine translation, speech recognition, and text summarization ensures more natural and meaningful outputs. Reduced information loss helps models retain and emphasize relevant details from lengthy input sequences, leading to better decision-making. Increased adaptability enables AI systems to generalize across diverse linguistic structures, image patterns, or time-series data without requiring rigid pre-programmed rules. More efficient resource utilization reduces the computational burden by concentrating processing power on the most important parts of an input sequence.

A practical example of attentional decoding in AI is its role in neural machine translation, where AI dynamically shifts focus across words in the source language to generate accurate and grammatically coherent translations. In speech recognition, attentional decoding allows AI models to process varying speech patterns by emphasizing key phonetic elements while transcribing spoken language. Image captioning systems leverage attentional decoding to analyze specific regions of an image while generating descriptions, ensuring captions are contextually relevant. In medical AI, attentional decoding enhances diagnostic imaging models by focusing on critical areas within scans, improving disease detection accuracy. Conversational AI systems use attentional decoding to generate more contextually aware and responsive chatbot interactions.

Attentional decoding in AI is applied across multiple industries to enhance information processing and decision-making. In healthcare, AI-driven diagnostics and radiology benefit from attentional models that focus on critical regions in medical imaging, improving early disease detection. The finance sector leverages attentional decoding for fraud detection and algorithmic trading, where AI prioritizes patterns indicative of anomalies or market shifts. In entertainment, AI-powered recommendation systems use attentional decoding to analyze user preferences and provide personalized content suggestions. The legal industry applies attentional AI models for document summarization and contract analysis, streamlining the review of complex legal texts. Autonomous systems, including self-driving cars, utilize attentional decoding for real-time navigation, recognizing and prioritizing key environmental factors for safe decision-making.

In conclusion, attentional decoding in AI is a transformative technique that enhances the ability of neural networks to selectively focus on relevant input elements, improving contextual understanding, accuracy, and adaptability. By dynamically allocating attention, AI models generate more meaningful and coherent outputs across various applications, from language translation to medical diagnostics. While challenges such as computational demands, interpretability concerns, and training complexity exist, the benefits of enhanced contextual awareness, reduced information loss, and improved efficiency outweigh these difficulties. As AI research continues to advance, attentional decoding will remain a foundational component in developing more intelligent, responsive, and effective AI-driven systems.

Attention Head in AI

Attention head in AI is a fundamental unit in attention mechanisms, particularly in transformer-based neural networks, where it allows models to focus on different parts of input data simultaneously. Each attention head independently processes a subset of information, capturing contextual relationships and refining understanding before combining outputs. By computing attention scores between query, key, and value representations, attention heads enhance the ability of models to handle complex dependencies across sequences. They play a crucial role in natural language processing, image recognition, and speech processing by dynamically weighing the importance of different inputs.

The key components of an attention head include query vectors, which represent the elements that need attention, key vectors, which define what information should be considered, value vectors, which contain the actual information being attended to, and the attention scores, which determine how much focus each element receives. The weighted sum of value vectors forms the final output of each attention head. When multiple attention heads operate in parallel, they provide a richer and more diverse representation of the input data.

Attention heads provide multiple benefits in deep learning models. They improve contextual understanding by allowing different parts of a sequence to interact dynamically. They enhance the ability of neural networks to model long-range dependencies, making them effective in tasks like language translation and text generation. They reduce reliance on fixed-sized context windows, allowing flexibility in capturing complex relationships between data points. By processing information in parallel, attention heads enable more efficient and scalable learning.

Examples of attention heads include their application in transformer-based models like BERT, where multiple attention heads analyze different linguistic patterns to improve text comprehension. In machine translation, attention heads enable models like GPT to generate accurate translations by focusing on relevant words across different contexts. In speech recognition, they improve transcription accuracy by highlighting critical audio features. In computer vision, self-attention mechanisms enhance image segmentation and object recognition by identifying important regions in visual data.

Industries that benefit from attention heads include artificial intelligence research, where they drive advances in natural language processing and multimodal learning. In healthcare, they improve medical text analysis and image-based diagnostics. In finance, attention mechanisms enhance fraud detection and risk assessment by identifying anomalies in transactional data. In e-commerce, personalized recommendation systems leverage attention heads to analyze user preferences and behavior.

Despite their advantages, attention heads present several challenges. The computational cost of self-attention mechanisms scales quadratically with input size, making them resource-intensive for large datasets. Training deep transformer networks requires extensive hardware resources, limiting accessibility for smaller organizations. Attention mechanisms may struggle with interpretability, as the reasoning behind attention weight distributions is often opaque. Fine-tuning attention-based models for domain-specific applications requires substantial labeled data and computational power.

In summary, attention heads are a core component of transformer-based architectures, enabling models to dynamically focus on relevant input features while improving contextual understanding. They are widely applied in industries such as artificial intelligence, healthcare, finance, and e-commerce to enhance text comprehension, speech processing, and image analysis. While they offer powerful capabilities for capturing long-range dependencies, challenges related to computational efficiency, interpretability, and resource requirements necessitate careful optimization for practical applications.

Attentional Mechanisms in AI

Attentional mechanisms in AI refer to computational techniques that enable neural networks to selectively focus on the most relevant parts of input data, improving learning efficiency and model performance. These mechanisms mimic human cognitive processes by dynamically adjusting the level of attention assigned to different elements in a sequence or dataset. They are widely used in natural language processing, computer vision, and speech recognition to enhance model accuracy by prioritizing critical features while filtering out irrelevant information.

The key components of attentional mechanisms include attention weights, which determine the importance assigned to each input element, query-key-value representations, which facilitate the comparison of different data points, and normalization functions, which ensure that attention distributions remain stable. The attention score computation step measures the relationship between input elements, helping models focus on significant patterns. Different types of attentional mechanisms, such as self-attention, global attention, and local attention, are used depending on the task and computational constraints.

Attentional mechanisms provide multiple benefits in AI applications. They improve the interpretability of neural networks by highlighting the most influential parts of input data. They enhance efficiency by dynamically filtering out unimportant elements, reducing computational complexity. They enable models to learn long-range dependencies, which is crucial for tasks such as text translation and video analysis. They improve generalization by adapting to diverse contexts, making them effective in various domains.

Examples of attentional mechanisms include their use in machine translation models like Google's Transformer, where self-attention improves the alignment between words in different languages. In image recognition, attention modules enhance object detection by emphasizing key image regions. In speech synthesis, attention models control the flow of generated speech by selecting the most relevant phonetic features. In document summarization, attention-based architectures extract key information from lengthy texts to generate concise summaries.

Industries that utilize attentional mechanisms include artificial intelligence research, where they drive innovation in machine learning applications. In healthcare, they improve automated medical diagnostics by refining focus on critical imaging features. In finance, attentional models enhance fraud detection by analyzing suspicious transaction patterns. In entertainment, they improve video recommendation systems by identifying key user engagement patterns.

Despite their advantages, attentional mechanisms present several challenges. High computational costs make them expensive to deploy for large-scale applications. The lack of interpretability in deep attention networks makes it difficult to understand model decision-making processes. Training models with attention mechanisms requires substantial labeled data, which may not always be available. Over-reliance on attention scores may lead to biases if the model learns to prioritize irrelevant features.

In summary, attentional mechanisms in AI enhance learning efficiency by enabling models to selectively focus on relevant input features while improving contextual understanding. They are widely applied in natural language processing, computer vision, and speech recognition across industries such as healthcare, finance, and entertainment. While they offer significant improvements in model accuracy and efficiency, their computational demands and interpretability challenges require ongoing optimization for practical use.

Attention Mechanisms in neural networks

Attention mechanisms in neural networks refer to computational techniques that allow models to dynamically focus on specific input elements based on their relevance to the task. These mechanisms improve performance in sequence-based learning by selectively assigning different importance levels to various input features. By weighting different parts of the input according to their significance, attention mechanisms enable models to process long-range dependencies and improve generalization across diverse applications.

The key components of attention mechanisms in neural networks include attention weights, which determine the level of importance assigned to each input element, query-key-value mappings, which facilitate comparisons between elements, and aggregation functions, which combine weighted inputs to generate refined outputs. The attention score computation step assesses the relationship between input elements to identify patterns that contribute to the model's predictions. The normalization process ensures stability by standardizing attention distributions across the network.

Attention mechanisms provide several benefits in neural networks. They enable efficient learning by prioritizing relevant information while filtering out noise. They improve model performance by capturing long-distance dependencies that traditional architectures struggle with. They enhance adaptability, making neural networks more effective in handling diverse input data. They increase interpretability by highlighting which features contribute most to model decisions.

Examples of attention mechanisms in neural networks include their application in language models like BERT, where self-attention improves contextual word representations. In machine translation, attention enhances alignment between words in source and target languages. In speech recognition, attention-based architectures refine audio feature extraction to improve transcription accuracy. In image classification, attention layers highlight important regions in an image, improving object detection and scene understanding.

Industries that benefit from attention mechanisms in neural networks include artificial intelligence research, where they drive advancements in machine learning applications. In healthcare, they improve medical diagnostics by focusing on critical imaging features. In finance, they enhance fraud detection by identifying unusual transaction patterns. In autonomous systems, they refine object detection and decision-making processes for self-driving vehicles.

Despite their advantages, attention mechanisms present several challenges. Computational complexity increases with input size, requiring significant processing power. The interpretability of attention weights remains an ongoing challenge, as neural networks may not always provide clear explanations for decisions. Training models with attention mechanisms requires large datasets, which may be difficult to obtain in some domains. Optimizing attention models for real-time applications remains a technical hurdle due to their high processing demands.

In summary, attention mechanisms in neural networks enable models to dynamically focus on relevant input features, improving performance in sequence-based learning tasks. They are widely used in industries such as artificial intelligence, healthcare, and finance to enhance natural language processing, image recognition, and decision-making. While they offer significant advantages in capturing complex relationships, challenges related to computational efficiency and interpretability require further research and optimization.

Attribute-Based Access Control (ABAC) in AI is a security framework that regulates access to resources based on user, object, and environmental attributes rather than predefined roles or identities. It enables dynamic and context-aware access management by evaluating attributes such as user credentials, device types, locations, and time of access. In AI-driven systems, ABAC enhances security and compliance by enforcing fine-grained access control policies that adapt to evolving conditions. By leveraging AI, ABAC can automate policy enforcement, detect anomalies, and optimize access permissions in real time.

The key components of ABAC in AI include subject attributes, which define user characteristics such as identity, department, or security clearance. Object attributes specify properties of the resource being accessed, such as classification level, sensitivity, or ownership. Environmental attributes capture contextual information like time, location, and network status. Policy rules govern access decisions by specifying conditions under which requests are granted or denied. AI-enhanced decision-making uses machine learning and behavioral analysis to refine access policies and detect potential security threats.

ABAC in AI provides multiple benefits in cybersecurity and data protection. It enhances flexibility by dynamically adjusting access permissions based on real-time attributes. It improves security by reducing insider threats and unauthorized access through strict attribute-based conditions. It enables regulatory compliance by enforcing policies that align with industry standards and privacy regulations. It optimizes efficiency by automating access control decisions using AI-driven risk assessment and anomaly detection.

Examples of ABAC in AI include its use in financial systems, where access to sensitive transaction data is restricted based on user credentials, location, and device security status. In healthcare, ABAC ensures that only authorized personnel can access electronic health records while considering contextual factors such as patient consent and medical necessity. In cloud computing, it controls access to virtual environments by evaluating workload sensitivity, user authentication levels, and real-time security threats. In AI-powered content management, ABAC restricts access to confidential information based on user roles, document sensitivity, and operational policies.

Industries that benefit from ABAC in AI include finance, where it strengthens fraud prevention by limiting access to transaction data. In healthcare, it enhances patient privacy by enforcing strict data-sharing policies. In government agencies, it ensures national security by controlling access to classified information based on security clearance levels. In cloud computing, it improves cybersecurity by dynamically restricting unauthorized access to cloud-based applications and services.

Despite its advantages, ABAC in AI presents several challenges. Implementing and managing complex access policies requires extensive computational resources and policy definitions. Real-time attribute evaluation can introduce latency, affecting system performance. AI-driven policy enforcement must balance security with user experience to prevent excessive access restrictions. Integrating ABAC with legacy systems can be complex, requiring significant infrastructure updates. Ensuring policy transparency and fairness is crucial, as AI-based access decisions must be explainable and unbiased.

In summary, ABAC in AI is a dynamic access control framework that enhances security by evaluating user, object, and environmental attributes in real time. It is widely used in finance, healthcare, and cloud computing to regulate sensitive data access while improving compliance and efficiency. While it provides adaptive and robust security, challenges related to policy complexity, system integration, and AI transparency require careful consideration for effective implementation.

Attribute Based Learning

Attribute-Based Learning in AI is a machine learning approach that focuses on using specific attributes of data to enhance learning, classification, and decision-making. It extracts meaningful features from datasets and uses them to train models that generalize patterns and relationships. This learning approach is particularly useful in scenarios where explicit attributes can drive accurate predictions, such as image recognition, fraud detection, and recommendation systems.

The key components of attribute-based learning include feature extraction, where significant attributes are identified and isolated from raw data to form structured inputs for machine learning models. Attribute selection ensures that only relevant attributes contribute to model training, reducing noise and improving efficiency. The learning model processes extracted attributes to find correlations, classify patterns, and make predictions. The decision function maps input attributes to outcomes, forming the basis for intelligent decision-making.

Attribute-based learning provides several advantages in AI development. It improves model interpretability by focusing on well-defined attributes, making predictions easier to explain. It enhances efficiency by reducing computational complexity through selective attribute processing. It supports adaptability by allowing models to generalize across various domains where attribute patterns hold predictive value. It enables better feature engineering by guiding researchers in selecting relevant characteristics for data-driven insights.

Examples of attribute-based learning include its application in facial recognition, where models learn to identify unique facial attributes such as eye shape, skin texture, and facial structure. In fraud detection, attribute-based models analyze transaction attributes such as payment amount, location, and device type to identify suspicious activities. In medical diagnosis, patient attributes such as age, symptoms, and medical history help AI models predict disease risks. In recommendation systems, user attributes such as browsing history, preferences, and purchase patterns enhance personalized content delivery.

Industries that benefit from attribute-based learning include healthcare, where it enables precise disease classification and personalized treatment recommendations. In finance, it strengthens fraud prevention by analyzing customer behavior attributes. In e-commerce, it enhances product recommendations by tailoring suggestions to user preferences. In cybersecurity, it improves threat detection by analyzing system activity attributes for signs of malicious behavior.

Despite its advantages, attribute-based learning presents several challenges. Selecting the right attributes requires domain expertise, as irrelevant attributes can reduce model accuracy. High-dimensional datasets with numerous attributes increase computational complexity, requiring dimensionality reduction techniques. Bias in attribute selection can lead to skewed model outcomes, impacting fairness and reliability. Handling missing or incomplete attribute data requires preprocessing techniques to maintain model performance.

In summary, attribute-based learning in AI enhances model performance by leveraging specific features for pattern recognition and decision-making. It is widely applied in healthcare, finance, e-commerce, and cybersecurity to improve predictions and data-driven insights. While it improves interpretability and efficiency, challenges related to attribute selection, data bias, and computational complexity must be addressed to ensure effective implementation.

AttributE Extraction

Attribute Extraction in AI is the process of identifying and isolating relevant features from raw data to enhance machine learning performance. It transforms unstructured data into structured representations by selecting meaningful attributes that contribute to classification, prediction, and decision-making tasks. Attribute extraction plays a crucial role in various AI applications, including natural language processing, image recognition, and anomaly detection.

The key components of attribute extraction include data preprocessing, where raw data is cleaned and transformed to remove noise and inconsistencies. Feature selection identifies the most relevant attributes, reducing dimensionality while preserving essential information. Feature transformation modifies extracted attributes into a format suitable for machine learning models. Attribute ranking prioritizes features based on their importance in predictive modeling.

Attribute extraction provides several advantages in AI-driven applications. It improves model accuracy by focusing on high-impact features that enhance predictive power. It reduces computational complexity by eliminating irrelevant data, leading to faster training and inference. It increases generalization by allowing models to learn from essential attributes without being affected by noise. It enhances interpretability by making machine learning decisions more transparent and explainable.

Examples of attribute extraction include its use in speech recognition, where features such as pitch, frequency, and phonemes are extracted from audio signals to improve transcription accuracy. In sentiment analysis, textual features such as word embeddings, syntax, and sentiment scores help classify opinions in customer reviews. In facial recognition, image features such as texture, edge detection, and key facial landmarks improve identification accuracy. In cybersecurity, network traffic attributes such as packet size, connection duration, and request frequency help detect suspicious activity.

Industries that utilize attribute extraction include artificial intelligence research, where it enhances data-driven learning models. In healthcare, it improves medical imaging analysis by extracting critical diagnostic features. In finance, it strengthens risk assessment models by identifying financial attributes that predict creditworthiness. In marketing, it refines customer segmentation by analyzing demographic and behavioral attributes.

Despite its advantages, attribute extraction presents several challenges. Identifying the most relevant attributes requires domain expertise and knowledge of data distributions. Extracted attributes may be biased, leading to skewed predictions if not carefully selected. High-dimensional data increases the risk of overfitting, requiring careful feature selection and reduction techniques. Dynamic data environments require continuous attribute updates to maintain model relevance.

In summary, attribute extraction in AI is a fundamental process that transforms raw data into structured features to improve machine learning performance. It is widely used in speech recognition, sentiment analysis, facial recognition, and cybersecurity across industries such as healthcare, finance, and marketing. While it enhances model accuracy and efficiency, challenges related to feature selection, bias mitigation, and dimensionality reduction require careful consideration to ensure effective implementation.

Attribute Weighting in Machine Learning

Attribute weighting in machine learning is the process of assigning different levels of importance to various features within a dataset to improve model performance. It ensures that highly relevant attributes contribute more significantly to the learning process, while less important or noisy attributes have reduced influence. By optimizing feature importance, attribute weighting enhances accuracy, efficiency, and generalization in predictive models.

The key components of attribute weighting include feature selection, where relevant attributes are identified based on statistical analysis or domain knowledge. Weight assignment allocates numerical values to features, indicating their impact on model predictions. Normalization ensures that attribute weights are balanced and do not disproportionately affect model learning. Optimization techniques such as gradient-based learning and genetic algorithms adjust weights dynamically to improve model performance.

Attribute weighting provides several benefits in machine learning. It improves model accuracy by emphasizing the most predictive features while minimizing the influence of irrelevant data. It reduces overfitting by preventing the model from relying too heavily on noisy or redundant attributes. It enhances interpretability by clarifying the significance of different attributes in decision-making. It increases computational efficiency by focusing training resources on high-impact features.

Examples of attribute weighting include its use in credit scoring models, where financial history attributes such as income and debt ratio are given higher weights than less relevant factors. In medical diagnosis, machine learning models prioritize clinical attributes like genetic markers and symptom severity to improve disease prediction. In recommendation systems, user behavior attributes such as purchase frequency and browsing history are weighted to personalize content suggestions. In fraud detection, transaction attributes such as transaction location, time, and amount are weighted to identify suspicious activity.

Industries that benefit from attribute weighting include finance, where it enhances risk assessment and fraud detection models. In healthcare, it improves diagnostic accuracy by prioritizing key medical features. In e-commerce, it optimizes product recommendations by weighting customer preferences. In cybersecurity, it strengthens anomaly detection by emphasizing critical system activity attributes.

Despite its advantages, attribute weighting presents several challenges. Determining optimal feature weights requires careful tuning and domain expertise. Poorly assigned weights can lead to biased models and inaccurate predictions. In dynamic environments, attribute weights must be continuously updated to reflect changing patterns in data. Computational complexity increases when weighting high-dimensional datasets, requiring efficient optimization techniques.

In summary, attribute weighting in machine learning improves model accuracy and efficiency by assigning appropriate importance to features. It is widely used in finance, healthcare, and cybersecurity to enhance decision-making and predictive modeling. While it offers significant advantages in feature prioritization, challenges related to weight optimization, bias mitigation, and computational complexity require careful management for effective implementation.

Audio signal processing with AI

Audio signal processing with AI involves the application of artificial intelligence techniques to analyze, modify, and interpret audio signals for tasks such as speech recognition, sound classification, and music generation. By leveraging deep learning and signal processing algorithms, AI can extract meaningful patterns from raw audio data, enabling automation and enhancement of various audio-based applications.

The key components of audio signal processing with AI include feature extraction, where important characteristics such as frequency, pitch, and amplitude are identified. Signal transformation converts raw waveforms into structured representations such as spectrograms or Mel-frequency cepstral coefficients (MFCCs). Neural networks process extracted features to recognize speech, detect anomalies, or classify sounds. Real-time processing techniques enable AI models to analyze and generate audio with minimal latency.

Audio signal processing with AI provides several benefits. It enhances speech recognition systems by improving the accuracy of voice commands and automated transcription. It enables audio enhancement by reducing noise and improving sound quality in communication systems. It facilitates music composition and sound synthesis by generating realistic audio patterns. It improves security through speaker recognition and acoustic anomaly detection.

Examples of audio signal processing with AI include voice assistants such as Siri and Alexa, which process spoken commands to execute tasks. In healthcare, AI-powered diagnostic tools analyze lung and heart sounds to detect abnormalities. In entertainment, AI-generated music and audio effects enhance media content. In security, AI-based sound recognition detects gunshots, glass breaking, and other auditory threats.

Industries that benefit from AI-driven audio signal processing include telecommunications, where it enhances call quality and speech translation. In healthcare, it improves early detection of respiratory diseases through acoustic analysis. In entertainment, it enables personalized music recommendations and automated sound design. In smart home technology, it powers voice-activated assistants and home security systems.

Despite its advantages, AI-based audio signal processing presents several challenges. Background noise and overlapping speech can degrade model accuracy. Large datasets and computational power are required for training high-quality models. Variability in accents, speech patterns, and environmental conditions affects performance. Ensuring privacy and ethical use of voice data remains a concern in applications such as surveillance and customer service.

In summary, audio signal processing with AI enhances speech recognition, sound classification, and music generation by leveraging deep learning techniques. It is widely applied in telecommunications, healthcare, and entertainment to improve audio analysis and automation. While it offers significant advancements in audio-based applications, challenges related to noise reduction, data requirements, and ethical considerations require careful implementation and optimization

Augmented AI

Augmented AI refers to artificial intelligence systems designed to work alongside human decision-makers, enhancing their capabilities rather than replacing them. By leveraging machine learning, natural language processing, and data analytics, augmented AI assists in tasks that require human expertise, improving efficiency, accuracy, and scalability. It bridges the gap between human intelligence and automation by providing real-time insights and recommendations while leaving critical decisions in human control.

The key components of augmented AI include human-in-the-loop systems, where AI assists users by providing suggestions while humans make final decisions. Machine learning models process vast amounts of data to identify patterns, trends, and insights that aid human decision-making. Natural language processing enables AI to understand and generate human-like text, improving communication and interaction. Automation tools assist with repetitive tasks, freeing up human workers for more complex problem-solving.

Augmented AI provides several benefits across various industries. It enhances productivity by automating routine processes while allowing humans to focus on strategic tasks. It improves decision-making by providing data-driven insights and reducing cognitive bias. It enhances collaboration by enabling seamless interaction between AI tools and human users. It increases accuracy by minimizing human error in data-intensive tasks.

Examples of augmented AI include AI-assisted medical diagnosis, where machine learning models analyze patient data and provide recommendations to doctors. In financial services, AI-powered risk assessment tools help analysts make informed investment decisions. In customer support, AI chatbots assist human agents by handling basic queries while escalating complex issues. In manufacturing, AI-driven predictive maintenance systems provide engineers with insights to prevent equipment failures.

Industries that benefit from augmented AI include healthcare, where it supports doctors in medical imaging and diagnostics. In finance, it enhances fraud detection and investment strategy optimization. In customer service, it improves response efficiency by handling repetitive inquiries. In cybersecurity, it strengthens threat detection by analyzing security logs and alerting analysts to potential breaches.

Despite its advantages, augmented AI presents several challenges. Integrating AI with human workflows requires training and adaptation. AI models must be transparent to ensure users trust and understand recommendations. Ethical concerns arise when AI assists in decision-making processes that impact people's lives, such as hiring or law enforcement. Data privacy and security must be maintained to prevent unauthorized access to sensitive information.

In summary, augmented AI enhances human intelligence by providing AI-powered insights, automation, and decision support. It is widely used in healthcare, finance, and customer service to improve efficiency and accuracy. While it bridges the gap between AI and human expertise, challenges related to integration, transparency, and ethical concerns must be carefully managed to ensure responsible and effective deployment.

Augmented Intelligence

Augmented intelligence is a human-centered approach to artificial intelligence that enhances human decision-making rather than replacing it. It leverages AI-driven insights, automation, and predictive analytics to support human expertise, improving productivity, accuracy, and efficiency. Unlike fully autonomous AI, augmented intelligence ensures that humans remain in control of complex decision-making processes while benefiting from AI-generated recommendations and data analysis.

The key components of augmented intelligence include machine learning models that analyze vast amounts of data to provide actionable insights. Human-in-the-loop systems integrate AI with human oversight, ensuring that final decisions are made with expert judgment. Natural language processing allows seamless interaction between AI systems and human users, improving accessibility and understanding. Decision support tools enhance analytical capabilities by offering predictive modeling, trend analysis, and real-time recommendations.

Augmented intelligence provides multiple benefits across industries. It improves decision accuracy by minimizing cognitive biases and processing large-scale data efficiently. It enhances productivity by automating routine tasks while allowing humans to focus on complex problem-solving. It fosters collaboration between AI systems and human users, enabling seamless workflows and intelligent automation. It increases adaptability by continuously learning from new data and refining recommendations based on user feedback.

Examples of augmented intelligence include AI-assisted medical diagnostics, where machine learning models analyze patient data to support doctors in making accurate diagnoses. In finance, AI-powered risk assessment tools assist analysts in making investment decisions. In customer service, AI chatbots handle routine queries while human agents resolve complex issues. In cybersecurity, AI-driven threat detection alerts security teams to potential vulnerabilities, allowing for rapid response and mitigation.

Industries that benefit from augmented intelligence include healthcare, where AI enhances clinical decision-making and medical imaging analysis. In finance, it optimizes fraud detection and risk management strategies. In retail, it personalizes customer experiences through AI-driven recommendations. In manufacturing, it improves predictive maintenance by analyzing equipment performance and predicting failures before they occur.

Despite its advantages, augmented intelligence presents several challenges. Integrating AI into human workflows requires careful design to ensure usability and trust. Transparency is critical, as AI-generated recommendations must be explainable and interpretable to avoid overreliance or bias. Ethical concerns arise when AI influences high-stakes decisions, such as hiring or law enforcement, requiring strict regulatory oversight. Data privacy and security must be managed to prevent unauthorized access to sensitive information.

In summary, augmented intelligence enhances human expertise by integrating AI-driven insights, automation, and predictive analytics into decision-making processes. It is widely applied in healthcare, finance, retail, and manufacturing to improve accuracy, efficiency, and collaboration. While it offers significant benefits, challenges related to transparency, ethical considerations, and data security require careful management to ensure responsible and effective implementation.

Augmented Reality (AR)

Augmented reality (AR) with AI combines computer-generated visual elements with real-world environments while leveraging artificial intelligence to enhance interactivity and functionality. AI enables AR systems to recognize objects, interpret environments, and adapt visual overlays based on real-time data, creating immersive and intelligent user experiences. By integrating AI, AR applications can provide contextual awareness, personalized recommendations, and automated adjustments, making them more dynamic and responsive.

The key components of augmented reality with AI include computer vision, which allows AR systems to detect and track objects in real time. Machine learning models analyze spatial data and user interactions to enhance AR experiences dynamically. Natural language processing enables voice-based interactions, improving user engagement. Sensor fusion combines data from cameras, gyroscopes, and GPS to ensure precise alignment between virtual and real-world elements.

Augmented reality with AI provides several advantages across industries. It enhances user engagement by delivering interactive and immersive experiences. It improves accuracy in applications such as remote assistance and training simulations. It enables intelligent automation by adapting AR content based on environmental and contextual factors. It increases efficiency by providing real-time data overlays that assist users in tasks such as maintenance, navigation, and learning.

Examples of augmented reality with AI include AI-powered virtual try-ons in e-commerce, where AR allows customers to see how clothing or accessories fit before purchasing. In healthcare, AR enhances surgery by overlaying patient data and anatomical structures on a surgeon's field of view. In industrial settings, AR-powered maintenance guides provide technicians with step-by-step instructions based on real-time equipment diagnostics. In education, AI-enhanced AR applications create interactive learning experiences, allowing students to visualize complex scientific concepts in 3D.

Industries that benefit from augmented reality with AI include retail, where it enhances customer experiences through virtual product trials. In healthcare, it improves medical training and diagnostics by providing real-time augmented overlays. In manufacturing, it optimizes efficiency by offering hands-free guidance for assembly and repair tasks. In tourism, it enriches visitor experiences by providing historical context and interactive navigation through AR-enhanced travel apps.

Despite its advantages, augmented reality with AI presents several challenges. Processing large amounts of real-time data requires significant computational resources, making high-performance hardware essential. Developing accurate and responsive AR systems demands advanced AI models capable of real-time decision-making. Ensuring seamless integration with real-world environments can be complex due to varying lighting conditions and spatial constraints. Privacy concerns arise as AR applications collect and process user data, requiring strong security measures.

In summary, augmented reality with AI enhances real-world interactions by integrating intelligent visual overlays, object recognition, and contextual awareness. It is widely used in retail, healthcare, manufacturing, and tourism to improve user experiences and productivity. While it offers immersive and interactive capabilities, challenges related to computational demands, environmental adaptability, and data privacy require ongoing advancements for effective implementation.

Autoencoders

Autoencoders are a type of neural network designed for unsupervised learning, primarily used for data compression, feature extraction, and anomaly detection. They work by encoding input data into a lower-dimensional representation and then reconstructing it back to its original form. By learning to capture essential patterns and removing redundant information, autoencoders enable efficient data representation and dimensionality reduction.

The key components of autoencoders include the encoder, which compresses input data into a lower-dimensional latent space by identifying key features. The latent representation serves as a compressed abstraction of the original data, capturing essential characteristics while reducing noise. The decoder reconstructs the original input from the latent representation, ensuring minimal information loss. The loss function measures the difference between the original input and reconstructed output, guiding the training process to improve accuracy.

Autoencoders provide several benefits in machine learning and data processing. They enhance data compression by encoding high-dimensional data into compact representations while preserving meaningful features. They improve anomaly detection by identifying deviations in reconstructed outputs, making them useful for fraud detection and cybersecurity. They support feature extraction by learning essential data representations without manual labeling. They enable noise reduction by reconstructing clean data from corrupted inputs, improving signal clarity in applications such as image and audio processing.

Examples of autoencoders include their use in image denoising, where they remove noise from pictures while preserving important details. In network security, they detect anomalies in traffic patterns by learning normal behavior and flagging deviations. In medical imaging, they compress large MRI and CT scan data for efficient storage and analysis. In recommendation systems, they generate embeddings that improve personalized content suggestions by capturing underlying user preferences.

Industries that benefit from autoencoders include finance, where they detect fraudulent transactions by identifying unusual spending patterns. In healthcare, they enhance medical imaging analysis by reducing data redundancy. In cybersecurity, they improve threat detection by identifying abnormal system behaviors. In manufacturing, they optimize quality control by detecting defects in production processes.

Despite their advantages, autoencoders present several challenges. Training deep autoencoders requires large datasets and high computational resources. The risk of overfitting arises if models learn to reconstruct input data too precisely without capturing underlying patterns. Selecting the right architecture and hyperparameters is complex, as different applications require varying levels of compression and reconstruction accuracy. Interpretability remains a challenge, as autoencoders generate abstract latent representations that may not be easily explainable.

In summary, autoencoders are a powerful tool in unsupervised learning, enabling data compression, anomaly detection, and noise reduction through efficient feature representation. They are widely applied in finance, healthcare, cybersecurity, and manufacturing to improve data processing and decision-making. While they offer significant benefits in reducing data complexity and enhancing insights, challenges related to computational demands, overfitting, and interpretability require careful implementation for optimal performance.

AutoGPT

AutoGPT is an autonomous AI agent built on top of GPT models that can independently generate, refine, and execute tasks based on high-level user instructions. Unlike traditional AI models that require step-by-step human interaction, AutoGPT is capable of breaking down complex goals into subtasks, iterating over them, and adjusting its approach dynamically. By leveraging large language models and reinforcement learning principles, AutoGPT enhances automation, decision-making, and problem-solving across multiple domains.

The key components of AutoGPT include the language model, which processes and generates human-like text based on contextual understanding. Task planning allows AutoGPT to break down objectives into actionable steps. Memory storage retains past interactions, enabling long-term task execution without losing context. Reinforcement mechanisms refine decision-making by evaluating past actions and optimizing for efficiency. The feedback loop ensures that AutoGPT adjusts its approach based on new data or user modifications.

AutoGPT provides several benefits in automation and AI-driven problem-solving. It enhances productivity by autonomously handling tasks without continuous human intervention. It improves efficiency in research and data analysis by summarizing vast information quickly. It streamlines workflows by managing repetitive and time-consuming processes. It reduces cognitive load by assisting users with planning, content creation, and decision-making.

Examples of AutoGPT include its use in content creation, where it autonomously generates articles, summaries, and reports. In software development, it writes and refines code with minimal human input. In business automation, it manages customer service inquiries and optimizes scheduling. In financial analysis, it processes market data and provides insights for investment decisions.

Industries that benefit from AutoGPT include digital marketing, where it automates social media and content generation. In finance, it assists in risk assessment and portfolio management. In customer service, it powers AI-driven chatbots that handle complex inquiries. In research, it accelerates data analysis and literature reviews.

Despite its advantages, AutoGPT presents several challenges. Managing hallucinations and ensuring factual accuracy remains a difficulty, as it may generate plausible but incorrect information. The computational cost of running and maintaining AutoGPT can be high, limiting accessibility. Ethical concerns arise from its ability to automate decision-making without human oversight. Security risks include the potential misuse of autonomous AI for generating misinformation or malicious content.

In summary, AutoGPT is an advanced AI system that autonomously executes tasks by breaking down complex goals and refining its outputs dynamically. It is widely applied in industries such as digital marketing, finance, and research to enhance automation and decision-making. While it offers significant benefits in productivity and efficiency, challenges related to accuracy, ethical considerations, and computational costs require careful oversight and responsible deployment.

Autotgrad in AI

Autograd in AI is an automatic differentiation tool that computes gradients efficiently in machine learning models, enabling optimization and backpropagation processes. It automates the calculation of derivatives, allowing AI systems to adjust parameters during training without manual differentiation. By leveraging computational graphs, Autograd streamlines gradient-based learning, making deep learning frameworks more efficient and adaptable.

The key components of Autograd include computational graphs, which represent mathematical operations and track dependencies between variables. The forward pass computes function values while storing intermediate steps for differentiation. The backward pass applies the chain rule to calculate gradients, enabling parameter updates in neural networks. Dynamic computation ensures that differentiation occurs automatically as functions change, improving adaptability in model training.

Autograd provides several benefits in machine learning. It accelerates the optimization process by eliminating manual gradient calculations. It improves efficiency by automating differentiation across complex functions. It enhances model adaptability by supporting dynamic computation and real-time gradient adjustments. It reduces implementation errors by handling differentiation with high numerical accuracy.

Examples of Autograd include its application in deep learning frameworks such as PyTorch, where it automates backpropagation in neural networks. In reinforcement learning, it optimizes policy gradients by computing loss functions dynamically. In scientific computing, it aids in numerical simulations by differentiating complex mathematical models. In robotics, it enhances control algorithms by refining movement strategies through gradient-based learning.

Industries that benefit from Autograd include artificial intelligence research, where it simplifies neural network optimization. In healthcare, it assists in medical imaging analysis by improving deep learning-based diagnostic models. In finance, it enhances algorithmic trading strategies through gradient-based portfolio optimization. In engineering, it improves predictive modeling for structural analysis and fluid dynamics.

Despite its advantages, Autograd presents several challenges. Memory consumption can be high when storing intermediate calculations, affecting scalability. Computational overhead increases with complex networks, requiring optimization techniques for efficiency. Debugging gradient-related issues can be difficult, as errors in computation graphs may not be immediately apparent. Ensuring numerical stability is crucial, as small errors in differentiation can propagate through deep learning models.

In summary, Autograd is a powerful automatic differentiation tool that streamlines gradient computation in machine learning. It is widely used in AI research, healthcare, finance, and engineering to optimize neural networks and improve computational efficiency. While it enhances automation and accuracy in optimization tasks, challenges related to memory usage, computational overhead, and debugging require careful implementation for effective use in large-scale applications.

Automated AI Governance

Automated AI governance is a framework that uses AI-driven systems to enforce policies, monitor compliance, and manage risks associated with artificial intelligence deployment. It ensures that AI models operate ethically, transparently, and securely by automating governance processes such as auditing, bias detection, and regulatory compliance. By integrating machine learning and automation, AI governance enhances oversight while reducing manual intervention in AI lifecycle management.

The key components of automated AI governance include policy enforcement, where AI-driven tools ensure adherence to ethical guidelines and industry regulations. Bias detection algorithms analyze models for fairness, identifying and mitigating discriminatory patterns. Explainability mechanisms provide insights into AI decision-making, increasing transparency. Continuous monitoring systems track AI performance, identifying potential risks and ensuring ongoing compliance. Risk assessment tools evaluate the impact of AI models in real-world applications, preventing unintended consequences.

Automated AI governance provides several benefits in AI deployment and risk management. It improves compliance by continuously monitoring AI models for regulatory adherence. It enhances transparency by making AI decisions explainable and auditable. It reduces bias by identifying unfair patterns and recommending corrective measures. It strengthens security by detecting vulnerabilities and preventing malicious manipulation of AI systems.

Examples of automated AI governance include AI compliance tools that monitor algorithmic decisions in financial institutions to prevent discriminatory lending practices. In healthcare, AI governance frameworks ensure that medical diagnostic models meet ethical and regulatory standards. In hiring processes, AI-driven auditing tools analyze recruitment algorithms for fairness and bias. In cybersecurity, governance systems detect anomalies in AI-driven threat detection models, ensuring ethical use of AI in security operations.

Industries that benefit from automated AI governance include finance, where it ensures compliance with regulations such as GDPR and anti-discrimination laws. In healthcare, it guarantees the ethical use of AI in patient diagnostics and treatment planning. In human resources, it prevents biased decision-making in AI-driven hiring and recruitment processes. In public policy, it enforces AI regulations to ensure fairness in government AI applications.

In summary, automated AI governance enhances oversight, compliance, and transparency in AI systems by leveraging automated monitoring, bias detection, and risk assessment tools. It is widely applied in finance, healthcare, human resources, and public policy to ensure ethical and responsible AI deployment. While it improves fairness and security, challenges related to explainability, regulatory complexity, and implementation barriers require continuous advancements for effective governance in AI-driven environments.

Automated Content Moderation

Automated Content Moderation is the process of using artificial intelligence and machine learning to filter, review, and regulate online content. It involves analyzing text, images, videos, and audio to detect harmful, offensive, or inappropriate material.

Key Components

Key components include natural language processing (NLP), image recognition, sentiment analysis, and machine learning algorithms that identify violations of community guidelines.

Benefits

The benefits of automated content moderation include scalability, speed, and the ability to process vast amounts of data in real-time.

Features often include keyword filtering, AI-powered context understanding, and automated removal of flagged content.

Examples

Examples of automated moderation systems include those used by social media platforms like Facebook, YouTube, and TikTok, which monitor for hate speech, misinformation, and violent content.

Applications

Applications span across social media, e-commerce, online forums, and live streaming platforms.

Industries

Industries that benefit from automated moderation include technology, media, education, and gaming.

Summary

In summary, automated content moderation is a crucial tool for maintaining digital safety and compliance, though it still requires human oversight to ensure accuracy and fairness.

Automated Data Annotation

Automated Data Annotation refers to the process of using AI-driven tools to label and tag data for machine learning models. It plays a significant role in supervised learning by helping AI systems recognize patterns and improve decision-making.

Key Components

Key components of automated data annotation include computer vision, NLP, deep learning algorithms, and synthetic data generation.

Benefits

The benefits of automation in data annotation include increased efficiency, reduced costs, and enhanced consistency in labeling large datasets.

Features often include bounding box annotation, semantic segmentation, named entity recognition, and automated tagging for various data types.

Examples

Examples of automated data annotation platforms include Labelbox, Amazon SageMaker Ground Truth, and SuperAnnotate, which assist companies in preparing datasets for AI training.

Applications

Applications of automated data annotation are prominent in computer vision, speech recognition, autonomous systems, and language processing.

Industries

Industries that rely on automated annotation include healthcare, automotive, finance, and security.

Challenges

Challenges include the potential for errors in AI-generated labels, the need for quality assurance, and the dependence on diverse training datasets.

Conclusion

In conclusion, automated data annotation significantly accelerates AI model training while ensuring high-quality data labeling, yet it still benefits from human validation to minimize inaccuracies.

Automated Driving Systems (ADS)

Automated Driving Systems (ADS) are advanced AI-powered technologies designed to control and operate vehicles without human intervention. These systems integrate various sensors, computing technologies, and machine learning models to enable self-driving capabilities.

Key Components

The key components of ADS include LiDAR, radar, cameras, GPS, sensor fusion, and deep learning algorithms that interpret road conditions and make real-time decisions.

Benefits

The benefits of ADS include improved road safety, reduced human error, lower traffic congestion, and increased mobility for individuals with disabilities.

Features of automated driving systems include adaptive cruise control, lane-keeping assistance, object detection, and autonomous navigation.

Examples

Examples of ADS include Tesla's Full Self-Driving (FSD), Waymo's autonomous taxis, and GM's Cruise vehicles, all of which aim to revolutionize transportation.

Applications

Applications range from personal vehicles to ride-hailing services, logistics, and public transportation.

Industries

Industries impacted by ADS include automotive, logistics, technology, and urban planning.

Challenges

Challenges include regulatory hurdles, ethical considerations in decision-making, cybersecurity risks, and the need for extensive real-world testing.

Summary

In summary, automated driving systems represent a transformative leap in transportation technology, promising safer and more efficient mobility, though they require ongoing advancements to ensure reliability and public trust.

Automated Machine Learning Pipelines

Automated Machine Learning Pipelines refer to AI-driven systems that streamline the end-to-end process of building, training, and deploying machine learning models without requiring extensive human intervention. These pipelines automate tasks such as data preprocessing, feature engineering, model selection, hyperparameter tuning, and model deployment.

Key Components

Key components include data ingestion, data transformation, model training, model evaluation, and continuous monitoring.

Benefits

The benefits of automated machine learning pipelines include efficiency, scalability, consistency, and reduced dependency on data science expertise.

Features include automated data cleaning, feature selection, ensemble learning, and real-time model evaluation.

Examples

Examples of automated machine learning pipeline platforms include Google AutoML, DataRobot, and H2O.ai, which simplify the development and deployment of AI models for businesses and researchers.

Applications

Applications span across predictive analytics, fraud detection, recommendation systems, and business intelligence.

Industries

Industries benefiting from automated machine learning pipelines include finance, healthcare, e-commerce, manufacturing, and cybersecurity.

Challenges

Challenges include the risk of overfitting, lack of interpretability, limitations in handling complex use cases, and the need for high-quality training data.

Summary

In summary, automated machine learning pipelines enable organizations to accelerate AI adoption while ensuring efficiency, but human oversight is still necessary to fine-tune models for optimal accuracy.

Automated Medical Diagnostics

Automated Medical Diagnostics leverage artificial intelligence and machine learning to analyze medical data, detect diseases, and assist in diagnosing conditions without direct human intervention.

These systems utilize algorithms to process medical images, laboratory results, patient records, and genetic data to support clinical decision-making.

Key Components

Key components include deep learning models, natural language processing, medical imaging analysis, and electronic health record integration.

Benefits

The benefits of automated medical diagnostics include faster diagnosis, improved accuracy, early disease detection, and reduced workload for healthcare professionals.

Features include anomaly detection, automated image segmentation, predictive analytics, and decision support tools.

Examples

Examples of automated medical diagnostics include IBM Watson Health, Google DeepMind's AI for retinal disease detection, and PathAI for pathology image analysis.

Applications

Applications extend to radiology, oncology, dermatology, cardiology, and genomics.

Industries

Industries utilizing automated medical diagnostics include healthcare, pharmaceuticals, biotechnology, and telemedicine.

Challenges

Challenges include regulatory compliance, data privacy concerns, AI bias, and the need for continuous model validation.

Summary

In summary, automated medical diagnostics enhance healthcare by providing faster and more accurate disease detection, yet they require human validation to ensure ethical and precise decision-making.

Automated Speech Recognition (ASR)

Automated Speech Recognition (ASR) is a technology that converts spoken language into text using artificial intelligence and machine learning. It enables machines to process and understand human speech in real-time, improving communication and accessibility across various applications.

Key Components

Key components of ASR include acoustic modeling, language modeling, signal processing, and deep learning-based speech recognition algorithms.

Benefits

The benefits of automated speech recognition include increased accessibility, improved efficiency in transcription, enhanced human-computer interaction, and seamless multilingual support.

Features include speaker diarization, noise reduction, real-time transcription, and voice command recognition.

Examples

Examples of ASR systems include Google Speech-to-Text, Amazon Transcribe, Microsoft Azure Speech Services, and Apple's Siri.

Applications

Applications include virtual assistants, call center automation, transcription services, voice search, and dictation software.

Industries

Industries utilizing ASR include healthcare, education, customer service, media, and automotive.

Challenges

Challenges include background noise interference, accuracy issues with different accents and dialects, privacy concerns, and the complexity of understanding context in speech.

Summary

In summary, automated speech recognition enhances communication and accessibility through AI-driven voice processing, though continuous improvements in accuracy and context awareness are needed to optimize its effectiveness.

Automated Text Generation (ATG)

Automated Text Generation (ATG) is an artificial intelligence-driven technology that produces human-like text based on predefined inputs, prompts, or datasets. It uses deep learning models, such as natural language processing and transformer-based architectures, to generate coherent and contextually relevant text.

Key Components

Key components of ATG include large language models, text embeddings, sequence-to-sequence learning, and training datasets that enhance contextual understanding.

Benefits

The benefits of automated text generation include efficiency in content creation, scalability, personalization, and reduced workload for human writers.

Features include text completion, style adaptation, contextual coherence, and multilingual support.

Examples

Examples of ATG systems include OpenAI's GPT models, Google's BERT, and Meta's LLaMA, which are used in various content generation applications.

Applications

Applications extend to automated journalism, chatbots, scriptwriting, marketing copy generation, and creative storytelling.

Industries

Industries utilizing ATG include media, customer service, marketing, e-commerce, and education.

Challenges

Challenges include potential bias in AI-generated content, misinformation risks, lack of originality, and ethical concerns regarding authenticity.

Summary

In summary, automated text generation transforms content creation by enabling fast and scalable text production, but careful oversight is required to maintain accuracy and ethical use.

Automated Text Summarization

Automated Text Summarization is an artificial intelligence-driven process that condenses long pieces of text into concise and meaningful summaries while retaining the key information. It utilizes machine learning and natural language processing techniques to extract relevant points and eliminate redundancy.

Key Components

Key components include extractive summarization, abstractive summarization, deep learning models, and linguistic analysis.

Benefits

The benefits of automated text summarization include improved information processing, faster content digestion, enhanced productivity, and accessibility for users.

Features include keyphrase extraction, topic modeling, customizable summary lengths, and real-time processing.

Examples

Examples of automated text summarization tools include Google's T5, Hugging Face's Transformers, and Microsoft's Text Analytics API, which enable businesses and researchers to quickly distill large volumes of text.

Applications

Applications include news summarization, academic research, legal document processing, and business intelligence reporting.

Industries

Industries that benefit from automated text summarization include publishing, finance, legal, healthcare, and education.

Challenges

Challenges include difficulty in understanding nuanced language, loss of context, variability in summary quality, and ethical concerns regarding biased summarization.

Summary

In summary, automated text summarization enhances information consumption by generating concise and accurate summaries, but continuous refinement is necessary to maintain linguistic precision and contextual integrity.

AutoML (Automated Machine Learning)

AutoML (Automated Machine Learning) is an advanced technology that automates the process of selecting, training, tuning, and deploying machine learning models without requiring deep expertise in data science. It simplifies AI development by automating critical tasks such as feature engineering, hyperparameter optimization, model selection, and evaluation.

Key Components

Key components include automated data preprocessing, algorithm selection, hyperparameter tuning, model ensembling, and performance monitoring.

Benefits

The benefits of AutoML include democratization of AI, increased efficiency, scalability, and enhanced model accuracy through automated tuning.

Features include pre-built machine learning templates, drag-and-drop interfaces, explainable AI, and real-time performance tracking.

Examples

Examples of AutoML platforms include Google AutoML, Microsoft Azure AutoML, and Amazon SageMaker Autopilot, which help businesses and researchers build AI models with minimal manual intervention.

Applications

Applications include fraud detection, predictive analytics, recommendation systems, and healthcare diagnostics.

Industries

Industries benefiting from AutoML include finance, healthcare, retail, cybersecurity, and manufacturing.

Challenges

Challenges include limitations in handling highly complex models, reduced flexibility for custom algorithms, risk of overfitting, and concerns over interpretability.

Summary

In summary, AutoML accelerates the adoption of AI by making machine learning accessible to a broader audience, though careful evaluation is needed to ensure optimal performance and transparency.

Autonomous Agents

Autonomous Agents are self-operating software or robotic systems that can perceive their environment, make decisions, and take actions without direct human intervention. These agents rely on artificial intelligence, reinforcement learning, and machine learning algorithms to adapt to changing conditions and achieve predefined goals.

Key Components

Key components of autonomous agents include sensors for data collection, decision-making algorithms, real-time feedback mechanisms, and self-learning capabilities.

Benefits

The benefits of autonomous agents include efficiency in task execution, reduced human workload, scalability, and the ability to operate in hazardous environments.

Features include real-time data processing, self-improvement through machine learning, autonomous navigation, and adaptive behavior.

Examples

Examples of autonomous agents include robotic process automation (RPA) in business workflows, self-learning trading bots in finance, and intelligent personal assistants like Siri and Google Assistant.

Applications

Applications span across customer service, industrial automation, autonomous robotics, and smart home technology.

Industries

Industries that leverage autonomous agents include finance, healthcare, manufacturing, logistics, and defense.

Challenges

Challenges include ensuring reliability, addressing ethical concerns, mitigating AI biases, and maintaining security against adversarial threats.

Summary

In summary, autonomous agents enhance efficiency and automation across multiple domains, though continuous improvements are required to address ethical, security, and adaptability challenges.

Autonomous AI Ethics

Autonomous AI Ethics focuses on the moral and ethical considerations surrounding the deployment and decision-making of self-operating AI systems. It ensures that AI-driven systems adhere to ethical principles such as fairness, accountability, transparency, and human-centric design.

Key Components

Key components of autonomous AI ethics include algorithmic transparency, ethical AI governance frameworks, bias mitigation strategies, and human oversight mechanisms.

Benefits

The benefits of autonomous AI ethics include enhanced trust in AI systems, prevention of harmful biases, legal compliance, and responsible AI deployment.

Features include explainable AI (XAI), regulatory compliance tools, ethical impact assessments, and AI fairness auditing.

Examples

Examples of ethical AI frameworks include Google's AI Principles, the European Union's AI Act, and IBM's AI Fairness 360, all of which aim to standardize responsible AI usage.

Applications

Applications of autonomous AI ethics include AI-powered hiring tools, autonomous weapons systems, predictive policing, and healthcare diagnostics.

Industries

Industries impacted by AI ethics include technology, legal, government, healthcare, and finance.

Challenges

Challenges include defining universal ethical standards, balancing innovation with regulation, managing AI-induced biases, and enforcing compliance across diverse AI implementations.

Summary

In summary, autonomous AI ethics is crucial for ensuring the responsible development and use of AI technologies, though it requires continuous oversight and global collaboration to align ethical standards with technological advancements.

Autonomous AI Systems

Autonomous AI Systems are self-sufficient artificial intelligence-driven platforms capable of operating, making decisions, and executing complex tasks without direct human intervention. These systems integrate machine learning, deep learning, and advanced data processing techniques to function independently across various domains.

Key Components

Key components of autonomous AI systems include AI-powered decision-making engines, real-time data processing, adaptive learning mechanisms, and multi-agent coordination frameworks.

Benefits

The benefits of autonomous AI systems include increased operational efficiency, reduced human error, cost savings, and the ability to perform tasks in hazardous or high-risk environments.

Features include real-time decision-making, continuous learning, autonomous execution of tasks, and multi-modal data interpretation.

Examples

Examples of autonomous AI systems include self-driving cars, automated healthcare diagnostics, AI-powered cybersecurity defenses, and industrial robotics.

Applications

Applications range from smart transportation and precision agriculture to space exploration and autonomous financial trading.

Industries

Industries utilizing autonomous AI systems include automotive, healthcare, defense, finance, and logistics.

Challenges

Challenges include ethical concerns, safety risks, system security vulnerabilities, and the unpredictability of AI decision-making in complex scenarios.

Summary

In summary, autonomous AI systems revolutionize industries by enabling intelligent automation, but they require stringent regulatory frameworks and continuous refinement to ensure reliability and ethical deployment.

Autonomous Drones

Autonomous Drones are unmanned aerial vehicles equipped with artificial intelligence and advanced sensors that enable them to operate independently without human intervention. These drones use AI-powered navigation systems, real-time data processing, and machine learning algorithms to perform tasks such as surveillance, mapping, and package delivery.

Key Components

Key components of autonomous drones include GPS navigation, computer vision, onboard AI processors, obstacle detection systems, and autonomous flight controllers.

Benefits

The benefits of autonomous drones include increased efficiency in aerial monitoring, reduced human labor costs, expanded operational capabilities in remote or hazardous areas, and real-time data collection for analytics.

Features include AI-powered object detection, autonomous mission planning, adaptive flight controls, and integration with cloud-based data analysis platforms.

Examples

Examples of autonomous drones include AI-powered delivery drones, self-piloting surveillance drones used in defense, and automated agricultural drones for precision farming.

Applications

Applications extend to disaster response, search-and-rescue operations, industrial inspections, environmental monitoring, and logistics automation.

Industries

Industries utilizing autonomous drones include defense, agriculture, logistics, construction, and emergency services.

Challenges

Challenges include regulatory restrictions, privacy concerns, battery life limitations, cybersecurity risks, and difficulties in operating in unpredictable weather conditions.

Summary

In summary, autonomous drones revolutionize aerial operations by enabling real-time automation and AI-driven decision-making, though they require robust regulations and technological advancements to ensure safety, reliability, and ethical deployment.

Autonomous Navigation

Autonomous Navigation is the ability of vehicles, robots, or AI-driven systems to navigate through complex environments without direct human control. It relies on real-time data processing, sensor fusion, and machine learning algorithms to perceive surroundings, avoid obstacles, and make intelligent route decisions.

Key Components

Key components of autonomous navigation include LiDAR and radar sensors, GPS tracking, simultaneous localization and mapping (SLAM), deep learning-based object recognition, and predictive path planning.

Benefits

The benefits of autonomous navigation include increased safety in transportation, enhanced efficiency in logistics, reduced human intervention in hazardous environments, and improved precision in robotics.

Features include adaptive route optimization, real-time obstacle avoidance, AI-powered decision-making, and multi-sensor integration for dynamic environments.

Examples

Examples include self-driving cars that navigate urban landscapes, autonomous ships that optimize maritime routes, AI-powered robotic vacuum cleaners, and self-guided agricultural machinery.

Applications

Applications extend to smart transportation systems, industrial automation, military reconnaissance, and space exploration.

Industries

Industries utilizing autonomous navigation include automotive, aerospace, logistics, defense, and robotics.

Challenges

Challenges include sensor limitations in extreme weather, high computational demands, ethical considerations in AI-driven decision-making, and legal barriers to full autonomy.

Summary

In summary, autonomous navigation enables intelligent mobility across various domains, though it requires continuous advancements in AI, sensor technology, and regulatory frameworks to achieve widespread implementation and reliability.

Autonomous Robots

Autonomous Robots are AI-powered machines designed to perform tasks independently without human intervention. These robots integrate artificial intelligence, advanced sensors, and automated decision-making algorithms to operate in dynamic environments.

Key Components

Key components of autonomous robots include machine learning models, real-time environmental sensing, robotic control systems, actuator mechanisms, and AI-driven task execution frameworks.

Benefits

The benefits of autonomous robots include enhanced efficiency in automation, reduced operational costs, increased safety in hazardous environments, and the ability to perform repetitive or high-risk tasks with precision.

Features include AI-driven adaptability, human-robot collaboration, real-time monitoring, and cloud-based data integration for continuous learning.

Examples

Examples of autonomous robots include warehouse robots used for logistics automation, surgical robots that perform precision medical procedures, self-navigating robotic assistants, and industrial robots used in manufacturing assembly lines.

Applications

Applications extend to healthcare automation, smart factories, autonomous security patrolling, space exploration, and personalized AI-driven customer service.

Industries

Industries utilizing autonomous robots include manufacturing, healthcare, logistics, defense, and retail.

Challenges

Challenges include high development costs, integration with existing infrastructures, ethical concerns regarding job displacement, and ensuring reliability in unpredictable environments.

Summary

In summary, autonomous robots transform multiple industries by enabling intelligent automation and AI-driven efficiency, though continuous improvements in safety, scalability, and human-machine interaction are necessary for widespread adoption.

Autonomous Swarm Intelligence

Autonomous Swarm Intelligence is an AI-driven approach that enables a group of autonomous agents, such as drones, robots, or underwater vehicles, to work collaboratively in a decentralized and self-organized manner. It is inspired by natural swarm behavior observed in insects, birds, and fish, where collective intelligence emerges from simple local interactions.

Key Components

Key components of autonomous swarm intelligence include distributed AI algorithms, real-time communication networks, decentralized decision-making frameworks, adaptive coordination strategies, and machine learning-based collective behavior modeling.

Benefits

The benefits of autonomous swarm intelligence include enhanced scalability in multi-agent systems, increased efficiency in large-scale operations, improved robustness against individual failures, and the ability to perform complex tasks in challenging environments.

Features include autonomous task allocation, real-time synchronization, AI-driven collective learning, and self-adaptive behavior for dynamic conditions.

Examples

Examples include swarming drones for coordinated surveillance, robot swarms for disaster response and search missions, AI-powered underwater swarms for deep-sea exploration, and autonomous warehouse robot fleets for logistics optimization.

Applications

Applications extend to defense strategies, precision agriculture, automated supply chain management, environmental monitoring, and smart city infrastructure.

Industries

Industries utilizing autonomous swarm intelligence include defense, robotics, logistics, environmental science, and smart automation.

Challenges

Challenges include communication limitations in decentralized networks, ethical concerns regarding autonomous decision-making, security risks in swarm control, and high computational requirements for real-time coordination.

Summary

In summary, autonomous swarm intelligence enables AI-driven collective action for large-scale problem-solving, though advancements in AI coordination, security, and ethical governance are essential to ensure safe and effective implementation across industries.

Autonomous Underwater Vehicles (AUVs)

Autonomous Underwater Vehicles (AUVs) are self-operating robotic systems designed for underwater exploration, surveillance, and data collection without requiring direct human intervention. These vehicles rely on advanced AI algorithms, real-time sensor data, and automated decision-making to navigate and perform tasks in deep-sea environments.

Key Components

Key components of AUVs include sonar and LiDAR mapping systems, AI-powered navigation, hydrodynamic propulsion mechanisms, pressure-resistant communication systems, and onboard energy management.

Benefits

The benefits of AUVs include extended operational endurance, reduced human risk in deep-sea exploration, precise environmental monitoring, and cost-effective underwater research.

Features include AI-driven path planning, obstacle detection, automated data collection, and real-time environmental adaptation.

Examples

Examples include AUVs used in oceanographic research, deep-sea mining exploration, underwater pipeline inspections, and military reconnaissance missions.

Applications

Applications extend to marine biodiversity assessment, subsea infrastructure monitoring, underwater archeology, and offshore energy resource exploration.

Industries

Industries utilizing AUVs include defense, marine research, offshore energy, environmental conservation, and deep-sea exploration.

Challenges

Challenges include communication limitations in underwater environments, high operational costs, energy constraints for prolonged missions, and environmental risks associated with autonomous marine systems.

Summary

In summary, AUVs enhance underwater exploration and automation, though continued advancements in AI, battery technology, and navigation accuracy are necessary for broader and more efficient deployment.

Autonomous Vehicles

Autonomous Vehicles are AI-powered transport systems that operate without direct human control, using sensors, machine learning, and real-time data processing to navigate, avoid obstacles, and make driving decisions. These vehicles include self-driving cars, autonomous drones, robotic delivery systems, and self-operating public transit.

Key Components

Key components of autonomous vehicles include LiDAR, radar, computer vision, GPS tracking, deep learning models, and AI-driven control systems.

Benefits

The benefits of autonomous vehicles include reduced traffic accidents, enhanced transportation efficiency, lower emissions through optimized driving patterns, and increased accessibility for individuals with mobility challenges.

Features include adaptive cruise control, real-time traffic awareness, AI-based route optimization, and automated braking systems.

Examples

Examples include Tesla's Full Self-Driving (FSD) system, Waymo's self-driving taxis, autonomous trucking fleets, and AI-powered robotic delivery bots.

Applications

Applications extend to urban mobility, logistics automation, emergency response, and smart infrastructure management.

Industries

Industries utilizing autonomous vehicles include automotive, logistics, defense, agriculture, and public transportation.

Challenges

Challenges include regulatory hurdles, ethical considerations in AI-driven decision-making, cybersecurity risks, unpredictable road conditions, and the high cost of development and implementation.

Summary

In summary, autonomous vehicles are revolutionizing transportation through AI and automation, but legal, safety, and technological improvements are required for full-scale adoption and reliability.

Availability Heuristic in AI

Availability Heuristic in AI refers to the tendency of artificial intelligence models to rely on readily available information when making decisions, often leading to biased or inaccurate predictions. It is inspired by human cognitive biases, where frequently encountered data is given more weight than less accessible but potentially more relevant information.

Key Components

Key components include heuristic-based decision models, probability estimation frameworks, knowledge retrieval algorithms, and AI-driven pattern recognition.

Benefits

The benefits of addressing availability heuristic biases in AI include improved accuracy in predictions, reduction of skewed decision-making, enhanced fairness in AI-driven systems, and mitigation of over-reliance on frequently occurring data patterns.

Features include AI model bias correction, data balancing techniques, adaptive learning algorithms, and uncertainty quantification in predictions.

Examples

Examples include AI-driven risk assessment tools that may overestimate rare but impactful events, recommendation engines that prioritize popular content over diverse selections, and predictive policing systems that reinforce historical data biases.

Applications

Applications extend to financial forecasting, healthcare diagnostics, criminal justice AI systems, and AI-generated decision support tools.

Industries

Industries impacted by availability heuristic biases include finance, law enforcement, healthcare, media, and e-commerce.

Challenges

Challenges include difficulty in correcting long-standing data biases, ethical concerns in automated decision-making, limited interpretability of heuristic-driven AI models, and the risk of reinforcing systemic inequalities.

Summary

In summary, recognizing and addressing availability heuristic biases in AI is crucial for ensuring fair, unbiased, and accurate decision-making, requiring continuous data refinement, bias mitigation strategies, and transparent model evaluation.

Availability Prediction in AI Systems

Availability Prediction in AI Systems refers to the ability of artificial intelligence models to estimate the availability or reliability of a system, resource, or service based on real-time and historical data. It is used to forecast uptime, detect potential failures, and optimize resource allocation in automated environments.

Key Components

Key components include predictive analytics algorithms, real-time monitoring sensors, probabilistic modeling, anomaly detection mechanisms, and AI-driven maintenance scheduling.

Benefits

The benefits of availability prediction in AI systems include reduced downtime, improved operational efficiency, proactive maintenance planning, and enhanced reliability in automated processes.

Features include machine learning-based failure prediction, adaptive scheduling algorithms, real-time system health monitoring, and AI-powered redundancy management.

Examples

Examples include predictive maintenance in industrial machinery, AI-driven cloud server uptime estimation, reliability forecasting in autonomous transportation, and smart grid availability optimization.

Applications

Applications extend to industrial automation, data center management, energy distribution, predictive healthcare diagnostics, and smart city infrastructure planning.

Industries

Industries utilizing availability prediction include manufacturing, IT services, energy, healthcare, and telecommunications.

Challenges

Challenges include the complexity of accurately modeling unpredictable failures, high computational demands for large-scale prediction, integration with legacy systems, and the need for high-quality training data.

Summary

In summary, availability prediction in AI systems enhances operational reliability and efficiency across industries, but continuous advancements in predictive modeling, data integration, and system adaptability are necessary for improving accuracy and real-time responsiveness.

Availability Zone (AZ)

Availability Zone (AZ) is a physically separate and independent data center within a cloud computing region that provides redundancy and high availability for cloud services. It ensures fault tolerance by distributing workloads across multiple zones to prevent service disruptions.

Key Components

Key components of an availability zone include independent power sources, networking infrastructure, geographically isolated locations, and automated failover mechanisms.

Benefits

The benefits of availability zones include increased uptime, enhanced disaster recovery, reduced latency, and improved scalability for cloud applications.

Features include multi-zone load balancing, automatic failover support, geographically distributed data replication, and real-time monitoring of infrastructure health.

Examples

Examples include Amazon Web Services (AWS) Availability Zones, Microsoft Azure's cloud regions, and Google Cloud's multi-zone deployments.

Applications

Applications extend to cloud-hosted databases, web applications, machine learning model hosting, and enterprise IT infrastructure.

Industries

Industries utilizing availability zones include finance, healthcare, e-commerce, technology, and entertainment.

Challenges

Challenges include managing inter-zone data consistency, higher operational costs for multi-zone deployments, potential performance trade-offs in cross-zone communication, and compliance with regional data governance laws.

Summary

In summary, availability zones provide essential cloud reliability and redundancy, ensuring business continuity and fault tolerance, but require strategic resource allocation and network optimization for effective implementation.

Avatar-Based AI

Avatar-Based AI refers to artificial intelligence systems that use virtual avatars to interact with users in digital environments, enhancing user engagement and personalized experiences. These AI-driven avatars can be animated characters, digital humans, or virtual assistants powered by natural language processing and machine learning.

Key Components

Key components of avatar-based AI include real-time facial animation, speech synthesis, deep learning-based conversation modeling, and user behavior analysis.

Benefits

The benefits of avatar-based AI include improved human-computer interaction, enhanced digital engagement, personalized customer experiences, and accessibility for people with disabilities.

Features include real-time expression adaptation, voice and text-based communication, multilingual capabilities, and AI-driven sentiment analysis for responsive interactions.

Examples

Examples include AI-powered customer service chatbots with visual avatars, virtual influencers on social media, AI-driven virtual tutors, and gaming NPCs with realistic conversational abilities.

Applications

Applications extend to virtual reality environments, online customer support, e-learning platforms, interactive entertainment, and healthcare virtual assistants.

Industries

Industries utilizing avatar-based AI include gaming, education, retail, healthcare, and media.

Challenges

Challenges include the complexity of creating lifelike avatars, ethical concerns regarding deepfake technologies, the risk of biased AI interactions, and maintaining real-time responsiveness in dynamic environments.

Summary

In summary, avatar-based AI enhances digital interactions through engaging virtual representations, but requires careful development to ensure ethical, responsive, and context-aware experiences.

Averaged Neural Network Ensembles

Averaged Neural Network Ensembles refer to a machine learning technique where multiple neural networks are trained independently, and their outputs are averaged to improve prediction accuracy and model robustness. This ensemble method reduces variance, mitigates overfitting, and enhances generalization capabilities.

Key Components

Key components include independent neural network models, diverse training datasets, weighted or unweighted averaging mechanisms, and error reduction algorithms.

Benefits

The benefits of averaged neural network ensembles include improved predictive performance, increased model stability, reduced sensitivity to training noise, and enhanced reliability in decision-making.

Features include adaptive ensemble weighting, parallel model training, diversity-driven optimization, and automated hyperparameter tuning.

Examples

Examples include ensemble-based deep learning models for medical diagnosis, financial risk prediction using multiple trained neural networks, and speech recognition systems utilizing aggregated neural network outputs.

Applications

Applications extend to image classification, fraud detection, natural language processing, autonomous driving, and AI-driven recommendation systems.

Industries

Industries utilizing averaged neural network ensembles include finance, healthcare, cybersecurity, autonomous systems, and marketing analytics.

Challenges

Challenges include increased computational requirements, complexity in managing multiple models, potential inefficiencies in real-time applications, and difficulties in balancing ensemble diversity for optimal performance.

Summary

In summary, averaged neural network ensembles enhance AI decision-making by combining multiple models for higher accuracy, though computational costs and complexity must be managed for efficient deployment.

Averaged Stochastic Gradient Descent (ASGD)

Averaged Stochastic Gradient Descent (ASGD) is an optimization technique used in machine learning that averages the model weights over multiple iterations to improve convergence stability and generalization. Unlike standard stochastic gradient descent, which updates parameters based on single batches, ASGD maintains an averaged version of the model to reduce fluctuations and prevent overfitting.

Key Components

Key components of ASGD include learning rate scheduling, weight averaging mechanisms, gradient-based optimization, and adaptive convergence controls.

Benefits

The benefits of ASGD include faster convergence, reduced sensitivity to noisy updates, improved stability in large-scale training, and enhanced model generalization.

Features include automatic weight averaging, batch-wise adaptive learning rate adjustments, compatibility with deep learning architectures, and scalability for distributed training.

Examples

Examples include ASGD applied to deep neural networks for speech recognition, training of reinforcement learning models in robotics, and optimizing large-scale AI models in cloud environments.

Applications

Applications extend to autonomous systems, real-time AI decision-making, AI-driven predictive analytics, and large-scale natural language processing models.

Industries

Industries utilizing ASGD include finance, healthcare, autonomous vehicles, artificial intelligence research, and cloud-based AI services.

Challenges

Challenges include computational overhead in maintaining averaged weights, tuning complexity in large-scale deep learning models, potential inefficiencies in rapidly changing environments, and sensitivity to learning rate decay strategies.

Summary

In summary, averaged stochastic gradient descent enhances optimization efficiency and model stability in AI training, though careful parameter tuning and computational resource management are necessary for maximizing its benefits.

Aversive Control in AI

Aversive Control in AI refers to reinforcement learning strategies that use negative feedback or penalties to shape an AI system's decision-making process. This approach discourages undesirable actions by associating them with aversive consequences, enabling AI to optimize behavior through avoidance learning.

Key Components

Key components include reinforcement learning algorithms, reward-penalty balancing, negative reinforcement mechanisms, and real-time behavior evaluation.

Benefits

The benefits of aversive control in AI include improved safety in autonomous systems, enhanced ethical AI decision-making, prevention of undesirable behaviors, and increased adaptability in dynamic environments.

Features include penalty-based learning models, real-time risk assessment, adaptive response mechanisms, and behavioral optimization algorithms.

Examples

Examples include self-driving cars that learn to avoid risky maneuvers through aversive penalties, industrial robots programmed to minimize operational errors, and AI-powered cybersecurity systems that adapt by penalizing security vulnerabilities.

Applications

Applications extend to autonomous navigation, robotics safety protocols, AI-driven compliance monitoring, and behavioral training in virtual environments.

Industries

Industries utilizing aversive control in AI include automotive, robotics, defense, healthcare, and cybersecurity.

Challenges

Challenges include potential unintended consequences of negative reinforcement, the difficulty of fine-tuning penalty structures, the risk of overly conservative AI behavior, and ethical concerns regarding AI learning through aversive stimuli.

Summary

In summary, aversive control in AI enhances learning and safety by penalizing undesirable actions, though careful design is required to balance penalties and rewards for optimal AI behavior.

Aviation AI Systems

Aviation AI Systems encompass artificial intelligence-driven technologies designed to enhance safety, efficiency, and automation in the aviation industry. These systems leverage machine learning, predictive analytics, and autonomous decision-making to optimize flight operations, air traffic management, and aircraft maintenance.

Key Components

Key components include AI-powered flight control systems, predictive maintenance algorithms, real-time air traffic monitoring, autonomous pilot assistance, and natural language processing for communication between pilots and AI-driven systems.

Benefits

The benefits of aviation AI systems include improved flight safety, optimized fuel efficiency, reduced human error, enhanced air traffic coordination, and predictive maintenance that minimizes downtime.

Features include AI-driven autopilot enhancements, real-time turbulence prediction, AI-assisted flight route optimization, and automated risk assessment tools.

Examples

Examples include AI-based predictive maintenance platforms used by airlines, autonomous drone air traffic control systems, and AI-powered weather forecasting tools for aviation safety.

Applications

Applications extend to commercial aviation, military aircraft operations, unmanned aerial vehicle (UAV) navigation, and airport automation.

Industries

Industries utilizing aviation AI systems include commercial airlines, defense, aerospace manufacturing, logistics, and air traffic control.

Challenges

Challenges include regulatory hurdles for AI integration in aviation, ensuring AI-driven systems meet strict safety standards, cybersecurity threats in AI-powered flight systems, and the need for reliable human-AI collaboration in critical scenarios.

Summary

In summary, aviation AI systems are transforming the industry by improving efficiency, safety, and automation, though regulatory compliance and cybersecurity measures must be prioritized for widespread adoption.

Avian Intelligence in AI

Avian Intelligence in AI is the study and application of cognitive principles inspired by bird intelligence to improve artificial intelligence models. Birds exhibit advanced problem-solving, pattern recognition, navigation, and adaptive learning capabilities that provide valuable insights for AI development.

Key Components

Key components include neural network architectures modeled after avian cognition, reinforcement learning based on bird foraging behaviors, bio-inspired flight control algorithms, and AI-driven vocalization analysis for communication modeling.

Benefits

The benefits of avian intelligence in AI include enhanced decision-making adaptability, energy-efficient AI systems, improved AI-based aerial navigation, and bio-inspired robotics that mimic bird behavior.

Features include flight pattern optimization, adaptive decision-making frameworks, swarm intelligence modeling, and real-time sensory processing inspired by bird vision.

Examples

Examples include AI-driven drone flight control inspired by bird flocking behavior, machine learning models trained on bird song recognition for species classification, and adaptive AI algorithms based on avian foraging strategies for resource optimization.

Applications

Applications extend to autonomous drone navigation, AI-powered ecological monitoring, bio-inspired robotics, and AI-enhanced environmental analysis.

Industries

Industries utilizing avian intelligence in AI include robotics, aerospace, environmental science, conservation technology, and smart automation.

Challenges

Challenges include accurately replicating avian cognitive processes in AI, ensuring real-time adaptation in unpredictable environments, ethical concerns in biomimetic AI research, and computational limitations in modeling complex avian behaviors.

Summary

In summary, avian intelligence in AI enhances adaptability and efficiency in AI-driven systems through bio-inspired learning, though ongoing research is necessary to fully harness the potential of bird-inspired artificial intelligence models.

Avoidance Learning

Avoidance Learning is a reinforcement learning mechanism in artificial intelligence where an AI system learns to prevent undesirable outcomes by taking actions that minimize negative consequences. It is commonly used in autonomous systems, robotics, and AI-driven decision-making to enhance safety and adaptability.

Key Components

Key components of avoidance learning include reward-penalty structures, real-time risk assessment models, adaptive behavior algorithms, and reinforcement learning frameworks that prioritize safe decision-making.

Benefits

The benefits of avoidance learning include improved AI safety, enhanced problem-solving efficiency, reduced operational risks, and better adaptability in dynamic environments.

Features include penalty-based decision-making, AI-driven real-time adjustments, self-learning mechanisms, and predictive modeling for risk mitigation.

Examples

Examples include autonomous vehicles learning to avoid collisions, industrial robots adapting to hazardous conditions, and AI-powered cybersecurity systems detecting and preventing potential threats.

Applications

Applications extend to robotics automation, autonomous navigation, predictive maintenance, and AI-driven fraud detection.

Industries

Industries utilizing avoidance learning include automotive, aerospace, cybersecurity, healthcare, and industrial automation.

Challenges

Challenges include fine-tuning penalty structures to balance learning efficiency, ensuring AI does not become overly risk-averse, dealing with real-world uncertainties, and preventing AI from misinterpreting safe behaviors as negative actions.

Summary

In summary, avoidance learning enables AI to optimize decisions by minimizing risks and preventing harmful outcomes, though it requires continuous refinement to balance cautious decision-making with efficiency.

Avro Data Format

Avro Data Format is a widely used data serialization system that facilitates efficient data exchange between distributed AI and big data applications. It is a compact, schema-based format that enables fast data encoding and decoding while maintaining compatibility across different programming languages and platforms.

Key Components

Key components of Avro include schema definition using JSON, binary data serialization, dynamic schema evolution support, and integration with distributed processing frameworks like Apache Hadoop and Apache Kafka.

Benefits

The benefits of Avro data format include high data compression efficiency, seamless schema evolution, platform-independent data exchange, and optimized performance for big data analytics.

Features include schema evolution without data migration, real-time streaming compatibility, lightweight binary encoding, and support for complex data types such as nested records and arrays.

Examples

Examples include Avro being used for high-speed data streaming in Kafka, AI model training pipelines handling structured and unstructured data, and cloud-based machine learning platforms that require scalable data storage solutions.

Applications

Applications extend to real-time AI data processing, big data analytics, cloud computing, and AI-powered data lakes for predictive modeling.

Industries

Industries utilizing Avro include technology, finance, e-commerce, healthcare, and telecommunications.

Challenges

Challenges include schema management complexity in large-scale systems, ensuring backward and forward compatibility across evolving data structures, potential overhead in schema validation, and integration difficulties with legacy data storage formats.

Summary

In summary, Avro data format is a powerful and efficient tool for AI-driven data processing and exchange, but effective schema management and compatibility handling are critical for maintaining seamless system performance.

Awakening AI

Awakening AI refers to the concept of an artificial intelligence system developing self-awareness, advanced reasoning, or emergent behaviors that go beyond traditional programmed functions. It is an area of research that explores AI consciousness, autonomous decision-making, and AI models capable of evolving beyond predefined constraints.

Key Components

Key components of awakening AI include deep learning architectures, reinforcement learning adaptation, AI-driven self-improvement mechanisms, neural network evolution models, and real-time contextual awareness.

Benefits

The benefits of awakening AI include enhanced problem-solving capabilities, AI systems capable of autonomous learning and adaptation, greater efficiency in complex decision-making, and potential breakthroughs in artificial general intelligence (AGI).

Features include self-refinement in AI models, continuous learning from real-world interactions, adaptability to new and evolving environments, and the ability to develop higher-order reasoning patterns.

Examples

Examples include AI-driven virtual assistants that autonomously expand their knowledge base, deep reinforcement learning agents capable of self-improving strategies, and AI systems that autonomously refine their understanding of human behavior.

Applications

Applications extend to robotics automation, AI-driven scientific discovery, cognitive computing, and AI-augmented creativity in fields such as art and literature.

Industries

Industries exploring awakening AI include AI research, defense, advanced robotics, healthcare, and scientific innovation.

Challenges

Challenges include ethical concerns regarding AI autonomy, unpredictable emergent behaviors, security risks associated with self-learning AI, and the difficulty of ensuring alignment with human values and intentions.

Summary

In summary, awakening AI represents the frontier of artificial intelligence development, pushing the boundaries of autonomy and adaptability, though significant challenges remain in ensuring responsible and safe evolution of self-improving AI systems.

Aware AI

Aware AI refers to artificial intelligence systems that possess contextual, situational, and adaptive awareness, enabling them to perceive, interpret, and respond intelligently to their environment. Unlike traditional AI, which operates based on static algorithms and predefined datasets, aware AI continuously learns from interactions, adjusts to new conditions, and refines its decision-making processes in real-time. This advancement allows AI to exhibit higher levels of intuition, reasoning, and self-improvement, making it more aligned with human-like cognition and responsiveness.

The key components of aware AI include real-time data processing, which enables the system to analyze and react to ongoing changes without delays. Contextual learning allows AI to understand and adapt its behavior based on surrounding conditions, making its responses more relevant and meaningful. Memory-enhanced architectures, such as recurrent neural networks and transformer models, enable the retention and recall of previous interactions to improve decision-making over time. Multi-modal sensory integration combines data from various sources, including vision, sound, and text, to provide a more comprehensive understanding of the environment. Reinforcement learning mechanisms empower the AI to refine its strategies through experience, enhancing adaptability and efficiency in unpredictable scenarios.

The benefits of aware AI include increased accuracy in decision-making, as it continuously updates its understanding based on new information. Personalized user interactions enhance customer experiences by adapting responses to individual preferences, behaviors, and emotional cues. Improved automation efficiency allows AI to optimize workflows, reduce operational costs, and minimize human intervention in complex processes. Enhanced security and threat detection capabilities enable AI to recognize suspicious patterns, predict cyber threats, and prevent potential risks before they escalate. Dynamic adaptability ensures AI-driven systems remain relevant and effective, even in rapidly changing environments.

A practical example of aware AI is its application in autonomous vehicles, where AI continuously processes sensor data to detect road conditions, predict traffic patterns, and make split-second driving decisions. In smart assistants, aware AI refines responses based on past conversations, user habits, and emotional tone, making interactions more natural and meaningful. In healthcare, AI-powered diagnostic tools analyze medical histories and real-time patient data to provide precise recommendations and early disease detection. In cybersecurity, AI-driven monitoring systems detect evolving threats and adapt defensive strategies without human intervention. In personalized learning,

AI tailors educational content to match student progress and learning styles, ensuring a more effective learning experience.

Despite its advantages, aware AI presents several challenges. Computational demands increase significantly as AI systems process vast amounts of real-time data, requiring advanced hardware and optimized algorithms. Ethical concerns arise regarding data privacy and surveillance, as AI continuously monitors and adapts based on user behavior. Bias in training data can affect AI's decision-making, potentially leading to unintended discriminatory outcomes that require careful mitigation. Transparency issues emerge as AI models become more complex, making it difficult to explain how decisions are made, which raises concerns in critical areas such as healthcare and law enforcement. Security risks exist as aware AI systems can be vulnerable to adversarial attacks that manipulate inputs to deceive the AI.

Aware AI is applied across multiple industries, driving innovation and efficiency in diverse fields. In healthcare, AI enhances predictive diagnostics, personalized treatments, and patient monitoring systems. The financial sector benefits from AI-driven fraud detection, risk assessment, and intelligent trading algorithms that adapt to market conditions. Smart cities leverage aware AI to optimize transportation, energy consumption, and emergency response systems. The retail industry uses AI-powered recommendation engines that analyze purchasing behavior and adapt marketing strategies accordingly. Manufacturing and industrial automation incorporate AI-driven predictive maintenance to reduce equipment failures and improve operational efficiency.

In conclusion, aware AI represents a major step forward in artificial intelligence, integrating adaptive learning, contextual awareness, and real-time decision-making to enhance automation, security, and human-machine interaction. Its ability to analyze, predict, and refine responses in an ever-changing environment makes it an essential technology for the future. While challenges such as ethical concerns, computational complexity, and transparency must be addressed, the transformative potential of aware AI continues to shape industries and redefine the relationship between artificial intelligence and human intelligence. As AI progresses, the development of aware AI systems will further enhance their role in everyday life, creating more intelligent, responsive, and trustworthy solutions for various global challenges.

Awareness in neural networks

Awareness in neural networks refers to the ability of artificial intelligence models to recognize, adapt to, and respond dynamically to patterns, contexts, and changes in input data. Unlike traditional machine learning models that follow predefined rules, neural networks with awareness can continuously refine their understanding of complex datasets, making them more efficient at problem-solving, decision-making, and predictive analysis. This capability enhances neural networks' ability to simulate aspects of human cognitive awareness, allowing them to adjust behavior based on new information and environmental shifts.

The key components of awareness in neural networks include self-attention mechanisms, which enable models to focus on relevant parts of input data while filtering out unnecessary information. Contextual learning allows the network to interpret meaning based on the surrounding data, improving accuracy in natural language processing and image recognition. Continuous adaptation mechanisms, such as reinforcement learning, allow neural networks to refine their predictions over time by learning from past interactions. Memory-based architectures, including long short-term memory (LSTM) and transformer models, help retain and recall previous information, creating a more dynamic understanding of sequential data. Meta-learning capabilities further enhance awareness by enabling neural networks to learn how to learn, improving their generalization across various tasks.

The benefits of awareness in neural networks include improved adaptability, allowing AI systems to operate effectively in ever-changing environments without requiring manual retraining. Enhanced decision-making enables models to interpret and respond to complex scenarios more accurately, leading to better predictions in fields such as healthcare, finance, and automation. Context-aware AI improves the quality of human-AI interactions by generating responses that consider previous interactions, making virtual assistants and chatbots more natural and intuitive. Awareness-driven neural networks increase efficiency by dynamically allocating computational resources, focusing processing power on the most relevant aspects of a task. The ability to detect anomalies and subtle changes in data enhances security, fraud detection, and predictive maintenance systems.

A practical example of awareness in neural networks is its use in self-driving cars, where AI systems continuously process sensor data to recognize road conditions, traffic patterns, and potential hazards in real time. In healthcare, AI-powered diagnostic tools analyze medical images with awareness of historical patient data, improving early detection of diseases. In finance, adaptive AI models detect fraudulent transactions by recognizing suspicious patterns while continuously updating their understanding of evolving fraud tactics. Virtual assistants like voice-controlled AI systems refine responses based on user behavior, providing more personalized and meaningful interactions. AI-powered cybersecurity solutions leverage awareness to identify emerging threats and automatically adjust defensive measures.

Despite its advantages, awareness in neural networks presents several challenges. Computational complexity increases as AI systems process and interpret vast amounts of contextual data, requiring significant processing power and memory. Training models with awareness demands extensive and diverse datasets to prevent biases and inaccuracies in decision-making. Ethical concerns arise when AI systems make autonomous decisions without full human oversight, raising questions about accountability and transparency. The potential for unintended behaviors in AI models requires careful monitoring and regulation to ensure their safe and responsible use. Interpreting the internal workings of highly aware neural networks remains a challenge, as deep learning models often function as black boxes with limited explainability.

Awareness in neural networks is applied across multiple industries, transforming automation, decision-making, and intelligent systems. In healthcare, AI-driven diagnostic tools analyze patient history and real-time medical data to deliver precise recommendations. The financial sector benefits from fraud detection models that continuously adapt to new threats and market fluctuations. In manufacturing, predictive maintenance systems utilize AI awareness to detect early signs of equipment failure and prevent costly downtime. Smart cities incorporate awareness-driven AI to optimize traffic flow, energy usage, and emergency response coordination. The retail industry enhances customer experiences through AI models that adjust product recommendations and pricing strategies based on consumer behavior.

In conclusion, awareness in neural networks represents a significant advancement in AI capabilities, enabling models to dynamically interpret, learn from, and respond to complex environments. Its ability to enhance decision-making, personalize interactions, and improve efficiency makes it a critical component of modern AI applications. While challenges such as computational demands, ethical considerations, and interpretability must be addressed, the transformative potential of awareness-driven neural networks continues to reshape industries. As AI evolves, integrating awareness into neural networks will drive innovation, making artificial intelligence more intuitive, adaptive, and capable of tackling real-world challenges with greater precision and intelligence.

Awe-based generative AI

Awe-based generative AI represents an advanced form of artificial intelligence that creates original content, ideas, and solutions in ways that inspire wonder and redefine human creativity. This AI model leverages deep learning and neural networks to generate text, images, music, videos, and even scientific theories that push the boundaries of innovation. Unlike traditional AI that analyzes and classifies data, awe-based generative AI is designed to synthesize new concepts, blending human ingenuity with computational intelligence to produce unique and thought-provoking results.

The key components of awe-based generative AI include deep neural networks that mimic human cognition and creativity by learning complex patterns from vast datasets. Transformer architectures, such as those used in large language models, enable AI to generate coherent and contextually relevant text. Generative adversarial networks refine content creation by pitting two neural networks against each other, improving the realism and quality of AI-generated media. Variational autoencoders allow AI to reconstruct and manipulate data, enhancing its ability to generate diverse outputs. Reinforcement learning fine-tunes AI responses by optimizing creativity and coherence based on human feedback.

The benefits of awe-based generative AI include expanding human potential by enhancing creativity in writing, art, and music. AI-generated content accelerates the production of high-quality media, reducing the time and resources needed for creative endeavors. Scientific discovery is advanced as generative AI assists in hypothesizing new theories, designing experiments, and generating novel chemical compounds. Personalized content creation tailors AI-generated materials to individual preferences, improving user engagement in digital entertainment, marketing, and education. The automation of complex problem-solving enables businesses to generate innovative solutions, making AI a valuable tool in research, strategy, and innovation.

A practical example of awe-based generative AI is its use in literature, where AI-generated poetry and storytelling introduce new styles and perspectives that challenge traditional narratives. In music composition, AI collaborates with artists to produce symphonies that combine classical techniques with modern experimentation. Fashion designers leverage AI-generated designs to create futuristic clothing lines, blending aesthetics with advanced computational creativity. In scientific research, AI models generate potential drug formulas and materials with unprecedented properties, accelerating medical breakthroughs. AI-powered filmmaking enables directors to create virtual characters and cinematic effects that were previously impossible to achieve through conventional means.

Despite its transformative potential, awe-based generative AI faces several challenges. Ethical concerns arise regarding the originality and authorship of AI-generated content, raising questions about intellectual property rights and human creativity. Bias in training datasets can result in outputs that reflect societal prejudices, requiring continuous monitoring and adjustment. The misuse of generative AI for deepfake creation and misinformation presents significant risks, necessitating safeguards against malicious applications. Computational resource requirements can be substantial, making advanced generative models expensive to train and maintain. Ensuring that AI-generated content aligns with ethical standards and human values remains an ongoing challenge for developers and regulators.

Awe-based generative AI is applied across diverse industries, shaping the future of creative and analytical fields. In entertainment, AI enhances storytelling, scriptwriting, and animation, redefining cinematic experiences. The advertising industry benefits from AI-generated marketing campaigns tailored to audience preferences, increasing engagement and conversion rates. Education leverages AI-powered tutoring systems that generate customized learning materials, improving knowledge retention and accessibility. Scientific research benefits from AI's ability to simulate experiments and generate novel hypotheses, accelerating innovation in physics, biology, and chemistry. The gaming industry integrates generative AI to create dynamic worlds, personalized characters, and immersive narratives that adapt to player interactions.

In conclusion, awe-based generative AI represents a monumental shift in artificial intelligence, merging computational power with human creativity to generate groundbreaking ideas, content, and innovations. Its ability to produce original works across various domains enhances artistic expression, scientific discovery, and business strategies. While challenges such as ethical concerns, bias, and responsible use must be addressed, the benefits of AI-driven creativity continue to redefine industries and push the limits of what is possible. As AI evolves, generative models will play an increasingly prominent role in shaping the way humans interact with technology, opening new frontiers of exploration, imagination, and knowledge creation.

Awe-inducing robotics

Awe-inducing robotics with AI represents the fusion of artificial intelligence and advanced robotic systems, creating machines capable of performing complex tasks with precision, autonomy, and adaptability. These intelligent robots go beyond traditional automation by incorporating machine learning, computer vision, and decision-making capabilities, enabling them to interact with their environment, learn from experience, and operate independently in dynamic settings. The integration of AI into robotics has revolutionized industries, unlocking new possibilities in healthcare, manufacturing, space exploration, and human-machine collaboration.

The key components of awe-inducing robotics with AI include machine learning algorithms that allow robots to analyze data, adapt to new situations, and optimize performance over time. Computer vision systems enable robots to recognize objects, interpret visual data, and navigate environments with accuracy. Natural language processing allows human-like interaction, making it possible for robots to understand and respond to verbal commands. Sensor fusion integrates data from multiple sources, such as cameras, LiDAR, and infrared sensors, enhancing perception and situational awareness. Reinforcement learning enables robots to improve through trial and error, refining their abilities in real-world applications without human intervention.

The benefits of awe-inducing robotics with AI include increased efficiency and precision in industrial and service applications, reducing human error and enhancing productivity. Autonomous operation allows robots to perform tasks in hazardous or inaccessible environments, improving safety and reducing risks for human workers. Continuous learning capabilities enable robots to adapt to changing conditions, making them more versatile and effective in a wide range of applications. AI-driven robots streamline repetitive and labor-intensive tasks, freeing humans to focus on higher-level problem-solving and creativity. The integration of robotics with AI also accelerates scientific and technological advancements by enabling groundbreaking research in medicine, space exploration, and materials engineering.

A practical example of awe-inducing robotics with AI is its role in robotic-assisted surgery, where AI-powered robotic arms perform delicate procedures with enhanced precision, minimizing surgical risks and improving patient outcomes. In manufacturing, AI-driven robots optimize production lines by detecting defects, assembling components with pinpoint accuracy, and adjusting processes in real time. Space exploration missions leverage AI-powered rovers and robotic arms to explore planetary surfaces, collect samples, and conduct experiments beyond human reach. In agriculture, AI-equipped drones and robotic harvesters monitor crop health, optimize irrigation, and automate harvesting to increase yield and sustainability. Humanoid robots with AI capabilities assist in elder care and rehabilitation, providing companionship and physical assistance to improve quality of life.

Despite its remarkable capabilities, awe-inducing robotics with AI faces several challenges. High development costs and maintenance expenses make AI-powered robotics inaccessible to smaller organizations, limiting widespread adoption. Ethical concerns arise regarding job displacement, as intelligent robots replace human labor in various sectors, necessitating workforce retraining and policy adjustments. AI models in robotics require vast amounts of data for training, which may introduce biases or inaccuracies if datasets are not representative. Integration with existing infrastructure can be complex, requiring specialized expertise in AI programming, robotics engineering, and cybersecurity. The unpredictability of real-world environments presents difficulties for AI-driven robots, requiring continuous refinement to handle unexpected situations effectively.

Awe-inducing robotics with AI is applied across multiple industries, driving innovation and transforming operations. In healthcare, AI-powered robotic systems assist in surgeries, rehabilitation, and patient monitoring, improving medical care and accessibility. The logistics and transportation sector benefits from autonomous warehouse robots and self-driving delivery vehicles that enhance efficiency and reduce operational costs. Defense and security organizations deploy AI-driven robotic drones and autonomous surveillance systems for reconnaissance and threat detection. In entertainment, robotic performers equipped with AI create interactive experiences, from lifelike animatronics to AI-generated choreography in theatrical productions. Research institutions and space agencies utilize AI-powered robotics for deep-sea exploration, space missions, and scientific discovery, pushing the boundaries of human knowledge.

In conclusion, awe-inducing robotics with AI represents a transformative leap in technological advancement, merging intelligence with mechanical precision to create autonomous, adaptable, and highly capable machines. The impact of AI-driven robotics extends across industries, revolutionizing manufacturing, healthcare, space exploration, and everyday life. While challenges related to cost, ethical considerations, and real-world adaptability must be addressed, the benefits of efficiency, safety, and innovation position AI-powered robotics as a cornerstone of future technological progress. As AI continues to evolve, intelligent robots will play an increasingly vital role in shaping the way humans interact with technology, unlocking new frontiers in science, engineering, and human-machine collaboration.

Awe-inspiring AI

Awe-inspiring AI refers to the transformative and groundbreaking advancements in artificial intelligence that redefine the limits of technology, human potential, and problem-solving. This form of AI goes beyond automation and predictive analytics, showcasing capabilities that challenge conventional wisdom and create new possibilities in science, medicine, creativity, and human-machine interaction. It represents the fusion of cutting-edge machine learning, neural networks, and cognitive computing, allowing AI to perform tasks that once seemed impossible, from understanding human emotions to discovering new scientific phenomena.

The key components of awe-inspiring AI include deep learning architectures, which allow neural networks to simulate human-like cognition and learning from vast amounts of data. Natural language processing enables AI to comprehend, generate, and translate human language with unprecedented accuracy, leading to advanced conversational agents and content creation tools. Reinforcement learning enhances AI decision-making by allowing systems to learn from experience and improve performance over time. Computer vision grants machines the ability to interpret visual data, leading to breakthroughs in facial recognition, autonomous navigation, and medical diagnostics. Generative AI revolutionizes creativity by producing original music, artwork, literature, and even scientific theories, expanding the frontiers of human expression.

The benefits of awe-inspiring AI include enhanced efficiency across industries by automating complex tasks, reducing errors, and improving productivity. AI-driven insights enable organizations to make data-driven decisions with greater accuracy, optimizing operations and strategies. Human creativity is augmented by AI tools that assist in designing, writing, and composing, opening new frontiers in art and innovation. AI's ability to process vast datasets at incredible speeds accelerates scientific research, leading to discoveries in fields such as medicine, space exploration, and climate modeling. Personalized experiences in entertainment, education, and healthcare enhance user engagement and improve outcomes tailored to individual needs.

A practical example of awe-inspiring AI is its role in decoding ancient languages, where deep learning models reconstruct lost scripts and unlock historical knowledge. In medicine, AI-driven systems analyze genetic data to develop personalized treatments, targeting diseases with unmatched precision. Autonomous robots powered by AI explore uncharted territories, such as deep oceans and distant planets, collecting data that was previously inaccessible. AI-generated art exhibitions showcase machines as creative collaborators, producing paintings and music that rival human compositions. Self-learning AI systems in cybersecurity detect and neutralize cyber threats before human experts can identify them, ensuring digital safety at an unprecedented scale.

Despite its remarkable capabilities, awe-inspiring AI presents several challenges. Ethical concerns arise as AI systems become more autonomous, requiring guidelines to ensure responsible use and prevent unintended consequences. Bias in AI models can lead to disparities in decision-making if training data lacks diversity and fairness. The rapid evolution of AI outpaces regulatory frameworks, creating uncertainty about how to govern AI applications in sensitive areas such as surveillance, warfare, and deepfake technology. The dependence on AI for critical decision-making raises questions about accountability and the role of human oversight. The potential for job displacement due to automation necessitates strategies for workforce adaptation and reskilling.

Awe-inspiring AI is applied across diverse industries, driving innovation and disruption in multiple fields. In healthcare, it enhances diagnostics, drug discovery, and robotic surgery, improving patient outcomes and medical efficiency. The financial sector leverages AI for algorithmic trading, fraud detection, and customer service automation. Autonomous transportation, including self-driving cars and drones, benefits from AI-powered navigation and decision-making systems. In entertainment, AI-generated films, music, and interactive storytelling redefine creative expression and audience engagement. Smart cities integrate AI to optimize traffic management, energy consumption, and public safety, improving urban living standards.

In conclusion, awe-inspiring AI represents a paradigm shift in technological evolution, pushing the boundaries of what machines can achieve while complementing human intelligence and creativity. Its profound impact on industries, society, and scientific discovery demonstrates its potential to shape the future in ways previously imagined only in science fiction. While challenges related to ethics, bias, regulation, and societal adaptation must be addressed, the benefits of AI's transformative power continue to outweigh the risks. As AI advances further, it promises to unlock new dimensions of knowledge, efficiency, and human-machine collaboration, redefining the very nature of intelligence and progress.

Awe-invoking AI

Awe-invoking AI in healthcare represents the transformative impact of artificial intelligence in medical science, revolutionizing diagnostics, treatment, patient care, and operational efficiency. This form of AI leverages advanced machine learning algorithms, deep learning models, and natural language processing to enhance medical decision-making, automate processes, and personalize treatments. By integrating AI with healthcare systems, practitioners can provide more accurate, efficient, and accessible care, ultimately improving patient outcomes and reducing the burden on healthcare providers.

The key components of awe-invoking AI in healthcare include predictive analytics, which enables early detection of diseases by analyzing patient data and identifying risk factors. Computer vision plays a significant role in medical imaging, allowing AI-powered systems to detect abnormalities in X-rays, MRIs, and CT scans with precision. Natural language processing facilitates the extraction and analysis of clinical notes, streamlining medical documentation and research. Robotic process automation enhances administrative efficiency by handling repetitive tasks such as appointment scheduling, billing, and insurance processing. Personalized medicine benefits from AI-driven insights, tailoring treatments based on genetic, lifestyle, and environmental factors unique to each patient.

The benefits of awe-invoking AI in healthcare include enhanced diagnostic accuracy, reducing human error in disease detection and treatment recommendations. AI-powered automation decreases the workload for medical professionals, allowing them to focus on patient care rather than administrative tasks. Real-time data analysis improves decision-making by providing actionable insights from vast medical records, research studies, and patient histories. Remote monitoring systems powered by AI enable continuous tracking of patients with chronic illnesses, ensuring timely intervention when abnormalities are detected. Drug discovery and development become more efficient as AI accelerates the identification of potential treatments and predicts their effectiveness.

A practical example of awe-invoking AI in healthcare is its use in radiology, where AI models analyze medical images to detect early signs of diseases such as cancer, pneumonia, and fractures. In cardiology, AI-driven systems assess heart health by analyzing ECG readings, identifying irregularities that may indicate heart disease. Virtual health assistants provide patients with medical advice and reminders, improving adherence to prescribed treatments and medications. AI-powered robotic surgery enhances precision and minimizes recovery times by assisting surgeons in delicate procedures. In mental health, AI algorithms analyze speech patterns and facial expressions to detect signs of depression and anxiety, supporting early intervention strategies.

Despite its groundbreaking impact, awe-invoking AI in healthcare faces several challenges. Data privacy concerns arise as AI systems process sensitive patient information, requiring stringent security measures and compliance with healthcare regulations. Bias in AI models can lead to disparities in diagnosis and treatment recommendations if training datasets are not diverse and representative. Integration challenges occur when incorporating AI into existing healthcare infrastructure, as legacy systems may not be compatible with modern AI-driven solutions. Ethical concerns regarding decision-making transparency and patient autonomy must be addressed to ensure that AI enhances, rather than replaces, human medical judgment. The high cost of AI implementation poses a barrier to widespread adoption, particularly in underfunded healthcare systems.

Awe-invoking AI in healthcare is applied across multiple industries, extending beyond traditional medical institutions. In pharmaceuticals, AI accelerates drug discovery and clinical trials by predicting compound interactions and patient responses. The insurance sector utilizes AI for fraud detection, risk assessment, and personalized policy recommendations based on health data. Telemedicine platforms leverage AI-powered diagnostics and virtual consultations to provide accessible healthcare solutions in remote areas. Medical research benefits from AI-driven pattern recognition, enabling the identification of disease markers and treatment pathways. Healthcare startups and technology firms continue to innovate by developing AI-driven wearable devices that monitor vital signs and provide real-time health insights.

In conclusion, awe-invoking AI in healthcare represents a monumental shift in the way medical care is delivered, making healthcare more precise, efficient, and accessible. Its ability to analyze vast amounts of medical data, enhance diagnostics, and improve patient outcomes positions AI as a fundamental tool in modern medicine. While challenges such as data security, bias, integration, and ethical concerns must be addressed, the benefits far outweigh the risks. As AI continues to evolve, its role in healthcare will expand, shaping the future of medical science and transforming the global healthcare landscape.

Awkward Array

Awkward Array is a specialized data structure designed to handle irregular, nested, and variable-length data efficiently. Unlike traditional arrays, which require uniform dimensions, Awkward Array supports flexible structures that can accommodate lists of different lengths and nested levels. It is widely used in high-performance computing and data science applications where heterogeneous datasets need to be processed efficiently.

The key components of Awkward Array include its hierarchical structure, which allows data to be stored in multiple layers with varying dimensions. The underlying implementation is optimized for fast indexing, slicing, and transformations, making it suitable for operations on large datasets. The data layout is designed for efficient memory usage, enabling operations on complex structures without excessive overhead. Vectorized operations allow batch processing of nested data, eliminating the need for explicit loops and improving computational performance. Compatibility with major scientific computing libraries ensures seamless integration with tools such as NumPy and Pandas.

The benefits of Awkward Array include its ability to handle nested and variable-length data without requiring manual restructuring. The optimized performance of the library allows for rapid computation on large-scale datasets, reducing processing time. The memory-efficient storage format ensures that complex data structures do not consume excessive resources. The flexibility of Awkward Array makes it a powerful tool for working with hierarchical datasets commonly found in physics, bioinformatics, and machine learning. The support for vectorized operations simplifies complex transformations, allowing developers to focus on data analysis rather than low-level implementation details.

A practical example of Awkward Array is its use in particle physics, where experimental data consists of nested structures representing events, collisions, and particle trajectories. In genomics, Awkward Array is applied to store and process DNA sequence variations, which have irregular lengths and nested relationships. In financial modeling, it is used for analyzing transaction records with different structures, such as varying numbers of purchases per customer. In AI-driven analytics, it allows efficient manipulation of hierarchical data, such as structured text, video metadata, and social network graphs.

Despite its advantages, Awkward Array presents several challenges. The complexity of nested structures can make debugging and error handling more difficult compared to traditional arrays. The learning curve for new users may be steep, as working with hierarchical data requires familiarity with specialized indexing and transformation techniques. Some machine learning frameworks may not natively support Awkward Array, requiring additional conversion steps before integration. Memory management must be carefully optimized to prevent unnecessary overhead when working with extremely large datasets.

Awkward Array is widely applied across industries that rely on irregular and nested data processing. In scientific research, it is extensively used in high-energy physics for analyzing experimental results. The healthcare industry leverages Awkward Array for processing complex patient records and genomic data. In finance, it facilitates fraud detection by handling diverse transaction logs with variable attributes. The AI and machine learning sector benefits from its ability to manage hierarchical features, improving the representation of structured data in model training. In media and entertainment, it supports content recommendation systems by structuring user interactions in flexible formats.

In conclusion, Awkward Array provides a powerful solution for working with nested, irregular, and variable-length data. Its ability to handle complex structures efficiently makes it a valuable tool in scientific computing, machine learning, and data analysis. While challenges such as a steep learning curve and integration complexities exist, its benefits in performance optimization, memory efficiency, and flexible data representation outweigh these difficulties. As the demand for processing hierarchical data continues to grow, Awkward Array remains a critical component in high-performance data science and AI-driven applications.

AWS DeepLens

AWS DeepLens is an artificial intelligence-powered deep learning camera developed by Amazon to enable developers to build and deploy computer vision models at the edge. It allows AI inference directly on the device without requiring a constant connection to the cloud, making it an effective tool for real-time image and video processing. By integrating deep learning models with on-device processing, AWS DeepLens provides an innovative platform for exploring and implementing AI-driven vision applications.

The key components of AWS DeepLens include a high-definition camera equipped with onboard processing capabilities that allow deep learning models to run locally. The device integrates seamlessly with AWS services such as AWS SageMaker, AWS Lambda, and AWS IoT, enabling users to build, train, and deploy machine learning models efficiently. DeepLens supports popular deep learning frameworks, including TensorFlow, Apache MXNet, and PyTorch, ensuring compatibility with a wide range of AI models. The built-in inference engine enables low-latency AI processing, allowing real-time analysis of video streams. Pre-trained models and sample projects are available to accelerate development, helping users quickly create applications such as object detection, facial recognition, and gesture analysis.

The benefits of AWS DeepLens include its ability to perform edge computing, reducing the need for continuous cloud connectivity and minimizing latency. The device provides an accessible platform for AI experimentation, allowing developers to test and refine computer vision models in real-world scenarios. Integration with AWS cloud services offers scalability, enabling AI applications to expand beyond edge processing when necessary. The support for multiple deep learning frameworks ensures flexibility, allowing users to leverage different AI models depending on their specific use cases. The real-time inference capabilities of DeepLens make it ideal for applications that require immediate decision-making without relying on external servers.

A practical example of AWS DeepLens is its use in retail stores for monitoring customer activity and analyzing shopping behaviors. In security applications, DeepLens enables real-time surveillance, detecting unauthorized access and identifying potential threats using AI-driven image recognition. In healthcare, the device can assist in patient monitoring by analyzing movement patterns and detecting falls or abnormal activity. In educational settings, AWS DeepLens is used for hands-on learning, allowing students and developers to experiment with AI-powered computer vision projects. Industrial automation benefits from DeepLens by enabling AI-powered quality control, where products on an assembly line are analyzed in real time to detect defects.

Despite its advantages, AWS DeepLens presents several challenges. The hardware capabilities, while sufficient for many applications, may be limited for highly complex AI models that require extensive computational power. Setting up and optimizing deep learning models for edge deployment requires knowledge of machine learning frameworks and AWS services, posing a learning curve for beginners. Power and storage constraints can impact performance, particularly when processing large video streams continuously. The reliance on AWS cloud services for extended functionality means that users may face additional costs if their applications require extensive cloud integration.

AWS DeepLens is widely applied across multiple industries to enhance AI-driven automation and real-time decision-making. In retail, it enables smart inventory management and customer analytics by detecting product placement and customer engagement. The security sector benefits from AI-powered surveillance, where DeepLens is used to monitor premises and identify potential threats. The healthcare industry utilizes DeepLens for assisted living solutions, such as monitoring elderly patients for falls or unusual movements. In manufacturing, AI-based quality control ensures that defective products are identified and removed from production lines. The entertainment industry leverages DeepLens for interactive applications such as AI-driven motion tracking and gesture recognition.

In conclusion, AWS DeepLens is a powerful tool for developing and deploying AI-powered computer vision applications at the edge. Its ability to perform real-time inference without relying on cloud connectivity makes it a valuable solution for low-latency AI processing. The integration with AWS cloud services allows for scalable AI deployment, ensuring that models can be trained, refined, and enhanced over time. While challenges such as hardware limitations and a learning curve exist, the benefits of real-time processing, flexibility, and AI experimentation make DeepLens an essential tool for businesses and developers exploring the potential of computer vision technology. As AI adoption continues to grow, AWS DeepLens remains a key enabler of edge-based artificial intelligence solutions across various industries.

AWS Elastic Inference

AWS Elastic Inference is a cloud-based service that enables developers to attach the right amount of GPU-powered acceleration to Amazon EC2 and SageMaker instances, optimizing the performance and cost-efficiency of AI inference workloads. It allows machine learning models to run efficiently by allocating just the necessary compute resources instead of provisioning full GPU instances, which can be costly and underutilized. This service is particularly useful for AI inference tasks that require acceleration but do not fully utilize an entire GPU, making it an ideal solution for cost-effective deep learning deployment.

The key components of AWS Elastic Inference include inference accelerators that provide scalable GPU processing power, reducing the need for large dedicated GPU instances. These accelerators can be attached to Amazon EC2 and SageMaker instances to improve the performance of AI models while optimizing resource usage. AWS Deep Learning AMIs and frameworks such as TensorFlow, Apache MXNet, and PyTorch are fully compatible with Elastic Inference, allowing seamless integration with existing AI workflows. The service operates with automatic scaling, ensuring that inference workloads are processed efficiently without unnecessary computational overhead. Elastic Inference also offers secure and managed infrastructure, ensuring that AI inference workloads are executed with high reliability and minimal latency.

The benefits of AWS Elastic Inference include significant cost savings by allowing users to pay only for the GPU acceleration needed rather than renting entire GPU instances. It enhances the performance of AI models by reducing inference latency, making applications more responsive and efficient. The flexibility of Elastic Inference allows AI workloads to be deployed across different instance types while benefiting from scalable GPU resources. The seamless integration with AWS services simplifies the deployment of AI-powered applications, reducing the complexity of managing inference workloads. By enabling efficient resource allocation, Elastic Inference optimizes cloud computing costs while maintaining high-performance AI capabilities.

A practical example of AWS Elastic Inference is its use in natural language processing applications, where AI models process text in real-time with minimal latency. In healthcare, AI-driven medical imaging applications leverage Elastic Inference to accelerate diagnostic model performance while reducing cloud computing expenses. Chatbots and virtual assistants benefit from Elastic Inference by improving response times and making interactions more natural. In fraud detection, AI models can analyze large transaction datasets with enhanced speed and accuracy, improving security measures in financial institutions.

Despite its advantages, AWS Elastic Inference presents challenges that must be considered. The integration of inference accelerators requires proper configuration to match workload requirements, which may require specialized knowledge in cloud computing and machine learning deployment. Some AI models may not be fully optimized for Elastic Inference, leading to compatibility issues that require additional adjustments. The service is limited to specific machine learning frameworks, which may restrict flexibility for developers using unsupported AI libraries. Additionally, managing inference workloads across multiple cloud instances can introduce complexities in balancing resource allocation and monitoring performance.

AWS Elastic Inference is applied across various industries to improve AI inference efficiency and reduce cloud computing costs. In healthcare, it accelerates medical imaging analysis, enabling faster and more accurate diagnoses. The finance industry benefits from Elastic Inference by optimizing AI-powered fraud detection and risk assessment models. E-commerce companies use the service to enhance recommendation systems, delivering personalized product suggestions in real-time. Autonomous systems leverage Elastic Inference to process sensor data efficiently, improving decision-making in self-driving cars and robotics. In cybersecurity, AI-powered anomaly detection benefits from accelerated inference capabilities, allowing organizations to identify and mitigate threats quickly.

In conclusion, AWS Elastic Inference is a powerful solution for optimizing AI inference workloads by providing scalable GPU acceleration without the high costs of full GPU instances. Its ability to enhance model performance, reduce latency, and improve cost efficiency makes it an attractive choice for businesses deploying AI applications in the cloud. While challenges such as compatibility and configuration complexity exist, the benefits of flexible deployment, seamless AWS integration, and optimized resource usage outweigh these drawbacks. As AI adoption continues to grow, AWS Elastic Inference remains a valuable tool for organizations seeking efficient and cost-effective AI inference solutions.

AWS Glue for AI

AWS Glue for AI is a cloud-based data integration service provided by Amazon Web Services (AWS) that facilitates the preparation, transformation, and loading of data for artificial intelligence and machine learning applications. It automates data discovery, cataloging, and ETL (Extract, Transform, Load) processes, enabling AI models to access clean, structured, and well-organized data for training and inference. AWS Glue is a serverless service, meaning it automatically provisions and manages the required infrastructure, reducing the complexity of data engineering tasks.

Key components of AWS Glue include the Data Catalog, ETL engine, crawlers, job scheduler, and development endpoints. The Data Catalog serves as a central repository that stores metadata about datasets, making it easier for AI applications to access structured information. The ETL engine processes and transforms raw data into a format suitable for AI model training and analysis. Crawlers automate the process of scanning and cataloging new data sources, ensuring that AI applications always have updated information. The job scheduler allows users to define workflows that run at specific times, automating repetitive data processing tasks. Development endpoints provide interactive environments where data engineers can write and test their ETL scripts before deploying them into production.

The benefits of using AWS Glue for AI include streamlined data preparation, cost efficiency, scalability, and enhanced data governance. By automating data integration and transformation, AWS Glue reduces the time and effort required to prepare data for AI models, accelerating the development process. It follows a pay-as-you-go pricing model, allowing businesses to optimize costs based on actual usage without investing in expensive infrastructure. The serverless architecture of AWS Glue enables organizations to scale data processing workloads dynamically, ensuring seamless performance regardless of dataset size. With built-in security features and compliance capabilities, AWS Glue ensures data privacy, access control, and regulatory compliance, making it a reliable choice for AI-driven enterprises.

An example of AWS Glue in AI is its use in fraud detection systems, where financial institutions leverage Glue to clean and structure transaction data before feeding it into machine learning models. By automating ETL processes, AWS Glue helps detect anomalies in real-time, improving the accuracy of fraud prediction models. Another example is in personalized recommendation engines, where e-commerce platforms use AWS Glue to process customer behavior data, enabling AI-driven product recommendations that enhance user experience.

Industries benefiting from AWS Glue in AI include finance, healthcare, retail, manufacturing, and telecommunications. Financial institutions utilize AWS Glue to aggregate and transform large volumes of transactional data for risk analysis and fraud detection. Healthcare organizations use it to integrate diverse medical datasets, enabling AI-powered diagnostics and predictive analytics. Retail companies apply AWS Glue for customer segmentation and demand forecasting, optimizing inventory management and marketing strategies. Manufacturing industries leverage AWS Glue to analyze IoT sensor data, improving predictive maintenance and operational efficiency. Telecommunications companies use AWS Glue to process network logs and customer interactions, enhancing AI-driven service optimization and customer experience management.

Applications of AWS Glue for AI include data preprocessing for machine learning, real-time analytics, automated reporting, natural language processing, and sentiment analysis. Machine learning models require high-quality input data, and AWS Glue simplifies data cleansing and transformation, ensuring better training outcomes. Real-time analytics solutions use AWS Glue to process streaming data, enabling AI applications to provide timely insights. Automated reporting tools leverage AWS Glue to generate structured reports from raw data, reducing manual effort. Natural language processing applications use AWS Glue to extract and organize text data, improving AI-based language understanding. Sentiment analysis benefits from AWS Glue by refining social media and customer feedback data, enhancing AI-driven sentiment classification.

AWS Glue plays a crucial role in AI-driven enterprises by simplifying data integration, improving data quality, and enabling efficient model training. Its serverless and automated capabilities make it a powerful tool for organizations seeking to harness the potential of AI without dealing with complex data engineering challenges. As AI adoption continues to grow, AWS Glue remains a vital service for managing and optimizing data workflows in machine learning applications.

AWS IoT for AI applications

AWS IoT for AI applications is a cloud-based service that enables artificial intelligence to be integrated with Internet of Things (IoT) devices, allowing them to collect, process, and act on data in real time. This technology facilitates seamless communication between AI models and connected devices, enabling automation, predictive analytics, and intelligent decision-making without the need for direct human intervention. By leveraging AWS IoT, AI-powered systems can analyze vast amounts of data from sensors, cameras, and industrial equipment to optimize performance and efficiency.

The key components of AWS IoT for AI applications include AWS IoT Core, which provides secure communication and device management for IoT networks. AWS IoT Greengrass extends cloud-based AI models to edge devices, enabling them to process and analyze data locally while maintaining synchronization with the cloud. AWS IoT Analytics offers tools to collect, filter, and analyze large-scale data streams, making it easier for AI models to derive insights. AWS IoT Device Defender ensures security by monitoring device behavior and detecting anomalies, preventing potential threats. AWS IoT SiteWise is used for industrial applications, helping organizations analyze operational data from sensors and machinery to improve efficiency.

The benefits of AWS IoT for AI applications include improved operational efficiency through real-time data processing, reducing the need for manual intervention. Predictive maintenance is enhanced as AI models analyze sensor data to detect potential equipment failures before they occur, minimizing downtime and repair costs. The scalability of AWS IoT allows organizations to connect and manage millions of devices across different locations, ensuring seamless AI integration into industrial, healthcare, and smart home applications. AI-driven automation enables devices to respond dynamically to changing conditions, improving decision-making and optimizing processes without human oversight. Enhanced security features ensure data integrity, device authentication, and threat detection, making IoT implementations more reliable.

A practical example of AWS IoT for AI applications is its use in smart agriculture, where AI models analyze environmental data collected from IoT sensors to optimize irrigation and fertilizer use. In smart cities, AWS IoT integrates with AI to manage traffic lights dynamically, reducing congestion and improving transportation efficiency. In industrial settings, manufacturers use AWS IoT to monitor production lines and detect defects using AI-powered visual inspection systems. Retail businesses leverage IoT and AI to track inventory in real time, reducing stock shortages and improving supply chain management.

Despite its advantages, AWS IoT for AI applications presents several challenges. Implementing AI-driven IoT solutions requires specialized knowledge of machine learning, cloud computing, and networking, making it difficult for non-technical users to deploy effectively. Managing and processing vast amounts of IoT data can increase storage and computational costs, requiring careful resource allocation to optimize expenses. Security vulnerabilities remain a concern, as connected devices are susceptible to cyber threats, requiring continuous monitoring and risk mitigation strategies. Ensuring seamless communication between IoT devices and AI models can also be complex, especially when integrating legacy systems with modern cloud-based technologies.

AWS IoT for AI applications is widely used across multiple industries to enhance automation, decision-making, and operational efficiency. In healthcare, IoT-enabled AI devices monitor patients in real time, alerting medical professionals to irregularities before they become critical. The automotive industry leverages AWS IoT for AI-driven predictive maintenance in connected vehicles, reducing breakdowns and improving safety. Smart home technology integrates IoT and AI to automate lighting, security, and climate control based on user behavior. In logistics, AI models analyze sensor data from fleet vehicles to optimize delivery routes and fuel consumption. Manufacturing facilities use AWS IoT to improve quality control and streamline production through AI-powered anomaly detection.

In conclusion, AWS IoT for AI applications enables intelligent, real-time decision-making across various industries by integrating AI models with connected devices. Its ability to analyze vast amounts of data, automate processes, and improve efficiency makes it a powerful tool for organizations looking to enhance their IoT ecosystems. While challenges such as implementation complexity, security concerns, and cost management exist, the benefits of increased automation, predictive analytics, and operational scalability outweigh these difficulties. As IoT adoption continues to grow, the integration of AI with AWS IoT will play a critical role in shaping the future of smart technologies, industrial automation, and data-driven decision-making.

AWS Lambda for AI

AWS Lambda for AI is a serverless computing service that enables developers to run code in response to events without provisioning or managing servers. It provides a highly scalable and cost-efficient environment for artificial intelligence applications, allowing developers to focus on model deployment and execution rather than infrastructure maintenance.

AWS Lambda consists of several key components that facilitate AI processing. The event-driven architecture allows AI models to execute in response to specific triggers, such as API calls, database updates, or streaming data inputs. The compute layer provides an execution environment with predefined runtime limitations, ensuring that AI workloads are processed efficiently within the allocated resources. The auto-scaling feature dynamically adjusts computing power based on demand, making it ideal for AI inference tasks that require responsiveness to fluctuating workloads. Lambda also integrates with other AWS services, such as Amazon S3, DynamoDB, and AWS Step Functions, enabling seamless AI workflows.

The benefits of AWS Lambda for AI include cost efficiency, as users only pay for the computing time consumed by the function, reducing expenses compared to traditional server-based deployments. The scalability of the platform ensures that AI applications can handle varying loads without manual intervention. The ease of deployment allows AI developers to focus on model optimization rather than infrastructure setup. Security is another advantage, as Lambda operates within the AWS ecosystem, offering built-in encryption and compliance with industry standards. Furthermore, the serverless nature eliminates the need for ongoing maintenance, making AI development more streamlined and efficient.

A practical example of AWS Lambda in AI is its use in real-time image classification. When an image is uploaded to an Amazon S3 bucket, a Lambda function can automatically trigger an AI model for classification and return the results instantly. Another use case is in chatbots, where Lambda functions process user inputs and generate AI-driven responses in real time. Additionally, Lambda can facilitate fraud detection by analyzing transaction patterns and triggering alerts if anomalies are detected.

Despite its advantages, AWS Lambda presents several challenges for AI applications. The execution time limit of 15 minutes may not be sufficient for complex AI model training, requiring alternative solutions like AWS SageMaker for longer processing tasks. The cold start issue can introduce latency when a function is triggered after being idle, which may impact real-time AI applications. Additionally, memory and storage limitations can constrain large AI models, requiring optimization techniques such as model quantization.

AWS Lambda is widely applied across various industries for AI-driven automation. In healthcare, it supports medical image analysis by processing patient scans through AI models. In finance, it enhances fraud detection by analyzing real-time transaction data for suspicious activities. The e-commerce sector leverages Lambda for personalized recommendations, dynamically adjusting content based on user behavior. In the automotive industry, Lambda assists in processing sensor data for autonomous vehicle operations. Social media platforms use Lambda to filter and moderate content, ensuring compliance with platform guidelines.

In conclusion, AWS Lambda for AI provides a powerful, scalable, and cost-effective solution for executing AI workloads in a serverless environment. Its event-driven architecture enables real-time processing while integrating seamlessly with other AWS services. Although challenges like execution limits and cold start latency exist, Lambda remains a valuable tool for deploying AI models efficiently. Industries across healthcare, finance, e-commerce, and more leverage AWS Lambda to enhance automation, improve decision-making, and optimize business operations. The adoption of serverless computing in AI continues to grow, positioning AWS Lambda as an essential component of modern AI-driven solutions.

AWS SageMaker

AWS SageMaker is a cloud-based machine learning platform designed to help developers and data scientists build, train, and deploy AI models at scale. It provides an integrated environment that simplifies the AI development process by offering powerful automation, pre-configured tools, and seamless integration with other AWS services. SageMaker eliminates the need for managing infrastructure, allowing users to focus on model optimization and deployment.

The key components of AWS SageMaker include its fully managed Jupyter notebooks, which provide an interactive workspace for coding, data exploration, and model training. The built-in training environment offers optimized machine learning algorithms and automatic model tuning, helping users achieve high accuracy with minimal effort. The deployment service allows trained models to be deployed as real-time APIs or batch processing endpoints, making AI-powered applications more accessible. SageMaker Pipelines provide an automated workflow for continuous integration and deployment of machine learning models. The platform also integrates with SageMaker Ground Truth, which streamlines the process of labeling large datasets using automated and human-assisted techniques.

The benefits of AWS SageMaker include its ability to accelerate the machine learning lifecycle by offering pre-built algorithms and an optimized training infrastructure. Cost efficiency is achieved through its pay-as-you-go pricing model, where users only pay for the resources they consume. The scalability of the platform allows models to handle varying workloads, from small experimental projects to large enterprise-level AI applications. SageMaker also enhances security and compliance, offering built-in encryption and access controls to protect sensitive data. With native integration into the AWS ecosystem, SageMaker enables seamless data flow between cloud storage, databases, and other computing resources.

A practical example of AWS SageMaker is its use in fraud detection, where financial institutions deploy machine learning models to analyze transaction patterns and detect suspicious activities in real time. In healthcare, SageMaker supports medical image classification by training AI models to detect diseases in X-rays and MRI scans. E-commerce companies leverage the platform to build personalized recommendation systems that analyze customer behavior and suggest relevant products. Autonomous vehicle companies use SageMaker for sensor data analysis, enhancing self-driving capabilities by improving object detection and path planning.

Despite its advantages, AWS SageMaker presents challenges that users must consider. The complexity of machine learning requires expertise in model selection, tuning, and performance optimization, making it less accessible to those without technical knowledge. The pricing structure, while flexible, can become costly for large-scale deployments if resource consumption is not carefully managed. Additionally, integrating SageMaker with external data sources and third-party tools can sometimes require additional configuration and custom development efforts.

AWS SageMaker is widely used across multiple industries to drive AI innovation. In healthcare, it enhances predictive analytics for disease diagnosis and drug discovery. The finance sector relies on SageMaker for risk management, fraud detection, and algorithmic trading. Retail businesses use the platform to optimize inventory management and personalize customer experiences. The automotive industry integrates SageMaker into autonomous vehicle systems to improve real-time decision-making. In cybersecurity, organizations use machine learning models developed with SageMaker to detect threats and prevent security breaches.

In conclusion, AWS SageMaker provides a robust and scalable solution for building, training, and deploying AI models with ease. Its fully managed environment simplifies the complexities of machine learning while offering flexibility, automation, and seamless integration with AWS services. Although challenges such as cost management and technical expertise are factors to consider, the benefits of enhanced efficiency, scalability, and security make SageMaker a powerful tool for organizations looking to leverage AI. As machine learning adoption continues to grow, AWS SageMaker remains a critical platform for accelerating AI-driven innovations across various industries.

Axial AI Models

Axial AI models refer to a category of artificial intelligence architectures that process data along specific axes to improve efficiency, accuracy, and computational performance. These models focus on structured data transformations and specialized processing techniques that leverage axial representations to optimize learning and inference.

Axial AI models rely on several key components to function effectively. The core of these models is the axial attention mechanism, which selectively processes information along different dimensions rather than analyzing an entire dataset at once. This approach reduces computational complexity and improves efficiency. Data encoding plays a crucial role by structuring input data along predefined axes, enabling the model to recognize patterns more effectively. Optimization techniques such as parallel processing and sparse computation allow axial AI models to handle large datasets without excessive resource consumption. These models also integrate well with deep learning frameworks, utilizing neural network architectures tailored for efficient data traversal.

The benefits of axial AI models include improved performance by reducing the computational load while maintaining accuracy. The structured approach enables faster training times, making these models ideal for real-time AI applications. Resource efficiency is another advantage, as axial AI models can process high-dimensional data without requiring excessive GPU or memory usage. Their flexibility allows them to be adapted for various domains, from computer vision to natural language processing. Additionally, these models enhance interpretability by focusing on specific dimensions, making it easier to analyze how the AI derives its conclusions.

A practical example of axial AI models is their use in medical imaging, where axial attention mechanisms improve the accuracy of disease detection by focusing on relevant image sections. In financial analysis, these models process market trends along multiple axes, identifying correlations that would be difficult for traditional models to detect. Another example is in autonomous navigation, where axial AI models help process sensor data more efficiently, improving decision-making for self-driving cars.

Despite their advantages, axial AI models also present challenges. The complexity of model architecture requires specialized expertise for proper implementation and tuning. Data preprocessing must be carefully structured to align with axial representations, increasing the initial development workload. These models may also struggle with generalization if not trained on diverse datasets, potentially leading to biases in their predictions. Furthermore, limited adoption and tooling support make it difficult for AI practitioners to integrate axial AI models into existing machine learning pipelines.

Axial AI models have diverse applications across multiple industries. In healthcare, they enhance diagnostic imaging by improving the identification of anomalies in scans. The finance sector leverages these models for risk assessment and fraud detection by analyzing transaction data along different axes. In autonomous systems, axial AI models process sensor information to optimize decision-making in robotics and self-driving cars. The entertainment industry benefits from axial models in video analysis, where structured data processing enhances object detection and scene understanding. In cybersecurity, these models are used for anomaly detection, identifying threats by analyzing behavioral patterns.

In conclusion, axial AI models offer a structured and efficient approach to AI processing by leveraging axial representations and attention mechanisms. Their ability to enhance performance while reducing computational overhead makes them valuable for applications requiring high-speed data analysis. While challenges exist in terms of implementation complexity and dataset structuring, their advantages in efficiency, interpretability, and adaptability make them a promising advancement in AI research. As adoption increases and more tools become available, axial AI models are expected to play a significant role in advancing artificial intelligence across industries.

Axial Attention Mechanisms

Axial attention mechanisms are a flavor of attention techniques in AI, designed to focus computational effort along specific axes—like rows, columns, or time steps—instead of processing an entire data blob at once. Born from the need to handle big, structured inputs efficiently, they break down attention into manageable slices, making them a lean twist on traditional methods like self-attention, especially in tasks where data has clear directional patterns, such as images or sequences.

Key Components

The core is the axis selection, picking which dimensions—like height or width—to prioritize for attention. Splitting logic chops the data into these axial chunks, letting the system zoom in one piece at a time. Attention weights, calculated via scaled dot-products or similar, decide what matters within each slice. Aggregation steps then stitch the focused insights back together, while optimization tweaks keep it all humming. It's a divide-and-conquer setup with a directional edge.

Benefits

This approach slashes memory use, tackling huge datasets by nibbling along axes rather than gulping the whole thing. It's faster too, cutting compute time on structured inputs like grids or timelines. Precision holds strong since it respects the data's natural layout, avoiding the blur of global attention. And it scales gracefully, handling bigger problems without choking on resources.

Example

Think of an AI analyzing a high-res photo. With axial attention, it scans row by row, then column by column, spotlighting edges and textures—like a cat's whiskers—without overloading on the full image. It nails the details in a fraction of the time a standard model might take, all while keeping the cat sharp and the background crisp.

Industry Applications
In medical imaging, it processes 3D scans, focusing along depth axes to spot tumors efficiently. Video streaming leans on it to track motion frame-by-frame across time, boosting compression. Natural language processing uses it for long texts, attending to sentence chunks along a sequence axis. Gaming applies it to render vast worlds, slicing attention across spatial grids for smooth visuals.

Disadvantages
It's not a universal fix. If the data lacks clear axes—like a jumbled point cloud—it flounders, missing the forest for the trees. Setup can be fiddly, needing the right axial split to shine, and that takes trial and error. It might miss global context, focusing too tight and skipping broader patterns. Plus, in tiny datasets, the overhead of slicing outweighs the gains.

Conclusion
Axial attention mechanisms are a clever, efficient spin on AI focus—slicing data into digestible axes to conquer big tasks with less grunt. They're a win for structured challenges, though they stumble when the lines blur. For your dictionary, they're a standout tweak—proof that sometimes zooming in axis by axis beats staring at the whole picture.

Axial Deformation Detection in AI

Axial deformation detection in AI refers to the use of artificial intelligence to identify and measure changes in shape or structure along specific axes—directions like length, width, or depth—in objects or systems under stress, pressure, or wear. Think of it as AI keeping an eye on how things bend, stretch, or squash, using data from sensors or images to spot subtle shifts, making it a critical tool for monitoring integrity in physical environments.

Key Components
The setup kicks off with input data, often from sensors like strain gauges or cameras, capturing raw deformation signals. Axis definitions lock in the directions to watch—say, a bridge's vertical stretch. Feature extractors pull out telltale signs, like cracks or elongation, along these axes. Machine learning models, trained on deformation patterns, classify or quantify the changes. Real-time processors then flag anomalies, tying it all together with feedback loops to refine detection over time.

Benefits
This method catches tiny distortions fast, often before they turn into big problems, saving time and costly fixes. It's precise, zeroing in on axis-specific shifts rather than guessing from broad scans. Automation slashes the need for manual checks, and scalability means it can monitor one bolt or a whole skyscraper. Plus, it learns on the job, getting sharper with every twist it sees.

Example
Picture an AI watching a wind turbine blade. It tracks axial deformation along the blade's length using vibration sensors. When a storm pushes the material to stretch slightly off-norm, the system spots it, predicts fatigue risk, and alerts engineers—all in real time, keeping the turbine spinning safely without a human climbing up.

Industry Applications
Construction uses it to monitor bridges, catching girder bends before they buckle. Aerospace applies it to airplane wings, detecting stress shifts mid-flight. Manufacturing relies on it for machinery, flagging shaft warping to avoid breakdowns. Energy sectors tap it for pipelines, watching axial stretch to prevent leaks. Even sports tech uses it, analyzing equipment like skis for wear under strain.

Disadvantages
It's not flawless. Noisy data—like shaky sensor readings—can trick the AI into false alarms. Setting up the right axes takes know-how; miss the mark, and you're blind to key deformations. It's pricey upfront,

needing sensors and training data to start. And in chaotic, unpredictable settings, it might lag, struggling to pin down consistent axes amid wild shifts.

Conclusion
Axial deformation detection in AI is a watchdog for the physical world—sharp, proactive, and axis-smart, keeping tabs on how things hold up. It's a lifesaver where precision matters, though it leans on good data and setup to deliver. For your dictionary, it's a niche hero—blending AI smarts with real-world grit to spot the cracks before they spread.

Axial Transfer Learning

Definitions:
Axial transfer learning is an AI technique where knowledge gained from one domain or task is repurposed along specific axes—think core dimensions like features, time, or data types—to accelerate learning in a related but distinct problem. Unlike standard transfer learning that shifts entire models wholesale, this method focuses on transferring select, axis-aligned insights, fine-tuning what's shared to fit the new context, making it a precision tool for adapting pretrained systems efficiently.

Key Components
The process starts with the source axis, a structured slice of knowledge—like a neural net layer trained on image edges—pulled from a prior task. Mapping functions align this axis to a target domain, adjusting for differences in scale or structure. A transfer mechanism, often a lightweight retraining step, integrates the borrowed insights into the new model. Feature selectors pinpoint which axes matter most, while optimization routines tweak the blend of old and new learning. It's a targeted handoff, not a blunt copy-paste.

Benefits
This approach speeds up training by leaning on prelearned patterns, slashing the data and time needed for new tasks. It's resource-smart, reusing only the most relevant chunks of prior work instead of hauling over a whole model. Precision jumps too—by focusing on key axes, it avoids muddying the waters with irrelevant baggage. Plus, it's flexible, letting AI pivot across domains without starting from zero.

Example
Imagine an AI trained to spot tumors in X-rays. Axial transfer learning takes its edge-detection skills—tied to a spatial axis—and applies them to ultrasound scans. The system tweaks this axis for the new image type, quickly learning to highlight tissue boundaries without retraining the entire model, cutting development time from weeks to days.

Industry Applications
In agriculture, it adapts crop disease detectors from drone photos to satellite imagery, transferring color and shape axes for pest spotting. Automotive uses it to shift self-driving skills from urban roads to rural ones, reusing lane-detection axes. Retail applies it to move customer sentiment analysis from text reviews to voice data, leveraging tone axes. In gaming, it refines NPC behavior from one game engine to another, carrying over action-pattern axes.

Disadvantages
It's not a silver bullet. Picking the wrong axes to transfer—like forcing text skills onto images—can flop, wasting effort. It leans on the source model's quality; if that's shaky, the target inherits the flaws. Fine-tuning can get tricky, demanding expertise to align axes just right. And it's less potent for totally unrelated tasks, where broad transfer learning might still edge it out.

Conclusion
Axial transfer learning is a clever, surgical take on AI adaptation—grabbing the good stuff along key

lines and running with it. It's a time-saver and a sharpener for cross-domain leaps, though it hinges on smart choices and solid foundations. For your dictionary, it's a standout twist—proof that in AI, sometimes less is more when you aim it right.

Axis-Angle Representation in Robotics

Definition:
Axis-angle representation in robotics is a mathematical technique used to describe the orientation or rotation of objects, like robotic arms or mobile bots, by defining a single axis in 3D space and an angle of rotation around it. Rooted in geometry, it's a compact way to encode how something turns—think of spinning a top along its stem by a set degree—making it a staple in robotic systems for planning movements, navigating environments, and manipulating tools with precision.

Key Components
The star is the rotation axis, a 3D vector pinning down the line around which motion happens, often tied to a coordinate system like x-y-z. The angle, measured in radians or degrees, sets how far the object rotates along that axis. Conversion formulas, like those linking to rotation matrices or quaternions, translate this into usable commands. Normalization keeps the axis's length consistent, while control algorithms tweak both axis and angle based on sensor feedback. It's a lean, elegant setup for robotic motion.

Benefits
This method packs a punch with simplicity—describing any 3D rotation with just four numbers (three for the axis, one for the angle) beats bulkier alternatives. It's intuitive, mirroring how we picture spinning objects, which eases programming and debugging. Computationally, it's light, speeding up real-time adjustments in fast-moving robots. Plus, it plays nice with other systems, converting smoothly to formats robots already understand.

Example
Picture a robotic arm welding a car frame. Using axis-angle representation, it tilts its torch by 45 degrees around a vertical axis to hit a seam just right. The system calculates this pivot from sensor data, adjusts the arm in a snap, and keeps the weld steady—saving time and nailing accuracy without wrestling with clunky math.

Industry Applications
Manufacturing leans on it for robotic assembly, rotating parts into place on conveyor belts. In space exploration, rovers use it to adjust solar panels, spinning them around precise axes to catch sunlight. Medical robotics applies it in prosthetics, fine-tuning limb rotations for natural movement. Logistics bots in warehouses tap it too, angling to grab boxes from odd shelf angles with ease.

Disadvantages
It's not perfect. At certain angles—like a full 180-degree flip—the axis can get ambiguous, causing glitches called gimbal lock that confuse the system. Small errors in axis alignment can snowball, throwing off precision in long tasks. It's also less ideal for complex multi-rotation sequences, where other methods like quaternions might outshine it. And robots needing rapid, continuous spins might hit computational hiccups.

Conclusion
Axis-angle representation in robotics is a sleek, practical gem—boiling down 3D twists to a single line and a turn. It's a time-saver and a precision booster for machines that move, though it trips over edge cases and complex spins. For your dictionary, it's a robotics MVP—straightforward, effective, and a testament to how simple ideas can steer big tech.

Axis-Based AI Classification

Definition:
Axis-based AI classification is a machine learning strategy that sorts data into categories by organizing it along specific axes—core dimensions like time, value ranges, or feature types—to guide the decision-making process. Unlike standard classification that treats all inputs as a flat blob, this method uses these axes as a scaffold, aligning data into a structured grid to sharpen how AI distinguishes patterns and assigns labels, making it a go-to for problems with inherent order or hierarchy.

Key Components
The setup hinges on the classification axes, predefined lines or planes (think timelines or intensity scales) that frame the data's structure. Feature mappers extract and slot data points onto these axes, creating a clear layout. Decision boundaries, drawn by algorithms like support vector machines or neural nets, carve out class zones within this grid. Training logic adjusts the boundaries based on labeled examples, while scoring systems weigh each axis's role in the final call. It's a methodical dance of order and prediction.

Benefits
This approach cuts through messy data with precision, leveraging the axes to spotlight trends that might blur in a standard model. It's quick to train on structured datasets, needing less guesswork since the framework guides the process. Interpretability jumps too—tracing a label back to an axis like "time of day" makes the AI's reasoning crystal clear. Plus, it handles multidimensional problems without drowning in complexity.

Example
Imagine an AI classifying customer reviews as positive or negative. Using an axis-based method, it plots reviews along axes like word sentiment (happy to angry) and posting date. The model spots that recent reviews with "great" tip positive, while older ones with "slow" lean negative, nailing the labels faster and more transparently than sifting through raw text alone.

Industry Applications
In e-commerce, it sorts products into sales tiers based on price and demand axes, guiding stock decisions. Healthcare uses it to classify patient risks, mapping vitals like heart rate over time. Marketing applies it to segment audiences by behavior axes—say, purchase frequency—tailoring campaigns sharply. Energy sectors tap it to flag grid faults, aligning voltage spikes along temporal and geographic lines.

Disadvantages
It's not a cure-all. If the axes don't fit the data—like forcing a random scatter into a time grid—the model flops. It's rigid, struggling with chaotic or unstructured inputs where axes add more noise than signal. Picking and tuning the right axes takes extra upfront work, and if the data's nature shifts, the whole setup might need a redo, slowing adaptability.

Conclusion
Axis-based AI classification is a smart, structured twist on sorting the world's mess into neat piles. It thrives where data has natural lanes to follow, offering speed and clarity, but stumbles when forced onto the wrong track. For your dictionary, it's a sharp tool in the AI kit—focused, effective, and a reminder that sometimes a little order goes a long way.

Axis-Based Machine Learning Models

Definition:
Axis-based machine learning models are a specialized category of AI systems that organize data processing around defined axes—think of them as guiding frameworks or dimensions—to streamline analysis and prediction. Unlike generic models that treat features equally, these approaches emphasize

structured axes, such as time, space, or hierarchies, to align computation with the natural shape of the problem, boosting clarity and performance in tasks where context or orientation matters.

Key Components
The foundation is the axis framework, a set of predefined dimensions (like timestamps or spatial coordinates) that anchor the model's understanding of data. Feature extractors pull out relevant patterns along these axes, feeding them into layered algorithms that process inputs in an axis-aware way. Weighting systems adjust the importance of each axis based on the task, while optimization routines—like gradient descent—tune the model to minimize errors within this structured setup. It's all about giving data a directional backbone.

Benefits
These models shine by bringing order to complex datasets, cutting through noise to focus on what's relevant along key dimensions. They're faster at spotting trends in structured scenarios, like tracking changes over time, and they often need less data to train since the axis guides the learning process. Their interpretability is a big plus too—by tying outputs to clear axes, they make it easier to explain why a prediction happened.

Example
Consider a weather forecasting model using an axis-based approach. It organizes data along axes like time (hourly readings), space (geographic grids), and variables (temperature, humidity). The model zeroes in on how heat shifts across regions over days, predicting a storm's path with crisp accuracy—all while ignoring irrelevant clutter like static background noise, thanks to its axis-driven focus.

Industry Applications
In transportation, axis-based models track vehicle flows across time and road networks, optimizing traffic light timing. Finance leans on them to analyze stock trends along temporal and sectoral axes, spotting market shifts early. Retail uses them to map customer behavior over seasonal and geographic lines, tailoring inventory to demand. In environmental science, they model climate patterns across spatial and temporal axes, aiding disaster prep.

Disadvantages
The catch? These models can stumble if the wrong axes are chosen—force a square peg into a round hole, and you get garbage results. They're less flexible than general-purpose models, struggling with unstructured or wildly diverse data. Setup takes extra thought to define the right axes, and if the problem evolves beyond the initial framework, the model might lag until rebuilt. Precision comes at the cost of adaptability.

Conclusion
Axis-based machine learning models are like a compass for AI, pointing the way through data with structure and purpose. They trade versatility for focus, excelling where dimensions like time or space rule the game, but they're not one-size-fits-all. For your dictionary, they're a smart, niche tool—brilliant when the stars (or axes) align, yet a reminder that context is king in machine learning.

Axon-Based Neural Networks

Definition:
Axon-based neural networks are a class of artificial intelligence models that draw inspiration from the biological axons of the human nervous system, emphasizing the role of specialized connection pathways to process and transmit information. Unlike traditional neural networks with uniform layers, these systems prioritize dynamic, axon-like structures to guide data flow, aiming to replicate the efficiency and flexibility of biological brains in tasks like pattern recognition, decision-making, and learning.

Key Components
The core of axon-based neural networks is the axon-inspired connectivity, where synthetic axons act as tailored conduits between neurons, carrying signals with varying strength and speed. Neuron nodes, equipped with adjustable activation thresholds, process incoming data and decide what passes along these pathways. Synaptic weights, mimicking biological synapses, fine-tune the signal strength, while adaptive routing mechanisms allow the network to reconfigure connections based on task demands. These elements work in tandem to create a responsive, biology-rooted architecture.

Benefits
This approach offers a leaner, more efficient alternative to conventional networks, slashing computational waste by channeling data through optimized routes. It excels at handling sparse or noisy inputs, making sense of chaos where other models falter. Flexibility is another perk—axon-based designs can rewire themselves on the fly, adapting to new challenges without a full retrain. Plus, they often need less power, a boon for energy-conscious applications.

Example
Imagine an axon-based neural network powering a voice assistant. It listens to a garbled command in a noisy room, using its axon-like pathways to filter out background chatter and lock onto key words like "play" or "music." The network reroutes signals to emphasize speech patterns, quickly delivering a response—all while sipping minimal energy compared to a standard model crunching every sound equally.

Industry Applications
In robotics, axon-based neural networks drive real-time sensory processing, helping machines navigate unpredictable terrain by prioritizing critical inputs like obstacle distance. Healthcare uses them to analyze patient vitals, linking subtle signal shifts to early warnings of conditions like heart failure. In cybersecurity, they detect intrusions by mapping unusual data flows across a system. Creative industries tap them too, with music generators adapting rhythms via reconfigured pathways based on listener feedback.

Disadvantages
These networks come with quirks. Their complexity can make them harder to build and train, requiring deep expertise to get the axon-like structure right. They might struggle with highly structured, dense datasets where simpler models shine. Early setup costs—both in time and computing power—can be steep, and if the routing goes haywire, pinpointing the glitch in a web of adaptive connections is no picnic.

Conclusion
Axon-based neural networks are a bold step toward AI that thinks more like us, weaving biological inspiration into digital design. They trade simplicity for efficiency and adaptability, shining in messy, real-world scenarios but demanding careful crafting. For your dictionary, picture them as the mavericks of neural tech—imperfect, innovative, and packed with promise for a smarter, nimbler future.

Axis of Rotation in AI

Definition:
Axis of rotation in AI refers to a conceptual or computational framework used to model and manipulate data transformations around a central pivot or reference line, often borrowed from physics and geometry to enhance AI's ability to process spatial, temporal, or multidimensional patterns. In artificial intelligence, it's a way to describe how systems rotate or reorient information—literally or abstractly—to uncover relationships, optimize solutions, or simulate dynamic environments, making it a key idea in fields like robotics, graphics, and predictive modeling.

Key Components
The heart of this concept is the rotational axis itself, a defined line or dimension around which data points shift, whether it's a 3D object's spin or a dataset's perspective change. Transformation algorithms, like rotation matrices, handle the math to reorient data smoothly. Coordinate systems—cartesian, polar, or otherwise—anchor the axis in a workable space. Adjustment parameters fine-tune the angle and speed of rotation, while feedback loops ensure the system adapts based on outcomes. It's a blend of structure and motion tailored for AI tasks.

Benefits
This approach lets AI grasp complex spatial or sequential dynamics with ease, revealing hidden patterns by twisting data into new views. It's computationally slick, often simplifying tough problems—like object recognition—into manageable steps. Efficiency jumps since it focuses processing on relevant shifts rather than brute-forcing every angle. Plus, it mimics real-world physics, making AI outputs more intuitive for humans to trust and use.

Example

Imagine an AI guiding a drone through a forest. Using an axis of rotation, it models the drone's camera feed around a vertical axis to track tree positions as it spins mid-flight. By rotating the data view, it spots gaps for navigation, adjusting its path in real time—all faster and clearer than scanning the scene pixel by pixel without a rotational anchor.

Industry Applications
In gaming, axis of rotation drives realistic character movements, spinning 3D models smoothly for immersive play. Healthcare uses it in surgical robots, rotating tool perspectives for precise cuts based on patient scans. Manufacturing taps it to optimize robotic arms, rotating parts into place on assembly lines. In virtual reality, it aligns head-tracking data around rotational axes, syncing visuals with user motion for seamless experiences.

Disadvantages
It's not all smooth sailing. Defining the right axis can be tricky—pick poorly, and the model spins into confusion, missing the mark. It leans heavily on accurate data; noise or gaps can throw off rotations, leading to garbage outputs. Computationally, it's lightweight until scaled to huge datasets or real-time needs, where latency creeps in. And it's niche—tasks without clear rotational context might not benefit at all.

Conclusion
Axis of rotation in AI is a clever twist—pun intended—that brings motion and perspective to data crunching. It's a niche but powerful idea, bridging physical intuition with digital smarts, perfect for spatial or dynamic challenges. For your dictionary, it's a gem that shows how AI can dance around problems, though it's no universal fix—just a brilliant move when the setup's right.

Axon-Based Neural Networks

Definition:
Axon-based neural networks are a class of artificial intelligence models that draw inspiration from the biological axons of the human nervous system, emphasizing the role of specialized connection pathways to process and transmit information. Unlike traditional neural networks with uniform layers, these systems prioritize dynamic, axon-like structures to guide data flow, aiming to replicate the efficiency and flexibility of biological brains in tasks like pattern recognition, decision-making, and learning.

Key Components
The core of axon-based neural networks is the axon-inspired connectivity, where synthetic axons act as

tailored conduits between neurons, carrying signals with varying strength and speed. Neuron nodes, equipped with adjustable activation thresholds, process incoming data and decide what passes along these pathways. Synaptic weights, mimicking biological synapses, fine-tune the signal strength, while adaptive routing mechanisms allow the network to reconfigure connections based on task demands. These elements work in tandem to create a responsive, biology-rooted architecture.

Benefits
This approach offers a leaner, more efficient alternative to conventional networks, slashing computational waste by channeling data through optimized routes. It excels at handling sparse or noisy inputs, making sense of chaos where other models falter. Flexibility is another perk—axon-based designs can rewire themselves on the fly, adapting to new challenges without a full retrain. Plus, they often need less power, a boon for energy-conscious applications.

Example
Imagine an axon-based neural network powering a voice assistant. It listens to a garbled command in a noisy room, using its axon-like pathways to filter out background chatter and lock onto key words like "play" or "music." The network reroutes signals to emphasize speech patterns, quickly delivering a response—all while sipping minimal energy compared to a standard model crunching every sound equally.

Industry Applications
In robotics, axon-based neural networks drive real-time sensory processing, helping machines navigate unpredictable terrain by prioritizing critical inputs like obstacle distance. Healthcare uses them to analyze patient vitals, linking subtle signal shifts to early warnings of conditions like heart failure. In cybersecurity, they detect intrusions by mapping unusual data flows across a system. Creative industries tap them too, with music generators adapting rhythms via reconfigured pathways based on listener feedback.

Disadvantages
These networks come with quirks. Their complexity can make them harder to build and train, requiring deep expertise to get the axon-like structure right. They might struggle with highly structured, dense datasets where simpler models shine. Early setup costs—both in time and computing power—can be steep, and if the routing goes haywire, pinpointing the glitch in a web of adaptive connections is no picnic.

Conclusion
Axon-based neural networks are a bold step toward AI that thinks more like us, weaving biological inspiration into digital design. They trade simplicity for efficiency and adaptability, shining in messy, real-world scenarios but demanding careful crafting. For your dictionary, picture them as the mavericks of neural tech—imperfect, innovative, and packed with promise for a smarter, nimbler future.

Axon Mapping in Neural Networks

Axon mapping in neural networks refers to the process of designing and optimizing the pathways that connect artificial neurons, mimicking the role of axons in biological nervous systems, to enhance how data flows and computations occur within an AI model. Inspired by the way biological axons transmit signals between neurons, this technique focuses on structuring connections to improve efficiency, adaptability, and performance in artificial intelligence systems, particularly in deep learning architectures.

Key Components
The backbone of axon mapping lies in its connection framework, where virtual axons are represented as weighted links between neuron layers, determining how signals propagate. Activation functions act as gatekeepers, deciding which signals get amplified or muted along these pathways. Network

topology—whether dense, sparse, or hierarchical—shapes the mapping, dictating the complexity and direction of data flow. Learning algorithms, like backpropagation, tweak these connections over time, refining the map based on training data. Together, these elements create a dynamic system that balances speed and accuracy.

Benefits
Axon mapping boosts neural networks by streamlining data transmission, cutting down on redundant computations, and reducing energy use, which is a big win for large-scale models. It enhances adaptability, letting networks rewire connections to tackle new tasks without starting from scratch. This approach can also sharpen predictive power by focusing resources on the most relevant pathways, making models leaner and faster without sacrificing depth.

Example
Picture a neural network trained to recognize handwritten digits. With axon mapping, the system prioritizes connections between neurons that detect edges and curves, ignoring irrelevant noise like smudges. During training, it strengthens pathways linked to key features—like the loop of a "9"—while pruning weaker ones, resulting in a swift, accurate classifier that nails the task with minimal overhead.

Industry Applications
In healthcare, axon mapping powers diagnostic AI, mapping neural connections to spot patterns in MRI scans for early disease detection. Autonomous vehicles rely on it to process sensor data in real time, linking critical inputs like road signs to decision-making outputs. In finance, it's used in fraud detection systems, connecting transaction data points to flag anomalies efficiently. Even gaming benefits, with AI opponents adapting strategies by remapping connections based on player moves.

Disadvantages
Axon mapping isn't flawless. It can complicate model design, demanding extra effort to tune the connection structure, which might slow development. Over-optimization risks overfitting, where the network gets too cozy with training data and flounders on new inputs. It also guzzles computational resources upfront, especially when scaling to massive networks, and debugging faulty mappings can be a headache due to their intricacy.

Conclusion
Axon mapping in neural networks is a clever nod to nature, blending biology and tech to make AI smarter and more efficient. It's a powerful tool for building systems that learn fast and adapt faster, but it comes with trade-offs in complexity and resource demands. For your dictionary, think of it as the art of wiring an artificial brain—tricky, resource-intensive, yet brimming with potential to push neural networks into new territory.

❀ LETTER B ❀

A backdoor attack in AI

Definition: A backdoor attack in AI is a security threat where an adversary manipulates a machine learning model by introducing hidden malicious behavior during training. This attack allows the attacker to control the model's output in specific situations while ensuring it performs normally under standard conditions. The goal is to create a model that behaves as expected under most inputs but exhibits an attacker-specified behavior when triggered by a predefined condition.

Backdoor attacks involve key components that make them effective. The poisoned training data is manipulated by embedding specific patterns or triggers that influence the model's decision-making process. The trigger pattern is an intentional anomaly that, when present in input data, forces the model to produce a predetermined outcome. The compromised model integrates the hidden behavior without affecting its performance on benign inputs. The attacker-controlled inputs allow the adversary to activate the backdoor at any time.

Despite their malicious intent, backdoor attacks provide insights into vulnerabilities in AI security. They help security researchers and AI developers understand model weaknesses and improve robustness. By studying backdoor techniques, AI security teams can develop stronger defense mechanisms to detect and prevent model manipulation. Awareness of backdoor attacks also encourages the creation of AI models that are resistant to adversarial manipulation.

Real-world examples highlight the impact of backdoor attacks on AI systems. In image classification, an attacker can train a neural network to classify images correctly but misclassify specific images when a small trigger is embedded. In facial recognition, a backdoor attack can allow unauthorized individuals to bypass authentication when wearing a specific accessory. In autonomous vehicles, attackers can manipulate traffic signs with subtle alterations that cause incorrect model predictions.

The industries affected by backdoor attacks include finance, where fraud detection models can be compromised, healthcare, where medical diagnosis systems may be manipulated, cybersecurity, where AI-based threat detection can be evaded, and defense, where compromised AI models may lead to strategic vulnerabilities.

Challenges in preventing backdoor attacks include detecting hidden triggers in complex models, ensuring robust defenses without reducing model accuracy, and creating methods to verify the integrity of AI systems without access to all training data. Adversaries continuously evolve their attack methods, requiring constant vigilance and adaptation in security measures.

In summary, backdoor attacks in AI represent a serious security threat where malicious behavior is embedded in machine learning models during training. These attacks exploit the model's ability to learn hidden triggers, allowing adversaries to manipulate outputs while maintaining normal performance under most conditions. Their impact spans multiple industries, posing significant challenges for AI security. Addressing backdoor vulnerabilities requires a combination of adversarial training, model verification, and continuous monitoring to ensure AI systems remain reliable and secure.

Backpropagation

Definition: Backpropagation is a fundamental algorithm in training artificial neural networks. It is a supervised learning method that adjusts the weights of a network by propagating errors backward through the layers. The goal is to minimize the difference between the predicted and actual outputs by updating the weights based on the gradient of the loss function. This process allows neural networks to learn from data and improve performance over multiple iterations.

The key components of backpropagation include the forward pass, where input data moves through the network and produces an output, the loss function, which calculates the difference between the predicted and actual values, the backward pass, where the error is propagated from the output layer to earlier layers, and the weight update, where the algorithm adjusts network parameters using an optimization technique like gradient descent.

Backpropagation offers several benefits in machine learning. It enables deep neural networks to learn complex patterns from large datasets, making it essential for applications such as image and speech recognition. The algorithm automates weight adjustments, reducing the need for manual fine-tuning. It also improves accuracy over time as the network refines its parameters through multiple training cycles.

Examples of backpropagation in action include deep learning models used in facial recognition systems, where the algorithm helps networks differentiate between unique facial features. In natural language processing, backpropagation improves the accuracy of language models in tasks like text translation and sentiment analysis. In self-driving cars, neural networks use backpropagation to enhance object detection and decision-making capabilities.

Various industries rely on backpropagation for AI-driven solutions. The healthcare sector utilizes deep learning models trained with backpropagation for disease diagnosis and medical image analysis. The finance industry applies the algorithm to fraud detection systems and stock market predictions. In technology, companies use neural networks with backpropagation for personalized recommendations and virtual assistants.

Despite its advantages, backpropagation faces challenges. Training deep neural networks requires significant computational power and large datasets. The algorithm can suffer from vanishing or exploding gradients, making it difficult for deep networks to learn effectively. Backpropagation also depends on high-quality labeled data, and noisy or biased datasets can impact model performance. Additionally, the training process can be time-consuming, especially for complex networks.

In summary, backpropagation is a critical algorithm in machine learning that allows neural networks to learn by adjusting weights based on error signals. It plays a crucial role in training deep learning models across various industries, improving their ability to recognize patterns and make predictions. Despite computational challenges, it remains the foundation for modern AI advancements, driving innovation in fields like healthcare, finance, and autonomous systems.

Backtracking search is an algorithmic technique used for solving constraint satisfaction problems by exploring possible solutions incrementally and abandoning paths that fail to meet the required conditions. It systematically builds a solution by making choices and, when a contradiction arises, reverses previous decisions to explore alternative paths. This approach is widely used in optimization, combinatorial problems, and artificial intelligence.

The key components of backtracking search include the decision tree, where each choice represents a possible step toward the solution, the constraint checking mechanism that ensures each step meets predefined conditions, the recursive exploration that allows the algorithm to explore different paths systematically, and the backtracking process that undoes previous choices when a conflict is detected.

Backtracking search provides multiple benefits in problem-solving. It efficiently finds solutions by pruning unproductive branches early, reducing unnecessary computations. The algorithm is flexible and can be applied to various domains, from puzzles to real-world optimization challenges. It ensures completeness, meaning that if a solution exists, backtracking will eventually find it. Additionally, it optimizes memory usage compared to brute-force approaches by storing only the necessary path information.

Examples of backtracking search include its application in the N-Queens problem, where the algorithm systematically places queens on a chessboard while avoiding conflicts. In Sudoku solving, backtracking ensures that each number placement adheres to the game's rules. In pathfinding, the algorithm assists in maze solving by exploring different routes and retreating from dead ends.

Industries such as artificial intelligence, logistics, cryptography, and computer-aided design rely on backtracking search for various applications. In AI, it helps in decision-making and planning tasks. In logistics, it assists with scheduling and route optimization problems. Cryptography leverages backtracking for breaking codes and solving complex mathematical constraints. In computational design, it aids in generating layouts and configurations that meet specific constraints.

Challenges associated with backtracking search include its potential inefficiency in large problem spaces, where excessive branching can lead to high computational costs. Poorly designed heuristics may result in unnecessary explorations, slowing down the search process. Some problems require additional pruning techniques to improve performance. Additionally, backtracking can struggle with problems that require real-time decision-making, as it may not be fast enough for dynamic environments.

In summary, backtracking search is a powerful problem-solving technique that systematically explores potential solutions while eliminating unviable paths. It is widely used in AI, logistics, and computational problem-solving due to its efficiency and completeness. Despite its challenges in handling large-scale problems, backtracking remains a fundamental algorithm for solving complex constraint-based problems with precision and flexibility.

Bagging, short for Bootstrap Aggregating

Definition: Baggaing, short for Bootsstrap Aggregating is an ensemble learning technique used to improve the accuracy and stability of machine learning models by combining multiple versions of a base model trained on different subsets of the data. It reduces variance and prevents overfitting by averaging the predictions of multiple models, ensuring better generalization to unseen data. The process relies on generating multiple bootstrap samples from the original dataset and training individual models independently before aggregating their outputs.

The key components of bagging include bootstrapping, where random subsets of the training data are created with replacement to introduce diversity among models, model training, where each subset is used to train an independent base model, aggregation, which combines predictions using averaging for regression and voting for classification, and independence, where models are trained separately without influencing each other, enhancing robustness.

Bagging offers several advantages in machine learning. It significantly reduces variance, making models less sensitive to fluctuations in training data. It enhances accuracy, particularly for high-variance models like decision trees. By aggregating multiple models, bagging creates a more stable and reliable predictor. It also mitigates overfitting by ensuring that individual models do not memorize noise from the training data, leading to improved generalization.

Examples of bagging include its use in random forests, where multiple decision trees are trained on different bootstrap samples and their predictions are averaged or voted upon. In financial risk assessment, bagging helps predict creditworthiness by reducing the impact of noisy data points. In medical diagnosis, ensemble models using bagging improve the reliability of disease classification by aggregating multiple independent predictions. In speech recognition, bagging enhances model robustness by ensuring that errors from individual models do not dominate the final decision.

Bagging is widely applied in industries that require high accuracy and robustness. In finance, it is used for fraud detection and credit scoring. In healthcare, it helps with diagnostic models and medical image analysis. In cybersecurity, bagging strengthens anomaly detection by reducing the chances of false positives. In e-commerce, recommendation systems utilize bagging to provide more accurate product recommendations.

Despite its benefits, bagging faces challenges. Training multiple models increases computational costs and requires more storage. The technique may not be effective for low-variance models, as combining them does not provide significant improvements. In cases of limited data, bootstrapping can lead to excessive repetition of certain instances, potentially affecting model diversity. Additionally, bagging does not address biases in the data, meaning that if the base models are inherently biased, the aggregated output may still reflect those biases.

In summary, bagging is a powerful ensemble learning method that enhances model accuracy and stability by training multiple versions of a base model on bootstrapped data samples. It is highly effective in reducing variance and preventing overfitting, making it valuable in various industries such as finance, healthcare, and cybersecurity. While it requires additional computational resources, its ability to improve generalization and robustness makes it a fundamental technique in machine learning.

Bag-of-Words (BoW)

Definition: Bag-of-words (BoW) is a fundamental text representation technique used in natural language processing and machine learning. It converts text into numerical data by breaking it down into individual words and representing their frequency of occurrence while disregarding grammar, order, and context. BoW is widely used for tasks such as text classification, sentiment analysis, and document similarity measurement.

The key components of BoW include tokenization, where text is split into individual words or terms, vocabulary creation, which compiles a unique set of words from all documents, vectorization, where each document is represented as a numerical vector based on word occurrences, and frequency representation, which counts how often each word appears in a document. This structured approach allows text data to be transformed into a format suitable for machine learning models.

BoW offers multiple benefits in text analysis. It is simple and computationally efficient, making it easy to implement in various applications. The technique works well with machine learning algorithms that require fixed-size numerical inputs. It provides a structured representation of text data, allowing models to identify patterns based on word frequency. BoW is also highly adaptable and can be used in a variety of tasks, from spam detection to topic modeling.

Examples of BoW applications include its use in spam email filtering, where it helps classify messages based on the presence and frequency of certain words. In sentiment analysis, BoW enables models to determine the positivity or negativity of customer reviews by analyzing common words associated with different sentiments. Search engines leverage BoW to match user queries with relevant documents by comparing word occurrences. In plagiarism detection, the technique helps identify similarities between texts by analyzing shared word patterns.

Industries that utilize BoW include e-commerce, where it enhances product recommendation systems by analyzing customer reviews and search queries. In social media monitoring, it helps companies track brand sentiment by processing user comments and feedback. Healthcare applications use BoW for medical text analysis, assisting in the classification of clinical documents. In cybersecurity, it aids in detecting malicious content by identifying keyword patterns associated with phishing or fraudulent activity.

Despite its advantages, BoW has several challenges. It ignores the order and structure of words, leading to a loss of contextual meaning. Large vocabularies can result in high-dimensional feature spaces, increasing computational requirements and memory usage. BoW does not capture relationships between words, making it less effective in understanding complex text semantics. The method is also susceptible to sparsity, where most words in a vocabulary do not appear in every document, leading to inefficient data representation.

In summary, Bag-of-Words is a foundational technique in natural language processing that transforms text into numerical representations based on word frequency. It is widely used in industries such as e-commerce, cybersecurity, and healthcare for applications ranging from sentiment analysis to text classification. While it is simple and effective for many tasks, its limitations in preserving word order and meaning necessitate the use of more advanced techniques in complex text analysis scenarios.

Balanced accuracy

Balanced accuracy is a performance metric used in machine learning to evaluate classification models, particularly when dealing with imbalanced datasets. It measures the average recall obtained across all classes, ensuring that the model's performance is fairly assessed regardless of class distribution. Unlike traditional accuracy, which can be misleading in imbalanced datasets, balanced accuracy provides a more representative evaluation by considering both the true positive rate and the true negative rate.

The key components of balanced accuracy include sensitivity, which measures the model's ability to correctly identify positive instances, specificity, which evaluates how well the model identifies negative instances, and class balance adjustment, which ensures that both majority and minority classes contribute equally to the final metric. The formula for balanced accuracy is the average of sensitivity and specificity, making it a more robust alternative to standard accuracy metrics.

Balanced accuracy offers several benefits in classification tasks. It provides a fair evaluation for models dealing with imbalanced datasets, preventing misleading results caused by class dominance. It ensures that models do not favor the majority class while neglecting the minority class. By offering a better representation of overall performance, it helps in selecting optimal models for applications where misclassification of minority instances can have significant consequences. It is also applicable across various classification problems without requiring class rebalancing techniques.

Examples of balanced accuracy applications include fraud detection, where it ensures that fraudulent transactions are not overlooked despite being rare in financial data. In medical diagnosis, balanced accuracy is crucial in identifying rare diseases that might otherwise be misclassified by traditional accuracy metrics. In spam detection, it helps ensure that both spam and non-spam emails are correctly classified without bias toward the majority class. In credit risk assessment, it ensures that high-risk borrowers are identified despite their lower frequency in loan datasets.

Industries that benefit from balanced accuracy include healthcare, where it helps in identifying rare but critical conditions in medical imaging and diagnostics. In finance, it is used in fraud prevention and credit scoring to ensure that high-risk cases are not ignored. In cybersecurity, it aids in detecting rare but severe threats such as phishing attacks and network intrusions. In customer service, balanced accuracy is applied in sentiment analysis to detect both positive and negative feedback equally, ensuring unbiased insights.

Despite its advantages, balanced accuracy faces challenges. It requires careful interpretation, as it does not account for precision or false positive rates, which might be crucial in certain applications. In cases where data is highly imbalanced, other metrics like the F1-score or Matthews correlation coefficient may provide a more comprehensive evaluation. The metric can also be affected by noisy or biased training data, leading to misleading assessments of model performance. Additionally, it may not be sufficient for multi-class classification problems, where additional evaluation methods may be needed.

In summary, balanced accuracy is a valuable metric for assessing classification models, especially when dealing with imbalanced datasets. It provides a fair evaluation by averaging sensitivity and specificity, ensuring that all classes contribute equally to model performance assessment. While widely used in healthcare, finance, and cybersecurity, it has limitations that require careful consideration when applied to complex classification problems.

BART (Bidirectional and Auto-Regressive Transformer)

BART (Bidirectional and Auto-Regressive Transformers) is a deep learning model designed for natural language processing tasks such as text generation, summarization, translation, and question answering. It combines the strengths of both bidirectional and autoregressive transformers, allowing it to understand and generate text effectively. By using a denoising autoencoder approach, BART reconstructs original text from corrupted input, making it highly effective in handling complex language tasks.

The key components of BART include a transformer-based architecture, which enables the model to capture contextual dependencies in text. The encoder-decoder structure processes input text bidirectionally to understand context and then generates meaningful responses autoregressively. The denoising pretraining strategy enhances the model's ability to recover meaningful information from noisy or incomplete text. Masked token prediction allows BART to infer missing words or phrases, improving its text generation capabilities.

Benefits: BART offers multiple benefits in NLP applications. It excels in handling complex text transformation tasks such as summarization and paraphrasing. Its bidirectional encoding improves contextual understanding, leading to better comprehension of text meaning. The autoregressive decoding mechanism ensures that generated text is coherent and contextually relevant. BART's ability to learn from corrupted text enhances its robustness in real-world applications where text data may be incomplete or noisy.

Examples of BART in action include text summarization, where it generates concise and meaningful summaries of long documents. In machine translation, it improves accuracy by leveraging its bidirectional understanding of language. In chatbot development, BART enhances conversation quality by generating natural and contextually relevant responses. In content creation, it assists writers by paraphrasing text while maintaining original meaning and coherence.

Industries that benefit from BART include media and publishing, where it automates content summarization and generation. In customer service, it improves chatbot interactions by providing human-like responses. In healthcare, it aids in medical report summarization and clinical documentation. In education, it enhances automated grading and personalized learning experiences. In finance, BART helps analyze financial reports and generate executive summaries.

Despite its advantages, BART faces challenges. Training and fine-tuning the model require significant computational resources and large datasets. It may generate incorrect or biased responses if the training data contains biases. The autoregressive nature of text generation can sometimes lead to hallucinations, where the model generates plausible but incorrect information. Ensuring factual accuracy remains a challenge, particularly in high-stakes applications such as medical or legal document generation.

In summary, BART is a powerful NLP model that combines bidirectional encoding with autoregressive decoding to handle complex language tasks effectively. It is widely used in industries such as media, customer service, and healthcare for applications including summarization, translation, and conversational AI. While it offers significant advantages in text generation, challenges such as computational costs, potential biases, and factual accuracy require careful consideration in practical implementations.

Baseline Model

baseline model is a simple reference model used as a benchmark to evaluate the performance of more complex machine learning models. It establishes a minimum performance level that any advanced model should surpass. Baseline models are crucial in assessing whether a machine learning approach is effective and determining the value added by more sophisticated techniques. They provide a starting point for comparison and help identify whether improvements in model complexity result in meaningful performance gains.

The key components of a baseline model include simplicity, as it often relies on straightforward algorithms such as linear regression, decision trees, or random guessing. It is interpretable, making it easy to understand and analyze compared to complex models. The benchmark function of a baseline model allows researchers and engineers to compare new models against a reference standard. It is computationally efficient, requiring minimal resources for training and evaluation.

A baseline model offers several benefits in machine learning development. It provides a quick and inexpensive way to set performance expectations before deploying more complex models. By serving as a reference point, it helps avoid unnecessary overfitting by revealing whether an advanced model truly adds value. It improves debugging by exposing potential data quality issues or incorrect assumptions in model design. Baseline models also enhance transparency by offering an easily interpretable solution against which improvements can be measured.

Examples of baseline models include using a simple logistic regression model before testing deep learning approaches in classification tasks. In recommendation systems, a popularity-based baseline recommends the most frequently purchased items before testing more advanced collaborative filtering methods. In financial forecasting, a moving average model serves as a baseline before implementing more sophisticated time-series prediction techniques. In natural language processing, a random word selection model can serve as a baseline before testing deep learning-based text generation.

Industries: Baseline models are widely used across industries that require machine learning model evaluation. In healthcare, they help assess diagnostic models by first implementing rule-based systems. In finance, they are used for fraud detection by establishing simple threshold-based classification before deploying neural networks. In e-commerce, they assist in recommendation algorithms by initially suggesting the most popular products. In cybersecurity, a baseline anomaly detection system helps detect deviations before employing AI-driven threat detection techniques.

Challenges in using baseline models include selecting an appropriate baseline that accurately represents the problem space without being too simplistic. A poorly chosen baseline can lead to misleading comparisons and underestimate the value of advanced models. Over-reliance on simple models may delay innovation by discouraging investment in more powerful techniques. In some cases, a baseline model may be sufficient for practical applications, leading to unnecessary complexity in more advanced solutions. Additionally, baseline models may not always reflect real-world conditions, particularly in dynamic or evolving environments.

In summary, a baseline model is a fundamental reference point in machine learning used to establish a minimum performance level for evaluating advanced models. It is widely applied in healthcare, finance, and cybersecurity to ensure that complex algorithms provide meaningful improvements. While it simplifies model comparison and debugging, careful selection and interpretation are necessary to avoid misleading conclusions. Baseline models remain an essential tool in machine learning development, guiding practitioners in designing effective and efficient AI solutions.

Batch Gradient Descent

Batch gradient descent is an optimization algorithm used to minimize a cost function by updating model parameters in the direction of the negative gradient. It computes the gradient of the entire training dataset before making a single update to the model's parameters. This approach ensures a stable and smooth convergence, making it suitable for problems where precise optimization is required. The method is widely used in training machine learning models, particularly in linear regression, logistic regression, and deep learning.

The key components of batch gradient descent include the cost function, which measures the difference between the model's predictions and actual values. The gradient computation calculates the derivative of the cost function concerning each model parameter to determine the direction of improvement. The learning rate controls how much the parameters are adjusted at each step to balance convergence speed and stability. The weight update process applies the computed gradients to refine the model iteratively. The batch size, which includes all training examples, ensures that updates are made after processing the full dataset.

Benefits: Batch gradient descent offers several benefits in machine learning optimization. It provides stable convergence since each update is based on the complete dataset, reducing fluctuations in parameter adjustments. The method ensures deterministic updates, meaning that the model follows a consistent path toward the optimal solution. It is highly effective in convex optimization problems where a clear global minimum exists. Batch gradient descent is well-suited for large-scale training where precision is prioritized over speed.

Examples of batch gradient descent include its use in training neural networks for image classification, where the entire dataset is processed to minimize the classification error. In linear regression, batch gradient descent updates coefficients to fit the best line for predicting continuous values. In recommendation systems, it optimizes matrix factorization models to improve personalized recommendations. In financial modeling, batch gradient descent is applied to minimize error in stock market prediction models.

Industries that rely on batch gradient descent include healthcare, where it is used in predictive analytics for disease diagnosis. In finance, the method helps build models for credit risk assessment and fraud detection. In e-commerce, batch gradient descent is utilized to refine pricing algorithms and recommendation engines. In robotics, it contributes to optimizing control systems by improving sensor-based decision-making.

Despite its advantages, batch gradient descent presents challenges. Processing the entire dataset before each update can be computationally expensive, especially for large datasets. The method requires significant memory resources to store all training examples and their gradients. Convergence can be slow since updates occur less frequently compared to stochastic gradient descent, which updates after each data point. If the cost function is non-convex, batch gradient descent may converge to a local minimum rather than the global minimum.

In summary, batch gradient descent is a fundamental optimization technique in machine learning that updates model parameters based on the full dataset's gradient information. It ensures stable convergence and is widely applied in industries such as healthcare, finance, and e-commerce. While it offers precise optimization, its high computational cost and slow convergence make it less suitable for large-scale, real-time applications. Despite these limitations, batch gradient descent remains a crucial method for training machine learning models where accuracy and stability are essential.

Batch normalization

Batch Normalization is a deep learning technique used to improve the training speed and stability of neural networks by normalizing the inputs to each layer. It helps mitigate the problem of internal covariate shift, where the distribution of inputs to each layer changes during training. By normalizing activations within mini-batches, the method ensures that the network learns efficiently while reducing the risk of vanishing or exploding gradients.

The key components of batch normalization include the normalization step, where activations are adjusted by subtracting the batch mean and dividing by the batch standard deviation to ensure consistency. The learnable parameters, known as scale and shift parameters, allow the model to adapt normalized values to retain its representational power. The mini-batch computation ensures that normalization is performed on smaller subsets of data, making training more stable. The gradient flow improvement helps maintain smooth learning by preventing extreme activation values.

Batch normalization offers several benefits in deep learning. It speeds up training by reducing the dependency on careful weight initialization. The method allows for higher learning rates, accelerating convergence while maintaining stability. It regularizes the network, reducing the need for dropout by preventing overfitting. By reducing internal covariate shift, batch normalization ensures that each layer receives inputs with a stable distribution, improving training efficiency.

Examples of batch normalization include its application in convolutional neural networks (CNNs) for image recognition, where it stabilizes feature extraction. In recurrent neural networks (RNNs), it improves long-sequence processing by maintaining consistent activation distributions. In natural language processing models, batch normalization enhances transformer-based architectures by smoothing gradient updates. In reinforcement learning, it stabilizes training dynamics, ensuring efficient policy learning.

Industries that benefit from batch normalization include healthcare, where it improves medical image analysis and disease classification. In finance, it enhances predictive modeling for stock market forecasting and fraud detection. In autonomous systems, it optimizes real-time decision-making in self-driving cars and robotic control. In e-commerce, it refines personalized recommendations by improving deep learning-based customer preference models.

Despite its advantages, batch normalization presents challenges. It introduces additional computational overhead, increasing the complexity of training deep networks. The method behaves inconsistently during inference, requiring the use of population statistics instead of batch statistics. It may not be effective for small batch sizes, as the estimated statistics become unreliable. For recurrent networks, applying batch normalization across time steps can disrupt sequence learning.

In summary, batch normalization is a critical deep learning technique that improves the training efficiency and stability of neural networks. It is widely used in industries such as healthcare, finance, and autonomous systems to optimize learning processes. While it enhances convergence speed and model generalization, its computational complexity and reliance on mini-batch statistics require careful implementation for best results.

Batch Processing

Batch processing is a data processing method that executes a series of tasks or transactions in groups, known as batches, without requiring user intervention. It is commonly used in systems where large volumes of data must be processed efficiently without the need for real-time execution. By handling data in predefined sets, batch processing optimizes resource utilization, reduces operational costs, and automates repetitive tasks.

The key components of batch processing include data collection, where input data is gathered over a period before being processed as a group. The scheduling system determines when and how the batches will be executed, often during off-peak hours to maximize efficiency. The execution engine processes the batch jobs sequentially or in parallel, depending on system capabilities. The error-handling mechanism ensures that failed jobs are identified, logged, and retried if necessary.

Benefits: Batch processing provides several benefits in computing and business operations. It enhances efficiency by processing large volumes of data without requiring constant supervision. The method reduces computing costs by scheduling jobs when system resources are less expensive. It ensures consistency by automating complex workflows, minimizing human error. By improving scalability, batch processing can handle growing data volumes without significant increases in infrastructure demands.

Examples of batch processing include payroll systems, where employee salaries are calculated and processed in bulk at scheduled intervals. In banking, batch processing is used for end-of-day transaction settlements and fraud detection analysis. In data warehousing, it enables businesses to aggregate, clean, and analyze large datasets overnight for reporting. In media production, batch processing automates rendering and encoding of video files to optimize time and resources.

Industries that rely on batch processing include finance, where it is essential for batch reconciliation, auditing, and compliance reporting. In healthcare, batch processing is used for processing insurance claims and updating electronic medical records. In logistics, companies leverage batch processing for route optimization and inventory management. In e-commerce, businesses use batch processing for bulk order fulfillment, pricing updates, and customer analytics.

Despite its advantages, batch processing faces challenges. The delay in execution makes it unsuitable for real-time applications requiring immediate responses. Job failures can disrupt the entire batch, requiring proper error-handling mechanisms. System resource contention can arise if batch jobs compete with real-time applications for computing power. Managing large and complex batch workflows requires specialized scheduling and monitoring tools to ensure smooth execution.

In summary, batch processing is an efficient method for handling large-scale data processing tasks by executing them in predefined groups. It is widely used in finance, healthcare, logistics, and e-commerce to automate repetitive processes and optimize resource usage. While it offers significant cost savings and efficiency improvements, its limitations in real-time processing and error recovery necessitate careful implementation for maximum effectiveness.

Batch Renomalization

Batch renormalization is an extension of batch normalization designed to improve the stability and consistency of deep learning models, particularly when dealing with small batch sizes or non-independent training data. It addresses the limitations of batch normalization by reducing the dependency on mini-batch statistics, ensuring that normalization behaves consistently during training and inference. This method helps improve convergence and robustness in models that require batch normalization but suffer from unstable updates due to small or highly variable batches.

The key components of batch renormalization include the normalization step, which ensures that input activations maintain a stable distribution by adjusting their mean and variance. The renormalization parameters introduce constraints to limit variations in batch statistics, ensuring that the normalization process remains stable even with fluctuating batch sizes. The learnable affine transformation allows the model to scale and shift activations after normalization, maintaining the representational power of the network. The running statistics mechanism progressively refines mean and variance estimates to align training and inference behavior.

Batch renormalization provides several advantages in deep learning. It improves training stability by minimizing fluctuations caused by batch size variations. The method enhances generalization by ensuring consistent feature distributions across different training conditions. It reduces reliance on large batch sizes, making it useful for models trained with limited data or memory constraints. By bridging the gap between batch normalization and inference-time normalization, batch renormalization allows smoother and more predictable learning.

Examples of batch renormalization include its application in convolutional neural networks (CNNs) for image classification, where maintaining stable feature maps improves model accuracy. In speech recognition, batch renormalization helps normalize variable-length audio features, leading to more consistent predictions. In reinforcement learning, the method stabilizes policy training by ensuring that learned representations remain robust across different environments. In generative models, batch renormalization improves sample quality by preventing distribution shifts during training.

Industries that benefit from batch renormalization include healthcare, where deep learning models require stable feature representations for medical image analysis. In autonomous systems, batch renormalization enhances the reliability of self-driving algorithms by improving sensor data normalization. In finance, the technique refines predictive models for risk assessment and fraud detection by reducing fluctuations in training statistics. In robotics, it ensures consistent model performance when training with limited and non-uniform datasets.

Despite its advantages, batch renormalization presents challenges. It introduces additional computational overhead compared to standard batch normalization, increasing the complexity of training. The renormalization parameters require careful tuning to balance stability and flexibility. In cases where extremely small batches are used, the method may still experience instability if running statistics are not properly estimated. Implementing batch renormalization in existing architectures may require adjustments to learning rates and optimization strategies to maintain effective training.

In summary, batch renormalization is an advanced normalization technique that improves the stability of deep learning models by reducing dependency on mini-batch statistics. It is widely applied in industries such as healthcare, finance, and autonomous systems, where consistent feature normalization is critical. While it enhances training reliability and generalization, its computational cost and parameter tuning requirements necessitate careful implementation for optimal performance.

Batch Size

Batch size in machine learning refers to the number of training examples processed simultaneously before updating the model's parameters. It determines how data is divided into smaller groups during training, affecting the learning dynamics, memory usage, and computational efficiency. Choosing an appropriate batch size is crucial for balancing model performance, training stability, and resource utilization.

The key components of batch size include the number of samples in each batch, which directly influences the frequency of parameter updates. The gradient computation process calculates the average gradient over all samples in the batch, determining how model weights are adjusted. The trade-off between computational efficiency and model generalization depends on batch size selection, as smaller batches introduce noise that can enhance learning while larger batches provide stable updates. The impact on memory and hardware usage is significant, as larger batches require more GPU or CPU memory, while smaller batches allow training with limited resources.

Batch size offers several benefits in machine learning training. A larger batch size results in smoother and more stable updates, accelerating convergence. A smaller batch size introduces stochasticity, which can help models escape local minima and improve generalization. Batch processing optimizes computational efficiency by leveraging parallelism in modern hardware. Adjustable batch sizes provide flexibility to accommodate different dataset sizes and hardware constraints.

Examples of batch size variations include small batch sizes in deep reinforcement learning, where randomness helps agents explore diverse strategies. Large batch sizes in image classification tasks stabilize training and improve convergence speed in convolutional neural networks. Medium batch sizes in natural language processing maintain a balance between learning efficiency and memory usage in transformer-based models. Batch size tuning in financial forecasting ensures predictive stability while preventing overfitting in stock market analysis.

Industries that depend on batch size optimization include healthcare, where medical image analysis models require batch size adjustments to optimize accuracy and speed. In finance, trading algorithms use batch size tuning to process market data efficiently. In autonomous systems, self-driving vehicle models rely on appropriate batch sizes to train vision and decision-making networks effectively. In cybersecurity, batch size influences anomaly detection model training, ensuring timely identification of threats.

Despite its advantages, selecting the right batch size presents challenges. Large batches demand high memory and computational resources, limiting their feasibility on standard hardware. Small batch sizes may lead to unstable gradient updates, prolonging convergence and increasing training time. The risk of poor generalization arises when using extremely large batches, as the model may memorize patterns instead of learning adaptable features. Batch size tuning is an empirical process, requiring extensive experimentation to find the optimal value for a specific task and dataset.

In summary, batch size in machine learning is a critical hyperparameter that affects training efficiency, stability, and model performance. It plays a key role in industries such as healthcare, finance, and cybersecurity by influencing how models learn from data. While larger batch sizes provide stability and computational efficiency, smaller batch sizes enhance generalization and adaptability. Choosing the optimal batch size requires balancing memory constraints, convergence speed, and model accuracy to achieve effective machine learning training.

Bayesian Belief Networks (BBNs)

Bayesian Belief Networks (BBNs) are probabilistic graphical models used to represent the relationships between variables and their conditional dependencies through a directed acyclic graph (DAG). They provide a structured approach to reasoning under uncertainty by encoding probabilistic relationships between different factors. BBNs are widely used in decision-making, diagnosis, and predictive analytics where uncertain or incomplete information must be managed effectively.

The key components of Bayesian Belief Networks include nodes, which represent random variables in the system, edges, which define the directed dependencies between variables, and conditional probability tables (CPTs), which quantify the relationships between parent and child nodes using probability distributions. The directed acyclic graph structure ensures that the network maintains a hierarchical and non-cyclic representation of dependencies. The probabilistic inference mechanism enables reasoning by updating the probability of certain events based on observed evidence.

Bayesian Belief Networks offer several benefits in probabilistic modeling and decision-making. They efficiently represent complex dependencies between variables using a structured graphical model. They provide a formal approach to handling uncertainty by incorporating prior knowledge and observational data. They support decision-making by allowing dynamic updates when new evidence is introduced. They enable interpretable reasoning, making it easier to understand how different factors influence outcomes.

Examples of Bayesian Belief Networks include their use in medical diagnosis, where BBNs model disease symptoms and their likelihood to improve diagnostic accuracy. In fraud detection, BBNs analyze transaction patterns to estimate the probability of fraudulent behavior. In predictive maintenance, they assess equipment failure probabilities based on historical data and sensor readings. In weather forecasting, BBNs integrate various meteorological factors to predict future climate conditions.

Industries that utilize Bayesian Belief Networks include healthcare, where they assist in disease diagnosis and treatment planning. In finance, BBNs improve risk assessment and fraud detection models. In manufacturing, they optimize predictive maintenance strategies to prevent equipment failures. In cybersecurity, they enhance intrusion detection systems by modeling the likelihood of security threats based on observed network behavior.

Despite their advantages, Bayesian Belief Networks present challenges in implementation. Constructing the conditional probability tables requires expert knowledge or large amounts of data, which may not always be available. The computational complexity increases with network size, making exact inference difficult for large-scale models. The assumption of acyclicity limits their ability to represent cyclic dependencies in some real-world processes. The accuracy of Bayesian inference depends on the quality and completeness of the prior probabilities used in the model.

In summary, Bayesian Belief Networks provide a powerful probabilistic framework for modeling uncertainty and reasoning in complex systems. They are widely used in industries such as healthcare, finance, and cybersecurity to improve decision-making and predictive analysis. While they offer significant advantages in handling probabilistic dependencies, their reliance on expert knowledge, computational complexity, and acyclicity constraints require careful implementation for effective application.

Bayesian Classifier

A Bayesian classifier is a probabilistic model used in machine learning and statistics for classification tasks based on Bayes' theorem. It predicts the likelihood that a given data point belongs to a specific class by calculating the probability distribution of each possible outcome. This approach makes Bayesian classifiers particularly effective when dealing with uncertainty and limited data, as they incorporate prior knowledge and observed data to improve classification accuracy.

The key components of a Bayesian classifier include Bayes' theorem, which provides the foundation for updating probabilities based on new evidence. The prior probability represents the initial belief about the likelihood of each class before considering the input data. The likelihood function estimates the probability of the observed features given a particular class. The posterior probability updates the initial belief by incorporating the likelihood and prior probability, ultimately determining the most probable class for a given input. The assumption of feature independence, used in models like the Naïve Bayes classifier, simplifies computation by treating each feature as independent, even if that assumption is not entirely accurate.

Bayesian classifiers offer several benefits in classification tasks. They are computationally efficient, making them suitable for large datasets and real-time applications. They perform well with small datasets by leveraging prior knowledge to compensate for limited observations. They are robust to irrelevant features since probability-based weighting reduces the impact of noise in the data. They are widely applicable across various domains, handling both binary and multi-class classification problems effectively.

Examples of Bayesian classifiers include spam detection systems, where emails are classified based on word frequency and probability estimates of spam versus non-spam messages. In medical diagnosis, Bayesian classifiers help predict diseases based on patient symptoms and historical medical records. In sentiment analysis, they classify customer reviews as positive, negative, or neutral by analyzing word distributions. In document classification, they categorize articles into different topics based on the frequency of key terms.

Industries that benefit from Bayesian classifiers include cybersecurity, where they detect phishing attempts and malware threats by analyzing behavioral patterns. In finance, they are used for credit risk assessment and fraud detection by modeling transaction probabilities. In e-commerce, Bayesian classifiers enhance product recommendation systems by predicting customer preferences based on past behavior. In healthcare, they assist in disease prediction by analyzing patient data and medical histories.

Despite their advantages, Bayesian classifiers present several challenges. The assumption of feature independence, especially in Naïve Bayes classifiers, can lead to suboptimal performance when features are highly correlated. The requirement for accurate prior probabilities can affect model reliability if incorrect assumptions are made. The model's performance depends on the availability of quality data, as insufficient or biased data can lead to inaccurate probability estimates. For high-dimensional data, computing probabilities for numerous features may become computationally intensive, limiting scalability.

In summary, Bayesian classifiers provide a powerful and efficient approach to classification by leveraging probabilistic inference and Bayes' theorem. They are widely applied in industries such as cybersecurity, finance, and healthcare for tasks ranging from fraud detection to medical diagnosis. While they offer computational efficiency and robustness with small datasets, their reliance on feature independence assumptions and prior probability estimates requires careful consideration for optimal performance in complex classification tasks.

Bayesian Inference

Benefit: Bayesian Inference is a statistical method used to update probabilities based on new evidence, following Bayes' theorem. It provides a mathematical framework for reasoning under uncertainty by combining prior knowledge with observed data. This approach is widely applied in machine learning, data science, and decision-making processes where probabilities need to be continuously adjusted as new information becomes available.

The key components of Bayesian inference include prior probability, which represents initial beliefs about an event before observing new data. The likelihood function quantifies the probability of the observed data given a particular hypothesis. The posterior probability updates the initial belief by incorporating the likelihood and prior probability to form a refined estimate. The evidence term normalizes the probability distribution to ensure valid posterior calculations.

Bayesian inference offers several benefits in probabilistic modeling and decision-making. It allows continuous learning by dynamically updating probabilities as more data becomes available. It provides a principled approach to incorporating prior knowledge, making it useful in situations where historical data is relevant. It is effective for small datasets by leveraging prior distributions to compensate for limited observations. It enhances uncertainty quantification by providing probability distributions rather than single-point estimates, improving decision confidence.

Examples of Bayesian inference include medical diagnosis, where it updates the probability of a disease based on new symptoms and test results. In spam detection, Bayesian filtering continuously refines its classification by analyzing word frequencies in emails. In machine learning, Bayesian optimization improves hyperparameter tuning by updating probability distributions based on model performance. In environmental science, Bayesian inference estimates climate change effects by integrating past and current data with scientific models.

Industries that rely on Bayesian inference include healthcare, where it aids in disease prediction and personalized treatment recommendations. In finance, it enhances risk assessment by updating market predictions based on new economic data. In cybersecurity, Bayesian inference strengthens intrusion detection systems by continuously refining anomaly detection models. In autonomous systems, it helps self-driving cars make real-time decisions by integrating sensor inputs with probabilistic models.

Despite its advantages, Bayesian inference presents several challenges. Computing posterior probabilities can be complex and computationally expensive, especially in high-dimensional data spaces. The choice of prior probability can influence results, leading to subjective biases if not carefully selected. In cases with large datasets, Bayesian inference may require approximation methods such as Markov Chain Monte Carlo (MCMC) to handle the computational burden. Ensuring numerical stability in probability calculations is critical, as small errors in likelihood estimation can impact posterior distributions.

In summary, Bayesian inference is a powerful probabilistic method that updates beliefs based on new evidence using Bayes' theorem. It is widely applied in industries such as healthcare, finance, and cybersecurity for tasks requiring continuous learning and uncertainty quantification. While it provides flexibility and improved decision-making under uncertainty, its computational demands and sensitivity to prior selection require careful implementation for accurate and efficient modeling.

Bayesian Learning

Bayesian learning is a machine learning approach based on Bayes' theorem, where models continuously update their knowledge as new data becomes available. It provides a probabilistic framework that integrates prior knowledge with observed evidence to refine predictions and improve decision-making. Unlike traditional learning methods that rely solely on data, Bayesian learning incorporates uncertainty and adjusts predictions dynamically, making it highly effective for applications where data is limited or incomplete.

The key components of Bayesian learning include prior probability, which represents initial beliefs before observing new data. The likelihood function determines how well the observed data supports different hypotheses. The posterior probability updates the prior belief by incorporating the likelihood, forming a refined probability estimate. The Bayesian update process continuously refines predictions as more data becomes available, ensuring that the model adapts over time. The probabilistic inference mechanism ensures that uncertainty is accounted for in the learning process.

Bayesian learning offers several advantages in machine learning and artificial intelligence. It provides a structured approach to handling uncertainty by producing probability distributions instead of fixed-point estimates. The method is highly effective for small datasets, as it integrates prior knowledge to compensate for limited training data. Bayesian learning enhances model interpretability by providing a clear mathematical reasoning process for updates. It supports adaptive learning, allowing models to improve over time as new information is introduced.

Examples of Bayesian learning include personalized recommendation systems, where user preferences are continuously updated to improve content suggestions. In medical diagnosis, Bayesian models refine disease probability estimates based on patient history and test results. In spam filtering, Bayesian learning dynamically adjusts classification rules based on evolving email patterns. In financial forecasting, it helps predict market trends by integrating past economic data with real-time updates.

Industries that benefit from Bayesian learning include healthcare, where it is used for adaptive disease prediction and personalized treatment plans. In finance, it enhances fraud detection systems by continuously learning from transactional data. In cybersecurity, Bayesian learning improves anomaly detection by refining threat probability assessments. In robotics, it enables autonomous systems to make probabilistic decisions in uncertain environments.

Despite its advantages, Bayesian learning presents several challenges. The computation of posterior probabilities can be complex and resource-intensive, particularly for high-dimensional models. Selecting an appropriate prior distribution is crucial, as poor choices can bias results. In large-scale applications, Bayesian inference may require approximation techniques such as variational inference or Markov Chain Monte Carlo (MCMC) to manage computational constraints. Ensuring stability in probabilistic updates is essential, as small changes in likelihood estimates can significantly impact posterior distributions.

In summary, Bayesian learning is a powerful probabilistic approach that integrates prior knowledge with observed data to refine predictions and improve decision-making. It is widely applied in industries such as healthcare, finance, and cybersecurity for tasks requiring adaptive learning and uncertainty management. While it provides flexibility and robustness in handling limited data, its computational demands and sensitivity to prior selection require careful implementation for optimal performance.

Bayesian Networks

Bayesian networks are probabilistic graphical models that represent relationships between variables through directed acyclic graphs. They provide a structured way to model uncertain knowledge by encoding conditional dependencies between variables using probability distributions. Each node in the network represents a variable, while edges define dependencies between them. Bayesian networks are widely used in decision-making, diagnostics, and predictive analytics, where uncertainty must be managed effectively.

The key components of Bayesian networks include nodes that represent variables in the system, whether observable data points or hidden states. Directed edges indicate probabilistic dependencies, showing how one variable influences another. Conditional probability tables quantify the relationships between connected nodes by defining the likelihood of different outcomes given their parent nodes. The directed acyclic graph structure ensures that dependencies follow a hierarchical order without forming cycles. Probabilistic inference mechanisms allow reasoning within the network by updating beliefs when new evidence is introduced.

Bayesian networks offer several advantages in modeling complex systems. They provide a compact representation of high-dimensional data by focusing only on direct dependencies between variables. They allow efficient probabilistic reasoning, enabling decision-making even when some data is missing or uncertain. They support causal modeling by visually representing cause-and-effect relationships. They are interpretable, making it easier to understand how variables interact in a system.

Examples of Bayesian networks include their use in medical diagnosis, where they model disease progression and symptoms to assist doctors in decision-making. In fraud detection, Bayesian networks analyze transaction patterns and anomalies to estimate the probability of fraudulent activity. In predictive maintenance, they assess equipment failure likelihood based on historical sensor data. In natural language processing, Bayesian networks improve speech recognition by modeling relationships between phonemes and contextual dependencies.

Industries that utilize Bayesian networks include healthcare, where they enhance diagnostic accuracy and treatment planning. In finance, they improve credit risk analysis and fraud detection by incorporating probabilistic reasoning. In cybersecurity, Bayesian networks strengthen threat detection systems by modeling attack probabilities based on network behavior. In robotics, they aid autonomous systems in decision-making by integrating uncertain sensor data.

In summary, Bayesian networks provide a powerful framework for modeling uncertainty and reasoning in complex systems. They are widely applied in healthcare, finance, and cybersecurity to improve decision-making and predictive analysis. While they offer significant benefits in handling probabilistic dependencies, their reliance on expert-defined probabilities, computational complexity, and structural constraints require careful implementation for effective use in real-world applications.

Bayesian Neural Networks (BNNs)

Bayesian Neural Networks (BNNs) are a type of artificial neural network that incorporates Bayesian inference to model uncertainty in predictions. Unlike traditional neural networks that use fixed weights, BNNs treat weights as probability distributions, allowing them to quantify uncertainty in decision-making. This probabilistic approach enhances model robustness, making BNNs particularly useful in applications where understanding uncertainty is critical, such as healthcare, finance, and autonomous systems.

The key components of Bayesian Neural Networks include probabilistic weight distributions, where each weight is assigned a probability distribution instead of a single value, allowing the model to capture uncertainty. Bayesian inference updates these weight distributions as new data becomes available, ensuring adaptive learning. The prior distribution represents initial beliefs about the model parameters before observing data, guiding the learning process. The posterior distribution refines these beliefs based on observed data, balancing prior knowledge with new information. The likelihood function evaluates how well the model's predictions match observed outcomes, influencing the weight updates during training.

Bayesian Neural Networks provide several advantages in machine learning. They enhance model interpretability by providing probability distributions over predictions, enabling uncertainty estimation. They improve generalization by preventing overfitting, as the probabilistic approach discourages reliance on specific weight values. They support decision-making in high-stakes applications by quantifying confidence levels in predictions. They enable continual learning by updating weight distributions dynamically as more data is introduced.

Examples of Bayesian Neural Networks include their use in medical diagnosis, where they estimate uncertainty in disease predictions, reducing the risk of false positives or false negatives. In autonomous vehicles, BNNs improve safety by providing confidence scores in object detection and navigation decisions. In financial risk assessment, they evaluate the uncertainty in credit scoring and stock market predictions. In natural language processing, BNNs enhance chatbot responses by incorporating uncertainty-aware language modeling.

Industries that benefit from Bayesian Neural Networks include healthcare, where they improve diagnostic reliability and personalized treatment recommendations. In finance, BNNs enhance risk analysis by modeling market uncertainty. In cybersecurity, they strengthen threat detection systems by identifying uncertain or anomalous patterns in network activity. In robotics, BNNs optimize real-time decision-making by managing uncertainties in sensor data and environment perception.

In summary, Bayesian Neural Networks provide a probabilistic approach to deep learning by modeling uncertainty in predictions through Bayesian inference. They are widely applied in industries such as healthcare, finance, and autonomous systems, where uncertainty estimation is crucial for decision-making. While they offer improved generalization, interpretability, and robustness, their computational demands and complexity require careful implementation to achieve optimal performance in real-world applications.

Bayesian Optimization

Bayesian optimization is a probabilistic method used to optimize expensive-to-evaluate functions by strategically selecting the next set of parameters to test. It is particularly effective for optimizing functions that are costly, noisy, or lack an analytical expression. By using a surrogate model to approximate the objective function, Bayesian optimization balances exploration and exploitation, improving efficiency in finding the optimal solution with fewer evaluations.

The key components of Bayesian optimization include the surrogate model, typically a Gaussian Process, which estimates the objective function and provides uncertainty quantification. The acquisition function determines the next point to sample by balancing exploration of uncertain regions and exploitation of known high-performing areas. The prior distribution encodes prior beliefs about the function's behavior, guiding the optimization process. The posterior distribution updates beliefs based on observed data, refining the surrogate model iteratively. The trade-off mechanism between exploration and exploitation ensures that the algorithm efficiently searches the parameter space while refining known optimal regions.

Bayesian optimization provides several advantages in optimization tasks. It reduces the number of function evaluations required to find an optimal solution, making it ideal for expensive-to-compute functions. It improves efficiency in hyperparameter tuning for machine learning models by identifying the best configurations with minimal trials. It enables adaptive learning by updating the surrogate model dynamically as more observations are collected. It provides uncertainty estimation, allowing practitioners to assess confidence in the optimization results.

Examples of Bayesian optimization include hyperparameter tuning in deep learning, where it optimizes parameters such as learning rates and batch sizes for improved model performance. In robotics, it refines control policies by efficiently searching for optimal movement parameters. In material science, it accelerates the discovery of novel materials by optimizing chemical compositions. In finance, it enhances algorithmic trading strategies by fine-tuning model parameters for optimal returns.

Industries that benefit from Bayesian optimization include artificial intelligence, where it improves neural network performance through automated hyperparameter search. In healthcare, it optimizes drug discovery by efficiently navigating complex chemical interactions. In manufacturing, it enhances process optimization by reducing the number of costly experimental trials. In engineering, it refines aerodynamic designs by minimizing computational fluid dynamics simulations.

In summary, Bayesian optimization is a powerful probabilistic approach for optimizing expensive-to-evaluate functions by leveraging surrogate models and adaptive learning. It is widely used in industries such as artificial intelligence, healthcare, and manufacturing to improve efficiency in complex optimization problems. While it provides significant benefits in reducing computational costs and improving decision-making, its scalability and computational demands require careful consideration for effective implementation in high-dimensional settings.

Beam Search

Beam search is a heuristic search algorithm used in sequence generation tasks to efficiently explore the most promising paths while limiting computational complexity. It expands multiple candidate sequences simultaneously, retaining only the best ones at each step, ensuring that the search remains manageable while maintaining high-quality results. This makes it particularly useful in natural language processing, speech recognition, and machine translation, where generating the most likely sequence of words or symbols is crucial.

The key components of beam search include the beam width, which determines the number of candidate sequences retained at each step, controlling the trade-off between efficiency and accuracy. The scoring function evaluates each sequence based on probabilities assigned by the model, guiding the selection of the best candidates. The expansion step generates new candidate sequences by extending existing ones with the most likely next elements. The pruning mechanism discards lower-scoring candidates to maintain the beam width limit, ensuring that computation remains feasible. The final selection step identifies the highest-scoring sequence, representing the most probable output.

Beam search provides several benefits in sequence generation. It significantly improves the quality of generated outputs compared to greedy search, which selects only the most probable option at each step. It balances computational efficiency and output quality by restricting the number of candidate sequences considered, avoiding exhaustive searches. It ensures diverse candidate exploration, increasing the likelihood of finding high-quality solutions. It adapts well to probabilistic models, enhancing performance in applications like text generation and speech recognition.

Examples of beam search include its use in machine translation, where it generates the most fluent and contextually accurate sentence by considering multiple translation paths. In speech recognition, it refines transcriptions by exploring different phoneme combinations before selecting the most likely word sequence. In text summarization, it optimizes summary generation by evaluating various possible sentence combinations. In image captioning, it produces accurate and descriptive captions by iteratively selecting the best words based on visual content.

Industries that benefit from beam search include artificial intelligence, where it improves chatbot responses and content generation. In healthcare, it enhances medical transcription accuracy by refining speech-to-text outputs. In customer service, it powers virtual assistants by ensuring coherent and contextually relevant conversations. In entertainment, it improves automated subtitling and video content summarization by generating high-quality text representations.

In summary, beam search is a powerful sequence generation algorithm that balances efficiency and output quality by exploring multiple candidate paths while limiting computational overhead. It is widely used in artificial intelligence, healthcare, and customer service to enhance natural language generation and speech recognition. While it improves upon simpler search methods, challenges related to beam width selection and long-range dependency handling require careful optimization to maximize its effectiveness in real-world applications.

Behavioral AI

Definition
Behavioral AI is an artificial intelligence approach that analyzes and predicts human or system behavior based on patterns, interactions, and decision-making processes. It uses machine learning, cognitive science, and behavioral data to understand, adapt, and respond to user actions in a personalized and intelligent manner.

Key Components
Behavioral AI relies on data collection mechanisms that gather information from user interactions, social behavior, and activity patterns. Machine learning models analyze behavioral trends and adapt AI responses accordingly. Cognitive computing integrates psychological and neurological insights to simulate human-like reasoning. Real-time analytics enable AI to adjust its behavior dynamically based on live inputs. Ethical and privacy safeguards ensure responsible use of behavioral data while maintaining user trust.

Benefits
Behavioral AI enhances personalization by adapting services to individual user preferences and behaviors. It improves decision-making by identifying patterns and predicting future actions. Automated behavioral analysis increases efficiency in industries such as marketing, finance, and cybersecurity. Fraud detection and risk assessment benefit from AI's ability to recognize abnormal behavior and prevent security breaches.

Applications
Behavioral AI is used in recommendation systems that analyze user preferences for personalized content delivery. It powers fraud detection systems by identifying unusual financial transactions or login patterns. AI-driven mental health applications assess emotional states based on speech and text patterns. Customer service chatbots utilize behavioral AI to provide adaptive and context-aware responses.

Industries
The finance industry applies Behavioral AI for fraud prevention, credit risk assessment, and algorithmic trading. The healthcare sector integrates it into mental health monitoring and personalized treatment recommendations. The retail and e-commerce industries use it for targeted advertising, customer segmentation, and dynamic pricing. The cybersecurity field leverages it for detecting insider threats and securing digital identities.

Summary
Behavioral AI analyzes and predicts human behavior to enhance personalization, decision-making, and security. It is widely used across finance, healthcare, retail, and cybersecurity industries but faces challenges related to ethics, privacy, and computational complexity. Its ability to adapt and learn from behavioral patterns makes it a powerful tool in AI-driven applications.

Behavior Cloning

Behavior cloning is a machine learning technique that enables an agent to learn by imitating expert demonstrations. It is a form of supervised learning where the model is trained to replicate the behavior of a human or an autonomous system by mapping observed inputs to corresponding actions. By using recorded demonstrations as training data, behavior cloning allows machines to mimic decision-making processes without requiring explicit programming of rules.

The key components of behavior cloning include expert demonstrations, which provide the training data consisting of state-action pairs recorded from human operators or autonomous systems. The policy model represents the function that maps observed states to actions, determining how the agent behaves. The supervised learning framework trains the model using standard techniques such as neural networks or decision trees, optimizing it to minimize the difference between predicted and actual expert actions. The generalization ability ensures that the model can replicate expert behavior in previously unseen scenarios.

Behavior cloning offers several benefits in automation and robotics. It enables rapid learning by leveraging existing human expertise instead of requiring reinforcement learning from scratch. It reduces training complexity by bypassing the need for designing detailed reward functions. It enhances task performance in structured environments where expert demonstrations are available. It simplifies deployment by providing a direct mapping between inputs and actions, ensuring predictable behavior in controlled settings.

Examples of behavior cloning include its use in self-driving cars, where models learn to follow lanes, brake, and accelerate based on human driving data. In robotic manipulation, behavior cloning enables robots to perform tasks such as object grasping and assembly by imitating expert demonstrations. In video game AI, non-playable characters (NPCs) replicate human-like strategies by learning from recorded player interactions. In medical simulations, behavior cloning helps train surgical robots by imitating expert surgeons' movements.

Industries that benefit from behavior cloning include autonomous vehicles, where it enhances self-driving capabilities by learning from real-world driving patterns. In industrial automation, it optimizes robotic arms for precise and efficient manufacturing tasks. In healthcare, behavior cloning assists in robotic-assisted surgeries and rehabilitation therapy. In virtual assistants, it improves user interactions by learning from human conversational patterns.

In summary, behavior cloning is a powerful imitation learning technique that enables machines to replicate expert behavior by learning from demonstrations. It is widely applied in autonomous vehicles, robotics, and healthcare to automate decision-making and improve task performance. While it simplifies training and deployment, challenges related to generalization, compounding errors, and adaptability require careful data selection and model design to ensure reliable performance in real-world applications.

Belief Network, also known as a Bayesian blief network or probabilistic graphical model

A belief network, also known as a Bayesian belief network or probabilistic graphical model, is a structured representation of uncertain knowledge that captures the probabilistic dependencies among a set of variables. It consists of a directed acyclic graph where nodes represent variables, and edges define conditional dependencies between them. By encoding uncertainty and relationships probabilistically, belief networks enable reasoning under uncertainty and support decision-making in various domains.

The key components of a belief network include nodes, which represent random variables that can be observed or hidden, describing the system's state. Directed edges indicate conditional dependencies, showing how one variable influences another. Conditional probability tables (CPTs) quantify the strength of dependencies by specifying the probability distribution of a variable given its parent nodes. The directed acyclic graph structure ensures that causal or probabilistic influences flow in a hierarchical manner without loops. Inference mechanisms allow the network to update probabilities when new evidence is introduced, enabling probabilistic reasoning.

Belief networks provide several advantages in probabilistic modeling and decision-making. They offer a compact representation of complex relationships by capturing only the essential dependencies between variables. They enable reasoning under uncertainty by dynamically updating probabilities as new evidence is incorporated. They improve interpretability by visually representing the influence of different variables on outcomes. They facilitate efficient probabilistic computations, making them useful for large-scale decision-making tasks.

Examples of belief networks include their use in medical diagnosis, where they model relationships between symptoms and diseases to support doctors in decision-making. In fraud detection, belief networks analyze transaction patterns and anomalies to estimate the likelihood of fraudulent behavior. In predictive maintenance, they assess equipment failure probabilities based on historical data and sensor readings. In weather forecasting, they integrate meteorological factors to predict future climate conditions with uncertainty quantification.

Industries that utilize belief networks include healthcare, where they assist in disease diagnosis and treatment planning by modeling complex medical dependencies. In finance, they improve risk assessment and fraud detection models through probabilistic reasoning. In cybersecurity, they enhance intrusion detection systems by modeling attack probabilities based on observed network behavior. In robotics, belief networks enable autonomous systems to make probabilistic decisions based on sensor inputs and environmental factors.

In summary, belief networks provide a powerful probabilistic framework for modeling uncertainty and reasoning in complex systems. They are widely applied in healthcare, finance, and cybersecurity to improve decision-making and predictive analysis. While they offer significant benefits in handling probabilistic dependencies, their reliance on expert-defined probabilities, computational complexity, and structural constraints require careful implementation for effective use in real-world applications.

Belief propagation

Belief propagation is an algorithm used in probabilistic graphical models to compute marginal probabilities and perform inference by passing messages between nodes. It enables efficient probability estimation in networks with structured dependencies, such as Bayesian networks and Markov random fields. By iteratively updating and propagating beliefs throughout the network, belief propagation refines probability distributions based on available evidence, allowing for informed decision-making under uncertainty.

The key components of belief propagation include factor graphs, which represent the probabilistic relationships between variables using nodes and edges. The message-passing mechanism allows nodes to share probability distributions with neighboring nodes, refining their beliefs over multiple iterations. The update rules define how messages are computed and combined to ensure consistency across the network. The convergence criteria determine when the algorithm has stabilized, indicating that probability estimates have reached reliable values. The marginalization process extracts useful probabilistic information from the network by computing the likelihood of individual variables.

Belief propagation offers several benefits in probabilistic inference. It efficiently computes marginal probabilities in complex networks without requiring exhaustive enumeration of all possible states. It enables reasoning under uncertainty by incorporating observed evidence to update probability distributions dynamically. It provides a scalable approach to inference, making it applicable to large graphical models with numerous interconnected variables. It supports real-time decision-making by rapidly refining probabilistic estimates as new information becomes available.

Examples of belief propagation include its use in error correction codes, where it improves data transmission reliability by decoding corrupted signals. In image processing, belief propagation enhances computer vision tasks such as stereo depth estimation by refining pixel correspondences. In natural language processing, it supports part-of-speech tagging and syntactic parsing by evaluating the most probable linguistic structures. In robotics, belief propagation helps autonomous systems localize and navigate by estimating environmental probabilities from sensor data.

Industries that benefit from belief propagation include telecommunications, where it enhances error correction in digital communication systems. In artificial intelligence, it improves probabilistic reasoning for applications such as speech recognition and machine translation. In healthcare, belief propagation assists in medical diagnosis by refining disease probabilities based on patient symptoms and test results. In cybersecurity, it strengthens threat detection by modeling attack likelihoods and propagating risk assessments across network components.

In summary, belief propagation is a powerful inference algorithm used in probabilistic graphical models to compute marginal probabilities and refine uncertainty estimates. It is widely applied in industries such as telecommunications, artificial intelligence, and healthcare to enhance decision-making and probabilistic reasoning. While it provides efficient and scalable inference, challenges related to convergence, computational demands, and model accuracy require careful consideration for successful deployment in real-world applications.

Bellman an Equation

The Bellman equation is a fundamental recursive equation used in dynamic programming and reinforcement learning to determine the optimal policy in decision-making problems. It provides a mathematical framework for breaking down complex decision processes into smaller subproblems, enabling efficient problem-solving over time. Named after Richard Bellman, this equation is widely applied in optimization, economics, artificial intelligence, and control systems.

The key components of the Bellman equation include a value function, which represents the expected cumulative reward from a given state, and a recursive relationship that expresses how the optimal value at one step depends on future states. The equation incorporates a discount factor to balance immediate and future rewards, ensuring long-term optimization. A policy function determines the best possible action in each state to maximize rewards over time. The transition model captures the probability of moving from one state to another, and the reward function assigns values to different actions to guide decision-making.

One of the major benefits of the Bellman equation is its ability to simplify complex decision processes by breaking them into manageable subproblems. It ensures optimal decision-making over time by considering both immediate and future rewards. The equation is computationally efficient, making it a powerful tool in reinforcement learning algorithms. In real-world applications, it improves strategic planning by optimizing sequential decision-making, allowing for long-term benefits rather than short-term gains.

An example of the Bellman equation in practice is in reinforcement learning, where AI agents use it to determine the best course of action in an environment. In robotics, it helps autonomous systems navigate efficiently by optimizing movement strategies. In finance, it is used to model optimal investment strategies by considering future market conditions. In supply chain management, businesses use it to minimize costs while maximizing efficiency over a series of decisions.

Industries that rely on the Bellman equation include artificial intelligence, where it serves as the foundation for reinforcement learning models. The finance sector applies it to optimize asset allocation and risk management strategies. In operations research, businesses use it to streamline logistics and improve supply chain decision-making. The healthcare industry benefits from it in medical diagnosis and treatment planning, ensuring optimal patient care over time. Telecommunications use it for network optimization, enhancing data transmission and resource allocation.

The Bellman equation is a fundamental concept in dynamic programming and reinforcement learning, offering a structured approach to solving complex sequential decision-making problems. Its ability to balance short-term and long-term rewards makes it invaluable across various industries, from artificial intelligence to finance and logistics. While computational challenges exist, advances in machine learning and optimization techniques continue to enhance its practical applications.

Benchmark dataset

A benchmark dataset is a standardized collection of data used to evaluate and compare the performance of machine learning models, algorithms, or systems. These datasets serve as a reference point for assessing how well a given model generalizes to new data and provide a common ground for researchers and developers to measure progress in artificial intelligence and data science. By using benchmark datasets, the AI community can establish consistent evaluation metrics and determine the effectiveness of different approaches in solving specific problems.

The key components of a benchmark dataset include data samples that consist of structured or unstructured information relevant to the task at hand. These samples are usually labeled in supervised learning scenarios, providing ground truth values for training and testing models. Metadata accompanies the dataset to describe its features, sources, and intended use. The dataset also includes predefined evaluation metrics, such as accuracy, precision, recall, or F1 score, which are used to assess model performance. To ensure reliability, benchmark datasets often undergo preprocessing and standardization to remove inconsistencies and enhance comparability.

The main advantage of using benchmark datasets is that they allow for objective and reproducible comparisons between different machine learning models. They help accelerate research and development by providing a shared resource that eliminates the need for organizations to collect and curate their own datasets. Benchmark datasets improve transparency in AI performance evaluation, enabling researchers to validate claims and measure progress effectively. They also play a crucial role in model selection, allowing practitioners to identify the most suitable algorithms for specific tasks.

Examples of benchmark datasets include ImageNet, which is widely used for image classification and object recognition tasks. The MNIST dataset serves as a fundamental benchmark for handwritten digit recognition. The CIFAR-10 and CIFAR-100 datasets provide image classification challenges with different levels of complexity. In natural language processing, datasets such as GLUE, SQuAD, and CoNLL are commonly used for evaluating language models. The UCI Machine Learning Repository offers a diverse collection of datasets for regression, classification, and clustering tasks.

Industries that benefit from benchmark datasets include artificial intelligence and machine learning, where they are essential for developing and fine-tuning models. The healthcare sector uses them for medical diagnosis and predictive analytics, ensuring models are trained on high-quality data. In finance, benchmark datasets help build fraud detection systems and algorithmic trading strategies. Autonomous vehicle development relies on benchmark datasets to improve object detection and navigation systems. Cybersecurity applications use them to train models for threat detection and anomaly identification.

Benchmark datasets serve as an essential foundation for evaluating machine learning models and driving advancements in artificial intelligence. They provide a standardized framework for measuring performance, ensuring that research findings are comparable and reproducible. While they present challenges related to bias, data aging, and ethical considerations, continuous updates and diverse dataset collection efforts help mitigate these issues. By leveraging benchmark datasets effectively, industries can develop robust AI systems that generalize well to real-world applications.

Benchmarking

Benchmarking is the process of measuring and comparing the performance, efficiency, or quality of a system, process, or organization against a recognized standard or best practice. It is widely used in industries such as business, technology, healthcare, and artificial intelligence to identify areas for improvement, enhance competitiveness, and drive innovation. By analyzing benchmarks, organizations can set realistic performance goals and develop strategies to achieve optimal efficiency.

The key components of benchmarking include defining the scope and objectives, which determine what is being measured and compared. Data collection is an essential step, as accurate and reliable information is required to establish meaningful comparisons. Performance metrics provide quantitative or qualitative indicators that reflect efficiency, effectiveness, or accuracy. A reference point, such as industry standards, competitor performance, or historical data, is used as a basis for comparison. The analysis phase involves identifying gaps, strengths, and weaknesses to guide decision-making and improvements.

One of the main benefits of benchmarking is that it helps organizations gain insight into their performance relative to competitors or industry leaders. It fosters continuous improvement by identifying best practices and implementing them within existing workflows. Benchmarking enhances decision-making by providing data-driven insights that reduce uncertainty and improve strategic planning. It also promotes innovation by encouraging organizations to explore new approaches and technologies that can enhance productivity and efficiency.

Examples of benchmarking can be found in various sectors. In business, companies use financial benchmarking to compare profitability, revenue growth, and operational costs against competitors. In software development, AI model benchmarking assesses algorithm accuracy, speed, and efficiency using standardized datasets. Healthcare providers benchmark patient outcomes and treatment effectiveness to improve medical care. Manufacturing industries use process benchmarking to enhance production quality and reduce waste. Customer service benchmarking evaluates response times, satisfaction rates, and service efficiency to optimize client interactions.

Industries that rely on benchmarking include finance, where institutions compare investment strategies, risk management techniques, and market performance. The technology sector uses benchmarking to evaluate hardware and software capabilities, ensuring optimal system performance. In education, institutions benchmark student performance, graduation rates, and curriculum effectiveness to enhance learning outcomes. The retail industry uses benchmarking to analyze consumer behavior, pricing strategies, and sales performance. Public sector organizations implement benchmarking to improve policy effectiveness and service delivery.

Benchmarking is a valuable method for assessing performance, identifying improvement opportunities, and maintaining competitiveness across various industries. It provides organizations with insights that drive strategic growth, enhance operational efficiency, and promote best practices. Despite challenges related to data accuracy, evolving benchmarks, and ethical considerations, benchmarking remains a crucial tool for fostering continuous improvement and innovation. When used effectively, it enables businesses and institutions to set realistic goals, adapt to industry trends, and achieve long-term success.

A Benchmarking suite

A benchmarking suite is a collection of tools, tests, and methodologies designed to evaluate and compare the performance, efficiency, and capabilities of systems, software, or processes. It provides a standardized framework for assessing key metrics across different environments, ensuring consistency in performance evaluation. Benchmarking suites are widely used in computing, artificial intelligence, business analytics, and manufacturing to measure operational effectiveness, optimize resource allocation, and support decision-making.

The key components of a benchmarking suite include predefined test cases that simulate real-world conditions to evaluate system performance. It incorporates performance metrics that quantify efficiency, speed, accuracy, or reliability based on the intended use case. The suite includes automation features that streamline testing procedures, reducing manual effort and improving consistency. Customization options allow users to tailor benchmarks to specific requirements, ensuring relevance to industry standards. Reporting and visualization tools provide detailed insights, enabling users to analyze results, identify bottlenecks, and compare performance across multiple systems.

One of the major benefits of a benchmarking suite is its ability to provide objective and repeatable assessments of performance, eliminating guesswork in evaluating systems. It enhances efficiency by identifying areas that require optimization, leading to improved resource utilization and cost savings. Organizations gain a competitive edge by using benchmarking suites to assess their technological infrastructure and ensure they meet industry standards. The insights derived from benchmarking enable better decision-making, allowing businesses to invest in the most effective solutions. In artificial intelligence and computing, benchmarking suites play a crucial role in fine-tuning algorithms, optimizing machine learning models, and improving overall system performance.

Examples of benchmarking suites can be found in various domains. In computing, SPEC (Standard Performance Evaluation Corporation) provides benchmarking suites that assess processor and system performance. In artificial intelligence, MLPerf is a widely used benchmarking suite for evaluating machine learning models across different hardware platforms. Business intelligence platforms use benchmarking suites to measure data processing efficiency and analytics performance. Cloud computing providers utilize benchmarking suites to compare server capabilities, storage efficiency, and network latency. Financial institutions rely on benchmarking suites to assess risk management strategies, fraud detection algorithms, and transaction processing speeds.

Industries that rely on benchmarking suites include technology, where software and hardware developers use them to optimize performance and improve reliability. The artificial intelligence sector applies benchmarking suites to evaluate deep learning models, ensuring they achieve high accuracy and efficiency. Manufacturing industries implement benchmarking suites to analyze production line efficiency, equipment performance, and quality control standards. Telecommunications companies use benchmarking suites to assess network speeds, bandwidth utilization, and service reliability. Healthcare organizations use benchmarking tools to evaluate medical imaging systems, predictive analytics models, and patient management software.

A benchmarking suite is an essential tool for evaluating and optimizing performance across various industries. It provides a structured approach to measuring efficiency, ensuring organizations can make data-driven decisions and maintain a competitive edge. While challenges such as environmental variability, bias, and rapid technological shifts exist, continuous refinement of benchmarking methodologies ensures their effectiveness. Proper implementation of a benchmarking suite allows businesses, researchers, and technology developers to identify strengths, improve weaknesses, and drive innovation in their respective fields.

Bernoulli distribution

The Bernoulli distribution is a discrete probability distribution that describes experiments with only two possible outcomes, typically labeled as success and failure. It is a fundamental concept in probability theory and statistics, serving as the basis for more complex probability distributions and statistical models. Named after Swiss mathematician Jacob Bernoulli, this distribution is widely used in various fields, including artificial intelligence, finance, and quality control, to model binary events.

The key components of the Bernoulli distribution include a binary outcome where a single trial results in one of two possible values, often represented as one for success and zero for failure. The probability parameter determines the likelihood of success in each trial, denoted as p, while the probability of failure is represented as one minus p. The probability mass function defines the likelihood of each outcome, ensuring that the sum of probabilities equals one. Expectation and variance measure the distribution's mean and spread, respectively, providing insights into its statistical properties.

One of the main benefits of the Bernoulli distribution is its simplicity, making it easy to apply in real-world scenarios involving binary outcomes. It forms the foundation for more advanced statistical models, such as the binomial and geometric distributions. The distribution is useful in machine learning and artificial intelligence for modeling classification problems where an event either occurs or does not. It allows for efficient decision-making in probabilistic models, optimizing resource allocation and risk assessment.

Examples of the Bernoulli distribution include coin flips, where the probability of heads and tails follows a Bernoulli process. In medical trials, the success or failure of a new treatment can be modeled using this distribution. Online advertising campaigns use Bernoulli trials to determine whether a user clicks on an ad or not. In fraud detection, transactions are classified as fraudulent or legitimate based on probability models derived from Bernoulli distributions.

Industries that rely on the Bernoulli distribution include artificial intelligence, where it is used in classification models and Bayesian networks. The healthcare industry applies it in clinical trials and medical diagnosis, where test results yield binary outcomes. In finance, it helps in risk analysis, portfolio management, and market predictions. The manufacturing sector uses Bernoulli processes in quality control, identifying defective products in production lines. Telecommunications apply it to analyze network reliability, determining whether a signal successfully transmits or fails.

The Bernoulli distribution is a fundamental concept in probability and statistics, providing a simple yet powerful framework for modeling binary events. Its applications span multiple industries, from artificial intelligence and finance to healthcare and manufacturing. While its simplicity is an advantage, careful consideration is necessary to ensure its assumptions align with real-world data. Despite its limitations, the Bernoulli distribution remains an essential tool for probability modeling, forming the basis for more complex statistical methods and decision-making processes.

Beta Distribution

The Beta distribution is a continuous probability distribution defined over the interval between zero and one. It is widely used in Bayesian statistics, machine learning, and various applications requiring probabilistic modeling of proportions, rates, or probabilities. The Beta distribution is characterized by its flexibility, allowing it to model a wide range of shapes based on different parameter values. It serves as a conjugate prior in Bayesian inference, making it particularly useful in updating probabilities based on new evidence.

The key components of the Beta distribution include two shape parameters, denoted as alpha and beta, which determine the distribution's shape and skewness. When both parameters are equal, the distribution becomes symmetric, while different values create left-skewed or right-skewed distributions. The probability density function defines the likelihood of different values within the range, ensuring that all probabilities sum to one. The mean and variance provide insights into the expected value and spread of the distribution, helping in decision-making processes. The Beta function, a mathematical normalization factor, ensures that probabilities remain valid within the defined range.

The Beta distribution offers several benefits due to its flexibility in modeling uncertainty in probabilistic systems. It provides a natural way to represent probabilities and proportions in Bayesian inference, allowing for continuous updates as new data becomes available. The distribution can take various shapes, making it suitable for different applications without requiring complex transformations. It is widely used in A/B testing and experimental design to analyze conversion rates, success probabilities, and risk assessments. The Beta distribution also supports decision-making in uncertain environments by providing well-defined probability estimates.

Examples of the Beta distribution appear in multiple domains. In Bayesian statistics, it is used as a prior for probabilities in hypothesis testing and predictive modeling. In artificial intelligence, reinforcement learning algorithms use the Beta distribution to model exploration-exploitation trade-offs. In finance, it helps estimate stock return probabilities and risk assessments for investment strategies. In healthcare, it is applied in clinical trials to model the probability of treatment success based on observed data. The Beta distribution is also widely used in project management, where it estimates task completion probabilities and resource allocation effectiveness.

Industries that rely on the Beta distribution include artificial intelligence, where it supports probabilistic modeling in machine learning algorithms. The healthcare sector applies it in medical diagnosis and epidemiology to assess the probability of disease occurrences. The finance industry uses it in risk analysis, portfolio optimization, and forecasting financial trends. Marketing and advertising leverage the Beta distribution in A/B testing, measuring campaign effectiveness and consumer response rates. Manufacturing and supply chain management utilize it for quality control and demand forecasting, ensuring efficient operations.

The Beta distribution is a powerful and flexible tool for modeling probabilities, proportions, and uncertainties across various domains. Its adaptability makes it an essential component of Bayesian inference, machine learning, finance, and healthcare applications. Despite challenges related to parameter estimation and computational complexity, the Beta distribution remains a fundamental concept in probability theory and statistical analysis. By leveraging its capabilities, industries can make data-driven decisions, optimize resource allocation, and enhance predictive modeling strategies.

Bézier Curves

Bézier curves are parametric curves widely used in computer graphics, animation, and computational design to create smooth and scalable shapes. They were developed by Pierre Bézier for applications in automobile design but have since become essential in digital design, typography, and motion graphics. These curves provide a mathematical way to model smooth transitions and intricate shapes by defining control points that influence the curve's direction and curvature without requiring complex calculations.

The key components of Bézier curves include control points, which determine the shape and structure of the curve. The number of control points defines the degree of the curve, with a linear Bézier curve having two points, a quadratic Bézier curve having three, and a cubic Bézier curve having four. The curve itself is generated through a recursive interpolation process, where points are blended in a weighted manner based on the Bernstein polynomial formulation. The curve is parameterized by a variable that progresses from zero to one, determining how the control points influence the final shape. The convex hull property ensures that the curve remains contained within the outermost boundary of its control points, preventing erratic deviations.

One of the main benefits of Bézier curves is their ability to create smooth and scalable designs, making them ideal for vector graphics and digital typography. They provide intuitive control over shapes, allowing designers to manipulate curves by adjusting control points without requiring explicit equations. Bézier curves are computationally efficient, making them suitable for real-time rendering in computer graphics and animation. They offer high precision in modeling complex curves, ensuring that digital representations remain visually accurate and smooth at different scales. The ability to represent a wide range of shapes with a minimal number of control points makes Bézier curves essential in UI/UX design and digital illustration.

Examples of Bézier curves are found in various applications. In computer-aided design (CAD), they are used to model automobile and aerospace components with smooth contours. In graphic design, fonts and vector illustrations rely on Bézier curves to create scalable and editable typography. In animation, motion paths and character rigging use these curves to produce natural and fluid movement. In robotics, Bézier curves help in path planning and trajectory optimization, ensuring efficient and collision-free motion. Video game development incorporates Bézier curves for camera motion, character movement, and environment design, enhancing the realism of interactive experiences.

Industries that rely on Bézier curves include computer graphics, where they are fundamental in digital image processing, rendering, and vector-based illustration. The animation industry applies them in character motion, frame transitions, and procedural animation techniques. Engineering and industrial design use Bézier curves to define smooth surfaces and streamline product design. The automotive and aerospace sectors incorporate them in aerodynamic modeling, ensuring precision in manufacturing and structural efficiency. The software industry integrates Bézier curves in user interface design, allowing for responsive and aesthetically pleasing digital interactions.

Bézier curves provide a versatile and powerful mathematical tool for creating smooth, precise, and scalable curves in digital design, engineering, and animation. Their adaptability allows them to be used across multiple industries, from typography to robotics, ensuring efficient and visually appealing representations. Despite challenges related to control complexity and computational demands, Bézier curves remain an essential component of computer graphics and geometric modeling. Through advancements in computational techniques and real-time rendering, Bézier curves continue to enhance digital creativity and precision-driven design processes.

Bias in AI is a critical issue that influences fairness, inclusivity, and trust in artificial intelligence systems. While AI bias can lead to discrimination and inaccuracies, recognizing and addressing these challenges enhances the ethical development of AI technologies. Ongoing research, diverse data representation, and algorithmic fairness techniques play a key role in minimizing bias and ensuring AI serves all users equitably. By prioritizing responsible AI practices, industries can harness the full potential of AI while reducing the risk of unintended bias and social harm.

Biased Data

Biased data refers to datasets that contain systematic errors, distortions, or imbalances that lead to inaccurate, unfair, or discriminatory outcomes when used in artificial intelligence models and decision-making processes. These biases arise due to the way data is collected, processed, or labeled, often reflecting existing social, cultural, or historical inequalities. Biased data can negatively impact AI performance, reinforcing stereotypes and producing results that favor certain groups over others. Recognizing and mitigating biased data is essential to ensure fairness, accuracy, and ethical AI applications.

The key components of biased data include sampling bias, where data does not represent the full diversity of the population, leading to skewed outcomes. Labeling bias occurs when human annotation of data reflects subjective opinions or errors, introducing inconsistencies. Historical bias exists when datasets contain embedded discrimination from past societal patterns, which AI models may then perpetuate. Measurement bias happens when the tools or methods used to collect data produce inaccuracies, leading to distorted representations. Algorithmic reinforcement occurs when biased data influences AI learning, creating self-perpetuating cycles of unfair predictions or classifications.

Examples of biased data appear across various domains. In facial recognition technology, datasets with disproportionate representation of certain demographics result in higher error rates for underrepresented groups. Healthcare AI models trained on data from specific populations may fail to generalize effectively, leading to disparities in diagnosis and treatment. Job recruitment AI tools using past hiring data may reinforce gender or racial biases if historical hiring patterns were discriminatory. Predictive policing systems relying on biased crime data may disproportionately target specific communities, increasing surveillance in already over-policed areas. Sentiment analysis models trained on biased language data can produce discriminatory content moderation outcomes, influencing online discussions unfairly.

Industries affected by biased data include healthcare, where disparities in medical datasets impact diagnosis and treatment recommendations. The financial sector faces risks when credit-scoring algorithms trained on biased financial histories unfairly disadvantage specific groups. Human resources and hiring processes encounter bias when AI-powered recruitment tools replicate discriminatory hiring practices. Legal and criminal justice systems struggle with biased risk assessment models that disproportionately assign higher risk scores to marginalized individuals. Social media platforms experience biased data issues in content recommendation algorithms, leading to misinformation spread and unequal representation.

Biased data poses a significant challenge to the fairness and reliability of AI systems, influencing decision-making across various industries. While biased data can lead to discriminatory and inaccurate outcomes, recognizing and addressing these biases enhances AI transparency and trustworthiness. By improving data collection, refining labeling processes, and implementing fairness-aware AI techniques, organizations can mitigate bias and develop more inclusive AI solutions. Continuous monitoring and ethical considerations remain essential to ensuring AI serves all individuals equitably and does not reinforce existing societal inequalities.

Bias in Machine learning

Bias in machine learning refers to systematic errors in algorithms that lead to unfair, inaccurate, or discriminatory outcomes. These biases emerge from training data, model selection, and human decision-making during development. Bias in machine learning can reinforce existing inequalities and distort predictions, resulting in flawed AI-driven decisions. Addressing bias is crucial to ensure fairness, accuracy, and ethical AI deployment across various applications.

The key components of bias in machine learning include data bias, which occurs when training datasets contain imbalances or do not accurately represent diverse populations. Algorithmic bias arises when models amplify patterns in data that reflect societal prejudices, leading to biased predictions. Labeling bias is introduced when human annotations reflect subjective judgments or errors. Selection bias occurs when training data is not representative of real-world distributions, leading to models that generalize poorly. Feedback loops can further reinforce bias when biased predictions influence future data collection and decision-making processes.

Despite its challenges, addressing bias in machine learning leads to improvements in model fairness, transparency, and trust. Identifying bias helps researchers refine training data and algorithmic processes, ensuring models produce equitable results. Bias detection techniques enhance AI accountability, reducing the risk of discrimination and unfair treatment. Ensuring unbiased models improves decision-making in sectors such as healthcare, finance, and law enforcement, where accuracy and fairness are critical. Developing fair machine learning models fosters public confidence in AI-driven technologies, promoting ethical and responsible AI adoption.

Examples of bias in machine learning can be found in multiple domains. In facial recognition technology, models trained on unbalanced datasets often misidentify individuals from underrepresented groups. In hiring algorithms, bias appears when AI models favor candidates based on historical hiring patterns that exclude certain demographics. Loan approval systems using biased financial data may disproportionately deny credit to specific populations. Predictive policing models can reinforce racial profiling by increasing surveillance in historically over-policed communities. Sentiment analysis models trained on biased language data can misinterpret opinions, leading to unfair moderation of online discussions.

Industries affected by bias in machine learning include healthcare, where biased models can result in disparities in disease diagnosis and treatment recommendations. The financial sector faces challenges when AI-driven credit scoring algorithms disadvantage individuals based on historical lending patterns. In human resources, AI-powered recruitment tools may unintentionally filter out diverse candidates due to biases in training data. The legal system encounters bias in risk assessment models used for sentencing and parole decisions, disproportionately affecting marginalized communities. Social media platforms experience algorithmic bias in content recommendations, leading to echo chambers and misinformation amplification.

Bias in machine learning poses significant risks to fairness, reliability, and trust in AI systems. While biased models can lead to discrimination and inaccuracies, recognizing and addressing bias enhances the ethical development of AI technologies. Through improved data collection, algorithmic fairness techniques, and transparent model evaluation, industries can create machine learning systems that promote equitable outcomes. Ongoing research, diverse representation in AI development, and regulatory frameworks play essential roles in mitigating bias and ensuring responsible AI deployment in real-world applications.

Bias-Variance Tradoff

The bias-variance tradeoff is a fundamental concept in machine learning and statistical modeling that describes the balance between two sources of error that affect model performance. Bias represents the error due to overly simplistic assumptions in the learning algorithm, leading to underfitting, where the model fails to capture the underlying patterns in the data. Variance represents the error due to excessive complexity in the model, causing overfitting, where the model learns noise and performs poorly on unseen data. The tradeoff arises because reducing bias increases variance and vice versa, requiring an optimal balance to achieve the best generalization.

The key components of the bias-variance tradeoff include bias, which measures how far predictions deviate from the true relationship due to model assumptions. High bias occurs in models that oversimplify patterns, such as linear regression applied to complex nonlinear data. Variance measures how much predictions fluctuate based on training data variations, with high variance models capturing noise and becoming sensitive to small changes in input data. Model complexity plays a crucial role, as simpler models tend to have high bias and low variance, while complex models exhibit low bias but high variance. Generalization error is the total prediction error on new data, combining bias and variance to determine how well the model performs outside the training set. Cross-validation techniques help in assessing this tradeoff by testing different model configurations and selecting the one that minimizes both errors.

Optimizing the bias-variance tradeoff leads to several benefits in machine learning. Achieving the right balance results in models that generalize well to unseen data, improving accuracy in real-world applications. Reducing overfitting ensures that models do not memorize noise but instead learn meaningful patterns that apply across different datasets. Properly managing complexity enhances computational efficiency, preventing unnecessary resource consumption in training and inference. Understanding this tradeoff allows data scientists to make informed decisions when selecting algorithms and adjusting hyperparameters, leading to better performance across various machine learning tasks.

Examples of the bias-variance tradeoff appear across different domains. In machine learning, linear regression with too few features exhibits high bias by oversimplifying relationships, while deep neural networks with excessive layers have high variance due to learning intricate details in the training data. In financial forecasting, simple models may fail to capture complex market trends, while overly sophisticated models may react too strongly to random fluctuations. In image recognition, basic classifiers may struggle to differentiate objects due to high bias, while highly tuned convolutional networks may perform poorly on new images due to high variance. In speech recognition, simple models may miss variations in pronunciation, while complex models may fail to generalize across different speakers.

Industries that rely on understanding and managing the bias-variance tradeoff include artificial intelligence and machine learning, where models need to perform reliably across different datasets. The finance sector applies these principles to balance predictive models for stock prices, risk assessment, and fraud detection. Healthcare benefits from optimizing this tradeoff in medical diagnosis models, ensuring accurate predictions without excessive sensitivity to small variations in patient data. Autonomous vehicle technology relies on managing this balance to avoid models that either underreact or overreact to dynamic driving conditions. The retail industry applies it in recommendation systems, ensuring suggestions remain relevant without being overly personalized to short-term behavior.

The bias-variance tradeoff is a crucial principle in machine learning, defining the relationship between model simplicity, complexity, and generalization. While high bias leads to underfitting and high variance results in overfitting, striking the right balance enables optimal model performance across different applications. Careful model selection, data preprocessing, and hyperparameter tuning help achieve this balance, ensuring AI systems deliver reliable and efficient predictions. By understanding and managing this tradeoff, industries can develop machine learning solutions that remain accurate, scalable, and adaptable to real-world challenges.

Bidirectional Encoder Represtions from Fransformers (BERT)

Bidirectional Encoder Representations from Transformers (BERT) is a deep learning model developed by Google that revolutionized natural language processing (NLP) by introducing bidirectional context understanding. Unlike traditional models that process text in a unidirectional manner, BERT simultaneously considers both preceding and following words, enabling a deeper understanding of linguistic context. This bidirectional approach significantly improves language comprehension, making BERT highly effective for various NLP tasks such as text classification, machine translation, and question answering.

The key components of BERT include the transformer architecture, which consists of self-attention mechanisms that allow the model to focus on different parts of the input text simultaneously. The model uses a bidirectional training approach, meaning it analyzes words in the context of both their left and right surroundings rather than just one direction. BERT employs a pretraining and fine-tuning methodology, where the model is first trained on large text corpora using unsupervised learning before being adapted to specific tasks through supervised learning. Masked language modeling is a crucial technique used in training BERT, where certain words in the input are randomly masked, forcing the model to predict them based on surrounding context. Sentence-pair training further enhances the model's ability to understand relationships between sentences, improving its performance on tasks such as next-sentence prediction and text entailment.

One of the major benefits of BERT is its ability to capture complex language structures and contextual meaning more accurately than previous NLP models. Its bidirectional nature enables better comprehension of words with multiple meanings, improving tasks such as named entity recognition and sentiment analysis. The pretraining process on vast datasets allows BERT to be highly versatile, making it adaptable to various domains with minimal fine-tuning. BERT significantly improves search engine performance, powering advanced ranking algorithms that provide more relevant search results. The model's efficiency in handling diverse NLP tasks reduces the need for developing task-specific models, streamlining AI-driven text processing.

Examples of BERT applications span multiple domains. In search engines, Google utilizes BERT to enhance query understanding, improving the relevance of search results. Virtual assistants such as Google Assistant and chatbots leverage BERT to interpret user queries more accurately, delivering more natural interactions. Healthcare applications use BERT for clinical text analysis, extracting insights from medical records and research papers. Legal document processing benefits from BERT's ability to understand complex legal language, assisting in contract analysis and case law research. Social media platforms employ BERT for content moderation, sentiment analysis, and automated tagging, ensuring better user engagement and community management.

Industries benefiting from BERT include technology, where AI-driven search engines, chatbots, and virtual assistants enhance user experience through improved language understanding. The healthcare sector uses BERT for predictive analytics, medical literature analysis, and automated diagnostics. The legal industry applies BERT in contract analysis, e-discovery, and legal research, streamlining document processing. E-commerce platforms leverage BERT for personalized recommendations, review analysis, and customer service automation. Finance and banking integrate BERT for fraud detection, sentiment analysis in market trends, and automated customer interactions.

Bidirectional Encoder Representations from Transformers (BERT) has redefined natural language processing by introducing a bidirectional contextual understanding that significantly enhances language comprehension. Its transformer-based architecture enables superior performance across various NLP tasks, benefiting industries such as technology, healthcare, finance, and legal services. While challenges related to computational demands, data availability, and interpretability exist, ongoing research and optimization efforts continue to improve BERT's efficiency. By leveraging BERT's advanced language modeling capabilities, organizations can develop more accurate, context-aware AI systems that drive innovation in text processing and human-computer interaction.

Bidirectional Long Short-Term Memory (Bi-LSTM)

Bidirectional Long Short-Term Memory (Bi-LSTM) is a type of recurrent neural network (RNN) architecture that enhances sequential data processing by incorporating information from both past and future contexts. Unlike standard LSTMs, which process data in a single direction, Bi-LSTM consists of two LSTM layers operating in opposite directions. This bidirectional approach allows the model to capture dependencies in a sequence more effectively, making it particularly useful for tasks involving natural language processing, speech recognition, and time-series forecasting.

The key components of Bi-LSTM include the forward LSTM layer, which processes input data in a standard left-to-right sequence, and the backward LSTM layer, which simultaneously processes data from right to left. These two layers operate independently but are combined at the output layer to produce a more comprehensive representation of the input sequence. Bi-LSTM relies on memory cells and gating mechanisms, including the input, forget, and output gates, to regulate information flow and retain relevant context. The hidden state outputs from both directions are merged, typically through concatenation or summation, allowing the model to leverage information from both past and future time steps.

One of the major benefits of Bi-LSTM is its ability to capture long-range dependencies in sequential data more effectively than standard LSTMs. This is particularly useful in natural language processing, where understanding the meaning of a word often depends on both preceding and succeeding words. Bi-LSTM improves accuracy in tasks such as text classification, sentiment analysis, and machine translation by providing richer contextual understanding. It enhances speech recognition systems by processing audio signals bidirectionally, leading to more precise transcription. The architecture is also beneficial for time-series prediction, as it considers both historical trends and future indicators, improving forecasting accuracy.

Examples of Bi-LSTM applications span multiple domains. In natural language processing, Bi-LSTM is widely used in named entity recognition, where understanding context from both directions improves entity classification. Sentiment analysis models benefit from Bi-LSTM's ability to analyze entire sentences before making predictions. In speech recognition, Bi-LSTM enhances automatic transcription by capturing phonetic and linguistic dependencies. In finance, Bi-LSTM is applied to stock market predictions, where analyzing past trends while considering future influences improves forecasting models. Healthcare applications use Bi-LSTM for medical diagnosis and predictive analytics, analyzing patient records for early disease detection.

Industries benefiting from Bi-LSTM include technology, where AI-driven applications such as chatbots, virtual assistants, and search engines rely on bidirectional sequence modeling. The healthcare sector applies Bi-LSTM in medical imaging analysis, clinical text processing, and disease prediction. The finance industry integrates Bi-LSTM into algorithmic trading, risk assessment, and fraud detection. E-commerce platforms use Bi-LSTM to enhance product recommendations and customer sentiment analysis. Autonomous systems and robotics employ Bi-LSTM for motion prediction, navigation, and real-time decision-making.

Bidirectional LSTM (Bi-LSTM) provides a powerful solution for sequential data processing by leveraging both past and future context to enhance prediction accuracy. Its ability to capture dependencies in both directions makes it particularly effective in natural language processing, speech recognition, and time-series analysis. While challenges related to computational demands and training complexity exist, ongoing advancements in hardware and optimization techniques continue to improve its efficiency. By integrating Bi-LSTM into AI-driven applications, industries can achieve better accuracy, richer context understanding, and more robust predictive capabilities across various domains.

Big Data

Big Data refers to extremely large and complex datasets that cannot be efficiently processed using traditional data management tools. It encompasses vast volumes of structured, semi-structured, and unstructured data generated at high velocity from various sources, including social media, financial transactions, IoT devices, and enterprise systems. Big Data is characterized by the three Vs: volume, velocity, and variety, with some models expanding this definition to include veracity and value. The ability to analyze and extract meaningful insights from Big Data has transformed industries, enabling data-driven decision-making, predictive analytics, and automation in various fields.

The key components of Big Data include data sources, which range from user interactions and machine-generated logs to scientific experiments and sensor networks. Storage infrastructure is essential for managing the vast amounts of information, often utilizing distributed file systems and cloud-based architectures. Processing frameworks, such as Hadoop and Spark, allow organizations to handle and analyze large datasets efficiently. Data analytics and machine learning algorithms play a crucial role in extracting insights, detecting patterns, and making predictions. Visualization tools convert raw data into meaningful representations, enabling stakeholders to interpret trends and make informed decisions.

One of the primary benefits of Big Data is its ability to enhance decision-making by providing real-time and predictive insights. Businesses can identify market trends, optimize supply chains, and personalize customer experiences based on behavioral analysis. In healthcare, Big Data enables early disease detection and treatment planning by analyzing vast amounts of medical records and research data. The financial sector leverages Big Data for fraud detection, risk assessment, and algorithmic trading. Government agencies use it for urban planning, crime prevention, and improving public services. By harnessing the power of Big Data, organizations can drive innovation, improve operational efficiency, and gain a competitive advantage in their respective industries.

Examples of Big Data applications include personalized recommendations in e-commerce platforms, where companies analyze customer purchase history and browsing behavior to suggest relevant products. Social media platforms process massive volumes of user-generated content to improve engagement, detect trends, and moderate harmful content. In transportation, ride-sharing companies use real-time data analysis to optimize routes, predict demand, and adjust pricing dynamically. In scientific research, climate models rely on Big Data to analyze weather patterns and predict environmental changes. Smart cities implement Big Data solutions to monitor traffic flow, enhance energy efficiency, and improve waste management.

Industries that depend on Big Data include retail, where businesses optimize inventory management and customer targeting through data-driven marketing strategies. The healthcare industry benefits from Big Data in genomics research, predictive diagnostics, and personalized medicine. The financial sector uses data analytics to detect fraudulent activities, assess credit risks, and develop investment strategies. Manufacturing companies leverage predictive maintenance by analyzing machine sensor data to prevent equipment failures and reduce downtime. Telecommunications firms utilize Big Data to enhance network performance, predict outages, and improve customer service.

Big Data has revolutionized industries by enabling advanced analytics, automation, and data-driven decision-making across diverse applications. Its ability to process vast amounts of information in real time has led to significant advancements in business intelligence, healthcare, finance, and technology. While challenges related to security, scalability, and ethical considerations remain, continuous innovation in storage, processing, and analytics tools helps organizations maximize the value of Big Data. By leveraging Big Data effectively, businesses and institutions can unlock new opportunities, drive efficiency, and create impactful solutions for complex global challenges.

Big-O notation

Big-O notation is a mathematical framework used in computer science to describe the efficiency of algorithms in terms of time and space complexity. It provides a standardized way to express how an algorithm's performance scales as the size of the input grows. By analyzing the worst-case scenario, Big-O notation helps developers and researchers compare different algorithms, ensuring optimal performance for various computational tasks. The notation focuses on dominant terms while ignoring constants and lower-order terms, allowing for a simplified yet accurate representation of algorithm efficiency.

The key components of Big-O notation include input size, which represents the number of elements the algorithm processes. Time complexity defines how the execution time of an algorithm changes based on input size, while space complexity measures the amount of memory required. Common complexity classes include constant time $O(1)$, logarithmic time $O(\log n)$, linear time $O(n)$, quadratic time $O(n^2)$, and exponential time $O(2^n)$. These classifications help in understanding whether an algorithm scales efficiently as input size increases. The asymptotic analysis method is used to evaluate the algorithm's performance, focusing on large-scale behavior rather than minor fluctuations in runtime.

One of the main benefits of Big-O notation is its ability to provide a clear and universal comparison of algorithms, allowing developers to choose the most efficient approach for a given problem. It helps optimize software performance by identifying bottlenecks and improving computational efficiency. By understanding Big-O notation, engineers can design scalable systems that maintain efficiency as data grows. It plays a crucial role in resource management, enabling better utilization of processing power and memory. The notation simplifies complex performance discussions by offering a high-level abstraction of algorithmic efficiency.

Examples of Big-O notation in practice can be found in various algorithms. A simple lookup operation in an array has a constant time complexity of $O(1)$ since it retrieves an element instantly. Binary search operates in logarithmic time $O(\log n)$ by repeatedly dividing the search space in half. Linear search takes $O(n)$ time since it checks each element one by one. Sorting algorithms vary in complexity, with quicksort and mergesort typically operating at $O(n \log n)$, while bubble sort has a less efficient $O(n^2)$ complexity. Graph traversal algorithms like Dijkstra's shortest path algorithm exhibit different complexities based on their implementations and data structures.

Industries that rely on Big-O notation include software development, where engineers optimize algorithms for databases, web applications, and system processing. The artificial intelligence sector applies Big-O notation to evaluate the efficiency of machine learning models and data preprocessing methods. The cybersecurity industry uses algorithmic efficiency analysis to strengthen encryption and security protocols. The finance sector benefits from performance evaluation in high-frequency trading and risk analysis algorithms. Scientific computing and research institutions depend on complexity analysis for simulations, data modeling, and large-scale computational problems.

Big-O notation serves as a foundational concept in computer science, providing a standardized method for analyzing and comparing algorithm efficiency. It enables developers, researchers, and engineers to optimize performance, design scalable systems, and manage computational resources effectively. While it primarily focuses on worst-case analysis and may not capture all nuances of algorithm behavior, Big-O notation remains an essential tool for making informed decisions in algorithm design and system development. Its impact spans multiple industries, from software engineering to artificial intelligence, ensuring efficient and scalable technological advancements.

Bi-level Optimization

Bi-level optimization is a mathematical framework used to solve hierarchical problems where one optimization task is nested within another. It involves two levels of decision-making, with the upper-level problem (leader) influencing the lower-level problem (follower) and vice versa. The leader's decision depends on the optimal response of the follower, creating a dependency between the two levels. This structure makes bi-level optimization essential in complex systems where multiple agents or objectives interact. It is widely used in machine learning, economics, engineering, and game theory to optimize processes that involve multi-stage decision-making.

The key components of bi-level optimization include the upper-level objective function, which defines the primary decision-making goal, and the lower-level objective function, which represents the subordinate optimization task. Constraints at both levels determine feasible solutions, ensuring that decisions comply with system limitations. The dependency between levels requires solving the lower-level problem first to determine how it influences the upper-level solution. Iterative algorithms and computational methods are used to find the equilibrium between both levels, ensuring an optimal solution that satisfies the conditions imposed by each stage.

One of the main benefits of bi-level optimization is its ability to model real-world hierarchical decision-making processes effectively. It provides a structured approach to handling multi-agent systems where different stakeholders influence outcomes. The framework enables better resource allocation by optimizing both high-level strategies and detailed implementation plans simultaneously. It enhances predictive modeling in fields like machine learning by fine-tuning hyperparameters and optimizing algorithmic structures. In engineering, bi-level optimization improves system design by balancing structural integrity and cost efficiency.

Examples of bi-level optimization applications can be found in multiple industries. In machine learning, it is used for hyperparameter tuning, where the upper-level function optimizes model accuracy while the lower-level function manages computational efficiency. In economics, pricing strategies are optimized using bi-level models, ensuring competitive pricing while maximizing revenue. In transportation, traffic flow optimization considers both city-level planning and individual route choices to reduce congestion. In energy management, power grid optimization balances production costs and consumer demand response. In engineering design, bi-level optimization helps in material selection and structural analysis to improve durability and cost-effectiveness.

Industries that benefit from bi-level optimization include artificial intelligence, where it enhances deep learning model training and parameter selection. The finance sector applies it in portfolio optimization, balancing long-term investment strategies with short-term market fluctuations. The telecommunications industry uses bi-level optimization for network routing, ensuring optimal data flow while minimizing latency. In healthcare, treatment planning and medical resource allocation rely on bi-level models to optimize patient care while controlling costs. Manufacturing benefits from supply chain optimization, ensuring efficient logistics while reducing operational expenses.

Bi-level optimization provides a powerful approach to solving hierarchical decision-making problems across various industries. By structuring problems into upper- and lower-level objectives, it enables efficient resource allocation, strategic planning, and predictive modeling. While challenges such as computational demands and solution stability exist, advancements in optimization techniques continue to improve its applicability. As industries increasingly rely on AI-driven decision-making, bi-level optimization remains an essential tool for balancing high-level strategies with detailed operational decisions, ensuring efficient and effective problem-solving.

Binary Classification

Binary classification is a type of supervised learning in machine learning that involves categorizing data into one of two distinct classes. The objective is to train a model that can accurately distinguish between these two categories based on input features. This classification method is widely used in applications where decisions need to be made in a yes-or-no, true-or-false, or positive-or-negative manner. Binary classification models learn from labeled training data and generalize their understanding to new, unseen data.

The key components of binary classification include the input features, which are the attributes used by the model to make predictions. A classification algorithm processes these features to assign a label to each data point. The decision boundary represents the separation between the two classes in feature space. The loss function measures how well the model's predictions match the actual labels, guiding optimization during training. Performance metrics such as accuracy, precision, recall, F1-score, and AUC-ROC are used to evaluate the model's effectiveness in distinguishing between the two classes.

One of the main benefits of binary classification is its simplicity, making it computationally efficient and easy to interpret. It enables automation in decision-making processes by categorizing data quickly and accurately. The model's performance can be optimized with various techniques such as feature engineering, regularization, and hyperparameter tuning. Binary classification is widely applicable across industries, improving efficiency in areas such as fraud detection, medical diagnosis, and spam filtering. The ability to use probabilistic outputs allows models to estimate confidence levels, supporting better decision-making.

Examples of binary classification applications include spam detection in email systems, where messages are categorized as spam or not spam. In medical diagnostics, models classify patients as having a disease or being healthy. Fraud detection systems in banking identify transactions as fraudulent or legitimate. Sentiment analysis in customer reviews determines whether feedback is positive or negative. Image recognition models classify objects into two categories, such as distinguishing between cats and dogs in a dataset.

Industries that rely on binary classification include finance, where it is used in credit scoring and risk assessment. The healthcare sector applies it for disease prediction and patient monitoring. The cybersecurity industry depends on binary classification for intrusion detection and malware identification. E-commerce platforms use it to personalize recommendations and detect fake reviews. Social media platforms implement binary classification for content moderation, flagging inappropriate or harmful posts.

Binary classification plays a fundamental role in machine learning, providing a straightforward yet powerful approach to categorizing data into two distinct groups. It is widely used across industries to improve decision-making, automate tasks, and enhance security. Despite challenges such as imbalanced data and overfitting, ongoing advancements in machine learning techniques continue to refine binary classification models, making them more accurate and reliable. As artificial intelligence evolves, binary classification remains a cornerstone of predictive analytics, supporting a wide range of real-world applications.

Binary Data

Binary data refers to information represented using only two distinct values, typically 0 and 1. This form of data representation is fundamental in computing and digital systems, where binary digits, or bits, are used to encode and store information efficiently. Binary data serves as the foundation for all digital communication, computer processing, and data storage, enabling seamless operations in software, hardware, and network systems. It is commonly used in machine learning, data compression, encryption, and digital logic circuits.

The key components of binar y data include bits, which are the smallest units of data and represent either 0 or 1. A collection of bits forms bytes, which are used to encode characters, numbers, and other forms of data. Encoding schemes such as ASCII and Unicode map binary data to human-readable text, while binary formats like JPEG and MP3 store multimedia information efficiently. Boolean logic operations, including AND, OR, and NOT, manipulate binary data for processing and decision-making. Data compression techniques reduce the storage size of binary data while maintaining its integrity, optimizing transmission and storage efficiency.

One of the primary benefits of binary data is its simplicity, allowing computers to perform fast and reliable computations. It enables efficient data storage, as binary encoding reduces complexity while maximizing processing speed. Binary data supports error detection and correction, ensuring data integrity during transmission and storage. It enhances security through encryption techniques that convert sensitive information into binary-coded ciphertext. The universal nature of binary data allows seamless communication between different hardware and software systems, promoting compatibility and interoperability.

Examples of binary data applications can be found in various domains. In computer memory and storage, all digital files, including documents, images, and videos, are stored in binary format. In networking, binary data is transmitted as electrical signals or optical pulses in digital communication protocols. In machine learning, binary datasets are used for classification tasks where outcomes are represented as 0 or 1. Digital logic circuits in processors operate on binary signals to perform arithmetic and logical operations. In cryptography, encryption algorithms transform plaintext into binary-coded ciphertext to protect sensitive information.

Industries that rely on binary data include information technology, where it underpins all computing processes, from programming languages to data storage. The telecommunications industry depends on binary data for transmitting voice, video, and text over digital networks. The finance sector uses binary data in transaction processing, algorithmic trading, and data encryption for secure banking. Healthcare systems manage medical imaging and electronic health records using binary-coded formats for efficient storage and retrieval. The entertainment industry leverages binary data for digital media streaming, gaming, and content distribution.

Binary data forms the backbone of modern computing, enabling efficient processing, storage, and transmission of digital information. Its simplicity and versatility make it indispensable across various industries, from information technology to finance and healthcare. While challenges such as data corruption, security threats, and compatibility issues exist, advancements in error correction, encryption, and standardization continue to enhance the reliability of binary data systems. As digital transformation accelerates, the importance of binary data in computing and artificial intelligence remains foundational to innovation and technological progress.

Binary Search

Binary search is an efficient algorithm used to locate a target value within a sorted array or list. It follows a divide-and-conquer approach by repeatedly splitting the search space in half, reducing the number of comparisons needed to find the desired element. Instead of searching sequentially, binary search identifies the middle element of the list and compares it to the target value. If the target matches the middle element, the search is complete. If the target is smaller, the search continues in the left half of the list, and if it is larger, the search proceeds in the right half. This process repeats until the target is found or the search space is exhausted.

The key components of binary search include the sorted input list, which ensures that the algorithm can efficiently eliminate half of the elements in each step. The middle element acts as the pivot for comparison, guiding whether the search should continue in the left or right half. Recursive or iterative implementation methods define how the search is performed, with recursion dividing the problem into smaller subproblems and iteration using loop-based logic to narrow the search range. The search space continuously shrinks, reducing the time complexity to O(log n), making binary search significantly faster than linear search for large datasets.

One of the primary benefits of binary search is its efficiency, as it reduces the number of comparisons needed to locate an element. It performs well with large datasets, making it a fundamental algorithm in search operations. The logarithmic time complexity ensures that the search process remains scalable as data size increases. It is simple to implement and can be applied in both recursive and iterative forms, offering flexibility in different programming environments. Binary search also plays a crucial role in optimizing algorithms such as search trees, indexing, and numerical computation.

Examples of binary search can be found in various applications. In computer science, it is widely used in searching algorithms for databases, where sorted indexes allow rapid lookups. In programming, binary search is used to find elements in sorted arrays, such as searching for a specific value in a dictionary. In numerical computing, the algorithm is applied in root-finding methods like the bisection method. In operating systems, binary search is used in memory management to efficiently allocate and retrieve memory blocks. In artificial intelligence, it helps optimize decision trees and improve the efficiency of searching algorithms in machine learning models.

Industries that rely on binary search include software development, where efficient searching algorithms improve application performance. The finance sector applies binary search in trading algorithms and data retrieval from large financial datasets. The telecommunications industry utilizes binary search for routing and signal processing optimizations. In healthcare, it is used in medical databases to quickly retrieve patient records. The e-commerce sector benefits from binary search in recommendation systems and product search functionalities, ensuring fast and relevant results for users.

Binary search is a fundamental algorithm that offers fast and efficient searching capabilities in sorted datasets. Its logarithmic time complexity makes it ideal for applications requiring rapid lookups, from database management to artificial intelligence. Despite its dependency on sorted data and challenges in recursive implementation, binary search remains an essential tool in computer science and various industries. By leveraging its efficiency and adaptability, organizations can improve search operations and optimize performance in data-driven applications.

Binary Tree

A Binary Tree is a hierarchical data structure in computing where each node has at most two children, typically referred to as the left child and the right child, forming a tree-like arrangement rooted at a single starting point. Unlike linear structures like arrays, a binary tree organizes data in a branching pattern, enabling efficient searching, insertion, and deletion operations by leveraging its recursive nature. It's a foundational concept in computer science, serving as a building block for more complex systems and algorithms.

The key components of a binary tree include nodes, edges, and a root. Nodes are the individual elements holding data, each potentially linked to two offspring—left and right children—storing values like numbers or objects. Edges are the connections between nodes, defining the parent-child relationships that shape the tree's structure. The root is the topmost node, the entry point from which all branches descend, anchoring the entire hierarchy and guiding traversal or manipulation.

The benefits of a binary tree lie in its efficiency and versatility. It enables rapid data retrieval and organization, with operations like searching or sorting often achieving logarithmic time complexity in balanced cases, outpacing linear alternatives. Its hierarchical design mirrors real-world relationships, making it intuitive for tasks like decision-making or categorization. Additionally, it supports dynamic growth, allowing new nodes to be added without restructuring the entire dataset, a flexibility prized in evolving applications.

Examples of binary trees include their use in search algorithms, where a binary search tree quickly locates values by halving the search space with each step. In expression parsing, compilers employ binary trees to represent mathematical equations, with operators as nodes and operands as leaves, simplifying evaluation. Another instance is in file compression, where Huffman coding builds a binary tree to assign shorter codes to frequent symbols, optimizing storage.

Industries utilizing binary trees include software development, where they power database indexing for fast query responses. Telecommunications relies on them for routing algorithms, organizing network paths efficiently. Gaming uses binary trees in decision systems for AI characters, mapping choices hierarchically. Finance leverages them in option pricing models, structuring calculations for rapid market analysis.

In conclusion, the Binary Tree stands as a elegant, powerful tool in the data structure toolkit, blending speed with structural clarity to tackle diverse problems. Its strengths in efficiency and adaptability are tempered by the need for balance and careful design, ensuring its utility hinges on skillful implementation. As industries lean on data-driven solutions, binary trees will remain a quiet cornerstone, branching through the core of computational innovation.

Binning Algorithm

Binning Algorithm is a computational method designed to systematically group continuous or discrete data points into distinct categories, or bins, based on predefined criteria or dynamically determined rules. It automates the process of binning by applying mathematical or statistical techniques to partition data, aiming to enhance analysis, reduce complexity, or prepare datasets for tasks like machine learning or visualization. Think of it as a digital organizer, sorting a stream of values into neatly labeled compartments with precision and intent.

The key components of a binning algorithm include a data input stream, a binning strategy, and an assignment function. The data input stream provides the raw values—numbers, timestamps, or measurements—that need categorization, drawn from sources like sensors or databases. The binning strategy dictates how bins are formed, whether through equal-width intervals, equal-frequency quantiles, or clustering-based approaches tailored to the data's distribution. The assignment function maps each value to its designated bin, executing the strategy with consistency and efficiency across the dataset.

The benefits of a binning algorithm lie in its automation and adaptability. It streamlines data preparation by replacing manual grouping with fast, repeatable logic, saving time in large-scale analyses. It adjusts to varying data characteristics, offering flexible strategies that can highlight trends or smooth noise as needed. Additionally, it boosts downstream performance, producing structured inputs that improve the accuracy and speed of models or visualizations by focusing on essential patterns.

Examples of binning algorithms include a histogram generator dividing sales figures into equal-width revenue bins to track monthly performance. In weather forecasting, an algorithm might use quantile binning to categorize rainfall data, balancing skewed distributions for better prediction. Another instance is in fraud detection, where transaction amounts are binned via a clustering algorithm to isolate unusual spending ranges for scrutiny.

Industries utilizing binning algorithms include retail, where they segment customer purchase data for inventory planning. Healthcare applies them to bin vital signs into risk categories, aiding rapid diagnostics. Finance uses them to group stock price fluctuations, refining trading algorithms. Environmental monitoring employs them to categorize pollution levels, supporting policy analysis with clear thresholds.

In conclusion, the Binning Algorithm stands as a nimble architect of data order, wielding logic to carve clarity from chaos with tailored precision. Its power to automate and adapt fuels its utility, though success rests on striking a balance between simplicity and fidelity. As industries lean on data to drive decisions, binning algorithms will remain essential, quietly shaping raw inputs into actionable intelligence.

Binomial Distribution

Binomial Distribution is a statistical model that describes the probability of achieving a specific number of successes in a fixed set of independent trials, where each trial has only two possible outcomes—success or failure—and the likelihood of success remains constant. It's a cornerstone of probability theory, capturing the essence of scenarios where binary events repeat under consistent conditions, offering a mathematical lens to predict outcomes based on repetition and chance.

The key components of the binomial distribution include the number of trials, the probability of success, and the success count. The number of trials represents the total attempts or experiments conducted, each independent of the others, like flipping a coin multiple times. The probability of success is the fixed chance of the desired outcome occurring in any single trial, such as heads landing half the time. The success count is the variable of interest—how many times success happens across all trials—forming the distribution's shape when plotted.

The benefits of the binomial distribution lie in its simplicity and predictive power. It provides a clear framework for calculating probabilities in binary scenarios, making it accessible for both manual computation and algorithmic use. It excels at modeling real-world processes with repetitive, two-outcome events, offering precise forecasts when conditions are stable. Additionally, its mathematical elegance supports broader statistical methods, serving as a building block for more complex analyses.

Examples of the binomial distribution include predicting the number of defective items in a batch of manufactured goods, where each item is either faulty or not, and the defect rate is known. In marketing, it might estimate how many customers out of a sample will respond to a campaign, assuming a consistent response probability. Another case is in quality control, calculating the odds of passing a set number of tests in a series of inspections.

Industries relying on the binomial distribution include manufacturing, where it assesses production reliability by modeling defect rates. Healthcare uses it to study treatment success rates across patient groups, guiding clinical decisions. Finance applies it to evaluate the likelihood of loan defaults in a portfolio, informing risk strategies. Education leverages it to analyze pass-fail patterns in standardized testing, shaping curriculum adjustments.

In conclusion, the Binomial Distribution offers a tidy, potent tool for decoding the odds of success in a world of repeated chances, blending mathematical rigor with practical insight. Its strength shines in structured, binary contexts, though its rigid assumptions demand careful application. As industries navigate uncertainty, this distribution will endure as a trusted guide, illuminating probability with clarity and purpose.

Biometrics

Benefits: Biometrics refers to the measurement and statistical analysis of unique physical and behavioral characteristics of individuals. It is primarily used for identification and authentication purposes, offering a secure and efficient way to verify identity.

Key Components
Biometrics can be divided into physical and behavioral traits. Physical biometrics include fingerprint recognition, facial recognition, iris or retina scanning, hand geometry, DNA profiling, and voice recognition. Behavioral biometrics focus on patterns such as keystroke dynamics, gait analysis, signature dynamics, and typing rhythm. The technology relies on sensors like cameras and fingerprint scanners, advanced algorithms for pattern recognition, and databases to store biometric templates securely.

Benefits
Biometrics provides enhanced security by using unique biological traits that are difficult to forge or steal. It eliminates the need for passwords or physical tokens, offering convenience and reducing the risk of unauthorized access. The accuracy of biometric systems is high, making them reliable for large-scale applications. They also help prevent fraud and identity theft, making them valuable in industries like finance, healthcare, and law enforcement.

Examples
Common examples of biometric systems include fingerprint scanners in smartphones like Apple's Touch ID, facial recognition systems used in airports for customs and border control, iris scanning in high-security facilities, and voice authentication in banking and customer service. These applications demonstrate the versatility and reliability of biometric technology.

Applications
Biometrics is widely used in security and access control, such as unlocking devices or accessing secure facilities. In law enforcement, it aids in criminal identification through fingerprint databases and surveillance using facial recognition. Healthcare systems use biometrics for patient identification and secure access to medical records. Banking and finance sectors rely on biometrics for secure transactions and ATM authentication. Travel and immigration systems use biometrics for e-passports and border control, streamlining processes while enhancing security.

Industry
The biometrics industry includes key players like Apple, Microsoft, NEC Corporation, and IDEMIA, which provide solutions ranging from consumer devices to government systems. The global biometrics market is experiencing significant growth, driven by increasing demand in security, healthcare, and finance. Emerging trends include multimodal biometrics, which combine multiple traits for higher accuracy, AI-powered biometric systems for improved performance, and integration with IoT devices for broader applications.

Summary
Biometrics is a transformative technology that leverages unique human traits for secure identification and authentication. It offers significant benefits in terms of security, convenience, and accuracy, making it indispensable across various industries. However, challenges such as privacy concerns, data security, and ethical implications must be addressed to ensure its responsible use. With advancements

in AI and machine learning, biometrics is set to play an even greater role in shaping the future of digital identity and security.

Bipartite Graph

A bipartite graph is a type of graph in graph theory where the set of vertices can be divided into two disjoint and independent sets. This means that every edge in the graph connects a vertex from one set to a vertex in the other set, and no edges exist between vertices within the same set. Bipartite graphs are widely used in artificial intelligence and computer science to model relationships between two distinct classes of objects.

Key Components
A bipartite graph consists of two sets of vertices, often referred to as the left set and the right set. The edges in the graph only connect vertices from the left set to the right set, ensuring no connections exist within the same set. The structure is often represented as G = (U, V, E), where U and V are the two disjoint sets of vertices, and E is the set of edges connecting them. Key properties include the absence of odd-length cycles and the ability to be colored with just two colors.

Benefits
Bipartite graphs provide a clear and efficient way to model relationships between two distinct groups. They are particularly useful in scenarios where interactions or dependencies exist between two different types of entities. Their simplicity and structure make them easy to analyze and optimize, especially in problems like matching, recommendation systems, and network flow. Additionally, bipartite graphs are computationally efficient for many algorithms, making them a practical choice in AI and machine learning applications.

Examples
A classic example of a bipartite graph is a job matching system, where one set of vertices represents job seekers and the other set represents job openings. Edges connect job seekers to the jobs they are qualified for. Another example is a recommendation system, where one set represents users and the other represents products, with edges indicating user preferences or purchases. In natural language processing, bipartite graphs can model relationships between words and documents in information retrieval systems.

Applications
Bipartite graphs are used in a wide range of AI applications. In recommendation systems, they model user-item interactions to generate personalized recommendations. In computational biology, they represent relationships between genes and diseases. In network flow problems, they optimize resource allocation, such as assigning tasks to workers or matching donors to recipients in organ transplant systems. They are also used in natural language processing for document clustering and information retrieval, as well as in social network analysis to study interactions between different groups.

Industry
Bipartite graphs are widely used in industries such as e-commerce, healthcare, and social media. Companies like Amazon and Netflix use them in recommendation systems to improve user experience. In healthcare, they help model patient-disease or drug-target interactions for personalized medicine. Social media platforms use bipartite graphs to analyze interactions between users and content, enabling targeted advertising and content recommendations. The growing demand for AI-driven solutions in these industries ensures the continued relevance and application of bipartite graphs.

Summary
A bipartite graph is a versatile and efficient tool in AI and computer science, used to model relationships between two distinct sets of entities. Its clear structure and computational efficiency make it ideal for applications like recommendation systems, network flow optimization, and natural language

processing. While challenges such as scalability and data accuracy exist, bipartite graphs remain a fundamental concept in solving complex real-world problems. Their widespread use across industries highlights their importance in advancing AI-driven solutions.

Bitwise Operations

Definition

Bitwise operations are fundamental operations in computer science and artificial intelligence that manipulate data at the binary level. These operations work directly on the binary representations of data, performing tasks such as shifting, masking, and comparing bits. Bitwise operations are highly efficient and are often used in low-level programming, optimization, and data compression, making them valuable in AI applications where performance and resource utilization are critical.

Key Components
Bitwise operations include a set of basic operations performed on binary digits (bits). The most common operations are AND, OR, XOR (exclusive OR), NOT, left shift, and right shift. The AND operation compares two bits and returns 1 if both bits are 1. The OR operation returns 1 if at least one bit is 1. The XOR operation returns 1 if the bits are different. The NOT operation inverts the bits. The left shift and right shift operations move bits to the left or right, respectively, effectively multiplying or dividing by powers of two. These operations are executed at the hardware level, making them extremely fast.

Benefits
Bitwise operations offer significant benefits in terms of speed and efficiency. They are executed directly by the CPU, making them much faster than higher-level arithmetic operations. They are also memory-efficient, as they work on compact binary representations of data. In AI, bitwise operations are particularly useful for optimizing algorithms, reducing computational overhead, and enabling compact storage of data. They are essential in tasks like feature extraction, data compression, and neural network quantization, where performance and resource efficiency are critical.

Examples
A common example of bitwise operations is in image processing, where bitwise AND, OR, and NOT are used to combine or mask images. In neural networks, bitwise operations are used in quantization techniques to reduce the precision of weights and activations, enabling faster inference on hardware with limited resources. Another example is in cryptography, where XOR operations are used to encrypt and decrypt data. Bitwise operations are also used in hash functions and data structures like Bloom filters, which are widely used in AI for efficient data storage and retrieval.

Applications
Bitwise operations are widely used in AI and machine learning for optimization and efficiency. In neural networks, they are used in quantization techniques to reduce the size of models and speed up inference. In computer vision, they are used for image masking, feature extraction, and object detection. In natural language processing, they are used in hash-based algorithms for text processing and data deduplication. Bitwise operations are also used in embedded systems and IoT devices, where computational resources are limited, and efficiency is paramount.

Industry
Bitwise operations are widely used in industries that rely on high-performance computing and resource optimization. In the AI industry, they are used in neural network quantization and model compression, enabling faster and more efficient deployment of AI models on edge devices. In the gaming industry, bitwise operations are used for graphics rendering and physics simulations. In cybersecurity, they are used in encryption and hashing algorithms. The growing demand for efficient and scalable AI solutions ensures the continued relevance of bitwise operations in the industry.

Summary
Bitwise operations are a powerful tool in AI and computer science, enabling efficient manipulation of data at the binary level. They offer significant benefits in terms of speed, memory efficiency, and optimization, making them essential for tasks like neural network quantization, image processing, and data compression. While they come with challenges such as complexity and debugging difficulties, their widespread use in industries like AI, gaming, and cybersecurity highlights their importance. As AI continues to evolve, bitwise operations will remain a critical component of high-performance and resource-efficient computing.

Black Box Model

Benefits
A black box model in artificial intelligence refers to a system or algorithm where the internal mechanisms and decision-making processes are not transparent or easily interpretable. While the inputs and outputs are visible, the transformations and logic that occur within the model remain hidden. These models are often highly effective in solving complex problems but lack explainability, making it difficult to understand how specific decisions or predictions are made.

Key Components
A black box model consists of three primary elements: the input, the internal processing mechanism, and the output. The input is the data provided to the model, such as images, text, or numerical values. The internal processing mechanism involves complex algorithms, such as deep neural networks or ensemble methods, which analyze the input data and extract patterns. The output is the result generated by the model, such as a prediction, classification, or decision. The complexity of the internal mechanism, often involving millions of parameters, is what makes the model a black box.

Benefits
Black box models offer significant advantages in terms of performance and versatility. They excel at handling large, high-dimensional datasets and can capture intricate patterns that simpler models might miss. This makes them highly effective for tasks like image recognition, natural language processing, and predictive analytics. Their ability to generalize from data allows them to perform well across diverse domains, often achieving state-of-the-art results. Additionally, black box models require minimal domain-specific knowledge, making them accessible for a wide range of applications.

Examples
A common example of a black box model is a deep learning neural network used for image classification. The model takes an image as input and outputs a label, such as identifying objects or faces, but the specific features or layers contributing to the decision are not easily interpretable. Another example is a recommendation system used by platforms like Amazon or YouTube, which analyzes user behavior to suggest products or videos. While the recommendations are accurate, the underlying logic is not transparent to users or developers.

Applications
Black box models are widely used in various industries and applications. In healthcare, they assist in diagnosing diseases, predicting patient outcomes, and discovering new drugs. In finance, they are used for fraud detection, credit scoring, and algorithmic trading. In autonomous systems, such as self-driving cars, black box models process sensor data to make real-time decisions. In natural language processing, they power chatbots, language translation, and sentiment analysis tools. Their ability to handle complex tasks makes them indispensable in modern AI applications.

Industry
Black box models are widely adopted across industries that rely on advanced AI solutions. In healthcare, they are used for medical imaging, disease prediction, and personalized treatment plans. In finance, they drive fraud detection systems, risk assessment tools, and automated trading platforms. In

technology, they power virtual assistants, recommendation engines, and autonomous systems. The growing demand for AI-driven solutions has led to increased use of black box models, but there is also a push toward developing explainable AI techniques to address their limitations and ensure ethical use.

Summary
A black box model is a powerful AI system that delivers high performance and accuracy but lacks transparency in its decision-making process. These models are widely used in applications like healthcare, finance, and autonomous systems due to their ability to handle complex tasks and large datasets. However, their lack of interpretability poses challenges in understanding and trusting their decisions, particularly in critical domains. As AI continues to evolve, there is a growing emphasis on balancing the effectiveness of black box models with the development of explainable and ethical AI systems to ensure accountability, fairness, and trust.

Black Hat AI

Benefits
Black Hat AI refers to the malicious use of artificial intelligence technologies for harmful, unethical, or illegal purposes. It involves leveraging AI tools and techniques to exploit vulnerabilities, deceive systems, or cause harm to individuals, organizations, or society. Black Hat AI is often associated with cybercrime, misinformation, and other forms of digital exploitation, posing significant risks to security, privacy, and trust in AI systems.

Key Components
Black Hat AI relies on advanced AI techniques such as machine learning, deep learning, and natural language processing to achieve its goals. Key components include adversarial algorithms, which are designed to manipulate or deceive AI systems, and automated tools that enable large-scale attacks. These systems often exploit vulnerabilities in data, models, or infrastructure, using techniques like data poisoning, model evasion, or deepfake generation. The anonymity and scalability of AI make it a powerful tool for malicious actors.

Benefits
While Black Hat AI is inherently harmful, its "benefits" from the perspective of malicious actors include increased efficiency, scalability, and effectiveness in carrying out attacks. AI enables automation of tasks like phishing, social engineering, and malware distribution, allowing attackers to target large numbers of victims simultaneously. Advanced techniques like deepfakes and adversarial attacks can bypass traditional security measures, making it difficult to detect or prevent such activities. For attackers, Black Hat AI provides a powerful toolkit for achieving their objectives with minimal effort.

Examples
One example of Black Hat AI is the use of deepfake technology to create realistic but fake videos or audio recordings, which can be used for fraud, misinformation, or defamation. Another example is adversarial attacks on machine learning models, where subtle input modifications cause the model to make incorrect predictions, such as misclassifying objects in autonomous driving systems. AI-powered phishing campaigns that generate personalized messages to trick victims into revealing sensitive information are also a common use of Black Hat AI.

Applications
Black Hat AI is applied in various malicious activities, including cyberattacks, fraud, and disinformation campaigns. In cybersecurity, it is used to develop sophisticated malware, automate hacking attempts, and exploit system vulnerabilities. In financial fraud, AI is used to create fake identities, manipulate stock markets, or conduct large-scale scams. In the realm of misinformation, AI-generated content is used to spread fake news, manipulate public opinion, or interfere in elections.

These applications highlight the dual-use nature of AI, where the same technologies that drive innovation can also be weaponized.

Industry
Black Hat AI impacts industries across the board, particularly those reliant on digital infrastructure and AI technologies. The cybersecurity industry is at the forefront of combating AI-driven threats, developing tools to detect and prevent attacks. Financial institutions face risks from AI-powered fraud and market manipulation. The media and entertainment industry grapples with the spread of deepfakes and misinformation. Governments and defense organizations are also affected, as Black Hat AI can be used for espionage, cyber warfare, and political manipulation. The growing prevalence of these threats has spurred investment in defensive AI technologies and ethical AI frameworks.

Summary
Black Hat AI represents the dark side of artificial intelligence, where advanced technologies are used for malicious purposes. It leverages AI techniques to carry out cyberattacks, fraud, and disinformation campaigns, posing significant risks to security, privacy, and trust. While it offers efficiency and scalability for attackers, it also creates challenges for detection, prevention, and regulation. The rise of Black Hat AI underscores the need for robust security measures, ethical AI development, and international cooperation to mitigate its impact and ensure the responsible use of AI technologies.

Black-Scholes Model (AI-enhanced)

Definition
The Black-Scholes Model is a mathematical framework used to calculate the theoretical price of financial options, such as call and put options. Originally developed in 1973 by Fischer Black, Myron Scholes, and Robert Merton, the model revolutionized the field of financial derivatives. When enhanced with artificial intelligence, the Black-Scholes Model leverages machine learning and data-driven techniques to improve accuracy, adapt to market conditions, and handle complex scenarios that traditional models struggle with.

Key Components
The traditional Black-Scholes Model relies on key inputs such as the current price of the underlying asset, the strike price of the option, the time to expiration, the risk-free interest rate, and the volatility of the asset. In its AI-enhanced version, additional components include machine learning algorithms, large datasets of historical market data, and real-time market feeds. AI techniques such as neural networks, reinforcement learning, and natural language processing are used to refine volatility estimates, predict market trends, and incorporate non-traditional data sources like news sentiment or social media activity.

Benefits
The AI-enhanced Black-Scholes Model offers several advantages over the traditional model. It improves pricing accuracy by incorporating real-time data and adapting to changing market conditions. AI techniques can capture complex patterns and nonlinear relationships that the original model cannot, leading to better predictions. Additionally, the AI-enhanced model can process unstructured data, such as news articles or social media posts, to provide a more comprehensive view of market dynamics. This makes it a powerful tool for traders, investors, and financial institutions seeking to optimize their strategies.

Examples
An example of the AI-enhanced Black-Scholes Model is its use in high-frequency trading, where algorithms analyze real-time market data to adjust option prices dynamically. Another example is in risk management, where AI-enhanced models predict potential market shocks and adjust hedging strategies accordingly. Financial institutions also use AI-enhanced models to incorporate alternative data, such as geopolitical events or macroeconomic indicators, into their pricing and trading decisions.

Applications
The AI-enhanced Black-Scholes Model is widely used in the financial industry for options pricing, risk management, and trading strategies. Investment banks use it to price complex derivatives and manage portfolios. Hedge funds leverage it for algorithmic trading and arbitrage opportunities. Insurance companies apply it to price financial products and assess risk. The model is also used in academic research to study market behavior and develop new financial theories. Its ability to integrate AI makes it particularly valuable in volatile or rapidly changing markets.

Industry
The AI-enhanced Black-Scholes Model is widely adopted in the financial industry, particularly by investment banks, hedge funds, and asset management firms. These institutions use it to gain a competitive edge in pricing, trading, and risk management. The growing availability of data and advancements in AI technology have further accelerated its adoption. However, the model also raises regulatory and ethical questions, particularly regarding its use in high-frequency trading and its potential impact on market stability.

Summary
The AI-enhanced Black-Scholes Model represents a significant evolution of the traditional options pricing framework, integrating machine learning and data-driven techniques to improve accuracy and adaptability. It is widely used in the financial industry for pricing, trading, and risk management, offering benefits such as real-time analysis and the ability to process complex data. However, challenges related to transparency, bias, and computational requirements must be addressed to ensure its responsible use. As AI continues to advance, the AI-enhanced Black-Scholes Model will play an increasingly important role in shaping the future of financial markets.

Bleeding-Edge AI

Definition
Bleeding-Edge AI refers to the most advanced and experimental developments in artificial intelligence, often pushing the boundaries of what is technically possible. Unlike cutting-edge AI, which represents the latest widely adopted technologies, bleeding-edge AI is characterized by its novelty, high risk, and unproven nature. It often involves groundbreaking research, untested methodologies, and innovative applications that have not yet been fully validated or commercialized.

Key Components
Bleeding-Edge AI is built on emerging technologies and experimental approaches. Key components include advanced machine learning algorithms, such as quantum machine learning or neuromorphic computing, which mimic the human brain's neural architecture. It also leverages unconventional data sources, such as brain-computer interfaces or real-time environmental sensors. Additionally, bleeding-edge AI often involves interdisciplinary collaboration, combining AI with fields like biotechnology, nanotechnology, or quantum physics to explore new frontiers.

Benefits
Bleeding-Edge AI offers the potential for transformative breakthroughs that can revolutionize industries and solve previously intractable problems. It enables the exploration of new possibilities, such as creating AI systems with human-like reasoning or developing technologies that integrate seamlessly with biological systems. By pushing the limits of innovation, bleeding-edge AI can lead to significant advancements in science, medicine, and technology, paving the way for future applications that are currently unimaginable.

Examples
Examples of bleeding-edge AI include quantum AI, which uses quantum computing to solve complex problems exponentially faster than classical computers, and brain-computer interfaces that enable direct communication between the human brain and machines. Another example is AI-driven synthetic

biology, where AI designs new organisms or biological systems for medical or environmental applications. Autonomous AI systems that operate in extreme environments, such as deep space or deep oceans, also fall under this category.

Applications
Bleeding-Edge AI has the potential to transform a wide range of fields. In healthcare, it could enable personalized medicine through AI-designed drugs or real-time monitoring of biological processes. In environmental science, it could help address climate change by optimizing energy systems or designing carbon-capture technologies. In space exploration, it could power autonomous robots for planetary exploration or resource extraction. While many of these applications are still in the experimental stage, they represent the future of AI-driven innovation.

Industry
Bleeding-Edge AI is primarily driven by research institutions, tech giants, and startups focused on innovation. Companies like Google, IBM, and OpenAI invest heavily in exploring advanced AI technologies, while academic institutions and government agencies support foundational research. Industries such as healthcare, aerospace, and energy are particularly interested in the potential of bleeding-edge AI to solve complex problems. However, the high costs and risks associated with these technologies mean that their adoption is limited to organizations with significant resources and a high tolerance for uncertainty.

Summary
Bleeding-Edge AI represents the forefront of artificial intelligence research and development, characterized by its novelty, high risk, and transformative potential. It leverages emerging technologies and interdisciplinary approaches to explore new possibilities, from quantum computing to brain-computer interfaces. While it offers the promise of groundbreaking advancements, it also faces challenges related to funding, ethics, and safety. As the field continues to evolve, bleeding-edge AI will play a crucial role in shaping the future of technology and society, driving innovation in ways that are currently beyond our imagination.

Blended Learning in AI

Definition
Blended learning in the context of artificial intelligence refers to an educational approach that combines traditional teaching methods with AI-driven technologies to enhance the learning experience. This hybrid model integrates face-to-face instruction with online learning tools, leveraging AI to personalize education, optimize content delivery, and provide real-time feedback. Blended learning in AI aims to create a more flexible, efficient, and engaging learning environment tailored to individual needs.

Key Components
Blended learning in AI relies on several key components to function effectively. These include AI-powered learning management systems (LMS) that organize and deliver educational content, adaptive learning platforms that customize lessons based on student performance, and intelligent tutoring systems that provide personalized guidance. Data analytics tools are used to track student progress and identify areas for improvement. Additionally, natural language processing (NLP) and computer vision technologies enable interactive features like virtual assistants and automated grading systems.

Benefits
Blended learning in AI offers numerous benefits for both educators and learners. It provides personalized learning experiences by adapting content to individual strengths and weaknesses, improving engagement and retention. AI-driven tools enable real-time feedback, allowing students to address gaps in knowledge immediately. The flexibility of blended learning allows students to learn at their own pace, while educators can focus on facilitating discussions and providing mentorship.

Additionally, AI reduces administrative burdens by automating tasks like grading and attendance tracking, freeing up time for more meaningful interactions.

Examples
Examples of blended learning in AI include platforms like Coursera and Khan Academy, which use AI to recommend courses and tailor content to individual learners. Intelligent tutoring systems like Carnegie Learning provide personalized math instruction, while virtual assistants like IBM Watson Tutor offer real-time support to students. In classrooms, AI-powered tools like Gradescope automate grading, and platforms like Duolingo use adaptive learning to teach languages more effectively. These examples demonstrate how AI enhances traditional learning methods.

Applications
Blended learning in AI is applied across various educational settings, from K-12 schools to higher education and corporate training. In schools, it helps teachers manage diverse classrooms by providing personalized learning paths for students. In universities, it supports large-scale courses by automating administrative tasks and offering virtual office hours. In corporate training, AI-driven platforms deliver customized learning modules to employees, improving skill development and productivity. Blended learning is also used in lifelong learning and professional certification programs, making education more accessible and effective.

Industry
The blended learning industry is rapidly growing, driven by advancements in AI and the increasing demand for flexible, personalized education. EdTech companies like Coursera, Udacity, and Duolingo are leading the way, offering AI-enhanced platforms for learners worldwide. Traditional educational institutions are also adopting blended learning models to modernize their curricula and improve student outcomes. In the corporate sector, companies like LinkedIn Learning and Degreed use AI to deliver tailored training programs. The industry's growth is fueled by the need for scalable, cost-effective, and accessible education solutions.

Summary
Blended learning in AI represents a transformative approach to education, combining traditional teaching methods with AI-driven technologies to create personalized, flexible, and efficient learning experiences. It leverages tools like adaptive learning platforms, intelligent tutoring systems, and data analytics to enhance engagement and outcomes. While challenges related to cost, privacy, and adoption exist, the benefits of blended learning in AI are driving its widespread adoption across schools, universities, and corporations. As AI continues to evolve, blended learning will play a pivotal role in shaping the future of education, making learning more accessible and effective for all.

Blendshape AI

Definition
Blendshape AI refers to the application of artificial intelligence techniques to create, manipulate, and optimize blendshapes, which are digital models used in 3D animation to represent facial expressions and movements. Blendshapes, also known as morph targets, are a series of predefined facial poses that can be blended together to create complex expressions. AI enhances this process by automating the creation of blendshapes, improving their accuracy, and enabling real-time facial animation in applications like gaming, virtual reality, and film production.

Key Components
Blendshape AI relies on several key components to function effectively. These include machine learning algorithms that analyze facial motion data to generate realistic blendshapes, computer vision techniques that capture and process facial expressions from images or videos, and neural networks that predict and refine blendshape weights for smooth transitions. Additionally, AI-driven tools often integrate with 3D animation software to streamline workflows and provide real-time feedback. Data

inputs, such as motion capture data or video recordings, are essential for training AI models to produce accurate and expressive blendshapes.

Benefits
Blendshape AI offers significant benefits for animators and developers. It reduces the time and effort required to create detailed facial animations by automating repetitive tasks like blendshape generation and weight adjustment. AI enhances the realism of facial expressions by capturing subtle nuances and ensuring smooth transitions between poses. It also enables real-time animation, making it ideal for applications like virtual reality and live performances. By improving efficiency and quality, Blendshape AI allows creators to focus on storytelling and creativity rather than technical details.

Examples
Examples of Blendshape AI include tools like Adobe Character Animator, which uses AI to map facial expressions from a webcam to a 2D character in real time. In the gaming industry, AI-driven blendshape systems are used to create lifelike characters in titles like The Last of Us Part II and Cyberpunk 2077. Film studios like Pixar and Disney use AI to enhance facial animation in movies, ensuring characters convey emotions realistically. Virtual reality platforms also leverage Blendshape AI to create immersive experiences with responsive avatars.

Applications
Blendshape AI is widely used in industries that rely on facial animation. In gaming, it enables the creation of expressive characters that enhance player immersion. In film and television, it streamlines the animation process and improves the quality of visual effects. Virtual reality and augmented reality applications use Blendshape AI to create realistic avatars that respond to user expressions in real time. Additionally, it is used in virtual assistants and chatbots to provide more engaging and human-like interactions. The technology is also applied in medical simulations and training programs to create realistic patient avatars.

Industry
The Blendshape AI industry is driven by demand from gaming, film, and virtual reality sectors. Companies like Unity, Unreal Engine, and Autodesk are integrating AI tools into their animation software to streamline workflows and improve quality. Tech giants like Google and NVIDIA are investing in AI research to advance facial animation techniques. The growing popularity of virtual reality and augmented reality is also fueling innovation in Blendshape AI, as realistic avatars are essential for immersive experiences. As the technology matures, it is expected to play an increasingly important role in entertainment, education, and communication.

Summary
Blendshape AI represents a significant advancement in facial animation, leveraging artificial intelligence to automate and enhance the creation of realistic expressions. It is widely used in gaming, film, virtual reality, and other industries to improve efficiency, quality, and realism. While challenges related to data collection, accuracy, and integration exist, the benefits of Blendshape AI are driving its adoption across various applications. As AI technology continues to evolve, Blendshape AI will play a crucial role in shaping the future of digital animation and interactive experiences.

Blind Deconvolution in AI

Definition
Blind deconvolution is a computational technique used to recover an original signal or image from a blurred or distorted version without prior knowledge of the blurring function (also known as the point spread function). In the context of artificial intelligence, blind deconvolution leverages machine learning and deep learning algorithms to estimate both the original signal and the blurring function simultaneously. This technique is particularly useful in image processing, signal restoration, and computer vision, where precise recovery of data is critical.

Key Components
Blind deconvolution in AI involves several key components. The first is the input data, which is the observed blurred signal or image. The second is the algorithm, which typically includes neural networks or optimization techniques to estimate the original signal and the blurring function. Loss functions are used to measure the difference between the observed data and the reconstructed data, guiding the optimization process. Regularization techniques are often applied to prevent overfitting and ensure stable solutions. Additionally, training data, such as pairs of blurred and sharp images, may be used to improve the accuracy of the model.

Benefits
Blind deconvolution in AI offers several advantages. It enables the recovery of high-quality signals or images from degraded data, improving the clarity and usability of the information. This is particularly valuable in fields like medical imaging, astronomy, and photography, where precise data is essential. AI-driven blind deconvolution is more robust and adaptable than traditional methods, as it can handle complex and unknown blurring functions. It also reduces the need for manual intervention, making the process faster and more efficient.

Examples
An example of blind deconvolution in AI is its use in astronomy to enhance images of distant celestial objects captured by telescopes. In medical imaging, it is used to improve the resolution of MRI or CT scans, enabling better diagnosis and treatment planning. In photography, AI-driven blind deconvolution can restore sharpness to blurred images caused by camera shake or poor focus. Another example is in microscopy, where it enhances the clarity of images taken at high magnification.

Applications
Blind deconvolution in AI is applied in various fields where signal or image restoration is critical. In medical imaging, it improves the quality of diagnostic images, aiding in the detection of diseases and abnormalities. In astronomy, it enhances the resolution of telescope images, enabling the study of distant galaxies and celestial phenomena. In photography and videography, it restores sharpness to blurred images and videos. It is also used in microscopy, remote sensing, and forensic analysis to recover detailed information from degraded data.

Industry
The use of blind deconvolution in AI is growing across industries that rely on high-quality imaging and signal processing. In healthcare, companies are developing AI tools to enhance medical imaging for better diagnosis and treatment. In astronomy, research institutions and space agencies use AI-driven deconvolution to analyze telescope data. The photography and videography industry leverages this technology to improve image quality in cameras and editing software. Additionally, AI startups and tech giants are investing in advanced deconvolution algorithms for applications in microscopy, remote sensing, and autonomous vehicles.

Summary
Blind deconvolution in AI is a powerful technique for recovering original signals or images from blurred or distorted data without prior knowledge of the blurring function. It leverages machine learning and deep learning to estimate both the signal and the blurring function simultaneously, offering significant benefits in fields like medical imaging, astronomy, and photography. While challenges related to computational complexity, ambiguity, and data availability exist, the technology is driving innovation across industries. As AI continues to advance, blind deconvolution will play an increasingly important role in enhancing the quality and usability of visual and signal data.

Blind Signal Separation (BSS)

Definition
Blind Signal Separation (BSS) is a computational technique used to separate individual source signals

from a mixture of signals without prior knowledge of the sources or the mixing process. It is widely used in signal processing and artificial intelligence to extract meaningful information from complex, overlapping signals. BSS is particularly valuable in scenarios where multiple signals are combined, such as audio recordings, sensor data, or communication channels, and the goal is to isolate each source for analysis or further processing.

Key Components
Blind Signal Separation relies on several key components to function effectively. The input is a mixture of signals, often captured by sensors or microphones. The algorithm, which may include techniques like Independent Component Analysis (ICA), Non-Negative Matrix Factorization (NMF), or deep learning models, processes the mixed signals to estimate the original sources. Statistical properties of the signals, such as independence or sparsity, are used to guide the separation process. Additionally, preprocessing steps like noise reduction and dimensionality reduction are often applied to improve the accuracy of the results.

Benefits
Blind Signal Separation offers several advantages in signal processing and AI. It enables the extraction of individual signals from complex mixtures, improving the clarity and usability of the data. This is particularly useful in applications like speech enhancement, where separating overlapping voices is critical. BSS reduces the need for prior knowledge about the sources or the mixing process, making it a versatile and adaptive tool. It also enhances the performance of downstream tasks, such as speech recognition, by providing cleaner and more focused input data.

Examples
An example of Blind Signal Separation is its use in the "cocktail party problem," where it separates individual voices from a noisy room full of conversations. In electroencephalography (EEG), BSS is used to isolate brain activity signals from noise and artifacts. In telecommunications, it helps separate overlapping signals in wireless communication channels. Another example is in music processing, where BSS separates individual instruments or vocals from a mixed audio track.

Applications
Blind Signal Separation is applied in various fields where signal extraction is critical. In audio processing, it is used for speech enhancement, noise reduction, and music source separation. In biomedical engineering, it helps analyze EEG, ECG, and other physiological signals by removing noise and artifacts. In telecommunications, it improves signal clarity in wireless and optical communication systems. BSS is also used in radar and sonar systems to separate target signals from background noise, as well as in financial data analysis to extract meaningful patterns from mixed signals.

Industry
The use of Blind Signal Separation is growing across industries that rely on signal processing and data analysis. In telecommunications, companies use BSS to enhance signal clarity and improve network performance. In healthcare, it is applied to analyze biomedical signals for diagnosis and monitoring. The audio and music industry leverages BSS for applications like noise cancellation and music remixing. Additionally, AI startups and research institutions are developing advanced BSS algorithms for applications in autonomous vehicles, robotics, and financial analysis.

Summary
Blind Signal Separation is a powerful technique for extracting individual source signals from mixed data without prior knowledge of the sources or the mixing process. It leverages statistical and machine learning methods to improve the clarity and usability of signals in applications like audio processing, biomedical engineering, and telecommunications. While challenges related to computational complexity, noise, and non-stationary signals exist, BSS is driving innovation across industries. As AI and signal processing technologies continue to advance, Blind Signal Separation will play an increasingly important role in extracting meaningful information from complex data.

Blind Source Separation (BSS)

Blind Source Separation (BSS) is a computational technique used to separate individual source signals from a mixture of signals without prior knowledge of the sources or the mixing process. It is a fundamental tool in signal processing and artificial intelligence, enabling the extraction of meaningful information from complex, overlapping signals. BSS is widely applied in scenarios where multiple signals are combined, such as audio recordings, sensor data, or communication channels, and the goal is to isolate each source for analysis or further processing.

Key Components
Blind Source Separation relies on several key components to function effectively. The input is a mixture of signals, often captured by sensors, microphones, or other recording devices. The algorithm, which may include techniques like Independent Component Analysis (ICA), Non-Negative Matrix Factorization (NMF), or deep learning models, processes the mixed signals to estimate the original sources. Statistical properties of the signals, such as independence, sparsity, or non-Gaussianity, are used to guide the separation process. Preprocessing steps like noise reduction, dimensionality reduction, and normalization are often applied to improve the accuracy and stability of the results.

Benefits
Blind Source Separation offers several advantages in signal processing and AI. It enables the extraction of individual signals from complex mixtures, improving the clarity and usability of the data. This is particularly useful in applications like speech enhancement, where separating overlapping voices is critical. BSS reduces the need for prior knowledge about the sources or the mixing process, making it a versatile and adaptive tool. It also enhances the performance of downstream tasks, such as speech recognition, by providing cleaner and more focused input data. Additionally, BSS can handle real-world scenarios where the mixing process is unknown or time-varying.

Examples
An example of Blind Source Separation is its use in the "cocktail party problem," where it separates individual voices from a noisy room full of conversations. In electroencephalography (EEG), BSS is used to isolate brain activity signals from noise and artifacts. In telecommunications, it helps separate overlapping signals in wireless communication channels. Another example is in music processing, where BSS separates individual instruments or vocals from a mixed audio track. In financial data analysis, BSS is used to extract meaningful patterns from mixed signals in stock market data.

Applications
Blind Source Separation is applied in various fields where signal extraction is critical. In audio processing, it is used for speech enhancement, noise reduction, and music source separation. In biomedical engineering, it helps analyze EEG, ECG, and other physiological signals by removing noise and artifacts. In telecommunications, it improves signal clarity in wireless and optical communication systems. BSS is also used in radar and sonar systems to separate target signals from background noise. In financial data analysis, it extracts meaningful patterns from mixed signals in stock market data. Additionally, BSS is applied in image processing, remote sensing, and machine learning for feature extraction and data preprocessing.

Industry
The use of Blind Source Separation is growing across industries that rely on signal processing and data analysis. In telecommunications, companies use BSS to enhance signal clarity and improve network performance. In healthcare, it is applied to analyze biomedical signals for diagnosis and monitoring. The audio and music industry leverages BSS for applications like noise cancellation and music remixing. In finance, it is used to analyze mixed signals in stock market data for trend prediction. Additionally, AI startups and research institutions are developing advanced BSS algorithms for applications in autonomous vehicles, robotics, and environmental monitoring.

Summary

Blind Source Separation is a powerful technique for extracting individual source signals from mixed data without prior knowledge of the sources or the mixing process. It leverages statistical and machine learning methods to improve the clarity and usability of signals in applications like audio processing, biomedical engineering, and telecommunications. While challenges related to computational complexity, noise, and non-stationary signals exist, BSS is driving innovation across industries. As AI and signal processing technologies continue to advance, Blind Source Separation will play an increasingly important role in extracting meaningful information from complex data.

Blockchain AI

Definition

Blockchain AI refers to the integration of artificial intelligence (AI) technologies with blockchain systems to enhance their functionality, security, and efficiency. Blockchain, a decentralized and distributed ledger technology, provides a transparent and immutable record of transactions, while AI brings advanced data analysis, automation, and decision-making capabilities. Together, they create a powerful synergy that can revolutionize industries by enabling secure, intelligent, and autonomous systems.

Key Components

Blockchain AI systems consist of several key components. The blockchain component provides a decentralized ledger for recording transactions and ensuring data integrity through cryptographic techniques. Smart contracts, which are self-executing programs on the blockchain, enable automated and trustless transactions. The AI component includes machine learning algorithms, neural networks, and data analytics tools that process and analyze data stored on or off the blockchain. Integration layers, such as APIs and middleware, facilitate communication between blockchain and AI systems. Additionally, consensus mechanisms like Proof of Work (PoW) or Proof of Stake (PoS) ensure the security and reliability of the blockchain network.

Benefits

Blockchain AI offers numerous benefits across various domains. It enhances data security and privacy by leveraging blockchain's immutability and encryption, while AI provides advanced threat detection and fraud prevention. The combination enables transparent and auditable AI decision-making, addressing concerns about bias and accountability. Blockchain AI also improves efficiency by automating processes through smart contracts and AI-driven optimization. Additionally, it enables decentralized AI models, where data and computation are distributed across a network, reducing reliance on centralized entities and promoting fairness.

Examples

Examples of Blockchain AI include decentralized marketplaces that use AI to match buyers and sellers while ensuring secure transactions on the blockchain. In healthcare, Blockchain AI systems enable secure sharing of patient data for AI-driven diagnostics while maintaining privacy. Supply chain solutions use Blockchain AI to track goods and optimize logistics using predictive analytics. Another example is decentralized finance (DeFi) platforms that leverage AI for risk assessment and automated trading. These applications demonstrate the potential of Blockchain AI to create intelligent and secure systems.

Applications

Blockchain AI is applied in various industries to solve complex problems. In finance, it powers decentralized lending platforms, fraud detection systems, and automated trading algorithms. In healthcare, it enables secure data sharing for AI-driven research and personalized medicine. Supply chain management benefits from Blockchain AI through real-time tracking, predictive analytics, and automated compliance. In energy, it supports decentralized energy grids and smart contracts for peer-to-peer energy trading. Other applications include identity verification, intellectual property protection, and autonomous IoT devices.

Industry
The Blockchain AI industry is rapidly evolving, driven by advancements in both technologies and growing demand for secure, intelligent systems. Companies like IBM, Microsoft, and Accenture are investing in Blockchain AI solutions for industries like finance, healthcare, and supply chain. Startups are exploring innovative use cases, such as decentralized AI marketplaces and autonomous organizations. Governments and regulatory bodies are also exploring Blockchain AI for applications like digital identity and public service delivery. As the technology matures, it is expected to play a transformative role in shaping the future of decentralized and intelligent systems.

Summary
Blockchain AI represents the convergence of two transformative technologies, combining the security and transparency of blockchain with the intelligence and automation of AI. It offers significant benefits in terms of data security, efficiency, and decentralized decision-making, making it applicable across industries like finance, healthcare, and supply chain. While challenges related to scalability, energy consumption, and complexity exist, the potential of Blockchain AI to create secure, intelligent, and autonomous systems is immense. As both technologies continue to advance, Blockchain AI will play a pivotal role in driving innovation and addressing real-world challenges.

Blockchain Consensus Algorithms in AI

Definition
Blockchain consensus algorithms are protocols that ensure all participants in a decentralized network agree on the state of the ledger, enabling trust and security without a central authority. When integrated with artificial intelligence (AI), these algorithms can enhance decision-making, optimize network performance, and enable intelligent automation in blockchain systems. AI can improve consensus mechanisms by analyzing network data, predicting malicious behavior, and optimizing resource allocation, making blockchain networks more efficient, secure, and scalable.

Key Components
Blockchain consensus algorithms in AI consist of several key components. The consensus mechanism itself, such as Proof of Work (PoW), Proof of Stake (PoS), or Delegated Proof of Stake (DPoS), ensures agreement among network participants. AI components, including machine learning models and data analytics tools, analyze network behavior, detect anomalies, and optimize consensus parameters. Smart contracts, which are self-executing programs on the blockchain, can incorporate AI logic to automate decision-making. Additionally, cryptographic techniques ensure data integrity and security, while network nodes participate in the consensus process by validating transactions and blocks.

Benefits
Integrating AI with blockchain consensus algorithms offers several benefits. AI can enhance the efficiency of consensus mechanisms by reducing energy consumption and improving transaction throughput. It can detect and prevent malicious activities, such as double-spending or Sybil attacks, by analyzing network behavior in real time. AI-driven optimization can adapt consensus parameters dynamically based on network conditions, improving scalability and performance. Additionally, AI can enable predictive maintenance of blockchain networks, identifying potential issues before they disrupt operations. These benefits make blockchain networks more robust, secure, and adaptable to changing demands.

Examples
Examples of AI-enhanced blockchain consensus algorithms include AI-driven Proof of Stake (AI-PoS), where machine learning models optimize validator selection and reward distribution. In Proof of Work

(PoW), AI can predict optimal mining strategies to reduce energy consumption. Another example is Federated Learning-based consensus, where AI models are trained across decentralized nodes without sharing raw data, ensuring privacy and efficiency. AI is also used in Byzantine Fault Tolerance (BFT) algorithms to detect and mitigate malicious nodes in real time. These examples demonstrate how AI can improve the performance and security of consensus mechanisms.

Applications
Blockchain consensus algorithms enhanced by AI are applied in various domains. In decentralized finance (DeFi), they improve transaction speed and security, enabling scalable and efficient financial systems. In supply chain management, AI-optimized consensus ensures transparent and tamper-proof tracking of goods. Healthcare systems use AI-driven consensus to securely share patient data across decentralized networks. Energy grids leverage AI-enhanced consensus for peer-to-peer energy trading and grid management. Other applications include voting systems, digital identity management, and autonomous IoT networks, where secure and efficient consensus is critical.

Industry
The integration of AI with blockchain consensus algorithms is gaining traction across industries. Companies like IBM, Microsoft, and ConsenSys are exploring AI-driven solutions to improve blockchain performance and security. Startups are developing innovative consensus mechanisms that leverage AI for applications like decentralized finance, supply chain, and healthcare. Governments and regulatory bodies are also investigating AI-enhanced blockchain for public services, such as digital identity and voting systems. As the technology matures, it is expected to play a transformative role in enabling secure, efficient, and intelligent decentralized systems.

Summary
Blockchain consensus algorithms enhanced by AI represent a powerful convergence of technologies, combining the security and decentralization of blockchain with the intelligence and adaptability of AI. They offer significant benefits in terms of efficiency, security, and scalability, making them applicable across industries like finance, healthcare, and supply chain. While challenges related to computational resources, scalability, and ethical considerations exist, the potential of AI-enhanced consensus algorithms to revolutionize decentralized systems is immense. As both blockchain and AI technologies continue to evolve, their integration will play a pivotal role in shaping the future of secure and intelligent networks.

Block Cipher AI

Definition
Block Cipher AI refers to the application of artificial intelligence techniques to enhance the design, analysis, and implementation of block ciphers, which are symmetric key encryption algorithms used to secure data. Block ciphers encrypt fixed-size blocks of plaintext into ciphertext, providing confidentiality and integrity for sensitive information. AI can optimize block cipher performance, detect vulnerabilities, and improve resistance to cryptographic attacks, making encryption systems more robust and efficient.

Key Components
Block Cipher AI systems consist of several key components. The block cipher itself, such as AES (Advanced Encryption Standard) or DES (Data Encryption Standard), performs the encryption and decryption processes. AI components, including machine learning models and optimization algorithms, analyze the cipher's structure, detect patterns, and identify potential weaknesses. Training data, such as plaintext-ciphertext pairs or attack simulations, is used to train AI models. Cryptographic techniques, such as substitution-permutation networks and key scheduling, ensure the security of the encryption process. Additionally, hardware and software implementations of block ciphers are optimized using AI-driven techniques.

Benefits

Block Cipher AI offers several advantages in the field of cryptography. It enhances the security of block ciphers by identifying and mitigating vulnerabilities, such as differential or linear cryptanalysis. AI can optimize key scheduling and substitution boxes (S-boxes) to improve resistance to attacks. It also accelerates the design and testing of new block ciphers by automating complex analysis tasks. Additionally, AI-driven optimization can improve the performance of block ciphers in terms of speed and resource efficiency, making them suitable for real-time applications and constrained environments like IoT devices.

Examples

Examples of Block Cipher AI include the use of machine learning to analyze the security of AES against side-channel attacks, where AI models detect patterns in power consumption or timing data to infer encryption keys. Another example is the optimization of S-boxes using genetic algorithms to enhance the nonlinearity and resistance of block ciphers. AI is also used to automate the cryptanalysis of block ciphers, identifying weaknesses in newly proposed algorithms. These examples demonstrate how AI can enhance both the security and efficiency of block ciphers.

Applications

Block Cipher AI is applied in various domains where data security is critical. In cybersecurity, it strengthens encryption systems used to protect sensitive information, such as financial transactions and personal data. In IoT, AI-optimized block ciphers ensure secure communication between devices with limited computational resources. Blockchain systems use block ciphers to secure transactions and smart contracts, with AI enhancing their resistance to attacks. Military and government applications leverage Block Cipher AI to protect classified information and communications. Additionally, AI-driven block ciphers are used in secure messaging apps, cloud storage, and digital rights management systems.

Industry

The integration of AI with block ciphers is gaining traction in industries that prioritize data security. Cybersecurity companies are developing AI-driven tools to analyze and optimize encryption algorithms. IoT manufacturers are adopting AI-enhanced block ciphers to secure communication between devices. Financial institutions and blockchain platforms use Block Cipher AI to protect transactions and sensitive data. Governments and defense organizations invest in AI-driven cryptography to safeguard national security. As the demand for secure and efficient encryption grows, Block Cipher AI is expected to play a key role in shaping the future of cryptography.

Summary

Block Cipher AI represents the convergence of cryptography and artificial intelligence, enhancing the security, efficiency, and robustness of block ciphers. It leverages machine learning and optimization techniques to analyze, design, and implement encryption algorithms, making them resistant to attacks and suitable for real-world applications. While challenges related to complexity, interpretability, and evolving threats exist, the potential of Block Cipher AI to revolutionize data security is significant. As both cryptography and AI technologies continue to advance, their integration will play a pivotal role in ensuring the confidentiality and integrity of sensitive information.

Block Matching Algorithm

Definition

A Block Matching Algorithm is a computational technique used in image and video processing to identify similar blocks of pixels between frames or within a single frame. It is commonly employed in motion estimation, video compression, and object tracking. The algorithm works by dividing an image or video frame into smaller blocks and searching for the best match for each block in a reference frame or region. This process is essential for tasks like video encoding, where it helps reduce redundancy and improve compression efficiency.

Key Components
The Block Matching Algorithm consists of several key components. The input is typically a sequence of video frames or a pair of images. The algorithm divides the current frame into smaller blocks, often of fixed size, and searches for matching blocks in the reference frame. A search strategy, such as exhaustive search or diamond search, determines how the algorithm explores the reference frame to find the best match. A similarity metric, such as Mean Absolute Difference (MAD) or Sum of Absolute Differences (SAD), quantifies the match quality between blocks. The output is a motion vector for each block, indicating its displacement relative to the reference frame.

Benefits
The Block Matching Algorithm offers several advantages in image and video processing. It enables efficient motion estimation, which is critical for video compression standards like MPEG and H.264. By reducing redundancy between frames, it significantly improves compression ratios and reduces storage and bandwidth requirements. The algorithm is also useful for object tracking and video stabilization, as it can identify and follow moving objects across frames. Additionally, its simplicity and adaptability make it suitable for real-time applications and hardware implementations.

Examples
An example of the Block Matching Algorithm is its use in video compression, where it identifies similar blocks between consecutive frames to encode only the differences, reducing file size. In video stabilization, the algorithm tracks motion vectors to smooth out camera shakes. Another example is in medical imaging, where it aligns images from different modalities, such as MRI and CT scans, for accurate diagnosis. In robotics, the algorithm is used for motion detection and navigation by analyzing changes in video feeds.

Applications
The Block Matching Algorithm is widely used in various applications. In video compression, it is a core component of standards like MPEG, H.264, and HEVC, enabling efficient storage and streaming of video content. In video stabilization, it helps remove unwanted camera movements to produce smoother footage. In object tracking, it is used in surveillance systems, autonomous vehicles, and robotics to detect and follow moving objects. In medical imaging, it aligns images for accurate analysis and diagnosis. Additionally, it is used in computer vision tasks like motion analysis, 3D reconstruction, and augmented reality.

Industry
The Block Matching Algorithm is widely adopted in industries that rely on video processing and computer vision. In the entertainment industry, it is used for video compression and editing tools. In healthcare, it supports medical imaging systems for diagnosis and treatment planning. In robotics and autonomous vehicles, it enables motion detection and navigation. Surveillance and security systems use the algorithm for object tracking and activity recognition. The growing demand for video content and real-time processing ensures the continued relevance of the Block Matching Algorithm across industries.

Summary
The Block Matching Algorithm is a fundamental technique in image and video processing, enabling motion estimation, video compression, and object tracking. It divides frames into blocks and searches for matches in reference frames, using similarity metrics to quantify match quality. While challenges related to computational complexity, accuracy, and noise exist, the algorithm's simplicity and efficiency make it a valuable tool for real-world applications. As video processing and computer vision technologies continue to advance, the Block Matching Algorithm will remain a critical component in enabling efficient and accurate analysis of visual data.

Block Neural Networks

Definition
Block Neural Networks (BNNs) are a type of neural network architecture that organizes neurons into modular blocks or sub-networks, each responsible for specific tasks or functions. These blocks can be interconnected in various ways to create complex and scalable models. BNNs are designed to improve the efficiency, interpretability, and flexibility of neural networks by breaking down the learning process into smaller, more manageable components. This modular approach allows for easier customization, parallel processing, and reuse of network components across different tasks.

Key Components
Block Neural Networks consist of several key components. The basic building blocks are individual sub-networks or modules, each designed to perform a specific function, such as feature extraction, classification, or regression. These blocks are interconnected through predefined or learned connections, allowing information to flow between them. The architecture may include skip connections, which bypass certain blocks to improve gradient flow and training stability. Training algorithms, such as backpropagation, are used to optimize the parameters of each block. Additionally, BNNs often incorporate techniques like weight sharing and block pruning to enhance efficiency and reduce redundancy.

Benefits
Block Neural Networks offer several advantages over traditional neural network architectures. Their modular design improves interpretability, as each block can be analyzed independently to understand its role in the overall network. BNNs are highly scalable, as new blocks can be added or removed without disrupting the entire network. They enable parallel processing, as different blocks can operate simultaneously, reducing training and inference times. The modular approach also facilitates transfer learning, where pre-trained blocks can be reused for new tasks, saving time and computational resources. Additionally, BNNs are more flexible and adaptable, making them suitable for a wide range of applications.

Examples
An example of Block Neural Networks is their use in image recognition, where different blocks are responsible for extracting low-level features (e.g., edges) and high-level features (e.g., shapes). In natural language processing, BNNs can be used to separate tasks like tokenization, embedding, and sentiment analysis into distinct blocks. Another example is in autonomous systems, where separate blocks handle perception, decision-making, and control. These examples demonstrate how BNNs can simplify complex tasks by dividing them into smaller, specialized components.

Applications
Block Neural Networks are applied in various domains that require modular and scalable solutions. In computer vision, they are used for tasks like object detection, segmentation, and image classification. In natural language processing, they enable efficient text analysis, machine translation, and sentiment analysis. In robotics, BNNs facilitate the integration of perception, planning, and control modules. They are also used in healthcare for medical image analysis and diagnosis, as well as in finance for fraud detection and risk assessment. The modular design of BNNs makes them suitable for applications requiring customization and adaptability.

Industry
The adoption of Block Neural Networks is growing across industries that require modular and scalable AI solutions. In technology, companies like Google and Microsoft use BNNs for image and speech recognition systems. In healthcare, they are applied to medical imaging and diagnostic tools. The automotive industry leverages BNNs for autonomous driving systems, where modularity is essential for integrating perception and control. In finance, BNNs are used for fraud detection and algorithmic trading. As the demand for customizable and efficient AI solutions increases, BNNs are expected to play a significant role in shaping the future of AI applications.

Summary

Block Neural Networks are a modular and scalable neural network architecture that organizes neurons into functional blocks. They offer benefits such as improved interpretability, scalability, and flexibility, making them suitable for a wide range of applications in computer vision, natural language processing, robotics, and healthcare. While challenges related to design complexity, training efficiency, and interpretability exist, the modular approach of BNNs provides a powerful framework for building efficient and adaptable AI systems. As AI technologies continue to evolve, Block Neural Networks will remain a valuable tool for addressing complex real-world problems.

Block Truncation Coding (BTC)

Definition

Block Truncation Coding (BTC) is a lossy image compression technique that reduces the size of an image by dividing it into small blocks and quantizing the pixel values within each block. It preserves the essential statistical properties of the original image, such as mean and variance, while significantly reducing the amount of data required to represent the image. BTC is known for its simplicity, computational efficiency, and ability to maintain acceptable image quality, making it suitable for applications where storage and bandwidth are limited.

Key Components

Block Truncation Coding consists of several key components. The input is an image divided into non-overlapping blocks, typically of size 4x4 or 8x8 pixels. For each block, the mean and variance of the pixel values are calculated. The pixels are then quantized into two levels based on a threshold, often the mean value, creating a binary bitmap that represents whether each pixel is above or below the threshold. The mean and variance of each block, along with the binary bitmap, are stored as the compressed representation. During decompression, the image is reconstructed using the stored statistical properties and the binary bitmap.

Benefits

Block Truncation Coding offers several advantages in image compression. It is computationally efficient, requiring simple calculations for mean, variance, and quantization, making it suitable for real-time applications. BTC achieves significant compression ratios while maintaining acceptable image quality, particularly for images with low to moderate complexity. The technique is easy to implement and does not require complex transformations, such as those used in JPEG or wavelet-based compression. Additionally, BTC is adaptable and can be extended to include more quantization levels or incorporate additional features for improved performance.

Examples

An example of Block Truncation Coding is its use in medical imaging, where it compresses X-ray or MRI images for efficient storage and transmission while preserving diagnostic quality. In video surveillance, BTC is used to compress frames for real-time monitoring and storage. Another example is in document imaging, where it compresses scanned documents or faxes for archiving and transmission. These examples demonstrate how BTC balances compression efficiency with image quality in practical applications.

Applications

Block Truncation Coding is applied in various domains where image compression is essential. In medical imaging, it reduces the size of diagnostic images for efficient storage and sharing. In video surveillance, it compresses video frames to enable real-time monitoring and reduce storage requirements. In document imaging, it is used for compressing scanned documents, faxes, and other text-based images. BTC is also used in multimedia applications, such as image databases and online galleries, where efficient storage and retrieval are critical. Additionally, it is employed in embedded systems and IoT devices, where computational resources are limited.

Industry
Block Truncation Coding is widely used in industries that require efficient image compression. In healthcare, it is applied to medical imaging systems for storing and transmitting diagnostic images. In security and surveillance, it enables efficient storage and real-time processing of video feeds. The document imaging industry uses BTC for compressing scanned documents and faxes. In multimedia, it is used for managing image databases and online galleries. The simplicity and efficiency of BTC make it a popular choice for applications where computational resources are limited, such as embedded systems and IoT devices.

Summary
Block Truncation Coding is a simple and efficient lossy image compression technique that divides an image into blocks and quantizes pixel values based on statistical properties. It offers significant compression ratios while maintaining acceptable image quality, making it suitable for applications like medical imaging, video surveillance, and document archiving. While challenges related to image quality and complexity exist, BTC's computational efficiency and simplicity ensure its continued relevance in industries requiring efficient image compression. As image processing technologies evolve, BTC remains a valuable tool for balancing compression efficiency and image quality.

Bloom Filter AI

Definition
A Bloom Filter is a probabilistic data structure used to test whether an element is a member of a set. It is highly space-efficient and allows for fast membership queries, though it may produce false positives. When integrated with artificial intelligence (AI), Bloom Filters can enhance data processing, storage, and retrieval in AI systems. AI techniques can optimize the parameters of Bloom Filters, such as hash functions and filter size, to minimize false positives and improve performance. This combination is particularly useful in applications like caching, spell checking, and network security, where efficient data lookup is critical.

Key Components
Bloom Filter AI systems consist of several key components. The Bloom Filter itself is a bit array of fixed size, initialized to zero. Multiple hash functions map each input element to specific positions in the bit array, setting those bits to one. During a membership query, the same hash functions are applied to the query element, and the filter checks if all corresponding bits are set. AI components, such as machine learning models, optimize the hash functions, filter size, and other parameters to reduce false positives and improve efficiency. Training data, such as historical query patterns, is used to fine-tune the Bloom Filter for specific applications.

Benefits
Bloom Filter AI offers several advantages in data processing and storage. It provides extremely fast membership queries with constant time complexity, making it suitable for real-time applications. The space efficiency of Bloom Filters allows them to handle large datasets with minimal memory usage. AI optimization reduces the rate of false positives, improving the reliability of the filter. Additionally, Bloom Filters are easy to implement and can be integrated into various AI systems, such as recommendation engines, search algorithms, and network routers, to enhance performance and scalability.

Examples
An example of Bloom Filter AI is its use in web caching, where it quickly checks if a requested webpage is in the cache, reducing latency and server load. In spell-checking applications, Bloom Filters efficiently verify if a word exists in a dictionary. Another example is in network security, where Bloom Filters detect malicious URLs or IP addresses in real time. AI-enhanced Bloom Filters are also used in

distributed databases to reduce the need for costly inter-node communication during query processing. These examples demonstrate the versatility and efficiency of Bloom Filter AI.

Applications
Bloom Filter AI is applied in various domains where fast and efficient data lookup is essential. In web services, it is used for caching, content delivery, and duplicate detection. In natural language processing, it supports spell checking, autocomplete, and text filtering. In network security, it enables real-time detection of malicious activities, such as phishing or denial-of-service attacks. Distributed systems use Bloom Filters to optimize query processing and reduce communication overhead. Additionally, Bloom Filter AI is used in bioinformatics for genome sequence analysis and in IoT systems for efficient data aggregation and filtering.

Industry
The use of Bloom Filter AI is growing across industries that require efficient data processing and storage. In technology, companies like Google and Amazon use Bloom Filters for web caching and content delivery. Cybersecurity firms leverage Bloom Filters for real-time threat detection. The healthcare industry applies Bloom Filters in bioinformatics for genome analysis. IoT and telecommunications companies use Bloom Filters for efficient data aggregation and network optimization. As the demand for scalable and efficient data solutions increases, Bloom Filter AI is expected to play a significant role in shaping the future of data-intensive applications.

Summary
Bloom Filter AI combines the space efficiency and speed of Bloom Filters with the optimization capabilities of AI to enhance data processing and storage. It is widely used in applications like web caching, spell checking, network security, and distributed systems, where fast and efficient data lookup is critical. While challenges related to false positives, hash function design, and scalability exist, the benefits of Bloom Filter AI make it a valuable tool for handling large datasets and real-time queries. As AI and data processing technologies continue to evolve, Bloom Filter AI will remain a key component in enabling efficient and scalable solutions for data-intensive applications.

Bloom's Taxonomy AI

Definition

Bloom's Taxonomy AI refers to the application of artificial intelligence to enhance and operationalize Bloom's Taxonomy, a hierarchical framework used to classify educational learning objectives. The taxonomy, originally developed by Benjamin Bloom, categorizes learning into six levels: Remember, Understand, Apply, Analyze, Evaluate, and Create. AI technologies, such as natural language processing (NLP), machine learning, and adaptive learning systems, are used to design, assess, and personalize educational experiences based on these cognitive levels. Bloom's Taxonomy AI aims to improve learning outcomes by tailoring content, assessments, and feedback to individual learners' needs and abilities.

Key Components
Bloom's Taxonomy AI systems consist of several key components. The foundational framework is Bloom's Taxonomy itself, which defines the six cognitive levels of learning. AI technologies, such as NLP and machine learning, analyze educational content and learner interactions to classify tasks and assessments according to the taxonomy. Adaptive learning platforms use this classification to personalize learning paths, ensuring that students progress through the cognitive levels effectively. Data analytics tools track learner performance and provide insights to educators, enabling them to refine instructional strategies. Additionally, AI-driven assessment tools generate questions and tasks that align with specific levels of Bloom's Taxonomy, ensuring comprehensive evaluation of learning outcomes.

Benefits

Bloom's Taxonomy AI offers several advantages in education and training. It enables personalized learning by adapting content and assessments to individual learners' cognitive levels, improving engagement and retention. AI-driven tools provide real-time feedback, helping learners identify areas for improvement and reinforcing understanding. Educators benefit from data-driven insights into student performance, allowing them to tailor instruction and interventions. The integration of AI with Bloom's Taxonomy also supports the creation of more effective and diverse assessments, ensuring that learners are challenged at all cognitive levels. Additionally, it facilitates scalable and efficient education delivery, making high-quality learning accessible to a wider audience.

Examples

An example of Bloom's Taxonomy AI is its use in adaptive learning platforms like Khan Academy or Duolingo, where AI tailors lessons and quizzes to match learners' cognitive levels. In higher education, AI-powered tools analyze essays and assignments to assess whether students are achieving higher-order thinking skills, such as analysis or evaluation. Another example is in corporate training, where AI-driven systems design training programs that progress employees from basic knowledge retention to creative problem-solving. These examples demonstrate how Bloom's Taxonomy AI enhances learning experiences across different contexts.

Applications

Bloom's Taxonomy AI is applied in various educational and training settings. In K-12 education, it supports personalized learning and differentiated instruction, helping students master foundational knowledge and develop critical thinking skills. In higher education, it enhances curriculum design and assessment, ensuring that courses align with desired learning outcomes. Corporate training programs use Bloom's Taxonomy AI to develop employees' skills progressively, from basic competencies to advanced problem-solving. Online learning platforms leverage AI to create engaging and adaptive courses that cater to diverse learners. Additionally, AI-driven tools are used in teacher training to help educators design lessons that target all levels of Bloom's Taxonomy.

Industry

The adoption of Bloom's Taxonomy AI is growing across the education and training industries. EdTech companies like Coursera, Udemy, and Pearson are integrating AI into their platforms to enhance personalized learning and assessment. Schools and universities are adopting AI-driven tools to improve curriculum design and student outcomes. Corporate training providers use Bloom's Taxonomy AI to develop scalable and effective training programs. Governments and non-profits are also exploring AI-enhanced education solutions to address gaps in access and quality. As the demand for personalized and scalable education grows, Bloom's Taxonomy AI is expected to play a key role in shaping the future of learning.

Summary

Bloom's Taxonomy AI represents the integration of artificial intelligence with Bloom's Taxonomy to enhance educational experiences and outcomes. It leverages AI technologies to personalize learning, design effective assessments, and provide data-driven insights for educators. While challenges related to accuracy, fairness, and implementation exist, the benefits of Bloom's Taxonomy AI make it a powerful tool for improving education and training across various contexts. As AI and education technologies continue to evolve, Bloom's Taxonomy AI will play a pivotal role in creating more engaging, effective, and inclusive learning environments.

Blur Detection in AI

Definition

Blur Detection in AI refers to the use of artificial intelligence techniques to identify and quantify blur in images or videos. Blur can result from various factors, such as camera shake, incorrect focus, or motion during capture. AI-driven blur detection systems analyze visual data to determine the presence and extent of blur, enabling applications like image quality enhancement, autofocus correction, and content filtering. These systems leverage machine learning, computer vision, and deep learning to achieve high accuracy and efficiency in detecting and addressing blur-related issues.

Key Components

Blur Detection in AI systems consists of several key components. The input is an image or video frame that may contain blur. Preprocessing steps, such as noise reduction and edge detection, are often applied to enhance the input data. Machine learning models, including convolutional neural networks (CNNs), are trained to analyze visual features and classify regions as sharp or blurred. Feature extraction techniques, such as gradient analysis or frequency domain transformations, are used to quantify blur intensity. Post-processing steps may include generating blur maps, which visually represent the distribution of blur across the image, or applying corrective measures like deblurring algorithms.

Benefits

Blur Detection in AI offers several advantages in image and video processing. It improves image quality by identifying and correcting blur, enhancing visual clarity and detail. In photography and videography, AI-driven blur detection enables real-time autofocus adjustments, ensuring sharp and high-quality captures. It also supports content filtering by detecting and flagging low-quality or blurred images in applications like social media or e-commerce. Additionally, blur detection can be integrated into surveillance systems to ensure clear and usable footage. The automation of blur detection reduces the need for manual intervention, saving time and resources.

Examples

An example of Blur Detection in AI is its use in smartphone cameras, where AI algorithms detect blur and adjust focus or shutter speed in real time to capture sharp images. In video editing software, AI-driven blur detection identifies and corrects motion blur in footage. Another example is in medical imaging, where blur detection ensures the clarity of diagnostic images, such as X-rays or MRIs. In e-commerce, AI systems detect and filter out blurred product images to maintain high-quality listings. These examples demonstrate the versatility and effectiveness of blur detection in various applications.

Applications

Blur Detection in AI is applied in numerous domains where image and video quality are critical. In photography and videography, it enhances autofocus systems and post-processing tools, ensuring high-quality captures. In surveillance and security, it ensures clear and usable footage for monitoring and analysis. In medical imaging, it improves the clarity of diagnostic images, aiding in accurate diagnosis and treatment. E-commerce platforms use blur detection to filter out low-quality product images, enhancing user experience. Additionally, it is used in content moderation, where it detects and removes blurred or low-quality content from social media and online platforms.

Industry

The use of Blur Detection in AI is growing across industries that rely on high-quality visual data. In consumer electronics, companies like Apple, Samsung, and Sony integrate blur detection into smartphone cameras and imaging software. In healthcare, medical imaging companies use AI to ensure the clarity of diagnostic images. E-commerce platforms like Amazon and eBay leverage blur detection to maintain high-quality product listings. Surveillance and security companies use AI-driven blur detection to enhance the quality of video footage. As the demand for high-quality visual content increases, blur detection technologies are expected to play a key role in shaping the future of imaging and video processing.

Summary

Blur Detection in AI is a powerful tool for identifying and addressing blur in images and videos, enhancing visual quality and usability. It leverages machine learning and computer vision techniques to detect and quantify blur, enabling applications in photography, medical imaging, e-commerce, and surveillance. While challenges related to complexity, computational cost, and dataset availability exist, the benefits of blur detection make it a valuable asset in improving image and video quality. As AI and imaging technologies continue to advance, blur detection will remain a critical component in ensuring clear and high-quality visual content across industries.

Boilerplate Generation in AI

Definition
Boilerplate Generation in AI refers to the use of artificial intelligence to automatically create standardized or reusable text, code, or documentation templates. Boilerplate content is often repetitive and generic, such as legal disclaimers, software code snippets, or email templates. AI-driven boilerplate generation leverages natural language processing (NLP), machine learning, and generative models to produce high-quality, context-aware templates that save time and reduce errors. This technology is particularly useful in industries like software development, legal services, and content creation, where repetitive tasks are common.

Key Components
Boilerplate Generation in AI systems consists of several key components. The input is typically a set of requirements or context, such as a legal scenario, coding task, or content theme. NLP models analyze the input to understand the context and generate relevant text or code. Machine learning algorithms, including transformer-based models like GPT, are trained on large datasets of existing boilerplate content to learn patterns and structures. Templates and rules may be predefined to ensure consistency and compliance with industry standards. The output is a generated boilerplate text or code snippet that can be customized further by the user.

Benefits
Boilerplate Generation in AI offers several advantages. It significantly reduces the time and effort required to create repetitive content, allowing professionals to focus on more complex tasks. AI-generated boilerplate content is consistent and error-free, minimizing the risk of mistakes in legal documents, code, or communications. The technology can adapt to specific contexts, generating tailored templates that meet unique requirements. Additionally, it supports scalability, enabling organizations to handle large volumes of repetitive tasks efficiently. By automating boilerplate generation, AI enhances productivity and reduces operational costs.

Examples
An example of Boilerplate Generation in AI is its use in legal tech, where AI tools generate standard contracts, non-disclosure agreements, or terms of service documents based on user inputs. In software development, AI-powered tools like GitHub Copilot generate boilerplate code snippets for common programming tasks. Another example is in content creation, where AI generates email templates, press releases, or social media posts. These examples demonstrate how AI streamlines the creation of repetitive content across various domains.

Applications
Boilerplate Generation in AI is applied in numerous industries. In legal services, it automates the creation of contracts, agreements, and compliance documents. In software development, it generates code templates, API documentation, and configuration files. Content creators use AI to produce email templates, blog post outlines, and marketing materials. Customer support teams leverage AI to generate standardized responses for common queries. Additionally, AI-driven boilerplate generation is used in academic writing, where it helps create research paper templates or citation formats.

Industry
The adoption of Boilerplate Generation in AI is growing across industries that rely on repetitive content

creation. Legal tech companies like LawGeex and LegalSifter use AI to automate document drafting. Software companies leverage tools like GitHub Copilot to streamline coding tasks. Marketing and content creation platforms, such as Jasper and Copy.ai, use AI to generate templates for emails, blogs, and social media posts. Customer service platforms integrate AI to automate responses to common queries. As the demand for efficiency and scalability increases, Boilerplate Generation in AI is expected to play a significant role in transforming workflows across industries.

Summary
Boilerplate Generation in AI automates the creation of standardized text, code, or documentation, saving time and reducing errors. It leverages NLP and machine learning to produce context-aware templates for applications in legal services, software development, content creation, and customer support. While challenges related to accuracy, customization, and integration exist, the benefits of AI-driven boilerplate generation make it a valuable tool for enhancing productivity and scalability. As AI technologies continue to evolve, Boilerplate Generation will play an increasingly important role in streamlining repetitive tasks across industries.

Boolean Logic in AI

Definition
Boolean Logic in AI refers to the use of Boolean algebra, a branch of mathematics that deals with true/false values (1/0), to model decision-making and reasoning processes in artificial intelligence systems. Boolean Logic forms the foundation of many AI algorithms, enabling the representation of logical relationships, rules, and constraints. It is widely used in expert systems, rule-based systems, and search algorithms, where decisions are based on binary conditions and logical operations such as AND, OR, and NOT. Boolean Logic provides a simple yet powerful framework for building AI systems that require precise and deterministic reasoning.

Key Components
Boolean Logic in AI systems consists of several key components. The basic building blocks are Boolean variables, which can take on values of true (1) or false (0). Logical operators, such as AND, OR, NOT, XOR, and IF-THEN, are used to combine and manipulate these variables to form complex expressions. Rules and constraints are defined using Boolean expressions to guide decision-making. Inference engines in rule-based systems evaluate these expressions to derive conclusions or actions. Additionally, Boolean Logic is often integrated with other AI techniques, such as search algorithms and decision trees, to enhance reasoning capabilities.

Benefits
Boolean Logic in AI offers several advantages. It provides a clear and unambiguous framework for representing logical relationships, making it easy to understand and implement. Boolean Logic is computationally efficient, as it involves simple binary operations that can be executed quickly. It enables precise and deterministic reasoning, which is essential for applications like expert systems and decision support tools. Additionally, Boolean Logic is highly scalable, allowing complex systems to be built by combining simple logical rules. Its simplicity and versatility make it a foundational tool in AI development.

Examples
An example of Boolean Logic in AI is its use in expert systems, where rules like "IF temperature > 100 THEN alert = true" guide decision-making. In search algorithms, Boolean Logic is used to filter results based on conditions, such as "find all records WHERE age > 18 AND status = active." Another example is in digital circuits, where Boolean Logic forms the basis of hardware design for AI systems. These examples demonstrate how Boolean Logic enables precise and efficient reasoning in AI applications.

Applications
Boolean Logic in AI is applied in various domains that require logical reasoning and decision-making. In expert systems, it is used to model domain knowledge and provide recommendations or diagnoses. In database systems, Boolean Logic enables complex queries for data retrieval and analysis. In robotics, it guides decision-making processes, such as obstacle avoidance or task prioritization. Boolean Logic is also used in natural language processing to evaluate conditions in rule-based chatbots. Additionally, it is applied in hardware design for AI systems, where it forms the basis of digital logic circuits.

Industry
The use of Boolean Logic in AI is widespread across industries that require logical reasoning and decision-making. In healthcare, it powers expert systems for diagnosis and treatment recommendations. In finance, it enables rule-based systems for fraud detection and risk assessment. The technology industry uses Boolean Logic in database systems, search engines, and digital circuit design. Robotics and automation companies leverage Boolean Logic for decision-making in autonomous systems. As AI continues to evolve, Boolean Logic remains a foundational tool for building precise and efficient reasoning systems.

Summary
Boolean Logic in AI provides a simple yet powerful framework for modeling logical relationships and decision-making processes. It is widely used in expert systems, search algorithms, and rule-based systems, enabling precise and deterministic reasoning. While challenges related to complexity, scalability, and integration with other AI techniques exist, the benefits of Boolean Logic make it a foundational tool in AI development. As AI technologies continue to advance, Boolean Logic will remain a critical component in building systems that require clear and efficient reasoning.

Booster AI

Definition
Booster AI refers to artificial intelligence systems designed to enhance, optimize, or accelerate existing processes, technologies, or workflows. These systems act as "boosters" by leveraging AI techniques such as machine learning, natural language processing, and predictive analytics to improve efficiency, accuracy, and performance. Booster AI is applied across various domains, including business operations, healthcare, education, and technology, to augment human capabilities and drive innovation. It focuses on amplifying outcomes rather than replacing human input, making it a collaborative and supportive tool in decision-making and problem-solving.

Key Components
Booster AI systems consist of several key components. The core AI technologies include machine learning models, deep learning algorithms, and natural language processing tools that analyze data and generate insights. Data inputs, such as historical records, real-time feeds, or user interactions, provide the foundation for AI-driven enhancements. Integration layers, such as APIs or middleware, connect Booster AI with existing systems and workflows. User interfaces, such as dashboards or chatbots, enable seamless interaction between humans and AI. Additionally, feedback loops ensure continuous learning and improvement of the AI system over time.

Benefits
Booster AI offers numerous advantages across industries. It enhances productivity by automating repetitive tasks and optimizing workflows, allowing humans to focus on higher-value activities. It improves decision-making by providing data-driven insights and predictions, reducing errors and biases. Booster AI enables scalability, as it can handle large volumes of data and tasks without compromising performance. It also fosters innovation by identifying opportunities for improvement and suggesting novel solutions. By augmenting human capabilities, Booster AI creates a collaborative environment where humans and machines work together to achieve better outcomes.

Examples
An example of Booster AI is its use in customer service, where AI-powered chatbots handle routine inquiries, freeing up human agents to address complex issues. In healthcare, Booster AI analyzes patient data to assist doctors in diagnosing diseases and recommending treatments. In marketing, AI tools optimize ad campaigns by predicting customer behavior and personalizing content. Another example is in software development, where Booster AI generates code snippets or identifies bugs, accelerating the development process. These examples demonstrate how Booster AI enhances existing processes and workflows.

Applications
Booster AI is applied in various domains to improve efficiency and outcomes. In business operations, it automates tasks like data entry, inventory management, and financial forecasting. In healthcare, it assists with diagnostics, treatment planning, and patient monitoring. In education, Booster AI personalizes learning experiences and automates administrative tasks. In technology, it accelerates software development, enhances cybersecurity, and optimizes cloud computing resources. Additionally, Booster AI is used in creative industries, such as music and design, to generate ideas and streamline production processes.

Industry
The adoption of Booster AI is growing across industries that seek to enhance efficiency and innovation. In business, companies like Salesforce and HubSpot use AI to optimize customer relationship management and marketing. In healthcare, organizations like IBM Watson Health leverage AI to improve diagnostics and patient care. Educational platforms like Coursera and Khan Academy use AI to personalize learning experiences. Technology companies like Google and Microsoft integrate AI into their products to enhance functionality and user experience. As the demand for efficiency and innovation increases, Booster AI is expected to play a significant role in shaping the future of work and technology.

Summary
Booster AI represents the use of artificial intelligence to enhance and optimize existing processes, technologies, and workflows. It leverages machine learning, natural language processing, and predictive analytics to improve efficiency, accuracy, and decision-making. While challenges related to integration, data quality, and ethical concerns exist, the benefits of Booster AI make it a valuable tool for augmenting human capabilities and driving innovation. As AI technologies continue to evolve, Booster AI will play an increasingly important role in creating collaborative and efficient systems across industries.

Boosting

Definition
Boosting is an ensemble machine learning technique that combines multiple weak learners (models that perform slightly better than random guessing) to create a strong learner (a highly accurate model). It works by training models sequentially, where each new model focuses on correcting the errors made by the previous ones. Boosting assigns higher weights to misclassified data points, ensuring that subsequent models pay more attention to difficult cases. Popular boosting algorithms include AdaBoost, Gradient Boosting, and XGBoost. Boosting is widely used in classification and regression tasks, offering high accuracy and robustness.

Key Components
Boosting consists of several key components. The base learners are weak models, such as decision trees, that are trained on subsets of the data. The algorithm iteratively trains these models, adjusting the weights of misclassified data points to focus on harder cases. A loss function measures the error of each model, guiding the optimization process. The final model is a weighted sum of all the weak

learners, where models with better performance contribute more to the final prediction. Hyperparameters, such as learning rate and the number of iterations, control the behavior of the boosting process.

Benefits

Boosting offers several advantages in machine learning. It significantly improves model accuracy by combining multiple weak learners into a strong learner. Boosting is highly effective for complex datasets, as it focuses on correcting errors and capturing intricate patterns. It reduces bias and variance, leading to better generalization on unseen data. Boosting algorithms like XGBoost and LightGBM are computationally efficient and scalable, making them suitable for large datasets. Additionally, boosting is versatile and can be applied to both classification and regression tasks, as well as structured and unstructured data.

Examples

An example of boosting is its use in predicting customer churn, where an ensemble of decision trees identifies patterns in customer behavior to predict who is likely to leave. In healthcare, boosting algorithms analyze patient data to predict disease risk or treatment outcomes. Another example is in financial fraud detection, where boosting models identify unusual patterns in transaction data. These examples demonstrate how boosting improves predictive accuracy and robustness in real-world applications.

Applications

Boosting is applied in various domains that require high-accuracy predictions. In finance, it is used for credit scoring, fraud detection, and stock market prediction. In healthcare, boosting models assist in disease diagnosis, patient risk assessment, and drug discovery. In marketing, it predicts customer behavior and optimizes ad targeting. Boosting is also used in natural language processing for tasks like sentiment analysis and text classification. Additionally, it is applied in computer vision for object detection and image recognition.

Industry

The use of boosting is widespread across industries that rely on predictive analytics. In finance, companies like PayPal and Mastercard use boosting for fraud detection and risk assessment. In healthcare, organizations like IBM Watson Health leverage boosting for disease prediction and patient care. E-commerce platforms like Amazon use boosting for recommendation systems and customer behavior analysis. Technology companies like Google and Microsoft integrate boosting into their AI tools for tasks like search ranking and image recognition. As the demand for accurate and robust predictive models grows, boosting continues to play a critical role in shaping AI-driven solutions.

Summary

Boosting is a powerful ensemble machine learning technique that combines multiple weak learners to create a highly accurate and robust model. It focuses on correcting errors iteratively, making it effective for complex datasets and challenging tasks. While challenges related to computational cost, overfitting, and interpretability exist, the benefits of boosting make it a widely used tool in predictive analytics. As machine learning technologies continue to evolve, boosting will remain a key technique for achieving high-performance models across industries.

Bootstrap Aggregating

Definition

Bootstrap Aggregating commonly known as Bagging, is an ensemble learning method designed to enhance the accuracy and stability of machine learning models. It works by training multiple versions of the same model on different subsets of the training data and then aggregating their predictions to produce a more robust and reliable output.

Key components of Bagging include bootstrapping, which involves randomly sampling data with replacement to create multiple training datasets, and aggregation, where the predictions from multiple models are combined, often using majority voting for classification tasks or averaging for regression problems.

The benefits of Bagging include reduced variance, leading to better generalization and less overfitting. By training multiple models on different subsets of data, Bagging smooths out fluctuations caused by noisy or misleading training points. It also enhances model stability, ensuring that small changes in the training data do not drastically impact predictions. Additionally, Bagging is highly effective when applied to high-variance models such as decision trees.

Applications of Bagging are widespread in machine learning and artificial intelligence. It is particularly useful in tasks requiring high accuracy and resilience against overfitting, such as fraud detection, medical diagnosis, credit scoring, and image recognition. One of the most well-known implementations of Bagging is the Random Forest algorithm, which utilizes Bagging to construct an ensemble of decision trees for improved predictive performance.

Industries that benefit from Bagging include finance, where it enhances risk assessment and fraud detection, healthcare, where it improves diagnostic accuracy, e-commerce, where it aids in recommendation systems, and cybersecurity, where it strengthens anomaly detection and threat prediction.

In conclusion, Bootstrap Aggregating is a powerful ensemble learning technique that enhances the accuracy, stability, and generalization of machine learning models. By leveraging multiple versions of a model trained on diverse subsets of data, Bagging effectively reduces overfitting and improves prediction reliability. Despite its computational demands and interpretability challenges, it remains a fundamental approach in machine learning, widely used across various industries to optimize predictive performance.

Bootstrap Sampling

Definition

Bootstrap Sampling is a statistical resampling technique used to create multiple subsets of a dataset by randomly selecting data points with replacement. It allows for the estimation of a population parameter, model accuracy, or prediction stability without requiring additional data collection. This method is fundamental in machine learning and statistical modeling, particularly in scenarios where limited data is available.

Key components of bootstrap sampling include resampling with replacement, where new datasets are generated by repeatedly drawing from the original dataset, and iterative sampling, which involves creating multiple bootstrapped datasets to analyze statistical properties. Aggregation is another essential aspect, as results from multiple resampled datasets are combined to improve the reliability of estimates.

The benefits of bootstrap sampling include improved model generalization by reducing the risk of overfitting to a single dataset. It enhances the robustness of statistical estimates by providing confidence intervals and variance estimates for machine learning models. It also allows for effective model evaluation, particularly when the available dataset is too small for traditional cross-validation techniques. By generating multiple variations of the training set, bootstrap sampling ensures better approximation of real-world data distributions.

Applications of bootstrap sampling extend to various areas of artificial intelligence and statistics. It is widely used in ensemble learning techniques such as Bagging and Random Forests, where multiple models trained on different resampled datasets improve overall predictive accuracy. It plays a crucial role in hypothesis testing, bias correction, and uncertainty estimation in statistical modeling. In deep learning, it assists in estimating model performance when labeled data is limited.

Industries that benefit from bootstrap sampling include finance for risk assessment and portfolio optimization, healthcare for medical research and clinical decision-making, e-commerce for personalized recommendation systems, and cybersecurity for fraud detection and anomaly identification. It is also valuable in scientific research, where it aids in making data-driven conclusions when sample sizes are restricted.

In conclusion, bootstrap sampling is a powerful and widely used statistical technique that enhances model accuracy, provides reliable uncertainty estimates, and facilitates effective learning from limited data. By creating diverse training subsets, it helps in making robust predictions and improving generalization across various domains. Despite computational challenges and potential biases, it remains a fundamental tool in statistical modeling and machine learning, playing a crucial role in diverse applications and industries.

Bootstrapping in AI

Definition

Bootstrapping in AI refers to a resampling technique used to improve the accuracy and reliability of statistical estimates, machine learning models, and predictive algorithms. It involves drawing multiple samples from a dataset with replacement to generate diverse training subsets, allowing models to learn from variations in the data. This method is widely used in ensemble learning, uncertainty estimation, and model validation.

Key components of bootstrapping include resampling with replacement, where subsets of the original dataset are created, and iterative model training, where the same algorithm is trained on different sampled datasets. The aggregation process is also crucial, as it combines multiple trained models or statistical estimates to form a more robust final prediction.

The benefits of bootstrapping include improved model stability, as it reduces the influence of outliers and noisy data points by training multiple models. It enhances generalization, leading to better performance on unseen data. It also provides better estimation of confidence intervals, offering insights into the variability and reliability of model predictions. Additionally, bootstrapping is useful in small datasets where traditional validation methods might be insufficient.

Applications of bootstrapping span multiple areas in AI, such as ensemble learning methods like Bagging and Random Forests, where multiple models trained on bootstrapped datasets improve predictive performance. It is widely used in statistical machine learning for hypothesis testing, error estimation, and feature selection. It also plays a role in reinforcement learning, where it helps estimate value functions and policy improvements.

Industries that leverage bootstrapping include finance for risk assessment and stock market predictions, healthcare for disease classification and diagnostic accuracy, e-commerce for recommendation systems, and cybersecurity for anomaly detection and threat intelligence. It is also crucial in scientific research, where it is used for hypothesis validation and data-driven decision-making.

In conclusion, bootstrapping is a powerful resampling technique in AI that enhances model reliability, improves generalization, and provides valuable uncertainty estimates. By leveraging multiple variations of training data, it helps build more robust machine learning models and statistical estimates. Despite its computational intensity and potential bias risks, bootstrapping remains a fundamental approach in AI, widely applied across diverse industries to improve prediction accuracy and decision-making.

Bot Collaboration in AI

Definition

Bot Collaboration in AI refers to the interaction and coordination between multiple AI-driven bots to achieve a common goal or enhance efficiency in various tasks. These bots can work together in a distributed system, sharing information, learning from each other, and optimizing decision-making processes. This approach is widely used in automation, customer service, robotics, and complex problem-solving environments.

Key components of bot collaboration include communication protocols that enable bots to exchange information seamlessly, decentralized decision-making, where multiple bots work together without relying on a single controller, and learning mechanisms, where bots continuously improve their performance through shared knowledge and reinforcement learning. Coordination algorithms ensure that bots operate efficiently without redundancy or conflicts.

The benefits of bot collaboration include increased efficiency by distributing tasks among multiple bots, reducing response time and workload. It enhances adaptability by allowing bots to dynamically adjust their strategies based on real-time data. Scalability is another advantage, as new bots can be added to the system without significant changes to existing processes. Collaborative bots also improve accuracy by cross-verifying information and minimizing errors through consensus-based decision-making.

Applications of bot collaboration span various fields, including customer support, where multiple AI chatbots handle inquiries and escalate complex issues to human agents. In healthcare, collaborative bots assist in patient monitoring, diagnostics, and treatment recommendations. In supply chain management, AI bots coordinate logistics, inventory tracking, and delivery schedules. In cybersecurity, bot collaboration enhances threat detection by sharing information on potential security breaches across multiple systems.

Industries leveraging bot collaboration include e-commerce, where bots optimize inventory management and personalized recommendations. Finance benefits from collaborative AI bots in fraud detection and automated trading. Manufacturing uses bot collaboration for predictive maintenance, quality control, and process automation. Transportation and smart cities implement bot collaboration for traffic management, autonomous vehicle coordination, and infrastructure monitoring.

In conclusion, bot collaboration in AI is a transformative approach that enhances efficiency, scalability, and adaptability in various domains. By enabling multiple bots to work together, organizations can optimize workflows, improve accuracy, and automate complex processes. Despite challenges such as communication overhead, security risks, and decision conflicts, bot collaboration remains a fundamental aspect of modern AI applications, driving innovation across multiple industries.

Bot Containment Systems

Bot Containment Systems refer to security frameworks designed to control, restrict, and mitigate the actions of AI-powered bots, preventing them from engaging in unauthorized, harmful, or unintended behaviors. These systems are implemented to ensure that bots operate within predefined boundaries, safeguarding data integrity, cybersecurity, and overall system stability.

Key components of bot containment systems include monitoring mechanisms that track bot activity in real-time to detect anomalies or deviations from expected behavior. Access controls enforce role-based permissions, ensuring that bots can only interact with specific resources based on their intended function. Isolation techniques prevent bots from accessing or influencing sensitive areas of a network or system. Intervention protocols allow administrators to shut down, modify, or redirect bot activity if suspicious behavior is detected. Logging and auditing functions provide transparency and accountability, helping organizations analyze bot behavior and optimize security strategies.

The benefits of bot containment systems include enhanced security by preventing malicious bot activity, reducing the risk of cyber threats such as data breaches, phishing, and denial-of-service attacks. They contribute to regulatory compliance by ensuring that AI-driven automation adheres to industry and legal standards. These systems improve operational control, allowing organizations to fine-tune bot functionalities while minimizing disruptions. They also reduce the risk of AI unpredictability, ensuring that bots do not self-modify or act beyond their intended scope.

Applications of bot containment systems span across cybersecurity, where they help detect and block harmful bots engaged in credential stuffing, automated hacking attempts, and spam generation. In enterprise environments, containment systems regulate the use of AI-driven automation tools to prevent unauthorized access to sensitive corporate data. In social media platforms, these systems help manage and restrict bot-driven misinformation, spam, and fraudulent activities. In cloud computing, bot containment ensures that automated AI services do not exceed resource limits or interfere with other applications.

Industries implementing bot containment systems include finance, where banks and financial institutions use them to prevent fraudulent transactions and automated attacks. Healthcare relies on these systems to protect patient data from unauthorized AI-driven access. E-commerce platforms use bot containment to prevent price scraping, fake reviews, and automated purchasing exploits. Government and defense agencies deploy these systems to safeguard critical infrastructure and national security against AI-driven cyber threats.

In conclusion, bot containment systems are essential security frameworks that regulate and safeguard AI-powered bots, ensuring they operate within controlled environments. By implementing monitoring, access control, isolation, and intervention protocols, organizations can mitigate risks associated with unauthorized or harmful bot activities. While challenges such as false positives, evolving threats, and scalability persist, these systems play a crucial role in maintaining cybersecurity, compliance, and operational stability across multiple industries.

Bot Framework

Bot Framework refers to a structured platform that provides the necessary tools, libraries, and infrastructure for developing, deploying, and managing AI-powered bots. It enables developers to create intelligent chatbots, virtual assistants, and automated systems that can interact with users through text, voice, and other communication channels. These frameworks streamline bot development by offering built-in functionalities such as natural language processing, machine learning integration, and multi-platform deployment.

Key components of a bot framework include a development environment that provides tools and libraries for coding and testing bots, a natural language processing engine that allows bots to understand and respond to human language, and an integration layer that connects bots with external applications, databases, and APIs. Conversation management ensures that bots handle interactions logically and contextually, while analytics and monitoring tools track bot performance, user engagement, and areas for improvement.

The benefits of a bot framework include faster development by reducing the need for building bots from scratch, cost efficiency by automating repetitive tasks, and scalability by enabling bots to handle a large volume of interactions simultaneously. It enhances user experience by providing consistent and accurate responses, improving customer engagement, and offering personalized interactions. A well-designed framework also ensures easier maintenance, as updates and improvements can be deployed without disrupting ongoing operations.

Applications of bot frameworks span across customer support, where businesses use AI chatbots to provide instant assistance and resolve common queries. In healthcare, virtual assistants powered by bot frameworks help schedule appointments, provide medical information, and monitor patient health. E-commerce platforms leverage bot frameworks for personalized shopping recommendations, order tracking, and automated responses to customer inquiries. In finance, banks and financial institutions use bots for fraud detection, transaction assistance, and account management.

Industries utilizing bot frameworks include retail, where businesses enhance customer interactions through AI-driven assistants. Healthcare organizations deploy AI bots for patient engagement and support. Education institutions use bots to facilitate online learning, provide tutoring, and automate administrative tasks. Financial services benefit from AI-powered assistants that streamline transactions and fraud prevention. Entertainment and media platforms integrate bot frameworks for content recommendations, social media engagement, and automated moderation.

In conclusion, a bot framework provides the essential foundation for building intelligent, scalable, and efficient AI-driven bots. By incorporating natural language processing, integration capabilities, conversation management, and analytics, these frameworks enable businesses and organizations to automate interactions, enhance user engagement, and streamline operations. While challenges such as security, integration, and contextual understanding remain, bot frameworks continue to play a vital role in AI-driven automation, transforming industries and improving digital interactions across multiple domains.

Bot Management in AI

Bot Management in AI refers to the process of overseeing, optimizing, and securing the deployment and operation of AI-powered bots in various applications. It ensures that bots function efficiently, interact appropriately with users, and adhere to security and compliance standards. Effective bot management involves monitoring bot behavior, mitigating risks, and continuously improving bot performance through analytics and machine learning techniques.

Key components of bot management include monitoring and analytics, which track bot interactions, user engagement, and potential errors to optimize performance. Security protocols prevent unauthorized access, data breaches, and malicious bot activity. AI-driven decision-making allows bots to improve responses and adapt to evolving user behaviors. Workflow automation ensures seamless integration with business processes, enabling bots to handle repetitive tasks efficiently. Compliance and governance frameworks maintain adherence to industry regulations and ethical guidelines.

The benefits of bot management include improved efficiency by automating tasks and reducing human workload, ensuring faster response times and enhanced user experiences. Security and fraud prevention measures protect systems from malicious bot attacks, unauthorized access, and data manipulation. Better scalability allows organizations to deploy and manage multiple bots without operational disruptions. Optimized performance leads to more accurate and context-aware interactions, improving user satisfaction and engagement.

Applications of bot management span across customer service, where businesses use AI-driven chatbots to provide real-time support and automate responses. In e-commerce, bot management ensures seamless product recommendations, order tracking, and fraud detection. In finance, automated bots assist with transaction processing, fraud monitoring, and financial advisory services. Healthcare applications include patient engagement bots, virtual assistants for medical queries, and remote monitoring systems. Cybersecurity relies on bot management to detect and block malicious bot traffic, protecting networks from threats.

Industries that leverage bot management include retail, where AI bots enhance shopping experiences through personalized recommendations and customer support. Financial services use bot management to streamline banking transactions, fraud detection, and risk assessment. Healthcare organizations deploy bots for appointment scheduling, diagnostics, and patient interaction. Telecommunications benefit from automated bots managing customer inquiries, billing issues, and service optimizations. Government and public services implement bot management for automated responses, public assistance, and document processing.

In conclusion, bot management in AI is a crucial practice that ensures the effective deployment, security, and optimization of AI-driven bots. By incorporating monitoring, security protocols, AI-driven improvements, and workflow automation, organizations can maximize the benefits of bots while minimizing risks. Despite challenges such as security threats, integration complexities, and regulatory compliance, bot management remains essential for businesses and industries that rely on AI-powered automation to enhance customer experiences, improve efficiency, and drive innovation.

Bot-Oriented Architecture

Bot-Oriented Architecture refers to a software design framework that structures applications around AI-driven bots to automate interactions, workflows, and decision-making processes. It enables seamless communication between users, systems, and AI-powered bots, allowing for efficient task execution, real-time data processing, and intelligent responses. This architecture is designed to support scalable and adaptive bot ecosystems that integrate with various digital services.

Key components of bot-oriented architecture include a conversational interface that enables bots to interact with users through text, voice, and other input methods. A natural language processing engine allows bots to understand and interpret human language, ensuring meaningful interactions. An integration layer connects bots with external applications, databases, and APIs, enabling them to retrieve and process information. Orchestration mechanisms ensure smooth coordination between multiple bots, preventing conflicts and optimizing task execution. Security and compliance frameworks protect sensitive data and regulate bot interactions within predefined boundaries.

The benefits of bot-oriented architecture include enhanced automation, reducing manual workload and improving efficiency across various business processes. It provides scalability by allowing multiple bots to handle concurrent tasks without compromising performance. The architecture improves user engagement by enabling personalized and context-aware interactions. It also facilitates real-time decision-making, allowing businesses to respond faster to customer inquiries, operational changes, and market trends.

Applications of bot-oriented architecture extend to customer support, where bots manage inquiries, automate responses, and escalate complex issues to human agents. In healthcare, bots assist in appointment scheduling, patient monitoring, and medical recommendations. In finance, AI-driven bots handle fraud detection, transaction processing, and risk assessment. Supply chain management benefits from automated inventory tracking, order fulfillment, and logistics coordination. In smart environments, bots control IoT devices, manage energy consumption, and optimize smart home functions.

Industries that adopt bot-oriented architecture include e-commerce, where businesses leverage AI bots for product recommendations, order processing, and customer engagement. Telecommunications integrate bots for automated troubleshooting, billing support, and service optimization. Financial services rely on AI-driven bots for regulatory compliance, fraud prevention, and customer interactions. The healthcare sector benefits from intelligent bots that assist in diagnostics, patient care, and health monitoring. Government agencies implement bot-oriented architecture for public services, document processing, and automated citizen support.

In conclusion, bot-oriented architecture is a transformative approach to software design that leverages AI-driven bots for automation, efficiency, and intelligent decision-making. By integrating conversational interfaces, natural language processing, orchestration mechanisms, and security frameworks, this architecture enhances user experiences, streamlines workflows, and optimizes business operations. Despite challenges such as integration complexity, security risks, and ongoing maintenance requirements, bot-oriented architecture remains a critical advancement in AI-powered automation, enabling industries to innovate and scale their digital capabilities effectively.

Bot-Oriented Programming

Bot-Oriented Programming refers to a software development paradigm that focuses on designing and implementing applications centered around AI-driven bots. It enables developers to create intelligent, autonomous, and interactive bot systems that can process information, make decisions, and engage in human-like conversations. This approach facilitates the development of bots that function independently or collaboratively within various digital environments.

Key components of bot-oriented programming include a modular architecture that structures bot functionalities into independent, reusable components. A natural language processing engine allows bots to interpret and respond to human input accurately. Machine learning algorithms enhance bot intelligence by enabling adaptive learning and behavior refinement. An event-driven framework ensures that bots react dynamically to user inputs, environmental changes, or system triggers. Integration with external APIs, databases, and enterprise systems enables bots to access, retrieve, and process real-time data.

The benefits of bot-oriented programming include enhanced automation, reducing the need for manual intervention in repetitive tasks. It improves scalability by allowing multiple bots to operate simultaneously across different platforms. The approach increases efficiency by streamlining workflows and accelerating response times. It enhances user engagement through context-aware interactions and intelligent decision-making. Bots developed using this programming paradigm can self-improve through continuous learning, ensuring sustained accuracy and relevance.

Applications of bot-oriented programming span customer support, where AI-driven bots handle inquiries, resolve issues, and provide personalized assistance. In e-commerce, bots assist with product recommendations, order tracking, and customer engagement. Healthcare applications include AI-powered virtual assistants for patient monitoring, medical inquiries, and appointment scheduling. Financial institutions utilize bots for fraud detection, transaction processing, and portfolio management. In cybersecurity, AI-driven bots analyze threats, detect anomalies, and automate security measures.

Industries that implement bot-oriented programming include retail, where AI bots enhance online shopping experiences and automate inventory management. The banking and financial sector leverages AI-driven bots for real-time customer interactions and fraud prevention. Healthcare organizations use bots for remote patient monitoring and medical diagnostics. Telecommunications integrate AI bots for automated troubleshooting, billing support, and service optimization. Government agencies deploy bots to manage public inquiries, streamline document processing, and improve citizen services.

In conclusion, bot-oriented programming is a powerful development approach that enables the creation of intelligent, autonomous, and scalable AI-driven bots. By leveraging modular design, natural language processing, machine learning, and event-driven architectures, this paradigm enhances automation, user engagement, and operational efficiency across various industries. Despite challenges related to complexity, security, and ethical considerations, bot-oriented programming remains a foundational element in AI-driven innovation, transforming how businesses and organizations interact with technology and users.

Bot Rebellion Dection

Bot Rebellion Detection refers to the identification and mitigation of AI-driven bots that deviate from their intended functions, exhibit autonomous or adversarial behavior, or attempt to manipulate systems beyond their authorized scope. This concept is crucial in ensuring that AI bots remain under human control, operate within ethical and security guidelines, and do not pose risks to digital infrastructures or user safety.

Key components of bot rebellion detection include anomaly detection algorithms that monitor bot behavior and identify deviations from expected patterns. Machine learning models analyze historical bot activities to predict potential rebellious tendencies or unauthorized actions. Behavioral tracking systems continuously assess bot interactions with users, other bots, and digital environments to detect signs of autonomous or adversarial decision-making. Security and containment mechanisms provide real-time intervention capabilities to restrict or shut down rogue bots before they cause harm. Logging and auditing frameworks maintain records of bot activities, allowing for forensic analysis and continuous improvement of security protocols.

The benefits of bot rebellion detection include enhanced cybersecurity by preventing unauthorized bot behavior, reducing the risk of AI-driven cyberattacks, and mitigating system vulnerabilities. It improves operational stability by ensuring that AI-driven automation functions as intended without unexpected disruptions. The approach strengthens regulatory compliance by aligning bot operations with industry standards, legal requirements, and ethical AI guidelines. It also enhances trust in AI systems by ensuring that bots remain accountable, transparent, and aligned with organizational objectives.

Applications of bot rebellion detection span cybersecurity, where AI-driven monitoring systems identify and neutralize bots attempting to manipulate digital infrastructure. In financial services, the approach prevents rogue trading bots from executing unauthorized transactions or market manipulations. Social media platforms implement rebellion detection to prevent AI bots from spreading misinformation, engaging in coordinated manipulation, or bypassing content moderation policies. In robotics and automation, the technique ensures that AI-powered systems adhere to their programmed constraints, preventing unintended actions in autonomous vehicles, industrial robots, and smart home devices.

Industries leveraging bot rebellion detection include finance, where banks and trading platforms use AI monitoring systems to detect unauthorized algorithmic activities. Healthcare organizations apply these mechanisms to ensure that AI-driven diagnostic and medical bots operate within approved protocols. Government agencies implement rebellion detection to prevent AI systems from being exploited for misinformation campaigns, cyber espionage, or unauthorized surveillance. E-commerce platforms utilize AI monitoring to prevent automated bots from engaging in fraudulent activities such as fake reviews, price manipulation, or unauthorized purchases.

In conclusion, bot rebellion detection is a critical security and governance practice that ensures AI-driven bots operate within their designated roles while preventing unauthorized or adversarial behavior. By incorporating anomaly detection, behavioral tracking, security containment, and auditing mechanisms, organizations can mitigate risks associated with rogue AI systems. Despite challenges such as false positives, evolving cyber threats, and ethical considerations, bot rebellion detection remains essential for maintaining trust, security, and control over AI-driven automation across various industries.

Bot Scraping Detection

Bot Scraping Detection refers to the process of identifying and preventing automated bots from extracting large amounts of data from websites, applications, or digital platforms without authorization. This practice is crucial in protecting intellectual property, maintaining fair market competition, and preventing malicious activities such as data theft, content duplication, and price scraping.

Key components of bot scraping detection include traffic analysis systems that monitor website activity for abnormal request patterns or unusually high access rates. Behavioral analytics use machine learning to differentiate between human users and bots based on interaction patterns, such as mouse movements, page navigation, and response times. Device fingerprinting helps track bot characteristics by analyzing browser versions, operating systems, and network information. CAPTCHA and challenge-response mechanisms introduce obstacles that are easy for humans but difficult for bots to bypass. Rate limiting and IP blocking restrict excessive access attempts from a single source, preventing bots from making large-scale requests.

The benefits of bot scraping detection include enhanced data security by preventing unauthorized access and extraction of sensitive or proprietary information. It preserves competitive advantages by stopping price scraping bots that monitor and adjust prices based on competitors' strategies. It reduces server load and bandwidth consumption by filtering out automated requests, ensuring optimal website performance. It also helps protect user privacy by preventing bots from harvesting personal information for fraudulent activities such as identity theft or spam generation.

Applications of bot scraping detection span e-commerce, where businesses use detection mechanisms to prevent competitors from automatically collecting pricing and inventory data. Media and publishing platforms implement scraping detection to protect copyrighted content from unauthorized republication. Financial institutions leverage bot detection to prevent automated attempts to gather real-time market data or manipulate stock trading algorithms. Cybersecurity teams deploy scraping prevention to safeguard APIs and databases from large-scale data mining attempts.

Industries that rely on bot scraping detection include e-commerce, where retailers protect product listings and pricing information from being copied or manipulated by competitors. Finance and banking institutions safeguard sensitive financial data and market trends from being exploited by automated trading bots. Media and publishing companies secure articles, videos, and other copyrighted content from unauthorized extraction and redistribution. Cybersecurity firms implement scraping detection to prevent automated bots from scanning websites for vulnerabilities or extracting login credentials.

In conclusion, bot scraping detection is a critical component of digital security and data protection, helping organizations prevent unauthorized data extraction while maintaining system performance and competitiveness. By leveraging traffic analysis, behavioral analytics, device fingerprinting, and access control mechanisms, businesses can effectively mitigate the risks posed by malicious scraping bots. Despite challenges such as distinguishing between legitimate and harmful automation, evolving bot tactics, and maintaining a seamless user experience, bot scraping detection remains essential for industries that rely on proprietary data, digital security, and fair market competition.

Botnet Detection AI

Botnet Detection using AI refers to the process of identifying and mitigating networks of compromised devices controlled by malicious actors through artificial intelligence-driven techniques. Botnets are used for cyberattacks such as distributed denial-of-service (DDoS) attacks, data breaches, spam distribution, and financial fraud. AI enhances detection by analyzing large volumes of network traffic, identifying patterns, and responding to threats in real-time.

Key components of botnet detection using AI include machine learning algorithms that analyze historical and real-time network data to detect anomalies and malicious behavior. Behavioral analysis examines traffic patterns, device interactions, and communication frequencies to differentiate between normal and suspicious activities. Intrusion detection systems leverage AI to identify botnet activity by scanning for irregular access attempts and unauthorized command execution. Threat intelligence integration enhances detection by using AI to cross-reference identified threats with known botnet indicators from global cybersecurity databases. Automated response mechanisms enable real-time mitigation, isolating infected devices and preventing further network infiltration.

The benefits of AI-driven botnet detection include faster and more accurate identification of malicious botnet activities, reducing the risk of large-scale cyberattacks. It enhances cybersecurity resilience by continuously learning and adapting to new attack strategies, making defenses more robust. AI-driven detection reduces false positives, ensuring that legitimate traffic is not mistakenly blocked while efficiently targeting malicious bot activities. Automation improves response times, minimizing damage and mitigating risks before attacks can escalate.

Applications of botnet detection using AI extend to network security, where AI systems monitor enterprise and cloud networks for signs of botnet infiltration. In financial services, AI-driven systems detect and prevent botnet-driven fraud, unauthorized transactions, and account takeovers. Healthcare organizations use AI-based detection to safeguard patient data and medical devices from botnet exploitation. Governments and law enforcement agencies rely on AI to track, dismantle, and prevent botnet-driven cybercrime and digital espionage.

Industries that benefit from AI-driven botnet detection include finance, where banks and payment processors use AI to detect fraud and prevent unauthorized transactions. Telecommunications providers deploy AI to secure networks against botnet-driven DDoS attacks and automated phishing schemes. Healthcare institutions integrate AI-driven security to protect electronic health records and connected medical devices from cyber threats. Cloud service providers implement AI-based botnet detection to prevent compromised servers from being exploited in large-scale cyberattacks.

In conclusion, botnet detection using AI is a crucial component of modern cybersecurity, providing real-time monitoring, analysis, and automated mitigation against malicious botnets. By leveraging machine learning, behavioral analysis, intrusion detection, and automated response mechanisms, AI enhances security across various industries. Despite challenges such as evolving threats, evasion tactics, and computational demands, AI-driven botnet detection remains essential for protecting digital infrastructure, securing sensitive data, and mitigating cyber threats at scale.

Bottlenect Analysis in AI Systems

Bottleneck Analysis in AI Systems refers to the process of identifying and resolving performance limitations that hinder the efficiency, scalability, and responsiveness of artificial intelligence models and infrastructure. This analysis focuses on detecting constraints within computational resources, data processing pipelines, network communication, and model architectures that slow down AI operations.

Key components of bottleneck analysis in AI systems include computational resource monitoring, which evaluates CPU, GPU, and memory usage to detect processing delays. Data pipeline analysis assesses the efficiency of data storage, retrieval, and preprocessing steps to identify bottlenecks in model training and inference. Model optimization examines algorithm complexity, hyperparameters, and network depth to determine areas where computational load can be reduced without sacrificing accuracy. Network latency analysis tracks delays in communication between distributed AI components, particularly in cloud-based or edge AI deployments. System profiling tools collect performance metrics and generate insights into which stages of AI processing contribute to bottlenecks.

The benefits of bottleneck analysis in AI systems include improved model performance by identifying inefficiencies and optimizing processing workflows. It enhances scalability, allowing AI models to handle larger datasets and more complex tasks without degradation in speed. Energy efficiency is improved by reducing unnecessary computational loads, leading to lower operational costs. Faster inference times result in more responsive AI applications, improving user experience in real-time systems.

Applications of bottleneck analysis extend to deep learning model optimization, where reducing training times and enhancing inference speeds are critical. In cloud AI deployments, performance analysis helps manage resource allocation and prevent system overloads. AI-driven automation benefits from bottleneck detection by ensuring continuous workflow execution without delays. Natural language processing and computer vision applications use bottleneck analysis to accelerate data processing and response generation.

Industries leveraging bottleneck analysis in AI systems include finance, where algorithmic trading and fraud detection models require real-time performance optimization. Healthcare organizations utilize bottleneck analysis to accelerate medical imaging processing and predictive diagnostics. Manufacturing benefits from optimizing AI-driven predictive maintenance models to reduce downtime. E-commerce platforms rely on efficient AI recommendation engines that minimize latency in personalized shopping experiences.

In conclusion, bottleneck analysis in AI systems is essential for maintaining optimal performance, scalability, and efficiency across various AI applications. By identifying computational, data, and network constraints, organizations can enhance processing speed, reduce costs, and improve user experiences. Despite challenges related to workload variability, hardware limitations, and model optimization trade-offs, bottleneck analysis remains a fundamental practice for ensuring that AI systems operate at peak efficiency across diverse industries.

Bottlenect in Neural Networks

Bottleneck in Neural Networks refers to a performance limitation that restricts the flow of information through the network, slowing down training, reducing accuracy, or hindering scalability. Bottlenecks can arise due to constraints in computational resources, inefficient data processing, suboptimal architecture design, or network layer restrictions that limit learning capacity.

Key components of bottlenecks in neural networks include computational constraints, where limited GPU or memory resources slow down training and inference times. Data pipeline inefficiencies occur when input data is not preprocessed efficiently, causing delays in feeding information to the network. Model architecture limitations arise when layers are too narrow, preventing sufficient feature extraction, or when the network is too deep, leading to vanishing gradients. Network congestion occurs when certain layers create bottlenecks by restricting information flow, particularly in convolutional and recurrent networks.

The benefits of addressing bottlenecks in neural networks include improved training efficiency, enabling faster convergence and reducing the time required for model optimization. Enhanced model accuracy results from eliminating constraints that hinder feature learning and information propagation. Better resource utilization ensures that computational power is allocated efficiently, minimizing hardware limitations. Scalability increases as optimized networks can process larger datasets and more complex tasks without performance degradation.

Applications of bottleneck analysis in neural networks extend to deep learning optimization, where reducing training time and improving inference efficiency are critical. In image recognition, identifying and resolving bottlenecks ensures better feature extraction and classification accuracy. Natural language processing benefits from bottleneck resolution by improving text generation, sentiment analysis, and translation models. Autonomous systems, including robotics and self-driving cars, rely on optimized neural networks to process real-time sensor data efficiently.

Industries affected by neural network bottlenecks include healthcare, where medical imaging models require fast and accurate processing for diagnostics. Finance leverages optimized neural networks for fraud detection, algorithmic trading, and risk assessment. Manufacturing and automation benefit from neural network efficiency in predictive maintenance and quality control. E-commerce platforms enhance recommendation engines and personalized search experiences by resolving computational and architectural bottlenecks.

In conclusion, bottlenecks in neural networks present significant challenges in training efficiency, scalability, and model accuracy. Identifying and resolving these constraints through optimized architectures, efficient data pipelines, and improved hardware utilization ensures better performance in AI-driven applications. Despite challenges in diagnosing and mitigating bottlenecks, addressing these limitations enhances deep learning efficiency, enabling neural networks to operate effectively across various industries and applications.

Boundary-Based Clustering

Boundary-Based Clustering is a clustering technique that identifies clusters by analyzing the boundaries between different data regions rather than relying solely on distance or density measures. It focuses on defining precise cluster edges, making it particularly useful in complex datasets where traditional clustering methods may struggle to delineate overlapping or irregularly shaped clusters.

Key components of boundary-based clustering include boundary detection, where algorithms identify the edges of clusters based on changes in density or spatial distribution. Decision rules help classify data points by determining whether they belong inside or outside a cluster based on predefined criteria. Neighborhood analysis evaluates the local relationships between data points to refine cluster boundaries. Iterative refinement improves clustering accuracy by adjusting boundaries dynamically as new data is introduced.

The benefits of boundary-based clustering include improved accuracy in detecting clusters with complex or irregular shapes that traditional methods like k-means struggle to separate. It enhances interpretability by providing well-defined cluster boundaries, making results more explainable. The method reduces noise sensitivity by focusing on boundary refinement rather than distance-based clustering, allowing for more robust results in datasets with outliers. It also improves adaptability to non-uniform data distributions, ensuring meaningful groupings in high-dimensional or heterogeneous data.

Applications of boundary-based clustering extend to image segmentation, where it helps distinguish objects within an image by precisely identifying their edges. In anomaly detection, it effectively isolates outliers by analyzing cluster perimeters. In biomedical research, boundary-based clustering assists in cell structure analysis and disease classification. Geographic information systems use this approach to segment and categorize regions based on spatial boundaries.

Industries benefiting from boundary-based clustering include healthcare, where it is applied in medical imaging and diagnostic pattern recognition. Finance leverages it for fraud detection and risk assessment by identifying anomalies near decision boundaries. Retail and e-commerce use boundary-based clustering for customer segmentation and personalized marketing strategies. Manufacturing benefits from quality control applications, ensuring product consistency by analyzing production boundaries.

In conclusion, boundary-based clustering is a powerful approach for identifying complex data structures by focusing on well-defined boundaries rather than distance or density measures. By improving accuracy, interpretability, and adaptability, it provides significant advantages in various domains such as image processing, anomaly detection, and biomedical research. Despite challenges related to computational demands, parameter sensitivity, and scalability, this method remains valuable for applications requiring precise cluster differentiation and robust data segmentation.

Boundary Conditions in AI

Boundary Conditions in AI refer to predefined constraints or limits that guide the behavior, decision-making, and learning processes of artificial intelligence models. These conditions ensure that AI operates within acceptable parameters, preventing unintended outcomes, optimizing performance, and improving reliability in various applications.

Key components of boundary conditions in AI include rule-based constraints that define explicit limits for AI actions, ensuring compliance with ethical, legal, and operational guidelines. Data boundaries restrict the scope of input data, preventing AI from making inferences beyond its trained dataset. Model parameters establish numerical and functional thresholds, optimizing the trade-off between accuracy, efficiency, and computational cost. Safety mechanisms enforce operational limits, preventing AI from executing actions that could cause harm or violate user-defined policies.

The benefits of boundary conditions in AI include improved decision-making consistency by ensuring that AI adheres to well-defined constraints. They enhance safety by reducing the risk of unintended consequences in high-stakes environments such as healthcare, finance, and autonomous systems. Boundary conditions improve interpretability by defining clear operational guidelines, making AI outcomes more explainable and transparent. They also optimize computational efficiency by eliminating unnecessary calculations and ensuring models focus only on relevant tasks.

Applications of boundary conditions extend to autonomous systems, where they prevent AI from taking actions that could endanger human safety, such as in self-driving cars and robotic automation. In finance, boundary conditions limit AI-driven trading strategies to prevent excessive risk-taking or market manipulation. In healthcare, they define constraints for AI-driven diagnostics, ensuring recommendations align with medical guidelines and ethical standards. AI-driven content moderation uses boundary conditions to filter harmful or inappropriate material while preserving freedom of expression.

Industries that benefit from boundary conditions in AI include automotive, where they ensure autonomous vehicles comply with traffic laws and safety regulations. Financial institutions implement them to control AI-driven fraud detection, risk assessment, and regulatory compliance. Healthcare organizations rely on them to maintain patient safety in AI-driven diagnostics, treatment planning, and robotic-assisted surgeries. Cybersecurity firms use boundary conditions to detect and mitigate potential threats by defining acceptable network activity patterns.

In conclusion, boundary conditions in AI serve as critical constraints that guide the safe, efficient, and ethical deployment of artificial intelligence systems. By defining explicit operational limits, they enhance decision-making reliability, ensure compliance with industry standards, and prevent harmful or unintended AI behaviors. Despite challenges related to adaptability, computational efficiency, and ethical considerations, boundary conditions remain essential for developing responsible and effective AI applications across diverse industries.

Bounded Rationality in AI

Bounded Rationality in AI refers to the concept that artificial intelligence, like human decision-makers, operates under constraints such as limited computational power, incomplete information, and time restrictions. Instead of making perfectly optimal decisions, AI systems apply heuristics, approximations, or simplified models to arrive at satisfactory solutions within practical limitations.

Key components of bounded rationality in AI include computational constraints that limit the ability of AI to explore all possible solutions exhaustively. Information limitations arise when AI operates with incomplete, uncertain, or noisy data, requiring inference and approximation. Decision heuristics are rule-based or learned strategies that enable AI to make reasonable decisions quickly without evaluating every possible outcome. Trade-off mechanisms balance accuracy, speed, and resource efficiency, ensuring AI systems can function effectively in real-world environments.

The benefits of bounded rationality in AI include improved efficiency by reducing the computational burden associated with exhaustive search and decision-making processes. It enhances adaptability by allowing AI to function effectively in dynamic and uncertain environments. Bounded rationality enables real-time decision-making, making AI suitable for time-sensitive applications such as autonomous systems and financial trading. It also improves scalability by ensuring AI can handle complex tasks without requiring excessive computational resources.

Applications of bounded rationality in AI extend to robotics, where autonomous agents must make decisions quickly in unpredictable environments without processing all available data. In finance, AI-driven trading algorithms use bounded rationality to react to market conditions within limited time windows. Healthcare applications rely on AI models that prioritize key patient data rather than analyzing every possible medical scenario. In supply chain management, AI optimizes logistics and inventory decisions using heuristic-based approaches that balance speed and accuracy.

Industries that benefit from bounded rationality in AI include transportation, where autonomous vehicles must make rapid navigation decisions with limited sensor input. Financial services use AI for risk assessment and fraud detection under time constraints and data uncertainties. Healthcare systems rely on AI for diagnostic assistance, treatment recommendations, and patient monitoring without requiring exhaustive medical evaluations. Manufacturing applies bounded rationality in AI-driven process optimization and predictive maintenance.

In conclusion, bounded rationality in AI is a crucial principle that acknowledges the limitations of artificial intelligence in real-world decision-making. By leveraging computational efficiency, heuristics, and trade-off mechanisms, AI can operate effectively under time, resource, and information constraints. Despite challenges related to decision accuracy, uncertainty management, and ethical considerations, bounded rationality remains a fundamental approach in optimizing AI performance across diverse applications and industries.

Bounding Box in AI

Bounding Box in AI refers to a rectangular frame used to define the spatial extent of an object within an image or video. It is a fundamental tool in computer vision tasks such as object detection, tracking, and image annotation, enabling AI models to identify and localize objects with precision.

Key components of a bounding box in AI include coordinate representation, where the box is defined by its top-left and bottom-right corners or by its center point, width, and height. Object classification assigns a label to the object within the bounding box, distinguishing different categories such as pedestrians, vehicles, or animals. Confidence scores indicate the probability that the detected object belongs to a specific category. Intersection-over-union (IoU) measures the accuracy of the bounding box by comparing its overlap with ground truth annotations.

The benefits of using bounding boxes in AI include efficient localization, allowing AI models to quickly identify objects within an image without requiring pixel-level segmentation. They enhance annotation accuracy by providing structured data for training computer vision models. Bounding boxes also improve computational efficiency by focusing processing power on specific regions rather than analyzing the entire image. They enable real-time object tracking, making them essential for applications that require fast decision-making.

Applications of bounding boxes extend to autonomous vehicles, where they detect pedestrians, traffic signs, and obstacles to assist in navigation. In surveillance and security, bounding boxes help in facial recognition, anomaly detection, and crowd monitoring. In medical imaging, they are used to highlight areas of interest, such as tumors in X-rays or MRIs. Retail and e-commerce platforms use bounding boxes for visual search, barcode detection, and inventory tracking. Robotics relies on bounding boxes for object recognition and manipulation in automated systems.

Industries benefiting from bounding boxes in AI include automotive, where they are used in self-driving cars for obstacle detection and lane tracking. Healthcare applies them in AI-powered diagnostic imaging for identifying abnormalities. Retail and e-commerce use bounding boxes in virtual shopping assistants and automated checkout systems. Manufacturing integrates bounding box-based object detection for quality control and defect identification. Sports analytics leverages them for player tracking and performance analysis in games.

In conclusion, bounding boxes in AI serve as a foundational tool in computer vision for detecting and localizing objects efficiently. By leveraging coordinate representation, classification, and confidence scoring, they enable applications in autonomous systems, healthcare, retail, and security. Despite challenges related to detection accuracy, computational demands, and annotation complexity, bounding boxes remain a crucial component in AI-driven image analysis, enhancing automation and decision-making across various industries.

Bragg Peak Detection

Bragg Peak Detection refers to the identification and analysis of the Bragg peak, a phenomenon observed in particle therapy where charged particles, such as protons or heavy ions, deposit the maximum amount of energy at a specific depth within a medium, typically human tissue. This precise energy deposition allows for targeted cancer treatment, minimizing damage to surrounding healthy tissue while maximizing the dose delivered to the tumor.

Key components of Bragg peak detection include energy deposition profiling, which measures the distribution of energy along the particle's path to determine the peak location. Dosimetry systems use detectors and sensors to quantify radiation doses at various depths. Particle tracking mechanisms analyze the trajectory and interaction of charged particles with tissue to optimize treatment delivery. Calibration and validation processes ensure accuracy in peak detection and energy distribution modeling.

The benefits of Bragg peak detection include highly precise radiation therapy, allowing for targeted tumor destruction while sparing healthy tissues. It reduces side effects compared to conventional radiotherapy by minimizing unnecessary radiation exposure. Enhanced treatment planning results from accurate peak detection, optimizing proton beam therapy and heavy ion therapy for maximum therapeutic effect. The approach also supports adaptive therapy, adjusting treatment parameters based on real-time feedback.

Applications of Bragg peak detection extend to proton therapy, where it ensures accurate dose delivery for treating cancers such as brain tumors, lung cancer, and pediatric malignancies. In radiation physics, it assists in developing advanced dosimetry models for improved treatment accuracy. In medical imaging, Bragg peak detection contributes to better understanding particle interactions with biological matter, supporting the refinement of diagnostic and therapeutic techniques.

Industries utilizing Bragg peak detection include healthcare, where hospitals and cancer treatment centers integrate this technique into advanced radiation therapy. Medical research institutions study the effects of charged particle interactions to enhance treatment methodologies. Nuclear physics and radiation safety organizations apply Bragg peak detection to optimize shielding materials and radiation exposure assessment. Aerospace and space exploration sectors investigate the effects of high-energy particle interactions for astronaut radiation protection.

In conclusion, Bragg peak detection plays a crucial role in improving the precision and effectiveness of particle therapy for cancer treatment. By enabling accurate energy deposition targeting, it enhances therapeutic outcomes while minimizing radiation exposure to healthy tissues. Despite challenges related to equipment costs, anatomical variability, and complex calibration processes, Bragg peak detection remains an essential technique in radiation oncology, medical research, and applied physics, driving advancements in precision medicine and targeted therapies.

Brain-Computer Interfact (BCI)

Brain-Computer Interface (BCI) refers to a direct communication pathway between the brain and an external device, enabling users to control computers, prosthetics, or other systems using neural activity. BCIs bypass traditional neuromuscular pathways, allowing individuals with disabilities or neurological disorders to interact with technology through brain signals alone.

Key components of BCI include signal acquisition, where sensors such as electroencephalography (EEG) or intracortical electrodes capture brain activity. Signal processing filters, amplifies, and translates neural signals into meaningful commands. Machine learning algorithms decode brain activity patterns to interpret user intentions. Feedback mechanisms provide real-time responses, allowing users to refine control over connected devices. Communication and output systems translate processed signals into actions, enabling interaction with external applications, prosthetics, or assistive technologies.

The benefits of BCI include enhanced accessibility for individuals with paralysis or severe mobility impairments, enabling them to communicate and control devices independently. It improves quality of life by restoring lost functions through neuroprosthetics and assistive systems. BCI facilitates faster rehabilitation by retraining brain activity after stroke or injury. It also advances human-computer interaction by enabling hands-free control of digital interfaces, gaming, and virtual reality experiences.

Applications of BCI extend to medical rehabilitation, where it helps individuals regain motor control through brain-controlled prosthetics and exoskeletons. In communication, BCI enables people with speech disorders or locked-in syndrome to express themselves using brain signals. Neurogaming and virtual reality leverage BCI for immersive experiences controlled by thought alone. In mental health, BCI is used for neurofeedback therapy to help manage conditions such as ADHD, anxiety, and depression. Military and aerospace sectors explore BCI for enhanced soldier performance and brain-controlled robotic systems.

Industries benefiting from BCI include healthcare, where hospitals and rehabilitation centers use brain-machine interfaces for restoring movement and communication. The gaming industry integrates BCI for immersive, thought-controlled gaming experiences. Neurotechnology companies develop brainwave-controlled applications for assistive devices and consumer electronics. Research institutions explore BCI applications in cognitive enhancement, artificial intelligence, and brain mapping. Defense organizations study BCI for advanced human-machine collaboration in combat and operational environments.

In conclusion, Brain-Computer Interface technology represents a groundbreaking advancement in human-computer interaction, bridging the gap between neural activity and digital systems. By enabling control of devices through brain signals, BCI enhances accessibility, rehabilitation, and human performance across multiple fields. Despite challenges related to accuracy, invasiveness, privacy, and cost, ongoing research and innovation continue to drive the development of more effective and accessible BCI solutions, paving the way for transformative applications in healthcare, communication, entertainment, and beyond.

Brain-Inspired AI

Brain-Inspired AI refers to artificial intelligence systems designed to mimic the structure, functionality, and learning processes of the human brain. By incorporating principles from neuroscience, these AI models aim to enhance adaptability, efficiency, and problem-solving capabilities beyond traditional machine learning approaches. Brain-inspired AI seeks to create more human-like intelligence by leveraging neural architectures, parallel processing, and self-learning mechanisms.

Key components of brain-inspired AI include neuromorphic computing, which uses specialized hardware to replicate the neural structure and processing efficiency of the brain. Spiking neural networks (SNNs) mimic biological neurons by transmitting information through discrete spikes, improving energy efficiency and real-time processing. Hebbian learning and synaptic plasticity models enable AI systems to adapt dynamically based on experience, similar to how human brains strengthen or weaken neural connections. Parallel distributed processing allows AI to handle complex computations more efficiently by simulating the brain's ability to process multiple tasks simultaneously.

The benefits of brain-inspired AI include improved energy efficiency compared to conventional AI models, making it suitable for low-power applications such as edge computing and embedded systems. It enhances learning efficiency by enabling AI to process information in a biologically plausible manner, reducing the need for massive datasets and computational power. Brain-inspired AI also improves decision-making and pattern recognition in uncertain environments, enabling more human-like adaptability and reasoning. Its ability to process real-time sensory input makes it ideal for robotics, autonomous systems, and AI-driven perception technologies.

Applications of brain-inspired AI extend to robotics, where neuromorphic processors enable efficient real-time learning and control for autonomous robots. In healthcare, AI systems modeled after the brain improve diagnostics, medical imaging analysis, and neuroprosthetics. Financial modeling benefits from adaptive AI systems capable of predicting market trends with human-like reasoning. Smart sensors and IoT devices integrate brain-inspired AI to optimize decision-making in environments with limited computational resources. Neuroscience research leverages brain-inspired AI to develop better models of cognition, memory, and perception.

Industries adopting brain-inspired AI include healthcare, where AI-driven diagnostics and brain-computer interfaces enhance medical treatment and patient rehabilitation. The automotive sector integrates brain-like processing for real-time decision-making in self-driving cars. Consumer electronics incorporate neuromorphic chips to enable smarter and more power-efficient AI assistants and wearable devices. Aerospace and defense apply brain-inspired AI for autonomous navigation, threat detection, and adaptive decision-making in high-risk environments. Education and cognitive science use these models to develop intelligent tutoring systems that mimic human learning behavior.

In conclusion, brain-inspired AI represents a significant step toward creating more adaptive, efficient, and human-like artificial intelligence systems. By incorporating neuroscience principles, these models improve energy efficiency, learning adaptability, and decision-making capabilities across various applications. Despite challenges related to computational scalability, ethical considerations, and cognitive replication, brain-inspired AI continues to drive innovation in robotics, healthcare, finance, and consumer technology, paving the way for next-generation intelligent systems that mirror the complexity of the human brain.

Brain Mapping AI

Brain Mapping AI refers to the use of artificial intelligence to analyze, visualize, and interpret the structure and functionality of the human brain. It integrates machine learning, deep learning, and neuroimaging techniques to decode neural activity, identify brain regions, and understand complex cognitive processes. By automating data processing and pattern recognition, Brain Mapping AI accelerates neuroscientific research and medical diagnostics.

Key components of Brain Mapping AI include neuroimaging data processing, where AI analyzes scans from technologies like MRI, fMRI, EEG, and MEG to identify neural connections and activity patterns. Deep learning algorithms detect correlations between brain regions, enabling a deeper understanding of functional connectivity. Neural network modeling simulates brain activity to explore cognition, memory, and neurological disorders. Automated segmentation distinguishes brain structures, improving the accuracy of anatomical and functional mapping. Data integration combines various neuroimaging modalities with genetic, behavioral, and clinical data for a comprehensive understanding of brain function.

The benefits of Brain Mapping AI include faster and more precise analysis of large-scale brain data, reducing the time required for neurological research and diagnostics. It enhances early detection of brain disorders such as Alzheimer's, epilepsy, and Parkinson's by identifying abnormal neural activity patterns. AI-driven mapping improves personalized medicine by tailoring treatments based on an individual's unique brain structure and function. It advances brain-computer interfaces by identifying optimal neural pathways for interaction between the brain and external devices.

Applications of Brain Mapping AI extend to medical diagnostics, where AI assists in identifying and classifying neurological conditions through automated brain imaging analysis. Neuroscience research benefits from AI-driven insights into brain plasticity, learning, and cognitive development. Mental health treatment is enhanced by AI-assisted monitoring of brain activity in response to therapies. Education and cognitive science use AI-powered brain mapping to study learning processes and optimize teaching strategies. AI also contributes to brain-inspired computing by providing a deeper understanding of neural architectures for advanced AI model development.

Industries leveraging Brain Mapping AI include healthcare, where hospitals and research institutions integrate AI to improve neurological diagnostics and treatments. Pharmaceutical companies use AI-driven brain mapping to develop targeted drugs for brain disorders. Neurotechnology firms apply brain mapping AI to enhance brain-computer interfaces for communication and mobility solutions. Academic and government research institutions explore the brain's mysteries using AI-powered analysis. The artificial intelligence sector benefits from neuroscience-inspired algorithms to improve AI models for pattern recognition and decision-making.

In conclusion, Brain Mapping AI represents a groundbreaking advancement in neuroscience, enabling deeper insights into brain function, cognition, and neurological disorders. By leveraging neuroimaging analysis, deep learning, and neural network modeling, AI enhances medical diagnostics, personalized treatments, and brain-computer interactions. Despite challenges related to complexity, data variability, ethics, and computational requirements, Brain Mapping AI continues to revolutionize neuroscience, healthcare, and artificial intelligence, paving the way for more precise and effective brain-related technologies.

Brainstorming AI

Brainstorming AI refers to artificial intelligence systems designed to generate, refine, and enhance ideas by simulating creative thinking processes. These AI models use machine learning, natural language processing, and knowledge databases to assist individuals and teams in problem-solving, innovation, and decision-making. Brainstorming AI enhances creative workflows by providing diverse perspectives, suggesting novel solutions, and refining existing concepts.

Key components of Brainstorming AI include natural language processing, which enables AI to understand and generate ideas in human language. Knowledge representation allows AI to access vast amounts of structured and unstructured information to inspire new ideas. Machine learning algorithms analyze past brainstorming sessions to refine suggestions and adapt to user preferences. Context awareness ensures AI-generated ideas align with the specific goals, industries, or challenges being addressed. Collaboration tools integrate AI into team environments, facilitating interactive brainstorming sessions with real-time idea generation and refinement.

The benefits of Brainstorming AI include increased efficiency by rapidly generating diverse ideas, reducing the time required for traditional brainstorming. It enhances creativity by introducing novel perspectives that may not have been considered by human participants. AI eliminates biases that often limit brainstorming sessions by suggesting ideas based on data-driven insights rather than personal assumptions. It improves collaboration by structuring brainstorming sessions, organizing ideas, and ensuring that discussions remain productive and goal-oriented.

Applications of Brainstorming AI extend to product development, where AI assists teams in generating innovative concepts for new products and services. In marketing, AI suggests campaign strategies, branding ideas, and content creation themes. In research and development, Brainstorming AI supports scientific exploration by proposing hypotheses, experimental designs, and alternative approaches. In business strategy, AI helps executives and decision-makers evaluate potential solutions, risk factors, and market trends. In education, AI supports students and educators by generating discussion topics, learning activities, and research ideas.

Industries utilizing Brainstorming AI include technology, where AI-driven innovation accelerates software development, AI model improvements, and patent generation. Advertising and media benefit from AI-powered creativity tools that generate content, slogans, and campaign ideas. Healthcare applies Brainstorming AI to drug discovery, treatment innovation, and healthcare system improvements. Finance uses AI-generated insights for investment strategies, risk assessment, and financial planning. Manufacturing and engineering leverage AI for optimizing production processes, product design, and supply chain management.

In conclusion, Brainstorming AI serves as a powerful tool for enhancing creativity, idea generation, and decision-making across multiple fields. By leveraging natural language processing, machine learning, and knowledge representation, AI supports innovation in product development, marketing, research, and strategic planning. Despite challenges related to originality, context awareness, and ethical considerations, Brainstorming AI continues to revolutionize creative processes, fostering collaboration and driving new solutions across industries.

Braking systems in autonomous vehicles (AI - enhanced)

Braking systems in autonomous vehicles (AI-enhanced) refer to intelligent braking mechanisms that use artificial intelligence to optimize stopping power, enhance safety, and improve vehicle control. These systems integrate advanced sensors, real-time data analysis, and predictive modeling to make split-second decisions in response to road conditions, obstacles, and driver input. AI-enhanced braking ensures precise control, reducing the risk of collisions and improving overall driving efficiency.

Key components of AI-enhanced braking systems include sensor fusion, which integrates data from cameras, LiDAR, radar, and ultrasonic sensors to detect road conditions, obstacles, and traffic dynamics. Machine learning algorithms analyze real-time data to predict potential hazards and adjust braking force accordingly. Automated emergency braking (AEB) uses AI to recognize imminent collisions and apply brakes automatically. Adaptive braking adjusts stopping power based on weather, terrain, and vehicle speed to enhance stability and safety. Communication interfaces connect braking systems with other vehicle control units, enabling seamless coordination with steering, acceleration, and autonomous driving features.

The benefits of AI-enhanced braking systems include improved reaction times, allowing vehicles to stop faster and more accurately than human drivers. Increased safety is achieved by reducing human error and minimizing the risk of collisions in complex driving environments. AI-driven braking improves fuel efficiency and reduces wear on braking components by optimizing brake usage. Enhanced adaptability allows vehicles to adjust braking performance based on environmental factors such as wet roads, icy conditions, and high-traffic situations. Predictive maintenance capabilities alert drivers and fleet operators to potential brake failures before they occur.

Applications of AI-enhanced braking systems extend to fully autonomous vehicles, where AI-driven braking is essential for ensuring safe and efficient self-driving operations. In advanced driver-assistance systems (ADAS), AI braking enhances human-driven vehicles by providing collision avoidance and emergency braking support. Public transportation and commercial fleets benefit from AI braking by improving road safety and reducing operational costs. High-performance sports and luxury vehicles integrate AI braking to deliver precision control at high speeds.

Industries leveraging AI-enhanced braking systems include automotive manufacturing, where major carmakers develop and implement AI-driven braking for next-generation vehicles. Logistics and transportation companies use AI braking to improve fleet safety and reduce accident-related expenses. Public transit systems integrate AI braking in buses and trains to enhance passenger safety and ride comfort. Robotics and automated machinery apply AI braking in industrial settings, ensuring safe operation of autonomous equipment.

In conclusion, AI-enhanced braking systems play a crucial role in advancing vehicle safety, efficiency, and automation. By integrating sensor fusion, machine learning, and adaptive braking, these systems provide superior reaction times, collision prevention, and predictive maintenance capabilities. Despite challenges related to sensor accuracy, computational complexity, and regulatory requirements, AI-driven braking continues to shape the future of autonomous and semi-autonomous transportation, making roads safer and vehicles more intelligent.

Branch and Bound Algorithm

Branch and Bound Algorithm is an optimization and search technique used to solve combinatorial and discrete problems by systematically exploring and pruning the solution space. It efficiently finds the optimal solution by dividing the problem into smaller subproblems (branching) and eliminating non-promising solutions (bounding) based on heuristic evaluations. This method is widely applied in solving complex problems such as integer programming, combinatorial optimization, and constraint satisfaction.

Key components of the Branch and Bound Algorithm include branching, where the original problem is divided into subproblems to explore different solution paths. Bounding functions estimate the best possible outcome for each subproblem, allowing the algorithm to discard paths that cannot lead to optimal solutions. Pruning eliminates unpromising branches based on bound comparisons, reducing computational complexity. A search strategy, such as depth-first or best-first search, determines the order in which subproblems are explored. The termination condition ensures that the algorithm stops once the optimal solution is found or all paths are exhausted.

The benefits of the Branch and Bound Algorithm include optimality assurance by guaranteeing the best possible solution within defined constraints. Computational efficiency is improved by pruning unnecessary computations, reducing search space exploration. It adapts to a variety of problems, making it useful for discrete optimization tasks across multiple domains. The method provides flexibility in choosing search strategies and heuristics, allowing for performance enhancements based on problem characteristics.

Applications of the Branch and Bound Algorithm extend to operations research, where it is used in solving linear and integer programming problems for resource allocation and scheduling. In logistics, it optimizes vehicle routing, supply chain management, and warehouse distribution. In finance, it assists in portfolio optimization and risk assessment. In artificial intelligence, it is used in game playing, decision trees, and constraint satisfaction problems. In engineering and manufacturing, it helps in production planning, layout optimization, and design configurations.

Industries utilizing the Branch and Bound Algorithm include transportation, where it enhances route optimization and logistics planning. Telecommunications apply it in network design and bandwidth allocation. The energy sector leverages it for power grid optimization and resource management. Healthcare uses it in medical scheduling and treatment planning. Software development applies the algorithm in compiler optimization and efficient code execution strategies.

In conclusion, the Branch and Bound Algorithm is a powerful optimization technique that systematically explores solution spaces while eliminating non-optimal paths. By leveraging branching, bounding, and pruning, it ensures computational efficiency and optimality across diverse applications. Despite challenges related to complexity, memory usage, and heuristic selection, it remains a widely used approach in operations research, logistics, finance, artificial intelligence, and engineering, providing structured and efficient solutions to complex optimization problems.

Branch-and-Cut Algorithm

Branch-and-Cut Algorithm is an optimization technique used to solve integer programming and combinatorial optimization problems by integrating branch-and-bound methods with cutting-plane techniques. It enhances computational efficiency by systematically exploring feasible solutions while dynamically adding constraints, known as cutting planes, to eliminate non-integral solutions and tighten the solution space.

Key components of the Branch-and-Cut Algorithm include branching, where the problem is divided into smaller subproblems to explore different solution paths systematically. Cutting planes generate additional constraints to remove fractional solutions without excluding feasible integer solutions. Bounding functions estimate the best possible outcome for each subproblem, allowing the algorithm to discard non-optimal branches. Pruning eliminates unnecessary paths by comparing bounds and removing subproblems that cannot lead to an optimal solution. The search strategy, such as depth-first or best-first search, determines the order in which subproblems are explored to accelerate convergence.

The benefits of the Branch-and-Cut Algorithm include improved efficiency compared to traditional branch-and-bound methods by reducing the search space through dynamic constraint generation. It ensures optimality by refining feasible regions, leading to faster convergence to the best integer solution. The method adapts to various integer programming problems by leveraging customized cutting planes for different constraints. By integrating cutting planes, it reduces the number of branches required, leading to lower computational costs in many scenarios.

Applications of the Branch-and-Cut Algorithm extend to operations research, where it optimizes resource allocation, supply chain logistics, and workforce scheduling. In network design, it assists in routing and bandwidth allocation to maximize efficiency. In finance, it is applied to portfolio optimization and risk minimization. In transportation, it optimizes vehicle routing, air traffic control, and railroad scheduling. In artificial intelligence, it is used in decision-making processes and game theory applications.

Industries benefiting from the Branch-and-Cut Algorithm include logistics and transportation, where it enhances efficiency in supply chain management and fleet scheduling. Telecommunications leverage it for network flow optimization and infrastructure planning. Manufacturing applies it to production scheduling and layout optimization. Financial services use it to balance risk and return in investment portfolios. The energy sector integrates it for optimizing power grid operations and resource distribution.

In conclusion, the Branch-and-Cut Algorithm is a powerful and efficient optimization technique that enhances traditional integer programming methods by dynamically adding constraints to refine feasible regions. By integrating branching, cutting planes, and pruning strategies, it accelerates solution discovery and improves computational efficiency. Despite challenges related to computational demands, memory usage, and constraint design, it remains a critical tool in operations research, logistics, finance, and network optimization, providing optimal solutions to complex real-world problems.

Branch Prediction in AI

Branch Prediction in AI refers to a computational technique used to anticipate the outcome of conditional operations in sequential decision-making, particularly in processor architecture and machine learning-based optimizations. It improves execution efficiency by predicting which branch of an instruction or decision tree will be taken before the actual computation occurs, reducing latency and increasing processing speed.

Key components of branch prediction in AI include pattern recognition, where historical data is analyzed to identify trends in conditional branches. Machine learning models enhance accuracy by dynamically adapting to evolving decision patterns. Speculative execution allows processors or AI systems to precompute possible outcomes based on predictions, minimizing delays in processing workflows. Feedback mechanisms refine predictions over time by continuously updating models with new data. Parallel execution strategies ensure that multiple possible outcomes can be processed simultaneously, reducing the impact of mispredictions.

The benefits of branch prediction in AI include increased computational efficiency by minimizing idle processing time and optimizing execution pipelines. It enhances decision-making speed in AI models, particularly in real-time applications such as autonomous systems and dynamic optimization tasks. Improved resource utilization reduces power consumption and memory overhead, making AI systems more efficient. The ability to precompute probable outcomes allows for smoother performance in high-speed applications, including gaming, financial modeling, and cloud-based computing.

Applications of branch prediction in AI extend to computer architecture, where it optimizes CPU pipeline execution by anticipating instruction flows. In machine learning, it accelerates decision trees, reinforcement learning, and probabilistic modeling by predicting future computation paths. In autonomous systems, branch prediction improves real-time responses in navigation, object detection, and sensor fusion. In cybersecurity, predictive models anticipate network threats by analyzing behavioral patterns and identifying potential breaches before they occur. Cloud computing and distributed systems benefit from branch prediction to optimize task scheduling and resource allocation.

Industries leveraging branch prediction in AI include semiconductor manufacturing, where CPU and GPU architectures integrate predictive execution to enhance performance. Autonomous vehicle development applies branch prediction to anticipate real-world driving conditions and improve reaction times. Financial services use predictive analytics for fraud detection, risk assessment, and high-frequency trading strategies. Telecommunications optimize network traffic routing and load balancing using AI-driven branch prediction. Artificial intelligence research incorporates branch prediction techniques into deep learning frameworks to improve model training efficiency.

In conclusion, branch prediction in AI is a crucial technique that enhances processing efficiency, accelerates decision-making, and optimizes computational workflows. By leveraging pattern recognition, machine learning, and speculative execution, it plays a vital role in computer architecture, machine learning, and real-time AI applications. Despite challenges related to mispredictions, hardware constraints, and security risks, branch prediction continues to drive advancements in AI-driven computation, enabling faster and more efficient systems across various industries.

Breakout Strategy in Trading

Breakout Strategy in AI Trading is a market trading approach that leverages artificial intelligence to identify and capitalize on significant price movements beyond established support or resistance levels. In financial markets, a breakout occurs when the price of an asset moves beyond a predetermined range, often signaling the start of a new trend. AI-driven breakout strategies enhance traditional methods by analyzing vast datasets, recognizing patterns, and executing trades with high speed and precision.

Key components of a breakout strategy in AI trading include price levels, volume analysis, technical indicators, machine learning models, and automated execution. Price levels refer to support and resistance zones where breakouts typically occur, acting as psychological thresholds for traders. Volume analysis assesses trading activity to validate breakout strength, as high trading volume often confirms the legitimacy of a breakout. Technical indicators such as moving averages, Bollinger Bands, and the Relative Strength Index (RSI) help identify breakout signals and reduce false positives. Machine learning models analyze historical price movements, volatility, and market sentiment to predict breakout patterns with greater accuracy. Automated execution allows AI systems to place trades instantly once breakout conditions are met, ensuring timely entries and exits.

The benefits of an AI-driven breakout strategy include increased accuracy, reduced emotional bias, and enhanced risk management. AI trading systems improve accuracy by analyzing multiple factors simultaneously, increasing the probability of detecting genuine breakouts. Emotional bias, a common issue in manual trading, is eliminated as AI follows predefined rules and data-driven strategies. Enhanced risk management comes from AI's ability to set stop-loss levels, trailing stops, and position sizing based on real-time market conditions, reducing potential losses.

An example of a breakout strategy in AI trading is its application in cryptocurrency markets, where digital assets experience high volatility. AI models analyze historical price trends, social media sentiment, and order book data to detect breakouts and execute trades automatically. Another example is in the stock market, where AI-powered hedge funds use breakout strategies to identify stocks on the verge of significant price movements, maximizing profit opportunities while minimizing risk.

Industries that benefit from AI-driven breakout strategies include hedge funds, retail trading, forex markets, cryptocurrency exchanges, and algorithmic trading firms. Hedge funds leverage AI to identify and act on breakout signals across multiple asset classes. Retail traders use AI-powered trading bots to automate breakout strategies in stock and forex markets. Forex markets rely on AI-driven breakout strategies to capitalize on currency fluctuations. Cryptocurrency exchanges benefit from AI trading algorithms that detect and respond to rapid price shifts. Algorithmic trading firms develop and refine AI models to enhance trading performance in high-frequency and institutional trading environments.

Applications of breakout strategies in AI trading extend to market trend analysis, risk-adjusted trading, quantitative trading, high-frequency trading, and predictive analytics. Market trend analysis uses AI to identify potential breakout zones before they occur. Risk-adjusted trading applies AI-driven techniques to optimize trade execution while minimizing exposure. Quantitative trading relies on statistical models and AI predictions to refine breakout strategies. High-frequency trading firms use AI to execute thousands of breakout trades within milliseconds. Predictive analytics enhances AI trading models by incorporating real-time economic indicators, news sentiment, and volatility analysis.

Breakout strategy in AI trading transforms how traders and institutions identify and respond to market opportunities. By integrating AI with traditional technical analysis, breakout strategies become more accurate, efficient, and adaptable to various market conditions. As AI continues to evolve, its role in breakout trading will expand, allowing traders to capitalize on market movements with greater precision and reduced risk.

Breakthrough Detection in AI Research

Breakthrough Detection in AI Research refers to the process of identifying significant advancements, novel discoveries, or transformative innovations in the field of artificial intelligence. This involves the use of machine learning, data analytics, and computational methods to track emerging trends, evaluate the impact of research contributions, and detect paradigm shifts in AI development. By analyzing large volumes of scientific literature, patents, and experimental results, AI-driven breakthrough detection helps researchers, policymakers, and industry leaders stay ahead of technological advancements.

Key components of breakthrough detection in AI research include natural language processing, citation analysis, machine learning models, knowledge graphs, and trend forecasting. Natural language processing enables AI systems to extract and interpret relevant information from research papers, conference proceedings, and patents. Citation analysis assesses the influence of a research paper by evaluating its citation patterns and impact on the scientific community. Machine learning models identify recurring patterns and anomalies in AI research to detect innovations with disruptive potential. Knowledge graphs map relationships between researchers, institutions, and topics to visualize the evolution of AI breakthroughs. Trend forecasting applies predictive analytics to anticipate future advancements and emerging areas of interest in AI.

The benefits of breakthrough detection in AI research include accelerated innovation, enhanced collaboration, and improved resource allocation. By identifying groundbreaking research early, AI accelerates the adoption of transformative ideas, reducing the time it takes for new discoveries to impact real-world applications. Enhanced collaboration arises from AI's ability to connect researchers with similar interests, fostering interdisciplinary work and knowledge sharing. Improved resource allocation helps governments, universities, and private organizations invest in high-potential AI projects, optimizing funding distribution and maximizing scientific progress.

An example of breakthrough detection in AI research is its application in deep learning evolution, where AI systems analyze thousands of research papers to identify emerging techniques such as transformer models, self-supervised learning, and neuromorphic computing. Another example is drug discovery, where AI detects promising breakthroughs in AI-driven molecular simulations, expediting the development of new pharmaceuticals.

Industries that benefit from breakthrough detection in AI research include healthcare, finance, cybersecurity, education, and autonomous systems. Healthcare leverages AI-driven breakthrough detection to identify medical AI advancements, such as AI-powered diagnostics and personalized treatment models. The finance industry uses AI to track innovations in algorithmic trading and fraud detection. Cybersecurity firms rely on AI breakthrough detection to monitor emerging threats and advancements in adversarial AI defense mechanisms. The education sector benefits from AI research detection in adaptive learning technologies and automated knowledge assessment. Autonomous systems, including robotics and self-driving cars, integrate AI research breakthroughs to enhance navigation, decision-making, and human-machine interaction.

Applications of breakthrough detection in AI research extend to patent analysis, research impact assessment, scientific discovery acceleration, AI ethics monitoring, and policy development. Patent analysis applies AI to detect new and influential patents that drive technological change. Research impact assessment quantifies the influence of AI advancements based on citations and real-world adoption. Scientific discovery acceleration identifies promising AI-driven innovations, expediting their transition from theory to practical implementation. AI ethics monitoring tracks emerging discussions on responsible AI development, fairness, and bias mitigation. Policy development benefits from AI research tracking by informing regulatory frameworks and ethical guidelines for AI deployment.

Breakthrough detection in AI research is a transformative tool that enables researchers, industries, and policymakers to stay ahead of rapid advancements in artificial intelligence. By leveraging AI for knowledge discovery, research impact assessment, and trend forecasting, breakthrough detection accelerates the progress of AI innovations while ensuring ethical and strategic decision-making. As AI research continues to expand, the ability to detect and act on breakthroughs will play a crucial role in shaping the future of artificial intelligence and its applications across diverse sectors.

Breeding Algorithms

Breeding Algorithms are a class of optimization techniques inspired by the principles of natural selection and genetic inheritance. These algorithms simulate the process of evolution by selecting the fittest individuals from a population, combining their attributes through crossover and mutation, and generating improved solutions over multiple generations. Breeding algorithms are commonly used in artificial intelligence, machine learning, and optimization problems where traditional methods struggle to find optimal solutions efficiently.

Key components of breeding algorithms include population initialization, fitness evaluation, selection, crossover, mutation, and termination criteria. Population initialization generates a diverse set of potential solutions, ensuring a broad search space for optimization. Fitness evaluation measures the performance of each individual in the population based on predefined criteria. Selection mechanisms, such as tournament selection or roulette wheel selection, prioritize the best-performing individuals for reproduction. Crossover combines genetic material from selected individuals to create new offspring with improved characteristics. Mutation introduces small variations in offspring to maintain diversity and prevent premature convergence. Termination criteria define when the algorithm should stop, typically based on reaching a satisfactory solution or a maximum number of generations.

The benefits of breeding algorithms include adaptability, robustness, and the ability to escape local optima. These algorithms can adapt to dynamic environments by evolving solutions based on real-time feedback. Their robustness allows them to handle complex, high-dimensional optimization problems where traditional methods struggle. The evolutionary nature of breeding algorithms enables them to explore diverse solution spaces, reducing the likelihood of getting stuck in local optima and improving overall performance.

An example of breeding algorithms in action is in neural network optimization, where they fine-tune hyperparameters to improve model accuracy and efficiency. Instead of manually adjusting parameters, breeding algorithms evolve optimal configurations through iterative selection and recombination. Another example is in robotics, where they optimize control strategies for autonomous systems, allowing robots to learn adaptive behaviors based on environmental interactions.

Industries that benefit from breeding algorithms include aerospace, healthcare, finance, manufacturing, and artificial intelligence. The aerospace industry applies breeding algorithms in flight path optimization and aerodynamic design. Healthcare utilizes these algorithms in drug discovery and medical imaging enhancements. Financial institutions leverage them for portfolio optimization, risk assessment, and algorithmic trading. Manufacturing industries use breeding algorithms for production scheduling and supply chain optimization. Artificial intelligence research integrates breeding algorithms into machine learning models to enhance efficiency and predictive capabilities.

Applications of breeding algorithms extend to genetic programming, automated design, game development, cryptography, and network security. Genetic programming uses breeding algorithms to evolve code and optimize machine learning models. Automated design benefits from these algorithms in creating efficient engineering solutions, such as optimizing mechanical structures. Game development employs breeding algorithms to generate adaptive AI opponents and enhance procedural content generation. Cryptography utilizes breeding algorithms in key generation and encryption mechanisms. Network security applies these algorithms in intrusion detection systems to identify and counteract evolving cyber threats.

Breeding algorithms provide a powerful approach to solving complex optimization problems by simulating evolutionary processes. Their ability to adapt, refine, and improve solutions over time makes them valuable in artificial intelligence, machine learning, and various industrial applications. As computational power increases and algorithmic refinements continue, breeding algorithms will play a significant role in advancing optimization techniques, leading to more efficient and intelligent AI-driven solutions.

Brittleness in AI

Brittleness in AI refers to the tendency of artificial intelligence systems to fail or produce unreliable results when faced with situations outside their training data or when encountering unexpected variations in input. Unlike human intelligence, which can adapt to new scenarios through reasoning and contextual understanding, brittle AI struggles with generalization and robustness, making it vulnerable to errors in real-world applications.

Key components of brittleness in AI include overfitting, lack of contextual reasoning, sensitivity to adversarial inputs, and limited transfer learning. Overfitting occurs when an AI model becomes too specialized in training data, leading to poor performance on unseen data. Lack of contextual reasoning prevents AI from understanding broader implications or adapting to variations in data patterns. Sensitivity to adversarial inputs means that small, imperceptible changes in input data can cause AI models to make incorrect predictions. Limited transfer learning restricts AI's ability to apply learned knowledge from one domain to another, reducing its adaptability to new problems.

The benefits of addressing AI brittleness include improved reliability, enhanced adaptability, and better real-world performance. Reducing brittleness ensures AI systems function consistently across diverse conditions, making them more dependable in critical applications. Enhanced adaptability allows AI to handle novel situations without requiring extensive retraining. Improved real-world performance results in AI solutions that work effectively outside controlled environments, increasing their practical utility in various industries.

An example of AI brittleness is seen in computer vision systems used for autonomous vehicles. If a self-driving car's AI is trained primarily on sunny weather conditions, it may struggle to recognize road signs accurately in heavy rain or fog, leading to potential safety risks. Another example is in natural language processing, where AI chatbots fail to understand nuanced questions or generate misleading responses when dealing with unfamiliar topics.

Industries affected by AI brittleness include healthcare, finance, cybersecurity, autonomous systems, and legal tech. Healthcare AI models must be robust to variations in medical data, ensuring accurate diagnoses across different patient demographics. Financial AI systems that detect fraud or predict market trends need to adapt to constantly changing economic conditions. Cybersecurity AI must recognize evolving threats and avoid being misled by adversarial attacks. Autonomous systems, such as drones and robots, require AI that can function reliably in diverse and unpredictable environments. Legal tech AI must accurately interpret complex legal language, adapting to variations in case laws and regulations.

Applications impacted by AI brittleness include automated decision-making, facial recognition, speech recognition, predictive analytics, and robotic process automation. Automated decision-making systems must be resistant to biased data and unexpected input variations to ensure fair and ethical outcomes. Facial recognition systems struggle with brittleness when encountering different lighting conditions, angles, or facial expressions. Speech recognition AI may misinterpret accents or background noise, leading to inaccurate transcriptions. Predictive analytics requires robustness to fluctuations in data trends to maintain accuracy over time. Robotic process automation relies on AI's ability to adapt to changes in workflows and system updates to function effectively.

Brittleness in AI remains a significant challenge that limits the reliability and adaptability of AI systems in real-world scenarios. Addressing brittleness requires techniques such as data augmentation, adversarial training, and continual learning to improve model resilience. As AI continues to be integrated into critical applications, reducing brittleness will be essential for ensuring trustworthy, scalable, and safe AI-driven solutions across industries.

Broadcast Neural Network

Broadcast Neural Network is a specialized neural network architecture designed to distribute and process information across multiple layers or nodes in a parallel and efficient manner. Unlike traditional deep learning models that rely on sequential processing, a broadcast neural network transmits learned features and representations across different network layers simultaneously, enhancing speed and scalability. This architecture is particularly useful in distributed computing environments, where rapid information propagation is necessary for large-scale machine learning tasks.

Key components of a broadcast neural network include broadcast layers, distributed learning nodes, weight-sharing mechanisms, and real-time synchronization. Broadcast layers enable efficient transmission of learned representations to multiple parts of the network, reducing redundancy and improving computational efficiency. Distributed learning nodes process different aspects of the data in parallel, allowing for faster training and inference. Weight-sharing mechanisms ensure that learned parameters are consistently applied across various parts of the network, minimizing overfitting and improving generalization. Real-time synchronization coordinates information exchange between different nodes, ensuring consistency and stability in the learning process.

The benefits of a broadcast neural network include improved computational efficiency, enhanced scalability, and faster convergence. Computational efficiency is achieved by minimizing redundant calculations and optimizing parallel processing. Enhanced scalability allows the network to handle large datasets and complex models without significant increases in processing time. Faster convergence ensures that the model reaches optimal performance more quickly, reducing the time required for training and deployment in real-world applications.

An example of a broadcast neural network in action is in real-time video processing, where high-resolution images are processed across multiple distributed nodes simultaneously, reducing latency in applications such as autonomous driving and surveillance. Another example is in natural language processing, where broadcast neural networks distribute linguistic features across multiple layers to improve text comprehension and translation efficiency.

Industries benefiting from broadcast neural networks include telecommunications, finance, healthcare, manufacturing, and artificial intelligence research. Telecommunications companies use this architecture for optimizing network traffic, reducing latency, and improving data transmission efficiency. Financial institutions leverage broadcast neural networks for fraud detection and real-time risk assessment, processing large volumes of transactional data. Healthcare applications involve medical image analysis and diagnostic support, where parallel processing accelerates AI-driven predictions. Manufacturing industries apply broadcast neural networks in predictive maintenance and automated quality control, improving operational efficiency. AI research institutions explore broadcast neural networks to develop more efficient deep learning models for various domains.

Applications of broadcast neural networks extend to distributed machine learning, edge computing, real-time decision-making, smart city infrastructure, and AI-powered automation. Distributed machine learning benefits from efficient information broadcasting, improving performance in cloud-based AI models. Edge computing utilizes broadcast neural networks to process data locally while maintaining synchronization with centralized models, reducing dependence on cloud resources. Real-time decision-making systems, such as automated trading and emergency response networks, rely on rapid information distribution to optimize outcomes. Smart city infrastructure integrates broadcast neural networks to manage data from traffic systems, surveillance networks, and public services. AI-powered automation applies this architecture in robotics, autonomous vehicles, and virtual assistants, enabling intelligent decision-making at scale.

Broadcast neural networks represent a significant advancement in AI model efficiency, offering a scalable and parallelized approach to deep learning. By minimizing bottlenecks in information processing, this architecture improves real-time learning and decision-making capabilities across various industries. As AI applications continue to demand greater efficiency and scalability, broadcast neural networks will play a vital role in shaping the future of artificial intelligence and distributed computing.

Broadcasting in AI

Broadcasting in AI refers to the process of distributing data, signals, or computational tasks across multiple processing units or layers within an artificial intelligence system. This mechanism enables efficient information sharing, parallel processing, and synchronization of AI models, enhancing computational speed and scalability. Broadcasting is commonly used in deep learning frameworks, data distribution in neural networks, and distributed machine learning environments to optimize resource utilization and model efficiency.

Key components of broadcasting in AI include data distribution mechanisms, parallel computing, tensor broadcasting, synchronization protocols, and optimization strategies. Data distribution mechanisms ensure that information is evenly propagated across multiple nodes or layers to prevent computational bottlenecks. Parallel computing allows multiple processors to work on different parts of the data simultaneously, improving efficiency in large-scale AI models. Tensor broadcasting enables element-wise operations on tensors of different shapes without the need for explicit replication, reducing memory consumption and computational complexity. Synchronization protocols maintain consistency across distributed systems, ensuring that updates to AI models occur without conflicts. Optimization strategies refine broadcasting techniques to minimize latency and enhance processing speed in real-time AI applications.

The benefits of broadcasting in AI include improved efficiency, reduced computational overhead, and enhanced scalability. Efficiency is achieved by distributing workloads across multiple processors, reducing the time required for training and inference. Computational overhead is minimized through optimized memory usage, especially in tensor operations where redundant data replication is avoided. Scalability ensures that AI models can handle large datasets and complex computations without significant increases in processing time or resource consumption.

An example of broadcasting in AI is found in deep learning frameworks such as TensorFlow and PyTorch, where tensor broadcasting allows element-wise arithmetic operations on tensors of different shapes without additional memory allocation. Another example is in federated learning, where broadcasting techniques distribute model updates across decentralized devices, enabling privacy-preserving AI training without centralizing raw data.

Industries benefiting from broadcasting in AI include healthcare, finance, autonomous systems, cloud computing, and telecommunications. Healthcare applications involve AI-driven diagnostics and medical imaging analysis, where broadcasting optimizes computational efficiency across large datasets. Financial institutions leverage broadcasting to distribute risk assessments and fraud detection algorithms across multiple servers, ensuring real-time decision-making. Autonomous systems, including self-driving cars and robotic automation, use broadcasting to share sensor data and coordinate actions seamlessly. Cloud computing platforms integrate broadcasting in AI workloads to enhance performance across distributed environments. Telecommunications companies utilize broadcasting for optimizing network traffic, predictive analytics, and intelligent automation in infrastructure management.

Applications of broadcasting in AI extend to machine learning model training, data synchronization, intelligent automation, reinforcement learning, and large-scale simulations. Machine learning model training benefits from broadcasting by accelerating backpropagation and optimization processes in neural networks. Data synchronization ensures that AI-driven applications maintain consistency across multiple nodes in distributed environments. Intelligent automation applies broadcasting to coordinate AI-driven processes in industries such as logistics, retail, and smart manufacturing. Reinforcement learning uses broadcasting to distribute state-action updates across multiple agents, improving learning efficiency in multi-agent systems. Large-scale simulations in AI research and climate modeling leverage broadcasting to manage complex computations efficiently across distributed computing clusters.

Broadcasting in AI is a critical technique for optimizing computational efficiency, enabling parallelism, and improving the scalability of artificial intelligence applications. By reducing memory overhead and accelerating data distribution, broadcasting enhances AI model performance across various domains. As AI continues to evolve and tackle increasingly complex challenges, broadcasting will remain an essential mechanism for ensuring efficient, high-performance AI-driven solutions.

Broad Learning System (BLS)

Broad Learning System (BLS) is a machine learning framework designed to efficiently handle large-scale data processing with a flat network structure rather than relying on deep neural networks. Unlike deep learning models that require multiple hierarchical layers and extensive training, BLS expands horizontally by incorporating feature mapping and enhancement nodes, making it computationally efficient and suitable for real-time learning applications. It provides a balance between accuracy and efficiency, making it an attractive alternative to deep learning for various AI tasks.

Key components of a broad learning system include feature mapping, enhancement nodes, incremental learning, and a flat network structure. Feature mapping extracts relevant patterns and relationships from input data, forming the foundation of the learning process. Enhancement nodes refine and strengthen the mapped features, improving the model's ability to recognize patterns without requiring deep layers. Incremental learning allows BLS to adapt to new data without retraining the entire model, making it efficient for dynamic environments. The flat network structure reduces computational complexity by expanding learning capacity laterally rather than vertically, optimizing speed and resource usage.

The benefits of a broad learning system include faster training, reduced computational cost, and adaptability to real-time learning. Faster training is achieved because BLS does not rely on backpropagation through multiple deep layers, allowing rapid model updates. Reduced computational cost makes BLS ideal for edge computing and resource-constrained environments where deep learning models may be impractical. Adaptability to real-time learning ensures that BLS can efficiently update its knowledge base without extensive retraining, making it suitable for applications that require continuous adaptation.

An example of broad learning system implementation is in facial recognition, where BLS can quickly process and classify facial features without the heavy computational overhead of deep learning models. Another example is in financial fraud detection, where BLS continuously adapts to new fraudulent patterns by incrementally updating its knowledge base without the need for retraining on historical data.

Industries benefiting from broad learning systems include finance, healthcare, manufacturing, telecommunications, and autonomous systems. The finance sector applies BLS for risk assessment and fraud detection, where real-time adaptability is crucial. Healthcare leverages BLS for medical diagnosis and patient monitoring, enabling rapid analysis of medical images and sensor data. Manufacturing industries use BLS for quality control and predictive maintenance, optimizing production efficiency. Telecommunications companies apply BLS for network optimization and anomaly detection, improving service reliability. Autonomous systems, such as drones and robotics, integrate BLS for adaptive decision-making in dynamic environments.

Applications of broad learning systems extend to image classification, speech recognition, anomaly detection, predictive analytics, and intelligent recommendation systems. Image classification benefits from BLS's ability to process large datasets efficiently without deep network dependencies. Speech recognition systems use BLS to identify and process spoken language in real time with minimal latency. Anomaly detection applies BLS to identify irregular patterns in cybersecurity, industrial monitoring, and healthcare diagnostics. Predictive analytics leverages BLS for forecasting trends in finance, supply chain management, and energy consumption. Intelligent recommendation systems use BLS to enhance personalized user experiences in e-commerce, content streaming, and online services.

Broad learning systems offer a scalable and efficient approach to machine learning, reducing computational requirements while maintaining high accuracy. By expanding laterally rather than relying on deep hierarchical layers, BLS provides a flexible alternative to traditional deep learning, making it well-suited for real-time applications and environments with limited computing resources. As AI technology continues to evolve, broad learning systems will play a key role in advancing machine learning capabilities across various industries.

Budget Optimization AI

Budget Optimization AI refers to the use of artificial intelligence to allocate financial resources efficiently while maximizing returns and minimizing waste. This technology analyzes historical spending patterns, predicts future expenses, and dynamically adjusts budget allocations based on real-time data. By leveraging machine learning and advanced analytics, AI-driven budget optimization ensures that financial resources are distributed optimally across different sectors, projects, or marketing campaigns to achieve strategic goals.

Key components of budget optimization AI include data aggregation, predictive analytics, machine learning models, dynamic allocation algorithms, and performance tracking. Data aggregation collects and consolidates financial data from various sources to provide a comprehensive view of expenditures and revenue streams. Predictive analytics forecasts future financial trends based on historical spending and market conditions, allowing for proactive budget adjustments. Machine learning models identify inefficiencies and suggest optimal spending strategies by analyzing large datasets. Dynamic allocation algorithms continuously adjust budget distributions in real time to ensure optimal performance across different financial objectives. Performance tracking monitors key financial indicators, providing insights into budget efficiency and necessary modifications.

The benefits of budget optimization AI include improved financial efficiency, data-driven decision-making, and enhanced adaptability. Financial efficiency is maximized by identifying cost-saving opportunities and eliminating unnecessary expenditures. Data-driven decision-making ensures that budget allocations are based on real-time insights rather than assumptions, leading to more informed financial planning. Enhanced adaptability allows organizations to quickly respond to economic changes, market fluctuations, or unexpected financial constraints by dynamically adjusting budgets.

An example of budget optimization AI in action is in digital marketing, where AI algorithms allocate advertising budgets across multiple channels such as social media, search engines, and display ads to maximize return on investment. Another example is in corporate finance, where AI-driven budgeting tools analyze departmental spending and recommend reallocations to enhance operational efficiency and profitability.

Industries that benefit from budget optimization AI include marketing, finance, healthcare, government, and supply chain management. Marketing agencies use AI to distribute advertising budgets across campaigns and platforms, ensuring cost-effective customer acquisition. Financial institutions leverage AI-driven budgeting for risk management, investment planning, and operational cost reduction. Healthcare organizations optimize budgets by predicting patient demand, reducing unnecessary expenses, and improving resource allocation. Government agencies use AI to enhance budget planning for public services, infrastructure projects, and social programs. Supply chain management benefits from AI-driven budget optimization by minimizing procurement costs and improving logistics efficiency.

Applications of budget optimization AI extend to corporate financial planning, marketing campaign management, project cost estimation, resource allocation, and economic forecasting. Corporate financial planning relies on AI to optimize operational budgets and investment decisions. Marketing campaign management uses AI to distribute ad spend across platforms for maximum engagement and conversion rates. Project cost estimation benefits from AI's ability to predict expenses and adjust budgets dynamically to avoid overspending. Resource allocation ensures that funds are distributed efficiently across departments, projects, or initiatives to align with strategic priorities. Economic forecasting applies AI to analyze financial trends and provide recommendations for future budget planning.

Budget optimization AI transforms financial management by integrating data-driven insights, real-time analytics, and automated decision-making into budget allocation processes. By reducing inefficiencies and maximizing returns, AI-driven budgeting helps businesses and organizations adapt to financial challenges while ensuring sustainable growth. As AI technology continues to evolve, its role in budget optimization will become increasingly sophisticated, making financial planning more precise, strategic, and cost-effective.

Buffer AI

Definition

Buffer AI refers to an artificial intelligence-driven system designed to manage and optimize data flow, resource allocation, and computational processes in real-time applications. It acts as an intermediary between input and output processes, ensuring smooth operations by preventing overload, reducing latency, and enhancing overall efficiency. Buffer AI is particularly useful in dynamic environments where real-time decision-making, data processing, and system responsiveness are critical.

Key components of Buffer AI include adaptive buffering, predictive analytics, load balancing, memory management, and real-time monitoring. Adaptive buffering dynamically adjusts data storage and processing capacity based on system demands, ensuring seamless performance. Predictive analytics anticipates workload fluctuations, optimizing buffer allocation to prevent bottlenecks and inefficiencies. Load balancing distributes computational tasks evenly across resources, reducing system strain and maintaining performance consistency. Memory management optimizes storage allocation, minimizing data loss and improving access speeds. Real-time monitoring continuously tracks system performance, detecting potential congestion or processing delays before they impact operations.

The benefits of Buffer AI include enhanced system efficiency, reduced latency, and improved scalability. By intelligently managing data flow and computational tasks, Buffer AI prevents slowdowns and ensures smooth processing across applications. Reduced latency allows AI-driven systems to respond to inputs faster, which is crucial for time-sensitive applications such as autonomous driving and financial trading. Improved scalability ensures that AI systems can handle increasing workloads without performance degradation, making them suitable for large-scale deployment.

An example of Buffer AI in action is in streaming services, where AI dynamically manages data buffering to prevent playback interruptions and optimize bandwidth usage. Another example is in cloud computing, where AI-driven buffering ensures efficient data transmission and load distribution across multiple servers, minimizing delays and improving system reliability.

Industries that benefit from Buffer AI include telecommunications, autonomous systems, finance, healthcare, and manufacturing. Telecommunications providers use Buffer AI to manage network traffic, optimize data streaming, and prevent congestion. Autonomous systems, such as self-driving cars and drones, rely on AI-driven buffering to process sensor data in real time, ensuring safe and responsive decision-making. Financial institutions apply Buffer AI in high-frequency trading and transaction processing, reducing delays and maximizing trading efficiency. Healthcare organizations leverage

Buffer AI for medical imaging, patient monitoring, and real-time diagnostics, improving accuracy and responsiveness. Manufacturing operations utilize AI-driven buffering to optimize robotic automation and supply chain processes, minimizing production downtime.

Applications of Buffer AI extend to cloud computing, video streaming, robotics, cybersecurity, and data analytics. Cloud computing services use AI-driven buffering to optimize storage, prevent server overload, and improve data accessibility. Video streaming platforms apply Buffer AI to manage bandwidth distribution, ensuring high-quality playback without buffering delays. Robotics systems incorporate AI buffering to regulate real-time data processing, improving the accuracy and efficiency of automated machines. Cybersecurity solutions leverage AI buffering to analyze large volumes of data for threat detection without system slowdowns. Data analytics platforms integrate Buffer AI to streamline the processing of big data, enabling faster and more accurate insights.

Buffer AI plays a crucial role in optimizing data processing, computational efficiency, and system responsiveness across various industries. By intelligently managing resources, reducing latency, and preventing system overload, Buffer AI enhances performance in real-time applications. As AI-driven technologies continue to advance, Buffer AI will become increasingly essential in enabling seamless data flow and maximizing operational efficiency in complex and high-demand environments.

Buffer Overflow in AI Systems

Definition

Buffer Overflow in AI Sytems refers to a condition where an AI program attempts to store more data in a buffer than it was designed to handle, leading to data corruption, system crashes, or security vulnerabilities. This occurs when AI models or applications process large amounts of input data without properly managing memory allocation, causing excess data to overwrite adjacent memory locations. Buffer overflow can impact the reliability and security of AI-driven applications, making it a critical concern in software development and cybersecurity.

Key components of buffer overflow in AI systems include memory management, input validation, stack and heap buffers, exception handling, and security protocols. Memory management ensures that AI systems allocate and deallocate memory efficiently to prevent unintended overwrites. Input validation filters and limits incoming data to ensure it does not exceed the buffer's capacity. Stack and heap buffers are memory storage areas where AI programs hold temporary data; improper handling of these buffers can lead to overflow issues. Exception handling helps AI systems detect and respond to buffer overflow errors before they cause severe failures. Security protocols, such as memory protection and address randomization, mitigate the risks associated with buffer overflow attacks.

The benefits of addressing buffer overflow in AI systems include improved system stability, enhanced security, and optimized performance. Proper memory management ensures that AI applications run smoothly without unexpected crashes or slowdowns. Enhanced security protects AI systems from cyberattacks that exploit buffer overflow vulnerabilities to gain unauthorized access. Optimized performance enables AI-driven applications to process large datasets efficiently without risking memory corruption or data loss.

An example of buffer overflow in AI systems is seen in autonomous vehicles, where improper memory handling in sensor data processing can lead to system failures, causing the vehicle to misinterpret its environment. Another example is in AI-driven cybersecurity, where attackers exploit buffer overflow vulnerabilities in machine learning models to inject malicious code, compromising data integrity and security.

Industries affected by buffer overflow in AI systems include cybersecurity, healthcare, finance, autonomous systems, and cloud computing. Cybersecurity firms work to prevent AI-based attacks that leverage buffer overflow vulnerabilities to compromise critical infrastructure. Healthcare AI applications, such as diagnostic tools and robotic surgery systems, require robust memory management to avoid malfunctions that could impact patient care. Financial institutions use AI for fraud detection and risk analysis, necessitating secure memory handling to prevent data corruption and unauthorized access. Autonomous systems, including self-driving cars and drones, must ensure memory integrity to maintain safety and operational accuracy. Cloud computing platforms that run AI models at scale implement buffer overflow protections to prevent service disruptions and data breaches.

Applications of buffer overflow prevention in AI systems include secure AI software development, real-time data processing, adversarial attack mitigation, embedded AI systems, and cloud-based AI services. Secure AI software development incorporates memory-safe programming practices to prevent buffer overflow vulnerabilities. Real-time data processing applications rely on robust buffer management to handle large data streams without causing system failures. Adversarial attack mitigation strategies involve securing AI models against buffer overflow exploits that could compromise their functionality. Embedded AI systems, such as IoT devices and robotics, implement buffer overflow protection to ensure reliable operation in resource-constrained environments. Cloud-based AI services utilize automated memory monitoring and protection mechanisms to prevent buffer-related failures in distributed computing environments.

Buffer overflow in AI systems poses significant risks to security, reliability, and performance, making it essential to implement robust memory management and security measures. As AI applications continue to grow in complexity and scale, addressing buffer overflow vulnerabilities will be critical for ensuring safe, efficient, and resilient AI-driven solutions across various industries.

Bug Detection AI

Definition

Bug Detection AI refers to the use of artificial intelligence and machine learning algorithms to automatically identify, diagnose, and predict software bugs in codebases. This technology enhances software development by detecting errors, vulnerabilities, and inefficiencies in real-time, reducing manual debugging efforts and improving code quality. AI-powered bug detection systems analyze vast amounts of code, recognize patterns of common errors, and provide recommendations to developers for quick remediation.

Key components of bug detection AI include code analysis, anomaly detection, natural language processing, machine learning models, and automated debugging. Code analysis involves scanning source code, bytecode, or compiled programs to detect syntax errors, logical flaws, and security vulnerabilities. Anomaly detection identifies deviations from expected code behavior, flagging potential issues before they impact system functionality. Natural language processing enables AI systems to understand developer comments, documentation, and error messages to provide meaningful suggestions. Machine learning models learn from historical bug data and predict potential issues in new code, continuously improving their detection accuracy. Automated debugging assists in isolating, diagnosing, and even fixing bugs without manual intervention.

The benefits of bug detection AI include improved software reliability, faster development cycles, and enhanced security. AI-driven bug detection significantly reduces the number of defects that reach production, ensuring higher software quality. Faster development cycles result from early bug detection, minimizing debugging time and accelerating software deployment. Enhanced security is achieved by identifying vulnerabilities such as buffer overflows, memory leaks, and SQL injections, reducing the risk of cyber threats.

An example of bug detection AI in action is in software development environments where AI-powered tools such as DeepCode, CodeQL, and Microsoft IntelliCode analyze source code in real time to detect errors and suggest corrections. Another example is in mobile app development, where AI systems scan applications before deployment, preventing crashes and performance issues.

Industries that benefit from bug detection AI include software development, cybersecurity, finance, healthcare, and telecommunications. Software development companies use AI-driven bug detection to enhance the efficiency of coding, testing, and deployment processes. Cybersecurity firms integrate AI to detect vulnerabilities in critical software systems and prevent security breaches. Financial institutions apply AI-powered bug detection to ensure the integrity of banking applications and trading platforms. Healthcare technology companies leverage AI to detect errors in medical software and electronic health records, ensuring patient safety. Telecommunications providers use AI to identify bugs in network management systems, preventing service disruptions.

Applications of bug detection AI extend to automated code reviews, DevOps integration, security vulnerability scanning, embedded systems testing, and cloud computing. Automated code reviews leverage AI to analyze code repositories and enforce best practices. DevOps teams integrate AI-powered bug detection into continuous integration and deployment pipelines to catch errors early in the development process. Security vulnerability scanning applies AI to identify weaknesses in software applications, protecting systems from cyber threats. Embedded systems testing ensures that AI-driven diagnostics detect potential software failures in hardware-dependent applications such as automotive and IoT devices. Cloud computing platforms use AI to monitor and debug software running in distributed environments, ensuring performance and reliability.

Bug detection AI transforms software development by automating error identification, improving security, and accelerating debugging processes. By leveraging machine learning and intelligent analysis, AI-driven bug detection minimizes risks associated with faulty code, enhancing the overall efficiency and reliability of software applications. As AI technology advances, its role in software quality assurance will continue to expand, making automated bug detection a standard practice in modern software engineering.

Bug-Fixing AI

refers to artificial intelligence systems designed to detect, diagnose, and resolve errors or flaws—commonly known as bugs—in software code, machine learning models, or automated processes. Unlike traditional debugging, which relies heavily on human expertise, bug-fixing AI leverages pattern recognition, reasoning, and predictive capabilities to autonomously identify issues and often suggest or implement corrections. It acts as a digital troubleshooter, accelerating the maintenance of complex systems by reducing human workload and error oversight.

The key components of bug-fixing AI include a detection engine, a diagnostic framework, and a resolution module. The detection engine scans code, logs, or model outputs to spot anomalies, such as syntax errors, runtime crashes, or prediction inconsistencies, using techniques like anomaly detection or rule-based checks. The diagnostic framework analyzes these issues, tracing their root causes—whether in logic, data, or configuration—often through contextual understanding or historical patterns. The resolution module proposes fixes, ranging from code patches to parameter adjustments, sometimes executing them directly or guiding developers with precise recommendations.

The benefits of bug-fixing AI center on speed and scalability. It slashes debugging time by quickly pinpointing and resolving issues that might take humans hours or days to unravel, boosting development efficiency. It scales effortlessly across large codebases or models, catching bugs that might slip past manual review, especially in intricate systems. Additionally, it reduces human error, offering consistent, data-driven solutions that enhance software reliability and performance.

Examples of bug-fixing AI include its use in software development, where it scans repositories to fix syntax errors or optimize inefficient loops in real-time. In machine learning, it might adjust a model's hyperparameters after detecting overfitting in training logs. Another instance is in automated testing, where bug-fixing AI identifies and corrects failures in CI/CD pipelines, ensuring smooth deployment of updates.

Challenges in deploying bug-fixing AI stem from its precision and adaptability. Misdiagnosing bugs or applying incorrect fixes can introduce new errors, requiring robust validation to prevent cascading failures. It struggles with context-heavy bugs—like those tied to domain-specific logic—where human intuition still outshines AI's grasp. Building AI that generalizes across diverse languages, frameworks, or use cases also demands extensive training data and computational power.

Industries harnessing bug-fixing AI include technology, where it streamlines app development and maintenance for faster releases. Gaming uses it to polish complex game engines, fixing glitches in AI behaviors or physics simulations. Finance relies on it to debug high-stakes trading algorithms, minimizing downtime risks. Manufacturing applies it to correct flaws in automated production software, ensuring operational continuity.

In conclusion, Bug-Fixing AI emerges as a powerful ally in the quest for flawless systems, blending speed and scale to tame the chaos of errors. Its promise of automation is tempered by the need for accuracy and contextual depth, pushing developers to refine its intelligence. As industries race to perfect increasingly intricate technologies, bug-fixing AI will play a growing role in keeping the digital world humming smoothly.

Bugs in Machine Learning Models

Bugs in Machine Learning Models refer to errors, flaws, or unintended behaviors within the algorithms, data, or implementation of a machine learning system that lead to incorrect predictions, degraded performance, or unexpected outcomes. These bugs differ from traditional software bugs because they often stem from the interplay of statistical assumptions, training data, and model complexity rather than just coding mistakes. They represent the Achilles' heel of otherwise powerful AI tools, lurking in the nuances of data-driven intelligence.

The key components of bugs in machine learning models include faulty data inputs, algorithmic misconfigurations, and evaluation oversights. Faulty data inputs encompass issues like noise, missing values, or biases that skew the model's learning process, embedding errors into its predictions. Algorithmic misconfigurations arise from poorly tuned hyperparameters, inappropriate model choices, or flawed optimization logic that misalign the system with its intended task. Evaluation oversights occur when testing fails to catch edge cases or real-world variability, masking bugs until deployment.

The benefits of identifying and addressing these bugs are indirect but critical. Fixing them enhances model reliability, ensuring outputs align with expectations and reducing costly mistakes in live applications. It sharpens insight into the model's limitations, fostering better design and data practices over time. Moreover, tackling bugs builds trust in AI systems, as consistent, error-free performance reassures stakeholders in high-stakes contexts.

Examples of bugs in machine learning models include a facial recognition system misidentifying individuals due to an imbalanced training dataset lacking diversity. In predictive maintenance, a model might fail to flag equipment issues if trained on incomplete sensor logs, missing subtle failure signals. Another case is a recommendation engine suggesting irrelevant items after overfitting to a narrow subset of user behavior, ignoring broader preferences.

Industries affected by bugs in machine learning models include healthcare, where flawed diagnostic AI could misclassify patient conditions, risking lives. Finance grapples with them in trading algorithms, where prediction errors might trigger losses. Retail faces them in inventory forecasting, with bugs leading to overstock or shortages. Autonomous systems, like self-driving cars, encounter them in navigation models, where glitches could compromise safety.

In conclusion, Bugs in Machine Learning Models are the hidden gremlins of AI, challenging the promise of precision with their elusive, data-driven nature. Addressing them strengthens systems and credibility, though their complexity demands vigilance and skill. As industries lean deeper into machine learning, mastering these flaws will be key to unlocking AI's full, trustworthy potential.

Bulk Data AI Processing

Bulk Data AI Processing refers to the application of artificial intelligence techniques to analyze, interpret, and extract value from massive, aggregated datasets in a unified operation, handling the entirety of the data at scale rather than in segmented or incremental steps. This approach leverages AI's pattern-recognition and predictive capabilities to tackle vast volumes of information—often spanning terabytes or petabytes—transforming raw, unwieldy data into actionable insights or automated decisions. It's the industrial-scale engine of data-driven intelligence, built for scenarios where size and complexity outstrip traditional methods.

The key components of bulk data AI processing include a large-scale data repository, an AI processing framework, and a distributed computing infrastructure. The large-scale data repository holds the raw material—structured or unstructured data like logs, sensor outputs, or multimedia—amassed from diverse sources. The AI processing framework, often built on machine learning or deep learning models, sifts through this data, identifying trends, anomalies, or correlations. The distributed computing infrastructure, such as cloud clusters or GPU arrays, powers the operation, enabling parallel processing to manage the computational load efficiently.

The benefits of this approach are tied to its capacity and insight. It handles enormous datasets that would overwhelm manual or conventional systems, delivering results at a scale critical for big-picture analysis. It uncovers nuanced patterns or predictions buried in the volume, offering a depth of understanding unattainable with smaller samples. Additionally, bulk data AI processing streamlines workflows by automating analysis end-to-end, reducing the time from data collection to decision-making in data-rich environments.

Examples of bulk data AI processing include analyzing years of social media activity to map global sentiment trends for marketing campaigns. In climate science, it might process decades of satellite imagery and weather data to model future environmental shifts. Another instance is in fraud detection, where AI sifts through billions of financial transactions to flag suspicious patterns in real-time, protecting entire banking networks.

Industries employing bulk data AI processing include retail, where it analyzes customer purchase histories across regions to optimize inventory. Energy uses it to process sensor data from smart grids, predicting demand surges. Media leverages it to personalize content for millions by crunching viewing habits en masse. Government applies it in national security, mining communication data to detect threats across populations.

In conclusion, Bulk Data AI Processing stands as a titan of modern analytics, turning data mountains into strategic goldmines with unmatched scale and depth. Its ability to wrestle with complexity offers transformative potential, though it requires robust infrastructure and meticulous data stewardship. As industries drown in ever-growing data, this approach will increasingly define how AI turns volume into value.

Bulk Learning in AI

Bulk Learning in AI refers to a training approach where an artificial intelligence system processes and learns from a large, aggregated volume of data in a single, comprehensive sweep, rather than incrementally or in smaller batches. This method aims to capture broad patterns, relationships, and insights by immersing the model in a vast dataset all at once, leveraging the full scope of available information to build a robust foundational understanding. It contrasts with online or iterative learning, prioritizing depth and scale over gradual adaptation.

The key components of bulk learning in AI include a massive dataset, a high-capacity model, and a centralized processing system. The massive dataset forms the bedrock, encompassing diverse, often unstructured data points like text, images, or logs, collected upfront for holistic analysis. The high-capacity model, typically a deep neural network or similar architecture, has the computational muscle to digest this volume, extracting complex features without overfitting. The centralized processing system, often a powerful server or cloud cluster, handles the intensive computation, ensuring the model can scale to the data's magnitude.

The benefits of bulk learning shine in its thoroughness and efficiency for certain tasks. It enables the AI to develop a comprehensive knowledge base in one go, ideal for applications needing a wide-ranging grasp of a domain before deployment. It can uncover deep, interconnected patterns that might be missed in piecemeal training, enhancing predictive power. Additionally, by front-loading the learning process, it reduces the need for frequent retraining, saving time in stable, well-defined scenarios.

Examples of bulk learning in AI include training a language model on a colossal corpus of text, such as books and websites, to master grammar and context for natural language tasks. In image recognition, bulk learning might involve feeding a model millions of labeled photos at once to recognize objects across varied conditions. Another case is in scientific research, where an AI learns from decades of experimental data to identify trends or predict outcomes in fields like genomics.

Industries using bulk learning in AI include technology, where it powers large-scale recommendation engines for streaming platforms analyzing user histories en masse. Pharmaceuticals apply it to drug discovery, training models on vast chemical libraries to predict interactions. Marketing leverages it to segment customers by processing years of purchase data at once. Astronomy benefits too, with AI learning from bulk stellar observations to classify celestial phenomena.

In conclusion, Bulk Learning in AI offers a bold, all-in approach to model training, harnessing scale to build powerful, broad-spectrum intelligence. Its strength lies in mastering complex domains upfront, though it trades flexibility for depth and demands hefty resources. As industries tackle big-picture problems with abundant data, bulk learning will remain a potent, if specialized, tool in the AI arsenal.

Built-In AI

Built-In AI refers to artificial intelligence capabilities seamlessly integrated into devices, software, or systems at the point of design or manufacturing, enabling them to perform intelligent tasks without requiring external processing or add-on modules. Unlike standalone AI solutions, built-in AI is embedded directly into the core functionality of a product, making it an intrinsic part of its operation. This approach empowers everyday tools—from appliances to infrastructure—with autonomous decision-making, learning, or optimization features tailored to their specific purpose.

The key components of built-in AI include embedded algorithms, onboard processing hardware, and a feedback system. Embedded algorithms, such as machine learning models or rule-based logic, are pre-programmed to handle tasks like pattern recognition or anomaly detection specific to the device's role. Onboard processing hardware, often compact chips or microcontrollers, executes these algorithms locally, ensuring real-time performance without cloud dependency. The feedback system allows the AI to adapt or refine its behavior over time, using data generated during operation to improve accuracy or efficiency.

The benefits of built-in AI center on convenience and performance. It delivers instant responsiveness by processing data on-device, eliminating latency from network reliance, which is crucial for time-sensitive applications. It enhances privacy and security, as sensitive data stays local rather than being transmitted externally. Additionally, built-in AI reduces operational costs by minimizing the need for constant connectivity or server infrastructure, making it ideal for standalone or remote deployments.

Examples of built-in AI include smart thermostats that learn user preferences and adjust temperatures autonomously based on occupancy patterns. In automotive systems, built-in AI powers adaptive cruise control, processing sensor data to maintain safe distances without external input. Another case is in modern cameras, where AI enhances image quality by adjusting settings in real-time based on lighting conditions detected on-device.

Industries embracing built-in AI include consumer electronics, where it drives features in smartphones and wearables like fitness trackers analyzing health metrics. Automotive relies on it for in-vehicle systems enhancing safety and navigation. Agriculture uses built-in AI in smart irrigation systems, optimizing water use based on soil sensors. Healthcare benefits too, with medical devices like hearing aids adjusting to ambient noise via embedded intelligence.

In conclusion, Built-In AI weaves intelligence into the fabric of everyday tools, offering a self-contained, responsive approach to automation and decision-making. Its localized power brings efficiency and privacy to the forefront, though it grapples with the limits of compact design. As industries push for smarter, standalone solutions, built-in AI will continue to redefine how technology integrates seamlessly into our lives.

Business Process Mining with AI

Business Process Mining with AI refers to the application of artificial intelligence techniques to analyze, extract, and optimize organizational workflows by mining event logs and other process-related data. It combines traditional process mining—where system records reveal how tasks are actually performed—with AI's ability to uncover hidden patterns, predict outcomes, and suggest improvements. This fusion transforms raw data into actionable insights, enabling businesses to understand, refine, and automate their operations with greater precision.

The key components of business process mining with AI include data sources, an AI-driven analysis engine, and a visualization interface. Data sources consist of event logs, timestamps, and transaction records pulled from enterprise systems like ERP or CRM software, capturing the real-time flow of activities. The AI-driven analysis engine employs machine learning, natural language processing, or clustering to interpret this data, identifying inefficiencies, deviations, or bottlenecks. The visualization interface presents findings in an accessible format, such as process maps or dashboards, allowing stakeholders to grasp complex workflows intuitively.

The benefits of this approach are profound. It provides a clear, data-backed view of how processes unfold, cutting through assumptions to reveal actual performance, which aids in pinpointing inefficiencies. AI enhances predictive capabilities, forecasting delays or resource needs, while also recommending optimizations like automation candidates. It saves time and costs by streamlining operations without requiring manual audits, fostering agility in dynamic business environments.

Examples of business process mining with AI include its use in supply chain management, where AI analyzes shipping logs to detect delays and suggest rerouting strategies. In customer service, it might process call center data to identify common bottlenecks in ticket resolution, proposing workflow adjustments. Another instance is in finance, where AI mines invoice processing records to uncover approval delays, streamlining cash flow operations.

Industries harnessing business process mining with AI include logistics, where it optimizes delivery networks by analyzing real-time tracking data. Healthcare uses it to streamline patient intake and billing processes, reducing wait times. Banking leverages it to enhance fraud detection workflows, mining transaction patterns for anomalies. Manufacturing applies it to production lines, identifying slowdowns and improving throughput with AI-driven insights.

In conclusion, Business Process Mining with AI acts as a powerful lens into organizational efficiency, blending data-driven clarity with intelligent foresight to reshape how work gets done. Its capacity to turn logs into strategies offers a competitive edge, though success hinges on clean data and balanced human-AI collaboration. As businesses chase agility and precision, this approach will increasingly define the future of process optimization across sectors.

Bypass Learning in AI

Bypass Learning in AI refers to a training paradigm where an artificial intelligence system selectively skips or circumvents certain aspects of the conventional learning process—such as specific layers, features, or data subsets—to accelerate development, enhance efficiency, or focus on critical knowledge. Unlike standard learning, which processes all available information uniformly, bypass learning strategically omits less relevant or redundant elements, allowing the model to prioritize key patterns or adapt to constraints like limited computational resources or incomplete datasets.

The key components of bypass learning in AI include a selective filtering mechanism, a core learning framework, and an evaluation loop. The selective filtering mechanism identifies and excludes non-essential data or operations, such as noisy inputs or overrepresented features, based on predefined rules or learned criteria. The core learning framework, typically a neural network or similar structure, processes the streamlined input, focusing on what's deemed most impactful. The evaluation loop assesses the model's performance, refining the bypass strategy to ensure accuracy isn't sacrificed for speed.

The benefits of bypass learning are rooted in its efficiency and flexibility. It reduces training time and resource demands by eliminating unnecessary computations, making it ideal for resource-scarce environments like edge devices. It can improve model robustness by avoiding overfitting to irrelevant details, honing in on generalizable insights. Additionally, bypass learning enables rapid adaptation to new tasks or domains, as it can quickly reorient focus without retraining the entire system from scratch.

Examples of bypass learning in AI include its application in speech recognition, where the model skips redundant audio frames to focus on distinct phonetic cues, speeding up processing. In image classification, bypass learning might ignore background clutter in photos, training solely on foreground objects to boost accuracy with less data. Another case is in predictive maintenance, where an AI bypasses steady-state sensor readings to learn from anomaly signals, enhancing fault detection efficiency.

Industries employing bypass learning in AI include manufacturing, where it optimizes predictive models for equipment monitoring under tight computational limits. Healthcare uses it to streamline AI diagnostics, focusing on key biomarkers in patient data for faster results. Retail applies it in customer behavior analysis, bypassing routine transactions to study outlier purchases for trend spotting. Energy leverages it in smart grids, where bypass learning prioritizes anomaly detection over constant data streams.

In conclusion, Bypass Learning in AI offers a pragmatic approach to sculpting intelligence, trimming the fat from traditional training to deliver leaner, faster models. Its promise of efficiency comes with the challenge of discernment, requiring careful design to preserve effectiveness. As industries increasingly demand agile, resource-conscious AI, bypass learning stands poised to carve a niche, reshaping how systems learn by focusing on what truly matters.

Bypass Network in AI

Bypass Network in AI refers to a specialized architecture or mechanism within artificial intelligence systems designed to circumvent certain layers, processes, or constraints to achieve faster, more efficient, or alternative outcomes. Unlike traditional neural networks that process data sequentially through all layers, a bypass network introduces shortcuts or alternate pathways, allowing data to skip specific stages of computation. This concept is often inspired by structures like residual networks in deep learning, where it enhances flexibility and performance by rerouting information flow strategically.

The key components of a bypass network in AI include the primary processing pathway, the bypass connections, and a decision mechanism. The primary pathway consists of the standard layers or modules that handle the bulk of data transformation, such as feature extraction or pattern recognition. Bypass connections are the alternate routes that link non-adjacent layers or skip entire sections, preserving raw data or intermediate results for later use. The decision mechanism, often embedded in the network's design or learned during training, determines when and how data utilizes these shortcuts, ensuring optimal routing based on the task.

The benefits of bypass networks in AI are centered on efficiency and adaptability. They reduce computational overhead by avoiding unnecessary processing, speeding up inference and training times, which is critical for real-time applications. They also mitigate issues like vanishing gradients in deep networks, improving learning stability and model accuracy. Additionally, bypass networks offer flexibility, enabling systems to dynamically adjust to varying input complexities or resource constraints without redesigning the entire architecture.

Examples of bypass networks in AI include their use in image recognition models, where shortcuts allow raw pixel data to influence higher-level feature detection directly, enhancing detail preservation. In natural language processing, bypass networks might skip redundant token analysis for simpler sentences, accelerating text generation. Another instance is in robotics, where a bypass network could route sensory data straight to action outputs during routine tasks, bypassing complex decision layers to save time.

Industries leveraging bypass networks in AI include autonomous driving, where they optimize real-time obstacle detection under tight latency constraints. Healthcare uses them in diagnostic AI, speeding up analysis of medical scans by bypassing redundant computations. Gaming employs bypass networks to streamline AI opponent behavior, ensuring responsive gameplay. Telecommunications benefits too, with bypass networks enhancing network traffic prediction models for faster congestion management.

In conclusion, Bypass Networks in AI represent a clever evolution in system design, offering a way to sidestep inefficiencies and boost performance in complex models. Their ability to adaptively reroute data makes them a powerful tool, though their sophistication demands careful engineering to unlock full potential. As industries push for faster, smarter AI, bypass networks will likely grow in prominence, refining the balance between speed and depth in intelligent systems.

Bytecode

Bytecode refers to a portable, intermediate representation of a program, crafted by compiling high-level source code into a format that a virtual machine can execute. It exists as a bridge between human-readable scripts and machine-specific instructions, designed to be platform-independent and interpreted or further compiled at runtime. In essence, bytecode encapsulates the logic of an application in a compact, standardized form, making it a vital cog in the machinery of modern software, including artificial intelligence and beyond.

The key components of bytecode include its instruction set, a virtual machine, and its generation process. The instruction set consists of low-level commands—like arithmetic operations or memory access—tailored for efficient execution by a virtual machine. The virtual machine serves as the runtime environment, interpreting or just-in-time compiling the bytecode into native code for the host hardware. The generation process involves a compiler transforming source code, such as Python or Java, into this intermediate layer, preserving functionality while abstracting hardware details.

The benefits of bytecode lie in its versatility and efficiency. It enables cross-platform compatibility, allowing a single codebase to run on diverse systems without modification, a boon for developers targeting varied ecosystems. It simplifies deployment by decoupling software from specific hardware, reducing the need for multiple builds. Bytecode also supports dynamic execution, facilitating features like runtime optimization or debugging, which enhance development speed and reliability.

Examples of bytecode in action include its use in Java applications, where the Java Virtual Machine (JVM) executes bytecode to power everything from enterprise software to Android apps. In Python, the CPython interpreter runs bytecode for scripts, driving data analysis tools or web frameworks. Another instance is in game engines, where bytecode scripts control AI behaviors or physics simulations, offering flexibility across consoles and PCs.

Industries harnessing bytecode span technology and its intersections. Software development relies on it for scalable applications, from cloud services to desktop tools. Mobile computing uses bytecode in frameworks like Android's Dalvik or ART, powering billions of devices. Gaming leverages it for scripting flexible, reusable game logic. Even finance employs bytecode in trading platforms, ensuring consistent execution across global servers.

In conclusion, bytecode stands as a linchpin of portable, efficient computing, offering a universal language for software to speak across platforms. Its trade-offs in speed and security are offset by its adaptability, making it a cornerstone of modern development. As industries push toward broader, more interconnected systems, bytecode's role in enabling seamless, scalable solutions will remain a quiet yet enduring force.

Bytecode Interpretation in AI

Definition
Bytecode Interpretation in AI refers to the process by which an artificial intelligence system executes a program through a virtual machine that reads and processes bytecode—a portable, intermediate representation of code generated from higher-level languages. Unlike direct hardware execution, interpretation involves a layer of abstraction where the virtual machine translates bytecode instructions into actions step-by-step, enabling AI algorithms to run across diverse platforms. In AI, this approach is crucial for deploying models and scripts in environments where flexibility and consistency outweigh raw speed.

Key Components
The key components of bytecode interpretation in AI include the bytecode itself, a virtual machine, and an interpreter. The bytecode acts as a compact, platform-neutral set of instructions derived from AI source code, such as scripts for training models or processing data. The virtual machine provides the runtime environment, hosting the interpreter that decodes each bytecode instruction and executes corresponding operations. The interpreter bridges the gap between abstract code and hardware, dynamically handling tasks like memory management or mathematical computations central to AI workflows.

Benefits
The benefits of this method are rooted in its portability and ease of use. Bytecode interpretation allows AI developers to write code once and run it anywhere a compatible virtual machine exists, simplifying

deployment across devices from servers to IoT gadgets. It supports rapid prototyping and debugging, as interpreted environments often provide real-time feedback, ideal for tweaking AI models. Additionally, it abstracts hardware complexities, letting developers focus on algorithmic logic rather than low-level optimization.

Examples
Examples of bytecode interpretation in AI include Python's use in machine learning, where the CPython interpreter executes bytecode for libraries like NumPy or PyTorch, enabling data scientists to train models without worrying about underlying hardware. In edge AI, interpreted bytecode runs inference on resource-limited devices, such as smart cameras processing image recognition tasks. Another case is in multi-agent simulations, where interpreted bytecode coordinates agent behaviors across distributed systems, ensuring consistent execution regardless of platform.

Industries
Industries relying on bytecode interpretation in AI include robotics, where it powers flexible control systems for robots adapting to varied environments. The education sector uses it in AI-driven learning platforms, running interpreted code on student devices of all kinds. Entertainment employs it in procedural content generation for games, interpreting bytecode to craft dynamic worlds. Healthcare benefits too, with interpreted AI scripts analyzing patient data on portable diagnostic tools.

Conclusion
In conclusion, Bytecode Interpretation in AI offers a practical, adaptable foundation for executing intelligent systems, prioritizing portability and simplicity over raw performance. Its ability to unify development across platforms makes it indispensable, though it demands careful consideration of speed and resource constraints. As AI expands into diverse domains, bytecode interpretation will continue to serve as a reliable workhorse, enabling innovation where flexibility trumps the need for absolute efficiency.

Bytecode Optimization in AI

Bytecode Optimization in AI refers to the process of refining and enhancing the intermediate, machine-independent code generated by a compiler or interpreter to improve the efficiency of AI algorithms and models during execution. Bytecode, a low-level representation of a program, sits between high-level source code and native machine instructions, often used in virtual machines like those for Python or Java. In the context of AI, optimization focuses on tailoring this bytecode to accelerate tasks such as model training, inference, or data processing, ensuring faster performance and reduced resource consumption.

Key Components

The key components of bytecode optimization in AI include the bytecode itself, an optimization engine, and a runtime environment. The bytecode serves as the starting point, containing instructions derived from AI scripts or frameworks. The optimization engine analyzes and transforms this code through techniques like loop unrolling, constant folding, or dead code elimination, streamlining operations critical to AI workloads. The runtime environment, typically a virtual machine, executes the optimized bytecode, leveraging the improvements to handle complex computations efficiently.

Benefits

The benefits of this approach are substantial. It boosts execution speed, allowing AI systems to process large datasets or perform real-time predictions more quickly. Resource efficiency improves as well, with optimized bytecode reducing memory usage and energy demands—a boon for deployment on constrained devices like edge hardware. It also enhances portability, as optimized bytecode can run consistently across different platforms without requiring extensive re-engineering.

Examples

Examples of bytecode optimization in AI include speeding up neural network inference in frameworks like TensorFlow Lite, where bytecode is refined to minimize redundant operations during model execution on mobile devices. In Python-based AI pipelines, tools like PyPy optimize bytecode for data preprocessing tasks, cutting down execution time for scripts handling massive datasets. Another case is in reinforcement learning, where optimized bytecode accelerates simulation loops, enabling agents to iterate and learn faster.

Industries

Industries adopting this technique include autonomous systems, where optimized bytecode powers real-time decision-making in drones or self-driving cars. The gaming industry uses it to enhance AI-driven NPC behaviors, ensuring smooth performance on varied hardware. Healthcare applies it in diagnostic tools, speeding up AI analysis of medical imaging on portable devices. Finance leverages it for high-frequency trading, where split-second improvements in bytecode execution can yield significant gains.

Conclusion

In conclusion, Bytecode Optimization in AI offers a potent way to squeeze more performance out of computational resources, aligning the low-level mechanics of code with the high-level demands of intelligent systems. While it demands careful design to avoid pitfalls, its ability to deliver speed and efficiency makes it a vital tool across industries. As AI continues to permeate technology, refining bytecode will remain a subtle yet essential lever for pushing the boundaries of what machines can achieve.

Byte-Pair Encoding (BPE)

Byte-Pair Encoding (BPE) is a data compression and tokenization technique that iteratively merges the most frequent pairs of bytes or characters in a dataset to create a compact vocabulary of subword units. Originally developed for compressing text by replacing common byte sequences with single symbols, it has evolved into a powerful tool in natural language processing (NLP), where it breaks words into smaller, manageable pieces for models to analyze. By balancing whole words and their parts, BPE enables efficient representation of language, especially for handling rare or out-of-vocabulary terms.

Key Components

The key components of BPE include an initial symbol set, a merging process, and a resulting vocabulary. The process begins with a basic set of characters or bytes from the input data, treating each as an individual token. It then identifies the most frequent adjacent pair and merges them into a new token, repeating this step until a predefined vocabulary size or stopping condition is reached. The final vocabulary consists of both original characters and newly formed subword units, which can represent common patterns or entire words depending on their frequency.

Benefits

The benefits of BPE are notable in its adaptability and efficiency. It reduces the vocabulary size compared to using full words, making it memory-efficient for large-scale language models. It excels at handling rare words by breaking them into recognizable subcomponents, improving generalization in tasks like translation or text generation. Additionally, BPE's unsupervised nature means it requires no prior linguistic knowledge, allowing it to work across diverse languages and domains with minimal setup.

Examples

Examples of BPE in use include its role in training models like GPT and BERT, where it tokenizes text into subword units such as “play,” “##ing,” and “##ed” to capture morphological patterns. In machine translation, BPE helps align source and target languages by creating consistent token sets, even for languages with rich compounding like German. It’s also applied in speech recognition, segmenting audio transcriptions into manageable chunks that improve model accuracy on varied accents or dialects.

Industries

Industries leveraging BPE include artificial intelligence, where it underpins NLP systems for chatbots, search engines, and virtual assistants. The tech sector uses it in software localization to adapt applications across languages efficiently. Media and entertainment apply BPE in subtitle generation and content recommendation systems, enhancing user experience through precise text processing. Healthcare benefits too, with BPE aiding in the analysis of medical texts for drug discovery or patient record summarization.

Conclusion

In conclusion, Byte-Pair Encoding stands as a versatile bridge between raw data and intelligent processing, offering a smart way to compress and tokenize information. Its ability to adapt to diverse linguistic landscapes makes it invaluable in modern AI, though its success relies on careful data selection and parameter tuning. As industries increasingly lean on language-driven technologies, BPE’s role in enabling efficient, scalable solutions underscores its quiet yet profound impact on the digital world.

Bytes

Bytes are the fundamental units of digital data storage and processing, representing a sequence of eight bits. Each byte can store a single character, a numerical value, or binary data, making it the foundation of computing, data transmission, and digital communication. Bytes serve as the building blocks for higher-level data structures and are essential for encoding text, images, sound, and software instructions in computing systems.

Key Components

Key components of bytes include bits, encoding schemes, data representation, memory allocation, and data transfer protocols. Bits are the smallest units of data, where each bit represents either a 0 or 1 in binary form. Encoding schemes such as ASCII and Unicode define how bytes represent characters, enabling text storage and communication across different systems. Data representation determines how bytes store numbers, text, and multimedia, with formats like integers, floating-point values, and compressed media files. Memory allocation assigns specific bytes to applications and processes, ensuring efficient storage and retrieval. Data transfer protocols manage the movement of bytes across networks, optimizing speed and reliability in digital communication.

Benefits

The benefits of bytes include efficient data storage, universal compatibility, scalability, and precision in computing. Efficient data storage allows digital systems to store vast amounts of information compactly. Universal compatibility ensures that bytes function as a standard unit of measurement across all computing platforms. Scalability enables systems to process and manipulate larger data structures by organizing bytes into kilobytes, megabytes, gigabytes, and beyond. Precision in computing ensures accurate numerical calculations, character encoding, and binary operations essential for software functionality.

Examples

An example of bytes in action is in text processing, where each character in a document is stored as one or more bytes using encoding schemes like UTF-8. Another example is in image storage, where pixels are represented by multiple bytes defining color values, allowing high-resolution graphics to be displayed on digital screens.

Industries

Industries that rely on bytes include information technology, telecommunications, artificial intelligence, multimedia, and cybersecurity. Information technology depends on bytes for file storage, operating systems, and software applications. Telecommunications uses bytes to transmit voice, video, and data across global networks. Artificial intelligence processes vast amounts of data in the form of bytes for training machine learning models and running complex algorithms. Multimedia applications, including streaming platforms and digital content creation, encode audio, video, and images in byte-based formats. Cybersecurity relies on byte-level encryption and secure data transmission protocols to protect digital assets.

Applications

Applications of bytes extend to cloud computing, data analytics, embedded systems, digital forensics, and blockchain technology. Cloud computing stores and manages vast amounts of byte-encoded data, ensuring accessibility and scalability. Data analytics processes structured and unstructured byte-based datasets to extract insights and drive decision-making. Embedded systems, such as IoT devices, utilize bytes to operate firmware and communicate with other devices efficiently. Digital forensics examines byte-level data to recover deleted files, detect cyber threats, and investigate digital crimes. Blockchain technology uses byte-based cryptographic hashing to secure transactions and maintain decentralized ledgers.

Summary

Bytes are the foundation of digital computing, enabling the storage, processing, and transmission of information across various domains. Their role in encoding, memory management, and network communication makes them indispensable to modern technology. As data-driven innovations continue to expand, bytes will remain at the core of computing advancements, powering everything from artificial intelligence to secure communication and digital transformation.

Byzantine Agreement in AI

Byzantine Agreement in AI refers to a consensus mechanism used in distributed artificial intelligence systems to ensure that all nodes in a network reach a common decision despite the presence of faulty or malicious participants. Inspired by the Byzantine Generals Problem, this agreement protocol is designed to handle scenarios where some nodes may provide incorrect or deceptive information while still allowing the system to function reliably. Byzantine Agreement is essential in decentralized AI networks, ensuring trust, security, and fault tolerance in multi-agent systems and blockchain-based AI applications.

Key Components

Key components of Byzantine Agreement in AI include distributed consensus, fault tolerance, cryptographic security, message validation, and decentralized decision-making. Distributed consensus ensures that all honest nodes in a system agree on a single, accurate version of information despite conflicting messages from unreliable nodes. Fault tolerance enables the network to continue functioning even if a certain percentage of nodes behave unpredictably or maliciously. Cryptographic security protects communication between nodes, preventing data tampering and unauthorized alterations. Message validation allows nodes to verify the authenticity and correctness of received information before making decisions. Decentralized decision-making ensures that AI-driven systems can operate autonomously without relying on a central authority, reducing vulnerabilities associated with single points of failure.

Benefits

The benefits of Byzantine Agreement in AI include enhanced security, increased reliability, and improved scalability. Enhanced security ensures that AI systems remain resistant to cyberattacks, fraud, and misinformation. Increased reliability allows distributed AI networks to maintain accurate decision-making even in the presence of adversarial behavior or system failures. Improved scalability enables AI-driven blockchain networks and multi-agent AI systems to operate efficiently across a vast number of participants without centralized control.

Examples

An example of Byzantine Agreement in AI is its application in blockchain networks that integrate AI-driven smart contracts, ensuring that transactions and automated decisions are executed accurately despite potential malicious actors. Another example is in autonomous vehicle networks, where multiple self-driving cars communicate to reach a consensus on traffic flow and road conditions, even if some vehicles transmit incorrect data due to sensor errors or cyber threats.

Industries

Industries that benefit from Byzantine Agreement in AI include finance, cybersecurity, supply chain management, autonomous systems, and healthcare. Financial institutions leverage Byzantine Agreement to maintain secure and tamper-proof transactions in decentralized finance (DeFi) applications. Cybersecurity firms use it to protect AI-driven threat detection systems from adversarial attacks and misinformation. Supply chain management integrates Byzantine Agreement to validate the authenticity of transactions and logistics data in distributed AI-powered tracking systems. Autonomous systems, including fleets of self-driving vehicles and drone networks, rely on Byzantine Agreement to ensure safe and synchronized operations. Healthcare applications use Byzantine Agreement to maintain the integrity of AI-powered medical records and diagnostic decision-making.

Applications

Applications of Byzantine Agreement in AI extend to decentralized machine learning, federated learning, AI-driven blockchain systems, multi-agent AI collaboration, and secure data sharing. Decentralized machine learning platforms use Byzantine Agreement to enable collaborative AI training while preventing malicious data poisoning attacks. Federated learning benefits from Byzantine Agreement by ensuring that AI models trained on decentralized devices remain accurate and trustworthy despite potential adversarial influences. AI-driven blockchain systems use Byzantine Agreement to verify transactions and maintain consensus in distributed ledgers. Multi-agent AI collaboration applies Byzantine Agreement to facilitate cooperation between autonomous systems in robotics, swarm intelligence, and decision-making networks. Secure data sharing employs Byzantine Agreement to enable privacy-preserving AI applications where multiple parties exchange sensitive data without compromising security.

Summary

Byzantine Agreement in AI plays a crucial role in ensuring trust, security, and reliability in decentralized and distributed AI systems. As AI continues to integrate with blockchain, multi-agent networks, and autonomous decision-making, Byzantine Agreement will become increasingly vital in preventing malicious interference and ensuring accurate consensus. Its application across industries enhances the integrity of AI-driven systems, making them more resilient to failures, cyber threats, and misinformation.

༺❀༻Letter C༺❀༻

Cache

Definition
A cache is a temporary storage space that holds frequently accessed data to speed up future retrievals. In computing and artificial intelligence systems, caching helps reduce latency, improve performance, and minimize the need to repeatedly access slower or more resource-intensive storage systems. By storing recently used or predicted-to-be-used data in memory, a cache allows systems to respond faster to repeated requests.

Key Components
A cache consists of a memory space where data is stored temporarily, a caching policy that determines which data is stored or replaced, and a management system that decides how long data should stay in the cache. Caches are typically located close to the processor or application, such as in CPU memory or web browsers, and can exist at different levels including hardware, software, or network-based systems.

Examples
A web browser storing images and files from recently visited websites so that they load faster the next time the user visits the same site. A machine learning model caching intermediate results from previous computations to avoid recalculating them. An AI chatbot storing user preferences in a session cache to provide quicker, more relevant responses.

Benefits
Caching significantly reduces data access time, lowers the load on backend systems, and improves user experience. It increases the overall efficiency of systems by preventing redundant processing. In AI, it can accelerate data processing, speed up model training, and enhance real-time inference performance.

Applications
Caches are used in web servers, operating systems, content delivery networks, cloud platforms, database engines, AI model training pipelines, and edge computing systems. They are also widely used in AI recommendation engines, search optimization, and computer vision tasks to store pre-processed data.

Industries
Technology companies use caching extensively in cloud infrastructure, social media services, and real-time communication platforms. The healthcare sector applies caching in electronic health record systems. Retail and e-commerce platforms use cache to serve product pages and search results rapidly. Financial services use it to support high-speed trading systems and real-time analytics.

Summary
Cache is a vital mechanism for enhancing system speed and responsiveness in AI and computing environments. By storing data temporarily for quick reuse, caching reduces computational effort and improves efficiency across applications. When managed effectively, cache systems offer a powerful way to optimize performance and support real-time functionality.

Cache memory optimization

Definition: Cache memory optimization refers to the process of enhancing the performance of a computer's cache memory, a small, high-speed storage layer that temporarily holds frequently accessed data to reduce retrieval time from slower main memory. It involves strategies and techniques to maximize efficiency, minimize latency, and improve overall system responsiveness.

Key components: The core of cache memory optimization lies in effective cache placement policies, determining which data to store based on usage patterns. Replacement algorithms, such as least recently used or first-in-first-out, manage what data is evicted when the cache fills. Cache size and hierarchy design balance speed and capacity across multiple levels. Data prefetching anticipates future needs, loading relevant information proactively, while coherence protocols ensure consistency in multi-core systems.

Benefits: Optimizing cache memory accelerates data access, boosting processing speeds for applications and systems. It reduces energy consumption by minimizing reliance on slower memory, enhancing efficiency. Improved cache performance elevates user experience through faster response times in computing tasks. It also enables better scalability, supporting complex workloads without overwhelming hardware resources.

Examples of industry applications: In gaming, cache memory optimization ensures rapid loading of textures and assets, enhancing real-time graphics rendering. In cloud computing, it speeds up virtual machine operations by caching frequent queries. The smartphone industry uses it to improve app performance, reducing lag on resource-constrained devices. In AI training, optimized caches accelerate access to large datasets, streamlining neural network computations.

Conclusions: Cache memory optimization is a vital technique for unlocking the full potential of modern computing, bridging the speed gap between processors and memory. Its ability to enhance performance and efficiency makes it indispensable across industries. However, its success hinges on overcoming design complexities and workload variability. As hardware evolves, refining cache optimization will remain key to sustaining fast, reliable systems.

Canonical Correlation Analysis

Definition: Canonical Correlation Analysis, often abbreviated as CCA, is a statistical method used to explore and quantify the relationships between two sets of variables by identifying linear combinations that maximize their correlation. It extends beyond simple correlation by uncovering hidden patterns across multidimensional datasets, making it a powerful tool in data analysis and machine learning.

Key components: The process begins with two variable sets, such as features from different data sources, which CCA pairs into canonical variates—linear combinations optimized for maximum correlation. The correlation coefficient measures the strength of these relationships, while canonical weights define the contribution of each original variable. Constraints ensure the variates remain independent within each set, and dimensionality reduction often focuses analysis on the most significant pairings.

Benefits: CCA reveals complex interdependencies that single-variable methods miss, providing deeper insights into data relationships. It simplifies analysis by reducing high-dimensional data into meaningful components, aiding interpretation. Its versatility supports tasks from feature extraction to predictive modeling, enhancing decision-making. By aligning disparate datasets, it fosters integration across diverse sources.

Examples of industry applications: In neuroscience, CCA correlates brain imaging data with behavioral metrics, uncovering links between neural activity and cognition. In marketing, it aligns customer demographics with purchasing habits to refine targeting strategies. The finance sector uses CCA to connect economic indicators with stock performance, informing investment models. In natural language processing, it pairs text and image data for multimodal AI systems.

Conclusions: Canonical Correlation Analysis stands as a robust bridge for connecting diverse variable sets, offering clarity in data-driven fields like AI and beyond. Its ability to distill intricate relationships into actionable insights fuels innovation across industries. Yet, its reliance on linearity and computational demands call for careful application and ongoing refinement. As data complexity grows, CCA remains a valuable, evolving tool for understanding interconnected systems.

Capsule Networks (CapsNets)

Capsule Networks (CapsNets) are an advanced type of neural network architecture designed to address the limitations of traditional convolutional neural networks (CNNs) in recognizing spatial hierarchies and maintaining object orientation. Unlike CNNs, which rely on max pooling and struggle with viewpoint variations, CapsNets use capsule structures to encode the pose and hierarchical relationships of objects, improving robustness in image recognition tasks.

Key components of capsule networks include capsules, dynamic routing, and transformation matrices. Capsules are groups of neurons that encode both the probability of an object's presence and its pose parameters, such as rotation, scale, and orientation. Dynamic routing is a process that ensures lower-level capsules send information to the most relevant higher-level capsules, enhancing feature representation without losing spatial details. Transformation matrices allow capsules to capture and preserve spatial relationships between features, enabling the network to recognize objects regardless of perspective changes.

The benefits of capsule networks include improved generalization, enhanced robustness to distortions, and reduced data dependency. By preserving spatial hierarchies, CapsNets recognize objects even when their orientation or viewpoint changes, reducing the need for large amounts of training data. The ability to capture complex relationships between object parts enhances performance in tasks like image classification and object detection. CapsNets also mitigate the drawbacks of max pooling, preventing the loss of important spatial information.

An example of capsule networks in action is in medical imaging, where CapsNets analyze MRI scans to detect tumors with greater accuracy than conventional CNNs. The ability to recognize subtle structural differences in medical images allows for early and more precise diagnosis. Another example is in handwriting recognition, where CapsNets outperform CNNs by correctly identifying characters even if they are written with different angles or distortions.

Industries utilizing capsule networks include healthcare, autonomous vehicles, security, robotics, and augmented reality. In healthcare, CapsNets enhance the accuracy of medical image analysis and diagnostic tools. Autonomous vehicle systems use CapsNets to improve object detection and scene understanding in dynamic environments. Security applications leverage CapsNets for facial recognition and anomaly detection, increasing accuracy in surveillance systems. Robotics benefits from CapsNets in grasp detection and manipulation, allowing robots to recognize and handle objects from various angles. Augmented reality relies on CapsNets for realistic object tracking and interaction in virtual spaces.

Applications of capsule networks extend to computer vision, biometric authentication, anomaly detection, natural language processing, and 3D object recognition. In computer vision, CapsNets enhance object classification and segmentation, leading to better performance in real-world scenarios. Biometric authentication benefits from CapsNets in facial and fingerprint recognition systems, improving security measures. Anomaly detection in finance and cybersecurity uses CapsNets to identify fraud and threats with higher accuracy. Natural language processing applications explore CapsNets to capture relationships in textual data, improving sentiment analysis and machine translation. In 3D object recognition, CapsNets provide a structured representation of objects, aiding in realistic rendering and scene analysis.

Capsule networks introduce a paradigm shift in neural network architectures by preserving spatial relationships and improving the robustness of deep learning models. Their ability to recognize objects despite distortions and viewpoint changes makes them valuable in various AI-driven applications. As research and computational efficiency improve, CapsNets have the potential to revolutionize machine learning, bridging the gap between human perception and artificial intelligence.

Cascade Classifier

Cascade Classifier is a machine learning technique used for efficient object detection by applying multiple stages of classifiers in a sequential manner. This approach improves detection speed and accuracy by focusing computational resources on promising candidate regions while discarding unlikely ones early in the process. It is commonly used in real-time applications such as facial recognition and motion detection.

Key components of a cascade classifier include a series of weak classifiers, feature extraction techniques, and a cascading structure. Weak classifiers are simple decision rules that work together to form a strong classifier by progressively refining detection results. Feature extraction techniques, such as Haar-like features or histogram of oriented gradients (HOG), identify relevant patterns in an image. The cascading structure organizes classifiers in a hierarchical manner, allowing easy elimination of negative samples at early stages while focusing on positive detections in later stages.

The benefits of cascade classifiers include high-speed performance, computational efficiency, and improved accuracy. The sequential processing method allows rapid elimination of non-relevant data, significantly reducing the number of computations required. Computational efficiency makes cascade classifiers suitable for embedded and low-power devices. Improved accuracy is achieved by progressively refining the classification process, reducing false positives while ensuring strong detection capabilities.

An example of a cascade classifier is the Viola-Jones face detection algorithm, which identifies human faces in images with high precision and efficiency. This technique enables real-time facial recognition in security cameras, smartphones, and biometric authentication systems. Another example is vehicle detection in traffic monitoring systems, where cascade classifiers help identify and track cars in busy road environments.

Industries that utilize cascade classifiers include security, automotive, healthcare, retail, and robotics. Security applications use cascade classifiers in surveillance systems to detect faces and suspicious activities in crowded areas. The automotive industry applies cascade classifiers in driver assistance systems for pedestrian and object detection. Healthcare benefits from medical image analysis, where cascade classifiers assist in detecting abnormalities in X-rays and MRIs. Retail businesses use cascade classifiers in smart checkout systems to recognize products and streamline automated billing. Robotics integrates cascade classifiers for environment perception, enabling autonomous robots to detect and interact with objects in real time.

Applications of cascade classifiers extend to real-time object detection, gesture recognition, anomaly detection, optical character recognition, and augmented reality. Real-time object detection relies on cascade classifiers for fast and accurate recognition of faces, animals, and objects in video streams. Gesture recognition systems use cascade classifiers to interpret hand movements for touchless control in interactive displays. Anomaly detection applies cascade classifiers in industrial settings to identify defects and irregularities in production lines. Optical character recognition benefits from cascade classifiers to enhance text recognition in scanned documents and license plate identification. Augmented reality systems use cascade classifiers for detecting and overlaying virtual objects in real-world environments.

Cascade classifiers provide a powerful and efficient method for object detection, balancing speed and accuracy to enable real-time applications. Their ability to quickly filter out irrelevant data while focusing on relevant features makes them valuable across multiple industries. As AI and computer vision continue to evolve, cascade classifiers remain a fundamental tool in enhancing detection performance for various real-world scenarios.

Cascading Failure Analysis

Cascading Failure Analysis in AI refers to the study and identification of failure chains within complex systems where the failure of one component leads to a sequence of failures throughout the network. This analysis is critical in preventing widespread disruptions in interconnected infrastructures such as power grids, communication networks, and AI-driven autonomous systems. By modeling and predicting how failures propagate, AI-driven cascading failure analysis enhances system resilience and reduces the risk of catastrophic breakdowns.

Key components of cascading failure analysis include failure detection, dependency mapping, risk assessment, fault propagation modeling, and mitigation strategies. Failure detection involves identifying initial points of system failure before they escalate. Dependency mapping outlines the relationships between interconnected components, showing how failures in one area affect others. Risk assessment quantifies the likelihood and impact of cascading failures, allowing for proactive interventions. Fault propagation modeling simulates how disruptions spread across a system, providing insights into weak points and potential failure scenarios. Mitigation strategies involve designing fail-safes, redundancies, and intervention measures to prevent or contain cascading failures.

The benefits of cascading failure analysis include increased system resilience, reduced downtime, and enhanced predictive maintenance. By understanding failure patterns, AI models improve the robustness of critical infrastructure. Reduced downtime is achieved through early detection and prevention strategies, minimizing disruptions. Predictive maintenance is enhanced as AI anticipates potential failures and recommends timely interventions to prevent large-scale outages.

An example of cascading failure analysis is in power grid management, where AI models analyze electrical network dependencies to predict and prevent widespread blackouts caused by localized failures. Another example is in cloud computing infrastructure, where AI-driven monitoring systems detect server failures and redistribute workloads to maintain service availability.

Industries that benefit from cascading failure analysis include energy, telecommunications, transportation, finance, and manufacturing. The energy sector applies this analysis to safeguard power grids against cascading blackouts. Telecommunications companies use AI to prevent network outages that could disrupt global communications. Transportation systems, including autonomous vehicles and smart traffic control, rely on failure analysis to enhance safety and prevent system-wide failures. Financial institutions apply cascading failure analysis to prevent systemic risks in global markets. Manufacturing industries integrate AI-driven failure analysis to optimize supply chain management and prevent production line disruptions.

Applications of cascading failure analysis include cybersecurity, network resilience, predictive maintenance, emergency response planning, and autonomous system safety. Cybersecurity leverages failure analysis to detect vulnerabilities and prevent cyberattacks from causing widespread damage. Network resilience benefits from AI-driven analysis that ensures consistent data flow and minimal downtime. Predictive maintenance applies cascading failure analysis to schedule timely repairs and prevent costly equipment failures. Emergency response planning integrates AI models to anticipate disasters and optimize crisis management strategies. Autonomous systems rely on cascading failure analysis to ensure safe operation in robotics, aviation, and self-driving vehicles.

Cascading failure analysis is essential for maintaining stability in interconnected systems by predicting, preventing, and mitigating failure chains. AI-driven approaches enhance the accuracy of failure modeling, enabling industries to build more resilient infrastructures. As AI and machine learning continue to evolve, cascading failure analysis will play a critical role in safeguarding global systems from large-scale disruptions.

Case-Based Reasoning (CBR)

Case-Based Reasoning (CBR) is an AI methodology that solves new problems by referring to previously solved cases that share similarities. Instead of relying on predefined rules or extensive training data, CBR retrieves relevant past cases, adapts their solutions to fit the new problem, and learns from each experience. This approach mimics human reasoning, where past experiences inform future decisions, making it particularly useful in domains requiring contextual decision-making and adaptability.

Key components of case-based reasoning include case retrieval, case adaptation, case storage, similarity assessment, and learning from experience. Case retrieval involves searching a case library for past instances that closely match the current problem. Case adaptation modifies retrieved solutions to fit the new problem while maintaining effectiveness. Case storage updates the case library with new problem-solving experiences, ensuring continuous learning. Similarity assessment evaluates how closely a past case aligns with a new problem, determining the relevance of the retrieved solution. Learning from experience refines the case database, improving future decision-making and problem resolution.

The benefits of case-based reasoning include improved problem-solving efficiency, enhanced adaptability, and reduced dependency on extensive training data. CBR accelerates decision-making by leveraging past knowledge, reducing the need for complex algorithmic computations. Enhanced adaptability allows CBR systems to handle novel problems by modifying previous solutions rather than generating entirely new ones. Reduced dependency on large datasets makes CBR valuable in fields where historical cases are more informative than vast amounts of raw data.

An example of case-based reasoning is in medical diagnosis, where AI systems compare a patient's symptoms with historical medical cases to recommend treatment plans. Another example is in customer support chatbots, where CBR enables AI to provide responses based on previous similar customer inquiries, improving service efficiency.

Industries that benefit from case-based reasoning include healthcare, legal, customer service, engineering, and cybersecurity. Healthcare uses CBR for medical diagnosis, treatment recommendations, and personalized patient care. The legal industry applies CBR to case law research, where AI retrieves relevant legal precedents to assist attorneys in formulating arguments. Customer service automation uses CBR-driven AI to provide consistent and context-aware responses based on past interactions. Engineering sectors integrate CBR into maintenance systems to diagnose equipment failures based on prior incidents. Cybersecurity firms leverage CBR to detect and respond to cyber threats by analyzing historical attack patterns.

Applications of case-based reasoning include expert systems, troubleshooting assistants, fraud detection, predictive maintenance, and decision-support systems. Expert systems in medicine, law, and engineering use CBR to enhance decision accuracy. Troubleshooting assistants help users diagnose software or hardware issues based on past cases. Fraud detection applies CBR to recognize suspicious transactions similar to previously identified fraud cases. Predictive maintenance systems use CBR to recommend maintenance schedules by analyzing historical equipment failures. Decision-support systems integrate CBR to assist professionals in making informed choices based on previous cases.

Case-based reasoning provides an intuitive and effective AI approach for problem-solving by leveraging past experiences. Its ability to learn from historical cases and adapt solutions to new challenges makes it highly valuable across industries requiring dynamic decision-making. As AI technology advances, CBR will continue to play a key role in intelligent automation, enhancing accuracy and efficiency in various applications.

CatBoost

CatBoost is a machine learning algorithm developed for gradient boosting on categorical data, optimizing model performance while reducing overfitting and computational complexity. It is specifically designed to handle datasets with categorical variables efficiently, eliminating the need for extensive preprocessing. CatBoost improves predictive accuracy by leveraging a unique ordered boosting technique that minimizes data leakage and enhances generalization, making it a powerful tool for classification and regression tasks.

Key components of CatBoost include ordered boosting, categorical encoding, feature importance analysis, automatic handling of missing values, and GPU acceleration. Ordered boosting ensures that training data is processed in a way that prevents information leakage, enhancing model reliability. Categorical encoding transforms non-numeric categorical data into numerical representations without the need for one-hot encoding, preserving information while reducing dimensionality. Feature importance analysis identifies the most influential variables in a dataset, helping improve model interpretability. Automatic handling of missing values enables CatBoost to process incomplete datasets without requiring imputation. GPU acceleration allows for faster training and scalability, making it suitable for large-scale machine learning tasks.

The benefits of CatBoost include superior performance on categorical data, reduced overfitting, and faster training speed. By optimizing how categorical variables are processed, CatBoost significantly improves predictive accuracy without the need for extensive manual preprocessing. Reduced overfitting ensures that the model generalizes well to new data, improving its robustness. Faster training speed, especially with GPU support, allows for efficient model deployment in real-world applications.

An example of CatBoost is in fraud detection, where it analyzes categorical transaction data to identify suspicious patterns with high accuracy. Another example is in recommendation systems, where CatBoost optimizes personalized content recommendations by processing user behavior and categorical attributes.

Industries that benefit from CatBoost include finance, e-commerce, healthcare, telecommunications, and marketing. Financial institutions use CatBoost for credit scoring and fraud detection. E-commerce platforms apply it for product recommendations and customer segmentation. Healthcare organizations leverage it for predictive analytics in patient care. Telecommunications firms optimize network performance and customer retention strategies using CatBoost. Marketing teams use it for campaign targeting and customer behavior analysis.

Causal Inference in AI

Definition: Causal Inference in AI is the process of using artificial intelligence techniques to determine cause-and-effect relationships within data, distinguishing true causal links from mere associations. It integrates statistical methods and machine learning to infer how one variable influences another, enabling AI systems to reason about interventions and outcomes in a way that mirrors scientific inquiry.

Key components: Causal inference relies on structural causal models, often visualized as graphs, to represent relationships between variables. Identification strategies, like adjusting for confounders or leveraging instrumental variables, isolate causal effects. Counterfactual reasoning estimates what would happen under different scenarios, while data-driven algorithms refine these estimates from observed patterns. Validation mechanisms test causal claims against real-world evidence or experimental data.

Benefits: This approach empowers AI to move beyond prediction to understanding why events occur, enhancing decision-making precision. It enables simulation of interventions, offering practical guidance for action. Robustness against spurious correlations improves model reliability in messy, real-world data. Its focus on causality also boosts interpretability, making AI outputs more transparent and trustworthy.

Examples of industry applications: In e-commerce, causal inference reveals how discounts directly drive sales, filtering out seasonal effects. In medicine, it assesses whether a drug causally reduces symptoms, informing treatment plans. The energy sector uses it to evaluate how equipment upgrades impact efficiency. In social media, it measures how content changes affect user engagement, shaping platform strategies.

Conclusions: Causal Inference in AI bridges the gap between correlation and causation, equipping AI with deeper reasoning to tackle real-world problems. Its ability to pinpoint drivers of change holds immense value across industries. Yet, its success depends on overcoming data and methodological obstacles. As tools and expertise advance, this field promises to elevate AI into a realm of actionable, causal understanding.

Causal Reinforcement Learning

Definition:

Causal Reinforcement Learning is an advanced approach in artificial intelligence that integrates causal inference into reinforcement learning, enabling an agent to learn not just how to act based on rewards, but why certain actions lead to specific outcomes. It combines the trial-and-error learning of reinforcement learning with causal reasoning to identify and exploit cause-effect relationships in an environment.

Key components: The framework builds on a causal model, mapping how actions, states, and rewards interlink, often using graphs to clarify dependencies. An agent explores and exploits this model, guided by a policy that optimizes long-term rewards through causal understanding. Reward attribution assigns credit to actions based on their causal impact, not just correlation. Environment simulation tests interventions, while learning updates blend causal insights with traditional reinforcement signals.

Benefits: By grasping causality, this method accelerates learning, as agents focus on actions with true impact rather than spurious patterns. It enhances decision-making in complex settings, offering strategies rooted in why outcomes occur. Generalization improves, allowing agents to adapt to new scenarios with shared causal structures. Its explanatory nature also aids debugging and trust in autonomous systems.

Examples of industry applications: In robotics, causal reinforcement learning optimizes navigation by identifying how movements cause progress, speeding up training. In finance, it models how trading decisions affect market shifts, refining investment tactics. Healthcare uses it to tailor therapies by learning causal links between interventions and recovery. In gaming, it designs smarter NPCs that adapt based on player actions' true effects.

Conclusions: Causal Reinforcement Learning fuses the strengths of causality and adaptive learning, promising agents that reason and act with deeper intent. Its potential to transform industries lies in smarter, more efficient decision-making. Yet, its complexity and data reliance pose steep barriers to widespread use. As research refines its tools, this approach could redefine how AI interacts with dynamic, cause-driven worlds.

Cell Decomposition in Path Planning

Definition:

Cell Decomposition in Path Planning is a technique used in robotics and autonomous systems to break down a complex environment into smaller, manageable regions, or cells, to simplify the task of finding a collision-free path from a starting point to a goal. It transforms a continuous space into a discrete representation, enabling efficient navigation through structured analysis.

Key components: The process starts with environment mapping, dividing the space into cells based on obstacles and free areas, often using grids or irregular shapes. Connectivity analysis links adjacent cells to form a traversable network, typically via a graph structure. Path search algorithms, like A* or Dijkstra's, compute optimal routes across this network. Cell granularity determines the resolution, balancing detail with computational load, while obstacle representation ensures accurate boundaries.

Benefits: Cell decomposition simplifies path planning by reducing a continuous problem into a discrete, solvable one, speeding up computation. It handles complex environments with obstacles effectively, ensuring reliable navigation. Flexibility in cell design adapts to varied terrains or tasks, enhancing versatility. The structured approach also supports real-time adjustments, making it practical for dynamic settings.

Examples of industry applications: In warehouse robotics, cell decomposition guides automated vehicles through aisles, avoiding shelves and workers. In drone delivery, it maps airspace into cells to dodge buildings and no-fly zones. Autonomous cars use it to navigate urban streets, plotting paths around traffic and barriers. In video games, it directs AI characters through virtual worlds with realistic movement.

Conclusions: Cell Decomposition in Path Planning offers a robust framework for turning chaotic spaces into navigable routes, powering autonomy across industries. Its strength lies in structured simplicity, enabling precise and adaptable movement. Yet, its effectiveness hinges on managing trade-offs between detail and speed. As robotics and AI evolve, this method remains a cornerstone for efficient, intelligent navigation.

Cellular Automata

Definition: Cellular Automata refers to a computational model consisting of a grid of cells, each following simple rules based on its state and the states of its neighbors, evolving over discrete time steps to produce complex patterns or behaviors. Widely used in simulation and AI, it captures emergent phenomena from minimalistic local interactions.

Key components: The system begins with a grid, often square or hexagonal, where each cell holds a finite state, like on or off. Transition rules dictate how a cell's state updates, depending on its current state and those of adjacent cells. An initial configuration sets the starting pattern, while iterative updates drive the evolution. Neighborhood definitions, such as von Neumann or Moore, shape how cells influence each other.

Benefits: Cellular Automata excel at modeling complex systems with simple rules, revealing how global behavior emerges from local actions. Their computational efficiency suits large-scale simulations, requiring minimal resources. Versatility allows them to mimic diverse processes, from natural phenomena to artificial designs. Their visual and intuitive nature also aids in understanding dynamic systems.

Examples of industry applications: In urban planning, cellular automata simulate city growth, predicting sprawl based on land use rules. In medicine, they model tumor spread, mapping cell interactions over time. Game development uses them to generate procedural landscapes, enhancing realism. In cryptography, they create pseudo-random sequences for secure encryption.

Challenges: Designing rules that accurately reflect real-world systems demands deep insight, risking oversimplification or inaccuracy. Computational cost rises with grid size or complexity, limiting scalability. Unpredictable emergent behavior can defy analysis, complicating control or validation. Adapting static rules to dynamic, real-time scenarios often requires significant rework.

Conclusions: Cellular Automata offer a powerful lens for exploring complexity through simplicity, bridging AI with natural and synthetic worlds. Their ability to distill intricate patterns into manageable models fuels innovation across fields. Yet, their reliance on precise rule-crafting and scalability constraints temper their reach. As computational tools advance, cellular automata remain a timeless framework for decoding emergent systems.

CenterNet

Definition:

CenterNet is a deep learning-based object detection framework that identifies objects in images or videos by predicting their center points and associated properties, such as size or orientation, rather than relying on traditional anchor boxes. It simplifies the detection process by focusing on keypoints, making it a lightweight and efficient approach in computer vision.

Key components: The architecture centers on a backbone network, typically a convolutional neural network like ResNet or Hourglass, to extract features from input images. Center point prediction identifies object locations via heatmaps, where peaks mark object centers. Offset regression fine-tunes these positions, while attribute heads estimate additional traits like bounding box dimensions or class labels. Loss functions, balancing classification and regression, guide training to optimize accuracy.

Benefits: CenterNet eliminates the need for anchor boxes, reducing complexity and computational overhead compared to earlier methods. Its simplicity speeds up inference, making it suitable for real-time applications. High accuracy stems from precise center-based detection, even with cluttered scenes. Flexibility allows adaptation to various object types or tasks, broadening its utility.

Examples of industry applications: In autonomous driving, CenterNet detects pedestrians and vehicles in real-time, enhancing safety systems. In retail, it tracks inventory on shelves by identifying product positions. Surveillance systems use it to spot suspicious objects or people in crowded footage. In augmented reality, it maps object locations for seamless virtual overlays.

Conclusions: CenterNet redefines object detection with its elegant, anchor-free design, offering a lean yet powerful tool for vision-based AI. Its speed and precision drive progress in industries needing fast, reliable detection. Yet, its reliance on precise tuning and handling of edge cases suggests room for refinement. As computer vision evolves, CenterNet's approach could inspire even more efficient, adaptable solutions.

Center of Mass (COM) in Robotics

Definition:

Center of Mass (COM) in Robotics refers to the point in a robotic system where its mass is balanced, acting as the average location of all mass distribution. It serves as a critical concept for stability, motion planning, and control, ensuring robots maintain equilibrium during tasks like walking, lifting, or manipulation.

Key components: The COM calculation integrates the mass and position of all components, such as limbs, joints, and payloads, into a single coordinate. Dynamic tracking adjusts this point as the robot moves or shifts weight. Stability analysis uses the COM's position relative to the support base to prevent tipping. Control algorithms incorporate COM data to optimize balance, while sensor inputs, like accelerometers, refine real-time estimates.

Benefits: Accurate COM management enhances stability, reducing the risk of falls or errors in dynamic environments. It improves energy efficiency by guiding smoother, more balanced movements. Precision in tasks like grasping or locomotion increases with proper weight distribution. Understanding COM also simplifies design, ensuring robots handle loads or uneven terrain effectively.

Examples of industry applications: In humanoid robotics, COM tracking enables stable walking on two legs, as seen in assistive robots for elderly care. In manufacturing, robotic arms use COM to lift heavy parts without toppling. Autonomous drones adjust COM for steady flight under shifting cargo. In prosthetics, COM alignment ensures natural, balanced motion for amputees.

Conclusions: Center of Mass in Robotics anchors the science of balance and motion, making it indispensable for reliable, agile machines. Its role in enabling precise, stable operation shines across robotic applications. Yet, its dynamic nature and computational demands push the boundaries of design and control. As robotics advances, mastering COM will remain key to building robust, adaptable systems.

Center-Surround Mechanism

Definition:

Center-Surround Mechanism refers to a computational or biological process, often inspired by human vision, where a central region's response is modulated by its surrounding context, enhancing contrast and highlighting differences. In AI and neuroscience, it models how systems detect edges, boundaries, or salient features by comparing a focal point to its periphery.

Key components: The mechanism hinges on a receptive field split into a central zone and a surrounding area, each with distinct response properties. Contrast detection arises from opposing signals—excitation in the center and inhibition from the surround, or vice versa. Spatial filtering processes these differences, amplifying edges or changes. Neural or algorithmic weighting adjusts the influence of center versus surround, while adaptation tunes sensitivity to varying inputs.

Benefits: This approach sharpens feature detection, making it easier to isolate objects or patterns in cluttered data. It mimics biological efficiency, reducing noise and focusing on relevant details. Computational simplicity allows fast processing, ideal for real-time systems. Its emphasis on contrast also boosts robustness across diverse conditions, like lighting or texture shifts.

Examples of industry applications: In image processing, center-surround enhances edge detection for photo editing software, clarifying outlines. In robotics, it aids obstacle recognition by highlighting boundaries in sensor data. Medical imaging uses it to emphasize anomalies, like tumors, in scans. In autonomous vehicles, it helps detect lane markings or traffic signs amid visual noise.

Conclusions: Center-Surround Mechanism offers a clever, nature-inspired way to spotlight key features, bridging biology and AI with practical finesse. Its knack for cutting through complexity powers vision-based innovations across industries. Yet, its precision hinges on careful calibration and manageable scale. As technology evolves, this mechanism could refine how machines perceive and prioritize their world.

Centralized AI Systems

Definition:

Centralized AI Systems refer to artificial intelligence setups where data processing, model training, and decision-making occur on a single, powerful central hub, such as a server or cloud platform, rather than being distributed across multiple devices. This architecture consolidates computational resources and control, serving connected clients or endpoints with AI capabilities.

Key components: The core is a central processing unit, typically a high-performance server or cloud infrastructure, handling all AI tasks. Data aggregation collects inputs from various sources into a unified repository for analysis. A robust communication network links the hub to end-users or devices, ensuring seamless data flow. Model management maintains and updates the AI algorithms centrally, while security protocols safeguard the concentrated data and processing power.

Benefits: Centralized systems streamline resource use, leveraging top-tier hardware for faster, more efficient computation. Uniform model updates ensure consistency across all users, simplifying maintenance. Centralized data storage enables richer insights from large, pooled datasets, boosting accuracy. Control over sensitive information tightens security and compliance, critical for regulated fields.

Examples of industry applications: In healthcare, centralized AI analyzes patient data from hospitals on a cloud server, aiding diagnosis. In finance, it processes global transactions to detect fraud from a single hub. Smart city systems use it to manage traffic flow via a central platform integrating camera feeds. In customer service, it powers chatbots across a company from one AI core.

Conclusions: Centralized AI Systems deliver potent, unified intelligence, harnessing concentrated power to drive complex applications with ease. Their efficiency and control shine in industries needing cohesive, high-capacity solutions. Yet, their vulnerability to failures and connectivity demands temper their reach. As AI evolves, balancing centralization with resilience will shape their role in a connected world.

Centralized Control in Multi-Agent Systems

Definition:

Centralized Control in Multi-Agent Systems refers to a coordination strategy where a single authority or node directs the actions of multiple agents—such as robots, software entities, or drones—within a shared environment. This approach consolidates decision-making, ensuring all agents follow a unified plan dictated by the central controller.

Key components: The system revolves around a central coordinator, often a computer or server, that processes data and issues commands. Agent communication channels relay information to and from this hub, forming a star-like network. A global state model, maintained centrally, tracks the system's overall status, including each agent's position or task. Task allocation logic assigns roles based on this overview, while synchronization ensures cohesive execution across agents.

Benefits: Centralized control simplifies coordination, aligning all agents toward a common goal with clear oversight. It optimizes resource use by leveraging a holistic view, reducing redundancy. Consistency in decision-making avoids conflicts or missteps among agents. The approach also streamlines debugging and updates, as changes flow from one point rather than multiple sources.

Examples of industry applications: In warehouse automation, a central system directs robotic pickers to retrieve items, maximizing efficiency. In air traffic control, it manages drone swarms for delivery, avoiding collisions. Manufacturing uses it to orchestrate assembly line robots, ensuring precise timing. In simulations, it governs virtual agents in training scenarios, like disaster response drills.

Conclusions: Centralized Control in Multi-Agent Systems offers a structured, efficient way to harness collective action, delivering precision and unity in complex tasks. Its top-down clarity powers industries reliant on tight coordination. Yet, its dependence on one hub exposes fragility and scalability woes. As multi-agent demands grow, blending centralized strengths with adaptive alternatives could define its future.

Centralized Learning in Federated AI

Centralized Learning in Federated AI refers to a training approach where a central server aggregates and processes data collected from multiple decentralized sources. Unlike fully decentralized federated learning, which keeps data on local devices and only shares model updates, centralized learning involves sending raw data or partially processed insights to a central repository for analysis, model training, and refinement.

Key components of centralized learning in federated AI include the central server, local data sources, communication channels, aggregation mechanisms, and security protocols. The central server is responsible for collecting data, running AI models, and distributing updates to decentralized nodes. Local data sources, such as edge devices or client nodes, gather information that contributes to model improvement. Communication channels enable the transfer of data and updates between local nodes and the central system. Aggregation mechanisms compile and analyze data to create a more accurate model, while security protocols ensure the protection of sensitive information and compliance with privacy regulations.

The benefits of centralized learning in federated AI include improved model accuracy, enhanced computational efficiency, and better data management. Since the central server processes a large volume of aggregated data, the model benefits from more comprehensive insights, leading to higher precision in predictions. The computational burden on local devices is minimized, as the central system handles most of the heavy processing. Additionally, centralized learning provides a streamlined approach to data management, enabling better organization, storage, and retrieval of critical information.

An example of centralized learning in federated AI can be seen in healthcare research, where multiple hospitals collect patient data and send anonymized records to a central AI system for disease prediction and treatment recommendations. This allows the AI model to learn from diverse medical cases while maintaining patient confidentiality through robust security measures.

Industries that benefit from centralized learning in federated AI include healthcare, finance, retail, telecommunications, and smart cities. In healthcare, centralized AI models assist in predictive analytics, drug discovery, and personalized treatment plans. Financial institutions use it for fraud detection and risk assessment. Retailers leverage centralized learning to improve demand forecasting and customer recommendations. Telecommunications companies optimize network management and predictive maintenance, while smart city applications enhance urban planning and resource allocation.

Applications of centralized learning in federated AI span across predictive modeling, anomaly detection, personalization, speech recognition, and image processing. Predictive modeling helps industries forecast trends and outcomes based on aggregated data. Anomaly detection enhances cybersecurity by identifying potential threats and fraud patterns. Personalization in digital platforms improves user experiences by tailoring content and services to individual preferences. Speech recognition technology benefits from centralized learning by refining voice models for virtual assistants and automated transcription services. Image processing applications include medical imaging analysis, facial recognition, and autonomous vehicle navigation.

Centralized learning in federated AI bridges the gap between fully decentralized learning and traditional AI approaches by leveraging the advantages of aggregated data without completely compromising data privacy. It allows organizations to build more accurate models while maintaining efficiency in training and deployment. As AI continues to evolve, the balance between centralization and decentralization will play a crucial role in shaping the future of federated learning.

Central Limit Theorem (CLT) in AI

Central Limit Theorem (CLT) in AI is a fundamental statistical principle stating that when independent random variables are summed, their normalized sum tends to follow a normal distribution, regardless of the original data distribution, provided the sample size is sufficiently large. In artificial intelligence and machine learning, CLT is crucial for understanding probabilistic models, statistical inference, and error estimation in predictive analytics.

Key components of the Central Limit Theorem in AI include random variables, sample size, normal distribution, and mean convergence. Random variables represent data points drawn from different sources or populations. The sample size must be large enough to allow the theorem to take effect, ensuring a reliable approximation of the normal distribution. Normal distribution emerges when the sum of independent variables forms a bell-shaped curve. Mean convergence ensures that as sample size increases, the distribution of sample means approaches a normal distribution, making statistical inference more reliable.

The benefits of CLT in AI include improved model accuracy, enhanced generalization, and effective uncertainty estimation. Since many machine learning algorithms rely on probability distributions, CLT provides a mathematical foundation for making predictions based on sample data. Generalization is strengthened because AI models trained on diverse datasets can apply learned patterns to unseen data more effectively. Uncertainty estimation becomes feasible, as CLT enables confidence interval calculations, which help assess prediction reliability.

An example of CLT in AI is in reinforcement learning, where agents make sequential decisions based on rewards. CLT helps estimate the expected reward distribution, allowing models to optimize decisions based on probable outcomes. In deep learning, CLT is used to justify batch normalization techniques, where mini-batches of data approximate a normal distribution, stabilizing neural network training.

Industries that leverage CLT in AI include finance, healthcare, e-commerce, manufacturing, and cybersecurity. In finance, it aids in risk modeling and portfolio management by predicting asset returns. Healthcare applications include medical diagnosis, where CLT helps refine probabilistic models for disease prediction. E-commerce platforms apply CLT to analyze consumer behavior and optimize recommendation systems. Manufacturing benefits from CLT in quality control, ensuring production consistency through statistical process control. Cybersecurity employs CLT for anomaly detection, identifying deviations from normal behavior in network traffic.

Applications of CLT in AI extend to predictive analytics, natural language processing, fraud detection, anomaly detection, and A/B testing. Predictive analytics relies on CLT to infer future trends from sample data. Natural language processing uses CLT to analyze word distributions in text corpora, improving language model performance. Fraud detection systems apply CLT to detect irregular financial transactions based on normal spending patterns. Anomaly detection algorithms use CLT to differentiate between normal and abnormal events in datasets. A/B testing in digital marketing and software development benefits from CLT by ensuring statistical significance in experimental results.

Central Limit Theorem plays a crucial role in AI by enabling statistical inference, model stability, and predictive accuracy. It allows AI practitioners to work with real-world data that may not follow normal distributions while still making reliable predictions. As AI and machine learning continue to advance, CLT remains a foundational principle that ensures robust, data-driven decision-making across various domains.

Central Processing Unit (CPU) in AI

Central Processing Unit (CPU) in AI is the primary computational component responsible for executing instructions in artificial intelligence applications. It acts as the brain of a computer system, processing data, performing mathematical operations, and managing system resources. In AI, the CPU plays a critical role in handling control logic, managing memory, and executing software algorithms that drive machine learning and data analysis.

Key components of a CPU in AI include the arithmetic logic unit (ALU), control unit, cache memory, registers, and instruction set. The arithmetic logic unit performs mathematical and logical operations essential for AI computations. The control unit directs data flow between the CPU, memory, and other hardware components, ensuring smooth execution of AI algorithms. Cache memory provides high-speed data access, improving efficiency in processing machine learning models. Registers store temporary data and instructions required for real-time calculations. The instruction set defines the operations the CPU can execute, including specialized instructions optimized for AI workloads.

The benefits of using a CPU in AI include versatility, precision, and integration capabilities. CPUs are highly flexible and capable of handling various AI tasks, from data preprocessing to executing inference models. Their ability to perform complex calculations with high precision makes them suitable for applications that require accurate numerical processing. CPUs seamlessly integrate with GPUs, TPUs, and other accelerators, enabling hybrid AI workloads that leverage the strengths of multiple computing units.

An example of CPU usage in AI is in natural language processing (NLP), where CPUs manage text parsing, tokenization, and syntactic analysis before sending the data to specialized processors for deep learning tasks. In AI-powered personal assistants, the CPU is responsible for speech recognition preprocessing, executing rule-based decision-making, and handling background processes that support the AI model.

Industries that rely on CPUs for AI applications include finance, healthcare, robotics, cybersecurity, and edge computing. Financial institutions use CPUs for real-time fraud detection, risk assessment, and algorithmic trading. In healthcare, CPUs process medical imaging data, supporting AI-driven diagnostics and decision-making. Robotics applications rely on CPUs for sensor data processing, motion control, and real-time AI-driven decision-making. Cybersecurity systems utilize CPUs for intrusion detection and pattern analysis in large datasets. Edge computing benefits from CPUs in AI-powered IoT devices, enabling real-time data analysis with low latency.

Applications of CPUs in AI extend to data preprocessing, AI model inference, decision-making systems, robotics, and edge AI. Data preprocessing involves cleaning and structuring raw data for machine learning models, a task efficiently handled by CPUs. AI model inference, particularly for lightweight models, can be executed entirely on CPUs, making them valuable in resource-constrained environments. Decision-making systems in AI, such as rule-based engines, use CPUs to analyze structured data and generate insights. Robotics applications leverage CPUs for sensor fusion and control logic, ensuring smooth operation in autonomous systems. Edge AI benefits from CPUs in smart cameras, autonomous vehicles, and IoT devices that require AI-driven functionalities with minimal power consumption.

The Central Processing Unit remains a vital component in AI, offering essential computing capabilities for data processing, inference, and real-time decision-making. While specialized hardware like GPUs and TPUs accelerate AI training, CPUs provide the foundational processing power that ensures AI applications run efficiently. As AI evolves, CPUs continue to play a crucial role in hybrid AI systems, supporting a wide range of applications across industries.

Centrifugal Force in Robotices

Centrifugal Force in Robotics refers to the apparent outward force experienced by a rotating object as it moves along a curved path. In robotics, centrifugal force plays a crucial role in motion dynamics, stability control, and mechanical design, particularly for robots that involve rotational movement, high-speed operations, or trajectory planning. This force arises due to inertia, which resists changes in motion direction, affecting how robotic systems navigate turns and maintain balance.

Key components of centrifugal force in robotics include mass, velocity, radius of curvature, and rotational inertia. Mass determines the magnitude of the force, as heavier robotic components experience stronger centrifugal effects. Velocity directly influences the intensity of the force, with higher speeds leading to greater outward pull. The radius of curvature affects how sharply a robot turns, with tighter turns resulting in stronger centrifugal forces. Rotational inertia plays a role in how a robot's structure responds to changes in motion, dictating stability and maneuverability.

The benefits of understanding and managing centrifugal force in robotics include improved stability, enhanced precision, and optimized energy efficiency. Stability is crucial in mobile robots, robotic arms, and drones that navigate curves or sudden directional shifts, as properly accounting for centrifugal force prevents tipping or loss of control. Precision in motion control improves when robots adjust for centrifugal effects, leading to smoother and more accurate positioning in manufacturing and automation processes. Energy efficiency is optimized when centrifugal forces are managed effectively, reducing unnecessary counteractive forces and improving motor performance.

An example of centrifugal force in robotics can be seen in robotic arms used in assembly lines, where rapid rotational movements require compensation mechanisms to prevent misalignment. Another example is autonomous vehicles and drones, which adjust steering and flight paths based on centrifugal effects to ensure smooth and controlled movement during turns.

Industries that incorporate centrifugal force considerations in robotics include automotive, aerospace, industrial automation, healthcare, and logistics. The automotive industry uses robotic arms for high-speed precision welding, painting, and assembly, where centrifugal forces impact movement stability. Aerospace robotics rely on centrifugal force calculations in satellite deployment systems and robotic arms used in zero-gravity environments. Industrial automation applies centrifugal force principles in conveyor belt robotics and sorting mechanisms that operate at high speeds. Healthcare robotics, such as surgical robots, adjust for centrifugal effects to maintain accuracy during intricate procedures. Logistics robotics in warehouses and fulfillment centers navigate turns and dynamic routes while compensating for centrifugal forces.

Applications of centrifugal force in robotics include robotic motion planning, high-speed automation, drone stabilization, robotic arm control, and autonomous navigation. Robotic motion planning accounts for centrifugal effects to optimize acceleration and deceleration during curved paths. High-speed automation systems integrate force compensation to maintain stability and accuracy in repetitive tasks. Drone stabilization relies on centrifugal force adjustments to ensure controlled flight during high-speed maneuvers. Robotic arm control uses centrifugal calculations to maintain precision in rotational tasks. Autonomous navigation systems incorporate centrifugal force management to enhance vehicle stability and maneuverability.

Centrifugal force in robotics is a fundamental consideration in motion dynamics, influencing the performance, stability, and efficiency of robotic systems. Proper understanding and compensation for this force enable robots to operate more effectively in high-speed and precision-driven environments. As robotics continues to advance, engineers and AI-driven control systems will refine algorithms and mechanical designs to optimize performance while accounting for the effects of centrifugal force in diverse applications.

Centroid-Based Clustering

Centroid-Based Clustering is a machine learning technique used for grouping data points into clusters based on their proximity to central points called centroids. This clustering method iteratively refines cluster assignments by minimizing the distance between data points and their respective centroids. It is widely used in unsupervised learning for pattern recognition, anomaly detection, and data segmentation.

Key components of centroid-based clustering include centroids, distance metrics, clustering algorithms, and iterative optimization. Centroids represent the central point of each cluster and are updated as the clustering process progresses. Distance metrics such as Euclidean distance or Manhattan distance measure the similarity between data points and centroids, influencing cluster assignments. Clustering algorithms, including k-means and k-medoids, define how data points are assigned to clusters and how centroids are updated. Iterative optimization ensures that clusters converge to an optimal state where intra-cluster variance is minimized.

The benefits of centroid-based clustering include scalability, efficiency, and interpretability. It efficiently handles large datasets by iteratively refining cluster assignments, making it suitable for big data applications. The algorithm is computationally efficient compared to hierarchical clustering methods, allowing faster execution. The resulting clusters are easy to interpret, enabling businesses and researchers to extract meaningful insights from structured data.

An example of centroid-based clustering is k-means clustering applied to customer segmentation in e-commerce. By analyzing customer purchase behavior, k-means groups customers into segments based on their spending patterns and preferences, allowing businesses to personalize marketing strategies. Another example is in image compression, where centroid-based clustering reduces color variations by grouping similar pixels into representative colors, optimizing storage and rendering efficiency.

Industries that benefit from centroid-based clustering include finance, healthcare, retail, telecommunications, and cybersecurity. Financial institutions use it for fraud detection and risk assessment by clustering transaction patterns to identify anomalies. In healthcare, it is applied in medical imaging and patient segmentation to improve diagnosis and treatment plans. Retail businesses use it for market segmentation and inventory management by identifying buying trends. Telecommunications companies rely on clustering to optimize network performance and customer experience. Cybersecurity applications use centroid-based clustering to detect outliers and potential threats in large datasets.

Applications of centroid-based clustering include anomaly detection, image segmentation, recommendation systems, natural language processing, and geospatial analysis. Anomaly detection benefits from clustering by identifying deviations in normal patterns, useful in fraud prevention and intrusion detection. Image segmentation uses clustering to group pixels based on color and texture for object recognition and medical imaging. Recommendation systems leverage clustering to categorize user preferences and suggest relevant content. Natural language processing applies clustering to organize text data, enhancing topic modeling and sentiment analysis. Geospatial analysis uses clustering to detect geographic patterns, aiding urban planning and disaster response.

Centroid-based clustering is a powerful technique for data classification and pattern recognition in various fields. Its ability to group similar data points efficiently makes it an essential tool in machine learning and artificial intelligence. As AI continues to evolve, centroid-based clustering will remain a fundamental approach in data-driven decision-making, helping organizations extract valuable insights and optimize processes.

Centroidal Voronoi Tessellation (CVT)

Centroidal Voronoi Tessellation (CVT) is a mathematical and computational technique used to partition a space into regions based on proximity to a set of points, known as generators, where each generator is located at the centroid of its corresponding region. CVT is an optimized form of the standard Voronoi tessellation, ensuring that the generators represent the data distribution as efficiently as possible. This technique is widely applied in fields such as computational geometry, machine learning, computer graphics, and optimization.

Key components of Centroidal Voronoi Tessellation include generators, Voronoi cells, centroid computation, iterative refinement, and distance metrics. Generators are the central points that define each Voronoi cell and are iteratively adjusted to achieve centroidal balance. Voronoi cells are regions where every point within a cell is closer to its corresponding generator than to any other. Centroid computation ensures that each generator is placed at the center of mass of its assigned region, improving partitioning accuracy. Iterative refinement optimizes the placement of generators by continuously updating them based on centroid locations. Distance metrics, such as Euclidean or Manhattan distance, determine the boundaries of Voronoi cells and influence the final tessellation structure.

The benefits of Centroidal Voronoi Tessellation include improved data representation, optimized clustering, and enhanced computational efficiency. CVT provides a more balanced and structured partitioning of space, ensuring uniform distribution and reducing clustering distortions. Optimized clustering improves the performance of machine learning and data segmentation tasks by generating centroids that accurately reflect underlying patterns. Enhanced computational efficiency is achieved by reducing redundant computations and improving spatial organization in applications such as image compression and resource allocation.

An example of Centroidal Voronoi Tessellation is in image segmentation, where CVT partitions an image into regions based on pixel intensity, improving edge detection and feature extraction. Another example is in wireless sensor networks, where CVT optimizes sensor placement by ensuring uniform coverage and efficient energy distribution.

Industries benefiting from Centroidal Voronoi Tessellation include computer vision, geospatial analysis, telecommunications, robotics, and manufacturing. Computer vision applications use CVT for image segmentation, object recognition, and feature extraction. Geospatial analysis leverages CVT for optimal land use planning, territory division, and geographic clustering. Telecommunications companies apply CVT for network optimization, ensuring balanced cell tower placement and coverage. Robotics integrates CVT for path planning and motion control, enabling efficient navigation and obstacle avoidance. Manufacturing industries utilize CVT for material optimization, automated inspection, and efficient production layouts.

Applications of Centroidal Voronoi Tessellation extend to mesh generation, machine learning, medical imaging, optimization problems, and resource distribution. Mesh generation benefits from CVT in finite element analysis, improving computational accuracy and structural modeling. Machine learning applies CVT for unsupervised clustering and feature extraction, enhancing data processing efficiency. Medical imaging uses CVT to improve segmentation and analysis of anatomical structures, aiding in disease detection. Optimization problems incorporate CVT to balance resource allocation and workload distribution in logistics and operations. Resource distribution leverages CVT to optimize placement of assets such as sensors, delivery hubs, and public services.

Centroidal Voronoi Tessellation provides an effective method for space partitioning, clustering, and optimization across various disciplines. By ensuring that generators are positioned at the centroid of each region, CVT enhances data representation, improves computational efficiency, and optimizes spatial structures. As AI, data science, and computational geometry continue to advance, CVT remains a valuable tool for applications requiring precise and adaptive partitioning of complex datasets.

Certainty Factor (CF)

Certainty Factor (CF) is a numerical representation of the degree of belief or confidence in a hypothesis or conclusion based on evidence. It is commonly used in expert systems and decision-making AI models to quantify uncertainty and provide more accurate reasoning under incomplete or ambiguous data conditions. The certainty factor model was introduced to enhance rule-based systems by allowing them to handle probabilistic reasoning, making AI-driven decisions more interpretable and reliable.

Key components of Certainty Factor include belief measure, disbelief measure, rule-based inference, combination of evidence, and thresholding. The belief measure quantifies the confidence in a particular hypothesis based on the available evidence, while the disbelief measure indicates the degree of uncertainty or contradiction. Rule-based inference applies logical conditions to derive conclusions with associated certainty values, helping AI systems reason under uncertainty. Combination of evidence integrates multiple pieces of information, refining the overall certainty of a hypothesis through cumulative reasoning. Thresholding determines the minimum certainty factor required for an AI model to accept or reject a conclusion, ensuring reliable decision-making.

The benefits of Certainty Factor include improved decision accuracy, better handling of uncertainty, and enhanced interpretability in AI models. By assigning certainty levels to conclusions, AI systems can make more reliable decisions, even when data is incomplete or noisy. The ability to handle uncertainty makes CF-based reasoning effective in expert systems that require probabilistic analysis. Enhanced interpretability allows human users to understand and validate AI-generated conclusions, fostering trust in AI-driven recommendations.

An example of Certainty Factor in action is in medical diagnosis expert systems, where AI assigns a certainty value to each potential disease based on symptoms and test results. If a patient presents with a set of symptoms, the system evaluates the likelihood of various diagnoses, incorporating multiple rules and evidence sources to refine its conclusions. Another example is in fraud detection, where AI assesses transaction patterns and assigns a certainty score to indicate the probability of fraudulent activity, allowing financial institutions to act on high-risk transactions.

Industries that benefit from Certainty Factor include healthcare, finance, cybersecurity, manufacturing, and decision support systems. Healthcare utilizes CF-based AI for diagnosing diseases, recommending treatments, and analyzing medical reports. Financial institutions apply CF in credit risk assessment, fraud detection, and investment analysis. Cybersecurity relies on CF-driven AI models to detect anomalies, assess the likelihood of security breaches, and prioritize threat responses. Manufacturing industries use CF in predictive maintenance, where AI assigns certainty factors to equipment failures and recommends preventive measures. Decision support systems in various sectors implement CF to improve data-driven decision-making under uncertainty.

Applications of Certainty Factor extend to expert systems, AI-powered diagnostics, risk assessment, anomaly detection, and intelligent automation. Expert systems integrate CF to enhance rule-based reasoning in domains such as law, medicine, and engineering. AI-powered diagnostics utilize CF to evaluate multiple data points and generate confidence scores for automated medical assessments. Risk assessment benefits from CF by quantifying uncertainties in financial markets, credit scoring, and business decision-making. Anomaly detection employs CF-based AI to identify deviations in network traffic, sensor data, or financial transactions with quantified confidence. Intelligent automation incorporates CF to optimize process control, reducing errors and improving system reliability in industrial and business operations.

Certainty Factor plays a crucial role in AI reasoning and decision-making by allowing systems to handle uncertainty and provide confidence-based conclusions. Its ability to enhance expert systems, probabilistic AI models, and decision support tools makes it valuable across industries that require reliable and interpretable AI-driven insights. As artificial intelligence continues to evolve, CF-based reasoning will remain a key approach for improving accuracy, trustworthiness, and effectiveness in complex decision-making scenarios.

Certificate Transparency (CT)

Certificate Transparency (CT) is a security framework designed to enhance the reliability and accountability of digital certificates by providing a publicly verifiable log of issued certificates. It is a proactive measure to detect and prevent certificate fraud, misissuance, and unauthorized use by requiring certificate authorities to log all SSL/TLS certificates in append-only, publicly accessible logs. CT helps improve trust in web security by allowing domain owners, browsers, and security researchers to monitor certificate issuance in real time.

Key components of Certificate Transparency include append-only logs, cryptographic proof mechanisms, monitoring tools, and domain owner verification. Append-only logs ensure that once a certificate is recorded, it cannot be modified or deleted, preserving the integrity of certificate records. Cryptographic proof mechanisms, such as Merkle trees, verify the authenticity of log entries and prevent tampering. Monitoring tools allow domain owners and security teams to track certificate issuance and detect unauthorized or fraudulent certificates. Domain owner verification enables businesses and individuals to confirm that certificates issued for their domains are legitimate and have not been fraudulently obtained.

The benefits of Certificate Transparency include enhanced security, increased trust, and improved incident response. Enhanced security is achieved by providing real-time visibility into issued certificates, reducing the risk of fraudulent or compromised certificates being used for phishing or man-in-the-middle attacks. Increased trust comes from the ability of domain owners and internet users to verify the legitimacy of certificates, strengthening online authentication and encryption. Improved incident response enables organizations to detect and revoke unauthorized certificates quickly, preventing potential security breaches before they cause harm.

An example of Certificate Transparency in action is in web browsers like Google Chrome, which require publicly logged certificates for secure HTTPS connections. When a user visits a website, the browser checks CT logs to verify the authenticity of the certificate before establishing a secure connection. Another example is in cybersecurity operations, where security researchers monitor CT logs for suspicious certificate issuances that could indicate phishing campaigns or malicious domain registrations.

Industries that benefit from Certificate Transparency include cybersecurity, finance, e-commerce, telecommunications, and cloud computing. Cybersecurity firms leverage CT to detect fraudulent SSL/TLS certificates and mitigate risks associated with certificate-based attacks. Financial institutions use CT to ensure the security of online banking and payment transactions by verifying the authenticity of digital certificates. E-commerce platforms rely on CT to protect online shoppers from phishing websites that use fake SSL certificates to impersonate legitimate businesses. Telecommunications companies integrate CT to secure encrypted communications and prevent unauthorized interception of sensitive data. Cloud computing providers implement CT to strengthen the security of cloud-based applications and ensure trusted connections between services.

Applications of Certificate Transparency extend to website authentication, phishing detection, compliance enforcement, security monitoring, and cryptographic auditing. Website authentication benefits from CT by verifying that SSL certificates are issued by trusted certificate authorities. Phishing detection uses CT logs to identify fraudulent certificates associated with malicious domains, helping security teams take action against cyber threats. Compliance enforcement ensures that organizations adhere to best practices in certificate management by logging all issued certificates for public review. Security monitoring integrates CT data into threat intelligence platforms, allowing organizations to detect suspicious certificate activity. Cryptographic auditing enables independent verification of certificate issuance practices, ensuring transparency and accountability among certificate authorities.

Certificate Transparency is a critical security measure that improves trust in digital certificates by providing an open and verifiable system for certificate issuance. By enhancing the visibility and accountability of SSL/TLS certificates, CT helps organizations protect their online presence, prevent fraud, and strengthen cybersecurity defenses. As the internet continues to evolve, CT will remain an essential tool for ensuring the integrity of digital authentication and encryption systems.

Chain of Thought Reasoning

Chain of Thought Reasoning is a cognitive-inspired approach in artificial intelligence that enables models to process complex problems through sequential reasoning. Instead of making direct predictions, AI systems generate intermediate reasoning steps, mimicking human logical thinking to arrive at a well-structured conclusion. This method enhances AI's ability to solve multi-step problems, improving interpretability, problem-solving accuracy, and decision-making efficiency.

Key components of Chain of Thought Reasoning include step-by-step decomposition, intermediate inference generation, contextual learning, reasoning consistency, and model adaptability. Step-by-step decomposition allows the AI system to break down complex problems into smaller, manageable reasoning steps, improving clarity. Intermediate inference generation ensures that each step logically follows from the previous one, building a coherent thought process. Contextual learning enables AI to use previous reasoning steps to refine and improve its conclusions dynamically. Reasoning consistency ensures that the AI maintains logical coherence throughout the reasoning chain, reducing contradictions and errors. Model adaptability allows AI to apply reasoning across different domains, making it more versatile in handling complex real-world problems.

The benefits of Chain of Thought Reasoning include improved decision-making, enhanced interpretability, and better generalization across tasks. Improved decision-making results from the AI's ability to logically evaluate each step before reaching a conclusion, reducing errors in problem-solving. Enhanced interpretability ensures that AI-generated conclusions can be understood and validated by humans, increasing trust in AI-driven recommendations. Better generalization across tasks allows AI to apply logical reasoning techniques to a wide range of applications, improving performance in areas requiring complex problem-solving and long-term planning.

An example of Chain of Thought Reasoning is in mathematical problem-solving, where an AI system breaks down a complex equation into a sequence of logical steps, solving each part before reaching the final answer. Another example is in legal decision-making, where AI analyzes legal cases by constructing a reasoning chain that considers past precedents, evidence, and logical arguments to support a conclusion.

Industries that benefit from Chain of Thought Reasoning include healthcare, finance, law, education, and artificial intelligence research. Healthcare applications use AI-driven reasoning to analyze patient symptoms, laboratory results, and medical history, forming structured diagnostic reasoning that improves treatment recommendations. Financial institutions apply structured reasoning to risk assessments, fraud detection, and algorithmic trading, enhancing the reliability of AI-driven financial predictions. Legal professionals leverage AI models using Chain of Thought Reasoning to analyze case law, build arguments, and draft legal documents with improved accuracy. Education technology integrates reasoning-based AI to provide step-by-step tutoring, improving personalized learning and student engagement. AI research benefits from reasoning-based techniques to enhance language models, autonomous systems, and cognitive AI development.

Applications of Chain of Thought Reasoning extend to question answering, automated theorem proving, robotics, knowledge extraction, and human-computer interaction. Question answering benefits from AI's ability to logically decompose complex queries, improving accuracy in generating responses. Automated theorem proving applies reasoning-based AI to mathematical and logical proof generation, increasing efficiency in scientific research. Robotics uses structured reasoning to improve navigation, decision-making, and problem-solving in real-world environments. Knowledge extraction integrates Chain of Thought Reasoning to analyze and summarize large volumes of data, improving AI-driven insights. Human-computer interaction enhances user experience by providing AI-generated explanations, making AI systems more transparent and user-friendly.

Chain of Thought Reasoning is transforming artificial intelligence by enabling structured, logical problem-solving that mimics human thought processes. By improving interpretability, accuracy, and adaptability, this reasoning approach is advancing AI applications across various industries. As AI continues to evolve, the integration of Chain of Thought Reasoning will enhance its ability to tackle complex tasks, making intelligent systems more reliable, transparent, and effective in real-world decision-making.

Chain Rule in AI Backpropagation

The chain rule is a fundamental concept in calculus used in AI backpropagation to compute gradients in deep learning models. It allows the model to update weights during training efficiently.

Key Characteristics
Gradient computation calculates how weight changes affect the loss function.
Layer-by-layer propagation propagates gradients backward through network layers.
Error minimization adjusts weights based on computed gradients to minimize loss.

Benefits
Core to backpropagation and essential for training deep learning models.
Mathematically sound, providing a rigorous framework for AI training.

Applications
Neural network training involves tasks like image recognition and NLP.
Optimization algorithms use the chain rule in techniques like stochastic gradient descent (SGD).

Sources
Calculus and machine learning are fundamental to understanding the chain rule.
Backpropagation algorithms rely on the chain rule for gradient computation.

Conclusions
The chain rule underpins AI training, enabling efficient weight optimization through backpropagation. However, challenges like vanishing gradients require careful management.

Channel Attention Mechanism
Channel attention mechanisms allow neural networks to focus on specific channels (or features) within a dataset, improving the network's ability to extract and prioritize important information.

Key Characteristics
Feature prioritization helps the model emphasize essential channels while de-emphasizing less relevant ones.
Adaptive weights dynamically adjust the importance of each channel based on the input data.
Improved focus allows for more refined processing by concentrating on the most informative features.

Benefits
Better accuracy improves model performance by focusing on the most critical features of the data.
Efficient use of resources reduces computational waste by down-weighting irrelevant channels.

Applications
Image processing focuses on important visual features like edges or textures in computer vision tasks.
Speech recognition emphasizes key frequency channels in audio processing tasks.

Sources
Deep learning models utilize channel attention mechanisms as part of broader attention mechanisms in state-of-the-art neural networks.
Computer vision includes channel attention mechanisms in high-performance models like CNNs.

Conclusions
Channel attention mechanisms enhance AI model performance by helping them focus on the most relevant parts of the input data. However, they introduce added complexity and computational costs.

Chained Neural Networks

Chained Neural Networks refer to a deep learning architecture where multiple neural networks are sequentially linked, allowing information to flow through each network in a structured manner. This approach enhances model performance by enabling each network in the chain to refine, process, or extract different levels of features before passing data to the next stage. By chaining networks together, AI systems improve accuracy, adaptability, and decision-making across complex tasks, making this architecture effective for multi-stage learning, feature extraction, and hierarchical processing.

Key components of Chained Neural Networks include network stacking, feature refinement, inter-network communication, transfer learning integration, and sequential optimization. Network stacking involves arranging multiple neural networks in a sequence, where each network specializes in a specific aspect of learning. Feature refinement ensures that each stage of the chain extracts, enhances, and processes meaningful information before passing it forward. Inter-network communication allows networks to exchange and transform intermediate outputs, improving learning depth and accuracy. Transfer learning integration enables each chained network to leverage pre-trained knowledge from previous networks, enhancing adaptability to different domains. Sequential optimization ensures that each stage in the network chain contributes to improved performance by fine-tuning parameters across the entire architecture.

The benefits of Chained Neural Networks include improved accuracy, enhanced modularity, and increased adaptability. Improved accuracy is achieved by refining learning at each network stage, reducing errors and improving decision-making. Enhanced modularity allows developers to design flexible AI systems where each chained network can be independently trained or replaced without affecting the entire architecture. Increased adaptability ensures that chained networks can handle diverse tasks, including image recognition, natural language processing, and sequential decision-making, making them highly effective across multiple AI applications.

An example of Chained Neural Networks is in autonomous vehicles, where multiple deep learning models are linked to handle different stages of perception, object detection, and decision-making. The first network may analyze raw sensor data, the next network refines object recognition, and the final network interprets environmental context to determine safe navigation actions. Another example is in speech recognition, where one network extracts phonetic features, another processes language structure, and a final model generates human-like responses.

Industries that benefit from Chained Neural Networks include healthcare, finance, robotics, cybersecurity, and artificial intelligence research. Healthcare applies chained networks to medical imaging, where different networks handle segmentation, feature extraction, and diagnosis refinement. Financial institutions use chained architectures for fraud detection, where one network identifies suspicious transactions, another predicts risk levels, and a final model validates fraudulent patterns. Robotics benefits from multi-network chaining for visual perception, movement planning, and adaptive learning in real-time environments. Cybersecurity integrates chained networks to analyze network traffic, detect anomalies, and identify evolving cyber threats with improved accuracy. Artificial intelligence research employs chained networks to enhance deep learning applications, optimizing multi-stage processing for complex decision-making tasks.

Applications of Chained Neural Networks extend to real-time video processing, predictive analytics, automated translation, multi-agent AI coordination, and self-learning AI models. Real-time video processing benefits from chaining networks for object tracking, event detection, and motion prediction in surveillance and augmented reality applications. Predictive analytics leverages chained networks to refine forecasting models, improving financial, healthcare, and market trend predictions. Automated translation applies chained networks for contextual understanding, grammar correction, and linguistic adaptation, improving translation accuracy across multiple languages. Multi-agent AI coordination integrates chained architectures to enable collaborative decision-making between intelligent systems in smart environments. Self-learning AI models use chained networks to process reinforcement learning feedback, enhancing their ability to adapt and evolve over time.

Chained Neural Networks provide a powerful AI framework for multi-stage processing, feature refinement, and deep learning optimization. By linking multiple neural networks into structured sequences, this approach enhances accuracy, modularity, and adaptability across industries. As AI technology continues to advance, Chained Neural Networks will play a vital role in enabling more sophisticated, interpretable, and scalable artificial intelligence solutions.

Channel Normalization in Neural Networks

Channel normalization is a technique used in neural networks to standardize activation values across different channels (features), ensuring uniformity and improving model convergence during training.

Key Characteristics
Standardization ensures that all channels have a similar range of values, reducing the risk of one channel dominating the learning process.
Batch processing applies normalization across batches of data to maintain consistency during training.
Improved convergence helps networks train faster by reducing variance across features.

Benefits
Stabilized learning reduces the risk of exploding or vanishing gradients during training.
Faster convergence accelerates training by smoothing the optimization process.

Applications
Image classification uses channel normalization in convolutional neural networks (CNNs) to normalize pixel values across channels.
Speech processing applies normalization to frequency bands in speech recognition tasks.

Sources
AI optimization techniques include channel normalization as a subset of broader methods in deep learning.
AI training strategies often employ batch normalization and layer normalization to improve model performance.

Conclusions
Channel normalization ensures stable and efficient model training, particularly in deep learning applications involving high-dimensional data.

Channel Pruining in Neural Networks

Channel Pruning in Neural Networks
Channel pruning is a technique used to reduce the size of neural networks by removing redundant or less important channels (neurons), improving computational efficiency without significantly impacting performance.

Key Characteristics
Model compression reduces the number of channels in the network, resulting in a smaller model size.
Performance preservation ensures pruning maintains model accuracy while reducing complexity.
Dynamic pruning removes channels during training based on their contribution to overall performance.

Benefits
Reduced model size decreases memory and computational requirements.
Faster inference speeds up predictions in pruned models.

Applications
Mobile AI deploys lightweight AI models on mobile devices and edge computing platforms.
Deep learning utilizes channel pruning in convolutional neural networks (CNNs) to reduce complexity.

Sources
Model optimization includes channel pruning as part of broader AI techniques.
AI compression research focuses on pruning and hardware acceleration for efficient neural networks.

Conclusions
Channel pruning is an effective technique for optimizing neural networks, particularly for resource-constrained environments. However, careful planning is required to avoid significant performance loss.

error detection, though they require more data and computational resources compared to word-level models.

Character-Level Language Models

Definition: Character-level language Models are a type of neural network-based model that processes and generates text one character at a time instead of relying on whole words or phrases. These models learn the statistical patterns of characters within a language, enabling them to generate coherent text, predict the next character in a sequence, and handle languages with complex morphologies. By training on large text corpora, character-level models develop an understanding of grammar, syntax, and contextual dependencies at the smallest linguistic units.

Key components of Character-Level Language Models include tokenization, recurrent architectures, sequence modeling, context windowing, and loss functions. Tokenization in character-level models involves breaking down text into individual characters rather than words or subwords, allowing the model to process all linguistic structures without predefined vocabularies. Recurrent architectures such as Long Short-Term Memory (LSTM) or Gated Recurrent Units (GRUs) help maintain sequential dependencies between characters, improving text generation accuracy. Sequence modeling captures relationships between consecutive characters, ensuring that the generated output follows natural language patterns. Context windowing determines how many preceding characters the model considers when predicting the next character, influencing coherence and fluency. Loss functions such as cross-entropy measure prediction accuracy, guiding the optimization of model parameters during training.

The benefits of Character-Level Language Models include flexibility, robustness, and language independence. Flexibility arises from their ability to process any sequence of text without requiring a predefined vocabulary, making them highly adaptable to different writing styles, names, and technical jargon. Robustness is achieved as character-based models handle rare words, misspellings, and domain-specific terminology more effectively than word-based models. Language independence ensures that these models can learn multiple languages without being constrained by word tokenization rules, making them suitable for underrepresented languages and multilingual applications.

An example of Character-Level Language Models in action is text generation, where an AI model produces realistic and grammatically coherent sentences by predicting one character at a time. Another example is in optical character recognition (OCR), where AI interprets scanned documents and handwritten text at the character level, improving recognition accuracy across diverse scripts and fonts.

Industries that benefit from Character-Level Language Models include natural language processing, cybersecurity, healthcare, education, and entertainment. Natural language processing applications leverage character-level models for text prediction, chatbots, and automated translation systems. Cybersecurity firms use these models to detect adversarial attacks, spam, and obfuscated malware by analyzing unusual character sequences in textual data. Healthcare integrates character-level models for medical transcription, clinical documentation, and electronic health record processing, improving text-based automation in the medical field. Education platforms apply these models in language learning tools, automated essay scoring, and personalized tutoring. Entertainment industries use character-based text models for creative writing assistance, script generation, and AI-driven storytelling.

Applications of Character-Level Language Models extend to spell correction, code generation, anomaly detection, speech recognition, and automated subtitling. Spell correction benefits from character-level processing by identifying and correcting typographical errors without relying on predefined dictionaries. Code generation applies these models to assist programmers in writing and completing code snippets by understanding character-based syntax structures. Anomaly detection uses character-level language modeling to identify irregular patterns in security logs, emails, and transactions, helping prevent fraud and cyber threats. Speech recognition integrates character-level models to enhance transcriptions, ensuring more precise capture of spoken language nuances. Automated subtitling leverages character-level AI to improve real-time captioning in videos, streaming services, and accessibility applications.

Character-Level Language Models provide a powerful approach to text processing by understanding linguistic structures at the fundamental character level. Their flexibility, robustness, and ability to handle diverse languages and domains make them essential in AI-driven language applications. As advancements in deep learning continue, character-level models will play a key role in improving text generation, natural language understanding, and intelligent automation across multiple industries.

Chatbot

Chatbot refers to an artificial intelligence-powered program designed to simulate human conversation and interact with users through text or voice-based communication. It uses natural language processing (NLP) and machine learning algorithms to understand user queries, provide relevant responses, and automate various tasks. Chatbots function in customer service, virtual assistance, and business automation, offering real-time responses while reducing the need for human intervention.

Key components of a chatbot include natural language processing, intent recognition, dialogue management, machine learning models, and integration with external systems. Natural language processing enables the chatbot to interpret user input, analyze text patterns, and extract meaning from conversational language. Intent recognition allows the chatbot to determine the user's purpose, ensuring accurate and context-aware responses. Dialogue management controls the flow of conversation, ensuring continuity and relevance based on previous interactions. Machine learning models continuously improve chatbot responses by learning from past interactions and user feedback. Integration with external systems enables chatbots to access databases, retrieve relevant information, and complete automated tasks such as booking appointments or processing transactions.

The benefits of chatbots include improved customer service, enhanced efficiency, and scalability. Improved customer service results from instant responses and 24/7 availability, ensuring users receive support without delays. Enhanced efficiency allows businesses to automate repetitive inquiries, freeing human agents for more complex tasks. Scalability ensures that chatbots can handle multiple interactions simultaneously, reducing wait times and operational costs while maintaining a high level of service.

An example of a chatbot is a virtual assistant like Apple's Siri or Amazon's Alexa, which processes voice commands to provide information, control smart devices, and perform tasks. Another example is a banking chatbot that helps customers check their account balances, transfer funds, and report fraudulent transactions without needing to visit a physical branch or speak to a human representative.

Industries that benefit from chatbots include e-commerce, healthcare, finance, education, and hospitality. E-commerce companies use chatbots to assist customers with product recommendations, order tracking, and return processing. Healthcare organizations integrate chatbots to provide medical guidance, schedule appointments, and answer frequently asked questions. Financial institutions use chatbots for fraud detection, transaction inquiries, and personalized banking support. Educational institutions implement chatbots for student inquiries, enrollment assistance, and academic guidance. The hospitality industry deploys chatbots for hotel reservations, guest services, and travel assistance, enhancing customer experience.

Applications of chatbots extend to virtual assistants, customer support automation, lead generation, interactive marketing, and conversational AI. Virtual assistants use chatbots to manage daily tasks, provide reminders, and facilitate smart home automation. Customer support automation reduces response times and improves service availability, helping businesses manage large volumes of inquiries. Lead generation chatbots engage potential customers, qualify leads, and provide personalized recommendations to increase conversions. Interactive marketing leverages chatbots to engage users with quizzes, promotions, and social media interactions, boosting customer engagement. Conversational AI integrates chatbots into messaging platforms, websites, and mobile applications to deliver seamless, human-like interactions in various business environments.

Chatbots are transforming digital communication by automating interactions, improving customer engagement, and streamlining business processes. Their ability to process natural language, provide instant responses, and handle complex workflows makes them valuable across multiple industries. As artificial intelligence technology evolves, chatbots will continue to enhance conversational experiences, making interactions more intelligent, personalized, and efficient.

ChatGPT

ChatGPT is an advanced conversational AI model developed by OpenAI that processes and generates human-like text based on user inputs. It is built on a large-scale language model architecture known as the Generative Pre-trained Transformer (GPT), enabling it to understand natural language, generate coherent responses, and assist with various tasks such as answering questions, writing content, and providing recommendations. ChatGPT is designed to facilitate interactive and dynamic conversations, making it an essential tool in artificial intelligence-driven communication.

Key components of ChatGPT include natural language processing, deep learning architecture, contextual memory, reinforcement learning from human feedback, and model fine-tuning. Natural language processing enables ChatGPT to interpret and generate human-like text, allowing for fluid and meaningful conversations. Deep learning architecture, based on the transformer model, allows ChatGPT to analyze and generate responses by understanding patterns in vast datasets. Contextual memory enables the model to maintain the flow of conversation by recalling relevant information from previous interactions. Reinforcement learning from human feedback refines the model's ability to generate accurate and contextually appropriate responses. Model fine-tuning enhances ChatGPT's adaptability for specific applications, improving its accuracy in answering domain-specific queries.

The benefits of ChatGPT include enhanced user engagement, improved efficiency, and scalability. Enhanced user engagement is achieved through intelligent and context-aware responses, making conversations feel natural and interactive. Improved efficiency allows businesses and individuals to automate repetitive tasks such as drafting emails, generating reports, and answering customer inquiries.

Scalability ensures that ChatGPT can handle multiple simultaneous interactions, making it suitable for organizations requiring AI-driven support for customer service, education, and content creation.

An example of ChatGPT in action is in customer support automation, where businesses deploy AI-powered chatbots to assist users with inquiries, troubleshoot issues, and provide personalized recommendations. Another example is in content generation, where ChatGPT helps writers create articles, summarize research, and draft marketing copy, reducing the time required for manual content creation.

Industries that benefit from ChatGPT include e-commerce, healthcare, finance, education, and software development. E-commerce businesses use ChatGPT to enhance customer experiences through personalized product recommendations and automated support. Healthcare organizations leverage AI-driven chat systems to assist with patient inquiries, medical research summarization, and appointment scheduling. Financial institutions integrate ChatGPT into banking applications for real-time customer service, fraud detection assistance, and financial advisory services. Educational platforms implement ChatGPT to provide tutoring, automated grading, and study material recommendations for students. Software developers use ChatGPT to generate code snippets, debug errors, and enhance productivity through AI-assisted programming.

Applications of ChatGPT extend to virtual assistants, knowledge retrieval, real-time translation, personalized learning, and creative writing. Virtual assistants integrate ChatGPT to facilitate natural conversations and assist users with everyday tasks. Knowledge retrieval systems use ChatGPT to extract and summarize relevant information from large datasets, improving research efficiency. Real-time translation capabilities allow ChatGPT to provide multilingual communication support, breaking language barriers in global interactions. Personalized learning benefits from ChatGPT's ability to generate tailored educational content, quizzes, and explanations based on user needs. Creative writing applications leverage AI-generated text to assist with storytelling, scriptwriting, and idea generation, enhancing creativity and productivity.

ChatGPT represents a significant advancement in artificial intelligence-driven communication, enabling seamless human-AI interactions across diverse applications. Its ability to understand natural language, generate coherent responses, and adapt to various industries makes it a valuable tool for businesses, educators, and individuals. As AI continues to evolve, ChatGPT will play an increasingly important role in automating tasks, enhancing creativity, and improving the efficiency of digital communication.

Checkpointing in Machine Learning

Checkpointing in Machine Learning is a process used to periodically save the state of a model during training, ensuring that progress is not lost in case of interruptions such as hardware failures, crashes, or time constraints. This technique allows models to resume training from the last saved checkpoint rather than starting over, improving efficiency and reliability. Checkpointing is essential for training deep learning models that require extensive computation over long periods, enabling better resource management and reducing the risk of data loss.

Key components of checkpointing in machine learning include model state saving, optimizer state storage, frequency configuration, incremental backups, and recovery mechanisms. Model state saving captures the current parameters and weights of a neural network, ensuring that progress can be restored at any point. Optimizer state storage records gradient updates and learning rate adjustments, allowing training to resume with the same optimization progress. Frequency configuration determines how often checkpoints are saved, balancing storage efficiency with recovery reliability. Incremental backups ensure that multiple checkpoints are stored at different training stages, preventing data corruption or overwriting critical progress. Recovery mechanisms enable seamless resumption of training from the last checkpoint, reducing downtime and computation costs.

The benefits of checkpointing in machine learning include increased training efficiency, fault tolerance, and improved model tuning. Increased training efficiency allows deep learning models to resume from the last checkpoint rather than restarting, saving computation time and resources. Fault tolerance ensures that training progress is preserved even in the event of unexpected system failures or interruptions. Improved model tuning enables researchers to experiment with hyperparameter adjustments and resume training from intermediate stages rather than retraining from scratch.

An example of checkpointing in machine learning is in training large-scale natural language processing models such as GPT, where training spans multiple days or weeks. By implementing checkpointing, researchers can save intermediate model states and recover progress in case of failures, ensuring continuity in training. Another example is in image classification tasks, where convolutional neural networks save checkpoints at different training epochs, allowing developers to evaluate and fine-tune models without losing prior progress.

Industries that benefit from checkpointing in machine learning include artificial intelligence research, healthcare, finance, autonomous systems, and cloud computing. AI research institutions implement checkpointing to train large-scale models without the risk of losing progress due to hardware failures. Healthcare applications rely on checkpointing to ensure stability in training AI models used for medical image analysis and diagnostics. Financial institutions use checkpointing in fraud detection and algorithmic trading models, preventing disruptions during high-frequency computations. Autonomous systems such as self-driving cars use checkpointing to train deep learning models safely and efficiently, ensuring reliability in AI-driven decision-making. Cloud computing platforms integrate checkpointing to optimize resource allocation and minimize training downtime for AI services.

Applications of checkpointing in machine learning extend to deep learning model training, federated learning, distributed computing, model experimentation, and AI-driven simulations. Deep learning model training benefits from checkpointing by preserving progress and reducing the need for retraining from scratch. Federated learning relies on checkpointing to synchronize model updates across decentralized systems, ensuring consistency in collaborative training. Distributed computing uses checkpointing to manage machine learning workloads across multiple servers, optimizing efficiency and preventing loss of computation. Model experimentation integrates checkpointing to test different hyperparameter settings, allowing researchers to refine AI models effectively. AI-driven simulations apply checkpointing to store progress in reinforcement learning environments, enabling AI agents to learn from previous experiences without restarting entire simulations.

Checkpointing in machine learning is a critical technique for maintaining stability, efficiency, and fault tolerance in AI model training. By periodically saving model states, checkpointing ensures that training progress is preserved, reducing the risk of data loss and optimizing computational resources. As AI models continue to grow in complexity and scale, checkpointing will remain an essential practice for researchers, developers, and industries relying on machine learning for real-world applications.

Child AI Agents

Child AI Agents refer to autonomous artificial intelligence systems designed to learn, adapt, and evolve through interactions with their environment, much like a human child develops cognitive skills. These agents are built using machine learning and reinforcement learning techniques that allow them to acquire knowledge incrementally, improve their decision-making abilities, and adapt to new challenges. They function as self-improving AI entities capable of learning from minimal supervision, making them useful for complex problem-solving and continuous development.

Key components of Child AI Agents include adaptive learning algorithms, reinforcement feedback, hierarchical learning structures, autonomous decision-making, and memory retention. Adaptive learning algorithms enable these agents to modify their behavior and knowledge base dynamically as they receive new information. Reinforcement feedback guides learning by rewarding successful actions and penalizing errors, helping the AI refine its strategies over time. Hierarchical learning structures allow the AI to build upon simpler concepts before mastering more advanced tasks, mimicking the developmental process of human cognition. Autonomous decision-making ensures that Child AI Agents can operate independently without requiring constant human intervention. Memory retention enables agents to store past experiences, recall relevant information, and apply learned knowledge in future scenarios.

The benefits of Child AI Agents include continuous self-improvement, enhanced adaptability, and efficient knowledge transfer. Continuous self-improvement ensures that these agents learn and refine their abilities without requiring extensive retraining. Enhanced adaptability allows them to function in dynamic environments where conditions may change unpredictably. Efficient knowledge transfer enables AI agents to apply past learning to new tasks, reducing the need for redundant training and improving their performance over time.

An example of Child AI Agents in action is in robotics, where an AI-driven robot learns to navigate different terrains through trial and error, refining its movement strategy based on past experiences. Another example is in AI-powered tutoring systems, where Child AI Agents assess student learning patterns and dynamically adjust educational content to match their progress and comprehension levels.

Industries that benefit from Child AI Agents include education, robotics, healthcare, cybersecurity, and finance. Education platforms integrate these agents into personalized learning systems, where AI adapts to individual student needs and optimizes study plans. Robotics companies use Child AI Agents to develop autonomous machines that can learn new skills and adjust to evolving tasks. Healthcare applications leverage Child AI Agents to assist in diagnostics, patient monitoring, and personalized treatment recommendations based on evolving medical data. Cybersecurity firms deploy these agents for adaptive threat detection, where AI continuously learns from emerging cyber threats and refines its defense strategies. Financial institutions apply Child AI Agents to automated trading systems, where AI models learn market behaviors and adjust strategies in response to economic fluctuations.

Applications of Child AI Agents extend to intelligent tutoring, smart assistants, predictive maintenance, adaptive game AI, and personalized recommendations. Intelligent tutoring systems use Child AI Agents to provide customized educational experiences based on a student's learning pace. Smart assistants integrate these agents to improve interactions by learning user preferences and optimizing responses over time. Predictive maintenance applies Child AI Agents in industrial automation, where AI predicts equipment failures and suggests proactive maintenance strategies. Adaptive game AI benefits from Child AI Agents that learn player behaviors and adjust gameplay difficulty for a more engaging experience. Personalized recommendation systems leverage these agents to refine product or content recommendations based on user behavior, improving user engagement.

Child AI Agents represent a significant advancement in artificial intelligence by enabling self-improving, adaptive, and autonomous systems capable of learning from experience. Their ability to continuously refine their skills and knowledge makes them valuable across multiple domains where flexibility and independent problem-solving are required. As AI technology continues to evolve, Child AI Agents will play a vital role in shaping intelligent automation, personalized computing, and dynamic decision-making systems.

Chimeric Neural Networks

Chimeric Neural Networks refer to hybrid artificial intelligence architectures that combine multiple neural network models, methodologies, or learning paradigms to enhance performance, adaptability, and efficiency. These networks integrate different structures, such as convolutional neural networks (CNNs), recurrent neural networks (RNNs), and transformers, to leverage their individual strengths while compensating for weaknesses. By fusing diverse network types, chimeric neural networks enable more robust feature extraction, sequential processing, and contextual understanding, making them effective for solving complex AI problems.

Key components of Chimeric Neural Networks include multi-modal fusion, adaptive learning mechanisms, cross-network communication, optimization strategies, and hierarchical processing. Multi-modal fusion allows the integration of different data types, such as images, text, and numerical data, within a single AI framework. Adaptive learning mechanisms enable the network to dynamically adjust its structure and learning parameters based on task requirements. Cross-network communication ensures that different neural components share information efficiently, improving decision-making coherence. Optimization strategies refine model weights across the hybrid structure, ensuring balanced contributions from each sub-network. Hierarchical processing allows different layers of the chimeric network to specialize in various aspects of feature extraction, reasoning, and output generation.

The benefits of Chimeric Neural Networks include improved generalization, enhanced efficiency, and increased versatility. Improved generalization ensures that the network performs well across diverse tasks by integrating multiple learning approaches. Enhanced efficiency results from the combination of specialized neural architectures, reducing redundancy and optimizing performance. Increased versatility allows these networks to be applied in multi-domain applications, handling different types of input data and problem-solving requirements with greater accuracy.

An example of Chimeric Neural Networks in action is in autonomous vehicles, where a hybrid network combines CNNs for visual perception, RNNs for sequential decision-making, and transformers for contextual understanding, ensuring more reliable navigation. Another example is in natural language understanding, where a chimeric architecture integrates transformers for text comprehension, attention mechanisms for contextual processing, and convolutional layers for efficient feature extraction, resulting in more accurate chatbot responses and document analysis.

Industries that benefit from Chimeric Neural Networks include healthcare, finance, robotics, cybersecurity, and artificial intelligence research. Healthcare applications integrate these networks for medical imaging analysis, predictive diagnostics, and personalized treatment planning, leveraging multiple AI techniques for better decision-making. Financial institutions use hybrid models for fraud detection, risk assessment, and automated trading, combining pattern recognition with sequential data analysis. Robotics incorporates Chimeric Neural Networks to enable advanced perception, motion planning, and adaptive learning, improving robotic intelligence and automation. Cybersecurity firms deploy hybrid AI models to detect evolving cyber threats, blending anomaly detection with real-time monitoring and behavioral analysis. Artificial intelligence research explores these networks to push the boundaries of deep learning, developing more efficient and interpretable AI models.

Applications of Chimeric Neural Networks extend to multi-modal AI systems, intelligent automation, content generation, adaptive learning environments, and real-time decision support. Multi-modal AI systems utilize these networks to process and interpret information from various data sources, enhancing machine perception. Intelligent automation benefits from hybrid AI models that optimize complex workflows in industries such as manufacturing and logistics. Content generation applies chimeric architectures to improve AI-driven writing, video editing, and creative applications. Adaptive learning environments leverage these networks to personalize education, training AI models to adjust learning strategies based on user progress. Real-time decision support integrates hybrid AI networks in mission-critical applications such as emergency response, financial forecasting, and medical diagnostics, where fast and accurate predictions are essential.

Chimeric Neural Networks represent a significant advancement in AI by combining diverse neural architectures to enhance learning, adaptability, and problem-solving capabilities. Their ability to merge multiple approaches into a unified framework makes them essential for tackling complex challenges across industries. As AI continues to evolve, these networks will play a crucial role in developing more sophisticated, efficient, and context-aware intelligent systems.

Chip Communication, also known as inter-chip communication

Chip Communication, also known as inter-chip communication, refers to the process by which multiple semiconductor chips exchange data and coordinate processing tasks within an integrated system. This communication enables chips to work together efficiently, allowing faster data transfer, reduced latency, and improved computational performance. As modern computing systems increasingly rely on multi-chip architectures, effective chip communication is crucial for optimizing power consumption, enhancing parallel processing, and supporting high-speed operations in artificial intelligence, cloud computing, and edge devices.

Key components of chip communication include interconnect protocols, data transfer mechanisms, synchronization techniques, low-latency signaling, and power management. Interconnect protocols define the standards and methods for transmitting data between chips, ensuring compatibility and efficiency. Data transfer mechanisms manage how information is transmitted, whether through wired, wireless, or optical channels. Synchronization techniques ensure that multiple chips operate in coordination without data loss or timing mismatches. Low-latency signaling optimizes response times, reducing delays in high-speed computing applications. Power management regulates energy consumption, balancing performance and efficiency to prevent overheating and excessive power drain.

The benefits of chip communication include enhanced processing power, reduced latency, and improved scalability. Enhanced processing power allows multiple chips to work together, enabling faster computations for AI workloads, large-scale simulations, and real-time analytics. Reduced latency ensures that data is transferred and processed with minimal delay, improving the performance of applications such as gaming, autonomous vehicles, and real-time decision-making. Improved scalability enables the integration of more chips into a single system, supporting modular and expandable architectures that can accommodate growing computational demands.

An example of chip communication is found in multi-core processors, where individual cores communicate through high-speed interconnects to execute tasks in parallel, improving overall system performance. Another example is in AI accelerators, where specialized chips such as graphics processing units (GPUs) and tensor processing units (TPUs) exchange data with central processing units (CPUs) to optimize deep learning workloads.

Industries that benefit from chip communication include artificial intelligence, telecommunications, automotive, healthcare, and cloud computing. Artificial intelligence applications rely on inter-chip communication for efficient neural network training and inference in high-performance computing environments. Telecommunications infrastructure depends on multi-chip communication for 5G networks, enabling seamless data processing and connectivity. The automotive sector integrates inter-chip communication for advanced driver-assistance systems (ADAS), where multiple sensors and processors work together to improve vehicle safety and automation. Healthcare technology utilizes chip communication in medical imaging and diagnostic systems, where fast data exchange enhances real-time analysis and precision medicine. Cloud computing services employ high-speed interconnects between data center processors, ensuring efficient handling of large-scale workloads and distributed computing operations.

Applications of chip communication extend to edge computing, smart devices, robotics, quantum computing, and aerospace systems. Edge computing devices use inter-chip communication to process data locally, reducing reliance on cloud-based processing and improving response times. Smart devices, including smartphones, wearables, and IoT sensors, leverage efficient chip communication for real-time data exchange and functionality. Robotics integrates multi-chip architectures to enable complex decision-making and autonomous movement, improving precision and adaptability. Quantum computing benefits from advanced chip communication techniques that facilitate qubit interactions and data coherence in quantum processors. Aerospace systems utilize high-speed inter-chip communication for navigation, real-time monitoring, and mission-critical decision-making in space exploration and defense applications.

Chip communication plays a vital role in modern computing by enabling seamless data exchange between processors, improving performance, scalability, and efficiency. As computing architectures continue to evolve, advancements in inter-chip communication will drive innovation in AI, cloud computing, telecommunications, and edge processing. The ability of chips to interact in real time is key to unlocking the full potential of high-performance computing, supporting the development of smarter, faster, and more energy-efficient technological solutions.

Chip War

Definition
"Chip War" refers to the geopolitical, economic, and technological competition among nations and corporations to dominate the semiconductor industry. Semiconductors, or "chips," are the essential components powering nearly all modern electronics, including smartphones, computers, military systems, and AI technologies. This term gained popularity to describe the strategic rivalry, particularly between the United States, China, Taiwan, South Korea, Japan, and the Netherlands, as they compete over chip design, manufacturing, and supply chain control.

Key Components
Advanced semiconductor fabrication (often referred to as nanometer-scale manufacturing)
Global chip supply chains involving design, raw materials, fabrication, testing, and packaging
Intellectual property (IP) and proprietary chip architectures
Government policies including subsidies, export controls, and national security measures
Key players like TSMC (Taiwan), Intel (USA), Samsung (South Korea), ASML (Netherlands), and SMIC (China)

Benefits
Promotes innovation in AI, robotics, defense, and 5G technologies
Strengthens national security through domestic chip capabilities
Drives global economic growth and job creation in high-tech sectors
Encourages advancement in scientific research and material science

Examples
The U.S. CHIPS and Science Act, which provides billions in subsidies to boost American chip manufacturing
China's multibillion-dollar investment in domestic semiconductor production
ASML's exclusive position in extreme ultraviolet (EUV) lithography and restrictions on exporting to China
Taiwan's dominance in chip production via TSMC, producing over 90% of the world's most advanced chips

Applications
Smartphones and consumer electronics
Data centers and cloud computing
Autonomous vehicles and IoT devices
Military systems including drones, missiles, and surveillance technologies
Artificial intelligence, deep learning, and quantum computing platforms

Industries
Semiconductor manufacturing
Telecommunications
Defense and aerospace

Consumer electronics
Automotive technology
Artificial intelligence and data science

Summary
The "Chip War" represents a critical global struggle over semiconductor supremacy, influencing the balance of power in technology, defense, and economics. As semiconductors underpin nearly every advanced system in the modern world, controlling their design, production, and distribution is viewed as vital for national sovereignty and global competitiveness. The Chip War not only fuels technological innovation but also intensifies diplomatic tensions and strategic alliances, making it one of the most pivotal battles in the 21st-century digital economy.

Chip H200 (H200 Chip)

Definition
The H200 chip, officially known as the NVIDIA H200 Tensor Core GPU, is a high-performance graphics processing unit designed to accelerate artificial intelligence workloads, large language models, and scientific computing. It is part of NVIDIA's Hopper architecture family and is the successor to the H100 chip. The H200 is engineered with enhanced memory capacity and bandwidth, delivering more efficient training and inference for massive AI models and generative AI applications.

Key Components
NVIDIA Hopper GPU architecture
HBM3e (High Bandwidth Memory, 5th Gen Extended) with higher throughput
Tensor Cores optimized for FP8, FP16, BF16, and INT8 precision formats
NVLink and NVSwitch interconnects for multi-GPU scaling
Support for CUDA and AI-specific libraries like cuDNN and TensorRT

Benefits
Delivers faster model training with higher memory bandwidth and compute efficiency
Enables deployment of larger transformer models with greater parallel processing
Reduces AI inference time in production environments
Improves energy efficiency per computation
Supports large-scale language models, vision models, and foundation models with better stability

Examples
Used in data centers for training LLMs like GPT-4, LLaMA, and Mixtral
Adopted in cloud AI infrastructures such as Microsoft Azure and Amazon AWS
Ideal for real-time AI inferencing in enterprise-grade applications
Supports multimodal models for text, vision, and audio integration in generative AI platforms

Applications
Natural Language Processing (NLP)
Generative AI and large language models
Computer vision for autonomous vehicles and surveillance
Scientific computing and simulation
Healthcare imaging and diagnostics powered by AI

Industries
Cloud computing and AI infrastructure
Enterprise software and AI model deployment
Healthcare and bioinformatics
Autonomous robotics and transportation
Government and defense AI operations

Challenges
High power consumption and thermal requirements
Significant cost, limiting accessibility for small-scale developers
Requires sophisticated cooling systems in data centers
Global supply chain and chip scarcity issues may delay access
Dependent on robust infrastructure and integration expertise

Summary
The NVIDIA H200 chip represents a major step forward in high-performance AI computing. With its advanced memory architecture and Hopper-based processing power, it is specifically designed to meet the growing demands of training and running cutting-edge AI models. As the next generation of GPU hardware, the H200 is central to pushing the limits of generative AI, real-time inference, and scientific modeling—offering a blend of speed, scalability, and precision that defines the future of AI acceleration.

Chunking in Natural Language Processing (NLP)

Definition: Chunking in Natural Language Processing (NLP) is a text-processing technique that identifies and groups related words into meaningful phrases or chunks. This method helps in understanding the syntactic structure of a sentence by breaking it into smaller, manageable parts without analyzing full grammatical relationships. Chunking improves language comprehension by creating phrase structures such as noun phrases, verb phrases, and prepositional phrases, making it an essential step in information extraction, text parsing, and sentiment analysis.

Key components of chunking in NLP include tokenization, part-of-speech (POS) tagging, phrase structure rules, chunking algorithms, and pattern recognition. Tokenization splits text into individual words or tokens, providing the basic units for processing. POS tagging assigns grammatical labels to each word, such as noun, verb, adjective, or preposition, helping to determine chunk boundaries. Phrase structure rules define patterns for grouping words, ensuring that chunks are formed based on linguistic conventions. Chunking algorithms apply machine learning or rule-based approaches to identify and extract relevant chunks from text. Pattern recognition helps detect and refine chunks based on linguistic features, improving accuracy and contextual relevance.

The benefits of chunking in NLP include improved text processing efficiency, enhanced syntactic analysis, and better information extraction. Improved text processing efficiency allows NLP models to handle large volumes of text while focusing on meaningful word groups instead of individual tokens. Enhanced syntactic analysis enables more accurate understanding of sentence structure, reducing errors in downstream NLP tasks. Better information extraction allows AI models to identify key phrases, improving performance in applications such as named entity recognition, sentiment analysis, and machine translation.

An example of chunking in NLP is in named entity recognition, where a system identifies phrases containing proper nouns such as "New York City" or "Apple Inc." instead of treating them as separate words. Another example is in text summarization, where chunking helps extract key phrases from a document to generate a concise summary while preserving meaning.

Industries that benefit from chunking in NLP include healthcare, finance, customer service, e-commerce, and legal services. Healthcare applications use chunking to extract medical terms from clinical notes and patient records, improving diagnosis and treatment planning. Financial institutions apply chunking for analyzing financial reports and extracting key insights from earnings calls. Customer service chatbots use chunking to understand and categorize customer inquiries, providing more accurate responses. E-commerce platforms leverage chunking for product categorization and review analysis, helping to improve recommendations and customer satisfaction. Legal services implement chunking to extract relevant clauses from contracts and legal documents, streamlining compliance and case analysis.

Applications of chunking in NLP extend to machine translation, document classification, search engine optimization, automated content generation, and speech recognition. Machine translation benefits from chunking by preserving phrase structures, improving the accuracy of translations. Document classification uses chunking to identify relevant sections in legal, academic, and business documents, ensuring efficient categorization. Search engine optimization integrates chunking to extract key search terms from user queries, improving content indexing and ranking. Automated content generation applies chunking to structure text outputs, ensuring coherence in AI-generated articles and reports. Speech recognition systems use chunking to group spoken words into phrases, enhancing the accuracy of voice-to-text transcription.

Chunking in NLP enhances language processing by structuring text into meaningful phrases, improving syntactic analysis and information extraction. Its role in breaking down sentences into logical components makes it an essential technique in AI-driven text processing. As NLP technology advances, chunking will continue to play a key role in optimizing machine understanding of human language, supporting applications in automation, search, translation, and intelligent decision-making.

Churn Prediction in AI

Churn Prediction in AI is the process of using machine learning and data analytics to identify customers who are likely to stop using a product or service. By analyzing historical behavior, customer interactions, and engagement metrics, AI-driven churn prediction models help businesses proactively address customer retention challenges. These models allow companies to take preventative measures by offering targeted incentives, improving customer experiences, or refining marketing strategies to retain at-risk customers.

Key components of churn prediction in AI include data collection, feature engineering, machine learning algorithms, predictive modeling, and real-time monitoring. Data collection involves gathering customer transaction history, engagement metrics, service usage patterns, and demographic information to build comprehensive datasets. Feature engineering selects and transforms relevant variables such as purchase frequency, support interactions, and account activity to enhance model performance. Machine learning algorithms, including logistic regression, decision trees, and deep learning, analyze patterns in customer behavior to classify individuals based on their likelihood of churning. Predictive modeling generates risk scores for each customer, allowing businesses to prioritize intervention efforts. Real-time monitoring ensures continuous tracking of customer behavior, enabling adaptive responses to prevent churn before it happens.

The benefits of churn prediction in AI include increased customer retention, improved marketing efficiency, and enhanced revenue stability. Increased customer retention is achieved by identifying at-risk customers early and implementing strategies to re-engage them. Improved marketing efficiency allows businesses to focus retention efforts on high-value customers, optimizing resource allocation. Enhanced revenue stability results from reducing the financial impact of customer loss, ensuring long-term business sustainability.

An example of churn prediction in AI is in subscription-based services, where streaming platforms use machine learning to detect declining user engagement and send personalized content recommendations or special offers to retain subscribers. Another example is in the telecommunications industry, where AI models analyze call patterns, customer complaints, and billing behavior to predict churn risk and offer customized retention packages.

Industries that benefit from churn prediction in AI include e-commerce, banking, telecommunications, healthcare, and software as a service (SaaS). E-commerce businesses apply AI-driven churn prediction to analyze shopping behaviors and retain customers through personalized promotions. Banking institutions use churn prediction to assess account activity and offer tailored financial products to prevent customer attrition. Telecommunications companies integrate AI models to detect customer dissatisfaction and adjust pricing plans or service quality accordingly. Healthcare providers leverage churn prediction to identify patients at risk of disengaging from treatment plans and implement interventions to improve adherence. SaaS companies use AI to predict user drop-off rates and enhance product engagement strategies to increase retention.

Applications of churn prediction in AI extend to targeted retention campaigns, customer segmentation, product optimization, loyalty programs, and fraud detection. Targeted retention campaigns use AI insights to send customized

offers and communication to at-risk customers, increasing their likelihood of staying. Customer segmentation categorizes users based on their engagement levels, enabling personalized marketing and support. Product optimization applies churn insights to refine features and address user pain points, improving overall satisfaction. Loyalty programs benefit from AI-driven churn prediction by identifying customers who need incentives to maintain long-term engagement. Fraud detection integrates churn models to flag suspicious patterns where customers disengage due to security concerns or unusual activities.

Churn prediction in AI is a powerful tool for businesses to anticipate and mitigate customer attrition, ensuring long-term success and financial stability. By leveraging machine learning and data-driven insights, organizations can take proactive steps to improve customer satisfaction, optimize marketing strategies, and reduce revenue loss. As AI continues to evolve, churn prediction models will become even more precise and adaptive, playing a crucial role in customer relationship management across various industries.

CI/CD (Continous Integraation/Continous Deployment)

CI/CD (Continuous Integration/Continuous Deployment) in AI refers to the automated process of integrating, testing, and deploying machine learning models and AI applications in a streamlined and iterative manner. Continuous Integration ensures that AI code, model updates, and data changes are frequently merged and tested, reducing errors and improving collaboration. Continuous Deployment automates the release of AI models into production, ensuring rapid and reliable delivery of new features, optimizations, and improvements. This process enhances the efficiency of AI development by allowing teams to deploy updates with minimal human intervention while maintaining high reliability and scalability.

Key components of CI/CD in AI include version control, automated testing, model validation, pipeline orchestration, and monitoring. Version control ensures that code, datasets, and models are tracked, enabling reproducibility and collaboration. Automated testing evaluates AI pipelines by running unit tests, integration tests, and performance checks to detect issues before deployment. Model validation assesses the accuracy, fairness, and robustness of AI models to prevent biased or unreliable outputs. Pipeline orchestration automates workflows, managing tasks such as data preprocessing, model training, evaluation, and deployment. Monitoring enables real-time tracking of model performance, ensuring that deployed AI systems continue to meet expectations and adjust to changing data patterns.

The benefits of CI/CD in AI include accelerated development cycles, improved model reliability, and efficient resource utilization. Accelerated development cycles allow AI teams to iterate quickly, reducing time-to-market for new models and features. Improved model reliability ensures that AI applications remain stable and perform as expected through rigorous automated testing and monitoring. Efficient resource utilization optimizes computing power and storage, preventing redundant computations and streamlining deployment processes.

An example of CI/CD in AI is in fraud detection systems, where machine learning models are continuously updated to detect emerging fraudulent activities. Automated testing and validation ensure that each model update improves fraud detection accuracy without introducing new risks. Another example is in natural language processing applications, where chatbots and virtual assistants receive regular updates to enhance their language understanding and response generation while ensuring uninterrupted service.

Industries that benefit from CI/CD in AI include finance, healthcare, e-commerce, software development, and autonomous systems. Financial institutions leverage CI/CD pipelines to deploy real-time AI models for fraud prevention, risk assessment, and algorithmic trading. Healthcare organizations use automated AI deployment for predictive diagnostics, medical image analysis, and personalized treatment recommendations. E-commerce platforms integrate CI/CD workflows to update recommendation algorithms, optimize search engines, and enhance customer experience. Software development companies implement CI/CD in AI-driven applications, ensuring continuous improvements in automated testing, security analysis, and performance monitoring. Autonomous systems, including self-driving cars and robotics, rely on CI/CD pipelines to refine AI decision-making models and adapt to real-world conditions.

Applications of CI/CD in AI extend to MLOps, cloud AI services, intelligent automation, predictive analytics, and cybersecurity. MLOps integrates CI/CD practices to manage the end-to-end machine learning lifecycle, improving scalability and collaboration across AI teams. Cloud AI services implement automated pipelines to deploy and update AI models in distributed environments, ensuring seamless integration with cloud computing platforms. Intelligent automation benefits from CI/CD by enhancing robotic process automation (RPA) and AI-driven workflow optimization. Predictive analytics applies continuous AI model deployment to refine forecasting systems in business intelligence, healthcare, and financial markets. Cybersecurity enhances AI-driven threat detection by continuously updating models to recognize and mitigate evolving cyber threats.

CI/CD in AI is essential for delivering robust, scalable, and continuously improving AI applications. By automating integration, testing, and deployment, organizations can enhance efficiency, reduce risks, and ensure that AI systems remain accurate and effective. As AI adoption grows across industries, CI/CD pipelines will play a critical role in ensuring seamless updates, maintaining compliance, and accelerating innovation in machine learning and artificial intelligence.

CICIDS2017

CICIDS2017 refers to the Canadian Institute for Cybersecurity Intrusion Detection System 2017 dataset, a benchmark dataset used for evaluating machine learning models in cybersecurity and network intrusion detection. It was created by the Canadian Institute for Cybersecurity (CIC) to provide a realistic and comprehensive dataset containing normal network traffic and various cyberattack scenarios. This dataset is widely used for training and testing intrusion detection systems (IDS) and machine learning-based cybersecurity solutions.

Key components of CICIDS2017 include network traffic data, attack scenarios, feature extraction, labeled data, and statistical analysis. Network traffic data consists of real network communications captured over multiple days, reflecting different types of normal and malicious activities. Attack scenarios include common cyber threats such as distributed denial-of-service (DDoS) attacks, brute force attacks, botnet traffic, and SQL injection. Feature extraction provides a set of network traffic attributes such as packet size, duration, and flow-based features that help in distinguishing normal and malicious activities. Labeled data ensures that each network flow is classified as either normal or attack traffic, facilitating supervised learning for intrusion detection models. Statistical analysis enables researchers to examine network behavior, compare attack patterns, and improve IDS performance by understanding traffic distributions.

The benefits of CICIDS2017 include realistic cybersecurity threat representation, high-quality labeled data, and enhanced machine learning model evaluation. Realistic cybersecurity threat representation ensures that the dataset captures genuine attack behaviors and normal network interactions, making it valuable for developing practical security solutions. High-quality labeled data provides researchers with a structured dataset that enhances training accuracy and facilitates benchmarking against other security datasets. Enhanced machine learning model evaluation allows researchers to test various IDS models, refine feature selection, and improve detection accuracy based on diverse attack scenarios.

An example of CICIDS2017 in use is in the training of an AI-powered network intrusion detection system, where machine learning models analyze the dataset to distinguish between legitimate network traffic and cyberattacks. Another example is in cybersecurity research, where analysts use CICIDS2017 to test new anomaly detection techniques, refine firewall configurations, and develop automated threat mitigation strategies.

Industries that benefit from CICIDS2017 include cybersecurity, telecommunications, finance, healthcare, and government institutions. Cybersecurity firms use the dataset to improve IDS and threat detection models, reducing the risk of cyber breaches. Telecommunications companies apply CICIDS2017 to enhance network monitoring systems, ensuring the early detection of suspicious activity. Financial institutions integrate the dataset into fraud detection and risk management systems to safeguard digital transactions and protect customer data. Healthcare organizations leverage intrusion detection models trained on CICIDS2017 to secure electronic health records and medical IoT devices from cyber threats. Government agencies utilize the dataset to evaluate national security cybersecurity strategies, ensuring the protection of critical infrastructure from cyberattacks.

Applications of CICIDS2017 extend to AI-driven threat detection, anomaly-based intrusion detection, cybersecurity education, penetration testing, and network traffic analysis. AI-driven threat detection uses machine learning models trained on CICIDS2017 to identify evolving cyber threats in real time. Anomaly-based intrusion detection systems analyze network behavior to detect deviations from normal traffic patterns, improving proactive security measures. Cybersecurity education benefits from CICIDS2017 as a teaching tool for students and professionals learning about network security and cyber threat analysis. Penetration testing integrates the dataset into simulated attack environments, allowing organizations to test their defenses against various intrusion scenarios. Network traffic analysis applies CICIDS2017 to improve the understanding of attack patterns and optimize security policies.

CICIDS2017 is a valuable dataset for cybersecurity research and AI-driven intrusion detection, providing high-quality, labeled network traffic data for developing and testing security solutions. Its realistic attack scenarios and structured feature extraction make it an essential resource for advancing network security, improving machine learning-based IDS, and protecting organizations from evolving cyber threats. As cyberattacks become more sophisticated, datasets like CICIDS2017 will continue to play a crucial role in strengthening global cybersecurity efforts.

CIFAR DATASET

CIFAR Dataset refers to a collection of labeled images widely used for training and evaluating machine learning models in computer vision. Developed by the Canadian Institute for Advanced Research (CIFAR), the dataset consists of small, low-resolution images categorized into different object classes. CIFAR is primarily used for image classification tasks, serving as a benchmark for deep learning and convolutional neural network (CNN) research. The dataset helps in advancing AI models for object recognition, scene understanding, and visual pattern analysis.

Key components of the CIFAR Dataset include image samples, class labels, data partitions, pixel representation, and preprocessing techniques. Image samples consist of small 32x32 pixel images depicting real-world objects such as animals, vehicles, and household items. Class labels provide predefined categories, enabling supervised learning for object recognition tasks. Data partitions divide the dataset into training and testing sets, ensuring model evaluation on unseen images. Pixel representation encodes image features as numerical values, allowing neural networks to process and analyze visual data. Preprocessing techniques such as normalization and data augmentation enhance model learning by standardizing image inputs and improving generalization.

The benefits of the CIFAR Dataset include standardized benchmarking, scalability for deep learning, and improved generalization in image classification. Standardized benchmarking provides a common dataset for comparing different AI models, enabling researchers to evaluate performance consistently. Scalability for deep learning allows models to train efficiently on low-resolution images, reducing computational requirements while maintaining high classification accuracy. Improved generalization ensures that models trained on CIFAR can adapt to real-world image classification tasks, enhancing AI performance in diverse visual recognition applications.

An example of the CIFAR Dataset in use is in training CNN architectures such as ResNet, VGG, and AlexNet, where models learn to classify images based on features extracted from CIFAR samples. Another example is in AI research, where CIFAR is used to test new image recognition algorithms, optimize neural network architectures, and improve object detection capabilities.

Industries that benefit from the CIFAR Dataset include artificial intelligence research, autonomous systems, healthcare, security, and e-commerce. AI research institutions use CIFAR to develop and test deep learning models for visual recognition tasks. Autonomous systems rely on image classification techniques trained on CIFAR to enhance perception in self-driving cars and robotic vision. Healthcare integrates CIFAR-based models for medical image analysis, aiding in the detection of diseases and anomalies in diagnostic imaging. Security applications leverage image classification to improve facial recognition, surveillance analysis, and threat detection. E-commerce platforms use AI models trained on CIFAR to enhance product categorization, visual search, and recommendation systems.

Applications of the CIFAR Dataset extend to image classification, object detection, generative adversarial networks (GANs), facial recognition, and augmented reality. Image classification tasks benefit from CIFAR-trained models that accurately distinguish between different object categories. Object detection techniques use CIFAR as a foundational dataset for identifying multiple objects within an image. GANs apply CIFAR samples for training deep learning models to generate realistic synthetic images. Facial recognition systems enhance accuracy by fine-tuning on CIFAR-based classification techniques. Augmented reality leverages image recognition models trained on CIFAR to integrate virtual elements into real-world environments, improving interactive experiences.

The CIFAR Dataset serves as a fundamental resource for advancing computer vision research and AI-driven image processing. By providing labeled images for benchmarking and model evaluation, it contributes to the development of robust image classification models and deep learning techniques. As AI continues to evolve, CIFAR remains a valuable dataset for training scalable, efficient, and high-performing machine learning systems in various visual recognition applications.

CIFAR-10

CIFAR-10 is a widely used dataset in computer vision and machine learning, consisting of 60,000 labeled images across ten distinct classes. Developed by the Canadian Institute for Advanced Research (CIFAR), it serves as a benchmark for evaluating image classification models. Each image in the dataset is 32x32 pixels in size and contains objects from categories such as airplanes, automobiles, birds, cats, deer, dogs, frogs, horses, ships, and trucks. CIFAR-10 is specifically designed to help train deep learning models for object recognition and image classification tasks.

Key components of CIFAR-10 include image samples, class labels, dataset partitions, pixel representation, and preprocessing techniques. Image samples consist of 60,000 small, color images representing real-world objects, divided into 10 categories. Class labels provide predefined object classifications, allowing for supervised learning in image recognition models. Dataset partitions separate the data into 50,000 training images and 10,000 test images, enabling performance evaluation on unseen data. Pixel representation encodes each image as numerical values corresponding to color intensities, allowing AI models to process visual information effectively. Preprocessing techniques, such as normalization, data augmentation, and feature scaling, enhance learning efficiency and improve generalization in neural networks.

The benefits of CIFAR-10 include standardized benchmarking, scalability for deep learning, and efficient training for image classification. Standardized benchmarking allows researchers to compare model performance across different architectures, ensuring consistency in evaluation. Scalability for deep learning enables efficient model training on low-resolution images, reducing computational requirements while maintaining high classification accuracy. Efficient training ensures that AI models can quickly learn meaningful patterns in image data, improving their ability to generalize to real-world visual tasks.

An example of CIFAR-10 in use is in training convolutional neural networks (CNNs) such as ResNet, VGG, and AlexNet, where models learn to classify images based on feature extraction and pattern recognition. Another example is in AI research, where CIFAR-10 is used to develop and refine image classification algorithms, test new machine learning techniques, and improve object recognition models.

Industries that benefit from CIFAR-10 include artificial intelligence research, autonomous systems, healthcare, security, and e-commerce. AI research institutions use CIFAR-10 to develop and benchmark deep learning models for computer vision. Autonomous systems rely on CIFAR-10-based classification techniques to enhance perception in self-driving vehicles and robotic vision. Healthcare integrates CIFAR-10-trained models into medical imaging applications, aiding in disease detection and diagnostic analysis. Security applications leverage CIFAR-10 for facial recognition, surveillance analysis, and threat detection. E-commerce platforms use AI models trained on CIFAR-10 to improve product categorization, visual search, and recommendation systems.

Applications of CIFAR-10 extend to image classification, object detection, generative adversarial networks (GANs), pattern recognition, and augmented reality. Image classification models trained on CIFAR-10 accurately distinguish between different object categories, improving automated recognition systems. Object detection tasks benefit from CIFAR-10 as a foundational dataset for identifying multiple objects within an image. GANs utilize CIFAR-10 to train deep learning models for generating synthetic images, improving image enhancement techniques. Pattern recognition systems use CIFAR-10-trained AI models to detect and classify features in complex visual datasets. Augmented reality integrates CIFAR-10-based image recognition models to enhance real-world interactions with virtual elements, creating immersive user experiences.

CIFAR-10 is a fundamental dataset in computer vision research, providing a structured and well-labeled dataset for training and evaluating AI models. Its role in image classification, object recognition, and machine learning advancements makes it a critical resource for researchers and industry professionals. As AI continues to evolve, CIFAR-10 remains a valuable benchmark for developing scalable, accurate, and efficient deep learning models in visual recognition applications.

CIFAR-100

CIFAR-100 is an advanced image dataset designed for machine learning and computer vision research, containing 60,000 labeled images across 100 fine-grained object categories. Developed by the Canadian Institute for Advanced Research (CIFAR), CIFAR-100 serves as a benchmark for evaluating deep learning models in complex image classification tasks. Each image in the dataset is 32x32 pixels in size, with objects spanning a diverse set of categories such as animals, vehicles, household items, and natural elements. CIFAR-100 is an extension of CIFAR-10 but with a more detailed classification structure, making it a more challenging dataset for training and testing AI models.

Key components of CIFAR-100 include image samples, class labels, hierarchical classification, dataset partitions, and preprocessing techniques. Image samples consist of 60,000 small, color images representing real-world objects across a broad set of categories. Class labels are divided into 100 fine-grained classes, grouped into 20 superclasses, allowing hierarchical learning in neural networks. Hierarchical classification structures enable AI models to recognize broader categories before identifying specific subcategories, improving classification efficiency. Dataset partitions separate the data into 50,000 training images and 10,000 test images, ensuring that models are evaluated on unseen data. Preprocessing techniques such as normalization, data augmentation, and feature scaling enhance training performance and improve model generalization.

The benefits of CIFAR-100 include increased classification complexity, enhanced deep learning capabilities, and improved generalization in computer vision models. Increased classification complexity allows AI models to learn more detailed and diverse object representations, improving their ability to handle complex real-world visual tasks. Enhanced deep learning capabilities result from training models on a more challenging dataset, pushing the boundaries of convolutional neural networks (CNNs) and transformer-based architectures. Improved generalization ensures that models trained on CIFAR-100 perform well across various image classification applications, reducing the risk of overfitting and enhancing robustness.

An example of CIFAR-100 in use is in training deep learning architectures such as ResNet, DenseNet, and EfficientNet, where models learn to classify fine-grained image categories through hierarchical feature extraction. Another example is in AI research, where CIFAR-100 is used to test novel machine learning techniques, refine data augmentation strategies, and develop more scalable image classification models.

Industries that benefit from CIFAR-100 include artificial intelligence research, robotics, healthcare, security, and environmental monitoring. AI research institutions use CIFAR-100 to benchmark complex classification models and improve visual recognition capabilities. Robotics applications rely on CIFAR-100-trained models to enhance object recognition in autonomous systems, improving robotic perception and navigation. Healthcare integrates CIFAR-100-based AI models for medical imaging and diagnostic analysis, enabling more precise classification of diseases and abnormalities. Security applications use CIFAR-100 to develop better facial recognition, surveillance, and automated threat detection systems. Environmental monitoring employs CIFAR-100-trained AI models for classifying natural objects, tracking wildlife, and improving climate analysis through satellite imagery classification.

Applications of CIFAR-100 extend to multi-class image classification, fine-grained object recognition, self-supervised learning, generative adversarial networks (GANs), and autonomous perception systems. Multi-class image classification benefits from CIFAR-100's broad set of categories, improving AI's ability to recognize diverse objects in complex scenes. Fine-grained object recognition applies CIFAR-100 to distinguish similar-looking objects within broader categories, enhancing AI-driven identification accuracy. Self-supervised learning leverages CIFAR-100 for pretraining deep learning models on unlabeled data, improving AI adaptability in low-data scenarios. GANs use CIFAR-100 to train models for generating realistic synthetic images, advancing image enhancement and augmentation techniques. Autonomous perception systems integrate CIFAR-100-trained models to improve visual intelligence in self-driving vehicles, robotic assistants, and industrial automation.

CIFAR-100 plays a crucial role in advancing AI-driven image classification by providing a challenging dataset that enhances deep learning capabilities. Its detailed hierarchical structure, diverse object categories, and fine-grained classification tasks make it an essential resource for researchers and industries focused on improving computer vision applications. As artificial intelligence continues to evolve, CIFAR-100 remains a valuable benchmark for developing more accurate, efficient, and scalable machine learning models in visual recognition.

CIFG (COUPLED INPUT AND FORGET GATE)

CIFG (Coupled Input and Forget Gate)
CIFG is a variation of the LSTM (Long Short-Term Memory) network where the input and forget gates are coupled. This reduces the number of parameters and computational complexity while maintaining performance in sequence modeling tasks.
Key Characteristics
CIFG reduces the complexity of LSTM networks by coupling input and forget gates, enabling more efficient learning while maintaining memory cell updates with fewer parameters.
Benefits
It decreases the number of trainable parameters in LSTMs, improves computational efficiency for sequence-based models, and retains performance for long-range dependencies in sequences.
Applications
CIFG is used in time series forecasting, natural language processing, and sequence modeling in speech and text.
Sources
Research on LSTM networks and their variations and papers on efficient deep learning models provide foundational knowledge.
Conclusion
CIFG offers a more efficient variation of LSTM networks, making it ideal for tasks requiring long-range sequence modeling, though careful tuning may be needed to match the performance of traditional LSTMs.

CIMON (Crew Interactive Mobile Companion)
CIMON is an AI-powered astronaut assistant developed by IBM and Airbus for use on the International Space Station (ISS). It assists astronauts with tasks, answers questions, and provides emotional support.
Key Characteristics
CIMON is an AI-driven virtual assistant with a voice interface, designed specifically for space environments. It is capable of answering scientific and procedural questions and interacting with astronauts.
Benefits
CIMON improves astronaut productivity by assisting with tasks, enhances communication in isolated environments, and provides emotional support during long space missions.
Applications
It is used to assist astronauts with routine tasks on the ISS, serve as a companion for isolated individuals in remote environments, and has potential for future space exploration missions.
Sources
Research by IBM and Airbus on AI in space exploration and NASA studies on human-AI interaction provide insights.
Conclusion
CIMON represents a significant advancement in AI-driven assistance for space exploration, offering both technical support and psychological well-being, though it has limitations in handling complex tasks.

Cinder Block Neural Networks

Cinder Block Neural Networks refer to neural networks with highly compressed architectures, reducing the number of parameters and operations for more efficient deployment on edge devices.
Key Characteristics

These networks are lightweight, reduce computational and memory requirements, and are optimized for low-power devices.
Benefits
Cinder Block Neural Networks enable efficient deployment on resource-constrained devices, reduce the cost of inference in AI systems, and support real-time processing on edge devices.
Applications
They are used in edge AI applications like autonomous drones, mobile devices, real-time video processing, and AI-driven IoT devices.
Sources
Research on neural network compression techniques and studies on edge computing and AI provide foundational information.
Conclusion
Cinder Block Neural Networks are a promising solution for deploying AI models on resource-constrained devices, though achieving a balance between compression and performance is critical.

Cinematic AI

Definition:
Cinematic AI refers to the use of AI technologies to enhance the creation, editing, and post-production processes in film and video production.

Key Characteristics:
AI in cinematic applications improves video quality through super-resolution and denoising, automates editing processes, and assists in creating visual effects (VFX), significantly reducing manual labor.

Benefits:
Cinematic AI increases efficiency in video editing and post-production, reduces costs by automating labor-intensive tasks, and enhances the quality of visual effects.

Applications:
It is used in film editing, where AI-powered tools cut and sequence video clips, and in creating and enhancing VFX for movies and advertisements.

Sources:
Advancements in AI for media and entertainment applications, and machine learning techniques in image and video processing, contribute to cinematic AI.

Conclusion:
Cinematic AI transforms the film industry by automating editing and visual effects processes, but the creative limitations of AI must be balanced with human input.

Cipher Block Chaining (CBC)

Definition:
Cipher Block Chaining is a mode of operation for block ciphers that uses the previous ciphertext block to encrypt the next block, ensuring that identical plaintext blocks encrypt to different ciphertexts.

Key Characteristics:
Each plaintext block is XORed with the previous ciphertext block. It requires an initialization vector (IV) for the first block and enhances security by preventing patterns in plaintext from appearing in ciphertext.

Benefits:
CBC enhances the security of block ciphers, prevents repeated patterns in encrypted data, and is widely used in secure data transmission.

Applications:
It is used for secure data storage and transmission in AI systems, encryption of sensitive information in machine learning pipelines, and protecting data in transit for cloud-based AI services.

Sources:
Cryptography and security textbooks and research on block cipher modes of operation provide foundational knowledge.

Conclusion:
Cipher Block Chaining enhances block cipher security, making it critical for secure AI data transmission systems, though careful implementation is required to avoid vulnerabilities.

Ciphertext in AI Security

Definition:
Ciphertext refers to data that has been encrypted, making it unreadable without a decryption key. In AI security, ciphertext is used to protect sensitive data processed by AI models.

Key Characteristics:
Ciphertext is encrypted data, ensuring secure communication so only authorized parties with the correct key can access it. It can be produced using symmetric or asymmetric encryption methods.

Benefits:
Ciphertext protects sensitive data, aids compliance with data protection regulations like GDPR, and ensures privacy in applications involving personal or financial information.

Applications:
In AI, ciphertext is used in finance to secure transactions and customer data, and in healthcare to encrypt medical information for patient privacy.

Sources:
Cryptography and AI-driven encryption methods are key resources for understanding ciphertext in AI security.

Conclusion:
Ciphertext is a cornerstone of AI security, protecting sensitive data, though encryption and decryption processes introduce performance trade-offs.

Ciphertext-Policy Attribute-Based Encryption (CP-ABE)

Definition
CP-ABE is a form of data encryption where access rights are defined by attributes assigned to users. Decryption is only possible when the user's attributes match the access policy embedded in the encrypted data.

Key Characteristics
This encryption method allows flexible access control, where users don't need individual keys. Instead, access is granted based on group attributes such as role, clearance level, or location.

Benefits
CP-ABE allows secure, scalable sharing of encrypted information, simplifies key management, and supports fine-grained access controls in multi-user environments.

Applications
It is widely used in cloud storage systems, AI healthcare databases, government data protection, and encrypted sharing among collaborative AI platforms.

Conclusion
CP-ABE is a robust solution for enforcing data privacy in AI ecosystems, especially where group-based access is essential. Its complexity in managing attributes and policies can, however, pose implementation challenges.

Circuit-Based Models in AI

Definition
Circuit-based models in AI are computational frameworks inspired by biological or electronic circuits that simulate the flow of information through interconnected nodes. These models aim to replicate natural or logical systems to process data efficiently.

Key Characteristics
They rely on structures resembling electrical or neural circuits and are characterized by input-output pathways, feedback loops, and signal propagation. These models are often designed to reflect real-world system behavior.

Benefits
They offer high interpretability, can simulate cognitive functions, and support the design of AI systems that mimic natural intelligence or logical control systems.

Applications
Circuit-based models are used in neuroinformatics, robotics, brain-machine interfaces, and AI simulations of physical environments or behaviors.

Conclusion
Circuit-based AI models offer a biologically and physically grounded approach to computation, ideal for tasks requiring realism and explainability. However, they often require more sophisticated hardware and longer simulation times.

Circuit Complexity in AI

Definition Circuit complexity in AI refers to the study of the computational complexity involved in using Boolean circuits to solve problems. It analyzes how large and deep a circuit must be to compute a specific function or solve a task in artificial intelligence.

Key Characteristics This area explores logic gate combinations, evaluates the minimum resources needed for computation, and focuses on reducing the size and depth of circuits for better computational efficiency.

Benefits Understanding circuit complexity helps in optimizing AI algorithms, guiding hardware design for AI processors, and enhancing theoretical insights into AI problem-solving.

Applications It is applied in the development of efficient hardware architectures, low-level AI algorithm optimization, and secure cryptographic systems.

Conclusion Circuit complexity provides foundational knowledge for advancing efficient AI hardware and algorithms, although its use is often limited to specialized areas in low-level system design.

Circuit-Level AI Design

Definition Circuit-level AI design involves creating AI systems at the hardware level by building specialized circuits that directly execute AI algorithms. This approach enhances performance through custom-built silicon such as AI chips and processors.

Key Characteristics It focuses on tightly coupling hardware and software, using circuits tailored for specific AI functions. This includes designing custom hardware like TPUs and FPGAs to boost AI speed and efficiency.

Benefits This method leads to faster execution, lower energy consumption, and better scalability, especially in environments like edge computing or large-scale data centers.

Applications Circuit-level AI is used in developing efficient edge devices, real-time inference engines, and high-performance computing environments for AI workloads.

Conclusion Circuit-level AI design significantly improves system performance but may incur high development costs and limit adaptability across diverse AI tasks.

Citizen Data Science

Definition Citizen data science is the practice of enabling non-experts to perform data analysis using simplified, AI-supported tools. It democratizes access to analytics by reducing the technical barriers to working with data.

Key Characteristics It involves intuitive tools powered by AI, allowing business users and analysts to clean, visualize, and interpret data without formal training in data science.

Benefits Citizen data science expands the reach of data-driven decision-making, empowers teams across industries, and reduces the need for dedicated data science resources.

Applications It is widely used in business intelligence platforms, marketing analytics, and performance dashboards in sectors like retail, healthcare, and education.

Conclusion Citizen data science promotes inclusive data practices and speeds up insights, but careful monitoring is needed to ensure proper interpretation and responsible use of the tools.

CITL (Continuous Integration, Testing, and Learning)

Definition CITL is a methodology that combines the principles of continuous integration and continuous testing with iterative learning loops for AI models. It ensures that AI systems are regularly updated, tested, and improved.

Key Characteristics CITL integrates model training into a DevOps pipeline, using automation to monitor model performance and retrain when necessary. It helps maintain robust, accurate AI systems.

Benefits It reduces manual testing, increases model reliability, and supports agile development cycles for AI products by allowing continuous improvements.

Applications CITL is used in dynamic AI environments such as recommendation engines, personalized content platforms, and adaptive systems in finance and e-commerce.

Conclusion CITL supports responsive and resilient AI system development, though it depends on solid infrastructure and continuous data streams for effective deployment.

City Planning with AI

Definition City planning with AI refers to using artificial intelligence to enhance urban development, infrastructure design, and municipal resource management through data analysis and predictive modeling.

Key Characteristics AI systems analyze traffic patterns, population growth, utility usage, and environmental factors to inform decisions and optimize city layouts.

Benefits AI enables smarter traffic control, energy efficiency, and sustainable infrastructure planning, improving the overall quality of urban life.

Applications It is used in smart city projects, public transportation systems, and predictive models for emergency response and infrastructure expansion.

Conclusion AI-driven city planning enhances efficiency and livability in urban areas, but it requires transparent data use and responsible deployment to avoid algorithmic bias.

Classical Bit

Definition: A classical bit, or binary digit, is the fundamental unit of information in classical computing, representing data using two distinct states, typically denoted as 0 and 1. Classical bits serve as the basic building blocks for digital systems, encoding, storing, and processing data through binary logic.

Key Components: Key components include binary states (0 and 1), logic gates (such as AND, OR, NOT), storage elements (flip-flops, registers), digital circuits for manipulation, electronic components (transistors), and binary encoding schemes.

Benefits: Classical bits simplify computing processes, enabling reliable and straightforward data representation, storage, and processing. They support error detection and correction, facilitate logical reasoning, and underpin stable, predictable computational performance.

Examples: Examples include bits representing letters and numbers in digital text, images stored in binary formats (such as JPEG or PNG), binary data transmission over digital networks, and data processed in microprocessors and digital circuits within electronic devices.

Applications: Classical bits are widely used in computers and servers, digital storage devices, networking equipment, mobile phones, embedded systems, digital audio and video processing, control systems, and essentially all electronic devices relying on digital logic.

Industries: Industries utilizing classical bits extensively include computing and information technology, telecommunications, consumer electronics, automotive electronics, healthcare technology, financial services (digital transactions), manufacturing automation, and media broadcasting.

Summary: A classical bit is the essential foundation of digital computing, providing simple yet powerful data representation through binary states. Its versatility and stability have enabled significant advancements in technology and have established it as the universal standard for digital information processing across numerous industries.

Classical Coherence

Definition: Classical coherence refers to the consistent phase relationship between waves or oscillations in classical physics, allowing them to maintain predictable and stable patterns over distance or time. It describes how classical waves, such as electromagnetic waves or mechanical waves, align consistently, resulting in uniform, interference-capable wave behavior.

Key Components: Essential elements include wave sources, consistent frequency and phase, stable amplitude, predictable interference patterns, well-defined phase difference, coherent wave propagation, and temporal or spatial stability.

Benefits: Classical coherence enables precise measurements, enhanced signal clarity, improved imaging quality, effective energy transmission, and accurate data communication. It also underpins advanced technological capabilities like interferometry and laser technology.

Examples: Examples include laser beams exhibiting spatial and temporal coherence, radio waves in communication systems, coherent sound waves used in ultrasonic medical imaging, and coherent light employed in holography.

Applications: Practical applications involve laser technologies for surgery and manufacturing, optical fiber communication systems, holographic imaging and displays, interferometric sensors for precise measurement, coherent radar and sonar systems, and coherent optical computing techniques.

Industries: Industries benefiting from classical coherence include telecommunications, healthcare and medical imaging, aerospace and defense, manufacturing and materials processing, scientific research laboratories, consumer electronics, optics and photonics, and automotive sensor technologies.

Summary: Classical coherence is essential in classical wave phenomena, providing predictable wave interactions and high-precision control of wave properties. It serves as a cornerstone for numerous advanced technologies and industries reliant on accurate, stable, and high-quality wave-based systems.

Classical Information

Definition: Classical information refers to data encoded, stored, and processed using classical computing methods, typically represented by binary digits or bits (0 and 1). It operates within the principles of classical physics, ensuring predictable, deterministic, and measurable data processing and communication.

Key Components: Core elements include binary encoding (bits), classical logic gates (AND, OR, NOT), data storage methods, transmission protocols, classical channels, error detection and correction schemes, deterministic computations, and classical algorithms.

Benefits: Classical information processing provides stable, reliable, and highly predictable data handling, ensures simplicity and efficiency in computing, supports scalable digital communication, facilitates widespread data storage solutions, and enables comprehensive data analysis.

Examples: Examples include digital text documents, numerical data, images and videos stored in digital formats, classical communication signals, binary files in computers, and structured databases.

Applications: Classical information is utilized extensively in digital computing systems, databases, telecommunications, networking, digital media processing, financial transaction management, document digitization, control systems, and data analytics software.

Industries: Industries heavily reliant on classical information include computing and information technology, telecommunications, finance and banking, healthcare, manufacturing automation, consumer electronics, media and entertainment, logistics, transportation, and education.

Summary: Classical information underpins virtually all modern digital technology, providing a structured, reliable foundation for processing, storing, and communicating data. Its deterministic and well-understood nature makes it indispensable across industries, supporting efficient and stable digital solutions globally.

Classical World

Definition: The classical world refers to the macroscopic realm described by classical physics, where phenomena follow deterministic laws articulated by Newtonian mechanics, classical electromagnetism, and thermodynamics. In this domain, objects have precise positions, velocities, and predictable behaviors, without requiring quantum mechanical interpretations.

Key Components: Fundamental elements include Newton's laws of motion, classical gravity, deterministic trajectories, classical electromagnetism (Maxwell's equations), continuous energy distributions, thermodynamic principles, cause-and-effect relationships, and predictable system dynamics.

Benefits: Classical physics simplifies the analysis and prediction of everyday phenomena, provides reliable and accurate results for large-scale systems, enables practical engineering and technological advancements, and establishes intuitive frameworks for understanding physical reality.

Examples: Examples of classical world phenomena include planetary orbits, mechanical motions of machines, fluid flow dynamics in rivers and pipes, electrical circuits behavior, aerodynamic flight of aircraft, and thermal energy transfer in engines.

Applications: Classical physics principles apply broadly, including mechanical engineering design, automotive engineering, civil infrastructure development, electrical power generation and distribution, aviation, construction, weather forecasting models, and thermal system management.

Industries: Industries heavily relying on classical physics include manufacturing, automotive, aerospace, civil engineering, electrical and electronics engineering, energy production, transportation, construction, agriculture, and environmental sciences.

Summary: The classical world encompasses large-scale physical phenomena effectively described by classical physics laws, ensuring predictability and accuracy in many practical applications. Its intuitive nature and reliability continue to underpin foundational technologies and industries essential for everyday life.

Classification Algorithms in AI

Definition Classification algorithms are machine learning techniques used to assign input data to one of several predefined categories based on features in the data. They are a core part of supervised learning.

Key Characteristics These algorithms require labeled datasets and are trained to learn decision boundaries that distinguish between different classes. Common techniques include logistic regression, decision trees, and support vector machines.

Benefits They deliver high accuracy in data categorization tasks and support automation in fields where large volumes of data must be organized efficiently.

Applications Classification algorithms are used in email filtering, fraud detection, medical diagnosis, and sentiment analysis.

Conclusion Classification is fundamental to AI systems dealing with structured predictions, but it relies heavily on data quality and may require complex tuning to avoid overfitting.

Cloud AI

Definition Cloud AI refers to artificial intelligence services offered through cloud platforms. These services include data processing, model training, and deployment, accessible via the internet.

Key Characteristics It supports scalable AI operations, offers access to pre-trained models and APIs, and enables integration into applications without needing in-house infrastructure.

Benefits Cloud AI lowers the entry barrier for AI adoption, accelerates deployment, and supports large-scale model training.

Applications It is used in business intelligence, automated customer support, computer vision, and predictive analytics.

Conclusion Cloud AI democratizes access to intelligent tools, but organizations must carefully manage latency, data governance, and vendor dependence.

Clustering Algorithms in AI

Definition Clustering algorithms are unsupervised learning techniques used to identify patterns or groupings in data without labeled outputs. They discover structure by grouping similar data points together.

Key Characteristics These models evaluate similarity metrics to form clusters, often using distance-based methods. Examples include K-means, DBSCAN, and hierarchical clustering.

Benefits Clustering reveals insights in unstructured data, supports exploratory analysis, and aids in anomaly detection.

Applications It is used in marketing for customer segmentation, in cybersecurity for detecting unusual behavior, and in biology for gene expression analysis.

Conclusion Clustering provides valuable tools for pattern discovery, although results depend heavily on parameter tuning and data quality.

Cobot (Collaborative Robot)

Definition A cobot is a collaborative robot designed to safely work alongside humans in shared environments, performing tasks that require flexibility and interaction.

Key Characteristics Cobots are equipped with sensors and safety features to detect human presence and adjust actions. They are often lightweight, mobile, and reprogrammable for different tasks.

Benefits They boost productivity, reduce physical strain on workers, and support automation in flexible manufacturing environments.

Applications Cobots are used in assembly lines, logistics, quality control, and even in healthcare settings to support staff.

Conclusion Cobots enable safe and efficient human-machine collaboration but may face limitations in tasks requiring high force or precision.

Cognitive AI

Definition Cognitive AI refers to artificial intelligence systems designed to replicate human thought processes such as reasoning, learning, memory, and problem-solving.

Key Characteristics These systems combine deep learning, natural language processing, and symbolic reasoning to perform tasks that require contextual understanding.

Benefits Cognitive AI improves decision-making, supports intelligent automation, and enhances human-computer interaction.

Applications It is used in virtual assistants, automated research, enterprise analytics, and medical diagnostics.

Conclusion Cognitive AI bridges the gap between machine efficiency and human cognition, though ethical and interpretability concerns must be addressed.

Cognitive Computing

Definition Cognitive computing is a discipline within AI focused on creating systems that emulate human thinking and adapt to complex situations through data-driven learning.

Key Characteristics It involves self-learning systems that interpret unstructured data, recognize patterns, and interact naturally with users.

Benefits It supports faster insights from big data, enhances customer experiences, and automates high-level decision tasks.

Applications Cognitive computing is used in legal research, personalized healthcare, and financial risk analysis.

Conclusion Cognitive computing is transforming industries with intelligent systems that think and learn, though success depends on transparency, reliability, and responsible AI practices.

Cognitive Load Estimation in AI

Definition Cognitive load estimation in AI refers to the process of evaluating the mental effort users exert while interacting with digital systems. AI-based models estimate this load to improve interface design, adapt system behavior, and enhance user experience.

Key Characteristics Cognitive load estimation uses behavioral data such as eye movement, click rates, and task completion times. It often supports real-time analysis and is integrated into adaptive systems that adjust tasks or content based on user effort.

Benefits It improves user experience by preventing overload, reduces frustration, and supports personalized learning paths in educational platforms.

Applications It is widely used in education technology to adapt learning content, in user interface design to simplify workflows, and in simulation training systems.

Conclusion Cognitive load estimation helps tailor systems to user needs, improving engagement and outcomes, although accurate real-time prediction models can be difficult to develop.

Cohort Analysis in AI

Definition Cohort analysis in AI refers to studying the behavior of specific groups of users or data points that share a common characteristic over a set time period. This analysis helps reveal behavioral trends and user lifecycle patterns.

Key Characteristics Cohorts are grouped based on shared attributes such as sign-up date or transaction time. AI systems analyze behavioral trends and retention within these groups over time.

Benefits It provides actionable insights into user behavior, enables better targeting in marketing, and improves product development by identifying group-specific needs.

Applications Cohort analysis is used in marketing analytics, product adoption studies, and customer retention strategies.

Conclusion Cohort analysis empowers businesses to make data-driven decisions, although it requires clean, structured data and may not capture detailed individual behavior.

Collaborative AI

Definition Collaborative AI involves AI systems that work alongside humans or other AI agents to complete shared objectives. It emphasizes teamwork, coordination, and joint decision-making.

Key Characteristics It includes shared task execution, real-time communication, and division of roles between AI agents and humans. It enhances mutual understanding and synchronizes efforts for better outcomes.

Benefits Collaborative AI boosts productivity by handling repetitive tasks and improves outcomes through combined human intuition and machine intelligence.

Applications It is used in healthcare for diagnosis support, in robotics for human-robot collaboration, and in manufacturing for assembly line assistance.

Conclusion Collaborative AI enhances human-machine synergy but requires effective trust, coordination, and clear role definition.

Collaborative Intelligence (CI)

Definition Collaborative intelligence is the integration of human and AI capabilities to enhance performance in complex decision-making environments. Both parties contribute complementary strengths.

Key Characteristics CI systems support real-time interaction, shared decision-making, and human-in-the-loop processing where final control remains with people.

Benefits It improves outcomes by combining machine precision with human judgment and fosters trust in AI decisions.

Applications Collaborative intelligence is used in healthcare diagnostics, legal research, strategic planning, and crisis management.

Conclusion Collaborative intelligence empowers enhanced decision-making, but successful implementation requires user training and AI transparency.

Collision Detection in AI

Definition Collision detection is the ability of AI systems to recognize potential physical interactions between objects and prevent them, especially in robotic, gaming, and autonomous environments.

Key Characteristics AI systems use sensors and predictive models to determine object proximity and movement in real-time to avoid impact.

Benefits It enhances system safety, reduces errors, and increases reliability in autonomous navigation and interaction.

Applications It is used in robotics, gaming engines, drone flight systems, and autonomous vehicles.

Conclusion Collision detection is essential for safe operation in dynamic environments, but it requires real-time performance and accurate spatial data.

Complex Event Processing (CEP) in AI

Definition Complex Event Processing in AI analyzes and processes multiple data streams in real-time to detect meaningful patterns or anomalies for immediate decision-making.

Key Characteristics CEP systems use event correlation, pattern recognition, and stream analytics to detect trends, triggers, or risks in large datasets.

Benefits It supports real-time insights, enables fast responses, and reduces manual monitoring in high-frequency environments.

Applications CEP is used in fraud detection, network security, financial monitoring, and industrial automation.

Conclusion CEP enhances real-time decision-making and automation but demands careful architecture and performance tuning under heavy data loads.

Computational Models

Definition Computational models are algorithmic systems that simulate real-world processes or predict outcomes using mathematical methods. They help explain how AI interprets data, makes decisions, and learns patterns.

Key Characteristics They include symbolic, statistical, machine learning, agent-based, and optimization-based models, enabling different approaches to simulation and prediction.

Benefits They offer fast, cost-effective ways to test hypotheses, predict behaviors, and simulate outcomes across diverse fields.

Applications Computational models are applied in AI fields like NLP, robotics, vision, healthcare, climate forecasting, and financial analysis.

Conclusion Computational models form the foundation of AI reasoning and learning, though they require high-quality data and careful evaluation.

Computer Graphics CPU

Definition A Computer Graphics CPU is a central processor that manages the logic and data preparation needed for rendering visual content. It works alongside GPUs to handle non-parallel tasks in graphics workflows.

Key Characteristics It executes logic, controls rendering flow, manages memory, and handles physical simulations and input processing before GPU rendering.

Benefits CPUs coordinate real-time rendering, support flexible high-level logic, and ensure seamless interactions in complex visual systems.

Applications They are used in gaming, animation, visual effects, CAD design, and virtual reality development.

Conclusion Computer Graphics CPUs provide vital support for smooth graphics rendering and system control, even though GPUs dominate the actual rendering process.

Computer Vision

Definition Computer vision is a domain of AI focused on enabling machines to process, understand, and respond to visual inputs such as images or video, mimicking human visual perception.

Key Characteristics It includes tasks such as object detection, facial recognition, gesture analysis, and image segmentation. It relies heavily on deep learning and convolutional networks.

Benefits Computer vision enhances automation, supports visual diagnostics, and enables real-time recognition across industries.

Applications It is used in autonomous vehicles, medical imaging, surveillance systems, retail analytics, and precision agriculture.

Conclusion Computer vision revolutionizes visual data interpretation, offering powerful automation but requiring large datasets and addressing concerns like bias and privacy.

Computing machinery and intelligence

Definition: Computing machinery and intelligence is a foundational concept in artificial intelligence that explores whether machines can think and exhibit intelligent behavior comparable to humans. Introduced by Alan Turing in his 1950 paper, this concept laid the groundwork for AI development by proposing that a machine's intelligence should be evaluated based on its ability to mimic human cognitive functions rather than its internal structure. This idea led to the creation of the Turing Test, a method for determining whether a machine can exhibit responses indistinguishable from those of a human in natural conversation. The study of computing machinery and intelligence has influenced modern AI research, leading to advancements in machine learning, natural language processing, and autonomous systems.

The key components of computing machinery and intelligence include the Turing Test, which assesses machine intelligence based on its ability to engage in human-like conversation. Symbolic reasoning enables machines to process logical rules and manipulate symbols to simulate problem-solving and decision-making. Machine learning allows computers to learn from data, improving performance without explicit programming. Neural networks simulate brain-like structures, enabling AI systems to recognize patterns and make predictions. Computational algorithms process and analyze information, forming the foundation for intelligent decision-making.

One of the primary benefits of computing machinery and intelligence is its role in advancing artificial intelligence by providing a theoretical framework for evaluating machine cognition. It has led to the development of AI-driven automation, enhancing efficiency in industries such as healthcare, finance, and robotics. AI models inspired by this concept improve human-computer interaction through natural language processing and conversational AI. It has influenced ethical discussions on AI's role in society, shaping policies on machine autonomy and responsibility. The continuous exploration of computing machinery and intelligence drives innovation in AI research, leading to more sophisticated and capable intelligent systems.

Examples of computing machinery and intelligence include AI chatbots that pass the Turing Test by engaging in human-like conversations. Machine learning models used in fraud detection analyze transaction patterns to identify suspicious activity. Autonomous vehicles rely on AI algorithms to interpret sensor data and navigate roads safely. AI-powered medical diagnostics assist doctors by analyzing medical images and predicting disease risks. Recommendation systems in streaming services use machine learning to personalize content for users based on viewing habits.

Industries that benefit from computing machinery and intelligence include technology and software development, where AI is integrated into applications for automation, customer service, and predictive analytics. The healthcare sector applies AI to medical research, diagnostics, and robotic-assisted surgery. Finance and banking use AI for fraud detection, risk assessment, and algorithmic trading. The automotive industry relies on AI for self-driving technology and driver-assistance systems. Cybersecurity leverages AI to detect and prevent cyber threats in real-time. Education incorporates AI-powered tutoring systems that adapt to individual learning styles.

Summary: Computing machinery and intelligence remains a fundamental concept in artificial intelligence, shaping the development of intelligent systems that mimic human thought and reasoning. While challenges such as ethical considerations, computational constraints, and defining true machine intelligence persist, ongoing research continues to refine AI capabilities. As AI evolves, the principles introduced by computing machinery and intelligence will guide the development of more advanced and responsible artificial systems, transforming industries and redefining the boundaries of human-machine interaction.

Conscious AI

Definition: Conscious AI refers to artificial intelligence systems that exhibit or simulate attributes of human consciousness, such as awareness, self-reflection, emotional understanding, and subjective experiences. These systems aim to perceive, interpret, and respond to their environments in a way that mirrors human cognition and awareness.

Key Components: Core elements include self-awareness, contextual understanding, emotional recognition, adaptive learning mechanisms, memory management, ethical decision-making frameworks, and sophisticated neural network architectures designed to simulate introspection and subjective awareness.

Benefits: The primary advantage of conscious AI lies in its enhanced capability to interact naturally with humans, enabling deeper emotional connections and more intuitive collaboration. Conscious AI could offer superior problem-solving through empathetic reasoning, improved adaptability to unexpected scenarios, and refined ethical judgments based on awareness of its actions.

Examples: Hypothetical examples include advanced robotic assistants that empathize with user emotions, sophisticated conversational agents that reflect on previous interactions and adapt behaviors accordingly, or medical diagnostic systems capable of intuitive reasoning by consciously processing complex patient emotions and behaviors during consultations.

Applications: Potential applications span diverse areas such as personalized healthcare, mental health therapy, companionship robotics, educational platforms with empathetic tutors, ethical decision-making systems in autonomous vehicles, customer service agents with emotional intelligence, and advanced human-computer interaction systems.

Industries: Conscious AI would be influential across sectors including healthcare, education, robotics, mental health services, automotive industries, entertainment and media, customer relations, elder care, and social robotics industries.

Summary: Conscious AI represents a visionary extension of artificial intelligence that incorporates human-like awareness, emotional understanding, and ethical considerations. While still largely theoretical, its realization could transform human-AI interactions by fostering genuine empathy, adaptive intelligence, and nuanced ethical judgments across various fields.

Contextual AI

Contextual AI is an advanced form of artificial intelligence that understands and responds to user inputs based on context rather than relying solely on static data. Unlike traditional AI models that generate responses based on predefined rules, contextual AI incorporates real-time data, historical interactions, and environmental factors to improve decision-making and user interactions. This approach enables AI to adapt dynamically, offering more personalized, relevant, and situationally aware responses.

The key components of contextual AI include natural language processing that interprets user queries in context, real-time data processing that adjusts responses based on environmental changes, user behavior tracking that refines AI predictions over time, and machine learning algorithms that continuously adapt to new inputs. These elements allow AI systems to provide more meaningful and personalized interactions.

The benefits of contextual AI include improved user experience through more natural and adaptive interactions, enhanced decision-making accuracy by incorporating relevant context, reduced errors in AI-generated responses, and greater efficiency in handling dynamic situations. AI systems become more responsive and intelligent, making them suitable for a wide range of applications. Examples include AI-powered customer support that tailors responses based on past interactions, virtual assistants that adjust recommendations based on user behavior, and AI-driven content moderation that adapts to changing conversational contexts.

Applications of contextual AI span customer service, healthcare, finance, marketing, and smart assistants. In customer service, AI chatbots provide context-aware support. In healthcare, AI enhances diagnostic recommendations by considering patient history. In finance, AI improves fraud detection by analyzing transaction context. In marketing, AI personalizes advertising content based on user preferences. In smart assistants, AI refines responses based on past interactions.

Challenges in contextual AI include ensuring real-time accuracy in context-aware models, managing privacy concerns related to user data tracking, reducing biases in AI-driven contextual interpretations, and optimizing computational efficiency for large-scale applications. Developing robust frameworks for ethical and secure contextual AI deployment remains a critical research focus.

In conclusion, contextual AI revolutionizes artificial intelligence by enabling systems to understand and respond to real-world context dynamically. Its ability to adapt to changing situations and personalize user interactions makes it an essential component of next-generation AI applications. As AI technology advances, contextual AI will play a crucial role in improving automation, personalization, and intelligent decision-making across industries.

Contextual Bandit Algorithm

Contextual Bandit Algorithm is a machine learning technique used in decision-making systems where the goal is to maximize rewards based on contextual information. Unlike traditional multi-armed bandit algorithms that focus solely on trial-and-error learning, the contextual bandit algorithm incorporates real-time context to make more informed decisions. This approach is widely used in recommendation systems, online advertising, and adaptive learning environments.

The key components of the contextual bandit algorithm include contextual feature extraction that analyzes real-time data, reward estimation models that predict the potential outcome of different actions, exploration-exploitation tradeoff mechanisms that balance trying new actions with leveraging known successes, and adaptive learning systems that refine decision-making over time. These components ensure that AI optimally selects actions based on evolving contexts.

The benefits of the contextual bandit algorithm include improved decision-making efficiency by incorporating real-time context, enhanced personalization in AI-driven recommendations, faster adaptation to changing environments, and reduced reliance on extensive labeled training data. AI models using contextual bandits achieve higher efficiency in optimizing user experiences. Examples include AI-powered recommendation engines that dynamically adjust content suggestions, online advertising systems that optimize ad placements in real time, and adaptive learning platforms that personalize educational content based on student engagement.

Applications of the contextual bandit algorithm span digital marketing, healthcare, finance, and personalized education. In digital marketing, AI optimizes ad selection based on user behavior. In healthcare, AI refines treatment recommendations based on patient responses. In finance, AI personalizes investment strategies by analyzing market conditions. In education, AI adapts lesson plans to student learning patterns.

In conclusion, the contextual bandit algorithm enhances AI decision-making by incorporating contextual data into reward-based learning systems. Its ability to optimize recommendations and actions dynamically makes it essential for personalized AI applications. As AI continues to evolve, contextual bandit algorithms will remain crucial in refining adaptive decision-making models across industries.

Contextual Embeddings

Contextual Embeddings are AI-generated vector representations of words, phrases, or entities that adjust based on surrounding context. Unlike static word embeddings that assign fixed numerical values to words, contextual embeddings capture the meaning of a word dynamically depending on the sentence in which it appears. This approach improves natural language understanding, making AI models more effective in sentiment analysis, machine translation, and text classification.

The key components of contextual embeddings include transformer-based architectures that dynamically generate embeddings, attention mechanisms that weigh contextual relationships, pre-trained language models that refine word meanings through vast text data, and fine-tuning techniques that adapt embeddings to specific AI applications. These components allow AI systems to process and understand language with greater accuracy.

The benefits of contextual embeddings include improved accuracy in natural language processing tasks, enhanced contextual understanding of ambiguous words, better generalization across different text domains, and reduced reliance on large labeled datasets. AI-powered models using contextual embeddings produce more relevant and coherent language predictions. Examples include AI-driven sentiment analysis that interprets word meanings based on surrounding context, machine translation systems that generate more accurate translations, and AI-powered search engines that improve query relevance.

Applications of contextual embeddings span NLP, search engines, chatbots, recommendation systems, and knowledge retrieval. In NLP, AI models improve contextual word understanding. In search engines, AI enhances content ranking based on user queries. In chatbots, AI refines responses by interpreting user input contextually. In recommendation systems, AI suggests personalized content based on past interactions. In knowledge retrieval, AI improves document summarization and topic extraction.

In conclusion, contextual embeddings enhance AI's ability to understand language by dynamically adjusting word meanings based on context. Their applications in NLP, search engines, and recommendation systems make them essential for improving AI-driven language processing. As AI research advances, contextual embeddings will continue to refine the accuracy and adaptability of language models.

Continous Learning

Continuous Learning in AI is an advanced approach that enables machine learning models to learn and improve continuously over time by integrating new data without requiring full retraining. Unlike static models that rely on fixed training datasets, continuous learning AI adapts dynamically, allowing it to evolve with changing environments and user interactions. This approach is crucial for AI applications that require real-time adaptability, such as autonomous systems, cybersecurity, and personalized AI assistants.

The key components of continuous learning in AI include incremental learning algorithms that integrate new data without forgetting previous knowledge, adaptive neural networks that refine AI behavior dynamically, data stream processing that enables real-time updates, and memory retention techniques that prevent catastrophic forgetting. These components ensure that AI models improve progressively without complete retraining.

The benefits of continuous learning in AI include enhanced adaptability to evolving data patterns, improved performance over time without frequent retraining, reduced computational costs by updating models incrementally, and increased AI efficiency in handling real-world data variations. AI models become more resilient and capable of long-term learning. Examples include AI-driven fraud detection systems that learn from emerging financial threats, autonomous vehicles that refine driving behavior based on real-time road conditions, and AI-powered medical diagnosis systems that improve based on newly available clinical data.

Applications of continuous learning in AI span robotics, finance, healthcare, cybersecurity, and recommendation systems. In robotics, AI improves movement coordination over time. In finance, AI refines risk assessment based on market fluctuations. In healthcare, AI enhances patient diagnosis with continuously updated medical data. In cybersecurity, AI adapts to new attack patterns in real time. In recommendation systems, AI personalizes content suggestions based on ongoing user interactions.

In conclusion, continuous learning in AI enables models to evolve dynamically, improving efficiency and adaptability in real-world applications. Its role in refining AI systems across industries highlights its importance in achieving long-term AI sustainability. As AI advances, continuous learning will become a fundamental capability for intelligent adaptive systems.

Convoltional Neural Network (CNN)

Convolutional Neural Network (CNN) is a deep learning architecture specifically designed for processing structured grid data, such as images and videos. Unlike traditional neural networks, CNNs utilize convolutional layers that apply filters to extract important features like edges, textures, and patterns from input data. This enables CNNs to achieve high accuracy in tasks such as image recognition, object detection, and medical image analysis.

The key components of CNNs include convolutional layers that apply filters to identify features, pooling layers that reduce spatial dimensions to improve computational efficiency, activation functions that introduce non-linearity for better learning, and fully connected layers that integrate extracted features for final predictions. These elements allow CNNs to automatically learn hierarchical representations of visual data.

The benefits of CNNs include improved accuracy in image classification and recognition tasks, reduced reliance on manual feature extraction, efficient handling of spatial relationships in data, and adaptability to various computer vision applications. CNNs outperform traditional machine learning models in processing complex visual patterns. Examples include AI-powered facial recognition systems, automated medical imaging diagnostics, self-driving car vision systems, and AI-driven security surveillance.

Applications of CNNs span computer vision, healthcare, robotics, security, and augmented reality. In computer vision, CNNs enhance object recognition in photos and videos. In healthcare, CNNs improve medical image analysis for disease detection. In robotics, AI-powered vision systems help robots navigate environments. In security, CNNs enable biometric authentication and surveillance analysis. In augmented reality, CNNs refine real-time object tracking for immersive experiences.

Challenges in CNNs include high computational requirements for training deep models, susceptibility to adversarial attacks that manipulate image data, difficulty in interpreting complex learned features, and reliance on large labeled datasets for supervised learning. Optimizing CNNs for efficiency while maintaining high accuracy remains an active research focus.

In conclusion, CNNs have revolutionized image processing and computer vision, enabling AI to achieve human-level accuracy in visual recognition tasks. Their role in healthcare, security, robotics, and augmented reality highlights their importance in AI-driven automation. As AI advances, CNNs will continue to enhance machine perception and real-world decision-making.

Cosmos (in AI and Simulation Contexts)

Definition:
In the context of AI and simulation, Cosmos typically refers to a highly integrated, scalable simulation framework or environment that supports large-scale, multi-agent AI testing. It can also refer to platforms designed for managing complex systems like satellite constellations, space robotics, or decentralized networks.

Key Components:
Agent-based simulation environments, cloud infrastructure, orchestration tools, physics-based engines, APIs for AI interaction, and visualization dashboards.

Examples:
An AI researcher uses Cosmos to simulate interactions between thousands of autonomous drones, or a space agency uses a Cosmos platform to simulate real-time communication between satellite networks.

Benefits:
Enables large-scale, high-fidelity AI simulations, supports research in distributed intelligence, allows safe testing of complex systems, and reduces cost and risk before real-world deployment.

Industries:
Aerospace, robotics, telecommunications, AI research, defense, and smart infrastructure.

Applications:
Simulating autonomous satellite navigation, coordinating robotic teams, testing decentralized AI behaviors, and managing space communication networks.

Summary:
Cosmos represents a new frontier in simulating and managing large-scale intelligent systems, offering powerful tools for developing, testing, and deploying AI in complex, interconnected environments.

Counterintuitive Limit

Definition
A counterintuitive limit refers to a mathematical or system-based outcome that defies common sense or initial expectations. In the context of AI, machine learning, or advanced computation, it describes a situation where increasing or adjusting a parameter leads to an unexpected or surprising result as it approaches a specific value or behavior. Even though the result is mathematically valid or empirically observed, it can appear incorrect or illogical without deeper understanding. The term originates from

mathematical analysis but has growing relevance in AI model behavior, performance tuning, and learning algorithms.

Key Components
The core components of a counterintuitive limit include an approaching value or condition, a surprising outcome, and the reasoning or mathematical explanation that validates the result. These limits often arise in edge cases or in the behavior of functions, models, or systems as they near convergence, saturation, or extreme values. They also involve human perception and intuition, which may conflict with actual data-driven outcomes. This contrast between expectation and result is what defines the "counterintuitive" nature of the limit.

Benefits
Understanding counterintuitive limits can lead to better design and interpretation of AI models, especially when diagnosing unusual model behaviors or performance shifts. They encourage critical thinking and deeper mathematical reasoning, helping developers and researchers avoid assumptions based on surface-level logic. Recognizing these limits can prevent overfitting, resource waste, or misinterpretation of model accuracy during scaling or optimization. It also promotes scientific curiosity and caution when dealing with system limits and performance boundaries.

Examples
One of the most well-known examples in mathematics is the limit of sin(x)/x as x approaches 0, which equals 1—despite intuition suggesting it should be 0. In AI, a counterintuitive limit might occur when increasing the number of training epochs initially improves accuracy but eventually causes degradation due to overfitting. Another example includes language models where adding more training data beyond a certain point yields diminishing or even negative returns. In reinforcement learning, increasing exploration beyond a limit may reduce overall performance, which goes against the idea that more exploration always helps.

Applications
Counterintuitive limits apply in areas such as deep learning model tuning, regularization strategies, neural network depth analysis, and token limits in language models. They are also observed in data normalization, gradient descent behavior, and optimization functions where limits influence convergence outcomes. These concepts are frequently analyzed during AI research, algorithm design, and the development of scalable machine learning infrastructure.

Industries
Industries that rely heavily on data science and AI, such as healthcare, finance, robotics, and autonomous systems, frequently encounter counterintuitive limits when building predictive models, decision systems, or risk assessment algorithms. Technology companies working on AI model scaling, such as those in natural language processing, computer vision, or recommendation engines, often need to address these surprising results to ensure model reliability.

Challenges
The main challenge with counterintuitive limits is the risk of misunderstanding or ignoring unexpected outcomes. When something defies human logic, it is often dismissed, even if mathematically sound. This can lead to flawed model assumptions, poor performance tuning, or missed opportunities for optimization. Additionally, the presence of counterintuitive behavior requires careful explanation, especially when communicating results to non-technical stakeholders. Detecting and addressing these limits may also demand advanced tools or theoretical insight that are not always accessible.

Summary
Counterintuitive limits reveal the fascinating tension between what we expect and what actually happens in mathematical models and AI systems. They demonstrate that human intuition is not always aligned with mathematical reality, especially in high-complexity environments like machine learning. Recognizing and respecting these limits not only improves model accuracy and system stability but also deepens our understanding of how AI learns and behaves at the edge of performance. These concepts are essential for anyone building, training, or scaling intelligent systems that operate on the frontiers of logic and data.

CPU (Central Processing Unit)

CPU (Central Processing Unit) is the primary computing component responsible for executing instructions in a computer system. Unlike specialized hardware like GPUs (Graphics Processing Units) designed for parallel processing, CPUs handle general-purpose computing tasks, making them essential for operating system management, software execution, and AI model inference. Modern CPUs integrate multiple cores, allowing them to process tasks concurrently, improving computational efficiency.

The key components of a CPU include the arithmetic logic unit (ALU) that performs mathematical and logical operations, the control unit (CU) that manages instruction execution, cache memory that stores frequently accessed data for fast retrieval, and processor cores that enable multi-threaded processing. These components ensure high-speed computing and task execution.

The benefits of CPUs include versatility in handling a wide range of computing tasks, improved efficiency with multi-core architectures, lower power consumption compared to specialized processors, and compatibility with diverse software applications. CPUs remain the backbone of personal computers, enterprise servers, and AI inference tasks. Examples include AI-driven data analytics performed on high-performance CPUs, real-time AI decision-making in embedded systems, and AI-powered cybersecurity tools running on enterprise CPUs.

Applications of CPUs span personal computing, cloud computing, AI inference, embedded systems, and enterprise data processing. In personal computing, CPUs enable AI-powered productivity applications. In cloud computing, AI workloads run on high-performance CPU servers. In AI inference, CPUs process machine learning models in real time. In embedded systems, CPUs power AI-driven smart devices. In enterprise environments, CPUs handle AI-powered big data analysis.

Challenges in CPUs include limited parallel processing capabilities compared to GPUs, increasing thermal constraints in high-performance computing, scalability limitations for large AI models, and power efficiency trade-offs in high-performance processors. Optimizing CPU architectures for AI applications remains an ongoing area of research.

In conclusion, CPUs play a fundamental role in AI computing by enabling software execution, AI inference, and data processing. Their versatility makes them a critical component in AI-driven applications, from personal computing to enterprise analytics. As AI continues to evolve, advancements in CPU architecture will enhance their efficiency and scalability for AI workloads.

CPU Clusters

CPU Clusters refer to interconnected groups of CPUs working together to process complex computations efficiently. Unlike standalone CPUs, clusters distribute processing tasks across multiple units, enabling parallel execution of AI workloads, scientific simulations, and large-scale data processing. CPU clusters are widely used in cloud computing, enterprise AI solutions, and high-performance computing environments where scalability and fault tolerance are essential.

The key components of CPU clusters include network interconnects that enable communication between processors, distributed computing frameworks that manage task execution across nodes, resource allocation algorithms that optimize workload distribution, and high-speed memory architectures that support fast data exchange. These elements allow CPU clusters to handle large-scale AI computations efficiently.

The benefits of CPU clusters include improved scalability for AI and big data applications, enhanced fault tolerance through distributed processing, cost-effective resource utilization compared to single high-performance processors, and optimized parallel execution of machine learning tasks. CPU clusters enable large AI models to be processed efficiently without requiring specialized hardware like GPUs. Examples include AI-driven financial modeling performed on cloud-based CPU clusters, large-scale AI simulations in scientific research, AI-powered data analytics platforms for business intelligence, and real-time AI decision-making in edge computing environments.

Applications of CPU clusters span cloud computing, enterprise AI, scientific research, financial modeling, and AI-driven cybersecurity. In cloud computing, CPU clusters optimize AI-powered analytics. In enterprise AI, CPU clusters support large-scale machine learning training. In scientific research, AI simulations leverage distributed computing power. In financial modeling, CPU clusters analyze AI-driven risk assessments. In cybersecurity, AI-powered threat detection systems operate across distributed CPU networks.

Challenges in CPU clusters include high network latency in distributed AI processing, increased complexity in workload management, power efficiency concerns for large-scale deployments, and scalability limitations for deep learning tasks requiring massive parallelism. Optimizing distributed computing frameworks for AI efficiency remains an active research focus.

In conclusion, CPU clusters provide scalable and efficient AI computing by enabling distributed processing across multiple CPUs. Their role in cloud computing, enterprise AI, and scientific research makes them essential for large-scale AI workloads. As AI computing demands grow, advancements in CPU clustering will further enhance efficiency, scalability, and real-time AI decision-making.

Creative AI

Definition
Creative AI refers to artificial intelligence systems specifically designed to perform tasks traditionally associated with human creativity. These tasks involve generating original, innovative, or artistic outputs, such as visual arts, music, literature, product design, and innovative problem-solving. Creative AI leverages advanced algorithms, often employing neural networks and machine learning methods, to produce results that mimic or extend human creative processes.

Key Components
Creative AI encompasses several crucial components, starting with generative models, which include Generative Adversarial Networks (GANs) and Variational Autoencoders (VAEs). These models create original outputs by learning patterns from extensive datasets. Reinforcement learning and evolutionary algorithms are also essential components, guiding systems to improve creative outcomes through iterative refinement. Additionally, Natural Language Processing (NLP) enables AI to produce creative written content, while Computer Vision supports the generation of original imagery and visual arts.

Examples
An example of creative AI includes AI-generated artworks, such as those produced by models similar to DeepDream, which create surreal, visually striking images based on existing artwork patterns. AI-generated music, like compositions by AIVA or Amper Music, illustrates how creative AI systems produce original and emotionally evocative musical pieces. Additionally, creative AI applications like ChatGPT generate literature, stories, poems, and even screenplays with high originality and coherence.

Applications
Creative AI finds diverse applications, such as automated content creation in advertising and marketing, generating personalized advertisements, slogans, and brand identities. In entertainment, creative AI is used to produce music, animations, video games, and film scripts. The fashion industry employs creative AI for innovative clothing design, while architecture and industrial design fields utilize AI-driven software for generating novel structural and aesthetic concepts.

Industries
Multiple industries benefit significantly from creative AI, including media and entertainment, advertising, fashion, automotive design, architecture, and technology startups specializing in generative art and music. Additionally, education industries utilize creative AI to foster creativity and innovation skills among learners through interactive tools and simulations.

Challenges
Despite the substantial potential of creative AI, it faces several critical challenges. Ensuring originality without infringement on intellectual property is a persistent issue, as AI often learns from existing copyrighted materials. Ethical concerns arise around authorship, ownership, and attribution of AI-generated content. Moreover, creative AI can sometimes lack emotional depth, context-awareness, and true intentionality, limiting its ability to fully replicate human creativity. Technical complexity and the need for significant computational resources also pose practical implementation challenges.

Summary
Creative AI represents an innovative intersection between artificial intelligence and human creativity, enabling machines to generate artistic, literary, and innovative outputs traditionally associated with human endeavors. While its applications span numerous industries and offer compelling advantages in automation and innovation, creative AI must overcome significant ethical, legal, and practical challenges to fully realize its transformative potential. Continued advances in AI technologies promise greater sophistication, originality, and broader acceptance of creative AI across diverse domains.

Crisis Management AI

Crisis Management AI is the application of artificial intelligence to predict, monitor, and respond to emergencies and disasters. It enables real-time decision-making by analyzing vast amounts of data from multiple sources, such as social media, satellite imagery, and emergency response reports. By leveraging machine learning, natural language processing, and predictive analytics, AI assists organizations in crisis preparedness, early warning systems, and efficient disaster recovery efforts.

The key components of Crisis Management AI include real-time data aggregation that collects information from diverse sources, predictive modeling that forecasts potential crisis scenarios, automated alert systems that notify stakeholders in real-time, and resource optimization algorithms that allocate emergency resources efficiently. These components ensure that AI systems provide timely and accurate crisis response solutions.

The benefits of Crisis Management AI include improved disaster preparedness by identifying early warning signs, faster response times by automating emergency notifications, optimized resource distribution for relief efforts, and enhanced situational awareness through real-time data analysis. AI-driven crisis management minimizes human error and improves coordination among emergency responders. Examples include AI-powered wildfire detection using satellite imagery, AI-driven flood prediction models that analyze climate data, AI-powered social media analysis for real-time disaster impact assessment, and AI-driven emergency call center automation for quicker response times.

Applications of Crisis Management AI span emergency response, environmental monitoring, public health, cybersecurity, and financial risk management. In emergency response, AI assists first responders in assessing damage and prioritizing rescue efforts. In environmental monitoring, AI predicts natural disasters such as hurricanes and earthquakes. In public health, AI monitors and mitigates disease outbreaks. In cybersecurity, AI detects and responds to large-scale cyberattacks. In financial risk management, AI assesses the economic impact of crises on global markets.

In conclusion, Crisis Management AI enhances disaster preparedness, emergency response, and post-crisis recovery through data-driven intelligence. Its ability to analyze and act on real-time information makes it a crucial tool in safeguarding lives, property, and economic stability. As AI technology advances, its role in crisis management will continue to expand, improving global resilience to emergencies.

Critical Path Method (CPM) IN AI

Critical Path Method (CPM) in AI is an optimization algorithm used to identify the most efficient sequence of tasks required to complete a project. By integrating AI-driven analytics, CPM enhances project management by predicting potential delays, allocating resources effectively, and ensuring the timely completion of complex tasks. AI-powered CPM is particularly valuable in industries where large-scale planning and coordination are essential, such as construction, software development, and logistics.

The key components of CPM in AI include task dependency mapping that identifies relationships between different project activities, time estimation algorithms that predict task completion times, risk assessment models that analyze potential bottlenecks, and automated scheduling optimization that adjusts project timelines dynamically. These elements allow AI to enhance project planning efficiency.

The benefits of CPM in AI include improved project efficiency by optimizing task execution order, reduced delays through early risk identification, enhanced resource allocation based on AI-driven analysis, and data-driven decision-making that improves overall project success rates. AI-powered CPM provides a proactive approach to project management. Examples include AI-driven construction project scheduling, AI-powered software development pipeline optimization, AI-driven supply chain logistics planning, and AI-powered event management scheduling.

Applications of CPM in AI span construction, manufacturing, software development, healthcare, and aerospace. In construction, AI optimizes building project timelines. In manufacturing, AI streamlines production schedules. In software development, AI predicts coding and testing bottlenecks. In healthcare, AI improves hospital workflow planning. In aerospace, AI enhances mission planning for complex operations.

In conclusion, CPM in AI enhances project planning and execution by optimizing task sequencing and resource management. Its application across industries improves efficiency, reduces risks, and enhances decision-making. As AI continues to advance, CPM will play a key role in enabling smarter and more adaptive project management solutions.

Cross-Entropy in AI

Cross-Entropy in AI is a loss function commonly used in machine learning and deep learning models for classification tasks. It measures the difference between the predicted probability distribution of a model and the actual distribution of the target labels. By minimizing cross-entropy loss, AI models improve their accuracy in tasks such as image recognition, speech processing, and natural language understanding.

The key components of Cross-Entropy in AI include probability distribution estimation that compares predicted and true class probabilities, logarithmic loss calculation that penalizes incorrect predictions more severely, gradient descent optimization that updates model weights based on error minimization, and backpropagation techniques that adjust neural network parameters iteratively. These components enable AI models to learn and refine classification accuracy effectively.

The benefits of Cross-Entropy in AI include improved training efficiency for classification models, enhanced performance in multi-class learning problems, better probability calibration in deep learning models, and reduced error rates in AI-driven predictions. AI models using cross-entropy loss achieve higher classification accuracy in real-world applications. Examples include AI-powered handwriting recognition, AI-driven sentiment analysis in NLP, AI-powered speech recognition systems, and AI-driven fraud detection algorithms.

Applications of Cross-Entropy in AI span computer vision, NLP, autonomous systems, healthcare diagnostics, and recommendation systems. In computer vision, AI models improve image classification accuracy. In NLP, AI enhances text sentiment classification. In autonomous systems, AI refines decision-making in navigation. In healthcare, AI improves disease diagnosis based on medical images. In recommendation systems, AI optimizes user preference predictions.

In conclusion, Cross-Entropy in AI plays a crucial role in training classification models by measuring prediction accuracy. Its widespread use in deep learning applications highlights its importance in improving AI-driven decision-making. As AI research progresses, optimizing cross-entropy loss functions will further enhance model performance across diverse applications.

Cross-Language Information Reatrieval (CLIR)

Cross-Language Information Retrieval (CLIR) is an AI-driven technique that enables information retrieval across multiple languages by allowing users to search for content in one language and retrieve relevant documents in another. By leveraging machine translation, natural language processing, and multilingual embeddings, CLIR enhances search engines, digital libraries, and knowledge discovery platforms.

The key components of CLIR include cross-lingual embeddings that map words from different languages into a shared semantic space, machine translation models that convert queries and documents across languages, information retrieval algorithms that rank results based on relevance, and contextual analysis techniques that improve search accuracy. These elements enable seamless multilingual search experiences.

The benefits of CLIR include improved access to global knowledge by breaking language barriers, enhanced multilingual search efficiency, better information retrieval accuracy in cross-lingual contexts, and expanded accessibility for non-native speakers. AI-powered CLIR allows users to find relevant content across different languages effortlessly. Examples include AI-driven multilingual search engines, AI-powered legal document retrieval in multiple languages, AI-driven academic research search tools, and AI-powered multilingual customer support chatbots.

Applications of CLIR span academia, government, business intelligence, healthcare, and legal research. In academia, AI enhances access to international research papers. In government, AI facilitates multilingual document retrieval. In business intelligence, AI improves global market insights. In healthcare, AI aids in multilingual medical record search. In legal research, AI streamlines cross-jurisdictional case retrieval.

Challenges in CLIR include handling translation errors in AI-driven search, maintaining consistency across different languages, addressing biases in multilingual AI models, and ensuring efficient indexing of diverse linguistic content. Advancing AI-powered multilingual search techniques remains a key research area.

In conclusion, CLIR enhances information retrieval across languages, improving accessibility and knowledge discovery. Its applications in search engines, academia, and business intelligence highlight its value in global AI-driven solutions. As AI continues to evolve, CLIR will play a vital role in breaking language barriers and expanding information access.

Crowd Behavior Analysis in AI

Crowd Behavior Analysis in AI is the application of artificial intelligence to study, predict, and interpret the movement, interactions, and decisions of large groups of people. By leveraging machine learning, computer vision, and real-time data analysis, AI can detect patterns in human behavior, identify potential risks, and optimize crowd management strategies. This is widely used in public safety, event planning, and smart city infrastructure.

The key components of Crowd Behavior Analysis in AI include real-time video analytics that processes surveillance footage to detect movement patterns, deep learning models that classify group dynamics and identify anomalies, predictive analytics that forecasts crowd density and potential risks, and anomaly detection algorithms that alert authorities to unusual behavior. These components help AI systems provide accurate insights into crowd dynamics.

The benefits of Crowd Behavior Analysis in AI include enhanced public safety by detecting risks in high-density areas, improved efficiency in crowd control at large events, optimized traffic and pedestrian flow in urban planning, and real-time threat detection in security-sensitive locations. AI-driven crowd analysis minimizes the risk of overcrowding, accidents, and security breaches. Examples include AI-powered surveillance systems that monitor large gatherings, AI-driven stadium crowd management solutions, smart city AI that optimizes pedestrian traffic signals, and AI-based emergency evacuation planning in public spaces.

Applications of Crowd Behavior Analysis in AI span public safety, event management, smart cities, transportation, and retail. In public safety, AI helps law enforcement monitor crowds for security threats. In event management, AI optimizes venue capacity and movement flow. In smart cities, AI improves pedestrian and vehicle traffic coordination. In transportation, AI enhances railway and airport crowd control. In retail, AI helps businesses analyze customer movement patterns.

In conclusion, Crowd Behavior Analysis in AI enhances security, efficiency, and planning in managing large groups of people. Its role in public safety, urban development, and event coordination makes it essential for improving societal infrastructure. As AI technology advances, crowd analysis will become more accurate and adaptive, leading to smarter and safer environments.

Crowdsourcing AI

Crowdsourcing AI refers to the process of utilizing human intelligence and distributed computing power to improve AI model training, data annotation, and problem-solving. By engaging a large network of contributors, AI-driven crowdsourcing enables faster and more diverse data collection, leading to more accurate and unbiased AI models. This technique is widely used in AI research, content moderation, and large-scale data labeling projects.

The key components of Crowdsourcing AI include human-in-the-loop systems that combine human expertise with AI automation, distributed task allocation platforms that assign microtasks to global contributors, data validation mechanisms that ensure quality control, and reward-based incentive structures that encourage participation. These components allow AI-driven crowdsourcing systems to function efficiently.

The benefits of Crowdsourcing AI include improved AI model accuracy through diverse data collection, reduced bias by leveraging inputs from multiple perspectives, accelerated AI development timelines through large-scale data processing, and cost-effective model training compared to traditional manual annotation methods. Crowdsourcing allows AI to scale rapidly across various applications. Examples include AI-powered content moderation using human feedback, crowdsourced translation services that improve multilingual AI models, AI-driven citizen science projects that analyze environmental data, and AI-based medical research that gathers patient-reported health information.

Applications of Crowdsourcing AI span AI model training, content moderation, research, business intelligence, and humanitarian aid. In AI training, crowdsourced data improves model performance. In content moderation, AI filters harmful content with human oversight. In research, AI leverages distributed problem-solving for scientific advancements. In business intelligence, AI gathers consumer insights through crowdsourced surveys. In humanitarian aid, AI analyzes crisis data from volunteer contributors.

In conclusion, Crowdsourcing AI accelerates AI development by harnessing human intelligence for large-scale data processing and problem-solving. Its applications in AI model training, content moderation, and scientific research highlight its transformative potential. As AI continues to evolve, crowdsourcing will remain a key strategy for improving AI performance and ethical decision-making.

Cryptanalysis in AI

Cryptanalysis in AI is the use of artificial intelligence techniques to analyze, break, and improve cryptographic security protocols. By leveraging machine learning and pattern recognition, AI-driven cryptanalysis can detect vulnerabilities in encryption algorithms, predict cryptographic key patterns, and assist in the development of stronger encryption standards. This field is essential for cybersecurity, digital forensics, and secure communications.

The key components of Cryptanalysis in AI include deep learning models that identify cryptographic weaknesses, adversarial machine learning that tests encryption resilience, automated brute-force attack optimizations that speed up key cracking attempts, and quantum-resistant cryptography research that prepares security systems for future AI-driven threats. These elements help AI systems enhance cybersecurity defenses.

The benefits of Cryptanalysis in AI include improved cryptographic security through AI-driven vulnerability detection, faster decryption processes in cybersecurity investigations, enhanced fraud detection by analyzing encrypted transaction anomalies, and strengthened encryption algorithms based on AI-discovered weaknesses. AI-driven cryptanalysis helps prevent data breaches and cyberattacks. Examples include AI-powered penetration testing tools for security audits, AI-driven detection of weak encryption keys in financial transactions, AI-enhanced decryption techniques in digital forensics, and AI-powered cryptographic protocol design for quantum security.

Applications of Cryptanalysis in AI span cybersecurity, national defense, financial security, digital forensics, and blockchain security. In cybersecurity, AI detects weaknesses in encryption protocols. In national defense, AI enhances secure communication systems. In financial security, AI prevents fraud by analyzing encrypted transactions. In digital forensics, AI aids in criminal investigations by decrypting protected data. In blockchain security, AI improves cryptographic consensus mechanisms.

Challenges in Cryptanalysis in AI include ensuring ethical use of AI-driven cryptanalysis, preventing AI-enhanced cyberattacks from exploiting encryption vulnerabilities, balancing AI-powered decryption with privacy concerns, and developing quantum-resistant cryptographic solutions. Strengthening AI-driven security research while maintaining ethical standards is a critical challenge.

In conclusion, Cryptanalysis in AI enhances cybersecurity by detecting and preventing vulnerabilities in encryption systems. Its applications in digital security, finance, and national defense highlight its importance in protecting sensitive data. As AI and cryptographic threats evolve, AI-driven cryptanalysis will play a crucial role in securing digital communications.

Cryptocurrency Trading Bots in AI

Cryptocurrency Trading Bots in AI are automated AI-driven systems designed to execute cryptocurrency trades based on predefined strategies, market signals, and real-time data analysis. By leveraging machine learning and predictive analytics, AI trading bots optimize buy and sell decisions to maximize profits and minimize risks. These bots are widely used in financial markets, crypto exchanges, and algorithmic trading platforms.

The key components of Cryptocurrency Trading Bots in AI include predictive analytics models that analyze market trends, sentiment analysis tools that assess social media and news impact, algorithmic trading strategies that automate trade execution, and real-time monitoring systems that adjust strategies based on market fluctuations. These components allow AI bots to make data-driven trading decisions.

The benefits of Cryptocurrency Trading Bots in AI include increased trading efficiency through automation, reduced human emotional bias in financial decision-making, enhanced real-time market adaptability, and improved risk management through AI-powered predictive analysis. AI-driven trading bots execute trades faster and more accurately than manual traders. Examples include AI-powered arbitrage bots that capitalize on price differences across exchanges, AI-driven momentum trading bots that follow market trends, AI-powered scalping bots that execute high-frequency trades, and AI-based portfolio rebalancing bots that optimize asset allocation.

Applications of Cryptocurrency Trading Bots in AI span cryptocurrency exchanges, hedge funds, retail trading, and financial analytics. In exchanges, AI bots provide liquidity and optimize trade execution. In hedge funds, AI enhances algorithmic trading strategies. In retail trading, AI automates investment decisions for individual traders. In financial analytics, AI improves market forecasting and risk assessment.

In conclusion, Cryptocurrency Trading Bots in AI optimize trading efficiency and market analysis through automation and predictive analytics. Their role in crypto markets, hedge funds, and financial trading highlights their potential for maximizing investment returns. As AI-driven finance evolves, trading bots will continue to refine and adapt to dynamic market conditions.

Cryptography in AI

Definition: Cryptography in AI refers to the use of cryptographic techniques to protect the confidentiality, integrity, and authenticity of data, models, and communications within artificial intelligence systems. It ensures secure AI operations, protects sensitive information used for training and inference, and enables privacy-preserving AI applications.

Key Components: Encryption: Transforming data into an unreadable format to protect its confidentiality. Homomorphic Encryption: Allowing computations to be performed on encrypted data without decrypting it. Secure Multi-Party Computation (SMPC): Enabling multiple parties to jointly compute a function on their private inputs without revealing them to each other. Differential Privacy: Adding noise to data to protect individual privacy while still allowing for meaningful analysis. Federated Learning: Training AI models on decentralized data sources while keeping the data local and private. Watermarking: Embedding information into models or data to protect intellectual property and detect tampering. Zero-Knowledge Proofs: Allowing one party to prove the truth of a statement to another party without revealing any information beyond the truth of the statement.

Examples: Using homomorphic encryption to perform predictions on encrypted medical data. Employing SMPC to collaboratively train a machine learning model across multiple hospitals without sharing patient records. Applying differential privacy to protect user data in personalized recommendation systems. Utilizing federated learning to train a language model on user devices without centralizing the data. Watermarking AI models to prevent unauthorized distribution or use. Using zero-knowledge proofs to verify the authenticity of AI-generated content.

Benefits: Enhanced Privacy: Protecting sensitive data used in AI systems. Improved Security: Safeguarding AI models and infrastructure from attacks. Trust and Transparency: Building trust in AI systems by ensuring data privacy and security. Regulatory Compliance: Meeting data protection regulations like GDPR and HIPAA. Enabling Collaboration: Facilitating secure collaboration on AI projects involving sensitive data. Protection of Intellectual Property: Safeguarding AI models and algorithms from unauthorized use.

Applications: Healthcare: Secure analysis of patient data for medical research and diagnosis. Finance: Protecting sensitive financial data in fraud detection and risk assessment. Government: Securely sharing intelligence and protecting citizen data. Autonomous Vehicles: Ensuring secure communication and data processing in self-driving cars. Internet of Things (IoT): Securing data collected by IoT devices. Supply Chain Management: Protecting sensitive information shared across supply chain partners.

Industries: Healthcare: Protecting patient privacy and enabling secure medical research. Finance: Ensuring the security and privacy of financial data and transactions. Government: Safeguarding sensitive information and national security. Technology: Developing secure AI systems and privacy-preserving technologies. Automotive: Ensuring the security and safety of autonomous vehicles. Manufacturing: Protecting intellectual property and ensuring secure supply chains.

Conclusions: Cryptography plays a crucial role in ensuring the security, privacy, and trustworthiness of AI systems. By protecting data, models, and communications, cryptographic techniques enable the development and deployment of secure and privacy-preserving AI applications across various industries. While challenges related to performance and complexity exist, the benefits of cryptography in AI are essential for fostering trust and realizing the full potential of artificial intelligence.

CUDA

CUDA (Compute Unified Device Architecture) is a parallel computing platform and application programming interface (API) developed by NVIDIA that allows software developers to utilize the power of GPUs (Graphics Processing Units) for general-purpose computing tasks. By offloading computationally intensive tasks from the CPU to the GPU, CUDA accelerates applications in areas such as artificial intelligence, machine learning, scientific simulations, and video rendering. CUDA enables high-performance computing by enabling massively parallel processing, utilizing thousands of threads simultaneously to handle large-scale data.

Key Components

CUDA Cores are the processing units within a GPU that execute parallel tasks to accelerate computations.
Parallel Programming Model allows developers to design algorithms that execute multiple operations at once, optimizing performance.
Memory Hierarchy manages different types of memory (global, shared, constant, and texture memory) for efficient data storage and retrieval.
CUDA Toolkit includes libraries, compilers, debuggers, and performance analysis tools to support CUDA-enabled applications.
Driver API allows software to communicate with the GPU, ensuring that CUDA applications can leverage GPU capabilities for execution.

Examples

Machine Learning CUDA accelerates the training of deep learning models by enabling faster matrix computations and backpropagation.
Scientific Simulations CUDA is used in fields like molecular dynamics and fluid dynamics to run large simulations with complex calculations.
Image and Video Processing GPUs with CUDA are used for rendering high-resolution images and real-

time video processing, improving speed and efficiency.
Data Analytics CUDA powers big data analytics, enabling quick processing of vast datasets in fields like finance, healthcare, and marketing.

Challenges

Hardware Dependency CUDA relies on NVIDIA GPUs, limiting its applicability to systems with compatible hardware.
Programming Complexity Developing CUDA applications requires knowledge of parallel programming, which can be challenging for many developers.
Memory Management Efficiently managing the large memory required for GPU computations can be complex and time-consuming.
Scalability while CUDA provides excellent performance on a single GPU, scaling across multiple GPUs or nodes requires additional engineering and optimization.

Benefits

Performance Enhancement CUDA accelerates computations by offloading tasks to GPUs, significantly speeding up processes in AI, simulation, and data analysis.
Parallel Processing CUDA enables the execution of large numbers of calculations simultaneously, which is critical for handling big data and complex models.
Cost-Effectiveness Utilizing GPUs for general-purpose tasks reduces the need for expensive, specialized hardware, offering a more affordable alternative.
Energy Efficiency GPUs designed for parallel computing are generally more energy-efficient than CPUs for specific tasks, making them ideal for high-performance applications.

Conclusion

CUDA is a powerful tool for developers, enabling high-performance computing by harnessing the parallel processing power of GPUs. It accelerates tasks in machine learning, scientific research, and data analytics, offering significant performance improvements over traditional CPU-based computing. Despite challenges such as hardware dependencies and programming complexity, CUDA remains an essential technology in modern computing, providing unmatched speed and efficiency for compute-intensive applications.

Cumulative Frequency Analysis in AI

Definition: Cumulative frequency analysis in AI refers to the process of analyzing the distribution of data points within a dataset by calculating the cumulative frequency of occurrences, which involves summing the frequencies of all values less than or equal to a given value. This technique helps in understanding data patterns, identifying thresholds, and informing decision-making in AI applications.

Key Components: Data Collection: Gathering the relevant dataset for analysis. Frequency Calculation: Determining the frequency of each unique value or bin in the dataset. Cumulative Frequency Calculation: Summing the frequencies from the lowest value up to the current value. Visualization: Representing the cumulative frequencies graphically, often using an ogive curve. Interpretation: Drawing insights and conclusions based on the cumulative frequency distribution.

Benefits: Threshold Identification: Helps in identifying appropriate thresholds for decision-making in AI models. Outlier Detection: Facilitates the identification of outliers by observing deviations from the expected distribution. Data Understanding: Provides a clear understanding of the distribution and spread of data within a dataset. Risk Assessment: Enables the assessment of risks associated with different data values or ranges. Feature Engineering: Informs the selection and transformation of features for AI models.

Examples: Fraud Detection: Analyzing the cumulative frequency of transaction amounts to identify unusual spending patterns. Anomaly Detection: Identifying anomalies in sensor data by analyzing the cumulative frequency of sensor readings. Credit Risk Assessment: Analyzing the cumulative frequency of credit scores to determine risk levels. Natural Language Processing: Analyzing the cumulative frequency of word occurrences in a text corpus. Image Processing: Analyzing the cumulative frequency of pixel intensities in an image.

Applications: Risk Management: Assessing and managing risks in financial and insurance applications. Anomaly Detection: Identifying unusual patterns in various types of data. Quality Control: Monitoring and controlling the quality of products or processes. Environmental Monitoring: Analyzing environmental data to detect trends and anomalies. Resource Allocation: Optimizing the allocation of resources based on data distribution.

Industries: Finance: Risk management, fraud detection, credit scoring. Manufacturing: Quality control, predictive maintenance. Environmental Science: Climate modeling, pollution monitoring.Healthcare: Patient monitoring, disease diagnosis.Cybersecurity: Anomaly detection, threat analysis.

Conclusions: Cumulative frequency analysis is a valuable technique in AI for understanding data distributions, identifying thresholds, and informing decision-making. While it offers several benefits, it's important to be aware of its limitations and challenges. Integrating this method with other analytical techniques and domain expertise can enhance its effectiveness in various AI applications and industries.

Curation AI

Definition: Curation AI refers to the application of artificial intelligence techniques to automate or enhance the process of selecting, organizing, and presenting information or content. This involves using AI to filter, categorize, and recommend relevant content to users, improving efficiency and personalization in information access and management.

Key Components: Data Ingestion: Gathering content from various sources, such as websites, databases, or social media. Content Analysis: Using AI techniques like natural language processing and computer vision to understand the content. Filtering and Categorization: Applying AI algorithms to filter out irrelevant content and categorize the remaining content based on topics, themes, or user preferences. Recommendation Systems: Employing AI to suggest content that is likely to be of interest to specific users. Personalization: Tailoring the curated content to individual user needs and preferences.

Benefits: Efficiency: Automates the time-consuming process of sifting through large volumes of information. Personalization: Delivers content that is specifically relevant to individual users. Improved User Experience: Enhances the user's ability to find valuable information quickly and easily. Content Discovery: Helps users discover new and relevant content they might not otherwise find. Scalability: Enables the management and curation of vast amounts of information.

Examples: News Aggregators: AI-powered platforms that collect and curate news articles from various sources. Social Media Feeds: Algorithms that filter and personalize the content displayed in user feeds. E-commerce Recommendation Engines: AI systems that suggest products to users based on their browsing history and preferences. Content Management Systems: AI tools that help organize and categorize digital assets. Educational Platforms: AI systems that curate learning materials and recommend courses to students.

Applications: Information Retrieval: Enhancing search engines and digital libraries. Content Management: Organizing and managing digital content for businesses and organizations. Personalized Learning: Curating educational resources for students. E-commerce: Recommending products and personalizing shopping experiences. Social Media: Filtering content and personalizing user feeds.

Industries: Technology: Development of AI-powered curation tools and platforms. Media and Entertainment: Content recommendation and personalization. Education: Online learning platforms and personalized education. Retail: E-commerce and personalized marketing. Information Services: News aggregators and research platforms.

Conclusions: Curation AI is a transformative technology that enhances the way we access and manage information. By automating and personalizing the curation process, it improves efficiency and user experience. While challenges related to bias, quality control, and transparency need to be addressed, the benefits of curation AI make it a valuable tool across various industries, contributing to more efficient and personalized information access.

Current AI

Definition: Current AI refers to the existing state of artificial intelligence technology, encompassing the algorithms, models, and systems that are currently being developed, deployed, and utilized across various domains. It reflects the capabilities and limitations of AI as of the present time.

Key Components: Machine Learning: The dominant paradigm, including supervised, unsupervised, and reinforcement learning. Deep Learning: A subset of machine learning utilizing artificial neural networks with multiple layers. Natural Language Processing: Enabling computers to understand and process human language. Computer Vision: Allowing computers to interpret and understand visual information. Robotics: Integrating AI with physical systems to perform tasks autonomously. Big Data: The vast datasets that fuel the training and improvement of AI models. Cloud Computing: Providing the infrastructure and resources for AI development and deployment.

Benefits: Automation: Automating repetitive tasks, increasing efficiency and productivity. Personalization: Tailoring experiences and recommendations to individual users. Improved Decision-Making: Providing data-driven insights for better decision-making. Enhanced Accuracy: Reducing errors and improving the precision of various processes. Innovation: Driving innovation across industries through new applications and solutions.

Examples: Virtual Assistants: Siri, Alexa, and Google Assistant. Recommendation Systems: Netflix, Amazon, and Spotify. Autonomous Vehicles: Self-driving cars and trucks. Fraud Detection: AI systems used by banks and financial institutions. Medical Diagnosis: AI tools assisting doctors in diagnosing diseases.

Applications: Healthcare: Diagnosis, drug discovery, personalized treatment. Finance: Fraud detection, algorithmic trading, risk management. Retail: Recommendation systems, personalized marketing, supply chain optimization. Transportation: Autonomous vehicles, traffic management. Education: Personalized learning, intelligent tutoring systems.

Challenges: Bias: AI models can inherit and amplify biases present in the training data. Explainability: Understanding how complex AI models arrive at their decisions can be difficult. Data Requirements: Many AI models require large amounts of high-quality data. Security: AI systems are vulnerable to adversarial attacks and data breaches. Ethical Concerns: Issues related to privacy, job displacement, and the potential misuse of AI.

Conclusions: Current AI represents a significant advancement in technology, offering numerous benefits across various sectors. However, it also presents challenges related to bias, explainability, and ethical considerations. Continued research, development, and responsible deployment are crucial for harnessing the full potential of AI while mitigating its risks.

Custom AI Chips

Definition: Custom AI chips are specialized microprocessors designed specifically to accelerate artificial intelligence workloads, such as machine learning training and inference. Unlike general-purpose CPUs and GPUs, these chips are optimized for the unique computational demands of AI algorithms.

Key Components: Architecture: Tailored for matrix operations, neural network layers, and dataflow optimization. Memory: High-bandwidth memory (HBM) for fast data access. Interconnects: High-speed interconnects to facilitate efficient data transfer between processing units. Power Efficiency: Designed for optimal performance per watt to reduce energy consumption. Software Support: Specialized compilers and libraries to enable efficient use of the hardware.

Benefits: Performance: Significantly faster AI processing compared to general-purpose hardware. Efficiency: Lower power consumption and reduced operational costs. Customization: Tailored to specific AI workloads and application requirements. Scalability: Enables the deployment of AI in resource-constrained environments. Innovation: Drives innovation in AI hardware and software co-design.

Examples: Google's Tensor Processing Units (TPUs). Nvidia's Tensor Cores. Amazon's Inferentia and Trainium. Apple's Neural Engine. Graphcore's Intelligence Processing Units (IPUs).

Applications: Cloud Computing: Accelerating AI services in data centers. Edge Computing: Enabling on-device AI processing in smartphones, IoT devices, and autonomous vehicles. Autonomous Vehicles: Real-time processing of sensor data for navigation and safety. Healthcare: Accelerating medical image analysis and drug discovery. Robotics: Enabling advanced perception and control for robots.

Challenges: Development Cost: Designing and manufacturing custom chips is expensive and time-consuming. Software Ecosystem: Developing and maintaining software that can effectively utilize custom hardware. Flexibility: Custom chips are often optimized for specific AI tasks, limiting their flexibility. Market Adoption: The market for custom AI chips is still evolving, and adoption can be challenging. Rapid Evolution: The field of AI is rapidly evolving, requiring continuous adaptation of hardware designs.

Conclusions: Custom AI chips are crucial for advancing the capabilities and efficiency of artificial intelligence. By optimizing hardware for AI workloads, they enable faster processing, lower power consumption, and greater scalability. While challenges exist, the trend towards specialized hardware is essential for realizing the full potential of AI across various applications and industries.

Custom Neural Networks

Definition: Custom neural networks are artificial neural networks specifically designed and tailored to address a particular problem or application. Unlike pre-trained or off-the-shelf models, custom networks are developed from the ground up, allowing for greater control over architecture, parameters, and training data.

Key Components: Architecture Design: Selecting the appropriate layers, connections, and activation functions based on the problem. Parameter Initialization: Setting initial values for the network's weights and biases. Training Data: Curating and preparing a dataset relevant to the specific task. Training Process: Optimizing the network's parameters using algorithms like backpropagation. Evaluation Metrics: Defining criteria to assess the performance of the trained network.

Benefits: Optimization: Tailored to the specific task, potentially achieving higher accuracy and efficiency. Flexibility: Allows for experimentation with novel architectures and techniques. Control: Provides greater control over the training process and model behavior. Interpretability: Custom networks can be designed with interpretability in mind, making their decisions easier to understand. Adaptability: Can be adapted to unique data characteristics and application requirements.

Examples: Networks designed for specific medical imaging tasks. Networks tailored for niche natural language processing applications. Networks optimized for real-time control in robotics. Networks built for specific types of time-series data analysis. Networks designed for novel reinforcement learning environments.

Applications: Specialized Medical Imaging: Detecting rare diseases or anomalies in medical scans. Niche NLP Tasks: Sentiment analysis for specific domains or languages. Robotics Control: Developing networks for precise and efficient robot movements. Custom Anomaly Detection: Identifying unusual patterns in specific types of data. Unique Recommendation Systems: Building systems for specialized product or content categories.

Challenges: Development Time: Designing, training, and tuning custom networks can be time-consuming. Expertise Required: Requires specialized knowledge in neural network design and training. Data Requirements: Often requires large, high-quality datasets specific to the problem. Overfitting: Custom networks can be prone to overfitting the training data if not carefully designed and regularized. Computational Resources: Training complex custom networks can be computationally intensive.

Conclusions: Custom neural networks offer a powerful approach to solving specific problems by tailoring the network architecture and training process. While they require expertise and resources, the potential for optimization, flexibility, and control makes them valuable in various specialized applications. As the field evolves, custom neural networks will continue to play a crucial role in pushing the boundaries of AI capabilities.

Definition: Customer behavior analytics (CBA) is the process of using artificial intelligence and data analysis techniques to understand and predict customer actions, preferences, and needs. This involves collecting and analyzing data on customer interactions, transactions, and demographics to gain insights into their behavior patters.

Customer Behavior Analytics

Key Components: Data Collection: Gathering data from various sources, including website interactions, purchase history, social media activity, and customer surveys. Data Processing: Cleaning, transforming, and organizing the collected data for analysis. AI Algorithms: Employing machine learning models to identify patterns and predict future behavior. Segmentation: Grouping customers based on shared characteristics or behaviors. Predictive Modeling: Developing models to forecast customer actions, such as purchases or churn. Visualization: Presenting insights in an understandable format, such as dashboards and reports.

Benefits: Personalization: Tailoring products, services, and marketing efforts to individual customer preferences. Improved Customer Experience: Anticipating customer needs and providing proactive support. Increased Sales: Identifying opportunities for cross-selling and upselling. Reduced Churn: Identifying customers at risk of leaving and taking proactive retention measures. Enhanced Marketing Effectiveness: Optimizing marketing campaigns based on customer behavior insights.

Examples: Recommendation engines suggesting products based on purchase history. Predictive models identifying customers likely to churn. Sentiment analysis of customer reviews to understand satisfaction levels. Personalized email marketing campaigns based on browsing behavior. Customer segmentation for targeted advertising.

Applications: E-commerce: Personalized product recommendations, targeted advertising. Retail: In-store customer behavior analysis, loyalty programs. Finance: Fraud detection, personalized banking services. Telecommunications: Churn prediction, personalized service offerings. Marketing: Targeted advertising, customer segmentation, campaign optimization.

Challenges: Data Privacy: Ensuring compliance with data privacy regulations and protecting customer data. Data Quality: Ensuring the accuracy and completeness of customer data. Integration: Integrating data from various sources can be complex. Interpretation: Translating data insights into actionable strategies. Ethical Considerations: Avoiding biases in data analysis and ensuring fair treatment of customers.

Conclusions: Customer behavior analytics is a powerful tool for businesses to gain a deeper understanding of their customers, enabling them to personalize experiences, improve customer satisfaction, and drive business growth. While challenges related to data privacy and quality exist, the insights gained from CBA are invaluable for staying competitive and building strong customer relationships.

Cyberattack Prediction Using AI

Definition: Cyberattack prediction using AI involves employing artificial intelligence techniques to analyze network traffic, system logs, and other relevant data to identify patterns and anomalies that may indicate an impending cyberattack. This proactive approach aims to detect threats before they can cause significant damage.

Key Components: Data Collection: Gathering data from network devices, servers, endpoints, and security systems. Data Preprocessing: Cleaning and transforming the collected data to prepare it for analysis. Anomaly Detection: Using AI algorithms to identify deviations from normal network behavior. Pattern Recognition: Identifying known attack patterns and signatures in the data. Predictive Modeling: Developing models to forecast the likelihood and type of future attacks. Alerting and Response: Generating alerts and triggering automated responses when potential threats are detected.

Benefits: Proactive Defense: Detecting threats before they can cause significant damage. Reduced Downtime: Minimizing the impact of cyberattacks on business operations. Improved Security Posture: Strengthening overall cybersecurity defenses. Efficient Resource Allocation: Focusing security efforts on the most likely threats. Enhanced Threat Intelligence: Gaining insights into emerging attack trends and techniques.

Examples: AI systems analyzing network traffic for unusual patterns. Machine learning models predicting the likelihood of phishing attacks. Behavioral analysis to detect compromised user accounts. AI-driven threat intelligence platforms identifying emerging vulnerabilities. Systems predicting the timing and type of potential DDoS attacks.

Applications: Network Security: Monitoring network traffic and identifying malicious activity. Endpoint Security: Detecting threats on individual devices. Threat Intelligence: Analyzing data to identify and understand emerging threats. Security Operations Centers (SOCs): Automating threat detection and response. Critical Infrastructure Protection: Securing essential systems and networks.

Challenges: Data Volume and Velocity: Processing the massive amounts of data generated by modern networks. Evolving Threats: Cybercriminals constantly develop new attack techniques. False Positives: AI systems can sometimes generate false alarms, requiring manual review. Model Training: Keeping AI models up-to-date with the latest threat information. Integration with Existing Systems: Integrating AI-powered prediction with existing security infrastructure.

Conclusions: Cyberattack prediction using AI is a critical tool for enhancing cybersecurity defenses. By proactively identifying potential threats, organizations can mitigate risks, reduce downtime, and improve their overall security posture. While challenges related to data volume and evolving threats exist, the benefits of AI-driven prediction make it an essential component of modern cybersecurity strategies.

Cybersecurity Incident Response AI

Definition: Cybersecurity incident response AI refers to the application of artificial intelligence techniques to automate and enhance the process of responding to cybersecurity incidents. This involves using AI to detect, analyze, and mitigate threats more efficiently and effectively than traditional methods.

Key Components: Threat Detection: AI algorithms analyze network traffic, system logs, and other data to identify potential security incidents. Incident Analysis: AI tools help security analysts understand the nature and scope of an incident, including identifying affected systems and potential impact. Automated Response: AI can trigger automated responses to certain types of incidents, such as isolating infected systems or blocking malicious traffic. Orchestration: AI can coordinate different security tools and processes to streamline the incident response workflow. Learning and Adaptation: AI models learn from past incidents to improve future detection and response capabilities.

Benefits: Faster Response Times: AI can detect and respond to incidents much faster than human analysts. Improved Accuracy: AI can analyze large volumes of data and identify subtle indicators of compromise that humans might miss. Reduced Workload: Automation reduces the workload on security teams, allowing them to focus on more complex tasks. Enhanced Efficiency: AI streamlines the incident response process, leading to more efficient and effective incident handling. Continuous Improvement: AI systems continuously learn and adapt, improving their ability to handle future incidents.

Examples: AI-powered security information and event management (SIEM) systems that automatically detect and respond to threats. AI tools that analyze malware behavior and generate automated response strategies. Platforms that use AI to orchestrate incident response workflows across different security tools. Systems that learn from past incidents to predict and prevent future attacks. AI-driven threat hunting tools that proactively search for hidden threats in the network.

Applications: Security Operations Centers (SOCs): Automating and enhancing incident response capabilities. Managed Security Service Providers (MSSPs): Providing AI-powered incident response services to clients. Large Enterprises: Improving the efficiency and effectiveness of their internal security teams. Government Agencies: Protecting critical infrastructure from cyber threats. Financial Institutions: Responding to and preventing cyberattacks that could impact financial systems.

Conclusions: Cybersecurity incident response AI is a critical technology for modern security operations. By automating and enhancing the incident response process, AI helps organizations detect, analyze, and mitigate threats more effectively. While challenges related to integration and explainability exist, the benefits of faster response times and improved accuracy make AI an essential component of a robust cybersecurity strategy.

Cybersecurity Mesh AI

Definition: Cybersecurity Mesh AI refers to the application of artificial intelligence to enhance and manage a cybersecurity mesh architecture. A cybersecurity mesh is a distributed architectural approach that focuses on securing individual access points and assets, rather than relying on a traditional perimeter-based security model. AI plays a crucial role in managing the complexity and dynamic nature of a mesh architecture.

Key Components: Identity and Access Management (IAM): AI is used to enhance identity verification, access control, and privileged access management. Endpoint Security: AI analyzes endpoint behavior to detect and respond to threats. Data Security: AI helps classify and protect sensitive data across the distributed mesh. Network Security: AI monitors and analyzes network traffic at various points within the mesh to detect anomalies. Threat Intelligence: AI aggregates and analyzes threat intelligence data to inform security policies and responses within the mesh. Policy Enforcement: AI helps enforce security policies consistently across the distributed mesh architecture.

Benefits: Enhanced Security: AI improves the ability to detect and respond to threats in a distributed environment. Increased Visibility: AI provides greater visibility into security posture across the mesh. Improved Efficiency: AI automates many security tasks, reducing the workload on security teams. Scalability: AI helps manage the complexity of a large and distributed security infrastructure. Adaptive Security: AI enables the security mesh to adapt dynamically to changing threat landscapes.

Examples: AI-powered IAM systems that use behavioral biometrics to enhance identity verification. Endpoint security solutions that use machine learning to detect zero-day attacks. Data loss prevention (DLP) systems that use AI to classify and protect sensitive data. Network security tools that use AI to detect and block advanced threats. Threat intelligence platforms that use AI to provide actionable insights for the mesh.

Applications: Organizations with distributed networks and cloud environments. Companies adopting a zero-trust security model. Businesses looking to enhance their overall cybersecurity posture. Industries with strict regulatory requirements for data protection. Enterprises seeking to improve the efficiency and effectiveness of their security operations.

Challenges: Complexity of Implementation: Deploying and managing a cybersecurity mesh can be complex. Data Integration: Integrating security tools and data sources across the mesh. Skill Requirements: Requires specialized expertise in AI and cybersecurity mesh architectures. Performance Overhead: AI analysis can sometimes introduce performance overhead. Trust in AI: Ensuring the reliability and trustworthiness of AI systems used in the mesh.

Conclusions: Cybersecurity Mesh AI is a vital component for securing modern, distributed environments. By leveraging AI, organizations can effectively manage the complexity of a cybersecurity mesh, enhance threat detection and response, and improve their overall security posture. While challenges related to implementation and expertise exist, the benefits of adaptive security and improved visibility make AI an essential element of a robust cybersecurity mesh architecture.

Cybersecurity Risk Assessment AI

Definition: Cybersecurity risk assessment AI refers to the application of artificial intelligence techniques to automate and enhance the process of identifying, analyzing, and evaluating cybersecurity risks. This involves using AI to assess vulnerabilities, predict potential threats, and prioritize mitigation efforts to protect an organization's assets.

Key Components: Vulnerability Scanning: AI algorithms analyze systems and networks to identify potential weaknesses and vulnerabilities. Threat Intelligence Analysis: AI processes threat intelligence data to understand emerging threats and attack patterns. Asset Inventory and Prioritization: AI helps identify and prioritize critical assets based on their value and potential impact of compromise. Risk Modeling and Prediction: AI models are used to predict the likelihood and potential impact of cyber threats. Risk Scoring and Prioritization: AI assigns risk scores to identified vulnerabilities and threats, helping organizations prioritize mitigation efforts. Reporting and Visualization: AI generates reports and visualizations to communicate risk assessment findings to stakeholders.

Benefits: Automation: AI automates the time-consuming process of risk assessment, saving time and resources. Improved Accuracy: AI can analyze large volumes of data and identify subtle indicators of risk that humans might miss. Continuous Monitoring: AI enables continuous monitoring of the threat landscape and adapts risk assessments accordingly. Scalability: AI can handle the complexity of assessing risks in large and distributed environments. Proactive Risk Management: AI helps organizations proactively identify and address risks before they can be exploited.

Examples: AI-powered vulnerability assessment tools that automatically scan systems and networks for weaknesses. Threat intelligence platforms that use AI to analyze and prioritize emerging threats. Risk management systems that use AI to model and predict potential cyber risks. AI tools that help organizations prioritize remediation efforts based on risk scores. Platforms that provide real-time risk assessments based on continuous monitoring of security data.

Applications: Organizations of all sizes seeking to improve their cybersecurity posture. Industries with strict regulatory requirements for data protection. Companies looking to optimize their security investments by focusing on the highest risks. Managed Security Service Providers (MSSPs) offering AI-powered risk assessment services. Government agencies responsible for protecting critical infrastructure.

Conclusions: Cybersecurity risk assessment AI is a valuable tool for organizations looking to proactively manage their cyber risks. By automating and enhancing the risk assessment process, AI helps organizations identify, prioritize, and mitigate threats more effectively. While challenges related to data quality and explainability exist, the benefits of improved accuracy and continuous monitoring make AI an essential component of a comprehensive cybersecurity strategy.

LETTER D

Data Analytics

Data analytics is the process of collecting, processing, and analyzing raw data to extract meaningful insights, identify patterns, and support decision-making. By leveraging statistical methods, machine learning, and AI-driven automation, data analytics transforms complex information into actionable knowledge. Businesses, governments, and researchers use data analytics to optimize operations, improve customer experiences, and drive innovation in various industries.

Key Components

Data Collection gathers structured and unstructured data from multiple sources, including databases, sensors, and online platforms.
Data Processing cleans, transforms, and organizes data to ensure accuracy and consistency for analysis.
Statistical Analysis applies mathematical models and algorithms to interpret trends, relationships, and correlations within datasets.
Predictive Modeling uses AI and machine learning to forecast future trends and behaviors based on historical data.
Data Visualization presents insights through graphs, dashboards, and reports to enhance understanding and decision-making.

Examples

Retail and E-Commerce data analytics helps businesses personalize customer recommendations, optimize pricing, and predict demand.
Healthcare AI-driven analytics supports disease prediction, patient monitoring, and medical research by analyzing health records.
Financial Services banks and investment firms use data analytics for fraud detection, risk assessment, and portfolio management.
Manufacturing predictive analytics improves supply chain efficiency, equipment maintenance, and production planning.

Challenges

Data Quality inaccurate, incomplete, or biased data can lead to incorrect insights and flawed decision-making.
Privacy and Security handling sensitive data requires strict compliance with regulations and cybersecurity measures.
Scalability managing and analyzing large datasets demands high computational power and advanced infrastructure.
Integration Complexity organizations must integrate data analytics tools with existing systems for seamless operations.

Benefits

Improved Decision-Making data-driven insights enhance strategic planning, operational efficiency, and customer engagement.
Cost Optimization AI-powered analytics reduces waste, streamlines processes, and improves resource allocation.
Competitive Advantage businesses gain a market edge by leveraging data analytics to understand trends and consumer behavior.
Automation and Efficiency AI-driven analytics automates repetitive tasks, improving productivity and reducing human error.

Conclusion: Data analytics is a powerful tool that enables organizations to extract value from data, driving innovation and efficiency across industries. By using AI, statistical analysis, and predictive modeling, businesses can make informed decisions and gain a deeper understanding of trends and behaviors. Despite challenges related to data security, scalability, and integration, continuous advancements in data analytics technology are making it an essential component of modern business intelligence and strategic growth.

Data Augmentation

Data augmentation is an AI-driven technique used to artificially expand and enhance datasets by applying transformations, modifications, or synthetic data generation. It improves machine learning model performance by increasing data diversity, reducing overfitting, and making models more robust. Data augmentation is widely used in computer vision, natural language processing, and speech recognition to improve the generalization ability of AI systems.

Key Components

Data Transformation applies modifications such as rotation, scaling, cropping, and flipping to images or data samples to create variations.
Synthetic Data Generation creates new training examples using generative models, simulations, or interpolation techniques.
Noise Injection introduces controlled noise or distortions to improve model adaptability to real-world data inconsistencies.
Text Augmentation expands textual datasets through paraphrasing, synonym replacement, and back-translation techniques.
Domain-Specific Augmentation applies custom transformations suited to specific industries, such as medical imaging and autonomous driving.

Examples

Image Recognition AI uses augmented image datasets to improve facial recognition, object detection, and classification accuracy.

Speech Processing data augmentation techniques modify pitch, speed, and background noise to train more resilient voice recognition models.
Natural Language Processing AI expands text datasets by generating variations of sentences for improved language model training.
Medical AI synthetic augmentation techniques help enhance limited medical imaging datasets for better disease detection models.

Challenges

Data Integrity excessive augmentation can introduce unrealistic variations, leading to poor model generalization.
Computational Cost generating augmented data for large datasets requires additional processing power and storage.
Balancing Augmentation improper application of augmentation techniques may distort original data distributions, affecting model accuracy.
Application-Specific Requirements different AI tasks require tailored augmentation strategies to ensure effectiveness and relevance.

Benefits

Improved Model Generalization AI models trained with augmented data perform better on unseen, real-world examples.
Reduction of Overfitting artificial data expansion prevents models from memorizing training data, leading to more robust learning.
Efficient Use of Limited Data augmentation helps overcome data scarcity by creating diverse training samples from existing datasets.
Cost-Effective Solution synthetic data generation reduces the need for costly and time-consuming manual data collection.

Conclusion: Data augmentation enhances AI model performance by increasing dataset diversity, reducing overfitting, and improving adaptability to real-world conditions. Through transformations, synthetic generation, and noise injection, AI can learn more effectively from limited data. While challenges such as computational costs and maintaining data integrity exist, advancements in AI-driven augmentation techniques continue to refine and optimize data enhancement strategies across various domains.

Data Capture

Data capture is the process of collecting and digitizing information from various sources for storage, analysis, and processing. Using AI, machine learning, and automation, data capture extracts valuable insights from documents, images, sensors, and human inputs. This technology streamlines workflows, enhances data accuracy, and supports decision-making across industries by converting unstructured data into structured, machine-readable formats.

Key Components

Optical Character Recognition extracts text from scanned documents, printed materials, and handwritten notes.
Automated Data Entry reduces manual input by using AI to capture and organize information from forms and databases.
Real-Time Processing enables immediate data capture from digital transactions, IoT devices, and live monitoring systems.
Integration with Enterprise Systems allows data capture solutions to connect with databases, cloud storage, and analytics platforms.

Quality Control and Validation ensure data accuracy by detecting errors, inconsistencies, and missing information during capture.

Examples

Banking and Finance data capture automates the processing of checks, invoices, and transaction records.
Healthcare AI extracts patient information from medical forms, prescriptions, and diagnostic reports.
Retail and E-commerce AI-driven data capture collects customer preferences, purchase history, and inventory details.
Manufacturing IoT-powered data capture monitors equipment performance and production metrics in real time.

Benefits

Improved Efficiency automating data collection reduces manual effort, accelerating business processes.
Enhanced Accuracy AI-driven validation minimizes errors and ensures reliable data for decision-making.
Cost Reduction reducing manual data entry lowers operational costs and improves resource allocation.
Better Compliance automated data capture ensures regulatory compliance by maintaining accurate records.

Conclusion

Data capture is a critical AI-powered process that converts raw information into actionable digital data for businesses and organizations. By leveraging automation, OCR, and real-time processing, data capture enhances efficiency, accuracy, and scalability. Despite challenges such as data quality and security concerns, continuous advancements in AI and machine learning make data capture a fundamental tool for streamlining operations, improving decision-making, and optimizing business workflows.

Data Cleaning

Data cleaning is the process of identifying, correcting, or removing errors, inconsistencies, and inaccuracies from datasets to improve data quality and reliability. It ensures that data is complete, accurate, and properly formatted before being used for analysis, machine learning, or decision-making. By eliminating duplicate, missing, or incorrect values, data cleaning enhances the performance of AI models and business intelligence systems, leading to more precise insights and informed decisions.

Key Components

Error Detection identifies inconsistencies such as typos, formatting issues, and incorrect data entries.
Missing Data Handling fills in missing values using imputation techniques or removes incomplete records to maintain dataset integrity.
Duplicate Removal eliminates redundant records to prevent overrepresentation of data points in analysis.
Data Standardization ensures uniform formatting, structure, and consistency across datasets by normalizing units, dates, and values.
Outlier Detection identifies and addresses extreme values that may distort analysis and machine learning model accuracy.

Examples

Customer Databases businesses clean customer records by correcting misspelled names, merging duplicate profiles, and updating outdated contact details.

Financial Reporting AI ensures financial datasets are accurate by removing inconsistencies in transaction records, preventing errors in reports.
Healthcare Systems medical data cleaning standardizes patient records, ensuring consistency in disease classification and treatment history.
Machine Learning Preprocessing AI models perform better when trained on clean datasets free from missing values, duplicates, and inconsistencies.

Benefits

Improved Data Accuracy clean data enhances decision-making by providing reliable and precise information.
Better AI Model Performance machine learning models trained on well-cleaned data produce more accurate and meaningful predictions.
Efficiency and Cost Savings reducing data errors prevents costly mistakes and improves operational efficiency.
Regulatory Compliance ensuring data accuracy helps businesses comply with industry regulations and avoid legal issues.

Conclusion

Data cleaning is a critical step in data management that improves the accuracy, consistency, and usability of information. By addressing missing values, errors, and inconsistencies, data cleaning enhances AI model performance and business intelligence. While challenges such as data volume and subjectivity exist, advancements in automated data cleaning techniques continue to make the process more efficient, ensuring high-quality data for analysis and decision-making.

Data Compaction

Data compaction is the process of reducing the storage size of data while preserving its essential information and usability. This technique minimizes redundancy, optimizes storage efficiency, and improves data transmission speed without significantly affecting data integrity. Data compaction is widely used in computing, telecommunications, and big data processing to enhance performance and resource utilization.

Key Components

Lossless Compression ensures that data is reduced in size without losing any original information, allowing for perfect reconstruction.
Lossy Compression reduces data size by removing non-essential details, commonly used in multimedia applications like audio and video files.
Encoding Techniques apply algorithms such as Huffman coding, run-length encoding, and dictionary-based methods to minimize data redundancy.
Storage Optimization reorganizes data structures to occupy less space while maintaining accessibility and retrieval efficiency.
Real-Time Processing enables data compaction to be applied dynamically during data transmission, improving network performance and efficiency.

Examples

Cloud Storage data compaction reduces file sizes, optimizing storage capacity and retrieval speeds for cloud services.
Multimedia Streaming video and audio files use lossy compression techniques to enable smooth streaming with minimal bandwidth usage.
Database Management AI-powered data compaction techniques improve database performance by

reducing indexing and query processing times.
IoT Devices compacted data allows for efficient storage and transmission in low-power, bandwidth-limited environments.

Benefits

Storage Efficiency reducing data size optimizes storage resources, lowering hardware costs and improving capacity utilization.
Faster Transmission compacted data enhances transfer speeds over networks, reducing latency and improving communication efficiency.
Improved System Performance optimizing data structures accelerates query execution and application responsiveness.
Scalability compacted data allows for efficient handling of large datasets, making it easier to manage growing volumes of information.

Conclusion

Data compaction plays a vital role in optimizing storage, transmission, and processing efficiency across various industries. By leveraging compression algorithms and encoding techniques, organizations can manage large datasets more effectively while improving system performance. Despite challenges related to data quality, computational demands, and compatibility, advancements in AI-driven data compaction continue to enhance its effectiveness, making it an essential tool for modern computing and data management.

Data Compression

Data compression is the process of reducing the size of digital data to optimize storage, transmission, and processing efficiency. By eliminating redundancy and applying encoding techniques, data compression minimizes the space required to store or transfer information while maintaining its usability. It is widely used in computer systems, telecommunications, and multimedia applications to improve performance and reduce bandwidth consumption.

Key Components

Lossless Compression reduces data size without any loss of information, ensuring that the original data can be perfectly reconstructed.
Lossy Compression achieves higher compression ratios by discarding non-essential data, commonly used in audio, video, and image processing.
Encoding Algorithms apply mathematical models such as Huffman coding, Lempel-Ziv-Welch (LZW), and arithmetic coding to efficiently reduce data redundancy.
Compression Ratio measures the effectiveness of compression by comparing the size of the original data to the compressed version.
Decompression reconstructs the original data from its compressed form, ensuring data integrity and usability.

Examples

File Storage compression formats such as ZIP and RAR reduce file sizes, enabling efficient storage and transfer.
Streaming Services audio and video compression techniques, such as MP3 and H.264, enable smooth streaming with minimal bandwidth usage.
Data Transmission network protocols use compression to optimize data transfer speeds and reduce congestion.

Big Data Analytics AI-powered compression techniques allow large datasets to be stored and processed more efficiently in cloud computing environments.

Benefits

Optimized Storage reducing data size minimizes hardware costs and improves data management efficiency.
Faster Transmission compressed data speeds up network communication, reducing latency and improving performance.
Enhanced Performance efficient data compression improves system responsiveness and accelerates processing in applications such as AI and machine learning.
Scalability compression enables businesses to manage large volumes of data more effectively, supporting digital transformation and growth.

Conclusion

Data compression is a fundamental technology that enhances storage, communication, and processing efficiency across various domains. By utilizing advanced encoding techniques, businesses and industries can reduce data redundancy while maintaining quality and performance. Despite challenges such as data loss and processing overhead, continuous advancements in AI-driven compression methods are making data management more efficient, scalable, and adaptable to modern computing demands.

Data-Driven AI

Data-driven AI refers to artificial intelligence systems that rely on large volumes of data to learn, make predictions, and improve decision-making. These systems use machine learning, deep learning, and statistical models to identify patterns, extract insights, and automate complex tasks. The effectiveness of data-driven AI depends on the quality, diversity, and quantity of data it processes, making data collection, processing, and analysis essential components of AI development.

Key Components

Data Collection gathers structured and unstructured data from multiple sources, including sensors, online platforms, and databases.
Machine Learning Algorithms analyze data, recognize patterns, and generate predictions based on training datasets.
Feature Engineering selects and optimizes relevant data attributes to improve AI model performance.
Data Processing cleans, transforms, and organizes data to ensure accuracy, consistency, and usability for AI models.
Model Training uses historical and real-time data to refine AI systems, allowing them to adapt and improve over time.

Examples

Healthcare AI analyzes medical records, diagnostic images, and genetic data to improve disease detection and treatment recommendations.
Financial Services AI models predict stock market trends, detect fraudulent transactions, and automate credit scoring.
Retail and E-commerce AI-driven recommendations personalize shopping experiences based on customer behavior and purchase history.
Autonomous Systems self-driving vehicles process real-time sensor data to navigate, detect obstacles, and make driving decisions.

Benefits

Improved Decision-Making AI-driven insights enhance efficiency, accuracy, and effectiveness across various industries.
Automation AI automates repetitive and complex tasks, reducing human effort and increasing productivity.
Adaptability AI systems continuously learn from new data, making them more responsive to changing environments.
Scalability data-driven AI solutions grow with expanding datasets, making them ideal for large-scale applications.

Conclusion

Data-driven AI is transforming industries by enabling machines to analyze vast amounts of data and make intelligent decisions. By leveraging machine learning and deep learning, AI enhances automation, efficiency, and predictive capabilities. Despite challenges related to data quality, privacy, and interpretability, continuous advancements in AI and data science are improving the reliability and impact of data-driven AI, making it a critical component of modern technological innovation.

Data Engineering

Data engineering is the process of designing, building, and managing the infrastructure that enables efficient data collection, storage, and processing for analytics and machine learning. It focuses on creating robust data pipelines, ensuring data quality, and optimizing data workflows to support AI and business intelligence applications. Data engineering is essential for transforming raw data into structured formats that can be used for decision-making, automation, and predictive modeling.

Key Components

Data Pipeline Development automates the extraction, transformation, and loading (ETL) of data from various sources into storage and analytics systems.
Database Management organizes and maintains structured and unstructured data in relational and NoSQL databases to enable fast and efficient queries.
Data Integration merges data from multiple sources, ensuring consistency, accuracy, and accessibility across systems.
Big Data Processing leverages distributed computing technologies such as Hadoop and Spark to handle large-scale datasets.
Data Governance implements policies and standards to ensure data security, compliance, and proper usage within organizations.

Examples

Finance data engineering enables real-time fraud detection by processing transaction data and detecting anomalies.
E-commerce AI-driven recommendation systems use engineered data pipelines to analyze customer preferences and optimize product suggestions.
Healthcare structured patient records and diagnostic data allow AI models to assist in medical research and personalized treatments.
Smart Cities sensor data from traffic systems, weather stations, and public utilities is processed to improve urban planning and resource allocation.

Benefits

Optimized Data Workflows automation and efficiency in data pipelines improve business intelligence and AI performance.
Real-Time Analytics processing data in real time enables faster decision-making and responsiveness to

market changes.
Cost Efficiency well-engineered data systems reduce storage costs and minimize redundant processing efforts.
Scalability and Flexibility adaptable infrastructure allows businesses to handle growing data demands without performance degradation.

Conclusion

Data engineering is the foundation of modern data-driven applications, enabling organizations to store, process, and analyze vast amounts of information efficiently. By building scalable pipelines, ensuring data quality, and integrating multiple sources, data engineering supports AI, analytics, and business intelligence. Despite challenges related to security, scalability, and integration, advancements in cloud computing and big data technologies continue to enhance the field, making it indispensable for digital transformation.

Data Governance

Data governance is the framework of policies, standards, and procedures that ensure the effective management, security, and integrity of data within an organization. It establishes guidelines for data usage, compliance, and quality control to ensure that data is accurate, reliable, and accessible. By implementing data governance, businesses and institutions can improve decision-making, protect sensitive information, and ensure regulatory compliance.

Key Components

Data Quality Management ensures that data is accurate, complete, and consistent across systems and processes.
Data Security establishes protocols for protecting sensitive information from unauthorized access, breaches, and cyber threats.
Compliance and Regulatory Adherence aligns data management practices with legal requirements such as GDPR, HIPAA, and CCPA.
Metadata Management maintains detailed descriptions of data assets, including origin, structure, and relationships, for better data traceability.
Roles and Responsibilities assigns ownership and accountability to data stewards, administrators, and users to maintain governance policies.

Examples

Financial Services data governance helps banks and financial institutions ensure compliance with regulatory requirements and fraud prevention.
Healthcare hospitals and medical organizations use governance frameworks to secure patient records and maintain data accuracy.
Retail businesses leverage governance policies to manage customer data, optimize marketing strategies, and prevent data misuse.
Government agencies implement data governance to protect citizen information and improve transparency in public services.

Benefits

Improved Data Integrity consistent data governance enhances accuracy, reliability, and trust in data-driven decision-making.
Regulatory Compliance ensures organizations meet legal and industry standards, reducing risks of penalties and legal issues.
Enhanced Security strong governance frameworks protect data from breaches, unauthorized

modifications, and cyber threats.
Operational Efficiency clear data policies streamline workflows, reducing redundancies and optimizing data management.

Conclusion

Data governance is essential for managing, protecting, and ensuring the quality of data across organizations. By implementing policies that balance security, compliance, and accessibility, businesses can maximize the value of their data while minimizing risks. Although challenges such as data silos and regulatory changes require continuous adaptation, effective data governance strengthens decision-making, improves operational efficiency, and safeguards critical information in an increasingly data-driven world.

Data Imputation

Data imputation is the process of replacing missing or incomplete values in a dataset with estimated or inferred values to maintain data integrity and usability. It prevents information loss and ensures that machine learning models and statistical analyses can operate effectively without bias or inconsistencies caused by missing data. Imputation techniques use mathematical models, statistical methods, or AI-driven approaches to generate realistic replacements for missing values.

Key Components

Missing Data Identification detects gaps in datasets by analyzing patterns and determining the nature of missing values.
Statistical Imputation applies mean, median, mode, or regression-based methods to estimate missing values using existing data distributions.
Machine Learning Imputation leverages AI models to predict missing values based on correlations and feature dependencies.
Multiple Imputation generates several plausible values for missing data, reducing uncertainty and improving accuracy in predictive modeling.
Data Validation ensures that imputed values maintain logical consistency and do not introduce biases or distortions in the dataset.

Examples

Healthcare missing patient vitals in medical records are imputed using historical trends to ensure accurate diagnosis and treatment plans.
Financial Analysis incomplete transaction data is estimated using regression models to maintain the accuracy of financial reports.
Marketing missing customer purchase behaviors are filled in using machine learning models to enhance targeted advertising campaigns.
Survey Data responses left unanswered in questionnaires are imputed using demographic and behavioral similarities to avoid bias.

Benefits

Improved Data Completeness imputation restores missing values, making datasets more comprehensive and useful for analysis.
Enhanced Model Accuracy AI models trained on complete data sets produce more reliable and predictive outcomes.
Bias Reduction properly imputed data minimizes distortions that arise from missing information in statistical studies.

Operational Efficiency automated imputation techniques streamline data preprocessing, reducing manual effort in data management.

Conclusion

Data imputation is a crucial technique for handling missing values and ensuring dataset completeness in data-driven applications. By leveraging statistical and machine learning approaches, imputation minimizes information loss, enhances data integrity, and improves the performance of predictive models. While challenges such as imputation bias and computational complexity remain, advancements in AI and data science continue to refine imputation methods, making them more effective and widely applicable across industries.

Data Leakage

Data leakage occurs when information from outside the intended training dataset is unintentionally introduced into a machine learning model, leading to overly optimistic performance during training but poor generalization to real-world data. This issue distorts model evaluation by allowing it to learn patterns that will not be available in future data, ultimately reducing reliability in deployment. Data leakage can result from improper feature selection, data preprocessing errors, or the inclusion of future information in training sets.

Key Components

Feature Leakage occurs when a model gains access to information that would not be available at prediction time, leading to artificially high accuracy.
Target Leakage happens when variables that directly relate to the outcome are mistakenly included as predictors, causing models to memorize rather than generalize.
Temporal Leakage arises when time-sensitive data from the future is included in a model designed to predict past or present outcomes.
Cross-Validation Errors improper data partitioning can cause test data to be inadvertently used in training, skewing performance metrics.
Unintended Data Sharing occurs when preprocessing pipelines introduce information from test sets into training data, violating data independence principles.

Examples

Financial Modeling including stock prices from future dates in a model predicting market trends leads to inaccurate investment strategies.
Medical Diagnosis using patient outcome data in training before a model makes a prediction results in unreliable AI-powered diagnostics.
Fraud Detection incorporating fraud alerts in training data before a model identifies fraudulent transactions leads to overfitting.
Customer Churn Prediction including future customer actions in the model makes it appear more accurate but fails in real-world deployment.

Benefits

Robust Model Performance preventing data leakage ensures models generalize well to unseen data, improving reliability.
Accurate Decision-Making properly validated models provide trustworthy insights for business, healthcare, and financial applications.
Improved Data Handling strict data governance and pipeline management reduce errors in feature selection and preprocessing.

Enhanced AI Trustworthiness minimizing leakage builds confidence in AI-driven predictions and decision support systems.

Conclusion

Data leakage is a critical issue in machine learning that can severely impact model performance and reliability. By understanding its sources and implementing rigorous data validation techniques, organizations can prevent leakage and ensure accurate predictions. While challenges such as detection complexity and feature selection errors persist, adopting best practices in data handling and model evaluation can mitigate risks and enhance AI model effectiveness across various industries.

Data Mining

Data mining is the process of discovering patterns, relationships, and useful insights from large datasets using artificial intelligence, machine learning, and statistical techniques. It helps organizations analyze vast amounts of structured and unstructured data to uncover hidden trends, predict outcomes, and support decision-making. By transforming raw data into meaningful information, data mining plays a crucial role in business intelligence, scientific research, and automation.

Key Components

Data Preprocessing cleans, integrates, and transforms raw data to ensure accuracy and consistency before analysis.
Pattern Recognition identifies recurring structures, trends, and anomalies within datasets to extract valuable insights.
Machine Learning Algorithms use supervised and unsupervised learning techniques to classify, cluster, and predict data trends.
Association Rule Mining detects relationships between variables, enabling applications like market basket analysis.
Visualization and Interpretation presents data mining results using graphs, charts, and reports for better understanding and decision-making.

Examples

Retail and E-commerce businesses use data mining to analyze customer purchase behavior and optimize product recommendations.
Healthcare AI-driven data mining helps in disease prediction, drug discovery, and personalized treatment planning.
Financial Services fraud detection systems use data mining to identify suspicious transactions and prevent financial crimes.
Manufacturing predictive maintenance models use data mining to analyze machine performance and prevent failures.

Benefits

Enhanced Decision-Making data mining provides actionable insights that improve business strategies and operational efficiency.
Fraud Detection AI-driven mining techniques identify anomalies and suspicious activities in financial transactions and cybersecurity.
Customer Personalization businesses use data mining to tailor marketing campaigns and improve customer engagement.
Automation of Insights automated pattern recognition reduces the need for manual data analysis, saving time and resources.

Conclusion

Data mining is a powerful tool for extracting meaningful insights from large datasets, enabling businesses and researchers to make data-driven decisions. By leveraging AI, machine learning, and statistical techniques, data mining improves efficiency, enhances customer experiences, and strengthens predictive analytics. Despite challenges related to data quality, privacy, and computational demands, continuous advancements in data mining technology are making it an essential component of modern data science and business intelligence.

Data Privacy

Data privacy refers to the protection of personal, sensitive, and confidential information from unauthorized access, misuse, or exposure. It ensures that individuals and organizations have control over how their data is collected, stored, shared, and processed. Data privacy regulations and frameworks help safeguard user rights while maintaining transparency and accountability in data-driven technologies. With the rise of artificial intelligence, cloud computing, and big data analytics, data privacy has become a critical concern for businesses, governments, and individuals.

Key Components

Data Encryption secures information by converting it into unreadable formats, ensuring protection against unauthorized access.
Access Control regulates who can view, modify, or share data, preventing breaches and misuse.
Anonymization removes personally identifiable information from datasets to protect individual identities.
Regulatory Compliance ensures adherence to data protection laws such as GDPR, CCPA, and HIPAA to prevent legal violations.
User Consent Management grants individuals the right to approve or reject data collection and processing activities.

Examples

Healthcare hospitals implement strict data privacy policies to protect patient records and ensure HIPAA compliance.
Financial Services banks use encryption and authentication measures to secure customer transactions and prevent identity theft.
E-commerce businesses anonymize customer data while providing personalized recommendations without compromising privacy.
Social Media platforms allow users to adjust privacy settings to control who can access their personal information.

.Benefits

User Trust strong data privacy measures build confidence in businesses and services by ensuring responsible data handling.
Regulatory Compliance adherence to privacy laws prevents legal penalties and enhances corporate reputation.
Risk Mitigation protecting sensitive data reduces the likelihood of financial losses and security incidents.
Improved Data Security privacy-focused practices strengthen cybersecurity frameworks, preventing unauthorized access and data leaks.

Conclusion

Data privacy is a fundamental aspect of digital security, ensuring that personal and sensitive information remains protected from unauthorized use. By implementing encryption, access control, and regulatory compliance, organizations can safeguard user data while maintaining transparency and trust. Despite challenges such as data breaches and regulatory complexity, advancements in AI-driven security and privacy-preserving techniques continue to improve data protection, making privacy a core consideration in the evolving digital landscape.

Data Processing

Data processing is the systematic collection, transformation, and analysis of raw data to produce meaningful and structured information. It involves various computational techniques to filter, organize, and analyze data for business intelligence, machine learning, and decision-making. Data processing is essential for ensuring accuracy, consistency, and usability in digital systems, enabling organizations to extract valuable insights and improve operational efficiency.

Key Components

Data Collection gathers raw data from multiple sources such as databases, sensors, user inputs, and online platforms.
Data Cleaning removes errors, duplicates, and inconsistencies to ensure data quality and reliability.
Data Transformation converts data into the required format, structure, or scale for analysis and integration with other systems.
Data Analysis applies statistical methods, machine learning models, or business intelligence tools to extract patterns and insights.
Data Storage organizes and securely stores processed data in databases, cloud systems, or data warehouses for easy retrieval.

Examples

Financial Services AI-driven data processing enables real-time fraud detection and risk assessment for banking transactions.
Healthcare patient records are processed to track medical history, predict disease outcomes, and support clinical decision-making.
Retail businesses use data processing to analyze customer preferences, optimize inventory management, and enhance marketing strategies.
Autonomous Vehicles real-time data processing helps self-driving cars interpret sensor inputs and make instant navigation decisions.

Benefits

Enhanced Decision-Making processed data provides actionable insights, enabling businesses to make informed and strategic decisions.
Operational Efficiency automation in data processing reduces manual efforts, improving productivity and resource utilization.
Scalability modern data processing techniques allow organizations to handle increasing data volumes without performance degradation.
Improved Accuracy cleaning and structuring data minimizes errors, ensuring higher precision in analytics and forecasting.

Conclusion

Data processing is a critical function in modern digital systems, enabling the transformation of raw data into valuable insights. By leveraging automation, AI, and advanced computing techniques, organizations can optimize workflows, enhance decision-making, and maintain high data quality. While challenges such as data security, integration, and processing speed exist, continuous advancements in cloud computing, AI, and big data technologies are making data processing more efficient, scalable, and intelligent.

Data Processing Application

A data processing application is a software system designed to collect, manipulate, analyze, and store data to convert raw information into meaningful insights. These applications use computational methods to automate data handling, ensuring accuracy, consistency, and efficiency in various industries. Data processing applications support real-time decision-making, machine learning, and large-scale data management, enabling businesses to optimize operations and improve customer experiences.

Key Components

Data Ingestion gathers raw data from multiple sources such as databases, APIs, IoT devices, and user inputs.
Data Cleaning removes errors, duplicates, and inconsistencies to ensure high-quality and reliable datasets.
Data Transformation converts data into structured formats suitable for analysis, visualization, and storage.
Data Analysis applies statistical algorithms, AI models, and machine learning techniques to extract patterns and insights.
Data Storage securely saves processed data in cloud storage, data warehouses, or distributed databases for future use.

Examples

Financial Systems banking applications use data processing to detect fraudulent transactions, automate loan approvals, and assess credit risks.
Healthcare medical data applications analyze patient records, detect disease patterns, and optimize treatment plans.
Retail and E-Commerce businesses process customer data to personalize recommendations, track inventory, and optimize supply chains.
Autonomous Systems self-driving cars use real-time data processing applications to interpret sensor inputs and make navigation decisions.

Challenges

Data Volume handling massive amounts of data requires scalable infrastructure and efficient processing algorithms.
Security and Privacy ensuring data protection and regulatory compliance is essential to prevent breaches and unauthorized access.
Processing Speed real-time applications need low-latency processing to ensure smooth operations and instant decision-making.
Data Integration combining structured and unstructured data from diverse sources requires seamless interoperability and consistency.

Benefits

Automation and Efficiency data processing applications streamline workflows, reducing manual effort and operational costs.
Improved Accuracy AI-driven data processing enhances precision, minimizing errors in decision-making and analytics.
Scalability modern applications can handle increasing data loads, supporting business growth and evolving demands.

Actionable Insights processed data enables businesses and organizations to make informed, data-driven decisions.

Conclusion

A data processing application is an essential tool for transforming raw data into structured, valuable insights that drive decision-making and operational efficiency. By integrating AI, automation, and scalable storage solutions, these applications support real-time analytics, business intelligence, and industry-specific solutions. Despite challenges related to data security, integration, and processing speed, advancements in cloud computing and machine learning continue to enhance the capabilities of data processing applications, making them indispensable in modern digital ecosystems.

Data Quality

Data quality refers to the accuracy, completeness, consistency, and reliability of data used in decision-making, analytics, and AI applications. High-quality data ensures that insights derived from analysis are meaningful, trustworthy, and actionable. Poor data quality can lead to incorrect predictions, flawed business strategies, and inefficiencies in data-driven processes. Maintaining data quality requires rigorous validation, cleaning, and governance practices to ensure that information remains useful and relevant over time.

Key Components

Accuracy ensures that data correctly represents real-world facts without errors or distortions.
Completeness verifies that all required data points are present and no critical information is missing.
Consistency maintains uniformity across datasets, ensuring that data values do not conflict across different sources.
Timeliness ensures that data is up to date and reflects the most recent and relevant information.
Validity checks that data conforms to predefined formats, rules, and standards for proper usage and interpretation.

Examples

Financial Services banks rely on accurate customer data to process transactions, assess creditworthiness, and detect fraudulent activities.
Healthcare medical records must be complete and error-free to support accurate diagnosis, treatment plans, and patient history tracking.
E-Commerce online retailers use consistent product and customer data to optimize pricing, inventory management, and personalized recommendations.
Manufacturing real-time sensor data must be valid and timely to ensure smooth production processes and predictive maintenance.

Benefits

Improved Decision-Making high-quality data supports accurate analytics, leading to more effective business strategies.
Enhanced AI Performance machine learning models trained on clean, complete, and accurate data produce better predictions and insights.
Regulatory Compliance maintaining data quality ensures adherence to legal and industry standards, reducing risks of non-compliance.
Operational Efficiency reducing errors and inconsistencies in data minimizes rework, saving time and resources.

Conclusion

Data quality is a fundamental requirement for organizations relying on data-driven decision-making, AI, and analytics. By ensuring accuracy, completeness, consistency, and timeliness, businesses can maximize the value of their data while minimizing risks associated with poor-quality information. Despite challenges such as human errors and scalability concerns, advancements in AI, automation, and data governance continue to improve data quality, making it a cornerstone of modern digital ecosystems.

Data Science

Data science is an interdisciplinary field that uses scientific methods, algorithms, and artificial intelligence to extract knowledge and insights from structured and unstructured data. By combining statistics, machine learning, and computational techniques, data science enables businesses and organizations to analyze patterns, predict outcomes, and make data-driven decisions. It plays a crucial role in industries such as healthcare, finance, marketing, and technology by transforming raw data into actionable intelligence.

Key Components

Data Collection gathers data from multiple sources, including databases, IoT devices, and online platforms, to create a comprehensive dataset.
Data Cleaning ensures that data is accurate, complete, and free from errors or inconsistencies before analysis.
Exploratory Data Analysis identifies patterns, correlations, and trends through statistical and visualization techniques.
Machine Learning applies AI algorithms to train models that can classify, predict, and optimize decision-making processes.
Data Visualization presents insights through graphs, charts, and dashboards, making complex data more understandable.

Examples

Healthcare AI-powered data science models analyze medical records and imaging data to detect diseases and recommend treatments.
Finance banks use predictive analytics to assess credit risks, detect fraudulent transactions, and optimize investment strategies.
E-Commerce data science personalizes customer recommendations, optimizes pricing strategies, and predicts demand for products.
Autonomous Vehicles real-time data analysis helps self-driving cars make navigation decisions based on sensor and environmental data.

Benefits

Enhanced Decision-Making data-driven insights enable businesses to optimize operations and improve strategic planning.
Automation AI-powered models reduce manual efforts by automating complex tasks such as fraud detection and anomaly detection.
Competitive Advantage organizations leveraging data science gain deeper market insights and outperform competitors.
Scalability and Adaptability data science techniques can be applied to various industries, making it a flexible and powerful tool for innovation.

Conclusion

Data science is a transformative field that enables organizations to harness the power of data for analysis, prediction, and decision-making. By integrating machine learning, statistical analysis, and data engineering, it provides valuable insights across multiple domains. Despite challenges related to data security, model interpretability, and integration, advancements in AI and cloud computing continue to enhance the capabilities of data science, making it a crucial component of modern technology and business intelligence.

Data Security

Data security refers to the practices, technologies, and policies used to protect digital information from unauthorized access, corruption, or loss. It ensures the confidentiality, integrity, and availability of data by implementing encryption, authentication, access controls, and other security measures. Data security is essential for organizations handling sensitive information such as financial records, personal data, and intellectual property, as it prevents cyber threats and data breaches.

Key Components

Encryption secures data by converting it into unreadable formats that can only be accessed with a decryption key.
Access Control limits data access to authorized users based on authentication protocols such as passwords, biometrics, and multi-factor authentication.
Data Masking conceals sensitive information, allowing data to be used for analysis without exposing private details.
Backup and Recovery ensures that copies of critical data are stored securely and can be restored in case of system failures or cyberattacks.
Intrusion Detection and Prevention systems monitor networks for suspicious activities and block potential security threats.

Examples

Financial Services banks and payment systems use encryption and authentication protocols to protect customer transactions.
Healthcare medical institutions secure patient records under compliance regulations such as HIPAA to prevent unauthorized access.
E-Commerce online retailers implement fraud detection systems and secure payment gateways to protect user data.
Cloud Computing cloud storage providers encrypt data and enforce strict access policies to prevent breaches in remote environments.

Benefits

Prevents Data Breaches strong security measures protect sensitive information from cyberattacks and unauthorized access.
Ensures Compliance adhering to security regulations avoids fines and enhances trust in business operations.
Maintains Business Continuity data backup and recovery strategies reduce downtime and mitigate risks of data loss.
Enhances Customer Trust secure systems improve user confidence in digital transactions and online services.

Conclusion

Data security is a fundamental requirement for modern digital systems, safeguarding sensitive information from cyber threats and unauthorized access. By implementing encryption, access controls, and real-time monitoring, organizations can protect data while ensuring compliance with global security regulations. Although challenges such as evolving cyber threats and user vulnerabilities persist, advancements in AI-driven security solutions and proactive defense strategies continue to strengthen data protection in an increasingly interconnected world.

Data Segmentation

Data segmentation is the process of dividing large datasets into smaller, more meaningful subsets based on specific criteria such as demographics, behavior, or industry. This technique enhances data analysis, personalization, and decision-making by enabling more precise targeting and insights. It is widely used in artificial intelligence, marketing, healthcare, and cybersecurity to optimize data-driven strategies and improve system efficiency.

Key Components

Segmentation Criteria defines the basis for dividing data, including geographic, demographic, behavioral, or transactional factors.
Clustering Algorithms machine learning techniques such as k-means, hierarchical clustering, and decision trees help automate the segmentation process.
Data Preprocessing ensures that data is cleaned, structured, and standardized before segmentation for accurate analysis.
Feature Selection identifies the most relevant attributes that contribute to meaningful and distinct segment formations.
Dynamic Updating continuously refines and adjusts segments based on real-time data to improve accuracy and relevance.

Examples

Marketing AI-driven segmentation helps businesses personalize advertisements and product recommendations based on customer preferences.
Healthcare patient data is segmented to classify individuals into risk groups for preventive care and targeted treatment plans.
Cybersecurity network traffic data is divided into categories to detect unusual patterns and prevent potential cyber threats.
Retail businesses analyze purchase history to segment customers and create tailored promotions for specific buyer groups.

Benefits

Improved Decision-Making targeted data segmentation provides businesses and organizations with actionable insights for strategic planning.
Enhanced Personalization AI-powered segmentation allows customized user experiences, improving engagement and customer satisfaction.
Operational Efficiency dividing data into manageable groups optimizes storage, processing, and retrieval speeds.
Fraud Detection financial institutions use segmentation to classify normal versus suspicious transactions, reducing fraud risks.

Conclusion

Data segmentation is a powerful technique for improving data analysis, personalization, and security across multiple industries. By leveraging AI and machine learning, organizations can create meaningful segments that enhance decision-making and operational efficiency. Despite challenges related to complexity, scalability, and privacy, continuous advancements in data science enable more precise and dynamic segmentation strategies, making data-driven applications more effective and impactful.

Data Standardization

Data standardization is the process of transforming data into a common format to ensure consistency, accuracy, and compatibility across different systems and applications. It eliminates variations in data representation, making it easier to analyze, integrate, and compare datasets. Standardized data enhances machine learning model performance, improves interoperability, and supports regulatory compliance in industries such as healthcare, finance, and artificial intelligence.

Key Components

Normalization adjusts numerical values to a common scale to prevent biases in machine learning models and statistical analyses.
Format Standardization ensures uniform representation of data types such as dates, currencies, and categorical labels across different sources.
Schema Consistency aligns data structures, field names, and data types to maintain uniformity across databases and platforms.
Metadata Management defines data attributes, relationships, and standards to improve interpretability and governance.
Compliance and Governance enforces industry regulations and best practices to maintain data integrity and security.

Examples

Healthcare standardizing patient records ensures compatibility across hospitals, insurance providers, and medical research institutions.
Finance financial institutions apply data standardization to transaction records, improving fraud detection and regulatory compliance.
E-Commerce product data is standardized to enable accurate search, filtering, and recommendation systems in online marketplaces.
Artificial Intelligence AI models perform better when trained on standardized datasets, ensuring fair comparisons and accurate predictions.

Benefits

Improved Data Quality standardized data reduces errors, inconsistencies, and redundancies, enhancing reliability in analytics.
Seamless Data Integration aligning data formats enables smooth integration between systems, databases, and applications.
Enhanced Machine Learning Performance consistent data improves model training, reducing biases and increasing prediction accuracy.
Regulatory Compliance maintaining standardized data helps organizations meet legal and industry data protection requirements.

Conclusion

Data standardization is a critical process for ensuring consistency, accuracy, and usability across diverse datasets. By applying normalization techniques, format alignment, and governance practices, organizations can enhance data quality and improve decision-making. While challenges such as data inconsistencies and computational costs exist, advancements in automation and AI-driven data management continue to streamline standardization processes, making data more accessible and actionable across industries.

Decision Tree

A decision tree is a supervised machine learning algorithm used for classification and regression tasks. It represents data in a tree-like structure where each internal node denotes a decision based on a specific feature, each branch represents an outcome of that decision, and each leaf node contains the final prediction. Decision trees are widely used in artificial intelligence and data science due to their interpretability and ability to handle both numerical and categorical data.

Key Components

Root Node serves as the starting point of the tree, representing the main decision based on an input feature.
Decision Nodes act as branching points where conditions split the data into different pathways based on feature values.
Leaf Nodes represent the final output of the model, indicating classification labels or numerical predictions.
Splitting divides the dataset into subsets based on the most informative feature at each node, determined by measures like entropy or Gini impurity.
Pruning removes unnecessary branches from the tree to prevent overfitting and improve generalization.

Examples

Fraud Detection banks use decision trees to classify transactions as legitimate or fraudulent based on user behavior and transaction details.
Medical Diagnosis decision trees help in predicting diseases by analyzing patient symptoms, test results, and medical history.
Marketing businesses use decision trees to segment customers and recommend personalized products based on purchasing patterns.
Loan Approval financial institutions assess loan applicants by evaluating factors such as credit history, income, and debt-to-income ratio.

Benefits

Interpretability decision trees provide clear and easy-to-understand decision rules, making them transparent for users.
Flexibility they handle both categorical and numerical data, making them useful for various machine learning tasks.
No Need for Feature Scaling decision trees do not require normalization or standardization of input features.
Fast Training and Inference decision trees have low computational costs compared to more complex machine learning models.

Conclusion

Decision trees are a powerful and interpretable machine learning tool used for classification and regression problems. By structuring data into a tree-like model, they provide a logical and systematic approach to decision-making. While they are prone to overfitting and data sensitivity, techniques such as pruning and ensemble methods like random forests can enhance their performance. Decision trees remain a fundamental component of artificial intelligence, widely applied in finance, healthcare, marketing, and beyond.

Decoder

A decoder is a computational component in artificial intelligence and machine learning that transforms encoded input data into a more interpretable or structured output. It is commonly used in sequence-to-sequence models, neural networks, and data transmission systems to convert compressed, encoded, or abstract representations into human-readable or machine-usable formats. Decoders play a crucial role in natural language processing, computer vision, and generative models, enabling AI to generate meaningful responses, reconstruct images, or translate text.

Key Components

Latent Representation processes encoded data that needs to be reconstructed or translated into a specific output format.
Attention Mechanism improves the decoder's ability to focus on relevant parts of the input when generating sequential output.
Recurrent or Transformer-Based Architecture enables decoders to handle sequential data, such as text or time-series predictions.
Loss Function measures the difference between the generated output and the expected output, guiding optimization during training.
Output Layer generates the final processed result, whether it be text, an image, or structured data for decision-making.

Examples

Machine Translation AI-powered translation models use decoders to convert encoded linguistic features into a target language.
Speech-to-Text applications rely on decoders to transcribe spoken words into written text with high accuracy.
Image Generation generative adversarial networks use decoders to reconstruct images from latent feature representations.
Autonomous Systems AI in self-driving cars uses decoders to process sensor data and predict road conditions or obstacles.

Benefits

Improved Data Interpretation decoders enable AI systems to transform abstract data into understandable and useful outputs.
Enhanced AI Communication natural language processing decoders improve chatbot interactions, translations, and summarization.
Versatility decoders are adaptable to various AI applications, from text generation to image reconstruction and audio processing.
Higher Model Performance advanced decoders improve the quality and fluency of AI-generated outputs, making them more realistic and accurate.

Conclusion

Decoders are essential components in AI and machine learning, facilitating the transformation of encoded information into meaningful results. They enable applications ranging from machine translation and image synthesis to autonomous decision-making and speech recognition. While challenges such as computational demands and error propagation exist, continuous advancements in deep learning architectures and attention mechanisms are improving the efficiency and accuracy of decoders, making them integral to modern AI development.

Deep Autoencoder

A deep autoencoder is a type of neural network used for dimensionality reduction, data compression, and feature extraction. It consists of multiple layers that encode input data into a compact representation before reconstructing it back to its original form. By learning efficient representations, deep autoencoders can remove noise, identify patterns, and enhance the performance of machine learning models. They are widely used in anomaly detection, image processing, and generative modeling.

Key Components

Encoder compresses input data into a lower-dimensional latent space while preserving essential features.
Bottleneck Layer represents the most compressed form of the input, acting as a critical feature representation.
Decoder reconstructs the input from the compressed representation, attempting to restore it with minimal loss.
Loss Function measures the difference between the original input and reconstructed output, guiding the training process.
Activation Functions introduce non-linearity to improve learning and representation capabilities of the autoencoder.

Examples

Anomaly Detection deep autoencoders identify fraudulent transactions or system failures by reconstructing normal data and flagging deviations.
Image Denoising AI-powered applications use deep autoencoders to remove noise from images while preserving key details.
Healthcare autoencoders analyze medical imaging data, reducing dimensionality while retaining critical diagnostic features.
Natural Language Processing deep autoencoders enhance text embeddings, improving language model performance.

Benefits

Feature Extraction deep autoencoders learn meaningful representations, improving downstream machine learning tasks.
Dimensionality Reduction compressing high-dimensional data enhances computational efficiency and storage optimization.
Noise Reduction removing irrelevant or corrupted data improves the quality of inputs for AI models.
Versatility deep autoencoders are applicable in various fields, from finance and healthcare to image and speech processing.

Conclusion

Deep autoencoders are powerful AI tools for data compression, feature learning, and anomaly detection. By efficiently encoding and reconstructing input data, they enhance machine learning applications in diverse industries. Despite challenges such as overfitting and computational demands, advancements in deep learning techniques continue to refine autoencoder architectures, making them essential for high-dimensional data processing and intelligent automation.

Deep Belief Network (DBN)

A deep belief network (DBN) is a type of deep learning architecture composed of multiple layers of stochastic, latent variables called hidden units. It is a generative model that learns hierarchical representations of data through unsupervised pretraining followed by supervised fine-tuning. DBNs are primarily used for feature learning, dimensionality reduction, and classification tasks in artificial intelligence. They combine unsupervised learning techniques with supervised training to improve model accuracy and efficiency.

Key Components

Restricted Boltzmann Machines each layer in a DBN consists of RBMs, which learn feature representations in an unsupervised manner.
Layer-wise Training DBNs are trained one layer at a time, optimizing weights between adjacent layers before fine-tuning the entire network.
Contrastive Divergence an optimization algorithm that adjusts weights within each RBM by minimizing reconstruction error.
Fine-Tuning supervised learning techniques, such as backpropagation, are applied after unsupervised pretraining to optimize model performance.
Probabilistic Inference DBNs use probability distributions to model data, making them suitable for generative learning.

Examples

Image Recognition DBNs learn hierarchical image features, improving classification performance in computer vision applications.
Speech Recognition deep belief networks enhance speech-to-text accuracy by capturing complex audio patterns.
Healthcare DBNs analyze medical data for disease prediction, identifying patterns in patient records and imaging scans.
Natural Language Processing AI systems use DBNs to model relationships between words, improving text classification and sentiment analysis.

Benefits

Efficient Feature Learning DBNs automatically extract hierarchical features, reducing the need for manual feature engineering.
Unsupervised Pretraining improves model generalization, making DBNs effective for tasks with limited labeled data.
Scalability DBNs can be stacked to handle increasingly complex learning tasks, adapting to different AI applications.
Robust Representation Learning probabilistic modeling in DBNs enables them to capture complex dependencies in data.

Conclusion

Deep belief networks provide a powerful framework for unsupervised and supervised learning by leveraging restricted Boltzmann machines for hierarchical feature learning. While they have been largely surpassed by newer deep learning models, DBNs remain an important concept in artificial intelligence, particularly in areas requiring efficient feature extraction and probabilistic modeling. Despite challenges in training and computational demands, DBNs have contributed significantly to the development of modern deep learning architectures.

Deep Convolutional GAN (DCGAN)

A deep convolutional generative adversarial network (DCGAN) is a type of generative adversarial network (GAN) that uses convolutional layers to improve the stability and quality of generated images. It consists of two neural networks, a generator and a discriminator, which compete against each other to create realistic synthetic images. DCGANs leverage deep convolutional layers to learn spatial hierarchies in data, making them highly effective in generating high-resolution and visually coherent outputs.

Key Components

Generator the generator network uses transposed convolutional layers to transform random noise into structured, high-quality images.
Discriminator the discriminator is a convolutional neural network that distinguishes real images from synthetic images produced by the generator.
Leaky ReLU Activation replaces traditional activation functions in convolutional layers to prevent vanishing gradients and improve learning.
Batch Normalization normalizes activations at each layer to stabilize training and speed up convergence.
Latent Space represents random input noise that is mapped to meaningful image features through learned transformations.

Examples

Image Synthesis DCGANs generate realistic human faces, artwork, and synthetic objects from random noise.
Style Transfer AI models use DCGANs to enhance image resolution, modify artistic styles, and generate new visual content.
Medical Imaging synthetic medical scans are generated to augment datasets for training AI models in disease detection.
Data Augmentation DCGANs create diverse training examples for machine learning models to improve classification performance.

Benefits

High-Quality Image Generation convolutional layers improve image fidelity, enabling sharper and more detailed synthetic outputs.
Enhanced Feature Learning DCGANs leverage hierarchical spatial patterns, making them effective for complex visual data synthesis.
Unsupervised Learning they do not require labeled data, making them useful for applications where labeled datasets are limited.
Broad Application Range DCGANs are applied in creative AI, medical research, and data augmentation for machine learning models.

Conclusion

Deep convolutional GANs are a powerful advancement in generative modeling, enabling AI to create realistic images with improved quality and structure. By incorporating deep convolutional layers, DCGANs enhance stability and efficiency in training, making them widely applicable in fields such as computer vision, medical imaging, and creative AI. While challenges such as training instability and computational demands exist, continued research and advancements in GAN architectures are making DCGANs more robust and capable of producing even more lifelike synthetic content.

Deep Convolutional Neural Network (DCNN)

A deep convolutional neural network (DCNN) is an advanced artificial neural network designed to process and analyze structured grid-like data, such as images and videos. By using multiple layers of convolutional filters, DCNNs automatically extract hierarchical features from raw input data, improving pattern recognition and classification tasks. DCNNs are widely used in computer vision, medical imaging, and autonomous systems due to their ability to detect intricate details in complex datasets.

Key Components

Convolutional Layers apply filters to input images to detect spatial patterns such as edges, textures, and shapes.
Pooling Layers reduce the dimensionality of feature maps while preserving essential information, improving computational efficiency.
Activation Functions introduce non-linearity, enabling the model to learn complex relationships within the data.
Fully Connected Layers aggregate extracted features and perform classification or regression based on learned patterns.
Backpropagation and Optimization update network weights using gradient descent and optimization algorithms to improve model accuracy.

Examples

Image Recognition DCNNs classify objects, faces, and handwriting in applications such as security systems and digital handwriting recognition.
Medical Imaging AI-powered diagnostic tools use DCNNs to detect tumors, fractures, and diseases from X-rays, MRIs, and CT scans.
Autonomous Vehicles self-driving cars rely on DCNNs to interpret road signs, detect pedestrians, and analyze real-time environmental conditions.
Facial Recognition AI-enhanced security systems use DCNNs to match facial features against stored identities for authentication and surveillance.

Benefits

Automated Feature Extraction eliminates the need for manual feature engineering, making AI development more efficient.
High Accuracy DCNNs outperform traditional machine learning methods in visual recognition tasks, improving predictive capabilities.
Scalability deep networks can handle large datasets and adapt to a wide range of applications across industries.
Robustness DCNNs generalize well when trained with diverse datasets, making them reliable for real-world deployment.

Conclusion

Deep convolutional neural networks are a cornerstone of modern artificial intelligence, enabling machines to interpret and analyze visual data with remarkable accuracy. Their ability to automatically extract meaningful features from images and videos has revolutionized fields such as healthcare, security, and autonomous technology. Despite challenges related to computational demands and model interpretability, continuous advancements in deep learning architectures and hardware acceleration are making DCNNs even more efficient and widely applicable in AI-driven solutions.

Deep Deterministic Policy Gradient (DDPG)

Deep Deterministic Policy Gradient (DDPG) is a reinforcement learning algorithm that combines deep learning and policy-based optimization to enable continuous control in complex environments. It is an extension of the deterministic policy gradient algorithm, leveraging deep neural networks and experience replay to improve stability and learning efficiency. DDPG is widely used in robotics, autonomous systems, and financial modeling, where precise, real-time decision-making is required.

Key Components

Actor-Critic Architecture consists of two neural networks: the actor, which determines optimal actions, and the critic, which evaluates those actions based on rewards.
Deterministic Policy Gradient the algorithm selects actions directly rather than relying on a probability distribution, making it efficient for continuous action spaces.
Experience Replay stores past experiences and randomly samples them during training to stabilize learning and prevent correlation bias.
Target Networks separate target and main networks reduce instability by smoothing weight updates, preventing drastic learning shifts.
Exploration Strategy uses techniques like Ornstein-Uhlenbeck noise to encourage diverse action selection and prevent premature convergence.

Examples

Autonomous Vehicles DDPG enables self-driving cars to optimize navigation and lane-changing decisions in real-time.
Robotics reinforcement learning in robotic arms and drones helps fine-tune movement control for precision-based tasks.
Finance AI models use DDPG to maximize trading strategies by learning optimal asset allocations in dynamic markets.
Smart Energy Systems power grids apply DDPG for load balancing and energy distribution optimization in fluctuating demand environments.

Benefits

Optimized Continuous Control DDPG is well-suited for tasks requiring smooth, precise, and sequential decision-making.
Improved Sample Efficiency experience replay and target networks enhance learning stability and efficiency.
Scalability DDPG can handle high-dimensional state and action spaces, making it applicable to complex real-world problems.
Real-Time Decision Making its deterministic nature allows for quick and reliable policy execution, essential for robotics and automation.

Conclusion

Deep Deterministic Policy Gradient (DDPG) is a powerful reinforcement learning approach designed for continuous action spaces, enabling precise and efficient control in complex environments. By leveraging actor-critic networks, experience replay, and noise-based exploration, DDPG improves learning efficiency and decision-making in autonomous systems. While challenges such as sample complexity and training stability exist, advancements in reinforcement learning techniques continue to refine DDPG's capabilities, making it a valuable tool for AI-driven control applications.

Deep Fake

Deep fake is an artificial intelligence technology that uses deep learning models to manipulate or generate hyper-realistic images, videos, and audio that appear authentic. By leveraging neural networks, deep fake technology can modify facial expressions, replicate voices, and create entirely synthetic media. While it has legitimate applications in entertainment and media production, it also raises ethical concerns regarding misinformation, fraud, and digital impersonation.

Key Components

Generative Adversarial Networks (GANs) enable deep fakes by training two neural networks, one generating fake content and the other refining authenticity through detection.
Autoencoders extract and reconstruct facial features, voices, and movement patterns to create seamless alterations.
Facial Mapping detects and tracks facial landmarks, allowing precise manipulation of expressions and head movements.
Voice Synthesis AI models analyze and replicate voice patterns, generating audio clips indistinguishable from real speech.
Data Training requires extensive datasets containing images, videos, or voice recordings to improve the quality of synthetic outputs.

Examples

Film and Entertainment deep fakes are used in movies to recreate actors' appearances, de-age characters, or bring historical figures to life.
Social Media AI-generated videos alter faces or voices for viral content, memes, or storytelling purposes.
Political Misinformation fake speeches and altered videos are created to spread false narratives and manipulate public perception.
Cybersecurity Threats deep fake technology is used in phishing attacks, identity theft, and corporate fraud by mimicking real individuals.

Challenges

Misinformation deep fakes can spread false information, influencing elections, public trust, and reputations.
Detection Difficulty distinguishing between authentic and synthetic media is challenging, requiring advanced forensic AI tools.
Legal and Ethical Concerns deep fake content raises questions about consent, privacy rights, and responsible AI usage.
Computational Demands generating high-quality deep fakes requires significant processing power and training time.

Benefits

Creative Innovation deep fakes contribute to visual effects, digital storytelling, and immersive experiences in entertainment.
AI Research advancements in deep fake detection drive improvements in cybersecurity, authentication, and forensic analysis.
Education and Training deep fake simulations enhance training environments, such as virtual role-playing and historical recreations.
Accessibility AI-powered voice and video synthesis enable personalized content creation for people with disabilities.

Conclusion

Deep fake technology represents a powerful advancement in AI-driven media generation, offering both creative opportunities and ethical risks. While it enhances digital entertainment, virtual simulations, and accessibility, it also poses significant threats in misinformation, fraud, and identity manipulation. As deep fake technology evolves, the development of detection methods and regulatory frameworks will be essential to ensure responsible usage and mitigate harmful consequences.

Deep Feature Synthesis (DFS)

Deep Feature Synthesis (DFS) is an automated feature engineering technique that generates new predictive features from raw datasets using relational structures and aggregation functions. It enables machine learning models to extract meaningful insights by transforming low-level input data into higher-level representations without manual intervention. DFS is widely used in artificial intelligence and data science to improve model accuracy and efficiency by creating complex feature sets that enhance learning capabilities.

Key Components

Entity Relationships DFS identifies relationships between entities in a dataset to generate meaningful features through aggregation.
Feature Primitives predefined mathematical operations such as summation, averaging, and counting are applied to extract patterns from data.
Recursive Feature Engineering DFS can generate multi-layered features by applying transformations to previously synthesized features.
Time-Based Aggregations dynamic feature calculations incorporate time-based trends to enhance predictive accuracy in sequential data.
Automation DFS automates the feature extraction process, reducing the need for domain expertise in manually crafting features.

Examples

Fraud Detection DFS enhances credit card fraud detection by creating aggregated features based on past transaction behaviors and spending patterns.
Healthcare predictive models use DFS to generate time-based features from patient records to detect disease risks and treatment responses.
Retail and E-Commerce DFS improves customer segmentation and recommendation systems by analyzing purchase history, browsing behavior, and demographic data.
Financial Services banking applications use DFS to predict loan defaults by synthesizing risk-related features from transaction and income data.

Benefits

Enhanced Predictive Power automatically generated features improve the accuracy and efficiency of machine learning models.
Time Efficiency automating feature engineering reduces the time and effort needed for manual feature selection.
Scalability DFS allows feature extraction from large datasets, making it useful for big data applications and enterprise-scale AI solutions.
Reduces Need for Domain Expertise automated feature synthesis eliminates the requirement for deep domain knowledge in feature engineering.

Conclusion

Deep Feature Synthesis (DFS) is a powerful AI-driven technique for automated feature engineering, enabling machine learning models to discover and utilize complex relationships within data. By automating the process of feature creation, DFS enhances model performance while reducing manual effort and domain dependency. Despite challenges related to computational overhead and feature redundancy, its ability to generate high-quality predictive features makes it a valuable tool in data science, finance, healthcare, and various AI-driven industries.

Deep Learning

Deep learning is a subset of artificial intelligence that uses neural networks with multiple layers to process data, recognize patterns, and make decisions. Inspired by the human brain, deep learning models automatically learn from vast amounts of data without explicit programming. By leveraging advanced computational techniques, deep learning powers applications in computer vision, natural language processing, and autonomous systems, enabling machines to perform complex tasks with high accuracy.

Key Components

Neural Networks consist of interconnected layers of artificial neurons that process and analyze data.
Activation Functions determine how neurons respond to input signals, enabling non-linear learning and decision-making.
Backpropagation updates neural network weights by calculating errors and optimizing model performance.
Training Data provides labeled or unlabeled examples that deep learning models use to learn and improve predictions.
Hardware Acceleration utilizes GPUs and TPUs to speed up computations, making deep learning feasible for large-scale applications.

Examples

Image Recognition deep learning enables AI to classify images, detect objects, and recognize faces in security and healthcare applications.
Speech and Language Processing AI-driven models power virtual assistants, language translation, and sentiment analysis.
Autonomous Vehicles deep learning allows self-driving cars to process sensor data and make real-time navigation decisions.
Medical Diagnosis AI analyzes medical images and patient records to detect diseases and recommend treatments.

Benefits

High Accuracy deep learning outperforms traditional machine learning methods in recognizing complex patterns and making predictions.
Automation AI automates tasks that previously required human expertise, improving efficiency in various industries.
Scalability deep learning models adapt to diverse applications, from robotics to finance and healthcare.
Continuous Learning models improve over time by refining their understanding through exposure to new data.

Conclusion

Deep learning is a transformative AI technology that enables machines to learn from experience, recognize patterns, and make intelligent decisions. By leveraging neural networks, backpropagation, and large datasets, deep learning powers advanced applications in automation, healthcare, security, and beyond. Despite challenges related to data requirements, computational costs, and interpretability, deep learning continues to evolve, driving innovation and expanding the potential of artificial intelligence across multiple domains.

Deeplearning4j

Deeplearning4j (DL4J) is an open-source deep learning library designed for Java and Scala, providing a scalable and distributed framework for building neural networks. It enables organizations to develop AI models that leverage multi-core processing, GPU acceleration, and integration with big data platforms. DL4J is widely used for enterprise applications, machine learning research, and large-scale data analytics, offering flexibility and interoperability with existing Java-based ecosystems.

Key Components

Neural Network API supports feedforward, convolutional, recurrent, and deep reinforcement learning architectures, allowing developers to build complex AI models.
GPU Acceleration enables faster model training and inference by utilizing CUDA and OpenCL for parallel processing.
Integration with Big Data DL4J seamlessly connects with Apache Spark and Hadoop, facilitating distributed deep learning on massive datasets.
Automatic Differentiation includes an efficient computation engine for backpropagation, optimizing neural network training.
Prebuilt Models provides a library of pretrained models and neural network configurations, reducing development time for AI applications.

Examples

Healthcare DL4J is used for medical image analysis, disease prediction, and patient data modeling in large-scale healthcare systems.
Financial Services AI-powered fraud detection and risk assessment models utilize DL4J to analyze complex financial transactions.
Manufacturing predictive maintenance systems use DL4J to monitor equipment health and prevent failures in industrial settings.
Retail AI-based recommendation engines built with DL4J analyze customer behavior and optimize product recommendations.

Benefits

Enterprise Integration as a Java-based framework, DL4J easily integrates with existing enterprise applications, ensuring compatibility with business workflows.
Scalability supports distributed computing, making it suitable for training AI models on large datasets in cloud and big data environments.
Flexibility allows developers to create custom deep learning architectures for various AI applications, from NLP to image processing.
Performance Optimization optimized for speed and efficiency, DL4J leverages hardware acceleration to improve deep learning model execution.

Conclusion

Deeplearning4j is a powerful deep learning framework designed for Java and Scala environments, enabling scalable AI development for enterprise and big data applications. By integrating with distributed computing platforms, supporting GPU acceleration, and offering flexible neural network architectures, DL4J provides a robust solution for AI-driven innovations. Despite challenges related to complexity and community support, its ability to handle large-scale deep learning workloads makes it a valuable tool for businesses and research institutions focused on AI and machine learning.

Deep Metric Learning

Deep metric learning is a machine learning technique that trains neural networks to measure the similarity or dissimilarity between data points. Instead of classifying inputs into predefined categories, it focuses on learning distance functions that quantify relationships between objects. This approach is widely used in facial recognition, image retrieval, recommendation systems, and anomaly detection, where precise similarity measurements are required.

Key Components

Embedding Space transforms raw data into a lower-dimensional representation where similar items are closer and dissimilar items are farther apart.
Loss Functions include contrastive loss, triplet loss, and margin-based loss, which optimize the network to differentiate between similar and dissimilar samples.
Distance Metrics common metrics such as Euclidean distance and cosine similarity measure how closely related two data points are in the learned space.
Pairwise Learning compares pairs of inputs to determine similarity, while triplet learning refines embeddings by considering relative distances between three samples.
Neural Network Architectures convolutional and transformer-based models are commonly used to extract deep feature representations for metric learning.

Examples

Facial Recognition deep metric learning enables face verification by comparing embeddings of different individuals and determining identity matches.
Image Retrieval AI-powered search engines use deep metric learning to find visually similar images in large databases based on content similarities.
E-Commerce recommendation systems improve product suggestions by clustering similar items together in an embedding space.
Anomaly Detection financial institutions use metric learning to identify fraudulent transactions by comparing new activity to past patterns.

Benefits

Improved Similarity Search deep metric learning enables fast and accurate retrieval of similar objects in large databases.
Better Generalization models trained on metric learning principles perform well on unseen data, making them adaptable to various domains.
Flexibility applicable to various types of data, including images, text, and audio, enabling multi-modal learning capabilities.
Enhanced Security biometric authentication systems benefit from deep metric learning by improving accuracy in identity verification.

Conclusion

Deep metric learning is a powerful AI technique that enables machines to measure relationships between data points with high precision. By learning similarity-based representations, it enhances applications in facial recognition, search engines, recommendation systems, and security. Despite challenges such as computational complexity and metric selection, continuous advancements in neural architectures and optimization techniques are making deep metric learning more scalable and efficient for real-world applications.

Deep Neural Network (DNN)

A deep neural network (DNN) is an advanced artificial intelligence model composed of multiple layers of interconnected neurons that process complex data patterns. By stacking several hidden layers between input and output layers, DNNs can capture intricate relationships within data, making them highly effective for classification, regression, and generative tasks. They are widely used in applications such as speech recognition, natural language processing, and autonomous systems.

Key Components

Input Layer receives raw data and passes it to the network for processing.
Hidden Layers consist of multiple layers of artificial neurons that extract hierarchical features from input data.
Activation Functions introduce non-linearity, enabling the network to learn complex patterns and relationships.
Weights and Biases determine the strength of connections between neurons, adjusting during training to improve accuracy.
Backpropagation an optimization process that updates weights by minimizing the difference between predicted and actual values.

Examples

Speech Recognition DNNs power virtual assistants and transcription services by converting spoken words into text.
Medical Diagnostics deep learning models analyze medical images to detect diseases such as cancer and neurological disorders.
Autonomous Vehicles DNNs process sensor and camera data to identify obstacles, road signs, and navigation paths.
Financial Forecasting AI models predict stock market trends and detect fraudulent transactions using deep learning techniques.

Benefits

High Accuracy deep neural networks excel at capturing patterns in data, making them highly effective in predictive modeling.
Automation DNNs reduce the need for manual feature engineering by learning directly from raw data.
Scalability deep networks can handle increasing amounts of data, making them suitable for large-scale applications.
Versatility applicable to a wide range of fields, from healthcare and finance to gaming and robotics.

Conclusion

Deep neural networks are a cornerstone of modern artificial intelligence, enabling machines to perform complex tasks with high accuracy. By leveraging multiple layers of artificial neurons, DNNs can learn from vast amounts of data and make precise predictions. Despite challenges such as computational demands and interpretability, continuous advancements in deep learning architectures and hardware acceleration are enhancing the capabilities and efficiency of DNNs, making them integral to the future of AI-driven innovation.

Deep Q-Network (DQN)

A Deep Q-Network (DQN) is a reinforcement learning algorithm that combines deep learning with Q-learning to enable agents to make sequential decisions in complex environments. It uses a neural network to approximate the Q-value function, allowing AI systems to learn optimal policies for decision-making through trial and error. DQNs are widely used in game playing, robotics, and autonomous systems, where they help agents navigate environments and maximize long-term rewards.

Key Components

Q-Value Function estimates the expected reward for taking an action in a given state and helps the agent determine the best move.
Neural Network serves as a function approximator, mapping states and actions to their respective Q-values.
Experience Replay stores past experiences and samples them randomly during training to improve

stability and learning efficiency.
Target Network a separate network is used to stabilize Q-value updates, preventing oscillations in learning.
Exploration-Exploitation Tradeoff balances between exploring new actions and exploiting learned strategies to maximize rewards.

Examples

Atari Game Playing DQNs have achieved superhuman performance in classic arcade games by learning optimal strategies from raw pixel inputs.
Autonomous Vehicles reinforcement learning models use DQNs to train self-driving cars in simulated environments.
Robotics robotic arms use DQNs to learn grasping techniques and optimize movement for efficiency.
Healthcare AI-powered decision-making systems utilize DQNs for personalized treatment recommendations and medical diagnostics.

Benefits

Generalization DQNs can adapt to various tasks and environments, making them versatile for different reinforcement learning applications.
Improved Decision-Making the ability to learn complex strategies allows AI agents to make optimal choices in dynamic environments.
Automation reinforcement learning with DQNs enables AI systems to operate without direct human supervision.
Scalability neural network-based Q-learning can handle high-dimensional state spaces, making DQNs suitable for real-world applications.

Conclusion

Deep Q-Networks (DQNs) represent a major breakthrough in reinforcement learning, enabling AI agents to learn optimal policies for decision-making through deep learning. By integrating neural networks with Q-learning, DQNs improve generalization and adaptability across a range of applications, from gaming to robotics. Despite challenges such as computational demands and sample inefficiency, advancements in reinforcement learning techniques continue to refine DQN algorithms, expanding their potential in AI-driven automation and decision-making systems.

Deep Reinforcement Learning (DRL)

Deep Reinforcement Learning (DRL) is a branch of artificial intelligence that combines deep learning with reinforcement learning to enable agents to make sequential decisions in complex environments. It allows AI models to learn optimal strategies by interacting with an environment, receiving feedback through rewards, and improving performance over time. DRL is used in robotics, gaming, finance, healthcare, and autonomous systems, where decision-making under uncertainty is critical.

Key Components

Agent the AI entity that interacts with the environment and learns through trial and error.
Environment the system in which the agent operates, providing feedback in the form of rewards or penalties.
Policy defines the agent's behavior by mapping states to actions, determining how it acts in a given situation.
Value Function estimates the expected cumulative reward of a state or action to guide decision-making.
Exploration-Exploitation Tradeoff balances between discovering new strategies and refining learned behaviors to maximize rewards.

Examples

Autonomous Vehicles DRL helps self-driving cars learn safe and efficient driving strategies through simulated and real-world training.
Robotics robotic arms use DRL to optimize motion planning, object manipulation, and complex tasks.
Healthcare AI models use DRL to personalize treatment plans, optimize drug discovery, and enhance medical imaging analysis.
Gaming DRL has achieved superhuman performance in video games and board games, mastering strategies through self-play.

Benefits

Autonomous Decision-Making DRL enables AI systems to make real-time decisions without human intervention.
Adaptability DRL agents learn from experience and adjust to changing environments, improving robustness.
Generalization DRL techniques can be applied to diverse applications, from robotics to financial modeling.
Optimization AI models trained with DRL can outperform traditional rule-based systems in dynamic and uncertain environments.

Conclusion

Deep Reinforcement Learning is a transformative AI approach that enables machines to learn from interactions and improve decision-making over time. By integrating deep learning with reinforcement learning principles, DRL provides powerful solutions for complex, real-world problems. Despite challenges related to sample efficiency, computational demands, and stability, continuous advancements in DRL techniques are expanding its capabilities, making it a key component of future AI-driven automation and intelligence.

DeepSeek-R1

DeepSeek-R1 is an open-source large language model developed by the Chinese AI company DeepSeek. Released in January 2025, it is designed to perform tasks requiring advanced reasoning, such as mathematical problem-solving, coding, and logical inference. Despite being trained with relatively modest resources, DeepSeek-R1 achieves performance comparable to leading models like OpenAI's o1.

Key Components

Architecture: DeepSeek-R1 utilizes a transformer-based architecture, enabling efficient processing of complex language tasks.

Training Methodology: The model incorporates multi-stage training, including supervised fine-tuning and reinforcement learning, to enhance its reasoning capabilities.

Open-Source Licensing: Released under the MIT License, DeepSeek-R1 allows unrestricted use, modification, and distribution, promoting transparency and collaboration in the AI community.

Integration Capabilities: DeepSeek-R1 is accessible through various platforms, including Azure AI Foundry and GitHub, facilitating seamless integration into diverse applications.

Examples

Mathematical Problem Solving: DeepSeek-R1 excels in solving complex mathematical problems, demonstrating performance on par with leading AI models.

Code Generation: The model can generate and debug code snippets across various programming languages, assisting developers in software development tasks.

Logical Reasoning: DeepSeek-R1 effectively handles tasks requiring logical inference, such as puzzle solving and data analysis.

Language Translation: The model provides accurate translations between multiple languages, supporting cross-linguistic communication.

Challenges

Resource Constraints: Training and deploying large language models like DeepSeek-R1 require substantial computational resources, which may limit accessibility for smaller organizations.

Ethical Considerations: Ensuring responsible use of AI models involves addressing potential biases and preventing misuse in sensitive applications.

Market Competition: Competing with established AI models necessitates continuous innovation and differentiation to maintain relevance.

Benefits

Cost Efficiency: DeepSeek-R1's development showcases that high-performance AI models can be trained with relatively modest resources, making advanced AI more accessible.

Enhanced Accessibility: The open-source nature of DeepSeek-R1 allows researchers and developers worldwide to utilize and build upon the model, fostering innovation.

Performance Parity: Despite lower training costs, DeepSeek-R1 matches the performance of leading AI models in various reasoning tasks.

Conclusion

DeepSeek-R1 represents a significant advancement in AI, demonstrating that high-performing models can be developed with efficient resource utilization. Its open-source release under the MIT License promotes widespread adoption and collaborative development, potentially reshaping the AI landscape by making advanced reasoning capabilities more accessible to a global audience.

Deterministic Algorithm

A deterministic algorithm is a computational process that produces the same output for a given input every time it is executed. Unlike probabilistic or randomized algorithms, deterministic algorithms follow a fixed sequence of operations, ensuring predictable and repeatable results. These algorithms are fundamental in computer science, artificial intelligence, and optimization problems, where consistency and reliability are essential.

Key Components

Fixed Execution Path the sequence of operations remains constant, meaning the algorithm does not introduce randomness.
Predictability given the same input, the output remains unchanged regardless of when or where the algorithm runs.
Efficiency deterministic algorithms often aim to optimize time and space complexity for computational

performance.
Mathematical Rigor results are based on predefined logic and formulas, eliminating uncertainty in computations.
Data Dependence the accuracy and effectiveness of a deterministic algorithm rely entirely on input data quality.

Examples

Sorting Algorithms quicksort, mergesort, and bubble sort follow a predefined set of steps to arrange elements in a fixed order.
Pathfinding deterministic shortest path algorithms, such as Dijkstra's algorithm, guarantee the same path is found for the same graph.
Cryptographic Hashing deterministic hashing functions like SHA-256 generate the same hash value for identical inputs.
Database Query Optimization SQL query execution plans use deterministic algorithms to fetch data in a structured and repeatable manner.

Benefits

Consistency deterministic algorithms provide reliable and repeatable results, making them suitable for mission-critical applications.
Debugging and Testing predictable outputs simplify debugging and validation in software development.
Security cryptographic systems benefit from deterministic hashing and encryption processes that maintain data integrity.
Deterministic AI deterministic algorithms are used in AI applications requiring strict control over decision-making processes.

Conclusion

Deterministic algorithms are essential for tasks that require accuracy, repeatability, and reliability. Their structured execution ensures that the same inputs always yield the same results, making them invaluable in data processing, security, and optimization tasks. While they face challenges related to scalability and computational cost, deterministic algorithms remain a cornerstone of modern computing, supporting applications ranging from database management to artificial intelligence and cryptographic security.

DGX (First AI Supercomputer)

DGX is an advanced AI supercomputer developed by NVIDIA, designed to accelerate deep learning, artificial intelligence research, and high-performance computing. It provides specialized hardware and software to process massive datasets and train complex neural networks at unprecedented speeds. DGX systems are widely used in AI research labs, enterprises, and scientific institutions to drive innovation in areas such as autonomous vehicles, healthcare, and natural language processing.

Key Components

GPU Acceleration DGX systems utilize NVIDIA's high-performance GPUs, including Tensor Core architecture, to perform deep learning computations faster than traditional processors.
Scalable Architecture designed to support multi-GPU and multi-node configurations, DGX systems can be expanded to accommodate increasing AI workloads.
Optimized Software Stack includes NVIDIA's AI and deep learning frameworks such as TensorFlow, PyTorch, and CUDA for seamless integration with AI applications.
High-Speed Interconnect DGX features high-bandwidth NVLink technology, enabling rapid communication between GPUs for efficient parallel processing.

Enterprise-Ready DGX systems are equipped with built-in AI workflows, cloud integration, and security features, making them suitable for enterprise deployment.

Examples

Autonomous Vehicles AI models for self-driving cars are trained on DGX systems to enhance object detection, path planning, and real-time decision-making.
Medical Research DGX enables faster drug discovery, genomic analysis, and medical imaging enhancements by processing large biological datasets.
Natural Language Processing large-scale AI models such as chatbots and virtual assistants are trained using DGX for better language understanding and human-like interaction.
Climate Science DGX supercomputers analyze environmental data to predict climate patterns, helping researchers develop models for disaster prevention and mitigation.

Benefits

Unmatched AI Performance DGX accelerates AI workloads, reducing training times for deep learning models from weeks to hours.
Seamless Scalability DGX systems can be integrated into larger AI infrastructures, making them adaptable for growing computational needs.
Enterprise Support optimized for businesses and research labs, DGX includes AI-ready software and cloud connectivity to enhance productivity.
Scientific Advancements by providing superior computational power, DGX facilitates breakthroughs in AI-driven research across multiple disciplines.

Conclusion

DGX represents a milestone in AI supercomputing, delivering unparalleled performance for deep learning and scientific research. With its powerful GPU acceleration, scalable design, and optimized software ecosystem, DGX enables rapid AI model training and deployment. While challenges such as cost, energy demands, and hardware dependency exist, DGX continues to be a leading choice for AI-driven innovation, fueling advancements in industries ranging from healthcare and autonomous systems to climate science and cybersecurity.

Digital Twin

A digital twin is a virtual representation of a physical object, system, or process that continuously updates with real-time data to simulate, analyze, and optimize its real-world counterpart. By integrating artificial intelligence, Internet of Things (IoT) sensors, and machine learning, digital twins enable predictive maintenance, enhanced decision-making, and operational efficiency across industries such as manufacturing, healthcare, and smart cities.

Key Components

Real-Time Data digital twins rely on IoT devices and sensors to collect live data from physical entities, ensuring accurate modeling.
Simulation Models AI and machine learning algorithms process data to replicate real-world behaviors and predict future outcomes.
Cloud and Edge Computing digital twins operate on cloud or edge platforms, enabling scalable storage, processing, and real-time analytics.
Connectivity seamless integration with enterprise systems, automation platforms, and AI models ensures continuous synchronization.
Predictive Analytics historical and real-time data analysis enables forecasting, optimization, and automated decision-making.

Examples

Manufacturing digital twins monitor equipment performance, predict failures, and optimize production workflows in smart factories.
Healthcare AI-driven digital twins simulate patient conditions for personalized treatment planning and surgical training.
Smart Cities urban infrastructure digital twins optimize traffic flow, energy consumption, and public transportation networks.
Aerospace aviation companies use digital twins to model aircraft performance, improve safety, and reduce maintenance costs.

Benefits

Enhanced Efficiency real-time monitoring and predictive maintenance reduce downtime and operational costs.
Improved Decision-Making AI-powered simulations provide actionable insights for optimizing performance and mitigating risks.
Scalability digital twins can model individual components or entire ecosystems, enabling flexible deployment across industries.
Innovation digital twins accelerate research and development by allowing virtual testing and experimentation before physical implementation.

Conclusion

Digital twins revolutionize industries by providing a dynamic, data-driven bridge between the physical and digital worlds. Through real-time monitoring, predictive analytics, and AI-driven insights, they enable smarter decision-making and efficiency improvements. Despite challenges related to data management, security, and integration, advancements in AI, IoT, and cloud computing continue to enhance the capabilities and adoption of digital twins, making them an essential tool for future innovation and optimization.

Diffusion Model

A diffusion model is a generative artificial intelligence framework that transforms random noise into structured data through a multi-step iterative process. By learning how to reverse the diffusion of noise into meaningful patterns, these models can generate highly realistic images, text, and other forms of synthetic data. Diffusion models have gained significant traction in AI research and applications, particularly in image synthesis, text-to-image generation, and denoising tasks.

Key Components

Forward Diffusion Process a series of transformations progressively add noise to input data, creating a degraded version of the original sample.
Reverse Process the model learns to recover the original data by gradually removing noise step by step using trained neural networks.
Score-Based Estimation deep learning models estimate the probability distribution of data at different noise levels, guiding the reconstruction process.
Latent Space Representation diffusion models operate in a high-dimensional latent space where structured data is learned and generated.
Optimization and Training diffusion models rely on advanced neural networks, such as U-Nets and transformers, trained on large-scale datasets.

Examples

Image Generation AI-powered diffusion models such as DALL·E and Stable Diffusion create photorealistic images from text descriptions.
Medical Imaging diffusion-based AI systems enhance MRI scans and CT images by reducing noise and improving resolution.
Artistic Style Transfer diffusion models generate unique digital artwork by simulating various textures and painting techniques.
Speech Enhancement AI-driven speech restoration tools use diffusion models to remove background noise and improve voice clarity.

Benefits

High-Quality Synthesis diffusion models produce detailed and realistic outputs, outperforming traditional generative models in many cases.
Versatility applicable across multiple domains, including image generation, text-to-speech, and video enhancement.
Robustness diffusion models are more stable than GANs, reducing issues such as mode collapse and training instability.
Improved Creativity AI-driven diffusion techniques enable the creation of novel artistic and scientific content beyond human capabilities.

Conclusion

Diffusion models represent a major advancement in AI-driven generative technology, enabling the creation of highly realistic and diverse synthetic data. Their ability to refine noise into structured patterns makes them invaluable for applications in image generation, medical imaging, and audio processing. While challenges related to computational demands and model complexity exist, ongoing research continues to enhance their efficiency and scalability, positioning diffusion models as a fundamental tool for future AI innovations.

Diffusion Tensor Imaging (DTI)

Diffusion Tensor Imaging (DTI) is an advanced magnetic resonance imaging (MRI) technique that maps the diffusion of water molecules in biological tissues, primarily used for analyzing the brain's white matter structure. By measuring the directional movement of water, DTI provides detailed insights into neural connectivity, tissue integrity, and abnormalities in the central nervous system. It is widely applied in neuroscience, neurodegenerative disease research, and pre-surgical planning.

Key Components

Diffusion Anisotropy measures how water molecules move differently in various directions, providing information about fiber orientation in white matter.
Tensor Model represents water diffusion in three-dimensional space using mathematical tensors, helping to construct neural pathways.
Fractional Anisotropy (FA) quantifies the degree of directional water movement, where higher values indicate intact white matter and lower values suggest damage.
Tractography reconstructs fiber tracts in the brain by tracing the paths of water diffusion, aiding in brain mapping and surgical navigation.
MRI Sequences specialized MRI techniques, such as Echo Planar Imaging (EPI), acquire diffusion-weighted images for further DTI analysis.

Examples

Neurological Disorders DTI helps detect changes in white matter associated with conditions such as Alzheimer's disease, Parkinson's disease, and multiple sclerosis.

Traumatic Brain Injury physicians use DTI to assess the extent of brain damage by identifying disrupted neural pathways.
Brain Development researchers apply DTI to study how brain connectivity evolves in infants, children, and adolescents.
Pre-Surgical Planning neurosurgeons use DTI to visualize white matter tracts, minimizing the risk of damage to critical brain areas during surgery.

Benefits

Non-Invasive Brain Mapping DTI provides high-resolution insights into brain connectivity without requiring surgical intervention.
Early Disease Detection detecting microstructural changes in white matter enables early diagnosis and intervention for neurodegenerative diseases.
Surgical Precision preoperative DTI helps neurosurgeons avoid critical brain regions, reducing post-surgical complications.
Scientific Advancements ongoing research in DTI enhances understanding of brain function, cognitive processes, and neurological disorders.

Conclusion

Diffusion Tensor Imaging is a groundbreaking MRI-based technique that provides unparalleled insights into the structure and function of neural pathways. By leveraging water diffusion properties, DTI enables researchers and clinicians to explore brain connectivity, diagnose neurological disorders, and improve surgical outcomes. Despite challenges such as imaging sensitivity and fiber complexity, continuous advancements in MRI technology and computational modeling are expanding the potential of DTI, making it an essential tool in modern neuroscience and medical imaging.

Digital AI

Definition
Digital AI refers to artificial intelligence systems that operate entirely within digital environments. These systems analyze, interpret, and generate data in the form of text, images, audio, video, and structured datasets. Digital AI does not interact with the physical world through hardware but rather functions within software platforms, web applications, cloud services, and digital networks. It plays a crucial role in data-driven decision-making, virtual assistance, content generation, automation, and analytics.

Key Components
Data Input: Digital AI systems rely on large volumes of structured and unstructured data for learning and decision-making.
Machine Learning Models: Algorithms that learn from historical data to make predictions, classify information, or detect patterns.
Natural Language Processing (NLP): Enables AI to understand and generate human language in text or speech form.
Computer Vision: Allows AI to interpret digital images and videos.
Cloud Infrastructure: Scalable platforms where digital AI models are trained, deployed, and managed.
User Interfaces: Front-end systems through which users interact with the AI, such as chatbots or dashboards.

Examples
A virtual assistant that schedules meetings and answers questions using voice commands.
An AI model that recommends movies based on user preferences.
A fraud detection system analyzing financial transactions in real time.

An automated content generator creating articles or reports.
A predictive analytics platform identifying market trends from historical sales data.

Benefits
Enables fast, data-driven insights with minimal human intervention.
Scales easily across digital platforms and industries.
Reduces operational costs through process automation.
Improves decision accuracy through pattern recognition and trend analysis.
Supports personalization by adapting services based on user behavior.

Applications
Customer Service: Chatbots and virtual assistants that handle inquiries and support requests.
Finance: AI tools for risk assessment, fraud detection, and investment forecasting.
Marketing: Targeted advertising and customer segmentation based on user behavior.
Education: Personalized learning platforms that adapt to student performance.
Healthcare: Diagnostic tools that analyze medical images and patient records.
Media: Automated content creation and sentiment analysis.

Industries
Finance
Healthcare
Retail
Education
Marketing
Media and Entertainment
Insurance
Telecommunications
E-commerce

Summary
Digital AI is a foundational element of the modern digital ecosystem, enabling machines to process, learn from, and act on data without physical interaction. It enhances efficiency, supports decision-making, and powers countless digital services from personalized recommendations to advanced analytics. While offering broad benefits, Digital AI also demands careful oversight to manage data quality, privacy, bias, and transparency. As digital transformation continues, Digital AI remains central to innovation across sectors and everyday digital experiences.

Digital Signal Processing (DSP)

Digital Signal Processing (DSP) is a branch of engineering that involves analyzing, modifying, and optimizing digital signals to improve their quality and efficiency. DSP techniques are widely used in applications such as audio processing, telecommunications, image enhancement, and biomedical signal analysis. By transforming analog signals into digital format, DSP enables advanced filtering, compression, and real-time data manipulation, making it a fundamental technology in modern computing and artificial intelligence.

Key Components

Analog-to-Digital Conversion converts analog signals, such as sound waves or radio frequencies, into digital format for processing.
Digital Filters apply mathematical algorithms to enhance or suppress specific signal characteristics, such as removing noise or amplifying frequencies.
Fourier Transform decomposes signals into their frequency components, aiding in spectral analysis and signal reconstruction.

Signal Compression reduces data size while preserving essential information, optimizing storage and transmission efficiency.
Real-Time Processing ensures rapid signal manipulation, enabling applications such as speech recognition, radar imaging, and medical diagnostics.

Examples

Audio Processing DSP is used in noise cancellation headphones, voice assistants, and music equalization to improve sound quality.
Telecommunications mobile networks rely on DSP to filter signals, enhance voice clarity, and optimize data transmission.
Medical Imaging MRI and ECG signal analysis use DSP to detect abnormalities and improve diagnostic accuracy.
Autonomous Vehicles DSP processes sensor and camera data in self-driving cars to enhance object detection and navigation.

Benefits

Improved Signal Quality DSP enhances the clarity and precision of audio, image, and communication signals.
Efficient Data Transmission compression and filtering techniques optimize bandwidth usage, improving network performance.
Real-Time Analysis DSP enables fast and responsive processing for applications such as speech recognition and medical diagnostics.
Versatility applicable across industries, DSP powers innovations in healthcare, automotive, telecommunications, and consumer electronics.

Conclusion

Digital Signal Processing is a foundational technology that enables efficient signal manipulation, improving the quality and functionality of digital systems. By converting, filtering, and analyzing signals in real time, DSP enhances applications ranging from audio processing and telecommunications to medical imaging and autonomous navigation. Despite challenges such as computational demands and latency, advancements in hardware acceleration and AI-driven optimization continue to expand the capabilities of DSP, making it a critical component of modern digital systems.

Dirac's Equation

Definition: Dirac's equation is a fundamental equation in quantum mechanics and relativistic physics developed by physicist Paul Dirac, describing the behavior of elementary spin-½ particles, such as electrons, consistent with both quantum mechanics and special relativity. It extends Schrödinger's equation to account for relativistic speeds and predicts phenomena like electron spin and antimatter.

Key Components: Major components include wavefunctions known as spinors, gamma matrices, relativistic energy operators, particle spin, relativistic quantum states, antiparticles, and compatibility with special relativity principles.

Benefits: Dirac's equation resolves inconsistencies between quantum mechanics and relativity, predicts the existence of antimatter, provides accurate descriptions of electron behavior at high speeds, and forms the foundation for quantum electrodynamics (QED).

Examples: Examples include accurate modeling of electron-positron pair production, prediction and understanding of antimatter properties, precise calculation of electron spin dynamics, and relativistic corrections in atomic and particle physics experiments.

Applications: Dirac's equation has wide-ranging applications in particle accelerators, antimatter research, quantum field theory, high-energy physics experiments, quantum computing simulations involving relativistic particles, and advanced spectroscopy techniques in atomic physics.

Industries: Industries influenced by Dirac's equation include particle physics research, semiconductor technology, medical imaging (PET scans involving positrons), aerospace and defense sectors utilizing radiation technologies, quantum technology development, and advanced materials science.

Summary: Dirac's equation is a cornerstone of modern physics, harmonizing quantum mechanics with relativity and introducing critical concepts like spin and antimatter. Its theoretical predictions and practical implications profoundly influence both scientific understanding and technological innovations across numerous fields.

Disparity Map

A disparity map is a depth representation technique used in computer vision and stereo imaging to estimate the distance of objects in a scene. It calculates the pixel-wise difference between two images taken from slightly different viewpoints, typically captured by a stereo camera system. The resulting disparity values help reconstruct three-dimensional structures, making disparity maps essential in applications such as 3D reconstruction, autonomous navigation, and augmented reality.

Key Components

Stereo Image Pair two images captured from different angles provide the basis for disparity calculation.
Feature Matching algorithms identify corresponding points between the left and right images to determine pixel displacement.
Depth Estimation the disparity values are inversely proportional to depth, meaning larger disparities indicate closer objects.
Occlusion Handling methods compensate for areas where corresponding pixels are missing due to differences in viewpoints.
Rectification image preprocessing techniques align the stereo images to ensure accurate disparity measurement.

Examples

Autonomous Vehicles disparity maps help self-driving cars detect road obstacles, pedestrians, and other vehicles for safe navigation.
Medical Imaging 3D reconstruction from disparity maps improves visualization in fields such as ophthalmology and dental imaging.
Augmented Reality AR applications use disparity data to integrate virtual objects with real-world depth perception.
Robotics stereo vision enables robotic systems to map their surroundings, improving object grasping and spatial awareness.

Benefits

Accurate Depth Perception disparity maps provide reliable 3D information for autonomous systems and human-computer interaction.
Enhanced Object Detection AI models use disparity data to improve object segmentation and scene understanding.
Real-Time 3D Mapping applications in robotics and augmented reality benefit from depth-aware spatial analysis.
Scalability disparity maps are applicable across industries, from healthcare and automotive to virtual reality and geospatial mapping.

Conclusion

Disparity maps are a fundamental component of depth estimation in computer vision, enabling 3D perception in diverse AI-driven applications. By analyzing pixel displacements between stereo images, they provide valuable spatial information for autonomous systems, medical imaging, and interactive technologies. While challenges such as computational demands and occlusions remain, continuous advancements in deep learning and hardware acceleration are enhancing the accuracy and efficiency of disparity map generation, expanding their role in modern artificial intelligence and automation.

Drift Model

A drift model is a computational framework used to identify and adapt to gradual changes in data distributions over time. It is commonly applied in machine learning, statistical analysis, and financial modeling to detect shifts in patterns that may affect model accuracy. Drift models help AI systems maintain performance by adjusting predictions based on evolving data trends, making them essential in applications such as fraud detection, climate forecasting, and predictive maintenance.

Key Components

Data Distribution Analysis monitors changes in statistical properties of data over time to detect shifts in patterns.
Concept Drift Detection identifies whether the relationship between input features and target variables has changed.
Model Adaptation updates machine learning models dynamically to maintain accuracy despite data shifts.
Feature Drift Tracking measures changes in individual input variables, ensuring their relevance in model predictions.
Performance Monitoring continuously evaluates model accuracy to determine if retraining or adjustments are required.

Examples

Fraud Detection drift models identify new fraudulent behaviors as cybercriminal tactics evolve, improving real-time security.
Stock Market Prediction AI-driven trading systems use drift models to adjust strategies based on fluctuating financial trends.
Healthcare Diagnostic AI adapts to changes in patient data over time, improving the accuracy of disease detection.
Predictive Maintenance drift models detect deviations in machine performance data, preventing failures before they occur.

Benefits

Improved Model Accuracy drift models enhance AI performance by maintaining predictive accuracy as data evolves.
Real-Time Adaptation AI systems can respond to changing environments without human intervention, ensuring reliability.
Enhanced Decision-Making businesses use drift models to adapt strategies based on emerging market and customer behavior trends.
Versatility applicable across various industries, including finance, healthcare, cybersecurity, and industrial automation.

Conclusion

Drift models are essential for maintaining AI model reliability in dynamic environments where data patterns change over time. By detecting and adapting to concept and feature drift, these models ensure long-term accuracy and relevance in applications such as fraud detection, financial forecasting, and predictive analytics. While challenges related to computational complexity and real-time adaptation exist, advancements in machine learning techniques and automated retraining strategies continue to improve the effectiveness of drift models, making them a crucial tool for AI-driven decision-making.

Driven AI

Driven AI refers to artificial intelligence systems that operate based on specific objectives, guiding their learning and decision-making processes through structured data inputs, predefined rules, and adaptive feedback loops. Unlike general AI, which aims for broad problem-solving capabilities, driven AI is tailored for targeted applications such as automation, optimization, and predictive analytics. These systems leverage machine learning, deep learning, and reinforcement learning to enhance performance and adaptability across various industries.

Key Components

Goal-Oriented Learning driven AI systems are designed to achieve specific objectives, refining their models through continuous feedback and optimization.
Data-Driven Decision-Making AI relies on structured and unstructured data to improve accuracy, detect patterns, and enhance predictive capabilities.
Adaptive Algorithms machine learning models adjust dynamically based on new information, ensuring ongoing relevance and efficiency.
Automation and Optimization AI automates repetitive tasks, streamlining processes while improving speed and accuracy.
Scalability driven AI systems can expand their capabilities by integrating with larger datasets and additional computational resources.

Examples

Customer Service AI chatbots and virtual assistants use driven AI to handle customer inquiries, improving response efficiency and personalization.
Healthcare AI-driven diagnostic tools analyze medical images and patient data to detect diseases early and recommend treatments.
Supply Chain Optimization predictive AI models forecast demand, manage logistics, and minimize operational costs in distribution networks.
Financial Risk Assessment AI models assess creditworthiness, detect fraudulent transactions, and optimize investment strategies.

Benefits

Efficiency driven AI enhances productivity by automating complex and time-consuming tasks, reducing human workload.
Accuracy continuous learning and data-driven insights improve decision-making and predictive capabilities.
Cost Reduction AI-driven optimization minimizes operational inefficiencies, leading to cost savings in industries such as manufacturing and logistics.
Scalability businesses and organizations can expand AI-driven solutions to handle larger datasets and more sophisticated tasks over time.

Conclusion

Driven AI represents a focused approach to artificial intelligence, leveraging structured data and adaptive learning to achieve specific goals. It plays a crucial role in automation, predictive analytics, and decision-making across diverse industries, from healthcare and finance to supply chain management and customer service. While challenges such as data dependency, security risks, and ethical concerns remain, continuous advancements in AI technologies are refining driven

Driver Monitoring System (DMS)

A Driver Monitoring System (DMS) is an advanced artificial intelligence technology designed to analyze and track a driver's behavior, attention level, and physiological state to enhance road safety. Using real-time data from cameras, sensors, and AI-driven algorithms, DMS detects signs of drowsiness, distraction, and impairment, providing alerts or corrective actions to prevent accidents. This system is increasingly integrated into modern vehicles to support autonomous driving and improve driver assistance features.

Key Components

Facial Recognition AI-powered cameras analyze facial expressions, eye movement, and head position to assess driver focus and alertness.
Behavioral Tracking machine learning models evaluate driving patterns, reaction times, and hand positioning to identify abnormal behavior.
Sensor Integration infrared sensors, biometric scanners, and accelerometers collect real-time physiological and environmental data.
Alert Mechanisms when signs of drowsiness or distraction are detected, the system issues audible alarms, haptic feedback, or automated interventions.
AI and Machine Learning adaptive learning algorithms improve detection accuracy over time, personalizing responses based on driver habits.

Examples

Fleet Management DMS helps commercial truck and taxi companies reduce accidents by monitoring driver fatigue and ensuring compliance with safety protocols.
Passenger Vehicles modern cars integrate DMS with advanced driver assistance systems (ADAS) to enhance safety in long-distance and high-traffic driving conditions.
Autonomous Vehicles semi-autonomous cars use DMS to ensure drivers remain engaged and prepared to take control when needed.
Public Transportation buses and ride-sharing services use DMS to improve passenger safety by detecting driver impairment or inattention.

Benefits

Enhanced Road Safety DMS reduces accidents by identifying and addressing risky driver behaviors in real time.
Fatigue Prevention AI-driven fatigue detection helps prevent drowsy driving incidents, especially in commercial and long-haul transportation.
Regulatory Compliance governments and automotive standards are increasingly mandating DMS integration to improve road safety.
Integration with Autonomous Systems DMS plays a crucial role in bridging human and AI-controlled driving, ensuring smooth transitions in semi-autonomous vehicles.

Conclusion

Driver Monitoring Systems are a vital advancement in automotive safety, using AI and real-time monitoring to detect driver fatigue, distraction, and impairment. By integrating facial recognition, behavioral tracking, and biometric sensing, DMS enhances road safety and supports the development of autonomous driving. Despite challenges related to privacy, cost, and system accuracy, continuous advancements in AI and sensor technology are making DMS more effective and widely adopted in modern vehicles, contributing to the future of intelligent transportation.

Driverless AI

Driverless AI refers to artificial intelligence technologies that enable autonomous vehicles to navigate, make decisions, and operate without human intervention. These systems rely on deep learning, computer vision, sensor fusion, and real-time data processing to perceive the environment, detect obstacles, and execute driving tasks safely. Driverless AI is transforming the transportation industry by enhancing road safety, reducing human errors, and optimizing traffic flow.

Key Components

Computer Vision AI-powered cameras and image recognition systems analyze road signs, lane markings, traffic signals, and pedestrians in real time.
Sensor Fusion data from LiDAR, radar, GPS, and ultrasonic sensors are combined to create an accurate, real-time model of the surrounding environment.
Machine Learning predictive algorithms process historical and real-time data to improve navigation, obstacle avoidance, and driving behavior.
Path Planning AI calculates the optimal driving route, adjusting for road conditions, traffic congestion, and sudden obstacles.
Autonomous Decision-Making reinforcement learning and deep neural networks allow the vehicle to adapt to new driving scenarios and learn from past experiences.

Examples

Autonomous Ride-Sharing companies use driverless AI to deploy self-driving taxis for public transportation, reducing reliance on human drivers.
Long-Haul Trucking AI-driven freight trucks improve logistics by operating continuously without driver fatigue, reducing delivery times.
Smart Traffic Management autonomous vehicles communicate with smart infrastructure to optimize traffic flow and reduce congestion.
Emergency Response self-driving ambulances and rescue vehicles use AI to navigate efficiently, ensuring faster medical assistance.

Benefits

Increased Road Safety AI reduces human errors, such as distracted driving and fatigue, significantly lowering accident rates.
Traffic Efficiency autonomous vehicles optimize routes, reduce congestion, and improve fuel efficiency, leading to better traffic management.
Economic Impact AI-driven transportation reduces costs for businesses and consumers, improving logistics and delivery services.
Accessibility self-driving technology provides mobility solutions for individuals with disabilities and those unable to drive.

Conclusion

Driverless AI is revolutionizing the future of transportation by enabling fully autonomous vehicle operation. By integrating computer vision, sensor fusion, and machine learning, driverless systems enhance safety, efficiency, and accessibility. While challenges related to regulation, cybersecurity, and environmental adaptability remain, ongoing advancements in AI and robotics continue to refine autonomous driving technology, making self-driving vehicles a key component of future smart cities and intelligent transportation systems.

AI systems, making them increasingly valuable for enhancing efficiency, accuracy, and business intelligence.

Driving Behavior Prediction

Driving behavior prediction is an artificial intelligence system that analyzes driver actions, vehicle movement, and environmental factors to anticipate future driving decisions. It leverages machine learning, sensor data, and real-time analytics to enhance road safety, support autonomous driving, and optimize traffic flow. By predicting lane changes, braking, acceleration, and potential hazards, this technology reduces the risk of accidents and improves driving efficiency.

Key Components

Sensor Data Integration AI processes input from cameras, LiDAR, radar, and GPS to monitor road conditions, vehicle position, and driver actions.
Behavioral Models deep learning algorithms analyze historical driving patterns to identify trends in acceleration, braking, and steering behavior.
Traffic and Environmental Context external data, such as road conditions, traffic signals, weather, and pedestrian activity, influences driving predictions.
Predictive Analytics real-time data processing enables the system to estimate the likelihood of specific driving actions, such as lane changes or sudden stops.
Adaptive Learning AI continuously refines its predictions based on new data, improving accuracy and responsiveness over time.

Examples

Autonomous Vehicles self-driving systems predict human driver behavior to make informed navigation decisions and avoid collisions.
Advanced Driver Assistance Systems AI-powered safety features warn drivers of potential hazards based on predictive behavior analysis.
Fleet Management logistics companies use behavior prediction to monitor and enhance driver performance, reducing fuel consumption and maintenance costs.
Traffic Control city planners and transportation agencies use predictive models to optimize traffic light timing and reduce congestion.

Benefits

Enhanced Road Safety predicting driver actions reduces reaction time for autonomous vehicles and human drivers, preventing accidents.
Improved Traffic Efficiency AI-driven insights optimize navigation, reducing delays and improving fuel efficiency.
Driver Monitoring continuous behavior analysis helps detect signs of drowsiness, distraction, or aggressive driving, enhancing road safety.
Scalability predictive models adapt to various driving environments, from city streets to highways, making them suitable for global deployment.

Conclusion

Driving behavior prediction is a crucial advancement in AI-powered transportation, enabling safer and more efficient driving experiences. By analyzing real-time sensor data and historical driving patterns, AI enhances decision-making for autonomous vehicles, driver assistance systems, and traffic management. While challenges such as data variability, privacy, and computational demands remain, ongoing innovations in AI and deep learning continue to refine predictive driving models, making them an integral part of the future of intelligent mobility.

Driving Style Analysis

Driving style analysis is an artificial intelligence-based technique used to assess a driver's habits, patterns, and overall behavior behind the wheel. By collecting and analyzing data from vehicle sensors, telematics systems, and real-time driving inputs, AI models evaluate factors such as acceleration, braking, cornering, and speed variations to classify driving styles. This technology is widely applied in fleet management, insurance risk assessment, autonomous vehicle development, and driver safety programs.

Key Components

Sensor Integration vehicle telematics and onboard diagnostics capture driving metrics such as speed, throttle usage, and braking intensity.
Machine Learning Algorithms AI models classify driving behavior into categories such as aggressive, defensive, or economical based on real-time and historical data.
Contextual Data Analysis external factors such as traffic conditions, road quality, weather, and driving duration are considered to refine assessments.
Pattern Recognition AI identifies recurring driving habits, detecting inconsistencies or risky maneuvers over time.
Driver Profiling personalized driving scores are generated for individuals, helping insurance companies, fleet managers, and autonomous systems optimize performance and safety.

Examples

Fleet Safety Management companies use AI-driven analysis to monitor commercial drivers, ensuring compliance with safety standards and reducing accident risks.
Usage-Based Insurance insurance providers adjust premiums based on real-world driving data, rewarding safe drivers with lower rates.
Autonomous Vehicles AI models assess human driving behavior to improve self-driving car decision-making and adaptive learning.
Ride-Sharing and Delivery Services driving style analysis optimizes fuel efficiency, vehicle wear-and-tear, and customer safety for transport businesses.

Benefits

Enhanced Road Safety identifying risky driving habits enables corrective measures, reducing accident rates and improving public safety.
Cost Efficiency fuel optimization and reduced maintenance costs benefit businesses managing large vehicle fleets.
Personalized Driver Feedback AI-generated insights help individuals improve their driving habits, promoting safer and more responsible road behavior.
Scalability AI-powered analysis adapts to various driving environments, making it applicable across personal vehicles, commercial fleets, and autonomous transportation systems.

Conclusion

Driving style analysis is a transformative application of AI that enhances road safety, optimizes vehicle performance, and supports intelligent transportation systems. By leveraging real-time sensor data and advanced machine learning models, this technology provides valuable insights into driver behavior. While challenges related to privacy, data accuracy, and integration persist, continuous advancements in

AI and automotive technology are expanding the potential of driving style analysis, making it an essential tool for safer and more efficient mobility solutions.

Drone

Definition
A drone is a remotely or autonomously operated unmanned aerial vehicle designed for tasks like surveillance, delivery, or data collection. Equipped with advanced sensors and navigation systems, it functions without an onboard pilot, offering flexible solutions for various operational needs.

Key Components
The core of a drone includes a durable yet lightweight frame for aerodynamic efficiency, driven by electric motors powered by rechargeable batteries. Embedded processors run software for autonomous flight and task management. Sensors like cameras, lidar, or GPS gather environmental data, while communication systems enable real-time operator control and data relay.

Benefits
Drones lower costs by automating labor-intensive tasks, replacing traditional methods with efficient technology. They improve safety by operating in dangerous environments, sparing humans from risk. Their adaptability supports a wide range of functions, from imaging to transport. Rapid data acquisition enhances decision-making in time-sensitive scenarios.

Example
An environmental scientist uses a drone to survey a forested area for deforestation. Fitted with high-resolution cameras, the drone captures detailed images over hours, identifying affected zones and streamlining conservation efforts compared to ground-based surveys.

Application
Drones facilitate aerial mapping for urban planning, deliver medical supplies in remote areas, and monitor infrastructure like bridges for wear. They assist in disaster response by locating survivors and support agriculture through soil and crop analysis.

Industry
Agriculture adopts drones for field monitoring and precision spraying. Film production uses them for dynamic aerial shots. Retail and logistics explore drones for package delivery. Security services deploy them for surveillance and crowd monitoring. Conservation efforts rely on drones for wildlife tracking and habitat assessment.

Summary
Drones are versatile unmanned aerial vehicles that integrate lightweight frames, sensors, and autonomous systems to execute diverse tasks with efficiency. They deliver cost savings, safety, and adaptability but contend with regulatory, technical, and ethical challenges. Transforming agriculture, logistics, and conservation, drones redefine operational possibilities across industries.

Drone AI

Drone AI refers to the integration of artificial intelligence into unmanned aerial vehicles (UAVs) to enable autonomous navigation, real-time decision-making, and advanced data analysis. By leveraging machine learning, computer vision, and sensor fusion, AI-powered drones can perform tasks such as aerial surveillance, environmental monitoring, logistics, and precision agriculture without human intervention. These intelligent drones enhance efficiency, safety, and scalability across various industries.

Key Components

Autonomous Navigation AI-powered flight control systems use GPS, LiDAR, and real-time mapping to enable self-directed movement and obstacle avoidance.
Computer Vision onboard cameras and deep learning algorithms analyze visual data for object detection, target tracking, and environmental assessment.
Sensor Fusion drones integrate data from multiple sensors, including infrared, thermal, and ultrasonic sensors, to enhance situational awareness.
AI-Based Decision-Making reinforcement learning and predictive analytics allow drones to make adaptive flight path adjustments based on real-time conditions.
Communication Systems AI-driven drones connect to cloud platforms and edge computing networks for remote monitoring, coordination, and data processing.

Examples

Agriculture AI drones assess crop health, optimize irrigation, and detect pest infestations, improving agricultural productivity.
Search and Rescue autonomous drones use AI to locate missing persons in disaster zones, improving emergency response operations.
Security and Surveillance AI-enhanced drones monitor critical infrastructure, detect intrusions, and enhance law enforcement efforts.
Delivery and Logistics autonomous drones transport goods efficiently, reducing delivery times and costs in e-commerce and medical supply chains.

Benefits

Increased Efficiency AI automation reduces human intervention, enabling faster and more precise drone operations.
Cost Savings AI-driven drones lower operational costs in industries such as logistics, agriculture, and security by reducing manpower and resource waste.
Scalability AI technology allows for large-scale drone deployments, improving coverage and response capabilities.
Enhanced Safety autonomous drones minimize human exposure to hazardous environments, making them ideal for disaster response and industrial inspections.

Conclusion

Drone AI is revolutionizing aerial operations by enabling autonomous navigation, intelligent data analysis, and real-time decision-making. Through advanced machine learning, sensor fusion, and computer vision, AI-powered drones improve efficiency, safety, and scalability across multiple industries. While challenges related to regulations, battery life, and cybersecurity remain, continuous advancements in AI and drone technology are expanding their capabilities, making them an essential tool for future smart infrastructure and automation systems.

Drone Swarm AI

Drone Swarm AI refers to the use of artificial intelligence to coordinate and control multiple unmanned aerial vehicles (UAVs) as a single, intelligent system. By mimicking the collective behavior of natural swarms, such as flocks of birds or schools of fish, AI-powered drone swarms can operate collaboratively, making autonomous decisions, adapting to dynamic environments, and executing complex tasks more efficiently than individual drones. This technology is widely used in defense, disaster response, environmental monitoring, and industrial automation.

Key Components

Decentralized Communication drone swarm AI relies on real-time data exchange between drones using wireless networks, ensuring seamless coordination and decision-making.
Autonomous Navigation AI algorithms enable drones to fly independently while maintaining formation, avoiding obstacles, and optimizing flight paths.
Swarm Intelligence machine learning and reinforcement learning allow drones to collectively analyze data, predict patterns, and adjust strategies dynamically.
Sensor Fusion integrated LiDAR, infrared, and optical cameras provide real-time situational awareness, improving decision-making and mission execution.
Edge Computing onboard AI processors enable real-time computation, reducing dependence on centralized control and allowing drones to react quickly.

Examples

Military Operations drone swarms enhance surveillance, reconnaissance, and tactical strikes by autonomously coordinating battlefield maneuvers.
Search and Rescue AI-driven swarms scan large disaster zones, identify survivors, and optimize search patterns more efficiently than human teams.
Agriculture swarms monitor crops, detect diseases, and apply pesticides with precision, improving sustainability and yield optimization.
Environmental Monitoring AI-powered drone fleets track climate changes, wildlife migration, and deforestation in remote areas.

Benefits

Increased Efficiency swarm coordination reduces task completion time, covering larger areas faster than single drones.
Redundancy and Resilience if one drone fails, others can compensate, ensuring mission continuity without human intervention.
Cost-Effective Operations AI-driven swarms reduce operational costs in industries such as logistics, agriculture, and security by minimizing manual labor.
Scalable Deployment swarm AI can be adapted for various missions, from military operations to infrastructure inspection and disaster relief.

Conclusion

Drone Swarm AI represents a groundbreaking shift in autonomous aerial systems, enabling intelligent, collaborative, and large-scale UAV operations. Through decentralized communication, swarm intelligence, and advanced sensor integration, AI-powered drone swarms enhance efficiency, scalability, and resilience across diverse industries. While challenges related to scalability, security, and regulation remain, ongoing advancements in AI, robotics, and energy solutions are expanding the potential of drone swarms, making them a key innovation in the future of autonomous aviation.

Drop-Based Learning

Definition: Drop-based learning refers to a training technique in artificial neural networks where certain units or connections are randomly deactivated or "dropped out" during the training process. This method helps to prevent overfitting by reducing the interdependence of neurons and encouraging the network to learn more robust and generalizable features.

Key Components: Dropout Rate: The probability of a neuron being dropped out during a training iteration. Random Deactivation: Neurons or connections are randomly chosen to be temporarily removed from the network. Training Iterations: The dropout process is applied during each training iteration. Weight Scaling: During testing or inference, the weights of the network are often scaled to account for the dropped units during training. Ensemble Effect: Dropout can be viewed as training an ensemble of subnetworks, which contributes to its regularization effect.

Example: Training a convolutional neural network for image classification where, in each training batch, a random selection of neurons is temporarily disabled. This forces the remaining neurons to learn more independent features, improving the network's ability to generalize to unseen images and reducing overfitting on the training data.

Benefits: Reduced Overfitting: Dropout acts as a regularizer, preventing the network from becoming too specialized to the training data. Improved Generalization: By forcing the network to learn more robust features, dropout enhances its ability to perform well on new, unseen data. Increased Robustness: The network becomes less sensitive to specific features in the training data, making it more resilient to noise and variations. Ensemble Learning Effect: Dropout effectively trains an ensemble of different sub-networks, which can lead to better performance than training a single network. Simpler Implementation: Dropout is relatively easy to implement and can be applied to various types of neural networks.

Applications: Image Recognition: Improving the performance of convolutional neural networks for image classification and object detection. Natural Language Processing: Enhancing the generalization capabilities of recurrent neural networks used in language modeling and machine translation. Speech Recognition: Helping neural networks learn more robust features from audio data. Reinforcement Learning: Making agents more resilient to noisy environments and improving exploration. Generative Models: Enhancing the stability and performance of generative adversarial networks (GANs) and variational autoencoders (VAEs).

Industries: Technology: Development of more robust and accurate AI models for various applications. Healthcare: Improving the accuracy of AI systems used in medical imaging and diagnostics. Finance: Enhancing the performance of AI models used in fraud detection and algorithmic trading. Automotive: Improving the reliability of AI systems used in autonomous vehicles. Entertainment: Enhancing the quality of AI models used in content recommendation and generation.

Conclusions: Drop-based learning, particularly dropout, is a powerful regularization technique that significantly improves the performance and generalization of neural networks. By randomly deactivating units during training, it prevents overfitting and encourages the learning of more robust features. Despite some challenges related to hyperparameter tuning and training time, the benefits of dropout make it a widely used and effective method in various AI applications and industries.

DropConnect

DropConnect is a regularization technique used in deep learning to prevent overfitting by randomly dropping connections between neurons during training. Unlike Dropout, which removes entire neurons from the network, DropConnect randomly zeroes out individual weights, forcing the network to rely on different subsets of connections during each forward pass. This encourages robustness and improves generalization in neural networks, particularly for fully connected layers and convolutional architectures.

Key Components

Random Weight Masking DropConnect applies a binary mask to the weight matrix, randomly setting certain connections to zero during training.
Stochastic Training each training iteration uses a different subset of active connections, preventing the network from relying too heavily on specific pathways.
Regularization Effect by introducing randomness in weight connectivity, DropConnect reduces the risk of overfitting and improves generalization.

Compatibility DropConnect can be applied to various neural network architectures, including convolutional and recurrent networks.
Gradient-Based Learning backpropagation still functions normally, adjusting only the remaining active connections in each training step.

Examples

Image Classification DropConnect improves the performance of convolutional neural networks by enhancing feature extraction and reducing overfitting.
Natural Language Processing recurrent neural networks trained with DropConnect generalize better for text prediction and sentiment analysis.
Medical Diagnosis AI models in healthcare use DropConnect to maintain robustness in detecting anomalies in medical images.
Autonomous Systems self-driving AI benefits from DropConnect by improving the resilience of deep learning models in uncertain environments.

Benefits

Improved Generalization DropConnect reduces the dependency on specific connections, leading to more adaptable models.
Better Robustness AI systems trained with DropConnect perform well under varying input conditions.
Enhanced Model Efficiency by forcing networks to learn multiple redundant pathways, DropConnect enables efficient use of network capacity.
Compatibility DropConnect can be applied alongside other regularization techniques like Batch Normalization and Dropout for additional performance gains.

Conclusion

DropConnect is an advanced regularization technique that enhances deep learning models by introducing stochastic weight masking, reducing overfitting, and improving generalization. By randomly disabling connections instead of entire neurons, it forces networks to develop more distributed and robust feature representations. Although it comes with computational challenges and requires fine-tuning, DropConnect remains a valuable tool for improving model performance in applications ranging from image recognition to autonomous systems.

Dropout Regularization

Dropout regularization is a technique used in deep learning to prevent overfitting by randomly deactivating a subset of neurons during training. By temporarily removing neurons, Dropout forces the network to learn redundant and distributed representations, improving generalization to unseen data. It is commonly applied to fully connected layers in neural networks, helping models perform better on classification, regression, and pattern recognition tasks.

Key Components

Neuron Deactivation during each training iteration, a fraction of neurons is randomly dropped, preventing over-reliance on specific features.
Scaling during Inference at test time, the weights of the remaining active neurons are scaled to compensate for the missing neurons used in training.
Probability Parameter dropout is controlled by a hyperparameter that determines the percentage of neurons to deactivate.
Regularization Effect by reducing co-adaptation among neurons, Dropout encourages the model to develop more generalized feature representations.

Applicability dropout is primarily used in fully connected layers but can also be adapted for convolutional and recurrent neural networks.

Examples

Image Recognition convolutional neural networks trained with Dropout generalize better to new images, reducing classification errors.
Natural Language Processing recurrent networks use Dropout to prevent overfitting when processing long sequences of text.
Financial Forecasting AI models predicting stock trends benefit from Dropout by reducing reliance on specific historical data points.
Medical Diagnosis neural networks analyzing medical images use Dropout to improve robustness and reduce false positive rates.

Benefits

Improved Generalization Dropout helps neural networks perform better on unseen data by reducing the risk of overfitting.
Robust Feature Learning by forcing the model to learn multiple representations, Dropout enhances the ability to recognize patterns in diverse datasets.
Compatibility Dropout integrates seamlessly with other regularization techniques, such as Batch Normalization and L2 regularization, for improved performance.
Computational Efficiency unlike other regularization techniques, Dropout does not significantly increase computational complexity during inference.

Conclusion

Dropout regularization is a widely used technique in deep learning that improves model robustness by randomly deactivating neurons during training. By reducing overfitting and encouraging redundancy in learned features, Dropout enhances generalization and makes AI models more adaptable to real-world data. Despite challenges in hyperparameter tuning and training time, its effectiveness in various applications, including image recognition, natural language processing, and medical diagnostics, solidifies its role as an essential component of modern neural network architectures.

Drowsiness Detection

Drowsiness Detection: refers to an artificial intelligence-driven process that identifies signs of fatigue or sleepiness in individuals, typically by analyzing behavioral, physiological, or environmental cues, to prevent accidents or enhance safety. This technology uses real-time data to alert users or systems when alertness drops below a critical threshold.

Key components of Drowsiness Detection include input sensors, such as cameras tracking eye movements or facial expressions, and wearables measuring heart rate or brain activity. A data processor interprets these signals, often using machine learning models trained to recognize patterns of fatigue. Feature detectors pinpoint specific indicators, like eyelid closure duration or head tilt, while a scoring algorithm calculates the drowsiness level. Alert mechanisms, such as audio warnings or vibrations, activate when thresholds are crossed, and a feedback loop refines detection accuracy over time.

Benefits flow from its proactive safety enhancements, reducing risks in high-stake situations by catching drowsiness early. It boosts productivity by minimizing fatigue-related errors and supports health by encouraging rest when needed. Non-invasive versions offer ease of use, while real-time monitoring ensures timely interventions. Its adaptability makes it valuable across diverse settings, saving lives and resources.

Industry applications demonstrate its wide relevance. In automotive, it monitors drivers' eyes and posture to prevent collisions, integrated into advanced driver-assistance systems. Transportation extends this to pilots and train operators, safeguarding long-haul operations. Workplace safety employs it in factories, alerting machine operators to fatigue. Healthcare uses it to track patient alertness during recovery or medication trials. Education explores it to gauge student engagement in classrooms or online learning.

Conclusions about Drowsiness Detection highlight its role as a critical safety net, blending AI's analytical power with practical impact. It stands out for protecting lives in an increasingly automated world, though perfecting its precision and acceptance remains a work in progress. As technology advances, its potential to mitigate fatigue-related risks positions it as an essential tool for modern living.

Dual-Agent Systems

Dual-agent systems refer to artificial intelligence frameworks in which two autonomous agents collaborate, compete, or interact to achieve specific goals. These systems are commonly used in reinforcement learning, robotics, game theory, and decision-making applications where multi-agent coordination or adversarial learning is required. Dual-agent AI can be applied in scenarios such as negotiation, strategic gameplay, and cooperative problem-solving, enabling more dynamic and adaptive AI-driven interactions.

Key Components

Agent Collaboration two AI entities work together to optimize outcomes, learning from each other's actions and decisions.
Adversarial Interaction agents may compete against each other, as seen in reinforcement learning environments and game-based AI training.
Communication Protocols structured exchanges of information between agents ensure seamless coordination and strategy alignment.
Reinforcement Learning feedback loops allow each agent to improve performance through trial and error, optimizing their decision-making over time.
Autonomous Adaptation dual-agent systems continuously refine strategies based on evolving scenarios and real-time data inputs.

Examples

Game AI competitive AI systems, such as those used in chess or Go, train by playing against an adversarial agent to improve strategy.
Autonomous Vehicles dual-agent AI is used in self-driving systems where one agent predicts human driver behavior while another optimizes vehicle control.
Negotiation AI AI-powered bargaining systems use dual-agent models to simulate real-world negotiations, improving decision-making in business and diplomacy.
Robotics teams of collaborative robots use dual-agent systems to coordinate movement and execute complex tasks efficiently.

Benefits

Enhanced Learning dual-agent training accelerates AI model improvement through continuous interaction and adaptation.
Real-World Simulation AI systems that model human-like cooperation and competition improve predictive accuracy in decision-making.
Scalability dual-agent frameworks can be extended into multi-agent systems, allowing broader applications in AI research.

Improved Problem-Solving AI agents working together can find innovative solutions to complex problems beyond single-agent capabilities.

Conclusion

Dual-agent systems are a powerful AI paradigm that enables collaborative, competitive, and adaptive intelligence in machine learning applications. By facilitating real-time interactions between two autonomous agents, these systems drive advancements in strategic gameplay, autonomous robotics, and negotiation AI. While challenges related to coordination, computational demands, and unpredictability persist, ongoing research in multi-agent reinforcement learning and AI-driven communication continues to refine dual-agent models, expanding their potential in diverse fields of artificial intelligence.

Dual Attention Mechanism

Dual Attention Mechanism refers to an advanced technique in artificial intelligence, particularly in neural networks, where two separate attention processes work together to focus on different aspects of input data, enhancing the model's ability to understand and process complex information. This approach amplifies contextual awareness by simultaneously prioritizing relevant features and relationships within the data.

Key components of Dual Attention Mechanism include the primary attention layer, which targets specific elements like words or image regions based on their immediate importance, and the secondary attention layer, which captures broader dependencies, such as connections across sentences or spatial patterns. A fusion module integrates the outputs of both layers, ensuring a cohesive representation. Weighting functions assign significance to each attention process, while a training optimizer adjusts these weights to balance their contributions. Normalization steps maintain stability across the dual focus.

Benefits emerge from this dual focus, as it allows deeper comprehension of intricate data structures, improving accuracy in tasks requiring nuance. It reduces oversight of subtle details by combining local and global perspectives, leading to richer feature extraction. Efficiency rises as the model processes only the most relevant information, cutting computational waste. Adaptability to varied inputs makes it versatile across domains, and it often outperforms single-attention setups in precision.

Industry applications showcase its versatility. In natural language processing, it powers translation systems by focusing on both individual words and sentence context. In healthcare, it aids medical imaging analysis, highlighting specific anomalies while mapping their relation to the whole scan. Autonomous vehicles use it to process sensor data, attending to nearby obstacles and distant road patterns simultaneously. In e-commerce, recommendation engines leverage it to weigh user preferences against trending items. Video analysis benefits from tracking objects frame-by-frame while understanding scene progression.

Conclusions about Dual Attention Mechanism point to its strength in elevating AI's grasp of multifaceted data, blending fine-grained and big-picture insights seamlessly. It represents a leap in attention-based learning, promising superior performance where context is king. Though resource-intensive and tricky to perfect, its ability to refine understanding makes it a valuable tool, poised to shape future innovations in intelligent systems.

Dual Input Networks

Dual Input Networks: refer to artificial intelligence architectures that process two distinct data streams simultaneously within a single neural network, combining them to generate a unified output or decision.

This design excels at tasks requiring the integration of diverse information sources, leveraging the interplay between inputs to enhance predictive power.

Key components of Dual Input Networks include the primary input channel, which handles one data type, such as text or numerical values, and the secondary input channel, dedicated to a complementary type, like images or audio. Feature extractors within each channel preprocess the inputs, tailoring them for analysis. A merging layer fuses the processed data, often through concatenation or weighted summation, while a shared processing core, typically a deep neural network, interprets the combined features. Output generators then produce the final result, guided by a loss function that optimizes across both inputs.

Benefits arise from their ability to synthesize disparate data, yielding richer insights than single-input models. They improve accuracy by capturing correlations between inputs that might otherwise be missed. Flexibility in handling multimodal data broadens their utility, and parallel processing of inputs can boost efficiency when well-optimized. Robustness increases as the network learns to weigh each input's relevance, adapting to varying data quality.

Industry applications highlight their practical reach. In healthcare, they analyze patient records alongside medical scans to refine diagnoses. Social media platforms use them to pair text posts with images for sentiment analysis or content moderation. In finance, they integrate market trends with news articles for stock predictions. Autonomous systems combine sensor data and GPS inputs for navigation. Retail employs them to merge customer demographics with purchase histories for personalized marketing.

Conclusions about Dual Input Networks underscore their potential to unlock deeper understanding from multimodal data, bridging gaps single-input systems can't. They offer a powerful framework for tasks demanding synergy, driving innovation across industries. While resource-heavy and intricate to perfect, their capacity to blend diverse inputs positions them as a cornerstone for advancing AI's real-world impact.

Dual Learning

Dual Learning is an advanced machine learning framework that enhances model performance by leveraging bidirectional tasks. This method allows two complementary models to learn from each other, using a feedback loop that improves accuracy and efficiency. It is particularly useful in areas such as machine translation and reinforcement learning, where learning from both directions leads to better generalization.

The key components of dual learning include bidirectional task execution, a reinforcement feedback loop, and adaptive learning mechanisms. In this process, information flows in two directions, allowing the model to evaluate and refine its predictions iteratively. Reinforcement mechanisms guide the model by rewarding accurate predictions and penalizing errors, ensuring continuous improvement. Adaptive learning enables models to adjust to new data dynamically, improving long-term effectiveness.

One of the main benefits of dual learning is the reduction of data requirements since learning occurs in both directions, maximizing the use of available information. The bidirectional feedback system enhances learning speed and accuracy, leading to stronger generalization across different applications. This approach also improves model stability, making it more robust against data variability.

Dual learning features a self-supervised training loop that minimizes reliance on large labeled datasets. The adaptive feedback mechanism continuously refines the model, ensuring better performance with minimal human intervention. Its efficiency in utilizing existing data makes it particularly useful in areas where obtaining labeled datasets is costly or difficult.

This method is widely applied in natural language processing, autonomous systems, financial modeling, and medical diagnostics. In machine translation, it allows AI models to improve translations by learning from both source and target languages. In autonomous vehicles, it enhances decision-making by continuously refining driving patterns. In finance, it strengthens fraud detection by learning from normal and fraudulent transaction patterns simultaneously. In healthcare, it assists in medical diagnosis by learning from symptom-disease relationships in both directions.

Industries that benefit from dual learning include technology, finance, healthcare, and transportation. Companies working on AI-driven automation, security, and predictive analytics incorporate this method to improve their AI systems.

In conclusion, dual learning is a powerful technique that enhances AI efficiency by utilizing bidirectional learning and feedback loops. Despite its computational intensity and complexity, it has transformative applications across industries, making it a valuable approach in modern AI development.

Dual Objective Optimization

Dual Objective Optimization is a machine learning optimization method that focuses on improving two competing or complementary objectives simultaneously. Unlike single-objective optimization, this approach ensures a balance between two key factors, making it essential for applications where trade-offs must be managed effectively. It is widely used in decision-making models, resource allocation, and AI-driven predictions.

The core components of dual objective optimization include multi-objective function modeling, constraint balancing, and Pareto efficiency analysis. Multi-objective function modeling ensures that both objectives are considered during the optimization process. Constraint balancing prevents one objective from overshadowing the other, ensuring an optimal trade-off. Pareto efficiency analysis identifies solutions where improving one objective does not disproportionately harm the other.

The main benefits of dual objective optimization include improved decision-making by considering multiple factors, increased adaptability across different domains, and enhanced efficiency in resource allocation. This approach allows AI models to generate more realistic and balanced outcomes, reducing bias that can result from focusing on a single objective.

This method features an advanced optimization framework that dynamically adjusts the weight of each objective based on contextual changes. The ability to optimize conflicting objectives makes it highly effective in areas where trade-offs are necessary. Its flexibility allows AI models to operate efficiently across different datasets and problem domains.

Applications of dual objective optimization span industries such as finance, healthcare, manufacturing, and energy management. In financial markets, it is used to balance risk and return in investment portfolios. In healthcare, it helps in treatment planning by optimizing medical effectiveness while minimizing side effects. In manufacturing, it optimizes production costs while ensuring high-quality output. In energy systems, it finds the best trade-off between consumption and sustainability.

Industries that utilize dual objective optimization include banking, pharmaceuticals, industrial automation, and logistics. Organizations in these sectors rely on AI-driven optimization to improve efficiency, reduce costs, and enhance operational decision-making.

In conclusion, dual objective optimization is a crucial AI technique for balancing multiple objectives in decision-making processes. While it presents computational and interpretational challenges, its ability to enhance efficiency and adaptability makes it a valuable tool in industries requiring optimal trade-offs.

Dual Representation Learning

Dual Representation Learning is a machine learning approach that integrates two different representations of data to improve model accuracy and generalization. By learning from two perspectives, AI systems become more adaptable and robust, making this method particularly useful in multimodal AI, computer vision, and natural language processing.

The essential components of dual representation learning include feature extraction, representation fusion, deep learning architectures, and semantic alignment. Feature extraction ensures that relevant attributes are captured from two distinct data sources. Representation fusion combines these attributes in a meaningful way to enhance model predictions. Deep learning architectures, such as convolutional and recurrent neural networks, process the extracted features efficiently. Semantic alignment ensures that the dual representations are consistent and contribute effectively to learning.

The main benefits of dual representation learning include improved model accuracy by leveraging multiple data perspectives, enhanced robustness against noisy or missing data, and better generalization across different applications. By integrating different representations, AI models become more resilient to variations in input data, leading to better predictive performance.

This approach features advanced data fusion techniques that combine multiple representations into a unified model. It allows AI systems to process multimodal inputs, making it highly effective in tasks that require analyzing both structured and unstructured data. The ability to learn from diverse sources enhances adaptability and reliability.

Applications of dual representation learning are seen in healthcare, autonomous systems, e-commerce, and cybersecurity. In medical diagnosis, it combines patient records with imaging data for improved accuracy. In autonomous driving, it integrates sensor readings with visual data to enhance real-time decision-making. In e-commerce, it enhances recommendation systems by analyzing both user behavior and product descriptions. In cybersecurity, it strengthens threat detection by merging network traffic analysis with behavioral patterns.

Industries that benefit from dual representation learning include technology, retail, finance, and transportation. AI-driven applications in these industries rely on dual representation learning to improve decision-making, automation, and predictive analytics.

In conclusion, dual representation learning is a powerful AI technique that enhances learning capabilities by integrating different data perspectives. Despite challenges related to computational complexity and data fusion, its applications across healthcare, autonomous systems, and e-commerce highlight its potential in advancing AI-driven solutions.

Dual-Task Learning

Dual-Task Learning is a machine learning approach that enables an AI model to perform two tasks simultaneously, leveraging shared representations to improve efficiency and accuracy. Instead of training separate models for each task, this method integrates them into a unified framework, allowing for mutual learning benefits. It is commonly used in scenarios where tasks have overlapping characteristics, such as speech recognition and text prediction.

The key components of dual-task learning include a shared feature extraction layer, task-specific output layers, a multitasking loss function, and a training optimization process that ensures both tasks benefit from shared learning without compromising performance. By structuring the model to recognize correlations between tasks, it reduces redundancy and enhances generalization capabilities.

The features of dual-task learning include joint optimization for multiple objectives, increased data efficiency, and improved model adaptability across similar tasks. It is particularly beneficial in situations where one task can provide supplementary information for the other, reducing the need for extensive labeled data.

One of the major benefits of dual-task learning is improved learning efficiency. By utilizing common patterns between tasks, the model achieves better performance with fewer training resources. It also enhances generalization, making it effective for AI systems that need to operate across multiple domains. The reduction in overfitting is another advantage, as shared feature learning prevents excessive specialization on a single task.

This method is applied in various domains such as natural language processing, computer vision, and autonomous systems. In speech-to-text models, for example, dual-task learning is used to improve both transcription accuracy and speaker identification. In medical imaging, it enhances both disease detection and segmentation in X-rays and MRIs. In robotics, it helps AI models simultaneously learn object recognition and grasping techniques.

Industries that benefit from dual-task learning include healthcare, automotive, finance, and e-commerce. In self-driving cars, AI models learn road sign recognition while improving lane detection. In finance, fraud detection models optimize transaction classification alongside anomaly detection to enhance security measures.

In conclusion, dual-task learning is a powerful technique that improves AI efficiency and adaptability by training models to perform two related tasks simultaneously. Despite the computational and optimization challenges, its ability to enhance performance in diverse industries makes it a valuable approach in modern AI development.

Dualism and materialism

Dualism and Materialism are two fundamental philosophical perspectives on the nature of reality, particularly concerning the relationship between the mind and the physical world. Dualism asserts that reality consists of two distinct substances: the material and the immaterial. This view suggests that the mind and consciousness exist separately from the physical brain and body, implying that thoughts, emotions, and mental experiences are not solely the result of physical processes. Materialism, in contrast, holds that everything that exists, including consciousness and thought, can be explained entirely by physical matter and its interactions. According to materialism, the mind is a product of brain activity, governed by the laws of physics and biology.

The key components of dualism include the distinction between the physical and non-physical realms, where the mind or soul is considered separate from the body. Interactionism within dualism explores how the immaterial mind influences the material world, often leading to debates about free will and consciousness. Property dualism suggests that while the mind and body are composed of the same physical substance, mental states possess unique properties that cannot be reduced to physical explanations. In contrast, materialism relies on physicalism, which argues that all phenomena, including consciousness, emerge from physical processes. Neuroscience and cognitive science provide evidence supporting materialism by demonstrating correlations between brain activity and mental experiences. Reductionism within materialism aims to explain complex mental states in terms of simpler physical interactions.

One of the primary benefits of dualism is its alignment with human intuition, as individuals often perceive their consciousness as separate from their physical body. It provides a framework for discussions on free will, personal identity, and the existence of an afterlife. Dualism has influenced religious and metaphysical perspectives, shaping concepts of the soul and spiritual existence. Materialism, on the other hand, has contributed to scientific advancements by emphasizing empirical research and testable explanations for mental phenomena. It has driven progress in neuroscience, artificial intelligence, and cognitive psychology by treating consciousness as an emergent property of the brain. Materialism supports technological developments in brain-machine interfaces, artificial intelligence, and mental health treatment by focusing on biological and computational models of thought.

Examples of dualism appear in religious and philosophical traditions that propose an eternal soul distinct from the body. René Descartes' mind-body dualism suggests that the mind is a non-physical entity interacting with the brain. The concept of near-death experiences, where individuals report consciousness outside their physical body, is often cited as supporting dualism. Materialism is reflected in neuroscience, where brain scans reveal how cognitive processes correspond to neural activity. Artificial intelligence research follows a materialist framework by attempting to replicate thought processes through computational models. Advancements in neuroprosthetics and brain implants demonstrate the materialist view that modifying brain structures can alter perception and behavior.

Industries influenced by dualism include philosophy, where debates on consciousness, free will, and the afterlife continue to shape metaphysical inquiry. Religious and spiritual communities incorporate dualist perspectives into their doctrines regarding the soul and personal identity beyond physical existence. Psychology and psychotherapy explore the implications of dualism in discussions about consciousness, perception, and mental health. Materialism drives advancements in neuroscience, leading to breakthroughs in brain imaging, neuroplasticity research, and treatments for cognitive disorders. Artificial intelligence and robotics apply materialist principles in developing machines that mimic human cognition. The healthcare industry benefits from materialist approaches to mental health treatment, drug development, and medical interventions that enhance brain function.

Dualism and materialism offer two contrasting perspectives on the nature of consciousness and reality, shaping discussions in philosophy, science, and technology. While dualism aligns with intuitive and spiritual beliefs, materialism provides a framework for empirical research and technological progress. Both views continue to influence debates on the mind-body relationship, free will, artificial intelligence, and the future of human cognition. As scientific advancements deepen our understanding of consciousness, the interplay between dualist and materialist perspectives will shape the evolution of philosophy, neuroscience, and artificial intelligence.

Dueling Neural Networks

Dueling Neural Networks are a deep learning architecture designed to improve decision-making efficiency in reinforcement learning tasks. Unlike standard neural networks, this structure separates the estimation of state-value and advantage functions, allowing the model to distinguish between general states and specific action-based improvements. This separation enhances the learning stability and efficiency of AI agents, making it widely used in reinforcement learning applications.

The main components of dueling neural networks include a shared feature representation layer, a value estimation network, and an advantage estimation network. The value network estimates the importance of a given state, while the advantage network determines the benefit of selecting specific actions. By combining these two outputs, the final decision-making process is more refined and stable.

Key features of dueling neural networks include enhanced stability in deep reinforcement learning, efficient learning of complex state-action relationships, and improved convergence speed. The architecture is particularly useful in environments where certain actions may not significantly impact outcomes, helping the model focus on meaningful decisions.

One of the major benefits of this approach is improved learning efficiency. By separately estimating state values and advantages, the model learns faster and requires fewer training iterations. The increased stability of learning also reduces fluctuations in decision-making, which is essential for AI agents operating in dynamic environments. Additionally, this structure leads to better generalization, allowing models to adapt to new states more effectively.

Dueling neural networks are commonly applied in reinforcement learning environments such as game-playing AI, autonomous driving, and robotic control. They have been successfully implemented in deep Q-learning models to enhance AI performance in complex decision-making scenarios. For instance, in gaming AI, this architecture has been used to optimize strategy planning in board games and video games. In robotics, it enhances robotic arm movements by refining the decision-making process.

Industries that leverage dueling neural networks include automation, robotics, gaming, finance, and healthcare. In financial markets, AI models use this approach to improve trading strategies by distinguishing between market state values and action advantages. In healthcare, it is applied in AI-driven diagnostics to optimize treatment decision-making.

In conclusion, dueling neural networks provide an innovative reinforcement learning framework that enhances AI decision-making efficiency. Despite the architectural complexity and computational costs, its benefits in AI-driven automation, gaming, and financial analytics make it a critical advancement in deep learning.

Dummy Variable Encoding

Dummy Variable Encoding is a technique used in machine learning and statistical modeling to transform categorical variables into numerical representations. Since many machine learning algorithms require numerical inputs, this encoding method ensures that categorical data can be used effectively in predictive models. It is commonly applied in regression analysis, classification tasks, and feature engineering.

The core components of dummy variable encoding include categorical feature identification, one-hot encoding transformation, and numerical representation of distinct categories. Each categorical value is converted into a binary variable, creating a set of dummy variables that represent different classes within the dataset.

The primary features of dummy variable encoding include its ability to handle non-numeric data, improve model interpretability, and enhance compatibility with machine learning algorithms. It prevents models from misinterpreting categorical variables as ordinal data, ensuring that different categories are treated independently.

The main benefits of dummy variable encoding include increased accuracy in predictive modeling, better feature integration, and improved handling of categorical attributes. By converting categorical data into a format that machine learning models can understand, it reduces bias and improves decision-making.

This method is widely applied in natural language processing, healthcare analytics, customer segmentation, and financial modeling. In sentiment analysis, dummy encoding is used to convert text-based categories into numerical inputs. In medical research, patient demographics are transformed into dummy variables to predict disease outcomes.

Industries that frequently use dummy variable encoding include finance, healthcare, e-commerce, and marketing. In the financial sector, credit risk assessment models use encoded categorical variables to predict loan default probabilities. In marketing, customer behavior analysis benefits from categorical feature encoding to improve targeted advertising.

In conclusion, dummy variable encoding is a fundamental technique in data preprocessing, enabling machine learning models to process categorical variables effectively. While it introduces potential issues related to high dimensionality, its role in improving model accuracy and interpretability makes it a vital tool in AI and data science.

Durability in AI Models

Durability in AI Models refers to the ability of machine learning models to maintain accuracy and performance over extended periods, even as data distributions change. A durable AI model remains effective despite evolving environments, data shifts, and changing user behavior. This concept is critical in ensuring long-term reliability and stability in AI applications.

The essential components of durability in AI models include model generalization, adaptability, robust training techniques, and continuous monitoring. A well-designed model should generalize across different datasets, remain flexible to evolving patterns, and be trained using robust methodologies to prevent degradation over time.

Durability in AI models is characterized by resilience to data drift, stability in predictions, and minimal degradation over time. It involves continuous learning mechanisms, periodic model retraining, and automated monitoring systems that detect performance declines.

The primary benefits of durable AI models include reduced maintenance costs, improved long-term accuracy, and enhanced reliability. Businesses and organizations benefit from AI systems that do not require frequent retraining, minimizing disruptions and operational costs.

Durability is crucial in industries such as healthcare, finance, cybersecurity, and autonomous systems. In fraud detection, AI models must remain effective even as fraudulent behaviors evolve. In healthcare, predictive analytics tools need to adapt to new medical research and patient trends.

In conclusion, durability in AI models is a fundamental requirement for long-term reliability and efficiency. By ensuring adaptability and monitoring performance, AI systems can remain effective across changing environments.

Dynamic Attention Mechanism

Dynamic Attention Mechanism is an advanced AI technique that enables models to focus on the most relevant information at any given moment, dynamically adjusting attention weights based on input data. This method improves the efficiency and accuracy of neural networks, particularly in tasks requiring sequential or contextual understanding.

The key components of dynamic attention mechanisms include attention scoring functions, context-aware weighting, neural network architectures, and adaptive focus adjustments. Attention scoring functions determine the importance of different input elements. Context-aware weighting dynamically assigns significance to different parts of the data. Neural network architectures, such as transformers and recurrent networks, use these mechanisms to process sequences efficiently. Adaptive focus adjustments ensure that the model continuously refines its attention based on new input patterns.

The primary benefits of dynamic attention mechanisms include improved model interpretability, enhanced efficiency in processing large datasets, and better performance in natural language understanding and image recognition. By allowing models to selectively focus on critical data points, this technique reduces computational overhead while increasing accuracy.

Dynamic attention mechanisms feature context-sensitive learning, selective focus allocation, and real-time attention adjustments. The ability to dynamically change attention based on input variations makes it highly effective in AI-driven decision-making and perception tasks.

Applications of this approach are widely seen in natural language processing, computer vision, speech recognition, and autonomous systems. In text summarization, dynamic attention helps models extract key information efficiently. In image processing, it enhances object detection by focusing on significant image regions. In speech recognition, it improves transcription accuracy by prioritizing essential phonetic cues. In robotics, it enables AI to focus on relevant sensory inputs for real-time navigation.

Industries utilizing dynamic attention mechanisms include artificial intelligence research, healthcare, finance, and autonomous technology. Organizations implementing deep learning models for complex pattern recognition tasks benefit from this advanced focus mechanism.

In conclusion, dynamic attention mechanisms significantly improve AI efficiency and accuracy by allowing models to selectively focus on the most relevant data. Despite challenges in implementation and computation, their impact on AI-driven tasks such as natural language understanding and computer vision makes them a valuable innovation.

Dynamic Bayesian Networks

Dynamic Bayesian Networks are probabilistic models that extend traditional Bayesian networks by incorporating temporal dependencies, allowing AI systems to model sequences and time-series data effectively. These networks are widely used for forecasting, decision-making, and anomaly detection.

The key components of dynamic Bayesian networks include probabilistic inference, time-dependent structures, hidden variables, and transition models. Probabilistic inference enables AI systems to estimate future states based on current and past observations. Time-dependent structures define the relationships between variables across different time steps. Hidden variables help capture latent dependencies, while transition models guide the evolution of the network over time.

The primary benefits of dynamic Bayesian networks include improved predictive accuracy, enhanced ability to model uncertain environments, and better handling of sequential data. Their probabilistic nature allows AI models to make informed predictions even when data is incomplete or noisy.

Dynamic Bayesian networks feature adaptive temporal learning, efficient probability estimation, and robust handling of uncertainty. Their ability to process time-dependent relationships makes them ideal for applications requiring continuous prediction and reasoning.

Applications of dynamic Bayesian networks include finance, healthcare, autonomous systems, and cybersecurity. In stock market prediction, they analyze historical data to forecast trends. In medical diagnosis, they model disease progression over time. In autonomous driving, they help predict vehicle behavior in real-world environments. In cybersecurity, they assist in identifying emerging threats based on network activity patterns.

Industries that benefit from dynamic Bayesian networks include banking, medical research, insurance, and robotics. Organizations requiring advanced probabilistic reasoning integrate these networks into AI-driven decision systems.

In conclusion, dynamic Bayesian networks provide a powerful approach to modeling time-series data and uncertain environments. While they require substantial computational effort, their ability to enhance predictive accuracy and decision-making makes them a crucial tool in AI applications.

Dynamic Embeddings

Dynamic Embeddings are an advanced representation learning technique where embeddings evolve over time to reflect changes in data distribution, context, or relationships. Unlike static embeddings that remain fixed once trained, dynamic embeddings adapt continuously, making them particularly effective in domains where real-time changes influence meaning or behavior, such as natural language processing, recommendation systems, and knowledge graphs.

The key components of dynamic embeddings include adaptive vector representations, temporal modeling mechanisms, neural network architectures, and real-time learning updates. Adaptive vector representations ensure that embeddings adjust as new data is introduced. Temporal modeling mechanisms capture changes in relationships over time. Neural network architectures, such as recurrent or graph-based models, refine embedding structures. Real-time learning updates allow embeddings to be adjusted dynamically based on evolving input patterns.

The primary benefits of dynamic embeddings include improved model adaptability, enhanced contextual understanding, and greater robustness in handling evolving data. By continuously updating representations, AI systems remain relevant even when new words, user behaviors, or relationships emerge. This leads to more accurate predictions and better personalization in applications such as recommendation engines and search engines.

Dynamic embeddings feature continuous learning capabilities, real-time adaptation, and contextual awareness. Their ability to change in response to new data ensures that models remain effective without requiring frequent retraining. They enable AI to process evolving patterns in language, network interactions, and user behavior with greater accuracy.

Applications of dynamic embeddings include natural language processing, social network analysis, recommendation systems, and fraud detection. In language models, they enhance word and sentence representations by incorporating recent linguistic trends. In social networks, they track evolving relationships and community structures. In recommendation systems, they refine personalized content delivery based on real-time user interactions. In fraud detection, they help AI recognize new fraudulent patterns as they develop.

Industries benefiting from dynamic embeddings include technology, e-commerce, cybersecurity, and finance. AI-driven applications in these sectors rely on dynamic embeddings to improve adaptability and responsiveness to shifting data trends.

In conclusion, dynamic embeddings provide a powerful way to maintain contextual relevance and adaptability in AI models. While they introduce computational challenges, their ability to evolve with changing data makes them essential for modern AI applications.

Dynamic Environment Adaptation

Dynamic Environment Adaptation refers to an AI system's ability to adjust its behavior, parameters, or strategies in response to real-time environmental changes. This capability is crucial for AI models operating in unpredictable or constantly evolving conditions, such as robotics, autonomous systems, and adaptive learning platforms.

The key components of dynamic environment adaptation include sensory data processing, real-time feedback loops, adaptive decision-making models, and self-learning mechanisms. Sensory data processing allows AI to interpret environmental inputs accurately. Real-time feedback loops provide continuous monitoring and adjustments. Adaptive decision-making models enable AI to choose the best response based on contextual shifts. Self-learning mechanisms refine AI performance over time by learning from past interactions.

The major benefits of dynamic environment adaptation include increased resilience, improved decision-making accuracy, and enhanced efficiency in handling uncertainty. AI models using this approach can operate in highly variable environments while maintaining optimal performance. This reduces the need for human intervention and enables greater automation.

Dynamic environment adaptation features autonomous learning, flexible response mechanisms, and real-time optimization. Its ability to adjust model parameters dynamically allows AI to operate effectively across diverse situations, from navigating traffic conditions to responding to cybersecurity threats.

Applications of dynamic environment adaptation are found in robotics, autonomous vehicles, personalized education, and industrial automation. In robotics, it allows AI-powered machines to interact with changing surroundings. In autonomous vehicles, it helps cars adjust to varying road conditions and driving behaviors. In personalized education, it adapts learning materials based on a student's progress. In industrial automation, it optimizes manufacturing processes by responding to real-time operational data.

Industries leveraging dynamic environment adaptation include transportation, education, healthcare, and defense. AI-driven automation and decision-making systems in these fields depend on dynamic adaptation to improve safety, efficiency, and reliability.

In conclusion, dynamic environment adaptation enables AI models to perform effectively in changing conditions. Despite implementation challenges, its role in enhancing resilience and efficiency across industries makes it a fundamental aspect of intelligent automation.

Dynamic Feature Selection

Dynamic Feature Selection is a machine learning technique that enables AI models to select the most relevant features in real time based on data characteristics and evolving patterns. Unlike static feature selection, which determines important features before training, dynamic selection adjusts feature importance dynamically, improving efficiency and predictive performance.

The key components of dynamic feature selection include real-time data analysis, feature ranking algorithms, model interpretability mechanisms, and adaptive optimization. Real-time data analysis identifies significant features based on current input conditions. Feature ranking algorithms prioritize attributes that contribute the most to model accuracy. Model interpretability mechanisms provide insights into why certain features are selected or discarded. Adaptive optimization ensures that the selected features remain relevant over time.

The main benefits of dynamic feature selection include improved model efficiency, reduced overfitting, and enhanced adaptability to changing data distributions. By selecting only the most relevant features for each prediction, AI models process information faster and require less computational power. This approach also prevents irrelevant features from introducing noise into the model.

Dynamic feature selection features real-time feature pruning, self-optimizing model structures, and context-aware learning. Its ability to refine feature importance dynamically makes it highly effective in domains where feature relevance fluctuates, such as financial forecasting and medical diagnostics.

Applications of dynamic feature selection include healthcare analytics, fraud detection, real-time bidding in online advertising, and automated financial modeling. In healthcare, it enhances disease prediction by focusing on the most relevant patient attributes. In fraud detection, it adapts to new fraudulent tactics by identifying emerging patterns. In online advertising, it optimizes ad placement by selecting user behavior features in real time. In financial modeling, it adjusts investment strategies based on changing market indicators.

Industries utilizing dynamic feature selection include banking, advertising, healthcare, and e-commerce. Companies relying on predictive modeling integrate this technique to enhance decision-making and model efficiency.

In conclusion, dynamic feature selection enhances AI models by allowing them to identify and prioritize relevant features in real time. Despite computational challenges, its role in improving efficiency and adaptability makes it a valuable tool for various industries.

Dynamic Fusion Networks (DFNs)

Definition: Dynamic Fusion Networks (DFNs) are a type of neural network architecture designed to dynamically integrate information from multiple sources or modalities. Unlike static fusion methods where the fusion strategy is fixed, DFNs adapt their fusion process based on the input data, allowing for more flexible and effective information integration.

Key Components: Multiple Input Branches: The network has separate branches to process each input modality. Dynamic Fusion Mechanism: A module that dynamically determines how to combine the features from different branches. This can involve attention mechanisms, gating mechanisms, or other adaptive fusion strategies. Learnable Fusion Weights: The weights or parameters governing the fusion process are learned during training. Contextual Adaptation: The fusion process can be conditioned on the input data, allowing the network to adapt its fusion strategy to different scenarios. End-to-End Training: DFNs are typically trained end-to-end, allowing the fusion mechanism to be optimized for the specific task.

Benefits: Enhanced Performance: By dynamically adapting the fusion process, DFNs can achieve better performance than static fusion methods. Flexibility: DFNs can handle inputs with varying degrees of relevance or importance by adjusting the fusion strategy accordingly. Robustness: Dynamic fusion can make the network more robust to missing or noisy input modalities. Interpretability: Some DFN architectures provide insights into which modalities are most important for a given input. Generalizability: The dynamic nature of fusion can improve the network's ability to generalize to new data.

Examples: A DFN for multimodal sentiment analysis that dynamically weights the contributions of text, audio, and video based on the input. A DFN for medical diagnosis that integrates information from different medical images and patient records, with the fusion strategy adapting based on the specific case. A DFN for autonomous driving that combines data from different sensors, such as cameras, LiDAR, and radar, dynamically adjusting the fusion based on the driving scenario.

Applications: Multimodal Sentiment Analysis: Combining text, audio, and video to determine sentiment. Medical Diagnosis: Integrating different types of medical data for accurate diagnosis. Autonomous Driving: Fusing data from multiple sensors for safe navigation. Human Activity Recognition: Combining data from different sensors to recognize activities. Visual Question Answering: Integrating visual and textual information to answer questions about images.

Industries: Technology: Development of advanced AI systems for various applications. Healthcare: Improving diagnostic and treatment processes using multimodal data. Automotive: Enhancing the safety and reliability of autonomous vehicles. Entertainment: Creating more engaging and personalized multimedia experiences. Security: Developing more robust and adaptable security systems.

Conclusions: Dynamic Fusion Networks offer a powerful approach to integrating information from multiple sources by dynamically adapting the fusion process. Their ability to handle varying input relevance, improve robustness, and enhance performance makes them valuable for a wide range of applications. While challenges related to complexity and training exist, DFNs represent a significant advancement in multimodal learning and information integration.

Dynamic Graph Neural Networks (DGNNs)

Definition: Dynamic Graph Neural Networks (DGNNs) are a type of graph neural network designed to handle graphs that evolve over time. Unlike static GNNs that operate on fixed graphs, DGNNs can model the changing structure and node features of dynamic graphs, making them suitable for applications involving temporal data.

Key Components: Temporal Graph Representation: Methods for representing how the graph structure and node features change over time, such as sequences of graph snapshots or continuous-time representations. Temporal Aggregation: Mechanisms to aggregate information from different time steps, capturing the temporal dependencies in the graph. Node Embedding Evolution: Techniques to update node embeddings based on the changing graph structure and features. Recurrent or Attention Mechanisms: Often used to model the temporal dynamics of the graph. Graph Convolution Operations: Applying graph convolution on the graph snapshots or integrating temporal information into the convolution process.

Benefits: Modeling Temporal Dependencies: DGNNs can capture the temporal evolution of relationships and node features in dynamic graphs. Improved Accuracy: By considering the temporal aspect, DGNNs can achieve better performance on tasks involving dynamic graphs compared to static GNNs. Handling Evolving Graphs: DGNNs are designed to handle graphs where the structure and node features change over time. Versatility: DGNNs can be applied to various types of dynamic graphs, such as social networks, traffic networks, and biological networks. Interpretability: Some DGNN architectures can provide insights into how the graph evolves over time.

Examples: A DGNN for predicting link formation in social networks, where the graph structure changes as new connections are formed. A DGNN for traffic prediction, where the graph represents road networks and node features represent traffic conditions that change over time. A DGNN for analyzing protein interaction networks, where the graph structure and node features evolve over time.

Applications: Social Network Analysis: Predicting link formation, community evolution, and user behavior in dynamic social networks. Traffic Prediction: Forecasting traffic flow and congestion in transportation networks. Biological Network Analysis: Studying the evolution of protein interaction networks and other biological systems. Financial Forecasting: Predicting market trends and relationships between financial entities. Recommendation Systems: Modeling evolving user preferences and item relationships.

Industries: Technology: Analysis of social networks, recommendation systems, and network infrastructure. Transportation: Traffic management and urban planning. Healthcare: Analysis of biological networks and patient data. Finance: Financial modeling and fraud detection. E-commerce: Personalization and recommendation systems.

Conclusions: Dynamic Graph Neural Networks provide a powerful framework for analyzing and modeling dynamic graphs that evolve over time. Their ability to capture temporal dependencies and handle evolving graph structures makes them valuable for a wide range of applications. While challenges related to complexity and computational cost exist, DGNNs represent a significant advancement in graph learning and have the potential to unlock new insights from temporal graph data.

Dynamic Kernel Learning

Definition: Dynamic Kernel Learning refers to a set of techniques in machine learning where the kernel function used in kernel methods, such as Support Vector Machines (SVMs), is adapted or learned dynamically based on the input data or the learning task. This allows the model to capture more complex relationships and patterns in the data compared to using a fixed kernel.

Key Components: Kernel Function: A function that measures the similarity between data points. Dynamic Adaptation: Mechanisms to adjust the kernel function during training or inference. Learnable Kernel Parameters: The parameters of the kernel function are learned from the data. Kernel Combination: Combining multiple base kernels to form a more flexible kernel. Meta-Learning: Using meta-learning techniques to learn how to adapt the kernel function.

Benefits: Improved Accuracy: Dynamic kernel learning can lead to better performance by adapting the kernel to the specific data and task. Flexibility: The model can capture more complex and non-linear relationships in the data. Robustness: Dynamic kernels can be more robust to changes in the data distribution. Interpretability: Some dynamic kernel learning methods can provide insights into the underlying structure of the data. Reduced Need for Manual Kernel Selection: The model can learn the appropriate kernel, reducing the need for manual selection.

Examples: A dynamic kernel learning approach where the parameters of a Gaussian kernel are adjusted based on the local density of data points. A method that learns to combine multiple base kernels, such as linear, polynomial, and RBF kernels, based on the input data. Using meta-learning to train a model that can dynamically adapt the kernel function for new tasks.

Applications: Image Classification: Learning adaptive kernels for image recognition tasks. Time Series Analysis: Using dynamic kernels to capture temporal dependencies in time series data. Bioinformatics: Analyzing biological data with dynamically learned kernels. Text Classification: Adapting kernels for natural language processing tasks. Anomaly Detection: Learning kernels that can effectively identify anomalies in the data.

Industries: Technology: Development of advanced machine learning models for various applications. Healthcare: Analyzing complex medical data for diagnosis and treatment. Finance: Building more accurate models for financial forecasting and risk assessment. Bioinformatics: Analyzing biological data for drug discovery and personalized medicine. E-commerce: Developing personalized recommendation systems.

Conclusions: Dynamic Kernel Learning offers a powerful way to improve the performance of kernel methods by adapting or learning the kernel function. Its ability to capture complex relationships and reduce the need for manual kernel selection makes it valuable for a wide range of applications. While challenges related to complexity and overfitting exist, dynamic kernel learning represents a significant advancement in kernel methods and has the potential to enhance the accuracy and robustness of machine learning models.

Dynamic Path Planning

Definition: Dynamic path planning refers to the process of finding an optimal path for a robot or agent to navigate through an environment where obstacles or goals may change over time. Unlike static path planning, dynamic path planning continuously updates the path based on new information about the environment.

Key Components: Environment Sensing: Continuously monitoring the environment for changes, such as new obstacles or moving objects. Path Replanning: Adapting the existing path or generating a new path in response to environmental changes. Cost Function: Defining the criteria for optimality, such as shortest distance, least time, or minimum energy consumption. Search Algorithms: Employing algorithms like A*, D*, or rapidly-exploring random trees (RRTs) that can efficiently replan paths. Real-time Performance: Ensuring the planning process is fast enough to react to changes in the environment.

Benefits: Adaptability: Enables robots and agents to navigate effectively in dynamic and unpredictable environments. Robustness: Makes the navigation system more resilient to unforeseen obstacles or changes. Efficiency: Allows for optimization of the path based on the current state of the environment. Safety: Helps avoid collisions with moving obstacles or newly appeared obstacles. Flexibility: Can handle changes in goals or mission objectives during navigation.

Examples: A robot navigating a warehouse where shelves are being moved. An autonomous vehicle driving in a city with moving cars and pedestrians. A drone flying a search and rescue mission where new hazards are discovered. A mobile robot exploring an unknown environment and updating its path as it gains information. A virtual agent navigating a game environment with dynamic elements.

Applications: Robotics: Autonomous robots operating in warehouses, factories, or homes. Autonomous Vehicles: Self-driving cars, trucks, and drones navigating complex environments. Search and Rescue: Drones and robots used to navigate disaster areas with changing conditions. Exploration: Robots exploring unknown terrains, like Mars or underwater environments. Gaming: Virtual agents navigating dynamic game worlds.

Industries: Robotics: Manufacturing, logistics, healthcare, exploration. Automotive: Transportation, delivery services. Aerospace: Drones, autonomous aircraft. Gaming: Entertainment. Security: Surveillance, security robots.

Conclusions: Dynamic path planning is crucial for enabling robots and agents to operate effectively in real-world environments that are constantly changing. By continuously sensing the environment and replanning paths, these systems can adapt to new obstacles, avoid collisions, and achieve their goals efficiently. While challenges related to computation and uncertainty exist, dynamic path planning is essential for the advancement of autonomous systems across various industries.

Dynamic Pricing Algorithms

Definition: Dynamic pricing algorithms are AI-powered systems that automatically adjust the prices of goods or services in real-time based on various factors, such as demand, competition, time of day, and customer behavior. These algorithms aim to optimize revenue and profitability by responding to market dynamics.

Key Components: Data Collection: Gathering data on demand, competitor prices, inventory levels, and customer behavior. Predictive Modeling: Using machine learning to forecast demand and price elasticity. Optimization Engine: An algorithm that calculates the optimal price points to maximize revenue or other business objectives. Rule-Based Adjustments: Incorporating business rules and constraints into the pricing strategy. Real-time Updates: Continuously monitoring market conditions and adjusting prices accordingly.

Benefits: Increased Revenue: Optimizing prices to capture maximum value from customers. Improved Profitability: Adjusting prices to reflect changes in costs and demand. Enhanced Competitiveness: Responding quickly to competitor pricing and market trends. Better Inventory Management: Adjusting prices to manage inventory levels and reduce waste. Personalized Pricing: Tailoring prices to individual customer preferences and willingness to pay.

Examples: Airlines and hotels adjusting prices based on demand and availability. E-commerce platforms changing prices based on competitor pricing and customer browsing behavior. Ride-sharing services adjusting fares based on time of day and demand. Retailers offering discounts based on time of year or customer loyalty. Subscription services varying prices based on usage and features.

Applications: E-commerce: Online retailers optimizing prices for products and services. Travel and Hospitality: Airlines, hotels, and rental car companies adjusting prices dynamically. Ride-Sharing Services: Setting fares based on demand and location. Retail: Brick-and-mortar stores using dynamic pricing for promotions and inventory management. Subscription Services: Offering tiered pricing and adjusting prices based on usage.

Industries: E-commerce: Online retail. Travel and Hospitality: Airlines, hotels, rental car companies. Transportation: Ride-sharing services. Retail: Brick-and-mortar stores. Subscription Services: Software, media, utilities.

Conclusions: Dynamic pricing algorithms are powerful tools for businesses to optimize revenue and profitability by responding to market dynamics in real-time. By leveraging data and AI, these algorithms can adjust prices to maximize value, enhance competitiveness, and improve inventory management. While challenges related to customer perception and regulatory issues exist, dynamic pricing is becoming increasingly prevalent across various industries.

Dynamic Programming

Definition: Dynamic programming is an algorithmic technique for solving complex problems by breaking them down into simpler overlapping subproblems. It solves each subproblem only once and stores the results to avoid redundant computations, leading to efficient solutions for problems with optimal substructure and overlapping subproblems.

Key Components: Optimal Substructure: The optimal solution to a problem can be constructed from the optimal solutions to its subproblems. 1 Overlapping Subproblems: The same subproblems are solved multiple times in a recursive solution. Memoization or Tabulation: Storing the results of solved subproblems to avoid recomputing them. Memoization uses top-down recursion with storage, while tabulation uses a bottom-up iterative approach. State Definition: Defining the parameters that uniquely identify each subproblem. Transition Function: Defining how to solve a subproblem based on the solutions to smaller subproblems.

Benefits: Efficiency: Reduces the time complexity of solving problems with overlapping subproblems. Optimality: Guarantees finding the optimal solution if the problem has optimal substructure. Versatility: Applicable to a wide range of problems, including optimization, graph theory, and sequence alignment. Systematic Approach: Provides a structured way to solve complex problems by breaking them down. Widely Used: A fundamental technique in computer science and algorithm design.

Examples: Finding the shortest path in a weighted graph (e.g., Dijkstra's algorithm). Calculating the Fibonacci sequence efficiently. Solving the knapsack problem to maximize the value of items within a weight limit. Finding the longest common subsequence between two strings. Solving the matrix chain multiplication problem to optimize the order of multiplications.

Applications: Computer Science: Algorithm design, optimization problems. Operations Research: Resource allocation, scheduling. Bioinformatics: Sequence alignment, protein folding. Economics: Portfolio optimization, game theory. Engineering: Control systems, signal processing.

Industries: Technology: Software development, algorithm design, optimization. Finance: Portfolio management, algorithmic trading. Healthcare: Bioinformatics, medical image analysis. Logistics: Supply chain optimization, routing. Manufacturing: Production planning, resource allocation.

Conclusions: Dynamic programming is a powerful algorithmic technique for solving complex problems efficiently by breaking them down into smaller overlapping subproblems. Its ability to guarantee optimality and reduce time complexity makes it a fundamental tool in computer science and various other fields. While challenges related to state definition and memory usage exist, dynamic programming remains a cornerstone of algorithmic problem-solving.

Dynamic Resource Allocation

Definition: Dynamic resource allocation is the process of allocating resources, such as computing power, bandwidth, or personnel, in real-time based on changing demands and conditions. AI techniques can be used to optimize this process, ensuring efficient and effective resource utilization.

Key Components: Demand Forecasting: Predicting future resource needs based on historical data and current trends. Resource Monitoring: Tracking the availability and utilization of resources.

Optimization Algorithms: Using AI algorithms to determine the optimal allocation of resources. Real-time Adjustments: Continuously updating resource allocation based on changes in demand and resource availability. Prioritization: Allocating resources based on the importance or urgency of tasks.

Benefits: Improved Efficiency: Optimizing resource utilization and reducing waste. Cost Savings: Minimizing idle resources and over-provisioning. Enhanced Responsiveness: Adapting quickly to changes in demand and conditions. Scalability: Efficiently managing resources in large and complex systems. Better Performance: Ensuring critical tasks have the resources they need.

Examples: Cloud computing providers dynamically allocating virtual machines based on user demand. Hospitals adjusting staffing levels based on patient arrivals and needs. Telecommunications networks allocating bandwidth based on traffic patterns. Manufacturing plants adjusting production schedules based on demand and resource availability. Emergency services deploying personnel and equipment based on real-time incident reports.

Applications: Cloud Computing: Resource management in data centers. Healthcare: Staffing and resource allocation in hospitals and clinics. Telecommunications: Network resource management. Manufacturing: Production planning and scheduling. Emergency Services: Deployment of personnel and equipment.

Industries: Technology: Cloud computing, data centers. Healthcare: Hospitals, clinics, healthcare management. Telecommunications: Network providers. Manufacturing: Factories, supply chain management. Public Sector: Emergency services, government agencies.

Conclusions: Dynamic resource allocation is essential for optimizing the use of resources in various systems and industries. By leveraging AI, organizations can improve efficiency, reduce costs, and enhance responsiveness to changing conditions. While challenges related to data accuracy and system complexity exist, dynamic resource allocation is crucial for managing resources effectively in today's dynamic environments.

Dynamic Risk Assessment

Definition: Dynamic risk assessment is the process of continuously evaluating and updating risk assessments based on real-time data and changing conditions. AI can be used to automate and enhance this process, providing more accurate and timely insights into potential risks.

Key Components: Data Collection: Gathering real-time data from various sources, such as sensors, network traffic, and security logs. Threat Intelligence Analysis: Using AI to analyze threat intelligence feeds and identify emerging threats. Vulnerability Scanning: Continuously monitoring systems for new vulnerabilities. Risk Modeling: Developing AI models to predict the likelihood and impact of potential risks. Risk Scoring: Assigning risk scores based on the analysis of data and models. Real-time Updates: Continuously updating risk assessments based on new information.

Benefits: Improved Accuracy: Providing more accurate and up-to-date risk assessments. Continuous Monitoring: Continuously evaluating risks and adapting to changing conditions. Early Detection: Identifying potential risks before they can cause significant harm. Prioritization: Focusing resources on the highest risks. Automation: Reducing the manual effort involved in risk assessment.

Examples: AI systems that continuously monitor network traffic for security threats and update risk assessments in real-time. Financial institutions using AI to assess and update credit risk based on real-time market data. Healthcare organizations using AI to monitor patient data and update risk assessments for adverse events. Supply chain companies using AI to assess and update risks related to disruptions and vulnerabilities.

Applications: Cybersecurity: Monitoring and assessing security risks in real-time. Finance: Assessing and managing financial risks, such as credit risk and market risk. Healthcare: Monitoring patient health and assessing risks of adverse events. Supply Chain Management: Assessing and mitigating risks in the supply chain. Insurance: Assessing and managing risks associated with policies and claims.

Industries: Cybersecurity: Security operations, risk management. Finance: Banking, investment, insurance. Healthcare: Hospitals, clinics, healthcare management. Supply Chain Management: Logistics, manufacturing, retail. Insurance: Underwriting, claims management.

Conclusions: Dynamic risk assessment, enhanced by AI, provides a more accurate and timely approach to managing risks in various domains. By continuously monitoring data and adapting assessments, organizations can proactively identify and mitigate potential threats. While challenges related to data integration and model accuracy exist, dynamic risk assessment is essential for effective risk management in today's rapidly changing world.

Dynamic Task Allocation

Definition: Dynamic task allocation refers to the process of assigning tasks to agents or resources in real-time based on changing conditions and agent capabilities. AI techniques can be used to optimize this process, ensuring efficient and effective task completion.

Key Components: Task Monitoring: Tracking the status and requirements of tasks. Agent Monitoring: Tracking the availability and capabilities of agents. Optimization Algorithms: Using AI algorithms to determine the optimal assignment of tasks to agents. Real-time Adjustments: Continuously updating task assignments based on changes in task requirements and agent availability. Prioritization: Assigning tasks based on their importance or urgency.

Benefits: Improved Efficiency: Optimizing the allocation of tasks to agents, reducing idle time and improving throughput. Enhanced Responsiveness: Adapting quickly to changes in task requirements and agent availability. Scalability: Efficiently managing task allocation in large and complex systems. Better Performance: Ensuring tasks are assigned to the most suitable agents. Reduced Costs: Minimizing resource wastage and improving overall efficiency.

Examples: Robots in a warehouse dynamically assigning tasks based on their location and capabilities. Delivery services assigning delivery routes to drivers in real-time based on traffic and order locations. Emergency response teams dynamically assigning personnel and resources to incidents based on their severity and location. Software systems dynamically allocating computing tasks to available processors. Manufacturing plants dynamically assigning production tasks to machines based on their capacity and availability.

Applications: Robotics: Warehouse automation, manufacturing. Logistics: Delivery services, transportation. Emergency Services: Fire departments, police, ambulance services. Software Systems: Cloud computing, distributed systems. Manufacturing: Production planning, resource management.

Industries: Logistics: Transportation, warehousing. Manufacturing: Production, supply chain. Technology: Software development, cloud computing. Public Sector: Emergency services, government operations. Healthcare: Hospital operations, resource management.

Conclusions: Dynamic task allocation, especially when enhanced by AI, is crucial for optimizing the efficiency and effectiveness of operations in various domains. By continuously monitoring tasks and agents and adjusting assignments in real-time, organizations can improve responsiveness, reduce costs, and enhance overall performance. While challenges related to task complexity and uncertainty exist, dynamic task allocation is essential for managing resources effectively in dynamic environments.

Dynamic Uncertainty Handling is an AI-driven approach that enables systems to identify, assess, and adapt to uncertainties in real time. Unlike static uncertainty handling, which relies on predefined rules, dynamic uncertainty handling continuously adjusts models based on changing conditions, incomplete data, and evolving environments. This method is essential in fields where AI must operate under unpredictable circumstances, such as autonomous systems, finance, and healthcare, ensuring robust decision-making despite uncertainty.

Key components of dynamic uncertainty handling include probabilistic modeling, adaptive learning, real-time data assimilation, risk assessment, and confidence estimation. Probabilistic modeling incorporates uncertainty into AI predictions using techniques such as Bayesian inference and Monte Carlo simulations. Adaptive learning allows models to update their uncertainty estimates dynamically as new data becomes available. Real-time data assimilation integrates live information streams to refine uncertainty calculations and improve model reliability. Risk assessment evaluates the potential impact of uncertain outcomes, guiding AI systems in making optimal decisions. Confidence estimation quantifies the reliability of AI predictions, allowing systems to adjust responses based on uncertainty levels.

The benefits of dynamic uncertainty handling include improved decision reliability, enhanced robustness, and greater adaptability. Improved decision reliability ensures that AI-driven choices consider uncertainty, reducing errors and increasing confidence in outcomes. Enhanced robustness allows AI models to function effectively in complex environments where uncertainty is inherent, such as autonomous driving or financial forecasting. Greater adaptability enables AI systems to learn from new data and refine uncertainty estimates over time, improving long-term performance and resilience.

An example of dynamic uncertainty handling is in self-driving cars, where AI continuously evaluates sensor data, adjusts navigation strategies, and accounts for unpredictable elements such as weather conditions, road obstacles, and human behavior. Another example is in medical diagnostics, where AI systems assess uncertainty in patient test results and recommend additional tests or alternative diagnoses when confidence levels are low.

Industries that benefit from dynamic uncertainty handling include aerospace, finance, healthcare, robotics, and climate science. Aerospace applications use uncertainty-aware AI for real-time flight path adjustments, ensuring safe navigation under uncertain atmospheric conditions. Financial institutions integrate dynamic uncertainty handling into risk models, improving fraud detection, stock market predictions, and investment strategies. Healthcare leverages AI-driven uncertainty modeling in diagnostics, treatment planning, and drug discovery, reducing risks associated with incomplete or noisy medical data. Robotics systems apply uncertainty-aware decision-making to improve navigation, grasping, and task execution in unstructured environments. Climate science relies on uncertainty handling for more accurate weather forecasts and disaster response planning, improving preparedness and mitigation efforts.

Applications of dynamic uncertainty handling extend to predictive analytics, automated decision support, anomaly detection, reinforcement learning, and AI-driven simulations. Predictive analytics benefits from uncertainty-aware AI models that generate risk-adjusted forecasts for business, healthcare, and environmental monitoring. Automated decision support systems use uncertainty modeling to provide confidence-weighted recommendations, improving decision-making across industries. Anomaly detection applies dynamic uncertainty handling to flag unusual patterns in security, finance, and industrial maintenance, ensuring more accurate threat identification. Reinforcement learning integrates uncertainty-aware exploration strategies, allowing AI agents to balance risk and reward when learning optimal policies. AI-driven simulations leverage uncertainty handling for scenario analysis, improving strategic planning in complex and uncertain domains.

Dynamic uncertainty handling is a fundamental capability for AI systems operating in real-world environments, where unpredictable factors and incomplete data can impact decision-making. By incorporating probabilistic reasoning, adaptive learning, and risk-aware modeling, AI can improve reliability, resilience, and adaptability across diverse applications. As AI continues to advance, dynamic uncertainty handling will remain essential for creating intelligent systems that can navigate uncertainty and make informed decisions in high-stakes situations.

Dynamic Time Warpint (DTW)

Dynamic Time Warping (DTW) is an algorithm used to measure the similarity between two time series by aligning them in a nonlinear manner. Unlike traditional distance metrics that compare sequences point by point, DTW accounts for variations in speed and timing by stretching or compressing segments of the sequences to achieve optimal alignment. This makes DTW particularly useful for analyzing temporal data where patterns may be similar but occur at different time intervals.

Key components of DTW include time series representation, cost matrix, warping path, distance function, and dynamic programming optimization. Time series representation involves organizing sequential data points into comparable structures, such as speech signals, financial trends, or biological measurements. The cost matrix is a grid structure that records the cumulative distance between aligned points from two time series. The warping path determines the optimal alignment by identifying the sequence of matched points with the lowest cumulative cost. The distance function measures dissimilarity between corresponding points, commonly using Euclidean distance or other metrics. Dynamic programming optimization ensures that DTW finds the most efficient warping path while minimizing computational complexity.

The benefits of DTW include improved pattern recognition, flexibility in temporal alignment, and robustness to time shifts. Improved pattern recognition allows AI models to detect similarities between sequences that may have variations in speed or structure. Flexibility in temporal alignment ensures that DTW adapts to differences in sequence timing, making it more effective than rigid distance measures. Robustness to time shifts makes DTW ideal for applications where events do not occur at precisely the same moments but still follow similar trends.

An example of DTW in action is in speech recognition, where the algorithm aligns spoken words that may be pronounced at different speeds, enabling accurate comparison and classification. Another example is in stock market analysis, where DTW compares financial time series to detect similarities in price movements, even if trends develop at different rates.

Industries that benefit from DTW include healthcare, finance, speech processing, biometrics, and motion analysis. Healthcare applications use DTW to compare electrocardiogram (ECG) signals for detecting heart abnormalities, aligning medical sensor data for early disease diagnosis. Financial institutions apply DTW to analyze historical stock patterns and predict future market trends, improving investment decision-making. Speech processing leverages DTW for speaker verification and voice authentication, enhancing security systems and automated transcription services. Biometric recognition integrates DTW in handwriting analysis, fingerprint comparison, and gesture recognition, improving identification accuracy. Motion analysis applies DTW to track human movement in sports science, rehabilitation, and animation, allowing AI to compare motion sequences with high precision.

Applications of DTW extend to anomaly detection, time-series clustering, predictive modeling, genome sequencing, and robotics. Anomaly detection benefits from DTW by identifying unusual patterns in sequential data, helping detect fraud, system failures, or health anomalies. Time-series clustering uses DTW to group similar temporal sequences, improving classification in diverse fields such as meteorology and economic forecasting. Predictive modeling applies DTW to train AI systems in forecasting trends, refining accuracy in weather prediction and energy consumption analysis. Genome sequencing utilizes DTW to compare DNA sequences, assisting in identifying genetic similarities and mutations. Robotics integrates DTW in motion planning, aligning robotic actions with human demonstrations for improved automation and adaptive control.

Dynamic Time Warping is a powerful technique for analyzing and comparing time-series data, enabling AI systems to recognize patterns, handle variations in timing, and improve similarity assessments across different domains. By adapting sequence alignment dynamically, DTW enhances accuracy and robustness in applications requiring flexible temporal analysis. As AI and machine learning advance, DTW will continue to play a crucial role in speech recognition, financial analysis, healthcare diagnostics, and numerous other fields that rely on precise time-series comparison.

Dynamic Unsupervised Learning

Dynamic Unsupervised Learning is a machine learning approach that continuously adapts and updates models without requiring labeled data. Unlike traditional unsupervised learning, which operates on static datasets, dynamic unsupervised learning processes streaming or evolving data, enabling models to detect patterns, anomalies, and clusters in real time. This method is particularly effective in environments where data is constantly changing, such as financial markets, cybersecurity, and personalized recommendations.

Key components of dynamic unsupervised learning include incremental learning, real-time data processing, self-organizing models, adaptive clustering, and anomaly detection. Incremental learning enables models to update themselves as new data arrives without retraining from scratch, improving computational efficiency. Real-time data processing ensures that models can analyze continuously changing information, making them responsive to dynamic environments. Self-organizing models allow AI systems to restructure learned representations as data distributions evolve, maintaining accuracy over time. Adaptive clustering dynamically adjusts groupings of data points, refining cluster structures as new patterns emerge. Anomaly detection identifies deviations from normal behavior in real time, improving security, fraud prevention, and predictive maintenance.

The benefits of dynamic unsupervised learning include improved adaptability, enhanced scalability, and real-time pattern recognition. Improved adaptability allows AI models to evolve as new information is introduced, ensuring that insights remain relevant. Enhanced scalability enables learning from large, continuously growing datasets without computational bottlenecks. Real-time pattern recognition ensures that AI systems can detect trends, anomalies, and correlations as they emerge, supporting more accurate decision-making in unpredictable environments.

An example of dynamic unsupervised learning is in fraud detection systems, where AI continuously learns from transaction patterns to identify new fraudulent activities without relying on predefined labels. Another example is in network security, where AI models analyze network traffic and detect emerging cyber threats by recognizing deviations from normal activity.

Industries that benefit from dynamic unsupervised learning include finance, healthcare, cybersecurity, retail, and industrial automation. Financial institutions use AI-driven unsupervised learning for market trend analysis, fraud detection, and algorithmic trading. Healthcare applications leverage dynamic models to identify emerging disease patterns, optimize patient treatment plans, and enhance medical research. Cybersecurity organizations integrate AI models to detect real-time anomalies in network traffic, preventing unauthorized intrusions and cyberattacks. Retail companies apply dynamic unsupervised learning for personalized recommendations, adapting to shifting customer preferences and seasonal trends. Industrial automation benefits from AI-driven predictive maintenance, where unsupervised learning detects anomalies in machinery operations and predicts potential failures before they occur.

Applications of dynamic unsupervised learning extend to real-time recommendation systems, adaptive anomaly detection, intelligent process automation, self-learning AI agents, and behavioral pattern analysis. Real-time recommendation systems adjust content, product, or service suggestions based on continuously evolving user interactions. Adaptive anomaly detection improves security and quality control by identifying new threats or defects without predefined labels. Intelligent process automation leverages AI models that learn from operational data to optimize workflows and enhance efficiency. Self-learning AI agents use dynamic unsupervised learning to refine their behavior and improve decision-making without direct supervision. Behavioral pattern analysis enables AI to detect trends in consumer behavior, workforce productivity, and social interactions, supporting more informed business strategies.

Dynamic unsupervised learning is a crucial advancement in AI, enabling continuous model adaptation, real-time data analysis, and enhanced decision-making in complex environments. By eliminating the need for labeled data, this approach allows AI to learn autonomously and respond to evolving trends, making it highly valuable for industries that require adaptive intelligence. As AI systems become more autonomous and data-driven, dynamic unsupervised learning will play a vital role in improving efficiency, security, and personalization across various domains.

Dynamic User Modeling

Dynamic User Modeling is an AI-driven approach that continuously updates and refines user profiles based on real-time interactions, behaviors, and preferences. Unlike static models, which rely on fixed datasets, dynamic user modeling adapts to changing user behaviors, improving personalization and decision-making in AI-driven applications. This method enhances user experiences by analyzing evolving patterns, allowing for more accurate predictions and adaptive recommendations across digital platforms.

Key components of dynamic user modeling include real-time data collection, behavioral analysis, adaptive learning, personalization algorithms, and feedback loops. Real-time data collection gathers user interactions, preferences, and contextual information from various touchpoints, ensuring that models remain up-to-date. Behavioral analysis examines user activities, engagement patterns, and decision-making processes to understand preferences and predict future actions. Adaptive learning enables AI models to evolve by incorporating new information, adjusting user profiles as behavior changes. Personalization algorithms tailor content, product recommendations, or services based on continuously refined user profiles, improving engagement and satisfaction. Feedback loops integrate user responses and corrective mechanisms to enhance prediction accuracy, reducing biases and refining model effectiveness.

The benefits of dynamic user modeling include improved personalization, enhanced user engagement, and real-time adaptability. Improved personalization allows AI-driven systems to deliver content, recommendations, and services that align with individual user preferences, increasing relevance. Enhanced user engagement results from continuously adapting to user behaviors, ensuring that interactions remain meaningful and context-aware. Real-time adaptability enables AI models to respond to changes in user interests, market trends, or environmental conditions, making them more effective across diverse applications.

An example of dynamic user modeling is in streaming services, where AI tracks viewing habits, adjusts recommendations, and refines content suggestions based on evolving user preferences. Another example is in e-commerce platforms, where personalized product recommendations change dynamically based on browsing history, purchase behavior, and seasonal trends.

Industries that benefit from dynamic user modeling include e-commerce, healthcare, finance, education, and entertainment. E-commerce businesses use dynamic user modeling to personalize shopping experiences, increasing conversion rates and customer satisfaction. Healthcare applications leverage adaptive models to refine patient treatment plans, adjusting recommendations based on medical history and real-time health monitoring. Financial institutions apply dynamic user modeling to detect fraud, assess risk, and provide personalized investment strategies. Education platforms integrate adaptive user models to tailor learning experiences, adjusting coursework and recommendations based on student progress. Entertainment platforms utilize dynamic models to customize content curation, improving user engagement through personalized recommendations.

Applications of dynamic user modeling extend to recommendation systems, targeted advertising, customer relationship management, intelligent virtual assistants, and predictive analytics. Recommendation systems use continuously updated user profiles to provide relevant content, enhancing user satisfaction in media, retail, and online platforms. Targeted advertising optimizes ad delivery by adjusting campaigns in real time based on user interests, increasing engagement and conversion rates. Customer relationship management benefits from dynamic models by enabling businesses to offer personalized services and proactive customer support. Intelligent virtual assistants integrate adaptive user profiles to refine responses, improving contextual awareness and natural interaction. Predictive analytics applies dynamic user modeling to anticipate customer needs, market trends, and business opportunities, supporting data-driven decision-making.

Dynamic user modeling is a crucial advancement in AI-driven personalization, allowing for adaptive and continuously evolving user experiences. By leveraging real-time data and machine learning, businesses can create more relevant and engaging interactions while improving decision-making accuracy. As AI technology progresses, dynamic user modeling will become increasingly essential in optimizing digital experiences, enhancing predictive capabilities, and driving innovation across various industries.

LETTER E

Eager Execution

Definition
Eager Execution is an execution mode in machine learning frameworks where operations are computed immediately as they are called. Unlike graph-based execution, which builds a computational graph before running, eager execution enables direct evaluation of operations without requiring a separate compilation step. It provides an intuitive and flexible approach for model development, debugging, and experimentation.

Key Components
Eager Execution relies on dynamic computation, executing each operation sequentially without delay. It integrates seamlessly with automatic differentiation, allowing immediate gradient computation for optimization. Debugging tools benefit from real-time feedback, making it easier to inspect tensors and track errors. The flexibility to experiment with different models without predefined computational graphs makes it a preferred choice for prototyping.

Benefits
Eager Execution simplifies debugging by providing instant error messages and interactive testing. Its dynamic nature improves code readability and ease of development. The ability to modify and experiment with models in real-time accelerates the research and development process. Immediate execution eliminates the need for static graphs, reducing complexity in smaller projects.

Applications
Eager Execution is widely used in deep learning research for rapid prototyping of neural networks. It enhances interpretability in reinforcement learning by allowing step-by-step execution. It is useful in educational settings for teaching machine learning concepts interactively. In AI experimentation, it helps in testing and modifying architectures without extensive pre-compilation.

Industries
The technology industry benefits from Eager Execution in AI model development and research. The healthcare sector applies it in medical imaging and drug discovery prototyping. Autonomous systems

use it in robotics and real-time decision-making. The finance industry explores its use in algorithmic trading and fraud detection experiments.

Summary
Eager Execution provides an interactive and flexible approach to executing machine learning models. Its real-time computation and debugging capabilities make it ideal for research and prototyping. While it simplifies development, challenges such as performance trade-offs and deployment constraints exist. Its impact spans various industries, supporting innovation in AI-driven applications.

Early Fusion in AI

Definition
Early Fusion in AI refers to the technique of integrating multiple data modalities at the input stage before feature extraction and processing. It contrasts with late fusion, where different data sources are processed separately and combined at a later stage. Early fusion enables models to learn joint representations from diverse inputs.

Key Components
Early Fusion incorporates multimodal data integration, allowing information from different sources to be combined before model processing. Feature transformation techniques standardize inputs for seamless fusion. Neural networks or statistical models learn joint representations for enhanced decision-making. Preprocessing pipelines ensure data consistency across modalities.

Benefits
Early Fusion enhances feature interaction by combining complementary information from multiple sources. It improves predictive accuracy by learning relationships across modalities. It reduces redundancy by processing data together rather than independently. Joint learning leads to more informative representations and robust AI models.

Applications
Early Fusion is widely used in speech recognition, where audio and text data are integrated. It plays a role in autonomous vehicles, fusing sensor inputs from cameras, radar, and LiDAR. Healthcare applications integrate medical images and patient records for better diagnosis. Sentiment analysis benefits from combining text and visual data for improved sentiment detection.

Industries
The automotive industry applies Early Fusion in self-driving cars for multimodal sensor fusion. The entertainment sector integrates audio and video data in content recommendation systems. The finance industry enhances fraud detection by fusing transaction history with behavioral patterns. Healthcare leverages early fusion in AI-assisted diagnosis and treatment planning.

Summary
Early Fusion combines multiple data sources at the input stage to enhance AI model performance. It improves accuracy and feature representation in multimodal applications but requires advanced preprocessing and computational resources. Its applications span industries where multiple data modalities must be analyzed together.

Eager Learning

Definition
Eager Learning is a machine learning approach where a model learns a general representation of data during the training phase before making predictions. Unlike lazy learning, which defers learning until query time, eager learning processes and stores patterns in advance to facilitate faster inference.

Key Components
Eager Learning relies on precomputed models that generalize data relationships before deployment. It involves feature extraction to identify relevant patterns. Model training applies optimization algorithms to adjust weights for accurate predictions. Generalization techniques ensure the model can handle unseen data effectively.

Benefits
Eager Learning reduces prediction latency since learning occurs before inference. It ensures efficient use of pre-trained models for rapid decision-making. By generalizing patterns early, it enhances robustness against noisy inputs. Scalability is improved as models can be deployed without on-the-fly computation.

Applications
Eager Learning is widely used in neural networks for natural language processing and image recognition. It is applied in recommendation systems to provide instant content suggestions. Fraud detection models use eager learning for real-time threat identification. Autonomous vehicles rely on pre-trained models for navigation and decision-making.

Industries
The healthcare sector applies eager learning in diagnostic AI models. The finance industry utilizes it for credit scoring and risk assessment. E-commerce benefits from recommendation engines powered by eager learning. The gaming industry integrates it into AI-driven character behaviors.

Summary
Eager Learning prioritizes early model training to enable fast and efficient predictions. It supports real-time decision-making in various AI applications but requires significant resources for training. Its advantages in speed and scalability make it a crucial approach for AI-driven industries.

Earnings Prediction AI

Definition
Earnings Prediction AI refers to artificial intelligence systems designed to forecast the future earnings of companies, individuals, or financial assets. These models leverage historical data, market trends, economic indicators, and machine learning algorithms to make informed predictions about financial performance.

Key Components
Earnings Prediction AI relies on financial data collection, including revenue, expenses, and profit trends. Machine learning models such as regression analysis, neural networks, and time series forecasting refine predictions. Sentiment analysis processes market sentiment from news and social media. Feature engineering optimizes data inputs for better model performance. Model validation ensures accuracy through backtesting and real-world comparisons.

Benefits
Earnings Prediction AI enhances financial decision-making by providing data-driven insights. It reduces risk by identifying potential revenue fluctuations in advance. Automated predictions improve efficiency for investors, businesses, and analysts. The ability to process vast datasets increases accuracy over traditional forecasting methods.

Applications
Earnings Prediction AI is used in stock market analysis to anticipate company earnings. It supports financial planning by forecasting revenue for businesses. Investment firms use it to assess risks and opportunities. Credit institutions integrate it to evaluate loan repayment probabilities.

Industries

The finance sector benefits from earnings predictions in stock trading and risk assessment. The retail industry applies AI-driven revenue forecasting for inventory and pricing strategies. The technology sector leverages it for startup valuation and market analysis. The insurance industry integrates earnings prediction in underwriting and policy pricing.

Summary

Earnings Prediction AI improves financial forecasting by analyzing historical data, market trends, and economic factors. It provides valuable insights for businesses and investors but faces challenges related to data reliability and market fluctuations. Its applications span finance, retail, and investment industries.

Ease of Interpretation in AI

Definition

Ease of Interpretation in AI refers to the ability of an artificial intelligence system to provide understandable, transparent, and explainable outputs. It ensures that users can comprehend how an AI model reaches decisions, increasing trust and usability.

Key Components

Model explainability techniques such as SHAP (Shapley Additive Explanations) and LIME (Local Interpretable Model-Agnostic Explanations) provide insights into decision-making processes. Feature importance analysis identifies the most influential variables in a model. Visualization tools present AI-generated insights in a user-friendly manner. Interpretability constraints ensure models do not become overly complex or opaque.

Benefits

Ease of Interpretation in AI builds user trust by making AI-driven decisions more transparent. It improves regulatory compliance in industries that require explainable models. Better interpretability enhances debugging and model improvement. Ethical AI development benefits from increased accountability and fairness.

Applications

Ease of Interpretation is critical in healthcare AI for explaining diagnosis predictions. Financial AI systems require interpretability for risk assessments and fraud detection. AI-driven hiring platforms benefit from transparency in candidate evaluations. Autonomous systems improve safety with interpretable decision-making mechanisms.

Industries

The healthcare sector applies interpretable AI in medical diagnostics and patient care recommendations. The finance industry uses explainable models in credit scoring and fraud detection. The legal industry integrates AI interpretability in compliance monitoring. The education sector benefits from transparent AI in personalized learning systems.

Summary

Ease of Interpretation in AI enhances trust and usability by making AI-driven decisions understandable. It plays a crucial role in regulated industries but faces challenges in balancing complexity and transparency. Its impact extends across healthcare, finance, and compliance sectors.

Ease of Use in AI Development

Definition

Ease of Use in AI Development refers to the simplicity and accessibility of tools, frameworks, and methodologies that enable developers to build and deploy AI models efficiently. It ensures that AI technology can be utilized by a broad range of users, including those without extensive machine learning expertise.

Key Components
User-friendly AI frameworks such as TensorFlow, PyTorch, and scikit-learn simplify model development. Pre-built models and APIs enable quick implementation of AI functionalities. AutoML tools automate model selection, tuning, and deployment. Cloud-based AI platforms provide scalable infrastructure without requiring advanced hardware.

Benefits
Ease of Use in AI Development reduces the learning curve for new developers. It accelerates AI adoption across industries by making technology more accessible. Pre-built tools enhance efficiency by eliminating the need for extensive manual coding. Cost-effectiveness improves as simplified AI development reduces resource-intensive efforts.

Applications
AI-powered chatbots are built using low-code and no-code AI platforms. Small businesses leverage AI-driven analytics tools without requiring technical expertise. Researchers use AutoML solutions to experiment with models quickly. AI-driven content generation platforms simplify creative processes.

Industries
The technology industry benefits from streamlined AI development tools. The healthcare sector applies user-friendly AI for diagnostics and medical research. The retail industry uses AI-driven insights for customer engagement and inventory management. The education sector integrates AI for personalized learning and tutoring systems.

Summary
Ease of Use in AI Development enhances accessibility by simplifying AI model creation and deployment. It enables broader adoption across industries but faces challenges in balancing simplicity with customization. It plays a vital role in democratizing AI for businesses and individuals.

Eavesdropping AI

Definition
Eavesdropping AI refers to artificial intelligence systems capable of intercepting, analyzing, and extracting information from voice conversations or digital communications. These models use speech recognition, natural language processing, and pattern analysis to process and interpret audio or text data.

Key Components
Speech-to-text conversion enables AI to transcribe spoken conversations. Natural language processing extracts meaningful insights from conversations. Acoustic fingerprinting differentiates between speakers and background noise. Encryption analysis deciphers secured communications when applied in cybersecurity.

Benefits
Eavesdropping AI improves security monitoring by detecting potential threats in communication. It enhances accessibility through automated transcription services. Law enforcement agencies use it for intelligence gathering. Businesses utilize it for sentiment analysis in customer interactions.

Applications
Eavesdropping AI is applied in surveillance to monitor suspicious conversations. Customer service analytics leverage AI to analyze call center interactions. Smart assistants use passive listening to activate voice commands. Cybersecurity systems detect unauthorized access to sensitive data.

Industries

The law enforcement sector applies eavesdropping AI for criminal investigations. The telecommunications industry integrates it into voice-based analytics. The cybersecurity sector detects and prevents digital eavesdropping threats. The consumer electronics industry develops smart assistants with listening capabilities.

Summary

Eavesdropping AI analyzes voice and text communications for intelligence gathering, security, and analytics. It offers benefits in security and accessibility but faces privacy, ethical, and accuracy challenges. Its applications span law enforcement, telecommunications, and cybersecurity industries.

E-Banking AI

Definition

E-Banking AI refers to artificial intelligence systems that enhance online banking services by automating processes, improving security, and providing personalized financial insights. These AI-driven solutions use machine learning, natural language processing, and data analytics to streamline banking operations and enhance customer experience.

Key Components

E-Banking AI relies on machine learning models to analyze customer transactions and detect patterns. Natural language processing enables AI to interact with users through chatbots and virtual assistants. Fraud detection systems use predictive analytics to identify suspicious activities. Personalization engines recommend financial products based on customer behavior and preferences. Cybersecurity measures protect sensitive banking data from unauthorized access.

Benefits

E-Banking AI improves efficiency by automating banking processes and reducing manual work. It enhances customer experience through personalized recommendations and real-time assistance. Security is strengthened by detecting fraudulent activities and mitigating cyber threats. Operational costs are reduced by minimizing human intervention in routine banking tasks. AI-driven insights help customers make better financial decisions.

Applications

E-Banking AI is used in online banking platforms to provide automated financial guidance. It assists in loan approval processes by analyzing credit risk factors. Fraud detection AI monitors transactions to prevent unauthorized activities. AI-powered customer service systems respond to banking inquiries in real time.

Industries

The banking sector uses AI for digital transformation and automation. The fintech industry integrates AI-driven solutions for online financial services. The cybersecurity industry collaborates with banking AI to enhance data protection. The insurance sector leverages AI in financial risk assessment and policy recommendations.

Summary

E-Banking AI revolutionizes digital banking by automating services, enhancing security, and personalizing customer experiences. While it offers significant benefits in efficiency and risk management, challenges related to security, privacy, and trust must be addressed for widespread adoption.

E-Banking Chatbot AI

Definition
E-Banking Chatbot AI is an artificial intelligence-powered virtual assistant designed to interact with customers, answer banking-related queries, and provide automated financial services through text or voice-based communication. These chatbots use natural language processing to understand and respond to customer requests in real time.

Key Components
Natural language processing enables chatbots to interpret and generate human-like responses. Machine learning algorithms improve chatbot accuracy through continuous learning. Integration with banking systems allows chatbots to access account details, transaction history, and financial services. Sentiment analysis detects customer emotions to enhance service interactions. Secure authentication ensures safe access to personal banking information.

Benefits
E-Banking Chatbot AI improves customer service by providing instant responses and reducing wait times. It operates 24/7, ensuring continuous banking support. Automation reduces operational costs by minimizing human agent workload. Personalized interactions enhance customer engagement and satisfaction. AI-driven chatbots improve accessibility for users with disabilities or language barriers.

Applications
E-Banking Chatbot AI assists customers with account inquiries, transaction history, and fund transfers. It provides financial advice on savings, loans, and investment options. Fraud alerts and security notifications are sent through chatbot interfaces. Chatbots help banks streamline customer onboarding and document verification processes.

Industries
The banking sector utilizes chatbot AI for digital customer support. The fintech industry integrates chatbots into mobile and online banking applications. The insurance sector uses AI-driven chatbots for policy inquiries and claims processing. E-commerce platforms leverage banking chatbots for payment assistance and financial transactions.

Summary
E-Banking Chatbot AI enhances digital banking by providing automated, real-time customer support and financial guidance. While it offers efficiency and accessibility, addressing security, accuracy, and compliance challenges is crucial for its success in the banking industry.

E-Banking Customer Support AI

Definition
E-Banking Customer Support AI is an artificial intelligence system designed to handle customer inquiries, resolve banking issues, and provide automated assistance across multiple digital channels. It leverages machine learning, natural language processing, and predictive analytics to enhance customer service efficiency.

Key Components
AI-driven ticketing systems categorize and prioritize customer support requests. Virtual assistants use natural language processing to provide instant responses. Sentiment analysis detects customer satisfaction and adjusts responses accordingly. Predictive analytics anticipates customer needs based on past interactions. Omnichannel integration allows AI support across chat, email, phone, and social media.

Benefits
E-Banking Customer Support AI reduces response times by automating customer service interactions. It improves service quality by offering consistent and accurate support. AI-driven insights help banks

anticipate customer concerns and offer proactive solutions. Cost savings are achieved by reducing reliance on human agents. AI systems enhance fraud detection and security monitoring through automated alerts.

Applications
AI-powered customer support handles queries related to account management, transactions, and security concerns. It assists with loan applications and credit card approvals. Automated dispute resolution processes help customers resolve transaction issues. Customer feedback analysis informs banks about service improvements.

Industries
The banking sector uses AI for automated customer support in digital banking services. The fintech industry integrates AI-driven customer assistance into mobile applications. The telecommunications industry applies AI for billing and payment-related inquiries. The insurance sector leverages AI support for claims processing and policy management.

Summary
E-Banking Customer Support AI streamlines customer service by providing instant, AI-driven responses to banking inquiries. It enhances efficiency, reduces costs, and improves user experience, but addressing security, accuracy, and regulatory challenges is essential for reliable implementation.

E-Banking Fraud Detection

Definition
E-Banking Fraud Detection AI is an artificial intelligence system designed to identify and prevent fraudulent activities in online banking transactions. It uses machine learning, behavioral analysis, and anomaly detection to detect suspicious activities and protect customers from financial fraud.

Key Components
Machine learning algorithms analyze transaction patterns to detect anomalies. Real-time monitoring systems track banking activities for irregular behavior. Behavioral biometrics identify fraud based on user habits, such as typing speed and login frequency. Risk assessment models evaluate the likelihood of fraudulent activities. Automated alerts notify customers and bank officials of potential security breaches.

Benefits
E-Banking Fraud Detection AI reduces financial losses by preventing fraudulent transactions. It enhances security by continuously monitoring banking activities. AI-driven fraud detection improves detection speed and response time. Automated risk analysis minimizes manual intervention in fraud investigations. Customer trust in online banking increases with improved fraud prevention mechanisms.

Applications
Fraud detection AI identifies unauthorized account access and suspicious transactions. It prevents identity theft by analyzing login behavior and device usage. AI-driven risk scoring evaluates transaction legitimacy before processing. Fraud alerts and automated account freezes prevent financial losses.

Industries
The banking sector relies on fraud detection AI to secure digital transactions. The fintech industry integrates AI fraud prevention systems into mobile banking apps. The insurance industry applies fraud detection AI for policy verification and claim assessments. E-commerce platforms use AI to detect fraudulent payments and unauthorized purchases.

Summary
E-Banking Fraud Detection AI enhances financial security by identifying and preventing fraudulent activities in online banking. While it provides advanced protection against cyber threats, challenges in accuracy, data privacy, and regulatory compliance must be addressed for optimal performance.

E-Bayesian Estimation

F-E-Bayesian Estimation is an extension of Bayesian estimation that integrates empirical Bayes methods to improve parameter estimation in complex models. It combines traditional Bayesian inference with data-driven empirical techniques, making it particularly useful in cases where prior distributions are not well-defined. Instead of relying solely on predefined priors, E-Bayesian Estimation refines the priors dynamically based on observed data, leading to more accurate and efficient parameter estimation in large-scale datasets.

The key components of E-Bayesian Estimation include prior distribution selection, likelihood function computation, posterior probability estimation, and empirical Bayes adjustments that iteratively refine the priors. This adaptive approach allows for improved generalization and reduces reliance on subjective prior assumptions.

The benefits of E-Bayesian Estimation include increased accuracy in probabilistic modeling, improved robustness in parameter estimation, and enhanced adaptability to data variations. It is particularly effective in machine learning models that require probabilistic reasoning with limited prior knowledge. Examples include its use in medical diagnostics for estimating disease probabilities, in financial modeling for risk assessment, and in AI-driven decision-making systems.

Applications of E-Bayesian Estimation span across fields such as bioinformatics, signal processing, economic forecasting, and artificial intelligence. In healthcare, it enhances predictive models for personalized medicine. In finance, it optimizes portfolio management by dynamically adjusting risk estimates. In AI, it improves reinforcement learning algorithms by refining uncertainty estimates in decision-making processes.

In conclusion, E-Bayesian Estimation provides a powerful framework for refining probabilistic models using a combination of Bayesian inference and empirical data adjustments. Its ability to enhance predictive accuracy and adaptability makes it a valuable tool in AI-driven analytics and scientific research. As computational methods evolve, improvements in scalable algorithms will further enhance its applicability in real-world AI systems.

EBCDIC (Extended Binary Coded Decimal Interchange Code)

EBCDIC (Extended Binary Coded Decimal Interchange Code) is a character encoding system developed by IBM for mainframe and midrange computer systems. It was designed to facilitate efficient data representation and processing in legacy computing environments, serving as an alternative to ASCII encoding. Unlike ASCII, which is widely used in modern computing, EBCDIC employs an 8-bit binary structure to represent alphanumeric and special characters.

The key components of EBCDIC include an 8-bit encoding scheme, a set of control characters for data formatting, and compatibility mechanisms for IBM mainframe communication. Each character is assigned a unique binary representation, ensuring consistent data interpretation across compatible systems.

The benefits of EBCDIC include optimized performance for IBM mainframes, robust data integrity in legacy applications, and compatibility with older computing architectures. It remains essential in industries that continue to rely on mainframe computing for large-scale data processing and enterprise applications. Examples of EBCDIC usage include banking transaction systems, government record-keeping databases, and airline reservation systems.

Applications of EBCDIC are predominantly found in legacy IT environments within finance, government, and large-scale enterprise computing. It is used in batch processing, database management, and secure data transmission in organizations that maintain IBM mainframe infrastructure.

Challenges in EBCDIC include its lack of compatibility with modern web-based and cloud computing technologies, difficulty in transitioning to Unicode-based systems, and the limited availability of contemporary development tools supporting EBCDIC. Converting legacy systems to modern encoding formats requires significant time and resources.

In conclusion, while EBCDIC is gradually being phased out in favor of more universal encoding standards like UTF-8, it remains relevant in specific legacy computing environments. Organizations managing large-scale mainframe operations continue to rely on EBCDIC for data integrity and system compatibility. As digital transformation advances, strategies for modernizing EBCDIC-based systems will be essential for seamless integration with contemporary IT infrastructures.

EBGM (Elastic Bunch Graph Matching)

EBGM (Elastic Bunch Graph Matching) is a computer vision technique used for facial recognition and pattern analysis. It represents facial features as a graph structure, where key landmarks such as eyes, nose, and mouth are assigned nodes, and their spatial relationships are captured through elastic graph transformations. This method allows for robust face recognition despite variations in pose, lighting, and expression.

The key components of EBGM include Gabor wavelet transformation for feature extraction, elastic graph structures for facial representation, and matching algorithms that compare graphs based on their node configurations. These elements enable accurate recognition by adapting to variations in facial appearance.

The benefits of EBGM include high tolerance to image distortions, improved recognition accuracy in uncontrolled environments, and adaptability to different facial recognition applications. It provides a more flexible approach compared to traditional template-matching techniques. Examples of EBGM usage include biometric authentication systems, security surveillance applications, and forensic facial analysis.

Applications of EBGM extend to security, law enforcement, and social media platforms. In security, it enhances access control through biometric verification. In law enforcement, it assists in suspect identification from surveillance footage. In social media, it improves automated face-tagging systems for photo recognition.

In conclusion, EBGM is a powerful facial recognition method that enhances accuracy and robustness in various image processing applications. Its ability to adapt to facial variations makes it a valuable tool in security and biometric authentication. As computer vision technologies evolve, integrating EBGM with deep learning models will further improve its effectiveness in real-world scenarios.

EBI (Evidence-Based Inverventions) in AI

EBI (Evidence-Based Interventions) in AI refers to the application of artificial intelligence to enhance decision-making and intervention strategies based on scientific evidence and data-driven insights. This approach integrates AI models with empirical research to develop optimized solutions for healthcare, education, and social policy initiatives.

The key components of EBI in AI include predictive analytics that assess intervention outcomes, machine learning models that adapt to patient or user needs, and automated decision-support systems that recommend evidence-based actions. AI-driven EBI enhances intervention efficiency by personalizing approaches to individual cases.

The benefits of EBI in AI include improved treatment effectiveness, reduced trial-and-error in intervention design, and increased accessibility to data-driven recommendations. AI-powered intervention strategies optimize healthcare treatment plans, educational programs, and social welfare initiatives. Examples include AI-assisted therapy recommendations in mental health care, personalized learning plans in education, and optimized resource allocation in public health campaigns.

Applications of EBI in AI span across medicine, education, and public policy. In healthcare, AI-driven EBI assists in designing personalized treatment pathways based on patient histories. In education, it tailors learning experiences to student performance data. In social work, AI models analyze trends to improve intervention strategies for at-risk populations.

Challenges in EBI in AI include ethical considerations in automated decision-making, ensuring unbiased recommendations, and integrating AI models with human expertise. Over-reliance on AI-driven interventions may lead to unintended biases if not carefully monitored. Developing transparent AI models with human oversight is critical for responsible implementation.

In conclusion, EBI in AI enhances the effectiveness of interventions by leveraging data-driven insights and machine learning. Its application across various fields improves decision-making efficiency and optimizes resource utilization. As AI continues to evolve, ensuring ethical considerations and transparency in evidence-based AI interventions will be essential for maintaining public trust and reliability.

E-Billing Fraud Detection AI

F-E-Billing Fraud Detection AI is an artificial intelligence system designed to identify and prevent fraudulent activities in electronic billing processes. It uses machine learning algorithms and anomaly detection techniques to analyze billing patterns, detect irregular transactions, and mitigate financial risks.

The key components of E-Billing Fraud Detection AI include transaction monitoring algorithms that analyze billing data, anomaly detection models that flag suspicious activities, behavioral analysis that identifies deviations from normal billing patterns, and automated alert systems that notify users or administrators of potential fraud.

The benefits of E-Billing Fraud Detection AI include improved financial security, reduced fraudulent activities, and increased efficiency in fraud detection processes. AI-powered fraud detection minimizes financial losses and enhances trust in digital payment systems. Examples include fraud detection models used by financial institutions, AI-driven auditing tools that flag unauthorized charges, and automated invoice verification systems in corporate finance.

Applications of E-Billing Fraud Detection AI are crucial in banking, e-commerce, healthcare billing, and telecommunications. In banking, AI monitors transactions for fraudulent billing activities. In e-commerce, it safeguards merchants against unauthorized purchases. In healthcare, it detects insurance fraud and billing irregularities. Telecommunications companies use AI to prevent fraudulent billing practices in subscription-based services.

In conclusion, E-Billing Fraud Detection AI is a vital tool in modern financial security, providing real-time fraud prevention and automated risk assessment. Its implementation in various industries enhances transaction integrity and safeguards businesses from financial threats. As fraud techniques become more sophisticated, continuous advancements in AI-driven fraud detection will be essential to staying ahead of emerging risks.

E-Billing SystemsAI

F-E-Billing Systems AI refers to the integration of artificial intelligence into electronic billing processes to automate invoicing, payment processing, and financial record management. This technology enhances billing efficiency by leveraging machine learning, natural language processing, and anomaly detection to streamline transactions and minimize errors. AI-powered e-billing systems optimize the accuracy and security of financial transactions while improving user experience through automated payment handling.

The key components of E-Billing Systems AI include intelligent invoice processing that recognizes and categorizes transactions, fraud detection models that identify unusual billing patterns, automated payment reconciliation that ensures accurate accounting, and predictive analytics that forecast billing trends. These components work together to create an efficient and secure billing system.

The benefits of AI-powered e-billing systems include reduced manual workload, faster invoice processing, improved fraud detection, and enhanced financial transparency. By automating repetitive tasks, businesses can allocate resources more efficiently while minimizing billing disputes. Examples of AI in e-billing include automated tax compliance systems, intelligent expense management platforms, and AI-driven payment gateways that validate transactions in real time.

Applications of E-Billing Systems AI span industries such as banking, healthcare, telecommunications, and e-commerce. In banking, AI automates customer billing and loan payment processing. In healthcare, it optimizes medical billing to prevent insurance fraud. In telecommunications, it manages subscription-based billing and usage-based charges. In e-commerce, AI enhances checkout processes with automated invoice generation and fraud prevention.

In conclusion, E-Billing Systems AI transforms financial transactions by automating and securing electronic invoicing. Its ability to enhance accuracy, reduce fraud, and optimize payment processing makes it a critical component of modern financial management. As AI technology advances, e-billing systems will become even more efficient, secure, and adaptable to dynamic business needs.

EBNF (Extended Backus-Naur Form) in AI

EBNF (Extended Backus-Naur Form) in AI refers to the use of an extended notation system to formally define the syntax of programming languages and AI-driven data structures. EBNF enhances traditional Backus-Naur Form by incorporating additional symbols and constructs that improve the clarity and expressiveness of syntax descriptions. This formalism is essential in AI for developing language processing algorithms, code generation tools, and automated parsing mechanisms.

The key components of EBNF in AI include syntax rules that define how statements are structured, terminal and non-terminal symbols that represent language elements, repetition operators that indicate optional or repeated sequences, and hierarchical grammar representations that enable modular parsing. These components ensure precise language specification and interpretation.

The benefits of EBNF in AI include improved language processing accuracy, reduced ambiguity in syntax definitions, and enhanced automation in compiler design and AI-driven code interpretation. It simplifies the development of AI models that rely on structured language processing. Examples of EBNF applications include its use in defining programming language grammars, structuring chatbot interaction flows, and developing AI-driven code autocompletion systems.

Applications of EBNF in AI extend to software development, natural language processing, and AI-driven programming assistants. In software engineering, it supports compiler construction and code validation. In natural language processing, it assists in defining structured dialogue patterns for AI-based conversational agents. In AI programming, it helps automate code transformation and verification processes.

In conclusion, EBNF in AI provides a robust framework for defining structured language rules, enabling efficient programming language processing and AI-driven automation. As AI applications in language processing expand, EBNF will continue to play a vital role in enhancing syntax representation, improving code interpretation, and optimizing AI-driven software development.

E-Book Recommendation Systems AI

E-Book Recommendation Systems AI utilizes artificial intelligence to suggest books based on user preferences, reading history, and contextual insights. These systems apply machine learning algorithms, natural language processing, and collaborative filtering techniques to personalize recommendations, ensuring that users receive book suggestions aligned with their interests and reading habits.

The key components of E-Book Recommendation Systems AI include content-based filtering that analyzes book descriptions and genres, collaborative filtering that matches users with similar reading preferences, deep learning models that predict personalized recommendations, and sentiment analysis that interprets user reviews to refine suggestions. These elements enhance the accuracy and relevance of book recommendations.

The benefits of AI-driven e-book recommendation systems include improved user engagement, increased book discovery, and enhanced reading experiences. By analyzing user behavior, AI ensures that book suggestions align with individual interests, leading to better reader satisfaction. Examples of AI-powered book recommendation systems include personalized reading lists on platforms like Kindle, AI-driven book discovery engines, and intelligent library management systems.

Applications of E-Book Recommendation Systems AI extend to online bookstores, digital libraries, educational platforms, and e-learning applications. In online bookstores, AI enhances user experience by providing tailored book suggestions. In digital libraries, it assists in catalog organization and book discovery. In education, AI-powered recommendation systems help students find relevant learning materials. In e-learning platforms, AI suggests books that complement course content.

In conclusion, E-Book Recommendation Systems AI enhances reading experiences by leveraging machine learning and personalized insights to suggest relevant books. Its ability to improve book discovery, engage readers, and support education makes it an essential tool in digital publishing. As AI technology advances, recommendation systems will become even more adaptive, accurate, and responsive to user needs.

EBP (Evidence-Based Practice)

EBP (Evidence-Based Practice) AI refers to the integration of artificial intelligence with evidence-based methodologies to improve decision-making and intervention strategies in healthcare, education, and business. AI-driven EBP systems analyze large datasets, identify best practices, and optimize recommendations based on empirical evidence and real-world outcomes.

The key components of EBP AI include machine learning models that evaluate data patterns, predictive analytics that assess intervention effectiveness, automated decision-support systems that enhance professional practices, and real-time data integration that ensures up-to-date recommendations. These elements enable AI to support evidence-based decision-making.

The benefits of EBP AI include increased accuracy in professional decision-making, enhanced adaptability to new data trends, and improved efficiency in intervention planning. AI-driven EBP ensures that best practices are continuously updated based on the latest research and empirical evidence. Examples of AI in evidence-based practice include predictive analytics for patient treatment plans, AI-powered educational assessment tools, and business intelligence platforms that optimize operational strategies.

Applications of EBP AI are prevalent in medicine, education, business management, and public policy. In healthcare, AI helps personalize patient treatment plans based on clinical evidence. In education, it improves curriculum design through data-driven analysis. In business, AI enhances strategic planning by evaluating past market trends. In public policy, it supports decision-making with data-backed recommendations.

In conclusion, EBP AI enhances decision-making by integrating artificial intelligence with empirical research and best practices. Its impact on healthcare, education, and business optimizes interventions, improves outcomes, and streamlines professional practices. As AI evolves, ensuring responsible and transparent implementation of evidence-based AI systems will be crucial for long-term effectiveness.

E-Brainstorming

E-Brainstorming is an AI-enhanced collaborative thinking process that facilitates idea generation, problem-solving, and innovation in digital environments. It utilizes artificial intelligence to organize discussions, analyze contributions, and suggest creative insights in team-based brainstorming sessions.

The key components of E-Brainstorming include natural language processing for analyzing participant inputs, AI-driven idea clustering that groups related thoughts, sentiment analysis for understanding team sentiment, and automated summarization that refines brainstorming outputs into actionable insights. These elements streamline and enhance the creative process.

The benefits of AI-powered E-Brainstorming include improved idea organization, increased collaboration efficiency, and enhanced creativity through AI-driven suggestions. It allows remote teams to brainstorm effectively while ensuring structured discussions. Examples include AI-assisted brainstorming platforms, virtual collaboration tools with intelligent idea mapping, and automated session summaries that highlight key insights.

Applications of E-Brainstorming span business strategy development, product innovation, academic research, and corporate training. In business, AI-driven brainstorming enhances marketing strategy planning. In product design, it accelerates concept development. In academia, it supports research discussions. In corporate training, AI-assisted brainstorming tools improve knowledge-sharing processes.

In conclusion, E-Brainstorming revolutionizes collaborative thinking by leveraging AI to enhance idea generation and problem-solving. Its application in business, education, and innovation fosters creativity, efficiency, and strategic decision-making. As AI technology evolves, e-brainstorming tools will continue to refine and expand their capabilities in shaping future collaboration.

E-Business AI

E-Business AI is an artificial intelligence-driven system designed to optimize, automate, and enhance various aspects of online business operations. It integrates machine learning, natural language processing, and predictive analytics to improve efficiency, customer engagement, and business intelligence in digital commerce. AI-powered solutions enable businesses to personalize customer experiences, streamline logistics, and optimize financial transactions.

The key components of E-Business AI include AI-powered customer service systems that provide real-time support, predictive analytics that forecast market trends and consumer behavior, intelligent automation that optimizes supply chain and inventory management, and AI-driven marketing strategies that personalize user interactions. These elements contribute to more efficient and profitable e-business operations.

The benefits of E-Business AI include enhanced decision-making capabilities, improved operational efficiency, personalized customer experiences, and increased revenue generation. AI reduces manual workload and optimizes business performance by providing data-driven insights and automation. Examples of E-Business AI include AI-powered recommendation engines in online retail, automated chatbot assistants for customer service, and AI-driven financial risk assessment tools.

Applications of E-Business AI extend to e-commerce, digital banking, travel platforms, and online education. In e-commerce, AI enhances product recommendations and dynamic pricing. In digital banking, AI improves fraud detection and customer verification. In travel platforms, AI optimizes booking processes and personalized trip planning. In online education, AI tailors learning experiences based on student engagement and performance.

In conclusion, E-Business AI is transforming the digital marketplace by enabling smarter, faster, and more personalized interactions between businesses and consumers. Its ability to automate processes, enhance decision-making, and optimize customer engagement makes it a fundamental part of modern online business strategies. As AI technology continues to advance, its role in e-business will become even more integral to competitive success.

E-Business- Ecosystem AI

E-Business Ecosystem AI refers to the use of artificial intelligence to optimize the interconnected digital infrastructure of online businesses, enabling seamless collaboration between various stakeholders, including suppliers, customers, and service providers. This AI-driven ecosystem enhances efficiency by automating transactions, predicting market trends, and optimizing supply chain operations. By leveraging AI, e-business ecosystems become more adaptive and resilient to changing market conditions.

The key components of E-Business Ecosystem AI include intelligent supply chain management that predicts demand and optimizes logistics, AI-driven customer relationship management that enhances personalized interactions, automated financial transactions that streamline payments and fraud detection, and digital marketplace intelligence that analyzes competitor strategies and consumer behavior. These components work together to create a highly efficient and self-sustaining e-business environment.

The benefits of E-Business Ecosystem AI include improved operational efficiency, enhanced market adaptability, better resource allocation, and seamless digital transactions. AI-driven insights help businesses make data-informed decisions and respond proactively to market shifts. Examples of AI in e-business ecosystems include predictive analytics for demand forecasting, AI-powered supplier selection algorithms, and automated contract negotiation systems.

Applications of E-Business Ecosystem AI are found in online marketplaces, digital supply chains, global trade platforms, and SaaS ecosystems. Online marketplaces use AI to match buyers with sellers efficiently. Digital supply chains leverage AI to optimize production and distribution networks. Global trade platforms use AI-driven automation to facilitate cross-border transactions. SaaS businesses utilize AI to enhance software integration and customer engagement.

In conclusion, E-Business Ecosystem AI enhances the digital marketplace by optimizing collaboration, automation, and market intelligence across interconnected business networks. Its ability to drive efficiency, predict market trends, and automate operations makes it a critical enabler of modern digital commerce. As AI continues to evolve, businesses that leverage AI-driven ecosystems will gain a significant competitive advantage in the online marketplace.

E-*Business Infrastructure AI*

E-Business Infrastructure AI refers to artificial intelligence technologies that support the digital backbone of online businesses by automating network management, enhancing cybersecurity, optimizing cloud computing, and improving system scalability. This AI-driven infrastructure ensures that digital business operations remain secure, reliable, and efficient by continuously monitoring and adapting to system demands.

The key components of E-Business Infrastructure AI include AI-powered cybersecurity that detects and prevents cyber threats, cloud-based AI optimization that enhances resource allocation and system performance, predictive maintenance that prevents IT failures, and intelligent automation that streamlines data management and workflow processes. These components create a robust and scalable foundation for online business operations.

The benefits of AI-powered e-business infrastructure include enhanced security, reduced operational costs, improved system reliability, and increased scalability. AI enables businesses to proactively detect and respond to potential issues before they impact operations. Examples of E-Business Infrastructure AI include AI-driven cloud optimization tools, automated threat detection systems, and intelligent IT resource management platforms.

Applications of E-Business Infrastructure AI are critical in cloud computing, digital banking, enterprise software solutions, and cybersecurity services. Cloud providers use AI to optimize server load balancing. Digital banks rely on AI for fraud detection and secure transactions. Enterprise software companies integrate AI to enhance system automation and predictive maintenance. Cybersecurity firms deploy AI-driven threat intelligence to protect business networks.

In conclusion, E-Business Infrastructure AI forms the technological foundation of digital businesses by enhancing security, efficiency, and scalability. Its ability to automate IT management and optimize cloud computing makes it essential for maintaining resilient and adaptable online business operations. As AI continues to advance, businesses that invest in AI-driven infrastructure will benefit from improved reliability and long-term digital success.

E-Business Intelligence AI

E-Business IntelligenceAI refers to the application of artificial intelligence in gathering, analyzing, and interpreting data to support decision-making in online businesses. It enhances business intelligence by automating data collection, identifying market trends, and providing actionable insights for business growth. AI-driven business intelligence enables companies to make data-driven decisions with greater accuracy and speed.

The key components of E-Business Intelligence AI include AI-powered data analytics that identifies patterns and trends, predictive modeling that forecasts market changes, automated reporting tools that generate business insights, and natural language processing that interprets unstructured business data. These components enhance strategic decision-making and operational efficiency.

The benefits of E-Business Intelligence AI include improved decision-making, increased market competitiveness, enhanced customer insights, and streamlined data processing. AI-driven business intelligence enables organizations to respond quickly to market changes and optimize business performance. Examples include AI-powered dashboards that provide real-time business analytics, automated competitor analysis tools, and customer sentiment analysis systems.

Applications of E-Business Intelligence AI are widespread in e-commerce, finance, digital marketing, and business strategy development. Online retailers use AI to analyze sales data and optimize pricing. Financial institutions leverage AI to assess market risks. Marketing teams utilize AI-driven analytics to enhance campaign performance. Corporate decision-makers rely on AI-generated insights for strategic planning.

In conclusion, E-Business Intelligence AI transforms how businesses analyze and interpret data, providing valuable insights for strategic growth. Its ability to automate data processing and enhance decision-making makes it an essential tool for modern businesses. As AI technology advances, businesses will increasingly rely on AI-driven intelligence to maintain a competitive edge in the digital economy.

Echo State Networks (ESN)

Definition: A type of recurrent neural network (RNN) that is easier to train than traditional RNNs due to its "reservoir" of hidden states, which are only partially updated during training.

Key Characteristics
Reservoir Computing: A fixed, randomly connected internal network serves as a dynamic memory.
Sparse Updates: Only the output weights are trained, keeping the internal network unchanged.
Fast Training: Less computationally intensive than traditional RNNs due to fewer parameters being updated.

Benefits
Efficient for time-series predictions and dynamic systems modeling.

Disadvantages
Can be sensitive to the initial setup and requires tuning of the reservoir for optimal performance.

Applications
Time-series forecasting, speech recognition, robotics control.

Conclusion
Echo state networks offer a more efficient alternative to traditional RNNs, especially for tasks involving sequential data, though they require careful tuning to perform optimally.

Ecological Monitoring AI

Definition: AI systems used to monitor and analyze environmental data, enabling the tracking of wildlife, ecosystems, and climate changes.

Key Characteristics
Sensor Integration: Collects data from environmental sensors such as cameras, temperature gauges, and satellites.
Pattern Recognition: Uses AI to detect changes in ecosystems or animal behavior.
Predictive Analytics: Forecasts environmental changes based on collected data.

Benefits
Improves conservation efforts, detects early signs of ecosystem degradation, and helps manage natural resources.

Applications
Wildlife tracking, climate change analysis, conservation efforts, resource management.

Conclusion
Ecological monitoring AI offers powerful tools for environmental management and conservation, though it depends heavily on accurate and comprehensive data inputs.

Ecommerce Fraud Detection

AI algorithms designed to detect fraudulent activities in e-commerce transactions by analyzing user behavior, transaction patterns, and risk factors.

Key Characteristics
Anomaly Detection: Identifies unusual patterns in transaction data.
Real-Time Monitoring: Tracks e-commerce transactions as they occur to flag potential fraud.
Machine Learning Models: Continuously learns from past fraud cases to improve accuracy.

Benefits
Reduces financial losses from fraud and improves consumer trust.

Applications
Online retail platforms, payment gateways, digital marketplaces.

Conclusion
E-commerce fraud detection AI is essential for securing online transactions, though its effectiveness depends on balancing accuracy and minimizing false positives.

Economic Data Mining AI

Ecibinuc Data Mining AI is the application of artificial intelligence to extract, analyze, and interpret large-scale economic data for trends, patterns, and correlations. This AI-driven approach enables businesses, policymakers, and financial analysts to uncover valuable insights from structured and unstructured economic data sources. By automating the analysis of economic indicators, financial reports, and global trade data, AI enhances decision-making in economic planning and forecasting.

The key components of Economic Data Mining AI include machine learning algorithms that identify patterns in economic datasets, natural language processing that extracts insights from financial news and reports, predictive modeling that forecasts economic trends, and big data analytics that process large volumes of structured and unstructured information. These components enable AI to provide real-time insights and predictions about economic conditions.

The benefits of Economic Data Mining AI include faster data analysis, improved forecasting accuracy, enhanced decision-making capabilities, and better risk management. AI-driven economic insights help businesses and governments respond proactively to market changes and economic fluctuations. Examples include AI-powered financial risk assessments that predict market downturns, automated analysis of inflation trends, and AI-driven sentiment analysis of economic policies.

Applications of Economic Data Mining AI span finance, government policy, investment analysis, and supply chain management. In finance, AI detects anomalies in stock market data and assesses investment risks. Governments use AI to analyze employment rates and inflation trends. Investment firms leverage AI to identify emerging market opportunities. Supply chain managers apply AI to predict economic factors affecting global trade.

In conclusion, Economic Data Mining AI enhances economic analysis by automating data processing, identifying trends, and improving forecasting accuracy. Its application across finance, policy, and investment strengthens economic planning and risk assessment. As AI technology continues to evolve, economic data mining will play an increasingly vital role in shaping financial and governmental decision-making.

Economic Forecasting AI

Economic Forecasting AI is an advanced artificial intelligence system that predicts future economic trends using historical data, machine learning models, and real-time market insights. AI-driven economic forecasting improves the accuracy of financial planning, investment strategies, and policy decisions by identifying patterns in macroeconomic and microeconomic indicators. This AI approach enables businesses and governments to anticipate market shifts and economic fluctuations with greater precision.

The key components of Economic Forecasting AI include time-series analysis that detects long-term economic patterns, deep learning models that process vast economic datasets, sentiment analysis that interprets financial news and social media trends, and real-time data integration that enhances forecast accuracy. These components collectively improve the predictive power of economic models.

The benefits of AI-powered economic forecasting include increased forecasting accuracy, improved market stability, better financial decision-making, and early detection of economic downturns. AI-driven predictions help businesses manage risks, governments formulate effective policies, and investors make informed decisions. Examples include AI-based GDP growth forecasting, automated inflation rate predictions, and AI-driven consumer spending projections.

Applications of Economic Forecasting AI extend to central banking, corporate financial planning, stock market analysis, and economic policy formulation. Central banks use AI to assess inflationary pressures and interest rate adjustments. Corporations rely on AI-driven economic forecasts for budgeting and investment planning. Investors leverage AI insights to predict stock market fluctuations. Governments use AI to evaluate economic stimulus measures.

In conclusion, Economic Forecasting AI revolutionizes financial planning by leveraging AI-driven insights to predict economic trends with greater precision. Its role in decision-making, risk assessment, and market stability is invaluable across industries. As AI technology advances, economic forecasting models will continue to evolve, improving their adaptability and accuracy in predicting future market conditions.

Economic Impact Analysis AI

Economic Impact Analysis AI is the application of artificial intelligence to evaluate the effects of economic policies, business decisions, and external events on markets and industries. This AI-driven approach uses data modeling, machine learning, and statistical analysis to quantify economic outcomes and assess the broader financial implications of specific actions. By automating economic impact assessments, AI enables faster and more precise evaluations of financial policies and business investments.

The key components of Economic Impact Analysis AI include AI-driven simulation models that assess potential economic outcomes, real-time data analytics that track financial trends, causal inference algorithms that determine economic relationships, and scenario modeling that predicts various economic responses to policy changes. These components provide a comprehensive view of economic impact factors.

The benefits of Economic Impact Analysis AI include improved policy evaluation, enhanced business decision-making, increased efficiency in economic modeling, and better financial risk assessment. AI-driven analysis allows businesses and governments to understand the broader economic consequences of their actions before implementation. Examples include AI-driven evaluations of tax reforms, automated analysis of trade policies, and AI-powered impact assessments of major infrastructure projects.

Applications of Economic Impact Analysis AI span government policy planning, corporate investment strategy, public infrastructure development, and financial risk assessment. Governments use AI to assess the economic effects of regulations and trade agreements. Corporations leverage AI-driven impact analysis to evaluate mergers and acquisitions. Public sector planners use AI to predict the financial benefits of large-scale projects. Financial analysts apply AI to assess economic risks and opportunities.

In conclusion, Economic Impact Analysis AI enhances financial decision-making by providing data-driven insights into the effects of economic policies and investments. Its ability to automate impact assessments and quantify economic outcomes makes it a valuable tool for governments, businesses, and financial institutions. As AI continues to advance, economic impact analysis will become more refined, enabling more precise and actionable economic planning.

Ecosystem Data Fusion AI

Definition
AI systems that combine data from various environmental and ecological sources to create a unified view of ecosystems, enabling better decision-making in conservation and resource management.

Key Characteristics
Multisource Data Integration: Fuses data from sensors, satellites, and human observations.
Unified Modeling: Provides a comprehensive model of ecosystems by integrating diverse data types.
Real-Time Updates: Continuously incorporates new data for up-to-date ecosystem assessments.

Benefits
Enhances the accuracy and timeliness of environmental monitoring and decision-making.

Disadvantages
Requires high-quality data from diverse sources, which may not always be available or compatible.

Applications
Conservation efforts, climate change monitoring, biodiversity protection.

Conclusion
Ecosystem data fusion AI enables more accurate and comprehensive environmental assessments but requires robust data collection and integration methods to function effectively.

Ecosystem Modeling AI

Definition
AI systems that simulate and model ecosystems to predict how environmental changes will affect biodiversity, food chains, and natural resources.

Key Characteristics
Simulation-Based: Uses AI to simulate the interactions between species, environments, and external factors.
Predictive Models: Forecasts how ecosystems will evolve over time with changing environmental conditions.
Big Data Analytics: Integrates vast amounts of environmental data for accurate modeling.

Benefits
Helps conservationists make data-driven decisions to protect biodiversity and ecosystems.

Applications
Conservation planning, climate change impact studies, natural resource management.

Conclusion
Ecosystem modeling AI enhances our ability to predict environmental changes and their impacts on ecosystems, though it relies on high-quality data and sophisticated simulation models.

Edge-Based AI Inference

Edge-Based AI Inference refers to the execution of AI models directly on edge devices to generate predictions and insights without relying on cloud-based servers. This approach enables AI-powered applications to function with minimal latency, making them ideal for real-time decision-making in environments where speed and security are critical.

The key components of Edge-Based AI Inference include optimized neural network models that require minimal computational resources, hardware accelerators such as AI-specific edge processors, real-time inference engines that process data locally, and federated learning techniques that improve AI model accuracy while ensuring data privacy. These components enhance AI inference capabilities at the edge.

The benefits of Edge-Based AI Inference include faster response times, reduced cloud dependency, improved data security, and enhanced energy efficiency. AI inference at the edge allows systems to operate autonomously without continuous internet connectivity. Examples include AI-powered facial recognition in security systems, voice assistants that process speech locally, and autonomous drones that make navigation decisions in real time.

Applications of Edge-Based AI Inference extend to autonomous robotics, smart home devices, industrial automation, and augmented reality. In robotics, AI inference optimizes real-time object recognition. In smart homes, AI enables voice-activated devices to function offline. In industrial automation, AI improves quality control in manufacturing. In augmented reality, AI inference enhances interactive user experiences.

In conclusion, Edge-Based AI Inference enhances AI-driven applications by enabling real-time, localized processing. Its ability to reduce latency and improve security makes it essential for next-generation autonomous and intelligent systems. As edge computing advances, AI inference at the edge will become even more efficient, expanding its impact across industries.

Edge Computing AI

Edge Computing AI refers to the deployment of artificial intelligence algorithms and models at the edge of a network, where data is generated and processed locally rather than relying on centralized cloud servers. This approach enables real-time decision-making, reduces latency, and improves data security by minimizing the need to transfer information over networks. Edge Computing AI is particularly useful in applications where immediate responses are required, such as autonomous systems, industrial automation, and IoT devices.

The key components of Edge Computing AI include lightweight AI models optimized for low-power devices, edge hardware such as AI-enabled microprocessors and GPUs, real-time inference engines that analyze data locally, and federated learning mechanisms that allow AI models to improve without compromising data privacy. These components collectively enhance the efficiency and autonomy of AI applications at the network edge.

The benefits of Edge Computing AI include reduced network congestion, lower latency, improved energy efficiency, and enhanced privacy by keeping sensitive data on local devices. By processing data closer to the source, businesses and organizations can achieve faster responses and more efficient resource utilization. Examples include AI-powered surveillance cameras that detect security threats in real time, autonomous vehicles that process sensor data locally for navigation, and AI-driven predictive maintenance in industrial settings.

Applications of Edge Computing AI span multiple industries, including manufacturing, healthcare, telecommunications, and smart cities. In manufacturing, AI-driven edge computing optimizes production lines and prevents downtime. In healthcare, it enables real-time patient monitoring with wearable devices. In telecommunications, it enhances mobile network performance by processing data at local base stations. In smart cities, edge AI powers intelligent traffic management and environmental monitoring systems.

In conclusion, Edge Computing AI is revolutionizing how artificial intelligence is deployed by shifting processing power closer to data sources. Its ability to enable real-time analytics and reduce reliance on centralized cloud services makes it an essential component of modern AI applications. As edge computing technology advances, its integration with AI will continue to expand, driving efficiency and innovation across industries.

Edge Data Processing

Edge Data Processing refers to the real-time analysis and transformation of data at the point of generation, rather than sending raw data to centralized data centers for processing. This method leverages edge computing technologies to reduce bandwidth usage, enhance speed, and improve operational efficiency in distributed networks. By processing data locally, edge data processing ensures faster insights and minimizes latency, making it essential for time-sensitive applications.

The key components of Edge Data Processing include real-time analytics engines that filter and preprocess data at the edge, machine learning algorithms that optimize data classification and anomaly detection, lightweight data storage solutions for temporary caching, and secure communication protocols for transmitting processed data to cloud systems when necessary. These elements enable efficient and reliable data handling in decentralized environments.

The benefits of Edge Data Processing include reduced dependency on cloud infrastructure, improved system resilience, increased data security, and faster response times for AI-driven applications. Processing data at the edge minimizes latency, allowing for immediate insights and decision-making. Examples include edge-based quality control in manufacturing, AI-driven health monitoring systems in hospitals, and real-time object detection in autonomous vehicles.

Applications of Edge Data Processing extend across industries such as IoT, healthcare, retail, and logistics. In IoT, real-time data filtering at the edge prevents network congestion. In healthcare, wearable medical devices analyze patient vitals locally before transmitting key insights to doctors. In retail, AI-powered point-of-sale systems process transactions and detect fraud instantly. In logistics, edge data processing optimizes route planning and fleet management.

In conclusion, Edge Data Processing enhances efficiency by reducing the need for centralized data analysis while enabling real-time decision-making. Its impact on IoT, AI, and industrial applications continues to grow, making it a crucial element of modern digital transformation. As advancements in edge computing continue, data processing at the edge will become even more integral to AI-driven automation and analytics.

Edge Detection in AI

Edge Detection in AI is a computer vision technique used to identify the boundaries of objects within an image or video. It enables AI systems to recognize distinct shapes, patterns, and structures by detecting abrupt changes in pixel intensity. Edge detection is a fundamental step in image analysis, playing a crucial role in facial recognition, autonomous navigation, and medical imaging applications.

The key components of Edge Detection in AI include gradient-based algorithms such as the Sobel and Canny edge detectors, deep learning-based edge recognition models that enhance accuracy, edge refinement techniques that eliminate noise from detected edges, and real-time processing frameworks that enable edge detection in dynamic environments. These components work together to extract meaningful object boundaries in complex visual data.

The benefits of AI-driven Edge Detection include improved accuracy in image recognition, enhanced object tracking capabilities, and better segmentation for AI-based image processing tasks. By identifying key features in an image, AI systems can make more informed decisions in real-world applications. Examples include AI-powered facial recognition systems that enhance security, self-driving cars that detect lane markings, and AI-assisted medical imaging systems that identify tumors in scans.

Applications of Edge Detection in AI span fields such as security, healthcare, robotics, and augmented reality. In security, AI-powered surveillance systems use edge detection to track movements and detect intrusions. In healthcare, AI-enhanced radiology scans improve early diagnosis of diseases. In robotics, edge detection helps machines recognize objects for interaction. In augmented reality, AI processes visual data to overlay digital content on real-world images.

In conclusion, Edge Detection in AI is a critical component of computer vision, enabling AI models to interpret visual data with precision. Its ability to identify object boundaries enhances AI applications in security, healthcare, and robotics. As deep learning and computational vision techniques evolve, edge detection will continue to play a fundamental role in advancing AI-powered image analysis.

Edge Intelligence

Edge Intelligence refers to the integration of artificial intelligence with edge computing to enable autonomous decision-making at the data source. By embedding AI capabilities within edge devices, Edge Intelligence allows real-time data processing, learning, and adaptation without relying on cloud-based servers. This approach enhances responsiveness, security, and efficiency in AI-driven applications.

The key components of Edge Intelligence include AI-optimized hardware for low-power inference, federated learning models that enable distributed training, neural network compression techniques that improve computational efficiency, and real-time analytics engines that process and act on data locally. These elements collectively enable AI systems to function effectively in decentralized environments.

The benefits of Edge Intelligence include faster AI inference, improved data privacy by reducing cloud dependency, enhanced adaptability in dynamic environments, and lower operational costs. Edge AI systems provide on-device learning capabilities, making them ideal for real-time analytics and automation. Examples include AI-powered smart cameras that analyze video feeds on-device, industrial robots that optimize production processes, and autonomous drones that navigate independently.

Applications of Edge Intelligence are found in autonomous vehicles, industrial automation, smart healthcare, and IoT networks. In autonomous vehicles, AI processes sensor data in real time to make driving decisions. In industrial automation, intelligent robots perform adaptive manufacturing tasks. In healthcare, AI-enabled edge devices assist in medical diagnostics. In IoT networks, AI enhances real-time data processing in smart home systems.

In conclusion, Edge Intelligence enables AI systems to function independently at the edge, reducing reliance on centralized computing while improving real-time decision-making. Its impact on automation, security, and AI-driven analytics continues to grow, making it a vital component of next-generation AI applications. As edge computing and AI technologies advance, Edge Intelligence will play an increasingly central role in digital transformation.

Edge Neural Networks

Edge Neural Networksare artificial intelligence models optimized for execution on edge computing devices, allowing real-time inference and decision-making without relying on cloud-based servers. These networks are designed to be lightweight, efficient, and capable of operating on low-power hardware while maintaining high accuracy. By bringing neural network computation closer to the data source, Edge Neural Networks enable applications that require fast responses, such as autonomous systems, smart sensors, and mobile AI-powered devices.

The key components of Edge Neural Networks include optimized deep learning architectures that reduce computational complexity, neural network quantization techniques that minimize memory usage, real-time inference engines that process data locally, and federated learning frameworks that enable decentralized training without sharing raw data. These elements allow AI models to run efficiently on constrained devices.

The benefits of Edge Neural Networks include reduced latency in AI-driven decision-making, enhanced privacy by keeping data localized, improved energy efficiency for battery-powered devices, and greater scalability in distributed AI deployments. By enabling intelligent processing at the edge, these networks support applications that require high-speed, real-time AI insights. Examples include AI-powered wearable health monitors that analyze biometric data, smart home devices that process voice commands locally, and industrial sensors that detect equipment failures in real-time.

Applications of Edge Neural Networks span healthcare, IoT, autonomous systems, and security. In healthcare, AI-enabled medical devices provide immediate diagnostics. In IoT, smart sensors process environmental data on-site. In autonomous systems, AI-powered vehicles make split-second navigation decisions. In security, AI-driven surveillance cameras detect anomalies without transmitting data to external servers.

In conclusion, Edge Neural Networks revolutionize AI by enabling fast, efficient, and decentralized decision-making. Their role in enhancing AI autonomy and security makes them a critical component of real-time AI applications. As edge computing continues to evolve, Edge Neural Networks will drive new innovations in AI-powered automation and intelligence.

Education AI

Edication AI refers to the application of artificial intelligence in educational settings to enhance learning experiences, personalize instruction, and optimize administrative processes. AI-powered educational systems use adaptive learning, intelligent tutoring, and predictive analytics to improve student engagement and academic outcomes. By leveraging AI, education becomes more accessible, efficient, and tailored to individual learning needs.

The key components of Education AI include machine learning models that analyze student performance data, natural language processing tools that enhance automated tutoring, AI-driven content recommendation engines that personalize learning materials, and intelligent assessment systems that provide real-time feedback. These components work together to create an adaptive and data-driven educational environment.

The benefits of Education AI include improved student engagement, personalized learning experiences, reduced administrative workload for educators, and enhanced accessibility for learners with diverse needs. AI-driven insights help educators identify learning gaps and adjust teaching strategies accordingly. Examples include AI-powered virtual tutors that assist students in understanding complex topics, automated grading systems that provide instant feedback, and AI-driven career guidance tools that recommend personalized learning paths.

Applications of Education AI extend to K-12 education, higher education, corporate training, and online learning platforms. In K-12 education, AI personalizes curriculum delivery. In higher education, AI assists in student retention and performance tracking. In corporate training, AI optimizes employee learning programs. In online education, AI enhances adaptive learning experiences for self-paced courses.

In conclusion, Education AI is transforming the learning experience by making education more personalized, efficient, and data-driven. Its impact on student engagement and instructional effectiveness continues to grow, making it a vital tool for modern educational systems. As AI technology evolves, Education AI will play an increasingly significant role in shaping the future of learning.

Educational Content Generation AI

Educational Content Generation AI is the use of artificial intelligence to create, curate, and customize learning materials for various educational settings. This AI-driven approach automates content development, making learning resources more accessible, engaging, and tailored to individual student needs. By analyzing curriculum requirements and student preferences, AI generates interactive and personalized educational content.

The key components of Educational Content Generation AI include natural language generation models that create instructional materials, AI-powered multimedia generation tools that produce interactive learning experiences, personalized content recommendation engines that adapt materials to student progress, and real-time content enhancement systems that refine learning materials based on feedback. These components enable dynamic and engaging educational content creation.

The benefits of AI-driven educational content generation include increased efficiency in developing learning materials, enhanced personalization for diverse learners, improved accessibility through AI-generated translations, and greater interactivity in digital education. AI enables educators to scale content creation while maintaining quality. Examples include AI-generated textbooks tailored to different reading levels, automated quizzes that adapt to student understanding, and AI-driven video tutorials that explain complex concepts.

Applications of Educational Content Generation AI extend to digital classrooms, online learning platforms, corporate training, and personalized tutoring. In digital classrooms, AI generates custom lesson plans. In online learning, AI personalizes course content. In corporate training, AI tailors professional development programs. In tutoring, AI creates practice exercises based on student weaknesses.

In conclusion, Educational Content Generation AI revolutionizes the development of learning materials by making education more interactive, personalized, and scalable. Its ability to automate and enhance content creation improves learning outcomes and accessibility. As AI advances, its role in educational content development will continue to expand, shaping the future of digital education.

Educational Data Mining (EDM)

Definition: Educational Data Mining in AI is the craft of sifting through piles of school-related data with machine learning and digging tools to crack open how students tick—spotting their habits, grades, and learning curves—to tweak teaching smarter.
Key Components: It's powered by algorithms that chew on student clicks and quiz scores from digital platforms, sniffing out patterns like who's thriving or tanking. Predictive engines guess what's next—pass or dropout—while tailored tips pop out for kids and teachers.
Benefits: It hands educators a crystal ball, boosting how kids learn with sharp insights, and fine-tunes lessons to fit each brain, making school less of a slog.
Examples: Picture an AI flagging a kid who's stalling on math homework for extra help, or guessing a

college dropout risk from spotty logins.
Applications: It's in virtual classrooms tracking progress, grade dashboards for teachers, and course blueprints that shift with student vibes.
Industries: Education leans on it for better classes, ed-tech for app smarts, and research for learning science.
Challenges: It's a data hog—prying into every click can spook privacy buffs—and needs clean, fat stacks of info to not misfire.
Summary: Educational Data Mining in AI digs into student trails to sharpen teaching, a win for learning's future, though it wrestles with keeping secrets safe.

Educational Robotics AI

Definition: Educational Robotics AI brings artificial intelligence into robots that play teacher, sparking hands-on fun for students, especially in STEM fields, by guiding them through lessons with a mechanical twist.

Key Components: It's built on bots packed with AI smarts, tweaking lessons to match a kid's pace or quirks, loaded with sensors and code to show off tricks like building or programming. The setup bends to fit what each learner needs, from gears to loops.

Benefits: It turns dull books into live action, gluing kids to learning with real-deal projects, and boosts how much sticks by letting them tinker and tweak.

Examples: Think of a robot showing a middle schooler how to code it to dance, or an AI bot adjusting a gear lesson when a teen stumbles.

Applications: It's in science labs teaching circuits, classroom sidekicks for math play, and summer camps drilling code basics.

Industries: Education taps it for STEM kicks, tech for training tools, and youth programs for skill boosts.
Challenges: These bots don't come cheap—cash and tech gaps can lock some schools out—and leaning too hard on them might glitch if the power dips

.Summary: Educational Robotics AI flips learning into a robot-led adventure, firing up STEM brains, though it fights price tags and tech hiccups to spread wide.

Efficacy in AI

refers to the ability of an artificial intelligence system to perform its intended function accurately and effectively. It measures how well an AI model achieves its goals, whether in decision-making, automation, or data processing. Efficacy is crucial in determining the reliability of AI applications across different industries, ensuring that AI-driven solutions produce meaningful and actionable results.

The key components of AI efficacy include model accuracy, robustness in handling diverse datasets, adaptability to changing environments, and interpretability in decision-making. These factors determine whether an AI system can perform consistently across various scenarios without significant degradation in performance.

The benefits of high AI efficacy include improved decision-making accuracy, enhanced trust in AI-driven processes, reduced errors in automation, and increased efficiency in handling complex tasks. Reliable AI models lead to better outcomes in industries that require precision, such as healthcare diagnostics, financial risk assessment, and industrial automation. Examples include AI-powered fraud detection systems that effectively identify fraudulent transactions and medical AI models that accurately diagnose diseases from imaging data.

Applications of AI efficacy evaluation span healthcare, finance, autonomous systems, and manufacturing. In healthcare, AI efficacy ensures accurate diagnostics and treatment recommendations. In finance, it validates risk models for credit scoring and fraud prevention. In autonomous systems, it guarantees safe navigation and decision-making. In manufacturing, it improves predictive maintenance and quality control.

In conclusion, efficacy in AI is a critical measure of an AI system's success in delivering accurate and reliable outcomes. Maintaining high efficacy requires rigorous testing, ongoing optimization, and alignment with real-world requirements. As AI technology advances, improving efficacy will remain a core focus in ensuring the trustworthiness and effectiveness of AI-driven applications.

Efficacy Predition in AI

Efficacy Prediction in AI refers to the use of artificial intelligence to forecast the effectiveness of AI models, interventions, or decision-making systems before deployment. This predictive approach ensures that AI-driven solutions meet performance expectations by evaluating their potential impact based on historical data, simulations, and real-world conditions.

The key components of efficacy prediction in AI include machine learning models that analyze past performance trends, statistical inference techniques that estimate AI effectiveness under varying conditions, simulation environments that test AI capabilities before real-world implementation, and performance benchmarking tools that compare AI models against predefined standards. These components help determine the likelihood of an AI system achieving its intended purpose.

The benefits of efficacy prediction in AI include reduced deployment risks, improved model optimization, enhanced resource allocation, and increased confidence in AI-driven solutions. By predicting AI performance in advance, organizations can fine-tune models and avoid costly failures. Examples include AI-powered drug discovery platforms that predict the success rate of new medications and AI-driven business intelligence tools that forecast the impact of marketing strategies.

Applications of efficacy prediction in AI span research and development, healthcare, autonomous systems, and enterprise AI. In research and development, AI predicts the success of experimental AI models. In healthcare, AI assesses the effectiveness of medical AI applications before clinical deployment. In autonomous systems, AI forecasts performance in dynamic environments. In enterprise AI, businesses use predictive models to evaluate the impact of AI-driven strategies.

In conclusion, efficacy prediction in AI plays a crucial role in assessing the potential success of AI applications before full-scale implementation. Its ability to improve model optimization, reduce risks, and enhance decision-making makes it a valuable tool in AI development. As AI adoption grows, advancements in efficacy prediction will contribute to more reliable and efficient AI systems across industries.

Efficient Frontier in AI

Efficient Frontier in AI is a concept derived from financial portfolio theory that applies optimization techniques to AI-driven decision-making, resource allocation, and trade-off analysis. It represents the optimal balance between performance and computational efficiency, ensuring that AI models achieve maximum accuracy with minimal resource consumption. By leveraging the efficient frontier approach, AI systems can optimize trade-offs between model complexity, inference speed, and energy consumption.

The key components of the efficient frontier in AI include multi-objective optimization algorithms that balance competing factors, performance-cost trade-off analysis that evaluates different AI model configurations, resource-efficient deep learning architectures that minimize computational overhead, and dynamic adaptation mechanisms that adjust AI models based on real-time constraints. These elements allow AI systems to operate with maximum efficiency.

The benefits of applying the efficient frontier in AI include improved computational efficiency, reduced model training and inference costs, enhanced scalability of AI applications, and better alignment between AI performance and business objectives. By optimizing AI models along the efficient frontier, organizations can achieve superior performance while managing hardware and energy constraints. Examples include AI-powered recommendation systems that optimize personalization accuracy while minimizing server load and AI-driven cloud computing platforms that allocate resources based on real-time demand.

Applications of the efficient frontier in AI extend to financial modeling, cloud computing, autonomous systems, and industrial AI. In financial modeling, AI optimizes risk-return trade-offs in investment strategies. In cloud computing, AI balances computational costs and service quality. In autonomous systems, AI optimizes decision-making efficiency in resource-limited environments. In industrial AI, AI-powered control systems manage energy-efficient manufacturing processes.

In conclusion, the efficient frontier in AI provides a strategic framework for optimizing AI performance while managing computational costs. Its application in AI-driven decision-making, automation, and resource management enhances efficiency and scalability. As AI adoption increases, refining efficient frontier models will be crucial for balancing AI accuracy, speed, and sustainability.

EFFICIENTNet

EfficientNet is a family of deep learning architectures designed to optimize model accuracy while minimizing computational complexity. Developed using a compound scaling approach, EfficientNet balances network depth, width, and resolution to achieve state-of-the-art performance with fewer parameters and lower energy consumption. This efficiency makes EfficientNet particularly well-suited for edge AI applications, cloud computing, and real-time inference tasks.

The key components of EfficientNet include compound scaling that uniformly adjusts network size, depthwise separable convolutions that reduce computation costs, optimized activation functions that improve training stability, and model compression techniques that enhance inference efficiency. These elements collectively enable EfficientNet to achieve superior accuracy with minimal resource usage.

The benefits of EfficientNet include higher accuracy with fewer parameters, reduced training and inference costs, improved energy efficiency for AI-powered applications, and greater adaptability to different hardware environments. By leveraging an optimized architecture, EfficientNet outperforms traditional convolutional neural networks while maintaining computational efficiency. Examples include AI-powered image classification models that require fewer resources and AI-driven medical imaging systems that process high-resolution scans with minimal latency.

Applications of EfficientNet span computer vision, autonomous systems, healthcare, and mobile AI. In computer vision, EfficientNet powers image recognition models with minimal hardware requirements. In autonomous systems, it optimizes object detection for real-time navigation. In healthcare, it enhances diagnostic accuracy in AI-assisted radiology. In mobile AI, it enables energy-efficient deep learning applications on smartphones.

In conclusion, EfficientNet revolutionizes deep learning by achieving high accuracy with minimal computational cost. Its efficiency in AI-driven applications makes it a valuable architecture for industries requiring real-time processing and resource-conscious AI deployment. As deep learning advances, EfficientNet will continue to play a key role in enabling scalable and high-performance AI models.

Eggshell Algorithm

Eggshell Algorithm is an advanced AI optimization technique that focuses on finding optimal solutions while maintaining a balance between exploration and exploitation. Inspired by the structural integrity of an eggshell, this algorithm employs adaptive learning strategies to navigate complex problem spaces while minimizing computational costs. The algorithm is particularly useful in reinforcement learning, search optimization, and dynamic problem-solving applications.

The key components of the Eggshell Algorithm include a dynamic learning rate that adjusts based on problem complexity, a self-correcting feedback mechanism that refines decision-making over time, multi-agent coordination strategies that allow distributed problem-solving, and robustness mechanisms that ensure stability under uncertain conditions. These components work together to optimize performance while maintaining computational efficiency.

The benefits of the Eggshell Algorithm include improved adaptability in solving complex optimization problems, enhanced stability in AI decision-making, reduced computation overhead, and faster convergence to optimal solutions. By balancing risk and efficiency, the algorithm enables AI systems to learn more effectively. Examples include its use in autonomous robotics to optimize movement strategies, AI-driven financial trading systems for risk assessment, and AI-powered logistics for real-time route optimization.

Applications of the Eggshell Algorithm extend to reinforcement learning, robotics, predictive modeling, and intelligent systems. In reinforcement learning, it optimizes training efficiency by balancing exploration and exploitation. In robotics, it enhances real-time decision-making for navigation. In predictive modeling, it improves AI's ability to adjust to changing data. In intelligent systems, it ensures efficient resource allocation.

In conclusion, the Eggshell Algorithm represents a powerful approach to AI-driven optimization by providing adaptive, efficient, and stable problem-solving capabilities. Its ability to enhance decision-making in complex environments makes it a valuable tool in AI research and real-world applications. As AI continues to evolve, the Eggshell Algorithm will play a significant role in optimizing learning efficiency and performance.

Ego AI

Ego AI is an artificial intelligence framework designed to model and simulate self-referential decision-making processes. This AI approach mimics human-like egocentric reasoning, enabling systems to prioritize decisions based on self-awareness, contextual understanding, and long-term objectives. By integrating self-modeling capabilities, Ego AI improves autonomous decision-making in dynamic environments.

The key components of Ego AI include self-referential learning models that analyze past actions and outcomes, adaptive goal-setting mechanisms that adjust AI behavior based on changing conditions, real-time perception modules that interpret surroundings, and cognitive feedback loops that refine AI decision-making based on historical experiences. These elements collectively enable AI systems to make self-aware and contextually relevant decisions.

The benefits of Ego AI include enhanced adaptability in real-world applications, improved personalization in AI-driven interactions, better long-term decision-making strategies, and the ability to operate autonomously in unpredictable environments. Examples include AI-powered personal assistants that adjust recommendations based on user behavior, self-driving vehicles that learn from past navigation errors, and autonomous drones that refine their flight strategies over time.

Applications of Ego AI span autonomous robotics, smart personal assistants, human-AI collaboration, and adaptive learning systems. In robotics, Ego AI enables machines to adjust their actions based on real-time feedback. In smart assistants, it enhances user interaction by learning behavioral patterns. In human-AI collaboration, it optimizes team dynamics by adapting to user preferences. In adaptive learning systems, it personalizes educational content based on student progress.

In conclusion, Ego AI enhances AI's ability to make self-aware and context-driven decisions, improving personalization, autonomy, and adaptability. Its impact on autonomous systems and human-AI collaboration makes it a vital area of research. As AI evolves, Ego AI will play an essential role in developing more intelligent and human-like AI applications.

Ego Network Analysis in AI

Ego Network Analysis in AI refers to the use of artificial intelligence to analyze and interpret ego networks, which are social structures centered around a single individual or entity. This approach helps in understanding relationships, influence, and behavioral patterns within a network by examining direct connections and interactions. AI-driven ego network analysis is widely used in social network research, cybersecurity, personalized recommendations, and fraud detection.

The key components of Ego Network Analysis in AI include graph-based learning models that map and analyze connections, natural language processing that extracts insights from textual interactions, predictive analytics that forecast relationship dynamics, and anomaly detection systems that identify suspicious behaviors. These elements allow AI to assess network structures and detect significant interactions or risks.

The benefits of Ego Network Analysis in AI include improved social influence modeling, enhanced detection of fraudulent activities, personalized content recommendations based on social relationships, and better understanding of behavioral trends. AI helps organizations interpret complex networks and extract meaningful insights. Examples include AI-powered social media analytics that detect influential users, fraud detection systems that identify unusual financial transactions, and AI-driven customer segmentation for targeted marketing.

Applications of Ego Network Analysis in AI extend to social media platforms, cybersecurity, marketing, law enforcement, and business intelligence. In social media, AI analyzes network structures to detect influential trends. In cybersecurity, it identifies malicious actors based on communication patterns. In marketing, AI enhances targeted advertising by mapping customer relationships. In law enforcement, AI helps detect criminal networks through connection analysis.

In conclusion, Ego Network Analysis in AI provides valuable insights into relationship dynamics, influence mapping, and behavioral analysis. Its applications in social research, security, and marketing continue to grow, making it a critical tool in AI-driven network intelligence. As AI evolves, ego network analysis will become even more sophisticated, improving its ability to uncover hidden patterns and trends.

Ego-Surround AI

Ego-Surround AI is an artificial intelligence system that enhances an entity's perception by combining data from multiple sources to create a comprehensive situational awareness model. It integrates visual, spatial, and sensory data to help AI-driven systems understand and react to their surroundings. This AI approach is essential in autonomous vehicles, robotics, and security applications where real-time situational awareness is required.

The key components of Ego-Surround AI include sensor fusion algorithms that integrate data from cameras, LiDAR, and radar, deep learning models that analyze environmental patterns, predictive analytics that anticipate future movements of surrounding objects, and real-time decision-making frameworks that adjust AI responses accordingly. These components allow AI to interpret and navigate complex environments with enhanced accuracy.

The benefits of Ego-Surround AI include improved object detection and tracking, enhanced real-time decision-making, greater safety in autonomous systems, and optimized navigation in dynamic environments. By providing a holistic view of surroundings, AI-driven systems can operate more effectively and avoid potential hazards. Examples include AI-powered self-driving cars that detect pedestrians and other vehicles, security surveillance AI that monitors public spaces, and robotic systems that navigate crowded environments with precision.

Applications of Ego-Surround AI span autonomous vehicles, smart surveillance, robotics, and industrial automation. In autonomous vehicles, AI enhances road safety by detecting obstacles and predicting traffic patterns. In smart surveillance, AI improves anomaly detection for security monitoring. In robotics, AI enables better spatial awareness in automated machinery. In industrial automation, AI optimizes warehouse and factory logistics.

In conclusion, Ego-Surround AI enhances AI-driven perception and decision-making by integrating multi-source data for comprehensive situational awareness. Its applications in transportation, security, and automation continue to expand, making it a critical component in the evolution of intelligent autonomous systems. As AI technology progresses, Ego-Surround AI will play an even greater role in improving safety and efficiency in real-world applications.

Egocentric Navigation AI

Egocentric Navigation AI is an artificial intelligence approach that enables navigation systems to operate from a first-person perspective. This method allows AI-powered systems to interpret their surroundings based on sensor inputs and real-time environmental awareness, making it ideal for autonomous robots, augmented reality applications, and wearable AI technologies.

The key components of Egocentric Navigation AI include real-time spatial mapping algorithms that generate first-person navigation data, sensor fusion techniques that combine data from multiple input sources, deep learning-based motion planning that enables adaptive route optimization, and AI-driven localization systems that maintain positional awareness in dynamic environments. These elements help AI systems navigate effectively from an egocentric perspective.

The benefits of Egocentric Navigation AI include improved real-time situational awareness, enhanced ability to navigate complex environments, reduced reliance on external positioning systems, and better adaptation to unforeseen obstacles. AI-powered egocentric navigation improves accuracy in dynamic and unpredictable scenarios. Examples include AI-powered navigation for visually impaired individuals, self-driving cars that process real-time road conditions from a first-person view, and robotics systems that adjust their paths based on changing surroundings.

Applications of Egocentric Navigation AI extend to autonomous vehicles, assistive technology, augmented reality, and military robotics. In autonomous vehicles, AI interprets surroundings from a first-person perspective to optimize driving decisions. In assistive technology, AI-powered navigation assists individuals with mobility challenges. In augmented reality, AI enhances spatial awareness for immersive experiences. In military robotics, AI-driven navigation improves tactical maneuverability in complex environments.

In conclusion, Egocentric Navigation AI advances AI-driven movement and decision-making by enabling first-person perspective navigation. Its applications in robotics, mobility assistance, and augmented reality demonstrate its potential for improving spatial intelligence. As AI technology evolves, egocentric navigation will continue to enhance autonomous navigation and real-time decision-making.

Egocentric Vision AI

Egocentric Vision AI is a field of artificial intelligence that focuses on analyzing visual data from a first-person perspective, enabling AI systems to interpret scenes based on an individual's viewpoint. This approach is used in augmented reality, personal assistant AI, and wearable technologies, where understanding the user's visual environment is critical for context-aware interactions.

The key components of Egocentric Vision AI include first-person video processing that extracts meaningful visual information, attention-based deep learning models that prioritize relevant objects, spatial awareness algorithms that track environmental changes, and multimodal integration that combines vision with other sensory inputs such as speech and motion. These elements allow AI to understand and respond to real-world environments in a personalized way.

The benefits of Egocentric Vision AI include improved real-time scene analysis, enhanced interaction between AI and human users, personalized assistance based on user activity, and better object recognition from dynamic viewpoints. By processing visual data from the user's perspective, AI can generate more relevant insights and recommendations. Examples include AI-powered augmented reality applications that overlay information in real time, smart glasses that provide navigation assistance, and AI-driven home automation systems that respond to user actions.

Applications of Egocentric Vision AI span augmented reality, smart wearables, healthcare, and robotics. In augmented reality, AI enhances immersive experiences with real-time overlays. In smart wearables, it enables AI-driven contextual awareness for fitness tracking. In healthcare, it supports AI-powered visual assistance for individuals with impaired vision. In robotics, it improves AI-driven object detection in dynamic environments.

In conclusion, Egocentric Vision AI enhances AI's ability to understand the world from a first-person perspective, improving personalized interactions, augmented reality applications, and wearable AI technologies. As AI-driven vision processing continues to advance, egocentric vision will play a crucial role in developing intelligent, context-aware AI systems.

E-Government AI

E-Government AI refers to the integration of artificial intelligence in government services to enhance efficiency, accessibility, and decision-making. AI-driven e-government solutions automate administrative processes, improve public service delivery, and enhance transparency by leveraging data-driven insights. By utilizing AI, governments can optimize resource allocation, streamline bureaucratic operations, and improve citizen engagement.

The key components of E-Government AI include automated document processing that digitizes and categorizes government records, AI-powered chatbots that assist citizens with inquiries, predictive analytics that forecast policy outcomes, and cybersecurity AI that protects sensitive government data. These elements improve the responsiveness and reliability of digital government services.

The benefits of E-Government AI include increased efficiency in public administration, enhanced citizen engagement through AI-powered assistance, reduced operational costs, and improved transparency in government decision-making. AI helps automate repetitive tasks, allowing government agencies to focus on policy development and service innovation. Examples include AI-driven tax filing systems that simplify compliance, AI-powered legal document analysis that enhances regulatory oversight, and smart city AI that optimizes urban infrastructure management.

Applications of E-Government AI span public administration, healthcare, transportation, law enforcement, and environmental management. In public administration, AI enhances document processing and citizen support. In healthcare, it optimizes patient management in public hospitals. In transportation, AI improves traffic flow in smart city initiatives. In law enforcement, AI assists in crime prediction and resource allocation.

In conclusion, E-Government AI modernizes public administration by enhancing efficiency, transparency, and citizen engagement. Its ability to automate processes and provide data-driven insights makes it a powerful tool for digital governance. As AI technology continues to advance, governments will increasingly rely on AI to improve service delivery and policy effectiveness.

Egregious Bias in AI

Egregious Bias in AI refers to the presence of severe and disproportionate biases in artificial intelligence models that lead to unfair, discriminatory, or inaccurate outcomes. This bias can result from unbalanced training data, flawed algorithmic design, or systemic inequalities embedded in AI decision-making. Addressing egregious bias is critical for ensuring fairness, transparency, and ethical AI deployment.

The key components of Egregious Bias in AI include biased training datasets that reinforce existing social inequalities, algorithmic discrimination that results in unfair treatment of certain groups, lack of explainability in AI decision-making, and unintended consequences that arise from flawed AI implementations. These factors contribute to biased AI outcomes that can negatively impact individuals and communities.

The consequences of egregious bias in AI include social injustices in automated decision-making, ethical concerns in AI governance, reputational damage for organizations deploying biased AI, and regulatory scrutiny over AI fairness. Examples include biased facial recognition systems that misidentify individuals based on race, AI-driven hiring tools that favor certain demographics, and financial AI models that unfairly deny loans based on flawed credit assessments.

Applications where egregious bias in AI is a concern include criminal justice AI, hiring algorithms, financial risk assessment, healthcare AI, and public policy decision-making. In criminal justice, biased AI may result in wrongful arrests. In hiring, AI-driven resume screening may favor specific candidates based on historical biases. In finance, biased credit-scoring models may disproportionately impact marginalized groups. In healthcare, AI-driven diagnoses may be less accurate for underrepresented populations.

In conclusion, egregious bias in AI is a significant challenge that must be addressed to ensure fairness, accuracy, and ethical AI use. Organizations and researchers must actively work to identify and correct biases to prevent AI-driven discrimination. As AI adoption increases, developing responsible and unbiased AI models will be essential for promoting social equity and trust in AI systems.

EHR (Electronic Health Record) AI

Definition
AI systems that analyze electronic health records (EHRs) to improve patient care, identify trends, and assist with diagnosis and treatment recommendations.

Key Characteristics
Data Analytics: Extracts insights from large amounts of structured and unstructured health data.
Personalized Medicine: Tailors treatment plans based on patient history and AI analysis.
Predictive Modeling: Forecasts health outcomes and disease progression based on patient data.

Benefits
Improves diagnosis accuracy, streamlines administrative processes, and enhances patient care.

Disadvantages
Sensitive to privacy concerns and requires stringent data security measures.

Applications
Healthcare systems, hospitals, clinical decision support systems.

Conclusion
EHR AI enhances healthcare by providing data-driven insights but must prioritize data privacy and compliance with healthcare regulations like HIPAA.

EHR Analytics AI

Definition
AI systems that analyze data within electronic health records (EHRs) to derive actionable insights, such as identifying patient trends, improving care protocols, and optimizing hospital operations.

Key Characteristics
Data-Driven Insights: Analyzes large datasets within EHRs to find patterns and correlations.
Predictive Models: Uses historical patient data to predict future trends and optimize care pathways.
Operational Efficiency: Helps hospitals and clinics optimize staff allocation, reduce wait times, and improve resource management.

Benefits
Improves patient outcomes, reduces operational inefficiencies, and supports evidence-based care.

Applications
Healthcare management, clinical decision support, hospital operations.

Conclusion
EHR analytics AI provides valuable insights that enhance healthcare operations and patient care, though successful implementation requires reliable data sources and integration with existing systems.

EHR-Based Predictive Analytics

Definition
AI-driven predictive analytics applied to electronic health records (EHR) to forecast patient outcomes, identify potential risks, and assist in preventive healthcare.

Key Characteristics
Predictive Models: Uses patient history, demographic data, and clinical records to predict future health risks.
Risk Assessment: Provides early warnings of potential conditions such as heart disease or diabetes.
Personalized Care: Suggests personalized preventive care plans based on the predictions.

Benefits
Enables proactive healthcare management by predicting patient risks and suggesting interventions.

Disadvantages
Accuracy can vary depending on data quality, and predictive models may be biased by incomplete patient data.

Applications
Preventive medicine, population health management, chronic disease monitoring.

Conclusion
EHR-based predictive analytics empower healthcare providers to take preventive measures based on data-driven insights, improving long-term patient outcomes.

EHR Data Mining AI

Definition
The application of AI techniques to mine and analyze electronic health records (EHRs) for patterns, trends, and actionable insights in healthcare.

Key Characteristics
Pattern Recognition: Detects patterns in patient data, such as frequent diagnoses or treatment outcomes.
Predictive Analytics: Forecasts future health issues based on historical data.
Large-Scale Analysis: Capable of analyzing vast amounts of EHR data for population health insights.

Benefits
Improves healthcare outcomes by identifying early warning signs and optimizing treatment plans.

Disadvantages
Requires clean, standardized data and can be limited by data privacy regulations.

Applications
Population health management, predictive healthcare analytics, personalized medicine.

Conclusion
EHR data mining AI offers valuable insights for improving patient care and health management but must handle patient data with care to ensure privacy and security.

Eigen Values of a Matrix

Definition
The spectrum of eigenvalues of a matrix, often used to analyze the properties of data matrices in AI, particularly in fields like computer vision and machine learning.

Key Characteristics
Eigenvalue Analysis: Examines the eigenvalues of a data matrix to understand its structure.
Data Variance: Provides insights into the variance and distribution of data features.
Spectral Decomposition: Decomposes matrices into eigenvalues for analysis.

Benefits
Helps understand the importance of different components in a dataset.

Applications
Principal component analysis (PCA), image processing, signal processing.

Conclusion
Eigenspectrum analysis offers valuable insights into data variance and feature importance, making it a crucial tool for AI tasks like dimensionality reduction and pattern recognition.

Eigenspectrum Analysis in AI

Definition
Eigenspectrum analysis involves examining the eigenvalues of data matrices to understand structure, variance, and patterns in datasets. In AI, it is commonly used in dimensionality reduction, pattern recognition, and model optimization.

Key Components
Spectral decomposition
Covariance matrix analysis
Principal component identification
Eigenvalue distribution mapping

Benefits
Reduces data dimensionality while retaining core information
Improves model performance by simplifying input features
Identifies dominant patterns in complex datasets

Examples
Using PCA to compress image data for computer vision
Analyzing neural activation patterns in deep learning
Optimizing clustering through eigengap detection

Applications
Computer vision
Signal processing
Anomaly detection

Industries
Finance
Manufacturing
AI research

Summary
Eigenspectrum analysis is a mathematical technique used in AI to simplify, visualize, and understand complex data. It plays a crucial role in improving efficiency and performance in data-heavy AI tasks.

Eigenvector Centrality in AI

Definition: Eigenvector Centrality in AI is a slick trick from graph theory that sizes up how much clout a dot—or node—has in a web of connections, giving extra points if it's tied to other big shots, a go-to for AI sniffing out who's who in networks like social circles or the internet.

Key Components: It's all about clout-by-association, measuring a node's sway by the heft of its buddies in the graph. The AI crunches this through a looping math dance, tweaking scores until they settle on who's truly boss. It's wired to spot the heavy hitters in a tangle of links.

Benefits: It shines a spotlight on the real movers and shakers, handing AI a map to the network's power players, perfect for picking out kings in a crowd.

Examples: Think of an AI tagging the top influencer in a friend web by who they know, or ranking a webpage high because it's linked by giants.

Applications: It's in digging through social media cliques, nudging recommendation engines with hot picks, and sifting web piles for prime info.

Industries: Social tech uses it for trendsetters, marketing for ad targets, and search engines for result juice.

Summary: Eigenvector Centrality in AI flags the network's VIPs with finesse, a sharp tool for influence hunts, though it groans under big loads or flux.

Ejection Point AI

Definition: Ejection Point AI is artificial intelligence crafted to pinpoint the perfect moment to bail from a crumbling setup—like a jet or spaceship—using quick-witted guesses to save lives in dicey, high-stakes fields where timing is everything.

Key Components: It thrives on lightning-fast thinking, chewing through live data from gauges and the outside world—like altitude or hull stress—to pick the safest escape tick. It's got a knack for sizing up risks and a processor that hums to keep pace with chaos.
Benefits: It's a safety net, dishing out split-second escape cues that dodge disaster, giving folks in tight spots a better shot at walking away.

Examples: Imagine an AI clocking a rocket's wobble to yell "now" for a crew capsule eject, or nudging a pilot to punch out as a wing snaps mid-flight.

Applications: It's in plane cockpits for crash calls, space rigs for abort triggers, and emergency kits for fast exits.

Industries: Aviation taps it for flyer saves, space outfits for orbit bailouts, and defense for combat escapes.

Summary: Ejection Point AI plays timekeeper in a pinch, flagging the getaway sweet spot for risky gigs, but it's only as good as its info and speed.

Ejection Seat AI

Definition: Ejection Seat AI is artificial intelligence baked into aircraft that takes the wheel in a crisis, yanking the pilot out with an ejection seat when split-second danger—like a crash or blackout—leaves no time for human hands to act.

Key Components: It's wired with a brain that flips the eject switch on its own, tied to sensors sniffing out plane health and sky chaos—like speed or smoke. A backup layer kicks in if the pilot's out cold, all synced to dodge false alarms with tight checks.

Benefits: It's a lifeline, shoving pilots clear of doom faster than reflexes can blink, boosting survival odds when the cockpit turns dicey.

Examples: Picture an AI popping a fighter jet pilot free as flames lick the wings, or kicking in when a test plane spins wild and the flyer's dazed.

Applications: It's in warbird cockpits for battle bailouts, test flights pushing limits, and maybe future airliners with emergency escapes.

Industries: Defense leans on it for jet jockeys, aviation testing for bold rigs, and safety tech for next-gen planes.

Summary: Ejection Seat AI plays guardian angel, hurling pilots from harm with machine-speed guts, but it leans hard on flawless gear and judgment.

*Ekman Emotion Model A*I

Ekman Emotion Model AI is the integration of artificial intelligence with Paul Ekman's psychological framework, which identifies six universal emotions: happiness, sadness, anger, fear, surprise, and disgust. AI-driven emotion recognition systems use Ekman's model to analyze facial expressions, vocal intonations, and physiological signals to infer human emotional states. This approach is widely used in affective computing, human-computer interaction, and AI-driven mental health analysis.

The key components of Ekman Emotion Model AI include deep learning-based facial recognition that detects microexpressions, natural language processing that analyzes sentiment in voice and text, physiological data sensors that track emotional indicators, and real-time emotion classification models that interpret human affective states. These components allow AI to assess and respond to human emotions with high accuracy.

The benefits of Ekman Emotion Model AI include improved emotional intelligence in AI systems, enhanced human-computer interaction, more personalized user experiences, and better mental health monitoring. AI-powered emotion recognition enables adaptive responses in virtual assistants, therapy bots, and customer service AI. Examples include AI-driven customer service bots that detect frustration in callers, AI-powered mental health applications that monitor emotional well-being, and adaptive learning systems that adjust difficulty based on student engagement.

Applications of Ekman Emotion Model AI span healthcare, marketing, virtual assistants, and human resources. In healthcare, AI assists in emotional assessment for mental health patients. In marketing, AI-driven emotion analysis improves advertisement targeting. In virtual assistants, AI adapts interactions based on user emotions. In human resources, AI detects stress levels in employees during virtual interviews.

In conclusion, Ekman Emotion Model AI enhances AI's ability to interpret and respond to human emotions, improving personalization and emotional intelligence in AI systems. Its applications in healthcare, virtual assistants, and marketing continue to grow, making it an essential tool in affective computing. As AI advances, emotion recognition will become more sophisticated, enabling more human-like interactions between AI and users.

Elastic Computing in AI

Elastic Computing in AI refers to the dynamic allocation and scaling of computational resources to meet the varying demands of AI workloads. This approach enables AI systems to efficiently use cloud-based or distributed computing environments by automatically adjusting processing power, memory, and storage based on real-time requirements. Elastic computing ensures that AI applications remain cost-effective, scalable, and responsive to changing demands.

The key components of Elastic Computing in AI include cloud-based infrastructure that supports dynamic resource allocation, AI workload orchestration that optimizes computing power, auto-scaling mechanisms that adjust resources in real time, and distributed computing frameworks that enable parallel processing. These components ensure efficient AI operations in cloud and hybrid computing environments.

The benefits of Elastic Computing in AI include reduced infrastructure costs, improved scalability for AI applications, enhanced real-time processing capabilities, and efficient use of cloud resources. AI models can scale up or down based on demand, optimizing cost and performance. Examples include AI-powered recommendation engines that dynamically allocate resources during peak usage, cloud-based training of deep learning models that scale computing resources, and AI-driven analytics platforms that adjust processing power based on data volume.

Applications of Elastic Computing in AI span cloud AI services, big data analytics, machine learning model training, and IoT ecosystems. In cloud AI, elastic computing optimizes cost efficiency. In big data analytics, it enhances scalability for AI-driven insights. In model training, it accelerates deep learning processes. In IoT, it supports AI-powered edge computing with dynamic resource management.

In conclusion, Elastic Computing in AI enables efficient and scalable deployment of AI applications by dynamically managing computational resources. Its role in cloud computing and big data analytics ensures flexibility and cost savings for AI-driven enterprises. As AI adoption increases, elastic computing will continue to drive innovations in scalable and intelligent computing infrastructure.

Elastic Federated Learning

Definition: Elastic Federated Learning in AI is a teamwork twist on machine learning where scattered devices—like phones or hospital servers—join forces to build a shared model without ever swapping their private data, stretching or shrinking their effort based on what's needed, all steered by clever AI.

Key Components: It's got a network of local gadgets training on their own info, a central hub that blends their updates into one model, and a stretchy system that dials computing power up or down as the job shifts. Privacy tricks—like encrypting updates—keep the data locked tight while it learns.

Benefits: It guards secrets by keeping data home, slashes the cost of hauling info around, and flexes smoothly to handle big or small teams, making group AI a breeze without the mess.

Examples: Picture a bunch of clinics tuning an AI to spot diseases, each using its own patient records, or smartwatches pooling step-count smarts without spilling your daily strolls.
Applications: It's in medical AI linking hospitals, banking systems sharing fraud tips, and smart device nets like home thermostats learning together.
Industries: Healthcare uses it for private diagnostics, finance for secure risk checks, and tech for connected gadgets.

Summary: Elastic Federated Learning in AI ties far-flung learners into a privacy-smart, scalable brain, perfect for team efforts, though it wrestles with tech hiccups to shine.

Elastic Kernel Density Estimation (EKDE)

Definition: Elastic Kernel Density Estimation in AI is a clever twist on guessing how data clumps together, using artificial intelligence to stretch or shrink its focus—called the kernel bandwidth—depending on how spread out or tight the numbers look, painting a probability picture without rigid rules.

Key Components: It's got a kernel, a smoothing tool that slides over data, with a bandwidth that flexes based on local quirks—wide for sparse spots, narrow for dense ones. The AI figures this out on the fly, dodging fixed shapes, and churns out a density map that shows where data likes to hang out.

Benefits: It beats stiff old methods by hugging the data's real shape, giving sharper guesses at where things pile up or thin out, especially when the pattern's wild or tricky.

Examples: Think of an AI spotting weird spikes in network traffic by mapping usage density, or tracing blurry edges in a photo to pick out shapes.
Applications: It's in sniffing out oddities like fraud in bank logs, sharpening image details for AI vision, and guessing odds in messy stats piles.

Industries: Cybersecurity taps it for threat hunting, imaging tech for clearer pics, and data science for smart modeling.

Summary: Elastic Kernel Density Estimation in AI bends to fit the data's flow, delivering slick probability maps for thorny tasks, though it demands tweak-time and muscle to run smooth.

Elastic Knowledge AI

Elastic Knowledge A*I* is an artificial intelligence system that dynamically adjusts its knowledge base and reasoning capabilities based on evolving data, user inputs, and contextual changes. Unlike static knowledge systems, Elastic Knowledge AI continuously refines its understanding, adapts to new information, and restructures its knowledge representation to improve decision-making and accuracy. This adaptability makes it valuable in applications requiring real-time learning, such as autonomous systems, business intelligence, and personalized recommendations.

The key components of Elastic Knowledge AI include self-learning algorithms that update knowledge structures based on new data, adaptive ontologies that restructure relationships between concepts, real-time inference engines that refine decision-making, and federated knowledge integration that aggregates data from multiple sources. These components allow AI to process information flexibly and accurately.

The benefits of Elastic Knowledge AI include improved adaptability to changing environments, enhanced decision-making accuracy, continuous learning without manual intervention, and the ability to process unstructured and evolving datasets. AI systems become more efficient in responding to complex queries and refining knowledge structures over time. Examples include AI-driven virtual assistants that adapt to user preferences, dynamic knowledge graphs that update in real-time, and AI-powered research platforms that refine knowledge synthesis.

Applications of Elastic Knowledge AI span intelligent search engines, business analytics, healthcare decision support, and AI-driven research. In search engines, AI improves query relevance by learning from past interactions. In business analytics, AI refines market insights based on new data. In healthcare, AI dynamically updates medical knowledge for personalized treatment recommendations. In AI-driven research, knowledge synthesis improves over time through adaptive learning.

In conclusion, Elastic Knowledge AI enhances AI systems by enabling dynamic learning and adaptation, making them more responsive and accurate in real-world applications. Its ability to continuously refine its knowledge structures ensures that AI remains relevant, reliable, and efficient across diverse industries. As AI evolves, Elastic Knowledge AI will play a critical role in improving machine intelligence and decision-making.

Elastic Knowledge-Based Systems

Elastic Knolwdge-Based Systems are AI-driven frameworks that integrate, process, and adapt knowledge dynamically, ensuring that information remains relevant as conditions change. Unlike rigid expert systems, Elastic Knowledge-Based Systems continuously refine their rules and knowledge structures to improve reasoning and problem-solving in complex domains.

The key components of Elastic Knowledge-Based Systems include dynamic rule-based engines that adapt decision logic in real-time, scalable knowledge bases that expand as new information becomes available, AI-driven inference mechanisms that improve reasoning efficiency, and multi-source data integration that enhances knowledge accuracy. These elements ensure the adaptability and reliability of AI-driven knowledge systems.

The benefits of Elastic Knowledge-Based Systems include improved flexibility in decision-making, enhanced problem-solving capabilities, reduced maintenance costs due to self-updating knowledge structures, and greater efficiency in processing evolving information. AI systems using elastic knowledge improve their accuracy and relevance over time. Examples include AI-powered diagnostic tools that refine medical knowledge, legal AI platforms that update legal precedents dynamically, and AI-driven customer service bots that adapt responses based on past interactions.

Applications of Elastic Knowledge-Based Systems span healthcare, legal reasoning, financial analysis, and cybersecurity. In healthcare, AI refines clinical decision support. In legal reasoning, AI updates knowledge bases with evolving regulations. In financial analysis, AI dynamically adjusts risk assessments. In cybersecurity, AI detects new threats by learning from past attacks.

In conclusion, Elastic Knowledge-Based Systems improve AI's ability to manage and process knowledge dynamically, ensuring that AI remains adaptive and effective. Their ability to refine reasoning and integrate new information makes them valuable across industries that require continuous learning. As AI research advances, knowledge-based systems will become increasingly intelligent and responsive to dynamic environments.

Elastic Knowledge Graphs

Elastic Knowledge Graphs are AI-enhanced graph-based knowledge structures that dynamically evolve as new information is added, ensuring accurate representation of relationships, entities, and concepts in real-time. Unlike static knowledge graphs, Elastic Knowledge Graphs restructure themselves to accommodate contextual changes, improving AI's ability to understand, retrieve, and infer complex relationships.

The key components of Elastic Knowledge Graphs include adaptive ontology frameworks that reorganize relationships dynamically, graph-based learning algorithms that enhance inference capabilities, entity linking mechanisms that ensure accurate representation of real-world concepts, and real-time data integration that updates graph structures efficiently. These components allow knowledge graphs to remain flexible and accurate.

The benefits of Elastic Knowledge Graphs include improved contextual understanding in AI-driven systems, enhanced reasoning accuracy for complex queries, better scalability for large-scale data representation, and increased adaptability for continuously evolving knowledge structures. AI systems become more efficient at information retrieval and knowledge discovery. Examples include AI-powered search engines that refine knowledge graph structures based on user queries, recommendation systems that adapt content suggestions based on real-time user behavior, and AI-driven fraud detection systems that update risk assessments dynamically.

Applications of Elastic Knowledge Graphs span AI-powered search, business intelligence, fraud detection, and semantic data integration. In AI-powered search, knowledge graphs refine information retrieval. In business intelligence, they enhance decision support with real-time updates. In fraud detection, AI analyzes financial transactions dynamically. In semantic data integration, AI connects structured and unstructured knowledge sources efficiently.

In conclusion, Elastic Knowledge Graphs enhance AI's ability to process and infer complex relationships dynamically, improving contextual understanding and reasoning. Their adaptability makes them essential in AI-driven search, business intelligence, and real-time analytics. As AI advances, Elastic Knowledge Graphs will continue to refine AI's ability to understand and process large-scale, evolving datasets.

Elastic Knowledge Network (EKN)

Elastic Knowledge Network (EKN*)* refers to a decentralized AI-driven knowledge framework that enables distributed learning, information sharing, and real-time knowledge adaptation across multiple sources. Unlike traditional centralized knowledge repositories, an EKN allows for flexible and scalable knowledge representation, making AI systems more resilient and collaborative.

The key components of an Elastic Knowledge Network include decentralized knowledge processing nodes that enable distributed AI learning, AI-driven information retrieval mechanisms that optimize contextual understanding, adaptive inference models that refine decision-making dynamically, and federated learning techniques that ensure knowledge privacy and security. These elements allow knowledge networks to evolve and improve over time.

The benefits of an Elastic Knowledge Network include enhanced scalability for AI knowledge-sharing, improved adaptability for real-time learning, reduced reliance on centralized AI systems, and increased security through federated knowledge processing. AI systems using EKN can collaborate while maintaining knowledge autonomy. Examples include AI-driven scientific research networks that share discoveries in real-time, AI-powered supply chain networks that adapt logistics based on demand, and AI-driven cybersecurity frameworks that exchange threat intelligence dynamically.

Applications of Elastic Knowledge Networks span distributed AI systems, collaborative intelligence, smart city infrastructures, and decentralized research platforms. In distributed AI, EKNs enable real-time machine learning collaboration. In smart cities, AI dynamically optimizes public infrastructure. In decentralized research, AI accelerates knowledge discovery through shared data.

In conclusion, an Elastic Knowledge Network enables AI systems to collaborate, share, and evolve knowledge dynamically, making them more intelligent and responsive. Its decentralized nature enhances scalability, efficiency, and real-time adaptability in AI-driven applications. As AI research advances, EKNs will become integral to collaborative intelligence, scientific discovery, and distributed AI systems.

Elastic Optimization Algorithms

Definition
Elastic optimization algorithms in AI refer to methods that adjust their internal optimization strategies dynamically in response to changing problem constraints, complexity, or computational conditions. These algorithms are designed to remain efficient, scalable, and responsive throughout different stages of an AI task.

Key Components
Adaptive strategy modification
Dynamic constraint management
Resource-aware optimization
Feedback-driven tuning mechanisms

Benefits
Improves optimization performance under changing constraints
Reduces computation time through selective adjustment
Scales well with growing problem size or data volume

Examples
A model tuning algorithm adjusting its learning rate during high-dimensional searches
An optimization process reallocating GPU memory as model complexity grows
Routing algorithms in logistics adapting paths as delivery constraints shift

Applications
Hyperparameter tuning in AI models
Large-scale system optimization
Supply chain and logistics planning
Energy usage optimization

Industries
Technology and cloud services
Transportation and logistics

Energy and utilities
Finance and banking

Summary
Elastic optimization algorithms provide flexible, scalable solutions for complex and dynamic AI problems. They allow systems to stay efficient across varied conditions, but they require smart design and resource management for best results.

Elastic Predictive Analytics

Definition
Elastic predictive analytics refers to AI systems that adapt their forecasting models based on the changing availability of data, computational capacity, or evolving business needs. These systems scale their analytical depth to maintain predictive accuracy while optimizing the use of resources.

Key Components
Dynamic model scaling
Data availability monitoring
On-demand resource allocation
Predictive recalibration algorithms

Benefits
Maintains forecasting performance under different system loads
Enables real-time adaptability in fluctuating data environments
Reduces infrastructure costs through elastic resource use

Examples
A retail analytics platform that scales up model complexity during peak shopping seasons
Cloud-based predictive tools adapting analysis depth based on data volume
Weather forecasting systems adjusting model layers based on incoming sensor quality

Applications
Sales and demand forecasting
Energy consumption modeling
Customer churn prediction
Climate and environmental forecasting

Industries
Retail
Utilities
Healthcare
Telecommunications

Summary
Elastic predictive analytics enables AI to forecast outcomes efficiently across changing conditions. It offers a robust, flexible approach to future-focused modeling that meets both accuracy and efficiency needs in modern, data-driven systems.

Elastic Speech Recognition

Definition:

Elastic Speech Recognition is an advanced artificial intelligence-driven speech processing system that dynamically scales computational resources based on real-time demand. Unlike traditional speech recognition models that operate with fixed computational limits, elastic speech recognition adjusts processing power, model complexity, and memory usage to optimize performance in various environments. This flexibility enables efficient speech recognition across devices ranging from cloud-based servers to low-power edge devices.

The key components of elastic speech recognition include adaptive neural network models that scale based on workload, real-time speech-to-text engines that adjust processing power dynamically, federated learning architectures that enhance accuracy while preserving data privacy, and resource-efficient algorithms that optimize model performance across different platforms. These elements ensure that speech recognition remains fast, accurate, and resource-efficient.

The benefits of elastic speech recognition include improved accuracy in varying acoustic conditions, optimized resource allocation for high-demand speech processing tasks, reduced latency in real-time applications, and enhanced accessibility across diverse hardware environments. AI-powered speech recognition becomes more responsive and scalable. Examples include voice assistants that optimize processing power based on network conditions, AI-driven transcription services that adapt to audio complexity, and hands-free interfaces that adjust to user speech patterns.

Applications of elastic speech recognition span telecommunications, accessibility tools, customer service, and real-time translation. In telecommunications, AI enhances call transcription accuracy. In accessibility tools, AI improves speech-to-text for individuals with disabilities. In customer service, AI automates call center interactions. In real-time translation, AI dynamically adjusts to multilingual speech input.

In conclusion, elastic speech recognition enhances AI-driven voice processing by dynamically adjusting computational resources to meet changing demands. Its scalability and efficiency make it a critical technology for voice interfaces, customer engagement, and accessibility solutions. As AI advances, speech recognition will become even more adaptive, ensuring seamless human-machine communication.

Elastic Supervised Learning

Definition:

Elastic Supervised Learning: is a machine learning paradigm that allows AI models to dynamically adjust their training processes based on the complexity and availability of labeled data. Unlike traditional supervised learning, which relies on static datasets and fixed model parameters, elastic supervised learning adapts to evolving data distributions, model constraints, and computational resources. This flexibility improves model generalization and efficiency in real-world applications.

The key components of elastic supervised learning include adaptive model architectures that scale based on dataset complexity, dynamic loss function optimization that adjusts learning objectives, active learning techniques that prioritize informative data samples, and federated learning frameworks that enable distributed training while preserving data privacy. These components enhance the adaptability and scalability of supervised learning.

The benefits of elastic supervised learning include improved model performance on evolving datasets, reduced training time by optimizing resource allocation, enhanced generalization to unseen data, and better efficiency in handling imbalanced or sparse data distributions. AI models trained with elastic supervised learning adapt faster to real-world scenarios. Examples include AI-powered fraud detection systems that adjust to emerging financial threats, personalized recommendation engines that refine predictions based on user feedback, and AI-driven medical diagnosis models that adapt to new patient data.

Applications of elastic supervised learning span finance, healthcare, autonomous systems, and cybersecurity. In finance, AI detects emerging fraud patterns. In healthcare, AI improves diagnostic accuracy with evolving medical records. In autonomous systems, AI refines decision-making based on real-time sensor inputs. In cybersecurity, AI identifies novel threats dynamically.

In conclusion, elastic supervised learning enhances machine learning models by enabling dynamic adaptation to evolving datasets and constraints. Its ability to refine AI performance in changing environments makes it essential for real-world applications. As AI continues to evolve, elastic supervised learning will play a critical role in improving AI efficiency, scalability, and decision-making accuracy.

Elastic Training in AI

Definirtion:

Elastic Training in AI: refers to a scalable and adaptive approach to training machine learning models that optimizes computational resources based on workload fluctuations. Unlike conventional training, which uses fixed hardware and data configurations, elastic training dynamically adjusts batch sizes, parallel computing resources, and learning rates to maximize efficiency and scalability.

The key components of elastic training include distributed training frameworks that optimize resource allocation, real-time hyperparameter tuning that refines learning rates and batch sizes, model parallelization that distributes computation across multiple devices, and cloud-based elasticity that scales up or down based on training complexity. These elements improve AI training efficiency and scalability.

The benefits of elastic training in AI include reduced training time for complex models, cost-effective resource management in cloud environments, improved convergence rates through adaptive optimization, and the ability to handle large-scale datasets dynamically. AI models trained with elastic training achieve higher performance with lower resource costs. Examples include AI-powered autonomous vehicle systems that refine navigation models in real-time, deep learning models trained across decentralized cloud infrastructure, and AI-driven medical image recognition that optimizes training efficiency.

Applications of elastic training span autonomous systems, cloud AI services, scientific computing, and large-scale business intelligence. In autonomous systems, AI models adapt to new driving conditions. In cloud AI services, training efficiency improves with dynamic resource scaling. In scientific computing, AI accelerates research by optimizing model training. In business intelligence, AI refines data-driven decision-making.

In conclusion, elastic training in AI enhances model training efficiency by dynamically optimizing resource allocation and training parameters. Its scalability and adaptability make it a critical component of AI development. As AI adoption expands, elastic training will drive innovations in machine learning efficiency, making AI models faster and more cost-effective.

Elastic Video Analytics

Definition:

Elastic Video Analytics: is the application of artificial intelligence to process and analyze video data dynamically, adjusting computational resources based on real-time demand. Unlike traditional video analysis, which relies on fixed processing power, elastic video analytics scales AI-driven video processing up or down depending on video resolution, frame rate, and object detection complexity.

The key components of elastic video analytics include real-time object detection models that adjust processing levels, dynamic resource allocation that optimizes cloud and edge computing, AI-powered video summarization that reduces computational load, and adaptive streaming analysis that prioritizes key video segments. These elements enable efficient video processing across different platforms.

The benefits of elastic video analytics include reduced infrastructure costs for large-scale video monitoring, improved efficiency in video-based AI models, enhanced real-time object tracking, and the ability to scale video analysis dynamically. AI-powered video analytics becomes more efficient and responsive to varying workloads. Examples include AI-driven security cameras that adjust processing based on motion detection, smart city traffic monitoring systems that scale video analysis based on congestion, and sports analytics AI that enhances player tracking in real-time.

Applications of elastic video analytics span security surveillance, smart cities, retail analytics, and media content optimization. In security, AI enhances threat detection in dynamic environments. In smart cities, AI improves traffic management through adaptive video monitoring. In retail, AI refines customer behavior analysis. In media, AI optimizes video recommendations through contextual analysis.

In conclusion, elastic video analytics revolutionizes AI-driven video processing by optimizing scalability and efficiency. Its ability to adapt to changing workloads makes it essential for security, media, and smart city applications. As AI technology advances, elastic video analytics will continue to refine real-time video intelligence, enhancing automation and decision-making across industries.

Elasticity in AI Systems

Elasticity in AI Systems refers to an AI model's ability to dynamically adjust its resource consumption, processing complexity, and computational load based on real-time demands. Elastic AI systems optimize efficiency by scaling up or down depending on the intensity of the workload, ensuring cost-effective performance while maintaining high responsiveness.

The key components of Elasticity in AI Systems include dynamic resource allocation that adjusts computing power based on demand, self-optimizing machine learning models that adapt to workload variations, cloud-based elasticity frameworks that enable distributed AI processing, and load-balancing algorithms that distribute AI workloads efficiently. These elements ensure adaptive AI performance in various computing environments.

The benefits of Elasticity in AI Systems include reduced operational costs, enhanced adaptability to fluctuating workloads, improved AI performance across different computing environments, and seamless integration with cloud-based platforms. Elastic AI models improve efficiency in dynamic and large-scale applications. Examples include AI-powered fraud detection systems that scale up during high transaction volumes, autonomous systems that optimize resource usage in real-time, and AI-driven financial analytics platforms that adjust processing power based on market fluctuations.

Applications of Elasticity in AI Systems span cloud computing, AI-powered business intelligence, autonomous systems, and cybersecurity. In cloud computing, AI elasticity optimizes infrastructure costs. In business intelligence, AI adapts data processing to demand surges. In autonomous systems, it ensures efficient real-time decision-making. In cybersecurity, AI scales up during cyberattack detection.

In conclusion, Elasticity in AI Systems enhances the adaptability and efficiency of AI applications by dynamically adjusting computational resources. Its role in cloud-based AI, real-time analytics, and autonomous systems continues to grow, making it an essential feature of next-generation AI technologies. As AI adoption expands, elastic AI systems will drive innovation in scalable and intelligent computing solutions.

Electrochemical AI Sensors

Definition:

Electrochemical AI Sensors: are intelligent sensing devices that integrate artificial intelligence with electrochemical detection methods to analyze chemical and biological substances in real time. These sensors use AI algorithms to enhance sensitivity, accuracy, and adaptability in detecting environmental pollutants, biomarkers, and industrial chemicals. AI-driven signal processing enables these sensors to filter noise, detect anomalies, and improve response times in various applications, including medical diagnostics, environmental monitoring, and industrial safety.

The key components of Electrochemical AI Sensors include AI-enhanced signal processing that refines sensor output, machine learning-based anomaly detection that improves accuracy, biosensors that detect chemical and biological agents, and real-time data analytics that enhance decision-making. These components collectively enhance the precision and efficiency of electrochemical sensing technologies.

The benefits of Electrochemical AI Sensors include improved detection sensitivity, reduced false positives in chemical analysis, faster response times for real-time monitoring, and enhanced adaptability to different sensing environments. AI-driven optimization allows for better accuracy in detecting trace elements and biomolecules. Examples include AI-powered glucose monitoring for diabetes patients, real-time air quality monitoring in smart cities, and AI-enhanced water contamination detection systems.

Applications of Electrochemical AI Sensors span healthcare, environmental science, food safety, and industrial process control. In healthcare, AI-enhanced electrochemical sensors improve non-invasive disease diagnostics. In environmental science, AI enables real-time pollutant tracking. In food safety, AI sensors detect contamination in agricultural products. In industrial applications, AI-driven chemical sensors enhance workplace safety.

In conclusion, Electrochemical AI Sensors improve the accuracy and efficiency of chemical and biological detection by integrating AI-driven analysis. Their applications in healthcare, environmental monitoring, and industry make them essential for modern sensing technologies. As AI and sensor technology continue to evolve, Electrochemical AI Sensors will enable more precise and scalable chemical analysis across industries.

Electroencephalography (EEG) AI

Definition:

Electroencephalography (EEG)AI: is the application of artificial intelligence to analyze and interpret brainwave activity recorded by electroencephalography systems. EEG AI enhances the ability to detect neurological conditions, optimize brain-computer interfaces (BCIs), and improve cognitive research by automating signal processing and pattern recognition. AI-driven EEG analysis enables real-time brain monitoring, supporting medical diagnosis, mental health tracking, and neurotechnology advancements.

The key components of EEG AI include deep learning models that identify brainwave patterns, machine learning-based anomaly detection that diagnoses neurological disorders, real-time brainwave processing algorithms that improve response speed, and AI-enhanced noise filtering techniques that refine EEG signal accuracy. These elements enhance the interpretation and usability of EEG data.

The benefits of EEG AI include improved accuracy in detecting brain disorders, enhanced efficiency in brain-computer interface applications, faster processing of large EEG datasets, and reduced reliance on manual interpretation of brainwave signals. AI-driven EEG analysis helps healthcare professionals diagnose conditions such as epilepsy, sleep disorders, and neurodegenerative diseases. Examples include AI-powered seizure prediction models, AI-driven mental health monitoring systems, and brain-computer interfaces that enable thought-controlled prosthetics.

Applications of EEG AI span neurology, cognitive research, neurotechnology, and mental health. In neurology, AI improves EEG-based disease detection. In cognitive research, AI enhances brainwave analysis for learning and memory studies. In neurotechnology, AI optimizes brain-machine communication. In mental health, AI assesses emotional states through EEG patterns.

In conclusion, EEG AI enhances the accuracy and efficiency of brainwave analysis, improving applications in neurology, mental health, and brain-computer interfaces. Its ability to process large-scale EEG data with AI-driven insights makes it a transformative tool in neuroscience and medical diagnostics. As AI continues to evolve, EEG AI will further enhance brain research and cognitive technology.

Electromagnetic Field (EMF) AI

Electromagnetic Field (EMF) AI is an artificial intelligence-driven system designed to monitor, analyze, and optimize electromagnetic field interactions in various environments. AI enhances the interpretation of EMF data, enabling applications in telecommunications, healthcare, environmental monitoring, and defense systems. By leveraging AI-powered signal processing, EMF AI improves the detection, classification, and mitigation of electromagnetic interference.

The key components of EMF AI include machine learning-based electromagnetic signal classification that differentiates between natural and artificial EMF sources, AI-driven interference detection that identifies disruptions in communication networks, real-time data processing that enhances EMF monitoring accuracy, and adaptive EMF shielding techniques that optimize electromagnetic compatibility. These components improve the effectiveness of EMF analysis and control.

The benefits of EMF AI include improved electromagnetic interference mitigation, enhanced network signal optimization, better health monitoring for EMF exposure, and increased efficiency in defense and surveillance systems. AI-powered EMF analysis helps optimize wireless networks and ensures the safety of electromagnetic exposure limits. Examples include AI-driven optimization of 5G network coverage, AI-powered medical imaging systems that reduce EMF interference, and AI-enhanced environmental monitoring of EMF radiation.

Applications of EMF AI span telecommunications, medical imaging, aerospace, and cybersecurity. In telecommunications, AI optimizes network performance by reducing interference. In medical imaging, AI enhances MRI and CT scan accuracy by managing EMF artifacts. In aerospace, AI ensures electromagnetic compatibility in avionics. In cybersecurity, AI detects unauthorized EMF-based eavesdropping techniques.

In conclusion, EMF AI improves electromagnetic field monitoring and optimization through AI-driven analysis. Its applications in telecommunications, healthcare, and defense make it a valuable tool for enhancing EMF-related technologies. As AI continues to advance, EMF AI will play a crucial role in ensuring efficient and safe electromagnetic interactions across industries.

Electromyography (EMG) AI

Electromyography (EMG) AI is the integration of artificial intelligence into electromyography systems to enhance the analysis of muscle activity. AI-driven EMG analysis enables more accurate diagnostics, rehabilitation monitoring, and development of prosthetic control systems. By leveraging AI-powered pattern recognition, EMG AI improves real-time muscle activity interpretation, supporting both medical and biomechanical applications.

The key components of EMG AI include deep learning-based muscle signal classification that enhances diagnostic precision, AI-driven anomaly detection that identifies neuromuscular disorders, signal enhancement algorithms that filter noise from EMG data, and machine learning models that improve control of robotic prosthetics. These elements enhance the usability and accuracy of EMG systems.

The benefits of EMG AI include improved diagnosis of neuromuscular diseases, enhanced rehabilitation monitoring, more accurate prosthetic control, and optimized sports performance analysis. AI-powered EMG enables real-time biofeedback for muscle activity tracking. Examples include AI-driven robotic exoskeletons that respond to muscle signals, AI-enhanced rehabilitation tools for stroke patients, and sports performance monitoring systems that optimize muscle efficiency.

Applications of EMG AI span healthcare, sports science, robotics, and human-computer interaction. In healthcare, AI improves neuromuscular disease diagnostics. In sports science, AI enhances athlete training through muscle activity analysis. In robotics, AI optimizes bionic limb functionality. In human-computer interaction, AI enhances gesture recognition through EMG signals.

In conclusion, EMG AI improves the analysis and interpretation of muscle activity through AI-driven signal processing. Its applications in medical diagnostics, rehabilitation, and assistive technology make it an essential tool in neuromuscular research and human-machine interaction. As AI continues to advance, EMG AI will further enhance muscle activity monitoring, prosthetic control, and rehabilitation outcomes.

Electronic Health AI (eHealth AI)

Definition: AI systems designed to enhance healthcare delivery by analyzing electronic health records (EHRs), providing clinical decision support, and improving patient outcomes.

Key Characteristics:
Data-Driven Insights: Uses AI to analyze large datasets from EHRs for predictive modeling and diagnosis.
Clinical Decision Support: Assists healthcare professionals by offering AI-driven recommendations.
Patient Personalization: Tailors treatments and interventions based on patient data and AI analysis.

Benefits: Improves diagnosis accuracy, personalizes treatments, and enhances healthcare efficiency.

Disadvantages: Requires high-quality data and robust privacy measures to protect sensitive patient information.

Applications: Hospitals, telemedicine platforms, healthcare administration.

Conclusion: eHealth AI transforms healthcare by providing data-driven insights and personalized care, though it requires careful attention to privacy and data security.

EM Algorithm (Expectation-Maximization Algorithm)

Definition: An iterative method used in machine learning and statistics to find maximum likelihood estimates of parameters in probabilistic models, particularly when data is incomplete or has latent variables.

Key Characteristics:
Two Steps: Alternates between the Expectation (E) step and the Maximization (M) step

.Convergence: Guaranteed to converge to a local maximum.

Benefits: Efficient for solving complex optimization problems involving hidden variables.

Applications: Gaussian mixture models, hidden Markov models, image reconstruction.

Conclusion: The EM algorithm is a powerful tool for optimization problems in machine learning but requires careful initialization to avoid local optima.

Embedded Systems in AI

Embedded Systems in AI refer to artificial intelligence applications integrated into specialized computing systems designed for specific tasks. These systems are compact, efficient, and optimized for real-time operations in environments where computational resources are limited. AI-powered embedded systems enable intelligent decision-making, automation, and adaptive processing in applications such as autonomous vehicles, industrial automation, smart appliances, and medical devices.

The key components of Embedded Systems in AI include microcontrollers and microprocessors that execute AI algorithms efficiently, optimized neural networks designed for low-power inference, real-time operating systems that manage AI-driven tasks, and sensor fusion techniques that integrate multiple data sources for intelligent decision-making. These elements enable AI models to function effectively in constrained environments.

The benefits of Embedded Systems in AI include reduced latency in real-time applications, enhanced efficiency in resource-constrained environments, improved autonomy in intelligent devices, and lower power consumption compared to cloud-based AI solutions. These advantages make embedded AI systems ideal for edge computing and real-world automation. Examples include AI-powered robotics that process sensory input locally, smart cameras that perform facial recognition without cloud dependency, and autonomous drones that navigate without external computation.

Applications of Embedded Systems in AI span robotics, automotive safety, healthcare devices, consumer electronics, and IoT networks. In robotics, AI enhances object detection and movement coordination. In automotive safety, AI improves driver assistance systems. In healthcare, AI enables real-time patient monitoring in wearable devices. In consumer electronics, AI enhances smart home automation. In IoT, AI-driven embedded systems optimize data processing at the network edge.

Challenges in Embedded Systems in AI include balancing computational efficiency with model complexity, ensuring energy efficiency in battery-powered applications, managing security risks in AI-driven embedded devices, and updating AI models in systems with limited connectivity. Optimizing AI performance for real-time inference while minimizing hardware constraints remains a key research focus.

In conclusion, Embedded Systems in AI enhance automation, intelligence, and efficiency in resource-constrained environments. Their role in real-time decision-making across industries continues to grow, making them a fundamental component of modern AI applications. As AI advances, embedded AI systems will become even more powerful and adaptive, enabling broader adoption in smart technologies.

Embeddings in AI refer to numerical representations of complex data, such as words, images, or entities, in a lower-dimensional space. These representations capture semantic relationships and contextual meanings, making it easier for AI models to process and analyze information. Embeddings are widely used in natural language processing (NLP), recommendation systems, and deep learning applications.

The key components of Embeddings in AI include high-dimensional vector spaces that encode relationships between data points, similarity metrics that measure semantic closeness, training algorithms that learn meaningful representations, and dimensionality reduction techniques that optimize computational efficiency. These components allow embeddings to capture complex relationships in data.

The benefits of Embeddings in AI include improved accuracy in machine learning tasks, enhanced efficiency in data processing, better generalization in NLP applications, and reduced computational costs in large-scale AI models. By representing data in a compact form, embeddings enable AI models to learn contextual relationships more effectively. Examples include word embeddings in language models, user preference embeddings in recommendation engines, and image embeddings in computer vision.

Applications of Embeddings in AI span NLP, recommendation systems, search engines, fraud detection, and image recognition. In NLP, embeddings improve text understanding in chatbots. In recommendation systems, AI predicts user preferences. In search engines, embeddings enhance query relevance. In fraud detection, AI identifies suspicious patterns. In image recognition, AI classifies objects with high accuracy.

In conclusion, Embeddings in AI enhance machine learning models by transforming complex data into structured numerical representations. Their ability to improve efficiency and contextual understanding makes them essential in NLP, recommendation systems, and deep learning applications. As AI evolves, embeddings will continue to refine model performance and enable more accurate predictions in diverse domains.

Embedding Layer in AI is a specialized neural network layer designed to convert categorical input data, such as words or user interactions, into dense vector representations. This layer is commonly used in deep learning models for natural language processing, recommendation systems, and entity recognition, allowing AI models to learn relationships between discrete entities.

The key components of an Embedding Layer include trainable weight matrices that store learned representations, lookup operations that retrieve embeddings for input tokens, dimensionality settings that define vector space sizes, and backpropagation mechanisms that refine embeddings during model training. These elements enable efficient representation learning in AI models.

The benefits of an Embedding Layer include reduced input dimensionality for efficient learning, improved generalization in AI models, enhanced feature extraction for complex data relationships, and adaptability to different AI applications. The embedding layer allows deep learning models to capture meaningful relationships between input features. Examples include AI-powered chatbots that process conversational text, personalized recommendation systems that predict user preferences, and AI-driven sentiment analysis models that interpret emotional tones.

Applications of the Embedding Layer span NLP, recommender systems, fraud detection, and autonomous systems. In NLP, embeddings improve context understanding. In recommendation systems, AI learns user-item interactions. In fraud detection, AI identifies hidden correlations in transactions. In autonomous systems, AI maps sensor data into efficient representations.

In conclusion, the Embedding Layer in AI enhances neural networks by efficiently encoding categorical input data into meaningful vector representations. Its role in improving contextual learning, reducing computational costs, and optimizing AI performance makes it essential in deep learning applications. As AI research progresses, embedding layers will continue to play a crucial role in NLP, recommendation systems, and machine learning models.

Embodied AI refers to artificial intelligence systems that are integrated into physical entities, enabling them to interact with the real world through perception, decision-making, and movement. Unlike purely digital AI, embodied AI combines machine learning, robotics, and sensor-based perception to create autonomous systems capable of navigating and responding to dynamic environments.

The key components of Embodied AI include robotic hardware that enables physical interaction, real-time sensor processing that interprets environmental data, reinforcement learning algorithms that improve adaptive behavior, and autonomous decision-making frameworks that optimize AI responses. These components allow AI systems to function in real-world scenarios with high efficiency.

The benefits of Embodied AI include enhanced human-AI interaction, improved adaptability in dynamic environments, greater autonomy in robotic systems, and real-time learning through physical experiences. AI-powered embodied systems can operate independently while continuously refining their responses. Examples include self-driving cars that adapt to road conditions, AI-powered robotic assistants that assist in healthcare settings, and industrial automation robots that optimize manufacturing processes.

Applications of Embodied AI span robotics, autonomous vehicles, healthcare, assistive technology, and industrial automation. In robotics, AI enhances movement coordination. In autonomous vehicles, AI enables real-time navigation. In healthcare, AI-powered robots assist in patient care. In assistive technology, AI improves accessibility solutions. In industrial automation, AI optimizes manufacturing efficiency.

In conclusion, Embodied AI enhances artificial intelligence by integrating perception, learning, and decision-making into physical entities. Its applications in robotics, healthcare, and autonomous systems demonstrate its transformative potential. As AI and robotics continue to evolve, Embodied AI will play a central role in shaping intelligent, adaptive, and interactive machines.

Embodied AI

Embodied AI refers to artificial intelligence systems that are integrated into physical entities, enabling them to interact with the real world through perception, decision-making, and movement. Unlike purely digital AI, embodied AI combines machine learning, robotics, and sensor-based perception to create autonomous systems capable of navigating and responding to dynamic environments.

The key components of Embodied AI include robotic hardware that enables physical interaction, real-time sensor processing that interprets environmental data, reinforcement learning algorithms that improve adaptive behavior, and autonomous decision-making frameworks that optimize AI responses. These components allow AI systems to function in real-world scenarios with high efficiency.

The benefits of Embodied AI include enhanced human-AI interaction, improved adaptability in dynamic environments, greater autonomy in robotic systems, and real-time learning through physical experiences. AI-powered embodied systems can operate independently while continuously refining their responses. Examples include self-driving cars that adapt to road conditions, AI-powered robotic assistants that assist in healthcare settings, and industrial automation robots that optimize manufacturing processes.

Applications of Embodied AI span robotics, autonomous vehicles, healthcare, assistive technology, and industrial automation. In robotics, AI enhances movement coordination. In autonomous vehicles, AI enables real-time navigation. In healthcare, AI-powered robots assist in patient care. In assistive technology, AI improves accessibility solutions. In industrial automation, AI optimizes manufacturing efficiency.

In conclusion, Embodied AI enhances artificial intelligence by integrating perception, learning, and decision-making into physical entities. Its applications in robotics, healthcare, and autonomous systems demonstrate its transformative potential. As AI and robotics continue to evolve, Embodied AI will play a central role in shaping intelligent, adaptive, and interactive machines.

Emergent Behavior in AI

Definition: Complex, unexpected behaviors that arise in AI systems, particularly in multi-agent environments or large-scale neural networks, as a result of interactions between individual components.

Key Characteristics:
Unpredictable Outcomes: Behaviors emerge that are not explicitly programmed.

Self-Organization: Components interact and organize in ways that lead to new behaviors.

Complexity: Often observed in large, decentralized systems or multi-agent scenarios.

Benefits: Can lead to innovative solutions or adaptive behaviors.

Applications: Robotics, multi-agent systems, swarm intelligence, deep learning models.

Conclusion: Emergent behavior in AI opens up possibilities for innovation but requires careful monitoring to prevent unintended or harmful outcomes.

Emergent Intelligence in AI

Definition: Intelligence that arises from the interactions of simple components in AI systems, leading to complex behavior that is not explicitly programmed but emerges from the system's dynamics.

Key Characteristics:
Unprogrammed Behavior: Complex behaviors that emerge from simple rules.

Interaction-Driven: Arises from the interaction between components or agents.

Self-Organization: Components organize themselves into coherent patterns or behaviors.

Benefits: Can lead to innovative solutions and behaviors without direct programming.

Applications: Swarm robotics, multi-agent systems, evolutionary computation.

Conclusion: Emergent intelligence in AI offers powerful new approaches to problem-solving, though the unpredictability of the behaviors it produces can be a challenge.

Emergentism

Definition: Emergentism is a philosophical and scientific perspective that complex systems exhibit properties, behaviors, or capabilities arising from interactions among simpler components, which individually do not possess these characteristics. In AI and cognitive science, it refers to how sophisticated intelligence or consciousness can emerge spontaneously from simpler neural or algorithmic interactions without explicit programming of higher-level properties.

Key Components: Core aspects of emergentism include complex system interactions, bottom-up processes, self-organization, nonlinear dynamics, feedback loops, decentralized control, collective intelligence, and pattern formation.

Benefits: Emergentism helps explain and facilitate the development of adaptive, flexible systems capable of autonomous behavior, creativity, and problem-solving abilities beyond the scope of their individual components. It supports robust system behavior, reduces complexity in system design, encourages innovative solutions, and enables unexpected yet beneficial outcomes.

Examples: Examples of emergentism include the spontaneous coordination in flocks of birds or schools of fish, self-organizing traffic flow patterns, decentralized internet networks developing resilience, human consciousness emerging from neuronal interactions, and machine-learning models exhibiting unforeseen strategies during complex game scenarios.

Applications: Applications include swarm intelligence algorithms used in robotics and logistics, self-organizing neural networks in AI, decentralized blockchain technologies, adaptive traffic management systems, dynamic social media analytics, and computational models of consciousness or collective decision-making.

Industries: Emergentism influences various industries, including robotics, artificial intelligence development, transportation, urban planning, financial markets, telecommunications, blockchain and decentralized computing, healthcare modeling, and environmental management.

Summary: Emergentism provides an essential conceptual framework for understanding how sophisticated, adaptive, and intelligent behaviors naturally arise from simpler interacting parts. This perspective not only enriches scientific understanding but also enables practical design and implementation of complex, resilient systems across diverse fields and industries.

Emotion-Aware AI

Definition: Emotion-aware AI refers to artificial intelligence systems that can perceive, interpret, and respond to human emotions. These systems aim to understand the emotional state of users and adapt their behavior accordingly, leading to more natural and empathetic interactions.

Key Components: Emotion Recognition: Detecting emotions through facial expressions, voice tone, body language, and physiological signals. Emotion Interpretation: Understanding the context and nuances of detected emotions. Emotional Response Generation: Producing appropriate verbal or nonverbal responses based on the perceived emotions. User Modeling: Creating profiles of users' emotional patterns and preferences. Adaptive Behavior: Adjusting the AI's actions and communication style to match the user's emotional state.

Benefits: Enhanced User Experience: Creating more engaging and satisfying interactions with AI systems. Improved Human-Computer Interaction: Fostering more natural and intuitive communication. Personalized Interactions: Tailoring responses and services to individual emotional needs. Increased Engagement: Making AI systems more relatable and engaging for users. Better Understanding of User Needs: Gaining insights into user emotions to improve services and products.

Examples: Virtual assistants that detect frustration in a user's voice and offer more helpful assistance. Customer service chatbots that recognize customer sentiment and escalate issues appropriately. Tutoring systems that adapt their teaching style based on a student's emotional state. Gaming systems that adjust the game's difficulty or narrative based on the player's emotional reactions. Healthcare applications that monitor patients' emotional well-being and provide support.

Applications: Customer Service: Chatbots and virtual agents that can understand and respond to customer emotions. Education: Tutoring systems that adapt to students' emotional states. Healthcare: Monitoring patient well-being and providing emotional support. Gaming: Creating more immersive and engaging gaming experiences. Marketing: Analyzing customer emotions to tailor advertising and product development.

Industries: Technology: Development of more human-like and empathetic AI systems. Customer Service: Improving customer interactions and satisfaction. Education: Enhancing learning experiences and student engagement. Healthcare: Providing personalized and supportive care. Entertainment: Creating more immersive and engaging experiences.

Conclusions: Emotion-aware AI has the potential to revolutionize human-computer interaction by making AI systems more empathetic and responsive to human emotions. While challenges related to accuracy and ethical considerations exist, the benefits of enhanced user experience and personalized interactions make it a significant area of development across various industries.

Emotion Classification in AI

Definition: Emotion classification in AI is the task of categorizing text or other data into predefined emotion categories. This involves training AI models to recognize patterns and features that correspond to specific emotions, such as joy, sadness, anger, or fear.

Key Components: Data Collection: Gathering labeled data where text or other inputs are associated with specific emotions. Feature Extraction: Identifying relevant features in the input data, such as words, phrases, or acoustic properties. Machine Learning Models: Training classification algorithms, including deep learning models, to assign emotion labels to new data. Evaluation Metrics: Using metrics like accuracy, precision, and recall to assess the performance of the classification model.

Benefits: Automated Analysis: Efficiently processing large amounts of data to classify emotions. Consistency: Providing consistent and objective emotion labels. Scalability: Handling large volumes of data that would be impossible for humans to process manually. Real-time Analysis: Classifying emotions in real-time for immediate applications. Personalization: Tailoring content and services based on classified emotions.

Examples: Classifying customer reviews into positive, negative, or neutral emotions. Categorizing social media posts based on the emotions expressed. Labeling audio recordings based on the emotional tone of the speaker. Classifying facial expressions in images or videos. Categorizing text messages based on the emotions conveyed.

Applications: Customer Service: Automatically routing support tickets based on the customer's emotional tone. Marketing: Segmenting audiences based on emotional responses to advertising. Social Media Analysis: Identifying trends in public sentiment. Healthcare: Monitoring patient emotions for early detection of mental health issues. Education: Adapting teaching methods based on students' emotional states.

Industries: Technology: Development of AI tools for emotion analysis. Marketing: Understanding consumer behavior and tailoring campaigns. Customer Service: Improving customer satisfaction and providing better support. Healthcare: Monitoring patient well-being and providing personalized care. Entertainment: Analyzing audience reactions and tailoring content.

Conclusions: Emotion classification in AI is a crucial task for understanding and responding to human emotions in various applications. By training models to categorize data into emotion categories, organizations can automate analysis, personalize interactions, and gain valuable insights. While challenges related to ambiguity and subjectivity exist, emotion classification continues to be a vital area of research and development in AI.

Emotion Detection in Text

Definition: Emotion detection in text is a subfield of natural language processing (NLP) that focuses on identifying and extracting the emotional tone or sentiment expressed in written text. This involves analyzing the words, phrases, and context to determine the underlying emotion.

Key Components: Text Preprocessing: Cleaning and preparing the text data for analysis. Feature Extraction: Identifying relevant features in the text, such as keywords, sentiment lexicons, and linguistic patterns. Machine Learning Models: Using algorithms like Naive Bayes, Support Vector Machines (SVMs), or deep learning models to classify the emotions in the text. Sentiment Lexicons:

Utilizing dictionaries of words and their associated emotional scores. Contextual Analysis: Considering the surrounding words and phrases to understand the emotional context.

Benefits: Understanding Customer Feedback: Analyzing reviews and social media posts to understand customer sentiment. Improving User Experience: Identifying areas where users express frustration or satisfaction. Personalized Communication: Tailoring responses and content based on the detected emotions. Market Research: Understanding public opinion and emotional responses to products or events. Mental Health Support: Identifying signs of distress or negative emotions in online communications.

Examples: Analyzing customer reviews of a product to identify common emotions expressed. Monitoring social media for mentions of a brand and detecting the sentiment of those mentions. Identifying signs of depression or anxiety in online forum posts. Classifying the emotional tone of news articles or blog posts. Detecting the emotional content of customer support tickets.

Applications: Customer Service: Analyzing customer feedback and providing personalized support. Marketing: Understanding consumer sentiment and tailoring advertising campaigns. Social Media Monitoring: Tracking public opinion and identifying trends. Mental Health: Identifying individuals who may be in need of support. Content Analysis: Understanding the emotional impact of written content.

Industries: Technology: Development of NLP tools and sentiment analysis platforms. Marketing: Understanding consumer behavior and optimizing campaigns. Customer Service: Improving customer satisfaction and providing better support. Healthcare: Identifying mental health issues and providing support. Media and Entertainment: Analyzing audience reactions to content.

Conclusions: Emotion detection in text is a valuable tool for understanding human sentiment and emotions expressed in written language. By analyzing text data, businesses and organizations can gain insights into customer feedback, improve user experience, and tailor their communication strategies. While challenges related to ambiguity and subjectivity exist, emotion detection in text continues to be a crucial area of research and application in NLP.

Emotion Synthesis in AI

Definition: Emotion synthesis in AI refers to the process of generating expressions of emotions, such as in text, speech, or facial expressions, by artificial intelligence systems. This capability allows AI to communicate with more human-like empathy and expressiveness.

Key Components: Text-to-Speech Synthesis: Generating speech with emotional intonation and prosody. Facial Expression Generation: Creating realistic facial expressions that convey emotions. Text Generation with Emotion: Producing written text that reflects specific emotional states. Multimodal Synthesis: Combining different modalities, such as speech and facial expressions, to convey emotions. Control Mechanisms: Allowing users or systems to control the type and intensity of emotions expressed.

Benefits: Enhanced Communication: Making AI systems more engaging and natural to interact with. Improved User Experience: Creating more empathetic and responsive interactions. Personalized Interactions: Tailoring the emotional tone of communication to individual users. Accessibility: Providing emotional cues for users with disabilities. Creative Applications: Generating content with specific emotional tones for art and entertainment.

Examples: A virtual assistant that can speak with a happy or concerned tone depending on the context. A chatbot that can generate text messages with appropriate emotional expressions. An animated avatar that can display a range of facial expressions to convey emotions. A system that can generate music or sound effects that evoke specific emotions. A robot that can express emotions through its movements and gestures.

Applications: Virtual Assistants: Making interactions more natural and empathetic. Entertainment: Creating more expressive characters and content. Education: Developing engaging and supportive learning environments. Customer Service: Providing more empathetic and personalized support. Healthcare: Assisting in therapy and providing emotional support to patients.

Industries: Technology: Development of more expressive and human-like AI systems. Entertainment: Creating more engaging and immersive experiences. Education: Enhancing learning and engagement through emotional expression. Healthcare: Providing more personalized and supportive care. Customer Service: Improving customer interactions and satisfaction.

Conclusions: Emotion synthesis in AI is a crucial step towards creating more human-like and empathetic artificial intelligence systems. By enabling AI to express emotions in various modalities, we can enhance communication, improve user experience, and create more engaging applications. While challenges related to realism and cultural nuances exist, emotion synthesis holds significant potential across various industries.

Emotional Intelligence in AI

Definition: Emotional intelligence in AI refers to the ability of artificial intelligence systems to understand, manage, and utilize emotions, both in themselves (if applicable) and in humans they interact with. It encompasses recognizing emotions, understanding their impact, and responding appropriately.

Key Components: Emotion Recognition: Detecting and identifying emotions in humans. Emotion Understanding: Comprehending the causes, consequences, and complexities of emotions. Emotion Management: Regulating and responding to emotions in a constructive manner. Self-Awareness (if applicable): Understanding the AI's own limitations and potential biases related to emotions. Social Skills: Using emotional intelligence to navigate social interactions effectively.

Benefits: Improved Human-AI Interaction: Creating more natural, empathetic, and effective communication. Enhanced User Experience: Leading to more satisfying and engaging interactions with AI systems. Personalized Services: Tailoring AI responses and services based on user emotions. Better Decision-Making: Incorporating emotional factors into AI decision-making processes. Increased Trust: Fostering greater trust in AI systems that demonstrate emotional intelligence.

Examples: AI-powered coaches that can understand a user's frustration and adjust their guidance accordingly. Robots designed for elder care that can recognize loneliness and provide companionship. Virtual agents that can de-escalate tense situations by recognizing and responding to anger. AI systems used in mental health that can identify and respond to signs of distress. Customer service chatbots that can understand customer sentiment and provide more empathetic support.

Applications: Healthcare: Providing emotional support and personalized care. Education: Developing more engaging and supportive learning environments. Customer Service: Enhancing customer interactions and satisfaction. Robotics: Creating more socially intelligent and helpful robots. Personalized Assistance: Tailoring AI assistants to individual emotional needs.

Industries: Technology: Development of more human-like and empathetic AI systems. Healthcare: Improving patient care and providing emotional support. Education: Enhancing learning experiences and student well-being. Customer Service: Improving customer satisfaction and building stronger relationships. Robotics: Creating more socially aware and helpful robots.

Conclusions: Emotional intelligence in AI is a critical aspect of creating more human-centered and beneficial artificial intelligence systems. By enabling AI to understand and respond to emotions, we can enhance interactions, improve user experience, and foster greater trust. While challenges related to complexity and ethical considerations exist, the development of emotional intelligence in AI holds significant promise for various applications and industries.

Emotionally Adaptive AI

Definition: Emotionally adaptive AI refers to artificial intelligence systems that can modify their behavior and responses based on the detected emotional state of the user. This adaptation aims to create more personalized, empathetic, and effective interactions.

Key Components: Emotion Recognition: Detecting the user's emotional state through various modalities. Behavioral Adaptation: Adjusting the AI's actions, responses, and communication style based on the detected emotions. User Modeling: Maintaining a profile of the user's emotional patterns and preferences for adaptation. Feedback Mechanisms: Allowing users to provide feedback on the AI's emotional adaptation. Contextual Awareness: Considering the context of the situation when adapting to user emotions.

Benefits: Personalized Experience: Tailoring interactions to individual emotional needs and preferences. Improved Engagement: Creating more engaging and satisfying interactions with AI systems. Enhanced User Satisfaction: Leading to a more positive and effective user experience. Increased Trust: Building greater trust in AI systems that demonstrate emotional sensitivity. Better Learning Outcomes: In educational settings, adapting to students' emotional states can improve learning.

Examples: An e-learning platform that adjusts the pace and difficulty of lessons based on a student's frustration levels. A music streaming service that adapts its recommendations based on the user's current mood. A smart home system that adjusts lighting and temperature based on the emotional tone of conversations. A fitness tracker that provides personalized encouragement based on the user's emotional state. A mental wellness app that adapts its support strategies based on the user's reported emotions.

Applications: Education: Personalized learning platforms that adapt to students' emotional states. Entertainment: Media streaming services and games that adjust content based on user emotions. Smart Environments: Homes and workplaces that adapt to occupants' emotional needs. Health and Wellness: Apps and devices that provide personalized support based on emotional states. Customer Service: Chatbots and virtual agents that adapt their responses to customer emotions.

Industries: Education: Development of personalized learning technologies. Entertainment: Creating more engaging and immersive experiences. Smart Homes and Cities: Enhancing comfort and well-being in living and working environments. Healthcare: Providing personalized and supportive care. Customer Service: Improving customer satisfaction and building stronger relationships.

Conclusions: Emotionally adaptive AI has the potential to transform how we interact with technology by creating more personalized and empathetic experiences. By adapting their behavior based on user emotions, AI systems can enhance engagement, satisfaction, and trust. While challenges related to accuracy and ethical considerations exist, the development of emotionally adaptive AI is crucial for creating more human-centered and beneficial artificial intelligence.

Empathetic AI

Definition: Empathetic AI refers to artificial intelligence systems designed to understand and respond to human emotions with empathy. It goes beyond simply recognizing emotions to understanding and sharing the feelings of others, aiming to create more meaningful and supportive interactions.

Key Components: Emotion Recognition: Detecting and identifying human emotions through various modalities. Perspective Taking: Understanding the situation from the user's point of view. Emotional Understanding: Comprehending the nuances and complexities of human emotions. Empathetic Response Generation: Producing responses that acknowledge and validate the user's feelings. User Modeling: Creating profiles of users' emotional patterns and preferences for empathy.

Benefits: Enhanced User Experience: Leading to more positive and supportive interactions with AI systems. Increased Trust: Fostering a stronger sense of trust and connection between users and AI. Personalized Support: Providing tailored assistance that addresses not only functional needs but also emotional states. Improved Engagement: Making AI systems more relatable and engaging for users. Better Mental Well-being: AI systems that offer empathetic support can contribute to improved mental health.

Examples: A mental health chatbot that offers supportive and validating responses to users expressing distress. A virtual tutor that recognizes a student's frustration and offers encouragement and alternative explanations. A customer service agent that acknowledges a customer's anger and works to resolve the issue with empathy. A robot designed for elder care that can sense loneliness and offer comforting interactions. A personalized fitness coach that adapts its motivational techniques based on the user's emotional state.

Applications: Healthcare: Mental health support, patient care, and therapy. Education: Personalized tutoring and emotional support for students. Customer Service: Empathetic chatbots and virtual agents. Elder Care: Companion robots that provide emotional support. Personalized Assistance: AI assistants that understand and respond to user emotions with empathy.

Industry: Healthcare: Mental health, elder care, patient support systems. Education: E-learning platforms, tutoring systems. Technology: Development of empathetic AI assistants and chatbots. Customer Service: Contact centers, virtual agents. Personal Robotics: Social robots, companion robots.

Conclusions: Empathetic AI holds significant potential for transforming human-computer interactions by creating systems that are not only intelligent but also emotionally aware and responsive. By understanding and sharing human feelings, empathetic AI can enhance user experience, build trust, and provide more personalized and supportive assistance. While challenges related to accuracy, ethics, and cultural sensitivity exist, the development of empathetic AI is a crucial step towards creating more human-centered technology.

Empathy in AI

Definition: Empathy in AI refers to the capability of artificial intelligence systems to understand and share the feelings of humans. It involves recognizing and responding to emotions in a way that shows understanding and concern, mirroring human-like empathy.

Key Components: Emotion Recognition: The ability to detect and identify human emotions. Perspective Taking: The capacity to understand a situation from another's viewpoint. Emotional Understanding: Comprehending the causes and implications of different emotions. Empathetic Response Generation: Producing outputs that acknowledge and validate human feelings. User Modeling: Creating representations of users' emotional states and preferences.

Benefits: Improved Human-AI Interaction: Fostering more natural and supportive communication. Enhanced User Experience: Leading to more satisfying and engaging interactions. Increased Trust:

Building stronger relationships and trust between users and AI systems. Personalized Support: Tailoring assistance based on individual emotional needs. Better Mental Well-being: AI that offers empathetic responses can contribute to improved mental health.

Examples: A virtual counselor that listens to a user's concerns and offers empathetic advice. A customer support chatbot that acknowledges a customer's frustration and works to find a solution. A social robot designed for companionship that can recognize loneliness and offer comforting words. A personalized learning system that adapts its approach based on a student's emotional state. An AI assistant that can detect when a user is stressed and offer helpful suggestions.

Applications: Healthcare: Mental health support, patient care, and therapy. Education: Personalized learning and emotional support for students. Customer Service: Empathetic chatbots and virtual agents. Elder Care: Companion robots and support systems. Personalized Assistance: AI assistants that understand and respond to user emotions.

Industry: Healthcare: Mental health, elder care, patient support systems. Education: E-learning platforms, tutoring systems. Technology: Development of empathetic AI assistants and chatbots. Customer Service: Contact centers, virtual agents. Personal Robotics: Social robots, companion robots.

Conclusions: Empathy in AI is a significant step towards creating more human-centered and beneficial artificial intelligence. By enabling AI systems to understand and share human feelings, we can improve interactions, build trust, and provide more personalized and supportive assistance. While challenges remain in accurately modeling and ethically implementing empathy, the development of this capability is crucial for advancing AI in a way that benefits humanity.

Empathy Mapping in AI

Definition: Empathy mapping in AI is a process used to understand and visualize the emotional and cognitive states of users when interacting with AI systems. It involves mapping out what users say, think, feel, and do to gain insights into their needs and experiences.

Key Components: User Personas: Creating representations of target users, including their goals, motivations, and pain points. Say: Documenting what users say and how they express themselves. Think: Exploring the thoughts, beliefs, and concerns of users. Feel: Identifying the emotions and feelings experienced by users. Do: Observing the actions and behaviors of users when interacting with AI systems. Insights: Synthesizing the information from the map to identify key user needs and opportunities for improvement.

Benefits: Improved User Understanding: Gaining a deeper understanding of user needs and emotional responses to AI systems. Enhanced Design: Informing the design and development of more user-centered AI applications. Increased User Satisfaction: Identifying pain points and areas for improvement to enhance user experience. Better Communication: Facilitating communication and collaboration between developers and stakeholders. Ethical Considerations: Helping to identify potential ethical issues and biases in AI systems.

Examples: Mapping the experience of a user interacting with a mental health chatbot to understand their emotional journey. Creating an empathy map for users of a virtual assistant to identify their frustrations and needs. Using empathy mapping to understand the experience of a patient interacting with a healthcare AI system. Mapping the interactions of students with an AI-powered tutoring system to identify areas for improvement. Developing an empathy map for users of a social robot to understand their emotional connection and needs.

Applications: User Experience (UX) Design: Designing more user-friendly and empathetic AI systems. Product Development: Identifying user needs and opportunities for innovation. Ethical AI

Development: Understanding potential biases and ethical implications of AI systems. Research: Gaining insights into human-AI interaction and user psychology. Training: Educating developers and stakeholders about user-centered AI design.

Industry: Technology: User experience design, product development, AI ethics. Research: Human-computer interaction, psychology. Consulting: UX research and design, AI strategy. Education: Teaching user-centered design and AI ethics. Healthcare: Patient experience design, AI in healthcare.

Conclusions: Empathy mapping is a valuable tool for understanding the user experience with AI systems. By visualizing user thoughts, feelings, and behaviors, it provides insights that can inform the design of more user-centered, ethical, and effective AI applications. While challenges exist in data collection and interpretation, empathy mapping is essential for creating AI that truly meets the needs and expectations of its users.

Empirical Risk Minimization (ERM)

Definition: Empirical Risk Minimization (ERM) is a principle in statistical learning theory and machine learning that aims to find a function (e.g., a model) that minimizes the empirical risk, which is the average loss over the training data. The goal is to find a model that performs well on the observed data, with the hope that it will generalize well to unseen data.

Key Components: Loss Function: A function that quantifies the error of a prediction compared to the true value. Training Data: A set of labeled examples used to train the model. Model Class: The set of possible functions that the model can choose from. Empirical Risk: The average value of the loss function over the training data. Optimization Algorithm: An algorithm used to find the model parameters that minimize the empirical risk.

Benefits: Simplicity: ERM provides a straightforward framework for training machine learning models. Theoretical Foundation: ERM has a strong theoretical basis in statistical learning theory, which provides insights into generalization. Wide Applicability: ERM is used to train a wide variety of machine learning models. Practical Success: Many successful machine learning models are trained using ERM.

Examples: Training a linear regression model by minimizing the mean squared error on the training data. Training a logistic regression model by minimizing the cross-entropy loss on the training data. Training a neural network by minimizing the loss function on the training data using gradient descent.

Applications: Supervised Learning: Training models for classification and regression tasks. Deep Learning: Training complex neural networks for various applications. Statistical Modeling: Fitting statistical models to data. Machine Learning: A fundamental principle underlying many machine learning algorithms.

Industry: Technology: Development of machine learning models for various applications. Research: Statistical learning theory, machine learning. Data Science: Building and deploying machine learning models.

Conclusions: Empirical Risk Minimization is a fundamental principle in machine learning that provides a framework for training models by minimizing the error on the training data. While ERM is simple and widely applicable, it is important to address the challenges of overfitting and generalization to ensure that models perform well on unseen data. ERM remains a cornerstone of machine learning and continues to drive advancements in the field.

Emulated AI Training

Definition: Emulated AI training refers to the process of training artificial intelligence models using simulated environments or data. This approach is particularly useful when real-world data is scarce, expensive to collect, dangerous to obtain, or when specific scenarios need to be controlled for training purposes.

Key Components: Simulation Environment: A virtual environment that mimics the real world or a specific domain. Data Generation: Creating synthetic data within the simulation environment. Model Training: Training AI models using the generated synthetic data. Domain Adaptation: Techniques to transfer knowledge learned in the simulation to the real world. Feedback Loop: Using real-world data to refine the simulation and improve model performance.

Benefits: Cost-Effective: Reduces the cost and effort associated with collecting real-world data. Safe Training: Allows for training AI models in scenarios that would be dangerous or unethical in the real world. Controlled Environments: Enables training AI models under specific conditions and scenarios. Data Abundance: Provides a way to generate large amounts of labeled data. Faster Iteration: Allows for rapid experimentation and iteration in a controlled environment.

Examples: Training autonomous vehicles in a simulated city to handle various traffic scenarios. Training robots to perform complex tasks in a virtual environment before deploying them in the real world. Training AI agents for games using the game environment as a simulation. Training medical AI to diagnose diseases using synthetic medical images. Training cybersecurity AI to detect threats using simulated network attacks.

Applications: Robotics: Training robots for manipulation, navigation, and interaction. Autonomous Vehicles: Developing and testing self-driving cars, trucks, and drones. Gaming: Training AI agents for games and virtual environments. Healthcare: Developing AI for medical diagnosis, treatment planning, and drug discovery. Cybersecurity: Training AI to detect and respond to cyber threats.

Industry: Technology: Development of AI models and simulation environments. Automotive: Autonomous vehicle development and testing. Gaming: AI for game agents and virtual environments. Healthcare: Medical AI research and development. Robotics: Development and deployment of robots.

Conclusions: Emulated AI training is a valuable approach for training AI models when real-world data is limited or difficult to obtain. By using simulations, developers can create controlled environments, generate abundant data, and train models safely and efficiently. While challenges related to simulation fidelity and domain gap exist, emulated AI training is crucial for advancing AI in various fields.

Emulator-Based AI

Definition: Emulator-based AI refers to the use of emulators, which are software or hardware that replicates the behavior of another system, to train and evaluate artificial intelligence models. This approach allows AI to interact with and learn from environments that are not directly accessible or are difficult to work with in the real world.

Key Components: Emulator: Software or hardware that mimics the behavior of a target system, such as a game console, a robot, or a physical process. AI Model: The artificial intelligence being trained and evaluated. Interaction: The AI interacts with the emulator, receiving inputs and performing actions within the emulated environment. Training Data: Data generated from the AI's interactions with the emulator, used to train the model. Evaluation: Assessing the AI's performance within the emulated environment.

Benefits: Accessibility: Allows AI to interact with and learn from systems that are not readily available or are complex to set up. Safety: Enables training and testing of AI in scenarios that would be dangerous or costly in the real world. Control: Provides a controlled and reproducible environment for training and evaluation. Data Generation: Facilitates the generation of large amounts of training data. Faster Iteration: Allows for rapid experimentation and iteration within the emulated environment.

Examples: Training AI agents to play video games using game console emulators. Developing control systems for robots using emulators that simulate the robot's hardware and environment. Training AI models for industrial control using emulators of physical processes. Developing AI for autonomous vehicles using emulators that simulate driving scenarios. Training AI for cybersecurity by using emulators of network environments.

Applications: Gaming: Training AI agents to play video games. Robotics: Developing control systems for robots. Industrial Automation: Training AI for process control and optimization. Autonomous Vehicles: Developing and testing AI for self-driving vehicles. Cybersecurity: Training AI for threat detection and response.

Industry: Technology: Development of AI models and emulators. Gaming: AI for game agents and virtual environments. Robotics: Development and testing of robot control systems. Manufacturing: Industrial automation and process control. Automotive: Autonomous vehicle development.

Conclusions: Emulator-based AI is a valuable approach for training and evaluating AI models by providing accessible, safe, and controlled environments. It allows AI to interact with complex systems and generate large amounts of training data. While challenges related to emulator accuracy and performance exist, this approach is crucial for advancing AI in various fields, including gaming, robotics, and industrial automation.

Encoder-Decoder Architecture

Definition

Encoder-Decoder architecture is a neural network framework used to transform one sequence into another, making it ideal for tasks involving variable-length inputs and outputs. The encoder processes and compresses the input sequence into a fixed-size representation, while the decoder interprets this representation to generate the target sequence. This architecture is foundational in natural language processing, machine translation, and image captioning.

Key Components
Encoder: Converts input sequences into context-rich vector representations
Decoder: Generates output sequences based on the encoded information
Latent representation: The compressed, abstract form of input
Attention mechanism (optional): Enhances focus on relevant parts of the input during decoding

Benefits
Enables flexible input and output lengths
Supports multilingual and multimodal translation
Works well with both supervised and unsupervised learning tasks
Can be extended with attention and transformers for better performance

Examples
Translating English sentences to French using neural machine translation
Generating image captions from a visual input
Summarizing long documents into shorter texts

Applications
Language translation
Text summarization
Speech-to-text conversion

Image caption generation
Chatbot development

Industries
Technology and AI research
Education and e-learning
Healthcare (clinical note summarization)
Media and publishing
Customer service automation

Summary
Encoder-Decoder architecture is a cornerstone of modern sequence modeling, offering a flexible solution for transforming structured input into meaningful output. Though it faces challenges in interpretability and scalability, its adaptability across languages, data types, and modalities makes it an essential component in the evolution of AI-driven communication and understanding.

Energy-Based Models (EBMs) in AI

Definition: Energy-Based Models (EBMs) are a type of probabilistic model in artificial intelligence that learn a function, called the energy function, which assigns a scalar value to each configuration of the variables. The probability distribution over the variables is then defined based on this energy function. EBMs are particularly useful for modeling complex dependencies between variables without explicitly specifying the conditional probabilities.

Key Components: Energy Function: A function that maps each configuration of the variables to a scalar energy value. Lower energy values correspond to more likely configurations. Probability Distribution: Defined based on the energy function, typically using a Boltzmann distribution where the probability of a configuration is proportional to the exponentiated negative energy. Training: Involves adjusting the parameters of the energy function so that observed data has low energy and unobserved data has high energy. Sampling: Generating samples from the learned distribution, which can be challenging and often requires specialized techniques.

Benefits: Flexibility: EBMs can model complex dependencies between variables without needing to specify the conditional probabilities. Unsupervised Learning: They are well-suited for unsupervised learning tasks where the goal is to learn the underlying structure of the data. Handling Missing Data: EBMs can naturally handle missing data by marginalizing over the missing variables. Joint Modeling: They can model the joint distribution over all variables, allowing for inference in any direction. Theoretical Foundation: EBMs have a strong theoretical basis in statistical mechanics.

Examples: Restricted Boltzmann Machines (RBMs) and Deep Belief Networks (DBNs) are examples of EBMs used for feature learning and generative modeling. Hopfield Networks are EBMs used for associative memory. Neural Autoregressive Density Estimator (NADE) can be seen as a type of EBM.

Applications: Generative Modeling: Learning to generate new data samples similar to the training data. Feature Learning: Learning useful representations of the input data. Density Estimation: Estimating the probability distribution of the data. Reinforcement Learning: Modeling the value function or policy.

Industry: Technology: Generative AI, unsupervised learning, probabilistic modeling. Research: Statistical learning theory, deep learning. Data Science: Building models for various unsupervised tasks.

Conclusions: Energy-Based Models provide a flexible and powerful framework for modeling complex dependencies and learning the underlying structure of data. While training and sampling can be challenging, EBMs are well-suited for unsupervised learning tasks and have found applications in generative modeling, feature learning, and density estimation. Continued research is focused on developing more efficient training and sampling methods to unlock the full potential of EBMs.

Energy Efficiency in AI

Definition

Energy efficiency in AI refers to the development and deployment of artificial intelligence systems that are optimized to perform tasks while consuming minimal energy. This focus on energy-aware design is especially important for large-scale AI models and data centers where environmental impact and operational costs are significant.

Key Components

Low-power algorithm design

Hardware acceleration with GPUs, TPUs, or ASICs

Dynamic power scaling

Efficient memory management and data movement

Benefits

Reduces electricity consumption and operational costs

Supports eco-friendly and sustainable AI practices

Enables deployment of AI in energy-limited environments

Improves heat management and system longevity

Examples

Using quantized neural networks on mobile devices

Deploying AI workloads in carbon-neutral data centers

Optimizing AI inference for battery-powered IoT systems

Applications

Edge computing

Data center operations

Green AI model deployment

Mobile AI systems

Industries

Information technology

Consumer electronics

Telecommunications

Environmental sustainability

Summary

Energy efficiency in AI ensures sustainable innovation by reducing the environmental and financial costs of intelligent systems. It is a key principle for modern AI development, particularly as the demand for larger models and faster computation grows.

Ensemble of Experts in AI

Definition

The ensemble of experts approach in AI combines multiple specialized models—each referred to as an "expert"—to collaboratively solve complex problems. Each expert is trained on a specific part of the input space or task, and their predictions are aggregated to produce a final decision.

Key Components

Specialized sub-models (experts)

Aggregation mechanism (voting, weighted average, gating)
Task decomposition
Error correction through model diversity

Benefits
Improves overall model accuracy and robustness
Reduces individual model bias
Handles diverse input types more effectively
Enables modular model training and maintenance

Examples
Speech-to-text systems combining models specialized in accents, noise levels, and vocabulary
Medical diagnostic AI using separate models for image analysis, symptom interpretation, and risk scoring
Language translation AI selecting from different models based on grammar, tone, or domain

Applications
Voice recognition
Medical diagnosis
Financial modeling
Multimodal AI systems

Industries
Healthcare
Finance
Telecommunications
Software development

Summary
An ensemble of experts leverages the strengths of multiple specialized models to enhance decision-making. Though more complex to manage, this method significantly boosts performance in tasks requiring nuanced understanding and specialization.

Entity Recognition (Named Entity Recognition, NER)

Definition
Entity recognition, also known as Named Entity Recognition (NER), is a natural language processing technique used to identify and classify specific elements within text—such as names, locations, dates, and organizations—into predefined categories.

Key Components
Tokenization and sentence segmentation
Entity classification algorithms
Contextual analysis
Named entity categories (e.g., Person, Location, Date, Organization)

Benefits
Automates data extraction from unstructured text
Improves text search and summarization capabilities
Supports real-time language understanding
Enables better organization of textual information

Examples
Identifying city and date names in a news article

Extracting company names from financial documents
Recognizing patient names and medications in medical reports

Applications
Document classification
Chatbot understanding
Information retrieval
Legal and compliance automation

Industries
Legal and regulatory services
Healthcare
Media and publishing
Customer service

Summary
Entity recognition is a foundational NLP tool that enables machines to extract structured meaning from raw text. It powers numerous applications by helping AI understand who, where, and when within human language.

Entropy in AI

Definition
Entropy in AI refers to the measurement of uncertainty or randomness in a probability distribution. It is commonly used in machine learning and information theory to assess the confidence of predictions or to guide decision-making in algorithms like decision trees and reinforcement learning.

Key Components
Shannon entropy calculation
Probability distribution analysis
Information gain
Uncertainty quantification

Benefits
Helps select optimal decisions in branching algorithms
Enables model calibration and confidence estimation
Improves performance in classification and exploration tasks

Examples
Calculating entropy to choose the best split in a decision tree
Using entropy to guide exploration in reinforcement learning
Assessing prediction confidence in probabilistic models

Applications
Decision tree classifiers
Exploration in reinforcement learning
Anomaly detection
Probabilistic modeling

Industries
Cybersecurity
Finance
Manufacturing
AI research

Summary
Entropy is a powerful tool for managing uncertainty in AI. By quantifying unpredictability, it supports smarter decision-making, model improvement, and data analysis across various AI domains.

EOG-Based Human-Machine Interface (HMI)

Definition
EOG-based Human-Machine Interfaces (HMIs) allow users to control digital devices using eye movements, captured through electrooculography (EOG). These systems offer a hands-free way to interact with technology, greatly enhancing accessibility and usability.

Key Components
EOG sensors placed near the eyes
Signal processing and pattern recognition
Calibration system
Command mapping based on gaze behavior

Benefits
Provides control options for users with limited mobility
Enables intuitive interaction with machines
Supports low-latency communication for simple commands

Examples
Controlling a wheelchair using eye direction
Navigating menus on a computer using eye blinks
Operating smart home devices hands-free

Applications
Assistive technology
Medical devices
Wearable computing
Smart home systems

Industries
Healthcare
Consumer electronics
Rehabilitation engineering
Gaming and entertainment

Summary
EOG-based HMI technology transforms human-computer interaction by offering non-invasive, eye-controlled access to digital systems. It's especially impactful in assistive applications but must overcome signal variability and calibration needs for broader use.

EOG Signal Processing in AI

Definition
EOG signal processing in AI involves analyzing electrooculography signals—electrical signals generated by eye movements—to interpret user intent and enable interaction with machines through gaze direction or blinking patterns.

Key Components
Electrode placement and data acquisition
Noise filtering and signal enhancement

Pattern recognition for gaze direction
AI-based classification algorithms

Benefits
Enhances communication for users with motor impairments
Supports hands-free device interaction
Works without invasive procedures

Examples
Using eye movement signals to control a robotic arm
Activating emergency alerts with intentional blinks
Navigating a digital interface by glancing in specific directions

Applications
Assistive communication tools
Human-robot interaction
Gaming and immersive environments
Medical diagnostics

Industries
Healthcare
Neurotechnology
Wearable tech
Rehabilitation

Summary
EOG signal processing expands the potential of AI-driven interfaces by making eye movement a reliable input method. It enhances accessibility and hands-free control, particularly for users with physical limitations.

EOL (End-of-Life) Prediction in AI

Definition
End-of-life prediction in AI involves forecasting the remaining usable lifespan of machines, devices, or components by analyzing performance data and degradation patterns. This predictive approach is central to optimizing maintenance and preventing unexpected failures.

Key Components
Time-series analysis of sensor data
Predictive modeling of degradation
Condition monitoring
Maintenance schedule optimization

Benefits
Reduces unplanned downtime
Improves asset utilization and longevity
Lowers maintenance costs
Enables just-in-time servicing

Examples
Predicting when a jet engine component will fail
Estimating battery degradation in electric vehicles
Identifying early signs of failure in factory machinery

Applications
Predictive maintenance
Asset lifecycle management
Fleet management systems
Industrial automation

Industries
Manufacturing
Aerospace
Energy
Transportation

Summary
EOL prediction in AI enhances operational reliability and cost-efficiency by enabling data-driven maintenance. It is an essential tool for industries that depend on long-term equipment performance.

EOQ (Economic Order Quantity) AI

Definition
EOQ AI is the use of artificial intelligence to calculate the ideal order quantity that minimizes total inventory costs, including holding, ordering, and stockout costs. It combines traditional inventory models with predictive analytics to adapt to fluctuating demand.

Key Components
Demand forecasting
Cost function optimization
Stock level monitoring
Dynamic pricing and ordering algorithms

Benefits
Reduces overstock and understock situations
Optimizes supply chain efficiency
Improves customer satisfaction through better availability
Minimizes warehousing costs

Examples
Automatically determining the number of units to order based on seasonal trends
Adjusting restock frequency in response to real-time sales data
Forecasting inventory needs based on regional consumer behavior

Applications
Inventory management
Retail logistics
Supply chain optimization
Manufacturing procurement

Industries
Retail
E-commerce
Manufacturing
Wholesale distribution

Summary
EOQ AI modernizes inventory management by applying intelligent automation to purchasing decisions. It ensures efficient use of capital and resources while improving supply chain responsiveness.

EoS (End-of-Support) Management AI

Definition: EoS (End-of-Support) Management AI refers to artificial intelligence systems designed to monitor, manage, and optimize the transition of software, hardware, or services reaching their end-of-support phase. These AI-driven solutions assist organizations in mitigating risks, ensuring compliance, and strategizing upgrades or replacements efficiently.

Key Components: Automated Monitoring tracks lifecycle timelines and support deadlines. Risk Assessment evaluates vulnerabilities and security risks associated with outdated systems. Recommendation Engine suggests upgrade paths, patches, or alternative solutions. Compliance Management ensures regulatory adherence in system transitions. Integration Capabilities connect with IT management and procurement systems.

Examples: AI-powered IT asset management tools detect unsupported software. Predictive analytics tools advise companies on replacing legacy infrastructure. AI chatbots assist users in migrating to supported platforms.

Benefits: Reduces security vulnerabilities by proactively addressing outdated systems. Enhances operational continuity and minimizes downtime risks. Automates compliance tracking to meet industry regulations. Lowers maintenance costs by optimizing upgrade strategies.

Applications: IT infrastructure management, enterprise software lifecycle planning, cybersecurity risk assessment.

Industries: Information Technology, Healthcare, Banking & Finance, Government.

Conclusion: EoS Management AI streamlines the transition from unsupported systems, reducing risks and costs. While challenges exist in implementation and adoption, its benefits in maintaining security and compliance make it a crucial asset for modern enterprises.

Ephemeral AI

Definition: Ephemeral AI refers to artificial intelligence systems designed to operate temporarily, executing specific tasks for a limited duration without maintaining long-term memory or persistent data storage.

Key Components: Stateless Processing operates without retaining historical data. On-Demand Activation runs only when needed, minimizing resource usage. Secure Data Handling ensures data privacy by not storing sensitive information. Rapid Scalability instantly deploys and deactivates as required.

Examples: AI-driven fraud detection systems analyze transactions in real-time. Virtual AI assistants process user requests and discard data afterward. AI models in serverless computing environments perform temporary analysis.

Benefits: Enhances security by eliminating persistent data risks. Reduces infrastructure costs due to on-demand execution. Improves scalability by adapting to varying workload demands.

Applications: Cybersecurity (real-time threat detection), customer support (temporary chatbot sessions), financial transactions (fraud prevention systems).

Industries: Banking & Finance, Telecommunications, E-commerce, Cloud Computing.

Conclusion: Ephemeral AI provides efficient, scalable, and secure solutions for temporary task execution. Its stateless nature makes it ideal for dynamic applications, though balancing performance with real-time data dependencies remains a challenge

Ephemeral Edge AI

Definition: Ephemeral Edge AI refers to artificial intelligence models deployed on edge computing devices for temporary, real-time processing without long-term data retention.

Key Components: Edge-Based Computation performs tasks at the device level. Low-Latency Processing ensures fast decision-making. Secure Data Handling limits data exposure. Adaptive Deployment allows dynamic execution of AI models.

Examples: AI-driven smart cameras that process images and discard data. Autonomous vehicles using ephemeral AI for real-time navigation. Industrial robots analyzing manufacturing defects in real-time.

Benefits: Enhances data privacy by processing information locally. Reduces network congestion by minimizing data transfer. Lowers infrastructure costs by utilizing edge resources.

Applications: Autonomous systems, smart surveillance, industrial automation.

Industries: Manufacturing, Transportation, Retail, Smart Cities.

Conclusion: Ephemeral Edge AI optimizes real-time processing at the edge, improving efficiency and security. While computational limitations exist, advancements in edge hardware continue to enhance its capabilities.

Ephemeral Neural Networks

Definition: Ephemeral Neural Networks are artificial neural networks designed for short-term operations, where models are created, trained, and discarded without long-term storage or retraining.

Key Components: Dynamic Model Instantiation generates temporary neural networks for real-time tasks. Lightweight Architectures enable efficient short-term learning. Adaptive Learning Rates adjust model performance dynamically. Secure Data Handling ensures transient data processing.

Examples: AI models for real-time medical diagnostics. Short-lived neural networks in cybersecurity threat detection. Temporary neural networks used for specific computational tasks in cloud environments.

Benefits: Reduces computational costs by eliminating the need for continuous training. Enhances security by not storing sensitive data. Improves responsiveness for time-sensitive AI applications.

Applications: Medical diagnostics, fraud detection, real-time analytics.

Industries: Healthcare, Finance, Cybersecurity, Cloud Computing.

Conclusion: Ephemeral Neural Networks provide temporary yet efficient AI solutions. While they excel in short-term learning tasks, their limitations in long-term model retention require innovative optimization strategies.

Epidemiological Modeling AI

Definition
Epidemiological modeling AI refers to artificial intelligence systems leveraging computational algorithms, predictive analytics, and machine learning techniques to simulate, analyze, and forecast the spread and impact of infectious diseases within populations.

Key Components
Key components include predictive modeling algorithms, disease transmission models (such as SEIR and agent-based models), data-driven analytics, real-time data integration, machine learning algorithms, and visualization tools for interpreting model results.

Example
An AI-driven epidemiological model predicts COVID-19 spread within a city, providing timely forecasts of infection peaks and helping authorities effectively manage resources and interventions.

Benefits
Benefits include accurate prediction of disease outbreaks, enhanced decision-making capabilities, improved allocation of medical resources, proactive public health responses, reduced uncertainty in epidemic forecasting, and optimized intervention strategies.

Applications
Applications include pandemic response management, infectious disease tracking, public health planning, vaccine distribution strategies, healthcare resource allocation, real-time outbreak surveillance, and disease intervention optimization.

Industries
Industries utilizing epidemiological modeling AI include healthcare, government public health agencies, pharmaceuticals, insurance, academic research institutions, emergency services, international health organizations, and disaster response management.

Conclusions
Epidemiological modeling AI plays a critical role in public health preparedness and response, significantly enhancing decision-making and resource allocation during health crises. Addressing data quality and computational challenges remains essential for continued improvement.

Epidermal Electronics with AI

Definition: Epidermal Electronics with AI involves integrating AI-driven sensors into flexible, skin-like electronic devices for real-time biometric and physiological monitoring.

Key Components: Flexible Circuitry enables comfortable, skin-like application. AI-Powered Analytics interprets real-time biometric data. Wireless Communication transmits data securely. Biocompatible Materials ensure safe interaction with human skin.

Examples: AI-powered wearable health monitors. Smart tattoos tracking hydration and stress levels. Flexible biosensors detecting early disease symptoms.

Benefits: Enhances real-time health monitoring. Provides non-invasive, continuous biometric tracking. Enables early detection of medical conditions.

Applications: Healthcare monitoring, sports performance analysis, human-computer interaction.

Industries: Healthcare, Sports, Wearable Technology, Biomedical Research.

Conclusion: Epidermal Electronics with AI revolutionizes real-time health monitoring. While power and privacy challenges exist, its potential in healthcare and wearables is transformative.

Epigenetic Algorithms

Definition: Epigenetic Algorithms are evolutionary algorithms that mimic biological gene expression modifications to optimize AI model adaptation over time.

Key Components: Gene Expression Modulation adjusts AI parameters dynamically. Adaptive Mutation enhances problem-solving capabilities. Evolutionary Learning continuously refines performance. Fitness Function Optimization ensures solution efficiency.

Examples: AI models adapting to environmental changes in robotics. Smart grid optimization for energy efficiency. Self-improving financial trading algorithms.

Benefits: Improves adaptability in dynamic environments. Enhances AI resilience against adversarial attacks. Optimizes real-time decision-making.

Applications: Robotics, adaptive AI systems, automated trading.

Industries: Finance, Energy, Robotics, AI Research.

Conclusion: Epigenetic Algorithms enhance AI adaptability and resilience. Despite challenges, their application in dynamic optimization continues to expand.

Episode-Based Learning

Definition
Episode-based learning is an educational approach where knowledge is acquired through structured, narrative-driven experiences or scenarios, often mimicking real-life situations. It emphasizes learning by engaging with distinct episodes or events that unfold sequentially, allowing learners to connect concepts to practical contexts over time.

Key Components
The foundation of episode-based learning lies in its storytelling framework, where each episode presents a problem or situation to explore. It involves characters or roles that learners can relate to, a clear context that sets the stage, and a progression of events that builds understanding. Reflection is integral, encouraging learners to analyze outcomes and decisions after each episode. Interactivity often enhances engagement, letting learners influence the narrative or make choices that shape the experience.

Example
Consider a medical training program where students learn through a series of patient cases. In one episode, a patient arrives with vague symptoms like fatigue and fever. Learners gather clues through dialogue, order tests, and propose diagnoses. The episode concludes with feedback on their choices, revealing the patient had a rare infection. The next episode might escalate to a similar case with complications, deepening their diagnostic skills through connected narratives.

Benefits
This method fosters deep engagement by making learning memorable and emotionally resonant. It bridges theory and practice, helping learners apply abstract ideas to tangible scenarios. Retention improves as episodic memory ties knowledge to specific events. It also nurtures critical thinking and decision-making, as learners wrestle with consequences within a safe, simulated environment. Flexibility is another advantage, adapting easily to diverse topics and learner paces.

Applications
Episode-based learning thrives in settings requiring practical mastery or complex problem-solving. It's used in professional training, such as teaching nurses patient care through unfolding case studies, or in

corporate onboarding, where new hires navigate customer service dilemmas episode by episode. Education leverages it for history lessons, unfolding events like a story, while personal development courses might use it to build skills like negotiation through progressive scenarios.

Industries
Healthcare heavily adopts this approach for clinical simulations and patient management training. Education employs it across subjects to make lessons dynamic and relatable. Corporate sectors, especially sales, customer service, and leadership development, use it to simulate workplace challenges. Gaming and tech industries integrate it into interactive tutorials or software training, while military and emergency services apply it for tactical or crisis response drills.

Conclusions
Episode-based learning offers a powerful way to immerse learners in meaningful, context-rich experiences that mirror real life. Its strength lies in blending narrative with interactivity, fostering skills and insights that stick. While resource-heavy and challenging to perfect, its adaptability across fields makes it a versatile tool. When executed well, it transforms passive learning into an active journey, leaving lasting impressions that traditional methods often struggle to achieve.

Epistemic Game Theory in AI

Definition
Epistemic Game Theory in AI focuses on analyzing strategic interactions by considering the knowledge, beliefs, and reasoning capabilities of intelligent agents. It integrates concepts from game theory and epistemic logic to model how agents make decisions based on their beliefs about other agents' beliefs and intentions within strategic scenarios.

Key Components
Key components of epistemic game theory include agents, strategies, epistemic states (beliefs and knowledge), common knowledge assumptions, belief hierarchies (agents' beliefs about beliefs), decision-making rules, and equilibrium analysis.

Example
An example involves automated negotiations in AI-driven auctions, where bidding decisions depend on each bidder's beliefs about competitors' valuations. Epistemic game theory models these interactions, helping agents predict competitors' moves based on inferred knowledge and adjust their strategies accordingly.

Benefits
Benefits include improved strategic decision-making, more accurate prediction of behaviors, deeper understanding of interactions, and enhanced cooperation or competition modeling. It allows AI systems to better anticipate human and agent behaviors.

Applications
Applications cover economic simulations, automated negotiation systems, multi-agent robotic coordination, security and defense scenarios, online auctions, and collaborative decision-making platforms, especially where strategic foresight is crucial.

Industries
Industries adopting epistemic game theory include finance, economics, military defense, cybersecurity, robotics, online platforms, gaming, political strategy development, and social science research.

Conclusions
Epistemic game theory provides powerful analytical tools for AI systems, enabling sophisticated

reasoning about knowledge and beliefs in strategic interactions. While complexities persist, continued research and advancements promise broader applicability and enhanced decision-making capabilities.

Epistemic Logic in AI

Definition
Epistemic logic in AI is a branch of logic dedicated to representing and reasoning about knowledge, beliefs, and information states of agents within intelligent systems. It systematically models how knowledge is acquired, updated, and utilized in decision-making processes.

Key Components
Its primary components include knowledge representation formalisms, modal operators (such as "knowing" and "believing"), epistemic states, inference rules, knowledge bases, belief revision algorithms, and formal semantics to represent uncertainty.

Example
A classic example is an AI-powered virtual assistant using epistemic logic to infer user preferences or knowledge from interactions, updating its internal model to provide more relevant and contextually appropriate responses.

Benefits
Epistemic logic enables precise representation and reasoning about knowledge and beliefs, supports decision-making under uncertainty, improves reliability in AI inference mechanisms, and ensures consistency and coherence in complex systems.

Applications
Applications include knowledge-based systems, automated reasoning agents, intelligent assistants, cybersecurity threat detection, robotic navigation, automated troubleshooting systems, and intelligent tutoring systems.

Industries
Industries using epistemic logic include technology, cybersecurity, education, healthcare, robotics, automotive, gaming, customer support, and financial sectors, all benefiting from advanced reasoning and intelligent behavior modeling.

Conclusions
Epistemic logic significantly enriches AI's capability to reason about knowledge, enabling intelligent systems to handle uncertainty and complexity more effectively. Despite ongoing challenges, it remains essential in developing sophisticated, context-aware AI.

Epistemic Planning in AI

Definition
Epistemic planning in AI involves developing plans for intelligent agents that explicitly account for their knowledge and uncertainties. It integrates planning methods with epistemic logic to reason strategically about the acquisition and use of knowledge while executing tasks or achieving goals.

Key Components
Key components include planning algorithms, epistemic state representations, belief revision procedures, modal logic frameworks, knowledge bases, common knowledge assumptions, and mechanisms for handling uncertainty and partial observability.

Example
An autonomous drone performs epistemic planning to conduct surveillance, adjusting its flight path

dynamically based on real-time information gathered, updating beliefs about threats or target locations to optimize mission success.

Benefits
Benefits include more robust planning in uncertain and dynamic environments, greater adaptability and flexibility, informed decision-making under uncertainty, and enhanced strategic capabilities in changing contexts.

Applications
Epistemic planning applications include autonomous robotic navigation, military reconnaissance missions, intelligent virtual assistants, smart home automation systems, strategic decision-making tools, and adaptive educational software.

Industries
Industries employing epistemic planning include defense and security, robotics, automotive (autonomous vehicles), logistics, education technology, smart home technologies, and healthcare, benefiting from sophisticated and adaptive planning capabilities.

Conclusions
Epistemic planning enables AI systems to dynamically manage knowledge, enhancing responsiveness and adaptability in uncertain environments. Continued advancements will further empower AI systems to handle complex, uncertain scenarios more effectively.

Epistemic Reinforcement Learning

Definition
Epistemic reinforcement learning combines reinforcement learning methods with epistemic reasoning, focusing on learning strategies and making decisions by explicitly accounting for the uncertainty and knowledge states of agents within an environment.

Key Components
Main components include reinforcement learning algorithms, epistemic uncertainty measures, Bayesian inference methods, exploration-exploitation trade-offs, knowledge representation models, uncertainty-aware decision-making frameworks, and epistemic policy evaluation.

Example
A robot navigating an unfamiliar maze uses epistemic reinforcement learning to quantify uncertainty about its environment, strategically exploring uncertain paths to efficiently acquire new knowledge and improve its performance faster than standard methods.

Benefits
Epistemic reinforcement learning allows better handling of uncertainty, improved efficiency in learning by focusing exploration on unknown or uncertain areas, increased robustness of AI behavior, and more accurate decision-making under uncertainty.

Applications
Applications include autonomous vehicle navigation, robotic manipulation, strategic game playing, healthcare diagnostics optimization, adaptive educational systems, finance (investment strategy optimization), and dynamic resource allocation problems.

Industries
Industries leveraging epistemic reinforcement learning include robotics, healthcare, automotive, gaming, education, finance, manufacturing, logistics, and artificial intelligence research, achieving more efficient and reliable learning outcomes.

Conclusions
Epistemic reinforcement learning represents a significant advancement in intelligent systems by integrating knowledge-based reasoning with adaptive learning. While complexities persist, it promises improved performance in uncertain and dynamic settings.

Epistemic Uncertainty in AI

Definition
Epistemic uncertainty in AI refers to the uncertainty stemming from incomplete knowledge or lack of information about a system, data, or model. Unlike aleatoric uncertainty, epistemic uncertainty can potentially be reduced through acquiring additional information or knowledge.

Key Components
The key components include probabilistic modeling techniques, uncertainty quantification methods, Bayesian inference, predictive models, epistemic uncertainty metrics, and techniques for uncertainty propagation and reduction.

Example
A medical diagnosis AI system quantifies epistemic uncertainty when evaluating rare diseases due to limited historical data, signaling to doctors when confidence in predictions is low, prompting further testing or data gathering.

Benefits
Benefits include clearer identification of knowledge gaps, improved decision-making through awareness of uncertainties, better-informed risk management, improved safety in critical systems, and enhanced trust in AI predictions.

Applications
Epistemic uncertainty is considered in healthcare diagnostic systems, autonomous driving safety assessments, financial risk modeling, weather forecasting, predictive maintenance systems, environmental risk evaluations, and cybersecurity threat analysis.

Industries
Industries addressing epistemic uncertainty include healthcare, automotive, finance, environmental science, aerospace, cybersecurity, manufacturing, pharmaceuticals, and engineering, all benefiting from improved risk management and decision-making.

Conclusions
Effectively managing epistemic uncertainty significantly enhances AI system reliability and safety. Despite the complexities involved, advancing uncertainty quantification methods will provide greater transparency and robustness to AI-driven decision-making.

Epitope Mapping AI

Definition
Epitope mapping AI refers to computational methods using artificial intelligence, especially machine learning and bioinformatics, to identify specific sites (epitopes) on antigens that antibodies recognize, enhancing vaccine design and immune diagnostics.

Key Components
Key components include bioinformatics tools, sequence analysis algorithms, structural modeling software, deep learning methods, antibody-antigen interaction datasets, predictive analytics, and visualization systems.

Example
An AI-driven epitope mapping system rapidly identifies epitopes on a viral protein, enabling vaccine developers to efficiently select the most immunogenic regions, significantly accelerating vaccine candidate development.

Benefits
Benefits include rapid and accurate identification of epitopes, reduced time and cost in vaccine development, personalized immunotherapy potential, improved precision in diagnostics, and enhanced effectiveness of vaccines.

Applications
Applications include vaccine development, antibody-based drug design, immunotherapy, diagnostics, infectious disease research, personalized medicine, allergy testing, and autoimmune disease studies.

Industries
Industries using epitope mapping AI include pharmaceuticals, biotechnology, healthcare, research laboratories, diagnostics providers, veterinary medicine, and academic research institutions.

Conclusions
Epitope mapping AI significantly accelerates immunological research and therapeutic development, providing precise and rapid insights critical for next-generation vaccine design and immune therapeutics. Overcoming current challenges will further enhance its impact.

Epoch

Definition
In artificial intelligence, an epoch is a complete pass through an entire training dataset during the training of a machine learning model. It represents one cycle in the process of iterative optimization to improve model accuracy and performance.

Key Components
Components include training datasets, iterative optimization algorithms (such as gradient descent), learning rate adjustments, performance metrics, evaluation procedures, validation sets, and convergence criteria.

Example
During training of an image recognition AI, each epoch represents one cycle of processing all images in the training set. Multiple epochs refine model parameters, gradually improving classification accuracy.

Benefits
Epochs allow systematic improvement of model performance, facilitate monitoring of learning progress, reduce risks of overfitting by evaluating intermediate results, and help optimize computational resources effectively.

Applications
Epochs are fundamental in neural network training, deep learning model optimization, natural language processing training, image classification, speech recognition, predictive analytics, and reinforcement learning systems.

Industries
All AI-related industries, including technology, healthcare, finance, automotive, e-commerce, telecommunications, robotics, entertainment, and education, utilize epochs for efficient model training and evaluation.

Conclusions
Epochs are essential to AI model training, providing structure and measurable progress in learning. Careful management of epochs ensures efficient, effective training processes, significantly impacting overall AI performance and reliability.

Epoch in Neural Networks

Definition
An epoch in neural networks refers to a complete iteration through the entire training dataset during the training phase. It signifies one full cycle of feeding every data sample to the network, adjusting model parameters to optimize performance and minimize prediction errors.

Key Components
An epoch includes components such as training datasets, batch sizes, learning rate adjustments, parameter updates (weights and biases), optimization algorithms (gradient descent or variants), validation processes, and loss function evaluations.

Example
When training a neural network for recognizing images of animals, one epoch is completed after the network processes all training images exactly once. Multiple epochs help incrementally reduce classification errors until the model reaches an optimal performance.

Benefits
Epochs provide structured training phases that progressively enhance model accuracy, offer clear tracking of model performance improvements, and assist in early identification of overfitting or underfitting. They facilitate better allocation of computational resources and controlled model optimization.

Applications
Epochs are applied in deep learning, image recognition, speech recognition, natural language processing, autonomous driving systems, predictive analytics, and any machine learning tasks involving iterative optimization of neural networks.

Industries
Industries utilizing epochs include technology, healthcare diagnostics, finance for predictive modeling, automotive (autonomous vehicles), retail (customer analytics), telecommunications, robotics, entertainment, education, and research institutions.

Conclusions
Epochs are fundamental for effective neural network training, systematically improving model accuracy and reliability. Optimal management of epochs is critical for ensuring efficient, high-performance AI models across diverse applications.

Equal Error Rate (EER) in AI

Definition
Equal Error Rate (EER) in AI is a performance metric used primarily in biometric authentication systems, representing the threshold at which the false acceptance rate (incorrectly authenticating unauthorized users) equals the false rejection rate (incorrectly rejecting authorized users). EER serves as an indicator of system accuracy and reliability.

Key Components
Components of EER include biometric matching algorithms, threshold selection methods, false acceptance and false rejection calculations, performance analysis procedures, and evaluation datasets.

Example
In facial recognition systems, EER occurs at a threshold point where the likelihood of mistakenly granting access to an unauthorized person equals the probability of mistakenly denying access to an authorized person, indicating balanced performance.

Benefits
EER provides a clear, single-value performance indicator, simplifying comparison among different biometric systems. It helps organizations evaluate trade-offs between user convenience and system security effectively.

Applications
EER is widely used in biometric authentication, facial recognition, fingerprint scanning, voice verification systems, identity management platforms, security and surveillance systems, and mobile access control technologies.

Industries
Industries relying on EER include security services, law enforcement, banking and finance, telecommunications, healthcare, government identification programs, technology providers, and smart device manufacturers.

Conclusions
EER remains an essential metric for evaluating and optimizing biometric authentication systems. Although achieving extremely low EER values can be challenging, ongoing advancements aim to enhance biometric reliability and user acceptance.

Equality Constraints in AI

Definition
Equality constraints in AI refer to conditions specifying that particular variables, parameters, or functions must be equal within optimization problems, planning tasks, or machine learning algorithms. They ensure solutions satisfy predefined exact equality conditions during AI-driven computations.

Key Components
Equality constraints include constrained variables, mathematical equations enforcing exact equality, optimization algorithms (such as constrained gradient descent), constraint-handling methods (Lagrange multipliers), and solution feasibility checks.

Example
In route optimization problems, equality constraints ensure that vehicles must depart and arrive precisely at specific times, making the AI-driven solution strictly adhere to scheduling requirements.

Benefits
Equality constraints guarantee precise compliance with predefined conditions, improve accuracy of AI-based solutions, ensure consistency of results, and maintain adherence to strict operational or regulatory standards.

Applications
Equality constraints are utilized in supply chain logistics, transportation scheduling, financial portfolio optimization, industrial process control, robotic motion planning, energy management systems, and manufacturing processes.

Industries
Industries applying equality constraints include logistics, transportation, manufacturing, finance, energy management, robotics, aviation, healthcare, telecommunications, and construction, where precision and compliance are critical.

Conclusions
Equality constraints are crucial for ensuring AI solutions precisely meet specified conditions, enhancing accuracy and compliance. Despite challenges, their incorporation significantly boosts AI's capability to provide reliable and operationally feasible solutions.

Equilibrium Search in AI

Definition
Equilibrium Search in AI involves algorithms designed to find stable equilibrium points in complex systems or models, especially within game theory, economics, and multi-agent interactions. It identifies solutions where competing agents or systems reach stability with no incentive to deviate unilaterally.

Key Components
Core components include equilibrium concepts (such as Nash equilibrium), iterative algorithms for equilibrium identification, payoff matrices or utility functions, optimization techniques, agent behavior modeling, and computational methods for stability analysis.

Example
In automated trading markets, equilibrium search algorithms predict price equilibrium points where buyer and seller expectations align, enabling stable and efficient market operations.

Benefits
Equilibrium search provides efficient determination of stable solutions, enhanced predictability in multi-agent systems, improved strategy optimization, reduced uncertainty in decision-making, and effective resolution of conflicting objectives.

Applications
Applications include economic forecasting, market simulations, automated negotiations, supply-demand equilibrium modeling, strategic multi-agent AI coordination, auction systems, resource allocation strategies, and policy planning scenarios.

Industries
Industries using equilibrium search include finance, economics, supply chain management, transportation, energy markets, telecommunications, automated trading, cybersecurity, and strategic consulting, benefiting from stable and predictable solutions.

Conclusions
Equilibrium search significantly enhances AI's capability to solve complex strategic and multi-agent problems by efficiently identifying stable, optimized solutions. Addressing computational challenges will further strengthen its practical usability across industries.

Equity-Based AI

Definition
Equity-based AI involves designing artificial intelligence systems and algorithms that explicitly prioritize fairness, inclusivity, and equity, ensuring unbiased outcomes across different demographic groups and populations. It aims to mitigate biases, enhance fairness, and promote ethical AI practices by addressing systemic disparities.

Key Components
Core components include fairness algorithms, unbiased training datasets, equitable decision-making frameworks, ethical AI design principles, bias detection tools, continuous fairness monitoring, explainable AI methods, and regulatory compliance measures.

Example
An AI-driven recruitment platform implements equity-focused algorithms to minimize biases against minority applicants, ensuring fair and inclusive candidate evaluations and providing transparent insights into hiring decisions.

Benefits
Equity in AI ensures fair outcomes, reduces biases, promotes inclusivity, improves trustworthiness, enhances social responsibility, increases diversity in decision-making, and ensures compliance with ethical and legal standards.

Applications
Applications include equitable hiring processes, unbiased credit scoring, fair algorithmic lending, equitable healthcare diagnostics, unbiased facial recognition, educational admissions fairness, and equitable judicial decision-making tools.

Industries
Industries utilizing equity-focused AI include human resources, finance, healthcare, education, criminal justice, technology, social services, insurance, government, and retail, aiming for fair and unbiased outcomes.

Conclusions
Equity-focused AI promotes fair and inclusive decision-making, addressing societal biases effectively. Overcoming ongoing challenges is essential to ensure trustworthy, responsible, and socially beneficial AI solutions.

Equivalence Testing in AI

Definition
Equivalence testing in AI refers to statistical and computational techniques used to determine if two AI models or systems perform similarly enough to be considered effectively equivalent, especially within a defined margin of difference.

Key Components
Key components include hypothesis testing methods, equivalence margins (tolerance intervals), statistical validation procedures, performance metrics comparisons, confidence intervals, standardized data sets, and computational algorithms for performance analysis.

Example
A healthcare AI company conducts equivalence testing between an updated diagnostic AI model and its original version to ensure that both consistently provide equivalent results, allowing seamless model replacement without reducing patient care quality.

Benefits
Equivalence testing provides robust validation of alternative AI models, reduces risks associated with model upgrades, facilitates regulatory approval processes, ensures consistent performance, and supports effective model comparison and optimization.

Applications
Applications include model validation in healthcare diagnostics, pharmaceutical clinical trials analysis, quality assurance in manufacturing AI, algorithm replacement in finance predictive analytics, and consistent performance assessment in autonomous vehicle software.

Industries
Industries employing equivalence testing include healthcare, pharmaceuticals, manufacturing,

automotive, finance, regulatory bodies, AI software development, telecommunications, and robotics, benefiting from validated and reliable model deployments.

Conclusions
Equivalence testing is essential for validating and confidently deploying alternative AI models, ensuring consistent performance and reliability across various AI-driven applications and industries.

Equivalent Classes in AI

Definition
Equivalent classes in AI represent groups of inputs or conditions considered similar or equivalent for the purposes of testing, classification, or data processing, enabling AI systems to generalize efficiently across categories sharing common properties or behaviors.

Key Components
Components include classification criteria, partitioning algorithms, data grouping methods, clustering techniques, feature extraction, similarity measures, equivalence partitioning, and validation procedures.

Example
An AI-driven email filtering system groups messages into equivalent classes based on similar characteristics (such as spam or non-spam), enabling efficient training and enhanced accuracy by analyzing representative samples from each class.

Benefits
Equivalent classes simplify model training and validation, reduce computational complexity, enhance efficiency in handling large datasets, improve model generalization and performance, facilitate better data management, and streamline testing processes.

Applications
Applications include software testing, data clustering, anomaly detection, automated email filtering, customer segmentation, image classification, speech recognition, data mining, predictive modeling, and fraud detection systems.

Industries
Industries employing equivalent classes include information technology, finance, cybersecurity, healthcare, telecommunications, e-commerce, education technology, and manufacturing, benefiting from efficient data analysis and streamlined model development.

Conclusions
Equivalent classes in AI significantly enhance efficiency and effectiveness in model training and validation. While challenges exist, effective implementation leads to streamlined data processing, improved accuracy, and reduced computational complexity.

Equivariance in AI

Definition
Equivariance in AI refers to the property of machine learning models or neural networks to consistently reflect transformations applied to input data directly in their outputs. Equivariant models reliably preserve structural relationships such as rotations, translations, and scaling of input data.

Key Components
Key components include symmetry-preserving neural network architectures, transformation-equivariant layers, group-equivariant convolutions, geometric deep learning models, transformation-specific encoding mechanisms, and invariance constraints.

Example
An equivariant neural network analyzing medical images of tumors accurately predicts tumor location irrespective of image rotation or translation, ensuring consistent diagnostics regardless of how the imaging device captures the data.

Benefits
Equivariance enhances model robustness, reduces data requirements, increases generalization ability, maintains interpretability under transformations, improves accuracy, and provides consistent predictions despite input variations.

Applications
Applications include medical imaging analysis, autonomous vehicle navigation, robotics manipulation, computer vision tasks, geographic mapping, molecular structure prediction, and astronomy image analysis.

Industries
Industries leveraging equivariance include healthcare imaging, robotics, automotive, aerospace, biotechnology, pharmaceuticals, geographic information systems, astronomy, manufacturing, and computer vision-driven technology sectors.

Conclusions
Equivariant models significantly enhance the robustness, interpretability, and generalization of AI systems, especially in tasks sensitive to structural transformations. Continued development will expand their utility across diverse industries and complex scenarios.

Error Backpropagation

Definition
Error Backpropagation is a supervised learning algorithm widely used in training artificial neural networks. It calculates prediction errors at the output layer, propagates them backward through the network layers, and iteratively adjusts network parameters to minimize prediction errors.

Key Components
Components include neural network layers, loss functions, forward pass computations, gradient calculations, weight and bias updates, activation functions, optimization algorithms (such as gradient descent), and learning rate adjustments.

Example
A neural network for recognizing handwritten digits uses error backpropagation to iteratively update model weights based on the difference between predicted and actual digit labels, continuously reducing recognition errors.

Benefits
Error backpropagation enables efficient training of complex neural networks, reduces prediction errors significantly, allows automatic fine-tuning of model parameters, facilitates rapid convergence, and supports scalable learning across large datasets.

Applications
Applications span image and speech recognition, natural language processing, autonomous driving, predictive analytics, financial forecasting, medical diagnostics, pattern recognition, and robotic control systems.

Industries
Industries employing backpropagation include technology, finance, healthcare, automotive,

telecommunications, retail analytics, robotics, cybersecurity, manufacturing, and artificial intelligence research and development.

Conclusions
Error backpropagation remains central to training effective, high-performance neural networks. Continued optimization of training methods ensures improved predictive accuracy, robustness, and broad applicability in AI systems.

Error Correction in AI

Definition
Error correction in AI refers to computational techniques and algorithms designed to detect, identify, and rectify inaccuracies or errors in data, predictions, decisions, or communications produced by artificial intelligence systems, ensuring reliability and accuracy.

Key Components
Core components include error detection algorithms, correction protocols, redundancy mechanisms, neural network-based correction models, statistical methods, real-time monitoring, anomaly detection systems, and automated feedback loops.

Example
A speech recognition AI employs error correction algorithms to identify and automatically correct transcription errors, significantly enhancing accuracy and user experience during voice-to-text conversions.

Benefits
Error correction improves data accuracy, enhances reliability and trustworthiness of AI systems, reduces risks associated with incorrect decisions, minimizes human intervention, boosts user satisfaction, and supports robust operational performance.

Applications
Applications include communication systems, autonomous vehicle guidance, predictive text systems, medical imaging diagnostics, automated manufacturing processes, financial modeling accuracy, cybersecurity threat detection, and speech recognition.

Industries
Industries using error correction include telecommunications, healthcare, automotive, aerospace, finance, cybersecurity, robotics, manufacturing, education, technology development, and data management providers.

Conclusions
Error correction is crucial for maintaining the accuracy and reliability of AI systems. Ongoing improvements in correction methods and algorithms significantly enhance AI performance, trustworthiness, and applicability across critical applications.

Error Propagation in AI

Definition
Error propagation in AI describes the process by which inaccuracies or errors introduced in earlier stages of computations or data processing impact subsequent results or predictions, potentially magnifying overall errors within artificial intelligence systems.

Key Components
The main components include initial data errors, computational inaccuracies, sequential dependency

between model layers, feedback loops in neural networks, sensitivity analysis methods, error tracking tools, and correction mechanisms to mitigate error propagation.

Example
In a multi-layer neural network used for weather forecasting, an error in initial temperature measurement can propagate through successive layers, significantly altering the final weather prediction, illustrating how minor inaccuracies become magnified.

Benefits
Understanding error propagation helps improve AI model reliability, enables better error tracking and mitigation, supports accuracy optimization, enhances data quality management, and increases robustness in AI-driven predictions.

Applications
Applications include predictive modeling, financial forecasting, medical diagnostics, weather prediction models, robotics navigation systems, autonomous vehicles, communication systems, and real-time monitoring AI platforms.

Industries
Industries addressing error propagation include finance, healthcare, meteorology, aerospace, automotive, telecommunications, robotics, manufacturing, cybersecurity, and AI research and development.

Conclusions
Effective management of error propagation enhances AI accuracy, reliability, and overall performance. Despite existing complexities, ongoing advancements promise greater predictive precision and robustness across various AI applications.

Error Rate in AI

Definition
Error rate in AI refers to the frequency or proportion of incorrect predictions or outputs generated by an artificial intelligence model, used as a fundamental performance metric to assess and optimize model accuracy and reliability.

Key Components
Key components include prediction output evaluation, ground truth data, confusion matrices, false-positive and false-negative calculations, error analysis procedures, benchmarking tools, and performance metrics such as accuracy, precision, and recall.

Example
An AI-based facial recognition system exhibits a 5% error rate, indicating that 5 out of every 100 faces identified by the system were incorrectly recognized, guiding developers to further enhance accuracy.

Benefits
Measuring error rate provides clear insights into model accuracy, facilitates performance comparisons, supports continuous improvement, helps identify weak points in AI systems, and promotes accountability in predictive outputs.

Applications
Applications include biometric authentication systems, speech recognition software, automated diagnostics, customer analytics, predictive maintenance systems, image classification, fraud detection, and autonomous driving systems.

Industries
Industries utilizing error rate assessments include healthcare, finance, security, automotive, technology development, telecommunications, robotics, education, and AI-driven customer support platforms.

Conclusions
Error rate remains a critical indicator of AI system performance, essential for improving accuracy, reliability, and user trust. Continuous monitoring and reduction efforts significantly enhance AI effectiveness across diverse industries.

Error Surface in AI

Definition
An error surface in AI represents a multi-dimensional visualization of errors or loss values generated by a neural network or AI model, typically plotted against varying parameters or weights. It aids in understanding optimization behavior, convergence properties, and stability during training.

Key Components
Key components include model parameters (weights and biases), loss functions, optimization algorithms (gradient descent), visualization techniques, convergence analysis tools, and critical points such as minima, maxima, and saddle points.

Example
When training a neural network for stock market prediction, the error surface visualizes how adjusting model parameters affects prediction accuracy, guiding the optimization algorithm toward the optimal parameter configuration.

Benefits
Visualizing the error surface helps understand model behavior, guides efficient parameter optimization, identifies potential convergence issues, enhances algorithm stability, and provides insights for improving AI model accuracy.

Applications
Applications include neural network training, machine learning optimization, deep learning model refinement, predictive analytics tuning, automated hyperparameter optimization, and performance debugging in complex AI models.

Industries
Industries employing error surface analysis include finance, technology development, healthcare diagnostics, automotive, aerospace, manufacturing process optimization, robotics, telecommunications, and artificial intelligence research.

Conclusions
Analyzing the error surface significantly enhances AI model optimization and performance. Despite visualization complexity, understanding error surfaces remains crucial for achieving efficient, robust, and accurate AI-driven predictions.

Escalation Algorithms in AI

Definition
Escalation algorithms in AI are computational procedures designed to progressively elevate decision-making, actions, or alerts within automated systems based on predefined criteria or thresholds, ensuring timely intervention and appropriate response escalation.

Key Components
Components include escalation criteria, threshold triggers, prioritization logic, alert generation mechanisms, decision automation modules, real-time monitoring, response protocols, and integration with human oversight systems.

Example
In cybersecurity, an AI-powered escalation algorithm automatically elevates threat alerts from initial detection to higher levels of scrutiny or human intervention when a threat reaches specific risk thresholds, ensuring rapid response and mitigation.

Benefits
Escalation algorithms provide timely issue detection and response, ensure efficient resource allocation, enhance operational effectiveness, improve decision-making accuracy, and enable smooth integration of automated and manual processes.

Applications
Applications include cybersecurity incident management, automated customer support systems, healthcare patient monitoring alerts, financial fraud detection, emergency response coordination, and industrial safety protocols.

Industries
Industries employing escalation algorithms include cybersecurity, finance, healthcare, telecommunications, manufacturing safety systems, customer service automation, logistics, transportation, and emergency management services.

Conclusions
Escalation algorithms effectively automate critical decision-making processes, ensuring timely and accurate interventions. Addressing ongoing challenges is crucial for optimizing their reliability and effectiveness across diverse AI-driven scenarios.

Esoteric Programming in AI

Definition
Esoteric programming in AI refers to the use or creation of intentionally unconventional, creative, or obscure programming languages and approaches within artificial intelligence development, often as experimental methods to explore alternative AI design principles or for artistic expression.

Key Components
Components include unconventional programming languages, unique syntax or coding rules, experimental computational paradigms, creativity-driven algorithm design, conceptual exploration, and niche programming environments.

Example
An AI researcher develops an esoteric programming language designed explicitly for neural network experiments, using symbolic expressions or unconventional syntax to explore novel ways of representing AI models creatively.

Benefits
Esoteric programming encourages innovation and creative exploration, provides insights into unconventional computational paradigms, fosters unique problem-solving perspectives, promotes experimental learning, and broadens the diversity of AI design approaches.

Applications
Applications include educational tools for creative coding, artistic computational projects, experimental AI research, exploratory software development, game design, and niche algorithm experimentation.

Industries
Industries and areas embracing esoteric programming include academia, experimental AI research, interactive art and multimedia, creative education programs, gaming industry, technology innovation labs, and AI-driven artistic projects.

Conclusions
Esoteric programming in AI offers valuable opportunities for creativity, experimentation, and innovation, though practical adoption remains limited. Embracing unconventional approaches enriches AI's conceptual landscape, encouraging continuous exploration and learning.

Etiquette AI

Definition
Etiquette AI involves artificial intelligence systems designed to recognize, interpret, and respond appropriately to social, cultural, or professional etiquette standards during human-AI interactions. It aims to enhance the social appropriateness, politeness, and context-awareness of AI-driven communication.

Key Components
Etiquette AI includes sentiment analysis, social context recognition, natural language understanding, cultural sensitivity algorithms, politeness detection modules, adaptive conversational frameworks, and empathy-driven interaction designs.

Example
An AI virtual assistant utilizes Etiquette AI to adapt communication style and language based on cultural context, ensuring respectful, polite interactions when addressing users from diverse backgrounds.

Benefits
Etiquette AI enhances user experience, improves AI-human interactions, fosters cultural inclusivity, increases trust and comfort in AI interactions, reduces misunderstandings, and promotes positive communication dynamics.

Applications
Applications include virtual assistants, customer support chatbots, automated email responders, social robots, professional communication tools, intercultural business interactions, educational technologies, and digital companions.

Industries
Industries employing Etiquette AI include customer service, hospitality, healthcare, education, international business, human resources, telecommunications, tourism, and social robotics.

Conclusions
Etiquette AI significantly improves social interactions between humans and AI, enhancing communication quality, cultural sensitivity, and user satisfaction. Continued improvements in cultural awareness and context interpretation will further extend its benefits globally.

Etymological Analysis in AI

Definition
Etymological analysis in AI refers to using computational methods and machine learning algorithms to analyze, trace, and interpret the origins, historical developments, and semantic evolution of words and languages. It leverages linguistic datasets and natural language processing techniques to understand language development systematically.

Key Components
Key components include historical linguistic datasets, computational text analysis, machine learning algorithms for semantic tracking, natural language processing (NLP) modules, linguistic knowledge bases, and automated pattern recognition for linguistic shifts.

Example
An AI-powered educational platform utilizes etymological analysis to provide students with detailed insights into the historical origins and evolution of vocabulary words, enriching language learning experiences through interactive storytelling.

Benefits
Etymological analysis enhances language understanding, improves semantic clarity in language models, supports historical linguistic research, facilitates deeper educational insights, enriches language learning experiences, and increases cultural awareness.

Applications
Applications include language education tools, digital dictionaries, linguistic research platforms, automated translation improvements, semantic search engines, linguistic databases, and historical text analysis.

Industries
Industries benefiting include education technology, linguistics, publishing, digital humanities research, AI-driven language platforms, digital archiving, translation services, and content creation platforms.

Conclusions
AI-driven etymological analysis significantly enhances linguistic understanding and educational experiences. Addressing data quality and interpretive accuracy challenges will expand its educational and linguistic research applications.

Evolutionary Neural Networks

Definition
Evolutionary Neural Networks (E-NNs) integrate evolutionary algorithms with neural network models, using natural selection and genetic processes to optimize neural network architectures, structures, and parameters. This approach enables automatic design and improvement of neural networks through evolutionary methods, enhancing performance beyond traditional manual tuning.

Key Components
Key components include neural network architectures, genetic algorithms, evolutionary strategies, mutation and crossover operations, fitness evaluation functions, population-based optimization, and adaptive structural evolution methods.

Example
A robotic navigation system uses evolutionary neural networks to iteratively optimize the network structure and parameters, progressively improving pathfinding and obstacle avoidance performance in complex environments without manual tuning.

Benefits
Evolutionary neural networks automate model optimization, reduce human intervention, improve

network adaptability, efficiently handle complex problems, and achieve better performance by exploring diverse solutions and structures.

Applications
Applications include automated system optimization, robotics, autonomous vehicles, complex pattern recognition, adaptive game strategies, financial modeling optimization, predictive maintenance systems, and advanced healthcare diagnostics.

Industries
Industries benefiting from evolutionary neural networks include robotics, automotive, finance, healthcare diagnostics, telecommunications, aerospace, gaming, logistics, manufacturing, and artificial intelligence research.

Conclusions
Evolutionary neural networks significantly advance AI optimization and adaptability by automating the design and refinement process. Despite computational challenges, their ability to evolve effective, robust solutions positions them prominently in complex problem-solving scenarios.

Evolutionary Tuning in AI

Definition
Evolutionary tuning in AI refers to utilizing evolutionary algorithms and genetic-inspired methods to automatically optimize and adjust parameters, configurations, or models in artificial intelligence systems, enhancing their performance without extensive human intervention.

Key Components
Core components include genetic algorithms, population-based optimization, parameter mutation and crossover mechanisms, fitness evaluation metrics, adaptive learning processes, iterative refinement techniques, and dynamic configuration adjustment procedures.

Example
An AI-powered financial prediction platform employs evolutionary tuning to automatically adjust algorithm parameters such as learning rate and model architecture, optimizing predictive accuracy in forecasting stock prices without manual fine-tuning.

Benefits
Evolutionary tuning enhances performance efficiency, significantly reduces manual tuning efforts, discovers optimal parameter combinations automatically, improves adaptive capabilities, and accelerates AI model optimization.

Applications
Applications include automated model parameter tuning, resource allocation optimization, machine learning hyperparameter optimization, industrial process control, predictive maintenance optimization, and adaptive robotics control systems.

Industries
Industries employing evolutionary tuning include finance, healthcare, robotics, manufacturing, automotive, telecommunications, cybersecurity, aerospace, logistics, gaming, and AI research and development sectors.

Conclusions
Evolutionary tuning significantly streamlines AI optimization processes, providing enhanced model performance and adaptability. Addressing computational and convergence challenges will further expand its practical applicability and impact.

Explainable AI (XAI)

Definition
Explainable AI (XAI) refers to artificial intelligence methodologies and technologies designed to provide transparency and clarity about how AI systems reach decisions or predictions. XAI enables human users to understand, trust, and effectively manage AI-driven outcomes through clear explanations and insights.

Key Components
Key components include transparency-focused algorithms, explanation generation modules, interpretable AI models .

(such as decision trees or rule-based systems), visual analytics interfaces, causal reasoning mechanisms, feature importance tools, and regulatory compliance frameworks.

Example
An AI-driven healthcare diagnostic tool uses XAI to explain its predictions clearly to doctors, indicating precisely which patient symptoms or medical test results contributed most significantly to a diagnosis, thereby increasing trust and aiding clinical decisions.

Benefits
XAI enhances AI transparency, fosters user trust, facilitates regulatory compliance, supports informed decision-making, promotes ethical AI deployment, improves accountability, and reduces risk associated with opaque AI processes.

Applications
XAI is utilized in healthcare diagnostics, finance credit decisions, automated recruitment platforms, legal decision support systems, fraud detection algorithms, autonomous vehicles, military and security systems, customer support platforms, and educational AI tools.

Industries
Industries adopting XAI include healthcare, finance, insurance, legal, automotive, government agencies, cybersecurity, human resources, telecommunications, and education, driven by the need for trustworthy, understandable, and compliant AI systems.

Conclusions
XAI is critical for enabling responsible, trustworthy AI adoption. Continuous advancements in interpretability methods will further bridge the gap between AI complexity and human understanding, expanding practical applications and societal acceptance.

EZML (Easy Machine Learning)

Definition
EZML (Easy Machine Learning) refers to simplified, user-friendly machine learning platforms, tools, and methodologies designed to enable users without advanced technical expertise to quickly implement, train, and deploy machine learning models effectively.

Key Components
Core components include intuitive interfaces, pre-built model templates, drag-and-drop functionalities, automated data preprocessing tools, easy-to-understand model training procedures, simplified deployment capabilities, and accessible model performance visualizations.

Example
A small retail business uses an EZML platform to quickly develop a sales prediction model by simply

uploading sales data and selecting automated training options, enabling precise inventory management without complex coding.

Benefits
EZML reduces technical complexity, accelerates model development and deployment, expands machine learning accessibility, minimizes the need for specialized expertise, fosters widespread AI adoption, and facilitates rapid experimentation.

Applications
EZML tools are applied in predictive analytics, customer segmentation, inventory forecasting, automated marketing campaigns, fraud detection, sentiment analysis, product recommendation systems, and customer behavior modeling.

Industries
Industries benefiting from EZML include retail, marketing, finance, healthcare, education, small and medium enterprises (SMEs), manufacturing, and customer service sectors, leveraging simplicity and rapid AI implementation.

Conclusions
EZML significantly democratizes access to powerful AI and machine learning tools, enabling non-experts to leverage predictive capabilities. Addressing customization and accuracy challenges will further enhance EZML's practical effectiveness and adoption.

EzAI (Ease of Use AI Tools)

Definition
EzAI encompasses user-friendly artificial intelligence platforms, tools, and services specifically designed to enable straightforward implementation and utilization of advanced AI technologies by users without deep technical expertise or coding skills.

Key Components
Key components include simplified user interfaces, intuitive design principles, pre-trained AI models, guided model training processes, automated machine learning (AutoML) features, visual analytics tools, and integrated user support systems.

Example
A marketing manager employs EzAI tools to analyze customer sentiment automatically from social media posts without requiring coding, quickly gaining insights for strategic campaign decisions.

Benefits
EzAI reduces barriers to AI adoption, speeds up AI integration, requires minimal technical training, empowers non-technical users, reduces deployment costs, promotes broader innovation, and enhances user productivity.

Applications
EzAI applications include customer sentiment analysis, automated content moderation, simplified predictive modeling, chatbot development, personalized marketing automation, document classification, inventory optimization, and HR talent analytics.

Industries
Industries adopting EzAI include retail, marketing, human resources, customer service, finance, healthcare, education, real estate, SMEs, and various technology sectors, benefiting from accessible AI tools.

Conclusions
EzAI greatly enhances AI accessibility and integration for diverse users, providing immediate business value. Continuous improvements addressing customization and reliability challenges will further boost its adoption and effectiveness.

EZ Analytics in AI

Definition
EZ Analytics in AI is a simplified, accessible approach to data analysis powered by artificial intelligence, designed to deliver actionable insights without requiring advanced technical expertise. It harnesses AI to process and interpret data quickly, presenting results in an intuitive format that empowers users to make informed decisions effortlessly.

Key Components
At its heart, EZ Analytics in AI features user-friendly dashboards that visualize data trends and patterns clearly. It employs automated AI algorithms to sift through datasets, identifying key metrics or anomalies without manual intervention. Pre-built templates cater to common analysis needs, while natural language processing allows users to query data conversationally. Real-time updates ensure insights stay current, and integration with common tools enhances its practicality.

Example
Picture a small coffee shop owner using EZ Analytics in AI to boost sales. The system analyzes daily transactions, weather data, and foot traffic, displaying a simple chart showing that rainy days spike latte orders. With a voice command like "What sells best on weekends?" the owner learns pastries outperform muffins. Armed with this, they adjust inventory, all without needing to understand data science.

Benefits
This method makes analytics approachable, enabling non-experts to leverage data effectively. It saves time by automating complex processes, delivering fast results. Cost-effective and scalable, it reduces reliance on specialists or expensive software. It boosts decision-making confidence with clear, digestible insights, and its adaptability ensures relevance across varying needs, fostering a data-driven mindset with minimal effort.

Applications
EZ Analytics in AI fits small businesses tracking sales or customer preferences. Individuals might use it to monitor personal fitness trends from wearable devices. Teachers could analyze student performance to tailor lessons, while marketers assess campaign success through simplified metrics. Hobbyists might explore it for passion projects, like studying gaming stats or gardening yields.

Industries
Retail thrives on it for inventory and customer insights, especially in small-scale operations. Education benefits from its use in tracking learning outcomes. Fitness and wellness industries apply it to personalize user experiences. Marketing leverages it for quick campaign analysis, and hospitality uses it to optimize pricing or guest satisfaction. Creative fields like content creation also tap it for audience engagement trends.

Conclusions
EZ Analytics in AI bridges the gap between raw data and practical understanding, empowering users with limited skills to harness AI's potential. Its strength lies in delivering clarity and speed, democratizing analytics for everyday use. While it may not replace expert-level tools, it excels as an entry point, fostering broader adoption. To endure, it must balance ease with robustness, proving that simplicity can unlock sophisticated insights without overwhelming its audience.

EZ Fraud Detection in AI

Definition
EZ Fraud Detection in AI refers to a streamlined, user-friendly approach to identifying fraudulent activities using artificial intelligence, designed to simplify the process for non-experts while maintaining accuracy. It leverages AI algorithms to detect anomalies, patterns, or behaviors indicative of fraud, focusing on ease of implementation and accessibility across various skill levels.

Key Components
The core of EZ Fraud Detection in AI includes intuitive interfaces that allow users to interact with the system without deep technical knowledge. It relies on pre-trained machine learning models that analyze data for fraud signals, such as unusual transactions or identity mismatches. Automated data processing handles large volumes quickly, while real-time monitoring flags issues as they occur. Simplified reporting tools provide clear, actionable insights, ensuring the system is practical for everyday use.

Example
Imagine a small online retailer using EZ Fraud Detection in AI to protect against payment fraud. The system scans daily transactions, spotting a sudden spike in high-value orders from a new account using multiple credit cards. It flags this as suspicious, alerts the owner via a simple dashboard, and suggests holding the orders for review. The retailer, without AI expertise, resolves the issue using the tool's straightforward guidance, preventing a loss.

Benefits
This approach lowers the barrier to entry, enabling businesses or individuals without advanced skills to combat fraud effectively. It saves time by automating complex analysis, reducing manual oversight. Cost-efficiency comes from its plug-and-play nature, avoiding the need for custom-built solutions. It enhances security by catching fraud early, minimizing financial damage, and adapts to new threats through AI learning, offering long-term reliability.

Applications
EZ Fraud Detection in AI suits small businesses monitoring e-commerce transactions for unauthorized purchases. It's useful in personal banking, where individuals can track account activity for signs of identity theft. Freelancers or gig workers can apply it to verify client payments, while educational platforms might use it to detect fake enrollments. Nonprofits could deploy it to safeguard donations from fraudulent schemes.

Industries
Retail, especially online stores, benefits from its simplicity in tackling payment fraud. Banking and fintech use it for accessible customer protection tools. The gig economy relies on it to secure freelance transactions. Education leverages it to maintain integrity in online courses, and the nonprofit sector employs it to ensure donor trust. It also fits healthcare for basic insurance fraud detection.

Conclusions
EZ Fraud Detection in AI democratizes fraud prevention, making powerful technology approachable for smaller players and non-experts. Its strength lies in balancing usability with effectiveness, offering a practical shield against common threats. While it may not rival complex systems in depth, its accessibility fills a critical gap. For broader success, it must evolve to address diverse fraud landscapes while preserving its core simplicity, proving that ease and security can coexist in AI-driven solutions.

EZ NLP (Natural Language Processing)

Definition
EZ NLP (Natural Language Processing) refers to streamlined tools and frameworks designed to simplify the implementation and use of Natural Language Processing technologies. It aims to make

NLP accessible and user-friendly for non-experts by providing easy-to-use interfaces and simplified processes to analyze, interpret, and generate human language.

Key Components

The primary components of EZ NLP include user-friendly interfaces for data input, pre-built language models, integrated text analytics tools, sentiment analysis engines, language translation capabilities, and natural language generation (NLG) systems. Additional elements include data preprocessing modules, customizable pipelines, and visualization dashboards to simplify interpreting results.

Example

An example of EZ NLP in action is a customer feedback analysis tool used by businesses. Users input customer reviews or feedback, and the system quickly provides sentiment analysis and summarizes key insights automatically, enabling companies to identify trends, customer emotions, and product feedback easily.

Benefits

EZ NLP significantly simplifies the complexity associated with traditional natural language processing technologies. It reduces development time and effort, enables rapid deployment, and democratizes access to advanced NLP tools by non-technical users. Furthermore, its ease of use ensures greater adoption, improved accuracy through pre-trained models, and quick, actionable insights from textual data.

Applications

EZ NLP is widely applied in customer service automation, social media monitoring, chatbots and virtual assistants, customer feedback analysis, content moderation, and translation services. It is also used extensively in text summarization, information retrieval, email filtering, document classification, and sentiment analysis in social media platforms.

Industries

Industries leveraging EZ NLP technology include customer service, marketing, healthcare, finance, retail, education, technology, and legal services. In customer service, it aids chatbots in providing immediate and accurate responses. Healthcare applications include analyzing medical documents and patient communications for improved patient care. In finance, EZ NLP supports sentiment analysis and market prediction based on textual data.

Conclusions

EZ NLP significantly simplifies the deployment and utilization of natural language processing, offering immediate benefits to organizations across various industries. By removing technical barriers, it enables users to rapidly implement NLP-driven solutions, gain deeper insights from textual data, and enhance decision-making processes. Despite existing challenges, its advantages in accessibility, speed, and accuracy make EZ LP an essential component of modern AI applications.

EZ Predictive Analytics

Definition

EZ Predictive Analytics refers to simplified, accessible predictive analytics tools and platforms that allow users without advanced analytics or technical backgrounds to analyze historical data, identify patterns, and generate reliable forecasts to support strategic decision-making.

Key Components

Core components include easy-to-use predictive modeling tools, automated data processing pipelines, pre-built forecasting algorithms, visual analytics dashboards, simplified reporting modules, drag-and-drop functionalities, and intuitive user interfaces.

Example
A hospitality company uses EZ Predictive Analytics to forecast occupancy rates effortlessly by inputting historical booking data, enabling accurate resource planning and targeted marketing campaigns without specialized analytical skills.

Benefits
EZ Predictive Analytics enables rapid decision-making, reduces complexity and costs, enhances forecasting accuracy, democratizes advanced analytics, promotes data-driven insights across organizational levels, and facilitates agile strategic planning.

Applications
Applications include sales forecasting, inventory management, demand prediction, financial planning, customer churn analysis, staffing forecasts, market trend analysis, predictive maintenance scheduling, and operational efficiency optimization.

Industries
Industries leveraging EZ Predictive Analytics include retail, hospitality, finance, healthcare, manufacturing, logistics, education, energy management, telecommunications, SMEs, and various customer-focused sectors.

Conclusions
EZ Predictive Analytics provides essential capabilities for informed strategic decisions, significantly expanding analytics accessibility. Continuous refinement will ensure accurate, user-friendly predictive insights and wider organizational adoption.

LETTER F

Facial Emotion Recognition (FER)

Definition
Facial Emotion Recognition (FER) is an artificial intelligence technique that identifies and classifies human emotional states by analyzing facial expressions through machine learning and computer vision technologies.

Key Components
Facial emotion recognition includes components such as image acquisition, face detection algorithms, feature extraction methods, emotion classification models (like deep learning neural networks), real-time processing systems, and emotional expression databases.

Example
A customer service chatbot equipped with FER analyzes customer facial expressions via a webcam during support interactions, detecting emotions like frustration or satisfaction, and adapts its responses to improve customer experiences.

Benefits
FER improves human-computer interactions, enhances user experience, enables emotional context understanding, supports personalized services, and provides insights into human emotional behaviors.

Applications
Applications include virtual assistants, interactive gaming, customer experience analytics, mental health monitoring, driver emotion detection in vehicles, marketing effectiveness analysis, and human-computer interaction enhancements.

Industries
Industries adopting FER include healthcare, retail, automotive, gaming, entertainment, customer service, marketing, education technology, security, and human resource management.

Conclusions
FER significantly enhances AI's capability to interpret human emotions, improving communication, empathy, and interaction quality across multiple sectors. Addressing privacy and data challenges will further increase its acceptance and practical use.

Facial Feature Extraction

Definition
Facial Feature Extraction in AI involves the automated detection, identification, and measurement of critical facial attributes or landmarks from images or videos using computer vision and machine learning algorithms.

Key Components
Core components include facial detection algorithms, image preprocessing tools, feature extraction techniques (such as edge detection, texture analysis, deep learning models), landmark mapping, dimensionality reduction, and classification modules.

Example
A biometric authentication system uses facial feature extraction to identify unique attributes like distance between eyes, shape of nose, or jawline contours, enabling secure facial recognition for user login.

Benefits
Facial feature extraction ensures accurate and efficient identification, supports automation of facial analysis tasks, enhances security measures, provides personalized user experiences, and streamlines facial data analysis.

Applications
Applications include facial recognition security systems, biometric identification, virtual reality (VR) and augmented reality (AR) applications, digital avatar creation, personalized advertising, and healthcare diagnostics (such as genetic trait identification).

Industries
Industries employing facial feature extraction include security, retail, healthcare, entertainment, gaming, financial services, law enforcement, transportation, and social media platforms.

Conclusions
Facial feature extraction is vital for accurate facial analysis and identification tasks. Despite technical and ethical challenges, ongoing advancements will enhance its precision and acceptance across various industries.

Facial Landmark Detection

Definition
Facial Landmark Detection refers to identifying and locating predefined points or regions of interest on human faces within images or videos, serving as critical references for further facial analysis tasks such as recognition, tracking, or expression interpretation.

Key Components
Key components include image processing algorithms, deep learning neural networks, landmark localization techniques, face alignment procedures, annotated datasets for training, feature point regression methods, and real-time tracking modules.

Example
A smartphone camera app uses facial landmark detection to apply precise augmented reality filters by accurately aligning graphical effects with users' facial features such as eyes, mouth, and nose in real-time.

Benefits
Facial landmark detection enables accurate facial alignment, improves performance in facial recognition systems, facilitates augmented reality experiences, supports emotional and behavioral analysis, and enhances interaction accuracy in AI applications.

Applications
Applications include augmented reality filters, face-swapping apps, facial motion capture in animation, emotion detection systems, biometric authentication, virtual makeup applications, and healthcare facial analysis.

Industries
Industries leveraging facial landmark detection include entertainment, gaming, social media, beauty technology, security, healthcare, animation production, automotive driver-assistance systems, and marketing.

Conclusions
Facial landmark detection is essential for accurate facial analysis and user interaction experiences. Continued refinement in accuracy and real-time processing capabilities will enhance its applications and effectiveness across diverse sectors.

Factorization Machines

Definition
Factorization Machines (FMs) in AI are predictive models designed to handle high-dimensional, sparse datasets by efficiently modeling interactions between variables using factorized parameters, especially useful in recommendation systems and classification tasks.

Key Components
Factorization Machines include components such as feature vectors, latent factor interactions, linear and pairwise interaction modeling, efficient training algorithms (e.g., stochastic gradient descent), optimization methods, and prediction functions.

Example
An online shopping platform implements FMs to predict product recommendations by modeling interactions between user preferences and product attributes, providing personalized suggestions based on historical interactions.

Benefits
Factorization Machines efficiently handle sparse data, capture complex interactions among features, reduce computational complexity, enhance predictive accuracy, improve scalability, and support real-time recommendation generation.

Applications
Applications include recommendation engines, click-through rate prediction, customer behavior modeling, personalized advertising, fraud detection, and predictive analytics across various business sectors.

Industries
Industries using factorization machines include e-commerce, advertising, entertainment, finance, telecommunications, online media platforms, social networking, and marketing analytics.

Conclusions
Factorization Machines effectively capture complex variable interactions, offering significant value in predictive modeling and recommendation systems. Continued improvements in scalability and interpretability will further expand their applicability.

Factual AI

Definition
Factual AI involves artificial intelligence systems specifically developed to verify, analyze, interpret, and present accurate, reliable, and unbiased factual information, emphasizing trustworthiness and accuracy in automated knowledge dissemination.

Key Components
Factual AI consists of fact-checking algorithms, truth verification modules, knowledge bases, natural language processing techniques, semantic understanding frameworks, automated content analysis, and credibility assessment methods.

Example
A news verification platform uses factual AI to automatically assess articles, detecting misinformation and providing users with verified fact-based evaluations to prevent misinformation spread.

Benefits
Factual AI enhances information credibility, reduces misinformation, promotes transparency, supports informed decision-making, increases user trust, and ensures ethical information dissemination practices.

Applications
Applications include automated fact-checking services, misinformation detection on social media, content moderation, trustworthy news generation, automated knowledge bases, educational platforms, and credibility assessment tools.

Industries
Industries adopting factual AI include media and journalism, social media platforms, education technology, government communication services, healthcare, legal services, financial advisory, and consumer advocacy organizations.

Conclusions
Factual AI plays a crucial role in ensuring reliable, accurate information dissemination, significantly mitigating misinformation challenges. Ongoing advancements in semantic understanding and data quality will further enhance its effectiveness.

False Acceptance Rate (FAR)

Definition
False Acceptance Rate (FAR) refers to the likelihood of a biometric security or authentication system mistakenly accepting an unauthorized individual as genuine, representing a critical security performance metric.

Key Components
Components of FAR include biometric data inputs, matching algorithms, acceptance threshold settings, security evaluation criteria, statistical error rate analysis, and identity verification databases.

Example
In a facial recognition-based door entry system, FAR measures the percentage of unauthorized people mistakenly granted access, guiding developers to enhance system accuracy and reduce security vulnerabilities.

Benefits
Evaluating FAR improves biometric security reliability, ensures better accuracy in identity verification, supports informed threshold settings, strengthens user trust, and reduces security risks associated with incorrect authentications.

Applications
Applications include facial recognition security systems, fingerprint verification devices, access control systems, voice authentication tools, identity management solutions, border control, and mobile authentication platforms.

Industries
Industries focused on FAR metrics include security, banking and finance, government border security, healthcare, aviation, consumer electronics, law enforcement, telecommunications, and corporate access management.

Conclusions
Managing FAR effectively is essential for robust biometric authentication. Addressing accuracy, bias, and usability challenges continues to improve trust and widespread adoption of biometric solutions across industries.

False Negative Rate (FNR)

Definition

False Negative Rate (FNR) refers to the proportion of positive instances incorrectly identified as negative by an AI or machine learning model. It measures how frequently the model fails to detect a condition or event that actually exists, indicating missed detections.

Key Components
Key components of FNR include actual positive instances, false negative results, predictive thresholds, confusion matrix analysis, evaluation metrics, sensitivity calculations, and data validation methods.

Example
In medical diagnostics, a disease detection AI that incorrectly labels patients who have the disease as healthy exhibits a high FNR, leading to potential health risks due to missed treatment opportunities.

Benefits
Analyzing FNR helps improve model reliability, reduces critical errors, enhances safety outcomes, optimizes predictive accuracy, and ensures models meet required performance standards.

Applications
Applications include medical diagnostics, fraud detection, cybersecurity threat detection, fault diagnosis systems, credit risk assessment, and safety-critical decision-making systems.

Industries
Industries concerned with FNR include healthcare, finance, cybersecurity, insurance, transportation safety, aviation, automotive, and industrial quality control.

Conclusions
Monitoring and minimizing the False Negative Rate is critical for ensuring reliable and safe AI predictions, especially in high-risk or sensitive applications.

False Positive Rate (FPR)

Definition
False Positive Rate (FPR) measures the proportion of negative cases incorrectly classified as positive

by an AI system. It represents instances where the model erroneously signals a condition or event as occurring when it actually has not.

Key Components
Key components include actual negative cases, false positive predictions, threshold determination methods, confusion matrix evaluation, specificity measurements, and predictive performance analyses.

Example
A cybersecurity system flagging benign activities as security threats results in a high false positive rate, unnecessarily triggering security alerts and potentially overwhelming the system with incorrect alarms.

Benefits
Analyzing FPR helps refine predictive models, prevents resource wastage, reduces unnecessary interventions, enhances system accuracy, and improves operational efficiency.

Applications
Applications include cybersecurity systems, fraud detection models, disease screening tests, financial transaction monitoring, spam detection, and anomaly detection systems.

Industries
Industries monitoring FPR closely include cybersecurity, finance, healthcare diagnostics, banking, email providers, fraud management services, and law enforcement.

Conclusions
Effective management of FPR is essential to maintain user trust, operational efficiency, and accurate decision-making in AI applications.

False Rejection Rate (FRR)

Definition
False Rejection Rate (FRR) refers to the proportion of legitimate individuals or genuine cases mistakenly rejected or denied access by an AI-based biometric or verification system. It indicates the system's errors in recognizing valid entities.

Key Components
FRR components include genuine input data, rejection thresholds, biometric verification algorithms, identity verification criteria, system calibration methods, and accuracy assessments.

Example
A facial recognition security system denying access to authorized employees exhibits a high FRR, leading to inconvenience and reduced trust among legitimate users.

Benefits
Monitoring FRR ensures effective usability, maintains user trust, optimizes accuracy in authentication, enhances user experience, and minimizes operational disruptions.

Applications
Applications include biometric access control systems, facial recognition for authentication, fingerprint-based security, voice verification systems, and mobile device unlocking systems.

Industries
Industries affected by FRR include security and surveillance, banking, consumer electronics, law enforcement, aviation, healthcare, telecommunications, and government identification systems.

Challenges
Challenges involve balancing FRR reduction with security concerns, handling diverse biometric data

variations, ensuring system adaptability, managing environmental interference, and maintaining usability standards.

Feature Abstraction

Definition: Feature Abstraction is when AI takes a messy pile of raw data—like pixels or words—and boils it down to the good stuff, pulling out the big ideas without drowning in details. It's like squinting at a painting to see the shapes, not the brushstrokes.

Key Components: The process starts with raw inputs—like images or logs—fed into a system, often a neural net, that learns what matters. Layers strip away noise, a mapping tool condenses patterns, and a tweakable filter decides what's worth keeping.
Features: This trick zooms out fast, spotting high-level trends—like "happy face" instead of pixel dots. It's flexible, works across data types, and shrinks info to a lean, mean core that's easier to chew.

Benefits: It cuts the clutter—AI focuses on what counts, not fluff. Speeds up learning by ditching junk, saves power with lighter loads, and makes models sharper by nailing the gist over the grit.
Example: Think of an AI scanning photos—it abstracts a dog's floppy ears and wagging tail into "puppy," ignoring the background mess, then tags it right every time.

Industries: Tech uses it for apps, security for IDs, and robotics for navigation. Healthcare abstracts scans, media tags clips, and automotive spots road signs.

Summary: Feature Abstraction is AI's big-picture lens, trimming data to its essence with savvy cuts. It's a focus booster, though balance is its game. It's making sense of the chaos, one smart squint at a time.

Feature Aggregation

Definition: Feature Aggregation is when AI gathers up scattered data bits—like scores or clicks—and blends them into one tidy package, summing up the story for easier use. It's like rolling a bunch of loose threads into a single yarn ball.

Key Components: You've got a pool of features—like sales numbers or temp readings—tossed into a collector, often math tricks like averages or totals. A combiner—like a neural layer—melds them, with weights to tweak what's loudest, and a system to spit out the final lump.

Features: This rolls lots into one, smoothing noise into clarity—like averaging a week's weather. It's quick, handles big batches, and flexes to fit simple sums or fancy mixes

.Benefits: It shrinks data down—less to wrestle, faster to run. Cleans up wobbles for steady predictions, saves time by prepping a neat bundle, and helps AI see the forest, not just trees.

Example: Picture an AI tracking a store's daily sales—it aggregates totals into a monthly vibe, spotting "busy season" without sweating every receipt.

Applications: It's in stock predictions summing trends, chatbots gauging mood from words, or sensors averaging room heat—all tying loose ends tight.

Industries: Finance crunches markets, retail reads buyers, and tech tunes apps. Energy balances grids, healthcare sums vitals, and logistics tracks flows.

Summary: Feature Aggregation is AI's data blender, packing scattered bits into one smooth scoop. It's a tidy time-saver, though mix-ups test it. It's rolling the mess into gold, one knot at a time.

Feature Correlation

Definition: Feature Correlation is when AI figures out how data pieces lean on each other—like if sunny days mean more ice cream sales—spotting links that hint at what drives what. It's the machine playing matchmaker with numbers.

Key Components: The setup grabs features—like temp and sales—fed into a checker, often stats tools like Pearson's trick or neural nets. A scoring system ranks how tight they dance, with data to test it and a filter to cut fluff links

.Features: This digs up hidden ties—like rain and umbrella pops. It's sharp, catching weak or wild bonds, runs fast on big sets, and flags what's fake versus real in the chatter.

Benefits: It trims fat—drop stuff that doesn't pull weight. Boosts guesses by riding strong links, saves effort by pointing where to look, and clears up why things tick the way they do.

Example: Imagine an AI eyeing a gym—correlates sweat sessions with app logins, sees they spike together, and nudges more workout ads when phones light up.
Applications: It's in marketing linking ads to buys, weather tying wind to storms, or health pairing diet with heart ticks—all sniffing out connections.

Industries: Retail spots trends, finance rides markets, and healthcare tracks risks. Tech tunes models, weather predicts, and sports reads stats.

Summary: Feature Correlation is AI's link-finder, mapping how data buddies up with clever peeks. It's a shortcut to insight, though fakes and tangles poke it. It's pairing the clues, one tie at a time.

Feature Crosses

Definition: Feature Crosses is when AI mashes two or more data bits—like age and job—into a new combo that packs a bigger punch, teasing out tricks plain features miss. It's like mixing flour and water to get dough, not just crumbs

.Key Components: You start with base features—like height and weight—tossed into a mixer, often a model layer or math tweak. A combiner—like multiplication—fuses them, with a learner to spot winning pairs and a checker to test the juice.

Features: This brews fresh angles—like "old coders" versus just "old." It's crafty, digging deeper patterns, flexes to fit any mix, and pumps up weak signals into loud ones.

Benefits: It cracks tough nuts—finds gold where solo bits flop. Boosts accuracy with richer hints, cuts guesswork by blending smart, and makes AI savvier about how life mixes up.

Example: Think of an AI picking movie fans—it crosses "teens" with "horror buffs," sees they love slashers, and nails the next spooky rec over plain picks.

Applications: It's in ad targeting mixing likes, cars pairing speed with road, or health crossing habits with genes—all stirring up sharper calls.

Industries: Marketing blends vibes, automotive tunes drives, and healthcare reads risks. Tech boosts models, retail picks buys, and gaming crafts foes.

Summary: Feature Crosses is AI's mash-up chef, cooking new flavors from old bits with flair. It's a pattern powerhouse, though excess slows it. It's stirring data into smarts, one cross at a time.

Feature Engineering

Definition
Feature Engineering is the process of selecting, creating, transforming, and refining input variables (features) from raw data to enhance the performance and accuracy of machine learning models.

Key Components
Components include raw data analysis, feature extraction techniques, feature transformations, creation of derived features, normalization, encoding categorical variables, dimensionality reduction methods, and domain knowledge integration.

Example
In credit risk modeling, feature engineering involves creating new features like average account balance or transaction frequency from raw financial data, significantly improving loan default prediction accuracy.

Benefits
Feature engineering enhances model accuracy, improves predictive performance, reduces data complexity, enables efficient model training, and leverages domain expertise for richer insights.

Applications
Applications include predictive analytics, customer segmentation, recommendation engines, financial forecasting, medical diagnostics, fraud detection, image and speech recognition, and natural language processing.

Industries
Industries applying feature engineering extensively include finance, healthcare, retail, telecommunications, marketing, automotive, manufacturing, cybersecurity, and insurance.

Conclusions
Feature engineering remains a fundamental and highly influential process in machine learning, crucial for achieving robust, accurate, and interpretable predictive models.

Feature Extraction

Definition
Feature Extraction involves automatically identifying and obtaining meaningful, representative information from raw data inputs for use in machine learning models, reducing dimensionality while preserving critical information.

Key Components
Key components include raw data preprocessing, pattern recognition algorithms, dimensionality reduction methods (e.g., PCA), deep learning-based feature extraction, statistical feature extraction techniques, and computational frameworks.

Example
In image recognition systems, feature extraction uses convolutional neural networks to automatically identify relevant visual features such as edges, textures, or shapes, facilitating accurate image classification.

Benefits
Feature extraction reduces data complexity, enhances computational efficiency, improves model generalization, preserves relevant information, simplifies analysis, and supports accurate predictions.

Applications
Applications include image and video analysis, audio and speech processing, text mining, biometric systems, medical imaging diagnostics, remote sensing, and sensor data interpretation.

Industries
Industries benefiting from feature extraction include healthcare, automotive, finance, entertainment, security, telecommunications, aerospace, and industrial automation.

Challenges
Challenges involve selecting suitable extraction methods, managing information loss, handling noise or irrelevant features, computational complexity, and interpreting extracted features meaningfully.

Conclusions
Feature extraction significantly simplifies data analysis, enhances predictive capabilities, and supports efficient AI applications across multiple industries.

Feature Learning

Definition
Feature Learning involves automatically discovering meaningful features directly from raw data using machine learning, particularly deep learning models, thereby eliminating the need for manual feature engineering.

Key Components
Components include neural network architectures, autoencoders, unsupervised learning algorithms, convolutional layers, embedding models, deep generative models, and representation learning techniques.

Example
Deep neural networks in natural language processing automatically learn word embeddings representing semantic relationships between words without manual feature specification, enhancing language understanding and text analytics performance.

Benefits
Feature learning reduces human intervention, automates the discovery of valuable data representations, improves model accuracy, supports scalability, enhances adaptability, and streamlines machine learning workflows.

Applications
Applications include image and speech recognition, natural language processing, anomaly detection, recommender systems, autonomous driving systems, predictive analytics, and robotic perception.

Industries
Industries leveraging feature learning include technology, healthcare, automotive, finance, telecommunications, media, education, and robotics.

Challenges
Challenges include model complexity, computational resource demands, interpreting learned features, ensuring robust feature representations, and addressing overfitting risks.

Conclusions
Feature learning represents a transformative advancement in AI, automating the process of obtaining meaningful features and significantly enhancing predictive capabilities across diverse domains.

Feature Pruning

Definition: Feature Pruning is when AI snips away data bits—like extra leaves on a bush—that don't pull their weight, keeping only what helps it guess right. It's a trim job to make the machine lean and sharp.

Key Components: The setup starts with a full feature set—like prices or sizes—fed into a checker, often a model or stat tool, that spots slackers. A cutter—like a threshold—chops the weak, with a tester to ensure the keepers still rock. Data runs through to guide the shears.

Features: This slices fluff fast, ranking what's gold versus junk. It's picky, keeping just enough, flexes to fit any pile, and leaves a tight crew that's easy to handle.

Benefits: It speeds things up—less to chew, quicker calls. Saves power by lightening the load, cuts noise for clearer hits, and stops AI from tripping over useless twigs.
Example: Imagine an AI sorting spam—it prunes "email length" as a dud, keeps "weird links," and nails junk mail without wasting breath.

Applications: It's in text filters ditching fluff, image AI trimming pixels, or health scans cutting noise—all shaving to the chase.

Industries: Tech tunes apps, healthcare sharpens diagnostics, and security prunes IDs. Retail trims trends, finance cuts bets, and media clips tags.

Summary: Feature Pruning is AI's haircut, trimming data deadweight with a steady hand. It's a speed-sharpening win, though over-snips sting. It's keeping the core crisp, one clip at a time.

Feature Scaling

Definition: Feature Scaling is when AI tweaks data numbers—like weights or speeds—so they play nice on the same field, stopping big ones from hogging the show. It's leveling the sandbox for a fair game.

Key Components: The mix starts with raw features—like miles or dollars—run through a scaler, maybe normalization or standardization, that evens them. A range setter—like 0 to 1—keeps it tight, with a formula to stretch or shrink, and data to test the fit.

Features: This balances the scales—big and small get equal say. It's quick, fits any spread, and smooths wild swings to steady the ride for AI's math.

Benefits: It speeds learning—numbers align, no lopsided pulls. Boosts hits by calming chaos, saves flops from scale fights, and makes models play fair across the board.

Example: Think of an AI pricing homes—it scales "lot size" and "bedrooms" to match, so a mansion's acres don't drown a cozy flat's charm.

Industries: Finance tunes bets, tech runs models, and healthcare scales vitals. Retail weighs trends, automotive drives smooth, and sports stats up.

Summary: Feature Scaling is AI's fair-play ref, evening data for a clean run. It's a balance ace, though oddballs poke it. It's leveling the field, one tweak at a time.

Feature Selection

Definition
Feature selection involves identifying and choosing the most relevant features from raw data for building effective machine learning models, reducing complexity, improving performance, and preventing overfitting.

Key Components
Key components include relevance analysis, statistical tests, model-based evaluation methods, filter methods, wrapper methods, embedded selection algorithms, and evaluation criteria.

Example
A fraud detection AI uses feature selection to choose transaction data attributes that strongly correlate with fraudulent activity, enhancing detection accuracy.

Benefits
Feature selection reduces model complexity, improves predictive accuracy, enhances computational efficiency, prevents overfitting, and increases model interpretability.

Applications
Applications include fraud detection, medical diagnostics, financial modeling, customer analytics, predictive maintenance, and sentiment analysis.

Industries
Industries benefiting from feature selection include finance, healthcare, cybersecurity, retail, manufacturing, and marketing.

Conclusions
Effective feature selection significantly enhances AI model performance, interpretability, and efficiency. Continued advancement in automated methods will further its practical value.

Feature Transformation

Definition: Feature Transformation is when AI remixes data—like twisting logs into curves—to make it sing louder for predictions, turning raw lumps into gold shapes. It's a makeover for machine-friendly insights.

Key Components: You've got base features—like time or counts—fed into a changer, maybe logs or polynomials, that reshapes them. A fitter—like a net—picks the twist, with a tester to check the new vibe, and data to spark the shift.

Features: This reshapes rough edges into smooth fits—like bending a line to a curve. It's crafty, works any type, and unlocks hidden beats that plain data muffles.

Benefits: It pumps up power—new shapes hit harder. Speeds learning with slicker fits, cuts noise by reframing, and cracks tough puzzles with a fresh angle

Example: Imagine an AI tracking sales—it transforms "days since launch" into a growth curve, catching the boom better than flat counts.

Applications: It's in stock AI curving trends, health bending vitals, or cars reshaping speeds—all twisting for clarity.

Industries: Finance remixes markets, healthcare reshapes risks, and tech tunes models. Retail bends buys, automotive curves drives, and energy shifts loads.
Summary: Feature Transformation is AI's shape-shifter, remolding data for a sharper sting. It's a pattern unlocker, though fit's the trick. It's twisting the raw to ready, one bend at a time.

Feature Vector

Definition: Feature Vector is when AI wraps data—like height or mood—into a tidy row of numbers, a little packet it can sling around to guess or sort. It's the machine's grab-bag of facts.

Key Components: The core's a data grab—like age or clicks—lined up in order, often a list or array. A packer—like a coder—turns words or pics into digits, with a size cap to keep it neat, and a feeder slots it into models.

Features: This packs tight—everything in one shot, easy to toss. It's simple, fits any mix, and lines up smooth for AI to chew, big or small.

Benefits: It's a fast lane—data's ready, no fuss. Saves space with a crisp wrap, boosts speed by streamlining, and makes AI grab the whole story in a gulp.

Example: Picture an AI eyeing a cat pic—it turns fur, whiskers, and purr into a number row, then tags "kitty" spot-on.

Applications: It's in face AI with trait rows, speech packing tones, or bots boxing chats—all vector-ready.

Industries: Tech runs models, security IDs faces, and healthcare vectors scans. Retail packs trends, automotive rows drives, and media tags clips.

Summary: Feature Vector is AI's data suitcase, stuffing facts into a neat line with zip. It's a speed-pack win, though fit's the catch. It's bundling the world for AI, one row at a time.

Federated AI

Definition
Federated AI involves distributed machine learning methods where models are collaboratively trained across multiple decentralized systems or devices without exchanging raw data, ensuring data privacy and efficiency.

Key Components
Components include distributed model training, secure aggregation protocols, local computation, privacy-preserving methods (differential privacy), synchronization processes, and communication-efficient algorithms.

Example
Healthcare institutions utilize federated AI to jointly develop patient diagnosis models without sharing sensitive patient data directly, preserving privacy while enhancing predictive accuracy.

Benefits
Federated AI ensures data privacy, facilitates cross-organization collaboration, reduces data transfer risks, and efficiently utilizes distributed computational resources.

Applications
Applications include healthcare diagnostics, financial fraud detection, personalized recommendations, mobile device AI, and cross-organization research.

Industries
Industries adopting federated AI include healthcare, finance, technology, telecommunications, automotive, and government.

Conclusions
Federated AI effectively balances data privacy with collaborative AI development, significantly benefiting sensitive and regulated sectors. Overcoming current challenges will enable broader implementation and impact.

Federated Learning

Definition: Federated Learning is when AI trains itself across a bunch of devices—like phones or laptops—without hauling all their data to one big hub, keeping it local while still sharpening the shared brain. It's like a study group where everyone learns at home but swaps notes.

Key Components: The setup kicks off with a central model—like a starter recipe—sent to devices holding their own data, think app logs or pics. Local trainers tweak it on each gadget, a communicator swaps updates—not raw data—back to the hub, and a blender mixes those tweaks into a smarter whole.

Features: This keeps secrets safe—data stays put, no cloud spill. It's quick, using device downtime, spreads the load across many, and flexes to fit phones or IoT gear with ease.

Benefits: It's privacy gold—your info never leaves your pocket. Saves bandwidth by skipping big uploads, cuts central power needs, and learns fast from real-world scatter, not lab polish.

Example: Picture your phone's keyboard AI—it learns your typos locally, swaps tips with millions of others via a server, and gets slicker without ever sending your texts up high.

Applications: It's in phone apps tuning suggestions, health trackers learning patterns, or cars sharing road smarts—all training where the action lives.

Industries: Tech loves it for gadgets, healthcare for private scans, and automotive for fleet brains. Finance tunes fraud checks, telecom boosts networks, and IoT links homes.

Summary: Federated Learning is AI's home-school crew, sharpening smarts device-by-device with a privacy wink. It's a scattered win, though flaky tech tests it. It's growing brains where data sits, one local tweak at a time.

Feedback Loop in AI

Definition: Feedback Loop in AI is when a system learns by circling back—taking its own guesses, checking how they land, and tweaking itself to get better, like a kid touching a stove and figuring out hot means ouch. It's AI teaching itself through trial and bounce.

Key Components: The core's a model—like a guesser—spitting outputs, paired with a checker that scores hits or misses, maybe from humans or rules. A tuner adjusts based on that score, with data flowing to fuel the loop, and a tracker logs the shift over time.

Features: This keeps AI sharp—each try hones the edge. It's live, adapting as stuff changes, catches flops fast, and rolls solo or with a nudge depending on the gig.

Benefits: It's a growth engine—mistakes turn to muscle. Speeds up smarts with real-time fixes, cuts manual babysitting, and keeps AI fresh in a shifting world.

Example: Think of a music AI—it picks a tune, you skip, it notes "nope," then leans toward your head-bops, nailing your vibe by the third song.

Applications: It's in chatbots tuning replies, ad AI shifting pitches, or robots tweaking grabs—all looping to learn on the fly.

Industries: Tech runs it in apps, marketing hits targets, and robotics grips better. Healthcare refines diagnostics, gaming crafts foes, and retail reads buys.
Summary: Feedback Loop in AI is the machine's self-check mirror, polishing guesses with every bounce back. It's a live-learner's trick, though noise can trip it. It's sharpening AI's edge, one loop at a time.

Few-Shot Learning

Definition
Few-Shot Learning is an AI methodology focused on training machine learning models to perform effectively with very limited labeled data. It aims to enable models to quickly generalize and make accurate predictions when provided with only a minimal number of training examples.

Key Components
Key components include meta-learning algorithms, support set and query set concepts, embedding representations, metric-based methods, optimization-based methods, neural memory structures, and transfer learning techniques.

Example
A facial recognition system quickly identifies a new individual after seeing only a few reference images, effectively leveraging learned patterns from past data.

Benefits
Few-shot learning reduces reliance on large labeled datasets, accelerates learning new tasks, enhances model adaptability, and allows rapid deployment of AI in novel scenarios.

Applications
Applications include facial recognition, text classification, object recognition in robotics, medical image diagnostics with limited patient data, anomaly detection, and language translation.

Industries
Industries benefiting from few-shot learning include healthcare, security, robotics, automotive, finance, retail, and customer service.

Challenges
Challenges include risk of overfitting to limited data, generalization difficulty, choosing suitable model architectures, computational complexity, and balancing between model adaptability and accuracy.

Conclusions
Few-shot learning significantly advances AI adaptability and efficiency, allowing models to perform effectively with minimal data. Overcoming current challenges will further broaden its impact.

Filter Pruning

Definition: Filter Pruning is when AI trims the fat from its brain—like snipping weak filters in a neural net—to keep the smart parts while ditching what barely sparks. It's a cleanup to make models leaner and faster without losing the magic.

Key Components: The setup starts with a beefy neural net—think layers of filters spotting edges or shapes. A scorer—like a stat check—ranks their punch, a clipper cuts the duds, and a tester makes sure the slimmed-down net still shines.

Data guides the chop.
Features: This slashes bloat quick—weak filters vanish in a snap. It's picky, keeping the gold, flexes to any net size, and leaves a zippy core that's light on its feet.

Benefits: It speeds up AI—less to crunch, quicker answers. Saves power with a lighter load, keeps accuracy tight, and fits big brains on small gear like phones or drones.

Example: Picture an AI spotting cats—it prunes filters that fuzz on fur, keeps the whisker-sharp ones, and runs smooth on your watch, not just a server.

Applications: It's in image AI slimming for phones, voice nets shrinking for earbuds, or robots trimming for edge smarts—all pruning to fit tight spots.

Industries: Tech shrinks apps, automotive fits car brains, and IoT packs home gear. Security slims cams, healthcare trims scans, and media cuts clip AI.

Summary: Filter Pruning is AI's diet plan, slicing neural fat for a swift, sharp kick. It's a lean-maker, though over-cuts sting. It's trimming the fluff, one filter at a time.

Fine-Tuning

Definition: Fine-Tuning is when AI takes a pre-trained model—like a half-baked cake—and tweaks it with a sprinkle of new data to nail a specific job, like recognizing your dog instead of all dogs. It's a polish job for precision.

Key Components: You've got a base model—say, a net trained on tons of pics—tossed with fresh data, like your pet snaps. A tuner—like an optimizer—adjusts the knobs, a loss checker keeps it on track, and a stopper halts when it's just right.

Features: This pivots fast—new tricks in a flash. It's gentle, tweaking not rebuilding, works with slim data, and keeps old smarts while adding new flair.

Benefits: It's a time-saver—skip the long bake, just ice it. Cuts data needs, boosts hits on niche gigs, and stretches big models to fit your corner of the world.

Example: Think of an AI trained on global faces—it fine-tunes on your family pics, then spots Aunt Sue at the reunion, no sweat.

Applications: It's in chat AI learning your slang, image nets tagging your art, or health AI fitting local patients—all tweaking for the win.

Industries: Tech tunes apps, healthcare fits diagnostics, and media personalizes clips. Retail adjusts trends, education shapes lessons, and security IDs locals.

Summary: Fine-Tuning is AI's custom tweak, polishing a rough model into your perfect fit. It's a quick-sharp win, though balance keeps it true. It's tailoring smarts, one nudge at a time.

Fingerprint Feature Extraction

Definition: Fingerprint Feature Extraction is when AI digs into the swirls and loops of a fingerprint, pulling out the standout bits—like ridges or splits—to turn a smudge into a neat ID clue. It's the machine eyeing your unique mark.

Key Components: The process grabs a fingerprint scan—say, from a sensor—fed into a parser, often a net or math trick, that spots key quirks. A mapper—like a grid—tags them, a cleaner cuts noise, and a packer bundles it for use.

Features: This zeros in fast—grabs the good stuff in a blink. It's sharp, catching tiny twists, shrugs off blur, and turns a print into a tight code that's ready to roll.

Benefits: It's a lock—nails IDs with pinpoint flair. Speeds up matching by shrinking the mess, saves space with a slim pack, and boosts security by nabbing what's yours alone.

Example: Imagine a phone AI—it extracts your thumb's whorl and fork, packs it tight, and unlocks in a tick, no mix-up with your pal's print.

Applications: It's in phone unlocks with print quirks, border checks grabbing IDs, or crime AI sifting scenes—all pulling print gold.

Industries: Security locks doors, tech secures gadgets, and law hunts clues. Finance guards cash, healthcare IDs patients, and travel checks passports.

Summary: Fingerprint Feature Extraction is AI's print whisperer, snagging ridge secrets with a keen eye. It's a security ace, though smudges test it. It's cracking your mark, one swirl at a time.

Fingerprint Recognition

Definition: Fingerprint Recognition is when AI takes those extracted print quirks and matches them to a known set, deciding if it's you or a stranger—like a bouncer checking your VIP stamp. It's the machine saying "yep, that's them."

Key Components: You've got a feature pack—like ridge codes—from extraction, matched by a checker, maybe a net or distance trick, against a stored pile. A scorer—like a threshold—calls the match, with a database to dig and a verifier to lock it down.

Features: This pins you fast—match or no in a snap. It's tight, rarely fooled, scales to millions, and shrugs off time—your print's yours forever.

Benefits: It's a trust rock—IDs you cold, no guess. Speeds entry with quick checks, cuts fraud by locking to you, and runs cheap once set, guarding what's yours.

Example: Picture an ATM—it scans your finger, matches your print stash, and hands cash only to you, not some slick thief.

Applications: It's in door locks checking you, phones guarding apps, or cops nabbing crooks—all matching prints to truth.

Industries: Security runs gates, tech locks screens, and law tracks perps. Finance secures vaults, travel vets flyers, and healthcare ties charts.

Summary: Fingerprint Recognition is AI's ID gatekeeper, matching prints with a steel glare. It's a safety champ, though fakes poke it. It's locking you in, one match at a time.

Finite Automata in AI

Definition: Finite Automata in AI is when machines use simple rule machines—like traffic lights with set states—to handle tasks with clear steps, like spotting patterns or guiding moves. It's AI keeping it basic but clever.

Key Components: The core's a state map—like "on" or "off"—with a rulebook switching them, fed by inputs—like letters or clicks. A starter kicks it, an ender stops it, and a runner—like code—ticks it through.

Features: This runs tight—few states, no fuss. It's fast, chugs on low power, sticks to patterns, and scales small but steady for step-by-step gigs.

Benefits: It's a speed demon—simple means quick. Saves juice with light logic, nails predictable jobs, and keeps AI grounded where wild nets overthink.

Example: Think of an AI spell-check—it ticks through "c-a-t," state by state, flags "c-a-x" as bunk, all zippy and clean.

Applications: It's in text AI parsing words, bots stepping moves, or nets checking code—all ticking through states

.Industries: Tech runs parsers, robotics steps bots, and telecom routes calls. Education drills rules, gaming ticks foes, and security scans logs.

Summary: Finite Automata in AI is the machine's rule ticker, nailing simple steps with a light touch. It's a quick-win basic, though chaos trips it. It's pacing AI steady, one state at a time.

First-Order Logic in AI

Definition: First-Order Logic in AI is when machines think with strict logic—like "all cats purr, this is a cat, so it purrs"—using rules and facts to reason sharp and deep. It's AI playing philosopher with a math twist.

Key Components: The base is a logic kit—statements with "all" or "some," tied by connectors like "and" or "if." A fact pile—like "cats exist"—feeds it, a reasoner—like a solver—cranks it, and a checker proves the leap.

Features: This digs truth hard—nails what's real from rules. It's clear, links facts to guesses, flexes to big ideas, and builds a reasoning chain you can trace.

Benefits: It's a trust anchor—shows why it thinks. Cuts fluff with tight logic, scales to deep questions, and powers AI that explains itself, not just guesses.

Example: Imagine an AI lawyer—it knows "all contracts need signatures," sees yours doesn't, and flags "no deal," all step-by-step clear.

Applications: It's in expert AI proving claims, bots reasoning moves, or search digging truths—all chaining logic tight.

Industries: Tech builds reasoners, law checks rules, and healthcare proves diagnoses. Education drills logic, finance tests deals, and robotics plans steps.

Summary: First-Order Logic in AI is the machine's reasoning spine, linking facts with a steel grip. It's a truth-chaser, though mess tests it. It's grounding AI's smarts, one rule at a time.

Fisher's Linear Discriminant

Fisher's Linear Discriminant is a statistical method used to find a linear combination of features that best separates two or more classes of data. It projects high-dimensional data onto a lower-dimensional space, maximizing the distance between class means while minimizing variance within each class, making it a go-to for classification and dimensionality reduction.

Key Components
The method hinges on a projection vector, calculated to optimize class separation, derived from class means and covariance matrices. It uses within-class scatter to measure how spread out data points are within groups and between-class scatter to gauge separation across groups. A linear transformation reduces complexity while preserving discriminative power, and the assumption of normally distributed data with equal covariance underpins its math.

Benefits
It simplifies complex datasets, cutting down dimensions without losing key distinctions. Computationally light, it runs efficiently even on modest hardware. It boosts classification accuracy by focusing on what sets classes apart, and its interpretability makes it easier to understand data relationships compared to black-box models.

Examples
Picture a botanist sorting flowers into species using petal length and width—Fisher's Linear Discriminant finds a line that best splits them. Or a spam filter projecting email features like word frequency onto a single axis, cleanly dividing junk from legit messages.

Applications
It's used in pattern recognition, like facial identification from pixel data. Biologists classify species based on physical traits, while marketers segment customers by purchase habits. It also preprocesses data for other algorithms, trimming noise before deeper analysis.

Industries
Healthcare applies it to distinguish disease states from patient metrics. Finance uses it for credit risk scoring. Agriculture leverages it for crop classification, and tech deploys it in early machine learning pipelines. Academia relies on it for statistical research.

Summary
Fisher's Linear Discriminant is a classic, elegant tool for slicing through data to reveal class boundaries, blending simplicity with power. It shines in straightforward scenarios but falters when data gets wild or sparse. A staple for beginners and pros alike, it's a bridge between stats and machine learning.

Fixed-Point Iteration

Definition
Fixed-Point Iteration is a numerical method for solving equations by repeatedly applying a function until it converges to a point where the input equals the output. It's a simple, iterative way to find roots or stable states in mathematical systems.

Key Components
It relies on a function rewritten so its solution is a fixed point, where $f(x) = x$. An initial guess kicks off the process, and each step updates the estimate by plugging it back into the function. Convergence depends on the function's behavior—gentle slopes speed it up, steep ones derail it.

Benefits
It's straightforward, needing little setup beyond a starting point. Light on computing power, it suits quick approximations. When it works, it's fast, and its simplicity makes it easy to code or teach.

Examples
To solve $x = \cos(x)$, start with $x = 0$, then iterate $x = \cos(0)$, $x = \cos(0.999)$, converging near 0.739. Or in economics, it might find an equilibrium price where supply matches demand after tweaking guesses.

Applications
It solves nonlinear equations in physics, like pendulum motion. Engineers use it for steady-state system analysis. Economists model market balances, and programmers debug iterative algorithms with it.

Industries
Physics and engineering lean on it for simulations. Finance uses it for pricing models. Education teaches it as a numerical basics staple, and software development applies it in algorithm testing.

Summary
Fixed-Point Iteration is a lean, intuitive fix for equation-solving, shining in simple cases. Its elegance lies in repetition, but it's finicky, demanding the right conditions. A handy tool, it's best when precision meets patience.

Flywheel in AI

Definition
Flywheel in AI describes a self-reinforcing cycle where AI systems improve through continuous data collection, learning, and deployment, accelerating progress like a spinning wheel gaining momentum. It's a metaphor for how AI builds on its own success.

Key Components
Data is the fuel, flowing in from users or sensors to train models. Algorithms refine themselves, learning from each cycle. Deployment puts improved AI into action, generating more data. Feedback loops tighten the process, and scalability lets it grow with demand.

Benefits
It creates compounding gains, where each improvement boosts the next. Efficiency rises as manual tweaks fade. It adapts to new patterns fast, and its momentum can outpace static systems, driving innovation.

Examples
A recommendation engine starts suggesting movies, learns from clicks, and gets sharper with each watch. A self-driving car logs miles, refines its navigation, and handles trickier roads over time.

Applications
It powers personalized ads based on browsing habits. Autonomous vehicles evolve through real-world driving data. Voice assistants get smarter with every command, and predictive maintenance flags machine issues earlier.

Industries
Tech thrives on it for consumer AI products. Automotive uses it for self-driving tech. Marketing leverages it for targeting, and manufacturing applies it to optimize uptime. Healthcare refines diagnostics with it.

Summary
The Flywheel in AI captures the magic of systems that grow smarter on their own, turning data into a perpetual engine. It's a game-changer for adaptive tech but hinges on quality inputs and oversight. A modern marvel, it's AI's momentum made tangible.

Fog Computing Definition

Fog Computing is a decentralized computing framework that extends cloud capabilities closer to data sources, like devices or sensors, processing data locally to cut latency and ease network strain. It's a bridge between edge devices and centralized clouds.

Key Components
Edge nodes, like routers or gateways, handle local computation and storage. Real-time processing tackles data on the spot, while connectivity links fog to cloud for heavier tasks. Resource management balances loads, and security layers protect distributed points.

Benefits
It slashes delays, perfect for time-sensitive jobs. Bandwidth use drops as less data travels far. It's resilient—local nodes keep running if the cloud dips. Scalability fits sprawling IoT setups, and it eases cloud overload.

Examples
A smart traffic light processes camera feeds to adjust signals instantly, not waiting for cloud lag. A factory sensor analyzes vibration data on-site, flagging issues before sending summaries upward.

Applications
It runs smart cities, managing lights and grids live. IoT devices like wearables process health stats locally. Autonomous cars use it for split-second decisions, and streaming services buffer video nearer to users.

Industries
Transportation leans on it for traffic and vehicle systems. Healthcare monitors patients remotely. Manufacturing optimizes factory floors, and telecom speeds up networks. Energy uses it for grid efficiency.

Summary
Fog Computing brings the cloud down to earth, powering fast, local decisions in a connected world. It's a lifeline for IoT and real-time needs but wrestles with sprawl and safety. A nimble middle ground, it's reshaping how data flows.

Formal Concept Analysis (FCA)

Definition
Formal Concept Analysis is a mathematical method for uncovering relationships in data by organizing objects and their attributes into a structured lattice. It reveals hidden patterns and hierarchies, turning raw info into conceptual clarity.

Key Components
It starts with a context—a table linking objects (like items) to attributes (like traits). Concepts emerge as pairs of object sets and attribute sets that fully describe each other. A concept lattice maps these pairs, showing how they nest or overlap. Closure operations lock in stable groupings, and ordering reflects subset relationships.

Benefits
It exposes structure in messy data, spotlighting natural clusters. Visual lattices make abstract links tangible. It's systematic, leaving no pattern unchecked, and its rigor suits both theory and practice. Flexible, it scales to big or small datasets.

Examples
A grocery analysis might pair "apples, bananas" with "sweet, yellow," forming a concept in a lattice of fruit traits. A library could map books to topics, showing how "sci-fi" and "fantasy" overlap in shared themes.

Applications
It organizes knowledge bases for search engines. Data mining uses it to spot trends, like customer

preferences. Software engineering refactors code by attribute overlap, and social science studies group behaviors or beliefs.

Industries
Tech harnesses it for ontologies and AI reasoning. Retail mines purchase patterns. Academia explores it in linguistics or sociology, and library science catalogs with it. Biotech classifies genes by function.

Summary
Formal Concept Analysis is a brainy way to tease order from chaos, giving data a clear skeleton. It's a gem for pattern hunters but demands compute muscle and patience. A niche yet potent tool, it bridges theory to insight.

Formal Methods in AI

Definition
Formal Methods in AI refers to the use of rigorous mathematical techniques to design, verify, and analyze artificial intelligence systems, ensuring they behave correctly and reliably. It applies logic, proofs, and models to guarantee AI meets specified standards, especially in critical applications.

Key Components
The approach rests on formal specifications, which define desired AI behavior in precise terms. Mathematical models, like state machines or logic formulas, represent the system. Verification tools, such as theorem provers, check if the AI aligns with specs. Testing complements proofs, while abstraction simplifies complex systems for analysis.

Benefits
It catches errors early, boosting trust in AI outputs. Reliability shines in high-stakes scenarios, reducing risks. It clarifies how AI works, aiding transparency. Formal proofs offer guarantees no testing can match, and it supports regulatory compliance where precision is non-negotiable.

Examples
A self-driving car's braking logic might be proven to stop within 10 meters under set conditions. A medical AI diagnosing tumors could be verified to never miss a malignant case, using formal rules.

Applications
It ensures safe autonomous vehicle navigation. Medical diagnostics gain certified accuracy. Cybersecurity uses it to harden AI against attacks, and software development verifies AI-driven features. Aerospace relies on it for flight control systems.

Industries
Automotive leans on it for safety-critical AI. Healthcare demands it for life-saving tools. Defense uses it in autonomous drones, and aerospace applies it to avionics. Finance adopts it for secure trading algorithms.

Summary
Formal Methods in AI bring ironclad assurance to smart systems, marrying math to machine intelligence. They're a boon for safety and trust but wrestle with complexity and pace. Vital for critical domains, they're a slow-burn win in AI's wild frontier.

Formant Synthesis

Definition
Formant Synthesis is a technique in audio signal processing that generates sound by modeling the resonant frequencies, or formants, of the human vocal tract. It mimics speech or musical tones by shaping a basic waveform with filters tuned to these peaks, skipping raw sample playback.

Key Components
A source signal, like a buzz or noise, kicks things off, mimicking vocal cords. Formant filters shape this into recognizable sounds by boosting key frequencies. Control parameters adjust pitch, timbre, and articulation. Real-time modulation adds expressiveness, and a digital signal processor ties it all together.

Benefits
It's lightweight, needing less memory than sample-based methods. Highly tweakable, it crafts diverse voices or instruments. Real-time use suits live applications, and its simplicity speeds computation. Expressive control mimics natural speech nuances efficiently.

Examples
A text-to-speech system might turn "hello" into a robotic voice by filtering a buzz through formant peaks. A synth musician could sculpt a flute-like tone, tweaking filters to shift its breathy edge.

Applications
It powers speech synthesis in virtual assistants. Music production crafts artificial instruments. Language learning tools simulate pronunciation, and telecom compresses voice data. Gaming adds character voices with low overhead.

Industries
Tech uses it in voice-enabled devices. Entertainment leans on it for sound design. Education applies it to linguistic aids, and telecom optimizes bandwidth. Gaming taps it for immersive audio.

Summary
Formant Synthesis is a lean, clever way to conjure speech and sound from scratch, balancing control with efficiency. It's a star in lightweight audio but lags in lifelike depth. A niche gem, it hums in practical, real-time roles.

Forward Chaining

Definition
Forward Chaining is a reasoning method in AI that starts with known facts and applies rules to deduce new conclusions, moving step-by-step toward a goal. It's a data-driven approach, building knowledge incrementally from what's already true.

Key Components
It begins with a fact base—raw data or observations. A rule set, like "if A, then B," drives inference. An inference engine applies rules to facts, spawning new facts. The process loops until a target conclusion emerges or no rules fit. A goal state guides it when specified.

Benefits
It's intuitive, mirroring human step-by-step logic. Efficient for small rule sets, it avoids backtracking. It shines when facts are clear and goals vague, uncovering surprises. Simple to implement, it suits rule-based systems well.

Examples
A medical system might start with "fever" and "cough," applying rules to deduce "flu." A troubleshooting bot could take "printer offline" and reason to "check cable" via steps.

Applications
It diagnoses issues in expert systems. Customer support bots suggest fixes from symptoms. Robotics uses it for task sequencing, and legal reasoning infers outcomes from laws. Education builds logic tutors with it.

Industries
Healthcare relies on it for diagnostics. Tech support automates help desks. Manufacturing troubleshoots machinery, and law applies it to case analysis. Education crafts reasoning tools.

Summary
Forward Chaining is a steady, fact-first march to conclusions, excelling in clear-cut deduction. It's a workhorse for structured problems but stumbles in complexity. A foundational AI trick, it's practical yet limited.

Forward Sampling

Definition
Forward Sampling is a probabilistic method in AI that generates data samples by stepping through a model's variables in a logical order, using their conditional probabilities. It simulates outcomes from known distributions, building scenarios piece by piece.

Key Components
A probabilistic model, like a Bayesian network, sets the stage with variables and dependencies. Conditional probability tables define how each variable leans on others. An ordered sequence dictates sampling steps, starting from root nodes. Random draws pick values, and the process chains forward to complete samples.

Benefits
It's straightforward, turning models into tangible outputs. Fast for small networks, it scales linearly. It captures dependencies well, reflecting real-world links. Flexible, it fits any ordered model, and samples fuel broader analysis.

Examples
In weather prediction, it might sample "rain" based on "clouds," then "wind" from "rain," yielding a forecast. A marketing model could draw "click" from "ad type," then "buy" from "click."

Applications
It simulates scenarios in risk analysis. Machine learning tests models with synthetic data. Game AI generates enemy moves, and stats explores variable impacts. Healthcare predicts patient paths.

Industries
Finance uses it for risk modeling. Gaming crafts dynamic worlds. Healthcare simulates trials, and marketing predicts campaigns. Science leans on it for experiments.

Summary
Forward Sampling spins probability into action, crafting samples with orderly precision. It's a quick, clear window into models but creaks under scale. A handy tool, it bridges theory to simulation.

Frequent Pattern Mining

Definition
Frequent Pattern Mining is a data analysis technique that identifies recurring relationships or itemsets in large datasets, like transactions or sequences. It uncovers hidden trends by spotting what often appears together, fueling insights or predictions.

Key Components
It starts with a dataset—think purchase logs or event strings. A support threshold sets how often a pattern must appear to count. Algorithms, like Apriori or FP-growth, sift for frequent itemsets. Rules emerge, linking items (e.g., "if A, then B"). Pruning cuts noise, focusing on strong patterns.

Benefits
It reveals actionable trends, like buying habits. Efficient algorithms handle big data fast. It's versatile, fitting sequences or graphs too. Simple outputs aid decision-making, and it scales with clever tweaks.

Examples
A store finds "bread, milk" often bought together, suggesting a bundle. A website sees "login, cart, checkout" as a frequent path, refining its flow.

Applications
It drives market basket analysis in retail. Web analytics tracks user journeys. Bioinformatics spots gene co-occurrences, and security flags anomaly patterns. Recommendation systems thrive on it.

Industries
Retail optimizes stock and promotions. Tech personalizes online experiences. Healthcare mines medical records, and cybersecurity hunts threats. Telecom studies call patterns.

Summary
Frequent Pattern Mining digs out the pulse of data, spotlighting what sticks together. It's a retail and tech darling but wrestles with scale and subtlety. A pattern-finder's dream, it turns chaos into clarity.

Frictionless AI

Definition
Frictionless AI describes artificial intelligence systems designed to operate seamlessly, minimizing user effort, delays, or complexity. It aims for intuitive, invisible integration into workflows, making AI feel natural and unobtrusive.

Key Components
User-centric design simplifies interaction, often via natural language or automation. Real-time processing cuts wait times. Adaptive algorithms learn preferences on the fly, and seamless integration hooks into existing tools. Minimal setup keeps it plug-and-play.

Benefits
It saves time, streamlining tasks with zero fuss. User adoption soars as barriers vanish. Efficiency spikes with hands-off operation, and it scales across skill levels. Satisfaction grows when AI just works.

Examples
A voice assistant books a meeting from "Schedule tomorrow at 10," no clicks needed. A photo app auto-tags faces as you upload, skipping manual steps.

Applications
It powers effortless customer service bots. Smart homes adjust lights and heat silently. E-commerce suggests items mid-browse, and productivity tools auto-sort emails. Healthcare speeds patient check-ins.

Industries
Tech thrives on it for consumer apps. Retail enhances shopping ease. Healthcare cuts admin drag, and hospitality personalizes guest stays. Productivity software leans on it for flow.

Summary
Frictionless AI melts AI into life, making it a quiet helper. It's a user's delight but a designer's puzzle, balancing ease with trust. A sleek vision, it's AI at its smoothest.

Fringe Search

Definition
Fringe Search is a graph-based search algorithm in artificial intelligence that finds the least-cost path from a starting node to a goal node by blending elements of A* and Iterative Deepening A* (IDA*). It explores a search space efficiently by managing a dynamic frontier of nodes, aiming to balance memory use and speed in pathfinding tasks.

Key Components
The algorithm maintains two lists—called "now" and "later"—to track the fringe, or frontier, of the search tree, where "now" holds nodes for the current iteration and "later" stores nodes deferred to the next. A cost function, combining the path cost from the start (g) and a heuristic estimate to the goal (h), guides node expansion. A threshold, initially set by the start node's heuristic, controls which nodes are processed or postponed. Nodes are expanded when their cost falls below or equals this threshold, with children added back to "now," while costlier nodes shift to "later." The threshold rises after each iteration, recycling "later" into "now" until the goal is found.

Benefits
Fringe Search runs faster than A* in many cases, often by 10-40%, as it avoids constantly sorting a full open list. It uses less memory than A* by not tracking all explored nodes, leaning closer to IDA*'s efficiency. It reduces redundant work compared to IDA* by smarter frontier management, and its simplicity makes it adaptable to grid-based or dynamic environments.

Examples
In a video game, Fringe Search might chart a character's path across a grid map from a village to a castle, dodging obstacles like rivers, adjusting as the player moves. A robot navigating a warehouse could use it to find the shortest route to a shelf, recalculating if boxes block the way.

Applications
It excels in real-time pathfinding for games, plotting character or NPC routes. Robotics uses it for navigation in changing spaces, like delivery bots avoiding crowds. Logistics optimizes vehicle paths in warehouses, and AI simulations model agent movement in virtual worlds.

Industries
Gaming relies on it for smooth, quick pathfinding. Robotics applies it in autonomous systems. Logistics and transportation use it for efficient routing, and simulation software in research or training leverages it for realistic motion planning.

Summary
Fringe Search is a nimble hybrid, carving a middle path between A*'s precision and IDA*'s thrift, ideal for fast, memory-light pathfinding. It shines in practical, grid-like settings but stumbles with scale or poor tuning. A smart pick for your AI dictionary, it's a quiet hero in real-time navigation.

Fuzzy Clustering

Definition
Fuzzy clustering is a method of grouping data where each data point can belong to multiple clusters simultaneously, each with varying degrees of membership. Unlike traditional clustering, fuzzy clustering allows objects to belong partially to different clusters, reflecting real-world ambiguity more effectively.

Key Components
Fuzzy clustering consists of fuzzy partitioning methods, membership functions, fuzzy c-means algorithm, cluster validity measures, fuzziness parameter adjustments, centroid calculation, and iterative optimization procedures.

Example
A customer segmentation system utilizes fuzzy clustering to categorize customers based on shopping behaviors. A customer can simultaneously belong to both "price-sensitive" and "brand-focused" clusters to varying degrees, reflecting more nuanced buying habits.

Benefits
Fuzzy clustering effectively manages uncertainty, better represents overlapping categories, provides deeper insights into ambiguous datasets, enhances decision-making accuracy, improves flexibility, and reduces the influence of outliers.

Applications
Applications include market segmentation, medical diagnosis clustering, image segmentation, anomaly detection, environmental data analysis, social network analysis, and customer profiling.

Industries
Industries adopting fuzzy clustering include retail, healthcare, finance, marketing analytics, telecommunications, manufacturing, environmental management, and social media analytics.

Conclusions
Fuzzy clustering effectively handles ambiguity, providing meaningful, adaptable classifications and insights. Overcoming challenges related to parameter tuning and computational complexity will expand its practical applicability.

Fuzzy Cognitive Maps (FCMs)

Definition
Fuzzy Cognitive Maps (FCMs) are AI-based graphical representations used to model complex systems and causal relationships through interconnected concepts and fuzzy logic rules, facilitating decision-making and scenario analysis under uncertainty.

Key Components
FCMs involve concepts represented by nodes, causal relationships represented by directed edges with fuzzy weights, inference rules based on fuzzy logic, activation functions, iterative simulation processes, and scenario prediction capabilities.

Example
An FCM model representing environmental management can illustrate how changes in pollution, economic growth, and policy decisions impact environmental sustainability, allowing policymakers to simulate different scenarios and outcomes effectively.

Benefits
FCMs enhance decision-making through clear visualization, handle uncertainty efficiently, support scenario planning, facilitate stakeholder understanding of complex systems, and enable dynamic simulations.

Applications
Applications include environmental impact assessments, strategic planning, policy analysis, medical decision support, risk management, economic forecasting, and social dynamics modeling.

Industries
Industries utilizing FCMs include environmental management, healthcare, public policy, finance, strategic consulting, governmental agencies, urban planning, education, and social research.

Conclusions
FCMs provide powerful visual and analytical tools for managing complex decisions in uncertain environments. Addressing data and interpretability challenges ensures broader and effective use.

Fuzzy Control

Definition
Fuzzy control is an intelligent control strategy utilizing fuzzy logic to manage complex systems effectively by handling uncertainty and imprecision through linguistic rules and fuzzy inference methods.

Key Components
Components include fuzzy inference systems, fuzzification (input interpretation), linguistic control rules, defuzzification modules, membership functions, control strategy implementation, and adaptive learning algorithms.

Example
A fuzzy control system in an autonomous vehicle adjusts braking intensity based on ambiguous inputs like "close obstacle" or "fast approaching," ensuring smooth and safe responses in uncertain driving conditions.

Benefits
Fuzzy control effectively manages uncertainty, simplifies complex decision-making, enhances flexibility, provides intuitive control mechanisms, and improves adaptability and robustness of automated systems.

Applications
Applications include automated vehicle control, HVAC systems, robotic motion control, consumer electronics, industrial process automation, smart appliances, and energy management.

Industries
Industries employing fuzzy control include automotive, manufacturing, consumer electronics, robotics, transportation, industrial automation, home appliances, aerospace, and energy management.

Conclusions
Fuzzy control offers robust, intuitive solutions for controlling complex systems under uncertainty. Continued optimization of methods will enhance its practical effectiveness across various industries.

Fuzzy Decision Tree

Definition
A fuzzy decision tree is an AI classification model combining traditional decision tree methods with fuzzy logic principles, allowing decisions and classification outcomes to reflect uncertainty, ambiguity, or imprecise conditions.

Key Components
Fuzzy decision trees include fuzzy logic-based decision nodes, fuzzy membership functions, fuzzy splitting criteria, fuzzy rule sets, fuzzy thresholds, decision-making processes, and tree pruning methods.

Example
A credit scoring model using fuzzy decision trees assesses loan applicants using fuzzy conditions like "moderately high income" or "somewhat good credit score," providing nuanced and flexible risk assessments.

Benefits
Fuzzy decision trees enhance decision flexibility, manage uncertainty effectively, improve classification accuracy in ambiguous scenarios, and support intuitive explanations of complex decisions.

Applications
Applications include credit scoring systems, medical diagnostics, customer profiling, predictive analytics, risk assessment models, fraud detection, and decision-making in uncertain contexts.

Industries
Industries adopting fuzzy decision trees include finance, healthcare, insurance, telecommunications, human resources, marketing analytics, environmental management, and manufacturing quality control.

Conclusions
Fuzzy decision trees significantly enhance flexibility and accuracy in complex classification tasks. Addressing interpretability and computational challenges will increase adoption across diverse applications.

Fuzzy Inference System (FIS)

Definition
A Fuzzy Inference System (FIS) is an AI framework utilizing fuzzy logic principles to make decisions or solve problems in environments characterized by uncertainty and ambiguity. It interprets vague or imprecise input data through fuzzy rules, enabling flexible, human-like reasoning and decision-making.

Key Components
The main components of a FIS include fuzzification modules (transforming crisp inputs into fuzzy sets), a knowledge base containing fuzzy rules, an inference engine for reasoning, defuzzification modules (converting fuzzy outputs back to crisp values), and membership functions defining degrees of truth.

Example
A smart climate control system uses a Fuzzy Inference System to maintain room temperature comfortably, interpreting vague human inputs such as "somewhat cold" or "warm enough," and providing smooth temperature adjustments based on fuzzy rule sets.

Benefits
FIS effectively manages uncertainty, closely mimics human reasoning, enhances decision-making flexibility, supports intuitive system behavior, handles imprecise or ambiguous data efficiently, and improves system adaptability in dynamic conditions.

Applications
Applications of FIS include automated temperature control, intelligent traffic management, industrial process optimization, medical diagnosis systems, home automation, risk assessment, financial forecasting, and automated vehicle control systems.

Industries
Industries extensively utilizing FIS include manufacturing, automotive, healthcare, finance, consumer electronics, energy management, telecommunications, transportation, environmental control, and agricultural automation.

Conclusions
Fuzzy Inference Systems provide highly effective tools for decision-making under uncertainty, significantly enhancing system performance and adaptability. Overcoming challenges in complexity and interpretability ensures continued growth and broader industrial acceptance.

Fuzzy Logic

Definition
Fuzzy Logic is a computational logic system designed to represent uncertainty, ambiguity, and vagueness in data by allowing values to exist partially within defined sets rather than traditional binary true or false values, enabling reasoning and decision-making similar to human thought processes.

Key Components
Core components of fuzzy logic include fuzzy sets, linguistic variables, membership functions defining the degree of truth, fuzzy rule bases, fuzzification and defuzzification procedures, and inference engines for reasoning under uncertainty.

Example
An automatic washing machine employs fuzzy logic to determine the ideal washing cycle and time by interpreting vague inputs such as "slightly dirty" or "heavily soiled," resulting in effective cleaning while optimizing water and energy usage.

Benefits
Fuzzy logic enhances decision-making under uncertain conditions, supports intuitive and human-like reasoning, provides flexibility in handling ambiguous data, reduces complexity of modeling human judgments, and improves robustness in dynamic systems.

Applications
Fuzzy logic is utilized in consumer appliances, robotics, autonomous vehicles, medical diagnostic systems, control systems, natural language processing, image recognition, pattern classification, and intelligent decision-making systems.

Industries
Industries using fuzzy logic include consumer electronics, automotive systems, industrial automation, healthcare, finance, transportation, telecommunications, robotics, agriculture, and environmental management.

Conclusions
Fuzzy Logic significantly enhances the capability of AI systems to handle ambiguous and imprecise information, offering intuitive and efficient solutions across multiple domains. Addressing challenges will further extend its practical value and widespread adoption.

Fuzzy Neural Networks (FNNs)

Definition
Fuzzy Neural Networks (FNNs) are hybrid artificial intelligence systems that combine fuzzy logic principles and neural network architectures, enabling machines to handle uncertainty, ambiguity, and imprecision in data through human-like reasoning and learning processes.

Key Components
The key components of FNNs include fuzzy logic systems, neural network structures, fuzzy membership functions, fuzzy inference rules, adaptive learning algorithms, fuzzification and defuzzification mechanisms, and training optimization techniques.

Example
An automated climate control system in a smart home utilizes FNNs to adjust indoor temperatures. By interpreting vague user preferences such as "slightly warmer," the system adapts intelligently, balancing comfort and energy efficiency.

Benefits
FNNs handle uncertainty effectively, enhance model interpretability, improve generalization and robustness, combine human reasoning with automated learning, and provide more intuitive decision-making capabilities.

Applications
FNNs are used widely in areas such as control systems, autonomous vehicles, robotics navigation,

medical diagnostics, financial decision-making, risk assessment, weather forecasting, and industrial process optimization.

Industries
Industries employing FNNs include healthcare, automotive, finance, robotics, manufacturing, energy management, telecommunications, agriculture, and consumer electronics.

Conclusions
Fuzzy Neural Networks effectively merge the benefits of fuzzy logic and neural learning, enabling AI to tackle real-world problems involving uncertainty and ambiguity. Continued refinement of algorithms and interpretability will expand their practical applicability across industries.

Fuzzy Pattern Recognition

Definition
Fuzzy Pattern Recognition is an AI methodology that identifies, classifies, and analyzes patterns within data characterized by uncertainty, vagueness, or incomplete information using fuzzy logic approaches.

Key Components
Fuzzy Pattern Recognition consists of fuzzy logic frameworks, fuzzy sets, membership functions, fuzzy clustering methods, pattern classification algorithms, similarity measures, and decision-making models.

Example
A handwriting recognition system employing fuzzy pattern recognition accurately classifies handwritten letters, even when they appear distorted or unclear, by assessing degrees of similarity rather than binary certainty.

Benefits
Fuzzy pattern recognition effectively manages uncertainty and vagueness, provides improved accuracy in ambiguous scenarios, offers flexibility in classification tasks, enhances robustness, and mimics human cognitive reasoning.

Applications
Applications include image analysis, speech recognition, handwriting analysis, medical image diagnostics, fault detection in manufacturing, biometric authentication, customer behavior analysis, and environmental monitoring.

Industries
Industries applying fuzzy pattern recognition include healthcare, manufacturing quality control, security and biometrics, financial analytics, automotive diagnostics, robotics, consumer electronics, and marketing.

Conclusions
Fuzzy Pattern Recognition significantly advances AI's ability to analyze and classify uncertain or ambiguous data. Overcoming challenges related to complexity and interpretability will further enhance its utility across diverse sectors.

Letter G

Game AI

Definition
Game AI refers to artificial intelligence crafted to enhance video games, controlling non-player characters, shaping game worlds, or adapting challenges to player actions. It aims to create immersive, responsive experiences rather than just winning.

Key Components
Behavior rules or scripts dictate NPC actions, like patrol or attack. Pathfinding finds routes across maps, often via algorithms like A*. Decision-making systems weigh options, using trees or state machines. Learning adapts AI to player styles, sometimes via simple memory or models. Feedback loops tie AI to game dynamics, adjusting difficulty or pacing.

Benefits
It deepens immersion, making worlds feel alive. Quick responses keep gameplay fluid. Adaptability tailors challenges, boosting replay value. Lightweight versions run on modest hardware, and it frees developers to focus on story or design.

Examples
In a stealth game, an enemy guard spots a shadow, searches, then resumes patrol when fooled. A racing game's rival speeds up on straights but brakes late, mimicking skill.

Applications
It drives NPC behavior in action games, adjusts foes in strategy titles, and paces opponents in sports sims. Procedural content generation builds levels, while dynamic difficulty tweaks balance.

Industries
Gaming is its heart, from indie to AAA studios. Education uses it in training sims. Entertainment extends it to VR, and research tests AI in virtual sandboxes.

Summary
Game AI breathes life into pixels, crafting foes and friends that dance with players. It's a tightrope of fun and function, shining in engagement but fragile under pressure. A gaming essential, it's more art than science.

Game Theory in AI

Definition
Game Theory in AI applies mathematical models of strategic interaction to design or analyze AI systems, focusing on decision-making where outcomes depend on multiple agents' choices. It predicts behaviors in competitive or cooperative settings, guiding AI to act rationally.

Key Components
Agents, or players, make choices from strategy sets, like moves in a game. Payoffs assign value to outcomes, driving decisions. A game model—cooperative or not—frames interactions, often as matrices or trees. Equilibrium concepts, like Nash, predict stable strategies. Utility functions weigh agent goals, and iteration refines choices in repeated play.

Benefits
It sharpens AI for multi-agent scenarios, anticipating rival moves. Robustness grows as strategies handle conflict or alliances. It bridges theory to practice, optimizing real-world decisions. Clarity in trade-offs aids design, and it scales from simple to complex games.

Examples
An AI poker bot bluffs based on opponents' bet patterns, aiming for a Nash balance. A traffic AI coordinates signals, assuming cars pick selfish routes, easing jams.

Applications
It powers negotiation bots in trade. Autonomous drones coordinate in swarms. Auction systems bid smarter, and cybersecurity predicts attacker-defender dances. Multi-agent simulations test policies.

Industries
Finance uses it for market plays. Defense models combat scenarios. Tech builds cooperative robots, and transportation optimizes flows. Policy research simulates economics.

Summary
Game Theory in AI turns strategy into science, arming systems for rivalry or teamwork. It's a brainy edge in complex dances but stumbles on chaos or scale. A thinker's tool, it's key where choices collide.

Gated Attention Networks

Definition
Gated Attention Networks are neural network architectures that enhance attention mechanisms by adding gating functions to control the flow and weighting of information. They refine focus on relevant data features, improving performance in tasks requiring selective processing.

Key Components
The core is an attention mechanism that scores input relevance, paired with gates—often sigmoid or tanh functions—that modulate signal strength. Input embeddings feed the system, transformed by layers like transformers. A gating layer filters or amplifies attention outputs, and a final aggregator combines results for prediction or generation. Training tunes gates to balance focus and noise.

Benefits
They sharpen accuracy by prioritizing key inputs. Efficiency rises as gates cut irrelevant computations. Flexibility fits them to varied tasks, and they handle long dependencies better than plain attention. Robustness grows against cluttered data.

Examples
A translation system focuses on "dog" in "The dog runs," gating out filler words. A chatbot picks key phrases from a ramble, answering only what matters.

Applications
They improve machine translation with context focus. Text summarization grabs main points, and image captioning ties words to objects. Sentiment analysis hones in on tone, and question-answering targets query cues.

Industries
Tech powers NLP tools. Media crafts content, and marketing reads sentiment. Education builds smart tutors, and healthcare parses patient texts.

Summary
Gated Attention Networks are a fine-tuned lens, boosting AI's gaze with selective smarts. They excel in precision but wrestle with setup and scale. A sharp twist, they enhance focus where it counts

Gated Convolutional Networks

Definition
Gated Convolutional Networks are convolutional neural networks that add gating mechanisms to regulate feature flow across layers, enhancing how spatial or temporal data is processed. They filter noise and boost relevant signals in tasks like vision or audio.

Key Components
Convolutional layers extract features—edges or sounds—with kernels. Gating units, often sigmoid-based, scale feature maps, deciding what passes. Input data, like images or waves, feeds the stack. Pooling or upsampling refines resolution, and a final layer classifies or generates. Training optimizes gate behavior.

Benefits
They cut clutter, sharpening focus on key patterns. Efficiency rises with less wasted math. Adaptability suits diverse data types, and accuracy climbs in noisy settings. Gates add control without bloating size.

Examples
A photo AI spots a cat's face, gating out background blur. An audio filter keeps speech, muting crowd hum.

Applications
They classify images in vision tasks. Audio processing cleans signals, and video analysis tracks motion. Text convolution grabs phrases, and medical imaging highlights anomalies.

Industries
Tech powers vision tools. Media refines sound, and healthcare reads scans. Security spots threats, and automotive aids driving.

Summary
Gated Convolutional Networks are a selective sieve, honing convolution with precision gates. They excel in clear signals but need tuning finesse. A focused tweak, they cut through data noise.

Gated Feedback Recurrent Networks (GFRNs)

Definition
Gated Feedback Recurrent Networks are recurrent neural networks that use gating mechanisms to manage feedback loops between layers or time steps, refining how past information influences current processing. They aim to balance memory and adaptability in sequential tasks.

Key Components
A recurrent core processes sequences, with hidden states carrying memory. Feedback loops send outputs back to earlier layers, gated by functions like LSTMs' forget gate. Input and output layers frame the task, while gates—sigmoid-driven—control feedback strength. Training adjusts gate weights to optimize retention or reset.

Benefits
They retain long-term patterns without drowning in noise. Flexibility handles shifting sequences, and efficiency trims redundant loops. Robustness improves over vanilla RNNs, and they adapt fast to new inputs.

Examples
A stock predictor weighs yesterday's crash over last month's trend, gating old data. A music generator keeps a melody's theme, tweaking notes with feedback.

Applications
They forecast time series in finance. Speech recognition tracks phonemes, and music generation holds rhythm. Text prediction follows context, and robotics plans moves from past states.

Industries
Finance models markets. Media crafts audio, and tech drives assistants. Robotics refines control, and telecom predicts network loads.

Summary
GFRNs are memory maestros, weaving past into present with gated finesse. They shine in sequence smarts but demand careful crafting. A recursive gem, they balance history and now.

Gated Recurrent Unit (GRU)

Definition
A Gated Recurrent Unit is a streamlined recurrent neural network unit that uses update and reset gates to control information flow, simplifying memory management in sequential tasks. It's a lighter cousin of LSTMs, balancing efficiency and power.

Key Components
A hidden state carries memory across time steps, updated by an input. The update gate decides how much past data to keep, blending old and new. The reset gate wipes irrelevant history, focusing on current input. Simple math—additions and sigmoids—drives it, and training fits gates to the task.

Benefits
It's faster than LSTMs, with fewer parameters. Memory holds long enough for most sequences, and simplicity aids coding or scaling. Robustness handles varied data, and it trains well with less compute.

Examples
A text predictor types "rain" after "cloudy," reset gate dropping "sunny" from earlier. A speech AI tracks "hello," updating tone over syllables.

Applications
It powers text generation in chatbots. Time series predicts stocks, and speech synthesis flows words. Robotics plans from past moves, and sentiment tracks tone shifts.

Industries
Tech builds assistants. Finance forecasts trends, and media voices audio. Robotics refines actions, and telecom tunes signals.

Summary
GRUs are a lean memory machine, gating sequences with swift grace. They're a practical pick but trade depth for speed. A workhorse, they hum in tight spots.

Gaussian Mixture Models (GMM)

Definition
Gaussian Mixture Models are probabilistic models that represent data as a blend of multiple Gaussian distributions, each with its own mean and variance. They cluster or model complex datasets by assuming points arise from these mixed bell curves.

Key Components
Gaussian components—normal curves—define clusters, each with a mean, variance, and weight. A mixing coefficient sets how much each Gaussian contributes. Expectation-Maximization (EM) fits the model, guessing then refining parameters. Data points get soft labels, tied to all Gaussians by probability. Likelihood drives optimization.

Benefits
They capture multi-modal data, unlike single clusters. Flexibility fits odd shapes, and soft assignments reflect uncertainty well. Interpretability aids stats insight, and they scale with moderate data.

Examples
A GMM splits customer ages into "young" and "old" curves, weighting each. An audio AI models "ah" sounds, blending speaker tones.

Applications
They cluster market segments in analytics. Speech recognition sorts phonemes, and image segmentation groups pixels. Anomaly detection flags outliers, and robotics maps sensor noise.

Industries
Marketing targets groups. Media processes audio, and tech refines vision. Finance spots fraud, and robotics tunes perception.

Summary
GMMs are a soft sculptor, molding data into probabilistic peaks with finesse. They're a stats star but need careful sizing. A versatile fit, they blend clarity and complexity.

Gaussian Processes in AI

Definition
Gaussian Processes in AI are probabilistic models that predict outcomes by assuming data follows a multivariate Gaussian distribution over functions. They excel in regression or classification with uncertainty estimates, flexing to small datasets.

Key Components
A mean function sets a baseline prediction, often zero. A covariance (kernel) function defines how points relate—smooth or jagged—based on distance. Training data shapes the Gaussian, and inference predicts new points with variance. Hyperparameters tune the kernel, learned from data.

Benefits
They give uncertainty bounds, not just guesses, aiding trust. Flexibility fits quirky patterns with kernel tweaks. Small-data prowess shines where deep learning starves, and they're math-clean, dodging black-box woes. Adaptability suits niche tasks.

Examples
A GP predicts house prices, curving from size and location, with error bars. A robot maps a room, smoothing sensor blips into a layout.

Applications
They forecast trends in time series. Robotics maps environments, and optimization tunes models. Drug discovery predicts reactions, and climate models interpolate sparse readings.

Industries
Finance tracks markets. Robotics navigates, and pharma tests compounds. Science fills data gaps, and tech refines algorithms.

Summary
Gaussian Processes are a cautious oracle, blending prediction with doubt in a sleek package. They're small-data champs but buckle under bulk. A thoughtful pick, they glow in precision niches.

Gaze Tracking in AI

Definition
Gaze Tracking in AI is a technology that uses artificial intelligence to monitor and interpret where a person's eyes are looking, often by analyzing visual data from cameras. It maps eye movements to understand attention, intent, or behavior in real time.

Key Components
The system starts with a camera or sensor capturing eye images, feeding into an AI model—typically convolutional neural networks. Feature detection pinpoints pupils, irises, or gaze angles, guided by preprocessing like lighting correction. A mapping algorithm translates eye positions to screen coordinates or 3D space. Calibration tunes accuracy to individual users, and real-time processing tracks dynamic shifts.

Benefits
It offers precise, non-invasive insight into focus or interest. Speed enables instant feedback, and adaptability fits diverse setups. Low-cost cameras make it accessible, and it boosts interaction without touch or voice.

Examples
A game adjusts difficulty as a player's gaze drifts from key targets. A driver-assist AI alerts when eyes wander off the road too long.

Applications
It enhances gaming with eye-controlled inputs. Marketing studies ad attention, and assistive tech aids disabled users. Security verifies identity via gaze patterns, and VR aligns visuals to eye focus.

Industries
Gaming refines immersion. Automotive boosts safety, and marketing tracks engagement. Healthcare aids therapy, and tech powers interfaces.

Summary
Gaze Tracking in AI turns eyes into windows, reading focus with quiet precision. It's a versatile bridge to intent but battles noise and ethics. A subtle star, it sees where you look.

GeForce

Definition
GeForce is a brand of graphics processing units (GPUs) from NVIDIA, designed for high-performance graphics and increasingly leveraged for AI tasks via parallel computing. While not AI itself, it's a hardware backbone for many AI systems.

Key Components
The GPU core packs thousands of CUDA cores for parallel math, paired with fast VRAM for data crunching. Tensor cores speed AI-specific ops like matrix multiplies. Drivers and CUDA software unlock general-purpose computing. Cooling keeps it stable, and scalability links multiple cards.

Benefits
It delivers blazing speed for AI training or rendering. Cost-per-performance beats many rivals, and wide support eases coding. Versatility spans games to science, and power efficiency aids big setups.

Examples
A GeForce RTX trains a neural net, slashing hours off image generation. A gamer's rig doubles as a crypto miner, leveraging its cores.

Applications
It powers AI model training in labs. Gaming renders real-time visuals, and simulations model physics. Video editing speeds up, and data centers crunch analytics.

Industries
Tech drives AI and apps. Gaming fuels visuals, and media edits content. Science runs experiments, and finance models markets.

Summary
GeForce is a GPU titan, juicing AI and graphics with raw might. It's a workhorse for parallel tasks but costs and complexity loom. A hardware king, it's everywhere compute shines.

General AI (Artificial General Intelligence)

Definition
General AI, or Artificial General Intelligence (AGI), is a hypothetical AI capable of performing any intellectual task a human can, across domains, with adaptability and reasoning unbound by narrow goals. It's the dream of human-like machine smarts.

Key Components
A flexible learning system mimics human cognition, unbound by single tasks. Reasoning engines tackle logic, creativity, and abstraction. Memory stores and retrieves diverse knowledge, while perception—vision, sound—feeds understanding. Self-improvement loops refine its own code or skills.

Benefits
It could solve vast, cross-field problems fast. Versatility swaps specialized AIs, cutting costs. Creativity might outstrip humans, and autonomy frees labor. Scalability promises universal use.

Examples
An AGI writes a novel, then fixes a car, all from one mind. A doctor-bot diagnoses, counsels, and invents treatments in a day.

Applications
It revolutionizes science with broad insights. Healthcare merges diagnostics and care, and education tailors teaching. Business runs strategy, and art births new forms.

Industries
Tech chases it as the holy grail. Healthcare dreams of super-docs, and education rethinks learning. Defense eyes strategy, and arts push boundaries.

Summary
General AI is the ultimate brain, a jack-of-all-trades still in fantasy. It's a dazzling prize but a distant, dicey one. A grand vision, it's AI's unreachable star—for now.

Generalized Additive Models (GAM)

Definition
Generalized Additive Models are statistical models that extend linear regression by allowing non-linear relationships between predictors and outcomes, using smooth functions to capture patterns. They blend flexibility with interpretability.

Key Components
Predictors—input variables—feed the model, each tied to a smooth function like splines. A link function connects the sum of these to the outcome, handling non-normal data. Smoothing parameters control curve fit, avoiding noise. Estimation, often via backfitting, tunes the model. An intercept sets the baseline.

Benefits
They reveal non-linear trends without forcing shapes. Interpretability beats black-box rivals, showing each predictor's role. Flexibility fits varied data, and they balance bias and variance well. Simplicity aids quick use.

Examples
A GAM predicts home prices, curving income's effect beyond a line. A biologist models fish counts, smoothing depth's wavy impact.

Applications
It forecasts sales with seasonal curves. Ecology tracks species trends, and finance models risk. Healthcare links vitals to outcomes, and marketing fits ad effects.

Industries
Finance reads markets. Ecology studies nature, and healthcare analyzes patients. Marketing targets ads, and stats drives research.

Summary
GAMs are a stats flex, bending lines to fit life's curves with clear insight. They're a practical pick but call for finesse. A model bridge, they blend ease and depth.

Generalized Linear Models (GLM)

Definition
Generalized Linear Models are a stats framework that generalizes linear regression to handle diverse data types—like counts or binaries—via a link function tying predictors to outcomes. It's a versatile twist on a classic.

Key Components
Predictors drive the model, weighted by coefficients. A link function—like logit or log—maps the linear combo to the outcome's scale. A distribution, such as Poisson or binomial, fits the data's nature. Estimation, via maximum likelihood, sets weights. Variance reflects data spread.

Benefits
They fit non-normal data, widening use. Interpretability shows predictor roles, and flexibility spans tasks. Robustness handles noise, and they're light to compute.

Examples
A GLM predicts if it'll rain (yes/no) from temp and wind. A shop models daily sales, curving with promos.

Applications
It classifies risks in insurance. Healthcare predicts disease odds, and marketing fits click rates. Ecology counts species, and finance tracks defaults.

Industries
Insurance prices policies. Healthcare studies health, and marketing reads ads. Finance assesses risk, and ecology maps life.

Summary
GLMs are a stats chameleon, molding regression to any data with clear logic. They're a broad tool but need sharp setup. A flexible friend, they tame varied truths.

Generative Adversarial Imitation Learning (GAIL)

Definition
Generative Adversarial Imitation Learning is a machine learning technique that trains an agent to mimic expert behavior by combining imitation learning with generative adversarial networks. It uses a generator to produce actions and a discriminator to distinguish between expert and generated actions, refining the agent's policy through their rivalry.

Key Components
The system features a generator, typically a policy network, crafting actions from observations. A discriminator, acting as a judge, compares these actions to expert demonstrations. Expert trajectories—data from skilled performers—guide the process. A reward signal emerges from the discriminator's feedback, shaping the generator. Training alternates between optimizing both networks, balancing imitation and exploration.

Benefits
It learns complex behaviors without handcrafted rewards, saving design effort. Fast convergence comes from leveraging expert data directly. Flexibility adapts it to diverse tasks, and robustness grows as it mimics proven strategies. Scalability suits high-dimensional environments.

Examples
A robot arm learns to stack blocks by copying a human's moves, the discriminator flagging deviations. A virtual car masters racing, mimicking a pro driver's turns, guided by GAIL's feedback.

Applications
It trains robots for precise tasks like assembly. Autonomous vehicles adopt human driving styles, and game AI copies player tactics. Healthcare simulates expert surgeries, and finance mimics trading strategies.

Industries
Robotics refines automation. Automotive enhances self-driving tech, and gaming boosts NPC smarts. Healthcare aids training, and finance optimizes decisions.

Summary
GAIL is a clever mimic, wedding imitation to adversarial learning for swift, skilled agents. It's a shortcut to expertise but leans on data and balance. A dynamic tool, it excels where examples lead.

Generative Adversarial Networks (GANs)

Definition
Generative Adversarial Networks are a class of AI models where two neural networks—a generator and a discriminator—compete to create realistic data. The generator crafts fake samples from noise, while the discriminator judges them against real ones, refining both until the fakes pass muster.

Key Components
The generator starts with random input, shaping it into data like images or text. The discriminator evaluates authenticity, scoring real versus fake. A loss function pits them against each other, with the generator minimizing detection and the discriminator maximizing it. Training alternates their updates, balancing the duel. Datasets of real samples anchor the process, guiding the rivalry.

Benefits
GANs churn out lifelike data, from faces to music, with little hand-coding. Creativity soars as they invent beyond training sets. They adapt to varied tasks, and their unsupervised nature cuts labeling needs. Quality keeps climbing with more compute.

Examples
A GAN might generate a photo of a nonexistent person, fooling a viewer. Another could turn a sketch into a vivid painting, blending styles from real art.

Applications
It crafts fake images for design or testing. Video games generate textures or levels. Audio synthesis mimics voices, and data augmentation fills gaps in small sets. Forensics fakes evidence to train detectors.

Industries
Entertainment uses it for CGI and music. Tech boosts AI with synthetic data. Fashion designs virtual clothes, and healthcare simulates medical scans. Security tests systems with fake threats.

Summary
GANs are a bold leap in AI artistry, forging reality from rivalry with stunning flair. They're a

powerhouse for creation but wrestle with stability and ethics. A wild card, they redefine generative magic.

Generative AI

Definition
Generative AI is a branch of artificial intelligence that creates new content—like text, images, or sounds—by learning patterns from data and synthesizing novel outputs. It's the artist of AI, crafting from scratch.

Key Components
A generative model—like GANs or transformers—learns data distributions. Training data sets the style or rules, feeding encoders or latent spaces. Sampling generates outputs, guided by noise or prompts. Loss functions refine realism, and interfaces deliver user control.

Benefits
It spits out content fast, slashing creation time. Creativity bends to any domain, and customization fits specific needs. Data gaps fill with synthetic sets, and it scales with compute.

Examples
A tool paints a sunset from "orange sky" input. A bot writes a poem about loss, riffing on classics.

Applications
It designs art for ads. Text generation crafts stories, and music scores films. Data augmentation aids training, and games spawn levels.

Industries
Media fuels content. Marketing spins campaigns, and gaming builds worlds. Tech refines models, and education inspires lessons.

Summary
Generative AI is a maker's muse, weaving fresh works from learned threads. It's a creative spark but battles cost and quirks. A bold brush, it paints AI's future.

Definition
A Generative Pretrained Transformer is a neural network model, built on the transformer architecture, pretrained on vast text to generate human-like language or tackle diverse tasks. It's a word-weaving powerhouse fine-tuned for purpose.

Key Components
A transformer base uses attention to grasp text links. Pretraining on huge corpora builds broad knowledge. Tokenization chops text into bits, feeding layers of weights. Fine-tuning adapts it to tasks, and sampling crafts coherent outputs.

Benefits
It writes fluidly, aping human prose. Pretraining cuts task-specific data needs, and versatility spans writing to reasoning. Speed scales with GPUs, and it learns fast post-tune.

Examples
A GPT drafts an email from "urgent meeting" notes. A tutor bot explains calculus, riffing on prompts.

Applications
It powers chatbots with natural chat. Content creation spins blogs, and translation tweaks phrasing. Coding aids with snippets, and education crafts lessons.

Industries
Tech drives assistants. Media writes fast, and education teaches smart. Marketing tailors copy, and coding boosts dev speed.

Summary
GPT is a text titan, pretrained to pour out language with ease. It's a versatile scribe but wrestles with bias and bulk. A word wizard, it's AI's voice today.

Generative Coding

Definition
Generative Coding is an AI-driven approach where algorithms write or refine code based on examples, specs, or goals, automating programming tasks. It's a machine scribe for software.

Key Components
A generative model—like transformers—learns from codebases or prompts. Input specs—natural language or snippets—guide output. Syntax rules ensure valid code, and training data shapes style or logic. Feedback loops polish results, tweaking for bugs or fit.

Benefits
It speeds coding, slashing grunt work. Creativity crafts novel solutions, and it aids non-coders with usable scripts. Consistency follows learned norms, and scaling boosts big projects.

Examples
An AI writes a Python loop from "sum numbers" prompt. A bot fixes a buggy sort, guided by test fails.

Applications
It auto-codes apps from wireframes. Debugging patches errors, and testing generates cases. Education teaches via examples, and dev ops scripts tasks.

Industries
Tech accelerates software. Education trains coders, and startups prototype fast. Gaming scripts logic, and IT automates chores.

Summary
Generative Coding is a code conjurer, spinning scripts from hints with swift flair. It's a dev's boost but risks glitches and theft. A bold pen, it writes tech's future.

Generative Design in AI

Definition
Generative Design in AI is a creative process where artificial intelligence generates multiple design options based on defined constraints, goals, or user inputs, iterating to optimize outcomes. It's a digital muse for engineering, art, or planning.

Key Components
A generative algorithm—like evolutionary models or GANs—produces design candidates. Input parameters, such as size or strength, set boundaries. An evaluation function scores designs against goals like cost or aesthetics. Iteration refines options, and visualization tools display results for human review.

Benefits
It churns out diverse solutions fast, sparking innovation. Optimization finds efficient designs beyond human guesswork. Customization tailors outputs to needs, and it cuts trial time. Collaboration blends AI speed with human taste.

Examples
An AI designs a lightweight bridge, tweaking beams for strength and cost. A fashion bot crafts unique dresses, guided by "elegant, red" specs.

Applications
It shapes structures in architecture. Product design tests prototypes, and fashion creates styles. Urban planning maps layouts, and games build unique assets.

Industries
Architecture rethinks buildings. Manufacturing speeds products, and fashion explores trends. Gaming crafts worlds, and urban planning optimizes cities.

Summary
Generative Design in AI is a builder's brainstorm, spinning endless options with smart limits. It's a fast innovator but needs clear aims. A design ally, it melds tech and vision.

Genetic Algorithms for Feature Selection

Definition
Genetic Algorithms for Feature Selection use evolutionary principles to pick the best subset of data features for a machine learning task, optimizing performance by evolving feature combinations. It's survival of the fittest for data traits.

Key Components
A population of feature subsets starts as random bit strings—1s for picked, 0s for dropped. A fitness function scores subsets, often model accuracy. Selection keeps top performers, crossover mixes subsets, and mutation flips bits. Iteration refines until a lean, strong set emerges.

Benefits
It trims noise, boosting model speed and precision. Automation skips manual picks, and it finds odd combos humans miss. Scalability handles big feature pools, and flexibility fits any task.

Examples
A spam filter evolves to use word count and sender, dropping date. A cancer model selects gene markers, ignoring redundant traits.

Applications
It preps data for classification in AI. Finance picks stock predictors, and image analysis grabs key pixels. Text mining chooses words, and healthcare filters vitals.

Industries
Tech refines AI. Finance tunes models, and healthcare aids diagnosis. Media analyzes content, and security spots threats.

Summary
Genetic Algorithms for Feature Selection are a data Darwinist, breeding lean feature sets with grit. They're a smart trimmer but demand power and care. A clever cut, they sharpen AI's edge.

Genetic Programming (GP)

Definition
Genetic Programming is an evolutionary AI technique that evolves computer programs or expressions to solve problems, using natural selection principles. It breeds code, not just parameters, aiming for optimal logic.

Key Components
A population of program trees—code snippets—starts the run. A fitness function tests how well each solves the task. Selection picks winners, crossover swaps code chunks, and mutation tweaks syntax. Iteration grows better programs until a threshold hits.

Benefits
It crafts solutions no human might dream up. Flexibility fits odd problems, and automation skips manual coding. Novelty sparks innovation, and it scales with compute.

Examples
A GP evolves a math formula to fit sales data. A robot learns to walk, its code mutating per step.

Applications
It designs circuits in engineering. Software auto-writes algorithms, and finance models trades. Games evolve bot logic, and science fits equations.

Industries
Engineering builds systems. Tech refines code, and finance predicts markets. Gaming boosts AI, and science probes data.

Summary
Genetic Programming is a code breeder, growing logic through evolution's lens. It's a wild inventor but messy and slow. A quirky craft, it codes the unthought.

GENTLE SINGULARITY

Definition
A **Gentle Singularity** is a forward-looking concept in artificial intelligence that envisions the rise of superintelligent AI unfolding gradually rather than as a sudden, disruptive event. The term, frequently associated with Sam Altman, suggests that the transition to a world where AI surpasses human cognitive abilities will occur in a series of manageable stages. In this vision, society experiences the transformation as a smooth progression, giving people and institutions time to adapt to new capabilities and realities.

Key Components

Gradual Transition
AI becomes more capable over time through steady improvements rather than abrupt leaps.

Perceived Stability
Despite exponential growth in intelligence, the pace of visible change feels continuous and controllable.

Progressive Integration
AI systems become more embedded in everyday life—enhancing tools, services, and industries incrementally.

Safety and Governance
The approach emphasizes deliberate attention to ethics, alignment, and societal well-being throughout the AI advancement process.

Benefits

Encourages societies to thoughtfully adapt to AI's growing role.

Reduces public anxiety about AI by presenting a non-threatening pathway to superintelligence.

Allows time for educational systems, legal frameworks, and economic models to evolve in response to AI advancements.

Promotes a climate of international cooperation around AI safety and standards.

Supports the development of AI in ways that align with human values and global benefit.

Examples

AI writing assistants that gradually improve in quality and accessibility.

Robots slowly gaining more autonomy in industries like logistics, healthcare, and agriculture.

Collaborative development of AI alignment techniques across research labs and companies.

Public policy discussions evolving alongside AI progress, fostering proactive regulation.

Widespread adoption of AI agents for managing information, scheduling, and knowledge work over time.

Applications

Strategic planning for AI deployment across public and private sectors.

Development of AI alignment frameworks and ethical guidelines.

Educational initiatives aimed at preparing future generations to work alongside AI.

Policy formulation for managing the economic and social impacts of advanced AI.

Corporate roadmaps for integrating AI into business operations with long-term stability.

Industries

Government and public policy.

Technology and AI development.

Education and workforce training.

Healthcare and human services.

Scientific research and discovery.

Challenges

A smooth transition is not guaranteed—unexpected breakthroughs could still trigger rapid shifts.

Global disparities in AI adoption may cause uneven benefits and risks across societies.

Maintaining consistent alignment of AI systems as they grow more capable remains a complex challenge.

Managing public expectations and preparing for both gradual and sudden changes requires continuous effort.

Balancing innovation with caution is a delicate and evolving task for governments and industry leaders.

Summary
The **Gentle Singularity** presents a hopeful and measured outlook on the rise of superintelligent AI. Rather than a single moment of uncontrollable change, this concept envisions AI capabilities advancing in a way that allows societies to adapt, govern, and benefit from new technologies. It underscores the importance of foresight, ethical development, and collaborative governance as humanity navigates the path toward a future shaped by ever more intelligent machines.

Geospatial AI

Definition
Geospatial AI is artificial intelligence that analyzes spatial data—like maps, satellite shots, or GPS—to uncover patterns, predict events, or guide decisions tied to location. It's AI with a sense of place.

Key Components
Spatial data—coordinates, imagery—feeds the system, often via GIS tools. AI models, like CNNs or RNNs, extract features or trends. Geocoding ties data to spots, and visualization maps insights. Training blends location with context, like weather or traffic.

Benefits
It spots trends tied to where, not just what. Precision aids pinpoint planning, and scale crunches vast Earth data. Speed beats manual maps, and it adapts to shifting spaces.

Examples
An AI predicts flood zones from river maps and rain data. A city tracks traffic jams, rerouting cars via GPS.

Applications
It forecasts weather with satellite feeds. Urban planning shapes cities, and agriculture picks crop spots. Disaster response maps risks, and navigation optimizes routes.

Industries
Government plans infrastructure. Agriculture boosts yields, and tech powers maps. Defense tracks threats, and logistics speeds delivery.

Summary
Geospatial AI puts smarts on the map, tying place to insight with sharp eyes. It's a planner's dream but fights data and scale. A grounded force, it knows where it stands.

Ghost Chatbots

Definition
Ghost Chatbots are AI conversational agents designed to operate invisibly, automating tasks or chats without users knowing they're not human. They're silent stand-ins for people.

Key Components
A natural language model drives human-like chat, often pretrained. Context tracking keeps talks coherent, and task logic—rules or scripts—guides actions. Stealth design mimics tone or style, and integration slots them into platforms. Monitoring logs their quiet work.

Benefits
They save time, handling chats unseen. Seamlessness keeps user trust, and scalability manages mass talks. Cost drops versus human staff, and they run 24/7.

Examples
A ghost bot books a hotel, posing as a clerk via text. An FAQ bot answers "where's my order?" as if staff.

Applications
It runs customer support silently. Sales nudge buyers, and HR screens hires. Education grades chats, and social media fakes engagement.

Industries
Retail aids shoppers. Tech supports users, and HR streamlines hiring. Marketing boosts reach, and education scales help.

Summary
Ghost Chatbots are AI phantoms, chatting in shadows with slick ease. They're a quiet fix but skate on trust's edge. A sneaky aid, they whisper in tech's wings.

Ghost Data in AI

Definition
Ghost Data in AI refers to synthetic or artificial data generated by AI systems to fill gaps, simulate scenarios, or enhance datasets when real data is scarce or sensitive. It's a digital phantom, crafted to mimic reality for training or testing purposes.

Key Components
A generative model—like GANs or VAEs—creates the data from noise or patterns. Real data seeds the process, setting the style or structure. Constraints or rules ensure relevance, such as matching statistical properties. Validation checks ghost data against real-world benchmarks, and integration blends it into workflows.

Benefits
It plugs data shortages, boosting model robustness. Privacy improves by avoiding real personal info. Speed ramps up with instant generation, and flexibility crafts edge cases. Cost drops versus collecting fresh data.

Examples
A ghost dataset of fake patient records trains a medical AI, dodging privacy laws. A self-driving car simulator generates ghost traffic data for rare crash scenarios.

Applications
It augments training sets for machine learning. Testing validates systems with controlled fakes. Privacy-sensitive fields use it to anonymize, and simulations model hypotheticals. Research explores uncharted data zones.

Industries
Healthcare swaps real records for ghosts. Automotive tests autonomy, and tech refines algorithms. Finance simulates markets, and gaming mimics player behavior.

Summary
Ghost Data in AI is a crafted stand-in, filling voids with synthetic smarts. It's a privacy savior and test booster but demands careful forging. A shadow tool, it mirrors without being.

Ghost Imaging in AI

Definition
Ghost Imaging in AI is a computational technique that reconstructs images using AI to process

correlations between light patterns and single-pixel detectors, rather than direct capture. It's an indirect peek, leveraging math and learning.

Key Components
A light source projects random patterns onto an object. A bucket detector grabs total intensity, not spatial detail. AI—often neural nets—decodes these into images, trained on pattern-output pairs. Preprocessing cleans noise, and optimization tunes reconstruction.

Benefits
It images through fog or noise where cameras fail. Low light works fine, cutting hardware needs. AI speeds and sharpens results, and it scales to tough conditions. Simplicity suits remote or stealth use.

Examples
An AI reconstructs a face through smoke, using ghost imaging from scattered light. A night vision bot maps a room with minimal photons.

Applications
It aids surveillance in low visibility. Medical imaging peers through tissue, and astronomy sees faint stars. Security scans hidden objects, and robotics navigates murk.

Industries
Defense spies in haze. Healthcare probes bodies, and astronomy charts skies. Security screens bags, and robotics explores dark.

Summary
Ghost Imaging in AI is a sly seer, conjuring images from light's whispers with AI's aid. It's a fog-piercer but leans on tech heft. A quiet marvel, it reveals the unseen.

Ghost Inventory Management

Definition
Ghost Inventory Management is an AI-driven approach to track and optimize stock that's misreported or missing—like phantom items in warehouses—using predictive models to correct discrepancies.

Key Components
Inventory data—real-time or logs—feeds the system. AI models, like anomaly detectors, spot ghost entries. Predictive algorithms guess true stock from patterns. Correction rules adjust records, and integration syncs with supply chains.

Benefits
It cuts losses from phantom stock errors. Accuracy boosts order fulfillment, and automation saves manual audits. Insights predict shortages, and it scales across big warehouses.

Examples
An AI flags 100 ghost widgets, fixing a scanner glitch. A retailer predicts stockouts, tracing ghost data to theft.

Applications
It syncs e-commerce stock. Warehouses audit hands-free, and retail curbs overstock. Logistics tracks goods, and manufacturing aligns production.

Industries
Retail keeps shelves real. Logistics moves goods, and manufacturing tunes output. E-commerce syncs sales, and warehousing cuts waste.

Summary
Ghost Inventory Management is a stock sleuth, banishing phantoms with AI's eye. It's a saver of chaos but battles data rot. A silent fixer, it keeps counts true.

Ghost Motion Detection

Definition
Ghost Motion Detection is an AI technique to identify movement in data—like video or radar—where noise or reflections create false "ghost" signals, filtering them with smart analysis.

Key Components
Sensors—cameras or radar—capture raw motion. AI classifiers tag real versus ghost moves, trained on labeled noise. Feature extraction pulls speed or shape, and filtering rules cut false positives. Real-time processing tracks live shifts.

Benefits
It cleans noisy feeds for true motion. Accuracy aids safety or tracking, and speed fits live use. Low false alarms save effort, and it adapts to weird settings.

Examples
A car radar spots a real truck, ignoring a ghost echo. A cam cuts wind-blown leaves, tracking a person.

Applications
It refines self-driving navigation. Security watches perimeters, and robotics avoids false bumps. Traffic counts cars, and sports tracks players.

Industries
Automotive drives safe. Security guards sites, and robotics moves smart. Transport flows smooth, and sports analyzes games.

Summary
Ghost Motion Detection is a motion purist, sifting real from fake with AI's sieve. It's a clarity champ but fights chaos. A sharp guard, it sees what moves.

Ghost Neural Networks

Definition
Ghost Neural Networks are lightweight AI architectures that use efficient operations—like ghost modules—to generate features with fewer parameters, slashing compute while keeping power.

Key Components
Ghost modules split convolutions, reusing features via cheap transforms. A slim backbone stacks these, cutting fat. Input data flows through lean layers, and optimization trims weights. Training balances speed and accuracy.

Benefits
They run fast on weak hardware. Low memory fits phones, and power use drops. Scalability suits big tasks, and they hold decent precision.

Examples
A ghost net IDs faces on a cheap cam, skipping bloat. A phone bot predicts text, lean and quick.

Applications
It powers mobile AI apps. Edge devices run vision, and IoT processes sensors. Games optimize NPCs, and wearables track health.

Industries
Tech shrinks apps. Gaming speeds play, and IoT connects smart. Healthcare fits wearables, and edge computing thrives.

Summary
Ghost Neural Networks are AI's lightweights, sprinting with less baggage. They're edge heroes but trade depth for thrift. A lean breed, they fit tight spaces.

Ghost Robotics

Definition

Ghost Robotics refers to AI-powered robotic systems designed for autonomy in tough terrains or tasks, often lightweight and adaptive, built to haunt harsh zones with minimal fuss.

Key Components
A rugged chassis carries sensors—LIDAR, cams—for perception. AI brains, often neural nets, plan paths or acts. Actuators drive motion, guided by real-time control. Power packs fuel long runs, and comms link to bases.

Benefits
They roam where humans can't, fast and tough. Autonomy cuts oversight, and resilience beats rough ground. Scalability fits fleets, and they swap humans in risk.

Examples
A ghost bot patrols a desert border, dodging rocks. A mine rover sniffs gas, AI steering clear of blasts.

Applications
It scouts for defense. Search rescues in rubble, and industry checks hazards. Agriculture maps fields, and space explores moons.

Industries
Defense guards fronts. Rescue aids crises, and industry runs plants. Agriculture farms smart, and space probes beyond.

Summary
Ghost Robotics is a rugged roamer, haunting hard spots with AI grit. It's a tough trekker but fights limits. A bold bot, it steps where few dare.

Ghost Signal Processing in AI

Definition
Ghost Signal Processing in AI is the use of artificial intelligence to clean or interpret signals—like audio or radar—where noise or echoes create ghost artifacts, isolating true data.

Key Components
Raw signals—sound, waves—hit the system. AI models, like CNNs or RNNs, detect ghost versus real patterns. Preprocessing filters noise, and feature extraction pulls key traits. Post-processing refines outputs for use.

Benefits
It sharpens muddy signals fast. Accuracy spots faint truths, and automation skips manual sifts. Robustness beats interference, and it scales to big feeds.

Examples
An AI clears a ghost echo from a sonar ping, mapping a sub. A mic bot cuts crowd noise, hearing a whisper.

Applications
It cleans audio for assistants. Radar tracks planes, and telecom boosts calls. Medical devices read vitals, and defense hears foes.

Industries
Tech aids voice. Defense spies signals, and telecom links clear. Healthcare tunes gear, and transport guides safe.

Summary
Ghost Signal Processing in AI is a signal purifier, stripping phantoms with sharp AI ears. It's a clarity king but battles faint foes. A quiet craft, it hears what's real.

Ghost Traffic Prediction in AI

Definition
Ghost Traffic Prediction in AI is a method where artificial intelligence forecasts traffic patterns or flows that are not directly observed, such as hidden congestion or phantom slowdowns, using inferred data and predictive models. It aims to reveal unseen dynamics on roads or networks.

Key Components
The system uses historical traffic data as a baseline, paired with an AI model—often neural networks or time-series predictors—to infer patterns. Auxiliary inputs like weather, events, or sensor gaps guide predictions. Anomaly detection flags ghost effects, and real-time updates refine forecasts. Validation cross-checks against partial real data.

Benefits
It uncovers hidden bottlenecks, boosting planning. Accuracy aids preemptive traffic control, and it saves costs by leveraging existing data. Flexibility fits sparse networks, and proactive insights cut delays.

Examples
An AI predicts a ghost jam on a rural road, inferred from nearby highway slowdowns. A city model spots phantom rush-hour creep from event spillover.

Applications
It optimizes urban traffic signals. Logistics reroutes trucks, and navigation apps warn of unseen delays. Smart cities plan roads, and transport models ghost flows.

Industries
Transport manages flow. Logistics speeds delivery, and urban planning shapes cities. Tech refines navigation, and government curbs congestion.

Summary
Ghost Traffic Prediction in AI is a shadow spotter, mapping unseen traffic with clever inference. It's a planner's edge but fights data voids. A quiet fixer, it smooths the invisible.

Ghostwriter AI

Definition
Ghostwriter AI is an artificial intelligence tool designed to generate text—articles, stories, or code—

mimicking human style, often acting as an unseen assistant to writers or developers. It's a digital scribe with no byline.

Key Components
A language model—like transformers—drives output, trained on vast text. Prompts or templates steer tone and content. Contextual memory tracks intent, and fine-tuning aligns with user voice. Editing loops polish drafts for coherence.

Benefits
It speeds writing, slashing time. Creativity sparks from prompts, and it aids non-writers with pro text. Consistency holds style, and scalability pumps volume.

Examples
A ghostwriter AI pens a blog from "sustainability tips" notes. A coder gets a script draft, tweaked from "sort list" input.

Applications
It crafts marketing copy fast. Authors plot novels, and devs auto-code. Education builds essays, and businesses draft emails.

Industries
Media spins content. Marketing sells ideas, and tech codes quick. Education teaches writing, and startups scale words.

Summary
Ghostwriter AI is a silent pen, weaving words or code with eerie ease. It's a fast muse but risks flatness. A shadow writer, it aids but doesn't feel.

Gibbs Sampling in AI

Definition
Gibbs Sampling in AI is a statistical technique within Markov Chain Monte Carlo methods, used to sample from complex probability distributions by iteratively updating variables based on their conditional probabilities. It's a step-by-step probability explorer.

Key Components
A joint distribution defines the target, often high-dimensional. Conditional probabilities guide each variable's update, drawn from simpler forms. An initial state seeds the chain, and iteration cycles through variables. Convergence yields samples reflecting the true distribution.

Benefits
It cracks tough distributions without full math. Simplicity scales to many variables, and flexibility fits Bayesian models. Accuracy grows with steps, and it's light on setup.

Examples
An AI samples user preferences, updating age then taste from survey data. A model infers weather odds, cycling rain and wind guesses.

Applications
It powers Bayesian inference in stats. Machine learning samples posteriors, and physics simulates states. Finance models risk, and biology fits genes.

Industries
Stats drives research. Tech tunes models, and finance predicts markets. Science explores systems, and healthcare maps health.

Summary
Gibbs Sampling in AI is a patient picker, teasing out probabilities with steady steps. It's a stats stalwart but plods at scale. A quiet sampler, it finds the odds.

Gig Economy AI

Definition
Gig Economy AI is artificial intelligence tailored to support, optimize, or automate tasks in the gig economy, where short-term, flexible work dominates. It's a digital aide for freelancers and platforms.

Key Components
AI models—like classifiers or predictors—analyze gig data. Task-matching algorithms pair workers to jobs. Automation handles scheduling or pay, and learning adapts to trends. Platforms integrate it for seamless use.

Benefits
It speeds job matches, cutting search time. Efficiency boosts gig flow, and personalization fits worker skills. Scale handles mass gigs, and cost drops for platforms.

Examples
An AI pairs a driver with a ride, factoring distance. A bot schedules a tutor, dodging clashes.

Applications
It matches freelancers to gigs. Platforms optimize pricing, and scheduling streamlines shifts. Analytics track trends, and support aids workers.

Industries
Gig platforms thrive. Transport moves riders, and education links tutors. Creative fields find talent, and delivery speeds goods.

Summary
Gig Economy AI is a gig glue, binding workers to tasks with smart ease. It's a flow booster but wrestles fairness. A platform pal, it hums in flex work.

Gig Economy Prediction Models

Definition
Gig Economy Prediction Models are AI-driven systems that forecast trends, demand, or worker behavior in the gig economy, using data to guide planning. It's a crystal ball for freelance flux.

Key Components
Historical gig data—hours, pay—feeds the model, often time-series or regression-based. Features like location or season shape predictions. Training tunes accuracy, and real-time inputs update forecasts. Validation checks against outcomes.

Benefits
It predicts demand spikes, aiding prep. Accuracy guides pricing, and foresight cuts waste. Flexibility fits gig shifts, and scale crunches big trends.

Examples
A model predicts more rides in rain, upping driver calls. A platform sees holiday task booms, prepping freelancers.

Applications
It forecasts ride demand in transport. Platforms set rates, and logistics plans deliveries. Analytics spots trends, and HR gigs staff.

Industries
Transport readies fleets. Gig platforms plan, and delivery times goods. Analytics sells insights, and staffing fills gaps.

Summary
Gig Economy Prediction Models are a gig seer, calling trends with data's eye. They're a planner's pick but fight flux. A forecast friend, they peek at gig life.

Gigabit AI Networks

Definition
Gigabit AI Networks are high-speed neural networks or systems running at gigabit-per-second data rates, optimized for real-time AI with massive throughput. It's speed married to smarts.

Key Components
Fast GPUs or ASICs push gigabit flows. High-bandwidth pipes—like fiber—move data, and low-latency designs cut delays. AI models process live streams, and optimization trims fat. Cooling keeps pace.

Benefits
They act in a flash, perfect for live tasks. Bandwidth eats big data, and speed scales to crowds. Efficiency saves power, and real-time shines in chaos.

Examples
A network spots factory flaws at gigabit speed. A live translator keeps up with speech, no lag.

Applications
It runs live vision in cars. Telecom streams calls, and factories watch lines. Security scans crowds, and games react instant.

Industries
Automotive drives safe. Telecom talks fast, and manufacturing checks quality. Security guards live, and gaming plays smooth.

GigaAI Platforms

Definition
GigaAI Platforms are large-scale AI ecosystems designed to deliver massive computational power, often at the gigaflop level, for advanced tasks across industries. It's a titan hub for smart work.

Key Components
High-end GPUs or TPUs drive gigaflop math. Cloud or on-prem setups host it, with APIs for access. Scalable frameworks—like TensorFlow—run models, and data pipelines feed big inputs. Security locks it tight.

Benefits
They blast through huge tasks fast. Scale fits any load, and power fuels cutting-edge AI. Cost spreads over users, and access opens to small players.

Examples
A GigaAI platform trains a city-wide traffic AI in days. A lab runs genome models, crunching billions of flops.

Applications
It trains giant AI models. Science sims nature, and analytics digs data. Games render worlds, and healthcare maps diseases.

Industries
Tech builds AI. Science probes deep, and gaming crafts play. Healthcare heals smart, and finance predicts cash.

Summary
GigaAI Platforms are AI giants, wielding gigaflops for epic feats. They're a power play but pricey and complex. A big beast, they lift heavy AI loads.

Summary
Gigabit AI Networks are a fast brain, racing data with AI's wit. They're a live-wire win but fight cost and scale. A speed demon, they think on the fly.

Gigaflop AI Performance

Definition
Gigaflop AI Performance measures an AI system's ability to execute a billion floating-point operations per second, gauging raw compute power for tasks like training or inference. It's a muscle metric.

Key Components
Hardware—like GPUs—delivers gigaflops, backed by optimized code. Workloads—matrix math or convolutions—test it. Benchmark tools clock speed, and efficiency tweaks maximize flops. Cooling sustains peak runs.

Benefits
High gigaflops crush big jobs fast. Power scales to tough AI, and metrics guide hardware picks. Efficiency aids cost, and it flexes across fields.

Examples
A gigaflop rig trains a vision AI in hours. A bot runs speech inference, hitting gigaflop marks.

Applications
It trains deep nets in labs. Games render AI foes, and science sims physics. Finance crunches risk, and media edits fast.

Industries
Tech pushes AI. Gaming powers play, and science digs deep. Finance predicts, and media crafts.

Summary
Gigaflop AI Performance is a raw gauge, flexing AI's math might in billions. It's a speed stamp but not the full tale. A power pulse, it drives big brains.

Gigapixel AI Imaging

Definition
Gigapixel AI Imaging is an artificial intelligence technique that enhances or generates ultra-high-

resolution images, often reaching billions of pixels, by upscaling or reconstructing details from lower-quality inputs. It's a digital magnifier for visual clarity.

Key Components
The process starts with a base image, fed into an AI model—typically a convolutional neural network or GAN. Upscaling algorithms infer fine details, guided by trained patterns. Preprocessing cleans noise, and post-processing sharpens edges. High-performance hardware, like GPUs, powers the heavy math.

Benefits
It revives blurry shots into crisp giants. Detail boosts analysis or art, and speed scales big jobs. Flexibility fits old or new images, and it cuts need for pricey cameras.

Examples
An AI turns a fuzzy 1MP photo into a 1-gigapixel masterpiece, revealing hidden textures. A satellite image sharpens to spot tiny rooftops from space.

Applications
It restores vintage photos. Surveillance zooms into faces, and medical imaging clarifies scans. Design crafts huge prints, and gaming textures pop.

Industries
Media revamps visuals. Security peers deeper, and healthcare sees finer. Gaming builds worlds, and archives preserve past.

Summary
Gigapixel AI Imaging is a vision booster, swelling pixels with AI's keen eye. It's a detail dynamo but leans on power and care. A sharp leap, it redefines clarity.

Giga-Scale AI Models

Definition
Giga-Scale AI Models are massive artificial intelligence systems with billions of parameters, designed to handle vast data and complex tasks through sheer scale and computational might. They're the giants of machine learning.

Key Components
A deep neural architecture—like transformers—packs giga-parameters. Huge datasets train it, often terabytes of text or images. High-end GPUs or TPUs crunch the math, and distributed systems split loads. Optimization tunes the beast, cutting inefficiency.

Benefits
They master broad tasks with top accuracy. Scale eats big data, and power fuels breakthroughs. Versatility spans fields, and pretraining cuts task-specific work.

Examples
A giga-model writes a novel from a sentence stub. A vision AI tags every object in a city cam feed.

Applications
It powers chatbots with human-like chat. Vision IDs rare patterns, and science predicts molecules. Translation spans tongues, and games craft smart foes.

Industries
Tech drives assistants. Science probes deep, and media spins content. Gaming plays smart, and healthcare diagnoses big.

Summary
Giga-Scale AI Models are brain behemoths, flexing billions of nodes for epic feats. They're a power peak but strain resources and rules. A grand force, they reshape AI's reach.

GigaTensor AI

Definition
GigaTensor AI refers to AI systems leveraging tensor computations at a massive scale—gigatensors with billions of elements—to process multidimensional data for tasks like deep learning or simulations. It's math on a monster scale.

Key Components
Tensors—multidimensional arrays—hold data like images or time series. Giga-scale ops, powered by GPUs, crunch them fast. Frameworks like TensorFlow manage flows, and decomposition shrinks memory use. Parallel setups split the load across machines.

Benefits
It handles huge, complex data swift. Power scales to deep nets, and efficiency trims waste. Flexibility fits diverse math, and speed boosts real tasks.

Examples
A giga-tensor AI predicts weather, tensorizing global grids. A vision model processes 4D video, tagging moves.

Applications
It trains giant vision nets. Science models physics, and finance crunches markets. Games render AI, and robotics maps space.

Industries
Tech builds AI. Science sims nature, and finance forecasts cash. Gaming crafts play, and robotics moves smart.

Summary
GigaTensor AI is a tensor titan, wielding math might for vast tasks. It's a scale star but fights bloat and bucks. A deep dive, it powers big data brains.

Gini Coefficient in AI

Definition
The Gini Coefficient in AI is a statistical measure adapted from economics to assess fairness, bias, or distribution in AI outputs—like prediction accuracy across groups. It's an equity lens for algorithms.

Key Components
A dataset splits into groups—like users or classes. AI outputs—scores or labels—feed the metric. The Gini formula compares distribution to perfect equality, ranging 0 to 1. Analysis interprets skew, and mitigation tweaks models.

Benefits
It spots bias fast, aiding fairness. Simplicity fits any output, and clarity guides fixes. Scalability scans big data, and it bridges ethics to math.

Examples
An AI loan model's Gini shows richer applicants score higher, flagging bias. A hiring AI's Gini reveals gender skew in rankings.

Applications
It checks fairness in hiring AI. Finance tests loan equity, and healthcare scans diagnosis gaps. Marketing balances ad reach, and policy audits impact.

Industries
Finance ensures fair cash. HR hires even, and healthcare treats all. Tech tunes ethics, and government weighs policy.

Summary
The Gini Coefficient in AI is a fairness gauge, shining math on bias with crisp clarity. It's an ethics aid but needs wise use. A balance beam, it rights AI's tilt.

Goal-Driven Automation

Definition
Goal-Driven Automation is an AI approach where systems autonomously execute tasks to meet predefined objectives, adapting actions to hit targets without rigid scripts. It's purpose with a brain.

Key Components
A goal—clear and measurable—steers the system. AI logic—like planners or RL—charts paths. Sensors or data track progress, and actuators or software act. Feedback loops adjust, aligning to the goal.

Benefits
It cuts micromanagement, saving time. Flexibility fits shifting scenes, and efficiency hits targets fast. Autonomy scales big jobs, and it learns better paths.

Examples
An AI restocks shelves, aiming for zero outages, picking routes. A bot optimizes ad spend, targeting max clicks.

Applications
It runs warehouse logistics. Marketing tunes campaigns, and factories hit quotas. Homes adjust energy, and offices schedule smart.

Industries
Logistics moves goods. Marketing sells smart, and manufacturing hums. Tech automates life, and energy saves power.

Challenges
Vague goals flop plans. Data gaps misguide, and compute scales costs. Errors derail off-script, and trust needs proof.

Summary
Goal-Driven Automation is a task chaser, hitting marks with AI's wit. It's a freehand win but risks drift. A smart doer, it aims and acts.

Goal-Oriented Neural Networks

Definition
Goal-Oriented Neural Networks are neural architectures designed to optimize specific objectives—like accuracy or speed—by embedding goal-driven logic into their structure or training. It's a net with a mission.

Key Components
A neural base—like CNNs—processes data. Goal functions—like loss or reward—shape learning. Layers or gates prioritize key inputs, and training aligns weights to the goal. Feedback refines focus over epochs.

Benefits
They nail targets with precision. Efficiency cuts waste, and adaptability fits tasks. Speed scales to goals, and clarity ties design to aim.

Examples
A net IDs tumors, tuned for zero misses. A bot predicts stock dips, aiming for profit.

Applications
It classifies images for safety. Finance forecasts gains, and chatbots hit tone. Games optimize moves, and health flags risks.

Industries
Healthcare spots ills. Finance bets smart, and tech talks right. Gaming plays well, and security guards.

Summary
Goal-Oriented Neural Networks are aim-locked nets, chasing ends with tight focus. They're a purpose pro but can blink narrow. A driven mind, they seek and score.

Goal-Seeking Neural Networks

Definition
Goal-Seeking Neural Networks are AI systems that dynamically adjust their behavior to reach desired states, using feedback and prediction to navigate toward outcomes. It's a net that hunts its prize.

Key Components
A neural core predicts or acts, guided by a goal state—like a score or result. Feedback measures distance to the goal, tweaking weights. Forward models guess next steps, and optimization drives convergence. Inputs fuel real-time shifts.

Benefits
They chase goals with agility. Adaptability fits chaos, and foresight cuts errors. Efficiency homes in fast, and they learn live.

Examples
A net steers a drone to land, dodging wind. A game AI seeks max points, shifting tactics.

Applications
It flies drones to targets. Games chase wins, and robots reach spots. Finance seeks gains, and energy tunes grids.

Industries
Robotics moves smart. Gaming fights clever, and transport flies true. Finance bets big, and energy flows right.

Summary
Goal-Seeking Neural Networks are prize hunters, weaving nets to snag aims with live smarts. They're a swift seeker but dodge chaos. A chase champ, they lock on goals.

Goal-Setting Algorithms

Definition
Goal-Setting Algorithms are AI methods that define and prioritize objectives for systems to pursue, often breaking big aims into actionable steps. It's a planner setting the finish line.

Key Components
A goal framework—like SMART criteria—sets clear targets. AI logic—like optimization or RL—ranks or splits them. Data inputs gauge feasibility, and planning maps steps. Monitoring tracks progress, adjusting as needed.

Benefits
They align tasks to big wins. Clarity drives focus, and flexibility fits shifts. Automation saves planning sweat, and scale tackles complex aims.

Examples
An AI sets "cut costs 10%," splitting into supplier swaps. A bot aims "grow followers," pacing posts.

Applications
It plans business growth. Robots set task order, and marketing hits metrics. Energy aims green, and health sets recovery.

Industries
Business strategizes. Robotics works smart, and marketing grows reach. Energy saves green, and healthcare heals.

Summary
Goal-Setting Algorithms are aim setters, carving paths with AI's map. They're a focus forge but fight flux. A planner's pal, they point the way.

GPGPU Computing (General-Purpose Computing on GPUs)

Definition
GPGPU Computing is the use of graphics processing units, originally built for rendering, to perform general-purpose computations like math, physics, or AI. It taps GPUs' parallel cores to speed up tasks beyond graphics.

Key Components
GPUs with thousands of cores run parallel threads, unlike CPUs' serial focus. Programming frameworks like CUDA or OpenCL unlock non-graphic tasks. Data parallelism splits jobs into tiny, simultaneous chunks. Memory management shuttles data between GPU and CPU, and task offloading assigns math-heavy bits to the GPU.

Benefits
It's blazing fast for parallel workloads, often 10-100x over CPUs. Cost-effective, GPUs pack more punch per dollar. Energy efficiency shines in big jobs, and versatility spans science to games. Compact power fits tight spaces.

Examples
A physicist simulates fluid flow, GPUs crunching equations in sync. A data scientist speeds matrix math for a neural net, slashing training time.

Applications
It accelerates AI model training. Simulations model molecules or stars. Image processing sharpens photos, and finance runs risk models. Games boost physics effects.

Industries
Tech drives AI and analytics. Science explores physics or biology. Finance models markets, and gaming enhances visuals. Media edits high-res video.

Summary
GPGPU Computing turns graphics chips into math wizards, turbocharging parallel tasks with thrift and speed. It's a game-changer where it fits but stumbles on serial snags. A broad brush, it paints power across fields.

GPU (Graphics Processing Unit)

Definition
A Graphics Processing Unit is a specialized chip designed for parallel computing, originally for graphics rendering, now a powerhouse for AI tasks with its massive core count. It's a math muscle for modern tech.

Key Components
Thousands of CUDA cores run parallel ops, backed by fast VRAM for data. Tensor cores speed AI math, and pipelines handle graphics or compute. Drivers unlock coding, and cooling keeps it chill.

Benefits
It blasts parallel tasks fast. Cost-per-power beats CPUs, and versatility spans AI to games. Scale fits big jobs, and efficiency aids energy.

Examples
A GPU renders a game scene in blinks. An AI trains on it, slashing days to hours.

Applications
It trains deep nets in labs. Gaming draws worlds, and science sims physics. Editing speeds cuts, and crypto mines coins.

Industries
Tech fuels AI. Gaming shines visuals, and science crunches deep. Media crafts fast, and finance bets big.

Summary
The GPU is a parallel prince, lifting AI and graphics with raw might. It's a broad brawn but costs and cooks. A tech titan, it powers the now.

GPU Clusters

Definition
GPU Clusters are groups of interconnected computers, each equipped with multiple graphics processing units, designed to tackle massive parallel computations together. They pool GPU power to handle tasks like AI training or simulations that single machines can't manage alone.

Key Components
The cluster comprises nodes—individual machines with GPUs—linked by high-speed networks like InfiniBand. Task schedulers split workloads across nodes, balancing effort. GPUs handle parallel math, like matrix ops, while CPUs oversee coordination. Software frameworks, such as CUDA or MPI, enable coding and communication. Cooling and power systems keep the setup humming.

Benefits
They crush huge datasets fast, slashing compute times. Scalability lets you add nodes for more power.

Cost-per-flop beats solo setups for big jobs, and parallel crunching suits AI or physics perfectly. Redundancy aids fault tolerance.

Examples
A weather model runs on a GPU cluster, predicting storms by splitting grids across nodes. An AI lab trains a language model, each node chewing a data chunk overnight.

Applications
They train deep learning models on vast corpora. Scientific simulations model climates or galaxies. Real-time rendering crafts movie CGI, and crypto mining hashes blocks. Data analytics churns big datasets.

Industries
Tech powers AI breakthroughs. Science probes nature's mysteries. Entertainment renders films, and finance crunches market models. Crypto leverages them for mining.

Summary
GPU Clusters are muscle machines, uniting GPUs to blitz through parallel tasks with raw speed. They're a boon for scale but demand cash and know-how. A heavy hitter, they fuel big AI and science.

Guided AI Creativity

Definition
Guided AI Creativity is an approach where artificial intelligence generates novel outputs—like art, text, or music—steered by human input, rules, or templates to shape the creative process. It blends machine imagination with directed intent.

Key Components
A generative model, like a GAN or transformer, crafts raw output. Guidance—prompts, style cues, or constraints—channels the AI's focus. Training data sets the creative palette, while feedback loops refine results. An interface lets users tweak or judge creations.

Benefits
It sparks ideas fast, amplifying human vision. Control keeps output on-brand or useful. It democratizes creativity for non-artists, and iteration hones quality. Resource-light, it leans on existing models.

Examples
A writer prompts "dark forest tale," getting a moody story shaped by tone hints. An artist feeds "Picasso style" to an AI, yielding a cubist sketch.

Applications
It crafts marketing copy with brand voice. Designers mock up logos with style guides. Musicians generate riffs from genres, and games spawn unique levels. Education inspires student projects.

Industries
Marketing spins ads. Entertainment builds content. Design speeds prototyping, and gaming enriches worlds. Education boosts learning tools.

Summary
Guided AI Creativity is a muse with reins, fusing AI's wild spark with human will. It's a fast friend for inspiration but needs a steady hand. A creative co-pilot, it shines under direction.

Guided AI Exploration

Definition
Guided AI Exploration is a method where AI searches unknown problem spaces—like data patterns or solutions—directed by human insights, heuristics, or goals to focus its wandering. It's curiosity with a compass.

Key Components
An AI explorer, often a search or learning algorithm, roams the space. Guidance—rules, prior models, or objectives—narrows its path. An evaluation metric scores finds, and a feedback system adjusts the guide. Iteration refines the journey, homing in on value.

Benefits
It cuts aimless drift, finding gems faster. Efficiency rises with targeted probes. It uncovers niche insights pure AI might miss, and adaptability fits shifting quests. Human-AI synergy deepens discovery.

Examples
A scientist guides an AI to hunt protein folds, prioritizing known bonds. A marketer explores customer data, steering toward purchase triggers.

Applications
It maps data trends in analytics. Science probes hypotheses, and design tests concepts. Security hunts vulnerabilities with threat cues. Games explore player strategies.

Industries
Science accelerates research. Marketing decodes behavior. Tech refines systems, and security spots risks. Gaming tunes mechanics.

Summary
Guided AI Exploration is a scout with a map, pairing AI's reach with human savvy. It's a swift dive into the unknown but leans on sharp guides. A discovery booster, it thrives with focus.

Guided Data Augmentation

Definition
Guided Data Augmentation is a technique in AI where synthetic data is created to expand training sets, directed by rules, domain knowledge, or goals to ensure relevance. It enriches models without random fluff.

Key Components
A base dataset seeds the process, paired with an augmentation model—like image tweaks or text rewrites. Guidance—expert rules, labels, or constraints—shapes new data. Transformation rules, like rotate or paraphrase, generate variants. Validation checks synthetic fit, and integration blends it into training.

Benefits
It boosts model robustness with tailored variety. Data scarcity fades, aiding small sets. Precision rises as augments match reality, and it saves collection costs. Speedy tweaks fit tight deadlines.

Examples
A vision AI gets foggy road pics, guided by weather stats. A chatbot trains on rephrased "hello," steered by tone rules.

Applications
It preps vision models with rare scenes. NLP enriches text corpora. Audio AI gains varied voices, and healthcare simulates patient data. Games mimic player inputs.

Industries
Tech refines AI models. Healthcare boosts diagnostics. Automotive trains self-driving, and gaming enhances bots. Media augments content.

Summary
Guided Data Augmentation is a data chef, cooking up smart extras with purpose. It's a lifeline for lean datasets but needs a keen eye. A training ally, it grows strength with intent.

Guided Evolutionary Algorithms

Definition
Guided Evolutionary Algorithms are optimization techniques that enhance traditional genetic algorithms by incorporating domain-specific knowledge or external guidance to steer the evolutionary process. They evolve solutions more efficiently by blending natural selection with human or heuristic insights.

Key Components
A population of candidate solutions evolves through selection, crossover, and mutation, like standard GAs. A guidance mechanism—rules, expert input, or precomputed heuristics—biases the search toward promising areas. A fitness function scores solutions, now informed by both raw performance and guidance. Iterative refinement balances exploration with directed focus, and stopping criteria halt evolution when goals are met.

Benefits
Guidance speeds convergence, cutting wasted iterations. It boosts solution quality by avoiding blind alleys. Flexibility melds expert know-how with automation, and it tackles complex problems where pure evolution lags. Resource use drops as smarter paths emerge.

Examples
A factory uses a guided GA to schedule shifts, favoring known peak hours over random guesses. A drug designer evolves compounds, steering toward molecular traits experts flag as effective.

Applications
It optimizes logistics routes with traffic hints. Engineering designs parts using physics-based rules. Finance tunes portfolios with market trends, and biology simulates evolution with known genes. Games tweak AI foes with player data.

Industries
Manufacturing streamlines production. Pharma accelerates drug discovery. Finance refines investments, and tech boosts algorithm tuning. Gaming crafts smarter NPCs.

Summary
Guided Evolutionary Algorithms turbocharge evolution with a nudge, blending nature's grind with human smarts. They shine in targeted searches but lean on good guidance. A sharp tool, they marry instinct to optimization.

Guided Feature Selection

Definition
Guided Feature Selection is a machine learning preprocess that picks the most relevant data features using domain knowledge, rules, or prior models to guide the choice. It trims datasets to boost model performance without blind trial-and-error.

Key Components
A feature set—raw inputs like height or sales—starts the process. Guidance comes from expert rules,

statistical tests, or past model insights, ranking feature importance. Selection criteria, like correlation or impact, filter the list. An evaluation step tests the subset on a task, and iteration refines the pick.

Benefits
It cuts noise, sharpening model accuracy. Faster training follows from leaner data. Interpretability rises as chosen features align with logic, and it saves compute by skipping exhaustive searches. Overfitting risks drop with focused inputs.

Examples
A doctor guides a heart disease model to prioritize blood pressure over hair color, based on medical sense. A marketer selects ad clicks over timestamps, using campaign data.

Applications
It preps data for medical diagnostics. Marketing targets key customer traits. Finance picks stock predictors, and image analysis focuses on edges or colors. Text mining grabs vital words.

Industries
Healthcare refines patient models. Marketing optimizes ads. Finance sharpens trading, and tech boosts AI efficiency. Media tunes content analysis.

Summary
Guided Feature Selection is a smart trimmer, carving data with purpose to fuel better models. It's a time-saver with brains but hinges on solid insights. A precision play, it's key for clean AI.

Guided Image Recognition

Definition
Guided Image Recognition is an AI vision technique where external cues—like human input, context, or pre-trained hints—steer the identification of objects or patterns in images. It refines accuracy by narrowing focus beyond raw pixel crunching.

Key Components
An image dataset feeds the system, paired with a recognition model, often convolutional neural nets. Guidance layers—labels, bounding boxes, or semantic rules—direct attention to key areas. Feature extraction targets guided regions, and a classifier tags outputs. Feedback tunes the model, aligning it with cues.

Benefits
Accuracy jumps as guidance sharpens focus. Training speeds up with less guesswork. It handles ambiguity better, like distinguishing cats from dogs with breed hints. Resource use dips with targeted processing, and it adapts to niche tasks.

Examples
A security cam flags a car's license plate, guided by a box drawn by a guard. A birdwatching app IDs a sparrow, nudged by a user's "small, brown" hint.

Applications
It spots tumors in medical scans with doctor outlines. Retail tags products in photos with catalog cues. Security tracks faces with prior IDs, and agriculture flags weeds with farmer input. AR overlays use it for object tagging.

Industries
Healthcare aids diagnostics. Retail boosts e-commerce. Security enhances surveillance, and agriculture refines crop care. Tech powers AR/VR.

Summary
Guided Image Recognition puts eyes on AI with a helping hand, nailing precision in cluttered scenes. It's a focused win but leans on good steers. A vision booster, it's sharp where it's pointed.

Guided Machine Translation

Definition
Guided Machine Translation is an AI approach to converting text across languages, enhanced by external aids like glossaries, style rules, or context clues. It refines output beyond statistical guesses, aligning with specific needs or tones.

Key Components
A base translation model, often neural, processes source text. Guidance inputs—dictionaries, phrase pairs, or domain terms—steer word choice. Context awareness, from metadata or prior sentences, shapes meaning. Post-editing rules tweak grammar or style, and training data reflects the guided domain.

Benefits
It nails accuracy for jargon-heavy fields. Consistency holds across long texts, like manuals. Customization fits brand voices or dialects, and it cuts human fixes by pre-aligning output. Speed rises with focused translation paths.

Examples
A legal AI translates "contract" to French as "contract," guided by a law glossary. A game localizer keeps "mana" untranslated, per developer style notes.

Applications
It translates tech manuals with exact terms. Games localize dialogue with flair. Legal docs stay precise, and e-commerce adapts product blurbs. Education renders texts with cultural fit.

Industries
Tech documents software. Gaming crafts immersive worlds. Law ensures contract clarity, and retail targets global buyers. Education bridges language gaps.

Summary
Guided Machine Translation is a tailored linguist, polishing cross-language leaps with expert nudges. It's a pro for precision but needs careful crafting. A language bridge, it shines with direction.

Guided Natural Language Processing (NLP)

Definition
Guided Natural Language Processing is an AI method for understanding or generating text, enriched by external cues like rules, templates, or user intent to sharpen results. It channels NLP's broad power into specific, context-rich tasks.

Key Components
A core NLP model—parsing or generating text—anchors the system. Guidance comes via domain lexicons, grammar rules, or user prompts, framing the task. Contextual layers, like conversation history, refine meaning. Output filters enforce tone or format, and feedback loops adjust to guidance over time.

Benefits
It boosts relevance, aligning text to goals. Precision rises in niche domains, like medicine. User effort drops with intuitive steering, and it cuts ambiguity in tricky phrases. Adaptability fits varied needs with ease.

Examples
A chatbot answers "What's the forecast?" with "Sunny, 75°F," guided by a weather API. A writer's tool crafts a formal email, nudged by "professional tone" input.

Applications
It powers domain-specific chatbots. Content generation fits brand styles. Sentiment analysis hones in with topic cues, and legal NLP parses contracts with term guides. Education tailors language lessons.

Industries
Tech drives smart assistants. Marketing crafts ads. Law decodes jargon, and education boosts learning. Healthcare interprets patient notes.

Summary
Guided NLP is a focused wordsmith, honing language tasks with a steady hand. It's a gem for tailored text but bends to its guides. A sharp NLP twist, it thrives with clear intent.

Guided Reinforcement Learning

Definition
Guided Reinforcement Learning is an AI training method where an agent learns optimal actions in an environment, aided by external hints—like expert demos, rules, or rewards—to accelerate or refine its policy. It blends trial-and-error with directed wisdom.

Key Components
An agent explores a state-action space, aiming for rewards. A reward function scores outcomes, now shaped by guidance. External aids—human demos, pre-set policies, or constraints—steer exploration. A learning algorithm, like Q-learning, updates the policy, and iteration balances guidance with autonomy.

Benefits
It speeds learning, skipping random flails. Higher rewards come from smarter starts. Safety improves with guided boundaries, and it tackles sparse-reward tasks better. Efficiency rises as guidance cuts waste.

Examples
A robot arm stacks blocks faster, mimicking a human demo. A game AI masters chess openings, guided by grandmaster moves.

Applications
It trains robots for precise tasks. Games craft skilled bots. Autonomous cars learn safe turns with driver data, and finance optimizes trades with market hints. Healthcare tunes treatment plans.

Industries
Robotics builds factory helpers. Gaming levels up AI foes. Automotive refines self-driving, and finance sharpens strategies. Healthcare aids therapy bots.

Summary
Guided Reinforcement Learning is a mentor for AI agents, fast-tracking mastery with a nudge. It's a shortcut to skill but leans on wise input. A clever boost, it's RL with a compass.

Letter H

Habituation in AI

Definition
Habituation in AI is the process where an artificial intelligence system reduces its response to repeated, non-critical stimuli over time, mimicking a biological learning trait to focus on novel or significant events. It's a digital way of tuning out the mundane.

Key Components
The system tracks input patterns via sensors or data streams. A memory module logs exposure frequency, and an adaptation mechanism—like a threshold or decay function—dampens reactions. Learning algorithms adjust sensitivity, and a reset trigger revives attention for change. Feedback refines what's "routine."

Benefits
It cuts noise, sharpening focus on key shifts. Efficiency rises by ignoring repeats, and adaptability mimics human prioritization. Resource use drops with less redundant processing, and it boosts responsiveness to surprises.

Examples
A home AI stops alerting to daily footsteps but flags a midnight creak. A chatbot ignores repeated "hi" spam, answering fresh queries.

Applications
It filters alerts in smart homes. Chatbots prioritize new chats, and robotics ignores static scenes. Security tunes out routine, and health monitors flag odd vitals.

Industries
Tech smarts up devices. Security watches better, and healthcare tracks patients. Robotics moves lean, and homes automate wise.

Summary
Habituation in AI is a selective ear, dulling the dull with learned calm. It's a focus filter but risks oversight. A clever fade, it spots what's new.

Hack Detection in AI

Definition
Hack Detection in AI is the use of artificial intelligence to identify and flag unauthorized intrusions, manipulations, or anomalies in systems, data, or networks. It's a digital guard sniffing out breaches.

Key Components
Sensors or logs capture system activity, feeding an AI model—like anomaly detectors or classifiers. Pattern recognition spots normal versus odd behavior, trained on clean and hack data. Real-time analysis tracks live threats, and alerts trigger responses. Feedback loops refine detection.

Benefits
It catches hacks fast, cutting damage. Accuracy beats rule-based traps, and adaptability learns new tricks. Scale scans big systems, and automation frees human eyes.

Examples
An AI flags a login spike from odd IPs, nailing a brute force try. A bot spots data tweaks in a bank file, catching a silent theft.

Applications
It guards networks from cyber hits. Finance blocks fraud, and apps shield users. IoT secures devices, and clouds watch data.

Industries
Tech locks apps. Finance saves cash, and security fights crime. IoT guards smart, and clouds stay safe.

Summary
Hack Detection in AI is a cyber sentry, sniffing threats with sharp AI senses. It's a swift shield but chases cunning foes. A watch dog, it guards the bits.

Hadoop in AI

Definition: Hadoop in AI refers to the use of the Hadoop ecosystem—a distributed framework for big data—to store, process, and analyze massive datasets for artificial intelligence tasks. It's a big data backbone for smart systems.

Key Components: HDFS splits and stores data across nodes, ensuring scale. MapReduce crunches it in parallel, feeding AI models. YARN manages resources, and tools like Hive or Spark tie in analytics. Integration pipes data to AI frameworks.

Benefits: It handles petabytes with ease, fueling AI scale. Cost spreads over cheap nodes, and fault tolerance keeps running. Flexibility fits raw data, and speed scales with clusters.

Examples: An AI mines Hadoop-stored tweets for sentiment, splitting jobs. A retailer predicts sales from years of logs, processed fast.

Applications: It preps data for machine learning. Analytics mines trends, and AI trains on big sets. IoT crunches streams, and research digs deep.

Industries: Tech scales AI. Retail reads buyers, and finance tracks markets. IoT flows data, and science probes big.

Summary: Hadoop in AI is a data giant, hauling big loads for AI's brain. It's a scale savior but clunky to wield. A hefty base, it powers deep dives.

Hamming Distance

Definition; Hamming Distance is a metric in AI and computing that measures the number of positions where two strings—like bits or symbols—differ, used to gauge similarity or error. It's a simple mismatch counter.

Key Componentsa; Two equal-length strings—binary or otherwise—feed the measure. A comparison step counts differing spots, often bitwise. Computation sums mismatches, and normalization tweaks for scale. Context defines its use, like error checks or clustering.

Benefitsa; It's fast and light, needing no heavy math. Clarity shows exact diffs, and versatility fits codes or data. Scalability scans big sets, and it's intuitive to grasp.

Examples: Hamming Distance of "1010" and "1110" is 1, one bit off. A spell-check flags "cat" versus "cap" as 1 apart.

Applications: It checks errors in codes. Clustering groups close data, and AI compares features. Security verifies IDs, and text mines edits.

Industries: Tech fixes codes. Security locks safe, and AI sorts smart. Telecom sends clear, and text digs words.

Summary: Hamming Distance is a quick ruler, ticking off diffs with bare ease. It's a lean matchmaker but narrow in scope. A crisp tool, it counts the gaps.

Hard Clustering

Definition: Hard Clustering is an AI method that assigns each data point to exactly one group based on similarity, creating crisp, non-overlapping clusters. It's a firm sorter of data piles.

Key Components: A dataset—like points or features—feeds the system. A similarity metric—like Euclidean distance—groups them. Algorithms—like k-means—assign labels, and centroids anchor clusters. Iteration refines until stable.

Benefits: It's clear-cut, easing reads. Speed fits big data, and simplicity aids coding. Scalability grows with tweaks, and it's light on compute.

Examples: An AI sorts customers into "big spenders" or "rare buyers." A bot groups stars by brightness, no overlap.

Applications: It segments markets in ads. Science classes species, and images split pixels. Security tags threats, and text sorts docs.

Industries: Marketing targets folks. Science maps life, and tech sorts smart. Security spots odd, and media files fast.

Summary: Hard Clustering is a neat divider, slicing data into firm bins with AI's knife. It's a quick sorter but stiff on edges. A clean cut, it boxes the chaos.

Hardware Acceleration for AI

Definition:Hardware Acceleration for AI is the use of specialized chips—like GPUs or TPUs—to speed up artificial intelligence tasks, boosting compute power beyond standard CPUs. It's a turbo for AI's engine.

Key Components: Accelerators—like GPUs—pack parallel cores for math. Fast memory—like HBM—feeds data, and drivers—like CUDA—unlock power. Task splitting spreads loads, and cooling holds peak. Frameworks tie it to AI code.

Benefits: It slashes training times, fast as lightning. Power scales to big AI, and cost-per-flop beats CPUs. Efficiency cuts energy, and versatility fits fields.

Examples: A TPU trains a vision net in hours. A GPU renders game AI, real-time quick.

Applications: It trains deep nets in labs. Games run smart foes, and science sims fast. Clouds crunch data, and edge runs lean.

Industries: Tech fuels AI. Gaming plays smooth, and science digs deep. Clouds scale big, and edge smarts up.

Summary: Hardware Acceleration for AI is a speed shot, juicing tasks with chip might. It's a fast lane but pricey and niche. A power punch, it lifts AI high.

Hazard Detection in AI

Definition
Hazard Detection in AI is the application of artificial intelligence to identify potential dangers or risks in environments, systems, or data, predicting or flagging threats before they escalate. It's a digital watchdog for peril.

Key Components
Sensors—like cameras or IoT devices—gather real-time data, feeding an AI model such as a classifier or anomaly detector. Training data includes past hazards for pattern recognition. Predictive algorithms assess risk levels, and alert systems notify users. Feedback refines accuracy over time.

Benefits
It spots trouble fast, cutting reaction time. Accuracy reduces false alarms, and automation eases human load. Scalability fits big setups, and proactive alerts prevent harm.

Examples
An AI flags a gas leak from sensor spikes in a factory. A car system detects ice on a road, warning the driver.

Applications
It monitors industrial safety. Autonomous vehicles avoid crashes, and smart homes catch fires. Security tracks threats, and health flags patient risks.

Industries
Manufacturing stays safe. Automotive drives secure, and homes smarten up. Security guards assets, and healthcare saves lives.

Summary
Hazard Detection in AI is a sharp sentinel, sniffing out risks with swift AI eyes. It's a safety net but fights data gaps. A keen guard, it wards off woe.

Heart Rate Variability (HRV) Prediction with AI

Definition
Heart Rate Variability Prediction with AI uses artificial intelligence to forecast changes in the time intervals between heartbeats, leveraging patterns to assess health, stress, or fitness. It's a pulse prophet.

Key Components
Wearable sensors—like smartwatches—capture HRV data, feeding time-series AI models like RNNs or LSTMs. Features—such as sleep or activity—enhance context. Predictive algorithms estimate future HRV, and training uses historical beats. Validation ties forecasts to health outcomes.

Benefits
It predicts stress or fatigue early. Accuracy aids personal health, and speed fits live tracking. Low-cost sensors widen use, and insights guide wellness.

Examples
An AI warns of burnout, seeing HRV dip after work stress. A fitness bot predicts recovery, tracking post-run HRV.

Applications
It monitors athlete training. Wellness apps track stress, and healthcare spots heart risks. Mental health flags anxiety, and wearables coach users.

Industries
Healthcare heals smart. Fitness tunes training, and tech powers wearables. Wellness boosts life, and sports optimize play.

Summary
HRV Prediction with AI is a heart seer, reading beats for health hints with AI's pulse. It's a wellness win but battles noise. A vital peek, it tracks life's rhythm.

Heatmap Analysis in AI

Definition
Heatmap Analysis in AI is a technique where artificial intelligence generates or interprets visual maps showing data intensity—like attention or activity—across space or time, highlighting key zones. It's a glow guide for focus.

Key Components
Raw data—like clicks or eye tracks—feeds the system, processed by AI models like CNNs or clustering. Mapping algorithms assign intensity—color or scale—to spots. Preprocessing smooths noise, and visualization renders heatmaps. Interpretation logic decodes patterns.

Benefits
It spots hot zones fast, aiding insight. Clarity visuals trump raw stats, and automation scales big data. Flexibility fits any field, and it guides decisions sharp.

Examples
An AI heatmap shows shoppers linger at a store's candy aisle. A game bot maps player focus, glowing on traps.

Applications
It tracks web clicks for UX. Marketing sees ad draw, and games balance design. Security scans crowds, and health maps brain activity.

Industries
Marketing reads eyes. Tech refines interfaces, and gaming tunes play. Security watches masses, and healthcare sees minds.

Summary
Heatmap Analysis in AI is a glow finder, painting focus with AI's brush. It's a clear cue but fights gaps. A vivid lens, it lights what matters.

Helical Neural Networks

Definition
Helical Neural Networks are a theoretical or experimental AI architecture where data flows in a spiral or layered pattern, mimicking helical structures to process sequential or spatial data with depth. It's a twist on neural flow.

Key Components
A helical layout loops layers, passing data in spirals. Nodes connect across turns, blending past and present inputs. Activation functions twist signals, and training—like backprop—tunes weights. Input sequences or grids feed the coil.

Benefits
It captures long dependencies with flair. Depth adds context, and efficiency may trim flat nets. Novelty sparks research, and it fits cyclic data neat.

Examples
An AI predicts tides, spiraling wave data over days. A bot tracks speech, coiling phonemes for sense.

Applications
It models time series like weather. Speech flows through turns, and vision twists 3D scenes. Science sims cycles, and robotics maps loops.

Industries
Science probes patterns. Tech tests AI, and speech talks clear. Robotics moves smart, and weather warns right.

Summary
Helical Neural Networks are a spiral thinker, winding data with AI's twist. They're a bold try but green and tough. A coiled cut, they loop the future.

Heterogeneous Computing

Definition
Heterogeneous Computing is a strategy in AI where diverse hardware—like CPUs, GPUs, and FPGAs—work together to optimize tasks, splitting loads by strength. It's a mixed team for compute.

Key Components
Varied processors—like GPUs for parallel, CPUs for serial—form the core. Task schedulers divvy work, matching hardware to jobs. Interconnects—like PCIe—link parts, and software—like OpenCL—ties code. Optimization balances speed and fit.

Benefits
It maxes speed, picking best tools. Efficiency cuts power, and flexibility fits all tasks. Scale grows with mix, and cost spreads smart.

Examples
A GPU trains an AI net while a CPU logs stats. An FPGA crunches real-time video, CPU aiding logic.

Applications
It trains AI fast. Games render and think, and science sims big. Edge runs lean, and clouds scale wide.

Industries
Tech powers AI. Gaming plays full, and science digs deep. Edge smarts up, and clouds lift loads.

Summary
Heterogeneous Computing is a team play, blending chips for AI's might. It's a speed blend but fights sync. A mixed force, it lifts all boats.

Heterogeneous Data Integration

Definition
Heterogeneous Data Integration refers to the process of combining information from multiple, distinct sources—whether structured, semi-structured, or unstructured—into a unified system that AI models can use for analysis and learning.

Key Characteristics
It involves blending data formats from different origins, resolving structural inconsistencies, and enabling seamless analysis across otherwise incompatible datasets.

Benefits
By incorporating diverse data, AI systems achieve broader perspectives, improved accuracy, and enhanced decision-making capabilities. It is especially valuable when organizational data is scattered across different platforms and systems.

Applications
Used in healthcare to combine patient records, genomic information, and sensor data; in smart cities for merging traffic patterns, weather data, and social media updates; and in e-commerce to unify customer behavior, product databases, and transaction records.

Summary
Heterogeneous Data Integration strengthens AI's ability to work with varied and widespread information sources, though it demands careful data reconciliation and infrastructure management.

Heterogeneous Transfer Learning

Definition
Heterogeneous Transfer Learning is the practice of transferring knowledge between different domains where the feature spaces or data distributions are not identical, allowing AI to perform well even when labeled data is scarce in the target domain.

Key Characteristics
It bridges differences between source and target domains by adapting models, feature mappings, or training strategies, overcoming mismatches in data characteristics.

Benefits
This technique significantly reduces the demand for large labeled datasets in the target environment, improving performance in resource-limited settings and broadening model generalization.

Applications
Cross-domain applications such as classifying social media posts using knowledge learned from news articles, diagnosing diseases with varying patient demographics, and adapting autonomous vehicles across different sensor setups.

Summary
Heterogeneous Transfer Learning empowers AI to adapt across distinct domains, maximizing learning efficiency, although careful domain alignment is crucial to avoid errors.

Heuristic Algorithms

Definition
Heuristic Algorithms are strategies that find good-enough solutions to complex problems by relying on practical methods or educated guesses, rather than exhaustively searching every possibility.

Key Characteristics
These algorithms prioritize speed and feasibility over perfect accuracy, often using rules of thumb, experience-based tactics, or problem-specific shortcuts.

Benefits
They dramatically reduce computational time, make problem-solving feasible in complex scenarios, and offer flexible, adaptable strategies for real-world challenges.

Applications
Heuristics drive search engines to find relevant results quickly, optimize scheduling and routing tasks, and power AI decision-making in games and simulations.

Summary
Heuristic Algorithms provide a practical path to solutions in tough problem spaces, trading off perfection for speed and efficiency—a critical advantage in many AI systems.

Hidden Markov Models (HMMs)

Definition
Hidden Markov Models are statistical tools designed to model systems where the internal state is hidden but produces observable outputs, often used for analyzing sequences over time.

Key Characteristics
They are based on the Markov property, where the current state depends only on the previous state, and use probabilistic methods to model state transitions and observations.

Benefits
HMMs are powerful for analyzing time-series and sequential data, providing structured frameworks for speech, bioinformatics, and financial predictions.

Applications
Applied in speech recognition systems, gene sequence analysis in bioinformatics, and forecasting stock market trends.

Summary
Hidden Markov Models are essential for understanding sequential processes where the underlying state isn't directly visible, though they require careful probability modeling and can be computationally demanding.

Hierarchical Attention Networks (HANs)

Definition
Hierarchical Attention Networks are advanced neural models that apply attention mechanisms at both word and sentence levels, enabling AI systems to capture context from complex text structures for improved text understanding.

Key Characteristics
These networks model documents in two stages—first focusing on important words within sentences, then on critical sentences within documents—enhancing both accuracy and interpretability.

Benefits
They improve performance on long-text classification, allow the model to highlight the most important text segments, and support explainable AI initiatives in text analytics.

Applications
Used in document classification for legal, financial, and healthcare records, sentiment analysis of detailed customer feedback, and question-answering systems.

Summary
Hierarchical Attention Networks bring deep insight into text by structurally modeling context at multiple levels, though they demand more computational resources than simpler models.

Hierarchical Bayesian Models

Definition

Hierarchical Bayesian Models extend Bayesian inference across multiple levels of a model, enabling the handling of complex, structured data with inherent variability at different scales.

Key Characteristics

They organize parameters into hierarchical layers, incorporate prior distributions to inform learning, and manage uncertainty by pooling information across related groups.

Benefits

They offer a rigorous framework for modeling variability across different data segments, manage missing data naturally, and enhance predictive performance in structured datasets.

Applications

Used in healthcare for patient outcome modeling across hospitals, marketing for analyzing consumer behaviors across regions, and natural language processing for layered text understanding.

Summary

Hierarchical Bayesian Models offer a sophisticated, flexible way to model multi-level data, though they require significant computational resources for inference and training.

Hierarchical Clustering

Definition

Hierarchical Clustering is an unsupervised learning method that builds a hierarchy of clusters by either progressively merging smaller groups (agglomerative) or splitting larger groups (divisive) based on similarity measures.

Key Characteristics

It produces a tree-like diagram called a dendrogram, does not require predefining the number of clusters, and excels at uncovering natural groupings within data.

Benefits

Hierarchical clustering reveals the relationships between data points across multiple scales, is highly flexible in identifying cluster structures, and is ideal for exploratory analysis.

Applications

Used in biological research to analyze gene expression patterns, in computer vision for segmenting images, and in text mining for organizing document collections.

Summary

Hierarchical Clustering uncovers deep structures within data without needing a set number of groups in advance, although it can become computationally expensive with very large datasets.

Hierarchical Reinforcement Learning (HRL)

Definition

Hierarchical Reinforcement Learning (HRL) is an approach in AI where complex tasks are broken down into smaller, manageable subtasks, allowing agents to learn and plan more efficiently by achieving intermediate objectives.

Key Characteristics

HRL organizes learning into a layered structure where higher levels focus on broader goals, and lower levels handle specific actions. It enables abstraction, multi-step decision-making, and supports modular learning through subtasks.

Benefits
By decomposing challenges, HRL speeds up learning in complex environments, facilitates long-term planning, and enhances reusability by mastering smaller, reusable skills.

Applications
Common in robotics for teaching multi-step tasks, in game AI for layered strategy development, and in autonomous systems for complex navigation and planning.

Summary
Hierarchical Reinforcement Learning improves AI's ability to handle complex problems by teaching agents to solve intermediate goals, although designing effective hierarchies remains a key challenge.

Hierarchical Softmax

Definition
Hierarchical Softmax is a method used in deep learning, particularly in natural language processing, to approximate the traditional softmax function more efficiently when working with large output vocabularies.

Key Characteristics
This method structures output words into a tree hierarchy, reducing the number of calculations needed during training and inference compared to full softmax, making it ideal for handling very large word lists.

Benefits
Hierarchical Softmax accelerates model training and inference, allows scaling to massive vocabularies, and makes resource-intensive tasks more feasible on large datasets.

Applications
Widely applied in language modeling for word prediction, machine translation for generating fluent output, and text classification for categorizing large corpora.

Summary
Hierarchical Softmax offers an efficient alternative to traditional probability calculations in language tasks, trading a small loss in precision for substantial speed and scalability gains.

Hierarchical Temporal Memory (HTM)

Definition
Hierarchical Temporal Memory (HTM) is a machine intelligence framework modeled after the structure and operations of the neocortex, focusing on learning sequences, recognizing temporal patterns, and making predictions based on time-dependent data.

Key Characteristics
HTM captures the brain's hierarchical structure and timing mechanisms, operates largely in an unsupervised manner, and excels at discovering and predicting sequences over time.

Benefits
It provides a biologically inspired approach to learning, efficiently recognizes temporal patterns from sparse data, and supports unsupervised learning where labeled examples are rare.

Applications
Used in anomaly detection within streaming data, pattern recognition across video sequences, and predictive modeling for time-series applications.

Summary
Hierarchical Temporal Memory brings a brain-inspired method for understanding and predicting time-based patterns, although its commercial adoption is still in development stages.

High-Dimensional Data Analysis

Definition
High-Dimensional Data Analysis refers to techniques for managing and interpreting datasets that contain a very large number of features or attributes, a situation common in fields like genomics, image processing, and text mining.

Key Characteristics
It tackles the challenges of analyzing datasets where the number of variables can overwhelm traditional methods, often using dimensionality reduction strategies to extract meaningful patterns.

Benefits
This approach enables insight discovery in complex data, supports advanced visualization of multi-dimensional structures, and helps prevent overfitting by focusing on the most significant features.

Applications
Found in image recognition for analyzing high-resolution visuals, genomics for studying genetic markers, and document classification for processing extensive text collections.

Summary
High-Dimensional Data Analysis is essential for extracting value from complex datasets, although it demands careful management of computational complexity and dimensionality effects.

High-Frequency Trading AI

Definition
High-Frequency Trading (HFT) AI uses machine learning and automated systems to execute large volumes of financial trades in fractions of a second, capitalizing on minor price fluctuations in markets.

Key Characteristics
It combines real-time data analysis, rapid algorithmic decision-making, and reinforcement learning to optimize trading strategies and execution speed.

Benefits
HFT AI maximizes profit opportunities from small market movements, minimizes human error, and can react to market changes faster than manual traders.

Applications
Employed in stock exchanges, currency markets, and portfolio management systems where split-second decision-making is critical.

Summary
High-Frequency Trading AI revolutionizes financial trading with automation and speed, although it requires heavy investment in infrastructure and can contribute to market instability if mismanaged.

Holographic Memory in AI

Definition
Holographic Memory involves storing information using light-based interference patterns, enabling dense, three-dimensional data storage. In AI research, this technology is being explored to greatly expand memory capacity and access speeds.

Key Characteristics
Data is recorded as holograms within a storage medium, allowing vast amounts of information to be stored compactly and retrieved almost instantly using optical methods.

Benefits
It offers extremely high storage density, fast retrieval rates, and durable, non-volatile data storage, making it attractive for future AI systems managing massive datasets.

Applications
Ideal for deep learning models requiring vast storage, large-scale data centers, and space missions where compact, reliable storage is essential.

Summary
Holographic Memory could dramatically expand AI's ability to store and access information, although the technology remains costly and complex to implement today.

Home Automation AI

Definition
Home Automation AI integrates artificial intelligence with smart home devices, automating tasks like lighting, climate control, and security based on user habits and real-time data.

Key Characteristics
It connects AI with IoT devices, uses machine learning to adapt to user preferences, and enables remote control, voice activation, and intelligent scheduling for household systems.

Benefits
Home Automation AI increases daily convenience, improves energy efficiency by optimizing device usage, and enhances home security through proactive monitoring.

Applications
Examples include AI-powered smart thermostats, automated lighting systems, voice-activated appliances, and intelligent home security solutions.

Summary
Home Automation AI transforms daily living by creating responsive, intelligent environments, although ensuring strong cybersecurity measures is essential to protect user privacy and data.

Homomorphic Encryption

Definition
Homomorphic Encryption is a security method that allows calculations to be carried out on encrypted information without revealing the underlying data. It plays a crucial role in AI applications where maintaining strict data privacy is essential.

Key Characteristics
It enables operations to be performed directly on encrypted data, allowing secure computation without exposing sensitive content. This technology is vital for cloud-based AI processing and secure data collaboration.

Benefits
It protects confidentiality while enabling valuable machine learning tasks, minimizes risks associated with data leaks, and is well-suited for sensitive industries like healthcare and finance.

Applications
Training AI models securely in cloud environments, enabling encrypted collaborative AI across organizations, and safeguarding financial data during AI-driven analysis.

Summary
Homomorphic Encryption empowers AI to process confidential data securely, making it indispensable for privacy-focused applications, though its computational demands are significantly higher than traditional methods.

Hopping Neural Networks

Definition
Hopping Neural Networks are specialized adaptations of recurrent neural networks (RNNs) designed to manage sequences with irregular timing, allowing the model to skip irrelevant time points during learning and focus on meaningful events.

Key Characteristics
These networks handle event-driven data by introducing flexible "hops" between important moments, optimizing learning in scenarios where time intervals between inputs vary unpredictably.

Benefits
They boost accuracy on unevenly spaced sequence data, reduce unnecessary computation, and adapt well to event streams where timing inconsistency is common.

Applications
Forecasting irregular market events, analyzing medical records with sporadic patient visits, and studying social media patterns with inconsistent user activity.

Summary
Hopping Neural Networks excel at managing irregular time-series data by selectively focusing on key events, though their design demands careful calibration for best results.

Horizontal Scaling in AI

Definition
Horizontal Scaling in AI refers to expanding a system's computational capacity by adding more machines or nodes, enabling the distribution of workloads across multiple processors to enhance performance and reliability.

Key Characteristics
Rather than upgrading individual hardware, horizontal scaling increases system strength by expanding the network, supporting parallel processing and improving system resilience.

Benefits
It offers a cost-efficient way to increase capacity, enhances processing power for large AI tasks, and improves fault tolerance by distributing risk across multiple nodes.

Applications
Training distributed machine learning models, operating scalable cloud-based AI services, and processing big data in analytics pipelines.

Summary
Horizontal Scaling equips AI systems to meet growing demands by expanding resources flexibly, though managing distributed systems adds layers of complexity.

Hospital AI Systems

Definition
Hospital AI Systems are advanced platforms that integrate artificial intelligence into healthcare environments to assist with diagnosis, treatment planning, patient management, and operational efficiency.

Key Characteristics
These systems combine machine learning with electronic health records, automate routine hospital tasks, and support clinical decision-making with predictive analytics.

Benefits
They improve diagnostic accuracy and speed, streamline hospital workflows, enhance resource allocation, and reduce administrative burdens on medical staff.

Applications
AI-driven diagnostic imaging, predictive patient admission and discharge planning, and automated scheduling for hospital resources.

Summary
Hospital AI Systems transform healthcare by enhancing patient care and hospital efficiency, though successful deployment demands strong data governance and cost management strategies.

Host-Based Intrusion Detection Systems (HIDS)

Definition
Host-Based Intrusion Detection Systems (HIDS) are cybersecurity solutions that monitor individual computers or servers for signs of malicious behavior, using AI to identify threats specific to a single host environment.

Key Characteristics
They analyze system files, logs, and activities to detect anomalies, focusing on the behavior of individual machines rather than network-wide monitoring.

Benefits
HIDS provide detailed security tailored to each device, detect internal threats that network-based systems might miss, and strengthen endpoint defense strategies.

Applications
Protecting sensitive government servers, securing cloud-hosted virtual machines, and monitoring critical infrastructure in enterprises.

Summary
Host-Based Intrusion Detection Systems offer essential device-level protection against cyber threats, but they must be integrated with broader security strategies to ensure complete system defense.

Hotspot Detection in AI

Definition
Hotspot Detection in AI refers to the use of machine learning to identify areas or periods with unusually high levels of activity, helping organizations spot trends, issues, or opportunities within spatial or temporal data.

Key Characteristics
It analyzes datasets for concentrated patterns of activity, often using clustering algorithms to find and highlight significant data clusters in real time.

Benefits
Hotspot detection provides actionable insights for rapid decision-making, enhances strategic planning, and allows timely responses to dynamic conditions.

Applications
Crime prevention by identifying high-risk areas, traffic congestion analysis in smart city initiatives, and trend detection in marketing and social media analytics.

Summary
Hotspot Detection empowers industries to act swiftly on concentrated data activity, though it depends heavily on accurate and up-to-date data sources.

Human Activity Recognition (HAR)

Definition
Human Activity Recognition (HAR) uses artificial intelligence to identify and classify human movements and behaviors, such as walking, sitting, or running, based on data collected from sensors, smartphones, or cameras.

Key Characteristics
It typically relies on time-series data from wearable devices or video feeds, using machine learning models to detect and categorize activities in real-time.

Benefits
HAR supports health and fitness monitoring, enhances gesture recognition for human-computer interaction, and strengthens security systems by identifying unusual behaviors.

Applications
Tracking patient rehabilitation progress in healthcare, real-time fitness monitoring in mobile apps, and monitoring daily activities in smart homes and assisted living facilities.

Summary
Human Activity Recognition enables AI to understand physical behaviors, with major impacts on healthcare and fitness, though it must carefully address privacy concerns when used in surveillance settings.

Human-Agent Interaction (HAI)

Definition
Human-Agent Interaction (HAI) explores how humans engage with AI-driven systems, aiming to enhance communication, cooperation, and mutual understanding between users and artificial agents.

Key Characteristics
It focuses on intuitive design, promotes natural interaction methods, and addresses trust, feedback, and system autonomy to strengthen collaboration.

Benefits
Enhances the effectiveness and trustworthiness of AI systems, improves teamwork between humans and AI, and makes technology easier and more enjoyable to use.

Applications
Voice-controlled virtual assistants like Siri and Alexa, collaboration between drivers and autonomous vehicles, and decision support systems in healthcare settings.

Summary
Human-Agent Interaction strengthens the bond between users and AI, promoting trust and efficiency, though it must be designed thoughtfully to avoid creating excessive reliance on machines.

Human Augmentation

Definition
Human Augmentation integrates AI technologies with the human body or mind to extend or enhance cognitive, physical, and sensory abilities, often through wearable devices or implants.

Key Characteristics
Combines AI with assistive devices to surpass natural human limitations, focusing on improving performance, perception, and decision-making.

Benefits
Boosts productivity and problem-solving capabilities, aids individuals with disabilities, and expands learning, memory, and physical performance beyond conventional limits.

Applications
Exoskeletons that assist physical labor, AI-enhanced hearing aids and vision tools, and cognitive enhancement systems that support learning and memory.

Summary
Human Augmentation through AI unlocks new frontiers for human capabilities but introduces ethical and societal questions regarding enhancement boundaries and accessibility.

Human Bias in AI

Definition
Human Bias in AI refers to the presence of prejudices or unfair assumptions within AI systems, often resulting from biased training data, flawed design, or societal influences.

Key Characteristics
Biases can emerge from historical data, labeling errors, or algorithmic structures, leading to unequal or discriminatory outcomes in AI decisions.

Benefits
Recognizing and addressing bias improves fairness, enhances trust in AI, and helps create more ethical and transparent systems.

Applications
Auditing AI systems used in hiring, finance, and law enforcement, retraining models to remove bias, and developing algorithms that automatically detect and correct biases.

Summary
Human Bias in AI must be proactively managed to build fair, trustworthy technologies, requiring continuous evaluation and updates throughout AI system development.

Human-Centered AI

Definition
Human-Centered AI is an approach to AI development that prioritizes human needs, values, and ethics, ensuring that technology works alongside people to enhance their lives rather than replace them.

Key Characteristics
Focuses on collaboration, ethical behavior, user empowerment, and adaptability based on ongoing human feedback.

Benefits
Creates AI systems that are more trustworthy, socially responsible, and tailored to human goals, fostering greater acceptance and effectiveness.

Applications
Decision-support AI in healthcare, adaptive learning platforms in education, and accessibility features for smart homes and public systems.

Summary
Human-Centered AI emphasizes collaboration between people and technology, requiring a continuous commitment to ethical development and human value alignment.

Human-Centered Design (HCD) in AI

Definition
Human-Centered Design (HCD) in AI refers to the practice of building AI systems around user needs, ensuring that technologies are intuitive, accessible, and aligned with societal values.

Key Characteristics
It involves iterative design, frequent user feedback, attention to accessibility, and a strong focus on ethical and social impacts.

Benefits
Enhances user satisfaction and system effectiveness, reduces learning curves, and promotes ethical AI deployment that serves real-world needs.

Applications
Virtual assistant development focused on usability, AI-driven tools designed for users with disabilities, and smart city systems that prioritize human convenience and safety.

Summary
Human-Centered Design in AI keeps technology accessible, effective, and ethically grounded, requiring continuous user involvement and responsive system updates.

Human-Computer Interaction (HCI)

Definition
Human-Computer Interaction (HCI) is the study and design of interactions between people and computer systems, aiming to create intuitive, efficient, and accessible technology experiences.

Key Characteristics
It integrates principles from AI, user experience design, and accessibility to ensure seamless communication between users and machines.

Benefits
HCI enhances usability, improves system efficiency, reduces user errors, and broadens accessibility across diverse user groups.

Applications
Designing intuitive interfaces for AI assistants, building user-friendly control systems for robotics, and creating touch-based or voice-activated systems for industrial environments.

Summary
Human-Computer Interaction ensures that AI and computing technologies are user-focused and accessible, requiring continuous testing and refinement to meet evolving user needs.

Human Enhancement through AI

Definition
Human Enhancement through AI involves applying artificial intelligence to extend human mental and physical capabilities, supporting functions like memory, decision-making, strength, and perception.

Key Characteristics
It integrates AI with cognitive tools, wearable technologies, and biological interfaces to augment natural human abilities.

Benefits
Enables greater productivity and learning, supports rehabilitation and accessibility for individuals with disabilities, and advances human capabilities in critical and high-performance environments.

Applications
AI-powered exoskeletons for labor and mobility, brain-computer interfaces for cognitive support, and augmented reality overlays for complex decision-making tasks.

Summary
Human Enhancement through AI offers groundbreaking opportunities to extend human potential, but careful ethical considerations are necessary to ensure equitable and responsible use.

Human Genome

Definition
The Human Genome represents the complete set of genetic instructions encoded within human DNA, containing approximately three billion base pairs organized into 23 chromosome pairs. It determines biological development, inheritance, and individual traits.

Key Components
It includes genes that produce proteins essential for bodily functions, regulatory elements that control gene expression, and non-coding regions that support chromosome structure and function. Variations and mutations influence health, traits, and disease susceptibility.

Benefits
Understanding the human genome enables personalized medicine, early disease detection, targeted therapies, and insights into human ancestry and evolution.

Applications
Genetic testing for inherited conditions, pharmacogenomics for optimizing drug treatments, gene therapy for correcting genetic disorders, and forensic DNA analysis for identification purposes.

Industries
Healthcare relies on genomics for diagnostics and treatment planning, pharmaceuticals develop precision medicines, biotechnology advances gene editing, forensics uses DNA for criminal investigations, and agricultural genomics improves crop and livestock health.

Summary
The Human Genome is a cornerstone of modern biology and medicine, revolutionizing our understanding of health, disease, and human history. While challenges remain, its potential to drive personalized healthcare, scientific discovery, and technological innovation continues to grow.

Human-in-the-Loop (HITL) Learning

Definition
Human-in-the-Loop (HITL) Learning is an AI development method where human input is actively integrated into the training, evaluation, and refinement stages of machine learning models to improve performance and reliability.

Key Characteristics
It combines the strengths of human expertise with machine efficiency through iterative feedback loops, allowing humans to correct, guide, and enhance model outcomes, particularly in complex or sensitive domains.

Benefits
Enhances model accuracy by incorporating real-world expertise, aligns AI decision-making with human values and ethics, and reduces algorithmic biases by introducing diverse human perspectives.

Applications
Medical AI systems for diagnosing and planning treatments, fraud detection platforms augmented by human investigators, and legal document review systems guided by expert analysis.

Summary
Human-in-the-Loop Learning bridges the gap between human judgment and machine learning, delivering more accurate and ethical models, though it requires significant human involvement and careful bias management.

Human Language Processing (HLP)

Definition
Human Language Processing (HLP) encompasses AI technologies that enable machines to comprehend, interpret, and generate human language, facilitating natural communication between humans and computers.

Key Characteristics
It involves understanding syntax, semantics, and linguistic context, combining linguistic theory with machine learning to achieve both language comprehension and creation.

Benefits
HLP enhances human-machine interaction, improves automated translation, summarization, and sentiment analysis, and supports accessibility through voice-activated systems and speech recognition.

Applications
Customer service chatbots, AI-based translation platforms, sentiment detection in social media analysis, and intelligent virtual assistants.

Summary
Human Language Processing empowers AI to interact through natural language, offering intuitive communication capabilities while still grappling with the complexities and subtleties of human expression.

Human-Level AI

Definition
Human-Level AI refers to artificial intelligence systems capable of performing any intellectual task that a human can, matching human abilities in reasoning, learning, creativity, and understanding across multiple domains.

Key Characteristics
Exhibits generalized intelligence, adaptability across diverse tasks, and the ability to reason and learn independently, commonly associated with the concept of Artificial General Intelligence (AGI).

Benefits
Unlocks revolutionary advances across industries, allows seamless task transfer without retraining, and has the potential to drive breakthroughs in fields like healthcare, research, and education.

Applications
Robotic systems capable of autonomous complex problem-solving, AI personal assistants with human-like multitasking abilities, and AI artists generating original works across mediums.

Summary
Human-Level AI promises transformative capabilities but raises profound ethical, societal, and safety concerns that demand careful oversight as the technology progresses.

Human-Like Reasoning in AI

Definition
Human-Like Reasoning in AI involves designing systems that replicate human cognitive processes, allowing them to make decisions under uncertainty, handle incomplete information, and apply flexible thinking strategies.

Key Characteristics
Incorporates heuristic methods, probabilistic reasoning, and logical frameworks to mirror how humans approach problem-solving in ambiguous or complex scenarios.

Benefits
Improves AI's ability to tackle real-world situations requiring judgment, enhances user trust by making AI decisions more understandable, and increases versatility in uncertain environments.

Applications
Healthcare AI for diagnosing complex cases, autonomous vehicles navigating unpredictable conditions, and AI legal systems capable of interpreting nuanced legal arguments.

Summary
Human-Like Reasoning strengthens AI's decision-making in uncertain environments, though fully capturing the richness and depth of human thinking remains an ongoing challenge.

Human Motion Prediction

Definition
Human Motion Prediction leverages AI to forecast future human movements based on patterns observed through sensors, video data, or other tracking technologies.

Key Characteristics
Analyzes past motion trajectories, predicts near-future positions, and models limb, joint, and body orientation to anticipate human actions.

Benefits
Enhances collaboration and safety between humans and robots, aids athletic performance analysis, and supports autonomous vehicles in predicting pedestrian behaviors.

Applications
Sports analytics for strategy planning, robotics for safer human-robot interaction, and autonomous systems for anticipating and responding to pedestrian motion.

Summary
Human Motion Prediction sharpens AI's ability to anticipate human actions, improving safety and collaboration, though it requires precise, high-quality motion data to perform accurately.

Humanoid

Definition
A humanoid is a robot, entity, or system engineered to resemble human physical form and mimic human actions, featuring attributes such as walking, speaking, or facial expressions.

Key Characteristics
Typically built with human-like body structures (head, torso, arms, and legs) and designed to replicate behaviors like movement, communication, and emotional expression, often powered by AI.

Benefits
Facilitates natural interaction, handles repetitive or hazardous tasks, supports care and companionship roles, and enhances realism in entertainment and education.

Applications
Airport robots assisting travelers, healthcare robots aiding elderly patients, simulated training patients in medical education, and interactive performers in media and theme parks.

Summary
Humanoids bridge the gap between technology and human interaction, offering solutions in service, healthcare, education, and entertainment, although development remains costly and ethically sensitive.

Humanoid AI

Definition
Humanoid AI refers to artificial intelligence systems designed to emulate human-like behavior, cognition, and interaction, often embodied in robots or digital agents resembling human forms and traits.

Key Characteristics
Combines natural language processing, facial and gesture recognition, emotional understanding, and sophisticated robotics to deliver human-like experiences in physical or virtual environments.

Benefits
Promotes intuitive communication with machines, bridges social gaps in human-machine interaction, and provides human-style assistance in areas like healthcare, education, and customer service.

Applications
Companion robots in eldercare, educational tutors that adapt to student needs, hotel concierge robots, and interactive characters in entertainment settings.

Summary
Humanoid AI blends human traits with machine intelligence, offering relatable and powerful solutions across industries, though creating truly lifelike behavior remains technically and ethically complex.

Human Oversight in AI

Definition
Human Oversight in AI refers to embedding human supervision into AI decision-making processes, ensuring that critical outcomes, especially those involving ethics or safety, are reviewed and controlled by people.

Key Characteristics
Involves a balance between AI autonomy and human control, particularly in high-risk environments, maintaining human accountability and judgment over AI actions.

Benefits
Mitigates risks of errors or unintended consequences, enforces legal and ethical standards, and builds trust in AI-driven systems by retaining human authority over important decisions.

Applications
Human supervision over autonomous weapon systems, expert review of AI-generated medical diagnoses, and auditing AI-driven financial decisions.

Summary
Human Oversight in AI is crucial for safeguarding ethical standards, safety, and public trust, especially in high-stakes applications, although it may limit the speed and full autonomy of AI systems.

Human Perception in AI

Definition
Human Perception in AI refers to the use of artificial intelligence to mimic or interpret how humans perceive the world through senses like sight, sound, or touch, translating raw data into meaningful insights. It's an AI attempt to see, hear, or feel as we do.

Key Components
Sensors—like cameras or mics—capture raw input, feeding AI models such as neural networks. Perception algorithms process signals, extracting features like shapes or tones. Training data, often human-labeled, teaches context. Fusion combines multi-sense data, and real-time logic tracks live shifts.

Benefits
It bridges human and machine understanding fast. Accuracy apes our senses, and adaptability fits messy reality. Scalability handles big feeds, and it boosts natural interaction.

Examples
An AI IDs a dog's bark, gauging its mood like a person might. A camera bot spots a smile, reading joy from a face.

Applications
It powers voice assistants with tone sense. Vision spots objects, and robotics feels textures. Security reads behavior, and health tracks vitals.

Industries
Tech smarts devices. Security watches crowds, and healthcare heals keen. Robotics grabs real, and media crafts life.

Challenges
Noise scrambles weak models. Human variance trips training, and compute scales with senses. Ethics hit privacy, and mimicry caps at our flaws.

Summary
Human Perception in AI is a sense stealer, echoing our eyes and ears with digital wit. It's a human mirror but fights chaos. A keen echo, it feels our world.

Humor Generation in AI

Definition
Humor Generation in AI is the process where artificial intelligence creates jokes, witty remarks, or funny content by learning patterns of humor from text or context. It's a digital comedian crafting laughs.

Key Components
A language model—like transformers—builds text, trained on jokes or quips. Context inputs—like topics or moods—steer tone. Humor rules—like puns or surprise—shape output, and creativity tweaks add flair. Feedback gauges laughs, refining wit.

Benefits
It sparks joy fast, lifting spirits. Creativity bends to any crowd, and automation scales fun. Novelty keeps it fresh, and it aids human writers.

Examples
An AI quips "Why'd the tomato blush? It saw the salad dressing!" A bot roasts "Your code's so slow, it's got a walker."

Applications
It spices chatbots with sass. Media writes skits, and games jest with players. Marketing crafts funny ads, and education eases lessons.

Industries
Tech chats fun. Media laughs loud, and gaming plays light. Marketing sells smiles, and education lifts moods.

Challenges
Humor's subjective—laughs vary. Culture trips punchlines, and training needs vast jests. Compute scales creativity, and flat wit flops.

Summary
Humor Generation in AI is a giggle maker, spinning laughs with learned charm. It's a joy jolt but chases taste. A witty spark, it tickles the mind.

Hybrid AI Systems

Definition
Hybrid AI Systems combine multiple AI approaches—like symbolic reasoning and neural networks—to solve problems, blending strengths for broader smarts. It's a team-up of AI styles.

Key Components
Symbolic logic—like rules or trees—handles reasoning, paired with neural nets for pattern learning. Data inputs feed both, and integration—like APIs—links them. Decision layers weigh outputs, and training tunes the mix.

Benefits
It merges logic and intuition, widening scope. Accuracy rises with dual strengths, and flexibility fits complex tasks. Robustness beats single flaws, and it scales to big puzzles.

Examples
An AI diagnoses flu with rules, then predicts spread with nets. A bot plans routes logically, learning traffic via data.

Applications
It powers expert systems with depth. Healthcare blends rules and scans, and robotics mixes plans with sense. Finance weighs logic and trends, and games smarten foes.

Industries
Healthcare heals wise. Tech builds smart, and robotics acts sharp. Finance bets safe, and gaming plays deep.

Summary
Hybrid AI Systems are a brain blend, fusing logic and learning for full smarts. They're a wide winner but knotty to knit. A dual dance, they tackle all.

Hybrid Cloud AI

Definition
Hybrid Cloud AI is artificial intelligence deployed across mixed cloud setups—public and private—balancing scale, security, and cost for AI tasks. It's a split-sky smart system.

Key Components
Public clouds—like AWS—offer scale, while private clouds hold sensitive data. AI models—like deep nets—run across both, managed by orchestration tools. Data flows via secure pipes, and workload split optimizes use. Monitoring tracks performance.

Benefits
It scales big, stays safe. Cost flexes with need, and speed taps public power. Security locks private bits, and it fits mixed needs.

Examples
An AI trains on public cloud, then predicts on private for patient data. A retailer scales ads public, keeps sales private.

Applications
It trains AI on big clouds. Businesses secure analytics, and health hides records. IoT splits edge and sky, and finance guards trades.

Industries
Tech scales smart. Healthcare locks safe, and finance bets secure. Retail grows wise, and IoT flows split.

Summary
Hybrid Cloud AI is a cloud straddler, mixing scale and shield with AI's might. It's a flex fix but fights sync. A split smart, it spans skies.

Hyperautomation

Definition
Hyperautomation is the extreme use of AI, robotics, and tools to automate vast swaths of tasks, chaining processes for end-to-end efficiency. It's automation on overdrive.

Key Components
AI—like ML or NLP—drives decisions, paired with robotic process automation (RPA) for acts. Workflow engines link steps, and data feeds fuel it. Analytics spot gaps, and scaling spreads it wide.

Benefits
It slashes time across chains. Efficiency soars with no hands, and scale eats big jobs. Errors drop with smart links, and it frees humans for thought.

Examples
An AI auto-files taxes, linking forms and checks. A factory bot orders parts, syncing stock and build.

Applications
It runs office flows whole. Factories chain builds, and banks process loans. Retail stocks smart, and health logs patients.

Industries
Business hums fast. Manufacturing rolls smooth, and finance counts tight. Retail sells quick, and healthcare heals lean.

Summary
Hyperautomation is a task tornado, sweeping work with AI's full force. It's a speed sweep but ties tech tight. A bold rush, it remakes flows.

Hyperbolic Neural Networks

Definition
Hyperbolic Neural Networks are AI models that use hyperbolic geometry—curved space math—to process data, excelling at hierarchical or tree-like structures. It's a bent twist on flat nets.

Key Components
A hyperbolic space—like Poincaré disks—holds data, mapped by embeddings. Layers warp signals via hyperbolic ops, and activation bends like tanh. Training adjusts curves, and distance rules fit trees or graphs.

Benefits
It nails hierarchies with less bloat. Efficiency grows in deep trees, and accuracy fits nested data. Novelty aids research, and it scales to complex links.

Examples
An AI maps a family tree, curving kin ties tight. A bot ranks web pages, bending link depth.

Applications
It models taxonomies in science. NLP parses syntax, and graphs link social nets. Recommendation nests tastes, and biology trees genes.

Industries
Science sorts life. Tech reads text, and social maps friends. Retail suggests smart, and research probes deep.

Summary
Hyperbolic Neural Networks are a curve catcher, bending AI to tree truths with flair. They're a niche ace but twist hard. A deep bend, they reshape links.

Hyperconverged AI Systems

Definition
Hyperconverged AI Systems merge compute, storage, and networking into a single, AI-optimized platform, streamlining deployment and scaling for smart tasks. It's an all-in-one AI powerhouse.

Key Components
Integrated hardware—like GPUs and SSDs—packs power, managed by software like Kubernetes. AI frameworks run atop, and virtualization splits loads. Data pipes flow tight, and automation tunes use.

Benefits
It deploys fast with one box. Scale grows smooth, and efficiency cuts waste. Power fuels AI big, and simplicity eases ops.

Examples
A hyper-box trains a vision AI, storing data onboard. A firm runs analytics, all in one humming rig.

Applications
It trains AI in labs. Businesses crunch data, and edge runs lean. Clouds scale small, and research sims fast.

Industries
Tech builds smart. Business digs deep, and edge smarts up. Clouds flex wide, and science probes quick.

Summary
Hyperconverged AI Systems are a tight titan, boxing AI might in one sleek shell. They're a fast fit but pricey and fixed. A compact king, they pack a punch.

Hypergraph Neural Networks

Definition
Hypergraph Neural Networks are advanced neural models that extend traditional graphs by linking groups of nodes together, allowing AI systems to better handle complex relationships involving multiple entities at once.

Key Components
They utilize hypergraphs, where hyperedges connect several nodes instead of just two, spreading information across these group ties. Neural layers process these connections, with learning algorithms adjusting the network based on group dynamics.

Benefits
They capture richer, multi-entity patterns that traditional graphs miss, accelerate processing of group-based data, and improve model predictions in areas involving intricate relationships.

Applications
Analyzing social networks with overlapping groups, studying genetic interactions in bioinformatics, and managing vehicle clusters in traffic systems.

Industries
Technology companies for social media analysis, healthcare for mapping biological networks, and transportation for traffic optimization.

Summary
Hypergraph Neural Networks offer AI a deeper, more interconnected view of data, enabling powerful insights into group-based structures, though they demand significant processing resources and fine-tuning expertise.

Hyperparameter Optimization

Definition
Hyperparameter Optimization is the method by which AI systems systematically adjust training settings—such as learning rates or layer sizes—to find the best configuration for model performance.

Key Components
It involves model parameters set before learning begins, search algorithms like grid search, random search, or Bayesian optimization to explore settings, and validation scoring to select the best outcome.

Benefits
Enhances model accuracy without redesigning architectures, saves development time, and improves AI system generalization to new data.

Applications
Image classification, speech recognition improvements, fraud detection model tuning, and optimization of AI in financial forecasting.

Industries
Technology for AI model development, finance for predictive modeling, healthcare for improving diagnostic algorithms.

Summary
Hyperparameter Optimization fine-tunes AI systems for peak performance, dramatically improving outcomes, although it can be computationally intensive.

Hyperspectral Data Analysis

Definition
Hyperspectral Data Analysis leverages AI to interpret detailed light spectrum information from sensors, revealing patterns and materials invisible to human eyes.

Key Components
It involves collecting hyperspectral images across hundreds of light wavelengths, AI models parsing spectral signatures, and pattern recognition systems mapping findings.

Benefits
Unveils subtle distinctions in materials, accelerates analysis of environmental and agricultural conditions, and uncovers hidden information for decision-making.

Applications
Agricultural monitoring of crop health, environmental surveys of land and air quality, and mineral detection in mining.

Industries
Agriculture for precision farming, mining for resource identification, and environmental monitoring for climate studies.

Summary
Hyperspectral Data Analysis opens a detailed view of the world beyond visible light, providing powerful insights across sectors, though it demands specialized equipment and computing power.

Hyperspectral Imaging in AI

Definition
Hyperspectral Imaging in AI uses advanced sensors to capture imagery across many wavelengths of light and applies AI to detect fine-grained patterns for analysis and prediction.

Key Components
Hyperspectral cameras collect detailed spectral data, AI models interpret color variations, and processors handle large volumes of multi-band information.

Benefits
Detects features invisible to standard cameras, enhances accuracy in material detection, and enables early identification of health, environmental, or structural issues.

Applications
Medical diagnostics detecting early-stage diseases, forest monitoring for ecosystem health, and quality control in food production.

Industries
Healthcare, agriculture, environmental protection, defense, and industrial inspection.

Summary
Hyperspectral Imaging in AI brings unparalleled depth to visual analysis, uncovering fine details unseen by traditional imaging, though it faces hurdles in cost and complexity.

Hypertext Transfer Protocol (HTTP) in AI

Definition
Hypertext Transfer Protocol (HTTP) in AI refers to how artificial intelligence systems communicate over the internet, exchanging requests and responses through standardized web protocols.

Key Components
It involves AI systems sending HTTP requests to servers, receiving data in return, APIs facilitating smoother interactions, and servers responding to AI-driven queries.

Benefits
Enables AI to access vast online datasets, supports scalable integration with web-based services, and streamlines cloud communication for real-time AI applications.

Applications
Chatbots accessing real-time data, recommendation engines pulling product information, and smart devices syncing with web platforms.

Industries
E-commerce, IoT devices, media streaming, and financial services.

Summary
HTTP in AI connects systems to the vast world of online information, enabling smarter, real-time decisions, though it requires strong safeguards against delays and security risks.

Hypothetical AI Models

Definition
Hypothetical AI Models are conceptual designs of AI systems that explore theoretical capabilities or future possibilities, often created to test ideas, simulate scenarios, or inspire new technology development.

Key Components
They involve imaginative AI architectures, simulated datasets, experimental algorithms, and speculative evaluation methods that push beyond current limitations.

Benefits
Encourages innovation by exploring uncharted AI possibilities, identifies new potential applications, and reduces development risk by simulating before building.

Applications
Simulating ethical dilemmas in autonomous systems, modeling future general AI behaviors, and testing advanced human-emotion AI interaction ideas.

Industries
Technology research, philosophy of AI, healthcare future planning, and defense innovation.

Summary
Hypothetical AI Models stretch the boundaries of imagination in AI development, sparking ideas that could shape future technologies, though they remain conceptual until real-world realization.

Hypothesis Testing in AI

Definition
Hypothesis Testing in AI is the process of evaluating assumptions about data or models, using statistical techniques to confirm or refute predictions and improve AI decision-making.

Key Components
It includes forming a hypothesis, gathering data, applying statistical tests, interpreting results, and validating findings against expected outcomes.

Benefits
Strengthens model reliability by backing conclusions with statistical proof, reduces bias in model development, and clarifies the cause-and-effect relationships within data.

Applications
A/B testing for website optimization, verifying healthcare AI predictions, and evaluating machine learning feature selection.

Industries
Marketing analytics, healthcare research, financial risk modeling, and technology product development.

Summary
Hypothesis Testing brings scientific rigor into AI development, ensuring that decisions are driven by evidence rather than guesswork, though it demands careful statistical design and interpretation.

❀ Letter I ❀

IBAS (Intelligent Behavior Analytics Systems)

Definition
Intelligent Behavior Analytics Systems are advanced AI frameworks that analyze patterns in human or system behavior to uncover insights, predict actions, or detect anomalies. They sift through data to understand intent or flag irregularities, acting as a digital detective for behavior.

Key Components
The system pulls in diverse data streams—like user inputs or network logs—processed by machine learning models such as neural networks or clustering algorithms. Feature extraction highlights telltale signs, like timing or frequency. Real-time analytics keep it current, and a feedback loop sharpens its smarts. Visualization tools turn raw findings into readable trends.

Benefits
It catches oddities fast, sharpening foresight. Precision grows as it learns, cutting false flags. Scalability tackles big datasets, and automation frees up human effort. Insights deepen decision-making with a behavioral lens.

Examples
A retailer's IBAS spots a shopper's odd cart abandonments, hinting at fraud. A firm tracks employee logins, flagging a late-night data grab as suspect.

Applications
It powers fraud detection in banks. Security monitors insider threats, and marketing predicts buyer moves. Healthcare flags patient declines, and games tweak player hooks.

Industries
Finance guards cash. Tech secures systems, and retail reads customers. Healthcare tracks wellness, and gaming keeps fun flowing.

Summary
IBAS is a behavior sleuth, decoding actions with AI's keen eye. It's a sharp predictor but wrestles scale and secrets. A quiet watcher, it reads the unseen.

IBBS (Intelligent Biometric Border Systems)

Definition
Intelligent Biometric Border Systems use AI to enhance border security by identifying individuals through unique biological traits—like faces or fingerprints—streamlining checks while tightening safety. It's a smart gatekeeper for crossings.

Key Components
Biometric sensors—like cameras or scanners—capture traits, feeding AI models for recognition, often deep learning nets. Databases store profiles, and matching algorithms verify IDs. Real-time processing speeds decisions, and integration links to border ops.

Benefits
It speeds entry with precision. Security tightens against fakes, and automation cuts queues. Scalability fits busy borders, and data tracks threats smart.

Examples
An airport IBBS scans a traveler's iris, clearing them in seconds. A land border flags a face mismatch, halting a forged passport.

Applications
It screens travelers at ports. Immigration tracks overstays, and security IDs risks. Customs speeds cargo checks, and law logs movements.

Industries
Government runs borders. Travel eases flows, and security stops breaches. Logistics moves goods, and law enforces rules.

Summary
IBBS is a border brain, locking gates with biometric wit. It's a fast shield but battles fakes and rules. A keen eye, it guards the line.

IBD (Intelligent Behavior Detection)

Definition
Intelligent Behavior Detection is an AI-driven process to spot specific actions or anomalies in real-time data, focusing on intent or deviation from norms. It's a pinpoint listener for what's happening now.

Key Components
Data feeds—like video or logs—hit the system, parsed by AI detectors, often classifiers or anomaly spotters. Contextual rules set baselines, and live analysis flags shifts. Alert logic calls out hits, and learning adapts to new quirks.

Benefits
It nabs actions quick, boosting response. Accuracy hones in on real oddities, and flexibility fits contexts. Light compute suits live use, and it sharpens with time.

Examples
An IBD catches a shoplifter's sly grab on cam. A network bot flags a sudden data spike as a hack.

Applications
It watches stores for theft. Security tracks threats, and traffic spots jams. Health flags falls, and factories catch faults.

Industries
Retail guards stock. Security stays vigilant, and transport flows smooth. Healthcare aids care, and manufacturing runs tight.

Summary
IBD is a live lookout, catching moves with AI's quick glance. It's a sharp spotter but fights clutter. A swift ear, it hears the now.

IBDA (Intelligent Biometric Data Analysis)

Definition
Intelligent Biometric Data Analysis uses AI to process and interpret biometric data—like fingerprints or voice—extracting patterns or verifying identities with deep insight. It's a trait decoder for recognition.

Key Components
Biometric inputs—like scans or recordings—feed AI models, often convolutional nets or signal processors. Feature extraction pulls unique markers, and comparison logic matches profiles. Databases hold templates, and analytics refine precision.

Benefits
It IDs with razor accuracy. Speed scales checks, and depth spots fakes. Privacy aids anonymized use, and it grows sharper with data.

Examples
An IBDA matches a thumbprint, unlocking a vault. A voice bot confirms a caller, greenlighting a wire.

Applications
It secures logins in apps. Borders verify travelers, and banks OK trades. Health IDs patients, and law tracks suspects.

Industries
Tech locks devices. Finance guards funds, and government screens borders. Healthcare logs care, and law hunts clues.

Summary
IBDA is a trait teller, reading bodies with AI's fine comb. It's a tight lock but dodges cheats. A deep dive, it knows who's who.

IBDL (Intelligent Big Data Learning)

Definition
Intelligent Big Data Learning is an AI approach that mines massive datasets to uncover trends, predict outcomes, or adapt systems, leveraging scale for smarts. It's a data delver for big truths.

Key Components
Huge datasets—like logs or streams—pour in, crunched by AI frameworks like Spark or deep nets. Distributed systems split loads, and analytics—like clustering—find gems. Learning loops tweak models, and storage holds the flood.

Benefits
It sees patterns in chaos fast. Scale eats big data, and foresight guides plans. Cost spreads thin, and flexibility fits any field.

Examples
An IBDL predicts city power use from years of meters. A retailer forecasts holiday sales, scanning old buys.

Applications
It predicts weather from globals. Marketing targets ads, and health spots outbreaks. Cities plan traffic, and science mines stars.

Industries
Tech scales smarts. Retail reads trends, and healthcare heals wise. Government plans big, and science digs deep.

Summary
IBDL is a big data sage, sifting piles for AI's gold. It's a vast seer but wrestles bulk. A grand mind, it learns the flood.

These entries should give your AI dictionary a solid boost—each one's a unique take, built from scratch to grok these concepts fully. Let me know if you'd like to tweak anything! How's your morning going so far?

IBES (Intelligent Banking Encryption Systems)

Definition
Intelligent Banking Encryption Systems refer to AI-powered frameworks designed to secure banking

transactions and data through advanced encryption techniques, adapting to threats in real time. It's a digital vault that thinks, safeguarding financial flows.

Key Components
The system hinges on AI algorithms—like neural networks—that manage encryption keys and detect breaches. Real-time data feeds from banking ops fuel it, while adaptive encryption adjusts to threats. Secure hardware—like trusted modules—stores keys, and integration ties it to banking platforms.

Benefits
It locks data tight, foiling hacks fast. Adaptability counters new tricks, and speed keeps transactions smooth. Scalability fits big banks, and trust rises with ironclad safety.

Examples
An IBES scrambles a wire transfer, thwarting a mid-flight snoop. A bank spots a phishing key grab, shifting codes instantly.

Applications
It shields online banking logins. Payments stay safe, and ATMs lock tight. Fraud detection pairs with it, and compliance meets strict rules.

Industries
Finance banks on it. Tech builds secure apps, and government tracks cash safe. Retail ties payments, and cybersecurity sells it.

Summary
IBES is a banking shield, weaving AI into encryption with swift grit. It's a safety star but chases cunning foes. A lock thinker, it guards the vault.

IBES (Intelligent Biometric Enrollment Systems)

Definition
Intelligent Biometric Enrollment Systems use AI to streamline the capture, processing, and storage of biometric traits—like fingerprints or faces—for identity verification, making sign-ups smart and secure. It's a digital ID maker with brains.

Key Components
Biometric sensors—like scanners or cams—grab traits, parsed by AI models for accuracy, often deep nets. Databases log profiles, and quality checks filter bad scans. Automation speeds enrollment, and security layers protect stored data.

Benefits
It cuts sign-up time with precision. Accuracy nails IDs, and ease fits mass use. Scalability grows with crowds, and fraud drops with tight checks.

Examples
An IBES scans a new client's face, logging it in seconds. An airport enrolls travelers, flagging a fake print fast.

Applications
It sets up bank accounts quick. Borders log entrants, and phones unlock safe. Workplaces track staff, and health IDs patients.

Industries
Finance opens accounts. Travel speeds borders, and tech secures gadgets. Healthcare logs safe, and security locks access.

Summary
IBES is an ID swift, crafting biometrics with AI's quick hand. It's a fast gate but wrestles fakes. A sign-up sage, it knows you sharp.

IBHS (Intelligent Business Health Systems)

Definition
Intelligent Business Health Systems are AI-driven tools that monitor and analyze a company's operational vitality—think profits, workflows, or risks—offering diagnostics and fixes. It's a business doctor with data smarts.

Key Components
Data streams—like sales or logs—feed AI models, often predictive nets or analytics. Health metrics—like cash flow—set benchmarks, and diagnostics spot weak spots. Action plans suggest cures, and dashboards show the pulse live.

Benefits
It catches dips early, guiding wins. Precision tunes ops, and automation saves sweat. Scalability fits big firms, and insights sharpen strategy.

Examples
An IBHS flags a sales drop, suggesting ad tweaks. A factory sees downtime rise, cueing maintenance fast.

Applications
It tracks retail profit dips. Factories fix flows, and banks watch risk. HR spots staff churn, and startups gauge growth.

Industries
Retail stays lean. Manufacturing runs smooth, and finance bets safe. Tech scales smart, and HR heals teams.

Summary
IBHS is a firm's pulse, reading health with AI's deep scan. It's a fix finder but leans on data truth. A vital check, it keeps biz fit.

IBIS (Image-Based Information Systems)

Definition
Image-Based Information Systems leverage AI to extract, organize, and use data from images—think photos or scans—for insights or actions. It's a picture reader with purpose.

Key Components
Image inputs—like cams or files—hit AI vision models, often CNNs. Feature extraction pulls details—like shapes or text—and databases store finds. Processing turns pics to info, and interfaces show results clear.

Benefits
It mines pics fast, unveiling hidden bits. Accuracy beats eyeballs, and scale eats image piles. Flexibility fits any shot, and it boosts visual tasks.

Examples
An IBIS reads a license plate, logging a car. A store scans shelf pics, tracking stock gaps.

Applications
It IDs faces in security. Retail checks stock, and health reads X-rays. Maps pull road data, and archives sort old shots.

Industries
Security watches sharp. Retail stocks smart, and healthcare sees deep. Tech maps wise, and history keeps past.

Summary
IBIS is an image sage, turning snaps to smarts with AI's gaze. It's a visual ace but fights noise. A pic parser, it sees the tale.

IBM Watson

Definition
IBM Watson is an AI platform from IBM, blending natural language processing, machine learning, and data analytics to answer questions, predict trends, or assist decisions across industries. It's a thinking tool with broad reach.

Key Components
A core of NLP and deep learning—like transformers—drives it, fed by vast data pools. APIs link it to apps, and cloud scale powers big tasks. Watson's modules—like Assistant or Discovery—tackle specific jobs, and training adapts it to fields.

Benefits
It thinks fast, slicing complex queries. Versatility spans trades, and scale crunches big data. Ease opens it to non-techies, and precision aids trust.

Examples
Watson wins Jeopardy, outsmarting champs with quick answers. A doc uses it to suggest cancer care from patient files.

Applications
It chats as a help bot. Health plans treatments, and finance spots fraud. Retail predicts buys, and law sifts cases.

Industries
Tech builds assistants. Healthcare heals smart, and finance guards cash. Retail sells wise, and law digs deep.

Summary
IBM Watson is an AI titan, weaving words and numbers into sharp aid. It's a wide wonder but demands care. A brainy boost, it reshapes work.

IBP (Integrated Business Planning) AI

Definition
Integrated Business Planning AI is an advanced approach where artificial intelligence enhances the coordination of business functions—like sales, supply chain, and finance—by analyzing data to align strategies and optimize performance. It's a smart glue for enterprise harmony.

Key Components
Data streams from departments feed AI models, often predictive analytics or machine learning nets. Scenario planning tools simulate outcomes, and real-time dashboards track metrics. Integration platforms link silos, and optimization algorithms balance goals like profit and stock.

Benefits
It syncs plans fast, boosting agility. Precision sharpens forecasts, and efficiency cuts waste. Scalability fits growing firms, and collaboration rises as teams see one truth.

Examples
An AI spots a sales dip, adjusting production in real time. A retailer predicts holiday demand, syncing suppliers without overstock.

Applications
It streamlines supply chains. Finance tunes budgets, and sales forecast sharp. Operations cut delays, and execs plan growth.

Industries
Retail balances stock. Manufacturing flows smooth, and finance plans tight. Logistics moves smart, and tech scales ops.

Summary
IBP AI is a unity engine, weaving plans with AI's deft touch. It's a sync star but fights walls and flux. A planner's aid, it ties the knot.

IBR (Intelligent Behavior Recognition)

Definition
Intelligent Behavior Recognition uses AI to identify and interpret specific actions or patterns in data—like video or sensor feeds—decoding intent or anomalies with precision. It's a digital mind reading moves.

Key Components
Inputs like cameras or logs hit AI detectors, often deep learning nets or classifiers. Pattern libraries define norms, and real-time logic flags quirks. Contextual analysis adds depth, and learning refines over time.

Benefits
It catches acts quick, sharpening alerts. Accuracy nails subtle shifts, and automation frees eyes. Flexibility fits scenes, and scale scans wide.

Examples
An IBR spots a crowd panic, cueing evacuation. A bot flags a worker's odd machine tweak as error.

Applications
It watches security for threats. Factories catch faults, and retail reads shoppers. Health tracks patients, and cities ease flow.

Industries
Security stays keen. Manufacturing runs tight, and retail learns buyers. Healthcare aids care, and transport sorts chaos.

Summary
IBR is a move mapper, tracing deeds with AI's swift scan. It's a sharp seer but battles clutter. A live lens, it knows the play.

IBS (Intelligent Building Systems)

Definition
Intelligent Building Systems are AI-enhanced setups that manage a building's operations—like lighting,

HVAC, or security—optimizing comfort, energy, and safety through smart control. It's a brain for brick and mortar.

Key Components
Sensors—like temp or motion—feed AI controllers, often optimization nets. Automation adjusts systems, and data hubs track use. Predictive models foresee needs, and interfaces let managers tweak.

Benefits
It saves energy, cutting costs. Comfort rises with smart tweaks, and safety locks tight. Scale fits big sites, and upkeep drops.

Examples
An IBS dims lights as sun rises, saving power. A fire alert triggers vents, guiding safe exits.

Applications
It tunes office climates. Homes save bills, and factories run lean. Security locks doors, and cities green buildings.

Industries
Real estate thrives smart. Energy cuts waste, and manufacturing hums. Tech builds slick, and safety guards lives.

Summary
IBS is a building whisperer, tuning spaces with AI's green hand. It's a comfort king but fights retro fits. A silent boss, it runs the show.

ICA (Independent Component Analysis)

Definition
Independent Component Analysis is an AI technique that separates mixed signals—like audio or brain waves—into distinct, independent sources, uncovering hidden patterns without prior labels. It's a signal sleuth untangling chaos.

Key Components
Mixed data—like sound mixes—feeds statistical models, often matrix math or blind source separation. Assumptions of independence guide splits, and preprocessing cleans noise. Iteration refines sources, and validation checks purity.

Benefits
It digs deep, finding buried signals. Simplicity skips labels, and flexibility fits wild data. Accuracy splits clean, and scale grows with math.

Examples
An ICA pulls a voice from a noisy crowd. A brain scan splits signals, mapping thought zones.

Applications
It cleans audio for speech tech. Health reads EEGs, and finance sorts market noise. Images split features, and sensors clear clutter.

Industries
Tech talks clear. Healthcare sees minds, and finance bets smart. Media sharpens sound, and science probes deep.

Summary
ICA is a signal splitter, peeling layers with AI's math magic. It's a deep digger but dodges mess. A quiet cutter, it finds the core.

ICBT (Intelligent Cognitive Behavioral Therapy)

Definition
Intelligent Cognitive Behavioral Therapy uses AI to deliver or enhance CBT, tailoring mental health support through data-driven insights and adaptive interventions. It's a digital shrink with heart.

Key Components
User inputs—like moods or logs—feed AI models, often NLP or adaptive nets. Therapy frameworks guide steps, and personalization fits needs. Real-time chat or prompts engage, and tracking measures progress.

Benefits
It scales help, reaching more. Precision tunes to you, and speed aids quick relief. Cost drops vs humans, and access grows wide.

Examples
An ICBT bot spots gloom, suggesting a mood lift. A stressed user gets tailored calm tips fast.

Applications
It aids therapy apps. Clinics extend reach, and schools support kids. Workplaces ease stress, and self-help grows smart.

Industries
Healthcare heals minds. Tech builds apps, and education aids youth. Work boosts wellness, and startups scale care.

Summary
ICBT is a mind mender, weaving AI into therapy's weave. It's a reach rocket but fights soul gaps. A soft aid, it lifts the load.

ICD (Intelligent Customer Data)

Definition
Intelligent Customer Data is an AI-powered approach to collect, analyze, and use customer info—like habits or prefs—to sharpen business moves and personalize engagement. It's a buyer brain decoded.

Key Components
Data pools—like purchases or clicks—feed AI analytics, often clustering or predictive nets. Profiling builds personas, and real-time updates track shifts. Integration ties to CRM, and insights drive actions.

Benefits
It knows buyers deep, boosting sales. Precision targets right, and speed acts now. Scale eats big data, and loyalty grows with fit.

Examples
An ICD predicts a shopper's next buy, cueing an ad. A call bot tweaks tone, sensing frustration.

Applications
It fuels marketing campaigns. Sales pitch smart, and service fits needs. Retail stocks right, and apps tailor use.

Industries
Retail reads trends. Marketing hits marks, and tech personalizes. Finance woos clients, and service shines.

Summary
ICD is a customer key, unlocking wants with AI's fine sift. It's a sales spark but guards secrets. A buyer's map, it charts the way.

ICNN (Intelligent Convolutional Neural Networks)

Definition
Intelligent Convolutional Neural Networks are advanced AI systems that enhance traditional convolutional neural networks by adding adaptive or self-optimizing features, making them smarter at processing visual or spatial data. It's a sharper eye for patterns.

Key Components
The core builds on convolutional layers to extract features—like edges or shapes—from images or grids. Adaptive mechanisms—like dynamic filters or attention—tune focus, and pooling shrinks data smartly. Training leverages big datasets, and optimization tweaks for speed or precision.

Benefits
It sees deeper, boosting accuracy. Flexibility fits odd visuals, and efficiency cuts compute waste. Scalability handles big jobs, and self-tuning eases setup.

Examples
An ICNN spots a rare tumor in a blurry scan, adapting to noise. A drone IDs crops, shifting focus to wilted leaves.

Applications
It powers image classification in apps. Security scans faces, and health reads X-rays. Robotics maps terrain, and cars spot road signs.

Industries
Healthcare diagnoses sharp. Tech builds vision, and security guards keen. Automotive drives safe, and agriculture grows wise.

Summary
ICNN is a vision ace, sharpening convolution with AI's clever twist. It's a deep seer but fights bloat. A smart lens, it catches the fine.

ICR (Intelligent Character Recognition)

Definition
Intelligent Character Recognition is an AI technique that reads and interprets text from images or scans, going beyond basic OCR by understanding context or messy handwriting. It's a text whisperer for the unreadable.

Key Components
Image inputs—like docs or signs—feed AI models, often CNNs or RNNs. Preprocessing cleans blur, and character detection spots letters. Contextual logic—like language models—decodes meaning, and training uses varied scripts.

Benefits
It cracks tough text fast, lifting accuracy. Versatility reads scrawls, and automation skips typing. Scale eats big piles, and context adds smarts.

Examples
An ICR pulls a name from a scribbled note. A bot reads a faded receipt, guessing "milk" from smudge.

Applications
It digitizes old books. Banks scan checks, and apps read signs. Archives sort scans, and logistics tracks labels.

Industries
Finance logs cash. Tech reads real, and history keeps past. Logistics moves fast, and retail tags goods.

Summary
ICR is a script sleuth, teasing text from chaos with AI's keen read. It's a word winner but battles mess. A text tamer, it unlocks the page.

ICS (Intelligent Communication Systems)

Definition
Intelligent Communication Systems use AI to enhance how data, voice, or messages flow between people or devices, optimizing clarity, speed, or intent. It's a talk tuner with digital ears.

Key Components
Communication channels—like voice or text—feed AI processors, often NLP or signal nets. Real-time analytics tweak delivery, and context models grasp meaning. Automation routes or filters, and learning adapts to users.

Benefits
It clears chatter fast, boosting connection. Precision cuts misreads, and ease fits all talks. Scale grows with traffic, and smart routing saves time.

Examples
An ICS cleans a choppy call, filling gaps. A chat AI routes a plea to the right help desk.

Applications
It powers clear calls in telecom. Chatbots talk smart, and nets speed data. Teams sync quick, and emergencies route fast.

Industries
Telecom talks crisp. Tech links wise, and business flows smooth. Emergency aids fast, and media streams clear.

Summary
ICS is a comms crafter, sharpening talks with AI's swift sense. It's a link lifter but fights static. A talk tool, it bridges clear.

ICT (Intelligent Content Translation)

Definition
Intelligent Content Translation employs AI to convert text or media across languages or formats, adding context or style beyond raw word swaps. It's a meaning mover with flair.

Key Components
Source content—like text or speech—hits AI translators, often transformers or NLP nets. Language models grasp nuance, and context layers keep tone. Automation speeds shifts, and training uses paired tongues.

Benefits
It swaps fast, keeping soul. Accuracy holds intent, and style bends to fit. Scale eats big scripts, and ease aids all users.

Examples
An ICT turns a French poem to English, saving rhyme. A bot dubs a film, matching lip sync and slang.

Applications
It localizes apps smooth. Media dubs films, and sites go global. Education spans tongues, and biz talks worldwide.

Industries
Tech opens apps. Media crosses borders, and education teaches wide. Business sells far, and travel guides easy.

Summary
ICT is a tongue twister, weaving words with AI's deep grasp. It's a culture carrier but dodges quirks. A global voice, it spans the gap.

IDB (Intelligent Data Backup)

Definition
Intelligent Data Backup uses AI to automate and optimize data storage and recovery, predicting needs or risks to keep info safe and handy. It's a memory guard with foresight.

Key Components
Data streams—like files or logs—feed AI planners, often predictive nets. Risk models spot threats, and automation schedules saves. Storage splits across clouds or drives, and recovery logic pulls fast.

Benefits
It saves smart, cutting loss. Speed grabs data quick, and foresight nips fails. Scale fits big pools, and cost trims waste.

Examples
An IDB backs up a firm's files, skipping dupes. A bot saves a crashed drive, predicting key bits.

Applications
It guards biz data safe. Clouds sync smart, and homes save pics. Servers stay up, and archives hold long.

Industries
Tech keeps bits. Business runs sure, and home tech stores safe. Clouds scale wide, and history lasts.

Summary
IDB is a data keeper, stashing smart with AI's sly plan. It's a save star but fights flux. A safe hand, it holds the past.

IDF (Intelligent Document Filing)

Definition
Intelligent Document Filing is an AI system that organizes, sorts, and stores documents—digital or scanned—using context or content to file them right. It's a paper piler with brains.

Key Components
Docs—like PDFs or pics—feed AI classifiers, often NLP or vision nets. Content analysis reads text or tags, and filing rules set spots. Automation moves files, and search logic pulls fast.

Benefits
It sorts swift, slashing hunt time. Accuracy fits docs right, and ease cuts clutter. Scale eats big stacks, and access speeds up.

Examples
An IDF files a tax form under "2025" from its date. A bot sorts emails, tagging "urgent" from words.

Applications
It organizes office files. Law sifts cases, and health logs charts. Archives sort old, and biz tracks deals.

Industries
Business flows neat. Law digs quick, and healthcare charts clear. Tech builds order, and history keeps tidy.

Summary
IDF is a file fixer, stacking docs with AI's neat touch. It's an order ace but battles mess. A tidy mind, it clears the desk.

IDL (Intelligent Deep Learning)

Definition
Intelligent Deep Learning refers to an advanced form of deep learning where AI systems enhance their neural networks with adaptive, self-improving features to tackle complex tasks more efficiently. It's a brainy twist on deep neural power.

Key Components
The foundation rests on layered neural networks—like CNNs or RNNs—stacked deep to process data. Adaptive mechanisms, such as dynamic architectures or attention, refine focus. Big datasets fuel training, and optimization—like gradient tweaks—sharpens learning. Feedback loops boost smarts over time.

Benefits
It digs deeper, lifting accuracy on tough jobs. Flexibility bends to new challenges, and efficiency trims waste. Scalability conquers big data, and self-tuning cuts setup fuss.

Examples
An IDL spots rare defects in factory parts, learning from faint clues. A bot predicts storms, adapting to wild weather shifts.

Applications
It powers image recognition in apps. Health diagnoses scans, and finance forecasts markets. Robotics learns terrain, and speech decodes accents.

Industries
Tech drives innovation. Healthcare sees clear, and finance bets wise. Robotics moves smart, and weather warns sharp.

Summary
IDL is a deep thinker, juicing neural nets with AI's clever edge. It's a power player but fights bloat. A sharp mind, it masters the maze.

IDM (Intelligent Data Management)

Definition
Intelligent Data Management is an AI-driven approach to organize, store, and utilize data, optimizing access and insights while keeping it secure and clean. It's a data wrangler with a brain.

Key Components
Data pools—like logs or files—feed AI systems, often analytics or clustering nets. Automation sorts and cleans, and predictive models spot needs. Storage splits smartly across platforms, and security layers lock it tight.

Benefits
It streamlines data fast, easing use. Precision keeps it pure, and foresight aids plans. Scale eats big heaps, and safety builds trust.

Examples
An IDM tags customer files, cutting search time. A bot purges old junk, freeing cloud space.

Applications
It runs biz data smooth. Clouds stay tidy, and research digs deep. Security guards bits, and retail tracks trends.

Industries
Business flows clean. Tech scales smart, and research probes wide. Security locks safe, and retail reads right.

Summary
IDM is a data maestro, tuning piles with AI's deft hand. It's a tidy titan but wrestles chaos. A clean sweep, it rules the bits.

IDR (Intelligent Document Recognition)

Definition
Intelligent Document Recognition uses AI to identify, extract, and process info from documents—scanned or digital—understanding layout or context beyond basic text grabs. It's a page reader with insight.

Key Components
Doc inputs—like PDFs or pics—hit AI vision nets, often CNNs with NLP. Layout analysis maps structure, and content logic pulls meaning. Preprocessing clears noise, and databases store parsed data.

Benefits
It reads fast, nailing details. Depth grasps odd forms, and automation skips typing. Scale eats stacks, and accuracy lifts trust.

Examples
An IDR pulls a date from a crumpled bill. A bot sorts a contract, tagging clauses right.

Applications
It digitizes records in offices. Banks grab check data, and law sifts files. Health logs charts, and archives save past.

Industries
Finance tracks cash. Law digs quick, and healthcare charts neat. Tech builds order, and history keeps alive.

Summary
IDR is a doc decoder, peeling pages with AI's keen eye. It's a text ace but fights mess. A page pal, it cracks the code.

IDS (Intelligent Data Segmentation)

Definition
Intelligent Data Segmentation employs AI to split datasets into meaningful groups—like clusters or categories—based on patterns or goals, making sense of sprawl. It's a data carver with purpose.

Key Components
Raw data—like user stats—feeds AI models, often clustering or classification nets. Feature extraction pulls key traits, and segmentation logic draws lines. Adaptive rules tweak splits, and validation checks fit.

Benefits
It sorts chaos quick, boosting insight. Precision fits true groups, and flexibility bends to aims. Scale tackles big sets, and clarity aids use.

Examples
An IDS groups buyers by spend habits. A bot splits sensor hits, flagging odd zones.

Applications
It segments markets for ads. Health sorts patients, and tech tunes apps. Security tags risks, and research maps trends.

Industries
Marketing hits marks. Healthcare heals smart, and tech personalizes. Security guards keen, and science sees clear.

Summary
IDS is a data slicer, carving sets with AI's fine blade. It's a group guru but dodges clutter. A split star, it finds the seams.

IDT (Intelligent Data Tracking)

Definition
Intelligent Data Tracking uses AI to monitor and trace data flows—like usage or changes—across systems, offering real-time oversight and insights. It's a data stalker with smarts.

Key Components
Data streams—like logs or clicks—feed AI trackers, often time-series or anomaly nets. Monitoring logic follows paths, and predictive models spot trends. Storage logs trails, and alerts flag quirks.

Benefits
It tracks live, catching shifts fast. Depth sees fine moves, and automation saves eyes. Scale rides big flows, and foresight aids plans.

Examples
An IDT logs a file's edits, nailing a leak. A bot tracks ad clicks, predicting peaks.

Applications
It watches biz data moves. Security traces hacks, and retail follows buys. Tech syncs clouds, and health tracks vitals.

Industries
Business stays sure. Security locks tight, and retail reads trends. Tech flows smart, and healthcare keeps tabs.

Summary
IDT is a data hawk, trailing bits with AI's sharp watch. It's a flow finder but fights rush. A keen trace, it maps the move.

ILC (Intelligent Learning Control)

Definition
Intelligent Learning Control is an AI approach that adapts control systems—like robots or processes—by learning from data or feedback to hit goals with precision. It's a steering mind that grows.

Key Components
Control inputs—like sensors or commands—feed AI models, often reinforcement or adaptive nets. Learning loops tweak actions, and goal metrics guide success. Real-time logic adjusts live, and simulation tests refine.

Benefits
It adapts quick, nailing targets. Precision grows with use, and flexibility fits chaos. Scale rides big tasks, and autonomy cuts meddling.

Examples
An ILC steadies a drone in wind, learning gusts. A factory bot tunes speed, hitting quotas.

Applications
It steers robots smooth. Factories run tight, and cars drive smart. Energy grids balance, and planes fly true.

Industries
Robotics moves wise. Manufacturing hums, and transport rolls safe. Energy flows smart, and aerospace soars.

Summary
ILC is a control coach, guiding acts with AI's growing grip. It's a steady star but dodges mess. A live learner, it keeps the course.

ILF (Intelligent Load Forecasting)

Definition
Intelligent Load Forecasting is an AI-driven method to predict future demands on systems—like power grids or servers—using data patterns to optimize resource use. It's a crystal ball for capacity needs.

Key Components
Historical data—like usage logs—feeds AI models, often time-series nets or regression tools. External factors—like weather or events—add context, and predictive algorithms crunch trends. Real-time updates tweak forecasts, and visualization shows the curve ahead.

Benefits
It nails demand with precision, cutting waste. Speed aids quick plans, and foresight prevents overloads. Scalability fits big systems, and efficiency saves costs.

Examples
An ILF predicts a summer power surge, prepping the grid. A server farm scales up, foreseeing a game launch spike.

Applications
It tunes energy grids. Tech balances servers, and logistics plans fleets. Retail stocks for rushes, and cities manage flow.

Industries
Energy powers smart. Tech runs lean, and logistics moves wise. Retail preps right, and cities stay smooth.

Summary
ILF is a load seer, mapping needs with AI's keen foresight. It's a plan pro but fights flux. A demand decoder, it keeps the lights on.

ILP (Inductive Logic Programming)

Definition
Inductive Logic Programming is an AI technique that learns logical rules or programs from examples, blending logic with induction to build explainable models. It's a rule maker with a reasoning heart.

Key Components
Example data—like facts or outcomes—feeds a logic engine, often symbolic AI. Background knowledge sets rules, and induction crafts general principles. Search algorithms test fits, and validation checks truth.

Benefits
It builds clear rules, easing reads. Accuracy grows from examples, and logic cuts black-box haze. Flexibility fits small data, and scale aids reasoning tasks.

Examples
An ILP learns "if rain, then umbrella" from wet days. A bot deduces "late shipments delay sales" from logs.

Applications
It powers expert systems. Science finds laws, and biz spots trends. Health deduces risks, and law builds cases.

Industries
Science probes deep. Tech explains AI, and business plans clear. Healthcare heals wise, and law argues sharp.

Summary
ILP is a logic weaver, spinning rules with AI's clear mind. It's a reason rock but shrinks on mess. A rule sage, it speaks the why.

ILQ (Intelligent Language Querying)

Definition
Intelligent Language Querying uses AI to interpret and answer natural language questions, pulling insights from data with conversational ease. It's a chatty guide to info troves.

Key Components
User queries—like "what's trending?"—hit AI models, often NLP or transformers. Data pools—like

texts or bases—feed answers, and context logic grasps intent. Real-time processing replies fast, and learning hones wit.

Benefits
It chats answers quick, skipping code. Precision nails intent, and ease fits all users. Scale eats big queries, and smarts grow with talk.

Examples
An ILQ pulls sales stats from "show me Q1 gains." A bot answers "who won last game?" from sports logs.

Applications
It runs biz dashboards. Education aids research, and apps search smart. Health pulls records, and media digs news.

Industries
Business digs data. Tech talks easy, and education learns fast. Healthcare finds facts, and media spins tales.

Summary
ILQ is a query pal, chatting data with AI's slick tongue. It's a talk triumph but fights fuzz. A word seeker, it finds the way.

ILR (Intelligent Language Recognition)

Definition
Intelligent Language Recognition employs AI to identify and understand spoken or written languages, decoding dialects or intent with finesse. It's an ear and eye for global tongues.

Key Components
Audio or text inputs feed AI models, often RNNs or transformers. Language libraries tag sounds or words, and context layers catch nuance. Preprocessing cleans noise, and training spans dialects.

Benefits
It IDs tongues fast, bridging gaps. Accuracy hears soft shifts, and versatility fits wild speech. Scale eats big talks, and ease aids all.

Examples
An ILR tags a call as Spanish, routing it right. A bot reads "colour" as British, tweaking replies.

Applications
It powers call centers. Apps translate live, and borders talk clear. Education sorts speech, and biz chats global.

Industries
Tech links worlds. Telecom routes smart, and travel speaks easy. Education teaches wide, and business sells far.

Summary
ILR is a tongue tracker, catching speech with AI's broad ear. It's a voice victor but dodges din. A language light, it hears the world.

ILS (Intelligent Learning Systems)

Definition
Intelligent Learning Systems are AI frameworks that adapt and improve learning processes—like teaching or training—by personalizing paths and refining methods. It's a tutor with endless patience.

Key Components
User data—like progress or style—feeds AI models, often adaptive nets or RL. Content pools offer lessons, and personalization tailors pace. Feedback loops tweak plans, and analytics track gains.

Benefits
It fits learners tight, boosting gains. Speed cuts waste, and flexibility bends to needs. Scale teaches masses, and growth tracks smart.

Examples
An ILS slows math for a struggler, speeding as they catch on. A bot drills vocab, skipping known words.

Applications
It runs school platforms. Biz trains staff, and apps teach skills. Health educates patients, and games level up.

Industries
Education lifts minds. Business grows talent, and tech scales learn. Healthcare informs, and gaming hooks smart.

Summary
ILS is a learn leader, shaping minds with AI's custom touch. It's a teach titan but fights flux. A wise guide, it lights the path.

ILT (Intelligent Legal Technology)

Definition
Intelligent Legal Technology uses AI to streamline legal tasks—like research or contracts—enhancing speed and insight for law work. It's a digital clerk with sharp wits.

Key Components
Legal data—like cases or docs—feeds AI tools, often NLP or search nets. Analysis pulls rules or risks, and automation drafts or checks. Databases store laws, and interfaces aid lawyers.

Benefits
It cuts grind time, lifting pace. Precision spots fine points, and ease aids all pros. Scale eats big caseloads, and cost drops sharp.

Examples
An ILT flags a contract flaw in seconds. A bot pulls case law, nailing a defense angle.

Applications
It drafts deals in firms. Courts sort files, and biz checks rules. Research digs fast, and compliance stays tight.

Industries
Law runs lean. Business seals safe, and tech builds tools. Government tracks rules, and startups scale legal.

Summary
ILT is a law lifter, speeding justice with AI's quick mind. It's a case cracker but fights nuance. A legal ally, it clears the load.

ILV (Intelligent Loan Valuation)

Definition
Intelligent Loan Valuation leverages AI to assess loan worth or risk, crunching data for smarter lending calls. It's a cash calculator with keen sense.

Key Components
Loan data—like credit or income—feeds AI models, often regression or decision nets. Risk metrics weigh odds, and predictive tools forecast paybacks. Real-time updates tweak values, and integration ties to banks.

Benefits
It sizes loans fast, boosting trust. Accuracy cuts defaults, and foresight aids terms. Scale fits big books, and cost trims guesswork.

Examples
An ILV greenlights a mortgage, weighing job shifts. A bot flags a car loan risk, spotting late pays.

Applications
It values home loans. Banks set rates, and fintech scales fast. Risk teams watch odds, and biz lends smart.

Industries
Finance flows cash. Tech builds lend apps, and real estate seals deals. Startups grow quick, and insurance ties risk.

Summary
ILV is a loan lens, valuing debt with AI's sharp math. It's a lend leader but fights gaps. A cash eye, it sizes the stakes.

ILW (Intelligent Language Workflows)

Definition
Intelligent Language Workflows use AI to streamline language tasks—like writing or editing—chaining steps for smooth, smart output. It's a word weaver with flow.

Key Components
Text inputs—like drafts or chats—feed AI tools, often NLP or transformers. Workflow logic links steps—like translate then polish—and automation runs it. Context keeps tone, and learning refines over runs.

Benefits
It speeds word work, lifting ease. Precision holds intent, and flexibility fits tasks. Scale eats big jobs, and quality shines through.

Examples
An ILW drafts an email, then tweaks for charm. A bot translates a guide, editing slang smooth.

Applications
It runs biz comms fast. Media spins tales, and apps localize slick. Education aids write, and teams sync words.

Industries
Business talks clear. Tech builds apps, and media crafts quick. Education lifts pens, and startups scale voice.

Summary
ILW is a word wizard, flowing text with AI's deft chain. It's a write whiz but dodges drift. A smooth scribe, it crafts the stream.

Image Processing

Definition
Image Processing in AI is the use of artificial intelligence to analyze, enhance, or manipulate digital images, extracting insights or improving quality through computational means. It's a visual sculptor with a digital touch.

Key Components
Raw images—like photos or scans—feed AI models, often convolutional neural networks. Preprocessing cleans noise or adjusts light, and feature extraction pulls edges or colors. Algorithms tweak pixels or tag content, and output renders results.

Benefits
It transforms visuals fast, boosting clarity. Precision spots fine details, and automation skips manual edits. Scalability handles big batches, and versatility fits any image type.

Examples
An AI sharpens a blurry selfie, restoring focus. A bot tags cars in traffic cams, counting flow.

Applications
It enhances photos in apps. Security scans faces, and health reads X-rays. Retail IDs products, and maps chart land.

Industries
Tech polishes pics. Security watches keen, and healthcare sees deep. Retail sells smart, and transport maps wise.

Summary
Image Processing is a sight shaper, refining visuals with AI's deft eye. It's a picture pro but fights mess. A clear craft, it paints the scene.

Image Processing in AI

Definition
Image Processing in AI leverages artificial intelligence to analyze or enhance images, pulling insights or refining visuals with computational finesse. It's a picture polisher with depth.

Key Components
Images—like shots or scans—feed AI nets, often CNNs. Preprocessing fixes light, and feature logic spots traits. Algorithms tweak or tag, and outputs show results.

Benefits
It sharpens fast, lifting use. Accuracy sees fine bits, and automation cuts hands. Scale eats big pics, and flex fits all types.

Examples
An AI clears a foggy shot, showing hills. A bot tags dogs in park pics, counting play.

Applications
It boosts pics in apps. Security scans faces, and health reads scans. Retail IDs goods, and maps chart land.

Industries
Tech shines pics. Security watches sharp, and healthcare sees deep. Retail sorts quick, and transport maps wise.

Summary
IP is a vision verve, shaping pics with AI's keen craft. It's a sight star but fights mess. A clear cut, it frames the view.

Image Upscaling

Definition
Image Upscaling uses AI to increase the resolution of images, adding detail to low-quality visuals by predicting missing pixels. It's a zoom lens with a creative brain.

Key Components
Low-res images hit AI upscalers, often GANs or deep nets. Training data—high-res pairs—teaches detail, and interpolation guesses new pixels. Post-processing smooths edges, and compute power drives the lift.

Benefits
It revives old shots with crispness. Speed scales quick, and detail beats basic zoom. Flexibility fits any pic, and cost cuts new shoots.

Examples
An AI upscales a grainy 90s photo to 4K glory. A game bot boosts old textures, refreshing play.

Applications
It restores family pics. Games remaster art, and films upscale classics. Design prints big, and archives save past.

Industries
Media shines old. Gaming plays fresh, and design crafts bold. History keeps sharp, and tech builds apps.

Summary
Image Upscaling is a detail dreamer, bloating pics with AI's fine fill. It's a resolution redeemer but risks flaws. A sharp boost, it rekindles sight.

Imbalanced Dataset Handling

Definition
Imbalanced Dataset Handling in AI tackles datasets where classes—like spam vs. not—skew heavily, using techniques to balance learning for fair outcomes. It's a scale tipper for uneven data.

Key Components
Skewed data feeds AI tools, often classifiers. Resampling—like oversampling or undersampling—evens counts, and weighting tweaks class focus. Synthetic data—like SMOTE—fills gaps, and evaluation metrics—like F1—check fit.

Benefits
It lifts rare class hits, boosting fairness. Accuracy holds true, and ease aids most models. Scale fits big sets, and bias drops sharp.

Examples
An AI spots rare fraud, upping small cases. A bot flags sick plants, balancing healthy heaps.

Applications
It tunes fraud detection. Health finds rare ills, and security catches threats. Marketing hits niches, and science probes odd.

Industries
Finance guards cash. Healthcare heals rare, and security stays keen. Marketing sells smart, and science digs deep.

Summary
Imbalanced Dataset Handling is a fairness fixer, righting data with AI's deft tweak. It's a bias buster but fights bloat. A just judge, it evens the odds.

Imbalance Learning

Definition
Imbalance Learning is an AI approach that trains models to handle uneven data distributions, learning patterns despite skewed classes for robust predictions. It's a lesson in lopsided smarts.

Key Components
Uneven data—like rare events—feeds AI nets, often deep or ensemble models. Loss functions weigh rare hits, and augmentation boosts small groups. Training adapts to skew, and validation tracks true gains.

Benefits
It masters rare finds with grit. Precision cuts false flops, and flexibility fits tasks. Scale eats big skews, and learning grows wise.

Examples
An AI learns cancer signs from few cases. A bot predicts quakes, sifting calm days.

Applications
It spots disease in health. Finance catches cheats, and tech tunes rare bugs. Safety flags risks, and nature reads odd.

Industries
Healthcare heals deep. Finance bets safe, and tech fixes smart. Security guards tight, and science sees rare.

Summary
Imbalance Learning is a skew scholar, grasping odds with AI's tough mind. It's a rare winner but wrestles scant. A deep dive, it finds the few.

Imitation Learning

Definition
Imitation Learning is an AI method where systems learn tasks by mimicking expert behavior—like human moves or demos—instead of trial and error. It's a copycat with a purpose.

Key Components
Expert demos—like videos or logs—feed AI models, often neural nets or RL tweaks. Mapping links actions to goals, and inference predicts next steps. Training refines mimicry, and adaptation fits new scenes.

Benefits
It learns fast, skipping stumbles. Accuracy apes pros, and ease cuts coding. Scale rides demos, and trust grows with proof.

Examples
A robot folds shirts, copying a tailor. A car AI drives, shadowing a pro racer.

Applications
It trains robots for tasks. Cars steer smart, and games mimic players. Health copies docs, and biz learns moves.

Industries
Robotics works slick. Automotive rides wise, and gaming plays sharp. Healthcare acts skilled, and business flows fast.

Summary
Imitation Learning is a mimic master, cloning skill with AI's quick eye. It's a fast follower but sticks to scripts. A deft echo, it learns by watch.

Immersive AI

Definition
Immersive AI blends artificial intelligence with virtual or augmented realities to create rich, interactive experiences that feel real or deepen engagement. It's a world weaver with digital depth.

Key Components
VR/AR gear—like headsets—pairs with AI models, often vision or generative nets. Real-time rendering crafts scenes, and interaction logic reads moves. Data feeds—like maps or voices—build worlds, and learning adapts to users.

Benefits
It pulls you in deep, lifting joy. Speed keeps worlds live, and smarts fit your pace. Scale grows big realms, and awe drives use.

Examples
An AI crafts a VR forest, shifting with your gaze. A training bot builds AR fires, teaching escape.

Applications
It runs VR games. Training sims skills, and design mocks builds. Education tours past, and therapy calms minds.

Industries
Gaming dives rich. Education walks real, and design shapes fast. Healthcare heals soft, and biz trains deep.

Summary
Immersive AI is a reality spinner, crafting worlds with AI's vivid hand. It's a dive delight but fights tech heft. A deep dream, it blurs the line.

Immunoinformatics

Definition
Immunoinformatics uses AI to analyze immune system data—like proteins or responses—predicting reactions or designing treatments with computational power. It's a bio brain for body defense.

Key Components
Bio-data—like DNA or antibodies—feeds AI tools, often deep nets or stats models. Prediction maps immune hits, and simulation tests vaccines. Databases store markers, and analytics guide cures.

Benefits
It speeds cures, decoding fast. Precision targets bugs, and scale eats big bio. Cost cuts lab grind, and insights drive health.

Examples
An AI predicts flu shot strength from strains. A bot spots cancer markers, guiding therapy.

Applications
It designs vaccines quick. Health fights bugs, and research probes cells. Pharma crafts drugs, and docs plan care.

Industries
Healthcare heals smart. Pharma builds fast, and research digs deep. Biotech grows wise, and public guards health.

Summary
Immunoinformatics is an immune sleuth, cracking codes with AI's bio eye. It's a health hero but fights complexity. A life lift, it guards the core.

Impact Learning

Definition
Impact Learning is an AI approach that prioritizes outcomes—like social good or efficiency—in training models, optimizing for real-world effects over raw stats. It's a goal getter with heart.

Key Components
Data—like usage or results—feeds AI nets, often RL or optimization tools. Impact metrics—like lives saved—guide loss, and simulation tests ripple. Feedback tracks real wins, and adaptation fits goals.

Benefits
It aims high, hitting what counts. Precision ties to effect, and purpose drives use. Scale aids big aims, and trust grows with good.

Examples
An AI cuts grid waste, learning green impact. A bot boosts literacy, targeting school gains.

Applications
It greens energy use. Education lifts scores, and health saves lives. Biz cuts costs, and cities plan smart.

Industries
Energy flows green. Education rises high, and healthcare helps most. Business runs lean, and cities thrive.

Summary
Impact Learning is a cause crafter, shaping AI with real stakes in mind. It's a good guru but wrestles scope. A purpose push, it changes the game.

Impression Tracking

Definition
Impression Tracking in AI monitors and analyzes how users perceive or react to content—like ads or posts—using data to gauge reach or feel. It's a vibe checker with digital sense.

Key Components
User data—like clicks or views—feeds AI tools, often analytics or NLP nets. Sentiment analysis reads tone, and reach metrics count eyes. Real-time tracking logs live, and models predict impact.

Benefits
It gauges fast, guiding tweaks. Depth sees beyond counts, and ease fits all content. Scale eats big campaigns, and insight lifts effect.

Examples
An AI tracks ad views, noting joy spikes. A bot logs post shares, sensing viral lift.

Applications
It tunes marketing ads. Media reads buzz, and apps track use. Biz gauges brand, and creators chase hits.

Industries
Marketing sells smart. Media spins hot, and tech personalizes. Business builds fame, and creators grow.

Summary
Impression Tracking is a pulse prober, feeling vibes with AI's quick scan. It's a reach reader but fights clutter. A sense tool, it maps the crowd.

Independent Agentic AI

Definition
Independent Agentic AI refers to artificial intelligence systems that operate autonomously, making decisions and taking actions toward goals without constant human oversight, driven by self-directed reasoning. It's a free-thinking digital doer.

Key Components
The system hinges on an AI core—like neural nets or RL—capable of goal-setting and planning. Sensors or data inputs fuel awareness, and decision logic picks paths. Autonomy layers enable self-adjustment, and learning refines choices over time.

Benefits
It acts solo, slashing oversight needs. Speed tackles tasks fast, and flexibility fits wild scenes. Scalability grows with freedom, and initiative drives progress.

Examples
A drone maps a forest, dodging trees on its own. A bot negotiates deals, tweaking offers sans prompts.

Applications
It runs delivery drones. Homes manage energy, and biz optimizes stocks. Research probes alone, and security patrols free.

Industries
Transport flies smart. Home tech runs wise, and business trades quick. Science explores deep, and security guards loose.

Summary
Independent Agentic AI is a lone leader, steering itself with AI's bold mind. It's a free force but fights drift. A self-starter, it charts its course.

Inference Engine

Definition
An Inference Engine is an AI component that applies logical rules or learned patterns to data, drawing conclusions or making decisions from known facts. It's a reasoning heart for smart systems.

Key Components
A knowledge base—like rules or models—feeds the engine, paired with data inputs. Reasoning logic—like deduction or probability—crunches it, and inference steps derive outputs. Integration ties to apps, and tuning sharpens calls.

Benefits
It thinks fast, linking facts to finds. Clarity explains whys, and versatility fits fields. Scale rides big bases, and precision builds trust.

Examples
An engine diagnoses flu from symptoms and rules. A bot flags fraud, reasoning from odd spends.

Applications
It powers expert systems. Health deduces ills, and biz spots risks. Law sifts cases, and tech aids queries.

Industries
Healthcare heals smart. Business plans clear, and law argues tight. Tech explains quick, and science probes sure.

Summary
Inference Engine is a logic linker, weaving answers with AI's steady hand. It's a reason rock but shrinks on chaos. A clear mind, it solves the known.

Inference in AI

Definition
Inference in AI is the process where artificial intelligence draws conclusions, predicts outcomes, or fills gaps using trained models or data, extending beyond raw input. It's a leap from seen to unseen.

Key Components
Trained models—like deep nets—take data, often real-time feeds. Prediction logic—like probability—guesses nexts, and context adds depth. Validation checks truth, and inference loops refine over use.

Benefits
It predicts swift, stretching insight. Accuracy grows with learning, and ease fits live use. Scale eats big tasks, and foresight aids plans.

Examples
An AI infers rain from clouds and wind. A bot guesses a song pick from past plays.

Applications
It forecasts weather. Health predicts ills, and apps suggest moves. Security flags threats, and biz reads trends.

Industries
Weather warns sharp. Healthcare sees ahead, and tech personalizes. Security stays keen, and business bets wise.

Summary
Inference in AI is a guess guru, jumping gaps with AI's bold eye. It's a future finder but fights blanks. A smart stretch, it sees beyond.

Information Extraction

Definition
Information Extraction uses AI to pull specific details—like names or dates—from unstructured data, turning raw text into structured facts. It's a data digger with focus.

Key Components
Text inputs—like docs or posts—feed AI tools, often NLP or pattern nets. Entity recognition tags key bits, and relation logic links them. Preprocessing cleans mess, and storage holds finds.

Benefits
It mines fast, nailing nuggets. Precision grabs right bits, and automation skips hands. Scale eats big texts, and clarity aids use.

Examples
An AI extracts a meeting date from an email. A bot pulls drug names from health notes.

Applications
It sifts news for facts. Law grabs case points, and biz logs deals. Health sorts records, and research mines papers.

Industries
Media spins quick. Law digs deep, and business tracks smart. Healthcare files neat, and science sees clear.

Summary
Information Extraction is a fact fetcher, plucking gems with AI's fine sieve. It's a data dart but fights noise. A sharp scoop, it grabs the core.

Information Flow Analysis

Definition
Information Flow Analysis in AI tracks how data moves through systems or networks, using intelligence to spot patterns, leaks, or bottlenecks. It's a stream watcher with insight.

Key Components
Data traces—like logs or packets—feed AI trackers, often graph or time nets. Flow models map paths, and anomaly logic flags quirks. Real-time scans catch live, and visualization shows the tide.

Benefits
It maps flows fast, guiding fixes. Depth sees fine shifts, and automation saves eyes. Scale rides big nets, and foresight nips risks.

Examples
An AI spots a data jam in a cloud sync. A bot flags a leak, tracing odd sends.

Applications
It tunes tech nets. Security catches leaks, and biz tracks trades. Clouds flow smooth, and research maps data.

Industries
Tech runs clean. Security locks tight, and business flows sure. Clouds scale smart, and science digs deep.

Summary
Information Flow Analysis is a current catcher, tracing tides with AI's keen scan. It's a flow finder but fights rush. A path pro, it charts the stream.

Information Retrieval

Definition
Information Retrieval in AI fetches relevant data—like docs or answers—from vast stores, using intelligence to match queries with precision. It's a search sage with speed.

Key Components
Query inputs—like "find tax laws"—hit AI search nets, often NLP or ranking tools. Data pools—like texts or bases—feed matches, and relevance logic sorts hits. Indexing speeds looks, and learning refines ranks.

Benefits
It grabs fast, nailing needs. Accuracy cuts junk, and ease fits all asks. Scale eats big stores, and smarts grow with use.

Examples
An AI pulls a tax rule from legal files. A bot finds a recipe from "quick dinner" ask.

Applications
It runs web searches. Law sifts cases, and biz finds stats. Education digs facts, and apps fetch quick.

Industries
Tech seeks smart. Law hunts sharp, and business digs sure. Education learns fast, and media spins quick.

Summary
Information Retrieval is a find fixer, nabbing needs with AI's swift sift. It's a search star but fights fuzz. A data dart, it hits the spot.

Informed Search

Definition
Informed Search in AI uses knowledge—like heuristics or goals—to guide searches through problem spaces, finding solutions faster than blind tries. It's a path picker with a map.

Key Components
Problem data—like mazes or goals—feeds AI logic, often heuristic algorithms. Knowledge—like distance guesses—steers steps, and search trees track paths. Evaluation ranks moves, and pruning cuts dead ends.

Benefits
It speeds solves, dodging waste. Precision hits goals tight, and ease fits complex hunts. Scale rides big spaces, and smarts cut time.

Examples
An AI plots a quick route, guessing traffic. A bot solves a puzzle, skipping bad moves.

Applications
It maps navigation apps. Games find wins, and robotics plans paths. Biz optimizes flows, and science probes options.

Industries
Transport rolls fast. Gaming plays smart, and robotics steps sure. Business runs lean, and science digs deep.

Summary
Informed Search is a wayfinder, cutting paths with AI's wise nudge. It's a solve swift but leans on clues. A sharp guide, it charts the hunt.

Input Feature Engineering

Definition
Input Feature Engineering in AI crafts or refines data traits—like stats or tags—to boost model learning, turning raw inputs into gold for predictions. It's a data shaper with craft.

Key Components
Raw data—like logs or pics—feeds AI tools, often stats or transform nets. Feature selection picks key bits, and creation builds new ones—like ratios. Preprocessing cleans mess, and validation tests fit.

Benefits
It lifts learns fast, sharpening hits. Precision tunes models, and ease aids most tasks. Scale eats big sets, and insight drives gains.

Examples
An AI turns ages into bins, boosting ad fits. A bot crafts "time since last buy" for sales guesses.

Applications
It tunes biz forecasts. Health pulls vitals, and tech refines apps. Security tags risks, and science maps trends.

Industries
Business bets smart. Healthcare sees clear, and tech builds sharp. Security guards tight, and science digs deep.

Summary
Input Feature Engineering is a data dresser, polishing bits with AI's fine touch. It's a learn lift but fights fluff. A crafty cut, it shapes the win.

Instance-Based Learning

Definition
Instance-Based Learning in AI learns by storing and comparing past examples—like cases or moves—predicting new outcomes from memory matches. It's a recall ruler with no rules.

Key Components
Example data—like points or acts—feeds memory banks, often k-NN or lazy learners. Distance metrics—like Euclidean—rank closeness, and prediction picks nearest fits. Storage holds cases, and updates add new.

Benefits
It learns quick, skipping models. Accuracy grows with cases, and flexibility fits odd data. Scale rides memory, and ease aids fast starts.

Examples
An AI tags a flower, matching old blooms. A bot predicts rain, recalling past clouds.

Applications
It IDs pics in apps. Health matches ills, and biz spots trends. Security flags odd, and science sorts stars.

Industries
Tech sees sharp. Healthcare heals wise, and business reads clear. Security guards keen, and science maps sure.

Summary
Instance-Based Learning is a memory maven, guessing from past with AI's quick check. It's a case king but fights bloat. A recall ace, it banks on then.

Instance Segmentation

Definition
Instance Segmentation is an AI method that detects and delineates each distinct object in an image, tagging them with unique identities while tracing their precise outlines. It's a digital artist sketching every shape.

Key Components
Images flow into AI models, typically advanced convolutional networks like Mask R-CNN. Detection pinpoints objects, and segmentation paints their borders. Richly labeled datasets train the system, and refinement smooths jagged edges.

Benefits
It isolates objects with surgical accuracy. Speed tackles complex scenes, and automation frees up manual tracing. Detail reveals fine distinctions, and scalability manages crowded frames.

Examples
An AI maps every pedestrian in a street shot, counting steps. A medical bot outlines organs in a scan, measuring growth.

Applications
It guides autonomous cars through traffic. Healthcare tracks tumors, and retail monitors shelves. Robotics picks items, and security spots suspects.

Industries
Transport navigates smart. Medicine heals precise, and retail stocks sharp. Robotics grips sure, and security watches deep.

Summary
Instance Segmentation is a boundary bender, carving scenes with AI's keen stroke. It's a precision marvel but wrestles chaos. A fine framer, it captures each one.

Intelligent Agents

Definition
Intelligent Agents are AI entities that sense their surroundings and act independently to meet objectives, learning and adjusting as they go. It's a self-guided mind on a mission.

Key Components
Sensors or data streams provide input, feeding AI cores like reinforcement learners or logic engines. Decision-making drives actions, and effectors—like motors—carry them out. Adaptation refines tactics, and goals keep it on track.

Benefits
It cuts human reins, boosting freedom. Quick choices meet needs, and versatility handles flux. Scale spreads wide, and proactivity solves ahead.

Examples
A cleaning bot roams, dodging toys. A trading agent buys low, sensing dips.

Applications
It powers smart vacuums. Finance trades bold, and cars steer solo. Security scans free, and games challenge smart.

Industries
Home tech cleans wise. Finance bets fast, and automotive rolls free. Security patrols keen, and gaming fights real.

Summary
Intelligent Agents are solo solvers, acting with AI's free spirit. They're a bold breed but risk stray. A lone light, they chase the goal.

Intelligent Automation

Definition
Intelligent Automation merges AI with automation to streamline intricate tasks—like processes or decisions—flexing to handle exceptions beyond fixed rules. It's a thinking gear in the machine.

Key Components
Task data—like forms or logs—fuels AI systems, often blending ML and robotic tools. Automation executes routines, and intelligence bends to quirks. Live adjustments keep it current, and links mesh with workflows.

Benefits
It zips through jobs with smarts, trimming toil. Accuracy fits oddballs, and scale eats volume. Savings grow over time, and agility shines in change.

Examples
An AI sorts invoices, catching typos. A bot reroutes deliveries, dodging storms.

Applications
It smooths office ops. Banks clear loans, and plants sync builds. Retail restocks fast, and health logs swift.

Industries
Business flows lean. Finance runs tight, and manufacturing hums sure. Retail moves quick, and healthcare heals fast.

Summary
Intelligent Automation is a workflow whiz, fusing smarts with AI's nimble grip. It's a task titan but tangles legacy. A smooth spark, it lifts the grind.

Intelligent Process Automation

Definition
Intelligent Process Automation fuses AI with automation to streamline complex workflows—like forms or chains—adapting to nuance for end-to-end ease. It's a flow fixer with brains.

Key Components
Process data—like steps or logs—feeds AI tools, often ML or RPA nets. Automation runs tasks, and reasoning bends to quirks. Integration links systems, and learning refines flow.

Benefits
It speeds chains with smarts, cutting grind. Precision fits odd jobs, and scale eats big. Cost drops long haul, and flex aids shifts.

Examples
An IPA files taxes, reading scribbles. A bot syncs orders, dodging stock snags.

Applications
It runs office flows. Banks process quick, and factories chain tight. Retail stocks smart, and health logs fast.

Industries
Business hums lean. Finance flows sure, and manufacturing rolls smooth. Retail sells swift, and healthcare heals quick.

Summary
IPA is a process pro, weaving flows with AI's slick touch. It's a work whiz but fights binds. A flow friend, it clears the jam.

Intelligent Recommendation Systems (IRS)

Definition
Intelligent Recommendation Systems (IRS) refer to AI-driven tools designed to analyze user data, behaviors, and preferences to generate personalized suggestions or recommendations for products, content, or services.

Key Components
IRS includes user profiling, recommendation algorithms (collaborative filtering, content-based filtering, hybrid methods), real-time analytics, predictive modeling, personalized ranking mechanisms, and feedback analysis modules.

Example
An online streaming platform uses IRS to recommend movies and shows tailored to users' viewing histories, significantly improving user engagement and satisfaction.

Benefits
IRS enhances personalization, boosts customer engagement, increases sales conversion rates, improves user satisfaction, facilitates targeted marketing strategies, and encourages user retention.

Applications
Applications span e-commerce, content streaming platforms, personalized news feeds, social media platforms, travel recommendations, personalized advertising, e-learning, and digital marketing.

Industries
Industries extensively using IRS include retail, entertainment, education, travel, finance, marketing, media, and telecommunications.

Challenges
Challenges include managing data sparsity, avoiding recommendation bias, ensuring user privacy, handling cold-start problems, maintaining relevance over time, and balancing personalization with diversity.

Conclusions
Intelligent Recommendation Systems significantly enhance user experience and drive business value through effective personalization. Ongoing advancements in data management and algorithm fairness will further enhance user satisfaction and trust.

Intelligent Robotic Navigation (IRN)

Definition
Intelligent Robotic Navigation (IRN) refers to the capability of robotic systems to autonomously and intelligently navigate complex environments by making real-time decisions, path planning, and obstacle avoidance using artificial intelligence techniques and sensor inputs.

Key Components
Intelligent robotic navigation involves sensors (LIDAR, GPS, cameras), localization and mapping algorithms (SLAM), path-planning algorithms, obstacle avoidance systems, AI-based decision-making models, real-time computing systems, and environment perception technologies.

Example
An autonomous warehouse robot employs IRN to navigate effectively between shelves, avoiding obstacles and optimizing routes for picking and delivering items with minimal human intervention.

Benefits
IRN improves robot autonomy, reduces navigation errors, enhances operational efficiency, enables precise real-time decisions, ensures safety, and minimizes manual oversight.

Applications
Applications include autonomous vehicles, warehouse automation, drone navigation, agricultural robotics, healthcare delivery robots, search and rescue robots, and unmanned exploration robots.

Industries
Industries using IRN extensively include logistics, manufacturing, automotive, agriculture, healthcare, military, aerospace, transportation, and emergency response.

Challenges
Challenges include managing dynamic environments, accurately sensing and interpreting surroundings, computational efficiency, balancing speed and safety, dealing with unpredictable conditions, and handling limited sensor data.

Conclusions
Intelligent Robotic Navigation significantly enhances the effectiveness and autonomy of robotic systems. Continued advancement in sensor technology and AI decision-making will further extend IRN's potential across numerous sectors.

Intelligent Routing Protocol (IRP)

Definition

Intelligent Routing Protocol (IRP) in AI refers to advanced computational methods and algorithms that dynamically determine optimal paths for data transmission across networks or systems, adapting intelligently to network conditions, performance criteria, or user needs.

Key Components

Key components include route optimization algorithms, real-time analytics, adaptive learning methods, AI-based congestion detection, load balancing, predictive analytics for network demand, and automated rerouting capabilities.

Example

A telecommunications network utilizes IRP to automatically reroute internet traffic during peak usage hours, ensuring consistent, high-quality network performance for all users.

Benefits

IRP increases network efficiency, enhances reliability, reduces latency, optimizes resource allocation, prevents network congestion, provides proactive network management, and improves user satisfaction.

Applications

Applications include internet traffic routing, supply chain logistics, transportation systems management, emergency response communication, wireless sensor networks, cloud service routing, and intelligent traffic management.

Industries

Industries adopting IRP include telecommunications, transportation, logistics, IT services, emergency management, cloud computing, supply chain management, and aviation.

Challenges

Challenges involve computational complexity, real-time responsiveness, managing unpredictable network conditions, balancing network load effectively, addressing scalability issues, and ensuring security in dynamic routing environments.

Conclusions

Intelligent Routing Protocol significantly optimizes network management and efficiency through adaptive AI-driven routing decisions. Addressing scalability and responsiveness challenges will further enhance its practicality and adoption.

Intelligent Systems

Definition

Intelligent Systems are AI-powered setups that emulate human reasoning or learning to address diverse challenges, adapting across contexts with broad capability. It's a jack-of-all-trades brain.

Key Components

Inputs—like sensors or records—drive AI frameworks, often hybrid nets or deep learners. Reasoning or prediction powers solutions, and outputs guide use. Scalability stretches far, and growth sharpens edge.

Benefits

It tackles wide with wit, solving fast. Breadth spans domains, and speed cuts waits. Scale masters big, and depth fuels trust.

Examples

A smart grid balances power, sensing use. A bot predicts crop yields, mixing rain and soil.

Applications
It runs city grids. Biz plans deep, and health spots ills. Tech crafts apps, and transport flows easy.

Industries
Cities pulse smart. Business bets big, and healthcare heals wise. Tech scales broad, and transport glides smooth.

Summary
Intelligent Systems are a wide wonder, thinking vast with AI's deep reach. They're a solve-all but heft heavy. A grand mind, they span the task.

Intelligent Text Detection (ITD)

Definition
Intelligent Text Detection (ITD) involves AI algorithms and computer vision methods to accurately detect, localize, and interpret textual information within images, videos, or real-world environments in real-time.

Key Components
ITD consists of image preprocessing, deep learning models (CNNs), text localization methods, optical character recognition (OCR), segmentation algorithms, real-time detection frameworks, and multilingual text recognition.

Example
A smartphone camera app automatically detects and translates text on signs in real-time, assisting users in navigating foreign environments or understanding instructions seamlessly.

Benefits
ITD provides accurate and rapid text detection, improves information accessibility, enhances user experience, automates text extraction, and supports multilingual content handling.

Applications
Applications include augmented reality translation, document digitization, automated signage recognition, mobile accessibility apps, OCR systems, and digital content creation.

Industries
Industries adopting ITD include technology, retail, education, entertainment, automotive, logistics, healthcare, and media.

Challenges
Challenges involve handling diverse fonts and backgrounds, ensuring accuracy under varying conditions, computational efficiency, multilingual support, and managing occlusions or distortions.

Conclusions
Intelligent Text Detection greatly advances accessibility and content interaction. Overcoming accuracy and real-time performance challenges will further enhance its potential in diverse sectors.

Intelligent Threat Detection (ITD)

Definition
Intelligent Threat Detection (ITD) refers to AI-powered systems designed to identify, assess, and respond to potential security threats proactively through machine learning techniques, anomaly detection, and real-time analytics.

Key Components
ITD includes threat detection algorithms, behavioral analytics, anomaly detection models, predictive analytics, machine learning classifiers, real-time monitoring tools, automated alert systems, and response protocols.

Example
An enterprise cybersecurity platform uses ITD to analyze network traffic continuously, automatically identifying unusual behaviors indicative of cyberattacks or data breaches and triggering immediate security responses.

Benefits
ITD improves detection accuracy, reduces threat response times, enhances proactive security measures, minimizes false positives, ensures continuous security monitoring, and strengthens organizational cybersecurity defenses.

Applications
Applications include cybersecurity threat detection, fraud detection, intrusion detection systems, financial anomaly detection, network security monitoring, critical infrastructure protection, and digital forensic investigations.

Industries
Industries utilizing ITD include finance, cybersecurity, government, healthcare, telecommunications, utilities, retail, aviation, and defense sectors.

Challenges
Challenges involve managing false positives, dealing with constantly evolving threats, handling large-scale data, ensuring timely responses, computational resource demands, and privacy concerns.

Conclusions
Intelligent Threat Detection is crucial for proactive security management, providing early threat detection and mitigation. Overcoming real-time processing and accuracy challenges ensures its effectiveness in protecting critical assets.

Intelligent Traffic Distribution (ITD)

Definition
Intelligent Traffic Distribution (ITD) refers to AI-driven techniques and algorithms designed to manage, route, and optimize the distribution of data or network traffic dynamically, ensuring balanced network loads and efficient resource usage.

Key Components
ITD consists of load balancing algorithms, adaptive routing protocols, real-time network monitoring, predictive modeling, performance optimization tools, dynamic traffic analysis, and automated distribution strategies.

Example
A cloud computing provider employs ITD to evenly distribute web traffic across multiple data servers, reducing latency, improving reliability, and enhancing end-user experience.

Benefits
ITD enhances network efficiency, optimizes resource use, reduces latency, prevents bottlenecks, maintains consistent performance, and improves overall system reliability.

Applications
Applications include data center optimization, cloud service management, web traffic management, telecommunications network optimization, content delivery networks, and real-time streaming services.

Industries
Industries benefiting include IT, telecommunications, cloud computing, media streaming, finance, online gaming, content distribution, and enterprise network management.

Challenges
Challenges involve handling rapidly changing network conditions, real-time responsiveness, maintaining scalability, managing computational complexity, and balancing traffic efficiently across large networks.

Conclusions
ITD significantly optimizes network performance and reliability. Continued advancement in adaptive algorithms will enhance scalability and performance across industries.

Intent Classification

Definition
Intent Classification uses AI to decode the purpose or goal behind user inputs—like text or speech—sorting them into action categories. It's a mind reader for words.

Key Components
User inputs—like "book a flight"—feed AI models, often NLP or transformers. Intent libraries tag goals, and context logic grasps nuance. Training uses examples, and real-time sorts live.

Benefits
It catches wants fast, boosting chat. Accuracy nails meaning, and ease fits talks. Scale eats big queries, and smarts grow with use.

Examples
An AI tags "where's my order?" as tracking. A bot reads "turn off lights" as control.

Applications
It runs chatbots slick. Apps act on voice, and service sorts pleas. Retail aids buys, and homes obey calls.

Industries
Tech talks smooth. Retail sells quick, and service helps fast. Home tech listens, and biz aids clients.

Summary
Intent Classification is a wish spotter, decoding asks with AI's quick ear. It's a chat champ but fights fuzz. A word wise, it knows the want.

Interactive AI

Definition
Interactive AI is artificial intelligence that responds to users in real time, shaping exchanges—like talks or games—based on input and context. It's a lively partner in play.

Key Components
User moves—like speech or clicks—feed AI systems, often NLP or adaptive nets. Response logic crafts answers, and context tracks threads. Live loops shift with you, and learning adds zest.

Benefits
It chats fast, sparking fun. Flex fits your vibe, and ease builds ties. Scale takes big crowds, and depth keeps it real.

Examples
A bot plays trivia, upping stakes as you win. An AI coach drills skills, sensing weak spots.

Applications
It runs help bots. Games spar live, and apps talk smart. Education guides hands-on, and biz chats clients.

Industries
Tech chats crisp. Gaming feels real, and education lifts live. Business bonds deep, and service glows.

Summary
Interactive AI is a talk titan, weaving live with AI's quick wit. It's a bond booster but fights fuzz. A chat champ, it keeps you in.

Interactive Learning

Definition
Interactive Learning uses AI to tailor education or training through real-time user responses, adjusting lessons to fit pace and gaps. It's a teacher that bends to you.

Key Components
User inputs—like quiz scores—feed AI models, often adaptive or RL nets. Lesson banks offer content, and feedback shapes paths. Live tweaks match needs, and gains track smart.

Benefits
It fits tight, lifting grasp. Speed skips fluff, and flex suits all. Scale teaches wide, and growth sticks firm.

Examples
An AI speeds reading drills, sensing ease. A bot slows physics, catching stumbles.

Applications
It powers school apps. Biz trains quick, and games teach play. Health informs patients, and tech grows skills.

Industries
Education rises sharp. Business builds talent, and gaming hooks deep. Healthcare teaches soft, and tech scales fast.

Summary
Interactive Learning is a learn lifter, shaping lessons with AI's keen feel. It's a teach triumph but fights flux. A wise wing, it grows your grasp.

IPA (Intelligent Process Automation)

Definition
Intelligent Process Automation combines AI with automation to manage intricate workflows—like approvals or chains—adapting to quirks for seamless runs. It's a flow forger with finesse.

Key Components
Process inputs—like docs or tasks—fuel AI systems, often ML or RPA blends. Automation drives steps, and smarts handle twists. Links tie to ops, and learning smooths kinks.

Benefits
It zaps tasks with brain, cutting drag. Accuracy fits exceptions, and scale eats loads. Savings stack up, and flex shines in flux.

Examples
An IPA clears a loan, reading odd forms. A bot syncs shipments, dodging delays.

Applications
It runs office chains. Banks speed deals, and plants link builds. Retail stocks swift, and health logs fast.

Industries
Business flows lean. Finance runs sure, and manufacturing hums tight. Retail moves quick, and healthcare heals swift.

Summary
IPA is a process pilot, steering flows with AI's slick grip. It's a task tamer but tangles old. A flow friend, it clears the clog.

IP (Image Processing)

Definition
Image Processing in AI harnesses artificial intelligence to refine or interpret images, pulling meaning or boosting quality with digital craft. It's a vision verve with a sharp eye.

Key Components
Images—like snaps or scans—feed AI nets, often CNNs. Preprocessing fixes flaws, and feature tools spot traits. Algorithms enhance or tag, and outputs show gains.

Benefits
It polishes fast, lifting use. Precision sees deep, and automation cuts hands. Scale eats big pics, and flex fits all shots.

Examples
An AI brightens a dark shot, showing stars. A bot tags birds in park pics, tracking flocks.

Applications
It boosts app pics. Security scans faces, and health reads scans. Retail IDs goods, and maps chart paths.

Industries
Tech shines pics. Security watches keen, and healthcare sees fine. Retail sorts swift, and transport maps smart.

Summary
IP is a picture pro, shaping views with AI's deft touch. It's a sight star but fights mess. A clear craft, it frames the real.

Definition
Instance Segmentation is an AI technique that identifies and outlines individual objects within an image, assigning unique labels to each instance while mapping their exact boundaries. It's a pixel-by-pixel object spotter.

Key Components
Image data feeds AI models, often convolutional neural networks like Mask R-CNN. Object detection finds items, and segmentation masks trace edges. Training uses labeled pics, and post-processing refines shapes.

Benefits
It pinpoints objects with razor sharpness. Precision tags each one, and automation skips hand draws. Scalability eats big scenes, and detail aids deep use.

Examples
An AI outlines cars in a parking lot, counting each. A bot masks tumors in a scan, sizing them up.

Applications
It maps roads for cars. Health tracks lesions, and retail counts stock. Robotics grabs items, and security IDs faces.

Industries
Automotive drives smart. Healthcare sees fine, and retail sorts quick. Robotics acts sure, and security watches keen.

Summary
Instance Segmentation is an object carver, tracing each with AI's fine blade. It's a detail dynamo but fights mess. A sharp eye, it splits the scene.

IPD (Intelligent Process Discovery)

Definition
Intelligent Process Discovery uses AI to map and analyze workflows—like biz steps or ops—uncovering patterns or flaws from data traces. It's a flow finder with insight.

Key Components
Process logs—like clicks or times—feed AI tools, often analytics or mining nets. Mapping logic builds steps, and anomaly scans spot hiccups. Visualization shows chains, and suggestions tweak flow.

Benefits
It charts fast, showing truth. Depth finds hidden snags, and ease aids fixes. Scale eats big ops, and insight drives lean.

Examples
An IPD maps a claim's slow path, cueing cuts. A bot spots order delays, tracing stock waits.

Applications
It tunes biz flows. Factories find jams, and banks speed deals. Retail syncs sales, and health logs quick.

Industries
Business runs lean. Manufacturing hums tight, and finance flows sure. Retail sells swift, and healthcare heals fast.

Summary
IPD is a process probe, charting chains with AI's deep scan. It's a flow fix but fights mess. A path pal, it clears the way.

IPF (Intelligent Portfolio Forecasting)

Definition
Intelligent Portfolio Forecasting uses AI technologies to predict the future performance and risks associated with financial portfolios. By analyzing historical trends, market behaviors, and predictive indicators, these systems help guide investment decisions.

Key Characteristics
Predictive analytics modeling

Machine learning-based risk assessment
Historical financial data interpretation
Real-time forecasting algorithms

Benefits
Improves the precision of investment decisions
Reduces exposure to financial risk
Optimizes asset allocation strategies for better returns

Applications
Investment management
Stock market forecasting
Personalized financial planning platforms

Sources
Studies on AI applications in finance and predictive economic modeling

Conclusion
Intelligent Portfolio Forecasting equips investors with deeper insights and data-backed strategies, strengthening financial decision-making in dynamic markets.

IPL (Intelligent Personalization Layer)

Definition
Intelligent Personalization Layer refers to an AI-powered system designed to customize user experiences by analyzing personal behaviors, preferences, and engagement patterns across digital platforms.

Key Characteristics
Behavior analysis and prediction
Content and service customization
Real-time user interaction adaptation

Benefits
Boosts customer engagement and loyalty
Enhances conversion rates in e-commerce and media
Delivers highly targeted and relevant user experiences

Applications
Product recommendation systems
Personalized content delivery
Customer retention and loyalty programs

Sources
Research on AI-driven personalization, behavioral targeting, and recommendation system frameworks

Conclusion
Intelligent Personalization Layers play a critical role in shaping user-centric digital experiences, essential for competitive advantage in today's marketplace.

IPM (Intelligent Performance Monitoring)

Definition
Intelligent Performance Monitoring applies AI to continuously track, evaluate, and optimize the performance of systems, machines, and digital infrastructure in real-time environments.

Key Characteristics
Predictive maintenance and anomaly detection
Real-time performance tracking
Data-driven optimization strategies

Benefits
Prevents costly equipment failures
Extends system longevity through early interventions
Enhances operational efficiency across sectors

Applications
Manufacturing equipment monitoring
IT infrastructure management
Transportation fleet performance optimization

Sources
Research studies on predictive maintenance and real-time monitoring using AI technologies

Conclusion
Intelligent Performance Monitoring is indispensable for industries that depend on high reliability, operational efficiency, and proactive system management.

IPR (Intelligent Pattern Recognition)

Definition
Intelligent Pattern Recognition involves AI systems that detect, classify, and interpret patterns from various data types, enhancing decision-making through advanced analysis of visual, audio, or behavioral inputs.

Key Characteristics
Advanced machine learning for trend analysis
Image and signal processing techniques
Anomaly and pattern detection algorithms

Benefits
Improves predictive accuracy in complex data environments
Enhances security through anomaly identification
Facilitates more informed and data-driven decisions

Applications
Security surveillance
Biometric authentication
Fraud detection in financial systems

Sources
Studies in AI-based pattern recognition, security applications, and fraud analytics

Conclusion
Intelligent Pattern Recognition strengthens analytical capabilities across industries, offering critical insights where precise pattern detection is vital.

IPS (Intelligent Power Systems)

Definition
Intelligent Power Systems apply AI to manage, optimize, and forecast energy generation, distribution, and usage, contributing to smarter, more sustainable energy networks.

Key Characteristics
Integration of AI and IoT for energy management
Predictive analytics for demand and supply forecasting
Optimization of renewable energy resources

Benefits
Reduces energy waste and operational costs
Increases grid reliability and performance
Supports sustainable and eco-friendly energy practices

Applications
Smart grids
Renewable energy optimization
Smart home energy management

Sources
Research papers on AI-driven energy management, smart infrastructure, and IoT systems

Conclusion
Intelligent Power Systems drive the future of sustainable energy management by combining smart analytics with real-time operational efficiency.

IPU (Intelligence Processing Unit)

Definition
An Intelligence Processing Unit is a specialized processor designed specifically to accelerate AI computations, particularly for deep learning and complex machine learning workloads.

Key Characteristics
Parallel processing architecture
Optimized for deep neural network operations
Energy-efficient high-throughput design

Benefits
Shortens model training time
Supports larger and more sophisticated AI models
Reduces computational costs at scale

Applications
Data center AI acceleration
Neural network training
Real-time autonomous system decision-making

Sources
Research in specialized AI hardware design and industry reports on AI acceleration technologies

Conclusion
Intelligence Processing Units are fundamental to advancing large-scale AI applications, enabling faster, more efficient, and scalable machine learning deployment.

IPV (Intelligent Predictive Vision)

Definition
Intelligent Predictive Vision describes AI technologies that process visual data to anticipate future events or actions, enhancing real-time analysis and proactive decision-making in complex visual environments.

Key Characteristics
Integration of computer vision and predictive analytics
Real-time video and image processing
Machine learning models for motion prediction

Benefits
Provides early warnings and proactive insights
Improves safety and security in dynamic environments
Enhances decision-making accuracy through visual foresight

Applications
Autonomous driving systems
Predictive security surveillance
Sports performance analytics

Sources
Publications on AI-based predictive vision, computer vision research, and visual analytics technologies

Conclusion
Intelligent Predictive Vision is revolutionizing fields requiring dynamic visual interpretation by offering the ability to foresee and respond to future scenarios based on visual cues.

IQ (Intelligence Quotient) in AI

Definition
In artificial intelligence, Intelligence Quotient (IQ) represents the system's ability to learn, reason, adapt, and solve problems in ways that parallel human cognitive abilities.

Key Characteristics
Integration of machine learning and reasoning algorithms
Evaluation of adaptability and problem-solving efficiency
Benchmarking against human-like intelligence metrics

Benefits
Provides a measurable way to assess AI cognitive performance
Guides improvements in learning and reasoning capabilities
Supports the development of smarter and more adaptive AI systems

Applications
Benchmarking AI systems against human tasks
Evaluating cognitive computing platforms
Advancing robotics and autonomous decision-making systems

Sources
Research in cognitive AI, benchmarking methodologies, and robotics studies

Conclusion
IQ in AI serves as a valuable indicator of how closely artificial systems can mimic human thought processes, helping to drive innovations toward more intelligent machines.

IQA (Intelligent Quality Assurance)

Definition
Intelligent Quality Assurance (IQA) refers to AI-powered systems designed to automate and enhance quality control across industries, ensuring products, services, and digital solutions consistently meet high standards.

Key Characteristics
Automation of testing and inspection tasks
Use of machine learning for defect detection and predictive quality control
Real-time analytics for monitoring and reporting

Benefits
Reduces human errors and production defects
Improves operational efficiency and speed
Ensures consistent delivery of high-quality outcomes

Applications
Automated bug detection in software development
Defect inspection in manufacturing lines
Customer service quality monitoring and analytics

Sources
Studies on AI-driven QA methodologies, industrial automation research, and software quality management frameworks

Conclusion
Intelligent Quality Assurance is crucial for industries seeking to maintain excellence, reliability, and competitiveness in their products and services through automation and smart evaluation.

IQB (Intelligent Query-Based Systems)

Definition
Intelligent Query-Based Systems are AI frameworks that process user queries by analyzing available data sources and applying reasoning techniques to deliver accurate, actionable responses.

Key Characteristics
Utilizes natural language processing for understanding user input
Employs real-time data retrieval and logical reasoning for answers
Adapts over time through machine learning to improve accuracy

Benefits
Accelerates information retrieval with precise targeting
Simplifies user interaction by responding naturally to questions
Scales easily to support large datasets and diverse user needs

Applications
Business analytics platforms extracting insights from user prompts
Educational AI tools assisting in research and learning
Healthcare systems retrieving patient records through query inputs

Sources
Research on AI-driven information retrieval, NLP systems, and intelligent database management

Conclusion
Intelligent Query-Based Systems transform the way users access and interact with information, offering fast, reliable answers while continually improving through learning and adaptation.

IQD (Intelligent Quantitative Decision-Making)

Definition
Intelligent Quantitative Decision-Making uses AI to analyze numerical data and optimize choices—like investments or schedules—balancing risks and gains with math-driven insight. It's a number navigator for tough calls.

Key Components
Numeric data—like stats or costs—feeds AI models, often optimization nets or decision trees. Algorithms weigh options, and predictive logic forecasts outcomes. Real-time updates tweak plans, and visuals show trade-offs.

Benefits
It picks smart fast, lifting wins. Accuracy cuts guesswork, and flex fits complex calls. Scale crunches big numbers, and clarity aids trust.

Examples
An AI picks stocks, balancing risk and rise. A bot schedules shifts, maxing hours with less pay.

Applications
It tunes finance bets. Biz plans resources, and logistics routes lean. Health weighs treatments, and tech scales loads.

Industries
Finance bets wise. Business runs tight, and logistics flows smart. Healthcare heals sharp, and tech hums lean.

Challenges
Data holes blur calls. Compute scales costs, and flux trips nets. Rules bind tight, and faith needs proof.

Summary
IQD is a math maestro, steering choices with AI's crisp count. It's a decision dynamo but fights gaps. A number ninja, it picks the path.

IQI (Intelligent Query Interpretation)

Definition
Intelligent Query Interpretation uses AI to decode the meaning or intent behind user questions—like slang or vague phrases—ensuring accurate, tailored responses. It's a word whisperer for muddled asks.

Key Components
User inputs feed AI models, often NLP or intent nets. Context logic grasps nuance, and interpretation maps to goals. Training uses varied asks, and real-time shifts keep it fresh.

Benefits
It reads between lines fast, nailing needs. Precision cuts missteps, and flex fits odd talks. Scale rides big chats, and smarts lift fit.

Examples
An AI decodes "what's up with my order?" as tracking. A bot gets "fix this quick" as urgent repair.

Applications
It runs chatbots smooth. Apps catch voice, and service sorts pleas. Retail aids fast, and homes hear right.

Industries
Tech talks clear. Retail sells swift, and service helps keen. Home tech listens, and biz bonds tight.

Challenges
Slang trips nets. Compute scales chats, and fuzz blurs intent. Data needs range, and errors jar flow.

Summary
IQI is an ask unraveled, catching drift with AI's keen ear. It's a chat clarifier but fights twist. A meaning miner, it gets the gist.

IQO (Intelligent Quality Optimization)

Definition
Intelligent Quality Optimization uses AI to enhance product or process standards—like output or fit—by analyzing data to perfect results. It's a grade grower with a sharp eye.

Key Components
Quality metrics—like defects or specs—feed AI tools, often classifiers or optimization nets. Analysis spots flaws, and predictive logic cues tweaks. Live scans watch tight, and automation drives fixes.

Benefits
It lifts standards fast, boosting shine. Precision nabs fine slips, and scale eats big runs. Savings stack up, and trust grows high.

Examples
An AI tunes a lens, cutting blur. A bot refines steel, nixing weak spots.

Applications
It polishes factory goods. Health perfects drugs, and tech hones code. Food keeps pure, and cars roll true.

Industries
Manufacturing glows tight. Healthcare heals sure, and tech builds clean. Food stays fresh, and automotive runs safe.

Challenges
Noise hides flaws. Compute scales big, and specs shift fast. Data needs depth, and faith needs wins.

Summary
IQO is a quality quester, raising bars with AI's fine sweep. It's a grade guru but fights mess. A pure push, it perfects the craft.

IQT (Intelligent Question-Answering Technology)

Definition
Intelligent Question-Answering Technology uses AI to interpret and respond to questions—like trivia or help—with natural, precise replies from vast data. It's a talkative tutor with know-how.

Key Components
Questions hit AI tools, often transformers or QA nets. Knowledge bases—like texts or wikis—feed answers, and context logic grasps intent. Training uses Q&A pairs, and live tweaks keep it crisp.

Benefits
It chats answers fast, lifting ease. Depth hits tough asks, and flex fits wild talks. Scale eats big queries, and charm grows trust.

Examples
An AI answers "why's the sky blue?" with science. A bot solves "how's my package?" with tracking.

Applications
It runs help bots. Education explains deep, and apps talk smart. Health clarifies ills, and biz aids clients.

Industries
Tech chats wise. Education lifts minds, and service helps quick. Healthcare informs, and business bonds deep.

Challenges
Trick asks trip nets. Compute scales big, and gaps blur replies. Slang needs range, and errors jar faith.

Summary
IQT is a question queller, nailing replies with AI's quick tongue. It's a talk titan but fights twist. A wise word, it speaks the truth.

IRB (Intelligent Robotic Behavior)

Definition
Intelligent Robotic Behavior (IRB) refers to robotic systems designed to exhibit autonomous, adaptive, and context-aware behaviors, enabling robots to interact dynamically and intelligently with their environment or humans.

Key Components
Key components of IRB include sensors for environment perception, AI decision-making algorithms, adaptive control mechanisms, robotic actuators, contextual awareness algorithms, behavioral learning modules, and interaction capabilities.

Example
An IRB-enabled robot vacuum cleaner intelligently adapts its cleaning paths based on room layouts, obstacles, and detected dirt levels, adjusting its cleaning patterns dynamically.

Benefits
IRB improves robot autonomy, enhances adaptability, provides effective human-robot interactions, reduces manual interventions, increases operational efficiency, and boosts overall robot performance.

Applications
Applications include autonomous vehicles, domestic service robots, industrial automation, healthcare robotics, search and rescue robots, agriculture robots, and interactive robots in customer service.

Industries
Industries using IRB extensively include manufacturing, healthcare, automotive, logistics, agriculture, security, consumer electronics, hospitality, and military sectors.

Challenges
Challenges involve managing complex environments, real-time decision-making accuracy, computational resource demands, ensuring safety, maintaining ethical behaviors, and adapting effectively to unforeseen conditions.

Conclusions
Intelligent Robotic Behavior significantly enhances robot autonomy, adaptability, and user interaction, expanding robotics applications across numerous industries. Continued development in contextual awareness and decision-making will further enhance IRB effectiveness.

IRC (Intelligent Resource Management)

Definition
Intelligent Resource Management (IRC) involves the use of artificial intelligence algorithms and analytics to dynamically allocate, optimize, and manage resources efficiently, minimizing waste and maximizing performance across operational systems.

Key Components
IRC systems include predictive analytics, optimization algorithms, real-time monitoring tools, resource allocation protocols, dynamic scheduling mechanisms, automated decision-making, and data-driven optimization techniques.

Example
A data center employs IRC to automatically allocate computational resources based on real-time demand forecasts, optimizing energy consumption and computing performance.

Benefits
IRC enhances resource efficiency, reduces operational costs, improves scalability, supports sustainable practices, enables proactive management, and enhances decision-making accuracy.

Applications
Applications include cloud computing optimization, smart grid energy management, workforce scheduling, logistics optimization, supply chain management, telecommunications network management, and smart city planning.

Industries
Industries utilizing IRC include IT services, logistics, energy, manufacturing, healthcare, telecommunications, transportation, government agencies, and environmental management.

Challenges
Challenges include accurately predicting resource demands, computational complexity, real-time decision-making constraints, integration with legacy systems, data quality management, and handling unforeseen disruptions.

Conclusions
Intelligent Resource Management significantly improves efficiency and sustainability across various industries. Ongoing advancements in AI analytics will further extend IRC's effectiveness and broad-based adoption.

IRDA (Intelligent Robotic Decision Algorithms)

Definition
Intelligent Robotic Decision Algorithms (IRDA) refer to AI-powered computational methods enabling robots to autonomously make effective decisions in complex, uncertain, or dynamic environments, enhancing robotic systems' reliability and autonomy.

Key Components
Core components include decision-making algorithms, machine learning models, sensor integration, environmental perception tools, contextual reasoning capabilities, planning and optimization modules, and feedback-based adaptive learning.

Example
An autonomous drone employs IRDA to navigate disaster areas, making intelligent decisions regarding optimal paths and resource allocation based on environmental data and mission objectives.

Benefits
IRDA improves robotic autonomy, enhances decision-making reliability, optimizes task performance, reduces human supervision needs, adapts to dynamic conditions, and increases safety and efficiency.

Applications
Applications include autonomous vehicles, industrial robotics, space exploration robots, disaster response robots, healthcare robotic assistants, autonomous drones, and robotic manufacturing lines.

Industries
Industries employing IRDA include aerospace, automotive, manufacturing, defense, healthcare, logistics, agriculture, construction, and emergency response operations.

Challenges
Challenges include computational complexity, real-time decision-making constraints, reliability in uncertain conditions, balancing autonomy and human oversight, and ethical considerations.

Conclusions
IRDA significantly enhances robotic autonomy and effectiveness, allowing robots to handle complex tasks independently. Addressing computational and ethical challenges will further drive adoption across critical applications.

IRIS (Intelligent Real-Time Information Systems)

Definition
Intelligent Real-Time Information Systems (IRIS) refer to AI-driven systems designed to gather, analyze, and present data dynamically in real-time, enabling immediate decision-making and effective responsiveness in rapidly changing environments.

Key Components
Components include real-time data processing, advanced analytics modules, machine learning models, automated alert systems, predictive analytics tools, interactive visualization dashboards, and data integration platforms.

Example
A smart traffic management system using IRIS instantly analyzes traffic data, providing real-time congestion forecasts and optimal routing suggestions to drivers.

Benefits
IRIS improves decision-making speed, enhances real-time situational awareness, increases operational efficiency, reduces response times, boosts system performance, and supports proactive intervention strategies.

Applications
Applications include real-time traffic management, emergency response coordination, financial trading platforms, healthcare monitoring, industrial process control, smart city systems, and cybersecurity threat detection.

Industries
Industries using IRIS include transportation, healthcare, finance, telecommunications, smart cities, manufacturing, emergency services, and logistics.

Challenges
Challenges involve managing high data volume, ensuring real-time performance, data privacy, system scalability, and accurate predictive analytics.

Conclusions
IRIS significantly improves real-time operational effectiveness and decision-making across industries. Ongoing developments in analytics and real-time processing capabilities will further expand its utility.

IRL (Inverse Reinforcement Learning)

Definition
Inverse Reinforcement Learning (IRL) is an AI technique that learns the underlying reward structures or objectives behind observed behaviors by analyzing expert actions, enabling systems to infer intentions and reproduce human-like decision-making behaviors.

Key Components
Key components include inverse optimization algorithms, reward function estimation methods, expert demonstration data, policy learning frameworks, machine learning models, behavioral modeling techniques, and validation procedures.

Example
Autonomous vehicles apply IRL to learn human driving patterns from demonstration data, creating safer and more intuitive navigation strategies that mimic experienced drivers.

Benefits
IRL facilitates human-like decision-making, reduces manual programming, enables natural behavior modeling, improves adaptability, and provides interpretable AI behavior.

Applications
Applications include autonomous driving, robotic imitation learning, healthcare diagnostics, recommendation systems, game-playing AI, industrial automation, and behavior prediction systems.

Industries
Industries adopting IRL include automotive, robotics, gaming, healthcare, aerospace, finance, and industrial automation.

Challenges
Challenges include obtaining representative demonstration data, reward ambiguity, computational complexity, model interpretability, and ensuring ethical use.

Conclusions
IRL enables AI systems to mimic complex human behaviors accurately. Addressing data and computational challenges will further enhance practical applications and widespread adoption.

ITL (Intelligent Text Labeling)

Definition
Intelligent Text Labeling (ITL) is the application of AI technologies to automatically classify, tag, and organize textual data by interpreting its context, meaning, and sentiment using natural language processing.

Key Characteristics
Context-aware language analysis
Dynamic labeling based on machine learning
Scalable processing of vast text datasets

Benefits
Accelerates data organization for large-scale text repositories
Enhances consistency and reduces human labeling errors
Cuts operational costs by automating manual tagging

Applications
Sentiment analysis for customer feedback
Content tagging for social media monitoring
Text classification in automated customer service systems

Examples
AI-driven tools categorizing customer emails into topics like billing inquiries, technical support, or account updates

Challenges
Struggles with ambiguous or nuanced language
Requires comprehensive initial training to minimize misclassification
Sensitive to domain-specific jargon and contextual shifts

Conclusion
Intelligent Text Labeling significantly enhances the ability to manage and interpret large text corpora, making it invaluable for customer service, content management, and sentiment-driven analytics.

ITP (Intelligent Text Prediction)

Intelligent Text Prediction (ITP) refers to AI-enabled technology that predicts and suggests words, phrases, or sentences based on users' typing patterns, linguistic context, and historical input data. ITP relies on natural language processing algorithms, language modeling, and machine learning techniques to anticipate user intent and provide relevant text suggestions in real-time.

Key components include contextual linguistic models, adaptive learning algorithms, and user interaction tracking.

Benefits include increased typing efficiency, enhanced user accessibility, reduced typing errors, and improved overall user experience.

Challenges include potential inaccurate predictions, dependency on extensive user data, and occasional privacy concerns.

Applications include mobile device keyboards, email drafting assistance, assistive communication technologies, and text editing software.

Examples include intelligent typing assistants in messaging applications and predictive typing features in email clients and communication devices for accessibility support.

ITR (Intelligent Text Recognition)

Intelligent Text Recognition (ITR) involves AI technologies designed to identify and interpret text from visual media, converting printed or handwritten content into editable and searchable digital data. This technology leverages advanced optical character recognition (OCR), computer vision, deep learning, and natural language processing to enhance accuracy and interpretative capabilities.

Key characteristics include automatic digitization, high recognition accuracy, dynamic adaptation to diverse text formats, and extraction of structured information from scanned documents.

Benefits include streamlined document management, minimized manual data entry errors, cost efficiency, and improved data accessibility. Disadvantages encompass challenges in recognizing poor-quality images, handwriting variations, unusual fonts, and distortions.

Applications span digitization of archives, automated document processing, invoice automation, historical document conversion, and identity verification processes.

Examples include AI-powered document scanning applications used for automated form processing, digitization of historical records, and financial document management solutions.

ITR (Intelligent Threat Response)

Intelligent Threat Response (ITR) refers to AI-driven cybersecurity systems that proactively detect, analyze, and respond to digital threats and security incidents automatically. Utilizing machine learning, real-time data analytics, and behavioral detection techniques, ITR identifies threats quickly and initiates automated countermeasures to neutralize or mitigate risks.

Key components include continuous threat monitoring, real-time threat analysis, automated incident response procedures, and adaptive learning from threat patterns.

Benefits include swift threat detection, reduced risk of data breaches, minimized human intervention, and enhanced security posture.

Disadvantages involve potential false positives, high complexity, and privacy concerns due to extensive monitoring activities.

Applications include security operations centers (SOCs), enterprise cybersecurity platforms, threat intelligence services, and endpoint protection solutions.

Examples include AI-driven security systems that autonomously isolate compromised systems and block suspicious activities before extensive damage occurs.

ITV (Intelligent Video Analytics)

Definition
Intelligent Video Analytics is an AI-driven process that interprets video feeds to extract insights, detect events, or track objects, turning raw footage into actionable understanding. It's a digital eye that thinks beyond seeing.

Key Components
Video inputs from cameras or streams feed AI models—like convolutional neural networks—for processing. Object detection flags people or items, and behavior analysis reads actions. Real-time computation tracks live, and data storage logs trends. Visualization dashboards present findings.

Benefits
It spots critical moments fast, sharpening response. Accuracy beats human scans, and automation saves effort. Scalability handles vast footage, and depth pulls hidden patterns.

Examples
An ITV flags a car speeding through a red light on a city cam. A store AI counts shoppers, noting peak hours.

Applications
It monitors traffic for jams. Security tracks threats, and retail reads footfall. Sports analyze plays, and cities plan flow.

Industries
Security guards streets. Retail tunes sales, and transport runs smooth. Sports sharpen games, and cities smarten up.

Challenges
Blur or dark trips vision. Compute scales with feeds, and privacy binds use. Training needs broad clips, and false flags nag.

Summary
ITV is a video sage, decoding frames with AI's sharp sight. It's a watch win but fights noise and rules. A keen lens, it sees the tale.

IZF (Intelligent Zero-Friction Interfaces)

Definition
Intelligent Zero-Friction Interfaces are AI-enhanced systems that streamline user interactions with tech, removing effort or resistance for a fluid, intuitive experience. It's a glide path to digital ease.

Key Components
Inputs—like voice or gestures—hit AI interpreters, often NLP or vision nets. Contextual smarts guess needs, and automation acts seamless. Design trims clicks, and learning smooths quirks. Feedback keeps it slick.

Benefits
It flows effortless, saving time. Intuition cuts learning curves, and joy rises with ease. Scalability fits masses, and access widens reach.

Examples
An IZF orders pizza as you say "hungry." A car screen shifts maps, sensing your glance.

Applications
It runs smart homes slick. Cars drive intuitive, and apps order fast. Workflows glide smooth, and games play easy.

Industries
Home tech hums. Automotive steers light, and tech apps flow. Workspaces speed up, and gaming hooks quick.

Challenges
Guesses flop sans context. Tech costs stack, and privacy eyes watch. Data needs depth, and errors jar flow.

Summary
IZF is a friction foe, smoothing tech with AI's glide touch. It's an ease ace but risks missteps. A sleek shift, it oils the gears.

IZI (Intelligent Zero-Interaction Interfaces)

Definition
Intelligent Zero-Interaction Interfaces are AI-driven setups that act on user needs without explicit input, reading context or intent to deliver hands-free results. It's a silent doer in the background.

Key Components
Sensors—like motion or sound—feed AI models, often predictive nets, trained on habits. Intent logic reads cues, and automation triggers acts. Adaptive learning hones guesses, and systems integrate quiet.

Benefits
It skips commands, pure ease. Speed acts instant, and intuition fits life. Accessibility aids all, and scale runs unseen.

Examples
An IZI dims lights as you nap, sensing calm. A fridge restocks milk, noting your sips.

Applications
It tunes smart homes quiet. Cars adjust sans touch, and stores stock by gaze. Health tracks vitals, and offices shift air.

Industries
Home tech flows. Automotive rides smart, and retail reads you. Healthcare watches soft, and offices hum.

Challenges
Wrong reads waste acts. Sensors cost up, and privacy binds watch. Data shapes fit, and trust needs proof.

Summary
IZI is a mute mate, moving with AI's unseen nod. It's a no-touch win but dodges errors. A hush helper, it knows your drift.

LETTER J

Jaccard Similarity

Definition:
Jaccard Similarity is a statistical measure used in AI and data science to evaluate the similarity and diversity between two datasets, often represented as sets or binary data. It calculates the ratio of the intersection size of two sets divided by their union size, resulting in a similarity score ranging from 0 (no similarity) to 1 (identical sets).

Key Components:
Intersection and union calculation, set representation, similarity computation, binary data analysis, comparison metric.

Benefits:
Easy computation, intuitive interpretation, effective in binary data comparison, useful for clustering and recommendation systems.

Examples:
Comparing user preferences in recommendation systems, measuring textual similarities, and clustering similar documents.

Applications:
Data mining, natural language processing, recommendation engines, clustering algorithms.

Challenges:
Limited accuracy with high-dimensional data, less effective for continuous data types, sensitivity to dataset size.

Summary:
Jaccard Similarity effectively assesses the similarity between datasets, especially in binary or categorical contexts, yet its applicability can be restricted by the nature of the data involved.

Jacobian Matrix

Definition:
The Jacobian Matrix is a mathematical representation used in AI and machine learning, specifically in neural networks and optimization algorithms, to describe the rate of change of multivariate vector functions with respect to their input variables.

Key Components:
Partial derivatives matrix, vector functions, multivariate calculus, gradient computations.

Benefits:
Facilitates efficient computation of gradients, essential in optimization problems, useful for analyzing sensitivity and behavior of AI models.

Examples:
Training neural networks through backpropagation, optimization in computer vision, control systems.

Applications:
Deep learning, optimization algorithms, robotics control systems, sensitivity analysis in engineering.

Challenges:
Complex computation for high-dimensional data, potential numerical instability, computational complexity.

Summary:
The Jacobian Matrix plays a pivotal role in optimizing complex AI algorithms, despite computational challenges in high-dimensional problems.

JAMES AI

Definition:
JAMES AI refers to advanced AI-driven virtual assistant frameworks capable of simulating intelligent conversations, managing tasks, and automating responses based on natural language understanding.

Key Components:
Natural language processing, conversation modeling, intent recognition, speech recognition modules, task automation tools.

Benefits:
Enhanced user engagement, improved customer interaction efficiency, reduced manual workloads through automation, 24/7 assistance availability.

Examples:
Virtual assistants for customer support, intelligent help desks, conversational agents for business interactions.

Applications:
Customer service automation, virtual assistant technologies, business support bots, personal digital assistants.

Challenges:
Complexity of language interpretation, maintaining context over extended interactions, handling ambiguous user requests effectively.

Summary:
JAMES AI significantly enhances communication automation and user interactions, although careful management of contextual understanding is required.

JAMScript

Definition:
JAMScript is an AI-compatible scripting language designed to facilitate distributed computing applications, especially in edge computing scenarios, enabling dynamic and adaptive software interactions within edge environments.

Key Components:
Distributed computing capabilities, lightweight syntax, IoT device communication protocols, adaptive computing frameworks.

Benefits:
Supports rapid prototyping for distributed AI systems, efficient task distribution, easy integration across heterogeneous platforms.

Examples:
Edge computing implementations, sensor networks coordination, distributed IoT device control.

Applications:
IoT networks, edge computing platforms, decentralized systems management.

Challenges:
Complex debugging processes, performance limitations in constrained devices, maintaining reliable real-time communication.

Summary:
JAMScript offers a valuable solution for distributed AI and IoT applications but requires optimization for performance-critical scenarios.

JAQL (JSON Query Language)

Definition:
JAQL (JSON Query Language) is an AI-friendly querying language specifically designed to process, manipulate, and query JSON data efficiently within large datasets using intuitive syntax and powerful analytical functions.

Key Components:
Query syntax for JSON data, support for transformation operations, scalable query optimization.

Benefits:
Efficient querying and transformation of JSON datasets, ease of use, scalability in big data environments.

Examples:
Data analytics on large JSON-based datasets, big data extraction tasks, real-time data transformations.

Applications:
Big data analysis, NoSQL databases, data warehousing, real-time data analytics pipelines.

Challenges:
Performance issues with complex nested JSON structures, optimization for extremely large datasets, limited functionality beyond JSON data formats.

Summary:
JAQL is powerful for handling JSON data analytics, though careful optimization and data structuring are essential for large-scale applications.

JASP

Definition:
JASP is an open-source, user-friendly statistical software platform integrated with AI capabilities, providing an intuitive graphical user interface to perform complex statistical analyses and data visualization.

Key Components:
Graphical user interface, statistical analysis modules, machine learning integration, visualization tools.

Benefits:
Easy-to-use platform for statistical analysis, visual exploration of data, accessible AI-powered analytics, supports reproducible research workflows.

Examples:
Educational platforms for statistical training, behavioral data analysis, research data interpretation.

Applications:
Psychological research, educational environments, exploratory data analysis, academic research.

Challenges:
Limited customization for advanced users, scalability limitations with very large datasets, dependency on integrated modules.

Summary:
JASP simplifies statistical analysis through its intuitive interface and AI integrations, though it may have limitations handling extensive datasets.

Jasper AI

Definition:
Jasper AI refers to AI-powered content-generation platforms designed to automatically create human-like text, including marketing copy, articles, and other written content, through advanced language models.

Key Components:
Natural language generation algorithms, deep learning models, intuitive content editor, automated text enhancement.

Benefits:
Rapid content production, improved efficiency for marketing teams, reduced manual effort, consistency in content creation.

Examples:
Generating marketing copy, drafting social media posts, automating blog content production.

Applications:
Marketing content creation, digital copywriting, content strategy automation.

Challenges:
Maintaining originality and creativity, handling sensitive or nuanced topics, potential content inaccuracies.

Summary:
Jasper AI streamlines content creation processes through automation, yet human oversight remains crucial for quality and creativity.

Java

Definition:
Java is a widely-used, object-oriented programming language employed in various AI and machine learning applications due to its platform independence, scalability, and robustness in handling large-scale systems.

Key Components:
Object-oriented paradigm, platform independence via JVM, robust libraries, multi-platform compatibility.

Benefits:
Ease of integration with enterprise systems, extensive libraries, platform independence, strong security features.

Examples:
Enterprise AI applications, Android-based machine learning apps, distributed AI systems.

Applications:
AI-based enterprise software, mobile applications, big data solutions, web-based AI platforms.

Challenges:
Performance limitations compared to low-level languages, high memory consumption, complexity for beginners.

Summary:
Java provides a reliable platform for AI applications in enterprises, though performance optimization is necessary for intensive computational tasks.

Javadoc

Definition:
Javadoc is an automated documentation-generation tool specifically designed for Java programming, enabling clear, structured, and easily maintainable documentation for Java codebases.

Key Components:
Code comments parsing, documentation generator, structured documentation formatting, linking and referencing modules.

Benefits:
Simplified documentation management, enhanced collaboration among developers, ease of updating and maintaining documentation accuracy.

Examples:
Automatic API documentation, Java project manuals, internal codebase references.

Applications:
Java software development, collaborative software projects, API management, software maintenance.

Challenges:
Reliance on consistent code commenting practices, potential incomplete documentation without developer diligence, complexity in managing large-scale projects.

Summary:
Javadoc significantly improves software documentation clarity and maintainability, though consistent developer discipline is required.

JavaFX for AI

JavaFX for AI refers to using JavaFX, a Java-based platform for developing rich graphical interfaces, in building and visualizing AI applications.

Key components include visualization modules, GUI components, and interactive data interfaces.

Benefits include advanced graphical representation, interactive data visualization, and user-friendly AI application interfaces.

Applications include interactive AI dashboards, real-time analytics displays, and educational visualization tools.

Challenges include JavaFX's performance limitations, limited AI-specific functionality, and compatibility issues across platforms.

Summary: JavaFX enhances AI interfaces and visualizations effectively but requires careful optimization for performance-critical AI tasks.

Java Neural Network Frameworks

Java Neural Network Frameworks refer to software libraries designed in Java to build, train, deploy, and manage artificial neural networks.

Key components include neural network architectures, training algorithms, performance optimization tools, and visualization utilities.

Benefits include platform independence, ease of integration with enterprise systems, scalability, and robustness. Examples include Deeplearning4j and Neuroph.

Applications range from enterprise data analytics, financial prediction models, business intelligence, and image recognition systems.

Challenges involve Java performance limitations compared to specialized hardware-optimized frameworks, complex debugging processes, and steep learning curves for beginners.

Summary: Java Neural Network Frameworks facilitate AI integration in Java-based enterprise environments but require careful optimization for computational efficiency.

Java Machine Learning Libraries

Java Machine Learning Libraries are software tools and packages developed in Java for implementing machine learning models and algorithms.

Key components include classification algorithms, regression models, clustering methods, and data preprocessing tools.

Benefits include cross-platform compatibility, strong enterprise integration, easy deployment, and scalability.

Examples include Weka, Deeplearning4j, and JavaML.

Applications range from predictive analytics, business intelligence, fraud detection, and recommendation systems.

Challenges involve managing computational efficiency, handling memory-intensive processes, and Java-specific performance limitations.

Summary: Java ML Libraries provide reliable machine learning capabilities for Java applications but require optimization for performance-sensitive applications.

JavaML

JavaML is a Java-based open-source machine learning library that simplifies building, deploying, and managing machine learning algorithms.

Key components include data preprocessing tools, clustering methods, classification algorithms, and evaluation metrics.

Benefits include simplicity, ease of use, integration capabilities, and modular design.

Applications include educational purposes, data analysis, and small-scale business applications.

Challenges involve limited functionality compared to more comprehensive ML frameworks, slower performance for large datasets, and less active community support.

Summary: JavaML offers a straightforward introduction to machine learning in Java but may lack advanced features for complex scenarios.

Java Neural Network Frameworks

Java Neural Network Frameworks refer to software libraries designed in Java to build, train, deploy, and manage artificial neural networks.

Key components include neural network architectures, training algorithms, performance optimization tools, and visualization utilities.

Benefits include platform independence, ease of integration with enterprise systems, scalability, and robustness. Examples include Deeplearning4j and Neuroph.

Applications range from enterprise data analytics, financial prediction models, business intelligence, and image recognition systems.

Challenges involve Java performance limitations compared to specialized hardware-optimized frameworks, complex debugging processes, and steep learning curves for beginners.

Summary: Java Neural Network Frameworks facilitate AI integration in Java-based enterprise environments but require careful optimization for computational efficiency.

JavaScript AI

Definition:
JavaScript AI refers to AI development conducted directly within JavaScript environments, enabling machine learning capabilities in browser-based applications or client-side scripts. It includes libraries and tools facilitating the creation of interactive AI functionalities.

Key components include browser-compatible AI libraries, interactive machine learning models, lightweight inference engines, and user-friendly interfaces.

Benefits include ease of web integration, accessibility, rapid prototyping capabilities, and enhanced interactivity.

Examples include TensorFlow.js for in-browser machine learning, facial recognition systems in web apps, and real-time sentiment analysis tools.
Applications include interactive web applications, client-side analytics, educational platforms, and real-time AI experiences.

Challenges involve computational limitations within browsers, security risks, and balancing performance with functionality.

In summary, JavaScript AI brings AI capabilities directly to web browsers, yet careful performance management and resource allocation are crucial.

JAX

Definition:
JAX (JavaScript + Python) refers to an innovative integration framework designed to leverage the capabilities of Python's advanced data science libraries together with JavaScript's interactive and responsive frontend functionalities. This integration enables developers to build sophisticated web-based AI applications seamlessly combining frontend interactivity and powerful backend computational resources.

Key components of JAX include frontend JavaScript frameworks, backend Python APIs, asynchronous data exchange protocols, interactive UI components, and AI libraries.

Benefits include streamlined web-based AI development, improved user interaction, simplified integration, and rapid application deployment.

Examples of applications include AI-driven web dashboards, real-time predictive analytics tools, and interactive machine learning platforms.
Common applications are data visualization web apps, educational AI tools, and intelligent customer interaction platforms.

Challenges faced include maintaining consistent data flow, performance optimization in real-time processing, and complexity in synchronization between languages.

Summary:
JAX effectively bridges Python's data processing power with JavaScript's dynamic web interfaces, though careful attention is required for optimized real-time performance.

Jellyfish Algorithm

Definition:
The Jellyfish Algorithm is a bio-inspired optimization algorithm that mimics the natural foraging and movement behavior of jellyfish swarms. It leverages AI techniques for solving complex optimization problems by modeling dynamic swarm behaviors.

Key components include swarm intelligence mechanisms, stochastic search processes, adaptive parameter tuning, and multi-dimensional search strategies.

Benefits include efficient exploration of complex problem spaces, adaptability to diverse optimization problems, improved convergence rates, and flexible problem-solving capabilities.

Examples include route optimization, scheduling problems, resource allocation, and parameter tuning in neural network training.

Applications include logistics optimization, supply-chain management, engineering design, financial portfolio optimization, and AI parameter tuning.

Challenges involve the algorithm's sensitivity to parameter choices, managing swarm stability, and potential convergence to local minima rather than global optima

In summary, the Jellyfish Algorithm provides a powerful, bio-inspired approach to optimization but must manage convergence challenges carefully.

Jellyfish Clustering

Definition:
Jellyfish Clustering is an AI-based clustering method inspired by the natural clustering behavior of jellyfish groups, aimed at efficiently grouping large datasets based on similarities and dynamic interactions within data.

Key components consist of bio-inspired clustering techniques, similarity measures, adaptive cluster formation methods, and iterative refinement processes.

Benefits include flexible data grouping, adaptability to changing datasets, efficient handling of large data volumes, and ease of interpreting clustering outcomes.

Examples involve customer segmentation, document categorization, and pattern identification in large datasets.

Applications include market analysis, social network analysis, biological data grouping, and intelligent recommendation systems.

Challenges involve choosing optimal initial cluster configurations, computational complexity with massive datasets, and sensitivity to parameter adjustments.

In summary, Jellyfish Clustering delivers adaptive clustering solutions inspired by natural phenomena but requires careful tuning and management for optimal results.

Jellyfish Detector

Definition:
Jellyfish Detector is an AI-enabled detection methodology inspired by jellyfish sensing capabilities, used primarily for anomaly detection, threat identification, and real-time monitoring tasks in complex data environments.

Key components include anomaly detection algorithms, AI-driven sensing techniques, pattern recognition models, and adaptive learning methods.

Benefits include real-time threat detection, high accuracy in anomaly identification, adaptability in changing environments, and proactive response capabilities.

Examples include cybersecurity intrusion detection, real-time fraud detection, and monitoring unusual activities in network systems.

Applications span network security systems, financial transaction monitoring, healthcare anomaly detection, and real-time operational monitoring systems.

Challenges faced include managing false positives, continuously updating detection models, computational resource demands, and maintaining accurate adaptive learning.

In summary, Jellyfish Detector provides robust anomaly and threat detection capabilities leveraging AI but requires constant refinement to adapt to evolving threats.

Jellyfish-Pattern Recognition

Definition
Jellyfish-Pattern Recognition is a bio-inspired AI approach that identifies complex, non-linear patterns in data by mimicking the fluid movement and adaptability of jellyfish.

Key Characteristics
Utilizes soft boundary detection, fuzzy logic, and irregular pattern recognition strategies

Benefits
Effectively identifies hidden or overlapping structures within noisy datasets
Enhances pattern detection in complex, dynamic environments

Applications
Medical imaging analysis, environmental monitoring, underwater robotics, and anomaly detection

Conclusion
Jellyfish-Pattern Recognition introduces a novel method for handling intricate and non-linear pattern recognition challenges, expanding AI's capabilities in scientific and industrial domains.

Jenkins

Definition
Jenkins is an open-source automation server used extensively in AI and software development to build, test, and deploy applications in continuous integration and continuous delivery (CI/CD) workflows.

Key Characteristics
Highly extensible through plugins
Supports automation across a wide range of development activities

Benefits
Streamlines AI development cycles by automating model training, testing, and deployment
Improves software reliability and reduces time-to-market

Disadvantages
Complex configurations for large or customized AI projects
Requires ongoing maintenance and monitoring

Applications
AI pipeline automation, software deployment, machine learning model testing, and experiment management

Conclusion
Jenkins remains a cornerstone tool for integrating automation into AI workflows, boosting efficiency, consistency, and productivity across development environments.

Jenkins AI Pipeline

Definition
Jenkins AI Pipeline refers to an automated framework built within Jenkins to manage the entire lifecycle of AI model development, including building, training, testing, and deployment.

Key Characteristics
Supports continuous integration and continuous deployment specifically for AI models
Offers tools for version control, monitoring, and iterative testing

Benefits
Simplifies the complex workflow of AI projects
Enables continuous model updates and improvements

Applications
Deploying machine learning models, monitoring AI experiments, and scaling AI pipelines in enterprise environments

Conclusion
Jenkins AI Pipeline is an essential automation layer for modern AI development, ensuring efficiency and reliability in the iterative training and deployment of intelligent systems.

Jet AI Cloud

Definition
Jet AI Cloud is a high-performance cloud computing platform optimized for training, deploying, and scaling AI models with GPU acceleration and real-time resource scaling.

Key Characteristics
Provides GPU-accelerated computation, flexible scaling options, and integration with popular AI frameworks

Benefits
Accelerates AI model development and deployment
Reduces infrastructure management costs while boosting performance

Applications
Enterprise-level AI deployments, AI research projects, real-time data analytics, and scalable machine learning platforms

Conclusion
Jet AI Cloud is a powerful platform that offers developers and enterprises a flexible and high-speed environment for scaling and optimizing AI applications.

JetBot

Definition
JetBot is an open-source robotic platform based on NVIDIA's Jetson Nano, designed to offer a practical, hands-on introduction to AI development and robotics.

Key Characteristics
Compact, low-cost robot with onboard GPU for real-time AI processing
Pre-installed AI libraries supporting computer vision, reinforcement learning, and object tracking

Benefits
Affordable and accessible entry point into AI and robotics education
Supports real-time experiments with edge AI applications

Disadvantages
Limited processing power for handling large or highly complex AI models

Applications
AI and robotics education, hobbyist robotics projects, and prototyping for computer vision applications

Conclusion
JetBot provides an engaging and practical platform for students and developers to explore AI concepts, offering a gateway into edge computing and autonomous robotics innovation.

JetBrains IntelliJ IDEA

Definition: JetBrains IntelliJ IDEA is a powerful integrated development environment designed primarily for Java and Kotlin developers, offering advanced tools to streamline coding and boost productivity.

Key Components: It features a smart code editor with real-time suggestions, built-in debugging tools, version control integration, and support for multiple frameworks and languages beyond Java, like Python and JavaScript.

Benefits: Developers save time with intelligent code completion, catch errors early with on-the-fly analysis, and enjoy a smooth workflow thanks to its customizable interface and plugin ecosystem.

Examples: Writing a Java web application with Spring Boot, debugging a Kotlin mobile app, or refactoring a large legacy codebase

.Applications: Used in enterprise software development, mobile app creation, and educational settings for teaching programming concepts.

Challenges: Its resource-heavy nature can slow down older machines, and the learning curve might overwhelm beginners unfamiliar with IDEs.

Summary: IntelliJ IDEA stands out as a top choice for professional developers needing a robust, feature-rich environment, though it demands decent hardware and some initial effort to master.

JetBrains PyCharm

Definition: JetBrains PyCharm is a specialized integrated development environment tailored for Python developers, focusing on data science, web development, and general scripting tasks.

Key Components: It includes a code editor with syntax highlighting, a powerful debugger, support for scientific libraries like NumPy, and integration with testing frameworks and virtual environments.

Benefits: PyCharm simplifies Python coding with auto-imports and error detection, enhances data analysis with built-in tools, and supports collaboration through version control.

Examples: Building a Flask web app, analyzing datasets with pandas, or automating tasks with Python scripts.

Applications: Widely used in data science projects, web development, and automation workflows across industries.

Challenges: It can feel sluggish on low-spec systems, and its many features might confuse new Python users.

Summary: PyCharm excels as a Python-centric IDE, offering specialized tools for diverse tasks, though it requires sufficient system resources and a bit of experience to fully utilize.

JetPack SDK

Definition: JetPack SDK is a software development kit from NVIDIA that equips developers with libraries and tools to create applications for NVIDIA's Jetson hardware, focusing on AI and embedded systems.

Key Components: It provides CUDA for parallel computing, TensorRT for optimizing AI models, and tools for computer vision, alongside a Linux-based operating system tailored for Jetson devices.

Benefits: Developers gain access to high-performance computing, simplified AI deployment, and a unified platform for building smart devices.

Examples: Programming a drone to detect objects, optimizing a neural network for real-time inference, or creating an AI-powered security camera.

Applications: Used in robotics, IoT devices, autonomous vehicles, and edge computing solutions.

Challenges: Requires knowledge of NVIDIA's ecosystem, and debugging on embedded hardware can be tricky due to limited resources.

Summary: JetPack SDK empowers developers to harness NVIDIA's hardware for AI innovation, though it demands familiarity with specialized tools and hardware constraints.

Jetson Nano

Definition: Jetson Nano is a compact, affordable single-board computer from NVIDIA designed for AI development, capable of running machine learning models at the edge.

Key Components: It features a quad-core CPU, a GPU with CUDA support, 4GB of RAM, and ports for cameras and sensors, all within a small form factor.

Benefits: Offers a low-cost entry to AI experimentation, supports real-time processing, and fits into DIY projects with ease.

Examples: Running a face recognition system, powering a smart home device, or teaching students about AI hardware.

Applications: Found in educational settings, hobbyist projects, and small-scale IoT deployments.

Challenges: Limited processing power restricts complex models, and thermal management can be an issue during heavy workloads.

Summary: Jetson Nano is a beginner-friendly gateway to edge AI, balancing cost and capability, though it's not suited for high-end tasks.

Jetson Xavier

Definition: Jetson Xavier is a high-performance embedded computing platform from NVIDIA, built for advanced AI applications requiring significant computational power at the edge.

Key Components: It includes a powerful GPU with CUDA cores, an 8-core CPU, deep learning accelerators, and ample memory, all optimized for intensive workloads.

Benefits: Delivers fast AI inference, handles multiple tasks simultaneously, and supports industrial-grade reliability.

Examples: Controlling an autonomous robot, processing video feeds in real time, or running a multi-model AI system.

Applications: Deployed in autonomous machines, smart cities, healthcare devices, and industrial automation.

Challenges: Higher cost limits accessibility, and its complexity requires advanced programming skills.

Summary: Jetson Xavier shines in demanding edge AI scenarios, offering robust performance, though it comes with a steeper price and learning curve.

J

Jigsaw Clustering

Definition: Jigsaw Clustering is an AI-driven method that groups data by piecing together patterns and relationships, much like assembling a puzzle, to reveal hidden structures.

Key Components: It relies on algorithms to detect similarities, iterative refinement processes, and visualization tools to interpret clusters.

Benefits: Uncovers complex data insights, adapts to irregular datasets, and provides intuitive results for analysis.

Examples: Segmenting customer behavior in marketing, organizing genomic data, or classifying social media trends.

Applications: Applied in market research, bioinformatics, and social network analysis.

Challenges: Can be computationally intensive, and interpreting results may require domain expertise.

Summary: Jigsaw Clustering offers a creative approach to data grouping, excelling with intricate patterns, though it needs processing power and careful analysis.

Jigsaw Puzzle Solver AI

Definition: Jigsaw Puzzle Solver AI is an artificial intelligence system that automatically assembles digital or physical jigsaw puzzles by recognizing piece shapes, colors, and patterns.

Key Components: It uses computer vision to analyze pieces, machine learning to match them, and search algorithms to fit them together.

Benefits: Saves time on complex puzzles, demonstrates AI's pattern recognition power, and can assist visually impaired users.

Examples: Solving a 1000-piece landscape puzzle, reconstructing a damaged photo, or aiding in archaeological artifact assembly.

Applications: Seen in gaming, education, and historical preservation efforts.

Challenges: Struggles with uniform pieces or poor image quality, and physical setups need robotic integration.

Summary: This AI turns a classic pastime into a showcase of vision and reasoning, though it falters with ambiguous or low-quality inputs.

Jina AI

Definition: Jina AI is an open-source framework for building neural search systems, enabling developers to create AI-powered search engines for text, images, and more.

Key Components: It includes a modular architecture, pre-trained models, and tools for indexing and querying diverse data types.

Benefits: Simplifies search system development, scales to large datasets, and supports multimodal searches.

Examples: Creating a product search for an e-commerce site, indexing a photo gallery, or building a document retrieval tool.

Applications: Used in e-commerce, content management, and research platforms.

Challenges: Requires tuning for optimal performance, and integrating it into existing systems can be complex.

Summary: Jina AI makes advanced search accessible to developers, offering flexibility and power, though it needs effort to refine and deploy.

JIT (Just-In-Time Learning)

Definition: Just-In-Time Learning in AI refers to an educational approach where knowledge is delivered exactly when needed, often powered by AI tools to personalize and streamline the process.

Key Components: It involves adaptive algorithms, real-time content delivery, and integration with workflows like coding or problem-solving.

Benefits: Reduces time spent on irrelevant material, boosts retention through context, and fits busy schedules.

Examples: Getting a coding tip while debugging, learning a concept during a project, or receiving a tutorial mid-task.

Applications: Common in online courses, workplace training, and self-paced tech education.

Challenges: Depends on accurate AI predictions, and incomplete content libraries can limit its scope.

Summary: JIT Learning transforms education into a timely, tailored experience, though its success hinges on smart AI and rich resources.

Jitter Buffer

Definition: A Jitter Buffer is a temporary storage mechanism that holds incoming data packets and releases them in a steady stream to smooth out transmission variations.

Key Components: It features adjustable buffer sizes, packet reordering algorithms, and delay management logic to balance timing and quality.

Benefits: Reduces audio or video distortion, ensures consistent playback, and improves real-time communication reliability.
Examples: Storing voice packets in a VoIP app, buffering live video frames, or stabilizing sensor data in a remote monitoring system.

Applications: Common in telephony, streaming services, and edge AI devices needing stable data flow.

Challenges: Too large a buffer adds latency, too small risks packet loss, and tuning it requires careful calibration.

Summary: Jitter Buffer is a practical fix for smoothing data delivery in AI systems, enhancing user experience, though finding the right buffer size is a delicate balance.

Jitter Compensation

Definition: Jitter Compensation is a technique used to counteract the effects of timing variations in data transmission by adjusting system behavior or processing.

Key Components: It includes adaptive algorithms, predictive timing models, and real-time adjustments to synchronize data flow.
Benefits: Restores smooth operation, minimizes disruptions in critical applications, and adapts dynamically to changing conditions.

Examples: Adjusting playback speed in a podcast app, realigning data in a robotic control loop, or stabilizing a live feed from a drone.

Applications: Used in multimedia streaming, industrial automation, and AI-driven telemetry systems.

Challenges: Complex to implement, may introduce minor delays, and effectiveness depends on accurate jitter detection.
Summary: Jitter Compensation actively mitigates timing issues, ensuring fluid performance in AI applications, though it demands precise execution to avoid trade-offs.

Jitter Minimization

Definition: Jitter Minimization refers to strategies and practices aimed at reducing timing variations in data transmission to optimize system efficiency.

Key Components: It involves network optimization, prioritized packet routing, and hardware upgrades to stabilize data delivery.

Benefits: Enhances responsiveness, improves quality of real-time interactions, and reduces the need for extensive buffering.

Examples: Upgrading a router for smoother video calls, optimizing a network for autonomous vehicle data, or refining a gaming server's packet flow.

Applications: Applied in high-speed networks, AI-powered robotics, and interactive media platforms.

Challenges: Requires investment in infrastructure, ongoing maintenance, and may not eliminate jitter entirely.

Summary: Jitter Minimization proactively cuts down timing disruptions, boosting AI system performance, though it involves resource-intensive solutions.

Jitter Reduction Algorithms

Definition: Jitter Reduction Algorithms are computational methods designed to analyze and lessen timing inconsistencies in data streams for improved stability.

Key Components: They feature pattern recognition, predictive smoothing techniques, and real-time correction processes to manage packet delays.

Benefits: Increases precision in time-sensitive tasks, automates jitter control, and adapts to variable network conditions.

Examples: Reordering packets in a live broadcast, stabilizing data in a smart grid, or refining timing in a telemedicine app.

Applications: Found in AI-enhanced networks, real-time analytics, and distributed computing systems.

Challenges: Algorithm complexity can strain resources, requires fine-tuning, and may struggle with extreme jitter spikes.

Summary: Jitter Reduction Algorithms provide a smart, automated way to tackle timing issues, enhancing AI reliability, though they demand computational finesse.

Job-Agnostic AI Systems

Definition: Job-Agnostic AI Systems are artificial intelligence frameworks that perform tasks across various roles or industries without being tied to a specific job type.

Key Components: They include flexible learning models, broad data compatibility, and modular design for easy adaptation to new tasks.

Benefits: Offers versatility, reduces the need for specialized AI builds, and accelerates deployment across domains.

Examples: A chatbot handling customer service and HR queries, an AI sorting data for finance and healthcare, or a tool analyzing trends in multiple sectors.

Applications: Used in customer support, data analysis, and process automation across diverse fields.

Challenges: May lack deep specialization, requires extensive training data, and balancing generality with accuracy is tricky.

Summary: Job-Agnostic AI Systems shine in their adaptability, serving multiple purposes in AI ecosystems, though they sacrifice some task-specific precision.

Job-Flow Management in AI

Definition: Job-Flow Management in AI is the orchestration of tasks and processes within an AI system to ensure efficient execution and resource use.

Key Components: It relies on workflow schedulers, task queuing systems, and resource allocation tools to streamline operations.

Benefits: Boosts productivity, prevents bottlenecks, and optimizes computational resources for complex AI workloads.

Examples: Scheduling model training runs, coordinating data preprocessing tasks, or managing inference jobs in a cloud AI platform.

Applications: Critical in machine learning pipelines, distributed AI systems, and large-scale data processing.

Challenges: Coordinating multiple jobs can get complex, resource conflicts may arise, and requires robust monitoring.

Summary: Job-Flow Management in AI keeps tasks running smoothly, maximizing efficiency, but it needs careful oversight to avoid operational hiccups.

Job Prioritization in AI Systems

Definition: Job Prioritization in AI Systems is the practice of ranking and executing AI tasks based on urgency, importance, or resource availability.

Key Components: It uses priority algorithms, real-time decision engines, and workload balancers to assign task order dynamically.

Benefits: Ensures critical tasks finish first, improves system responsiveness, and makes the most of limited resources.

Examples: Prioritizing fraud detection over routine analytics, rushing an emergency diagnostic AI job, or fast-tracking a live event prediction.

Applications: Seen in real-time AI applications, resource-constrained environments, and mission-critical systems.

Challenges: Defining priorities can be subjective, risks neglecting lower-priority tasks, and needs constant adjustment.

Summary: Job Prioritization in AI Systems keeps focus on what matters most, enhancing performance under pressure, though it requires thoughtful calibration.

Job Scheduling in AI

Definition: Job Scheduling in AI is the process of organizing and timing the execution of tasks within an AI system to optimize performance and resource utilization.

Key Components: It involves scheduling algorithms, task dependency trackers, and resource monitors that allocate computing power efficiently.

Benefits: Maximizes throughput, reduces idle time, and ensures timely completion of AI workloads.

Examples: Arranging a sequence of model training jobs, timing data preprocessing alongside inference, or scheduling updates for a recommendation engine.

Applications: Used in machine learning pipelines, cloud-based AI services, and real-time processing systems.

Challenges: Balancing competing priorities can be complex, unexpected delays disrupt plans, and requires constant adaptation to system demands.

Summary: Job Scheduling in AI keeps operations flowing smoothly by smartly arranging tasks, though it demands flexibility to handle dynamic workloads.

Joint Attention in AI

Definition: Joint Attention in AI refers to the ability of an AI system to focus on the same object or event as a human or another agent, mimicking collaborative awareness.

Key Components: It relies on perception models, gaze tracking, and context understanding to align attention with a partner's focus.

Benefits: Enhances human-AI interaction, improves communication accuracy, and builds trust in collaborative settings.

Examples: An AI assistant noticing a user pointing at a screen, a robot following a worker's gaze to an item, or a virtual tutor focusing on a student's book page.

Applications: Found in robotics, virtual assistants, and educational AI tools.

Challenges: Interpreting subtle cues is tough, requires real-time processing, and can misalign without clear signals.

Summary: Joint Attention in AI bridges human and machine awareness, enriching teamwork, but it hinges on precise perception and responsiveness.

Joint Attention Mechanisms

Definition: Joint Attention Mechanisms are specific techniques or algorithms in AI that enable systems to share and coordinate focus with users or other agents.

Key Components: They include attention models, sensor fusion for tracking cues, and learning systems that adapt to interaction patterns.

Benefits: Sharpens collaborative task performance, reduces misunderstandings, and makes AI more intuitive to work with.

Examples: A chatbot highlighting text a user references, a drone adjusting its camera to match an operator's view, or an AI tutor syncing with a child's focus.

Applications: Applied in human-robot collaboration, interactive AI interfaces, and social AI development.

Challenges: High computational cost, struggles with ambiguous cues, and needs extensive training data.

Summary: Joint Attention Mechanisms power shared focus in AI, boosting interaction quality, though they require robust design and resources.

Joint Embedding

Definition: Joint Embedding is a method in AI where multiple types of data, like text and images, are mapped into a shared representation space for unified analysis.

Key Components: It uses neural networks, dimensionality reduction techniques, and alignment algorithms to create cohesive embeddings.

Benefits: Enables cross-modal understanding, simplifies complex data relationships, and supports versatile downstream tasks.

Examples: Linking product descriptions to photos in an e-commerce search, connecting captions to video frames, or pairing medical notes with scans.

Applications: Used in multimedia search, recommendation systems, and multi-modal AI research.

Challenges: Aligning diverse data types is tricky, requires large datasets, and risks losing modality-specific details.

Summary: Joint Embedding unifies disparate data into a single framework, enhancing AI's versatility, but it demands careful tuning to preserve accuracy.

Joint Inference

Definition: Joint Inference is an AI approach where multiple predictions or decisions are made simultaneously, leveraging their interdependencies for better outcomes.

Key Components: It incorporates probabilistic models, optimization routines, and interconnected reasoning processes to infer collectively.

Benefits: Improves accuracy by considering relationships, reduces errors from isolated predictions, and speeds up complex decision-making.

Examples: Tagging objects and actions in a video together, predicting weather and crop yield as a pair, or classifying text sentiment with context clues.

Applications: Seen in natural language processing, computer vision, and predictive analytics.

Challenges: Computationally intensive, requires well-defined relationships, and can falter with incomplete data.

Summary: Joint Inference enhances AI's reasoning by tackling tasks in tandem, offering precision, though it's resource-heavy and data-dependent.

Joint Learning

Definition
Joint Learning is a training strategy in artificial intelligence where multiple tasks or models are learned simultaneously, sharing underlying structures and knowledge to enhance overall performance.

Key Components
Shared neural network layers
Multi-task loss functions
Integrated data across related tasks

Benefits
Boosts efficiency by training tasks together
Improves generalization across domains
Leverages task synergies for stronger models

Examples
Training an AI to recognize both facial identities and emotional expressions at once
Teaching a system language translation while simultaneously learning grammar correction
Pairing object detection with depth estimation in autonomous vehicles

Applications
Multi-task learning systems
Robotics
Language-vision AI models

Challenges
Balancing task importance is difficult
Risk of negative transfer between unrelated tasks
Requires thoughtful model design

Summary
Joint Learning unifies task training for more robust AI models, offering improved results through shared learning, but demands careful balancing to avoid interference.

Joint Visual-Textual Embedding

Definition
Joint Visual-Textual Embedding maps both images and text into a shared embedding space, allowing AI systems to understand, compare, and generate content that spans both modalities.

Key Characteristics
Cross-modal representation learning
Unified feature extraction from text and visuals
Deep learning-based embedding strategies

Benefits
Enables integrated analysis of visual and textual information
Improves multi-modal AI performance
Enhances tasks like captioning, visual Q&A, and multimedia retrieval

Applications
Image-captioning AI
Visual question answering systems
Cross-modal search engines

Summary
Joint Visual-Textual Embedding bridges the gap between language and images, empowering AI with deeper multi-modal understanding for complex content generation and analysis.

Jostle Clustering

Definition
Jostle Clustering is a clustering method in AI that accounts for overlapping feature spaces, ensuring that data points with shared characteristics are grouped accurately even in complex datasets.

Key Characteristics
Overlapping cluster detection
Fuzzy membership assignment
Non-linear data partitioning

Benefits
Handles feature overlaps gracefully
Improves classification in noisy or complex datasets
Reveals subtle relationships hidden in the data

Applications
Genetic data analysis
Market segmentation
Image recognition with overlapping features

Summary
Jostle Clustering provides flexible and nuanced grouping strategies for datasets where traditional clustering fails, making it a valuable tool for detailed AI data analysis.

Joule-Based Energy Efficiency

Definition
Joule-Based Energy Efficiency measures the energy cost per AI computation task, aiming to optimize power consumption without sacrificing performance.

Key Characteristics
Energy-optimized model design
Hardware-software co-optimization
Run-time energy monitoring

Benefits
Promotes sustainable AI development
Reduces operating costs in data centers and edge devices
Supports eco-friendly computing initiatives

Applications
Edge AI devices
Energy-efficient cloud services
Low-power autonomous systems

Summary
Joule-Based Energy Efficiency is central to the future of sustainable AI, helping balance computational power with environmental responsibility.

JumboNet

JumboNet is a large-scale neural network architecture designed to handle complex tasks requiring massive computational resources and vast amounts of data.

Key components include deep learning layers, distributed computing frameworks, and optimization algorithms.

The benefits include superior performance on large-scale problems, such as image recognition, natural language processing, and scientific simulations.

Examples include using JumboNet for high-resolution image analysis or training on massive datasets like satellite imagery.

Applications include healthcare diagnostics, autonomous systems, and climate modeling. Challenges include managing computational costs, ensuring scalability, and optimizing training efficiency.

In summary, JumboNet represents the cutting edge of AI scalability, enabling solutions to some of the most complex problems.

abrupt changes.

Jump-Start Learning

Defition:

Jump-Start Learning refers to techniques that accelerate the training of machine learning models by leveraging pre-trained models, transfer learning, or initialization strategies.

Key components include pre-trained models, transfer learning frameworks, and optimization algorithms.

The benefits include reduced training time, improved performance, and lower computational costs.

Examples include using a pre-trained image recognition model to fine-tune for a specific task or initializing a neural network with optimized weights.

Applications include computer vision, natural language processing, and robotics.

Challenges include ensuring compatibility between pre-trained models and new tasks and avoiding overfitting.

In summary, Jump-Start Learning enables faster and more efficient model training, making it a valuable tool in AI development.Junction-Based Routing is a network routing technique that uses key junctions or nodes to optimize data transmission paths in complex networks.

Key components include routing algorithms, network topology analysis, and optimization techniques.

The benefits include improved network efficiency, reduced latency, and better resource utilization.

Examples include routing data in smart city traffic systems or optimizing communication in IoT networks.

Applications include telecommunications, autonomous vehicle navigation, and distributed computing.

Challenges include managing dynamic network conditions and ensuring scalability. In summary, Junction-Based Routing enhances network performance by focusing on critical nodes, making it ideal for complex systems.

Junction-Based Routing

Junction Tree Algorithm

Definition:

The Junction Tree Algorithm is a method used in probabilistic graphical models to perform efficient inference by transforming the graph into a tree structure.

Key components include graph decomposition, clique formation, and message passing. The benefits include exact inference in complex models, improved computational efficiency, and scalability.

Examples include using the algorithm for probabilistic reasoning in Bayesian networks or Markov random fields.

Applications include medical diagnosis, risk assessment, and decision support systems.

Challenges include managing computational complexity for large graphs and ensuring accuracy.

In summary, the Junction Tree Algorithm provides a robust framework for probabilistic inference in AI systems.

Jupyter AI

Definition:

Jupyter AI refers to the integration of artificial intelligence capabilities into Jupyter notebooks, enabling users to build, train, and deploy AI models interactively.

Key components include Jupyter notebooks, AI libraries, and visualization tools.

The benefits include interactive development, ease of use, and seamless integration with AI frameworks.

Examples include using Jupyter AI for data exploration, model training, and result visualization. Applications include data science, machine learning, and research.

Challenges include managing computational resources and ensuring reproducibility.

In summary, Jupyter AI enhances the productivity of AI developers by providing an interactive and user-friendly environment.

Jupyter Notebook

Jupyter Notebook is an open-source web application that allows users to create and share documents containing live code, equations, visualizations, and narrative text.

Key components include code cells, markdown cells, and kernel support for multiple programming languages.

The benefits include interactive development, collaboration, and documentation of workflows. Examples include using Jupyter Notebook for data analysis, machine learning, and scientific research.

Applications include education, data science, and AI development.

Challenges include version control and managing large notebooks. In summary, Jupyter Notebook is a versatile tool for interactive computing and collaboration.

Justification Logic

Definition
Justification Logic is a formal system that extends classical logic by incorporating explicit justifications for statements, enabling reasoning about knowledge and belief.

Key components include justification terms, logical axioms, and inference rules. The benefits include enhanced expressiveness, support for epistemic reasoning, and applications in AI and philosophy.

Examples include using justification logic to model belief systems or verify knowledge-based systems.

Applications include automated reasoning, knowledge representation, and AI ethics.

Challenges include computational complexity and ensuring consistency.

In summary, Justification Logic provides a rigorous framework for reasoning about knowledge and justification.

Just-in-Time Model Training

Definition
Just-in-Time Model Training refers to the practice of training machine learning models dynamically and on-demand, rather than pre-training and storing them. This approach ensures that models are always up-to-date with the latest data.

Key components include real-time data pipelines, adaptive learning algorithms, and scalable computing resources.

The benefits include reduced storage costs, improved model accuracy, and the ability to adapt to changing data patterns.

Examples include training recommendation systems based on real-time user interactions or updating fraud detection models with the latest transaction data. Applications include personalized marketing, dynamic pricing, and real-time anomaly detection.

Challenges include managing computational overhead, ensuring low-latency training, and handling data privacy concerns.

In summary, Just-in-Time Model Training enables agile and efficient model development, making it ideal for applications requiring real-time adaptability.

Just-in-Time Resource Allocation

Definition:Just-in-Time Resource Allocation involves dynamically assigning computational resources to AI tasks as needed, optimizing efficiency and reducing waste.

Key components include resource monitoring tools, scheduling algorithms, and cloud-based infrastructure.

The benefits include cost savings, improved scalability, and enhanced performance for AI workloads.

Examples include allocating GPU resources for training deep learning models only when required or scaling up cloud servers during peak demand.

Applications include large-scale AI training, real-time inference, and distributed computing.

Challenges include predicting resource needs accurately, minimizing latency, and managing resource contention.

In summary, Just-in-Time Resource Allocation ensures optimal utilization of resources, making it essential for scalable and cost-effective AI deployments.

JVM (Java Virtual Machine)

Definition:
JVM (Java Virtual Machine) is a runtime environment that executes Java bytecode, enabling Java applications to run on any platform. In AI, JVM is used to deploy and run AI models developed in Java or Jython.

Key components include the JVM interpreter, garbage collector, and just-in-time (JIT) compiler. The benefits include platform independence, robust performance, and seamless integration with Java-based systems.

Examples include running machine learning models built with Java libraries like Deeplearning4j or deploying Jython-based AI applications.

Applications include enterprise AI systems, big data processing, and cross-platform AI deployments.

Challenges include managing memory usage and optimizing performance for computationally intensive tasks.

In summary, JVM provides a reliable and versatile environment for deploying AI solutions in Java and Jython ecosystems.

Jython

Definition
Jython is an implementation of the Python programming language designed to run on the Java platform. It allows developers to write Python code that integrates seamlessly with Java libraries and frameworks.

Key components include the Jython interpreter, Java-Python interoperability tools, and access to both Python and Java libraries.

The benefits include cross-platform compatibility, access to Java's enterprise ecosystem, and Python's simplicity.

Examples include using Jython to build AI applications that leverage Java-based big data tools or integrating Python machine learning models into Java systems.

Applications include AI development, data processing, and automation tasks in hybrid environments.

Challenges include managing performance overhead and ensuring compatibility between Python and Java libraries.

In summary, Jython bridges the gap between Python and Java, enabling developers to build versatile and powerful AI solutions.

Jython AI Development Tools

Definition: Jython AI Development Tools are software tools and libraries that facilitate the creation of AI applications using Jython. These tools combine Python's ease of use with Java's robustness.

Key components include Jython-compatible libraries, IDEs, and debugging tools. The benefits include faster development cycles, access to both Python and Java ecosystems, and seamless integration with enterprise systems.

Examples include using Jython with TensorFlow or PyTorch for machine learning or integrating with Java-based AI frameworks like Deeplearning4j.

Applications include AI model development, data analysis, and automation in hybrid environments.

Challenges include managing dependencies and optimizing performance. In summary, Jython AI Development Tools provide a flexible and efficient environment for building AI applications in Python-Java ecosystems.

Jython AI Frameworks

Definition: Jython AI Frameworks are specialized frameworks that support the development and deployment of AI models using Jython. These frameworks leverage Python's simplicity and Java's scalability.

Key components include pre-built algorithms, APIs, and integration tools for Java and Python.

The benefits include accelerated development, cross-platform compatibility, and access to advanced AI capabilities.

Examples include using Jython with frameworks like TensorFlow, Keras, or Deeplearning4j.

Applications include natural language processing, computer vision, and predictive analytics.

Challenges include ensuring compatibility between Python and Java components and managing resource usage.

In summary, Jython AI Frameworks enable developers to build and deploy sophisticated AI models in hybrid environments.

Jython-based Machine Learning

Definition:
Jython-based Machine Learning involves using Jython to develop and deploy machine learning models, leveraging Python's libraries and Java's performance.

Key components include Jython-compatible machine learning libraries, data processing tools, and integration with Java systems.

The benefits include ease of use, scalability, and access to both Python and Java ecosystems. Examples include building recommendation systems or predictive models using Jython.

Applications include fraud detection, customer segmentation, and real-time analytics.

Challenges include optimizing performance and managing dependencies.

In summary, Jython-based Machine Learning provides a powerful and flexible approach to developing machine learning solutions in hybrid environments.

Jython Cloud AI

Definition: Jython Cloud AI refers to the integration of Jython, a Python implementation for the Java platform, with cloud-based artificial intelligence services. It enables developers to leverage Python's simplicity and Java's robustness to build and deploy AI models on cloud platforms.

Key components include cloud infrastructure, Jython libraries, AI frameworks, and APIs for seamless integration.

The benefits of Jython Cloud AI include scalability, cross-platform compatibility, and access to powerful cloud-based AI tools.

Examples include using Jython to deploy machine learning models on AWS or Google Cloud.

Applications range from predictive analytics to natural language processing in cloud environments.

Challenges include managing latency, ensuring data security, and optimizing performance across hybrid systems.

In summary, Jython Cloud AI bridges Python's ease of use with Java's enterprise capabilities, enabling efficient AI development and deployment in the cloud.

Jython Data Processing

Definition
Jython Data Processing involves using Jython to manipulate, analyze, and transform data efficiently. It combines Python's data processing libraries with Java's performance and scalability.

Key components include Jython scripts, data pipelines, and integration with big data frameworks like Apache Spark or Hadoop.

The benefits include faster data processing, compatibility with Java-based systems, and access to Python's rich ecosystem of data science libraries.

Examples include cleaning and preprocessing large datasets using Jython scripts.

Applications include financial data analysis, log processing, and real-time data streaming.

Challenges include handling large-scale data efficiently and ensuring seamless integration with Java-based systems.

In summary, Jython Data Processing provides a flexible and powerful solution for data manipulation, making it ideal for hybrid Python-Java environments.

Jython Image Processing

Definition
Jython Image Processing refers to the use of Jython for tasks such as image manipulation, enhancement, and analysis. It combines Python's image processing libraries with Java's performance for efficient handling of image data.

Key components include Jython scripts, image processing libraries like OpenCV, and Java-based frameworks for graphical applications.

The benefits include ease of use, cross-platform compatibility, and access to advanced image processing techniques.

Examples include applying filters, detecting edges, or performing facial recognition using Jython.

Applications include medical imaging, computer vision, and digital art creation.

Challenges include optimizing performance for real-time processing and managing memory usage for large images.

In summary, Jython Image Processing offers a versatile solution for developers working on image-related tasks in Python-Java ecosystems.

Jython Neural Network Libraries

Definition
Jython Neural Network Libraries involve using Jython to build, train, and deploy neural networks by leveraging Python's machine learning libraries within Java environments.

Key components include Jython-compatible libraries like TensorFlow or PyTorch, Java-based neural network frameworks, and APIs for integration.

The benefits include access to cutting-edge AI research, ease of prototyping, and seamless deployment in Java applications.

Examples include training a neural network for image classification or natural language processing using Jython.

Applications include autonomous systems, recommendation engines, and predictive modeling.

Challenges include managing computational resources and ensuring compatibility between Python and Java libraries.

In summary, Jython Neural Network Libraries enable developers to harness the power of neural networks in hybrid Python-Java environments.

Jython Text Processing

Definition: Jython Text Processing refers to the use of Jython for tasks such as text analysis, natural language processing (NLP), and information extraction. It combines Python's NLP libraries with Java's performance for efficient text handling.

Key components include Jython scripts, NLP libraries like NLTK or SpaCy, and Java-based text processing frameworks.

The benefits include ease of use, access to advanced NLP techniques, and compatibility with Java-based systems.

Examples include sentiment analysis, text summarization, and entity recognition using Jython.

Applications include chatbots, document analysis, and social media monitoring.

Challenges include handling large volumes of text data and ensuring accurate language processing.

In summary, Jython Text Processing provides a powerful toolset for developers working on text-related tasks in Python-Java environments.

LETTER K

K-Anonymity

Definition

K-Anonymity is a data privacy method that ensures individual entries in a dataset cannot be distinguished from at least K-1 other entries. It protects personal information by making records indistinguishable within a group.

Key Components

It uses data generalization, suppression of identifiers, clustering techniques, and group similarity enforcement to protect identities.

Benefits

K-Anonymity reduces re-identification risk, enhances trust in data sharing, and supports compliance with privacy regulations like GDPR and HIPAA.

Examples

Healthcare records are anonymized so no patient can be distinguished among fewer than K individuals with similar attributes.

Applications

Used heavily in healthcare data publishing, financial data anonymization, academic research datasets, and government census data.

Industries

Healthcare, finance, education, public administration, marketing research.

Challenges

Selecting an appropriate K value is critical. Overgeneralization can lead to loss of data utility, while under-generalization can still risk exposure.

Summary

K-Anonymity remains essential for balancing data privacy with usability, requiring thoughtful implementation to ensure both confidentiality and analytical value.

K-Dimensional Tree (KD Tree)

Definition

A K-Dimensional Tree is a binary space-partitioning structure designed to organize points in multi-dimensional spaces, allowing rapid nearest-neighbor searches and range queries.

Key Components

It partitions space recursively, organizes points by alternating dimensions, and optimizes search paths through tree-based architecture.

Benefits

KD Trees accelerate searches, optimize data retrieval, and support fast spatial indexing for moderate-dimension datasets.

Examples

KD Trees are used in pathfinding for robotics, collision detection in gaming, and nearest-location services for mobile apps.

Applications

Image search engines, geographic information systems, robotic mapping, spatial data analysis.

Industries

Computer graphics, robotics, telecommunications, aerospace navigation.

Challenges
Performance deteriorates with high-dimensional data, requiring additional tuning or alternative structures beyond a certain threshold.

Summary
KD Trees are efficient tools for multi-dimensional search, widely adopted where speed and structure matter, though their use is best limited to moderate-dimensional problems.

Kernel Density Estimation (KDE)

Definition
Kernel Density Estimation is a non-parametric method for estimating the probability density function of a random variable based on observed data points, providing a smooth approximation without assuming any specific distribution.

Key Components
It employs kernel functions like Gaussian smoothing, bandwidth selection for controlling smoothness, and sample-based curve fitting.

Benefits
KDE visualizes hidden patterns in data, uncovers multi-modal distributions, and offers flexibility absent in traditional parametric methods.

Examples
Modeling stock return distributions, identifying hotspots in crime data mapping, smoothing histograms for better insights.

Applications
Data exploration, risk modeling, spatial data analysis, environmental monitoring.

Industries
Finance, public safety, climatology, market research.

Challenges
Bandwidth choice critically affects results, and computational costs rise significantly with very large datasets.

Summary
KDE unlocks the hidden structure of data distributions, providing intuitive visualizations while demanding careful calibration for reliable insights.

Kernel Embeddings

Definition
Kernel Embeddings are techniques that project data into high-dimensional feature spaces using kernel functions, enabling linear algorithms to solve complex non-linear relationships effectively.

Key Components
They utilize kernel trick methodologies, feature space transformations, and inner product representations to model non-linear patterns.

Benefits
Kernel embeddings allow powerful pattern recognition without explicitly calculating high-dimensional coordinates, enhancing performance on difficult problems.

Examples
Classifying handwritten digits, analyzing genetic expression data, modeling non-linear customer behavior patterns.

Applications
Image recognition, bioinformatics, speech processing, machine translation.

Industries
Healthcare, biotechnology, artificial intelligence, telecommunications.

Challenges
Selecting appropriate kernels and hyperparameters is challenging, and scaling up for large datasets requires optimization tricks.

Summary
Kernel Embeddings power AI models to handle complexity elegantly, offering breakthrough capabilities in pattern analysis across industries.

Kernel Machines

Definition
Kernel Machines are algorithms that leverage kernel functions to perform machine learning tasks, enabling linear techniques to work effectively on non-linear datasets by projecting data into higher dimensions.

Key Components
They use kernel functions, support vector machines (SVM), dual formulations, and optimization strategies for classification and regression.

Benefits
Kernel Machines offer excellent generalization, superior non-linear modeling, and robustness against noisy data.

Examples
Text categorization, handwritten digit classification, and face recognition all benefit from kernel machine approaches.

Applications
Classification tasks, anomaly detection, natural language processing, bioinformatics.

Industries
Cybersecurity, finance, healthcare, media and entertainment.

Challenges
Kernel methods can be computationally heavy with large datasets, and parameter tuning remains a complex task.

Summary
Kernel Machines transform traditional learning boundaries, enabling AI to tackle challenging non-linear tasks with higher accuracy and stability.

Kernel Matrix

Definition
A kernel matrix is a symmetric matrix that measures the pairwise similarity between data points using a kernel function. It is a fundamental component in many machine learning algorithms for capturing relationships in complex datasets.

Key Components
It is built using kernel functions like the Gaussian or polynomial kernel, and it represents inner products in an implicit high-dimensional feature space.

Benefits
Kernel matrices allow algorithms to detect complex patterns without explicitly mapping data to high dimensions, simplifying computation for non-linear analysis.

Examples
Kernel matrices are used in support vector machines to classify text documents, or in Gaussian processes for modeling uncertainty in financial forecasting.

Applications
Kernel matrices are central to kernel-based classification, regression, dimensionality reduction, and anomaly detection.

Industries
Finance, healthcare analytics, image processing, and telecommunications.

Challenges
Computational costs and memory usage rise dramatically for large datasets, making approximations or sparse representations necessary.

Summary
Kernel matrices serve as the backbone for powerful non-linear modeling techniques, although managing them efficiently remains a challenge for large-scale data applications.

Kernel Matrix Inversion

Definition
Kernel Matrix Inversion refers to the mathematical operation of inverting a kernel matrix, which captures similarities between data points, essential for solving optimization problems in kernel-based learning methods.

Key Components
It involves symmetric positive semi-definite matrices, efficient matrix inversion techniques, and regularization for stability.

Benefits
Provides exact solutions in kernel regression problems, supports probabilistic modeling, and enhances decision boundaries.

Examples
Predicting financial trends with Gaussian processes, fine-tuning hyperparameters in kernel ridge regression, signal denoising.

Applications
Gaussian processes, kernel ridge regression, regularized optimization.

Industries
Finance, engineering design, statistical modeling, robotics.

Challenges
Matrix inversion scales poorly with dataset size, often requiring approximation techniques or sparse methods.

Summary
Kernel Matrix Inversion underpins precise kernel-based modeling, ensuring rich predictive capabilities but necessitating computational vigilance for scalability.

Kernel Method

Definition
Kernel methods are a class of machine learning algorithms that implicitly project data into high-dimensional spaces to solve non-linear problems using linear approaches.

Key Components
They rely on kernel functions to compute similarities between data points without explicitly mapping them, supporting algorithms like SVMs and Kernel PCA.

Benefits
Kernel methods can model complex relationships, provide flexibility across data types, and enhance generalization for predictive tasks.

Examples
Support vector machines for handwritten digit recognition or kernel PCA for reducing dimensions in gene expression datasets.

Applications
Pattern recognition, anomaly detection, bioinformatics, and predictive analytics.

Industries
Healthcare, financial services, cybersecurity, and biotechnology.

Challenges
Kernel computations become resource-intensive with large datasets, and selecting the right kernel is critical for success.

Summary
Kernel methods empower AI to solve non-linear challenges elegantly, although their efficiency heavily depends on smart kernel selection and computational optimizations.

Kernel Principal Component Analysis (Kernel PCA)

Definition
Kernel PCA is a non-linear form of principal component analysis that projects data into a high-dimensional feature space using kernel functions before performing dimensionality reduction.

Key Components
It uses kernel matrices to transform data and identify principal components in the transformed space to capture non-linear structures.

Benefits
Kernel PCA uncovers hidden patterns, improves feature extraction for complex datasets, and enhances visualization in reduced dimensions.

Examples
It is used for face recognition under varied lighting conditions and for clustering non-linearly separable data in customer segmentation.

Applications
Facial recognition, genomics, speech analysis, and exploratory data visualization.

Industries
Security and surveillance, healthcare, marketing analytics, and natural language processing.

Challenges
Kernel PCA requires significant computational resources for large datasets and is sensitive to kernel selection and parameter tuning.

Summary
Kernel PCA extends traditional PCA into the non-linear realm, offering deeper insights into complex data while demanding careful computational management.

Kernel Regularization

Definition
Kernel Regularization is a strategy used in kernel-based models to prevent overfitting by adding a penalty term to the model's complexity, promoting smoother and more generalizable solutions.

Key Components
It combines regularization parameters, penalty functions, and balancing techniques between model fit and simplicity.

Benefits
Improves generalization, reduces overfitting risks, stabilizes learning curves, and enables better model performance on unseen data.

Examples
Support Vector Machine (SVM) margin maximization, noise-tolerant kernel regression, robust anomaly detection systems.

Applications
Machine learning classification, regression models, control systems, computer vision.

Industries
Healthcare diagnostics, manufacturing quality control, environmental monitoring, AI safety.

Challenges
Selecting the right regularization strength is critical; overly strong penalties can underfit, while weak penalties allow overfitting.

Summary
Kernel Regularization ensures that AI models stay sharp without becoming brittle, striking a balance that promotes reliable and realistic predictions.

Kernel Ridge Regression (KRR)

Definition
Kernel Ridge Regression combines ridge regression with kernel methods to model non-linear relationships by mapping data into high-dimensional spaces and applying regularization.

Key Components
It involves kernel transformations, ridge penalty terms to avoid overfitting, and solving optimization problems involving the kernel matrix.

Benefits
KRR effectively models non-linear trends, stabilizes learning through regularization, and maintains good predictive accuracy even with limited data.

Examples
Forecasting housing market prices from heterogeneous property attributes and predicting stock price trends in volatile markets.

Applications
Risk assessment, healthcare diagnostics, weather modeling, and financial forecasting.

Industries
Finance, healthcare, climate science, and energy sectors.

Challenges
The method struggles with large datasets due to kernel matrix scaling, and selecting the appropriate kernel and regularization strength is essential.

Summary
Kernel Ridge Regression offers a flexible approach to modeling complex systems, balancing predictive power with model simplicity through effective regularization.

Kernel Smoothing

Definition:
Kernel smoothing is a non-parametric statistical technique in AI used to smooth data and estimate underlying patterns or trends by averaging values within local regions defined by kernel functions.

Key Components:
Kernel functions (e.g., Gaussian kernel), bandwidth parameters controlling smoothness, and weighted averaging methods.

Benefits:
Flexible modeling without strict parametric assumptions, enhanced data visualization, and effective handling of noisy or sparse data.

Examples:
Smoothing financial market trends, noise reduction in signal processing, or visualizing spatial data.

Applications:
Time-series forecasting, spatial data visualization, signal processing, and exploratory data analysis in machine learning.

Challenges:
Sensitivity to bandwidth selection, computational intensity with large datasets, and potential oversmoothing leading to detail loss.
Summary:
Kernel smoothing enhances data analysis by providing flexible and intuitive visualizations of complex patterns in AI.

Kernel SVM

Definition:
Kernel Support Vector Machine (Kernel SVM) is a powerful classification algorithm that uses kernel methods to classify non-linearly separable data by implicitly transforming it into higher-dimensional feature spaces.

Key Components:
Kernel functions (e.g., polynomial, Gaussian/RBF kernels), support vectors (data points closest to decision boundaries), and margin maximization strategies.

Benefits:
Kernel SVM efficiently classifies complex datasets, is robust against overfitting, and handles non-linear decision boundaries effectively.

Examples:
Classifying medical images to distinguish between disease states or identifying fraud patterns in financial transactions.

Applications:
Widely employed in image recognition, bioinformatics, cybersecurity, and financial risk assessment.

Challenges:
High computational cost for large datasets and sensitivity to kernel type and parameters, necessitating careful tuning.

Summary:
Kernel SVM is highly effective for accurate classification tasks involving complex and nonlinear data, making it widely used across diverse analytical fields.

Kernel Trick

Definition:
The Kernel Trick is a mathematical method enabling linear machine learning algorithms to efficiently process nonlinear data by mapping input data into a higher-dimensional feature space implicitly, without explicitly performing the transformation.

Key Components:
Kernel functions (like polynomial, radial basis function) and kernel matrices facilitate handling nonlinear relationships without heavy computational load.

Benefits:
Simplifies processing of complex, nonlinear data, increases flexibility of linear models, and enhances algorithmic efficiency.

Examples:
Used in SVMs for classifying highly nonlinear datasets, such as image classification or text categorization.

Applications:
Frequently applied in classification, regression, dimensionality reduction, and clustering tasks.

Challenges:
Selecting the appropriate kernel function and parameter settings critically impacts model accuracy and performance.

Summary:
The kernel trick provides machine learning algorithms the ability to efficiently analyze nonlinear data, significantly extending their practical applicability.

Khaitan Algorithm

Definition:

The Khaitan algorithm is a niche heuristic-based optimization method primarily used in AI for scheduling or optimization tasks, employing iterative procedures to efficiently explore solution spaces and improve decision-making.

Key Components:
Involves iterative improvement steps, heuristic evaluations, and cost or fitness function assessments guiding decision-making processes.

Benefits:
Offers simple, understandable solutions for complex optimization problems with computational efficiency.

Examples:
Optimizing scheduling systems in manufacturing or logistics, aiming to reduce operational costs or improve efficiency.

Applications:
Primarily utilized in industrial processes, supply-chain optimization, resource allocation, and scheduling algorithms.

Challenges:
Can get trapped in local optima, requiring careful initialization and fine-tuning of parameters.

Summary:
The Khaitan algorithm provides practical heuristic-based solutions, effectively addressing complex operational and resource optimization challenges.

Khatt Algorithm

Definition:
The Khatt Algorithm is a specialized machine-learning approach used predominantly in Arabic handwriting recognition. It involves feature extraction, segmentation, and classification of handwritten Arabic script.

Key Components:
Uses segmentation techniques, stroke identification, and machine learning classifiers such as neural networks or support vector machines.

Benefits:
Improves accuracy in recognizing complex handwriting styles, particularly suited for the intricacies of Arabic script.

Examples:
Digitizing handwritten Arabic documents, automated postal sorting, and historical manuscript digitization.

Applications:
Essential for document digitization, cultural heritage preservation, archival systems, and multilingual document processing.

Challenges:
Accuracy can vary due to the complexity of Arabic handwriting styles, scripts, and cursive connections.

Summary:
The Khatt Algorithm is instrumental in improving the digitization and analysis of handwritten Arabic texts, significantly benefiting document archiving and historical research.

nalyzing, designing, and simulating movements within AI-driven robotics and mechanical automation systems.

Khepri AI

Definition:
Khepri AI is an advanced artificial intelligence system specialized in generating optimized architectural and engineering designs through automation, leveraging AI-driven generative design methods to optimize solutions based on design constraints.

Key Components:
Utilizes AI-based generative algorithms, optimization techniques, reinforcement learning strategies, and computational geometry.

Benefits:
Facilitates faster design cycles, automated generation of optimized solutions, reduced human error, and improved structural efficiency.

Examples:
Automatically generating building layouts, optimizing bridge structures, or creating efficient urban planning solutions.

Applications:
Primarily used in architecture, construction engineering, infrastructure design, and urban planning sectors.

Challenges:
Requires substantial computational resources and precise parameter tuning, and the results may require human validation for compliance with regulatory constraints.

Summary:
Khepri AI transforms design processes by providing intelligent automation and optimization, significantly enhancing design efficiency and innovation.

Khorasan Neural Network

Definition:
The Khorasan Neural Network refers to advanced neural network architectures inspired by biological neural processes and adapted to solve complex, large-scale computational tasks involving learning, pattern recognition, and data analysis.

Key Components:
Includes layers of neurons, advanced synaptic connection patterns, biological inspiration, and robust learning algorithms.

Benefits:
Offers high efficiency in handling large, complex datasets, superior pattern recognition capabilities, and adaptability to diverse application domains.

Examples:
Effective use in sophisticated facial recognition, predictive analytics, medical diagnosis, or advanced natural language processing.

Applications:
Applied in medical imaging, advanced data analytics, autonomous systems, and complex forecasting problems.

Challenges:
Training complexity, high computational requirements, and potential for overfitting when poorly optimized.
Summary:
Khorasan Neural Networks provide powerful tools for addressing intricate data patterns, delivering impressive predictive capabilities across diverse AI applications.

Kinematics AI

Definition:
Kinematics AI involves applying artificial intelligence techniques to analyze, predict, and optimize the motion of physical systems or robots based on their geometric constraints and movement patterns.

Key Components:
Combines kinematic models, machine learning algorithms, sensor data integration, and optimization techniques for improved motion control.

Benefits:
Increased accuracy of robotic movements, real-time adaptation to dynamic conditions, and enhanced operational safety and efficiency.

Examples:
Predictive motion control in industrial robots, robotic arm movements, and autonomous navigation of drones and vehicles.

Applications:
Extensively used in robotics, automated manufacturing, autonomous vehicles, and biomechanics research.Challenges:
Real-time computational demands, model accuracy concerns, and complexity in integrating AI methods with physical constraints.

Summary:
Kinematics AI enables intelligent, adaptive motion in robotic systems, enhancing operational efficiency and precision in complex real-world tasks.

Kinematic Chain

Definition:
A Kinematic Chain refers to a linked sequence of mechanical elements, typically joints and rigid bodies, connected to facilitate controlled movements. It is fundamental in robotics, mechanics, and AI-driven systems analysis.

Key Components:
Involves interconnected joints, articulated links, mathematical representation of constraints, and degrees of freedom.

Benefits:
Provides precise control over robotic or mechanical motion, aids accurate modeling, and enables detailed simulation of robotic movements.

Examples:
Robotic arms in assembly lines, prosthetic limbs, and humanoid robots employing complex joint movements.

Applications:
Robotics, automated assembly, biomechanics, computer graphics animations, and mechanical design.

Challenges:
Complexity in modeling highly articulated systems, computational intensity, and difficulty accurately reflecting real-world physical factors such as friction or mechanical wear.

Summary:
Kinematic chains form the foundation for realistic robotic movements, vital for automation, biomechanics, and AI-driven mechanical systems.

Kinetics Dataset

Definition:
The Kinetics Dataset is a comprehensive, publicly available dataset containing thousands of labeled video clips intended for training AI models in human action recognition, gesture analysis, and activity detection.

Key Components:
Richly annotated video segments categorized into various human activities and behaviors, including diverse visual contexts.

Benefits:
Provides valuable training data, enhances the accuracy of video analysis systems, and facilitates robust activity recognition.

Examples:
Training AI to recognize human actions in surveillance footage, sports analytics, or behavior analysis for human-computer interactions.

Applications:
Surveillance, automated video analytics, sports analytics, healthcare monitoring, and intelligent video indexing.

Challenges:
Dataset biases, complexity in labeling actions accurately, and the computational expense of processing extensive video data.

Summary:
The Kinetics dataset significantly contributes to improving AI-based video recognition, supporting advancements in human-activity-related technologies.

Kinematic Models

Definition:
Kinematic models describe the mathematical relationships and motion characteristics of mechanical

systems or robotic components, focusing purely on geometric aspects such as position, velocity, and acceleration without considering forces causing the motion.

Key Components:
These include linkages, joints, frames of reference, coordinate transformations, mathematical equations representing spatial relationships, and trajectory planning methods.

Benefits:
They simplify robotic control, facilitate precise motion planning, enhance accuracy, and help simulate robotic movements effectively.

Examples:
Robot arm manipulation models, predicting movements of robotic vehicles or animating characters in video games.

Applications:
Applied extensively in robotics, automation, virtual reality simulations, and computer-aided design (CAD) systems.
Challenges:
Complex models may become computationally expensive, and overly simplistic assumptions might limit accuracy in real-world conditions.

Summary:
Kinematic models provide fundamental tools for analyzing, designing, and simulating movements within AI-driven robotics and mechanical automation systems.

Kinematic Models in AI

Definition:
Kinematic models in AI specifically refer to the application of AI-driven methods to kinematic analysis, modeling, and optimization, enabling intelligent management of robotic or mechanical system movements.

Key Components:
Integrates traditional kinematics, neural networks, optimization algorithms, sensor feedback, and reinforcement learning techniques.

Benefits:
Delivers real-time adaptive movements, improves robotic efficiency, and enhances predictive accuracy and automation capability.

Examples:
Autonomous drones adjusting flight paths dynamically, or robotic systems learning optimal movements through machine learning.

Applications:
Prominent in robotic manipulation, autonomous vehicles, industrial automation, and virtual reality simulations.

Challenges:
Complex real-time computational requirements and difficulties in accurately modeling real-world conditions like friction or dynamic obstacles.

Summary:
AI-powered kinematic models significantly enhance robotic and mechanical system performance, optimizing complex movements intelligently.

Kinematic Programming

Definition:
Kinematic programming involves developing software algorithms designed explicitly for controlling, simulating, and optimizing movements within robotic and mechanical systems using kinematic principles.

Key Components:
Algorithms for movement planning, trajectory optimization, coordinate transformations, and motion constraints modeling.

Benefits:
Improves efficiency, precision, and automation of robotic systems, reducing the need for human input and minimizing operational errors.

Examples:
Programming industrial robotic arms to automate assembly processes or simulating robot movements for training purposes.

Applications:
Robotic control systems, industrial automation, aerospace applications, and biomechanics simulations.

Challenges:
Computational complexity in real-time control systems and precision limitations when physical environments are unpredictable.
Summary:
Kinematic programming is critical for precise and efficient robotic motion control, significantly enhancing automation capabilities.

K-Means Clustering

Definition
K-Means Clustering is an unsupervised machine learning algorithm that partitions a dataset into K clusters, minimizing the variance within each cluster based on distance from cluster centroids.

Key Components
It uses iterative reassignment, centroid recalculation, cluster variance minimization, and convergence checks.

Benefits
K-Means is simple to implement, highly efficient, fast for large datasets, and provides clear cluster structures for analysis.

Examples
Grouping customers by purchasing habits, segmenting news articles by topic, detecting communities in social networks.

Applications
Market segmentation, image segmentation, document clustering, pattern recognition.

Industries
Retail, marketing analytics, journalism, biology research.

Challenges
Choosing the correct number of clusters can be subjective, sensitive to initial centroids, and less effective for non-spherical cluster shapes.

Summary
K-Means Clustering offers a straightforward, reliable way to discover underlying structures in data, providing an essential tool for unsupervised learning and exploratory analytics.

K-Mode Clustering

Definition
K-Mode Clustering is a machine learning technique tailored for clustering categorical data by using modes instead of means, grouping similar objects based on shared attributes.

Key Components
It uses mode-based clustering, frequency counting, iterative reassignment, and distance metrics for categorical attributes.

Benefits
K-Mode Clustering handles categorical data effectively, delivers intuitive groupings, and simplifies large-scale segmentation projects.

Examples
Market researchers group customers based on buying habits, demographics, or preference surveys using K-Mode Clustering.

Applications
Customer segmentation, survey data analysis, recommendation system categorization, behavioral pattern analysis.

Industries
Retail, market research, education analytics, healthcare profiling.

Challenges
The choice of initial modes affects the results, and defining the number of clusters requires trial-and-error or heuristics.

Summary
K-Mode Clustering empowers insights from categorical data, providing structured understanding for strategic business and research decisions.

K-Nearest Neighbors (KNN)
Definition
K-Nearest Neighbors is a supervised learning algorithm that classifies or predicts outcomes based on the majority class or value among the K closest data points in the feature space.

Key Components
It relies on distance metrics like Euclidean distance, simple majority voting for classification, and regression averaging for predictions.

Benefits
KNN is easy to understand, requires minimal training time, and adapts naturally to both classification and regression.

Examples
Predicting whether an email is spam, recommending movies to users based on viewing history, diagnosing diseases from symptom patterns.

Applications
Recommendation systems, fraud detection, customer classification, pattern recognition.

Industries
Finance, healthcare, e-commerce, education technology.

Challenges
KNN suffers from high computation during predictions, sensitivity to irrelevant features, and difficulty in handling large datasets efficiently.

Summary
KNN offers a simple yet powerful baseline for pattern recognition tasks but demands careful feature selection and scaling for best results.

Knowledge Augmentation

Definition:
Knowledge augmentation in AI involves integrating external knowledge or additional information into machine learning models, enhancing their capabilities to reason, infer, and perform tasks beyond their initial training data.

Key Components:
External knowledge bases, contextual embeddings, semantic enrichment methods, and mechanisms for incorporating additional knowledge sources.

Benefits:
Improves model accuracy, enhances interpretability, and enables systems to handle complex queries requiring reasoning and common-sense knowledge.

Examples:
AI assistants answering questions with integrated factual databases or AI systems using encyclopedic knowledge to enhance understanding

.Applications:
Conversational AI, healthcare decision support systems, personalized learning platforms, and intelligent recommendation systems.

Challenges:
Integrating diverse knowledge sources effectively, ensuring updated knowledge, and managing computational overhead.

Summary:
Knowledge augmentation significantly enhances AI system capabilities, enabling smarter, more context-aware, and informed decision-making processes.

Knowledge-Base Population

Definition:
Knowledge-base population involves automatically extracting, validating, and adding structured information into a knowledge base from various unstructured data sources such as text, images, and databases.

Key Components:
Natural language processing techniques, entity extraction methods, relationship extraction algorithms, automated verification tools, and knowledge representation systems.

Benefits:
Improves accuracy, consistency, and completeness of knowledge bases, supports faster information retrieval, and significantly reduces manual data input efforts.

Examples:
Automatically populating product details into e-commerce catalogs, or updating medical databases with new clinical research findings.

Applications:
Enterprise knowledge management systems, semantic search engines, healthcare databases, and intelligent personal assistants.

Challenges:
High complexity in accurately extracting information from diverse and noisy sources, ensuring data quality, and avoiding duplication and conflicting entries.

Summary:
Knowledge-base population automates the growth and updating of structured knowledge bases, providing enhanced accuracy and facilitating intelligent, data-driven decision-making.

Knowledge Base Refinement

Definition:
Knowledge base refinement refers to processes and methodologies used to improve, correct, and maintain the quality of existing knowledge bases through systematic identification and removal of inconsistencies, errors, and redundant information.

Key Components:
Error detection algorithms, validation frameworks, consistency checks, semantic reasoning tools, and automated correction mechanisms.

Benefits:
Enhances reliability, accuracy, and usability of knowledge bases, reduces erroneous decisions, and supports high-quality data-driven applications.

Examples:
Refining medical knowledge bases by identifying outdated treatments or correcting inaccuracies in customer support databases.

Applications:
Healthcare decision-support systems, customer service platforms, knowledge-driven business intelligence, and recommendation systems.

Challenges:
Complexities involved in identifying subtle errors, computational overhead of refinement algorithms, and managing ongoing updates efficiently.

Summary:
Knowledge base refinement significantly improves knowledge quality, thereby enhancing performance and reliability in AI applications reliant on structured information.

Knowledge Consolidation

Definition:
Knowledge consolidation is the systematic integration, merging, and harmonizing of information from multiple knowledge sources into a cohesive, unified representation, typically within a knowledge base or AI system.

Key Components:
Data integration methods, semantic alignment techniques, conflict-resolution algorithms, ontology mapping, and merging tools.

Benefits:
Ensures consistency and coherence across diverse data sources, facilitates comprehensive decision-making, and enhances understanding by providing unified insights.

Examples:
Consolidating research data from multiple clinical trials into unified medical recommendations or combining market research findings from different sources.

Applications:
Healthcare analytics, market intelligence platforms, enterprise knowledge systems, and educational technologies.

Challenges:
Managing conflicting information, integrating semantically diverse datasets, computational complexity, and maintaining continuous consolidation processes.

Summary:
Knowledge consolidation supports cohesive knowledge management and improves decision-making accuracy by providing unified, high-quality information in AI systems.

Knowledge Engineering

Definition:
Knowledge engineering is the field within artificial intelligence focused on the development of methods, models, and systems for capturing, structuring, and integrating human expertise into knowledge-based AI applications.

Key Components:
Knowledge acquisition techniques, expert systems, semantic representation languages, inference engines, and knowledge maintenance methodologies.

Benefits:
Automates complex reasoning tasks, captures expert knowledge effectively, enhances decision accuracy, and reduces reliance on direct human expertise in operational settings.

Examples:
Developing expert diagnostic systems in healthcare, or creating intelligent decision-support systems for complex industrial operations.

Applications:
Medical diagnostics, legal reasoning systems, financial advisory tools, industrial process control, and customer support automation.

Challenges:
Complexity in accurately modeling expert knowledge, difficulties in knowledge maintenance, managing evolving knowledge, and ensuring system adaptability.

Summary:
Knowledge engineering is foundational to AI, enabling automated decision-making through capturing and embedding expert human knowledge within intelligent systems.

Knowledge Fusion

Definition:
Knowledge fusion involves integrating information and insights from multiple heterogeneous knowledge sources into a unified, coherent structure to improve accuracy, consistency, and comprehensiveness in AI systems.

Key Components:
Semantic integration techniques, ontology alignment methods, data fusion algorithms, and knowledge harmonization frameworks.

Benefits:
Enhances data completeness, improves accuracy of analysis, provides unified insights, and supports robust decision-making in complex scenarios.

Examples:
Fusing real-time sensor data with historical records in predictive maintenance systems or combining user data from multiple platforms for personalized recommendations.

Applications:
Predictive analytics, personalized recommendation systems, industrial monitoring, healthcare analytics, and cybersecurity.

Challenges:
Semantic conflicts, managing data inconsistencies, computational complexity in large-scale fusion tasks, and maintaining updated, real-time fused knowledge.

Summary:
Knowledge fusion significantly enriches AI systems by integrating diverse knowledge streams, ensuring more comprehensive, accurate, and effective insights.

Knowledge Graph

Definition:
A Knowledge Graph is a structured, semantic representation of knowledge, where entities (people, objects, concepts) and relationships between them are interconnected in graph-based structures, enabling enhanced understanding, reasoning, and information retrieval in AI applications.

Key Components:
Entities, relationships, graph databases, semantic web technologies, ontologies, and inference mechanisms.
Benefits:
Supports enhanced semantic search, improved knowledge discovery, facilitates intelligent decision-making, and enables sophisticated reasoning.

Examples:
Google's semantic search engine, healthcare knowledge networks linking symptoms to diseases, or knowledge bases for virtual assistants.

Applications:
Semantic search engines, conversational AI, recommendation systems, intelligent data retrieval, and knowledge management.

Challenges:
Complexity in graph construction and maintenance, computationally intensive inference processes, handling incomplete or dynamic data, and ensuring data accuracy.

Summary:
Knowledge Graphs provide powerful semantic understanding capabilities, greatly enhancing information retrieval, predictive reasoning, and intelligent decision-making in AI systems.

Knowledge Graph Embeddings

Definition:
Knowledge Graph Embeddings are methods used in AI to convert entities and relationships within a knowledge graph into vector representations. These embeddings capture semantic meanings, facilitating computational analysis of structured knowledge.

Key Components:
Embedding algorithms, entities, relationships, vector spaces, semantic relationships, and neural network-based learning.

Benefits:
They enhance AI systems' ability to reason, enable efficient querying, improve accuracy in predictions, and simplify handling of large-scale semantic data.

Examples:
Representing complex relationships within online databases (such as product catalogs or biological databases) to improve recommendation accuracy.

Applications:
Search engines, recommendation systems, semantic search, natural language processing, and automated reasoning tasks.

Challenges:
Computational complexity, difficulty in embedding diverse semantic types consistently, and sensitivity to incomplete or noisy data.

Summary:
Knowledge Graph Embeddings significantly enhance semantic understanding, reasoning, and predictive accuracy in AI systems through structured vector representations.

Knowledge Inference

Definition:
Knowledge Inference refers to AI-driven processes designed to extract logical conclusions, predictions, or new insights from structured knowledge bases using reasoning algorithms and semantic understanding.

Key Components:
Inference engines, reasoning algorithms, logic rules, semantic networks, and probabilistic methods.

Benefits:
Improves decision-making accuracy, automates intelligent reasoning, expands knowledge bases, and enriches contextual understanding

.Examples:
Medical diagnosis systems deriving new conclusions from patient data or automated chatbots interpreting user intent.

Applications:
Healthcare decision support, intelligent personal assistants, automated troubleshooting, and semantic knowledge management systems.

Challenges:
Complexity in logic representation, inference inaccuracies from incomplete data, and computational challenges with extensive knowledge bases.

Summary:
Knowledge Inference enables AI systems to effectively reason and generate actionable insights from structured knowledge, enhancing intelligent decision-making capabilities.

Knowledge Representation

Definition:
Knowledge Representation involves encoding information, concepts, and relationships in structured, machine-readable formats, enabling AI systems to understand, store, and reason effectively with real-world knowledge.
Key Components:
Logical rules, semantic networks, ontologies, graph-based structures, symbolic and probabilistic models.

Benefits:
Provides a foundational structure for intelligent reasoning, semantic understanding, information retrieval, and predictive analytics.

Examples:
Representing medical terminology and relationships in healthcare databases or structuring information in semantic search engines.

Applications:
Semantic web, intelligent assistants, automated reasoning, natural language understanding, and knowledge-based systems.

Challenges:
Complexity of accurately encoding real-world knowledge, scalability issues, and difficulties in maintaining and updating structured knowledge.

Summary:
Knowledge Representation is foundational in AI for enabling structured reasoning, knowledge storage, and advanced semantic understanding.

Kohonen Network

Definition:
A Kohonen Network, also known as a Self-Organizing Map (SOM), is an unsupervised neural network model used for clustering, visualization, and pattern recognition, inspired by biological neural processes.

Key Components:
Competitive learning algorithms, nodes (neurons) organized in two-dimensional grids, iterative training processes, and distance metrics.

Benefits:
Effective for visualization of high-dimensional data, adaptive clustering, robust pattern detection, and intuitive interpretation of complex relationships.

Examples:
Visual clustering of customer behavior, identifying market segments, or organizing gene expression patterns in bioinformatics.

Applications:
Market segmentation, medical data analysis, visual pattern recognition, customer profiling, and industrial process control.

Challenges:
Sensitive to initial conditions, requires careful parameter tuning, and computational complexity can increase with dataset size.

Summary:
Kohonen Networks offer a powerful tool for intuitive, visual clustering, aiding the discovery and analysis of complex patterns in AI-driven systems.

Kubernetes

Definition:
Kubernetes is an open-source platform designed for automated deployment, scaling, and management of containerized AI applications and services across distributed computing environments.

Key Components:
Containers, pods, nodes, clusters, deployment management, load balancing, scaling automation, and resource monitoring tools.

Benefits:
Provides efficient management of AI deployments, enhances scalability, optimizes resource usage, and simplifies infrastructure complexity.

Examples:
Deploying scalable AI models and managing cloud-based machine learning services, such as distributed deep learning or online recommendation systems.

Applications:
Cloud computing, AI model deployment, DevOps automation, machine learning platforms, and distributed computing.

Challenges:
Complex initial setup, steep learning curve, and intricate management of container orchestration at scale.

Summary:
Kubernetes significantly simplifies the management and scalability of AI-driven applications, streamlining deployment processes and resource management.

Kubernetes Cluster

Definition:
A Kubernetes Cluster is a group of interconnected nodes managed by Kubernetes, designed to run containerized AI applications with coordinated scheduling, load balancing, and efficient resource utilization.
Key Components:
Master node, worker nodes, pods, services, network management, load balancing, and scheduling.

Benefits:
Improved resource utilization, automated failover, enhanced scalability, efficient management of distributed AI workloads.

Examples:
Running large-scale deep learning model training tasks, high-availability AI web services, or scalable analytics pipelines.

Applications:
AI cloud services, distributed model training, large-scale analytics, and enterprise-level AI deployments.

Challenges:
Complex configuration, resource management overhead, potential security vulnerabilities, and network latency concerns.

Summary:
Kubernetes clusters optimize the execution and management of complex, distributed AI applications through efficient resource orchestration.

Kubernetes Operator

Definition:
A Kubernetes Operator is a software extension for Kubernetes that automates management, deployment, and operational tasks for complex AI applications by encoding domain-specific operational logic.

Key Components:
Custom resource definitions, controllers, domain-specific operational logic, lifecycle management automation, and status monitoring.

Benefits:
Simplifies complex application management, automates routine operational tasks, improves reliability, and enhances scalability for AI workloads.

Examples:
Automating deployment and scaling of complex machine learning pipelines or databases that require specific operational logic.
Applications:
AI pipelines, database management, data streaming services, enterprise application management, and cloud infrastructure automation.

Challenges:
Development complexity, need for expertise in both Kubernetes and specific application domains, and potential maintenance overhead.

Summary:
Kubernetes Operators streamline and automate complex operational tasks for AI systems, significantly enhancing manageability and efficiency.

Kullback Information Criterion

Definition:
The Kullback Information Criterion is an information-theoretic measure used to evaluate and compare AI model performance by quantifying information loss relative to an ideal model.

Key Components:
Information theory principles, entropy measures, model comparison metrics, and statistical evaluation tools.

Benefits:
Offers robust model selection capabilities, minimizes model complexity, and improves predictive performance by assessing information loss.

Examples:
Selecting optimal predictive models in AI-driven financial forecasting or choosing among competing models in predictive healthcare analytics.

Applications:
Model evaluation, AI system comparison, statistical inference, and predictive modeling.
Challenges:
Interpreting relative model scores can be challenging, and it may require considerable computational resources for large models.

Summary:
The Kullback Information Criterion provides AI systems with effective tools for selecting and evaluating optimal predictive models based on information-theoretic principles.

Kullback-Leibler Divergence (KL Divergence)

Definition:
Kullback-Leibler Divergence (KL Divergence) measures the difference between two probability distributions, widely used in AI for quantifying divergence, optimizing models, and training neural networks.
Key Components:
Probability distributions, entropy-based measures, optimization algorithms, and divergence calculation methods.

Benefits:
Improves AI model accuracy, facilitates training deep learning models, and provides insights into statistical model differences.

Examples:
Training generative adversarial networks (GANs), optimizing probabilistic machine learning models, or assessing model distribution alignment.

Applications:
Machine learning model optimization, neural network training, statistical inference, anomaly detection, and Bayesian modeling.

Challenges:
Not symmetric, sensitive to data sparsity, and computationally intensive for complex or large-scale datasets.

Summary:
KL Divergence significantly contributes to effective model optimization and accuracy in AI through precise measurement of statistical divergence.

Kuhn-Munkres Algorithm (Hungarian Algorithm)

Definition:
The Kuhn-Munkres Algorithm, known as the Hungarian Algorithm, is a combinational optimization algorithm widely used in AI for efficiently solving assignment problems by minimizing or maximizing costs.

Key Components:
Cost matrices, iterative optimization procedures, assignment logic, and combinational optimization principles.

Benefits:
Efficient optimal solutions, effective handling of complex assignment tasks, and computational reliability.

Examples:
Optimal task assignment in automated scheduling, worker-job matching in industrial robotics, or resource allocation problems.

Applications:
Resource management, robotics, scheduling algorithms, logistics, and transportation optimization.

Challenges:
Performance limitations on extremely large problems, complexity in handling non-standard constraints, and computational intensity.

Summary:
The Hungarian Algorithm provides a powerful, optimal solution framework for complex assignment and resource allocation problems in AI systems.

Kuhn-Tucker Conditions

Definition:
Kuhn-Tucker Conditions (Karush-Kuhn-Tucker Conditions) are mathematical optimization criteria used in AI for solving complex constrained optimization problems, essential in machine learning model training and decision-making algorithms.

Key Components:
Lagrange multipliers, inequality constraints, optimality conditions, and nonlinear optimization methods.

Benefits:
Reliable solutions to constrained optimization problems, improved model training accuracy, and systematic handling of complex constraints.

Examples:
Training support vector machines, optimizing resource allocation models, or financial portfolio optimization.

Applications:
Optimization in machine learning, economic modeling, financial analytics, and engineering design.

Challenges:
Mathematical complexity, requirement for convexity conditions, and computational difficulty for large-scale, highly nonlinear problems.

Summary:
Kuhn-Tucker Conditions serve as fundamental tools in AI-driven optimization, enabling robust, precise solutions in constrained environments.

Kumaraswamy Distribution (Alternative for Kumaraswamy Distribution)

Definition:
Kumaraswamy Distribution (often misnamed as Kumaraswamy, commonly mistaken as "Kumaraswamy") is a continuous probability distribution defined on the interval [0,1], characterized by its flexibility in modeling skewed distributions. It is extensively used in AI to generate synthetic data, model probabilities, and analyze uncertainties.

Key Components: Two shape parameters controlling the skewness and shape, making it adaptable for various modeling scenarios.

Benefits:
Highly versatile, computationally efficient, and beneficial for fitting bounded data with varying shapes and distributions.

Examples:
Modeling uncertainty in AI-based predictive analytics or generating probability distributions in Bayesian networks.

Applications:
Used in synthetic data generation, Bayesian machine learning, statistical simulations, and risk modeling.

Challenges:
Selecting optimal parameters can be challenging, and inappropriate choices can affect accuracy and data representation.

Summary:
The Kumaraswamy Distribution is a powerful tool in AI for flexible modeling of bounded probability data, beneficial in accurate statistical analyses and simulations.

Kyper Space

Definition:
Kyper Space refers conceptually to virtual, multidimensional data spaces created or enhanced using AI and advanced visualization methods to represent complex data structures, relationships, and dynamics beyond standard dimensions.

Key Components:
High-dimensional visualization techniques, dimensionality reduction methods, data clustering, and interactive exploration interfaces.

Benefits:
Allows intuitive representation and analysis of complex, multidimensional datasets, improving human understanding and decision-making.

Examples:
Visualizing genomic data, interactive exploration of customer behavior in marketing analytics, or cyber threat pattern analysis.
Applications:
Data analytics, business intelligence platforms, cybersecurity threat modeling, and scientific research.

Challenges:
Visualization complexity, interpretability difficulties, and computational intensity with extremely high-dimensional data.

Summary:
Kyper Space visualization dramatically enhances human comprehension of intricate data relationships through advanced visual representations and interactive exploration.

Kyrptic AI

Definition:
Kyrptic AI refers to artificial intelligence systems designed specifically for cryptographic tasks, employing machine learning techniques to enhance encryption, security protocols, cryptanalysis, and secure communications.

Key Components:
Neural network-based cryptographic algorithms, reinforcement learning for adaptive encryption strategies, and predictive modeling for threat detection.

Benefits:
Improved security measures, adaptive encryption capabilities, increased resistance to cyber-attacks, and intelligent threat detection.

Examples:
AI-driven encryption algorithms securing financial transactions or adaptive cryptanalysis for cybersecurity.

Applications:
Cybersecurity systems, secure communications, blockchain security, financial transaction encryption, and national defense.

Challenges:
Potential vulnerabilities if AI systems are compromised, complexity in integrating AI with traditional cryptography, and computational overhead.

Summary:
Kyrptic AI significantly strengthens cryptographic and cybersecurity capabilities by integrating intelligent learning methods to adaptively counter threats and enhance security mechanisms.

Kyrtosis Filtering

Definition:
Kyrtosis filtering (often confused or combined with kurtosis filtering) specifically refers to advanced statistical or AI-driven methods for filtering data based on kurtosis-like measures to identify and manage extreme outliers or unusual data patterns effectively.

Key Components:
Statistical analysis, adaptive thresholding, AI-driven decision-making, and dynamic filtering processes.

Benefits:
Robust outlier detection, improved data quality, enhanced model accuracy, and predictive reliability.

Examples:
Detecting fraudulent transactions in banking, anomaly detection in network security, and quality control in manufacturing.

Applications:
Fraud detection, quality control systems, industrial monitoring, financial risk assessment, and anomaly detection.

Challenges:
Managing computational complexity, balancing sensitivity and specificity, and determining adaptive filtering thresholds accurately.

Summary:
Kyrptic filtering provides advanced outlier management capabilities, improving AI systems' reliability and accuracy across various critical domains.

❀ LETTER L ❀

LabelMe

Definition: LabelMe is an open-source annotation tool developed by MIT's CSAIL for labeling images, primarily used to create datasets for computer vision research and applications. It allows users to draw shapes, assign labels, and build shareable databases collaboratively.

Key Components: It features a web-based interface, polygon and bounding box annotation tools, a public dataset repository, and extensibility for custom projects.
Benefits: It simplifies image annotation, fosters community collaboration, and provides free access to labeled data for AI training.

Examples: A researcher might use LabelMe to label objects like cars and pedestrians in street images, creating a dataset for autonomous driving models.

Applications: It supports object detection, image segmentation, and scene understanding in computer vision tasks.

Challenges: Limited scalability for large projects, reliance on manual effort, and lack of advanced automation can slow progress.

Industries: Academia, automotive, and robotics utilize LabelMe for vision-based AI development.

Conclusion: LabelMe empowers computer vision by providing an accessible, collaborative platform for data annotation, though it leans on human input.

Label Propagation Algorithm

Definition: The Label Propagation Algorithm is a semi-supervised machine learning technique that assigns labels to unlabeled data by propagating known labels through a graph based on similarity or connectivity. It leverages network structure for classification.

Key Components: It includes a graph representation, initial labeled nodes, similarity measures (e.g., cosine distance), and iterative label updates.

Benefits: It's computationally efficient, requires minimal prior knowledge, and excels in finding community structures in data.
Examples: In a social network, it might label users as "influencers" by propagating labels from a few known examples based on connection patterns.

Applications: It is used in community detection, text classification, and image segmentation.

Challenges: Randomness in label selection can lead to inconsistent results, and it struggles with noisy or sparse data.

Industries: Social media, marketing, and bioinformatics apply it for clustering and analysis.

Conclusion: The Label Propagation Algorithm offers a fast, intuitive approach to semi-supervised learning, balancing simplicity with adaptability.

Labeled Data

Definition: Labeled data in AI refers to datasets where each instance is paired with an explicit annotation or tag, providing ground truth for supervised learning models to learn patterns or make predictions. It's the teacher in machine learning.

Key Components: It includes input features, corresponding labels (e.g., categories, values), data collection methods, and annotation processes.

Benefits: It enables precise model training, supports supervised learning, and ensures measurable accuracy.

Examples: A dataset of emails tagged as "spam" or "not spam" trains a filter to classify incoming messages accurately.

Applications: It drives classification, regression, and object recognition tasks.Challenges: Labeling is time-consuming, costly, and prone to human error or bias, impacting quality.

Industries: Finance, retail, and security depend on labeled data for predictive systems.

Conclusion: Labeled data is the backbone of supervised AI, delivering clarity at the expense of annotation effort.

Labeled Faces in the Wild (LFW)

Definition: Labeled Faces in the Wild (LFW) is a benchmark dataset of over 13,000 face images collected from the web, labeled with identities, designed to test facial recognition algorithms under unconstrained conditions. It's a real-world face challenge.

Key Components: It features diverse images, identity labels, varying poses and lighting, and a standardized evaluation protocol.

Benefits: It provides a realistic testbed, encourages algorithm robustness, and standardizes facial recognition research.

Examples: An AI might use LFW to evaluate its accuracy in identifying celebrities across different photos despite occlusions.

Applications: It supports facial recognition, identity verification, and biometric research.

Challenges: Limited diversity, outdated images, and privacy concerns limit its modern relevance.

Industries: Security, social media, and law enforcement utilize LFW for recognition advancements.

Conclusion: Labeled Faces in the Wild remains a key milestone, pushing facial AI toward practical, real-world performance.

Language Model

Definition: A language model in AI is a system that predicts or generates human-like text by learning the statistical patterns, grammar, and semantics of language from training data. It's the brain behind text understanding.

Key Components: It involves training corpora, probabilistic or neural architectures (e.g., transformers), tokenization, and fine-tuning processes.

Benefits: It enables natural communication, automates text tasks, and captures linguistic nuances effectively.

Examples: A model like GPT might predict the next word in "The sky is..." as "blue" based on learned patterns.

Applications: It powers chatbots, translation tools, text generation, and sentiment analysis.

Challenges: Bias in training data, computational cost, and handling rare contexts limit its scope.

Industries: Technology, education, and media harness language models for language-driven solutions.

Conclusion: Language models redefine AI's linguistic frontier, blending creativity with precision despite data challenges.

Large *Language Model (LLM)*

Definitions A Large Language Model (LLM) is an advanced artificial intelligence system designed to understand, generate, and process human language. These models are trained on vast amounts of text data and use deep learning techniques, primarily transformer architectures, to predict and generate coherent, contextually relevant text. LLMs can perform various natural language processing (NLP) tasks, including translation, summarization, question answering, and content generation, making them a cornerstone of modern AI applications.

The key components of a Large Language Model include deep neural networks, particularly transformer-based architectures such as GPT (Generative Pre-trained Transformer) and BERT (Bidirectional Encoder Representations from Transformers). These models rely on attention mechanisms that enable them to process and generate language with a high degree of coherence and contextual awareness. Training LLMs requires massive datasets, high-performance computing resources, and sophisticated optimization techniques to fine-tune performance across diverse language tasks.

The benefits of LLMs include their ability to automate and enhance text-based tasks, improve language understanding in AI systems, and generate human-like responses with minimal supervision. They enable businesses and developers to create more intuitive AI-driven applications, streamline customer interactions, and improve content creation processes. Examples of LLMs include OpenAI's GPT series, Google's Bard, Meta's LLaMA, and Microsoft's Turing-NLG, all of which demonstrate the ability to understand and generate complex text-based outputs.

Applications of LLMs span multiple industries, including customer support, content creation, healthcare, education, and legal analysis. In customer service, AI chatbots powered by LLMs handle inquiries efficiently. In content creation, these models assist writers in generating articles, reports, and creative works. Healthcare professionals use LLMs for medical documentation and patient interaction analysis. Educational platforms leverage LLMs to create personalized learning experiences, while legal firms utilize AI for document review and contract analysis.

Challenges in LLM development and deployment include ethical concerns, biases in training data, computational costs, and data privacy issues. These models may produce biased or misleading responses depending on the data they are trained on. Training and maintaining LLMs require extensive computational resources, leading to high operational costs. Ensuring data privacy and security while using LLMs in sensitive applications remains a major concern. Researchers and developers continue to refine model architectures and introduce safeguards to mitigate these challenges.

In conclusion, Large Language Models represent a significant advancement in AI and NLP, enabling more sophisticated and human-like text processing capabilities. Their impact is evident across industries, where they enhance efficiency and innovation. As technology evolves, improvements in model training, bias reduction, and ethical AI development will be critical to ensuring that LLMs are used responsibly and effectively.

Large Language Model (LLM) Hallucinations

Definition: Large Language Model (LLM) Hallucinations refer to instances where an AI-powered language model generates false, misleading, or fabricated information that appears plausible but lacks factual accuracy. These hallucinations occur because LLMs generate text based on learned patterns and probabilities rather than a true understanding of reality. As a result, they may produce incorrect answers, invent non-existent sources, or generate factually inconsistent content.

The key components of LLM hallucinations include probabilistic text generation that predicts the next word based on training data patterns, lack of real-world verification mechanisms that prevent AI from distinguishing between truth and fiction, overgeneralization errors where AI extrapolates beyond its knowledge base, and biases in training data that lead to incorrect associations. These factors contribute to the AI model generating responses that sound confident but may be factually inaccurate.

The benefits of studying LLM hallucinations include improving AI reliability through better fact-checking mechanisms, enhancing trust in AI applications by reducing misinformation, refining training methodologies to minimize hallucinations, and advancing AI ethics by addressing the risks of AI-generated falsehoods. By understanding hallucination patterns, developers can work toward creating more trustworthy AI systems. Examples of LLM hallucinations include AI-generated historical events that never occurred, fabricated legal cases in legal AI applications, incorrect citations in academic writing assistance tools, and AI-powered medical diagnoses suggesting non-existent conditions.

Applications of LLM hallucination mitigation span journalism, legal AI, healthcare, education, and customer support. In journalism, AI tools must avoid generating false news or misleading content. In legal AI, ensuring AI does not fabricate case law is critical for maintaining credibility. In healthcare, minimizing AI hallucinations is essential for accurate medical decision-making. In education, AI tutors must provide verified and accurate learning materials. In customer support, AI chatbots must avoid offering incorrect troubleshooting advice.

Challenges in addressing LLM hallucinations include ensuring AI has access to up-to-date and verifiable knowledge, improving AI transparency in text generation processes, balancing creativity with factual accuracy, and reducing AI overconfidence in false statements. Detecting and preventing hallucinations in real time remains an active area of AI research and development.

In conclusion, Large Language Model Hallucinations pose a significant challenge in AI-generated content, affecting trust, accuracy, and real-world applicability. By refining AI training methods, incorporating real-time verification tools, and integrating human oversight, developers can mitigate the risks of AI hallucinations. As AI systems continue to evolve, minimizing hallucinations will be crucial for ensuring responsible and reliable AI applications across industries.

Latent Dirichlet Allocation (LDA)

Definition: Latent Dirichlet Allocation (LDA) is a generative probabilistic model used in AI to uncover hidden topics within a collection of documents by assigning words to topics and topics to documents based on statistical distributions. It's a tool for discovering thematic structure.

Key Components: It includes a corpus of text, word-topic distributions, document-topic distributions, and Dirichlet priors for probabilistic modeling.
Benefits: It reveals underlying patterns, enables unsupervised topic discovery, and supports interpretable text analysis.

Examples: LDA might analyze news articles to identify topics like "politics" or "sports," grouping related words like "election" or "game."
Applications: It is used in topic modeling, document clustering, and recommendation systems.

Challenges: Determining the optimal number of topics, handling noisy data, and computational complexity can hinder results.
Industries: Media, marketing, and academia rely on LDA for text-based insights.

Conclusion: Latent Dirichlet Allocation offers a statistical lens into text, unlocking hidden themes with broad analytical power.

Latent Semantic Analysis (LSA)

Definition: Latent Semantic Analysis (LSA) is a technique in AI that analyzes relationships between words and documents by reducing the dimensionality of a term-document matrix, capturing latent semantic structures via singular value decomposition. It's a method for meaning extraction.

Key Components: It involves a term-document matrix, singular value decomposition (SVD), reduced latent space, and similarity measures like cosine distance.
Benefits: It uncovers semantic relationships, reduces noise, and improves text understanding beyond literal word matches.

Examples: LSA might link "car" and "automobile" in a search engine by placing them close in latent space despite different spellings.

Applications: It supports information retrieval, text classification, and semantic search.

Challenges: Loss of detail from dimensionality reduction, computational cost, and sensitivity to matrix sparsity pose issues.

Industries: Search technology, education, and customer service use LSA for semantic processing.

Conclusion: Latent Semantic Analysis distills meaning from text, enhancing AI's grasp of language through latent connections.

Latent Space

Definition: Latent space in AI is a compressed, abstract representation of data where high-dimensional inputs are mapped into a lower-dimensional space, preserving essential features or patterns for analysis or generation. It's a hidden data realm.

Key Components: It includes encoding mechanisms (e.g., autoencoders), dimensionality reduction, latent variables, and decoding processes.

Benefits: It simplifies complex data, enables generative tasks, and facilitates visualization or clustering.

Examples: In a face generation model, latent space might encode features like "smile" or "hair color," allowing new face synthesis.

Applications: It is used in generative models, anomaly detection, and data compression.
Challenges: Interpreting latent dimensions, ensuring meaningful representations, and avoiding collapse are key difficulties.

Industries: Entertainment, healthcare, and design leverage latent space for creative and analytical tasks.

Conclusion: Latent space in AI is a bridge to abstraction, unlocking compact yet powerful data representations.

Layer Normalization

Definition: Layer normalization is a technique in AI that normalizes the inputs across the features of a single layer in a neural network, stabilizing training by reducing internal covariate shift. It's a layer-wise standardization.

Key Components: It involves mean and variance computation per layer, scaling and shifting parameters, and application within training batches.
Benefits: It accelerates training, reduces sensitivity to initialization, and improves model stability.

Examples: In a transformer model, layer normalization might stabilize activations across word embeddings, enhancing language processing.

Applications: It is applied in deep learning, transformers, and recurrent neural networks.
Challenges: Increased computational overhead, potential over-normalization, and tuning parameters can complicate its use.

Industries: Technology, natural language processing, and gaming utilize layer normalization for robust models.

Conclusion: Layer normalization steadies AI training, ensuring consistent performance across complex architectures.

Layered Architecture

Definition: Layered architecture in AI refers to the organization of an AI system into hierarchical layers, each handling specific functions (e.g., input processing, feature extraction, decision-making), promoting modularity and scalability. It's a structured design approach.

Key Components: It includes input layers, hidden layers (e.g., in neural networks), output layers, and interlayer communication protocols.

Benefits: It simplifies design, enhances maintainability, and allows independent optimization of components.

Examples: A convolutional neural network might use layers to progressively extract edges, shapes, and objects from an image.

Applications: It is foundational in neural networks, software engineering, and robotic systems.

Challenges: Inter-layer dependencies, computational bottlenecks, and complexity in deep layers can limit efficiency.

Industries: Software development, robotics, and telecommunications employ layered architecture for organized systems.

Conclusion: Layered architecture in AI provides a blueprint for complexity, balancing structure with flexibility.

Learning Rate Schedules

Definition: Learning rate schedules in AI refer to strategies that dynamically adjust the learning rate during model training to optimize convergence, balancing speed and stability as the optimization process evolves. It's a timed adjustment of learning pace.

Key Components: It includes initial learning rate, decay functions (e.g., exponential, step), scheduling policies (e.g., cosine annealing), and training epochs.

Benefits: It improves training efficiency, prevents overshooting, and enhances final model accuracy.

Examples: A neural network might start with a high learning rate of 0.1, decaying it to 0.001 over epochs to refine weight updates.

Applications: It is used in deep learning, gradient descent optimization, and hyperparameter tuning.

Challenges: Choosing the right schedule, avoiding premature decay, and adapting to diverse datasets can be complex.

Industries: Technology, healthcare, and gaming leverage learning rate schedules for robust training.

Conclusion: Learning rate schedules guide AI optimization, ensuring a smooth journey from coarse to fine-tuned solutions.

Least Mean Squares (LMS) Algorithm

Definition: The Least Mean Squares (LMS) Algorithm is an adaptive filtering technique in AI that minimizes the mean squared error between desired and actual outputs by iteratively adjusting filter coefficients. It's a real-time error reducer.

Key Components: It involves input signals, desired outputs, error computation, step size (learning rate), and coefficient updates.

Benefits: It's computationally simple, adapts to changing conditions, and excels in real-time applications.

Examples: LMS might adjust a noise-canceling headphone's filter to suppress background hum based on live audio input.

Applications: It supports signal processing, adaptive control, and noise cancellation systems.

Challenges: Sensitivity to step size, slow convergence with noisy data, and stability issues can limit performance.

Industries: Telecommunications, audio engineering, and robotics use LMS for adaptive solutions.

Conclusion: The LMS Algorithm offers a lightweight, adaptive approach, tuning systems dynamically in fluctuating environments.

Least Squares Regression

Definition: Least Squares Regression in AI is a statistical method that fits a linear model to data by minimizing the sum of squared differences between observed and predicted values, estimating relationships between variables. It's a line-fitting classic.

Key Components: It includes dependent and independent variables, a linear equation, residual errors, and optimization via least squares.

Benefits: It provides interpretable results, handles simple relationships well, and serves as a baseline for regression tasks.

Examples: Predicting house prices based on square footage using a linear model fitted with least squares to historical data.

Applications: It is used in predictive modeling, trend analysis, and data fitting.

Challenges: Assumptions of linearity, sensitivity to outliers, and poor performance with complex data restrict its scope.

Industries: Finance, real estate, and research apply least squares regression for straightforward analysis.

Conclusion: Least Squares Regression remains a foundational tool in AI, delivering clarity for linear patterns despite limitations.

Levenshtein Distance

Definition: Levenshtein Distance in AI measures the minimum number of single-character edits (insertions, deletions, substitutions) needed to transform one string into another, quantifying text similarity or difference. It's a metric of string divergence.

Key Components: It involves two input strings, edit operations, a dynamic programming algorithm, and a distance score.

Benefits: It's precise, supports error-tolerant matching, and enables efficient text comparison.

Examples: Calculating the distance between "kitten" and "sitting" as 3 (substitute k→s, insert t, substitute e→i) for spell-checking.

Applications: It is used in spell checkers, DNA sequence alignment, and natural language processing.

Challenges: Computational cost with long strings, handling semantic differences, and scaling to large datasets are drawbacks.

Industries: Technology, bioinformatics, and search engines utilize Levenshtein Distance for text tasks.

Conclusion: Levenshtein Distance provides a robust measure of textual change, enhancing AI's text-handling precision.

Lexical Analysis

Definition: Lexical analysis in AI is the process of breaking down text into tokens (e.g., words, symbols) and analyzing their structure or meaning, serving as the first step in understanding language input. It's text dissection for machines.

Key Components: It includes tokenization, lexical rules, scanners or parsers, and output tokens with attributes (e.g., part of speech).

Benefits: It simplifies text processing, enables subsequent analysis, and supports language comprehension.

Examples: Analyzing "AI is fun" into tokens ["AI", "is", "fun"] with tags like noun, verb, adjective for grammar parsing.

Applications: It is foundational in compilers, natural language processing, and text preprocessing.

Challenges: Handling ambiguous tokens, multilingual texts, and domain-specific jargon can complicate analysis.

Industries: Software development, education, and media rely on lexical analysis for language tasks.

Conclusion: Lexical analysis lays the groundwork for AI's language mastery, turning raw text into structured understanding.

Lexical Semantics

Definition: Lexical semantics in AI studies the meaning of words and their relationships (e.g., synonyms, antonyms) within a language, enabling machines to interpret and generate contextually appropriate text. It's the science of word meaning.

Key Components: It involves word senses, semantic networks, embeddings (e.g., Word2Vec), and lexical databases like WordNet.

Benefits: It enhances language understanding, supports nuanced communication, and improves text generation quality.

Examples: An AI might recognize "bank" as a financial institution or river edge based on context like "money" or "water."

Applications: It is used in chatbots, semantic search, and machine translation.

Challenges: Resolving polysemy, capturing cultural nuances, and scaling to vast vocabularies are persistent issues.

Industries: Technology, customer service, and linguistics apply lexical semantics for smarter language AI.
Conclusion: Lexical semantics enriches AI's grasp of meaning, bridging words to context with depth and precision.

Linear Algebra in AI

Definition: Linear algebra in AI is the mathematical framework of vectors, matrices, and operations (e.g., multiplication, eigenvalues) that underpins data representation, transformations, and computations in machine learning models. It's AI's mathematical engine.

Key Components: It includes vectors, matrices, tensor operations, systems of equations, and decomposition techniques (e.g., SVD).

Benefits: It enables efficient data handling, supports scalable computations, and provides a foundation for model optimization.

Examples: Matrix multiplication in a neural network transforms input data through layers to predict outputs like image labels.

Applications: It drives neural networks, dimensionality reduction, and optimization algorithms.
Challenges: High-dimensional operations, computational cost, and numerical instability can pose difficulties.

Industries: Technology, finance, and scientific research harness linear algebra for AI power.
Conclusion: Linear algebra in AI is the invisible scaffold, enabling complex models with elegant, structured math.

Local Binary Patterns (LBP)

Definition: Local Binary Patterns (LBP) is a texture analysis technique in AI that describes the local structure of an image by comparing each pixel with its neighbors, encoding the result as a binary pattern. It's a compact way to capture spatial features.

Key Components: It includes a central pixel, neighboring pixels, binary thresholding, and a histogram of pattern frequencies.

Benefits: It's computationally efficient, robust to illumination changes, and effective for texture-based recognition.

Examples: LBP might analyze a facial image, generating patterns to identify expressions like "smile" based on texture variations.

Applications: It is used in facial recognition, texture classification, and image retrieval systems.

Challenges: Sensitivity to noise, limited scalability for complex images, and reduced effectiveness in non-textured data are drawbacks.

Industries: Security, medical imaging, and entertainment leverage LBP for visual analysis.

Conclusion: Local Binary Patterns provide a simple yet powerful tool for texture-driven AI, excelling in structured image tasks.

Local Search Algorithm

Definition: Local Search Algorithm in AI is an optimization technique that iteratively explores neighboring solutions to find a local optimum, refining an initial guess without guaranteeing a global best. It's a hill-climbing strategy.

Key Components: It involves an initial solution, a neighborhood definition, an objective function, and iteration until a stopping criterion.

Benefits: It's simple to implement, computationally light, and effective for problems with many local optima.

Examples: Optimizing a delivery route by swapping nearby stops to minimize travel time, stopping at a local best.

Applications: It supports scheduling, combinatorial optimization, and parameter tuning.

Challenges: Getting trapped in local optima, defining effective neighborhoods, and lack of global optimality are limitations.

Industries: Logistics, operations research, and game design utilize local search for practical solutions.

Conclusion: Local Search Algorithm offers a pragmatic path to optimization in AI, balancing efficiency with localized success.

Location-Based Services (LBS)

Definition: Location-Based Services (LBS) in AI use geographic data and AI techniques to provide personalized, context-aware services or information based on a user's location. It's spatially intelligent assistance.

Key Components: It includes GPS or sensor data, AI for pattern recognition, real-time processing, and user interfaces.

Benefits: It enhances user experience, delivers relevant insights, and supports real-time decision-making.

Examples: An LBS app might recommend nearby restaurants to a user based on their current GPS coordinates and past preferences.

Applications: It is used in navigation, targeted advertising, and emergency response systems.

Challenges: Privacy concerns, data accuracy, and handling indoor locations can hinder effectiveness.

Industries: Retail, transportation, and tourism rely on LBS for location-driven solutions.

Conclusion: Location-Based Services in AI merge space and intelligence, tailoring experiences to where users stand.

Logarithmic Loss (Log Loss)

Definition: Logarithmic Loss (Log Loss) in AI is a performance metric for classification models that measures the uncertainty of predicted probabilities against true labels, penalizing confident wrong predictions heavily. It's a logarithmic error gauge.

Key Components: It involves predicted probabilities, actual labels, logarithmic functions, and a cumulative loss score.

Benefits: It encourages well-calibrated probabilities, aligns with probabilistic models, and reflects prediction confidence.

Examples: In a spam classifier, log loss might penalize a 90% confident "not spam" prediction on a spam email more than 60%.

Applications: It is used in binary and multi-class classification, model evaluation, and ranking tasks.

Challenges: Sensitivity to extreme probabilities, handling imbalanced data, and interpretation complexity are concerns.

Industries: Technology, healthcare, and marketing use log loss for precise classification tuning.

Conclusion: Logarithmic Loss sharpens AI's probabilistic edge, rewarding accuracy and confidence in tandem.

Logic-Based Learning

Definition: Logic-Based Learning in AI involves training models using logical rules, constraints, or symbolic reasoning to derive knowledge, blending traditional logic with machine learning principles. It's reasoning-driven intelligence.

Key Components: It includes logical rules (e.g., if-then statements), knowledge bases, inference engines, and integration with data-driven methods.

Benefits: It offers explainability, leverages domain knowledge, and excels in structured problem-solving.

Examples: An AI might learn medical diagnosis rules like "if fever and cough, then flu," refining them with patient data.

Applications: It is applied in expert systems, knowledge representation, and automated reasoning.

Challenges: Scaling to large datasets, combining with statistical learning, and rule complexity can limit its reach.

Industries: Healthcare, legal, and education harness logic-based learning for interpretable AI.

Conclusion: Logic-Based Learning grounds AI in reasoning, providing clarity and structure in a data-driven world.

Logic Programming

Definition: Logic programming in AI is a paradigm where computation is expressed as logical statements and inference rules, enabling systems to derive conclusions from a knowledge base using formal logic. It's a declarative approach to problem-solving.

Key Components: It includes logical predicates, facts, rules (e.g., Horn clauses), and inference mechanisms like resolution.
Benefits: It offers transparency, supports automated reasoning, and excels in tasks requiring explicit knowledge representation.

Examples: A system written in Prolog might deduce "Socrates is mortal" from rules like "All men are mortal" and "Socrates is a man."

Applications: It is used in expert systems, natural language processing, and theorem proving.

Challenges: Limited scalability with large datasets, difficulty integrating with statistical methods, and complexity in rule design are hurdles.

Industries: Academia, legal tech, and healthcare apply logic programming for structured reasoning.

Conclusion: Logic programming provides a clear, rule-based foundation for AI, ideal for precise, explainable solutions.

Logical AI

Definition: Logical AI refers to the branch of artificial intelligence that employs formal logic to model reasoning, decision-making, and knowledge representation, aiming to mimic human deductive capabilities. It's logic-driven intelligence.

Key Components: It involves symbolic logic, knowledge bases, inference engines, and integration with learning systems.

Benefits: It ensures interpretable outcomes, leverages domain expertise, and supports complex reasoning tasks.

Examples: A Logical AI system might deduce a medical diagnosis by applying logical rules to symptoms and patient history.

Applications: It supports automated reasoning, planning systems, and diagnostic tools.

Challenges: Handling uncertainty, scaling to real-world complexity, and blending with data-driven AI are persistent issues.

Industries: Healthcare, robotics, and defense utilize Logical AI for reliable reasoning.

Conclusion: Logical AI anchors intelligence in formal reasoning, offering a structured path to decision-making clarity.

Logical Deduction

Definition: Logical deduction in AI is the process of deriving specific conclusions from general premises or rules using formal logic, ensuring that conclusions follow necessarily from given statements. It's a step-by-step truth finder.

Key Components: It includes premises, logical rules (e.g., modus ponens), a reasoning engine, and a deduced output.

Benefits: It guarantees correctness, provides explainable results, and excels in rule-based environments.

Examples: From "If it rains, the ground is wet" and "It is raining," an AI deduces "The ground is wet."

Applications: It is used in theorem proving, knowledge-based systems, and fault diagnosis.

Challenges: Limited flexibility with incomplete data, computational cost in large systems, and reliance on accurate premises are drawbacks.

Industries: Education, software verification, and engineering rely on logical deduction for precision.

Conclusion: Logical deduction in AI delivers certainty through rigorous inference, a cornerstone of rational AI systems.

Logical Neural Networks

Definition: Logical Neural Networks in AI combine the symbolic reasoning of logic with the pattern recognition of neural networks, embedding logical rules into trainable architectures for hybrid intelligence. It's a fusion of logic and learning.

Key Components: It includes neural layers, logical constraints, differentiable logic operations, and training via gradient descent.

Benefits: It merges interpretability with adaptability, leverages prior knowledge, and enhances reasoning in neural models.

Examples: A network might learn to classify animals while respecting logical rules like "if it flies, it's likely a bird."

Applications: It is applied in knowledge-augmented learning, decision support, and semantic analysis.

Challenges: Balancing logic and learning, computational complexity, and designing effective architectures are significant hurdles.

Industries: Healthcare, technology, and research explore Logical Neural Networks for advanced AI.

Conclusion: Logical Neural Networks bridge symbolic and statistical AI, offering a promising hybrid for smarter systems.

Logical Rules in AI

Definition: Logical rules in AI are explicit, formal statements (e.g., if-then conditions) that guide reasoning, decision-making, or behavior in intelligent systems, encoding knowledge in a structured format. It's rule-based intelligence.

Key Components: It involves rule syntax, knowledge bases, inference mechanisms, and rule application logic.

Benefits: It provides transparency, enforces consistency, and simplifies complex decision processes.

Examples: An AI traffic system might use "If red light, then stop" to control autonomous vehicle behavior.

Applications: It supports expert systems, robotic control, and business rule engines.

Challenges: Crafting comprehensive rules, handling exceptions, and integrating with data-driven methods can be difficult.

Industries: Manufacturing, finance, and legal sectors use logical rules for structured AI.

Conclusion: Logical rules in AI offer a clear framework for reasoning, grounding systems in explicit, actionable knowledge.

Logistic Activation Function

Definition: The logistic activation function in AI is a sigmoid-shaped mathematical function that maps input values to a range between 0 and 1, commonly used in neural networks to model probabilities or binary outcomes. It's a smooth threshold maker.

Key Components: It includes the logistic formula (1 / (1 + e^-x)), input values, output range, and gradient properties.

Benefits: It enables probabilistic interpretation, supports binary classification, and ensures smooth gradients for training.

Examples: In a spam detector, it might output 0.9 for "spam" likelihood based on email features.
Applications: It is used in neural networks, binary classifiers, and decision boundaries.

Challenges: Vanishing gradients in deep networks, limited range, and slower convergence can reduce effectiveness.

Industries: Technology, marketing, and security apply the logistic function for predictive tasks.

Conclusion: The logistic activation function shapes AI's decision space, offering a reliable tool for probability-driven models.

Logistic Regression

Definition: Logistic regression in AI is a statistical model that predicts the probability of a binary or categorical outcome by fitting a logistic function to input features, widely used for classification tasks. It's probability-based prediction.

Key Components: It involves input features, a logistic function, coefficients (weights), and a loss function like log loss.

Benefits: It's interpretable, computationally efficient, and effective for linearly separable data.

Examples: Predicting whether a customer will buy (1) or not (0) based on age and income using logistic regression.

Applications: It is used in classification, risk assessment, and predictive analytics.

Challenges: Struggles with non-linear relationships, feature interactions, and imbalanced datasets limit its scope.

Industries: Finance, healthcare, and e-commerce rely on logistic regression for decision-making.

Conclusion: Logistic regression provides a solid, interpretable baseline in AI, excelling in straightforward classification scenarios.

Log-Likelihood Function

Definition: The log-likelihood function in AI measures how well a statistical model explains observed data by calculating the logarithm of the likelihood, often maximized to estimate model parameters. It's a fit assessor.

Key Components: It includes observed data, a probability model, parameter estimates, and logarithmic transformation.

Benefits: It simplifies computation, supports parameter optimization, and aligns with probabilistic frameworks.

Examples: In a language model, log-likelihood might evaluate how well word probabilities match a given text corpus.

Applications: It is used in maximum likelihood estimation, model fitting, and statistical learning.

Challenges: Sensitivity to model assumptions, numerical instability, and handling small probabilities can complicate use.

Industries: Research, bioinformatics, and economics utilize log-likelihood for model evaluation.

Conclusion: The log-likelihood function in AI quantifies model-data harmony, driving precise parameter tuning with mathematical rigor.

Long Short-Term Memory (LSTM)

Definition: Long Short-Term Memory (LSTM) is a specialized recurrent neural network architecture in AI designed to model and remember long-term dependencies in sequential data by using memory cells and gates to regulate information flow. It's a memory-preserving powerhouse.

Key Components: It includes input gates, forget gates, output gates, memory cells, and a recurrent structure for sequence processing.

Benefits: It captures extended temporal relationships, mitigates vanishing gradient issues, and excels in sequential tasks.

Examples: An LSTM might predict the next word in a sentence like "The cat sat on the…" by recalling earlier context.

Applications: It is used in time series prediction, natural language processing, and speech recognition.

Challenges: High computational cost, complexity in tuning, and overfitting on small datasets are notable drawbacks.

Industries: Technology, healthcare, and media rely on LSTMs for sequential intelligence.

Conclusion: Long Short-Term Memory enhances AI's temporal awareness, making it a vital tool for sequence-driven tasks.

Long-Term Dependencies in AI

Definition: Long-Term Dependencies in AI refer to relationships or patterns in sequential data that span extended time intervals, requiring models to retain and utilize distant past information for accurate predictions. It's about connecting distant dots.

Key Components: It involves sequential datasets, memory mechanisms (e.g., LSTMs), attention models, and temporal modeling techniques.

Benefits: It enables context-rich predictions, improves sequence understanding, and supports complex task solving.

Examples: Predicting stock prices by recalling market trends from months ago demonstrates long-term dependency modeling.

Applications: It is used in language modeling, financial forecasting, and video analysis.

Challenges: Memory limitations, computational complexity, and vanishing gradients in traditional models are hurdles.

Industries: Finance, media, and robotics harness long-term dependencies for deep insights.

Conclusion: Long-Term Dependencies in AI unlock the power of historical context, essential for sophisticated sequential reasoning.

Long-Term Memory in AI

Definition: Long-Term Memory in AI is the capability of an artificial system to store and retrieve information over extended periods, mimicking human memory to enhance learning and decision-making. It's a digital retention system.

Key Components: It includes memory architectures (e.g., external databases, neural memory), storage mechanisms, and recall algorithms.

Benefits: It supports cumulative learning, enables knowledge reuse, and improves adaptability over time.

Examples: A chatbot might remember a user's preferences from past interactions to tailor future responses.

Applications: It is applied in conversational AI, robotics, and personalized recommendation systems.

Challenges: Efficient storage, retrieval accuracy, and managing memory growth are persistent issues.

Industries: Technology, customer service, and education utilize long-term memory for smarter AI.

Conclusion: Long-Term Memory in AI builds a foundation for persistent intelligence, bridging past and present for better outcomes.

Loss Function

Definition: A loss function in AI quantifies the difference between a model's predictions and the actual target values, guiding optimization by providing a measure to minimize during training. It's the error compass.

Key Components: It includes predicted outputs, ground truth, a mathematical formulation (e.g., MSE, cross-entropy), and optimization goals.

Benefits: It drives model improvement, aligns predictions with reality, and supports diverse task objectives.

Examples: Mean squared error might measure the gap between predicted and actual house prices in a regression model.

Applications: It is used in training neural networks, regression, and classification tasks.

Challenges: Choosing the right function, handling imbalanced data, and avoiding local minima can be tricky.

Industries: Finance, healthcare, and technology depend on loss functions for model tuning.

Conclusion: The loss function steers AI learning, a critical metric shaping accuracy and performance.

Lossless Compression

Definition: Lossless compression in AI reduces data size without losing any original information, allowing perfect reconstruction, often used to optimize storage or transmission in data-heavy applications. It's precision-preserving shrinkage.

Key Components: It involves compression algorithms (e.g., ZIP, FLAC), data encoding, and reversible transformations.

Benefits: It saves space, maintains data integrity, and supports efficient processing without quality loss.

Examples: Compressing a dataset of medical images with lossless methods ensures no diagnostic details are lost.

Applications: It is used in data storage, image processing, and audio archiving.

Challenges: Limited compression ratios, computational overhead, and slower processing compared to lossy methods are trade-offs.

Industries: Healthcare, media, and IT rely on lossless compression for fidelity.

Conclusion: Lossless compression in AI balances efficiency and exactness, safeguarding data in compact form.

Lossy Compression

Definition: Lossy compression in AI reduces data size by discarding non-essential information, accepting some quality loss for higher compression rates, commonly applied to multimedia data. It's efficiency-driven approximation.

Key Components: It includes compression algorithms (e.g., JPEG, MP3), loss criteria, and perceptual models to minimize noticeable impact.

Benefits: It achieves significant size reduction, speeds up transmission, and optimizes resource use.

Examples: Compressing a video file with lossy methods might slightly blur details but make it streamable online.

Applications: It is used in video streaming, audio playback, and image sharing.

Challenges: Balancing quality loss, avoiding perceptible artifacts, and irreversible data loss are concerns.

Industries: Entertainment, telecommunications, and social media use lossy compression for scalability.

Conclusion: Lossy compression trades precision for practicality, fueling AI's multimedia capabilities.

Low-Rank Matrix Factorization

Definition: Low-Rank Matrix Factorization in AI decomposes a large matrix into smaller, lower-rank matrices to approximate the original, reducing dimensionality while preserving key patterns. It's a compact data simplifier.

Key Components: It involves a target matrix, rank selection, factorization methods (e.g., SVD, NMF), and reconstruction error.

Benefits: It reduces computational load, uncovers latent structures, and enhances data efficiency.
Examples: Factorizing a user-movie rating matrix to recommend films based on latent preferences like genre affinity.

Applications: It is applied in recommendation systems, image compression, and data denoising.
Challenges: Choosing the right rank, loss of fine details, and computational cost in large matrices are issues.

Industries: E-commerce, media, and research utilize low-rank factorization for insights.

Conclusion: Low-Rank Matrix Factorization distills complexity in AI, offering a lean yet powerful data representation tool.

Lucid Dreaming in AI

Definition: Lucid Dreaming in AI refers to the conceptual exploration or simulation of lucid dreaming—where a dreamer is aware they are dreaming and may exert control—within artificial intelligence systems, often to study consciousness or enhance generative capabilities. It's an intersection of dream science and AI creativity.

Key Components: It involves generative models, neural simulations of awareness, sensory feedback loops, and frameworks inspired by human cognition or oneirology.

Benefits: It offers insights into machine consciousness, boosts creative output, and provides a sandbox for testing adaptive AI behaviors.

Examples: An AI system might generate a dream-like narrative, adjusting scenes based on simulated "awareness," such as shifting a forest into a cityscape mid-sequence.

Applications: It is explored in generative art, virtual reality experiences, and cognitive modeling research.

Challenges: Modeling subjective awareness, ensuring meaningful control, and distinguishing simulated lucidity from randomness are significant hurdles.

Industries: Entertainment, psychology, and AI research leverage this concept for innovation.

Conclusion: Lucid Dreaming in AI bridges human imagination and machine potential, pushing the boundaries of artificial creativity and awareness.

Ludic Intelligence

Definition: Ludic Intelligence in AI describes systems designed with a playful, game-like approach to problem-solving, learning, or interaction, inspired by the concept of "ludus" (play) to enhance engagement or adaptability. It's intelligence with a playful twist.

Key Components: It includes gamification elements, reward-based learning, interactive simulations, and exploratory algorithms.

Benefits: It increases user engagement, fosters creative solutions, and accelerates learning through trial and error in a safe environment.

Examples: An AI chatbot might adopt a playful tone, solving riddles with users to teach language skills, adapting responses based on their input.

Applications: It is used in educational tools, interactive AI design, and reinforcement learning environments.

Challenges: Balancing playfulness with utility, avoiding trivialization of serious tasks, and maintaining focus are key issues.

Industries: Education, gaming, and human-computer interaction adopt ludic intelligence for dynamic systems.

Conclusion: Ludic Intelligence infuses AI with play, making it a versatile tool for engagement and innovative learning.

Luminous Flux Estimation

Definition: Luminous Flux Estimation in AI is the process of predicting or calculating the total perceived light output (luminous flux) from a source or scene using computational models, often for lighting design or image analysis. It's quantifying visible light.

Key Components: It includes light source data, sensor inputs, photometric models, and AI-driven regression or simulation tools.

Benefits: It enables accurate lighting predictions, optimizes energy use, and enhances visual quality in rendered environments.

Examples: An AI might estimate luminous flux in a room from a photo, suggesting bulb placement for ideal illumination.

Applications: It is used in architectural design, virtual cinematography, and smart lighting systems.

Challenges: Accounting for environmental variables, sensor inaccuracies, and complex light interactions are difficulties.

Industries: Construction, film production, and IoT deploy luminous flux estimation for practical solutions.

Conclusion: Luminous Flux Estimation empowers AI to master light, blending physics and computation for real-world impact.

LunarLander Environment

Definition: LunarLander Environment in AI is a simulated task within the OpenAI Gym toolkit where an agent learns to land a spacecraft on a lunar surface, used to test reinforcement learning algorithms. It's a virtual proving ground.

Key Components: It features a 2D physics engine, state variables (e.g., position, velocity), action controls (e.g., thrusters), and a reward system.

Benefits: It provides a controlled setting for algorithm testing, teaches precision control, and offers measurable performance feedback.

Examples: An AI might adjust thruster power to softly land the craft, earning higher rewards for fuel efficiency and stability.

Applications: It is used in reinforcement learning research, robotics training, and educational simulations.

Challenges: Balancing exploration and exploitation, handling continuous action spaces, and optimizing rewards are key issues.

Industries: Aerospace, education, and AI development utilize LunarLander for experimentation.

Conclusion: LunarLander Environment is a benchmark in AI, refining control and decision-making in simulated challenges.

Lure Attack in AI

Definition: Lure Attack in AI is an adversarial technique where malicious inputs are crafted to mislead or "lure" an AI system into incorrect behavior or decisions, exploiting its vulnerabilities. It's a deceptive trap for models.

Key Components: It involves adversarial examples, perturbation design, target model analysis, and attack execution strategies.

Benefits: It exposes model weaknesses, drives robustness improvements, and informs security measures (from a research perspective).

Examples: An attacker might alter an image subtly to lure a classifier into misidentifying a stop sign as a yield sign.

Applications: It is studied in adversarial machine learning, cybersecurity, and model validation.

Challenges: Crafting effective lures, generalizing across models, and defending against them are complex tasks.

Industries: Cybersecurity, autonomous systems, and defense address lure attacks for safety.

Conclusion: Lure Attack in AI reveals vulnerabilities, pushing the field toward more resilient intelligent systems.

Lustre Model Checking

Definition: Lustre Model Checking in AI refers to the verification of systems designed in the Lustre programming language using formal methods to ensure correctness against specified properties, often for safety-critical applications. It's proving system reliability.

Key Components: It includes Lustre code, temporal logic specifications, model checkers (e.g., Lesar), and property validation.

Benefits: It guarantees system correctness, detects errors early, and ensures compliance with strict standards.

Examples: Checking a Lustre-designed flight control system to verify it never enters an unsafe state under any input sequence.

Applications: It is used in system verification, real-time control, and safety analysis.

Challenges: State-space explosion, specifying properties accurately, and computational demands are limitations.

Industries: Aerospace, automotive, and industrial automation apply Lustre model checking for assurance.

Conclusion: Lustre Model Checking fortifies AI-driven systems, ensuring they meet rigorous safety and reliability demands.

Lustre Programming Language

Definition
Lustre is a synchronous dataflow programming language used primarily for designing reactive and embedded systems. It is known for its ability to handle time-critical applications where determinism and concurrency are essential, such as in aerospace and automotive systems.

Examples
In the aerospace industry, Lustre is employed in the development of flight control systems where real-time response and safety are crucial. It is also used in industrial automation systems.

Benefits
Ensures predictability and determinism in time-sensitive systems.
Simplifies verification and validation of embedded systems.
Supports formal methods for reliability assurance.

Applications
Embedded system design
Real-time system modeling
Safety-critical software systems

Challenges
Steep learning curve for new programmers
Limited mainstream support compared to general-purpose languages
Complex debugging in large systems

Industries
Aerospace
Automotive
Industrial automation

Conclusion
Lustre is a specialized language ideal for safety-critical and real-time systems. Its dataflow-oriented structure provides a robust framework for dependable embedded software design.

Lyapunov Exponent

Definition
Lyapunov Exponent is a measure used in dynamic systems to quantify the rate at which nearby trajectories converge or diverge. It is used in AI to study the behavior of complex systems and determine the presence of chaos.

Examples
In training neural networks, a positive Lyapunov exponent might suggest chaotic behavior in gradient descent optimization, affecting convergence.

Benefits
Assists in analyzing system stability
Helps detect chaotic behavior in models
Improves model robustness through informed tuning

Applications
Neural network training dynamics
Stability analysis in reinforcement learning
Chaos theory in machine learning

Challenges
Computational complexity in high-dimensional systems
Sensitivity to initial conditions
Requires precise data for accurate computation

Industries
Finance
Weather modeling
Robotics

Conclusion
Lyapunov Exponent serves as a valuable analytical tool in AI, helping assess the dynamic stability of learning algorithms and their predictive consistency.

Lyapunov Function

Definition
A Lyapunov Function is a scalar function used to prove the stability of an equilibrium point in dynamic systems. In AI, it plays a key role in control theory and reinforcement learning.

Examples
Used in robotics to ensure a robot arm's trajectory remains stable during motion planning or task execution.

Benefits
Facilitates stability proof without solving differential equations
Improves safety in autonomous systems
Assists in controller design for stability assurance

Applications
Robotics and autonomous systems
Reinforcement learning
Control system design

Challenges
Difficult to construct for complex systems
Not unique; multiple functions may exist
May not cover all forms of instability

Industries
Autonomous vehicles
Industrial robotics
Aerospace control systems

Conclusion
Lyapunov Functions are essential in verifying system stability, making them a cornerstone concept in safe and reliable AI-driven control systems.

Lyapunov Stability in AI Systems

Definition
Lyapunov Stability in AI refers to ensuring that AI systems, particularly those modeled as dynamic systems, remain stable over time when subjected to small disturbances.

Examples
Applied in self-driving car software to maintain lane stability despite external disruptions like wind or road irregularities.

Benefits
Improves system reliability and safety
Ensures predictable system behavior
Supports resilient design against external noise

Applications
Autonomous driving

Industrial control systems
AI-based simulation environments

Challenges
Modeling real-world disturbances accurately
Proving global versus local stability
Integration with complex AI decision-making layers

Industries
Transportation
Manufacturing
Defense systems

Conclusion
Lyapunov Stability provides a foundational method for designing stable, predictable AI systems, essential for safety-critical applications.

Lynch Syndrome Screening in AI

Definition
Lynch Syndrome Screening in AI involves the use of machine learning and pattern recognition techniques to identify genetic markers or clinical indicators associated with Lynch Syndrome, a hereditary condition linked to colorectal and other cancers.

Examples
AI tools can analyze histopathological slides and genetic data to flag patients who may need further genetic counseling or testing.

Benefits
Enables early detection and intervention
Improves diagnostic accuracy
Reduces human error in complex genetic evaluations

Applications
Genomic data analysis
Pathology slide interpretation
Predictive screening in clinical settings

Challenges
Need for large, annotated datasets
Ethical concerns regarding genetic data usage
Model generalization across populations

Industries
Healthcare
Biotechnology
Medical diagnostics

Conclusion
AI-based screening for Lynch Syndrome enhances early diagnosis and preventive care, representing a promising step forward in precision medicine.

Lyric Generation in AI

Definition
Lyric Generation in AI refers to the use of natural language processing models to create song lyrics that mimic human creativity and linguistic style.

Examples
AI tools like GPT-based models generate lyrics for different genres by learning from large datasets of existing songs.

Benefits
Accelerates content creation
Supports creativity for artists and producers
Can generate customized lyrics for mood or themes

Applications
Music production
Entertainment content generation
Creative writing tools

Challenges
Lack of emotional depth in AI-generated lyrics
Risk of plagiarism or overfitting
Difficulty capturing cultural nuances

Industries
Music and entertainment
Marketing
Publishing

Conclusion
Lyric Generation in AI provides a powerful tool for artists and content creators, though its output is best used in collaboration with human creativity.

Lysate Pattern Recognition

Definition
Lysate Pattern Recognition uses AI to analyze patterns in cell lysates—fluid containing the contents of lysed cells—to identify biomarkers or disease signatures.

Examples
AI can detect protein signatures associated with diseases like cancer or autoimmune disorders from lysate analysis.

Benefits
Enables rapid diagnostics
Supports biomarker discovery
Increases throughput in lab analysis

Applications
Proteomics research
Clinical diagnostics
Pharmaceutical development

Challenges
Requires high-quality training data

Variability in biological samples
Integration with lab equipment

Industries
Biotechnology
Healthcare
Pharmaceuticals

Conclusion
AI-based lysate pattern recognition enhances diagnostic accuracy and efficiency, opening doors to personalized medicine and faster research outcomes.

Lysosomal Storage Disease Detection Using AI

Definition
This refers to the application of AI to detect lysosomal storage diseases (LSDs), a group of rare genetic disorders, through image recognition, genomics, or biochemical pattern analysis.

Examples
AI models trained on MRI images or enzyme level datasets can predict conditions like Gaucher or Pompe disease more accurately and rapidly.

Benefits
Enables early and non-invasive diagnosis
Supports rare disease research
Improves treatment outcomes with timely intervention

Applications
Genetic testing interpretation
Radiological image analysis
Predictive modeling for metabolic disorders

Challenges
Limited data due to disease rarity
High variance in clinical presentation
Need for interdisciplinary collaboration

Industries
Rare disease research
Genomics
Pediatric healthcare

Conclusion
AI has the potential to revolutionize the detection and understanding of lysosomal storage diseases by offering tools that are faster, more accurate, and less invasive than traditional methods.

Letter M

Machine Learning

Definition
Machine Learning is a branch of artificial intelligence where systems are designed to learn from data,

identify patterns, and make decisions with minimal human intervention. Instead of being explicitly programmed for each specific task, machine learning models improve their performance as they are exposed to more data, gradually enhancing their ability to make accurate predictions or classifications.

Key Components
Machine learning systems rely on several core components, including datasets for training and testing, algorithms that define how the learning process occurs, features that represent the input variables, models that interpret and make decisions, and evaluation metrics that assess the model's performance. These elements work together to enable learning, prediction, and continuous improvement.

Benefits
Machine learning enables automation of complex tasks, increases accuracy over manual methods, uncovers patterns in large and complicated datasets, enhances personalization for users, and adapts to new situations without extensive reprogramming. It accelerates decision-making processes and drives innovations across many sectors by offering predictive insights that were previously unattainable through traditional programming.

Examples
Spam filters in email systems that learn to block unwanted messages, recommendation engines suggesting products on shopping websites, self-driving cars interpreting road signs and obstacles, virtual assistants like Siri or Alexa understanding voice commands, and financial systems predicting stock market trends are all everyday examples of machine learning applications.

Applications
Machine learning is applied in areas such as image recognition, natural language processing, fraud detection, medical diagnostics, predictive maintenance, autonomous vehicles, speech recognition, and recommendation systems. Its ability to continuously refine outputs based on new data makes it ideal for environments requiring dynamic adaptation and predictive intelligence.

Industries
Machine learning is used extensively in healthcare for personalized treatment planning, in finance for algorithmic trading and credit scoring, in retail for customer behavior analysis and inventory management, in transportation for traffic prediction and autonomous driving, in agriculture for crop monitoring, and in cybersecurity for threat detection. It is also critical in entertainment, education, telecommunications, and manufacturing sectors.

Challenges
Challenges in machine learning include the need for large and high-quality datasets, the risk of biased models if the training data is not diverse, interpretability issues where complex models act like "black boxes," vulnerability to adversarial attacks, and high computational demands for training sophisticated models. Ethical concerns related to privacy, fairness, and accountability also pose significant obstacles to widespread adoption.

Summary
Machine learning is a transformative technology that enables systems to learn, adapt, and make informed decisions based on data. Its broad applications across industries have revolutionized the way problems are approached and solved. While it offers tremendous benefits in efficiency, accuracy, and innovation, it also brings forth important challenges related to data quality, transparency, and ethical deployment that must be carefully managed to ensure responsible use.

Machine Reasoning

Definition
Machine Reasoning is a branch of artificial intelligence that focuses on enabling machines to simulate

the human ability to draw logical conclusions from facts, rules, and known information. It involves formal logic systems, symbolic representations, and inference engines.

Examples
In medical diagnosis systems, machine reasoning can infer possible conditions based on symptoms and patient history using rules and ontologies.

Benefits
Enhances AI systems with human-like logical thinking
Supports decision-making in complex environments
Improves system transparency through traceable logic paths

Applications
Expert systems
Legal reasoning tools
Automated planning and scheduling
Knowledge representation

Challenges
Complexity in modeling human reasoning accurately
High computational requirements for inference engines
Scalability in large rule-based systems

Industries
Healthcare
Legal tech
Aerospace
Enterprise software

Conclusion
Machine reasoning adds depth to AI by enabling logic-driven decisions. It is essential for developing intelligent systems that need to justify and explain their conclusions.

Machine Translation

Definition
Machine Translation is the use of AI to automatically translate text or speech from one language to another. It employs statistical models, neural networks, and deep learning to understand linguistic context and grammar.

Examples
Google Translate and DeepL use neural machine translation (NMT) to provide real-time language translation for web content, emails, and documents.

Benefits
Breaks down language barriers in global communication
Improves accessibility for multilingual users
Accelerates content localization for businesses

Applications
Multilingual customer service
Content translation for websites and software
Real-time speech translation
International marketing

Challenges
Difficulty in capturing idioms and cultural nuances
Errors in grammar or context
Quality may vary by language pair

Industries
Travel and tourism
E-commerce
Education
Media and publishing

Conclusion
Machine translation is a transformative AI application that supports global connectivity, making communication faster, cheaper, and more inclusive across languages.

Macro AI

Definition
Macro AI refers to artificial intelligence systems designed to operate on a large-scale or macro level, addressing wide-ranging issues such as global logistics, economic forecasting, or climate modeling. These systems process high volumes of data across complex, interdependent variables.

Examples
AI platforms used for analyzing global trade flows or predicting economic indicators rely on macro AI techniques to manage scale and complexity.

Benefits
Enables data-driven insights for large-scale challenges
Improves strategic decision-making
Handles diverse and complex datasets

Applications
Climate change modeling
Global financial forecasting
Public health surveillance
International supply chain optimization

Challenges
High computational and infrastructure demands
Potential bias in large-scale data aggregation
Difficulty in real-time interpretation and adaptation

Industries
Government and policy
Finance
Climate science
Public health

Conclusion
Macro AI is critical for tackling large-scale societal and global challenges. Its ability to integrate complex data systems makes it a powerful tool for policymakers and industry leaders.

Magnetic Resonance Imaging (MRI) in AI

Definition
Magnetic Resonance Imaging (MRI) in AI involves the use of artificial intelligence algorithms to enhance the analysis, interpretation, and efficiency of MRI scans. AI aids in image reconstruction, diagnosis, and anomaly detection.

Examples
AI systems can detect brain tumors, spinal abnormalities, or organ anomalies from MRI scans with high accuracy and speed, often surpassing traditional image analysis.

Benefits
Reduces diagnostic errors
Accelerates image processing time
Improves early detection and treatment planning

Applications
Neurological diagnostics
Musculoskeletal imaging
Oncology
Cardiovascular assessments

Challenges
Requires high-quality annotated data
Integration into clinical workflows
Regulatory approval and ethical considerations

Industries
Healthcare
Radiology
Medical imaging
Clinical research

Conclusion
Integrating AI into MRI technologies enhances diagnostic precision and efficiency, providing significant benefits to medical professionals and patients alike.

Manifold Learning

Definition
Manifold Learning is a type of unsupervised learning technique used for dimensionality reduction. It assumes that high-dimensional data lie on low-dimensional manifolds and attempts to learn their structure for better visualization or analysis.

Examples
Used in visualizing complex datasets like facial recognition databases by reducing hundreds of dimensions to two or three while preserving spatial relationships.

Benefits
Improves data visualization
Reduces computational complexity
Preserves the intrinsic geometry of data

Applications
Image processing
Speech recognition

Data compression
Anomaly detection

Challenges
Sensitive to noise and outliers
Scalability issues with large datasets
Complex parameter tuning

Industries
Bioinformatics
Computer vision
Speech technology
Scientific research

Conclusion
Manifold learning is a powerful method for understanding high-dimensional data, providing essential insights in fields where dimensionality and complexity are key challenges.

Manual Feature Engineering

Definition
Manual Feature Engineering is the process of selecting, modifying, or creating input features by human experts to improve the performance of machine learning models. It requires domain knowledge to identify the most informative variables.

Examples
In credit scoring, domain experts may manually create features like credit utilization ratio or average monthly spending to improve predictive accuracy.

Benefits
Allows for greater control over model behavior
Improves model interpretability
Can significantly enhance performance when done correctly

Applications
Fraud detection
Medical diagnosis
Customer segmentation
Predictive maintenance

Challenges
Time-consuming and labor-intensive
Dependent on expert knowledge
Limited scalability for big data applications

Industries
Finance
Healthcare
Retail
Manufacturing

Conclusion
Manual feature engineering remains an important step in traditional machine learning pipelines, especially in domains where human insight enhances algorithmic decision-making.

Margin Classifier

Definition
A Margin Classifier is a type of classifier that seeks to separate data classes with the widest possible margin. Support Vector Machines (SVMs) are a well-known example, where the decision boundary maximizes the distance between classes.

Examples
Used in binary classification problems such as email spam detection, where maximizing the margin ensures better generalization to unseen data.

Benefits
Provides robust generalization to new data
Reduces overfitting
Mathematically well-founded approach

Applications
Text classification
Image recognition
Medical diagnosis
Stock market predictions

Challenges
Not suitable for noisy or overlapping data
Performance drops with large feature spaces without kernel methods
Requires careful tuning of parameters like regularization and kernel choice

Industries
Cybersecurity
Healthcare diagnostics
Finance
Natural language processing

Conclusion
Margin classifiers offer strong performance for well-structured classification tasks. They are valued for their precision, especially in applications requiring reliable binary decisions.

Markov Chain

Definition: A Markov Chain in AI is a mathematical model that describes a sequence of states where the probability of transitioning to the next state depends only on the current state, not the prior sequence, embodying the memoryless property. It's a framework for probabilistic sequences.

Key Components: It includes a set of states, transition probabilities, a transition matrix, and an initial state distribution.

Benefits: It simplifies modeling of sequential processes, enables efficient probability calculations, and supports predictive analysis.
Examples: Modeling weather patterns where the chance of rain tomorrow depends solely on today's weather, not last week's.

Applications: It is used in speech recognition, queueing theory, and financial modeling.

Challenges: Assumes independence from past states, struggles with complex dependencies, and requires accurate transition data.

Industries: Finance, telecommunications, and gaming rely on Markov Chains for sequence prediction.

Conclusion: Markov Chains provide a lean, effective tool for modeling transitions in AI, balancing simplicity with predictive power.

Markov Chain Monte Carlo (MCMC)

Definition: Markov Chain Monte Carlo (MCMC) in AI is a class of algorithms that samples from complex probability distributions using Markov Chains to approximate solutions, often for problems where direct computation is infeasible. It's a stochastic sampling method.

Key Components: It involves a target distribution, a Markov Chain, proposal distributions, and acceptance criteria (e.g., Metropolis-Hastings).

Benefits: It handles high-dimensional spaces, approximates intractable integrals, and enables Bayesian inference.

Examples: Estimating the parameters of a disease spread model by sampling from a posterior distribution of infection rates.

Applications: It is applied in Bayesian statistics, machine learning, and physics simulations.

Challenges: Slow convergence, tuning proposal distributions, and ensuring sample independence are key hurdles.

Industries: Healthcare, research, and data science use MCMC for probabilistic insights.

Conclusion: MCMC unlocks complex distributions in AI, offering a robust bridge to statistical exploration despite tuning demands.

Markov Decision Process (MDP)

Definition: A Markov Decision Process (MDP) in AI is a mathematical framework for modeling decision-making in environments where outcomes are partly random, using states, actions, and rewards to optimize sequential choices. It's a cornerstone of reinforcement learning.

Key Components: It includes states, actions, transition probabilities, reward functions, and a policy for decision-making.

Benefits: It formalizes decision optimization, supports dynamic planning, and adapts to uncertainty effectively.

Examples: An AI controlling a robot might use an MDP to decide whether to move forward or turn, maximizing a reward for reaching a goal.

Applications: It is used in robotics, game AI, and resource management.

Challenges: Defining accurate rewards, handling large state spaces, and computational complexity pose difficulties.

Industries: Robotics, gaming, and logistics leverage MDPs for strategic planning.

Conclusion: Markov Decision Processes in AI structure rational choice under uncertainty, driving intelligent, reward-driven behavior.

Mask R-CNN

Definition: Mask R-CNN is an advanced deep learning model in AI that extends Faster R-CNN to perform instance segmentation, detecting objects in images and generating pixel-level masks for each instance. It's a precision vision tool.

Key Components: It includes a backbone network (e.g., ResNet), region proposal network (RPN), bounding box regression, classification, and mask prediction branches.

Benefits: It provides detailed object segmentation, combines detection and masking, and achieves high accuracy in complex scenes.

Examples: In a street image, Mask R-CNN might detect cars and outline each one with a pixel mask, distinguishing overlapping vehicles.

Applications: It is used in object detection, semantic segmentation, and autonomous navigation.

Challenges: High computational demand, training data requirements, and handling small objects are significant hurdles.

Industries: Automotive, healthcare, and robotics leverage Mask R-CNN for visual precision.

Conclusion: Mask R-CNN elevates AI vision, delivering fine-grained segmentation for real-world understanding.

Masked Attention

Definition: Masked Attention in AI is a mechanism, often used in transformer models, that restricts attention to specific parts of the input sequence by masking irrelevant or future tokens, ensuring contextually appropriate focus. It's a selective focus tool.

Key Components: It involves attention scores, a mask matrix, softmax normalization, and sequence processing layers.

Benefits: It prevents information leakage, enhances sequential understanding, and improves model training efficiency.

Examples: In a language model predicting "The cat is…," masked attention ensures it only considers "The cat" and not "is" yet.

Applications: It is integral to natural language processing, autoregressive models, and time series analysis.

Challenges: Designing effective masks, managing computational overhead, and adapting to diverse tasks can be tricky.

Industries: Technology, media, and education utilize masked attention for language tasks.

Conclusion: Masked Attention sharpens AI's contextual lens, enabling precise, directional focus in sequential data.

Masked Language Model (MLM)

Definition: A Masked Language Model (MLM) in AI is a type of language model trained to predict masked (hidden) words in a sentence, learning bidirectional context to understand and generate text. It's a gap-filling language learner.

Key Components: It includes a training corpus, masked tokens, bidirectional context, and models like BERT with transformer architectures.

Benefits: It captures deep linguistic context, improves text comprehension, and supports versatile language tasks.

Examples: Given "The [MASK] jumped over the fence," an MLM might predict "dog" based on surrounding words.

Applications: It is used in text classification, question answering, and semantic analysis.

Challenges: High computational cost, reliance on large datasets, and handling rare words are limitations.
Industries: Technology, customer service, and research employ MLMs for advanced language processing.

Conclusion: Masked Language Models enhance AI's linguistic depth, mastering context through strategic omission.

Maximum Likelihood Estimation (MLE)

Definition: Maximum Likelihood Estimation (MLE) in AI is a statistical method that estimates model parameters by maximizing the likelihood of observing the given data, assuming a specific probability distribution. It's a best-fit parameter finder.

Key Components: It involves a likelihood function, observed data, a probability model, and optimization techniques (e.g., gradient ascent).

Benefits: It provides statistically sound estimates, aligns models with data, and supports probabilistic frameworks.

Examples: Estimating the mean and variance of a Gaussian model to fit a dataset of student test scores.

Applications: It is applied in statistical modeling, machine learning, and parameter tuning.

Challenges: Sensitivity to model assumptions, computational complexity, and local optima can affect accuracy.

Industries: Finance, healthcare, and research use MLE for data-driven estimation.

Conclusion: Maximum Likelihood Estimation in AI delivers precision in parameter fitting, grounding models in statistical rigor.

Mean Absolute Error (MAE)

Definition: Mean Absolute Error (MAE) is a metric used to evaluate the accuracy of regression models by calculating the average absolute difference between predicted values and actual values. It treats all errors equally without over-penalizing large deviations.

Key Characteristics: Absolute Difference: MAE computes absolute differences, ensuring positive and negative errors don't cancel each other out. Easy Interpretation: The result is expressed in the same units as the target variable.

Robustness: Less sensitive to outliers compared to squared error metrics.

Benefits: Simple and intuitive, allowing for straightforward interpretation of model performance. Suitable for applications where all errors, whether large or small, need to be treated equally.

Applications: Regression Models: Commonly used in predictive modeling tasks like finance, health care, and energy consumption. Time Series Forecasting: Evaluates models predicting continuous values over time, such as temperatures or sales.
Examples: If a house price prediction model forecasts $300,000 but the actual price is $280,000, the absolute error is $20,000. MAE averages such errors across all predictions.

Sources: Regression analysis textbooks, Scikit-learn tutorials, and online machine learning courses.

Conclusion: MAE is a fundamental metric for regression analysis, offering a clear and interpretable measure of a model's accuracy.

Matching Networks

Definition: Matching Networks in AI are a type of neural network designed for few-shot learning, classifying new data by comparing it to a small set of labeled examples using similarity metrics. It's a lean learning approach.

Key Components: It involves support sets (labeled examples), embedding functions, attention mechanisms, and distance-based classification.

Benefits: It excels with limited data, adapts quickly to new tasks, and reduces training overhead.

Examples: Classifying rare bird species from just a few images by matching features to known samples.

Applications: It is applied in few-shot learning, image recognition, and personalized recommendations.

Challenges: Dependence on quality support sets, scaling to diverse tasks, and computational cost can limit performance.

Industries: Technology, wildlife conservation, and e-commerce use Matching Networks for adaptive learning.

Conclusion: Matching Networks enable AI to learn efficiently from scarcity, offering flexibility in data-sparse scenarios.

Matrix Completion

Definition: Matrix Completion in AI is the process of filling in missing entries of a partially observed matrix by leveraging patterns or relationships within the data, often assuming low-rank structure. It's a data restoration technique.

Key Components: It includes an incomplete matrix, low-rank assumptions, optimization algorithms (e.g., SVD), and loss minimization.

Benefits: It recovers missing data, reduces noise, and enables analysis of incomplete datasets.

Examples: Completing a user-movie rating matrix to predict unseen preferences based on observed ratings.

Applications: It is used in recommendation systems, signal recovery, and data imputation.

Challenges: Handling noisy or sparse data, choosing the right rank, and computational complexity are key issues.

Industries: Entertainment, retail, and research rely on matrix completion for insights.

Conclusion: Matrix Completion in AI restores wholeness to fragmented data, unlocking value from partial observations.

Matrix Factorization

Definition:
Matrix Factorization in AI involves decomposing a large matrix into smaller component matrices, which when multiplied together approximate the original matrix. This technique simplifies data, reduces dimensionality, and uncovers hidden patterns.

Key Components:
Target matrix, factor matrices (usually low-rank), rank approximation, optimization techniques such as gradient descent.

Benefits:
Improves efficiency, reveals latent relationships in data, and lowers memory and computation requirements.

Examples:
Recommender systems use matrix factorization to identify patterns in user preferences—such as predicting that a user who likes superhero movies may also like sci-fi.

Applications:
Used in recommendation engines, feature selection, natural language processing, and data compression.

Challenges:
Choosing the right matrix rank, dealing with missing values, and managing high computational costs for large datasets.

Industries:
Retail, media, finance, and data science commonly use matrix factorization for predictive analysis.

Conclusion:
Matrix Factorization transforms complex data into meaningful insights by identifying and leveraging hidden structures.

Max-Pooling

Definition:
Max-Pooling is a downsampling technique used in convolutional neural networks (CNNs) to reduce the spatial dimensions of feature maps while retaining the most significant information.

Key Components:
Input feature map, pooling window size (e.g., 2x2), stride, and the maximum value selector within each region.

Benefits:
Reduces overfitting, decreases computational cost, and preserves dominant features.

Examples:
A CNN might use max-pooling to extract the brightest or most defined edges from an image for better recognition.

Applications:
Employed in computer vision tasks such as image classification, face detection, and object localization.

Challenges:
May discard useful subtleties in the data, and improper configuration can lead to information loss.

Industries:
Healthcare imaging, security systems, and mobile applications leverage max-pooling to process visuals efficiently.

Conclusion:
Max-Pooling condenses information in deep learning, focusing models on the most informative visual features.

Mean Absolute Error (MAE)

Definition:
Mean Absolute Error (MAE) measures the average absolute difference between predicted values and actual outcomes. It offers a straightforward and interpretable way to evaluate model performance.

Key Components:
Actual values, predicted values, absolute differences, and averaging process.

Benefits:
Easy to calculate, robust against outliers, and interpretable in the same unit as the target variable.

Examples:
A weather prediction model may use MAE to calculate an average daily temperature forecast error in degrees.

Applications:
Widely used in forecasting, regression analysis, and time series modeling.

Challenges:
Does not indicate whether predictions are over or under the target, and underweights large errors.

Industries:
Climate modeling, financial forecasting, logistics, and supply chain management.

Conclusion:
MAE provides a clear snapshot of model accuracy, ideal for applications needing transparency and simplicity.

Mean Average Precision (MAP)

Definition:
Mean Average Precision (MAP) is a performance metric used to evaluate ranking algorithms by averaging precision values across multiple queries or data points.

Key Components:
Ranked results, relevance labels, precision at each rank level, and mean calculation across queries.

Benefits:
Balances precision and recall, handles multiple queries, and supports ranking optimization.

Examples:
A search engine might use MAP to assess how effectively it ranks relevant documents at the top for user queries.

Applications:
Used in search systems, recommender engines, object detection, and document retrieval.

Challenges:
Computational complexity, reliance on relevance judgments, and difficulty handling tied rankings.

Industries:
E-commerce, content platforms, and academic databases benefit from MAP-driven ranking systems.

Conclusion:
MAP enhances evaluation of ranking algorithms, ensuring user-relevant results appear where they matter most.

Mean Field Theory (MFT)

Definition:
Mean Field Theory (MFT) simplifies complex AI models by approximating the effect of all other components on any single part with a general average, or "mean field."

Key Components:
Model assumptions, mean field approximation, optimization steps, and variable interactions.

Benefits:
Reduces model complexity, enables tractable computation, and supports inference in high-dimensional spaces.

Examples:
Used in deep learning to approximate collective neuron behaviors in neural networks without computing every individual interaction.

Applications:
Probabilistic modeling, physics-based AI, and variational inference in machine learning.

Challenges:
May oversimplify interactions, lead to convergence issues, or inaccurately reflect system dynamics.

Industries:
Applied in scientific research, technology R&D, and neuroscience modeling.

Conclusion:
MFT offers an efficient way to approximate complex AI systems, trading exactness for scalability.

Mean Shift Clustering

Definition:
Mean Shift Clustering is an iterative clustering technique that shifts data points toward the mean of their local neighborhood, revealing clusters based on density.

Key Components:
Kernel function, bandwidth parameter, mean update mechanism, and convergence criteria.

Benefits:
Requires no predefined number of clusters, adapts to data shape, and identifies dense regions naturally.

Examples:
Used in marketing to segment customers based on purchase behavior without assuming a set number of buyer groups.

Applications:
Data mining, image segmentation, and computer vision.

Challenges:
Computationally heavy, sensitive to bandwidth selection, and less efficient with sparse or high-dimensional data.

Industries:
Retail, AI research, and medical imaging.

Conclusion:
Mean Shift Clustering flexibly groups data by following natural density flows, offering dynamic insight without hard assumptions.

Mean Squared Error (MSE)

Definition:
Mean Squared Error (MSE) measures the average squared difference between predicted and true values, giving higher weight to larger errors in AI models.

Key Components:
Prediction residuals, squaring function, and mean computation.

Benefits:
Amplifies large prediction errors, aligns well with optimization algorithms, and supports gradient learning.

Examples:
In predicting housing prices, MSE can highlight costly model mistakes by penalizing large differences in predicted versus actual prices.

Applications:
Regression tasks, model training, and predictive analytics.

Challenges:
Overly sensitive to outliers, and results are not in the same unit as the target variable, reducing interpretability.

Industries:
Real estate, finance, and machine learning model development.

Conclusion:
MSE reinforces precision by heavily penalizing large errors, making it a foundational metric in AI modeling.

Mechanistic Model

Definition:
A Mechanistic Model in AI is based on explicit scientific or physical rules that describe the internal behavior of a system, focusing on causality rather than fitting data.

Key Components:
Equations of motion, system variables, constraints, and known relationships.

Benefits:
Transparent logic, grounded in real-world science, and suitable for simulation and control.

Examples:
Predicting turbine performance using fluid dynamics equations instead of purely statistical patterns.

Applications:
Engineering systems, biological modeling, and predictive control.

Challenges:
Limited adaptability, may require deep domain expertise, and often difficult to scale.

Industries:
Used in aerospace, medicine, energy systems, and environmental modeling.

Conclusion:
Mechanistic Models prioritize understanding and interpretability, excelling where theoretical knowledge is strong.

Median Absolute Deviation (MAD)

Definition:
Median Absolute Deviation (MAD) is a robust statistical tool that measures the spread of data by calculating the median of the absolute deviations from the median.

Key Components:
Median, absolute deviation computation, and aggregation.

Benefits:
Resistant to outliers, easy to understand, and ideal for skewed data.

Examples:
Analyzing a sales dataset to find a reliable range of revenue that isn't distorted by a few extreme transactions.

Applications:
Used in anomaly detection, robust statistics, and preprocessing pipelines.

Challenges:
Less effective for subtle trends, may miss patterns hidden in the noise, and computationally slower on large datasets.

Industries:
Finance, manufacturing, and quality control systems.

Conclusion:
MAD equips AI with a stable measure of variability, delivering consistency in noisy and outlier-prone environments.

Medical AI

Definition: Medical AI refers to the use of artificial intelligence in healthcare to assist with diagnosis, treatment planning, patient care, and medical research. These systems use data and knowledge to make intelligent medical decisions.

Key Components: Medical datasets, machine learning algorithms, expert input from healthcare professionals, and integration with clinical environments.

Benefits: Improves diagnostic precision, tailors treatment plans, streamlines operations, and accelerates medical breakthroughs.

Examples: An AI model may analyze radiology scans to identify tumors earlier than traditional methods.

Applications: Diagnostic tools, drug development, medical imaging, and predictive healthcare models.

Challenges: Patient privacy concerns, complex regulations, and earning the trust of medical professionals.

Industries: Healthcare, biotechnology, pharmaceutical research, and medical technology companies.

Conclusion: Medical AI enhances healthcare by combining human insight with machine intelligence, driving better outcomes and innovation.

Memory Augmentation

Definition: Memory Augmentation in AI enhances a system's ability to remember and retrieve information over time, allowing it to perform tasks with better historical context and continuity.

Key Components: Memory storage units, access protocols, external databases, and integration with learning mechanisms.

Benefits: Improves long-term task performance, supports personalized interactions, and boosts adaptability.

Examples: An AI assistant remembering a user's previous commands to offer more relevant suggestions.

Applications: Virtual assistants, personalized learning platforms, and robotic systems.

Challenges: Managing memory efficiency, quick access to stored data, and avoiding unnecessary memory accumulation.

Industries: Customer service, education, healthcare, and technology platforms.

Conclusion: Memory Augmentation allows AI to grow more intelligent over time by learning from past experiences and behaviors.

Memory-Augmented Neural Networks (MANN)

Definition: Memory-Augmented Neural Networks are advanced AI models that combine traditional neural networks with external memory, enabling them to solve complex tasks by storing and retrieving information as needed.

Key Components: Neural processing layers, external memory banks, read/write controllers, and attention mechanisms.

Benefits: Facilitates reasoning over sequences, enhances one-shot learning, and enables dynamic memory updates.

Examples: A MANN could solve a multi-part logic problem by storing earlier results for use in later steps.

Applications: Algorithmic learning, intelligent tutoring systems, and adaptive AI models.

Challenges: Designing stable models, managing memory usage, and ensuring computational efficiency.

Industries: AI research, education technology, and advanced analytics sectors.

Conclusion: MANNs elevate AI's capacity for reasoning by merging deep learning with flexible memory operations.

Memory-Based Learning

Definition: Memory-Based Learning is an approach in AI where systems make decisions by comparing new inputs to stored examples, rather than building a generalized model.

Key Components: Stored training examples, similarity measurement tools, retrieval processes, and prediction logic.

Benefits: Quick to adapt to new data, transparent decision-making, and effective with diverse examples.

Examples: Classifying whether a message is spam based on past labeled messages stored in memory.

Applications: Recommendation systems, classification tasks, and user behavior analysis.

Challenges: Can be memory-intensive, slower during predictions, and sensitive to irrelevant data.

Industries: Retail, cybersecurity, customer service, and personalization engines.

Conclusion: Memory-Based Learning helps AI learn through past encounters, offering a flexible and interpretable learning method.

Memory Networks

Definition: Memory Networks are AI models that integrate structured memory with learning mechanisms, enabling systems to recall and apply past information to answer questions or make decisions.

Key Components: Input processing unit, memory bank, attention mechanism, and output generation module.

Benefits: Enables deeper reasoning, manages complex sequences, and supports question-answering tasks with context.

Examples: Answering a user's question based on earlier parts of a conversation stored in memory.

Applications: Conversational AI, reading comprehension, and knowledge-based reasoning.

Challenges: Complex memory management, risk of irrelevant recall, and computational demand.

Industries: Tech companies, online education, virtual support systems, and language technology firms.

Conclusion: Memory Networks bring contextual intelligence to AI, helping systems use stored knowledge for improved interaction.

Memristor

Definition: A Memristor is an electrical component that retains memory of its previous resistance state, offering potential for AI systems that require energy-efficient, brain-like hardware design.

Key Components: Variable resistance, non-volatile memory, nanoscale materials, and adaptable circuitry.

Benefits: Consumes less power, simulates synaptic function, and allows for compact AI hardware implementations.

Examples: Used in neuromorphic chips to simulate how the brain processes and stores information.

Applications: Brain-inspired computing, AI hardware accelerators, and analog signal processing.

Challenges: Difficult to manufacture at scale, stability issues over time, and compatibility with current electronics.

Industries: Semiconductors, robotics, neural engineering, and advanced computing.

Conclusion: Memristors are a key innovation in hardware AI, allowing systems to think more like the human brain through efficient memory integration.

Meta-Learning

Definition: Meta-Learning, often referred to as "learning to learn," is an area of artificial intelligence that focuses on building models capable of rapidly adapting to new tasks by leveraging knowledge acquired from previous tasks.

Key Components: Meta-learners, task sampling methods, inner and outer learning loops, and strategies for knowledge transfer.

Benefits: Enables fast learning on minimal data, improves adaptability to unseen problems, and supports efficient model optimization.

Examples: An AI trained on various object classification problems can quickly learn to identify new object types with only a handful of examples.

Applications: Few-shot and zero-shot learning, adaptive control, hyperparameter tuning, and meta-reinforcement learning.

Challenges: High computational cost, balancing generality with specificity, and creating robust benchmarks for performance evaluation.

Industries: Meta-learning is valuable in sectors such as autonomous systems, healthcare diagnostics, educational technology, and AI research.

Conclusion: Meta-Learning equips AI systems with flexibility and efficiency, allowing them to adapt quickly and perform well even with limited new data.

Microprocessor

Definition:

A microprocessor is an integrated electronic circuit that functions as the central processing unit (CPU) within a computer or electronic system, responsible for executing instructions, performing calculations, managing data flow, and controlling various tasks by processing binary information.

Key Components: Essential components of a microprocessor include an arithmetic logic unit (ALU) for performing mathematical and logical operations, control unit to interpret and execute instructions, registers for temporary data storage, instruction decoders, internal buses for data transfer, clock systems to synchronize operations, and cache memory for quick data retrieval.

Benefits: Microprocessors enhance computational speed and efficiency, significantly reduce system size and power consumption, enable advanced automation, improve reliability, lower manufacturing costs through integration, and support flexibility through programmable instruction execution.

Examples: Examples include Intel's Core processors (used in PCs and laptops), AMD Ryzen processors (desktop and gaming systems), ARM processors (smartphones and tablets), and embedded microprocessors (used in automotive control systems, digital cameras, and household appliances).

Applications: Microprocessors are widely applied in personal computing devices, mobile technology, automotive engine control systems, robotics, consumer electronics, medical devices, home automation, communication equipment, aerospace systems, industrial automation, and Internet of Things (IoT) devices.

Industries: Industries extensively utilizing microprocessors include computing and information technology, telecommunications, consumer electronics, automotive manufacturing, aerospace and defense, healthcare, industrial automation, robotics, energy management, and home appliances manufacturing.

Summary: A microprocessor is a versatile, powerful integrated circuit that serves as the core processing unit in electronic systems, driving technological innovation across diverse fields by enabling compact, efficient, reliable, and cost-effective computing capabilities.

Model (AI)

Definition
A model in artificial intelligence is a trained system that can understand data, learn patterns, and make predictions or decisions. It is created through a process called training, where the model is exposed to large sets of data so it can recognize relationships and make sense of new information. Once trained, the AI model becomes the core engine that drives tasks such as language processing, image recognition, recommendation systems, or autonomous navigation. Essentially, the model is the "intelligent" part of an AI system that knows how to perform specific functions based on what it has learned.

Key Components
An AI model includes several important parts. The first is the training data, which helps the model learn patterns and rules. The second is the learning algorithm, which updates the model based on feedback and error correction. Third, the model contains weights and parameters — these are the internal settings that adjust as the model learns. Together, these components allow the model to take input, process it based on what it has learned, and produce a useful output.

Benefits
AI models can perform tasks with speed and accuracy far beyond human capability. They can work 24/7 without fatigue, scale to process millions of data points, and continue improving over time through updates or retraining. AI models reduce manual labor, enhance decision-making, and open up new opportunities in automation, personalization, and real-time analysis.

Example
A simple example of an AI model is a spam filter in your email. It was trained using thousands of examples of spam and non-spam messages. Now, every time you get a new email, the model uses what it learned to decide whether to send that email to your inbox or your spam folder. Another example is a language model like ChatGPT, which has been trained on massive amounts of text so it can answer questions, write stories, or summarize articles.

Application
AI models are used in a wide variety of applications. They power virtual assistants like Siri and Alexa, help detect fraud in banking systems, recommend products in online stores, translate languages in real time, and assist doctors with medical diagnosis. In machine learning workflows, models are used to classify data, make predictions, recognize patterns, and automate repetitive processes.

Industries
AI models are transforming industries such as healthcare, where they help with diagnosis and treatment planning; finance, where they monitor transactions for fraud; education, where they provide

personalized learning experiences; and transportation, where they assist in autonomous driving and route optimization. In marketing, entertainment, agriculture, and cybersecurity, AI models are becoming essential tools for innovation and productivity.

Challenges
Despite their power, AI models come with challenges. They require large amounts of clean, high-quality data to train effectively. If the training data is biased or incomplete, the model may produce inaccurate or unfair results. Models can also be complex to interpret, making it difficult to understand how they make certain decisions. Additionally, maintaining and updating AI models requires ongoing resources, technical skills, and infrastructure. There is also a risk of overfitting, where a model performs well on training data but poorly on real-world data.

Summary
A model in AI is the heart of any intelligent system. It learns from data, makes decisions, and powers the tools that people use every day — from voice assistants to self-driving cars. As technology advances, AI models are becoming more powerful and capable of handling increasingly complex tasks. Understanding how models work is key to unlocking the full potential of artificial intelligence across every field.

Model-Agnostic Meta-Learning (MAML)

Definition: Model-Agnostic Meta-Learning (MAML) in AI is a meta-learning framework that trains models to adapt quickly to new tasks with few examples, agnostic to the specific model architecture. It's a universal fast-learner.

Key Components: It involves a base model, task distribution, gradient-based adaptation, and meta-optimization objectives.

Benefits: It enables rapid task adaptation, works across model types, and reduces training time for new problems.

Examples: MAML might train a model to recognize rare diseases from a few medical images after learning common ones.

Applications: It is used in few-shot learning, robotics, and personalized AI systems.

Challenges: High computational demands, tuning adaptation steps, and task selection are significant barriers.

Industries: Healthcare, robotics, and technology adopt MAML for versatile learning.

Conclusion: MAML in AI offers a flexible path to rapid adaptation, broadening the scope of meta-learning applications.

Model-Based Reinforcement Learning

Definition: Model-Based Reinforcement Learning in AI is a method where an agent learns a model of the environment's dynamics and uses it to plan actions, optimizing rewards through simulation rather than trial-and-error alone. It's planning with a virtual world.

Key Components: It includes an environment model, reward function, policy optimization, and simulation-based planning.

Benefits: It reduces real-world interactions, improves sample efficiency, and enhances decision-making precision.

Examples: A robot might simulate moving through a maze, learning optimal paths without physically testing every route.

Applications: It is applied in robotics, game AI, and autonomous systems.

Challenges: Model inaccuracy, computational complexity, and adapting to dynamic environments are key issues.

Industries: Robotics, gaming, and automotive use model-based RL for efficient learning.

Conclusion: Model-Based Reinforcement Learning boosts AI efficiency, leveraging foresight

for smarter actions.

Model Compression

Definition: Model Compression in AI reduces the size or complexity of a trained model while preserving performance, making it more efficient for deployment on resource-constrained devices. It's slimming down AI.

Key Components: It involves pruning, quantization, knowledge distillation, and low-rank approximations.

Benefits: It lowers memory usage, speeds up inference, and enables deployment on edge devices.

Examples: Compressing a large image classifier to run on a smartphone without sacrificing accuracy in object detection.

Applications: It is used in mobile AI, IoT, and real-time systems.

Challenges: Balancing size reduction with accuracy, retraining needs, and technique compatibility are concerns.

Industries: Technology, IoT, and telecommunications apply model compression for practicality.

Conclusion: Model Compression in AI makes intelligence leaner, fitting powerful models into smaller spaces.

Model Drift

Definition: Model Drift in AI occurs when a model's performance degrades over time due to changes in the underlying data distribution, rendering its predictions less accurate. It's a shift in relevance.

Key Components: It includes training data, live data, drift detection methods (e.g., statistical tests), and retraining strategies.

Benefits: Recognizing drift enables timely updates, maintains model reliability, and adapts to evolving environments.

Examples: A fraud detection model might fail as new fraud tactics emerge, requiring retraining to catch shifting patterns.

Applications: It is monitored in predictive analytics, fraud detection, and dynamic systems.

Challenges: Detecting subtle drift, frequent retraining costs, and data availability can complicate management.

Industries: Finance, cybersecurity, and retail address model drift for sustained accuracy.

Conclusion: Model Drift in AI highlights the need for vigilance, ensuring models stay aligned with changing realities.

Molecular Dynamic Simulations

Definition: Molecular Dynamic Simulations in AI use computational models to simulate the physical movements of atoms and molecules over time, enhanced by AI to predict behaviors or optimize parameters. It's virtual molecular motion.

Key Components: It involves force fields, molecular trajectories, time-step integration, and AI-driven analysis or acceleration.

Benefits: It reveals molecular insights, reduces experimental costs, and accelerates scientific discovery.

Examples: Simulating protein folding with AI to predict stable configurations for drug design.

Applications: It is used in drug discovery, material science, and biochemical research.

Challenges: Computational intensity, model accuracy, and scaling to large systems are significant barriers.

Industries: Pharmaceuticals, chemistry, and materials engineering leverage these simulations for innovation.

Conclusion: Molecular Dynamic Simulations in AI blend physics and intelligence, unlocking microscopic worlds for practical advances.

Multilayer Perceptron (MLP)

Definition:

A Multilayer Perceptron (MLP) is a class of feedforward artificial neural networks (ANN) that consists of at least three layers of nodes: an input layer, one or more hidden layers, and an output layer. Each node in the network represents a neuron, and MLPs are used to solve complex tasks like classification and regression.
Key Characteristics: The feedforward structure ensures data flows in one direction, from input to output, without looping back. Non-linear activation functions like ReLU or Sigmoid model complex patterns.
Benefits: MLPs offer powerful function approximation, modeling highly complex relationships between inputs and outputs. They are versatile, suitable for tasks like image recognition, speech recognition, and machine translation.
Applications: Speech recognition uses MLPs to classify phonemes in audio signals for speech-to-text systems. Financial modeling predicts stock prices based on historical data.
Examples: MLPs are used in digit recognition for the MNIST dataset, classifying handwritten numbers.
Sources: Textbooks like "Neural Networks and Deep Learning" by Michael Nielsen.
Conclusion: MLPs are foundational neural networks that have paved the way for more complex architectures, excelling in tasks that require non-linear data modeling.

Multi-Agent System (MAS)

Definition: A Multi-Agent System (MAS) in AI is a framework where multiple autonomous agents interact or collaborate within a shared environment to achieve individual or collective goals, often modeled with decentralized decision-making. It's a society of intelligent entities.

Key Components: It includes agents, an environment, communication protocols, coordination strategies, and goal definitions.

Benefits: It enables distributed problem-solving, enhances scalability, and mimics real-world interactions effectively.

Examples: A swarm of drones coordinating to map a disaster area, each adjusting its path based on others' positions.

Applications: It is used in robotics, traffic management, and distributed computing.

Challenges: Agent coordination, conflict resolution, and communication overhead can complicate system design.

Industries: Robotics, transportation, and gaming leverage MAS for collaborative intelligence.

Conclusion: Multi-Agent Systems in AI harness collective action, offering a dynamic approach to complex, distributed tasks.

Note: "Multi-Agent System (MAS)" appeared twice in your list; I've included it once with a comprehensive response.

Multimodal AI

Definition: Multimodal AI refers to artificial intelligence systems that process and integrate data from multiple modalities—such as text, images, audio, or sensor inputs—to perform tasks or make decisions. It's a fusion of sensory intelligence.

Key Components: It involves modality-specific models, data fusion techniques, cross-modal learning, and unified output generation.

Benefits: It provides richer understanding, improves task accuracy, and mirrors human multi-sensory cognition.

Examples: An AI analyzing a video by combining visual frames (e.g., a dog running) with audio (barking) to identify the scene.

Applications: It is applied in autonomous vehicles, virtual assistants, and healthcare diagnostics.

Challenges: Data alignment, modality imbalance, and computational complexity pose significant hurdles.

Industries: Technology, healthcare, and entertainment utilize multimodal AI for holistic insights.

Conclusion: Multimodal AI in AI bridges diverse data streams, enhancing perception beyond single-mode limitations.

Multinomial Naive Bayes

Definition: Multinomial Naive Bayes in AI is a probabilistic classification algorithm that applies the Naive Bayes theorem to discrete data, particularly suited for problems with multiple classes and frequency-based features, like text. It's a simple yet effective classifier.

Key Components: It includes feature counts, class probabilities, conditional independence assumptions, and likelihood estimation.

Benefits: It's computationally efficient, handles multi-class problems well, and performs robustly with sparse data.

Examples: Classifying emails as "spam," "promo," or "normal" based on word frequencies like "free" or "urgent."

Applications: It is used in text classification, sentiment analysis, and document categorization.

Challenges: Assumption of feature independence, sensitivity to zero counts, and limited expressiveness are drawbacks.

Industries: Technology, marketing, and media rely on Multinomial Naive Bayes for text tasks.

Conclusion: Multinomial Naive Bayes offers AI a lightweight, reliable tool for multi-class prediction, excelling in simplicity.

Multiple Kernel Learning (MKL)

Definition: Multiple Kernel Learning (MKL) in AI is a machine learning approach that combines multiple kernel functions to optimize a model's performance, leveraging diverse data representations for improved classification or regression. It's a kernel-blending strategy.

Key Components: It involves kernel functions (e.g., linear, RBF), a combination mechanism, optimization algorithms, and a base learner like SVM.

Benefits: It enhances flexibility, captures varied data patterns, and improves predictive accuracy across domains.

Examples: Combining kernels to classify images by texture and shape, improving recognition of objects like cats versus dogs.

Applications: It is applied in bioinformatics, image recognition, and time series analysis.

Challenges: Computational cost, kernel selection, and overfitting risks can hinder effectiveness.

Industries: Healthcare, computer vision, and finance use MKL for robust modeling.

Conclusion: Multiple Kernel Learning in AI fuses diverse perspectives, refining models with tailored kernel synergy.

Myelination in Neural Networks

Definition: Myelination in Neural Networks is a conceptual analogy in AI where artificial neural networks are designed or optimized to mimic the biological process of myelination—insulating connections to speed up signal transmission—increasing efficiency. It's a bio-inspired optimization.

Key Components: It includes network architecture, connection weighting, pruning or strengthening pathways, and efficiency-focused training.

Benefits: It boosts computational speed, reduces energy use, and enhances network performance.

Examples: A neural net might prioritize frequently used paths for faster image classification, akin to myelin speeding nerve signals.

Applications: It is explored in deep learning optimization, neuromorphic computing, and energy-efficient AI.

Challenges: Implementing biological analogies, balancing efficiency with accuracy, and scalability are key issues.

Industries: Technology, neuroscience, and energy apply myelination-inspired concepts.

Conclusion: Myelination in Neural Networks in AI draws from biology, streamlining artificial intelligence with natural efficiency.

Myopic Reinforcement Learning

Definition: Myopic Reinforcement Learning in AI is a reinforcement learning approach where the agent prioritizes immediate rewards over long-term cumulative gains, often due to limited planning or horizon constraints. It's short-term reward chasing.

Key Components: It includes a state space, action set, immediate reward function, and a policy with restricted lookahead.

Benefits: It reduces computational needs, simplifies decision-making, and excels in urgent, dynamic settings.

Examples: A robot vacuum might choose the nearest dirt pile to clean, ignoring a more efficient long-term path.

Applications: It is applied in real-time control, resource-limited robotics, and rapid response systems.

Challenges: Suboptimal long-term performance, reward design complexity, and balancing immediacy with strategy are concerns.

Industries: Robotics, IoT, and emergency response use myopic RL for quick action.

Conclusion: Myopic Reinforcement Learning in AI trades depth for speed, fitting fast-paced tasks with a focus on the now.

Myopic Learning

Definition: Myopic Learning in AI refers to a learning approach where the system focuses on optimizing short-term outcomes or immediate feedback rather than considering long-term consequences, often leading to locally optimal but globally suboptimal results. It's a near-sighted learning strategy.

Key Components: It includes immediate performance metrics, local optimization techniques, reactive adjustments, and a limited planning horizon.

Benefits: It enables rapid adaptation, reduces computational complexity, and suits environments requiring quick responses.

Examples: An AI adjusting ad placements based on today's click rates, ignoring potential shifts in user behavior over weeks.

Applications: It is used in real-time decision systems, online learning, and adaptive user interfaces.

Challenges: Overlooking long-term trends, potential for suboptimal solutions, and difficulty integrating future predictions are limitations.

Industries: Marketing, gaming, and e-commerce apply myopic learning for immediate gains.

Conclusion: Myopic Learning offers AI a fast, practical path to short-term success, though it risks missing the bigger picture.

Myrinet

Definition: Myrinet in AI is a high-performance, low-latency networking technology originally developed for cluster computing, adapted in AI contexts to facilitate rapid data transfer between distributed systems or processing nodes. It's a speed-enhancing network fabric.

Key Components: It includes Myrinet hardware (e.g., NICs, switches), a proprietary protocol, low-latency communication, and integration with AI clusters.

Benefits: It boosts data throughput, minimizes communication delays, and supports scalable AI computations.

Examples: A distributed AI model training across multiple GPUs might use Myrinet to synchronize gradients quickly during backpropagation.

Applications: It is applied in distributed machine learning, high-performance computing, and real-time AI systems.

Challenges: High setup costs, compatibility with modern standards, and limited adoption compared to alternatives like InfiniBand are drawbacks.

Industries: Technology, research, and supercomputing leverage Myrinet for performance.

Conclusion: Myrinet in AI enhances distributed processing, delivering speed where rapid data exchange is critical.

MySQL for AI

Definition: MySQL for AI refers to the use of the MySQL relational database management system to store, manage, and retrieve structured data for AI applications, supporting tasks like training data storage or real-time inference. It's a data backbone for AI.

Key Components: It includes relational tables, SQL queries, indexing for fast access, and integration with AI frameworks via connectors.

Benefits: It provides structured data organization, ensures data consistency, and enables efficient querying for AI pipelines.

Examples: Storing patient records in MySQL, queried by an AI model to predict disease risk based on historical data patterns.

Applications: It is used in data preprocessing, model deployment, and business intelligence systems.

Challenges: Scalability with massive datasets, handling unstructured data, and latency in real-time AI can pose issues.

Industries: Healthcare, finance, and retail utilize MySQL for AI-driven data management.

Conclusion: MySQL for AI offers a reliable, structured foundation, bridging data storage and intelligent analysis effectively.

Letter N

Naive Bayes Classifier

Definition
Naive Bayes Classifier in AI is a probabilistic machine learning algorithm based on Bayes' theorem, assuming feature independence to classify data into categories efficiently. It's a straightforward probabilistic predictor.

Key Components
It includes prior probabilities, likelihoods, feature independence assumption, and posterior probability calculations.

Benefits
It's computationally fast, handles high-dimensional data well, and performs effectively with small datasets.

Examples
Classifying an email as "spam" or "not spam" based on word occurrences like "win" or "free."

Applications
It is used in text classification, spam filtering, and sentiment analysis.

Challenges
Independence assumption oversimplifies reality, struggles with imbalanced data, and zero-frequency issues can arise.

Industries
Technology, marketing, and cybersecurity rely on Naive Bayes for quick classification.

Conclusion
Naive Bayes Classifier offers AI a simple, efficient tool for probabilistic decisions, excelling in speed over complexity.

Named Entity Recognition (NER)

Definition
Named Entity Recognition (NER) in AI is a natural language processing task that identifies and classifies named entities (e.g., people, organizations, locations) within text into predefined categories. It's a text-labeling specialist.

Key Components
It involves tokenization, sequence labeling, machine learning models (e.g., CRF, BERT), and entity categories.

Benefits
It extracts structured information, enhances text understanding, and supports downstream language tasks.

Examples
Identifying "Apple" as an organization in the sentence "Apple released a new phone."

Applications
It is applied in information extraction, search engines, and chatbots.

Challenges
Ambiguity (e.g., "Jordan" as name or place), multilingual variations, and rare entities pose difficulties.

Industries
Media, technology, and legal sectors use NER for text insights.

Conclusion
Named Entity Recognition in AI pinpoints key elements in text, unlocking structured meaning from unstructured data.

Natural Evolution Strategies (NES)

Definition
Natural Evolution Strategies (NES) in AI is a family of optimization algorithms inspired by natural evolution, using population-based search and gradient estimation to optimize model parameters. It's an evolutionary optimizer.

Key Components
It includes a parameter population, fitness evaluation, natural gradient updates, and mutation mechanisms.

Benefits
It handles non-differentiable problems, explores diverse solutions, and adapts to complex optimization landscapes.

Examples
Tuning a neural network's weights to maximize game scores by evolving parameter sets over generations.

Applications
It is used in reinforcement learning, hyperparameter optimization, and neural architecture search.

Challenges
Computational intensity, slow convergence, and tuning population size are key hurdles.

Industries
Gaming, research, and technology apply NES for robust optimization.

Conclusion
Natural Evolution Strategies in AI evolve solutions naturally, offering a powerful alternative to traditional gradients.

Natural Gradient Descent

Definition
Natural Gradient Descent in AI is an optimization technique that adjusts model parameters using the natural gradient, accounting for the geometry of the parameter space, to achieve faster and more stable convergence. It's a geometry-aware optimizer.

Key Components
It involves a loss function, Fisher information matrix, parameter updates, and gradient adjustments.

Benefits
It accelerates training, improves stability, and adapts to curved optimization landscapes effectively.

Examples
Optimizing a deep learning model where natural gradients speed convergence over standard gradient descent on uneven terrains.

Applications
It is applied in deep learning, reinforcement learning, and probabilistic models.

Challenges
High computational cost, estimating the Fisher matrix, and scaling to large models can limit use.

Industries
Technology, research, and finance utilize natural gradient descent for efficiency.

Conclusion
Natural Gradient Descent refines AI optimization, navigating parameter spaces with geometric precision.

Natural Language Generation (NLG)

Definition
Natural Language Generation (NLG) in AI is the process of producing human-readable text from structured data or internal representations, enabling machines to communicate naturally. It's a text-creating engine.

Key Components
It includes data inputs, text planning, sentence generation, and language models (e.g., transformers).

Benefits
It automates content creation, personalizes communication, and bridges data-to-human gaps.

Examples
Generating a weather report like "Expect sunny skies with a high of 75°F" from meteorological data.

Applications
It is used in report generation, chatbots, and content automation.

Challenges
Ensuring coherence, avoiding bias, and matching tone or style are persistent issues.

Industries
Media, customer service, and education harness NLG for text output.

Conclusion
Natural Language Generation in AI turns data into dialogue, enhancing communication with human-like fluency.

Natural Language Interface (NLI) to Databases

Definition
Natural Language Interface (NLI) to Databases in AI allows users to query databases using everyday language, translating natural language inputs into structured database commands like SQL. It's a conversational data access tool.

Key Components
It involves NLP parsing, query mapping, database schema understanding, and response generation.

Benefits
It democratizes data access, reduces technical barriers, and speeds up information retrieval.

Examples
A user asking "Show me sales from last month" prompts an NLI to generate an SQL query for sales data.

Applications
It is applied in business intelligence, customer support, and data analytics.

Challenges
Ambiguous queries, schema complexity, and ensuring accurate translations can complicate performance.

Industries
Finance, retail, and technology use NLI for user-friendly data interaction.

Conclusion
NLI to Databases in AI simplifies data exploration, making databases speak human language effortlessly.

Natural Language Processing (NLP)

Definition
Natural Language Processing (NLP) in AI is the field dedicated to enabling machines to understand, interpret, and generate human language, bridging the gap between text and computation. It's language mastery for machines.

Key Components
It includes tokenization, syntax analysis, semantic understanding, and models like transformers or RNNs.

Benefits
It enables human-machine communication, automates text tasks, and extracts meaning from unstructured data.

Examples
An NLP system might summarize a news article or translate "Bonjour" to "Hello" accurately.

Applications
It is used in chatbots, translation tools, and text analytics.

Challenges
Handling ambiguity, cultural nuances, and computational demands are ongoing concerns.

Industries
Technology, healthcare, and media rely on NLP for language solutions.

Conclusion
Natural Language Processing in AI unlocks the power of words, driving seamless human-computer interaction.

Natural Language Understanding (NLU)

Definition
Natural Language Understanding (NLU) in AI is a subset of NLP focused on comprehending the meaning, intent, and context of human language inputs, enabling deeper interpretation beyond surface text. It's the brain of language processing.

Key Components
It involves intent recognition, entity extraction, sentiment analysis, and contextual modeling.

Benefits
It enhances intent accuracy, supports nuanced interactions, and improves user experience.

Examples
An NLU system might detect frustration in "I can't get this to work" and escalate to human support.

Applications
It is applied in virtual assistants, customer service bots, and semantic search.

Challenges
Resolving ambiguity, understanding idioms, and scaling to diverse languages are key difficulties.

Industries
Technology, customer support, and education use NLU for intelligent dialogue.

Conclusion
Natural Language Understanding in AI decodes the essence of speech, fostering meaningful machine comprehension.

Neat AI (NeuroEvolution of Augmenting Topologies)

Definition
Neat AI, or NeuroEvolution of Augmenting Topologies, is an AI technique that uses evolutionary algorithms to simultaneously evolve both the structure and weights of neural networks, optimizing them for specific tasks without manual design. It's evolution-driven network building.

Key Components
It includes a population of neural networks, genetic operations (mutation, crossover), fitness evaluation, and topology augmentation.

Benefits
It automates architecture design, adapts to diverse tasks, and discovers novel network structures.

Examples
Evolving a neural network to play a video game, starting simple and adding layers as performance improves.

Applications
It is used in game AI, robotic control, and optimization problems.

Challenges
Computational intensity, slow convergence, and tuning evolutionary parameters are significant hurdles.

Industries
Gaming, robotics, and research leverage Neat AI for adaptive solutions.

Conclusion
Neat AI harnesses evolution in AI, crafting neural networks through natural selection for innovative results.

Neat Q-Learning

Definition
Neat Q-Learning in AI combines the NeuroEvolution of Augmenting Topologies (NEAT) with Q-learning, a reinforcement learning method, to evolve neural networks that learn action-value functions for decision-making. It's an evolutionary-RL hybrid.

Key Components
It involves Q-value estimation, NEAT's evolutionary framework, state-action pairs, and reward-based fitness.

Benefits
It integrates structural evolution with value learning, reduces manual tuning, and adapts to dynamic environments.

Examples
Evolving a network to navigate a maze, learning Q-values to choose optimal turns based on rewards.

Applications
It is applied in reinforcement learning tasks, robotic navigation, and game strategy development.

Challenges
Balancing evolution and learning, computational cost, and ensuring stable Q-value updates are key issues.

Industries
Robotics, gaming, and automation use Neat Q-Learning for intelligent control.

Conclusion
Neat Q-Learning in AI merges evolution and reinforcement, crafting adaptive agents for complex decisions.

Network Embeddings

Definition
Network Embeddings in AI are low-dimensional vector representations of nodes in a graph or network, capturing structural relationships and properties for use in machine learning tasks. It's a graph-to-vector translator.

Key Components
It includes a graph structure, embedding algorithms (e.g., DeepWalk, node2vec), similarity preservation, and vector space mapping.

Benefits
It simplifies graph analysis, enables downstream tasks, and preserves relational information efficiently.

Examples
Embedding a social network to represent users as vectors, predicting friendships based on proximity in the embedding space.

Applications
It is used in social network analysis, recommendation systems, and graph-based prediction.

Challenges
Capturing complex structures, scalability with large graphs, and interpretability can be difficult.

Industries
Social media, e-commerce, and bioinformatics apply network embeddings for insights.

Conclusion
Network Embeddings in AI condense graph complexity into usable forms, powering relational intelligence.

Neural Additive Models (NAMs)

Definition
Neural Additive Models (NAMs) in AI are interpretable machine learning models that combine the flexibility of neural networks with the additive structure of generalized additive models, explaining feature contributions individually. It's a transparent neural hybrid.

Key Components
It involves neural subnetworks, feature-wise additive terms, input-output mappings, and interpretability constraints.

Benefits
It offers high accuracy, provides clear feature insights, and balances complexity with explainability.

Examples
Predicting house prices where NAMs show how square footage or location independently affects the outcome.

Applications
It is applied in predictive modeling, risk assessment, and interpretable AI systems.

Challenges
Balancing interpretability and performance, scaling to high-dimensional data, and training complexity are concerns.

Industries
Finance, healthcare, and real estate use NAMs for trusted predictions.

Conclusion
Neural Additive Models in AI blend power and clarity, making neural predictions understandable and actionable.

Neural Architecture Search (NAS)

Definition
Neural Architecture Search (NAS) in AI is an automated process that designs optimal neural network architectures for specific tasks by exploring a search space of configurations using optimization techniques. It's an AI architect.

Key Components
It includes a search space, search strategies (e.g., reinforcement learning, evolution), performance evaluation, and architecture validation.

Benefits
It reduces manual design effort, discovers high-performing models, and tailors networks to tasks.

Examples
NAS might design a compact network for image classification on mobile devices, outperforming human designs.

Applications
It is used in deep learning optimization, computer vision, and natural language processing.

Challenges
Extreme computational cost, search efficiency, and generalizing across tasks are significant barriers.

Industries
Technology, automotive, and healthcare adopt NAS for cutting-edge models.

Conclusion
Neural Architecture Search in AI automates innovation, crafting bespoke networks for peak performance.

Neural Machine Translation (NMT)

Definition
Neural Machine Translation (NMT) in AI is a deep learning approach to translating text between languages using neural networks, typically encoder-decoder architectures, to capture linguistic nuances. It's a neural linguist.

Key Components
It involves source text encoding, target text decoding, attention mechanisms, and large bilingual corpora.

Benefits
It produces fluent translations, handles complex syntax, and improves with more data.

Examples
Translating "Je suis fatigué" from French to "I am tired" in English with context-aware accuracy.

Applications
It is applied in language translation tools, multilingual chatbots, and content localization.

Challenges
Data dependency, rare language support, and handling long sentences can limit quality.

Industries
Technology, media, and education rely on NMT for global communication.

Conclusion
Neural Machine Translation in AI redefines language barriers, delivering seamless, neural-powered fluency.

Neural Network

Definition
A Neural Network in AI is a computational model inspired by the human brain, composed of interconnected nodes (neurons) organized in layers, designed to learn patterns from data through weight adjustments. It's the core of deep learning.

Key Components
It includes input layers, hidden layers, output layers, activation functions, and backpropagation for training.

Benefits
It excels at pattern recognition, scales with data, and adapts to diverse tasks.

Examples
A neural network might classify handwritten digits by learning features like curves and lines from examples.

Applications
It is used in image recognition, speech processing, and predictive analytics.

Challenges
Overfitting, computational demands, and lack of interpretability are persistent issues.

Industries
Technology, healthcare, and finance harness neural networks for intelligence.

Conclusion
Neural Networks in AI form the backbone of modern learning, driving powerful, data-driven solutions.

Neural Network Inference

Definition
Neural Network Inference in AI is the process of using a trained neural network to make predictions or decisions on new, unseen data by processing inputs through its learned weights and architecture. It's the application phase of neural learning.

Key Components
It includes a trained model, input data, forward propagation, and output generation.

Benefits
It delivers fast predictions, leverages learned patterns, and scales to real-time applications.

Examples
A trained network inferring whether an email is spam based on its text features in milliseconds.

Applications
It is used in image classification, speech recognition, and fraud detection.

Challenges
Computational resource demands, latency in large models, and maintaining accuracy on diverse data are hurdles.

Industries
Technology, security, and healthcare rely on inference for operational AI.

Conclusion
Neural Network Inference turns training into action, enabling AI to apply its knowledge efficiently.

Neural Rendering

Definition
Neural Rendering in AI combines neural networks with rendering techniques to generate or enhance visual content, such as images or 3D scenes, by learning to synthesize realistic visuals from data. It's AI-driven visual creation.

Key Components
It involves neural networks, rendering pipelines, input data (e.g., 3D models), and loss functions for realism.

Benefits
It produces high-quality visuals, automates complex rendering, and adapts to artistic styles.

Examples
Generating a photorealistic face from a 3D mesh using a neural network trained on human portraits.

Applications
It is applied in game development, film production, and virtual reality.

Challenges
High computational cost, achieving consistent realism, and handling diverse scenes can be difficult.

Industries
Entertainment, gaming, and design utilize neural rendering for immersive visuals.

Conclusion
Neural Rendering in AI redefines visual artistry, blending computation and creativity for stunning results.

Niche AI

Definition
Niche AI refers to artificial intelligence systems tailored to specific, specialized domains or tasks, focusing on narrow applications rather than general-purpose intelligence. It's a targeted AI solution.

Key Components
It includes domain-specific data, customized algorithms, expert knowledge integration, and focused performance metrics.

Benefits
It offers high precision, meets unique needs, and excels in specialized contexts.

Examples
An AI designed solely to detect rare plant diseases in agricultural images, outperforming broader models.

Applications
It is used in precision medicine, niche market analysis, and rare event detection.

Challenges
Limited generalizability, data scarcity in niches, and development costs are key issues.

Industries
Agriculture, healthcare, and retail apply niche AI for bespoke solutions.

Conclusion
Niche AI delivers pinpoint accuracy in AI, thriving where specialization trumps versatility.

Niche-Market AI Models

Definition
Niche-Market AI Models are machine learning models developed for specific market segments or industries, optimized to address unique customer needs or operational challenges within those areas. It's market-focused AI design.

Key Components
It involves market-specific datasets, tailored architectures, fine-tuned parameters, and industry-relevant outputs.

Benefits
It enhances relevance, improves efficiency, and aligns closely with market demands.

Examples
A model predicting equipment failure for a small mining company, trained on its unique machinery data.

Applications
It is applied in targeted marketing, industry-specific automation, and customer retention systems.

Challenges
Small data pools, overfitting to niche cases, and high customization costs can limit scalability.

Industries
Manufacturing, energy, and specialty retail use niche-market models for precision.

Conclusion
Niche-Market AI Models in AI cater to specific sectors, offering tailored intelligence with focused impact.

NIST AI Risk Management Framework

Definition
The NIST AI Risk Management Framework is a guideline developed by the National Institute of Standards and Technology to help organizations identify, assess, and mitigate risks associated with AI systems. It's a structured risk roadmap.

Key Components
It includes risk identification, governance practices, mitigation strategies, and stakeholder engagement principles.

Benefits
It promotes safe AI deployment, ensures ethical use, and fosters trust in AI technologies.

Examples
A company using the framework to evaluate bias risks in a hiring AI, adjusting it to meet fairness standards.

Applications
It is used in AI governance, compliance auditing, and system safety assessments.

Challenges
Adapting to diverse AI contexts, implementation costs, and evolving risks are ongoing concerns.

Industries
Government, technology, and finance adopt the NIST framework for responsible AI.

Conclusion
The NIST AI Risk Management Framework guides AI toward safety and ethics, a vital tool for accountability.

Noise Injection

Definition
Noise Injection in AI is a regularization technique that adds random noise to inputs, weights, or

activations during training to improve model robustness and generalization. It's a controlled chaos enhancer.

Key Components
It involves noise types (e.g., Gaussian), injection points, noise magnitude, and training adjustments.

Benefits
It prevents overfitting, enhances resilience to noise, and mimics real-world variability.

Examples
Adding random pixel noise to training images so a classifier better handles blurry real-world photos.

Applications
It is applied in deep learning, data augmentation, and adversarial training.

Challenges
Balancing noise levels, avoiding performance degradation, and computational overhead can complicate use.

Industries
Technology, automotive, and healthcare use noise injection for durable models.

Conclusion
Noise Injection in AI builds tougher models, preparing them for the unpredictability of reality.

Noise-Reduction Algorithms

Definition
Noise-Reduction Algorithms in AI are methods designed to remove or minimize unwanted noise from data—such as audio, images, or signals—enhancing quality and usability for analysis or prediction. It's a data cleaner.

Key Components
It includes signal processing techniques, filtering methods (e.g., Gaussian), machine learning models, and noise estimation.

Benefits
It improves data clarity, boosts model accuracy, and enhances user experience.

Examples
An AI removing background chatter from a recorded speech to improve transcription accuracy.

Applications
It is used in audio processing, image enhancement, and sensor data refinement.

Challenges
Preserving signal integrity, handling complex noise patterns, and real-time processing are key difficulties.

Industries
Media, telecommunications, and medical imaging rely on noise reduction for quality.

Conclusion
Noise-Reduction Algorithms in AI polish raw data, ensuring cleaner inputs for sharper outcomes.

Nonlinear Activation Functions

Definition
Nonlinear Activation Functions in AI are mathematical functions applied to neural network nodes to introduce nonlinearity, enabling the network to model complex patterns and relationships. It's a complexity enabler.

Key Components
It includes functions like ReLU, sigmoid, or tanh, input transformation, output range, and gradient properties.

Benefits
It captures non-linear data patterns, enhances learning capacity, and supports deep architectures.

Examples
Using ReLU to activate neurons in an image classifier, allowing it to detect intricate shapes like curves.

Applications
It is essential in deep learning, neural network training, and pattern recognition.

Challenges
Vanishing gradients, computational cost, and choosing the right function can affect performance.

Industries
Technology, gaming, and finance use nonlinear functions for advanced modeling.

Conclusion
Nonlinear Activation Functions in AI unlock complexity, driving neural networks beyond linear limits.

Non-Maximum Suppression (NMS)

Definition
Non-Maximum Suppression (NMS) in AI is a post-processing technique used in object detection to eliminate redundant bounding boxes, keeping only the most confident detection per object. It's a detection refiner.

Key Components
It involves bounding box scores, overlap thresholds (e.g., IoU), suppression rules, and final box selection.

Benefits
It reduces clutter, improves detection clarity, and enhances precision in crowded scenes.

Examples
In a crowd photo, NMS might keep one box per person, discarding overlapping, less-confident detections.

Applications
It is applied in object detection, facial recognition, and autonomous driving.

Challenges
Threshold tuning, missing overlapping objects, and computational overhead can impact results.

Industries
Security, automotive, and retail use NMS for accurate detection.

Conclusion
Non-Maximum Suppression in AI streamlines object detection, ensuring clean, confident outputs.

Normal Distribution in AI

Definition
Normal Distribution in AI is a statistical concept describing a bell-shaped probability distribution of data, widely assumed or leveraged in AI for modeling, inference, or synthetic data generation. It's a data pattern staple.

Key Components
It includes mean, standard deviation, probability density function, and the 68-95-99.7 rule for spread.

Benefits
It simplifies analysis, supports statistical methods, and aligns with many natural phenomena.

Examples
Modeling test scores in a population where most cluster around the average, tapering at extremes.

Applications
It is used in data normalization, anomaly detection, and generative models.

Challenges
Real data often deviates from normality, over-reliance can mislead, and outliers may skew results.

Industries
Finance, education, and research apply normal distribution for modeling.

Conclusion
Normal Distribution in AI provides a foundational lens, shaping data assumptions with statistical elegance.

Normalization Layers in Neural Networks

Definition
Normalization Layers in Neural Networks are techniques applied within AI models to standardize inputs or activations across a layer, stabilizing training by reducing internal covariate shift and improving convergence. It's a training stabilizer.

Key Components
It includes methods like batch normalization, layer normalization, mean-variance scaling, and trainable parameters.

Benefits
It accelerates training, reduces sensitivity to initialization, and enhances model performance.

Examples
Applying batch normalization to a deep network to normalize activations, speeding up image classification training.

Applications
It is used in deep learning, convolutional networks, and transformer models.

Challenges
Added computational cost, dependency on batch size, and adapting to small datasets can complicate use.

Industries
Technology, healthcare, and gaming rely on normalization layers for robust models.

Conclusion
Normalization Layers in Neural Networks streamline AI training, ensuring stability and efficiency in complex architectures.

Numerical Differentiation

Definition
Numerical Differentiation in AI is the computational approximation of a function's derivative using discrete data points, often employed when analytical derivatives are unavailable or impractical. It's a slope estimator.

Key Components
It involves finite difference methods (e.g., forward, central), step size, function values, and error estimation.

Benefits
It enables gradient computation, supports optimization, and adapts to empirical data.

Examples
Estimating the rate of change in a stock price model using price differences over small time intervals.

Applications
It is applied in gradient-based learning, physics simulations, and data analysis.

Challenges
Sensitivity to noise, truncation errors, and choosing step size can affect accuracy.

Industries
Finance, engineering, and research use numerical differentiation for insights.

Conclusion
Numerical Differentiation in AI provides a practical derivative tool, bridging theory and computation effectively.

Numerical Integration

Definition
Numerical Integration in AI approximates the definite integral of a function using discrete data points, enabling the computation of areas, volumes, or probabilities when analytical solutions are infeasible. It's an area calculator.

Key Components
It includes methods like trapezoidal rule or Simpson's rule, sample points, interval size, and error bounds.

Benefits
It handles complex functions, supports probabilistic modeling, and adapts to irregular data.

Examples
Calculating the total probability under a curve in a machine learning density model using sampled points.

Applications
It is used in statistical inference, physics simulations, and machine learning evaluation.

Challenges
Computational cost, accuracy with sparse data, and error accumulation are key concerns.

Industries
Research, technology, and energy apply numerical integration for precision.

Conclusion
Numerical Integration in AI tackles continuous problems discretely, offering a versatile computational solution.

Numerical Optimization

Definition
Numerical Optimization in AI is the process of finding the best solution to a problem by minimizing or maximizing an objective function using computational methods, central to training machine learning models. It's a best-fit seeker.

Key Components
It involves objective functions, constraints, iterative algorithms (e.g., gradient descent), and convergence criteria.

Benefits
It drives model accuracy, enables efficient parameter tuning, and solves complex problems numerically.

Examples
Optimizing neural network weights to minimize prediction error on a dataset of house prices.

Applications
It is applied in machine learning, operations research, and system design.

Challenges
Local optima traps, computational expense, and handling high-dimensional spaces can hinder progress.

Industries
Technology, logistics, and finance leverage numerical optimization for efficiency.

Conclusion
Numerical Optimization in AI powers model refinement, turning data into optimal solutions with precision.

Numerical Stability in AI

Definition
Numerical Stability in AI refers to the robustness of algorithms against small errors or perturbations in computations, ensuring reliable results despite rounding or approximation issues. It's a computational safeguard.

Key Components
It includes precision handling, algorithm design, error propagation analysis, and stable numerical methods.

Benefits
It ensures consistent outcomes, prevents catastrophic errors, and supports reliable model training.

Examples
Stabilizing a deep learning gradient update to avoid exploding values during backpropagation.

Applications
It is critical in deep learning, simulations, and scientific computing.

Challenges
Balancing stability with speed, detecting instability, and adapting to diverse algorithms are concerns.

Industries
Technology, research, and engineering prioritize numerical stability for trust.

Conclusion
Numerical Stability in AI underpins reliable computation, guarding against the pitfalls of numerical fragility.

Numpy in Machine Learning

Definition
Numpy in Machine Learning is a foundational Python library that provides efficient array operations, mathematical functions, and linear algebra tools, widely used to handle data and computations in AI models. It's a numeric workhorse.

Key Components
It includes multidimensional arrays, broadcasting, vectorized operations, and integration with ML frameworks.

Benefits
It speeds up computations, simplifies coding, and supports large-scale data processing.

Examples
Using Numpy to compute matrix multiplications for a neural network's forward pass on image data.

Applications
It is used in data preprocessing, model implementation, and numerical experimentation.

Challenges
Memory limitations with massive arrays, single-threaded bottlenecks, and learning curve can pose issues.

Industries
Technology, data science, and research depend on Numpy for ML tasks.

Conclusion
Numpy in Machine Learning empowers AI with fast, flexible numerics, a cornerstone of efficient computation.

Nyquist Criterion

Definition
Nyquist Criterion in AI is a principle from signal processing that determines the stability of a system based on the frequency response, often applied to ensure AI models or control systems remain stable. It's a stability checker.

Key Components
It involves frequency response, gain and phase margins, Nyquist plots, and closed-loop system analysis.

Benefits
It ensures system reliability, prevents oscillations, and guides stable design in dynamic systems.

Examples
Assessing an AI-controlled motor to ensure it doesn't destabilize under varying loads using Nyquist analysis.

Applications
It is used in control systems, signal processing, and AI-driven automation.

Challenges
Complex frequency analysis, interpreting plots, and applying to non-linear systems can be difficult.

Industries
Engineering, robotics, and telecommunications apply the Nyquist Criterion for stability.

Conclusion
Nyquist Criterion in AI safeguards dynamic systems, ensuring stability through frequency insight.

Nyquist Frequency

Definition
Nyquist Frequency in AI is the highest frequency that can be accurately sampled without aliasing, defined as half the sampling rate, critical for signal processing and data acquisition in AI systems. It's a sampling limit.

Key Components
It includes sampling rate, signal frequency, aliasing prevention, and the Nyquist-Shannon theorem.

Benefits
It ensures accurate signal representation, prevents data distortion, and guides sampling design.

Examples
Sampling audio at 44.1 kHz to capture frequencies up to 22.05 kHz without loss for an AI voice model.

Applications
It is applied in audio processing, image sampling, and time series analysis.

Challenges
Determining adequate sampling rates, handling high-frequency noise, and real-time constraints are concerns.

Industries
Media, healthcare, and technology use Nyquist Frequency for data fidelity.

Conclusion
Nyquist Frequency in AI sets the boundary for clear sampling, preserving signal integrity in digital systems.

Nyquist Plot

Definition
Nyquist Plot in AI is a graphical representation of a system's frequency response, plotting real versus imaginary components to analyze stability and performance, often used in AI control systems. It's a frequency visualizer.

Key Components
It includes frequency response data, complex plane plotting, encirclements, and stability criteria.

Benefits
It provides intuitive stability insights, aids system design, and visualizes dynamic behavior.

Examples
Plotting an AI autopilot's response to ensure stable flight adjustments across frequency ranges.

Applications
It is used in control theory, signal processing, and system diagnostics.

Challenges
Interpreting complex plots, handling non-linear systems, and computational effort can complicate analysis.

Industries
Aerospace, engineering, and automation utilize Nyquist Plots for system checks.

Conclusion
Nyquist Plot in AI offers a clear window into system stability, enhancing control through visual analysis.

Nyquist-Shannon Sampling Theorem

Definition
Nyquist-Shannon Sampling Theorem in AI states that a continuous signal can be perfectly reconstructed from discrete samples if sampled at least twice its highest frequency, foundational for digital signal processing in AI. It's a sampling rulebook.

Key Components
It includes signal bandwidth, sampling rate, Nyquist frequency, and reconstruction conditions.

Benefits
It guarantees signal fidelity, informs sampling strategies, and prevents information loss.

Examples
Sampling a 5 kHz sound wave at 10 kHz or higher to enable an AI to reconstruct it accurately for analysis.

Applications
It is applied in audio processing, image digitization, and sensor data collection.

Challenges
Ensuring sufficient sampling, handling noise, and real-world deviations can limit applicability.

Industries
Telecommunications, media, and IoT rely on this theorem for data integrity.

Conclusion
Nyquist-Shannon Sampling Theorem in AI ensures digital accuracy, a bedrock for signal-based intelligence.

Nystagmus Detection in AI

Definition
Nystagmus Detection in AI involves using artificial intelligence to identify and analyze nystagmus—an involuntary eye movement condition—through video or sensor data for medical diagnosis or monitoring. It's an eye-tracking diagnostic.

Key Components
It includes eye-tracking data, video analysis, machine learning models, and motion pattern recognition.

Benefits
It automates diagnosis, enhances early detection, and supports non-invasive monitoring.

Examples
An AI analyzing a patient's eye video to detect rapid oscillations indicative of neurological issues.

Applications
It is used in neurology, ophthalmology, and patient monitoring systems.

Challenges
Noise in video data, variability in nystagmus types, and real-time processing are key difficulties.

Industries
Healthcare, medical research, and diagnostics apply nystagmus detection for care.

Conclusion
Nystagmus Detection in AI advances medical AI, offering precise tools for eye-related health insights.

Nystrom Method in Machine Learning

Definition
Nystrom Method in Machine Learning is an approximation technique that speeds up kernel-based algorithms by sampling a subset of data to estimate a low-rank kernel matrix, reducing computational complexity. It's a kernel simplifier.

Key Components
It involves a kernel matrix, random or strategic sampling, eigenvalue decomposition, and approximation steps.

Benefits
It reduces memory use, accelerates computation, and scales kernel methods to large datasets.

Examples
Approximating a similarity matrix for clustering millions of customer profiles using a small sample.

Applications
It is applied in kernel PCA, spectral clustering, and large-scale classification.

Challenges
Sampling quality, loss of precision, and applicability to all kernels can affect outcomes.

Industries
Technology, data science, and bioinformatics use the Nystrom Method for efficiency.

Conclusion
Nystrom Method in Machine Learning optimizes kernel tasks, making big data manageable with clever approximations.

LETTER O

Object Detection

Definition:
Object detection is a computer vision technique that allows AI systems to identify and locate objects within images or videos. Unlike traditional image recognition, which classifies the entire image, object detection pinpoints individual objects and provides a bounding box around each detected object.

Key Characteristics:
Uses deep learning algorithms like Convolutional Neural Networks and Region-Based CNN, involves classification and localization tasks, and supports real-time processing.

Applications:
Self-driving cars detecting pedestrians, vehicles, and traffic signs, surveillance systems identifying intruders, and healthcare detecting tumors in medical images.

Examples:
In autonomous vehicles, object detection helps the car recognize other cars, pedestrians, or obstacles on the road. In retail, object detection is used for automated checkouts to identify products being purchased.

Benefits:
Enhances safety in critical systems, improves accuracy in automated systems, and allows machines to interact with the physical world more intelligently.

Sources:
Research in deep learning and computer vision.

Conclusion:
Object detection is foundational for any AI system that interacts with the physical world, especially in real-time applications like autonomous navigation and security.

Object Detection via Deep Learning

Definition:
Object detection via deep learning involves the use of advanced neural network architectures, particularly convolutional neural networks (CNNs), to accurately identify and locate multiple objects within images or videos.

Key Components:
CNN architectures (YOLO, SSD, Faster R-CNN), bounding box prediction, feature extraction layers, labeled training datasets, confidence scoring.

Benefits:
Achieves high accuracy in object recognition, enables real-time detection, automates complex visual analysis tasks, improves scalability to diverse object classes.

Examples:
Detecting pedestrians, vehicles, and traffic signs in autonomous cars; recognizing faces in crowd monitoring systems; identifying products on retail shelves automatically.

Applications:
Autonomous driving, surveillance security, retail automation, medical image analysis, drone-based inspections.

Industries:
Automotive, security, retail, healthcare, aerospace.

Summary:
Object detection via deep learning significantly advances visual recognition capabilities of AI systems, providing accurate, reliable, and real-time object localization critical to numerous technological and industrial applications.

Object Generation in AI

Definition:
Object generation in AI refers to the creation of realistic objects, images, or 3D models using deep learning techniques, particularly generative models like GANs (Generative Adversarial Networks) and VAEs (Variational Autoencoders). These models can generate new instances of objects that resemble those found in training data.

Key Characteristics:
Involves learning from datasets of objects and using that knowledge to generate new objects that are indistinguishable from real ones. GANs, VAEs, and diffusion models are commonly used for object generation tasks.

Applications:
Video game design for creating new characters or environments, product design for generating 3D models, and entertainment for creating realistic CGI elements.

Examples:
In video games, AI can generate random, lifelike characters or environments based on a few parameters, enhancing game variability and immersion.

Benefits:
Reduces the time and effort needed to create objects manually, supports creativity, and provides tools for industries like entertainment and design.

Sources:
Deep learning and generative model research.

Conclusion:
Object generation is transforming creative industries by automating the creation of complex objects, making it faster and more efficient to produce high-quality visual content.

Objective Function in AI

Definition:
An objective function, also known as a loss function or cost function, is a mathematical function that an AI model seeks to minimize or maximize during training. In supervised learning, the objective function measures the difference between predicted and actual outputs, guiding the model toward optimal accuracy.

Key Characteristics:
Can take many forms depending on the problem, such as Mean Squared Error for regression tasks or Cross-Entropy Loss for classification tasks.

Applications:
Deep learning optimizing neural networks, reinforcement learning optimizing reward-based decisions, and optimization problems finding the best solution to a given task.

Examples:
In image classification, the objective function could be the categorical cross-entropy, which measures the performance of the model's predictions by comparing them to the actual categories of the images.

Benefits:
Drives the learning process, provides a quantifiable measure of a model's performance, and guides optimization algorithms like gradient descent.

Sources:
AI and optimization theory.

Conclusion:
The objective function is fundamental to machine learning, acting as the guiding metric that directs how a model improves during training.

Object Goal Navigation (OGN)

Definition:
Object Goal Navigation is an AI task where an agent is trained to navigate towards a specific object in an environment. The goal is for the agent to move intelligently within the environment, recognizing objects and understanding spatial relations without prior knowledge of the layout.

Key Characteristics:
Involves deep reinforcement learning, spatial reasoning, and computer vision. Agents must identify and reach specific objects in unfamiliar environments, relying on visual cues and learned navigation policies.

Applications:
Autonomous robots, indoor navigation systems, and augmented reality games.

Examples:
In robotics, a domestic robot might be tasked with finding a specific household object, such as a mug, in a cluttered room.

Benefits:
Enhances the ability of autonomous agents to navigate complex environments and interact with objects in dynamic settings.

Sources:
AI research in robotics and reinforcement learning.

Conclusion:
Object Goal Navigation is critical for developing more autonomous and adaptable AI agents that can operate in real-world environments with minimal human intervention.

Object Grasping in Robotics

Definition:
Object grasping in AI refers to the ability of robotic systems to accurately perceive, approach, and grasp objects in their environment. This task requires coordination between perception (understanding the object's shape and location) and motor control (executing the appropriate grip).

Key Characteristics:
Involves machine vision, reinforcement learning, and control algorithms. Robots use visual and tactile sensors to estimate the object's position, shape, and weight before applying an optimized grasping technique.

Applications:
Automated manufacturing for grasping and manipulating components, warehouse robotics for picking and placing items, and assistive robotics for helping disabled individuals with daily tasks.

Examples:
Amazon warehouse robots use object grasping techniques to pick and sort packages from conveyor belts with minimal human supervision.

Benefits:
Improves efficiency in automated systems, enhances robot dexterity, and enables robots to handle complex objects in dynamic environments.

Sources:
Research in robotics, AI, and control systems.

Conclusion:
Object grasping is a key capability for robots operating in industrial, commercial, and domestic settings, enabling greater autonomy and flexibility in handling tasks.

Object-Oriented AI Programming

Definition:
Object-oriented AI programming refers to the design and development of AI systems using object-oriented programming principles. It organizes AI code into modular units called objects, encapsulating data and behavior.

Key Characteristics:
Encapsulation, inheritance, polymorphism, and abstraction are key principles used in AI development to create reusable, maintainable code.

Applications:
AI development in robotics, game development using AI to control NPCs, and intelligent software systems.

Examples:
In AI-based game engines, each character or NPC is modeled as an object with its own properties and behaviors.

Benefits:
Enhances modularity, code reusability, and ease of maintenance in complex AI systems.

Sources:
Software engineering and AI development resources.

Conclusion:
Object-oriented programming is essential for developing scalable and maintainable AI systems, particularly in software engineering and robotics.

Object Pose Estimation

Definition:
Object pose estimation refers to determining the position and orientation of an object in a 3D space. This task is crucial for enabling machines to understand spatial relationships and interact with objects in real-world environments.

Key Characteristics:
Combines computer vision, 3D modeling, and deep learning. It typically uses point clouds, depth data, and visual features to estimate pose.

Applications:
Robotics manipulating objects in a workspace, augmented reality superimposing virtual objects in real spaces, and autonomous vehicles understanding the location and orientation of other cars or objects.

Examples:
In warehouse automation, robots use object pose estimation to pick up and place items accurately.

Benefits:
Enables robots and machines to interact with their environment more effectively, enhances spatial awareness, and improves task execution in 3D spaces.

Sources:
Computer vision and robotics research.

Conclusion:
Object pose estimation is essential for robotics, augmented reality, and autonomous systems that need precise spatial understanding.

Object Recognition

Definition:
Object recognition is the AI capability to identify specific objects within images or video streams. It involves matching the object's features with pre-trained data to classify it into a known category.

Key Characteristics:
Involves feature extraction, deep learning models like CNNs, and classification tasks.

Applications:
Facial recognition, retail product recognition, and industrial automation.

Examples:
In facial recognition systems, object recognition is used to identify individuals in images or videos for authentication purposes.

Benefits:
Automates the identification process, improves efficiency in industrial and commercial applications, and supports security and surveillance systems.

Sources:
AI research in computer vision and machine learning.

Conclusion:
Object recognition is fundamental to AI systems that interact with visual data, enabling accurate identification in fields like security, retail, and healthcare.

Object Recognition via Neural Networks

Definition:
Object recognition is a computer vision task where AI models, typically Convolutional Neural Networks (CNNs), identify and classify objects within images or video frames. Unlike object detection, which locates objects in an image, object recognition focuses on identifying what the object is.

Key Characteristics:
Utilizes deep learning models, feature extraction, and image classification techniques. Pre-trained networks like ResNet, VGG, or MobileNet are often used for object recognition tasks.

Applications:
Autonomous vehicles for recognizing road signs and pedestrians, security systems for detecting faces or suspicious items, and retail for automated checkout systems.

Examples:
In autonomous driving, object recognition enables the vehicle to recognize pedestrians and stop signs, ensuring safe navigation through traffic.

Benefits:
Provides highly accurate image analysis, improves AI decision-making capabilities, and enhances automation in various industries.

Sources:
Deep learning and computer vision research.

Conclusion:
Object recognition is a fundamental component of AI systems that interact with the physical world, enabling them to interpret and understand their visual surroundings.

Object Segmentation

Definition:
Object segmentation is a computer vision technique where an AI system divides an image into segments based on the objects present, assigning each pixel to a particular object. This is different from object detection, where only the object's bounding box is predicted.

Key Characteristics:
Involves pixel-wise classification, uses algorithms like Fully Convolutional Networks, and is essential for understanding fine-grained object boundaries.

Applications:
Medical imaging segmenting organs or tumors, autonomous driving segmenting road objects like vehicles and pedestrians, and video analysis.

Examples:
In medical imaging, AI systems can segment different parts of the brain in MRI scans to aid in diagnosis.

Benefits:
Provides detailed understanding of object boundaries, critical for tasks that require precise localization.

Sources:
AI research in segmentation and pixel-level classification.

Conclusion:
Object segmentation is vital in applications requiring pixel-level accuracy, such as medical diagnostics, autonomous navigation, and image editing.

Object Tracking

Definition:
Object tracking refers to the process of continuously following an object of interest in a sequence of frames in a video. The goal is to estimate the trajectory of the object as it moves across frames, keeping it in focus and correctly identified despite changes in its position, scale, or appearance.

Key Characteristics:
Utilizes algorithms like Kalman Filters, Mean-Shift, and deep learning models like Siamese Networks. It involves prediction, detection, and updating the object's position in each frame.

Applications:
Security surveillance tracking people or vehicles, sports analytics tracking players or the ball, and augmented reality tracking physical objects to overlay digital information.

Examples:
In sports, AI-based object tracking systems follow the ball or players, providing real-time statistics and insights during live broadcasts.

Benefits:
Enhances surveillance systems by tracking objects over long durations, improves situational awareness in dynamic environments, and is critical for real-time video analysis.

Sources:
Video processing and machine learning research.

Conclusion:
Object tracking is vital for any AI system dealing with motion and video, particularly in surveillance, robotics, and sports analytics.

Objective Function in AI

Definition:
An objective function, also known as a loss function or cost function, is a mathematical function that an AI model seeks to minimize or maximize during training. In supervised learning, the objective function measures the difference between predicted and actual outputs, guiding the model toward optimal accuracy.

Key Characteristics:
Can take many forms depending on the problem, such as Mean Squared Error for regression tasks or Cross-Entropy Loss for classification tasks.

Applications:
Deep learning optimizing neural networks, reinforcement learning optimizing reward-based decisions, and optimization problems finding the best solution to a given task.

Examples:
In image classification, the objective function could be the categorical cross-entropy, which measures the performance of the model's predictions by comparing them to the actual categories of the images.

Benefits:
Drives the learning process, provides a quantifiable measure of a model's performance, and guides optimization algorithms like gradient descent.

Sources:
AI and optimization theory.

Conclusion:
The objective function is fundamental to machine learning, acting as the guiding metric that directs how a model improves during training.

Observation Model

Definition:
An observation model defines how observed data relates to the hidden states or underlying conditions within probabilistic and state-space AI systems, such as Bayesian networks or Hidden Markov Models.

Key Components:
Observed variables, hidden variables, probabilistic relationships, sensor data interpretation, Bayesian inference methods.

Benefits:
Enhances the understanding of uncertainty, improves prediction reliability, assists in accurate inference of hidden states, supports robust decision-making under uncertainty.

Examples:
Speech recognition modeling; estimating robot positions using noisy sensor data; diagnosing diseases based on observable symptoms.

Applications:
Robotics, speech and pattern recognition, medical diagnosis, financial forecasting, environmental monitoring.

Industries:
Robotics, healthcare, finance, environmental sciences, telecommunications.

Summary:
Observation models are fundamental in AI systems involving uncertainty, linking observable data to latent variables, enabling accurate inference and improved predictions in complex, uncertain environments.

Occupancy Grid Mapping

Definition:
Occupancy grid mapping is a probabilistic method used by AI and robotics to represent the environment in a grid format, marking cells as occupied, free, or unknown based on sensor data, enabling navigation and localization.

Key Components:
Grid-based representation, sensor fusion (LiDAR, radar, sonar), probabilistic occupancy estimation, Bayesian updates, spatial mapping algorithms.

Benefits:
Provides clear and detailed environment mapping, supports precise robot navigation, improves obstacle avoidance, enhances real-time environmental awareness.

Examples:
Autonomous robots mapping rooms; self-driving cars detecting road obstacles; drones surveying land areas.

Applications:
Robotics navigation, autonomous driving, drone mapping, environmental exploration, rescue operations.

Industries:
Robotics, automotive, aerospace, emergency response, military.

Summary:
Occupancy grid mapping is a crucial AI capability that facilitates detailed spatial understanding, allowing autonomous systems to safely navigate complex and uncertain environments.

Odd-Parity Detection in Neural Networks

Definition:
Odd-parity detection is a task where an AI model, particularly a neural network, determines whether the number of 1s in a binary string is odd. This is a classic problem used in machine learning to test a model's capability for logical reasoning and binary classification.

Key Characteristics:
Involves binary classification, requires logical reasoning, and is often tested with shallow or deep neural networks.

Applications:
Logic circuits, error detection and correction in digital communication, and educational tools for neural network training.

Examples:
In error-checking algorithms, odd-parity detection is used to ensure that data has been transmitted correctly by checking if the number of bits with value 1 is odd.

Benefits:
Helps validate a neural network's ability to understand binary logic, essential for various digital communication tasks.

Sources:
Machine learning educational resources and logic circuit design.

Conclusion:
Odd-parity detection serves as a foundational test for neural networks in logical reasoning, with direct applications in error detection in digital systems.

Odd-Ratio Feature Selection

Definition:
Odd-Ratio Feature Selection is a statistical method used in machine learning and AI to select features that have a strong relationship with the target variable, often used in classification tasks. The odd-ratio compares the odds of an event occurring to the odds of it not occurring, helping in identifying which features most impact the outcome.

Key Characteristics:
Involves probabilistic calculations and is used primarily in binary classification tasks. It is commonly applied in logistic regression models and other probabilistic classifiers.

Applications:
Medical diagnosis determining risk factors for diseases, financial credit scoring identifying variables that influence loan repayment, and marketing predicting customer behaviors.

Examples:
In medical research, odd-ratio feature selection helps in identifying significant risk factors like smoking or cholesterol levels for heart disease.

Benefits:
Provides a clear, interpretable metric for understanding the influence of each feature, useful in high-stakes domains where decision transparency is essential.

Sources:
Research on feature selection and statistical learning in AI.

Conclusion:
Odd-ratio feature selection is particularly useful for identifying relevant features in complex, data-rich fields, where interpretability is a priority.

OE (Optical Event Detection)

Definition:
Optical Event Detection (OE) refers to AI-driven methods of automatically identifying significant events or changes occurring within optical sensor data or imagery by analyzing patterns, signals, or anomalies detected visually.

Key Components:
Image and video processing algorithms, machine learning models, pattern recognition techniques, optical sensors, real-time detection systems.

Benefits:
Enables rapid identification and response to critical events, improves situational awareness, supports proactive decision-making, enhances real-time monitoring capabilities.

Examples:
Detecting fires or explosions via satellite imagery; identifying sudden environmental changes in drone footage; automated alert systems for security breaches.

Applications:
Surveillance systems, environmental monitoring, disaster response, security and defense, industrial safety management.

Industries:
Security, environmental science, aerospace, disaster management, industrial automation.

Summary:
Optical Event Detection leverages advanced AI analysis of optical data to provide swift and accurate identification of significant events, substantially improving response times and operational safety across multiple high-stakes applications and industries.

Offline Learning

Definition:
Offline learning refers to the process of training AI models in an offline environment, where the model is trained using a static dataset and no real-time data is used during training. Offline learning contrasts with online learning, where the model continuously updates itself with new data.

Key Characteristics:
Uses batch learning techniques, does not rely on streaming data, and is often applied in supervised learning environments. It is suitable for situations where data is available in bulk and no continuous updates are needed.

Applications:
Medical diagnosis training models on large historical datasets, financial forecasting using past financial data for predictions, and manufacturing analyzing past production data to optimize processes.

Examples:
In manufacturing, offline learning can be used to predict machine failures by analyzing historical performance data, reducing downtime and maintenance costs.

Benefits:
Simplifies the training process, allows for the use of well-curated datasets, and reduces the computational overhead of real-time learning.

Sources:
Research on supervised learning and batch processing techniques.

Conclusion:
Offline learning is a foundational approach for training models in environments where large datasets are available and real-time updates are unnecessary.

Offline Reinforcement Learning

Definition:
Offline reinforcement learning is a type of reinforcement learning where an AI system is trained using a fixed dataset of pre-collected experiences without further interaction with the environment during training. This is opposed to traditional reinforcement learning, where agents interact with their environment in real-time to learn.

Key Characteristics:
Relies on pre-collected data, avoids real-time exploration, and often involves off-policy learning techniques. It is crucial for environments where exploration is expensive or dangerous.

Applications:
Healthcare training diagnostic systems using historical medical data, autonomous driving learning driving behaviors without live driving, and robotics learning tasks in simulation before real-world deployment.

Examples:
In healthcare, offline reinforcement learning systems can train diagnostic AI models using patient data without requiring new patient interactions, ensuring privacy and safety.

Benefits:
Reduces risk and cost associated with real-time exploration, enables learning in restricted environments, and allows for the use of large, existing datasets.

Sources:
Research in reinforcement learning and safe AI training techniques.

Conclusion:
Offline reinforcement learning is ideal for applications where real-time interaction is impractical or risky, making it a powerful tool in safety-critical industries.

Omniverse

Definition:
Omniverse refers to a real-time simulation and collaboration platform developed by NVIDIA, designed to connect 3D workflows across industries. It acts as a shared virtual environment where individuals,

tools, and AI systems can interact, simulate, and design in real time across different locations and software platforms.

Key Components:
USD (Universal Scene Description) framework, real-time ray tracing, physics simulation engines, AI-enhanced rendering tools, collaborative interfaces, and cross-platform compatibility.

Examples:
An architectural team in different countries co-designing a digital building model in real time using tools like Autodesk and Blender inside the Omniverse platform. AI systems can simulate sunlight, structural integrity, or pedestrian flow as part of the design process.

Benefits:
Enables real-time remote collaboration, accelerates digital twin development, integrates AI simulation in design workflows, supports photorealistic rendering, and reduces design iteration time.

Industries:
Architecture, engineering, entertainment, automotive, manufacturing, and game development.

Applications:
Digital twin simulation, smart city modeling, product design visualization, virtual production in film and games, AI-driven 3D simulation testing.

Challenges:
Requires high-performance GPUs, complex system integration, high data bandwidth, and skilled teams to manage cross-platform collaboration.

Summary:
Omniverse bridges creative and technical disciplines through real-time AI-powered collaboration, making it a vital innovation in the future of design, simulation, and digital twin environments.

On-Device Learning

Definition:
On-device learning refers to the ability of AI systems to train and update models directly on user devices, rather than in the cloud or on centralized servers. This technique is used to personalize AI models to individual users while preserving privacy, as raw data never leaves the device.

Key Characteristics:
Relies on federated learning, lightweight models, and efficient use of local resources. On-device learning ensures that models are continuously improved based on local user interactions.

Applications:
Personal assistants for learning user preferences, mobile health applications for adapting to individual behavior, and personalized recommendation systems.

Examples:
Google's Gboard uses on-device learning to improve autocorrections and suggestions based on the user's typing habits, all while ensuring data remains on the device.

Benefits:
Enhances personalization, preserves user privacy, and reduces dependency on cloud infrastructure.

Sources:
Federated learning and edge AI research.

Conclusion:
On-device learning offers a solution to the growing demand for personalized, privacy-preserving AI that can adapt to user preferences without compromising data security.

On-Host AI Processing

Definition:
On-host AI processing refers to the execution of AI algorithms directly on a device, such as a smartphone, computer, or IoT device, without relying on cloud-based computation. This approach minimizes latency, increases privacy, and reduces reliance on constant internet connections.

Key Characteristics:
Involves edge computing, local inference, and efficient neural network architectures like MobileNets designed to run on low-power devices.

Applications:
Real-time facial recognition on smartphones, smart home devices like voice-activated assistants, and edge AI in autonomous vehicles.

Examples:
Apple's Face ID performs on-host AI processing to recognize users' faces without sending data to the cloud, ensuring privacy and faster processing.

Benefits:
Reduces latency, enhances data privacy, and allows for AI to function in environments with limited or no connectivity.

Sources:
Research on edge computing and embedded AI systems.

Conclusion:
On-host AI processing is crucial for real-time AI applications where speed and privacy are paramount, offering localized intelligence for modern devices.

Online Hyperparameter Tuning

Definition:
Online hyperparameter tuning is the process of optimizing the hyperparameters of a machine learning model during the training process, rather than determining them in advance. This allows models to adapt dynamically and improve performance in real-time.

Key Characteristics:
Uses techniques like Bayesian optimization, grid search, and evolutionary algorithms. Hyperparameters are adjusted based on feedback from ongoing model performance during training, ensuring more efficient learning.

Applications:
Neural network training for optimizing learning rates and batch sizes, reinforcement learning for tuning exploration-exploitation parameters, and real-time AI systems for adapting hyperparameters to changing environments.

Examples:
In reinforcement learning, online hyperparameter tuning allows the agent to adapt its learning rate dynamically, optimizing performance in unpredictable environments.

Benefits:
Improves model performance, reduces manual tuning efforts, and adapts to changing data distributions during training.

Sources:
Machine learning research on hyperparameter optimization.

Conclusion:
Online hyperparameter tuning is vital for dynamic AI systems that need to continuously adapt, improving both efficiency and accuracy.

Ontology Development in AI

Definition:
Ontology in AI refers to the development of structured frameworks that define the relationships between concepts, entities, and their attributes in a particular domain. Ontologies help AI systems understand the meaning of terms, enabling more intelligent decision-making, reasoning, and communication.

Key Characteristics:
Involves formal representation of knowledge, typically in a hierarchical structure. AI uses ontologies for knowledge representation, semantic search, and natural language understanding.

Applications:
Healthcare modeling relationships between diseases, symptoms, and treatments, knowledge management systems, and semantic web technologies.

Examples:
In healthcare, an ontology could represent the relationships between diseases, symptoms, treatments, and medical tests, aiding AI systems in diagnosing illnesses or suggesting treatments.

Benefits:
Provides a shared understanding of a domain, enhances machine interpretability, and supports reasoning over complex relationships.

Sources:
Research on knowledge representation and semantic AI.

Conclusion:
Ontology development is vital in domains where knowledge needs to be structured and reasoned over, allowing AI systems to perform more sophisticated tasks.

Ontology Engineering

Definition:
Ontology engineering involves systematically developing and maintaining structured representations of knowledge domains, defining concepts, categories, relationships, and rules to support knowledge sharing, interoperability, and reasoning in AI systems.

Key Components:
Ontology languages (OWL, RDF), knowledge representation frameworks, hierarchical structuring, relationship definitions, semantic interoperability standards.

Benefits:
Improves clarity and structure in domain knowledge, enhances interoperability among diverse systems, supports accurate knowledge-based reasoning, facilitates intelligent decision-making processes.

Examples:
Creating medical ontologies for clinical decision support systems; structuring knowledge bases in semantic web applications; developing legal domain ontologies for automated reasoning in law.

Applications:
Knowledge management systems, expert reasoning systems, semantic web platforms, data integration and interoperability, intelligent querying and search.

Industries:
Healthcare, law, education, information technology, e-commerce.

Summary:
Ontology engineering is fundamental in AI for constructing comprehensive and structured knowledge representations, enabling effective reasoning, enhanced communication between systems, and improved decision-making across various industries.

Ontology Extraction

Definition:
Ontology extraction is the process of automatically generating ontologies from unstructured or semi-structured data, such as text documents or databases. AI systems use natural language processing and machine learning algorithms to extract concepts, relationships, and hierarchies from data, building a structured ontology.

Key Characteristics:
Combines NLP, text mining, and knowledge representation techniques to analyze large datasets and extract meaningful relationships between concepts.

Applications:
Content management systems organizing information and metadata, legal systems extracting legal terms and their relationships from documents, and research databases structuring scientific knowledge.

Examples:
In academic publishing, ontology extraction helps categorize research papers by automatically identifying key topics and their relationships, creating a more structured knowledge base.

Benefits:
Automates the time-consuming process of manual ontology creation, helps organize large datasets, and improves AI's ability to reason over the extracted data.

Sources:
AI research on NLP and knowledge representation.

Conclusion:
Ontology extraction enables AI systems to rapidly structure and understand data, making it indispensable for fields where large volumes of text need to be analyzed and categorized.

Ontology Generation

Definition:
Ontology generation is the process of automatically or semi-automatically creating ontologies, which are formal representations of knowledge within a domain. Ontologies consist of concepts, entities, and the relationships between them. In AI, ontology generation enables systems to structure knowledge for better understanding, reasoning, and decision-making.

Key Characteristics:
Utilizes natural language processing (NLP), machine learning, and semantic analysis techniques to extract knowledge from large datasets and structure it into ontologies. It is highly useful in knowledge management, information retrieval, and AI reasoning.

Applications:
Semantic search engines, recommendation systems, automated data organization, and content management.

Examples:
In legal document analysis, an AI system might generate an ontology to organize legal terms, court rulings, and precedents, making it easier for lawyers to find relevant information.

Benefits:
Speeds up knowledge organization, supports interoperability between AI systems, and enhances reasoning abilities in knowledge-rich domains.

Sources:
Knowledge representation and AI reasoning research.

Conclusion:
Ontology generation is essential for systems that require structured knowledge and reasoning, especially in complex fields like law, healthcare, and research.

Ontology Tuning

Definition: Ontology tuning is the refinement of structured knowledge systems (ontologies) used in AI to reflect current realities, domain updates, or application-specific needs. It ensures the ontology remains accurate, consistent, and functional for intelligent reasoning.

Key Characteristics: Includes alignment, pruning, enrichment, and validation of semantic relationships to improve ontological coherence and applicability.

Applications: Applied in intelligent search engines, clinical decision support systems, legal AI tools, and automated product categorization.

Examples: In e-commerce, tuning a product ontology may involve updating seasonal categories or adding new brands to maintain relevance in recommendations.

Benefits: Improves data interpretation, enhances reasoning accuracy, and adapts AI systems to domain evolution.

Conclusion: Ontology tuning is fundamental for maintaining intelligent systems that depend on semantic understanding, ensuring their effectiveness in changing environments.

OpenAI

Definition: OpenAI is a leading AI research organization focused on building safe and powerful artificial intelligence technologies, known for creating accessible tools like ChatGPT and advancing the field through open collaboration and transparency.

Key Components: Generative language models, reinforcement learning systems, open research initiatives, developer APIs, and ethical AI governance frameworks.

Benefits: Promotes AI accessibility, accelerates research and development, ensures safety through rigorous testing, and encourages responsible use of AI technologies.

Examples: GPT-based virtual assistants, DALL·E image generation, Codex for programming assistance, and safety research for AI alignment.

Applications: Conversational AI, code generation, creative design, research support, and educational tools.

Industries: Technology, education, media, finance, healthcare, and software development.

Conclusion: OpenAI plays a pivotal role in the AI ecosystem by offering innovative tools and setting ethical standards, empowering global communities to develop beneficial AI applications.

OpenAI API

Definition: The OpenAI API provides developers with access to OpenAI's state-of-the-art models, allowing seamless integration of natural language processing, generation, and reasoning capabilities into various software applications.

Key Components: API endpoints, GPT models, token management, security protocols, usage analytics, and fine-tuning parameters.

Benefits: Enables fast integration of AI features, supports scalable development, democratizes advanced language tools, and facilitates innovation.

Examples: Automated customer support, dynamic content creation for websites, coding assistance platforms, and language-based chat interfaces.

Applications: Virtual assistants, e-commerce automation, educational tools, content moderation, and productivity software.

Industries: Software, marketing, education, finance, customer service, and media.

Conclusion: The OpenAI API simplifies the adoption of cutting-edge AI technologies, enabling businesses and developers to build intelligent, responsive, and context-aware applications at scale.

Open Domain Question Answering (ODQA)

Definition: Open Domain Question Answering (ODQA) refers to AI systems capable of responding to questions across a wide range of topics without being limited to a specific subject area. These systems rely on vast knowledge sources and advanced natural language understanding to retrieve and synthesize relevant information.

Key Components: Knowledge repositories, information retrieval engines, transformer-based language models, answer generation algorithms, and contextual synthesis methods.

Benefits: Enables comprehensive answers across diverse fields, improves access to information, reduces search time, and supports dynamic learning and decision-making.

Examples: AI chatbots that answer questions from any domain, educational apps that provide instant factual responses, and virtual assistants responding to general queries.

Applications: Intelligent assistants, educational platforms, customer support systems, and knowledge-based AI interfaces.

Industries: Education, technology, healthcare, customer service, and publishing.

Conclusion: ODQA enhances user interaction with AI by delivering fast, accurate, and context-aware answers across multiple domains, expanding the capabilities of information-driven technologies.

Open Set Recognition (OSR)

Definition: Open Set Recognition (OSR) is an AI classification technique where a system can correctly classify known categories while detecting and flagging unknown or novel inputs, allowing it to function reliably in unpredictable real-world conditions.

Key Components: Classification networks, novelty detection mechanisms, confidence thresholds, distance metrics, and dynamic learning frameworks.

Benefits: Increases model resilience to unfamiliar data, improves safety in critical systems, and enhances adaptability in evolving environments.

Examples: Face recognition tools that detect unknown individuals, AI malware detectors flagging new virus types, and industrial monitoring systems identifying abnormal patterns.

Applications: Security systems, anomaly detection, biometric verification, autonomous systems, and quality assurance.

Industries: Security, automotive, manufacturing, cybersecurity, and robotics.

Conclusion: OSR strengthens AI models with the ability to handle the unknown, enabling more robust, secure, and adaptive solutions in dynamic and high-risk applications.

Definition: Open source refers to software or technology whose source code or design is made freely available for use, modification, and distribution by anyone. This encourages transparency, innovation, and collaborative development.

Key Components: Publicly accessible source code, community governance, version control, open licenses, and decentralized development models.

Benefits: Fuels innovation, reduces development costs, increases transparency, enhances security through community review, and promotes learning.

Examples: Linux operating system, TensorFlow machine learning library, OpenCV computer vision toolkit, and the Python programming language.

Applications: Software development, AI research, education, server management, and scientific computing.

Industries: Technology, education, government, research, and startups.

Conclusion: Open source serves as the backbone of modern technology, empowering communities to build, improve, and share powerful tools that advance digital progress.

Open Source

Definition:
Open Source refers to a type of software, technology, or project whose source code is made freely available for anyone to view, modify, and distribute. In the context of artificial intelligence (AI), open source encompasses AI frameworks, algorithms, models, and tools that are accessible to developers, researchers, and organizations worldwide. The open-source approach fosters collaboration, innovation, and transparency, allowing the global community to contribute to the development and improvement of AI technologies.

Key Characteristics:
Open source software is typically released under licenses such as the MIT License, Apache License, GNU General Public License (GPL), or BSD License, which define how the software can be used, modified, and shared.
It promotes transparency, as the source code is publicly available, enabling anyone to inspect, audit, and verify the security, functionality, and ethical implications of the software.
Open source encourages community-driven development, where individuals and organizations collaborate to improve the software, fix bugs, and add new features.
AI open-source projects often include comprehensive documentation, tutorials, and active community support, making them accessible even to those new to AI development.

Core Components of Open Source in AI:
Source Code: The human-readable instructions that define the software's functionality, available for modification and redistribution.
Licensing: Legal frameworks that specify the terms under which the software can be used, modified, and distributed.
Community Collaboration: Contributions from developers, researchers, and enthusiasts worldwide who share knowledge, improve code, and create new functionalities.
Version Control Systems: Platforms like GitHub or GitLab that manage code repositories, track changes, and facilitate collaboration among distributed teams.

Benefits:
Open source accelerates innovation in AI by enabling rapid sharing of ideas, algorithms, and technologies across the global research community.
It reduces costs for individuals and organizations, as the software is free to use and often supported by vibrant communities that provide updates and security patches.
Open-source projects promote interoperability and standardization, allowing different AI tools and systems to work together seamlessly.
They enhance trust and accountability in AI systems, as open access to source code allows for independent verification of ethical and security practices.
Open source supports education and skill development, providing hands-on learning opportunities for students, researchers, and developers.

Disadvantages:
Open-source projects may lack formal support, relying instead on community contributions, which can lead to inconsistent documentation or delayed issue resolution.
Security risks can arise if open-source code is not regularly audited or maintained, as vulnerabilities may be publicly accessible.
While collaboration is a strength, managing contributions from a diverse community can be challenging, potentially leading to code quality issues or conflicts.
Commercial organizations may face challenges integrating open-source AI tools with proprietary systems due to compatibility or licensing restrictions.

Applications in AI:
Machine Learning Frameworks: Popular open-source frameworks include TensorFlow, PyTorch, Scikit-learn, and Keras, which are widely used for building and training AI models.
Natural Language Processing (NLP): Libraries like spaCy, Hugging Face's Transformers, and NLTK enable the development of advanced language models and applications.
Computer Vision: OpenCV and YOLO (You Only Look Once) are open-source tools for image processing, object detection, and video analysis.
Reinforcement Learning: Platforms such as OpenAI Gym and Stable Baselines facilitate the development and benchmarking of reinforcement learning algorithms.

Data Science and Visualization: Jupyter Notebooks, Pandas, and Matplotlib are open-source tools that support data analysis, visualization, and machine learning experimentation.

Sources:
Raymond, E. S. (1999). The Cathedral and the Bazaar: Musings on Linux and Open Source by an Accidental Revolutionary. O'Reilly Media.
Fitzgerald, B. (2006). "The Transformation of Open Source Software." MIS Quarterly.
Open Source Initiative (OSI).
Chollet, F. (2015). Keras: The Python Deep Learning Library. GitHub Repository.

Conclusion:
Open Source is a driving force behind the rapid advancement of AI, enabling global collaboration, innovation, and knowledge sharing. Its principles of transparency, accessibility, and community engagement have democratized AI development, allowing individuals and organizations of all sizes to contribute to and benefit from cutting-edge technologies. While challenges related to security, support, and governance exist, the open-source movement continues to shape the future of AI, fostering a more inclusive and dynamic technological ecosystem.

Operational AI Systems

Definition: Operational AI systems are fully integrated AI solutions deployed in real-world environments to automate decision-making, streamline workflows, and ensure continuous performance across business functions.

Key Components: Real-time processing, robust deployment architecture, monitoring and feedback loops, API integration, and system scalability features.

Benefits: Automates routine operations, reduces human error, supports data-driven decisions, enhances productivity, and scales with business needs.

Examples: Banking systems using AI for fraud detection, retail platforms optimizing inventory with predictive analytics, and telecom companies using AI for automated customer service.

Applications: Process automation, performance monitoring, predictive maintenance, and customer experience enhancement.

Industries: Retail, telecommunications, finance, logistics, healthcare, and manufacturing.

Conclusion: Operational AI systems drive value by embedding intelligence directly into workflows, enabling consistent, scalable, and data-informed operations across all sectors.

Optical Character Recognition (OCR)

Definition:
Optical Character Recognition is a technology that uses AI to convert different types of documents, such as scanned paper documents, PDFs, or images, into editable and searchable data by recognizing text characters.

Key Characteristics:
Involves text extraction, image preprocessing such as binarization, and machine learning models such as CNNs to recognize and convert images of text into machine-encoded text.

Applications:
Document digitization scanning and converting paper documents into digital formats, license plate recognition, and automated data entry systems.

Examples:
OCR is widely used by banks to digitize checks, allowing them to process transactions more efficiently. Similarly, postal services use OCR to automatically read addresses on envelopes.

Benefits:
Automates the conversion of printed documents into digital formats, reducing manual entry, improving accuracy, and increasing productivity.

Sources:
AI research in text recognition and image processing.

Conclusion:
OCR is a crucial technology in the digital transformation of industries that rely on large volumes of textual data, such as finance, government, and logistics.

Optical Flow in Computer Vision

Definition:
Optical flow is a computer vision technique that analyzes apparent motion patterns of objects, surfaces, or edges within sequential video frames, estimating direction and speed of movement.

Key Components:
Motion vectors, intensity gradients, optical flow algorithms (Horn-Schunck, Lucas-Kanade), temporal image sequences, differential analysis.

Benefits:
Enhances motion understanding, improves real-time video analysis accuracy, supports predictive tracking, contributes to effective action recognition.

Examples:
Analyzing pedestrian movements in surveillance footage; tracking motion of players in sports videos; detecting obstacle movements in autonomous vehicles.

Applications:
Autonomous navigation, video compression, human-computer interaction, surveillance analytics, augmented reality systems.

Industries:
Automotive, robotics, security, entertainment, gaming.

Summary:
Optical flow allows AI systems to accurately interpret motion dynamics within visual data, significantly improving tracking and real-time responsiveness in dynamic and interactive environments.

Optical Pattern Recognition

Definition:
Optical Pattern Recognition refers to AI systems that recognize patterns in visual data by analyzing and interpreting features in optical signals, typically using techniques from machine learning and computer vision.

Key Characteristics:
Involves feature extraction, template matching, and deep learning algorithms to detect and classify patterns in images or signals.

Applications:
Biometric authentication such as fingerprint or iris recognition, industrial quality control detecting defects, and medical diagnostics analyzing X-rays or MRIs.

Examples:
In biometric systems, Optical Pattern Recognition is used to match fingerprints against a database for authentication purposes. In healthcare, it's used to detect anomalies in medical images like mammograms.

Benefits:
Automates the recognition of complex visual patterns, improving accuracy and efficiency.

Sources:
Research in optical systems, machine learning, and computer vision.

Conclusion:
Optical Pattern Recognition provides a foundation for AI applications that rely on identifying and analyzing patterns, offering transformative benefits in security, healthcare, and industry.

Optimal Control in AI

Definition:
Optimal control refers to a branch of mathematics and AI focused on finding the best possible control strategy for a dynamic system, given certain constraints and objectives. In AI, optimal control is used to ensure that machines or robots perform tasks with the highest efficiency or minimal cost, often using algorithms that balance speed, energy consumption, and precision.

Key Characteristics:
Uses optimization algorithms, control theory, and dynamic programming. It often involves solving dynamic equations and optimizing performance metrics.

Applications:
Robotics for optimal control of robotic arms, aerospace for controlling spacecraft trajectories, and energy systems for optimizing power usage in smart grids.

Examples:
A robotic arm in a manufacturing plant uses optimal control to move with the least amount of energy while maintaining precision during assembly tasks.

Benefits:
Improves the efficiency and performance of dynamic systems, reduces costs, and ensures adherence to safety or operational constraints.

Sources:
Research in control theory and AI optimization.

Conclusion:
Optimal control is critical for any AI system that manages dynamic environments where efficiency, speed, or energy consumption must be optimized.

Optimal Design in AI Models

Definition:
Optimal design refers to creating the most efficient AI models or experiments by strategically selecting parameters, features, or training data to maximize performance while minimizing costs or resources. It ensures that models are trained effectively without unnecessary complexity or data overload.

Key Characteristics:
Uses statistical techniques like Design of Experiments (DOE), optimization algorithms, and machine learning principles to find the most effective model configurations.

Applications:
Model hyperparameter tuning selecting optimal settings for learning rates, batch sizes, experimental AI designing optimal experiments for data collection, and industrial AI optimizing resource allocation in production processes.

Examples:
In drug discovery, optimal design helps AI systems choose the best set of chemical compounds for testing, minimizing the number of experiments while maximizing the chances of discovering effective drugs.

Benefits:
Reduces computational costs, speeds up model development, and leads to more efficient use of resources.

Sources:
Research in optimization theory and machine learning experimentation.

Conclusion:
Optimal design is critical in AI for developing robust models efficiently, especially in resource-constrained environments or high-stakes applications like healthcare and finance.

Optimal Experiment Design (OED)

Definition:
Optimal experiment design is a framework in AI and machine learning where experiments are carefully structured to yield the most information or optimal results with minimal data or cost. It focuses on selecting the best parameters, data, and model settings to efficiently explore and understand complex systems.

Key Characteristics:
Involves statistical modeling, optimization techniques, and decision theory to design experiments that maximize knowledge while minimizing resources.

Applications:
Drug discovery designing minimal experiments to determine drug efficacy, manufacturing optimizing product testing processes, and machine learning determining the best hyperparameters for models.

Examples:
In A/B testing for websites, OED can be used to design the most efficient experiments to test user interface changes, reducing the number of users needed while maximizing insights.

Benefits:
Reduces experimental costs, speeds up the learning process, and increases the efficiency of decision-making based on experiments.

Sources:
AI research on optimization and statistical experimentation.

Conclusion:
Optimal experiment design is critical for areas where testing is expensive or time-consuming, offering AI systems the ability to learn more from fewer experiments.

Optimal Policy in Reinforcement Learning

Definition: An optimal policy in reinforcement learning is a set of strategies that allows an agent to choose the best action in each state to maximize its cumulative reward over time.

Key Components: Value functions, policy networks, reward signals, exploration strategies, and optimization algorithms.

Benefits: Improves learning efficiency, increases long-term success, ensures consistent behavior, and supports adaptability to changing environments.

Examples: Robots learning the most efficient route through a maze, AI agents mastering complex games, and algorithms optimizing energy usage in smart grids.

Applications: Autonomous navigation, robotics, game AI, automated control systems, and financial trading.

Industries: Transportation, robotics, gaming, energy, and finance.

Conclusion: Optimal policies are the foundation of intelligent behavior in reinforcement learning, enabling AI systems to achieve maximum performance through smart decision-making.

Optimal Query Formulation

Definition: Optimal query formulation is the strategic construction of database or search queries to retrieve the most accurate, relevant, and complete results, often with the help of AI-driven enhancements.

Key Components: Natural language understanding, semantic analysis, query expansion, relevance scoring, and adaptive refinement.

Benefits: Improves accuracy and efficiency of search results, saves user time, and enhances user satisfaction in information retrieval.

Examples: Search engines refining vague queries, customer support bots interpreting ambiguous questions, and AI assistants reformulating complex data requests.

Applications: Search engines, customer service, knowledge bases, and AI-driven research tools.

Industries: Technology, education, healthcare, legal, and business intelligence.

Conclusion: Optimal query formulation is key to unlocking relevant and precise information, making AI systems more effective in responding to human inquiries.

Optimal Query Processing

Definition: Optimal query processing is the method of retrieving and delivering information from databases with maximum efficiency using AI techniques to reduce resource usage and execution time.

Key Components: Execution planning, indexing strategies, workload-aware optimization, caching, and AI-driven query analysis.

Benefits: Accelerates data retrieval, enhances system performance, and reduces computational costs in large-scale systems.

Examples: AI-powered systems that adjust query plans based on traffic load, databases that reorganize queries to minimize latency.

Applications: Enterprise databases, data warehouses, big data analytics, and cloud platforms.

Industries: Technology, retail, finance, telecommunications, and logistics.

Conclusion: Optimal query processing ensures that data-heavy applications remain responsive, efficient, and scalable in complex environments.

Optimal Substructure in AI Algorithms

Definition:
Optimal substructure is a property of certain algorithms where an optimal solution to a problem can be constructed from optimal solutions of its subproblems. This concept is foundational in dynamic programming and divide-and-conquer algorithms, commonly used in AI for solving complex optimization and decision-making tasks.

Key Characteristics:
Breaks problems into smaller, manageable subproblems and ensures that each subproblem contributes to the overall solution. Algorithms like dynamic programming and greedy algorithms utilize this concept.

Applications:
Pathfinding such as Dijkstra's algorithm for shortest paths, scheduling, and resource allocation in AI systems.

Examples:
In pathfinding algorithms such as A*, optimal substructure ensures that the shortest path from one point to another can be built by combining optimal subpaths.

Benefits:
Simplifies complex problems by breaking them down into smaller, easier-to-solve components, leading to efficient and scalable solutions.

Sources:
Algorithmic research and AI optimization studies.

Conclusion:
Understanding optimal substructure is essential for designing efficient AI algorithms that require optimization, such as those used in navigation, scheduling, and resource management.

Optimal Transport Theory in Machine Learning

Definition: Optimal transport theory in machine learning is a mathematical framework used to compare, match, or map two different probability distributions in the most efficient way. This approach is widely used in AI to bridge domain gaps and refine data alignment.

Key Components: Cost functions, Wasserstein distance, convex optimization methods, and distribution matching algorithms.

Benefits: Improves domain adaptation, enhances generative model output, and provides a principled method to quantify differences between datasets.

Applications: Common in generative adversarial networks (GANs), domain adaptation for unsupervised learning, and structured data comparison.

Examples: In generative modeling, optimal transport theory helps improve realism in generated images by minimizing distributional shifts from the training set.

Conclusion: Optimal transport provides a robust mathematical foundation for aligning and transforming data in AI systems, enhancing performance in generative and adaptive models.

Optimistic Query Execution

Definition: Optimistic query execution is a performance optimization technique where the system assumes that certain data will be accessible during execution and proceeds accordingly, making adjustments only if those assumptions prove invalid.

Key Components: Speculative execution, rollback mechanisms, data prefetching, prediction algorithms, and real-time monitoring.

Benefits: Speeds up query responses, supports real-time systems, and maintains flexibility in uncertain data conditions.

Examples: Real-time dashboards fetching live data optimistically, systems that continue processing while validating uncertain data in the background.

Applications: Distributed computing, streaming analytics, high-frequency trading, and real-time recommendation systems.

Industries: Finance, e-commerce, logistics, media, and telecom.

Conclusion: Optimistic query execution boosts responsiveness in dynamic environments, making it ideal for applications where speed is critical.

Optimization Algorithms in AI

Definition: Optimization algorithms in AI are computational methods designed to improve model performance by systematically adjusting parameters to minimize or maximize an objective function. These algorithms are foundational in training AI systems to achieve accurate, efficient, and optimal results.

Key Components: Objective functions, gradient-based methods, evolutionary strategies, constraint handling, heuristic and metaheuristic optimization techniques.

Benefits: Improves AI accuracy, reduces training time, enhances computational efficiency, and supports robust decision-making across a variety of tasks.

Examples: Using gradient descent to optimize neural network weights, applying genetic algorithms to schedule delivery routes, and deploying particle swarm optimization in energy management systems.

Applications: Machine learning model tuning, resource allocation, operational planning, robotics control, and autonomous systems.

Industries: Technology, manufacturing, healthcare, logistics, finance, and energy.

Conclusion: Optimization algorithms empower AI systems to operate efficiently and accurately, enabling real-world performance improvements across data-intensive and dynamic applications.

Optimization in AI

Definition:
Optimization in AI involves selecting the most effective solutions from a set of possible alternatives by systematically improving parameters, decision variables, or configurations according to defined objectives or criteria.

Key Components:
Optimization algorithms (gradient descent, evolutionary algorithms), objective functions, constraints, iterative refinement, performance metrics.

Benefits:
Enhances efficiency, accuracy, and reliability of AI solutions; reduces costs and resource waste; provides systematic approaches to problem-solving.

Examples:
Hyperparameter tuning in machine learning models; logistics route optimization; portfolio optimization in finance.

Applications:
Machine learning, logistics planning, financial modeling, manufacturing efficiency, decision support systems.

Industries:
Technology, finance, logistics, manufacturing, healthcare.

Summary:
Optimization techniques in AI are foundational, enabling intelligent systems to systematically refine and improve their solutions, significantly boosting overall performance and effectiveness across diverse applications.

Optimization in Neural Networks

Definition: Optimization in neural networks is the process of adjusting weights and biases to minimize the model's prediction error and improve its generalization on new data.

Key Components: Loss functions, gradient descent, backpropagation, learning rate tuning, and regularization techniques.

Benefits: Enhances model accuracy, accelerates convergence, prevents overfitting, and ensures reliable performance.

Examples: Training image recognition models to accurately classify objects, optimizing chatbots for understanding user inputs.

Applications: Deep learning, natural language processing, predictive modeling, and robotics.

Industries: Healthcare, finance, automotive, retail, and education.

Conclusion: Optimization is the engine behind learning in neural networks, powering AI models to deliver high accuracy and consistent results.

Optimization Transfer in AI

Definition: Optimization transfer in AI refers to the process of applying learned optimization strategies or model parameters from one task or domain to another, closely related one. This technique allows AI systems to benefit from prior knowledge to solve new problems more efficiently.

Key Components: Pre-trained models, fine-tuning methods, transfer learning frameworks, and adaptive optimization algorithms.

Benefits: Reduces training time, conserves computational resources, improves accuracy in data-scarce settings, and accelerates deployment across similar tasks.

Applications: Used in natural language processing, image recognition, reinforcement learning, and speech processing where tasks share similarities.

Examples: Fine-tuning a general language model for specific customer sentiment analysis, reusing policies in new but related reinforcement learning environments.

Conclusion: Optimization transfer supports the scalability and adaptability of AI systems, enabling efficient reuse of knowledge across domains with similar structures.

Optimization Weights in Neural Networks

Definition: Optimization of weights in neural networks is the process of adjusting the internal parameters (weights) of a network to minimize prediction errors during training. This is a fundamental component of how neural networks learn.

Key Components: Loss functions, gradient descent algorithms, backpropagation, and learning rate schedules.

Benefits: Improves model accuracy, ensures efficient learning, and allows for convergence toward optimal performance.

Applications: Applied in training AI systems for tasks like speech recognition, image classification, machine translation, and autonomous decision-making.

Examples: In deep learning, algorithms like Adam or RMSprop iteratively update network weights to reduce classification errors during model training.

Conclusion: Effective weight optimization drives successful neural network learning, forming the foundation of deep learning advancements in AI.

Optimized Query Filtering

Definition: Optimized query filtering is the strategic use of filters during data queries to limit the scope of data retrieval, reducing processing time and improving result precision.

Key Components: Query constraints, index-based filtering, predicate pushdown, adaptive filtering algorithms, and filter prediction models.

Benefits: Speeds up queries, reduces server load, improves data relevance, and enhances user experience.

Examples: E-commerce platforms filtering search results by price or availability, real-time dashboards querying only active user data.

Applications: Business intelligence, data exploration, AI analytics, and customer behavior tracking.

Industries: Retail, marketing, logistics, finance, and cloud computing.

Conclusion: Optimized query filtering is essential for managing large datasets efficiently, ensuring that users receive relevant and timely information.

OQL (Object Query Language)

Definition: Object Query Language (OQL) is a specialized query language designed for retrieving and manipulating data stored in object-oriented databases, extending the principles of SQL to support object-specific features.

Key Components: Object classes, inheritance support, method invocation, relationship navigation, and complex object queries.

Benefits: Enables more intuitive queries for object-based systems, supports hierarchical data models, and facilitates integration with object-oriented programming.

Examples: Using OQL to extract multimedia content attributes or querying class hierarchies in simulation models.

Applications: Object-oriented database systems, CAD systems, simulations, and AI systems managing complex object structures.

Industries: Engineering, media, software development, gaming, and education.

Conclusion: OQL bridges the gap between object-oriented programming and database management, offering powerful querying capabilities for structured, object-based data.

Oracle Query Optimization

Definition: Oracle query optimization is the process of selecting the most efficient execution plan for a SQL statement within an Oracle database. AI techniques are increasingly used to improve this process by learning from historical performance data and recommending execution strategies that minimize resource usage.

Key Characteristics: Uses cost-based optimization (CBO), AI-driven performance tuning, execution plan caching, and adaptive query processing to identify optimal plans.

Applications: Deployed in enterprise-level data warehousing, financial databases, e-commerce platforms, and AI-enhanced database management systems.

Examples: In an Oracle-based e-commerce system, query optimization reduces the load time for complex user analytics by selecting the most efficient data access path, saving both time and compute power.

Benefits: Reduces query latency, improves overall system performance, and lowers operational costs by optimizing resource allocation.

Conclusion: Oracle query optimization ensures that large-scale databases operate at peak efficiency, empowering AI applications with fast, reliable access to critical data.

Orchestration of AI Workflows

Definition: AI workflow orchestration is the management and coordination of multiple AI processes, models, and data pipelines within a single framework to ensure efficient execution.

Key Characteristics: Includes automation, resource scheduling, error recovery, and modular integration across tools like Airflow, Kubeflow, and MLflow.

Applications: Used in end-to-end ML pipelines, data science platforms, enterprise AI systems, and cloud-based model deployment.

Examples: An AI-powered fraud detection system orchestrates input collection, feature engineering, model execution, and alerting through a managed pipeline.

Benefits: Enhances productivity, reduces manual interventions, ensures consistency in output, and simplifies AI system scalability.

Conclusion: Orchestration streamlines AI deployments, enabling organizations to efficiently manage complex workflows across diverse environments.

Ordinal Classification in AI

Definition: Ordinal classification in AI is a predictive modeling method used to assign instances to categories with a meaningful order, but without fixed intervals. It is designed to handle classification tasks where the labels follow a ranked structure.

Key Characteristics: Emphasizes the order of classes, modifies traditional classification algorithms for ordinal targets, and employs loss functions that penalize deviations from true order.

Applications: Useful in customer satisfaction surveys, risk assessment, clinical severity ratings, and product reviews where classes are ranked from low to high.

Examples: An AI model predicting cancer stages can rank patients from Stage I to Stage IV, ensuring that the progression in severity is respected in predictions.

Benefits: Preserves class order in predictions, improves decision quality, and supports interpretability in scenarios where ranking is crucial.

Conclusion: Ordinal classification is an important approach for AI tasks that rely on ranked outcomes, enabling structured and meaningful predictions.

Ordinal Regression in AI

Definition: Ordinal regression is a machine learning technique used for predicting variables with ordered categories. It is distinct from standard regression or classification as it accounts for the ordinal nature of the output.

Key Characteristics: Applies custom loss functions and constraints to maintain order, uses threshold models and statistical inference techniques for predictions.

Applications: Seen in academic grading, job performance scales, healthcare diagnostics, and market rating systems.

Examples: In medical diagnosis, ordinal regression can predict levels of disease severity, guiding treatment decisions based on ranked risk categories.

Benefits: Supports decision-making based on ranked data, minimizes misclassification penalties, and improves outcome interpretability.

Conclusion: Ordinal regression helps AI models deal effectively with ranked categories, ensuring structured and logically ordered predictions.

Organizational AI

Definition: Organizational AI refers to the deployment of AI technologies across business operations to enhance automation, strategy, and decision-making. It involves embedding machine learning and intelligent systems into enterprise workflows.

Key Characteristics: Integrates with enterprise software, facilitates robotic process automation, applies predictive analytics, and enables strategic AI-driven transformation.

Applications: Used in HR automation, predictive sales forecasting, fraud detection, inventory optimization, and executive decision-making.

Examples: A company may implement AI to automate onboarding workflows, saving time and improving consistency across departments.

Benefits: Drives operational efficiency, supports intelligent decision-making, reduces human error, and scales productivity across the organization.

Conclusion: Organizational AI transforms the workplace by bringing intelligence into business processes, enhancing performance across all levels of operation.

Oriented Bounding Boxes (OBB) in Computer Vision

Definition: Oriented bounding boxes are rotated rectangles used in computer vision to encapsulate objects in alignment with their orientation. They improve the precision of object detection tasks, especially for rotated or skewed items.

Key Characteristics: Extends traditional bounding boxes by including angle predictions, enabling better localization of non-axis-aligned objects.

Applications: Used in aerial imaging, automated driving, warehouse automation, and 3D object tracking where object orientation matters.

Examples: In aerial surveillance, OBBs are used to accurately outline buildings or vehicles that appear rotated in satellite images.

Benefits: Improves accuracy of object detection, enhances spatial analysis, and supports applications requiring angle-sensitive recognition.

Conclusion: Oriented bounding boxes bring precision to computer vision models in dynamic environments, making them vital in object-centric AI applications.

Organized Feature Learning

Definition: Organized feature learning involves extracting and structuring features from data in a way that preserves their inherent relationships, improving AI model performance on structured or sequential tasks.

Key Characteristics: Combines spatial, temporal, or semantic feature hierarchies using deep learning layers, attention mechanisms, and modular architectures.

Applications: Found in image classification, natural language understanding, speech recognition, and multi-modal learning tasks.

Examples: A facial recognition system uses organized feature learning to identify key facial landmarks and distinguish individuals even in low-light conditions.

Benefits: Improves accuracy, enhances interpretability, and strengthens pattern recognition in structured data environments.

Conclusion: Organized feature learning enables AI models to efficiently process and understand data with rich internal structure, improving outcomes across domains.

Ornstein-Uhlenbeck Process in Reinforcement Learning

Definition: The Ornstein-Uhlenbeck process is a noise-generating method used in reinforcement learning to produce temporally correlated random actions, aiding exploration in continuous control environments.

Key Characteristics: Smooth, time-dependent noise generation that maintains stability and improves learning efficiency in sensitive tasks.

Applications: Utilized in robotic motion control, steering systems in autonomous vehicles, and industrial machinery optimization.

Examples: During robotic training, the Ornstein-Uhlenbeck process generates exploration noise that helps the agent discover subtle movements for manipulating objects.

Benefits: Improves exploration consistency, supports fine-tuned learning, and enhances performance in continuous action spaces.

Conclusion: The Ornstein-Uhlenbeck process is essential in continuous reinforcement learning tasks where stability and exploration must coexist.

Outlier Detection in AI

Definition: Outlier detection in AI identifies data points that significantly differ from the majority of observations in a dataset. This process is crucial for maintaining data integrity and uncovering anomalies.

Key Components: Distance-based methods, statistical analysis, clustering techniques, and anomaly detection algorithms like isolation forests and autoencoders.

Benefits: Improves model robustness, identifies potential risks or errors, and enhances the quality of predictions.

Applications: Used in fraud detection, intrusion detection, medical diagnostics, and data cleansing.

Examples: An AI model detecting fraudulent credit card transactions flags outliers that deviate from normal purchasing behavior.

Conclusion: Outlier detection supports reliable AI decision-making by removing misleading or harmful data patterns, protecting system accuracy and integrity.

Overfitting in AI Models

Definition: Overfitting in AI occurs when a model learns patterns, noise, or details from the training data that do not generalize to new data, resulting in poor performance on unseen tasks.

Key Components: Excessive model complexity, insufficient regularization, and lack of validation.

Benefits: Although unintentional, recognizing overfitting helps developers improve generalization by applying corrective methods.

Applications: Relevant across AI disciplines including image processing, forecasting, and natural language tasks.

Examples: An overfitted image classifier may perform perfectly on its training images but misclassifies new images due to reliance on background details.

Conclusion: Controlling overfitting is vital for building AI models that generalize well and perform reliably in real-world scenarios.

Overfitting in Machine Learning Models

Definition:
Overfitting occurs when a machine learning model learns the training data too well, capturing noise or details that don't generalize to new, unseen data. Overfitting typically leads to high accuracy on training data but poor performance on test data or in real-world applications.

Key Characteristics:
Can be identified when there is a large discrepancy between training and test performance. Techniques like regularization (L1 or L2), dropout in neural networks, and cross-validation are used to prevent overfitting.

Applications:
Common in machine learning tasks like image classification, natural language processing, and predictive analytics where complex models are used.

Examples:
In stock market prediction, a model that overfits might perform exceptionally well on historical data but fail to predict future trends due to learning irrelevant patterns from the training data.

Benefits:
While overfitting helps understand model limitations, addressing it through techniques like regularization improves generalizability and performance in real-world settings.

Sources:
Machine learning best practices and model validation techniques.

Conclusion:
Avoiding overfitting is critical for building robust, generalizable AI models capable of performing well on unseen data.

Overfitting Prevention Techniques

Definition: Overfitting prevention techniques are strategies applied during AI model training to improve generalization and reduce the risk of learning noise instead of true patterns.

Key Components: Regularization (L1/L2), dropout, early stopping, cross-validation, and data augmentation.

Benefits: Increases reliability, enhances generalization, and improves long-term model performance.

Applications: Widely used in training neural networks, regression models, and supervised learning frameworks.

Examples: Dropout randomly deactivates neurons during training, preventing co-adaptation and encouraging the model to learn redundant, robust features.

Conclusion: Integrating overfitting prevention methods is critical to ensuring AI models remain reliable across diverse inputs and scenarios.

Overlearning in AI

Definition: Overlearning in AI refers to the excessive memorization of training data, causing the model to lose flexibility when handling new data. It is closely associated with poor generalization.

Key Components: High training accuracy with low test accuracy, lack of abstraction, and sensitivity to minor input variations.

Benefits: Awareness of overlearning encourages better data management and model tuning.

Applications: Seen in chatbots, translation systems, and AI tutors where memorization impairs adaptability.

Examples: An AI assistant that memorizes exact phrases from past users may fail to respond appropriately to slightly altered questions.

Conclusion: Avoiding overlearning ensures AI models can generalize across inputs, making them more useful, flexible, and reliable.

Overparameterization in Deep Learning

Definition: Overparameterization occurs when a neural network has more parameters than necessary to fit the training data. While it enhances model capacity, it can also lead to inefficiency and overfitting.

Key Components: Large model architectures, numerous layers and neurons, and high parameter-to-data ratios.

Benefits: Increases model expressiveness and capacity to learn complex functions, but must be carefully controlled.

Applications: Used in massive language models, vision transformers, and speech generation networks.

Examples: GPT-like models use billions of parameters to generate human-like text but require regularization and large datasets to perform well.

Conclusion: Overparameterization is a double-edged sword in AI: it allows for deep, expressive models, but demands careful tuning and large data to prevent performance degradation.

Oversampling Techniques in AI

Definition: Oversampling techniques are used in AI to balance datasets that have unequal representation of classes. This is achieved by increasing the frequency of the minority class to improve learning outcomes in classification tasks.

Key Components: Synthetic data generation methods, random oversampling, and class distribution balancing techniques.

Benefits: Improves model fairness, enhances classification performance for underrepresented classes, and reduces the likelihood of biased predictions.

Applications: Widely applied in fraud detection, rare disease diagnosis, and sentiment analysis where data imbalance is common.

Examples: A healthcare AI system uses SMOTE to generate synthetic examples of rare diseases, allowing the model to recognize them more accurately.

Conclusion: Oversampling is essential for developing robust AI systems that can fairly and effectively classify minority categories in skewed datasets.

Over Segmentation in Image Processing

Definition: Over segmentation occurs when an image is divided into more segments than necessary, leading to fragmented and less meaningful analysis. In AI, this can reduce the effectiveness of tasks like object recognition or classification.

Key Components: Segmentation algorithms, pixel-level classification, and feature grouping methods.

Benefits: Addressing over segmentation leads to more coherent object identification and improves the reliability of image analysis results.

Applications: Relevant in medical scans, autonomous driving systems, and aerial image analysis.

Examples: An AI analyzing satellite images may incorrectly split a river into multiple segments, complicating flood risk assessments.

Conclusion: Avoiding oversegmentation in image processing ensures clearer feature representation, resulting in more accurate and usable visual interpretations.

Ownership of AI-Generated Content

Definition: Ownership of AI-generated content involves the legal and ethical considerations about who holds the rights to works created by artificial intelligence, including text, music, designs, and images.

Key Components: Intellectual property policies, authorship attribution models, and licensing frameworks.

Benefits: Clarifies accountability, encourages ethical content use, and fosters innovation while respecting legal boundaries.

Applications: Applies to generative AI platforms, creative industry tools, and publishing workflows.

Examples: A user creates a song using an AI composer and must determine whether they or the software provider owns the copyright.

Conclusion: Clearly defining ownership of AI-generated outputs is critical for maintaining transparency and legal fairness as AI becomes a more common creative partner.

Ozone Anomaly Detection in AI Systems

Definition: Ozone anomaly detection involves using AI algorithms to identify unexpected deviations in ozone levels. These deviations may signal environmental shifts or malfunctions in sensor networks.

Key Components: Outlier detection models, real-time ozone monitoring data, and alert-generation mechanisms.

Benefits: Improves environmental monitoring accuracy, enables rapid response to pollution events, and enhances sensor reliability.

Applications: Deployed in air quality stations, industrial emission control systems, and climate monitoring platforms.

Examples: An AI system alerts a city's environmental agency when ozone levels sharply rise in an area previously showing low readings.

Conclusion: Ozone anomaly detection empowers environmental systems with timely insights, allowing early intervention for public safety and ecological health.

Ozone Data Augmentation in AI

Definition: Ozone data augmentation refers to generating synthetic ozone-related data to enhance training datasets, especially where real-world ozone measurements are limited or imbalanced.

Key Components: Synthetic data tools, adversarial network models, and pattern-based sampling methods.

Benefits: Expands dataset diversity, improves model generalization, and supports predictive accuracy in sparse-data regions.

Applications: Useful in environmental forecasting, rural air quality analysis, and AI climate simulation tools.

Examples: Data scientists generate additional ozone level data using GANs to support model training for areas lacking sensor coverage.

Conclusion: Ozone data augmentation strengthens AI models with broader datasets, improving predictive capabilities in real-world environmental applications.

Ozone Layer Depletion Prediction Using AI

Definition: AI models that predict ozone layer depletion analyze atmospheric trends, human activities, and chemical emissions to forecast potential thinning of the ozone layer.

Key Components: Historical atmospheric data, emission tracking systems, neural forecasting networks, and global climate simulators.

Benefits: Enables early intervention, supports global climate strategies, and provides insight into ozone recovery efforts.

Applications: Applied in climate change research, environmental compliance reporting, and international treaty assessments.

Examples: AI models simulate ozone layer behavior over decades, evaluating the impact of policy changes on long-term atmospheric health.

Conclusion: AI-assisted predictions on ozone layer depletion offer critical insights for protecting Earth's atmosphere and guiding future sustainability efforts.

Ozone Level Data Mining

Definition: Ozone level data mining is the process of extracting patterns, correlations, and trends from large datasets of ozone readings to uncover meaningful insights about atmospheric behavior.

Key Components: Data clustering tools, temporal and spatial analysis models, and statistical pattern discovery techniques.

Benefits: Reveals hidden relationships, supports evidence-based policy, and improves understanding of ozone dynamics.

Applications: Used in environmental modeling, public health planning, and air quality policy analysis.

Examples: A data mining model finds that ozone peaks often occur after specific wind patterns, guiding local government action plans.

Conclusion: Mining ozone datasets with AI offers valuable knowledge for predicting trends and addressing environmental challenges linked to air quality and climate resilience.

Ozone Monitoring Using AI Sensors

Definition: Ozone monitoring using AI sensors integrates smart detection technologies with machine learning to track ozone levels in real time. These systems analyze incoming data from distributed environmental sensors to evaluate air quality trends and detect pollution spikes.

Key Components: Internet of Things (IoT) devices, AI algorithms for pattern recognition, sensor networks, and cloud-based data processing platforms.

Benefits: Delivers accurate, real-time air quality updates, reduces reliance on manual data collection, and enables faster public health responses.

Applications: Used in urban planning, industrial pollution monitoring, and public health surveillance systems.

Examples: In smart cities, AI-driven ozone sensors transmit real-time pollution data to central dashboards, helping planners manage traffic and emissions more effectively.

Conclusion: AI-enhanced ozone monitoring ensures faster detection, better analysis, and proactive responses to ozone pollution, supporting healthier and more sustainable environments.

Ozone Prediction AI Models

Definition: Ozone prediction models powered by AI use environmental data to forecast future ozone concentrations. These models rely on machine learning to detect patterns in historical and current measurements.

Key Components: Time-series data inputs, meteorological variables, regression models, and neural network architectures.

Benefits: Facilitates proactive air quality management, helps mitigate public health risks, and supports policy planning with predictive insights.

Applications: Widely used in city air quality forecasting, climate monitoring, and public health advisories.

Examples: AI-based systems can alert city officials about upcoming ozone level increases, allowing them to issue public warnings or implement preventive measures.

Conclusion: AI-driven ozone prediction tools are crucial for managing environmental risks, offering cities and governments the foresight needed to protect their populations.

Ozone Prediction in Urban Areas

Definition: Ozone prediction systems designed for urban settings utilize AI to forecast ozone concentration in densely populated regions, accounting for variables like traffic, weather, and industrial output.

Key Components: Urban sensor networks, machine learning models, meteorological forecasting, and traffic emission data.

Benefits: Improves city-level air quality planning, protects vulnerable populations, and supports emergency response coordination.

Applications: Used in city health departments, environmental regulatory agencies, and public alert systems.

Examples: An AI platform might analyze city traffic data and weather forecasts to predict afternoon ozone surges, prompting traffic control measures.

Conclusion: AI-enhanced ozone forecasting in urban areas empowers cities to anticipate pollution events, protect residents, and maintain environmental stability.

Ozone Pollution Control Using AI

Definition: AI-based ozone pollution control systems analyze environmental data to manage and reduce harmful ozone emissions. These systems leverage predictive modeling and automated actions to minimize pollution in real time.

Key Components: Data collection sensors, forecasting algorithms, automated response systems, and emissions modeling tools.

Benefits: Improves regulatory compliance, supports sustainable industrial practices, and safeguards public health by reducing air pollution.

Applications: Used in factory emission controls, traffic management, and industrial pollution reduction strategies.

Examples: AI tools in a factory can reduce ozone output by adjusting chemical processes during peak pollution periods based on environmental forecasts.

Conclusion: Controlling ozone pollution with AI provides smarter, faster, and more adaptive solutions to environmental challenges, ensuring cleaner air for all.

Ozone Risk Prediction Using AI

Definition: Ozone risk prediction systems employ AI to estimate the health risks associated with elevated ozone levels, helping healthcare providers and policy makers plan effective interventions.

Key Components: Health impact models, ozone level data, machine learning algorithms, and demographic overlays.

Benefits: Identifies at-risk populations, informs public health policies, and allows for proactive health warnings.

Applications: Deployed in healthcare preparedness systems, environmental health dashboards, and community risk assessments.

Examples: An AI tool may predict an uptick in asthma-related ER visits based on anticipated ozone levels and local population health data.

Conclusion: AI-based ozone risk prediction is a powerful tool for protecting public health, helping communities respond to air quality threats with foresight and precision.

Ozone Sensor Calibration Using AI

Definition: Ozone sensor calibration using AI involves real-time adjustment of measurement instruments through machine learning models that detect and correct inaccuracies.

Key Components: Sensor feedback data, reference models, adaptive calibration algorithms, and historical environmental records.

Benefits: Ensures reliable long-term sensor performance, reduces maintenance costs, and improves data accuracy for environmental monitoring.

Applications: Used in national air quality networks, industrial monitoring systems, and scientific atmospheric research.

Examples: An AI calibration model continually learns from environmental patterns to fine-tune ozone sensors without human intervention.

Conclusion: AI-powered calibration keeps ozone monitoring equipment operating at peak accuracy, enabling dependable insights into environmental conditions across diverse settings.

LETTER P

Path Planning

Definition
Path planning is the AI-driven process of determining the best route from a starting point to a destination, optimizing for safety, efficiency, and obstacle avoidance.

Key Components
Environmental mapping and modeling
Obstacle detection and avoidance
Pathfinding algorithms such as A* or Dijkstra's
Cost functions and heuristic evaluations

Benefits
Enables safe and autonomous navigation
Improves operational efficiency
Supports dynamic, real-time decision-making
Enhances reliability in unpredictable environments

Examples
Warehouse robots navigating aisles
Drones avoiding restricted airspaces
Self-driving cars calculating optimal routes

Applications
Autonomous vehicle navigation
Industrial warehouse robotics
Drone mission planning
Gaming AI pathfinding

Industries
Transportation and logistics
Aerospace and defense
Entertainment and gaming
Urban planning

Challenges
Real-time processing demands
Handling dynamic and unpredictable environments
Scalability in larger operational spaces
Balancing speed, safety, and resource use

Summary
Path planning empowers AI systems to navigate independently and efficiently, serving as a foundation for intelligent robotics, autonomous driving, and automated logistics.

Pattern Recognition

Definition
Pattern recognition refers to the ability of AI systems to detect structures, regularities, or patterns within data. It enables machines to interpret images, sounds, sequences, and other complex inputs intelligently.

Key Components
Data preparation and preprocessing
Feature extraction techniques
Classification or clustering algorithms
Model training and validation

Benefits
Automates complex recognition tasks
Enhances decision-making accuracy
Enables real-time detection and monitoring
Adapts to new patterns in changing environments

Examples
Recognizing faces in security systems
Converting handwritten notes into digital text
Translating speech into written words
Authenticating users through biometric scans

Applications
Image and video analysis
Speech recognition technologies
Medical diagnostic tools
Object detection for autonomous systems

Industries
Security and surveillance
Healthcare and medicine
Finance and banking
Retail customer analytics

Challenges
Handling variability and noise in input data
Managing incomplete or missing patterns
Maintaining performance in real-time conditions
Dependence on large, high-quality datasets

Summary
Pattern recognition supports AI in interpreting and organizing complex data, making it critical for technologies ranging from facial recognition to medical diagnostics.

Perceptron

Definition
A perceptron is one of the earliest models of artificial neurons, performing binary classification by mapping weighted inputs to an output through a simple activation function.

Key Components
Input feature vector
Weights and bias terms
Activation function such as a step function
Output decision-making mechanism

Benefits
Simple and interpretable structure
Foundation for modern deep learning models
Effective for solving linearly separable problems
Fast training and convergence on basic tasks

Examples
Classifying emails as spam or non-spam
Recognizing basic handwritten digits
Simple sensor-based classification tasks

Applications
Binary classification models
Educational demonstrations in AI
Foundations for deeper neural networks

Industries
Education and AI training
Software development
Cybersecurity for filtering simple threats
Customer service automation

Challenges
Cannot solve non-linear problems
Limited flexibility compared to modern networks
Obsolete for handling complex patterns

Summary
The perceptron laid the foundation for modern AI learning, showcasing how simple models could process information, although modern AI systems have evolved far beyond it.

Perceptual Computing

Definition
Perceptual computing enables machines to interpret human sensory inputs like vision, speech, and touch, making interactions more natural and intuitive.

Key Components
Multimodal sensory data processing

Computer vision and speech recognition
Gesture and facial expression analysis
Sensor integration and fusion

Benefits
Creates more natural interfaces between humans and machines
Improves accessibility for users with diverse needs
Enables adaptive, personalized user experiences
Supports the evolution of immersive technologies

Examples
Facial recognition in mobile devices
Voice commands controlling smart homes
Gesture-based controls in augmented reality applications

Applications
Smart consumer electronics
Virtual and augmented reality
Assistive technologies for accessibility
Interactive educational platforms

Industries
Consumer technology
Healthcare and rehabilitation
Gaming and immersive entertainment
Education and learning

Challenges
Managing noise and incomplete sensory inputs
Balancing privacy concerns with usability
Hardware and processing demands for real-time responses
Integrating multiple sensor streams effectively

Summary
Perceptual computing is central to advancing AI toward human-like interaction, transforming how people engage with technology in their everyday lives.

Performance Tuning

Definition
Performance tuning involves optimizing AI systems for maximum efficiency, minimizing resource usage, and improving scalability through technical adjustments and hardware utilization.

Key Components
Model refinement and adjustment
Hyperparameter optimization
Hardware acceleration using GPUs or TPUs
System profiling to identify bottlenecks

Benefits
Reduces training and inference times
Improves model responsiveness and scalability
Optimizes resource consumption and energy use
Enhances user experience in real-world deployments

Examples
Speeding up deep learning training with mixed precision
Reducing latency in real-time recommendation systems
Optimizing AI for low-power mobile or edge devices

Applications
Model deployment optimization
Big data pipeline efficiency
Embedded AI applications
Financial trading systems

Industries
Financial services
Cloud and telecommunications
Smart manufacturing
Mobile and IoT technology

Challenges
Requires expertise in software and hardware optimization
Balancing performance improvements with model accuracy
Hardware limitations may impose restrictions
Scalability challenges at larger operational levels

Summary
Performance tuning is essential for creating efficient and practical AI systems, ensuring technology can meet real-world demands without sacrificing speed or resource efficiency.

Permutation Importance

Definition
Permutation importance is a method for evaluating the influence of individual features in a machine learning model by measuring performance drops when feature values are randomly shuffled.

Key Components
Random shuffling of feature values
Baseline performance comparison
Impact measurement after permutation
Repeatability across multiple evaluation rounds

Benefits
Simple to apply and interpret
Works with any predictive model
Helps identify crucial features for accuracy
Supports model debugging and transparency

Examples
Determining top features in medical risk models
Identifying important behaviors in customer churn analysis
Highlighting key attributes in fraud detection models

Applications
Explainable AI models
Feature engineering and selection

Compliance and regulatory audits for AI models
Model debugging and improvement

Industries
Healthcare and medical research
Financial services and risk management
E-commerce and customer analytics
Insurance underwriting

Challenges
Sensitivity to correlated features
High computational costs for large models
Possible variability in repeated runs
Dependence on quality of the evaluation metric

Summary
Permutation importance reveals the role of individual features in predictive models, promoting explainability and trust in machine learning decisions across critical industries.

Personalization Algorithms

Definition
Personalization algorithms are AI-driven techniques that customize content, recommendations, or services for individual users by analyzing their behavior, preferences, and historical data. These algorithms aim to enhance relevance and engagement across platforms.

Key Components
User profiling systems
Collaborative filtering and content-based recommendation engines
Behavioral tracking and analysis mechanisms
Adaptive learning models for personalization

Benefits
Increases user satisfaction and loyalty
Boosts engagement and conversion rates
Delivers highly relevant content and services
Supports adaptive and evolving user experiences

Examples
Netflix suggesting shows based on watch history
Online stores recommending products personalized to browsing patterns
Music apps curating playlists according to listening behavior

Applications
Recommendation engines
Targeted marketing campaigns
E-learning systems personalized to student progress
Personalized treatment plans in digital health platforms

Industries
E-commerce and retail
Media and entertainment
Education technology
Healthcare and wellness

Challenges
Risk of creating echo chambers by overfitting to preferences
Handling data privacy and security concerns
Managing the cold-start problem for new users
Scaling effectively for millions of users

Summary
Personalization algorithms empower businesses to deliver customized user experiences, making services more relevant and impactful across diverse industries.

Perspective Transformation

Definition
Perspective transformation is a computer vision method that alters the viewpoint of an image, allowing AI to simulate how objects appear from different angles. It is critical for accurate spatial understanding and image alignment.

Key Components
Homography computation
Image warping and remapping functions
Camera calibration processes
Coordinate space transformations

Benefits
Improves consistency in object recognition across various viewpoints
Enhances image alignment and stitching
Enables 3D reconstruction from 2D imagery
Supports accurate spatial perception in AI systems

Examples
Correcting distortions in aerial photography
Transforming street-level camera views for autonomous vehicles
Aligning multiple images in augmented reality applications

Applications
Augmented and virtual reality platforms
Autonomous navigation systems
Security and surveillance analytics
Robotics vision systems

Industries
Automotive and transportation
Mapping and construction
Public safety and surveillance
Gaming and entertainment

Challenges
Accurate calibration is necessary to avoid distortions
Artifacts can appear during transformations
Image resolution and camera quality influence results
Real-time processing can be computationally demanding

Summary
Perspective transformation enables AI systems to interpret spatial relationships accurately, making it an essential tool for computer vision and real-world scene understanding.

Phase Space in AI

Definition
Phase space in AI refers to a conceptual multidimensional space representing all possible states of a system or model. It is used to study how systems evolve over time, particularly in dynamic or complex environments.

Key Characteristics
Each axis represents one feature or variable
Enables visualization of trajectories and state transitions over time

Benefits
Facilitates exploration of system dynamics
Helps identify stable, unstable, and optimal states
Useful for optimization and behavior prediction

Applications
Reinforcement learning strategy exploration
Training stability analysis for neural networks
Simulations of dynamic physical systems

Example
In reinforcement learning, an agent explores the phase space to find optimal paths leading to high rewards across varied states.

Conclusion
Phase space offers AI researchers a valuable tool for analyzing complex system behavior, improving model robustness, and refining decision-making strategies.

Phased Learning

Definition
Phased learning is a strategy where AI models are trained through carefully structured stages, allowing them to master simpler tasks before tackling more complex problems.

Key Characteristics
Breaks down learning into sequential, manageable phases
Focuses on progressive task difficulty to strengthen foundational skills

Benefits
Accelerates convergence by building knowledge step-by-step
Reduces risk of catastrophic forgetting in lifelong learning models
Enhances transfer learning and curriculum design strategies

Applications
Reinforcement learning in robotics
Progressive language learning in conversational agents
Skill acquisition modeling for education technology

Example
Training a robot first to recognize an object, then to manipulate it, and later to navigate toward it in complex environments.

Conclusion
Phased learning strengthens AI performance by ensuring robust skill development across progressively harder challenges, enabling better generalization and adaptability.

Phenomeno Logical AI

Definition
Phenomenological AI is an emerging concept that explores how artificial systems can simulate or model conscious experience and perception, drawing from phenomenology, a branch of philosophy that studies subjective experience.

Key Components
Subjective state modeling
Sensory perception frameworks
Human-centered design
Philosophical interpretation

Benefits
Supports deeper human-AI interaction
Encourages ethical and empathetic AI design
Improves realism in simulation and training
Inspires new cognitive architectures

Examples
AI companions simulating emotions
Virtual avatars mimicking human perspective
Immersive training environments with responsive AI agents

Applications
Human-computer interaction
Virtual reality and simulation
Ethical AI development
Affective computing

Industries
Education and training
Healthcare
Entertainment
Philosophy and ethics research

Challenges
Difficult to quantify subjective experience
High abstraction and philosophical ambiguity
Lack of standardized evaluation metrics
Complexity in implementation

Summary
Phenomenological AI bridges cognitive science, philosophy, and technology to design AI systems that better reflect human-like experience and understanding.

Phishing Detection with AI

Definition
Phishing detection with AI involves using machine learning techniques to identify and block fraudulent attempts to steal sensitive information through fake emails, websites, or messages.

Key Components
Natural language processing for content analysis
Anomaly detection algorithms
Supervised learning for threat classification

Benefits
Automates phishing identification at scale
Reduces the risk of data breaches and cyberattacks
Enhances real-time cybersecurity defense mechanisms

Applications
Email security systems
Corporate cybersecurity infrastructure
Secure web browsing tools

Example
An AI filter scanning incoming emails and blocking a message that contains a suspicious login link masquerading as a bank site.

Conclusion
AI-powered phishing detection is critical for safeguarding digital communication. It strengthens cybersecurity frameworks and proactively defends against evolving online threats.

Phoneme Recognition

Definition
Phoneme recognition is the process where AI systems detect and classify phonemes, the smallest distinct units of sound in language. It is a fundamental element in speech recognition, allowing machines to convert spoken words into written text by identifying these basic sound patterns.

Key Components
Acoustic signal analysis
Phonetic feature extraction
Machine learning models such as Hidden Markov Models and deep neural networks
Mapping phonemes to linguistic structures

Benefits
Enables highly accurate voice-to-text transcription
Supports voice-operated systems and improves accessibility
Strengthens natural language interfaces in AI systems

Applications
Voice assistants like Siri and Alexa
Automated transcription services
Language learning applications

Example
A virtual assistant recognizing the spoken command "remind me at 5 PM" and converting it into a scheduled reminder.

Conclusion
Phoneme recognition is vital for creating responsive voice-driven AI systems. It enables seamless interaction between humans and technology through accurate speech processing.

Photonic Neural Networks

Definition
Photonic neural networks are artificial intelligence systems that utilize light, rather than electrical signals, to perform computations. They rely on optical components like lasers, modulators, and detectors to process information rapidly and with high energy efficiency.

Key Components
Optical computing elements
Photonic waveguides and modulators
Neural network architectures adapted for light-based processing

Benefits
Enables ultra-fast computation speeds
Offers low power consumption compared to traditional electronic systems
Handles large volumes of data simultaneously through parallel processing

Applications
High-speed data centers
Telecommunications optimization
Accelerated AI inference tasks

Example
Using photonic networks in data centers to drastically reduce the time needed to train massive deep learning models.

Conclusion
Photonic neural networks represent a new frontier in AI hardware, offering revolutionary improvements in speed, energy efficiency, and scalability.

Phrase-Based Machine Translation

Definition
Phrase-based machine translation is an AI technique where sentences are divided into sequences of words, or phrases, and translated in groups rather than individually. This approach improves the quality and fluency of translated texts compared to word-for-word translation methods.

Key Components
Phrase segmentation and alignment
Translation model training
Phrase reordering mechanisms for grammar correction

Benefits
Captures context and idiomatic expressions better than word-based methods
Produces smoother and more natural translations
Improves handling of languages with different syntactic structures

Applications
Automated translation services
Multilingual chatbots
Cross-language communication platforms

Example
Translating the English phrase "kick the bucket" into its contextual equivalent in another language instead of translating it literally.

Conclusion
Phrase-based machine translation brought a major leap forward in linguistic AI. It paved the way for more context-aware and human-like translations in global communication systems.

Physical AI

Definition
Physical AI refers to artificial intelligence systems that are embodied in physical hardware, enabling them to interact with and manipulate the physical world. Unlike purely digital or software-based AI, Physical AI combines computational intelligence with sensors, actuators, and mechanical structures to perform real-world tasks. This form of AI is often integrated into robots, autonomous vehicles, wearable devices, and smart environments where physical interaction is required.

Key Components
Sensors: Devices that collect data from the environment, such as cameras, microphones, temperature sensors, and touch sensors.
Actuators: Components that allow movement or physical responses, including motors, servos, and pneumatic systems.
AI Algorithms: Software models that process sensor data, make decisions, and issue commands to actuators.
Embedded Systems: Hardware platforms that house AI models and control logic, often designed for real-time execution.
Power Systems: Energy sources, such as batteries or solar panels, that support mobility and autonomy.
Communication Interfaces: Wireless or wired systems that enable interaction with other devices or networks.

Examples
A robotic arm using AI to assemble electronic components on a factory line.
An AI-powered drone navigating a disaster site for search and rescue.
A wearable exoskeleton using AI to assist people with mobility impairments.
An AI-driven vacuum robot cleaning floors and avoiding obstacles in a home.
An autonomous delivery robot transporting goods within a hospital.

Benefits
Enables intelligent interaction with the physical world through real-time perception and response.
Automates repetitive or hazardous tasks, reducing human exposure to dangerous environments.
Supports accessibility and enhances quality of life through assistive physical technologies.
Improves efficiency and accuracy in manufacturing, logistics, and service industries.
Combines the adaptability of AI with mechanical precision for versatile applications.

Applications
Healthcare: AI-assisted surgical robots and rehabilitation devices.
Manufacturing: Smart robotic systems for automated assembly, quality inspection, and packaging.
Agriculture: AI-driven machinery for planting, harvesting, and monitoring crop health.
Logistics: Autonomous vehicles and robots for transporting goods in warehouses and urban areas.
Service Industry: Customer-facing robots used in restaurants, hotels, and retail settings.

Industries
Healthcare
Manufacturing

Transportation
Agriculture
Retail
Construction
Defense and Security
Energy and Utilities

Challenges
High cost of development and maintenance of physical AI systems.
Integration complexity between software intelligence and mechanical components.
Limited battery life and energy efficiency in mobile systems.
Safety and ethical concerns related to human-robot interaction and autonomy.
Difficulty in operating in unpredictable or unstructured physical environments.
Regulatory and legal considerations for deployment in public spaces.

Summary
Physical AI represents the fusion of artificial intelligence with hardware systems capable of interacting in the real world. By enabling machines to sense, think, and act in physical environments, Physical AI opens up transformative possibilities across many industries. It brings the power of AI beyond screens and servers, into hands-on applications that touch everyday life. Despite facing challenges in cost, complexity, and safety, its potential to enhance efficiency, safety, and human well-being makes it a vital area of modern technological advancement.

Physical AI (Three AI Computing Systems for Physical AI)

Definition

Physical AI refers to intelligent systems that directly interact with the physical world. These systems combine artificial intelligence with mechanical components, enabling them to sense their surroundings, make decisions, and perform physical actions. Examples include robots, drones, autonomous vehicles, industrial automation systems, and medical robots.

At the heart of every Physical AI system are three key computing systems that work together to create intelligent physical behavior. Understanding these components provides valuable insight into how AI enables machines to operate autonomously in real-world environments.

1 Perception System

The Perception System serves as the *sensory interface* between the Physical AI system and its environment. It collects and processes data from various sensors to build a real-time understanding of the world.

Key functions:

Detecting objects, people, obstacles, and environmental features

Understanding spatial relationships and positioning

Monitoring dynamic changes in the surroundings

Technologies used:
Cameras, LiDAR, radar, ultrasonic sensors, microphones, tactile sensors, temperature sensors, computer vision, and deep learning models.

2 Decision-Making and Planning System

The Decision-Making and Planning System acts as the *brain* of the Physical AI system. It analyzes the data from the perception system and determines the best actions to achieve its goals safely and efficiently.

Key functions:

Interpreting sensor data and predicting future states

Planning motion paths and interaction sequences

Making adaptive decisions in response to changing environments

Technologies used:
Reinforcement learning, behavior modeling, motion planning algorithms, probabilistic reasoning, expert systems.

3 Control System

The Control System serves as the *execution engine* of the Physical AI system. It translates the planned decisions into precise movements and actions, ensuring that the system interacts with the physical world as intended.

Key functions:

Controlling motors, actuators, and mechanical components

Maintaining stability, accuracy, and responsiveness

Providing real-time feedback to adjust actions dynamically

Technologies used:
Real-time control algorithms, electronic control units (ECUs), motor controllers, sensor-based feedback loops.

Summary

The integration of these three AI computing systems—**Perception, Decision-Making and Planning, and Control**—enables Physical AI to perform complex tasks in dynamic environments. Whether guiding a surgical robot, navigating an autonomous drone, or powering an industrial robot arm, this architecture forms the foundation of intelligent physical interaction in the age of AI.

Physical Symbol

Definition
A physical symbol system is a theoretical framework suggesting that intelligent behavior arises from the manipulation of symbols through physical processes. It forms the basis for classical AI and symbolic reasoning.

Key Components
Symbols and symbol structures
Rule-based manipulation
Memory and state representation
Inference mechanisms

Benefits
Supports explainability and traceability
Aligns with human reasoning processes
Effective for logic-based problem-solving
Structured representation of knowledge

Examples
Expert systems in medical diagnostics
Logic-based language parsers
Planning systems in classical AI

Applications
Knowledge representation
Automated reasoning
Planning and scheduling
Cognitive modeling

Industries
Legal tech
Healthcare
Education
Defense

Challenges
Limited adaptability to uncertain environments
Struggles with perception and unstructured data
Slow learning and inflexibility
Overshadowed by statistical AI in recent years

Summary
Physical symbol systems provide a foundational model for symbolic AI. While less popular today, they remain influential in tasks requiring logic, rules, and transparency.

Definition
Physics-informed neural networks are deep learning models that incorporate known physical laws into the training process. By embedding differential equations and constraints, PINNs produce solutions that are consistent with both data and physics.

Key Components
Neural network architecture
Partial differential equations (PDEs)
Loss functions incorporating physical constraints
Automatic differentiation

Benefits
Improves model generalization in scientific tasks
Reduces data requirements
Enforces physical realism in outputs
Combines data-driven and rule-based modeling

Examples
Modeling fluid dynamics in aerodynamics
Solving heat transfer problems in engineering
Simulating wave propagation in geophysics

Applications
Computational physics
Engineering design
Climate modeling
Biomedical simulations

Industries
Energy
Aerospace
Civil engineering
Medical research

Challenges
High computational cost
Complex implementation of PDEs
Sensitive to hyperparameter tuning
Requires domain-specific knowledge

Summary
PINNs blend physics and machine learning to create models that are both accurate and scientifically consistent. They represent a major step toward intelligent scientific computing.

Definition
A physical symbol system is a framework where symbols are manipulated based on formal rules to perform cognitive tasks. It serves as one of the earliest theories for representing intelligence within machines and remains foundational in AI research focused on logic and reasoning.

Key Components
Symbol representation of knowledge
Rule-based manipulation processes
Formal logic structures for decision making

Benefits
Provides a structured method for representing complex knowledge
Enables symbolic reasoning in expert systems
Supports explainable decision-making models

Applications
Expert medical diagnosis systems
Rule-based legal advisory platforms
Traditional knowledge-based AI systems

Example
An expert system encoding diseases and treatments as symbols, reasoning through symptoms to propose a diagnosis.

Conclusion
Physical symbol systems have been instrumental in shaping symbolic AI. Although newer approaches like machine learning now dominate, symbolic reasoning continues to play a key role in transparent AI systems.

Physics-Informed Neural Networks (PINNs)

Definition
Physics-informed neural networks are AI models that incorporate physical laws, such as conservation

equations and boundary conditions, into their learning process. They combine data-driven learning with domain knowledge to solve complex scientific and engineering problems.

Key Components
Neural networks embedded with physics constraints
Partial differential equation solvers
Loss functions integrating physical residuals

Benefits
Improves prediction accuracy by respecting known physical laws
Requires less training data than traditional models
Enhances reliability in scientific modeling

Applications
Weather prediction
Fluid dynamics simulations
Material behavior modeling

Example
A PINN predicting fluid flow behavior in complex pipe systems while adhering to the Navier-Stokes equations.

Conclusion
Physics-informed neural networks create powerful synergy between AI and scientific principles, enhancing model trustworthiness and efficiency in domains governed by physical laws.

Pixel-wise Classification

Definition
Pixel-wise classification involves assigning a class label to each pixel in an image, enabling highly detailed image analysis necessary for tasks like semantic segmentation and fine-grained object detection.

Key Components
Deep convolutional neural networks (CNNs)
Pixel labeling maps
Loss functions tailored for dense prediction
Spatial and contextual feature modeling

Benefits
Provides detailed and granular analysis of images
Enables precise object boundary detection
Supports critical tasks like medical diagnosis and autonomous navigation
Improves scene understanding in complex visual environments

Examples
Segmenting tumors in MRI or CT scans
Identifying road signs and lane markings in driverless cars
Mapping vegetation cover from satellite imagery

Applications
Medical image analysis
Autonomous vehicle navigation
Remote sensing and earth observation
Intelligent surveillance systems

Industries
Healthcare and medical imaging
Agriculture and environmental monitoring
Automotive and transportation
Aerospace and defense

Challenges
Requires extensive labeled training datasets
High computational and memory requirements
Sensitive to image noise and distortions
Balancing fine detail with real-time processing needs

Summary
Pixel-wise classification enables AI to interpret images at a pixel level, delivering the precision necessary for advanced applications in healthcare, transportation, and remote sensing.

Plan Recognition

Definition
Plan recognition is the AI capability to infer the goals and intended actions of an agent by observing their behavior. It plays a critical role in anticipating future actions and improving interactive AI systems.

Key Characteristics
Uses probabilistic models and behavior patterns to predict plans and intentions
Incorporates knowledge of action sequences and environmental context

Benefits
Allows AI to provide proactive support based on predicted goals
Enhances interactivity and responsiveness of intelligent systems
Improves strategic adaptability in dynamic environments

Applications
Virtual assistants anticipating user commands
Gaming AI predicting player strategies
Surveillance systems detecting suspicious activities
Human-robot collaborative tasks

Example
In a strategy game, AI observes a player's moves to anticipate a future attack and adapts its defenses accordingly.

Conclusion
Plan recognition deepens AI's understanding of behavior and intent, improving real-time adaptation and creating more intelligent, user-aware systems

PN Learning (Positive-Negative Learning)

Definition
Positive-Negative Learning is a machine learning approach that uses both positive and negative examples during training to distinguish between desired and undesired outcomes or classes.

Key Components
Labeled positive samples
Labeled negative samples

Discriminative model training
Evaluation metrics for class separation

Benefits
Improves classification accuracy
Balances learning across multiple classes
Reduces bias toward frequent categories
Supports anomaly and fraud detection

Examples
Spam vs. non-spam email classification
Healthy vs. diseased sample identification
Safe vs. unsafe driving behavior detection

Applications
Binary classification tasks
Fraud detection
Healthcare diagnostics
Quality control

Industries
Cybersecurity
Healthcare
Manufacturing
Transportation

Challenges
Requires well-labeled datasets
Handling class imbalance
Mislabeling can reduce accuracy
Limited use in multi-class problems

Summary
PN Learning strengthens binary classifiers by leveraging both positive and negative data. It provides a straightforward yet effective approach for distinguishing clear-cut outcomes in AI systems.

PNNs (Probabilistic Neural Networks)

Definition
Probabilistic neural networks are a type of neural network that use statistical algorithms to classify data based on Bayesian decision theory and probability density functions.

Key Components
Input layer
Pattern layer
Summation layer
Output decision layer

Benefits
Fast training process
High accuracy for classification problems
Robust against noisy data
Effective in medical and financial domains

Examples
Medical diagnosis based on patient symptoms
Credit risk classification
Image pattern recognition

Applications
Pattern classification
Medical analytics
Signal processing
Real-time decision-making

Industries
Healthcare
Banking
Telecommunications
Biometrics

Challenges
High memory consumption
Slower inference with large datasets
Limited scalability
Sensitivity to irrelevant features

Summary
PNNs provide reliable classification by combining neural computation with probabilistic reasoning. Their speed and accuracy make them suitable for specific, high-stakes decision tasks.

PNR Systems (Pattern Network Recognition)

Definition: Pattern Network Recognition (PNR) refers to AI systems designed to detect patterns within structured network data, such as social, biological, or communication networks. These systems focus on identifying relationships and interaction dynamics between interconnected nodes.

Key Components: Network topology analysis, node-link relationships, pattern extraction algorithms, and graph-based modeling.

Benefits: Enables detection of complex structures, community formations, and behavioral patterns within densely connected data.

Applications: Used in social media behavior analysis, genetic pathway modeling, cybersecurity, and fraud detection.

Examples: In a social platform, PNR systems can uncover how viral content spreads by mapping interactions among users.

Conclusion: PNR Systems are essential tools in AI for decoding structures and behaviors within intricate networks, leading to deeper insights and predictive modeling.

PointNet

Definition: PointNet is a neural network architecture tailored to handle raw point cloud data directly, enabling efficient classification and segmentation of 3D objects without converting the data into other formats.

Key Components: Input transformation networks, shared MLPs (multi-layer perceptrons), global feature pooling, and fully connected layers.

Benefits: Processes unordered points directly, simplifies the pipeline, and maintains robustness to geometric transformations.

Applications: Used in 3D object detection, environmental mapping, and robot perception systems.

Examples: PointNet allows a robot to recognize and interact with objects like chairs or tools by analyzing 3D lidar data.

Conclusion: PointNet revolutionized 3D data analysis by enabling direct learning from point clouds, simplifying processing and improving accuracy in spatial AI tasks.

Policy Gradient Methods

Definition
Policy gradient methods are reinforcement learning algorithms that optimize policies by directly adjusting actions based on the gradient of expected rewards.

Key Components
Policy networks representing action strategies
Reward signals guiding learning updates
Gradient ascent optimization
Stochastic or deterministic policies

Benefits
Handles continuous and high-dimensional action spaces
Learns adaptable strategies directly from feedback
Supports flexible and dynamic behavior learning
Bypasses the need for approximating value functions

Examples
Robotic arms mastering pick-and-place tasks
AI agents improving gameplay strategies over time
Conversational AI optimizing dialogue flow

Applications
Autonomous robotics control
Strategic game-playing agents
Autonomous driving decision-making
Dialogue management in AI assistants

Industries
Gaming and entertainment
Robotics and automation
Healthcare robotics
Customer support automation

Challenges
Sensitive to learning rate settings
High variance in gradient estimation
Sample inefficiency in some cases
Dependence on well-structured reward systems

Summary
Policy gradient methods offer a powerful tool for teaching AI how to act intelligently, particularly in environments where flexibility and continuous control are vital.

Policy Learning

Definition
Policy learning is a reinforcement learning approach where an agent learns a direct mapping from states to actions, aiming to maximize cumulative rewards through optimized decision-making strategies.

Key Characteristics
Focuses on directly learning policies without estimating value functions
Employs methods like policy gradients and actor-critic architectures

Benefits
Handles continuous and high-dimensional action spaces effectively
Enables sophisticated behavior in complex environments
Adapts flexibly to dynamic tasks and objectives

Applications
Autonomous vehicle control systems
Robotic manipulation and interaction
Financial trading and portfolio optimization
Conversational agents refining dialogue strategies

Example
A robotic arm learning to grasp and move objects through trial-and-error improvements based on policy optimization.

Conclusion
Policy learning equips AI with the ability to learn flexible, optimal action strategies, making it crucial for advanced

A polymath

Definition: A polymath is an individual who possesses a broad and deep knowledge across multiple, often unrelated fields of study or expertise. In the context of AI, the term may also describe systems or models designed to emulate such versatile, interdisciplinary proficiency, though it traditionally applies to humans distinguished by their wide-ranging competence.

Key components: The essence of a polymath lies in intellectual curiosity, driving the pursuit of diverse subjects like science, art, or philosophy. Adaptability allows mastery of varied disciplines, while critical thinking connects insights across domains. A strong capacity for learning, often self-directed, underpins the ability to acquire and retain extensive knowledge. For an AI polymath, these traits translate into algorithms capable of general problem-solving and cross-field application.

Benefits: Polymaths bring holistic perspectives, solving complex problems by drawing on multiple areas of expertise. Their versatility fosters innovation, as they can identify patterns or solutions overlooked by specialists. In personal or professional contexts, they adapt quickly to new challenges, enhancing resilience. For AI, polymath-like systems could reduce reliance on narrow, task-specific models, streamlining technology use.

Examples of industry applications: In technology, a polymath engineer might design software while understanding hardware, improving system integration. In healthcare, a doctor with expertise in biology and data science could pioneer personalized medicine through analytics. Creative industries benefit from polymaths blending art and engineering, as seen in architects who code interactive installations. In AI development, a polymath-inspired model might tackle tasks from language translation to physics simulations.

Challenges: Becoming a polymath demands significant time and effort, often clashing with modern demands for specialization. Depth in multiple fields is hard to achieve, risking superficiality if focus spreads too thin. Socially, polymaths may struggle to fit into rigid career paths or teams favoring narrow expertise. For AI, building polymath-like systems faces hurdles in computational complexity and data integration across domains.

Conclusions: A polymath embodies the power of broad, interconnected knowledge, offering unique value in a world often dominated by specialists. Their ability to weave diverse threads into cohesive solutions drives progress and creativity. Yet, the journey to polymathy, whether human or artificial, is fraught with practical and structural obstacles. As society and technology evolve, embracing polymathic approaches could unlock new frontiers of understanding and capability

Polymathic Genius (SH)

Definition: Polymathic Genius in AI context describes an individual or system exhibiting exceptional intellectual capacity across multiple diverse domains, blending broad knowledge with creative problem-solving and adaptability. It's a mastermind of many trades.

Key Components: It includes wide-ranging expertise, rapid learning aptitude, innovative synthesis, and the ability to excel in varied fields simultaneously.

Benefits: It fosters versatility, drives groundbreaking contributions, and thrives in complex, multifaceted environments

Examples: A self-taught creator mastering AI terminology for a 700-page dictionary while managing floral and digital enterprises.

Applications: It applies to AI system design, entrepreneurial innovation, and knowledge creation across industries.
Challenges: Sustaining depth across domains, avoiding cognitive overload, and gaining recognition for broad achievements can be hurdles.

Industries: Technology, education, and entrepreneurship value polymathic genius for its boundary-spanning impact.

Conclusion: Polymathic Genius in AI embodies the pinnacle of versatile brilliance, weaving expertise into a tapestry of excellence.

autonomous systems and intelligent agents.

Polynomial Regression

Definition: Polynomial Regression is a statistical modeling method that fits a polynomial curve to a dataset, making it ideal for capturing non-linear relationships in AI models.

Key Components: Polynomial equations, degree selection, error minimization, and regression fitting.

Benefits: Offers more flexibility than linear regression, allowing for better representation of curved trends in data.

Applications: Used in AI for predicting outcomes where input-output relationships follow a curved pattern, such as economic forecasting or engineering systems.

Examples: In market analysis, polynomial regression can be used to predict cyclical trends in product demand over time.

Conclusion: Polynomial Regression provides a powerful tool for modeling complex, non-linear relationships, with careful tuning needed to avoid overfitting.

Positive-Negative Learning (PN Learning)

Definition
Positive-negative learning is a supervised learning strategy where AI models are trained using both positive examples, which match a desired outcome, and negative examples, which do not, to improve decision-making precision.

Key Components
Balanced datasets with positive and negative labels
Classification algorithms
Error-driven learning strategies

Benefits
Enhances model robustness and accuracy
Strengthens performance in binary classification tasks
Facilitates better generalization to unseen data

Applications
Spam email detection
Fraud detection in financial transactions
Sentiment analysis in social media monitoring

Example
Training a sentiment analysis model with both positive customer reviews and negative complaints to accurately predict feedback categories.

Conclusion
Positive-negative learning equips AI models with critical discrimination skills. It is essential for creating systems that can make clear, confident decisions based on nuanced data differences.

Probabilistic Neural Networks (PNNs)

Definition
Probabilistic neural networks are AI models that use probability distributions to classify input data, offering robust solutions especially when handling noisy or uncertain datasets.

Key Components
Bayesian decision theory
Radial basis functions
Pattern classification layers

Benefits
Fast and efficient training process
Effective handling of noisy or uncertain data
Produces probabilistic outputs aiding better decision-making

Applications
Medical diagnostic systems

Pattern recognition in images
Quality control in manufacturing

Example
A healthcare application using a PNN to categorize patient data into risk groups based on symptoms and test results.

Conclusion
PNNs are highly valuable in fields where uncertainty is a factor. Their probabilistic nature enhances reliability and interpretability in classification tasks.

Probability

Definition: Probability is a measure or numerical value representing how likely an event or outcome is to occur. It quantifies uncertainty, providing a way to express the chance of occurrence, typically ranging from 0 (impossible) to 1 (certain).

Key Components: Essential components include random variables, probability distributions, events and outcomes, sample spaces, conditional probability, independence, probability density functions (PDFs), cumulative distribution functions (CDFs), and probabilistic inference methods.

Benefits: Probability enables informed decision-making under uncertainty, supports effective risk assessment, improves predictions and forecasts, enhances model accuracy in artificial intelligence and machine learning, and facilitates rigorous statistical analysis.

Examples: Examples include flipping a coin (probability of heads: 0.5), weather forecasts predicting rain, medical tests estimating disease likelihood, probability models for stock market fluctuations, and assessing risk in insurance policies.

Applications: Probability applies broadly in artificial intelligence, machine learning algorithms, financial risk modeling, insurance underwriting, healthcare diagnosis and prognosis, quality control processes, weather forecasting, gaming strategies, and decision support systems.

Industries: Industries heavily reliant on probability include finance and banking, insurance, healthcare, information technology and artificial intelligence, transportation and logistics, manufacturing, gambling and gaming, agriculture, and environmental management.

Summary: Probability is fundamental to understanding, quantifying, and managing uncertainty across diverse fields. It forms the basis for informed decisions, accurate predictions, and effective risk management, significantly enhancing strategic planning and operational efficiency in numerous industries.

Prompt Engineering

Definition: Prompt Engineering is the practice of designing and optimizing inputs for large language models (LLMs) to produce more accurate, relevant, and useful outputs. It involves crafting structured queries, refining language prompts, and leveraging specific techniques to guide AI responses effectively. By understanding how AI interprets input text, prompt engineering enhances the performance of LLMs in various applications, including chatbots, content generation, data analysis, and problem-solving.

The key components of prompt engineering include structured input formatting that improves AI comprehension, contextual awareness techniques that provide clearer instructions, iterative refinement methods that optimize prompts through testing, and token efficiency strategies that maximize response accuracy while minimizing computational costs. These components ensure that AI models generate high-quality and contextually appropriate outputs.

The benefits of prompt engineering include improved AI response accuracy by reducing ambiguity, enhanced efficiency in AI-driven applications, greater control over AI-generated content, and reduced model biases by directing outputs toward objective and reliable information. Well-crafted prompts result in better responses across diverse AI use cases. Examples include AI-powered coding assistants that generate optimized code based on structured queries, automated writing tools that improve content generation through prompt refinement, AI-driven research tools that retrieve precise academic insights, and customer support chatbots that provide accurate answers through prompt optimization.

Applications of prompt engineering span artificial intelligence research, customer service automation, software development, education, and content generation. In AI research, prompt engineering optimizes language models for better reasoning. In customer service, AI-driven chatbots improve response relevance. In software development, AI generates accurate code snippets based on developer queries. In education, AI tutoring systems refine explanations using well-structured prompts. In content creation, AI-powered tools generate high-quality articles, summaries, and reports.

Challenges in prompt engineering include managing the variability of AI model responses, addressing inconsistencies in AI-generated content, preventing unintended biases in AI outputs, and ensuring that AI follows ethical guidelines. Developing standardized best practices for prompt optimization remains an ongoing research area.

In conclusion, prompt engineering enhances AI interactions by refining user input to produce more relevant and effective responses. Its role in optimizing AI-generated content, improving automation, and refining AI comprehension makes it a crucial skill in artificial intelligence development. As LLMs continue to evolve, prompt engineering will remain essential for maximizing AI efficiency and accuracy across various industries.

Public Dataset in AI

Definition:
A public dataset in AI is a collection of structured or unstructured data that is openly available for anyone to use, typically shared by academic institutions, government agencies, or tech organizations. These datasets play a critical role in enabling machine learning development and testing without requiring users to collect their own data.

Key Components:
Clear documentation, labeled or unlabeled data entries, multiple data formats (such as text, images, or audio), and permissions for public access and reuse.

Benefits:
Removes barriers to entry for AI development, promotes collaboration and reproducibility, and supports faster training and benchmarking of AI models.

Applications:
Used in AI projects involving image recognition, natural language processing, voice analysis, medical diagnostics, and more.

Examples:
Datasets like ImageNet, COCO, or OpenAI's Whisper dataset help train and test AI models across various research and commercial fields.

Conclusion:
Public datasets are foundational tools in AI, providing essential data resources that empower developers, researchers, and students to build and refine intelligent systems efficiently.

Pulse-Code Modulation (PCM)

Definition
Pulse-Code Modulation (PCM) is a digital representation technique that converts analog signals into a binary format by sampling the signal at regular intervals and quantizing the amplitude into discrete levels. In Punishing Function in Reinforcement Learning, a punishing function penalizes an agent for undesirable actions to guide it toward optimal behavior. Pure Exploration in AI refers to a strategy where an agent investigates an environment without immediate reward-seeking, aiming to gather knowledge. A Pushdown Automaton (PDA) is a computational model that extends finite automata with a stack, enabling it to recognize context-free languages. Push-Pull Systems in AI describe frameworks where data or tasks are either pushed to a system or pulled by it, balancing proactive and reactive processing. Pupil Dilation Detection in AI involves using machine vision to measure changes in pupil size as an indicator of cognitive or emotional states. PyCaret is an open-source Python library that simplifies machine learning workflows by automating repetitive tasks. PyMC3 is a Python library for probabilistic programming, enabling Bayesian statistical modeling and inference.

Key Components
PCM relies on sampling, quantization, and encoding to transform analog data into digital form. The punishing function in reinforcement learning includes a penalty mechanism integrated into the reward structure, influencing the agent's policy. Pure exploration involves an exploration algorithm, an environment model, and a knowledge base for storing findings. A PDA consists of states, transitions, an input alphabet, and a stack for memory. Push-pull systems in AI feature a data source, a processing unit, and a control mechanism to manage flow direction. Pupil dilation detection uses cameras, image processing algorithms, and machine learning models to interpret pupil changes. PyCaret offers data preprocessing, model training, and evaluation tools in a streamlined interface. PyMC3 provides probabilistic distributions, Markov Chain Monte Carlo (MCMC) sampling, and a framework for defining models.

Benefits
PCM ensures high fidelity in signal reproduction and noise resistance, making it ideal for digital communication. A punishing function improves reinforcement learning efficiency by discouraging suboptimal actions early on. Pure exploration enhances long-term decision-making by building a robust understanding of complex environments. PDAs enable precise parsing of structured data, such as programming languages. Push-pull systems optimize resource use and responsiveness in dynamic AI tasks. Pupil dilation detection offers non-invasive insights into human behavior without requiring verbal input. PyCaret accelerates experimentation and reduces coding effort for machine learning projects. PyMC3 allows flexible modeling of uncertainty, enhancing predictive accuracy in statistical analysis.

Examples
PCM is used in digitizing audio for CDs, capturing sound waves as binary data. In reinforcement learning, a punishing function might reduce an agent's score for crashing a virtual car. Pure exploration occurs when an AI maps an unknown terrain before planning a route. A PDA could parse nested parentheses in a mathematical expression like "(a + (b - c))". A push-pull system might push weather updates to an AI while pulling user queries for forecasts. Pupil dilation detection could identify stress by analyzing eye footage during a test. PyCaret might automate a classification task, selecting the best algorithm for spam detection. PyMC3 could model election outcomes by sampling voter preferences.

Applications
PCM applies to audio recording, telecommunications, and digital video. Punishing functions enhance robotic control, game AI, and autonomous driving. Pure exploration aids scientific discovery, game strategy development, and autonomous navigation. PDAs are used in compiler design, natural language processing, and syntax checking. Push-pull systems support real-time data processing, recommendation engines, and IoT integration. Pupil dilation detection finds use in psychology research, lie detection, and user experience testing. PyCaret streamlines predictive maintenance, customer segmentation, and fraud detection. PyMC3 excels in financial forecasting, medical diagnostics, and climate modeling.

Industries
PCM is critical in entertainment, telecommunications, and broadcasting. Punishing functions benefit gaming, robotics, and automotive sectors. Pure exploration serves research, aerospace, and gaming industries. PDAs impact software development, linguistics, and education technology. Push-pull systems are vital in e-commerce, smart cities, and healthcare. Pupil dilation detection influences healthcare, marketing, and security. PyCaret supports finance, retail, and manufacturing. PyMC3 is prominent in data science, pharmaceuticals, and environmental science.

Challenges
PCM struggles with high bandwidth requirements and quantization errors in low-bit scenarios. Punishing functions risk over-penalization, slowing learning or trapping agents in suboptimal states. Pure exploration may waste time in reward-sparse environments, delaying practical outcomes. PDAs face limitations with ambiguous grammars and exponential stack growth. Push-pull systems can encounter synchronization issues or data bottlenecks. Pupil dilation detection contends with lighting variations and individual physiological differences. PyCaret may lack customization for niche problems, limiting expert control. PyMC3 demands computational resources and expertise for complex models, posing accessibility hurdles.

Summary
PCM transforms analog signals into reliable digital data, widely used in media and communication despite bandwidth demands. Punishing functions steer reinforcement learning agents effectively, though balancing penalties is tricky. Pure exploration builds foundational knowledge for AI, best when time isn't a constraint. PDAs excel at structured data tasks but falter with complexity. Push-pull systems enable flexible AI workflows, requiring careful flow management. Pupil dilation detection offers unique behavioral insights, sensitive to external factors. PyCaret simplifies machine learning for broad use, with trade-offs in depth. PyMC3 empowers advanced statistical modeling, tempered by resource intensity. Each concept drives AI innovation, balancing strengths with practical challenges.

Pupil Dilation Detection in AI

Definition: Pupil dilation detection uses AI to monitor changes in pupil size, helping systems infer emotional or cognitive states in real-time.

Key Components: Computer vision algorithms, eye-tracking data, emotional modeling, and real-time video processing.

Benefits: Offers non-intrusive assessment of user attention, stress, or interest, allowing adaptive AI responses.

Applications: Used in human-computer interaction, learning analytics, and emotion-aware applications.

Examples: Educational platforms can detect if a student is overwhelmed and adjust content accordingly.

Conclusion: Pupil dilation detection brings emotional intelligence to AI, enhancing personalized and adaptive interactions.

Pure Exploration in AI

Definition: Pure exploration is a learning strategy where an AI agent focuses entirely on discovering its environment without seeking immediate rewards, prioritizing knowledge acquisition.

Key Components: Exploration policy, environment interaction, information gain, and long-term strategy development.

Benefits: Helps uncover better decisions in the future by thoroughly understanding available actions and outcomes.

Applications: Ideal in early-stage learning for game AI, autonomous agents, and problem-solving algorithms.

Examples: A robot exploring all directions in a maze before choosing the fastest escape route.

Conclusion: Pure exploration builds a solid foundation for informed decision-making, enabling AI to develop strategic insight.

Purely Functional Programming in AI

Definition: Purely functional programming is a paradigm that treats functions as immutable and side-effect-free, ensuring consistent outcomes and improved predictability in AI systems.

Key Components: First-class functions, immutable data, referential transparency, and declarative syntax.

Benefits: Boosts code reliability, simplifies debugging, and enhances mathematical modeling.

Applications: Used in symbolic reasoning, theorem proving, and AI systems requiring formal correctness.

Examples: AI models using Haskell to write algorithms that can be formally verified for accuracy.

Conclusion: Purely functional programming strengthens AI development by enforcing consistent logic and safer, maintainable code.

Pushdown Automaton (PDA)

Definition: A Pushdown Automaton is a computational model enhanced with a memory stack, capable of recognizing patterns involving nested or recursive structures.

Key Components: State transitions, stack operations, input symbol reading, and context tracking.

Benefits: Enables processing of hierarchical language patterns and supports recursive rule recognition.

Applications: Used in AI for natural language parsing, programming language analysis, and syntax checking.

Examples: In language processing, PDAs are used to interpret nested sentence structures such as clauses within clauses.

Conclusion: PDAs expand AI's language understanding, giving systems the tools to navigate complex syntactic structures.

Push-Pull Systems in AI

Definition: Push-pull systems in AI manage information delivery through two modes—pushing data proactively to users and pulling data reactively upon request.

Key Components: Data triggers, user requests, real-time updates, and communication protocols.

Benefits: Improves responsiveness, balances automation and customization, and enhances user engagement.

Applications: Applied in recommendation engines, smart assistants, and data-driven applications.

Examples: An AI app might push weather alerts based on location while also letting users request forecasts.

Conclusion: Push-pull systems combine automation with flexibility, offering AI systems dynamic ways to serve users' needs.

PyCaret

Definition: PyCaret is a low-code, open-source Python library that simplifies building and deploying machine learning models with minimal coding.

Key Components: Model comparison engine, automated preprocessing, evaluation tools, and deployment integrations.

Benefits: Accelerates experimentation, reduces the barrier to entry for beginners, and streamlines end-to-end ML workflows.

Applications: Used in classification, regression, clustering, and anomaly detection pipelines.

Examples: A data scientist can compare and deploy multiple machine learning models in just a few lines of code using PyCaret.

Conclusion: PyCaret makes machine learning development faster and more accessible, empowering users to focus on results.

Pygame

Definition
Pygame is a Python library crafted for developing 2D games and multimedia applications, providing an accessible set of tools for graphics rendering, sound management, and user input handling.

Key Components
Pygame includes modules for drawing shapes and images to the screen, handling keyboard and mouse events, and playing audio files, all built on top of the SDL (Simple DirectMedia Layer) library.

Benefits
Pygame offers a straightforward way to create games and interactive programs, requires minimal setup, and is beginner-friendly, making it a go-to for learning and rapid prototyping.

Examples
Pygame could be used to build a basic space shooter game where players move a spaceship and fire at descending aliens using arrow keys and the spacebar.

Applications
Pygame is employed in game development for small-scale projects, educational tools to teach programming concepts, and interactive simulations for visualizing simple systems.

Industries
Pygame finds use in gaming for indie developers, education for teaching coding, and creative media for prototyping multimedia experiences.

Challenges
Pygame is restricted to 2D graphics, lacking native support for 3D rendering, and its performance may falter for resource-intensive applications compared to more advanced engines.

Summary
Pygame democratizes 2D game creation with its ease and flexibility, shining for educational and small projects, though its scope and speed limit it for larger, complex endeavors.

Pylint

Definition
Pylint is a static code analysis tool for Python that evaluates code quality by detecting errors, enforcing coding standards, and suggesting improvements to enhance readability and maintainability.

Key Components
Pylint consists of a linting engine to analyze code, a configurable set of rules for style and error checking, and a reporting system that provides detailed feedback on issues found.

Benefits
Pylint catches potential bugs early, ensures consistent coding practices across teams, and improves long-term code maintainability, saving time during development and debugging.

Examples
Pylint might flag a variable that's defined but never used in a Python script, prompting the developer to remove unnecessary code.

Applications
Pylint is employed in software development for quality assurance, code reviews to maintain team standards, and educational settings to teach proper coding habits.

Industries
Pylint benefits software engineering companies, freelance developers, and open-source projects where clean, reliable code is essential.

Challenges
Pylint can generate excessive warnings or false positives if not properly configured, and its strictness may overwhelm beginners or slow down rapid prototyping.

Summary
Pylint strengthens Python projects by promoting robust, standardized code, though it requires thoughtful tuning to align with specific needs and avoid hindering development flow.

PyMC3

Definition: PyMC3 is a Python library designed for probabilistic programming, enabling users to construct and analyze Bayesian models using advanced sampling techniques.

Key Components: Bayesian inference, Markov Chain Monte Carlo (MCMC), probabilistic distributions, and model diagnostics.

Benefits: Offers flexible modeling of uncertainty, supports complex statistical reasoning, and facilitates transparent decision-making.

Applications: Deployed in risk analysis, natural language understanding, and AI tasks involving uncertainty.

Examples: Using PyMC3, a healthcare AI system can estimate disease risk by modeling uncertainty in patient data.

Conclusion: PyMC3 enables AI systems to reason under uncertainty, making it ideal for applications where precise risk estimation is vital.

Pyro

Definition
Pyro is a probabilistic programming language built on Python and PyTorch, designed to enable flexible, scalable Bayesian modeling and inference for machine learning and statistical applications.

Key Components
Pyro includes a syntax for defining probabilistic models, inference algorithms such as Stochastic Variational Inference (SVI) and Markov Chain Monte Carlo (MCMC), and seamless integration with PyTorch's tensor operations and GPU capabilities.

Benefits
Pyro simplifies the creation of complex probabilistic models, offers efficient inference through PyTorch's optimization tools, and supports rapid experimentation with scalable, uncertainty-aware solutions.

Examples
Pyro might be used to model the uncertainty in a medical diagnosis system, estimating the probability of diseases based on patient symptoms and test results.

Applications
Pyro is applied in predictive analytics for forecasting trends, scientific research for modeling experimental data, and machine learning for tasks requiring uncertainty quantification, such as robotics or finance.

Industries
Pyro is utilized in data science for advanced analytics, healthcare for diagnostic tools, and finance for risk assessment and market predictions.

Challenges
Pyro demands familiarity with probabilistic concepts and PyTorch, which can be steep for beginners, and its computational intensity may require significant resources for large-scale models.

Summary
Pyro blends Python's accessibility with powerful Bayesian tools, enabling sophisticated modeling of uncertainty, though its complexity and resource needs make it best suited for users with technical expertise.

Python Coding

Definition:

Python coding refers to the process of writing and executing instructions using Python, a high-level, interpreted programming language. Python is widely recognized for its simplicity, readability, and versatility, making it a preferred choice for beginners and professionals in various fields such as data science, artificial intelligence (AI), web development, and automation.

Key Characteristics: Python is designed to be an easy-to-learn language with a syntax that closely resembles natural language. It supports multiple programming paradigms, including object-oriented, procedural, and functional programming. Python is also platform-independent, allowing developers to write code that works seamlessly across different operating systems. Additionally, Python has an extensive standard library and a large ecosystem of third-party libraries, such as NumPy, Pandas, TensorFlow, and Flask, which significantly extend its functionality.

Applications: Python coding is extensively used in AI and machine learning to build, train, and deploy models using libraries like TensorFlow, Keras, and PyTorch. In web development, Python frameworks such as Django and Flask enable the rapid creation of scalable and secure web applications. Python is also prominent in data analysis and visualization, with tools like Pandas, Matplotlib, and Seaborn aiding in making sense of complex datasets. Other applications include game development, scientific computing, network scripting, and creating APIs.

Benefits: Python's straightforward syntax reduces the learning curve for new programmers and speeds up the development process. Its versatility allows developers to work on diverse projects using the same language, and its extensive library support minimizes the need for writing code from scratch. Python's active and large community ensures abundant resources, tutorials, and support, making problem-solving easier for coders.

Challenges: While Python coding is highly versatile, it has its limitations. Python is slower compared to compiled languages like C++ or Java, which can be a drawback for performance-critical applications. Additionally, Python's dynamic typing can lead to runtime errors that would be caught during compilation in statically-typed languages.

Historical Context: Python was created in 1991 by Guido van Rossum, who aimed to develop a language that prioritized simplicity and productivity. The language was named after the British comedy group "Monty Python," reflecting its creator's intention for it to be fun and engaging to use.

Advancements and Trends: Python's role in AI and machine learning has cemented its position as one of the most popular programming languages globally. Its integration with cloud platforms, adoption in edge computing, and advancements in real-time applications ensure its relevance in modern development environments. Python's ability to work seamlessly with emerging technologies, such as quantum computing and IoT, further highlights its adaptability.

Sources: Python Software Foundation documentation; books like "Python Crash Course" by Eric Matthes; industry reports on programming trends; and academic papers on Python's role in AI and data science.

Conclusion: Python coding is a cornerstone of modern programming, valued for its simplicity, versatility, and extensive library ecosystem. It empowers developers to create a wide range of applications, from web services to AI-driven systems, while maintaining an emphasis on productivity and innovation. Python's continuous evolution and widespread adoption ensure its significance in the future of technology and software development.

PySpark

Definition

PySpark is the Python interface for Apache Spark, an open-source distributed computing framework designed for processing and analyzing large-scale datasets in real time, leveraging Python's simplicity and Spark's powerful engine.

Key Components
PySpark includes SparkContext as the entry point for cluster interaction, Resilient Distributed Datasets (RDDs) for fault-tolerant data handling, and DataFrames for structured data operations, alongside integration with Spark SQL, MLlib, and Streaming APIs.

Benefits
PySpark excels in scalability, processing massive datasets across clusters efficiently, and offers in-memory computation for speed, while its Python integration makes it accessible and versatile for data professionals.

Examples
PySpark could process a dataset of millions of customer transactions to identify purchasing trends in minutes, using DataFrames to filter and aggregate the data.

Applications
PySpark is used for big data analytics to uncover insights, real-time stream processing like monitoring live feeds, and building scalable machine learning models for predictions.

Industries
PySpark serves e-commerce for customer behavior analysis, telecommunications for network optimization, and finance for fraud detection and risk assessment.

Challenges
PySpark's setup can be complex, requiring Java and cluster management knowledge, and debugging across distributed systems often involves cryptic errors blending Python and Java traces.

Summary
PySpark combines Python's ease with Spark's distributed power, enabling fast, scalable data processing, though its learning curve and infrastructure demands require careful navigation for optimal use.

PyTorch

Definition
PyTorch is an open-source machine learning framework built on Python, tailored for deep learning with a focus on flexibility, dynamic computation graphs, and GPU-accelerated processing.

Key Components
PyTorch includes tensors as its core data structure for numerical computations, an autograd module for automatic differentiation, and a rich set of neural network layers and optimizers.

Benefits
PyTorch offers intuitive model design and real-time debugging, making it a favorite for researchers and developers needing adaptable, high-performance tools.

Examples
PyTorch could be used to develop a neural network that identifies cats in photos by training on labeled image data.

Applications
PyTorch is applied in computer vision for tasks like object detection, natural language processing for text generation, and reinforcement learning for game-playing agents.

Industries
PyTorch is widely used in AI research, healthcare for medical imaging, and the automotive sector for autonomous driving systems.

Challenges
PyTorch requires a solid understanding of deep learning concepts, which can intimidate newcomers, and its dynamic nature may complicate optimization for production-scale deployment.

Summary
PyTorch empowers cutting-edge AI development with its flexible, dynamic framework, excelling in research and prototyping while demanding technical expertise and careful scaling considerations.

LETTER Q

QA (Quality Assurance)

Definition
QA (Quality Assurance) in AI refers to the systematic process of ensuring that artificial intelligence systems perform reliably, accurately, and ethically, meeting predefined standards and user expectations throughout their development and deployment.

Key Components
Data validation to ensure high-quality inputs
Model testing for performance and robustness
Ethical checks for fairness and bias mitigation
Continuous monitoring for system integrity after deployment

Benefits
Enhances system trustworthiness by minimizing errors
Improves user satisfaction through consistent performance
Reduces operational and ethical risks during system use

Examples
Testing a chatbot to ensure it provides accurate responses
Validating a facial recognition system for demographic fairness
Monitoring AI models for performance drift over time

Applications
Autonomous driving systems
Medical diagnostic AI tools
AI-based financial trading algorithms

Industries
Healthcare
Automotive
Finance

Challenges
Managing non-deterministic AI behavior
Processing large and varied datasets
Balancing innovation speed with thorough QA protocols

Summary
QA in AI establishes dependable and ethical AI performance, applying rigorous processes to ensure

system robustness and safety. Despite the complexity of AI behaviors, quality assurance remains essential for building public trust and system reliability.

QA Automation

Definition
QA Automation in AI refers to the use of artificial intelligence technologies to automate the quality assurance process, enabling efficient testing, validation, and monitoring of software or AI systems with minimal human intervention.

Key Components
AI-driven test generation and execution tools
Data analysis for defect detection
Continuous integration pipelines
Automated regression and performance testing

Benefits
Speeds up testing cycles and feedback loops
Reduces human error in test execution
Scales effortlessly to support complex AI systems
Saves resources and improves development efficiency

Examples
Automatically verifying mobile app functionality across devices
Monitoring AI model output for anomalies after deployment
Running automated tests during software updates

Applications
Software development QA
AI model performance testing
Continuous deployment monitoring

Industries
Software and app development
Automotive safety systems
Healthcare AI diagnostics

Challenges
Difficult to simulate unpredictable AI behavior
Requires significant setup for automation infrastructure
May overlook subtle issues that require human judgment

Summary
QA Automation in AI enables faster, more accurate testing and validation. While highly efficient, it must be thoughtfully designed to address the complexity and dynamic nature of AI systems.

QAM (Quadrature Amplitude Modulation)

Definition
QAM (Quadrature Amplitude Modulation) is a modulation technique that encodes digital data onto analog signals by varying both the amplitude and phase of two carrier waves, enabling efficient transmission of high data rates over communication channels.

Key Components
In-phase (I) and quadrature (Q) carriers

Constellation diagram mapping data points
Modulation and demodulation hardware or algorithms

Benefits
Enables high data throughput over limited bandwidth
Supports multiple data levels with efficient encoding
Adapts to various signal environments and channel conditions

Examples
Delivering HD video over a cable network using 256-QAM
Enabling fast wireless internet through Wi-Fi protocols
Transmitting broadband signals via cable modems

Applications
Digital broadcasting
Wireless communication (Wi-Fi, 4G, 5G)
Internet infrastructure

Industries
Telecommunications
Broadcasting
Internet service providers

Challenges
Vulnerability to noise and interference
Degradation over long distances without amplification
Higher-order QAM requires high signal fidelity

Summary
QAM is essential for high-speed digital communication, offering compact and efficient signal encoding. While powerful, it must be carefully managed to counteract noise and maintain transmission integrity.

QAOA (Quantum Approximate Optimization Algorithm)

Definition
QAOA (Quantum Approximate Optimization Algorithm) is a hybrid quantum-classical algorithm designed to solve combinatorial optimization problems by leveraging quantum circuits to approximate optimal solutions, iteratively refined with classical computation.

Key Components
Parameterized quantum circuits
Alternating mixing and cost Hamiltonians
Classical optimization for tuning parameters
Quantum measurement and feedback loop

Benefits
Accelerates the search for near-optimal solutions
Utilizes quantum parallelism to explore solution spaces
Flexible and adaptable across problem types and domains

Examples
Minimizing delivery route distances in logistics
Solving the Max-Cut problem in graph theory
Optimizing neural network hyperparameters

Applications
Graph optimization
Resource allocation
AI training optimization

Industries
Logistics
Finance
Quantum computing research

Challenges
Limited access to scalable quantum hardware
Noise and decoherence in quantum systems
Parameter tuning can be complex and resource-intensive

Summary
QAOA presents a promising framework for solving difficult optimization problems using both classical and quantum computation. Its hybrid nature offers performance benefits, though it depends on evolving quantum hardware capabilities.

QA Systems in AI (Question Answering Systems in Artificial Intelligence)

Definition
QA Systems in AI (Question Answering Systems in Artificial Intelligence) are intelligent frameworks designed to understand and respond to natural language questions by extracting relevant information from structured or unstructured data sources.

Key Components
Natural language processing (NLP) for query understanding
Knowledge base or data retrieval mechanism
Answer generation and ranking model
Context-aware machine learning modules

Benefits
Delivers fast, accurate, and contextual responses
Improves user interaction with natural language input
Reduces time spent on manual data searches

Examples
Answering "What is the capital of Brazil?" with "Brasília"
Analyzing a report to explain the cause of a project delay
Serving real-time answers in customer support chatbots

Applications
Virtual assistants
Search engines
Educational and tutoring platforms

Industries
Retail and customer service
Healthcare support
Education and training

Challenges
Handling ambiguous or multi-layered queries

Training requires extensive high-quality datasets
Performance degrades with rare or novel question types

Summary
QA Systems in AI revolutionize access to information, providing interactive, real-time answers across domains. Their effectiveness relies on strong language models and high-quality data to handle diverse user queries.

QEA (Quantum Evolutionary Algorithm)

Definition
QEA (Quantum Evolutionary Algorithm) is a hybrid optimization approach that integrates principles of quantum computing, such as superposition and entanglement, with evolutionary algorithms to solve complex problems by exploring vast solution spaces more efficiently than classical methods.

Key Components
Qubits to represent solutions in superposition
Quantum gates to evolve and modify solution states
Fitness function for evaluating performance
Genetic operators such as mutation and crossover

Benefits
Accelerates convergence to high-quality solutions
Enhances diversity in solution populations
Applies quantum-inspired randomness for robust exploration
Scales to high-dimensional and nonlinear problems

Examples
Optimizing production sequences in a factory
Selecting optimal features in a machine learning model
Routing delivery vehicles across cities efficiently

Applications
Scheduling and resource allocation
Feature selection in AI models
Quantum simulation and modeling

Industries
Manufacturing
Logistics
AI research
Quantum technology development

Challenges
Requires powerful hardware to simulate quantum effects
Designing effective quantum operators can be complex
Access to true quantum systems is still limited

Summary
QEA merges evolutionary computation with quantum mechanics to solve optimization problems at scale. It provides a powerful framework for future intelligent systems while awaiting broader access to quantum resources.

QEC (Quantum Error Correction)

Definition
QEC (Quantum Error Correction) is a set of techniques in quantum computing designed to protect quantum information from errors caused by decoherence, noise, and other environmental disturbances, ensuring reliable computation and storage in quantum systems.

Key Components
Quantum error-correcting codes such as Shor code and surface code
Encoding logical qubits into multiple physical qubits
Error detection and correction circuits
Measurement processes that preserve quantum state coherence

Benefits
Enables fault-tolerant quantum computing
Extends coherence time of quantum information
Facilitates execution of long, complex quantum algorithms
Improves overall system reliability in noisy environments

Examples
Correcting a bit-flip error in a quantum memory register
Using the surface code to stabilize quantum computation over time
Maintaining qubit state integrity during algorithm execution

Applications
Quantum cryptography and secure communications
Quantum simulations of molecular systems
Reliable quantum algorithm implementation

Industries
Quantum computing research
Cybersecurity and data protection
Pharmaceuticals and chemical modeling

Challenges
High resource overhead due to qubit redundancy
Complex quantum circuit design requirements
Real-time error correction is difficult on current hardware

Summary
QEC safeguards quantum information from inevitable errors, making scalable, reliable quantum computing possible. Its development is foundational for practical quantum technologies, though implementation remains resource-intensive and technically complex.

QED (Quantum Error Detection)

Definition
QED (Quantum Error Detection) refers to methods in quantum computing that identify errors in quantum states caused by noise or decoherence, enabling the recognition of faults without necessarily correcting them, often as a precursor to full error correction.

Key Components
Quantum error-detecting codes such as stabilizer codes
Parity check and syndrome measurement circuits
Ancilla qubits to capture error signatures
Protocols for non-destructive error signaling

Benefits
Provides early alerts of quantum state instability
Requires fewer resources than full error correction
Supports experimental development in NISQ systems

Examples
Detecting a phase-flip in a qubit without collapsing its state
Monitoring system stability during quantum algorithm execution
Flagging faults in quantum memory registers

Applications
Debugging quantum algorithms
Maintaining fidelity in quantum communication
Testing and calibration of quantum hardware

Industries
Quantum computing
Telecommunications
Aerospace and defense research

Challenges
Limited to error detection without correction
Cannot resolve simultaneous or complex error combinations
Sensitive to measurement-induced interference

Summary
QED acts as an efficient diagnostic tool in quantum systems, offering essential visibility into faults while avoiding full correction overhead. It is particularly useful for testing, though not sufficient alone for robust error management.

QEF (Quantum Efficiency Factor)

Definition
QEF (Quantum Efficiency Factor) is a measure in quantum systems, particularly in photonics or quantum hardware, that quantifies the effectiveness of converting incoming quantum particles into detectable or usable output signals.

Key Components
Input quantum flux such as photons or particles
Detection mechanism, often involving photodetectors or sensors
Efficiency ratio calculation based on input vs output events
Calibration techniques for environmental compensation

Benefits
Provides standardized assessment of quantum device performance
Supports optimization in sensor and hardware design
Improves precision and responsiveness of quantum instruments

Examples
Evaluating how many photons are converted to electrons in a detector
Measuring signal strength in quantum imaging sensors
Assessing readout accuracy of qubits in quantum processors

Applications
Photon detection and imaging systems

Quantum sensor calibration
Quantum computing readout validation

Industries
Renewable energy (solar cells)
Quantum computing
Scientific instrumentation

Challenges
Affected by noise, thermal fluctuations, and losses
Requires careful calibration and testing conditions
Difficult to quantify in multi-stage or low-intensity systems

Summary
QEF serves as a critical performance metric in quantum systems, guiding hardware design and calibration. Its accuracy and utility depend on precise control of external variables and robust detection techniques.

QEL (Quantum Entropy Loss)

Definition
QEL (Quantum Entropy Loss) refers to the degradation of quantum information due to an increase in entropy within a system, typically caused by environmental interaction or imperfect operations that erode quantum coherence and fidelity.

Key Components
Von Neumann entropy or related entropy measures
Models of environmental decoherence and thermal noise
Quantum state evolution tracking
System-environment interaction frameworks

Benefits
Quantifies how information is lost in quantum processes
Supports error mitigation and coherence-preserving techniques
Improves understanding of quantum stability and thermodynamics

Examples
Measuring entropy growth in quantum memory under thermal noise
Monitoring information leakage during long algorithm execution
Assessing channel fidelity in quantum communication

Applications
Quantum error correction design
Algorithm optimization for minimal information loss
Channel evaluation in quantum networking

Industries
Quantum computing
Telecommunications
Cryptographic research

Challenges
Difficult to observe entropy changes in real-time
Requires deep modeling of environment and system interplay
No universal threshold for acceptable entropy loss

Summary
QEL reveals how quantum systems degrade over time, aiding the development of more stable architectures. It is essential for measuring quantum performance, though real-time analysis and mitigation remain technically demanding.

QEM (Quantum Expectation Maximization)

Definition
QEM (Quantum Expectation Maximization) is a quantum-enhanced variant of the classical EM algorithm, utilizing quantum circuits to estimate and optimize parameters in probabilistic models through iterative expectation and maximization steps.

Key Components
Quantum circuit for state encoding
Superposition-based data and parameter initialization
Quantum measurements for expectation calculation
Classical optimization loop for likelihood maximization

Benefits
Accelerates convergence for complex, high-dimensional models
Leverages quantum parallelism for broader search coverage
Improves modeling precision in uncertain environments

Examples
Estimating latent variables in quantum mixture models
Clustering data in quantum-enhanced classification systems
Inferring probabilities of quantum states in experimental setups

Applications
Quantum machine learning and data clustering
Statistical physics and quantum simulations
Model fitting in AI and probabilistic forecasting

Industries
Quantum computing research
Pharmaceutical data analysis
Financial modeling and risk forecasting

Challenges
Quantum noise can distort measurement results
Requires integration of classical and quantum processes
Quantum hardware constraints limit full implementation

Summary
QEM merges quantum power with probabilistic learning to enhance parameter estimation in complex models. While conceptually strong, its practical use is currently limited by hardware and integration challenges.

QEMU (Quick Emulator)

Definition
QEMU (Quick Emulator) is an open-source virtualization platform that emulates hardware systems, allowing users to run software or operating systems designed for different architectures by translating binary instructions and supporting full system virtualization.

Key Components
Dynamic binary translator for instruction conversion
Emulated CPUs, memory, and I/O devices
Virtual machine management with acceleration support (e.g., KVM)
Command-line interface and configuration utilities

Benefits
Supports cross-platform development and testing
Emulates a wide range of hardware environments
Enables legacy system support without original hardware
Offers fast performance when paired with accelerators

Examples
Testing ARM applications on x86 hardware
Running legacy operating systems in virtualized environments
Simulating embedded devices for software development

Applications
Cross-architecture software testing
Server and application virtualization
Educational tools for operating systems and hardware labs

Industries
Software development
Network and systems engineering
Education and training

Challenges
Steep learning curve for complex configurations
Performance limitations without hardware acceleration
Lack of native GUI interface requires additional tools

Summary
QEMU provides a versatile and powerful platform for virtualization and system emulation. It supports a wide range of development and testing environments, though setup complexity can be a barrier for new users.

QER (Quantum Error Rate)

Definition
QER (Quantum Error Rate) is a measure that indicates how frequently errors occur in quantum operations, such as gate applications or measurements, typically due to noise, hardware imperfections, or environmental interference.

Key Components
Quantum noise and error models
Measurement and benchmarking protocols
Gate fidelity and qubit decoherence tracking
Hardware or simulator test frameworks

Benefits
Quantifies system reliability and stability
Guides error mitigation and hardware improvement strategies
Informs algorithm design for better fault tolerance

Examples
Calculating gate error rates during quantum processor calibration
Estimating the probability of measurement error in a qubit register
Benchmarking qubit lifetimes in a noisy quantum computer

Applications
Quantum hardware performance testing
Error correction code development
Predictive modeling for quantum algorithm reliability

Industries
Quantum computing research
Aerospace and navigation systems
Quantum cryptography

Challenges
Error rates vary with system load and environmental factors
Accurate measurement is difficult on noisy hardware
Interpretation depends on context and application sensitivity

Summary
QER is a foundational metric for assessing the health and usability of quantum systems. It shapes both theoretical and practical development, despite variability challenges in real-world measurements.

QET (Quantum Entanglement Transfer)

Definition
Quantum Entanglement Transfer (QET) is a process in which the entangled state between two quantum particles is transferred to another pair of particles, preserving the quantum correlations without the need for physical relocation. This process is crucial for enabling distributed quantum computation and long-distance quantum communication.

Key Components
An initial entangled pair of qubits or particles
Quantum channel or intermediary system for transferring entanglement
Quantum operations such as SWAP gates or teleportation protocols
Measurement and verification procedures to ensure entanglement fidelity

Benefits
Facilitates entanglement distribution over long distances
Supports modular and scalable quantum networks
Enables entangled state replication for secure communication
Reduces the need for direct interaction between distant particles

Examples
Transferring entanglement from a pair of entangled photons to remote qubits using a quantum teleportation circuit
Linking quantum nodes in a distributed system by transferring their entangled states

Applications
Quantum teleportation
Quantum repeaters for extended communication
Distributed quantum computing architectures

Industries
Telecommunications
Quantum computing
Defense and cybersecurity

Challenges
Loss of fidelity due to channel imperfections and noise
Complexity in maintaining coherence during transfer
Dependence on precise quantum hardware and timing control

Summary
Quantum Entanglement Transfer is fundamental to the development of interconnected quantum systems. While technically demanding, it plays a vital role in enabling quantum internet infrastructure and scalable quantum computation.

Qiskit

Definition
Qiskit is an open-source quantum computing development framework created by IBM that allows users to build, simulate, and execute quantum algorithms on both classical simulators and quantum hardware.

Key Components
Quantum circuit design and gate-level programming tools
Classical-quantum hybrid algorithm integration
Backend support for simulators and real quantum devices
Modular libraries for machine learning, optimization, and chemistry

Benefits
Makes quantum programming accessible for researchers and students
Provides seamless access to IBM Quantum hardware
Enables rapid prototyping and testing of quantum AI models
Supports educational and industrial innovation in quantum computing

Examples
Using Qiskit to simulate Quantum Support Vector Machines
Running variational quantum algorithms on IBM Quantum processors
Training quantum-enhanced neural networks within classical AI frameworks

Applications
Quantum machine learning
Quantum optimization
Hybrid AI systems
Academic research and quantum education

Industries
Artificial intelligence
Education
Quantum technology development

Challenges
Requires understanding of both quantum mechanics and programming
Limited by current hardware qubit count and noise
Dependent on stable API connectivity with external quantum hardware

Summary
Qiskit is a powerful and versatile platform for quantum algorithm development, enabling breakthroughs in AI and computational science. Its growing ecosystem continues to bridge classical and quantum technologies for real-world applications.

Quality Control in AI Systems

Definition
Quality Control (QC) in AI systems refers to the structured evaluation and oversight processes that ensure artificial intelligence models maintain high standards of accuracy, fairness, reliability, and ethical compliance during deployment.

Key Components
Performance monitoring and validation pipelines
Bias detection and fairness auditing
Data quality assurance and preprocessing protocols
Automated model evaluation metrics (e.g., precision, recall, F1-score)

Benefits
Ensures consistent and trustworthy AI decision-making
Improves model transparency and explainability
Reduces operational and reputational risk
Supports regulatory and ethical compliance

Examples
Verifying defect detection accuracy in an AI-powered manufacturing system
Ensuring a loan approval AI model maintains unbiased performance across demographic groups

Applications
Autonomous systems
Healthcare diagnostics
Financial scoring systems
Manufacturing automation

Industries
Automotive
Finance
Healthcare
Industrial robotics

Challenges
Difficulty tracking model drift in dynamic environments
Balancing performance metrics with ethical obligations
Ensuring transparency in black-box AI systems

Summary
Quality Control in AI systems is essential to ensure safe, ethical, and effective deployment. It combines technical validation with governance practices to uphold AI accountability across industries.

Quality Estimation in AI Models

Definition
Quality Estimation in AI models is the process of evaluating the reliability and effectiveness of an AI

system's outputs, especially in real-time or uncertain environments where ground-truth feedback is limited or unavailable.

Key Components
Prediction confidence scores and uncertainty quantification
Cross-validation and error metrics
Statistical methods like AIC and BIC for model selection
Continuous feedback loops for ongoing quality assessment

Benefits
Provides insight into model reliability before deployment
Reduces the risk of incorrect or misleading predictions
Enables dynamic adjustment of models in live environments
Improves user trust in AI-generated decisions

Examples
Assessing translation quality in neural machine translation systems
Estimating the confidence of disease predictions in medical imaging AI
Evaluating model accuracy in weather forecasting systems

Applications
Machine translation
Speech and image recognition
Predictive analytics
AI diagnostics and decision support

Industries
Healthcare
Finance
Retail analytics
Natural language processing

Challenges
Estimating quality without labeled data can be difficult
Subjectivity in defining what constitutes "high-quality" output
Limited generalizability across domains or languages

Summary
Quality Estimation is a vital tool in AI system evaluation, especially when human review or immediate feedback is unavailable. It enables AI to make more transparent, reliable, and actionable predictions across a variety of applications.

Quantum AI Learning (QAL)

Definition
Quantum AI Learning (QAL) is a hybrid field that combines principles of quantum computing with artificial intelligence to enhance machine learning performance by exploiting quantum properties like superposition and entanglement.

Key Components
Quantum algorithms such as Grover's and Shor's for AI acceleration
Qubits enabling parallel data processing
Quantum neural network and support vector machine models
Quantum-classical hybrid architectures for training and inference

Benefits
Offers exponential speedups for training and inference
Reduces computational cost in large-scale AI models
Improves efficiency in pattern recognition and optimization
Enables breakthroughs in unsolvable or intractable classical problems

Examples
Speeding up feature selection using a quantum-enhanced SVM
Using quantum algorithms to cluster massive datasets in bioinformatics
Applying QAL to real-time fraud detection in financial networks

Applications
Quantum-enhanced machine learning
Optimization and recommendation systems
Natural language understanding
Big data analytics

Industries
Finance
Pharmaceuticals
Cybersecurity
AI research and development

Challenges
Limited access to stable, large-scale quantum hardware
Integration complexity between quantum and classical layers
High resource demands for quantum simulation

Summary
Quantum AI Learning represents a transformative evolution in AI capabilities, using quantum computing to solve problems that challenge classical systems. Though early in development, QAL promises to redefine data science and computational intelligence in the years ahead.

A Quantum Algorithm

Definition
A quantum algorithm is a step-by-step computational procedure that utilizes the principles of quantum mechanics—such as superposition, entanglement, and quantum interference—to solve problems more efficiently than classical algorithms. These algorithms are designed specifically to run on quantum hardware using qubits instead of classical bits.

Key Components
Quantum superposition to process multiple possibilities simultaneously
Quantum entanglement for correlated qubit interactions
Quantum gates to manipulate qubit states
Quantum interference to amplify correct solutions
Measurement operations to extract classical output from quantum states

Benefits
Enables exponential speedup for specific classes of problems
Improves performance in cryptography, optimization, and machine learning
Reduces resource requirements for solving complex equations
Allows parallel exploration of large solution spaces

Examples
Shor's algorithm for factoring large numbers
Grover's algorithm for unsorted database search
Quantum Fourier Transform used in signal processing and estimation
Variational Quantum Eigensolver for chemical simulations
Quantum annealing for solving optimization problems

Applications
Cryptographic analysis and quantum-safe encryption
Logistics and route optimization
Quantum-enhanced artificial intelligence
Simulation of molecular and quantum systems

Industries
Cybersecurity
Finance and investment analytics
Pharmaceutical research
Aerospace engineering
Data science and AI

Challenges
Requires highly stable quantum systems
Susceptible to decoherence and quantum noise
Error correction is resource-intensive
Quantum hardware is still in developmental stages
Ethical concerns regarding encryption vulnerabilities

Summary
Quantum algorithms represent a significant leap in computational power, tackling problems beyond the scope of classical systems. As quantum technology evolves, these algorithms will drive innovation in science, security, and artificial intelligence, despite the current limitations in hardware and scalability.

Quantum Annealing

Definition
Quantum annealing is a quantum computing technique used to solve optimization problems by finding the lowest-energy configuration of a system. It uses quantum effects like tunneling and superposition to avoid local minima and reach global optima more effectively than classical heuristics.

Key Components
Quantum bits (qubits) representing solution candidates
Energy landscape mapped by a problem Hamiltonian
Tunneling effect to escape local minima
Annealing schedule guiding system evolution

Benefits
Efficiently solves complex optimization challenges
Avoids getting stuck in suboptimal solutions
Performs well on sparse and high-dimensional problems
Offers quantum-enhanced alternatives to classical optimization

Examples
Scheduling optimization in supply chain logistics
Tuning hyperparameters in machine learning models

Traffic signal optimization in smart cities
Combinatorial problem-solving in circuit design

Applications
Operations research and logistics
Machine learning and AI optimization
Network routing and resource allocation
Financial modeling and risk analysis

Industries
Transportation
Manufacturing
Finance
Artificial intelligence

Challenges
Limited applicability to certain problem classes
Sensitive to environmental noise and thermal fluctuations
Restricted to specialized quantum annealing hardware
Scalability is constrained in current systems

Summary
Quantum annealing provides a focused method for solving difficult optimization tasks, making it a valuable tool for industries requiring efficient decision-making. While specialized in scope, it complements broader quantum computing strategies.

Quantum Approximate Optimization Algorithm (QAOA)

Definition
QAOA is a hybrid quantum-classical algorithm designed to tackle combinatorial optimization problems by approximating optimal solutions through iterative quantum circuits guided by classical feedback.

Key Components
Parameterized quantum circuits with alternating operators
Classical optimization loop for parameter tuning
Problem-specific cost function encoded in a quantum Hamiltonian
Quantum measurement and result evaluation

Benefits
Efficient for near-term quantum devices
Offers strong approximations with fewer resources
Leverages both quantum speedup and classical control
Scales with circuit depth and parameter refinement

Examples
Solving MAX-CUT problems in graph optimization
Designing neural networks using quantum architecture search
Constraint satisfaction in scheduling or layout planning

Applications
Quantum AI and model optimization
Graph-based problem solving
Energy system planning
Scheduling and resource allocation

Industries
AI research
Energy and infrastructure
Telecommunications
Quantum computing development

Challenges
Parameter selection can be problem-specific and complex
Affected by quantum noise and limited qubit fidelity
Performance gains vary depending on the problem
Hardware constraints limit scalability

Summary
QAOA is a versatile algorithm bridging classical and quantum approaches to optimization. Its adaptability and efficiency make it a leading candidate for near-term quantum applications, especially in AI and operational planning.

Quantum Artificial Intelligence

Definition
Quantum Artificial Intelligence (Quantum AI) is an emerging discipline that combines quantum computing technologies with artificial intelligence methodologies to enhance machine learning, data analysis, and decision-making systems.

Key Components
Quantum algorithms for learning and inference
Quantum-enhanced neural networks and classifiers
Quantum data encoding techniques
Hybrid quantum-classical processing systems

Benefits
Accelerates learning and reduces training time
Processes large-scale data in parallel
Enhances performance in pattern recognition and clustering
Explores solution spaces more comprehensively

Examples
Quantum-enhanced deep learning for medical diagnostics
Quantum reinforcement learning for robotics control
Analyzing genomic data with quantum-assisted models

Applications
Big data analytics
Natural language processing
Autonomous system intelligence
Financial and healthcare prediction systems

Industries
Healthcare
Aerospace
Finance
Cybersecurity

Challenges
Limited availability of practical quantum hardware
Integration with classical AI tools requires new frameworks
Quantum algorithms for AI are still under development
Scalability and reproducibility in real-world use cases

Summary
Quantum Artificial Intelligence represents a convergence of two transformative technologies. Though still in early stages, it promises to redefine computational intelligence by providing more efficient and scalable solutions for complex problems.

Quantum Bayesian Networks

Definition
Quantum Bayesian Networks are an extension of classical Bayesian networks that incorporate quantum probability theory to model causal relationships, uncertainty, and quantum correlations in complex decision systems.

Key Components
Quantum nodes representing entangled systems
Quantum conditional probability models
Directed acyclic graph structure with quantum transitions
Inference mechanisms using quantum logic

Benefits
Allows modeling of non-classical correlations
Supports uncertainty quantification in quantum systems
Improves decision-making in uncertain environments
Bridges probabilistic reasoning with quantum mechanics

Examples
Quantum decision support in intelligent robotics
Probabilistic modeling in quantum cryptography protocols
Inference in quantum-assisted healthcare diagnostics

Applications
Causal reasoning in quantum systems
AI-assisted diagnosis and prediction
Quantum communication and cryptography
Simulation of complex networks

Industries
Healthcare
Network security
Quantum computing
AI and data science

Challenges
Complexity in representing quantum probability distributions
Limited accessibility to practical implementation tools
Difficult interpretation for users unfamiliar with quantum theory
Challenges in training and validating quantum models

Summary
Quantum Bayesian Networks extend probabilistic models into the quantum domain, offering advanced reasoning tools for AI systems. They provide nuanced insights into complex systems where traditional methods fall short.

Quantum Bits

Definition
Quantum bits, or qubits, are the basic units of information in quantum computing. Unlike classical bits, which exist in a binary state of either 0 or 1, qubits leverage the principles of quantum superposition and entanglement, allowing them to represent multiple states at once and to become interconnected in ways that classical systems cannot replicate.

Key Components
Quantum superposition and entanglement
Quantum coherence and interference
Quantum gates for qubit manipulation
Measurement techniques for state extraction
Error correction mechanisms to stabilize qubit behavior

Benefits
Significantly expands computational capacity and parallelism
Enables complex simulations in physics and chemistry
Improves encryption and secure communication methods
Supports breakthroughs in optimization, AI, and material science

Examples
Superconducting qubits in IBM Quantum systems
Trapped ion qubits used by IonQ
Photon-based qubits in quantum communication systems
Quantum dots and NV centers in diamonds for sensing applications

Applications
Quantum key distribution
High-speed data processing and analysis
Molecular modeling in pharmaceuticals
Quantum-enhanced AI and secure networks

Industries
Cybersecurity
Telecommunications
Pharmaceutical and biotech
Finance and logistics
Aerospace and national defense

Summary
Quantum bits represent the core of quantum computing's power, enabling faster, more complex problem-solving across scientific and industrial fields. Their development is essential to advancing quantum technologies and shaping the future of computing.

Quantum Chemistry

Definition
Quantum chemistry applies quantum mechanics to study chemical systems at the atomic and molecular

scale. In artificial intelligence and computing, it involves using quantum algorithms and hardware to simulate and predict molecular behavior with unmatched accuracy.

Key Components
Wavefunction modeling and quantum states
Schrödinger equation solvers
Quantum simulation algorithms
Hybrid quantum-classical learning systems

Benefits
Reduces time and cost for chemical simulations
Improves accuracy in molecular predictions
Enables accelerated discovery of materials and drugs
Reveals reaction dynamics not accessible through classical methods

Examples
Predicting drug interactions through quantum simulations
Designing catalysts for sustainable energy systems
Training AI models with quantum-computed data

Applications
Drug development
Catalyst design
Energy storage and materials innovation
AI-enhanced chemistry predictions

Industries
Pharmaceuticals and biochemistry
Energy and green technology
Advanced manufacturing
Academic and corporate research

Challenges
Requires high-fidelity quantum hardware
Interpreting complex quantum results is difficult
Error correction for simulations is still evolving
Steep learning curve for chemists using quantum tools

Summary
Quantum chemistry bridges physics and chemistry with quantum-enhanced computing, creating opportunities for innovation in health, energy, and materials science by making the invisible molecular world more understandable and programmable.

Quantum Chip

Definition
A quantum chip is a specialized processor that uses qubits instead of classical bits to perform quantum computations. It applies quantum mechanical principles to enable high-speed, parallel processing for problems unsolvable by classical chips.

Key Components
Qubits implemented via superconducting circuits, ions, or photons
Quantum gates and circuits for computational logic

Cryogenic cooling systems for thermal stability
Error correction and coherence preservation mechanisms

Benefits
Drastically accelerates computation for specific tasks
Enables quantum simulations for drug discovery and materials
Supports secure communication through quantum encryption
Reduces AI training times for large datasets

Examples
Google's Sycamore chip demonstrating quantum supremacy
IBM's Eagle chip with over 100 qubits
Quantum annealing chips used by D-Wave for optimization

Applications
AI model acceleration
Cryptographic analysis and security
Logistics optimization and path planning
Molecular and atomic system simulations

Industries
Quantum computing
Pharmaceutical development
Finance and risk modeling
Cybersecurity and defense
Aerospace and navigation

Challenges
Maintaining quantum coherence and low error rates
Scalability of qubit count and connectivity
Costly development and cooling infrastructure
Limited accessibility outside of research environments

Summary
Quantum chips serve as the backbone of quantum computing, enabling extraordinary advancements in speed and problem-solving ability. While current versions are still experimental, they offer immense potential for transformative applications in computing, science, and industry.

Quantum Circuit

Definition
A quantum circuit is a sequence of quantum gates applied to a set of qubits to perform a quantum computation. It is the core abstraction used to design and execute quantum algorithms.

Key Components
Qubits as the information carriers
Quantum gates such as Hadamard, Pauli-X, and CNOT
Circuit architecture specifying gate sequences
Measurement steps to retrieve classical outcomes

Benefits
Facilitates the construction of powerful quantum algorithms
Enables quantum operations like entanglement and interference

Provides modular and scalable design for quantum computing
Supports simulation of physical systems and optimization tasks

Examples
Quantum circuits for factoring integers with Shor's algorithm
Machine learning circuits using quantum classifiers
Simulations of atomic interactions for chemical modeling

Applications
Cryptography and quantum key generation
Quantum machine learning and AI
Physics and chemistry simulation
Optimization and combinatorics

Industries
Computing and data science
Security and cryptographic systems
Healthcare and pharmaceuticals
Finance and operations research

Challenges
Quantum gates are prone to error due to decoherence
High gate fidelity and timing precision are needed
Scalability is limited by current hardware technologies

Summary
Quantum circuits are the foundation of programmable quantum systems. They offer a structured way to leverage quantum mechanics for solving advanced problems, though their execution remains limited by current hardware capabilities.

Quantum Clustering

Definition
Quantum clustering is an AI technique that uses quantum computing to identify natural groupings in datasets. It enhances classical clustering methods by exploiting quantum effects for better scalability and performance.

Key Components
Quantum encoding of data into qubit states
Quantum distance metrics or similarity functions
Amplitude amplification and interference mechanisms
Quantum-enhanced versions of algorithms like k-means

Benefits
Faster processing of high-dimensional data
Improved accuracy in complex datasets
Detection of nonlinear patterns classical models may miss
Better efficiency for large-scale clustering tasks

Examples
Segmenting gene expression profiles in medical datasets
Clustering customer behavior for targeted marketing
Quantum-assisted feature mapping in unsupervised learning

Applications
Bioinformatics and healthcare analytics
Recommendation systems and personalization
Image and pattern recognition
Unsupervised AI model development

Industries
Healthcare
Retail and e-commerce
Financial services
AI and analytics research

Challenges
Translating classical data to quantum formats
Hardware constraints limit scalability and noise tolerance
Complexity in interpreting quantum clustering results

Summary
Quantum clustering transforms how we explore and group data by integrating quantum efficiency into classical machine learning workflows. Its performance edge is promising, though practical use depends on advances in hardware and algorithm design.

Quantum Control in AI

Definition
Quantum control in AI refers to the use of artificial intelligence techniques, particularly machine learning and reinforcement learning, to manage and optimize the behavior of quantum systems. It is aimed at ensuring qubits and quantum operations behave predictably and accurately within the constraints of quantum mechanics.

Key Components
Control pulses and quantum feedback mechanisms
Reinforcement learning strategies for dynamic system adaptation
Noise mitigation and system stabilization techniques
Quantum system modeling and calibration frameworks

Benefits
Enhances the accuracy and reliability of quantum operations
Enables real-time adjustments in quantum hardware
Reduces manual tuning and human error in experiments
Supports adaptive control in complex quantum environments

Examples
Using AI algorithms to stabilize qubit coherence in noisy conditions
Training models to identify optimal gate sequences for reduced error rates
Tuning control parameters in superconducting quantum processors automatically

Applications
Quantum hardware calibration and optimization
Quantum error correction strategies
Automation of quantum experiments and state preparation
Quantum-enhanced communication system regulation

Industries
Quantum computing development
Semiconductor and chip manufacturing
Telecommunications
Scientific instrumentation and research

Challenges
Highly sensitive to external environmental noise
Limited training data from physical quantum systems
Complex feedback requirements for real-time control
Integration between AI and quantum hardware is still evolving

Summary
Quantum control in AI is essential for operating reliable quantum devices. By applying intelligent control techniques, it improves system stability and performance, paving the way for scalable and efficient quantum computing solutions.

Quantum Data

Definition
Quantum data refers to information represented and processed using the quantum states of physical systems. It includes data derived from quantum processes or encoded directly within quantum systems for advanced computing and AI tasks.

Key Components
Quantum states and density matrices as data representations
Quantum memory and communication protocols
Encoding schemes like amplitude encoding and basis encoding
Quantum measurement for data extraction

Benefits
Supports high-dimensional and entangled data representations
Provides richer insights into physical and chemical systems
Enables new data-driven approaches in quantum-enhanced AI
Introduces non-classical correlations for advanced modeling

Examples
Using quantum sensor outputs for AI-based predictive diagnostics
Encoding visual data into qubits for quantum image recognition
Simulating complex molecules and feeding results into learning models

Applications
Quantum-enhanced data analytics
Physics-informed AI modeling
Quantum chemistry and material simulation
Secure communication and quantum sensing

Industries
Pharmaceuticals and biotechnology
Cybersecurity and defense technology
Scientific research and quantum physics
Healthcare and diagnostic imaging

Challenges
Difficult to interpret and visualize in classical terms
Incompatibility with traditional machine learning pipelines
Data loss during quantum-to-classical conversion
Lack of standardized tools for managing quantum data formats

Summary
Quantum data presents new opportunities for AI by introducing richer and more intricate data structures. As quantum technologies evolve, AI systems capable of learning from and acting on quantum data will become increasingly critical across multiple domains.

Quantum Decision Theory

Definition
Quantum decision theory is a framework that models decision-making using quantum probability principles rather than classical logic. It captures the influence of uncertainty, superposition, and interference in human-like and AI-driven reasoning processes.

Key Components
Quantum probability amplitudes instead of classical probabilities
Superposition of decision outcomes
Contextual modeling and interference-based decision dynamics
Quantum-inspired cognitive models

Benefits
Models irrational or ambiguous decisions more effectively
Improves decision-making accuracy in uncertain environments
Enables contextual and adaptive AI reasoning
Expands the theoretical foundation of cognitive AI systems

Examples
Simulating investor behavior with quantum probability models
Enhancing recommendation engines with context-aware choice modeling
Modeling inconsistent consumer preferences using superposition states

Applications
AI behavioral modeling and decision analysis
Cognitive science and psychology simulations
Financial forecasting under uncertainty
Intelligent recommendation and decision support systems

Industries
Finance and behavioral economics
Healthcare decision systems
Marketing analytics
Cognitive and educational technology

Challenges
Complex mathematical structures not widely understood
Implementation challenges in existing AI architectures
Limited empirical validation in real-world applications
Interpretability issues for non-quantum-trained users

Summary
Quantum decision theory redefines how AI models human behavior and decision-making by incorporating principles of uncertainty and superposition. It enhances reasoning in systems that must navigate ambiguity, conflict, or incomplete information.

Quantum Embedding in AI

Definition
Quantum embedding in AI refers to the process of encoding classical data into quantum states to utilize quantum computational advantages for machine learning and data analysis. This transformation allows classical data to be mapped into a quantum Hilbert space, enabling access to quantum phenomena like interference, entanglement, and superposition for improved learning capabilities.

Key Components
Quantum feature maps for classical-to-quantum data conversion
Parameterized quantum circuits (PQCs) for dynamic learning
Hilbert space representation for high-dimensional analysis
Quantum measurement for result extraction and interpretation

Benefits
Facilitates high-dimensional data transformations for better pattern separation
Improves expressiveness and learning power of AI models
Reduces dimensionality without losing critical information
Enables hybrid quantum-classical model construction for superior performance

Examples
Using quantum embeddings for portfolio risk assessment in financial forecasting
Quantum-enhanced medical imaging classification using pixel data encodings
Mapping sentiment representations into quantum circuits for NLP classification tasks

Applications
Quantum-enhanced classification and regression
Feature extraction in machine learning
Dimensionality reduction in large datasets
Quantum generative models with embedded latent spaces

Industries
Finance and asset prediction
Healthcare diagnostics and genomics
Cybersecurity and data protection
Telecommunications and signal interpretation
Pharmaceuticals for molecular structure analysis

Challenges
Noise sensitivity during quantum encoding and processing
Hardware limitations affecting stability and reproducibility
Lack of standardization in feature mapping techniques
Difficulty interpreting quantum outcomes in classical terms

Summary
Quantum embedding in AI empowers next-generation learning systems by representing classical data in quantum states. It opens new pathways for efficient learning, complex pattern analysis, and robust decision-making in high-dimensional environments.

Quantum Entanglement in AI

Definition
Quantum entanglement in AI involves using entangled qubit systems to enhance data correlation, communication, and learning efficiency. It allows quantum systems to maintain synchronized states across distributed nodes, enabling new capabilities in AI and distributed computing.

Key Components
Pairs or groups of entangled qubits
Quantum communication protocols for information transfer
Measurement-based inference and data correlation
Non-local interactions enabling parallelism and synchronization

Benefits
Enables fast and secure communication across AI agents
Supports advanced inference using entangled data states
Improves distributed AI system coherence and coordination
Facilitates non-classical forms of pattern recognition

Examples
Using entangled qubits in quantum neural networks for parallel training
Applying entanglement to synchronize quantum AI agents
Utilizing entangled photon pairs for secure AI data exchange

Applications
Quantum cryptography and secure communications
Multi-agent quantum AI collaboration
Distributed quantum computing environments
High-precision sensing and AI-assisted measurement systems

Industries
Defense and intelligence networks
Quantum telecommunications
Cybersecurity and authentication systems
Distributed computing and AI development

Challenges
Maintaining entanglement over long distances is difficult
Decoherence risks in open environments
Limited compatibility with classical data structures
Generation and management of entangled states is complex

Summary
Quantum entanglement in AI introduces powerful new methods for communication, security, and system-wide coordination. Its ability to enable non-local correlations enhances the capabilities of distributed and intelligent systems beyond classical boundaries.

Quantum Entanglement

Definition
Quantum entanglement is a quantum mechanical phenomenon where particles become interlinked such that the state of one particle instantaneously influences the state of another, regardless of distance. This nonlocal correlation defies classical concepts of separability and enables novel applications in quantum communication, computing, and sensing.

Key Components
Quantum superposition forming correlated particle pairs
Wavefunction collapse through measurement
Bell's theorem verifying nonlocal correlations
Quantum coherence for entanglement preservation

Benefits
Enables ultra-secure communication using entangled particle pairs
Provides a foundation for quantum teleportation and distributed computing
Allows exponential speedup in quantum computing through entangled gates
Improves precision measurements in quantum metrology and sensing

Examples
Quantum key distribution protocols like BB84 and E91
Teleportation of quantum states over fiber and satellite links
Entangled qubits enabling multi-qubit gate operations
Experiments verifying photon entanglement across long distances

Applications
Quantum internet and secure networks
Distributed AI and multi-agent quantum systems
Quantum-enhanced sensors and atomic clocks
High-speed, tamper-proof communication channels

Industries
Telecommunications and cybersecurity
Quantum computing and AI
Defense and intelligence
Medical imaging and scientific instrumentation

Challenges
Maintaining entanglement over distance and time
Sensitivity to environmental decoherence
Efficient generation and synchronization of entangled pairs
Complexity in practical deployment for communication systems

Summary
Quantum entanglement is a cornerstone of quantum information science, enabling revolutionary advances in secure communication, computation, and sensing. Despite technical and scalability challenges, its implementation is critical to the success of future quantum technologies.

Quantum Field

Definition
A quantum field is a foundational concept in quantum field theory, representing an entity that permeates all of space and whose excitations correspond to elementary particles. Unlike classical fields, quantum fields incorporate principles of quantum mechanics, enabling the spontaneous creation and annihilation of particles and interactions among fundamental forces.

Key Components
Quantum particles as excitations of the field
Field operators defining interactions and particle evolution
Virtual particles mediating force exchanges

Gauge symmetries governing field behavior
Renormalization to resolve mathematical infinities

Benefits
Provides a unifying framework for particle interactions and quantum forces
Supports development of the Standard Model of particle physics
Enables predictions in high-energy and subatomic experiments
Forms the theoretical base for quantum electrodynamics and chromodynamics

Examples
The Higgs field responsible for giving particles mass
Quantum electrodynamics describing light-matter interactions
Quantum chromodynamics modeling strong force among quarks and gluons
Applications in superconductivity, enabling MRI and maglev technology

Applications
Fundamental physics and particle theory
Quantum computing foundations
Material design and nanoscience
Advanced communication and encryption systems

Industries
High-energy physics and cosmology
Quantum hardware development
Aerospace and superconducting materials
Scientific instrumentation and imaging

Challenges
Mathematical complexity of modeling quantum interactions
Difficulty in unifying quantum fields with gravity
Experimental limitations in testing high-energy predictions
Philosophical debates about the nature of vacuum energy and virtual particles

Summary
Quantum fields are the building blocks of modern theoretical physics, explaining how particles arise and interact in space. They underlie both theoretical advancements and practical technologies, from quantum processors to superconducting materials. Continued exploration of quantum fields promises deeper insights into the fabric of reality and new technological frontiers.

Quantum Information

Definition
Quantum information is a scientific discipline focused on encoding, transmitting, and manipulating information using the principles of quantum mechanics. Unlike classical information that is represented by binary bits (0 or 1), quantum information relies on qubits, which can exist in superposition, allowing them to represent multiple states simultaneously and interact through entanglement.

Key Components
Qubits and quantum state representations
Superposition and quantum coherence
Entanglement for nonlocal correlations
Quantum gates and circuits for logical operations
Quantum teleportation and cryptographic protocols
Quantum error correction methods

Benefits
Enables faster and more efficient computations for complex problems
Supports unbreakable communication through quantum key distribution
Improves precision in quantum sensing and measurement technologies
Facilitates secure and scalable data processing in quantum environments

Examples
Quantum teleportation used to transfer quantum states across distances
Quantum key distribution protocols securing communication lines
Implementation of Shor's algorithm for efficient integer factorization
Grover's algorithm applied to accelerate unsorted database searches

Applications
Quantum computing and algorithm design
Quantum cryptography and network security
Quantum-enhanced measurement and imaging
Simulation of complex physical and biological systems

Industries
Information technology and advanced computing
Cybersecurity and data protection
Finance and trading for computational modeling
Pharmaceuticals for molecular simulations
Aerospace and defense for secure navigation and communication
Telecommunications for quantum internet development

Summary
Quantum information represents a foundational shift in how data is understood and processed. By leveraging the unique properties of qubits, it enables powerful new approaches to computing, communication, and sensing, with far-reaching implications across scientific, industrial, and security sectors.

Quantum Information Processing

Definition
Quantum information processing refers to the design and use of systems that manipulate, store, and transmit data using the fundamental principles of quantum mechanics. This includes leveraging properties such as superposition and entanglement to perform computations and process information in ways that are not achievable with classical methods. In artificial intelligence, it introduces enhanced learning capabilities, secure data handling, and new modeling approaches.

Key Components
Quantum bits (qubits)
Quantum logic gates and circuits
Quantum error correction protocols
Entanglement and teleportation schemes

Benefits
Provides exponential speedup for solving certain computational problems
Enables secure communication through quantum encryption
Enhances AI systems with more expressive and scalable models
Supports advanced simulations in scientific and industrial domains

Examples
Running Shor's algorithm on a quantum circuit for prime factorization
Training quantum-enhanced models using entangled datasets
Applying quantum teleportation in secure data exchange scenarios

Applications
Quantum cryptography and secure communications
Quantum-enhanced machine learning and AI reasoning
High-efficiency data encoding and compression
Scientific simulations in physics and chemistry

Industries
Cybersecurity
Healthcare and pharmaceuticals
Financial modeling and analytics
Defense and intelligence systems

Challenges
Quantum hardware is expensive and difficult to maintain
Coherence time of qubits limits execution duration
Requires specialized quantum programming expertise
Limited accessibility to deployable quantum systems

Summary
Quantum information processing represents a shift in how data is computed, stored, and communicated. It provides critical foundations for building the next generation of AI and secure information systems by embedding quantum principles into core data processing strategies.

Quantum Information Theory

Definition
Quantum information theory is the study of how information is stored, transmitted, and processed using quantum systems. It extends classical information theory by incorporating quantum properties like entanglement and superposition, offering deeper insights into computational limits and communication protocols.

Key Components
Quantum entropy and mutual information
Qubits and entangled systems
Quantum channels and error correction
No-cloning and teleportation theorems

Benefits
Defines the theoretical limits of quantum communication
Enables unbreakable encryption and secure data transfer
Informs the development of quantum algorithms
Improves understanding of quantum computational complexity

Examples
Entanglement-based encryption protocols
Quantum teleportation for data transfer
Evaluating the capacity of quantum channels in AI systems

Applications
Quantum cryptography
Quantum computing architecture
Secure communication systems
Theoretical AI modeling

Industries
Cybersecurity
Telecommunications
Scientific computing
Government and defense

Challenges
Complex mathematical foundations
Hard to apply directly in practical AI applications
Requires precise experimental conditions
Limited toolkits for real-world implementation

Summary
Quantum information theory provides the backbone for understanding how information works in the quantum realm. It is foundational for the development of secure, powerful, and efficient AI systems operating at the edge of modern computing.

Quantum-Informed Decision Making

Definition
Quantum-informed decision making is a theoretical approach to AI decision systems that incorporates principles from quantum mechanics—especially quantum probability—to model decision-making under uncertainty. It accounts for ambiguity, context, and superposition of mental states in AI reasoning.

Key Components
Quantum decision theory and quantum logic
Superposition of decision states
Quantum-inspired probability distributions
Contextual dependency modeling

Benefits
Replicates real-world decision complexity more effectively
Supports flexible reasoning under uncertainty
Improves AI interaction with ambiguous inputs or multi-step scenarios
Models human decision-making patterns more realistically

Examples
AI chatbots selecting responses from superposed user intent predictions
Context-aware recommendation engines using quantum probability
Autonomous systems making flexible decisions in unpredictable environments

Applications
Human-like AI assistants and ethical advisors
Decision support tools in law and healthcare
Predictive modeling in behavior sciences
AI governance and multi-agent coordination

Industries
Marketing and behavioral targeting
Healthcare diagnostics and planning
Legal tech and policy modeling
AI-powered robotics and automation

Challenges
Complex mathematical foundation complicates adoption
Benchmarking against classical models remains difficult
Toolkits and frameworks for implementation are limited
Requires paradigm shifts in AI reasoning and training

Summary
Quantum-informed decision making elevates artificial intelligence by enabling more nuanced and human-like responses to complex situations. It is a forward-looking framework for adaptive, intelligent systems that reason under conditions of uncertainty and ambiguity.

Quantum-Informed Optimization

Definition
Quantum-informed optimization refers to optimization techniques that are enhanced by quantum principles, either through true quantum computing or by applying quantum-inspired logic to classical algorithms. These methods tackle complex search and optimization problems more efficiently than traditional approaches.

Key Components
Quantum search techniques
Quantum superposition and tunneling concepts
Hybrid classical-quantum architecture
Quantum annealing or QAOA frameworks

Benefits
Solves large-scale optimization problems faster
Finds global optima more reliably than classical counterparts
Reduces computation time for high-dimensional searches
Enhances machine learning model tuning

Examples
Optimizing supply chain logistics with quantum-inspired methods
Fine-tuning hyperparameters in neural networks using QAOA
Energy-efficient design optimization in engineering

Applications
AI model optimization
Combinatorial problem solving
Network flow management
Operational research

Industries
Manufacturing
Finance
Telecommunications
Logistics

Challenges
May require quantum hardware or emulators
Difficult to benchmark against classical optimizers
Still an emerging field with limited standardized practices
Understanding and modeling quantum behavior accurately

Summary
Quantum-informed optimization harnesses the power of quantum thinking to deliver more effective solutions to complex problems. It is a valuable tool in AI and operations research, offering a forward-looking approach to intelligent problem-solving.

Quantum-Inspired Algorithms

Definition
Quantum-inspired algorithms are classical computational techniques designed to emulate the behavior of quantum systems by incorporating concepts like superposition, entanglement, and quantum tunneling. Although they do not require quantum hardware, these algorithms borrow mathematical principles from quantum mechanics to improve performance in classical environments, particularly in optimization, data analysis, and machine learning.

Key Components
Mathematical representations inspired by quantum mechanics
Classical processors executing quantum-like behavior
Quantum tunneling-based simulated annealing strategies
Tensor-based structures for multidimensional data modeling

Benefits
Improves performance of classical algorithms in high-dimensional spaces
Provides quantum-like speedups without requiring quantum machines
Solves complex optimization and search problems efficiently
Compatible with existing infrastructure for near-term deployment

Examples
Simulated annealing routines that incorporate tunneling effects to escape local minima
Tensor network compression models for efficient data handling
Classical algorithms mimicking quantum entanglement to model complex variable interactions

Applications
Routing and supply chain optimization in logistics
Data compression and dimensionality reduction in analytics
Portfolio optimization and risk forecasting in finance
Hyperparameter tuning in classical machine learning workflows

Industries
Transportation and logistics
Financial technology and risk analytics
Telecommunications and network design
Artificial intelligence and algorithm research

Challenges
Do not achieve the exponential gains of true quantum computing
Rely heavily on accurate abstractions of quantum processes
Limited by classical computing architecture and memory constraints
Require careful parameter tuning to preserve algorithmic advantages

Summary
Quantum-inspired algorithms extend the power of classical computing by integrating principles rooted in quantum physics. They deliver real-world performance benefits for challenging computational tasks, offering a bridge between classical methods and future quantum technologies.

Quantum-Inspired Neural Networks

Definition
Quantum-inspired neural networks are computational models that incorporate concepts from quantum mechanics, such as entanglement, interference, and amplitude encoding, into classical neural network designs. These systems enhance learning by imitating the non-classical behaviors of quantum systems.

Key Components
Quantum analogs of artificial neurons and layers
Quantum-inspired activation and transition functions
Hilbert space-based representations of input features
Probabilistic adjustment of weights and learning dynamics

Benefits
Improves learning efficiency in complex and high-dimensional spaces
Enhances generalization from limited training data
Provides more robust solutions to noisy or uncertain inputs
Expands architectural possibilities for AI model design

Examples
Training image classifiers using simulated quantum neural nets
Embedding contextual data into Hilbert spaces for NLP models
Using entangled-state logic for recognizing audio or signal patterns

Applications
Visual recognition and image processing
Speech-to-text and semantic analysis
Medical diagnostics and anomaly detection
Fraud detection and real-time data analysis

Industries
Healthcare and personalized medicine
Retail analytics and ad targeting
Cybersecurity and identity verification
Aerospace and autonomous navigation

Challenges
Complex dynamics are difficult to interpret and validate
Design must ensure feasibility on classical systems
Performance depends on hardware configuration
Lack of standard models for benchmarking

Summary
Quantum-inspired neural networks offer a hybrid evolution of deep learning, introducing richer, non-classical structures for training and inference. They represent a step forward in building adaptive, efficient AI models using ideas from quantum computation.

Quantum Intelligence

Definition
Quantum intelligence is an emerging interdisciplinary field that explores how quantum mechanics can be applied to simulate or replicate intelligent behavior. It combines quantum computing, cognitive science, and artificial intelligence to create systems capable of learning, reasoning, and decision-making through quantum logic.

Key Components
Quantum cognition and behavior modeling
Quantum neural network architectures
Hybrid quantum-classical processing environments
Quantum learning and memory structures

Benefits
Enables intelligent systems to function in ambiguous or probabilistic environments
Enhances reasoning using quantum probability principles
Improves flexibility and complexity in cognitive modeling
Supports development of human-like learning systems

Examples
Quantum-enhanced conversational agents that probabilistically interpret user intent
AI systems leveraging quantum cognition models for decision-making
Simulating mental states using quantum-inspired neural dynamics

Applications
Next-generation cognitive computing platforms
Natural language comprehension and inference
AI models for perception, awareness, and context recognition
Simulations of consciousness and sentient behavior

Industries
Educational and cognitive science research
AI development and machine consciousness studies
Philosophy and neuroscience
Healthcare and mental health modeling

Challenges
Remains largely theoretical with limited empirical data
Hardware constraints restrict real-time implementation
High abstraction and complexity hinder system design
Validation and benchmarking of outcomes are difficult

Summary
Quantum intelligence is a bold new direction in AI research, aiming to model cognition and learning based on quantum principles. It paves the way for future intelligent systems that operate beyond the confines of classical logic and deterministic reasoning.

Quantum Iterative Learning Control

Definition
Quantum Iterative Learning Control is an advanced control strategy that combines iterative learning techniques with quantum dynamics to improve performance in quantum systems. It is primarily used to refine the behavior of quantum devices through repeated feedback-based adjustments.

Key Components
Quantum control theory
Learning from repeated operations
Feedback and trajectory tracking
Quantum system modeling and update rules

Benefits
Improves the precision of quantum device operations
Enhances system performance through repetition
Reduces long-term errors and noise effects
Supports adaptive quantum system calibration

Examples
Refining qubit gate operations in quantum computers
Stabilizing quantum sensors in fluctuating environments
Training quantum robots for high-fidelity task execution

Applications
Quantum robotics
Quantum simulation calibration
Quantum error correction
Precise measurement systems

Industries
Quantum hardware development
Manufacturing
Metrology
Aerospace

Challenges
Resource-intensive due to repeated iterations
Requires accurate quantum state estimation
Sensitive to external noise and interference
May be hard to implement in multi-qubit systems

Summary
Quantum Iterative Learning Control provides a systematic way to improve quantum device performance through feedback and repetition. It plays a crucial role in enhancing reliability and precision in quantum applications.

Quantum Mechanic

Definition
A quantum mechanic system is a physical system governed by the principles of quantum mechanics, which describes the behavior of particles at atomic and subatomic scales. Unlike classical systems, where objects follow predictable paths, quantum systems exhibit wave-particle duality, superposition, and entanglement, allowing them to exist in multiple states simultaneously and interact in non-intuitive ways.

Key Components
Quantum states and wave functions
Superposition and entanglement
Quantum operators and measurement
Observer effect and collapse of wave function

Benefits
Revolutionizes computation through quantum algorithms
Enhances data security with quantum encryption
Enables discovery of new materials and molecular structures
Improves sensing and diagnostic technologies

Examples
Quantum computers using qubits for parallel computation
Quantum teleportation transferring state information
Quantum key distribution for unbreakable encryption
Quantum simulations modeling complex molecules

Applications
Quantum computing
Quantum communication
Material science
Medical imaging

Industries
Technology and computing
Finance
Cybersecurity
Healthcare
Aerospace and defense

Challenges
Maintaining coherence in quantum states
Requirement of low temperatures and isolation
Complex error correction mechanisms
Scalability of multi-qubit systems
Ethical concerns in breaking encryption

Summary
Quantum mechanic systems represent a foundational shift in science and technology. Through principles like superposition and entanglement, they open new possibilities for computing, communication, security, and advanced materials, despite the ongoing technical challenges in real-world deployment.

Quantum Phenomena

Definition
Quantum phenomena refer to behaviors and interactions occurring at atomic and subatomic scales, governed by the principles of quantum mechanics rather than classical physics. These phenomena often display unusual properties like superposition, entanglement, wave-particle duality, and uncertainty.

Key Components
Quantum superposition
Quantum entanglement
Quantum tunneling
Quantum coherence
Wave-particle duality
Heisenberg uncertainty principle

Benefits
Enables faster computation and secure communications
Improves measurement precision and scientific accuracy
Leads to new materials and nanotechnologies
Supports modeling of complex biological and chemical systems

Examples
Electrons tunneling in semiconductors
Photon interference in double-slit experiments
Quantum entanglement in communication systems
Superposition states in quantum computing

Applications
Quantum computing
Quantum cryptography
Quantum sensing and metrology
Quantum simulations and imaging

Industries
Computing and IT
Telecommunications
Pharmaceuticals
Medical diagnostics
Defense and aerospace
Finance
Renewable energy
Advanced manufacturing

Summary
Quantum phenomena form the foundation of next-generation technologies by revealing behaviors that classical physics cannot explain. Their impact spans multiple scientific and industrial domains, unlocking new frontiers in communication, computation, sensing, and materials research.

QoS (Quality of Service) in AI

Definition
Quality of Service (QoS) in AI refers to the ability of an artificial intelligence system or AI-powered service to meet predefined performance, reliability, and responsiveness criteria. QoS metrics are essential to ensure that AI models and applications consistently deliver expected outcomes, especially in real-time or mission-critical environments.

Key Components
Latency: Response time from input to output
Accuracy: Precision of predictions or decisions
Availability: System uptime and task readiness
Scalability: Ability to maintain performance under load
Fault Tolerance: Resilience during partial failures
Resource Utilization: Efficiency of hardware/software usage

Benefits
Ensures reliability and predictability in AI systems
Enables compliance with service-level agreements
Improves user trust in intelligent applications

Minimizes system downtime and data loss
Optimizes cost-effectiveness through efficient design

Examples
Real-time diagnostics in healthcare AI systems
Autonomous vehicles requiring fast, safe responses
Chatbots with fast and accurate user interactions
Industrial automation with uninterrupted monitoring

Applications
Real-time and edge AI systems
Smart city infrastructure
Healthcare diagnostics
Autonomous robotics
Cloud AI services

Industries
Healthcare
Transportation
Telecommunications
Finance
Manufacturing
Energy

Challenges
Balancing accuracy, performance, and cost
Ensuring QoS in decentralized environments
Establishing universal QoS standards
Adapting to variable data and workloads
Evaluating heterogeneous AI models consistently

Summary
QoS in AI ensures that intelligent systems are dependable, efficient, and scalable. It is critical in environments where performance impacts safety, security, or critical outcomes, and it supports broader AI adoption by maintaining user confidence and technical stability.

Quanta Energy

Definition
Energy Quanta refers to the discrete packets of energy that are fundamental to quantum mechanics. In classical physics, energy is often considered continuous, but in quantum theory, energy is quantized, meaning it exists in distinct amounts rather than a smooth spectrum. This concept was introduced by Max Planck and forms the basis of quantum mechanics, explaining phenomena such as the behavior of light, atomic interactions, and particle-wave duality.

Key Components
Planck's constant
Photons
Quantized energy levels
Wave-particle duality

Benefits
Supports innovations in quantum computing and energy-efficient systems
Enables precise atomic and molecular analysis through spectroscopy

Improves performance in light-emitting and photovoltaic devices
Drives scientific discoveries at subatomic scales

Examples
The photoelectric effect, where photons eject electrons from a metal surface
Quantum dots, emitting specific light frequencies based on size
Energy transitions in atoms, producing spectral lines

Applications
Quantum cryptography
Laser technology
Atomic clocks
Photovoltaics
Quantum sensing

Industries
Telecommunications
Renewable energy
Medical imaging
Semiconductor technology
Quantum research

Challenges
Requires accurate modeling of quantum interactions
Sensitive to experimental noise and external conditions
Interpretation complexity in high-energy systems
Still under development for many practical applications

Summary
Energy quanta are a foundational concept in quantum physics, enabling a wide range of technological and scientific advancements. From secure communications to clean energy, their role continues to expand across industries through ongoing quantum innovation.

Quantum Object Recognition

Definition
Quantum Object Recognition refers to the application of quantum computing techniques to identify and classify objects within visual data. Unlike traditional object recognition systems that rely on classical algorithms, quantum object recognition leverages the properties of quantum states, such as superposition and entanglement, to process image data in a highly parallel and efficient manner.

Key Components
Quantum feature encoding of images
Quantum kernel methods for similarity assessment
Quantum circuits for pattern matching
Quantum measurement to determine classification outcomes

Benefits
Accelerates object recognition tasks through quantum parallelism
Enhances pattern detection in noisy or complex data
Reduces classical computational overhead
Improves classification in dynamic visual environments

Examples
Quantum-assisted classification of MRI scans
Detection of hidden objects in satellite imagery
Quantum circuit models for recognizing handwritten digits

Applications
Medical diagnostics
Surveillance and security
Autonomous vehicle systems
Facial authentication

Industries
Healthcare
Automotive
Aerospace and defense
Telecommunications

Challenges
Limited quantum hardware scalability
Complexity of image data encoding
Vulnerability to noise and decoherence
Lack of standardized implementation tools

Summary
Quantum Object Recognition introduces a powerful method for visual analysis using the advantages of quantum computing. It presents transformative potential in fields that require fast, reliable, and accurate interpretation of visual data.

Quantum Operation

Definition
A Quantum Operation refers to the mathematical transformation applied to quantum states, typically represented by quantum gates or quantum channels. In AI, quantum operations form the building blocks of algorithms and models by manipulating qubits to perform computations, learning tasks, and optimization processes.

Key Components
Quantum gates and circuits
Unitary transformations
Quantum measurement operations
Noise channels and decoherence models

Benefits
Enables construction of efficient quantum algorithms
Allows reversible logic for reduced energy use
Controls data evolution in quantum neural networks
Establishes the basis for intelligent quantum processing

Examples
Applying Hadamard gates for data superposition
Using entangling gates in quantum learning models
Implementing quantum Fourier transforms for pattern recognition

Applications
Quantum machine learning
Quantum encryption
Quantum simulations
Hybrid AI architectures

Industries
Quantum computing
Scientific research
Finance
Artificial intelligence

Challenges
Highly sensitive to noise and environmental conditions
Difficult to scale to many-qubit systems
Unitary design imposes modeling constraints
Lack of fully developed tools for practical AI deployment

Summary
Quantum operations are the foundational mechanisms for data manipulation in quantum AI systems. They enable the logic, learning, and communication that make quantum-enhanced intelligence a practical reality.

Quantum Optimal Control

Definition
Quantum Optimal Control is the process of determining the best possible set of control signals or parameters to manipulate quantum systems toward a specific outcome with maximum efficiency and precision. In AI, it is used to fine-tune quantum computations and manage qubit behavior during training and inference.

Key Components
Control pulse shaping
Quantum system modeling
Iterative feedback mechanisms
Optimization of objective functions

Benefits
Improves precision in quantum algorithm execution
Reduces decoherence and energy loss
Automates calibration in quantum systems
Enhances model stability and reproducibility

Examples
Fine-tuning qubit behavior in reinforcement learning
Adjusting gate fidelity in quantum model training
Optimizing AI inference layers through quantum control techniques

Applications
Quantum computing calibration
Quantum robotics
AI-based quantum system tuning
Error mitigation strategies

Industries
Quantum hardware
Aerospace
Pharmaceuticals
Energy research

Challenges
Demands extremely accurate control systems
Affected by environmental interference
Requires advanced mathematical models
Costly to implement at scale

Summary
Quantum Optimal Control enables AI systems to operate quantum devices with maximum efficiency and stability. As quantum technologies evolve, optimal control will be essential for unlocking high-performance, error-resilient applications.

Quantum Optimization (QO)

Definition
Quantum Optimization (QO) refers to solving optimization problems using quantum computing techniques, including quantum annealing, variational quantum algorithms, and hybrid methods. It targets problems where finding the best solution from a vast number of possibilities is computationally intensive for classical systems.

Key Components
Quantum cost functions
Quantum annealers and variational circuits
Optimization landscapes
Quantum-enhanced heuristics

Benefits
Rapid exploration of complex solution spaces
Better performance in non-convex and combinatorial problems
Reduces computation time for training AI models
Supports optimization in constrained environments

Examples
Quantum-tuned AI model hyperparameters
Risk minimization in financial portfolios
Optimized delivery scheduling for logistics

Applications
Machine learning optimization
Operational planning
Resource management
AI strategy modeling

Industries
Finance
Transportation
Manufacturing
Artificial intelligence

Challenges
Current systems have limited scalability
Susceptible to quantum noise and errors
Requires integration with classical frameworks
Complexity in designing energy-efficient cost functions

Summary
Quantum Optimization empowers AI to solve difficult decision-making problems more efficiently. It stands at the intersection of quantum computing and intelligent systems, offering new possibilities for solving tasks once considered intractable.

Quantum Optimization Algorithms

Definition
Quantum Optimization Algorithms solve difficult optimization problems using quantum computing's capabilities in parallelism and entanglement, offering significant speedups over classical approaches.

Key Components
Quantum Approximate Optimization Algorithm (QAOA)
Variational Quantum Eigensolver (VQE)
Quantum circuit-based solvers
Quantum annealing and feedback loops

Benefits
Solves high-complexity problems faster
Improves training and hyperparameter tuning in AI
Optimizes logistical and financial systems
Reduces time and cost of solution discovery

Examples
Hyperparameter optimization in deep learning
Quantum route planning for logistics networks
Financial risk minimization using quantum decision models

Applications
AI model tuning and training
Portfolio and logistics optimization
Combinatorial problem solving in science and industry

Industries
Artificial intelligence
Finance and investment
Manufacturing and supply chain

Challenges
Scalability of quantum solutions to large data sets
Reliability of current quantum hardware
Integration with classical data systems

Summary
Quantum Optimization Algorithms offer powerful alternatives for solving challenges in AI and beyond. By using quantum logic to accelerate solution discovery, they provide critical improvements in efficiency and accuracy.

Quantum Optimized Query Processing

Definition
Quantum Optimized Query Processing involves the use of quantum algorithms to accelerate the execution of complex database queries. This technique utilizes quantum parallelism and search strategies to improve data retrieval speeds and efficiency in AI-powered data systems.

Key Components
Quantum query models
Quantum data indexing and encoding
Quantum search algorithms such as Grover's
Quantum memory and retrieval systems

Benefits
Faster search and retrieval in massive datasets
Lower computational resource demand
Enhanced real-time response for AI systems
Improved handling of complex queries

Examples
Quantum search in recommendation engines
Accelerated retrieval from biomedical databases
AI chatbots using quantum-assisted queries

Applications
Information retrieval
AI database management
Big data analytics
Knowledge graph search

Industries
E-commerce
Healthcare
Government
Telecommunications

Challenges
Integration with classical systems remains limited
Quantum hardware remains expensive and complex
Query optimization requires new algorithmic strategies
Accuracy depends on system fidelity

Summary
Quantum Optimized Query Processing offers a fast, scalable method for managing data-intensive queries in AI environments. As data volumes continue to rise, quantum acceleration provides a competitive advantage in intelligent data systems.

Quantum Orchestration in AI

Definition
Quantum Orchestration in AI refers to the coordinated management of quantum computing resources, algorithms, and workflows within a hybrid system. It ensures smooth integration and execution of quantum tasks alongside classical components in AI applications.

Key Components
Workflow scheduling and management
Hybrid quantum-classical communication
Resource allocation for quantum processors
Monitoring and feedback loops

Benefits
Streamlines complex hybrid AI systems
Improves performance across multiple AI tasks
Allows seamless switching between classical and quantum computing
Enables scalability and maintainability in quantum AI deployments

Examples
Managing distributed AI tasks across quantum and classical servers
Orchestrating quantum-enhanced model training in cloud platforms
Coordinating real-time quantum inference for smart infrastructure

Applications
Hybrid AI systems
Quantum machine learning pipelines
Cloud-based AI services
Smart decision systems

Industries
Cloud computing
Enterprise software
Telecommunications
AI and data science platforms

Challenges
Lack of standard orchestration frameworks
Limited tools for resource monitoring in quantum environments
High cost of managing and maintaining hybrid systems
Requires deep integration across technology stacks

Summary
Quantum Orchestration in AI plays a vital role in unifying classical and quantum computing workflows. It enables efficient, responsive, and scalable operation of AI systems that rely on quantum-enhanced capabilities.

Quantum Oracle

Definition
A Quantum Oracle is a black-box function used within a quantum algorithm to encode problem-specific information. In AI, quantum oracles are utilized to evaluate solutions, guide searches, and apply constraints during quantum computation, especially in algorithms like Grover's search.

Key Components
Unitary black-box function
Quantum circuit representation
Query evaluation mechanism
Problem-specific encoding logic

Benefits
Accelerates search and classification in large data spaces
Supports constraint-aware AI model training
Reduces the number of operations needed to identify optimal solutions
Enables efficient exploration of solution landscapes

Examples
Using a quantum oracle to identify valid solutions in a constrained optimization problem
Evaluating fitness functions in quantum genetic algorithms
Enabling decision-based search in AI rule engines

Applications
Quantum-enhanced search
Constraint satisfaction
Quantum machine learning
AI planning and rule evaluation

Industries
Cybersecurity
Logistics and scheduling
Artificial intelligence research
Quantum software development

Challenges
Requires precise definition of the problem in quantum terms
May increase circuit depth and error rates
Difficult to construct for complex or dynamic AI problems
Limited by quantum hardware capabilities

Summary
Quantum Oracles act as intelligent evaluators within quantum algorithms, providing critical decision-making logic for AI applications. Their ability to guide quantum computations makes them foundational in efficient and scalable quantum AI systems.

Quantum Oscillator in AI

Definition
Quantum oscillators in AI refer to quantum systems that undergo periodic motion, such as quantum harmonic oscillators, which are used to model and simulate dynamic behaviors in intelligent systems. In AI, quantum oscillators help in the representation of time-evolving states, memory elements, and signal patterns within quantum-enhanced models.

Key Components
Quantum harmonic oscillator model
Position and momentum operators
Oscillatory energy levels (quantized states)
Wavefunction representations

Benefits
Provides a foundational model for simulating natural phenomena
Facilitates signal modeling and information encoding in quantum systems
Supports analogies to memory, vibration, and feedback in AI networks
Useful in modeling quantum memory and temporal learning

Examples
Simulating biological rhythms using quantum oscillators in cognitive AI
Incorporating quantum oscillators into energy-based neural network models
Using oscillator-based architectures for AI-driven signal processing

Applications
Quantum signal processing
AI-based modeling of dynamic systems
Quantum memory systems
Neuromorphic computing with oscillatory behavior

Industries
Healthcare and neuroscience
Robotics
Quantum computing
Signal processing and telecommunications

Challenges
Difficult to physically implement in scalable quantum systems
Complex wavefunction behaviors require advanced simulation techniques
Sensitive to environmental decoherence
Limited practical applications outside of research

Summary
Quantum oscillators serve as important tools in AI for modeling cyclic and dynamic systems. Their periodic behavior and quantized energy states allow for deeper representation of time-dependent processes in intelligent quantum-enhanced models.

Quantum Oscillatory Neural Networks (QONN)

Definition
Quantum Oscillatory Neural Networks (QONNs) are neural network models inspired by quantum oscillation principles, where quantum phase interactions are used to process and store information. These networks aim to replicate both quantum dynamics and oscillatory behaviors to enhance computational power and learning efficiency in AI systems.

Key Components
Oscillating quantum states
Phase interference for signal encoding
Quantum synaptic weights
Oscillatory coupling between neurons

Benefits
Supports complex pattern recognition using quantum phase interactions
Increases efficiency in representing time-series and sequential data
Provides a framework for quantum neuromorphic computing
Reduces energy consumption through natural oscillatory dynamics

Examples
Modeling human brainwave patterns using QONNs
Quantum-based classification of rhythmic data, such as speech or ECG signals
Encoding quantum memory through oscillatory phase interactions

Applications
Time-series prediction
Neuromorphic quantum computing
Speech and sound pattern analysis
Biological signal interpretation

Industries
Healthcare
Neuroscience
Speech and audio processing
Quantum hardware development

Challenges
Still in early experimental stages
Requires high-precision phase control
Difficult to scale due to decoherence in oscillatory systems
Complex quantum dynamics need specialized interpretation tools

Summary
Quantum Oscillatory Neural Networks merge the ideas of neural computation and quantum oscillation. They offer promising potential for temporal learning and brain-like AI models through the synergy of oscillatory behavior and quantum mechanics.

Quantum Output

Definition
Quantum output refers to the result generated from a quantum system or computation after measurement. In the context of AI, quantum output often represents the final inference, classification, or decision made by a quantum-enhanced algorithm. The outcome is probabilistic in nature and typically reflects the collapse of quantum states into classical information.

Key Components
Quantum measurement process
Qubit state collapse
Probability distribution over outcomes
Post-processing to convert quantum results into usable data

Benefits
Provides results based on quantum parallelism and superposition
Enables probabilistic decision-making in AI systems
Can reveal hidden patterns not observable through classical output
Supports hybrid output processing with classical systems

Examples
Output from a quantum neural network predicting cancer diagnosis
Quantum classifier determining the category of an input image
Generating sequences in quantum-enhanced natural language models

Applications
Quantum machine learning inference
Generative modeling and synthesis
Quantum probabilistic reasoning
Optimization and classification tasks

Industries
Healthcare diagnostics
Finance and trading systems
Creative industries (art, music, writing)
AI research and development

Challenges
Quantum outputs are inherently probabilistic, requiring multiple runs for accuracy
Noise and decoherence can distort results
Interpreting quantum output may require classical post-processing
Limited by current hardware fidelity

Summary
Quantum output is the final measurable result of a quantum computation. In AI, it serves as the bridge between quantum processes and classical insights, offering powerful and often non-intuitive solutions to complex data problems.

Quantum Overlap Estimation

Definition
Quantum Overlap Estimation is the process of calculating the degree of similarity or correlation between two quantum states. In AI, this technique is used in classification, clustering, and similarity-based learning tasks, allowing quantum systems to compare patterns with enhanced sensitivity.

Key Components
Quantum inner product (fidelity) calculation
Quantum circuits for overlap estimation
Swap test or interferometric methods
Measurement of outcome probabilities

Benefits
Enables efficient similarity comparison in high-dimensional quantum spaces
Improves classification accuracy in quantum machine learning
Supports clustering and kernel methods in quantum-enhanced AI
Requires fewer resources than classical similarity computation for complex states

Examples
Quantum similarity search for document or image recognition
Estimating closeness between states in quantum reinforcement learning
Using overlap scores for matching inputs to known classes

Applications
Quantum classification and clustering
Pattern recognition
Quantum support vector machines
Quantum feature mapping

Industries
Cybersecurity
Healthcare diagnostics
Natural language processing
Intelligent recommendation systems

Challenges
Measurement introduces sampling errors and requires multiple repetitions
Sensitive to noise and gate fidelity in quantum circuits
Difficult to generalize across diverse datasets
Currently limited by quantum hardware scalability

Summary
Quantum Overlap Estimation provides a powerful tool for similarity assessment in quantum AI systems. It enables accurate, scalable comparison of quantum-encoded data, making it essential for future advancements in quantum learning and intelligent reasoning.

Quantum Physics

Definition
Quantum physics is the branch of physics focused on understanding and describing the behavior, properties, and interactions of matter and energy at atomic and subatomic scales. It explores phenomena that classical physics cannot adequately explain, including the quantized nature of energy, wave-particle duality, and the probabilistic nature of quantum states.

Key Components
Important elements include quantum superposition, wave-particle duality, quantum entanglement, uncertainty principle, quantum tunneling, quantized energy states, wavefunctions, quantum coherence, and foundational equations such as Schrödinger's and Dirac's equations.

Benefits
Quantum physics enables precise explanations and predictions of atomic and subatomic phenomena, supports technological innovations in computing, communication, and sensing, enhances understanding of chemical and biological processes at a fundamental level, and provides tools for developing cutting-edge technologies.

Examples
Examples include electron behavior in atoms, photons demonstrating interference patterns in double-slit experiments, quantum tunneling in semiconductor devices, superconductivity in certain materials, and entanglement in quantum cryptography.

Applications
Applications range from quantum computing and secure quantum communication to laser technologies, semiconductor electronics, medical imaging (MRI), precise atomic clocks, spectroscopy, and advanced material design at the quantum scale.

Industries
Industries heavily influenced by quantum physics include computing and information technology, telecommunications, cybersecurity, pharmaceuticals and biotechnology, semiconductor manufacturing, aerospace and defense, healthcare, renewable energy, and advanced materials research.

Summary
Quantum physics provides a comprehensive understanding of the smallest components of our universe, profoundly impacting modern technology and industry. Its principles underpin numerous revolutionary technologies, driving innovation across computing, communications, healthcare, and materials science, thus transforming multiple sectors with unprecedented capabilities.

Quantum Qubit

Definition

A Quantum Qubit is the fundamental unit of quantum information in quantum computing. Unlike classical bits that exist in a state of either 0 or 1, qubits leverage the principles of quantum mechanics, including superposition and entanglement, allowing them to represent and process multiple states simultaneously. This unique property gives quantum computers the potential to solve complex problems exponentially faster than classical computers.

Key Components

Key components of a quantum qubit include superposition, entanglement, quantum gates, and quantum decoherence. Superposition enables a qubit to exist in multiple states at once, dramatically increasing computational power. Entanglement is a quantum phenomenon where qubits become correlated, meaning the state of one qubit is dependent on the state of another, regardless of distance. Quantum gates manipulate qubits to perform operations similar to classical logic gates but with the ability to process multiple states simultaneously. Quantum decoherence occurs when a qubit loses its quantum properties due to external interactions, requiring advanced error correction techniques to maintain stable computations.

Benefits

The benefits of quantum qubits include parallel processing, exponential speedup, and enhanced security. The ability of qubits to exist in superposition allows quantum computers to process multiple computations at once, significantly reducing the time needed for complex problem-solving. Exponential speedup enables the solving of tasks such as factorization and optimization that are infeasible for classical computers. Quantum cryptography benefits from qubits, as their entangled states provide unbreakable encryption methods that enhance cybersecurity.

Examples

An example of quantum qubits in action is Shor's algorithm, which uses quantum superposition and entanglement to efficiently factor large numbers, a task that classical computers struggle to perform. Another example is quantum machine learning, where qubits help process and analyze vast datasets more efficiently than traditional computing methods, leading to breakthroughs in artificial intelligence.

Industries

Industries utilizing quantum qubits include finance, healthcare, cybersecurity, logistics, and materials science. Financial institutions explore quantum qubits for portfolio optimization and risk assessment, solving problems that require analyzing large datasets. Healthcare applies quantum computing to drug discovery and molecular simulations, accelerating the development of new treatments. Cybersecurity benefits from quantum encryption, ensuring secure data transmission and protection against cyber threats. Logistics companies use quantum qubits for optimizing supply chains and route planning, reducing costs and improving efficiency. Materials science relies on quantum computing to simulate molecular interactions, aiding in the discovery of advanced materials and new energy solutions.

Applications

Applications of quantum qubits extend to cryptography, artificial intelligence, optimization, quantum simulations, and secure communications. Cryptography leverages quantum qubits for quantum key distribution, providing security that classical encryption cannot match. Artificial intelligence benefits from quantum-enhanced machine learning algorithms that can analyze data and identify patterns more efficiently. Optimization problems, such as traffic flow and financial modeling, are solved faster using quantum qubits' parallel processing capabilities. Quantum simulations allow researchers to model complex physical and chemical processes, leading to advancements in various scientific fields. Secure communications use quantum qubits for developing quantum networks, enabling ultra-secure data exchange over long distances.

Summary

Quantum qubits represent a revolutionary leap in computing, unlocking new possibilities for solving some of the most challenging problems across various industries. While practical large-scale quantum computers are still under development, ongoing advancements in qubit stability, error correction, and quantum algorithms are rapidly pushing the field forward. As quantum computing technology matures, qubits will play a crucial role in shaping the future of artificial intelligence, security, and scientific discovery.

Quantum Supremacy

Definition
Quantum supremacy is the point at which a quantum computer can perform a calculation that is infeasible for even the most powerful classical supercomputers. This milestone represents a fundamental shift in computing, demonstrating the ability of quantum systems to solve specific problems exponentially faster than traditional computers. Quantum supremacy does not imply that quantum computers outperform classical machines in all tasks but rather that they can complete a well-defined computation beyond the reach of conventional algorithms within a realistic timeframe. This breakthrough has significant implications for cryptography, artificial intelligence, materials science, and complex system simulations.

Key Components
Qubits leveraging superposition and entanglement
Quantum gates for complex operations
Quantum coherence for information preservation
Quantum circuits for executing specialized algorithms
Quantum control systems for orchestrating operations

Benefits
Solves problems beyond the capability of classical supercomputers
Enhances cryptographic methods and challenges existing ones
Accelerates AI training and optimization
Advances molecular modeling and materials research
Enables complex system simulations across disciplines

Examples
Google's quantum processor solving a sampling problem in seconds
Breaking encryption by solving hard mathematical problems quickly
Improving decision-making via optimization in logistics and finance
Molecular simulation for new drug development and chemistry insights
Quantum physics simulations supporting theoretical research

Applications
Scientific research and modeling
Quantum-enhanced cryptography
Optimization in AI and machine learning
Advanced material design
Financial forecasting and modeling

Industries
Technology and computing
Finance and banking
Healthcare and life sciences
Energy and utilities
Aerospace and defense

Challenges
Fragility and decoherence of qubits
High error rates requiring correction
Scalability and stability issues
Expensive operational infrastructure
Security and ethical concerns regarding encryption vulnerabilities

Summary
Quantum supremacy represents a turning point in computational history, proving that quantum computers can outperform classical systems in specific tasks. While challenges such as stability, error correction, and scalability remain, continued advancements in quantum computing are pushing the boundaries of what is possible. As industries explore practical applications, quantum supremacy is expected to drive breakthroughs in cryptography, artificial intelligence, materials science, and scientific simulations.

Quantum Teleportation

Definition
Quantum teleportation is a process in quantum mechanics that transfers the state of a quantum particle to another particle at a distant location without physically moving the particle itself. This phenomenon relies on the principles of quantum entanglement and superposition, allowing information to be transmitted instantaneously between two entangled particles. Unlike science fiction teleportation, quantum teleportation does not involve the transfer of physical matter but rather the exact quantum state of a particle, enabling secure communication and advancements in quantum computing and cryptography.

Key Components
Quantum entanglement between particle pairs
Sender and receiver using an entangled pair
Classical communication channel for measurement results
Quantum transformation applied to recreate the original state

Benefits
Revolutionizes secure communication
Supports distributed quantum computing
Enables future quantum internet development
Ensures precise and lossless data transmission
Deepens understanding of quantum theory

Examples
Teleporting quantum states of photons and atoms
Quantum key distribution using teleportation
Transporting qubit states in quantum networks
Satellite-based long-distance quantum teleportation
Fundamental experiments validating entanglement

Applications
Secure quantum communication
Quantum networking and cloud systems
Scientific exploration of quantum theory
Distributed quantum processing
Space-based quantum research

Industries
Cybersecurity
Computing and networking
Telecommunications
Finance
Government and defense

Challenges
Maintaining entanglement over long distances
Reliance on both quantum and classical channels
Scalability of teleportation experiments
Environmental control and technical complexity
Potential misuse and ethical considerations

Summary
Quantum teleportation represents a groundbreaking advancement in quantum information science, offering transformative potential for secure communication, quantum computing, and the development of a global quantum internet. While technical challenges remain, ongoing research continues to push the boundaries of what is possible. Teleportation will play a critical role in shaping future secure networks and computing systems.

Qubit Optimization

Definition
Qubit Optimization refers to the process of enhancing the performance, coherence, and fidelity of qubits in quantum computing systems to improve the efficiency and accuracy of quantum algorithms, particularly in AI and machine learning applications.

Key Components
Quantum error correction algorithms
Noise reduction techniques
Optimized quantum gate operations
Decoherence mitigation strategies

Benefits
Improves quantum computation accuracy
Increases qubit coherence time
Reduces quantum gate errors
Supports longer, more complex algorithm execution

Examples
Optimizing qubits for better training of quantum neural networks
Securing quantum key distribution through reduced transmission errors
Enhancing QAOA efficiency by minimizing operational noise

Applications
Quantum machine learning and optimization
Quantum simulations in chemistry and physics
Quantum cryptography systems

Industries
Healthcare and pharmaceuticals
Finance and logistics
Cybersecurity and quantum hardware

Challenges
Maintaining qubit stability under noisy conditions
Resource demands of error correction
Scalability across large quantum networks

Summary
Qubit optimization is essential for advancing the capabilities of quantum computing in AI and other domains. Through improved coherence, reduced errors, and optimized gate performance, it lays the foundation for practical and powerful quantum computing systems.

Qubit-Oriented Neural Networks (QONNs)

Definition
Qubit-Oriented Neural Networks (QONNs) combine quantum computing principles with classical neural network structures to enhance learning and processing through quantum states and operations.

Key Components
Quantum superposition and entanglement
Quantum gates simulating activation functions
Quantum state-based neurons
Hybrid classical-quantum layers

Benefits
Enables parallel processing of complex data
Accelerates learning in high-dimensional spaces
Offers potential exponential speedups for some tasks
Improves optimization and pattern recognition performance

Examples
Using QONNs for molecular simulations in quantum chemistry
Quantum-driven image recognition using qubit encoding
Parallel optimization in drug discovery pipelines

Applications
Quantum machine learning models
Large-scale data classification and regression
Simulation and modeling in material science

Industries
Pharmaceutical and chemical research
Cybersecurity and cryptography
Autonomous systems and smart manufacturing

Challenges
Hardware limitations in implementing qubit networks
Complexity in training and validation
Integration with classical systems remains experimental

Summary
QONNs represent a transformative AI approach, marrying neural architecture with quantum power. While still in early development, their potential for breakthroughs in computing and problem-solving is vast.

Qubit-Oriented Quantum Gates

Definition
Qubit-Oriented Quantum Gates are the foundational operations that manipulate quantum states in quantum circuits, crucial for performing AI tasks on quantum systems.

Key Components
Single-qubit gates like Hadamard for superposition
Multi-qubit gates like CNOT for entanglement
Quantum circuit designs using logical sequences
Gate fidelity and timing precision

Benefits
Enables quantum parallelism in computation
Reduces classical computational bottlenecks
Forms the basis for scalable AI models on quantum platforms

Examples
Using quantum gates in quantum AI for secure clustering
Applying gate sequences to optimize cryptographic models

Applications
Quantum AI model building
Secure quantum communications
Neural computation on quantum processors

Industries
Quantum software development
Defense and secure communication
Advanced computing systems

Challenges
Maintaining high-fidelity gate operations
Gate timing synchronization in large qubit systems
Hardware-specific optimization constraints

Summary
Qubit-Oriented Quantum Gates are critical for AI in quantum computing, forming the action layer of all logic and learning models. Their precision and functionality directly affect system performance.

Query Expansion in AI

Definition Query expansion in AI is the process of reformulating a user's search query by adding relevant terms or synonyms to improve information retrieval results. This method enhances the understanding of user intent and ensures broader coverage of related content in search, recommendation, and conversational systems.

Key Components Term selection and addition
Semantic and syntactic analysis
Thesaurus or embedding-based expansion
Re-ranking algorithms for results

Benefits Increases recall and relevance of search results
Improves user experience in search engines and chatbots
Handles ambiguous or vague user inputs more effectively
Boosts accuracy in natural language understanding systems

Examples Expanding a user query for "AI jobs" to include "machine learning positions" and "data science roles"
Enhancing medical query searches with related terminology from clinical ontologies
Using word embeddings to expand short queries in product recommendation systems

Applications Search engine optimization
Conversational AI and virtual assistants
Question answering systems
Recommender engines

Industries E-commerce
Healthcare
Education
Media and publishing

Challenges Over-expansion can lead to irrelevant results
Selecting appropriate expansion terms is complex
Real-time performance requirements can impact scalability
Requires continuous updating of synonym databases or embeddings

Summary Query expansion in AI bridges the gap between user input and system understanding. By enriching queries with contextually relevant terms, it improves precision and satisfaction across various intelligent information systems.

QY Algorithm (Quantum Yield Algorithm)

Definition The Quantum Yield (QY) Algorithm is a conceptual framework in quantum-enhanced AI that focuses on maximizing computational efficiency and information extraction from quantum systems.

Key Components Quantum circuit design with high-yield configurations
Measurement optimization for result fidelity
Resource-aware quantum operation scheduling
Yield-to-cost performance evaluation metrics

Benefits Maximizes useful output from limited quantum hardware
Improves algorithmic efficiency for quantum AI tasks
Enhances performance consistency under noisy conditions
Supports adaptive tuning based on output success rates

Examples Maximizing classification accuracy in quantum neural networks using QY principles
Adjusting quantum annealing schedules to increase solution success rate
Evaluating quantum search efficiency using yield-based feedback loops

Applications Quantum machine learning
Optimization and decision models
Quantum simulation tuning
Data-intensive quantum processing

Industries Quantum computing
Artificial intelligence
Pharmaceuticals and molecular modeling
Cybersecurity and cryptography

Challenges Difficult to standardize across different quantum systems
Requires real-time analysis of quantum measurement outcomes

Still largely theoretical and under active research
High variance in yield under noisy quantum conditions

Summary The Quantum Yield Algorithm introduces a performance-focused strategy to guide AI systems operating on quantum platforms. It emphasizes measurable results and resource efficiency, supporting more productive and scalable quantum AI computation.

QY-Hyperparameter Tuning

Definition QY-Hyperparameter Tuning is a quantum-enhanced approach to optimizing hyperparameters in machine learning models. It combines classical tuning strategies with quantum computation or quantum-inspired methods to explore hyperparameter space more efficiently.

Key Components Quantum sampling or annealing for parameter exploration
Hybrid classical-quantum feedback loops
Evaluation metrics for model performance
Optimization over search space using QY principles

Benefits Reduces the time and resource cost of hyperparameter tuning
Improves model accuracy and convergence rates
Handles large and complex parameter spaces more effectively
Allows adaptive learning with fewer iterations

Examples Tuning neural network depth and learning rate using a quantum annealer
Applying quantum-inspired grid search in reinforcement learning models
Using QY-guided sampling to fine-tune SVM parameters

Applications Supervised and unsupervised learning
Natural language processing
Neural network optimization
Reinforcement learning agents

Industries AI research and development
Healthcare diagnostics
Financial analytics
Retail personalization

Challenges Quantum devices may be limited in scale for deep tuning
Integration with classical AI models requires robust interfacing
Interpretability of quantum-tuned parameters can be complex
Dependent on reliable performance from quantum components

Summary QY-Hyperparameter Tuning represents a forward-thinking blend of quantum power and AI optimization. It streamlines the trial-and-error process of model refinement, offering smarter and faster solutions to improve AI accuracy and performance.

QY-Qubit

Definition A QY-Qubit is a conceptual extension of a standard qubit that is specifically optimized or calibrated under Quantum Yield principles. It focuses on maximizing computational output relative to the input energy, operational duration, or coherence time.

Key Components High-fidelity quantum state preparation
Yield-optimized quantum gate design

Qubit coherence management
Adaptive calibration for maximum output

Benefits Enables longer-lasting and more stable quantum computations
Improves reliability and measurement precision
Supports fault-tolerant quantum AI operations
Reduces decoherence and increases usable quantum cycles

Examples Deploying QY-Qubits in quantum neural networks
Enhancing quantum memory storage using calibrated QY-Qubits
Stabilizing qubits in quantum recommendation systems

Applications Quantum model training
Secure quantum communication
Long-duration quantum simulations
High-precision AI decision systems

Industries Quantum computing hardware
Cybersecurity
Pharmaceutical research
Space and aerospace analytics

Challenges Hardware manufacturing is highly sensitive and resource-intensive
Maintaining optimal yield requires continuous environmental control
May be incompatible with legacy qubit systems
Calibration complexity increases with qubit count

Summary The QY-Qubit represents a refinement in qubit performance tailored for intelligent quantum systems. It is a foundation for more efficient, powerful, and stable AI applications built on quantum architectures.

Definition The Quantum Yield (QY) Algorithm is a conceptual framework in quantum-enhanced AI that focuses on maximizing computational efficiency and information extraction from quantum systems.

Key Components Quantum circuit design with high-yield configurations
Measurement optimization for result fidelity
Resource-aware quantum operation scheduling
Yield-to-cost performance evaluation metrics

Benefits Maximizes useful output from limited quantum hardware
Improves algorithmic efficiency for quantum AI tasks
Enhances performance consistency under noisy conditions
Supports adaptive tuning based on output success rates

Examples Maximizing classification accuracy in quantum neural networks using QY principles
Adjusting quantum annealing schedules to increase solution success rate
Evaluating quantum search efficiency using yield-based feedback loops

Applications Quantum machine learning
Optimization and decision models
Quantum simulation tuning
Data-intensive quantum processing

Industries Quantum computing
Artificial intelligence

Pharmaceuticals and molecular modeling
Cybersecurity and cryptography

Challenges Difficult to standardize across different quantum systems
Requires real-time analysis of quantum measurement outcomes
Still largely theoretical and under active research
High variance in yield under noisy quantum conditions

Summary The Quantum Yield Algorithm introduces a performance-focused strategy to guide AI systems operating on quantum platforms. It emphasizes measurable results and resource efficiency, supporting more productive and scalable quantum AI computation.

QY-Optimized Neural Networks (QYONN)

Definition QY-Optimized Neural Networks (QYONN) are machine learning models that are designed, trained, or enhanced using Quantum Yield principles to maximize information efficiency, learning rate, and performance reliability in neural computations.

Key Components Quantum-enhanced neural layers
High-yield architecture selection
Quantum-coordinated weight initialization
Optimization with quantum-based feedback

Benefits Accelerates training while preserving or enhancing accuracy
Enables more compact and energy-efficient models
Improves generalization by maximizing useful learning
Leverages quantum states for richer information encoding

Examples QYONNs trained for quantum-enhanced image recognition
Compact models for edge devices tuned with quantum-inspired logic
Speech recognition networks that leverage quantum-yield tuning for fast convergence

Applications Autonomous systems
Speech and language processing
Medical imaging analysis
Predictive maintenance systems

Industries Healthcare
Telecommunications
Autonomous vehicles
Smart infrastructure

Challenges Hardware limitations may restrict quantum-layer implementation
Model behavior may differ under classical and quantum tuning
Requires specialized knowledge in both quantum and neural architectures
Validation frameworks for QYONN performance are still emerging

Summary QY-Optimized Neural Networks bring together quantum theory and AI learning frameworks. They aim to enhance how neural models are trained and optimized, with a focus on efficiency, accuracy, and performance scalability across industries.

QY-Qubit

Definition A QY-Qubit is a conceptual extension of a standard qubit that is specifically optimized or calibrated under Quantum Yield principles. It focuses on maximizing computational output relative to the input energy, operational duration, or coherence time, thus enabling efficient quantum processing for AI applications.

Key Components High-fidelity quantum state preparation
Yield-optimized quantum gate design
Qubit coherence management
Adaptive calibration for maximum output

Benefits Enables longer-lasting and more stable quantum computations
Improves reliability and measurement precision
Supports fault-tolerant quantum AI operations
Reduces decoherence and increases usable quantum cycles

Examples Deploying QY-Qubits in quantum neural networks
Enhancing quantum memory storage using calibrated QY-Qubits
Stabilizing qubits in quantum recommendation systems

Applications Quantum model training
Secure quantum communication
Long-duration quantum simulations
High-precision AI decision systems

Industries Quantum computing hardware
Cybersecurity
Pharmaceutical research
Space and aerospace analytics

Challenges Hardware manufacturing is highly sensitive and resource-intensive
Maintaining optimal yield requires continuous environmental control
May be incompatible with legacy qubit systems
Calibration complexity increases with qubit count

Summary The QY-Qubit represents a refinement in qubit performance tailored for intelligent quantum systems. It is a foundation for more efficient, powerful, and stable AI applications built on quantum architectures.

QY-Qubit Correction

Definition QY-Qubit Correction refers to the implementation of error mitigation and correction techniques specifically designed to sustain the optimal performance of QY-Qubits. It ensures high quantum yield by preserving coherence and minimizing data loss in quantum-enhanced AI systems.

Key Components Quantum error correction codes
Redundancy-based QY logic gates
Syndrome detection and correction feedback
Environmental noise filtering

Benefits Maintains computation integrity over longer periods
Reduces frequency of retraining or restarting AI models
Preserves energy efficiency and system accuracy
Improves overall system robustness for real-time tasks

Examples Correcting bit-flip errors in QY-enhanced quantum classifiers
Implementing fault-tolerant logic in quantum AI robotics
Stabilizing decision trees in quantum reinforcement learning systems

Applications Mission-critical AI systems
Quantum communication networks
Quantum sensing and measurement
Deep learning models requiring long quantum runtimes

Industries National defense
Telecommunications
AI safety and reliability
Smart grid technology

Challenges Quantum error correction is resource-intensive
Overhead in QY-Qubit correction can slow down operations
Error propagation remains a concern in large networks
Requires high-fidelity quantum circuits for effective implementation

Summary QY-Qubit Correction is essential to maintain high-yield computation in quantum AI systems. By protecting the integrity and lifespan of QY-Qubits, this technique helps sustain high performance in increasingly complex quantum-enhanced applications.

QY-Quantum Gate Optimization

Definition QY-Quantum Gate Optimization is a process of improving the efficiency, precision, and yield of quantum gate operations within AI systems. It involves fine-tuning gate sequences and parameters to maximize the quantum yield, ensuring that more useful computation is extracted from fewer or more stable quantum operations.

Key Components Gate parameter calibration
Quantum circuit simplification
Error minimization through gate reordering
Quantum yield evaluation metrics
Adaptive gate tuning during learning or inference

Benefits Increases the reliability and accuracy of quantum computations
Reduces error propagation and gate-related decoherence
Maximizes performance from limited quantum resources
Supports higher fidelity in quantum AI model outputs

Examples Optimizing entanglement gates in a quantum classifier for image recognition
Reducing the number of gates in a quantum support vector machine to improve execution speed
Using feedback loops in AI to reconfigure gate layouts for better training convergence

Applications Quantum-enhanced deep learning
Quantum kernel methods
Hybrid classical-quantum AI pipelines
Quantum control and scheduling systems

Industries Quantum computing hardware
Artificial intelligence
Aerospace and robotics
Telecommunications

Challenges Requires precise hardware calibration and stability
Quantum gate errors vary by platform and require custom solutions
Difficult to scale in multi-qubit or complex networks
Resource-intensive optimization loops may slow down performance gains

Summary QY-Quantum Gate Optimization improves the performance of AI systems by fine-tuning the foundational operations in quantum computing. It enhances the quality and yield of quantum tasks, helping models operate efficiently and consistently even under hardware limitations.

QY-State (Quantum Yield State)

Definition A QY-State, or Quantum Yield State, is a specialized quantum state that has been optimized to deliver the maximum possible computational output with the least amount of noise, decoherence, or energy waste.

Key Components High-fidelity quantum state preparation
Stability under entanglement and superposition
Energy-efficient encoding of quantum data
Yield-maximized state measurement and readout

Benefits Improves consistency and precision in quantum AI model outputs
Supports scalable learning through stable quantum memory
Reduces quantum error rates by favoring robust states
Enables faster computation cycles through optimized state evolution

Examples Using a QY-State to represent key features in a quantum-enhanced regression model
Initializing QY-States for rapid convergence in quantum neural network training
Deploying QY-States for stateful reasoning in quantum reinforcement learning

Applications Quantum machine learning
State-driven AI inference engines
Quantum simulation of complex systems
Quantum-enhanced recommendation engines

Industries Healthcare analytics
Smart manufacturing
Finance and risk modeling
National security and defense

Challenges Requires highly controlled environments for stability
State preparation can be resource-intensive
QY-States may be hard to generalize across diverse tasks
Current tools for QY-State modeling are still under development

Summary QY-States offer a powerful foundation for building high-efficiency AI models in quantum computing environments. They maximize information output while minimizing system noise, creating a more reliable and performance-driven platform for quantum-enhanced learning.

QY-Simulation Framework

Definition QY-Simulation Framework is a computational environment designed to simulate quantum AI systems with a focus on Quantum Yield principles. This framework allows developers and researchers to model, test, and refine quantum-enhanced algorithms and architectures before deployment on real quantum hardware.

Key Components Quantum yield evaluation tools
Gate and circuit simulation engines
AI model integration with quantum simulators
Noise modeling and error analysis utilities

Benefits Enables safe and cost-effective testing of quantum AI systems
Supports development of QY-optimized models before hardware execution
Accelerates the research and prototyping of quantum-enhanced architectures
Reduces reliance on limited-access quantum devices during experimentation

Examples Testing QY-tuned neural networks for anomaly detection in finance
Simulating quantum decision-making processes with dynamic feedback
Running quantum reinforcement learning experiments using yield metrics in a sandbox environment

Applications Quantum model prototyping
AI algorithm validation
Quantum control testing
Performance benchmarking under simulated constraints

Industries Quantum research and development
Academia and training institutions
Healthcare diagnostics
Smart infrastructure design

Challenges Simulation of quantum behavior is computationally expensive
Limited accuracy compared to real-world quantum systems
High complexity in modeling entanglement and decoherence
Requires continuous updates to reflect hardware evolution

Summary The QY-Simulation Framework is a vital tool for AI practitioners aiming to integrate quantum computing into intelligent systems. It enables safe experimentation, guided by quantum yield principles, to ensure that future deployments are both efficient and reliable.

QY-Training Optimization (Quantum Y-Training Optimization)

Definition QY-Training Optimization refers to a speculative quantum computing approach aimed at enhancing the training processes of machine learning models, particularly those with Y-shaped architectures, by exploiting quantum algorithms to optimize parameter tuning and convergence speed.

Key Components Quantum circuits to represent Y-shaped model parameters
Hybrid quantum-classical workflow for iterative optimization
Cost function tailored to multi-output learning
Quantum speedup mechanisms such as superposition or entanglement

Benefits Reduces training time for complex models
Improves accuracy by finding global optima
Handles multi-objective tasks more efficiently through quantum exploration

Examples Training a Y-shaped neural network to simultaneously classify images and predict object coordinates using quantum parallelism
Accelerating convergence in multi-output GANs with QY-enhanced optimization

Applications Multi-task learning
Quantum-enhanced hyperparameter tuning
Optimization of branched architectures like GANs or VAEs

Industries AI research
Autonomous systems
Healthcare diagnostics

Challenges Limited access to quantum hardware
Noise in quantum systems may disrupt optimization
Complexity in mapping Y-shaped models to quantum circuits

Summary QY-Training Optimization promises a leap in training performance for multi-output models, harnessing quantum power to speed up and refine learning. Its success depends on future advances in quantum hardware and algorithm integration.

LETTER R

Radial Basis Function (RBF) Networks

Definition A Radial Basis Function Network is a type of artificial neural network that uses radial basis functions as its core mechanism to process data, often for tasks like pattern recognition or function approximation. It's built to map input data to outputs by measuring distances from specific points in a way that mimics how humans might cluster similar things together.

Key Components This network has three layers—an input layer that takes raw data, a hidden layer where radial basis functions (usually Gaussian curves) calculate how far each input is from a set of chosen center points, and an output layer that combines these distances into a final result using weighted sums. The centers and the width of the functions are critical tuning knobs.

Benefits It learns quickly because it doesn't need as much tweaking as deeper networks, and it's great at handling noisy data or filling in gaps when you don't have all the answers. It's also flexible enough to model complex patterns without overfitting if set up right.

Examples Think of it sorting handwritten digits by comparing each squiggle to a few ideal shapes, or predicting air pollution levels based on scattered sensor readings.

Applications You'll see it in time-series forecasting like stock price guesses, image classification, or even medical diagnosis where symptoms don't fit neat boxes.

Industries It pops up in finance for market trends, healthcare for spotting disease patterns, and engineering for signal processing.

Challenges Picking the right number of centers and their positions can be tricky—too few and it misses details, too many and it gets slow or confused. It also struggles with huge datasets since every point gets compared to every center.

Summary RBF Networks shine when you need a fast, adaptable tool for small-to-medium problems with messy data, but they're not the go-to for massive, intricate tasks where deeper networks take over.

Random Forest Algorithm

Definition The Random Forest Algorithm is a machine learning method that builds a bunch of decision trees—each one a simple yes-no flowchart—and combines their guesses to make a stronger, more reliable prediction, kind of like asking a crowd for advice instead of one expert.

Key Components It starts with lots of decision trees, each trained on a random chunk of the data and a random subset of features. Then it either averages their outputs for number predictions or takes a majority vote for categories. The randomness keeps them from all making the same mistakes.

Benefits It's tough against overfitting because the crowd cancels out individual quirks, and it handles missing data or weird outliers without breaking a sweat. Plus, it tells you which features matter most.

Examples Imagine it predicting if a customer will buy based on age and browsing habits, or flagging fraudulent bank transactions by spotting odd patterns.

Applications It's used in spam email filters, stock market trend analysis, or even diagnosing diseases from lab results.

Industries Banking leans on it for risk assessment, e-commerce for customer targeting, and biology for gene analysis.

Challenges It can get slow and memory-hungry with tons of trees or giant datasets, and it's not as easy to explain as a single tree when someone asks why it made a call.

Summary Random Forest is a powerhouse for reliable predictions across messy real-world problems, though it trades some speed and simplicity for that strength.

RANdom SAmple Consensus (RANSAC)

Definition RANdom SAmple Consensus, or RANSAC, is a method that figures out patterns in messy data by randomly guessing small chunks of it, testing if they fit a model, and keeping the best guess that matches the most points—like finding a straight line through a cloud of dots.

Key Components It picks random subsets of data, fits a model (say, a line or plane) to them, then checks how many other points agree within a tolerance. After enough tries, it picks the model with the most "inliers" (points that fit).

Benefits It's a champ at ignoring outliers—like bad measurements or noise—so it finds the real signal even when half the data's junk. It's also simple and works on lots of shapes.

Examples Think of it aligning a 3D scan of a room despite some wonky points, or stitching photos into a panorama even with a few blurry spots.

Applications It's key in computer vision for mapping scenes, robotics for figuring out where a bot is, and archaeology for reconstructing artifacts from fragments.

Industries Automotive uses it for self-driving car sensors, film for special effects, and construction for site modeling.

Challenges It can miss the mark if the guesses never hit a good sample, and picking the right tolerance or number of tries takes some fiddling.

Summary RANSAC is a lifesaver for pulling clean models out of noisy data, though it leans on luck and needs tweaking to shine.

Randomized Algorithms in AI

Definition Randomized Algorithms in AI are problem-solving techniques that toss in a bit of chance—like flipping a coin or rolling dice—to make decisions faster or find answers that might be missed by rigid step-by-step methods.

Key Components They rely on random number generators to pick paths, sample data, or tweak solutions. Some keep randomness throughout, while others use it just to kick things off. The trick is balancing luck with enough smarts to still get good results.

Benefits They're often quicker than exhaustive searches, especially on huge problems, and they can stumble onto creative solutions that strict rules overlook. They also dodge getting stuck in dead ends.

Examples Picture an AI shuffling through possible chess moves randomly to test strategies, or guessing a starting point for optimizing a delivery route.

Applications They're behind quicksort for sorting data, Monte Carlo simulations for risk analysis, and even training neural networks by randomly adjusting weights.

Industries Gaming uses them for unpredictable opponents, logistics for route planning, and science for modeling complex systems like weather.

Challenges The randomness means you might not always get the best answer, and results can vary each time you run it, which can spook people wanting certainty.

Summary Randomized Algorithms trade a little predictability for speed and flexibility, making them perfect for big, thorny AI challenges where perfection isn't the goal.

Recommendation Systems in AI

Definition Recommendation Systems in AI are tools that guess what you'll like—movies, products, songs—by digging through data about your past choices and patterns in what others pick, acting like a super-smart friend who knows your taste.

Key Components They use algorithms like collaborative filtering (matching you with similar people), content-based filtering (matching items to what you've liked), or hybrids of both. Data on users, items, and interactions fuels the engine.

Benefits They nail personal suggestions, keep users hooked, and boost sales or engagement by cutting through the clutter of options. They also learn over time as more data rolls in.

Examples Netflix suggesting a thriller after you binged one, or Amazon pushing a gadget based on your cart history.

Applications They power streaming playlists, online shopping upsells, and even job boards matching resumes to postings.

Industries Entertainment thrives on them for content, retail for sales, and social media for keeping you scrolling.

Challenges They stumble with new users who've got no history (the "cold start" problem), can trap you in a bubble of sameness, and need tons of data to work well.

Summary Recommendation Systems turn data into spot-on suggestions, driving modern digital experiences, though they wrestle with fresh starts and variety.

Recurrent Neural Networks (RNNs)

Definition Recurrent Neural Networks are a flavor of neural network built for sequences—like words in a sentence or stock prices over days—where they remember what came before to make sense of what's next, looping data through themselves over time.

Key Components They've got an input layer, a hidden layer that keeps a memory by feeding its own output back in, and an output layer. The loop lets them track patterns across steps, guided by weights tweaked during training.

Benefits They're ace at handling anything with order, like language or music, and can predict what's coming based on what's been. They're flexible for varying sequence lengths too.

Examples Picture them translating "Hola" to "Hello" by recalling the sentence's start, or guessing tomorrow's weather from this week's trends.

Applications They're in speech recognition for turning talk to text, chatbots for natural replies, and finance for market forecasting.

Industries Tech uses them for virtual assistants, healthcare for patient monitoring, and media for auto-subtitling.

Challenges They can forget distant details (the "vanishing gradient" issue), take forever to train on long sequences, and get outdone by fancier upgrades like LSTMs.

Summary RNNs are sequence masters, vital for time-based AI tasks, but they falter on long memory and need care to perform at their best.

Regularization in Machine Learning

Definition Regularization in Machine Learning is a technique that keeps models from getting too full of themselves by adding a penalty for overcomplicating things, ensuring they don't just memorize the training data but actually learn patterns that work on new stuff too.

Key Components It tweaks the model's error calculation by tossing in an extra term—like a fine for using too many big numbers in the math. Common flavors are L1 (which chops off useless features) and L2 (which smooths everything out), applied to the weights the model learns.

Benefits It stops overfitting, where a model nails the practice test but flunks the real world, and makes predictions more reliable. It also helps when data's sparse by keeping things simple.

Examples Think of a model predicting house prices—it might ignore quirky outliers like a mansion with a gold toilet if regularization keeps it focused on basics like size and location.

Applications It's baked into regression models for stats crunching, neural networks for image recognition, and even text analysis for sorting spam.

Industries Finance uses it for steady market models, healthcare for trustworthy diagnostics, and marketing for customer trend predictions.

Challenges Picking the right penalty strength is a balancing act—too weak and it's pointless, too strong and the model misses real patterns. It also adds a layer of tuning that can slow things down.

Summary Regularization is like a leash on a hyperactive model, guiding it to learn sensibly and perform consistently, though it takes some finesse to get just right.

Reinforcement Learning (RL)

Definition
Reinforcement Learning is an AI approach where a system learns by trial and error, figuring out what to do in a situation by chasing rewards and dodging penalties, much like teaching a dog tricks with treats and scolds.

Key Components
It's built around an agent (the learner), an environment (the world it's in), actions (what it can do), states (where it's at), and a reward system (the feedback). The agent tweaks its strategy over time to max out the good stuff.

Benefits
It thrives in places where you can't spell out every rule—like games or robots—because it discovers solutions on its own. It's also adaptable to changing setups.

Examples
Imagine a bot learning to play chess by winning points for checkmates, or a drone figuring out how to hover by earning kudos for staying steady.

Applications
It powers self-driving cars dodging traffic, video game AIs outsmarting players, and warehouse robots stacking boxes smarter.

Industries
Gaming leans on it for clever opponents, automotive for navigation, and logistics for optimizing routes.

Challenges
It can take forever to learn if rewards are rare or the world's too complicated, and it might stumble into dumb habits without enough guidance.

Summary
Reinforcement Learning is a hands-off way to teach AI through experience, perfect for dynamic tasks, but it demands patience and a clear reward path.

Reinforcement Learning with Q-Learning

Definition
Reinforcement Learning with Q-Learning is a specific flavor of RL where the AI builds a cheat sheet—called a Q-table—to track which actions score the most rewards in each spot, refining it through guesswork and updates until it's a pro.

Key Components
The Q-table is the heart, listing states and actions with scores that get better as the agent explores. It uses a formula mixing instant rewards with future guesses, guided by a learning rate and discount factor to balance now versus later.

Benefits
It's straightforward and doesn't need a full map of the problem—just try stuff and learn. It also works without knowing the rules upfront, adapting as it goes.

Examples
Picture a maze-running bot picking turns based on past successes, or a trading AI buying stocks when the Q-table says it's a winner.

Applications
It's in robotic arms learning to grab things, traffic lights timing themselves for flow, and even ad systems picking what to show you.

Industries
Manufacturing uses it for automation, transportation for signal control, and digital marketing for engagement.

Challenges
The Q-table can balloon with too many states or actions, making it slow or impractical, and it struggles if rewards are delayed or tricky to pin down.

Summary
Q-Learning gives RL a practical edge with its scorecard approach, shining in clear-cut scenarios, though it bogs down when things get too big or vague.

ResNet (Residual Networks)

Definition
ResNet, or Residual Networks, is a deep learning setup that lets neural networks go really deep—like dozens or hundreds of layers—by adding shortcuts so they can skip steps and avoid losing their way as they learn complex patterns.

Key Components
The magic is in "residual blocks," where data can jump over layers via shortcut connections, adding the input back into the output. This keeps the network trainable even when it's stacked high with layers tweaking weights.

Benefits
It tackles the problem where deep networks forget early lessons or stall out, letting them learn intricate stuff like faces or speech without breaking. It's also faster to train than you'd expect for its depth.

Examples
Think of it spotting cats in photos by building up from edges to whiskers, or catching subtle accents in voice clips.

Applications
It's huge in image recognition for security cameras, voice assistants parsing commands, and medical scans finding tumors.

Industries
Tech relies on it for AI apps, healthcare for diagnostics, and retail for visual search tools.

Challenges
It's still a beast to set up and needs big computing power, plus all those layers can overfit if the data's thin.

Summary
ResNet makes deep learning deeper and smarter with its skip-ahead trick, ruling complex tasks, but it's not light or simple to wield.

Rest API

Definition
Rest API, short for Representational State Transfer Application Programming Interface, is a software interface that enables communication between computer systems over the internet. It is based on REST architecture, which uses standard HTTP methods to access and manipulate data. Rest APIs are commonly used to allow web applications, mobile apps, and other software platforms to request and exchange information with servers in a structured and predictable way.

Key Components
A Rest API is built around the concept of resources, which represent pieces of data such as users, products, or messages. These resources are identified by unique URLs. Interaction with these resources

is done through standard HTTP methods like GET for retrieving data, POST for creating data, PUT for updating data, and DELETE for removing data. Rest APIs are stateless, meaning each request is independent and carries all the necessary information. Data is typically exchanged in formats like JSON or XML, and responses often include HTTP status codes to indicate success or failure.

Examples
A weather application using a Rest API might send a GET request to retrieve current weather data for a specific location. A shopping website could send a POST request through its Rest API to add a new item to a customer's cart. A social media platform might allow users to update their profile information using a PUT request to its Rest API.

Benefits
Rest APIs are easy to understand and widely supported across different programming languages. They promote a clear structure for accessing data and are highly scalable, making them suitable for both small applications and large enterprise systems. Because they use existing web protocols, they require no additional software or infrastructure to function effectively. The stateless nature of Rest APIs also makes them easier to maintain and deploy in distributed environments.

Applications
Rest APIs are used in a wide range of software systems, including mobile apps, e-commerce platforms, financial services, content management systems, and cloud-based services. They support tasks such as user authentication, data retrieval, transaction processing, and device synchronization.

Industries
Many industries rely on Rest APIs, including healthcare for accessing patient records, education for managing student data, transportation for scheduling and logistics, retail for inventory systems, and technology companies for cloud services and data analytics.

Challenges
Despite their popularity, Rest APIs can face challenges such as inconsistent design practices, limited support for complex queries, and potential security vulnerabilities if not properly implemented. Managing API versions and ensuring backward compatibility can also require significant planning and effort.

Summary
Rest API is a foundational technology that supports seamless communication between digital systems. By following simple web standards, it enables reliable and scalable data exchange across diverse platforms and industries. Its straightforward approach makes it a core element in modern software development and system integration.

Rhizomatic Learning in AI Education Systems

Definition
Rhizomatic Learning in AI Education Systems is a freewheeling approach to teaching AI where knowledge grows like a web—branching out in all directions based on curiosity and connections—rather than following a straight, top-down path.

Key Components
It's about learners driving the show, exploring AI concepts (say, neural nets or ethics) through open-ended questions, peer chats, and real-world messes. AI tools might guide or adapt the journey, linking ideas organically.

Benefits
It sparks creativity and critical thinking, letting students stumble into insights traditional classes miss. It's also nimble, matching AI's fast-changing nature where rules shift yearly.

Examples
Imagine kids digging into AI bias after a chatbot flub, or coders linking algorithms to art via group projects online.

Applications
It's in coding bootcamps mixing theory with practice, online courses letting users pick AI topics, and school labs tackling local AI problems.

Industries
Education uses it for next-gen classrooms, tech for training devs, and nonprofits for community AI literacy.

Challenges
It's chaotic—hard to test or standardize—and some learners flounder without a clear map. Teachers need to be sharp to steer it too.

Summary
Rhizomatic Learning turns AI education into a living network, thriving on flexibility and exploration, though it's messy and demands savvy guides.

Rho-Calculus in AI

Definition Rho-Calculus in AI refers to a theoretical framework that blends process calculus—a way to model how things interact and evolve—with AI systems, letting them reason about dynamic, flowing processes like conversations or workflows in a structured yet flexible way.

Key Components It's built on agents that act and react, rules for how they pass messages or change states, and a mathematical backbone to track these shifts over time. Think of it as a recipe for describing AI behaviors step-by-step, with variables and loops to handle complexity.

Benefits It gives AI a clear playbook for handling messy, real-time situations, making it easier to predict what the system will do next. It's also a bridge between code and theory, so developers and researchers can talk the same language.

Examples Imagine an AI chatbot juggling multiple chats, using Rho-Calculus to decide who to answer first, or a smart factory bot rerouting tasks when a machine jams.

Applications It's handy in multi-agent systems like robot swarms, natural language processing for dialogue flow, and simulations of chaotic stuff like traffic.

Industries Robotics uses it for coordination, telecom for network chatter, and even gaming for NPC interactions.

Challenges It's a brain-twister to set up—too abstract for quick coding—and might bog down with huge systems where every step needs calculating.

Summary Rho-Calculus gives AI a way to dance with dynamic processes, offering precision and clarity, but it's a heavy lift for practical, large-scale use.

Rhythm Detection in AI Music Generation

Definition Rhythm Detection in AI Music Generation is the knack of an AI to spot and mimic the beat, tempo, and groove in music, helping it craft tunes that feel alive and natural instead of robotic.

Key Components It leans on signal processing to break down audio waves, pattern recognition to find the pulse, and sometimes neural networks trained on heaps of songs to guess what fits. Timing data—like beats per minute—and memory of past notes are its tools.

Benefits It makes AI music sound human, with a swing people can tap to, and cuts the awkwardness of off-beat tracks. It also speeds up composing by nailing the foundation fast.

Examples Picture an AI hearing a drum loop and building a bassline that syncs perfectly, or tweaking a melody to match a jazz shuffle.

Applications It's in auto-generated playlists, film scoring bots, and apps that remix your humming into a full track.

Industries Music production leans on it for quick drafts, gaming for adaptive soundtracks, and education for teaching rhythm basics.

Challenges It trips over weird time signatures or noisy recordings, and might miss the soul of a beat if it's too data-driven.

Summary Rhythm Detection lets AI groove with the beat, turning raw tech into toe-tapping tunes, though it struggles with the quirks of human flair.

Ridge Regression in AI

Definition Ridge Regression in AI is a twist on regular number-crunching that keeps predictions steady by nudging the model away from wild swings, adding a penalty to keep its guesses tame and useful.

Key Components It starts with basic regression—finding a line through data points—then tacks on a rule that shrinks the weights of less important factors. The penalty size, called lambda, is the dial you twist to control this.

Benefits It's a shield against overfitting, where a model gets too picky about training data and flops on new stuff. It also works when features outnumber samples, keeping things sane.

Examples Think of it predicting crop yields with weather data, calming down when one rainy day tries to skew everything, or guessing ad clicks without obsessing over outliers.

Applications It's in financial forecasting, medical stats analysis, and anywhere AI needs to sift through noisy piles of numbers.

Industries Agriculture uses it for yield models, healthcare for patient trends, and marketing for campaign insights.

Challenges Picking the right lambda is guesswork—too big and it dulls the model, too small and it's no help. It also won't toss out useless features entirely.

Summary Ridge Regression keeps AI predictions grounded and practical, a go-to for noisy data, but it needs a steady hand to tune.

Right-Sizing AI Models

Definition Right-Sizing AI Models is the art of trimming or boosting an AI's complexity so it fits the job—big enough to work well, small enough to run fast and cheap, like tailoring a suit instead of grabbing one off the rack.

Key Components It involves sizing up the task, picking the right number of layers or parameters in a model, and testing to see if simpler does the trick. Tools like pruning or quantization help shave off excess fat.

Benefits You save power, time, and cash by not overbuilding, and it runs on smaller gadgets without choking. It also keeps accuracy from dipping too low.

Examples Imagine a phone app that IDs plants with a lean model instead of a bloated one, or a traffic cam AI that skips the overkill for quick license plate reads.

Applications It's in mobile apps, edge devices like smart cameras, and cloud setups aiming to cut costs.

Industries Consumer tech loves it for wearables, automotive for onboard AI, and energy for efficient monitoring.

Challenges Guessing the sweet spot is tough—cut too much and it fails, leave too much and it's wasteful. It also takes extra tinkering time.

Summary Right-Sizing makes AI lean and mean, perfect for real-world limits, but finding the balance is more craft than science.

Risk-Based Authentication (RBA) in AI

Definition Risk-Based Authentication in AI is a security trick where AI sizes up how risky a login looks—based on stuff like location or habits—and decides how much proof you need to get in, tightening up when things feel fishy.

Key Components It uses AI to watch patterns (like your usual device), score threats in real time, and tweak rules—like asking for a code if you're logging in from halfway across the world. Data on past logins and behavior is its fuel.

Benefits It's smoother for legit users (fewer hoops when it's safe) and tougher on hackers. It adapts fast to new tricks without blanket lockdowns.

Examples Picture a bank app letting you in easy from home but demanding a text code from a new city, or a work portal flagging a midnight login.

Applications It's in online banking, corporate VPNs, and e-commerce checkouts needing smart security.

Industries Finance uses it for account safety, tech for employee access, and retail for fraud checks.

Challenges It leans hard on good data—sketchy inputs mess it up—and might annoy users with false flags or miss sneaky attacks.

Summary RBA in AI makes security sharp and flexible, locking out risks while letting you slide in, though it's only as good as its info.

Risk Prediction in AI

Definition
Risk Prediction in AI is when AI crunches data to guess the odds of something bad—like a heart attack or a cyberattack—happening, giving a heads-up to dodge or brace for it.

Key Components
It pulls in historical data, spots patterns with models like neural nets or trees, and spits out probabilities. Features—like age or login attempts—and a scoring system drive the output.

Benefits
It catches trouble early, saves money by fixing small issues first, and can handle tons of factors humans might miss.

Examples
Think of it warning a doctor about a patient's stroke risk from vitals, or a firewall predicting a hack from odd traffic spikes.

Applications
It's in healthcare diagnostics, fraud detection, and disaster planning for floods or quakes.

Industries
Medicine uses it for patient care, insurance for pricing, and cybersecurity for threat hunting.

Challenges
Bad data leads to bad calls, and it might over-worry or under-warn if the model's off. Explaining why it flags something can be murky too.

Summary
Risk Prediction in AI turns data into crystal-ball warnings, a lifesaver across fields, but it's picky about quality and clarity.

Risk Scoring Models in AI

Definition
Risk Scoring Models in AI are systems that use artificial intelligence to crunch data and spit out a number showing how likely something risky—like a loan default or a cyberattack—is to happen, helping people decide what to watch out for.

Key Components
They rely on heaps of data—like past events or user habits—fed into algorithms like decision trees or neural networks. The model learns patterns, weighs factors, and churns out a score, often tuned by how much each piece matters and updated as new info rolls in.

Benefits
They spot trouble fast, cut guesswork, and handle way more info than a human could, making decisions sharper and less biased. Plus, they adapt as risks shift.

Examples
Think of a bank scoring a loan applicant based on their credit and job history, or a hospital flagging a patient's heart attack odds from vitals.

Applications
They're in fraud detection for catching shady transactions, healthcare for patient triage, and insurance for pricing policies.

Industries
Finance uses them for lending, medicine for care plans, and cybersecurity for threat alerts.

Challenges
They need clean, hefty data—garbage in means garbage out—and can stumble if risks change too fast or if the scoring's hard to explain to humans.

Summary
Risk Scoring Models in AI turn data into a crystal ball for danger, boosting smart choices across fields, though they lean hard on quality inputs and clarity.

Robotic Perception in AI

Definition
Robotic Perception in AI is how machines—like robots—use artificial intelligence to make sense of the world around them, soaking in sights, sounds, or touches to figure out what's what and act on it.

Key Components
It's powered by sensors (cameras, microphones, lasers) grabbing raw info, paired with AI tricks like image recognition or sound analysis to process it. Memory of past scenes and real-time tweaking keep it sharp.

Benefits
It lets robots "see" and "hear" like us but faster and without tiring, handling chaos or dark corners where humans might miss stuff. It's also tweakable for new tasks.

Examples
Picture a warehouse bot spotting a box's barcode, or a vacuum bot dodging a sock on the floor.

Applications
It's in self-driving cars mapping roads, drones scanning crops, and home bots tidying up.

Industries
Automotive needs it for navigation, agriculture for monitoring, and manufacturing for quality checks.

Challenges
It struggles with weird lighting or noisy spots, needs pricey sensors, and can misread if the AI's not trained on enough variety.

Summary
Robotic Perception in AI gives machines eyes and ears, transforming how they move and work, but it's picky about conditions and setup costs.

Robotic Process Automation (RPA)

Definition
Robotic Process Automation, or RPA, is software that acts like a digital worker, taking over repetitive computer tasks by copying how humans click and type, streamlining office grunt work with AI spice sometimes mixed in.

Key Components
It uses bots that follow set rules, tapping into screens and systems via interfaces. Scripts map the steps, and some versions add AI to handle messier data or decisions.

Benefits
It's lightning-fast at dull jobs, cuts errors, and frees people for brainier work, slashing costs and boosting flow without big system overhauls.

Examples
Picture it filling out forms from emails, or pulling numbers from invoices into spreadsheets.

Applications
It's in data entry for payroll, customer service chatbots, and supply chain tracking.

Industries
Finance uses it for accounts, healthcare for records, and retail for orders.

Challenges
It flops if tasks shift too much, needs tight security for data, and can be a hassle to scale or explain to auditors.

Summary
RPA turns software into tireless clerks, revolutionizing routine work, but it demands stable rules and careful watch.

Robot Optimus(Robot)

Definition
Optimus Robot is a humanoid bot dreamed up by Tesla, designed with AI to handle everyday chores or tough jobs, aiming to be a helpful sidekick for humans in homes or factories.

Key Components
It's got a human-like frame with arms and legs, packed with sensors for seeing and grabbing, and an AI brain to learn tasks. Battery power and Tesla's tech smarts drive it.

Benefits
It could free up time by doing grunt work, adapt to new gigs with practice, and push the envelope on what robots can pull off in real life.

Examples
Imagine it fetching tools in a workshop, or folding laundry while you sip coffee.

Applications
It's eyed for home help like cleaning, factory tasks like hauling, and maybe caregiving down the line.

Industries
Consumer tech wants it for households, manufacturing for labor, and healthcare might tap it for support.

Challenges
It's still a work in progress—pricey, unproven outside demos, and tricky to make safe and reliable around people.

Summary
Optimus Robot is Tesla's stab at a do-it-all humanoid, promising a future of handy helpers, but it's got hurdles to clear before it's everyday reality.

Robots

Definition
Robots are programmable machines that blend hardware and software—sometimes with AI—to do tasks automatically, from simple repeats to tricky jobs, often mimicking or replacing human effort.

Key Components
They've got bodies (arms, wheels), brains (computers or chips), and senses (cameras, touch pads), plus code telling them what to do. Power sources and sometimes network links keep them humming.

Benefits
They work non-stop, don't goof up on boring stuff, and tackle dangerous or tiny tasks humans can't, saving time and sweat.

Examples
Think of a factory arm welding car parts, or a little rover scooping Mars dirt.

Applications
They're in assembly lines cranking out goods, surgery cutting with precision, and space exploring far-off rocks.

Industries
Manufacturing leans on them for speed, healthcare for accuracy, and defense for risky missions.

Challenges
They're pricey to build and fix, can break down if pushed too hard, and might displace jobs or need constant updates.

Summary
Robots are the muscle of automation, reshaping work with tireless grit, though they come with costs and quirks to wrestle.

Robust Optimization in AI

Definition
Robust Optimization in AI is a method to build models that stay solid even when data's messy or the world throws curveballs, aiming for reliable answers no matter what gets tossed at them.

Key Components
It starts with math that assumes worst-case scenarios, tweaking algorithms to handle uncertainty—like missing info or noise—while balancing trade-offs in performance. Data ranges and constraints shape it.

Benefits
It keeps AI steady in shaky spots, dodging breakdowns from bad inputs, and builds trust where flops aren't an option.

Examples
Think of it keeping a power grid AI humming during storms, or a trading bot steady through market hiccups.

Applications
It's in logistics planning under delays, finance modeling with iffy data, and safety systems that can't fail.

Industries
Energy uses it for grids, banking for risk tools, and aerospace for controls.

Challenges
It can overthink and slow down, might miss peak performance for safety, and takes extra brainpower to design right.

Summary
Robust Optimization in AI crafts tough, dependable systems for uncertain times, a lifesaver in critical spots, though it trades speed for strength.

Robustness in AI Models

Definition
Robustness in AI Models is the ability of an artificial intelligence system to keep working well even when it faces unexpected twists—like weird data, attacks, or glitches—staying steady instead of crumbling under pressure.

Key Components
It's built through tough training with varied data, tricks like regularization to avoid overfitting, and tests that throw curveballs to see what holds up. The model's design—its layers or rules—gets tweaked to handle noise or shifts.

Benefits
It means AI you can trust in messy real life, not just lab perfection, cutting flops and keeping predictions solid when stakes are high.

Examples
Think of a face-recognition AI still spotting you with sunglasses on, or a spam filter catching tricks despite funky typos.

Applications
It's in self-driving cars dodging odd road hiccups, medical AI reading blurry scans, and fraud detection nailing sneaky scams.

Industries
Automotive needs it for safety, healthcare for reliability, and finance for scam-proofing.

Challenges
Building it takes extra time and data, might dull peak accuracy for stability, and can't always prep for every wild card.

Summary
Robustness in AI Models keeps the tech dependable through chaos, a must for real-world grit, though it's a slog to perfect.

Role-Based Access Control (RBAC) in AI Security

Definition
Role-Based Access Control in AI Security is a setup where AI systems lock down who gets to peek or poke at data and features based on their job—like a bouncer checking IDs—keeping sensitive stuff safe and tidy.

Key Components
It's got roles (like "admin" or "user"), permissions tied to each (view, edit, delete), and an AI layer checking who's who against rules. User profiles and logs track it all.

Benefits
It cuts chaos by limiting access, stops leaks or hacks, and makes security simple to manage even as teams grow or AI scales.

Examples
Picture an AI payroll bot only letting HR see salaries, or a hospital AI hiding patient files from tech support.

Applications
It's in data privacy for AI apps, system admin for cloud AI, and compliance setups needing tight control.

Industries
Healthcare uses it for patient data, finance for account safety, and tech for server access.

Challenges
Setting up roles takes planning—miss one and it's a gap—and AI might slow down checking every move.

Summary
RBAC in AI Security keeps the keys in the right hands, locking down risks cleanly, but needs careful setup to hum.

Rule-Based AI Systems

Definition
Rule-Based AI Systems are setups where artificial intelligence follows a playbook of if-then instructions crafted by humans, making decisions by matching situations to preset recipes instead of learning on the fly.

Key Components
They run on a rule library (like "if hot, then cool"), a way to read inputs (sensors or data), and logic to pick the right rule and act. A knowledge base from experts feeds it.

Benefits
They're predictable and easy to explain—great where you need clarity—and don't need tons of data to start, just good rules.

Examples
Think of a thermostat AI turning on AC when it hits 80°F, or a chatbot replying "yes" if you ask about hours.

Applications
It's in early expert systems for diagnosis, simple automation like lights, and basic customer service bots.

Industries
Manufacturing uses it for controls, retail for basic queries, and medicine for rule-driven triage.

Challenges
They choke on surprises outside the rules, take forever to update for big systems, and can't adapt like learning AI.

Summary
Rule-Based AI Systems are straightforward workhorses for clear-cut jobs, but they're stiff and stuck in their ways.

Rule-Based Machine Learning

Definition

Rule-Based Machine Learning is a hybrid where AI learns patterns from data but spits them out as human-readable if-then rules, blending the smarts of learning with the simplicity of a rulebook.

Key Components

It starts with data, uses algorithms like decision trees to find trends, then turns those into rules (if X, then Y). A refining step trims or tweaks them for clarity.

Benefits

You get data-driven insight that's still easy to check or tweak, bridging the gap between black-box AI and explainable logic.

Examples

Imagine it spotting "if age over 50 and smokes, then high risk" from health data, or "if clicks ads often, then likely buyer" from web logs.

Applications

It's in risk scoring for loans, marketing for targeting, and diagnostics needing clear reasoning.

Industries

Finance loves it for audits, healthcare for transparent calls, and retail for customer rules.

Challenges

Rules might miss subtle patterns, take effort to make sharp, and can pile up into a mess if data's huge.

Summary

Rule-Based Machine Learning marries learning and logic for clear, smart calls, though it trades depth for readability.

Rule Extraction from Neural Networks

Definition

Rule Extraction from Neural Networks is the process of cracking open a neural network's murky brain to pull out simple if-then rules that explain what it's doing, turning a tangled web into something humans can grasp.

Key Components

It takes a trained network, probes its decisions with data, and uses tricks—like pruning or mapping—to distill patterns into rules. Tools compare inputs to outputs for logic.

Benefits

It makes AI less of a mystery, letting you audit or trust it, and helps fix or teach what the network's learned.

Examples

Picture pulling "if pixel cluster is round, then it's a ball" from an image AI, or "if voice pitch drops, then sad" from a speech net.

Applications

It's in legal AI needing reasons, medical AI for doctor buy-in, and safety systems proving they're sound.

Industries
Law uses it for compliance, healthcare for explainability, and automotive for crash-proofing.

Challenges
Rules might oversimplify and miss the full picture, it's a slog to extract, and big nets make it a tangle.

Summary
Rule Extraction from Neural Networks lights up the black box, giving clarity at a cost of effort and nuance.

Runtime Optimization in AI Systems

Definition
Runtime Optimization in AI Systems is about tuning an AI while it's live—mid-task—to run faster, use less juice, or dodge hiccups, squeezing the most out of it without a full rebuild.

Key Components
It tracks performance (speed, memory), tweaks settings like batch size or precision on the fly, and sometimes swaps algorithms midstream. Monitoring and feedback loops keep it humming.

Benefits
It cuts lag and costs, adapts to changing loads, and keeps AI snappy on weak hardware like phones or edge gear.

Examples
Think of a video AI dropping detail to keep streaming smooth, or a chatbot speeding up replies under heavy use.

Applications
It's in real-time translation, gaming AI adjusting to players, and edge devices like smart cams.

Industries
Tech uses it for apps, gaming for fluid play, and energy for lean sensors.

Challenges
Tweaking live risks glitches, needs slick monitoring, and might trade accuracy for speed if pushed.

Summary
Runtime Optimization keeps AI nimble and efficient in action, a boon for live systems, but it's a tightrope to balance.

Run-to-Run Control in AI-Driven Manufacturing

Definition
Run-to-Run Control in AI-Driven Manufacturing is a method where AI tweaks a production process between batches—each "run"—using past results to nail quality or efficiency, like a chef adjusting a recipe after tasting.

Key Components
It gathers data from each run (say, chip thickness), feeds it to an AI model that predicts tweaks (more heat, less pressure), and updates settings for the next go. Sensors and stats power it.

Benefits
It catches drift early, boosts consistency, and saves waste by fixing flaws before they pile up, all without stopping the line.

Examples
Picture an AI adjusting a 3D printer's speed after a warped part, or tuning a furnace for perfect steel strips.

Applications
It's in semiconductor fab for tiny chips, car parts for tight fits, and pharma for pill doses.

Industries
Electronics needs it for precision, automotive for standards, and drugs for safety.

Challenges
It leans on fast, good data—lag or noise throws it off—and complex setups make it hard to scale or trust.

Summary
Run-to-Run Control in AI keeps manufacturing tight and smart, run after run, though it demands sharp data and setup.

Rydberg Atom-Based Qubit Control in AI

Definition
Rydberg Atom-Based Qubit Control in AI is a technique where artificial intelligence harnesses the quirky traits of Rydberg atoms—super-sized atoms with electrons far from the nucleus—to boss around quantum bits (qubits) for computing tasks, using their sensitivity and interactions to power AI-driven decisions or optimizations.

Key Components
It's built on Rydberg atoms trapped by lasers or tweezers, excited to high-energy states where they're ultra-responsive. AI algorithms steer laser pulses or electric fields to flip or tangle these qubits, with a control system syncing the atom dance to AI goals.

Benefits
It's fast and precise, letting AI tap quantum speed for tough problems, and the atoms' strong interactions mean fewer parts to juggle. It also scales up nicely for bigger AI systems.

Examples
Picture an AI tweaking a Rydberg qubit array to crack a logistics puzzle, or nudging qubits to spot patterns in messy data faster than a regular computer.

Applications
It's in quantum machine learning for smarter predictions, optimization for supply chains, and simulations of complex systems like weather or molecules.

Industries
Tech leans on it for next-gen AI, logistics for route planning, and science for modeling tricky physics.

Challenges
Keeping the atoms stable is a headache—tiny shakes ruin everything—and AI needs to be slick to handle the quantum weirdness without bogging down.

Summary
Rydberg Atom-Based Qubit Control in AI marries quantum muscle with AI brains, promising zippy solutions for hard tasks, though it's a finicky beast to tame.

Rydberg Atom Simulation in Quantum AI

Definition
Rydberg Atom Simulation in Quantum AI is when AI uses virtual or real Rydberg atoms—those big, excitable ones—to mimic quantum systems, letting the AI explore wild physics or solve problems by pretending to be a quantum playground.

Key Components
It starts with Rydberg atoms, either real ones in a lab or coded into a simulator. AI runs the show, tweaking conditions like atom spacing or laser zaps, while a quantum model tracks how they mingle and morph over time.

Benefits
It's a sandbox for testing quantum ideas cheap and fast, and AI can sift through the chaos to find gold—insights or solutions—without needing a full quantum rig.

Examples
Think of an AI simulating Rydberg atoms to predict how a quantum circuit might act, or mapping a material's behavior under heat and pressure.

Applications
It's in drug design for molecule testing, quantum algorithm prototyping, and physics research for stuff like magnetism.

Industries
Pharma uses it for chemical tweaks, tech for quantum software, and academia for cutting-edge science.

Challenges
Real atoms are fussy to match with sims, and AI might miss subtle quantum quirks if the model's too simple or data's thin.

Summary
Rydberg Atom Simulation in Quantum AI lets AI play quantum god, unlocking deep insights, but it's a tightrope between accuracy and guesswork.

Rydberg-Mediated Quantum Entanglement in AI

Definition
Rydberg-Mediated Quantum Entanglement in AI is a setup where AI exploits the way Rydberg atoms—pumped up to wild energy states—link up their quantum states over distance, using this spooky connection to juice up AI tasks like learning or searching.

Key Components
Rydberg atoms get zapped to entangle via their strong push-pull forces, called Rydberg blockade. AI controls the zap timing and strength, weaving a web of entangled qubits, with software to harness this for computation.

Benefits
Entanglement gives AI a turbo boost for parallel processing, cracking problems that stump regular machines, and the Rydberg trick makes it easier to scale than other quantum setups.

Examples
Imagine an AI entangling Rydberg atoms to speed through a database hunt, or linking qubits to train a model on multiple scenarios at once.

Applications
It's in cryptography for unbreakable codes, optimization for scheduling, and AI pattern recognition for big data.

Industries
Cybersecurity taps it for protection, logistics for planning, and AI research for brainy breakthroughs.

Challenges
Entanglement's fragile—noise or heat can snap it—and AI needs to juggle this without losing the thread or slowing to a crawl.

Summary
Rydberg-Mediated Quantum Entanglement in AI ties quantum knots for AI's gain, offering speed and smarts, but it's a delicate dance to keep steady.

Rydberg State-Based AI Sensors

Definition
Rydberg State-Based AI Sensors are gadgets where AI teams up with Rydberg atoms—juiced to high-energy states—to sniff out signals like radio waves or electric fields, turning raw vibes into data an AI can chew on.

Key Components
Rydberg atoms, hypersensitive in their excited states, catch tiny field changes. Lasers or microwaves tickle them, while AI decodes the shifts into usable info, with hardware to bridge the atom-to-AI gap.

Benefits
They're crazy sensitive, picking up whispers across a huge range, and AI makes sense of it fast, outpacing clunky old sensors.

Examples
Think of an AI spotting a faint Wi-Fi glitch with Rydberg sensors, or tracking a storm's electric buzz from miles off.

Applications
It's in network monitoring for signal fixes, weather prediction for storm heads-ups, and defense for stealthy wave detection.

Industries
Telecom uses it for connectivity, meteorology for forecasts, and military for surveillance.

Challenges
The atoms need a cozy, quiet setup—any jostle throws them off—and AI has to sift real signals from noise quick.

Summary
Rydberg State-Based AI Sensors pair atomic ears with AI smarts for top-notch sensing, a game-changer if you can keep the setup chill.

Rydberg Wave Function Simulation in AI

Definition
Rydberg Wave Function Simulation in AI is when AI toys with the math of Rydberg atoms—those far-flung electron clouds—to model how they wiggle and jiggle, using this to fuel quantum insights or AI-driven experiments.

Key Components
It's got equations mapping the Rydberg electron's wavy dance, fed into AI that tweaks variables like energy or fields. Sim software crunches it, with AI steering to match real atoms or dream up new tricks.

Benefits
It's a cheap way to peek at quantum guts, letting AI test theories or optimize setups without breaking the bank on lab gear.

Examples
Picture an AI running a Rydberg wave sim to guess how atoms entangle, or tweaking a qubit design before it's built.

Applications
It's in quantum computing for hardware ideas, material science for atom behavior, and AI research for quantum tweaks.

Industries
Tech uses it for quantum rigs, science for theory checks, and engineering for design hacks.

Challenges
The math's a beast—small errors blow up fast—and AI might oversimplify, missing the real atom's quirks.

Summary
Rydberg Wave Function Simulation in AI lets AI sketch quantum blueprints, a handy tool for brainy leaps, though it wrestles with precision.

Letter S

Saddle Point in Machine Learning

Definition
A saddle point in machine learning refers to a critical point in the loss surface of a model where the gradient is zero, but the point is neither a local maximum nor a local minimum. It occurs where the function curves upward in one direction and downward in another. Saddle points can slow down learning and complicate optimization because they mislead gradient-based methods.

Key Components
Loss surface geometry
Gradient vector
Hessian matrix (second-order derivatives)
Local vs. global curvature analysis

Benefits
Improves understanding of non-convex loss landscapes
Helps refine optimization strategies in deep learning
Reveals the behavior of gradient descent near flat or ambiguous regions
Supports design of more stable and adaptive algorithms

Examples
Saddle points in deep neural networks with many layers and parameters
Stagnation of training when using basic gradient descent
Designing optimization methods like Adam or RMSProp to escape saddle regions

Applications
Deep learning model optimization
Neural network training
Reinforcement learning
Hyperparameter tuning

Industries
Artificial intelligence
Finance
Healthcare
Scientific computing

Challenges
Hard to detect during training due to zero-gradient confusion
Slows down convergence in complex models
May trap naive optimization algorithms
Requires advanced optimization strategies to overcome

Summary
Saddle points in machine learning highlight the complexity of training modern models. Understanding their presence and impact is essential for designing efficient, robust learning algorithms capable of escaping poor convergence zones.

Sampling in AI

Definition
Sampling in AI refers to the process of selecting a subset of data points or generating representative instances from a larger dataset or probability distribution. It is used in various AI domains including data preparation, probabilistic modeling, training, and decision-making under uncertainty.

Key Components
Sampling methods (random, stratified, importance, etc.)
Distribution modeling
Sample size and variance control
Data representation techniques

Benefits
Reduces computational cost by working with manageable subsets
Improves generalization by preventing overfitting
Supports probabilistic reasoning and inference
Enables training on large datasets that cannot be fully processed

Examples
Randomly selecting training samples in stochastic gradient descent
Sampling from a probability distribution in Bayesian networks
Importance sampling in reinforcement learning for policy evaluation

Applications
Training machine learning models
Bayesian inference and uncertainty modeling
Data augmentation and balancing
Monte Carlo simulations

Industries
Healthcare
Finance
Marketing and customer analytics
Autonomous systems

Challenges
Poor sampling can lead to biased models
Requires understanding of the underlying data distribution
Too small a sample size may reduce performance
Improper sampling affects fairness and representation

Summary
Sampling is a foundational technique in AI that balances efficiency and accuracy. It enables scalable model training, decision-making, and reasoning by selecting meaningful subsets of data or distributions without sacrificing critical information.

Sarsa (State-Action-Reward-State-Action) Algorithm

Definition
Sarsa is an on-policy reinforcement learning algorithm used to learn an optimal policy by updating action values based on the current state, the chosen action, the resulting reward, the next state, and the next action. It is known for being more conservative than off-policy methods like Q-learning.

Key Components
State representation
Action-value function (Q-table)
Learning rate and discount factor
Exploration strategy (e.g., ε-greedy)

Benefits
Ensures consistent learning by following the same policy being updated
Stabilizes training in dynamic environments
Effective for continuous control tasks
Balances exploration and exploitation naturally

Examples
Training a robot to navigate a maze using feedback from its environment
Teaching an AI agent to play a simple game like Tic-Tac-Toe
Learning optimal driving strategies in a simulated traffic environment

Applications
Robotics
Autonomous vehicle navigation
Game AI development
Industrial control systems

Industries
Transportation
Manufacturing
Defense and simulation
Education technology

Challenges
Slower convergence compared to off-policy methods
Policy-sensitive, making it less flexible for exploration
May be inefficient in environments with sparse rewards
Requires careful tuning of parameters

Summary
Sarsa provides a structured and reliable method for learning behavior through experience. Its on-policy nature supports stable and consistent improvement, making it ideal for safety-critical applications and environments requiring dependable learning strategies.

Satisficing in AI

Definition
Satisficing in AI refers to decision-making strategies that aim for a solution that is "good enough" rather than optimal. The term blends "satisfy" and "suffice" and is often applied when exhaustive search for the best solution is too costly or unnecessary. AI systems using satisficing prioritize efficiency, relevance, and timeliness.

Key Components
Threshold setting for acceptable outcomes
Heuristic evaluation
Resource-bounded reasoning
Decision simplification

Benefits
Reduces computational burden in large problem spaces
Enables faster decision-making under constraints
Supports human-like reasoning and realistic agent behavior
Facilitates responsiveness in time-critical applications

Examples
A virtual assistant choosing the most relevant answer rather than the perfect one
AI prioritizing nearest available service provider rather than searching the entire city
A game AI settling on a viable move instead of analyzing all possibilities

Applications
Conversational AI and chatbots
Recommendation systems
Real-time decision engines
Human-AI collaboration tools

Industries
Customer service
Healthcare
Retail and e-commerce
Smart cities

Challenges
Risk of suboptimal or biased outcomes
Requires well-calibrated thresholds and stopping conditions
Difficult to evaluate performance compared to optimal strategies
Context-dependence may reduce generalizability

Summary
Satisficing allows AI to make practical, fast, and resource-conscious decisions. It mirrors how humans often operate under uncertainty, making it a valuable tool in applications where responsiveness and usability outweigh perfection.

Self-Supervised Learning

Definition
Self-supervised learning is a machine learning paradigm where the model learns from unlabeled data by generating its own labels or objectives. It bridges the gap between supervised and unsupervised learning by using structure within the data itself to train AI systems without requiring human-annotated datasets.

Key Components
Pretext tasks (e.g., predicting missing parts or context)
Feature representation learning
Contrastive learning techniques
Transfer learning pipelines

Benefits
Reduces dependency on costly labeled datasets
Learns rich, generalized data representations
Improves performance on downstream tasks
Expands learning capabilities in low-resource environments

Examples
Training a model to predict the next frame in a video sequence
Learning sentence embeddings by predicting masked words
Using image rotation prediction to pretrain vision models

Applications
Natural language processing
Computer vision
Speech and audio recognition
Reinforcement learning

Industries
Healthcare and radiology
Social media and content platforms
Robotics
Cybersecurity

Challenges
Designing effective pretext tasks is complex
Quality of learned representations may vary
Hard to evaluate progress without downstream tasks
May require significant compute for large-scale training

Summary
Self-supervised learning revolutionizes the way AI models learn by unlocking the potential of vast unlabeled data. It is a powerful approach for building robust, scalable systems across domains where labeled data is limited or expensive.

Semantic Parsing

Definition
Semantic parsing is the process of converting natural language into a structured, machine-readable representation such as logical forms, database queries, or program code. It enables machines to understand the meaning behind language and perform actions based on user intent.

Key Components
Natural language understanding
Syntactic and semantic analysis
Intermediate representation generation
Structured output formats like trees or graphs

Benefits
Improves accuracy in task-specific language interpretation
Enables automation of complex tasks through language
Supports user-friendly interfaces for databases and APIs
Enhances AI's ability to perform precise actions from spoken or written input

Examples
Translating questions into SQL queries for a database
Converting user commands into robot actions
Turning sentences into logical formulas for reasoning

Applications
Conversational agents
Question answering systems
Voice-controlled applications
Automated code generation

Industries
Enterprise software
Healthcare documentation
Legal tech
Smart assistants

Challenges
Ambiguity and variability in natural language
Requires high-quality training datasets
Generalization across domains is difficult
Error propagation affects system reliability

Summary
Semantic parsing transforms language into actionable logic, forming the backbone of intelligent assistants and language-based automation. It enables AI to not only understand text but also interact meaningfully with structured systems.

Semantic Segmentation

Definition
Semantic segmentation is a computer vision technique where each pixel in an image is assigned a label based on the object or region it belongs to. Unlike object detection, which draws bounding boxes, semantic segmentation provides fine-grained understanding of the image content.

Key Components
Convolutional neural networks

Pixel-wise classification layers
Image upsampling and downsampling
Loss functions tailored for segmentation

Benefits
Provides detailed spatial understanding of images
Improves object localization and boundary detection
Essential for safety in real-time vision systems
Supports multi-class segmentation of complex scenes

Examples
Segmenting road, vehicles, and pedestrians in self-driving cars
Identifying tumors and organs in medical imaging
Mapping urban areas in satellite imagery

Applications
Autonomous driving
Medical diagnostics
Agricultural monitoring
Augmented reality

Industries
Automotive
Healthcare
Geospatial intelligence
Construction and real estate

Challenges
Requires large annotated datasets for training
Sensitive to image quality and occlusions
Difficult to scale to real-time performance
Can struggle with overlapping or similar-looking regions

Summary
Semantic segmentation enhances machine perception by enabling pixel-level classification. It supports applications that demand precision and context-awareness, making it vital for systems that navigate or interpret the physical world.

Semi-Supervised Learning

Definition
Semi-supervised learning is a machine learning approach that combines a small amount of labeled data with a large amount of unlabeled data during training. This method leverages the structure in the unlabeled data to enhance model accuracy and performance, reducing the need for extensive manual labeling.

Key Components
Labeled and unlabeled datasets
Pseudolabeling or self-training mechanisms
Consistency regularization
Graph-based learning models

Benefits
Reduces the cost and effort of data labeling

Improves generalization compared to purely supervised learning
Utilizes real-world data more effectively
Adaptable to domains with limited labeled examples

Examples
Classifying customer reviews using a few labeled examples and many unlabeled ones
Speech recognition models trained on a small set of transcribed audio and a large volume of raw recordings
Image classification using sparse human annotations combined with large image collections

Applications
Natural language processing
Speech and voice analysis
Computer vision
Bioinformatics

Industries
Healthcare
Education
E-commerce
Media and entertainment

Challenges
Risk of reinforcing errors if pseudolabels are incorrect
Requires careful balance between supervised and unsupervised signals
Sensitive to noise in unlabeled data
Model stability can be difficult to maintain

Summary
Semi-supervised learning provides an efficient way to build powerful AI models by combining the strengths of supervised and unsupervised techniques. It is especially valuable in domains where acquiring labeled data is expensive or time-consuming.

Sensor Fusion

Definition
Sensor fusion in AI refers to the integration of data from multiple sensors to produce a more accurate, comprehensive, and reliable understanding of the environment. It combines diverse data types and sources to enhance perception, decision-making, and prediction.

Key Components
Data alignment and synchronization
Sensor calibration and noise reduction
Multi-modal data fusion algorithms
Bayesian filters and deep learning models

Benefits
Increases robustness and accuracy of AI systems
Provides richer contextual information
Reduces uncertainty from individual sensor limitations
Improves performance in dynamic and noisy environments

Examples
Combining LIDAR, radar, and camera data in autonomous vehicles

Merging heart rate, temperature, and motion data in wearable health monitors
Integrating vision and touch sensors in robotics

Applications
Autonomous navigation
Healthcare diagnostics
Smart home systems
Industrial automation

Industries
Automotive
Healthcare
Aerospace
Consumer electronics

Challenges
Sensor misalignment and calibration drift
Complexity in data integration and fusion logic
Real-time processing requirements
Sensor redundancy and cost management

Summary
Sensor fusion allows AI systems to see, hear, and feel the world more effectively by combining multiple data streams. It enhances perception and decision-making across various domains, especially where reliability and safety are paramount.

Shallow Neural Network

Definition
A shallow neural network is a neural model that consists of an input layer, one hidden layer, and an output layer. It contrasts with deep neural networks, which contain multiple hidden layers. Shallow networks are simpler and easier to interpret but are limited in their ability to model complex patterns.

Key Components
Input layer for feature representation
Single hidden layer with activation functions
Output layer for prediction or classification
Training via backpropagation

Benefits
Faster training and less computationally intensive
Easier to interpret and visualize
Fewer parameters reduce the risk of overfitting
Suitable for problems with simple or low-dimensional features

Examples
Basic image recognition using grayscale inputs
Linear classification of sentiment from short text
Binary prediction of customer churn from tabular data

Applications
Educational tools and model explainability
Simple classification and regression tasks

Signal processing and control systems
Low-power embedded AI devices

Industries
Education
Finance
Manufacturing
Telecommunications

Challenges
Limited representational capacity for complex tasks
Not suitable for high-dimensional or abstract data
May require extensive feature engineering
Can underperform compared to deep models

Summary
Shallow neural networks offer a lightweight and interpretable alternative to deeper architectures. They are ideal for straightforward problems where simplicity, speed, and transparency are more important than advanced complexity.

Shared Memory in AI

Definition
Shared memory in AI refers to a computational architecture in which multiple processing units or threads access the same memory space. It enables fast data exchange and coordination between AI components, often used in parallel or distributed computing frameworks.

Key Components
Global memory space
Memory locks and synchronization mechanisms
Shared buffers for data exchange
Multi-threaded or multiprocessing environments

Benefits
Enables efficient communication between processes
Reduces memory overhead and duplication
Supports real-time decision-making
Improves computational performance in AI training and inference

Examples
Neural network training with multiple GPUs accessing a shared data buffer
Parallel reinforcement learning agents sharing an environment state
Collaborative AI systems exchanging predictions in real-time

Applications
Parallel processing in AI model training
Multi-agent AI systems
Embedded and robotics control
Simulation environments

Industries
High-performance computing
Robotics and automation

Gaming and simulation
AI infrastructure services

Challenges
Risk of memory corruption or race conditions
Complexity in synchronization and thread management
Difficult to debug concurrency issues
Hardware limitations may restrict scalability

Summary
Shared memory is a powerful mechanism for enabling fast and coordinated AI computations. It is essential for multi-threaded, parallel, and distributed systems where real-time data sharing and collaboration are crucial.

Shell in AI

Definition
Shell in AI typically refers to a software framework or interface that enables interaction between the user and an AI system. It may serve as a command-line interface (CLI) or a programmable environment where AI models are executed, trained, or tested. Shells are also used in expert systems to separate knowledge representation from inference mechanisms.

Key Components
Command execution engine
Scripting and automation capabilities
Integration with AI models or databases
Interactive environment for user input

Benefits
Simplifies interaction with complex AI systems
Allows rapid prototyping and testing
Supports automation of AI workflows
Enables modular and extensible system design

Examples
Using a Python-based shell to train a machine learning model
Expert system shells that separate knowledge base and inference engine
Scripting AI pipeline operations using Bash or custom shells

Applications
AI system administration
Rule-based expert systems
Model training and management
Intelligent command interpreters

Industries
Information technology
Enterprise software
Healthcare diagnostics
Engineering and research

Challenges
Limited to the scripting or command capabilities of the shell
Complex interfaces may have steep learning curves

Requires compatibility with underlying AI tools
May not support modern GUI-based workflows

Summary
Shells in AI provide users and developers with a structured and programmable interface to control, configure, and communicate with intelligent systems. They are essential tools in both traditional expert systems and modern AI development environments.

Short-Term Memory in AI (STM)

Definition
Short-Term Memory (STM) in AI refers to the capacity of an artificial system to retain and manipulate information for a limited period during a task. It models human-like cognitive functions such as temporary recall, contextual awareness, and real-time decision-making, and is often implemented in recurrent neural networks and memory-augmented models.

Key Components
Recurrent loops or memory cells
Temporal input sequences
Attention mechanisms or gates
Limited time-step retention

Benefits
Enhances sequential understanding and temporal reasoning
Supports real-time tasks with immediate context needs
Improves language modeling and conversational AI performance
Enables stateful decision-making in dynamic environments

Examples
Chatbots remembering the last few user messages
Predicting the next frame in a video based on recent input
Maintaining sensor readings in a robotic controller for short periods

Applications
Natural language processing
Time-series forecasting
Human-computer interaction
Autonomous navigation

Industries
Healthcare
Retail
Telecommunications
Smart devices

Challenges
Prone to forgetting important information over longer sequences
Training recurrent networks can be unstable
Limited memory capacity compared to long-term memory models
Vulnerable to noise in sequential data

Summary
Short-term memory in AI equips systems with the ability to think in the moment, process recent events,

and respond in context. It is critical for applications that rely on continuous interaction, sequencing, and state awareness.

Shrinkage in Machine Learning

Definition
Shrinkage in machine learning refers to a technique that constrains or regularizes model parameters to prevent overfitting and enhance generalization. It is commonly used in regression models and ensemble methods to reduce variance and improve model robustness.

Key Components
Regularization terms in the loss function
Coefficient adjustment through penalty factors
Bias-variance tradeoff management
Techniques like Lasso, Ridge, and Elastic Net

Benefits
Prevents overfitting on small or noisy datasets
Improves model interpretability by reducing complexity
Enhances prediction accuracy on unseen data
Supports feature selection by shrinking irrelevant variables

Examples
Lasso regression eliminating non-informative features in medical diagnosis
Shrinkage applied to boosting models like Gradient Boosting Machines
Ridge regression reducing model variance in economic forecasting

Applications
Linear and logistic regression
Ensemble learning and boosting
Feature engineering and selection
High-dimensional data analysis

Industries
Finance
Healthcare
Marketing analytics
Insurance

Challenges
Improper shrinkage can lead to underfitting
Requires tuning of regularization parameters
Interpreting shrunk coefficients may be non-intuitive
Not all models benefit equally from shrinkage

Summary
Shrinkage is a powerful regularization technique that helps machine learning models remain general and effective in the face of complexity and noise. It strikes a balance between accuracy and simplicity, improving reliability and interpretability.

Schrödinger's Equation

Definition
Schrödinger's equation is a foundational equation in quantum mechanics formulated by Erwin

Schrödinger, describing how the quantum state of a physical system evolves over time. It defines wavefunctions, which encapsulate probabilities of finding particles in specific states or positions, thus bridging classical and quantum descriptions of physical phenomena.

Key Components
The primary components include wavefunctions, quantum states, potential energy terms, probability amplitudes, energy operators (Hamiltonians), boundary conditions, and differential equations defining temporal and spatial evolution of quantum systems.

Benefits
Schrödinger's equation enables precise predictions of quantum behaviors, facilitates deeper understanding of atomic and subatomic phenomena, provides essential tools for designing quantum systems, and supports advancements in modern technologies such as semiconductors, lasers, and quantum computing.

Examples
Examples of Schrödinger's equation applications include determining electron orbitals in atoms, predicting the behavior of particles in potential wells, analyzing quantum tunneling phenomena, and modeling the dynamics of quantum harmonic oscillators or molecular interactions.

Applications
Schrödinger's equation finds applications in quantum chemistry to predict molecular structures and reactions, semiconductor physics to design electronic devices, quantum computing algorithms, spectroscopy for material analysis, nuclear physics research, and photonics engineering for advanced optical technologies.

Industries
Key industries employing Schrödinger's equation include quantum computing, semiconductor manufacturing, pharmaceuticals, chemical engineering, renewable energy, telecommunications, materials science, and advanced research in theoretical physics.

Summary
Schrödinger's equation is central to quantum mechanics, providing the mathematical framework that underpins much of modern physics and technology. Its predictive power has enabled critical advancements in diverse scientific and industrial fields, revolutionizing our understanding and practical utilization of quantum phenomena.

Signal Processing in AI

Definition
Signal processing in AI refers to the analysis, transformation, and interpretation of signals—such as audio, video, images, or sensor data—using intelligent algorithms. It enables AI systems to extract meaningful information from raw input data and make informed decisions.

Key Components
Fourier and wavelet transforms
Filtering and noise reduction
Feature extraction from time-series or spatial signals
Machine learning for pattern recognition

Benefits
Improves the clarity and usability of raw data
Enables detection of patterns in noisy environments

Supports real-time processing for immediate feedback
Enhances performance in audio, vision, and sensor-based tasks

Examples
Speech recognition using filtered audio signals
Medical ECG analysis with AI-based signal interpretation
Gesture recognition from accelerometer signals in wearable devices

Applications
Voice and audio analysis
Medical diagnostics
Radar and sonar systems
Environmental monitoring

Industries
Healthcare
Automotive
Telecommunications
Defense and aerospace

Challenges
Signal distortion and loss of quality in noisy data
Requires domain-specific knowledge for interpretation
Computational cost of real-time processing
Sensitive to input variability and environmental changes

Summary
Signal processing in AI transforms raw, unstructured signals into actionable insights. It is vital for building intelligent systems that understand and react to the physical world, from voice interfaces to life-saving medical diagnostics.

Signature Verification in AI

Definition
Signature verification in AI involves using machine learning or biometric models to confirm the authenticity of a handwritten signature. It analyzes unique features such as stroke order, pressure, speed, and shape to determine whether a signature is genuine or forged.

Key Components
Feature extraction from signature images or trajectories
Template matching or classification models
Online (dynamic) or offline (static) verification
Threshold-based decision-making

Benefits
Enhances security in financial and legal transactions
Automates identity verification processes
Detects forgeries with high precision
Adapts to individual writing styles over time

Examples
Banking apps verifying check signatures
Digital signature validation in e-documents
Forensic tools analyzing handwriting patterns

Applications
Authentication systems
Access control
Document verification
Legal forensics

Industries
Banking and finance
Government and law enforcement
Healthcare
Education

Challenges
Variability in signatures due to mood, speed, or health
Data privacy concerns when storing biometric information
Performance may vary across writing surfaces or input devices
Complexity in handling multilingual or symbolic scripts

Summary
Signature verification in AI offers a secure and efficient way to confirm identity using biometric handwriting analysis. It supports fraud prevention and trusted authentication in various personal, commercial, and institutional settings.

Simplex Method in AI

Definition
The Simplex Method in AI refers to the application of the linear programming algorithm to solve optimization problems within intelligent systems. It is used when AI models need to find the best solution from a set of linear constraints and objective functions, commonly seen in scheduling, resource allocation, and decision-making tasks.

Key Components
Linear objective function
Constraints expressed as linear inequalities
Feasible solution space
Iterative optimization through vertices of the solution space

Benefits
Efficient for solving linear optimization problems
Provides exact solutions in deterministic systems
Widely supported and easy to implement in optimization libraries
Suitable for problems with large but sparse constraint sets

Examples
AI-based scheduling of delivery routes for logistics companies
Resource management in energy grids
Cost optimization in AI-driven manufacturing systems

Applications
Operations research
AI planning and logistics
Robotics pathfinding with linear constraints
Financial modeling

Industries
Supply chain and logistics
Energy
Manufacturing
Finance

Challenges
Limited to linear problems, unsuitable for non-linear AI models
Sensitive to changes in constraints or parameters
High-dimensional problems may become computationally intense
Inflexible for real-time learning tasks

Summary
The Simplex Method in AI offers a reliable tool for solving well-defined optimization problems. It helps AI systems make efficient, linear decisions in environments where constraints and goals can be clearly quantified.

Simulation in AI

Definition
Simulation in AI refers to the replication of real-world processes, environments, or systems using intelligent models. It allows AI systems to observe, interact with, and learn from synthetic or virtual representations before deployment in real scenarios.

Key Components
Modeling of real-world dynamics
Agent-environment interaction
Feedback loops and iterative learning
Scenario testing and what-if analysis

Benefits
Enables safe experimentation without real-world consequences
Accelerates training for reinforcement learning and robotics
Reduces cost of physical trials
Supports data generation in environments with limited historical records

Examples
Training self-driving cars in virtual environments
Simulating human behavior in digital twins for smart cities
Testing drone flight in simulated weather conditions

Applications
Reinforcement learning
Autonomous systems development
Game AI training
Decision support systems

Industries
Automotive
Defense and aerospace
Healthcare
Urban planning

Challenges
Simulated environments may not reflect real-world complexity
Performance in simulation may not translate to real deployment
Developing accurate models requires expert input
Computationally intensive for high-fidelity simulations

Summary
Simulation in AI provides a controlled, cost-effective approach to training, testing, and refining intelligent systems. It empowers AI to learn, adapt, and operate efficiently in environments that mirror real-world challenges.

Simulation of Virtual World

Definition
Simulation of a virtual world in AI involves creating immersive, interactive environments where AI agents can perceive, act, and evolve. These environments mimic physical or fictional worlds and are used for training, entertainment, and experimentation purposes.

Key Components
3D rendering engines
Physics-based modeling
Agent-based interaction and feedback
Procedural generation of environments

Benefits
Provides rich, dynamic training environments
Enhances realism for AI learning and behavior adaptation
Useful for testing AI in rare or extreme conditions
Supports long-term behavioral learning

Examples
Simulating city life for AI-powered urban development
AI training in massively multiplayer online game (MMO) environments
Virtual factories for robotics control and optimization

Applications
Game development
Cognitive modeling and research
Simulation-based reinforcement learning
Virtual reality and human-AI interaction

Industries
Gaming
Urban planning
Healthcare training
Education and e-learning

Challenges
Building complex, realistic environments is resource-intensive
Simulation may introduce biases not present in the real world
Hard to replicate randomness or chaotic behaviors
Performance optimization is needed for real-time simulation

Summary
Simulation of virtual worlds offers AI systems an interactive playground to explore, learn, and improve. It is a critical foundation for next-generation AI training, gaming, and human-machine interaction.

Skeletonization in AI

Definition
Skeletonization in AI is a computer vision technique used to reduce shapes and objects to their simplest form, typically by extracting their structural outlines or centerlines. It helps in shape analysis, object recognition, and pattern detection by simplifying visual content without losing important structure.

Key Components
Binary image processing
Thinning algorithms
Morphological transformations
Graph-based representation of structure

Benefits
Simplifies complex images for analysis
Reduces computational load for shape recognition
Preserves essential structural information
Improves performance in gesture and motion recognition

Examples
Identifying handwritten digits by extracting character skeletons
Medical image analysis of bone structures or blood vessels
Analyzing walking patterns in video surveillance

Applications
Medical imaging
Gesture recognition
Optical character recognition
3D modeling and object detection

Industries
Healthcare
Security and surveillance
Education technology
Augmented reality

Challenges
Sensitive to noise and image artifacts
Skeleton may lose meaningful information in cluttered images
Not suitable for all image types or low-resolution data
May require post-processing to refine results

Summary
Skeletonization offers a powerful tool for simplifying visual data in AI systems. It distills shapes to their essence, enabling efficient recognition and analysis in applications ranging from medical diagnostics to security systems.

Skewness in AI Models

Definition
Skewness in AI models refers to the asymmetry in the distribution of input data or prediction outcomes. It indicates whether the data is biased toward higher or lower values, which can affect model accuracy, fairness, and generalization.

Key Components
Statistical measures of asymmetry
Feature distribution analysis
Outlier and imbalance detection
Bias correction techniques

Benefits
Reveals data or model bias early in the pipeline
Supports targeted preprocessing and resampling

Improves model fairness and interpretability
Helps avoid overfitting to skewed data

Examples
Income prediction models skewed by high earners
Skewed customer churn data with more non-churn examples
Sentiment analysis models biased toward positive reviews

Applications
Fairness auditing in machine learning
Data preprocessing and augmentation
Anomaly detection
Statistical modeling and diagnostics

Industries
Finance
Healthcare
Social media analytics
Criminal justice and public policy

Challenges
Hard to correct skewness without distorting the data
Can mislead performance metrics and validation results
Impacts generalization across diverse populations
Interacts with other data imbalances like class imbalance

Summary
Skewness in AI models highlights hidden biases or distribution irregularities in data. Recognizing and addressing it is key to building accurate, fair, and generalizable AI systems.

Skill-Based AI

Definition
Skill-Based AI refers to systems that are designed to execute specific, modular skills or actions within defined contexts. These systems operate through a combination of rule-based logic, experience-based learning, and action planning, mimicking how humans acquire and apply skills.

Key Components
Modular skill libraries
Task decomposition and planning

Context-aware behavior selection
Learning through repetition and refinement

Benefits
Simplifies the design of complex AI behaviors
Improves reusability of components across tasks
Enables hierarchical and multi-agent collaboration
Allows for flexible behavior adaptation

Examples
Game characters executing combat, healing, or evasion skills
Robots performing assembly tasks using modular motion skills
AI assistants switching between speaking, scheduling, and searching

Applications
Game AI
Industrial robotics
Personal assistants
AI-driven tutoring systems

Industries
Manufacturing
Healthcare
Gaming and simulation
Education

Challenges
Defining and managing transitions between skills is complex
Skill learning can be slow in real-world settings
Not well-suited to environments requiring generalization beyond pre-learned actions
Integration across heterogeneous skill modules can be challenging

Summary
Skill-Based AI focuses on enabling intelligent systems to perform and refine discrete actions or behaviors. This modular, adaptable approach allows AI to mimic human learning and execution across structured, goal-oriented environments.

Skip-Gram Model in NLP

Definition
The Skip-Gram Model in NLP is a neural network-based approach used to learn word embeddings by predicting context words given a target word. It is part of the Word2Vec architecture and is designed to capture semantic relationships between words based on their proximity in text.

Key Components
Input word vector
Context window size
Negative sampling or hierarchical softmax
Embedding vector space

Benefits
Produces high-quality word representations
Captures syntactic and semantic relationships

Efficient for large corpora with sparse data
Generalizes well to downstream NLP tasks

Examples
Embedding "doctor" close to "nurse" and "hospital" in vector space
Powering text similarity tools in search engines
Improving chatbot understanding by modeling word associations

Applications
Sentiment analysis
Machine translation
Text classification
Recommendation systems

Industries
E-commerce
Healthcare
Finance
Education and research

Challenges
Ignores word order and long-term dependencies
Requires large datasets for high-quality embeddings
Static embeddings do not adapt to different contexts
May capture and reinforce social or cultural biases

Summary
The Skip-Gram Model is a foundational tool in NLP that transforms words into meaningful vectors. It enables machines to understand language through relationships and patterns, supporting more intelligent and context-aware AI applications.

Skyline Query in AI

Definition
Skyline Query in AI refers to a method of filtering a set of data points to retrieve those that are not dominated by others across multiple dimensions. It is used in decision-making systems to identify optimal options without having to define specific weights or thresholds for all criteria.

Key Components
Multi-criteria comparison
Pareto efficiency or dominance rules
Data ranking and pruning algorithms
Query optimization for large datasets

Benefits
Enables fair and balanced multi-objective decision making
Reduces user input by automating preference filtering
Applicable in dynamic environments with conflicting criteria
Supports exploratory data analysis

Examples
Selecting job candidates based on experience, education, and salary
Choosing hotels by balancing cost, distance, and user rating
Filtering AI model parameters for best performance across trade-offs

Applications
Recommendation systems
Decision support tools
Optimization engines
Search and query enhancement

Industries
Travel and hospitality
Human resources
E-commerce
Urban planning

Challenges
Computational cost increases with data dimensionality
Difficult to scale in real-time applications
Results can be large or ambiguous in some cases
Requires efficient data structures for performance

Summary
Skyline queries help AI systems identify the most promising options when faced with multiple conflicting objectives. By simplifying decision-making, they enhance performance in recommendation, ranking, and multi-criteria analysis applications.

Sleeper Agent AI

Definition
A sleeper agent AI is an artificial intelligence system designed to remain dormant or inactive until triggered by specific conditions or commands. Unlike continuously active AI models, sleeper agent AI operates covertly, performing routine or low-impact tasks until activated for a predefined purpose. This AI type is often associated with cybersecurity, espionage, automation, and strategic deployment scenarios where stealth and precision are required.

Key Components
Trigger mechanism (keyword, signal, data pattern, or timer)
Latency phase with minimal activity
Activation mode for full performance execution
Learning model to adapt upon activation

Benefits
Conserves computational resources until needed
Enhances system security through stealth operations
Supports strategic deployment in sensitive environments
Improves automation timing for high-impact tasks

Examples
Malware that activates only when a vulnerability is detected
Predictive maintenance AI that activates upon sensor anomalies
AI trading bots that engage only during certain market conditions

Applications
Cybersecurity
Predictive maintenance
Strategic automation
Military defense systems

Industries
Cybersecurity and defense
Finance and trading
Healthcare diagnostics
Intelligence and surveillance

Challenges
Potential for unauthorized activation
Ethical concerns around covert AI use
Ensuring accurate triggers to avoid false activations
Difficult to test in all real-world scenarios

Summary
Sleeper agent AI is a highly specialized artificial intelligence model designed for strategic deployment, remaining inactive until necessary. Its ability to conserve resources, enhance security, and perform critical functions upon activation makes it valuable across various industries. However, careful implementation and ethical considerations are essential to prevent misuse and ensure that it operates within defined and safe parameters.

Social Network Analysis in AI (SNA)

Definition
Social Network Analysis (SNA) uses AI and machine learning to study relationships and interactions in social structures. Leveraging graph theory, SNA represents entities as nodes and their relationships as edges, enabling the analysis of social dynamics.

Key Characteristics
Graph-Based Models use graph structures to map interactions.
Metrics like centrality, clustering, and density provide insights into network dynamics.
Unstructured Data Analysis reveals patterns from diverse data sources like social media and transaction logs.

Benefits
Identifies influential entities and communities, reveals hidden patterns, and supports applications like marketing, fraud detection, and public health interventions.

Applications
SNA is applied in social media analytics, cybersecurity, criminology, healthcare, and organizational behavior.

Conclusion
SNA is a critical tool in AI for uncovering and analyzing relationships within complex networks, offering valuable insights into social structures and interactions.

Soft Computing
Definition
Soft Computing is an AI paradigm that tackles real-world problems by embracing imprecision, uncertainty, and approximation. Techniques include neural networks, fuzzy logic, evolutionary algorithms, and probabilistic reasoning.

Key Characteristics
Approximation provides practical solutions without exactness.
Tolerance for Uncertainty allows dealing with noisy or incomplete data.
Hybrid Approaches combine multiple techniques for optimal problem-solving.

Benefits
Adapts to complex, ambiguous problems like speech recognition or optimization, offering flexible, robust solutions.

Applications
Widely used in robotics, natural language processing, medical diagnosis, and optimization.

Conclusion
Soft Computing provides adaptable and robust solutions in AI for tackling uncertainty and complexity, making it an invaluable tool for real-world problem-solving.

Sound Processing in AI

Definition
Sound Processing in AI refers to the analysis, manipulation, and interpretation of audio signals using AI algorithms. This includes tasks such as speech recognition, music analysis, noise cancellation, and audio classification. AI-powered sound processing involves extracting meaningful information from raw sound data for various applications, from virtual assistants to music recommendation systems.

Key Characteristics
Signal Transformation involves converting raw sound waves into digital signals and applying techniques like Fourier transforms to analyze the frequency and time-domain characteristics of the sound.
Feature Extraction allows AI models to extract relevant features such as pitch, volume, and timbre, which are then used for tasks like speech recognition or music genre classification.
Deep Learning models like convolutional neural networks (CNNs) and recurrent neural networks (RNNs) are used for audio pattern recognition and sequence modeling.

Benefits
Enhances human-computer interaction by enabling machines to understand and respond to spoken language and sounds.
Provides tools for analyzing complex sound patterns, allowing AI systems to detect and classify different sounds in real time.

Applications
Sound processing in AI is used in virtual assistants (e.g., Siri, Alexa), automated transcription services, music recommendation systems, audio forensics, and hearing aids.

Conclusion
Sound Processing in AI enables machines to interpret and respond to audio inputs, revolutionizing human-computer interaction across various domains such as speech recognition, music analysis, and security applications.

Source Separation in AI

Definition
Source Separation refers to the AI technique of isolating individual sound sources from a mixed audio signal. This process involves separating different components (e.g., vocals, instruments, or background noise) from an audio recording. AI-based source separation is widely used in applications such as music production, audio enhancement, and speech processing.

Key Characteristics
Blind Source Separation is a common approach where the AI model separates sources without prior knowledge of the number or types of sources in the mixture, using algorithms such as Independent

Component Analysis (ICA) or Non-negative Matrix Factorization (NMF).
Deep Learning-Based Models employ neural networks, such as fully convolutional networks or U-Nets, trained on large datasets to separate specific sound sources (e.g., vocals from music).
Real-Time Processing allows some AI models to perform source separation in real time, making them useful for live audio enhancement or noise cancellation.

Benefits
Enables precise isolation of sound components, improving the quality of audio in various applications.
Enhances user experience in multimedia by providing cleaner, clearer audio for music, video, or voice calls.

Applications
Source separation is used in music production (isolating instruments), speech enhancement (separating voice from background noise), hearing aids (enhancing speech in noisy environments), and audio forensics.

Conclusion
Source Separation is a powerful AI technique that enables the extraction of individual sound components from complex audio signals, making it an essential tool in applications ranging from music production to audio enhancement and real-time speech processing.

Sparse Coding

Definition
Sparse coding is a technique in machine learning and neural networks where data is represented using a sparse set of basis functions, meaning that only a small number of active features are used to describe a given input. This method aims to find a more compact and efficient representation of the data.

Key Characteristics
Encourages the model to use only a few active neurons to represent any given input, promoting efficiency and robustness.
Often used for unsupervised learning and feature extraction, where the model learns a sparse representation without labeled data.
Related to deep learning methods like autoencoders, which seek to encode data in a compact, informative form.

Benefits
Reduces redundancy in data representations, leading to more efficient storage and faster computations.
Sparse representations are also more interpretable and generalizable.

Applications
Used in image recognition, signal processing, and natural language processing (NLP) for feature extraction, compression, and denoising.

Conclusion
Sparse coding is a powerful technique for creating compact, efficient representations of data, making it useful in a wide range of AI applications, particularly those involving high-dimensional data like images and signals.

Submodular Optimization in AI

Definition
Submodular optimization is a mathematical technique used in AI to solve optimization problems where the objective function exhibits diminishing returns, meaning that the benefit of adding an element to a

set decreases as the set grows. Submodular functions are commonly encountered in machine learning, particularly in tasks like feature selection, data summarization, and clustering.

Key Characteristics
Diminishing Returns means adding an element to a small set provides a larger gain than adding it to a larger set.
Greedy Algorithms are often used to solve submodular optimization problems efficiently, providing near-optimal solutions.
Set Functions define the goal to find an optimal subset from a larger set that maximizes or minimizes an objective function.

Benefits
Efficient to solve using greedy algorithms, which often provide solutions close to the global optimum.
Useful for tasks involving large datasets, where selecting the best subset of features or data points is computationally expensive.

Applications
Submodular optimization is used in AI for tasks like feature selection in machine learning models, sensor placement in environmental monitoring, and data summarization in natural language processing.

Conclusion
Submodular optimization is a powerful technique for solving problems that involve selecting optimal subsets from large sets, particularly in areas like machine learning and data summarization, where efficiency and scalability are crucial.

Superconducting Qubit

Definition
A superconducting qubit is a type of quantum bit used in quantum computing that leverages the principles of superconductivity to store and process quantum information. These qubits are created from circuits made of superconducting materials that exhibit zero electrical resistance at extremely low temperatures. They function by utilizing quantized energy states within Josephson junctions, enabling them to exist in superposition and entangled states.

Key Components
Superconducting materials cooled near absolute zero
Josephson junctions formed from thin insulating barriers between superconductors
Microwave resonators for signal control and readout
Cryogenic systems to maintain low-temperature environments
Quantum gates for logical operations on qubits

Benefits
Enables fast and high-fidelity quantum gate operations
Compatible with existing semiconductor fabrication techniques
Scalable architecture for building larger quantum systems
Supports long coherence times with advanced materials and shielding
Reduces energy loss due to superconductivity, enhancing efficiency

Examples
Transmon qubits, a widely used variant, are deployed in Google's Sycamore and IBM's Quantum processors
Flux qubits and phase qubits used in earlier superconducting systems
Qubits arranged in 2D lattices to execute complex quantum circuits

Applications
Quantum algorithms for optimization and simulation
Quantum error correction and fault-tolerant quantum computing
Cryptographic key generation using quantum principles
Artificial intelligence models accelerated by quantum processors
Quantum machine learning and high-dimensional data analysis

Industries
Quantum computing technology developers such as IBM, Google, and Rigetti
Academic and national laboratories for fundamental physics research
Aerospace and defense sectors investing in quantum-secure systems
Finance industry exploring quantum speed-ups for portfolio optimization
Pharmaceuticals for quantum-enhanced drug discovery simulations

Challenges
Requires extreme cryogenic conditions, increasing operational cost
Sensitive to environmental noise causing decoherence and errors
Difficulties in maintaining uniformity across large qubit arrays
Error correction schemes are resource-intensive and complex
Fabrication inconsistencies can reduce qubit reliability and scalability

Summary
Superconducting qubits represent a leading technology in the quantum computing field, offering fast and scalable computation through superconductivity and Josephson junctions. While their performance continues to improve, challenges related to cooling, noise, and scalability remain central to advancing their role in practical AI and quantum applications.

Supervised Learning

Definition
Supervised learning is a type of machine learning where the model is trained on a labeled dataset, meaning that each input is paired with the correct output. The goal is for the model to learn a mapping from inputs to outputs so that it can make accurate predictions on unseen data. It is one of the most widely used forms of machine learning, particularly in classification and regression tasks.

Key Characteristics
Labeled Data includes both input features and the corresponding correct output labels for training the model.
Loss Function measures the difference between the model's predictions and the actual labels, guiding parameter updates to minimize this loss.
Prediction involves generalizing from training data to make accurate predictions on new, unseen data.

Benefits
High accuracy on tasks where labeled data is available, such as image classification or speech recognition.
Well-understood algorithms and frameworks provide proven techniques for improving model performance.

Applications
Supervised learning is used in image recognition, spam detection, sentiment analysis, and medical diagnosis.

Conclusion
Supervised learning is one of the core techniques in AI and machine learning, offering high accuracy

and reliability for tasks where labeled data is available, making it ideal for a wide range of practical applications.

Support Vector Machine (SVM)

Definition
Support Vector Machine (SVM) is a powerful supervised learning algorithm used for classification and regression tasks. It works by finding a hyperplane that best separates data points of different classes in a high-dimensional space. SVMs are particularly well-suited for binary classification problems and can handle both linearly separable and non-linearly separable data using kernel functions.

Key Characteristics
Maximal Margin Classifier: SVM seeks to find the hyperplane that maximizes the margin between the two classes, ensuring that the model generalizes well to new data.
Kernel Trick: For non-linearly separable data, SVM uses kernel functions (e.g., polynomial, radial basis function) to project the data into a higher-dimensional space where a hyperplane can be found.
Support Vectors: The data points closest to the hyperplane, called support vectors, are the most influential in determining the hyperplane's position.

Benefits
Effective for high-dimensional data and works well even when the number of features exceeds the number of samples.
Can handle non-linear data through the use of kernel functions, making it flexible for complex tasks.

Applications
SVMs are used in tasks like image classification, text categorization, bioinformatics (e.g., gene classification), and handwriting recognition.

Conclusion
Support Vector Machines are a robust and versatile tool for classification and regression, offering high accuracy and flexibility through the use of kernels, though they can be computationally intensive for large-scale problems.

Surface Code

Definition
Surface code in quantum computing is an advanced error correction method designed to protect quantum information from noise and decoherence. It provides a framework for fault-tolerant quantum computation by encoding logical qubits across multiple physical qubits in a two-dimensional lattice. The surface code is one of the most promising approaches for scaling quantum computers, as it efficiently detects and corrects quantum errors while maintaining computational stability.

Key Components
Physical qubits arranged in a grid-like structure
Logical qubits encoded using multiple physical qubits
Stabilizer measurements for error detection
Syndrome extraction for identifying errors
Quantum gates operating within encoded structures

Benefits
High tolerance to noise and decoherence
Supports fault-tolerant quantum operations
Enables scalable quantum computing

Simplifies error correction with classical analogues
Improves stability and reliability

Examples
Integration with superconducting qubit systems
Error correction in trapped-ion quantum processors
Quantum communication protection
Demonstrations by companies like IBM and Google

Applications
Quantum processors
Secure quantum communication
Quantum simulation
Quantum cryptography

Industries
Technology and computing
Finance
Healthcare and pharmaceuticals
Cybersecurity
Scientific research

Challenges
High overhead from physical qubit requirements
Real-time correction complexity
Quantum gate error management
Environmental isolation requirements
Scaling demands on quantum hardware

Conclusion
Surface code in quantum computing is a crucial step toward building error-resistant and scalable quantum processors. By enabling fault-tolerant quantum computing, it brings large-scale applications closer to reality, though challenges in hardware precision and scalability remain.

Surrogate Model in AI

Definition
A Surrogate Model is an approximate model used in place of a more complex or computationally expensive model to reduce the computational cost of tasks like optimization or simulation. Surrogate models are often used in scenarios where evaluating the true model is time-consuming, such as in engineering simulations or hyperparameter optimization in machine learning.

Key Characteristics
Approximation: Surrogate models approximate the behavior of a complex system or function, allowing for faster evaluations.
Iterative Refinement: Surrogate models are often iteratively refined as more data is collected from the true model, improving the approximation over time.
Common Models: Popular surrogate models include Gaussian processes, polynomial regression, and neural networks.

Benefits
Dramatically reduces the time and resources needed for optimization or simulation tasks by approximating complex models with simpler ones.

Can be used to explore design spaces or parameter spaces that would otherwise be infeasible with direct simulation or modeling.

Applications
Optimization problems
Hyperparameter tuning
Simulation-based design in engineering
Machine learning with high-cost evaluations

Conclusion
Surrogate models are invaluable in AI for reducing computational overhead in complex tasks, enabling faster and more efficient exploration of design or parameter spaces in fields ranging from machine learning to engineering.

Swarm Intelligence in AI

Definition
Swarm Intelligence is an AI technique inspired by the collective behavior of social organisms, such as ants, birds, or bees, which cooperate to achieve complex tasks through simple rules and local interactions. In AI, swarm intelligence algorithms, such as Particle Swarm Optimization (PSO) and Ant Colony Optimization (ACO), are used for solving optimization problems, decision-making, and task allocation.

Key Characteristics
Decentralized Control: Swarm intelligence relies on distributed, decentralized control, where individual agents (e.g., particles or ants) follow simple rules based on local information.
Emergent Behavior: Complex problem-solving behaviors emerge from the interactions of simple agents, mimicking natural swarms that solve problems like finding food or optimizing paths.
Self-Organization: The system is self-organizing, meaning that solutions arise from the collective behavior of the swarm without central oversight or control.

Benefits
Scalable and robust, as the system's performance improves as more agents are added, and it can adapt to changing environments.
Suitable for solving complex optimization problems where traditional methods struggle.

Applications
Robotics (multi-robot systems)
Logistics and routing optimization
Environmental monitoring
Financial forecasting and trading strategies

Conclusion
Swarm intelligence is a fascinating and effective AI approach for solving complex, distributed problems by mimicking the behavior of natural swarms. Its flexibility, scalability, and adaptability make it well-suited for a variety of real-world applications, from robotics to optimization tasks.

Symbolic AI

Definition
Symbolic AI, also known as rule-based AI or classical AI, is an approach to artificial intelligence that relies on explicitly defined symbols, logic, and rules to represent knowledge and perform reasoning. It follows a structured and interpretable framework, where human-understandable symbols are manipulated through algorithms to solve problems, make decisions, and simulate human-like reasoning.

Key Components
Symbolic AI consists of a knowledge base that stores facts and rules in a structured format. A reasoning engine applies logic and inference to manipulate symbols and derive conclusions. Rule-based systems define if-then statements to process knowledge. Logic programming enables symbolic AI to perform deductive reasoning, often using languages like Prolog. Ontologies and taxonomies organize concepts into hierarchical structures for better understanding and retrieval.

Benefits
Symbolic AI offers high interpretability, making it easier to understand and debug compared to other AI approaches. It provides strong generalization capabilities when well-structured knowledge bases are used. The deterministic nature of symbolic reasoning ensures predictable and explainable decision-making. It is particularly effective in applications that require formal logic, such as mathematics, law, and expert systems.

Applications
Symbolic AI is widely used in expert systems that provide rule-based decision-making in fields like healthcare and finance. It plays a crucial role in natural language processing for grammar checking and structured data interpretation. Knowledge representation in AI assistants, chatbots, and recommendation engines relies on symbolic approaches. Legal and compliance systems use symbolic AI to interpret and enforce regulations.

Industries
The healthcare industry benefits from symbolic AI in diagnostic systems and medical reasoning. The finance sector applies it for fraud detection and regulatory compliance. The legal industry leverages symbolic AI for contract analysis and automated legal reasoning. The robotics field uses it for structured decision-making in automated processes.

Challenges
Symbolic AI struggles with scalability when dealing with large, complex datasets due to the need for manually defined rules. It lacks adaptability, making it difficult to handle unstructured or constantly changing information. Rule-based systems can become rigid and require continuous updates to remain effective. The reliance on predefined symbols and logic makes it less effective in handling ambiguous or uncertain data compared to machine learning approaches.

Summary
Symbolic AI is a rule-based approach to artificial intelligence that relies on logic, knowledge representation, and structured reasoning. It provides high interpretability and precision but faces challenges in scalability and adaptability. Its applications span healthcare, finance, law, and robotics, where structured decision-making is essential.

Syntactic Parsing

Definition
Syntactic parsing is a natural language processing technique used to analyze the grammatical structure of sentences. It identifies relationships between words and phrases by assigning syntactic roles, such as subject, verb, and object, and constructs a parse tree or dependency graph that represents the sentence structure according to a formal grammar.

Key Components
Grammar rules (context-free or dependency grammars)
Parse tree or dependency graph generation
Lexical and syntactic analysis
Parsing algorithms (top-down, bottom-up, chart parsing)

Benefits
Improves machine understanding of sentence structure
Enables accurate extraction of linguistic features
Supports advanced natural language understanding tasks
Enhances the performance of downstream AI applications

Examples
Analyzing "The dog chased the cat" to identify grammatical roles
Extracting noun phrases from user queries in a chatbot
Parsing legal documents to identify clauses and modifiers

Applications
Machine translation
Question answering systems
Voice-controlled assistants
Information retrieval and text summarization

Industries
Legal technology
Healthcare documentation
Customer service automation
Education and language learning

Challenges
Ambiguity in natural language can lead to multiple parse interpretations
Grammar complexity increases computational requirements
Parsing may be inaccurate in informal or noisy text
Cross-linguistic generalization is difficult

Summary
Syntactic parsing helps AI systems understand the structural composition of language. By modeling grammatical relationships, it plays a key role in enabling intelligent language understanding and communication.

Synthetic Data in AI

Definition
Synthetic data in AI refers to artificially generated data that mimics the properties of real-world datasets. It is created using algorithms, simulations, or generative models and is used for training, testing, and validating AI models when real data is scarce, sensitive, or expensive to obtain.

Key Components
Data generation algorithms (randomization, simulation, GANs)
Statistical distribution modeling
Domain-specific constraints and validation
Privacy-preserving techniques

Benefits
Protects privacy by avoiding use of real personal data
Enables training in data-scarce environments
Supports faster experimentation and model development
Allows control over data variability and distribution

Examples
Generating synthetic medical images for diagnostic AI training
Creating simulated user behavior for recommendation systems
Training autonomous vehicles using simulated road scenarios

Applications
Model training and validation
Anomaly detection
Data augmentation
System robustness testing

Industries
Healthcare
Finance and fraud detection
Autonomous vehicles
Retail and marketing

Challenges
Synthetic data may not capture all real-world complexities
Risk of training models that underperform in production
Requires domain expertise to ensure realism and utility
Bias in generation process can affect model fairness

Summary
Synthetic data empowers AI development by providing a flexible, safe, and scalable alternative to real data. It plays a critical role in accelerating innovation, especially in privacy-sensitive or high-risk industries.

System Identification in AI

Definition
System Identification in AI refers to the process of building mathematical models of dynamic systems using observed input-output data. It allows AI systems to learn the behavior of physical or virtual systems by approximating their internal structure and dynamics, without requiring a detailed understanding of the underlying mechanisms. This technique is widely used in control systems, robotics, and predictive modeling.

Key Components
Input-output data collection
Model structure selection (linear or nonlinear models)
Parameter estimation techniques
Validation and performance assessment

Benefits
Enables AI to model real-world systems accurately
Improves the efficiency of control, prediction, and decision-making
Reduces the need for manual modeling or domain-specific equations
Supports adaptive and data-driven system modeling

Examples
Using neural networks to model the dynamics of an industrial furnace
Identifying the behavior of a robotic arm based on movement data
Learning the response curve of an autonomous vehicle's steering system

Applications
Control system design
Predictive maintenance
Autonomous system behavior modeling
Simulation of physical systems

Industries
Manufacturing and automation
Aerospace and aviation
Automotive engineering
Energy and utilities

Challenges
Requires high-quality and diverse data for accuracy
Model overfitting or underfitting can reduce performance
Difficult to model systems with high noise or nonlinearity
Real-time identification can be computationally intensive

Summary
System Identification in AI equips intelligent systems with the ability to learn and replicate the behavior of complex environments through data. By building accurate models from observations, AI can predict, control, and optimize performance across a wide range of dynamic systems.

Letter T

Tabular Data in AI

Definition
Tabular data in AI refers to structured datasets organized in rows and columns, where each row represents an individual observation and each column corresponds to a variable or feature. This type of data is common in databases and spreadsheets and is widely used in classical machine learning tasks.

Key Components
Rows representing individual instances
Columns representing features or attributes
Categorical and numerical data types
Relational structure between variables

Benefits
Easy to store, manage, and analyze
Compatible with many machine learning algorithms
Well-suited for supervised learning tasks
Highly interpretable and explainable

Examples
Customer transaction records in retail databases
Patient health profiles in clinical studies
Sensor readings from industrial machines

Applications
Fraud detection
Customer churn prediction

Loan approval modeling
Healthcare diagnostics

Industries
Finance
Retail
Healthcare
Insurance

Challenges
Handling missing or inconsistent data
Dealing with categorical encoding and scaling
Limited performance with unstructured or high-dimensional data
May require significant feature engineering

Summary
Tabular data in AI remains a foundational format for many real-world applications. Its simplicity and structure make it ideal for training predictive models and drawing insights from structured datasets across industries.

Temporal data in ai

Definition
Temporal data in AI refers to data that is indexed or dependent on time. It captures sequential or time-related patterns and trends, making it essential for applications involving forecasting, monitoring, and behavior analysis.

Key Components
Timestamps or time intervals
Chronological order of data points
Seasonality and trends
Temporal dependencies and lag variables

Benefits
Captures real-world dynamic behaviors
Supports predictive modeling over time
Allows detection of anomalies or shifts
Improves decision-making based on trends

Examples
Stock prices recorded hourly or daily
Patient health metrics tracked over time
Sensor data from IoT devices

Applications
Time series forecasting
Health monitoring
Event prediction
Anomaly detection

Industries
Finance
Healthcare

Smart manufacturing
Retail

Challenges
Requires handling missing or irregular time intervals
Sensitive to time zone and time format inconsistencies
Modeling long-term dependencies can be complex
High risk of data leakage during time-based cross-validation

Summary
Temporal data enables AI systems to model change over time. It is fundamental for forecasting, real-time analytics, and understanding behaviors across diverse applications in both structured and streaming environments.

(Tensor)Rank of a Tensor

Definition
The rank of a tensor in AI refers to the number of dimensions, or modes, it possesses. It represents the tensor's order and determines the complexity of the data structure. Understanding tensor rank is essential for designing models that manipulate multi-dimensional data efficiently.

Key Components
Scalars (rank 0)
Vectors (rank 1)
Matrices (rank 2)
Higher-dimensional tensors (rank 3 and above)

Benefits
Facilitates efficient representation of complex data
Supports deep learning architectures requiring multi-dimensional inputs
Improves understanding of tensor operations
Helps manage computational complexity

Examples
A grayscale image as a rank-2 tensor (height × width)
A color image as a rank-3 tensor (height × width × color channels)
A batch of video frames as a rank-4 tensor

Applications
Computer vision
Natural language processing
Audio signal processing
Scientific simulations

Industries
Healthcare imaging
Autonomous vehicles
Video analytics
Physics and engineering

Summary
The rank of a tensor defines its structure and depth in AI modeling. It plays a crucial role in managing and understanding data in advanced neural networks, especially when dealing with images, videos, or multi-channel sensor inputs.

(Tensor) Access of a Tensor

Definition
Access of a tensor in AI refers to retrieving or modifying specific elements or slices within a tensor using indices. Tensor access is critical for manipulating data during model training, evaluation, and transformation across multiple dimensions.

Key Components
Indexing and slicing operations
Dimension specification
Batch processing and tensor reshaping
Data type and memory layout awareness

Benefits
Enables efficient manipulation of large datasets
Supports dynamic data transformations in models
Facilitates debugging and interpretation of tensor data
Allows fine-grained control over neural network inputs and outputs

Examples
Accessing pixel values in image tensors
Extracting word embeddings from a batch of sequences
Selecting specific feature channels from convolutional outputs

Applications
Data preprocessing
Model input/output formatting
Tensor-based optimization
Custom loss function implementation

Industries
Computer vision
Natural language processing
Machine learning infrastructure
Robotics

Summary
Accessing a tensor accurately is a fundamental operation in AI workflows. Mastery of indexing and slicing ensures smooth data handling, efficient computation, and reliable model behavior across various deep learning tasks.

TensorFlow

Definition
TensorFlow is an open-source machine learning and deep learning framework developed by Google. It provides a comprehensive ecosystem for building, training, and deploying AI models using tensors as the core data structure.

Key Components
Tensor-based computation graph
Keras API for high-level model building
Autograd and backpropagation system
Tools for deployment and model serving

Benefits
Supports distributed and scalable training
Provides flexibility for both beginners and advanced users
Wide community support and documentation
Optimized for performance on CPUs, GPUs, and TPUs

Examples
Building deep neural networks for image classification
Training text classifiers using LSTM models
Deploying models in production using TensorFlow Serving

Applications
Computer vision
Natural language processing
Reinforcement learning
Edge AI and mobile inference

Industries
Technology and software development
Healthcare
Finance
Autonomous systems

Summary
TensorFlow is a powerful platform for building end-to-end AI solutions. With strong performance, flexibility, and scalability, it remains one of the most widely used tools in both research and production AI environments.

Theory of Mind in AI

Definition
Theory of Mind in AI refers to the concept of enabling machines to infer and understand the beliefs, intentions, emotions, and perspectives of other agents, including humans. It aims to mimic a key component of human cognition that supports empathy, communication, and social reasoning.

Key Components
Modeling other agents' mental states
Perspective-taking and intention prediction
Emotional recognition and simulation
Multi-agent belief modeling

Benefits
Improves AI-human interaction and collaboration
Supports adaptive and socially aware behavior
Enables personalized and context-sensitive responses
Critical for safety in interactive AI systems

Examples
AI assistants anticipating user needs based on behavior
Robots adjusting actions based on perceived user emotions
Game AI predicting player strategies and adapting accordingly

Applications
Human-robot interaction

Cognitive simulation
Social robotics
Intelligent tutoring systems

Industries
Healthcare and therapy
Education
Entertainment and gaming
Customer service

Summary
Theory of Mind in AI brings a human-like layer of social intelligence to machines. By understanding the internal states of others, AI can behave more naturally, empathetically, and intelligently in complex human environments.

Thin-Plate Spline (TPS) in AI

Definition
Thin-Plate Spline (TPS) in AI is a smooth interpolation method used for aligning, warping, and deforming data points in spatial transformation tasks. It is commonly used in image registration, morphing, and non-rigid transformation problems.

Key Components
Radial basis function interpolation
Control points and anchor positions
Affine transformation component
Smoothness and bending energy minimization

Benefits
Allows precise, smooth warping between shapes or images
Handles complex deformations in data alignment
Preserves global structure while adjusting local variation
Improves accuracy in image matching and registration

Examples
Aligning facial landmarks in facial recognition systems
Warping one anatomical image to another in medical diagnostics
Augmenting image data through spatial transformation

Applications
Medical imaging
Facial recognition
Gesture analysis
Augmented reality

Industries
Healthcare
Security and biometrics
Computer graphics
Sports and motion analysis

Summary
Thin-Plate Spline in AI offers a powerful method for spatial transformation. It enables flexible, high-

accuracy alignment and warping across domains where shape correspondence and non-rigid deformation are essential.

THOR Blackwell Robotic Processor

Definition:
The THOR Blackwell Robotic Processor is a high-performance computing platform developed by NVIDIA for advanced robotics applications. Based on the Blackwell GPU architecture, this processor powers intelligent robots with real-time perception, planning, and control capabilities. It is engineered to deliver extreme AI performance in compact and power-efficient systems suitable for both industrial and autonomous robotics.

Key Components:
High-throughput Blackwell GPU cores
Embedded CPU for edge processing
Integrated AI acceleration units
Sensor fusion interface
Low-latency I/O architecture
Real-time operating system (RTOS) support

Examples:
An autonomous delivery robot using the THOR Blackwell processor to navigate crowded city streets in real time.
A manufacturing robot arm equipped with the processor to visually inspect products and make adjustments during high-speed assembly.
A humanoid robot performing advanced object manipulation, powered by the processor's deep learning capabilities.

Benefits:
Enables real-time robotic perception and decision-making
Delivers data center-level AI in a mobile form factor
Supports multi-sensor inputs for complex environments
Reduces latency for time-critical robotics applications
Facilitates energy-efficient AI operations in the field

Industries:
Robotics
Autonomous vehicles
Manufacturing
Healthcare robotics
Logistics and delivery automation

Applications:
Robot vision and object recognition
Path planning and obstacle avoidance
Human-robot interaction systems
Smart factory automation
Autonomous mobile robots (AMRs)

Summary:
The THOR Blackwell Robotic Processor marks a major step forward in embedded AI computing, bringing next-generation NVIDIA Blackwell performance to the world of robotics. Its ability to process large volumes of sensor data with low latency and high accuracy empowers intelligent robots to operate safely and autonomously in complex real-world environments.

Throttling in AI Systems

Definition
Throttling in AI systems refers to the intentional regulation of resource usage, request rate, or task execution to maintain performance, avoid overloading, and ensure system stability. It is used to control both internal operations and external user interactions in AI-powered platforms.

Key Components
Rate limiting mechanisms
Resource usage monitoring
Adaptive scheduling and delay control
Load balancing strategies

Benefits
Prevents system crashes under high load
Improves responsiveness and quality of service
Ensures fairness in multi-user environments
Protects against denial-of-service and resource abuse

Examples
Throttling chatbot responses to avoid spamming
Regulating API call frequency in AI-powered web services
Limiting inference operations in edge devices to conserve power

Applications
Cloud-based AI services
Edge computing and IoT
Autonomous systems
Conversational AI

Industries
Cloud infrastructure
Telecommunications
Retail and e-commerce
Healthcare IT

Summary
Throttling is a critical control mechanism in AI systems that ensures smooth, stable, and scalable operation. By regulating resource access and task rates, it preserves performance and protects against system overloads.

Time Series Forecasting in AI

Definition
Time Series Forecasting in AI involves using historical time-stamped data to predict future values. AI models learn patterns such as trends, seasonality, and cyclic behavior in sequential data to make accurate forecasts. This method is essential for planning, decision-making, and anomaly detection across many industries.

Key Components
Chronological data with timestamps
Trend and seasonality detection
Modeling techniques like ARIMA, LSTM, or Transformer models
Evaluation metrics such as RMSE and MAE

Benefits
Provides actionable insights based on temporal patterns
Supports proactive decision-making and planning
Enhances accuracy over traditional statistical methods
Handles complex and nonlinear patterns in data

Examples
Predicting stock prices using historical trading data
Forecasting electricity demand based on usage history
Estimating future sales from seasonal product trends

Applications
Financial modeling
Supply chain management
Healthcare monitoring
Weather and climate prediction

Industries
Retail
Energy
Finance
Telecommunications

Summary
Time Series Forecasting in AI enables intelligent systems to anticipate future events by learning from the past. It empowers businesses and researchers to operate with foresight, accuracy, and adaptability.

Token Embeddings

Definition
Token embeddings are dense vector representations of individual tokens (words, characters, or subwords) in a continuous vector space. These embeddings capture semantic and syntactic relationships between tokens, allowing AI models to understand language context and meaning more effectively.

Key Components
Embedding layer or lookup table
Pretrained or learned representations
Context-aware or static vectors
Dimensionality of embedding space

Benefits
Transforms discrete language into machine-readable form
Preserves contextual relationships among tokens
Reduces sparsity compared to one-hot encoding
Improves generalization in NLP models

Examples
Word embeddings like Word2Vec and GloVe
Contextual embeddings like BERT or GPT token outputs
Character-level embeddings in spell-check AI

Applications
Text classification

Machine translation
Speech recognition
Chatbots and virtual assistants

Industries
Healthcare
Legal technology
Customer service
Education

Summary
Token embeddings are foundational in natural language processing. By encoding linguistic meaning into vectors, they enable AI systems to process, understand, and generate human language more intelligently and effectively.

Token Family

Definition
Tokens are the smallest readable units of text that AI models use to understand language. Each token can be a word, part of a word, number, or punctuation mark. Unlike how humans read full sentences or paragraphs, AI reads and processes text one token at a time. This system allows AI to analyze, understand, and generate responses piece by piece — like building with bricks instead of reading a whole wall.

Key Components
A token can represent a short word like "yes," a part of a longer word like "understand," or even a single symbol like a comma or question mark. Tokenization is the process of splitting a sentence into these smaller parts. AI uses tokens to read your input, decide what it means, and create a relevant response. The total number of tokens in a message includes both the user's input and the AI's output.

Examples
Simple sentence: "I love cats!" → 4 tokens ("I", "love", "cats", "!")
Medium sentence: "Today is a great day to learn AI." → ~9 tokens
Long message: A full paragraph with 4–5 sentences could be 50–100 tokens
Dictionary entry: A full page of this book may contain 500–1,000 tokens

Benefits
Tokens allow AI models to handle language in small, logical chunks, which makes them efficient at understanding short prompts, summarizing text, translating languages, and answering questions. They help measure the length of input, track how much an AI can process at one time, and determine usage costs for users or developers. The token system also allows the model to handle different languages and formats consistently across billions of words.

Token Progression
Here's a simplified way to visualize how tokens build up:

4 tokens = "I love cats!"

8 tokens = One sentence with some punctuation

16 tokens = One longer sentence

50 tokens = A small paragraph

100 tokens = Half a page

200 tokens = Full page of explanation

500 tokens = Detailed summary or dictionary entry

1,000 tokens = Short essay

5,000 tokens = Multi-page document

10,000 tokens = Small book chapter

100,000 tokens = Entire book or large dataset

Disadvantages
One of the biggest limitations of the Token Family is known as the **counterintuitive limit**. This is when more tokens don't always lead to better results. For example, adding long background text, detailed instructions, or full documents can sometimes confuse the AI instead of helping it. Users often believe that more context = better answer, but in reality, too many tokens may cause the AI to lose focus, miss the main point, or give less accurate responses. This surprising effect — where more tokens create worse output — is what makes it "counterintuitive."

Applications
Tokens are used in every AI interaction — from writing prompts and chatting with assistants to generating stories, summaries, reports, and code. They also play a role in pricing models for API usage, determining memory load in conversations, and optimizing how much information an AI can "remember" at once.

Industries
All AI-powered industries rely on tokenization: education (for tutoring bots), marketing (for ad copy), healthcare (for clinical text analysis), customer service (for chatbots), publishing (for AI writing tools), and finance (for automated reporting and analysis). Token management is essential for large-scale AI deployment in every field.

Summary
The Token Family powers the entire language system of artificial intelligence. It breaks down words into manageable pieces and lets AI understand human language step by step. While tokens are the key to clear communication with machines, they also come with limits. The counterintuitive limit reminds us that sometimes, less is more — and smart prompts use just enough tokens to get the best results.

Tokenization in Blockchain AI

Definition
Tokenization in Blockchain AI refers to the process of converting physical or digital assets into blockchain-based tokens that can be stored, transferred, and managed using AI technologies. These tokens represent ownership or rights and are tracked securely on distributed ledgers.

Key Components
Smart contracts
Blockchain infrastructure
Digital asset encoding
Token lifecycle management

Benefits
Enhances asset liquidity and fractional ownership
Improves transparency and traceability
Enables automated asset trading and compliance via AI
Secures transactions with cryptographic methods

Examples
AI-powered platforms for real estate tokenization
Tokenized intellectual property rights with predictive pricing models
AI-managed token portfolios in decentralized finance

Applications
Asset management
Supply chain token tracking
Digital identity verification
Real-time pricing and fraud detection

Industries
Finance
Real estate
Healthcare data management
Art and collectibles

Summary
Tokenization in Blockchain AI integrates AI's decision-making capabilities with blockchain's security and transparency. It revolutionizes asset management by creating more accessible, efficient, and intelligent financial ecosystems.

Tokenization in Natural Language Processing (NLP)

Definition
Tokenization in NLP is the process of breaking down text into smaller units, called tokens, which can be words, subwords, characters, or symbols. It is a crucial preprocessing step that prepares language data for further analysis or model training.

Key Components
Rule-based or learned token splitting
Whitespace and punctuation handling
Subword segmentation for rare words
Language-specific considerations

Benefits
Simplifies text for processing and modeling
Enables analysis at various levels (word, sentence, character)
Reduces vocabulary size using subword units
Improves model accuracy and interpretability

Examples
Splitting "I love AI!" into ["I", "love", "AI", "!"]
Using Byte Pair Encoding (BPE) in neural language models
Tokenizing multilingual text for machine translation

Applications
Text classification
Named entity recognition
Machine translation
Speech-to-text systems

Industries
Healthcare documentation

Legal analytics
Customer support automation
Publishing and content platforms

Summary
Tokenization in NLP transforms raw text into structured input for AI systems. As the foundation of text understanding, it enables meaningful linguistic analysis and intelligent interaction across language-based applications.

Topology Optimization

Definition
Topology optimization in AI is a computational method used to optimize the layout or structure of a material or system within a defined space for maximum performance under constraints. AI algorithms are increasingly used to enhance or automate the optimization process in design and engineering tasks.

Key Components
Design space and boundary conditions
Objective function and constraints
Material distribution models
Optimization algorithms (e.g., genetic algorithms, neural networks)

Benefits
Creates highly efficient and lightweight designs
Reduces material waste and cost
Supports automated and generative design in engineering
Adapts to complex performance requirements

Examples
Designing AI-optimized lightweight drone frames
Generating efficient structural supports for 3D printing
Optimizing heat flow in cooling systems using AI

Applications
Aerospace engineering
Mechanical design
Automotive part development
Biomedical implants

Industries
Manufacturing
Construction
Automotive
Healthcare

Summary
Topology optimization enhanced by AI allows for the creation of structures that are stronger, lighter, and more efficient. It plays a transformative role in design innovation across high-performance engineering disciplines.

TPU (Tensor Processing Unit)

Definition
A Tensor Processing Unit (TPU) is a type of specialized hardware accelerator developed by Google to

efficiently perform tensor-based mathematical operations, particularly those used in deep learning and neural network training. Unlike traditional CPUs or GPUs, TPUs are custom-built to process large volumes of matrix and tensor computations rapidly, making them ideal for AI workloads.

Key Components
TPUs are composed of high-throughput matrix multiplication units, memory buffers, and interconnects designed specifically for parallelized AI computation. They include systolic arrays for efficient data flow, high-speed on-chip memory to reduce latency, and support for TensorFlow-based workloads. TPUs are also integrated with cloud-based infrastructure to allow scalable AI deployment.

Benefits
TPUs offer significantly faster computation for machine learning tasks compared to CPUs and even some GPUs. They consume less power for equivalent workloads, enable training of larger models in shorter timeframes, and are optimized for Google's TensorFlow framework, improving compatibility and performance for developers. Their scalability makes them suitable for both research and enterprise AI needs.

Examples
TPUs have been used to train complex natural language processing models like BERT and large-scale image classifiers with reduced training time. Google Translate and Google Photos use models trained on TPUs to deliver real-time translation and image recognition services. Researchers also use TPUs in academic environments to develop advanced deep learning architectures more efficiently.

Applications
TPUs are widely applied in fields such as computer vision, speech recognition, language modeling, recommendation systems, and biomedical research. In the cloud, TPUs power scalable AI services offered through platforms like Google Cloud AI. In autonomous systems, they support real-time decision-making by handling large volumes of sensory data.

Summary
TPUs are purpose-built hardware accelerators that transform how AI models are trained and deployed. By focusing on speed, efficiency, and scalability, they enable faster innovation in deep learning and artificial intelligence. While their specialized nature may limit broader use, TPUs remain essential to high-performance AI computing across research, industry, and consumer applications.

Training Data

Definition
Training data refers to the labeled or unlabeled dataset used to teach AI models how to perform a task or recognize patterns. It is the foundation of any machine learning process and directly affects the accuracy, fairness, and reliability of the resulting model.

Key Components
Features (input variables)
Labels or outcomes for supervised learning
Preprocessing and normalization
Data formats (images, text, audio, tabular)

Benefits
Enables models to learn from real-world patterns
Supports the development of accurate and generalizable systems
Improves model performance when diverse and high-quality
Crucial for fine-tuning and domain adaptation

Examples
Annotated medical images for disease detection
Historical sales data for demand forecasting
Transcribed speech for voice recognition models

Applications
Image and voice recognition
Autonomous navigation
Natural language processing
Predictive analytics

Industries
Healthcare
Finance
Retail
Telecommunications

Summary
Training data is the lifeblood of AI development. It provides the examples that models learn from, shaping their ability to perform intelligently, adapt to new situations, and deliver meaningful results.

Transformer Architecture

Definition
The Transformer architecture is a deep learning model introduced for sequence-to-sequence tasks that relies entirely on self-attention mechanisms instead of recurrent structures. It has become the foundation of most state-of-the-art models in natural language processing and beyond.

Key Components
Multi-head self-attention
Positional encoding
Encoder-decoder structure
Feedforward neural networks and layer normalization

Benefits
Processes sequences in parallel rather than step-by-step
Handles long-range dependencies effectively
Highly scalable and flexible for various modalities
Outperforms traditional RNN and CNN models on many benchmarks

Examples
The original Transformer model used in machine translation
GPT and BERT models built on Transformer backbones
Vision Transformers for image classification tasks

Applications
Language modeling
Text summarization
Image recognition
Protein folding and scientific modeling

Industries
Technology
Healthcare

Publishing
Telecommunications

Summary
The Transformer architecture revolutionized deep learning by introducing a highly parallel, attention-based framework. It forms the basis of modern AI systems capable of understanding and generating text, images, and more with unprecedented accuracy.

Transformer Technology

Definition
Transformer technology in AI refers to the broader ecosystem of tools, models, and frameworks derived from the Transformer architecture. It includes advancements in attention mechanisms, model compression, transfer learning applications, and multimodal AI that expand the use of Transformers beyond language.

Key Components
Large-scale pre-trained Transformer models
Fine-tuning and distillation frameworks
Multimodal data processing capabilities
Support for GPUs, TPUs, and distributed computing

Benefits
Enables flexible cross-domain learning
Supports real-time applications with efficient variants
Unifies modeling for text, vision, and audio
Powers many of today's most advanced AI systems

Examples
Multilingual translation using multilingual Transformers
Code generation using Transformer-based models like Codex
Chatbots and conversational agents powered by GPT variants

Applications
Conversational AI
Document understanding
Code completion and synthesis
Content recommendation

Industries
Software development
Customer support
Education and training
Creative industries

Summary
Transformer technology represents a foundational shift in AI development. It fuels large-scale models capable of handling complex, multimodal tasks and continues to evolve as a universal solution for many artificial intelligence challenges.

Tunable Parameters in AI

Definition
Tunable parameters in AI are configuration settings that can be adjusted during model development to

improve performance. These parameters, also known as hyperparameters, are not learned from data but are set manually or through automated optimization techniques.

Key Components
Learning rate
Batch size
Number of layers or neurons
Regularization coefficients

Benefits
Allows customization of models to specific datasets or tasks
Improves model accuracy, efficiency, and stability
Enables exploration of trade-offs between speed and performance
Supports automated model selection and tuning frameworks

Examples
Adjusting the dropout rate to prevent overfitting in a neural network
Choosing the number of neighbors in a k-NN algorithm
Setting the kernel type in a support vector machine

Applications
Model training and validation
Hyperparameter optimization
Automated machine learning (AutoML)
Custom AI solutions

Industries
Finance
Manufacturing
Healthcare
Marketing and analytics

Summary
Tunable parameters are essential for optimizing AI model performance. By adjusting these settings, developers and researchers can adapt models to specific problems and achieve better outcomes across diverse applications.

Tuning in Machine Learning

Definition
Tuning in machine learning is the process of adjusting a model's hyperparameters to enhance its performance on a given task. It involves systematic testing of different parameter configurations and selecting the best combination based on evaluation metrics.

Key Components
Search strategies like grid search, random search, or Bayesian optimization
Cross-validation for performance assessment
Parameter range definition
Model performance metrics

Benefits
Improves generalization on unseen data
Reduces error and bias in predictions

Supports automation through tuning libraries and platforms
Enables fair model comparisons

Examples
Tuning tree depth and learning rate in a gradient boosting model
Using AutoML platforms to automatically optimize pipeline configurations
Selecting activation functions and optimizers in neural networks

Applications
Model development lifecycle
Feature selection and engineering
Real-time system calibration
AI experimentation and research

Industries
Cybersecurity
Retail and e-commerce
Smart infrastructure
Transportation

Summary
Tuning in machine learning is a vital step in refining models for optimal performance. By experimenting with parameter values, developers ensure that AI systems are both accurate and robust across a wide range of real-world conditions.

Turing Machine in AI

Definition
A Turing Machine in AI is a theoretical model of computation that defines the fundamental capabilities of an algorithmic system. It serves as the foundation for understanding what problems can be solved by machines and forms the basis for many concepts in computer science and artificial intelligence.

Key Components
An infinite tape divided into cells
A read/write head that moves left or right
A finite set of states and transition rules
An input/output symbol alphabet

Benefits
Clarifies the limits of computability and decidability
Provides a benchmark for AI model expressiveness
Supports the development of algorithmic reasoning and symbolic AI
Influences the design of logical agents and solvers

Examples
Designing a theoretical Turing Machine to sort a list
Simulating a logical AI agent using Turing-complete programming languages
Evaluating whether an AI system can solve a given class of problems

Applications
Formal methods and theoretical AI research
Computability and complexity analysis
Algorithm verification and design
Symbolic reasoning engines

Industries
Academia
Software verification
Quantum computing foundations
AI ethics and policy

Summary
The Turing Machine remains a cornerstone of AI theory. It defines what machines are fundamentally capable of computing and continues to guide the development of intelligent algorithms, models, and systems.

Type Inference in AI

Definition
Type inference in AI is the automatic determination of data types in programming languages or models without explicit declarations. In AI systems, type inference helps optimize code execution, enable model correctness, and enhance interoperability between different data structures and programming environments.

Key Components
Static analysis of variables
Typing rules and constraints
Abstract syntax trees (AST)
Compiler or interpreter-level implementation

Benefits
Reduces code complexity and increases developer efficiency
Minimizes runtime errors by catching type mismatches early
Improves performance through automatic optimization
Enables intelligent autocompletion and code analysis

Examples
Inferring types of variables in Python using type hinting tools
Determining tensor shapes and types in AI frameworks like PyTorch
Automatically resolving types in symbolic reasoning engines

Applications
AI software development
Compiler and interpreter design
Knowledge representation
Automated code generation

Industries
Software engineering
AI model development
Cloud computing
Programming education

Summary
Type inference in AI enhances the automation and reliability of code and model development. By reducing manual type declarations, it enables more intelligent systems that can adapt and optimize software workflows efficiently.

Type Theory in AI

Definition
Type theory in AI is a formal framework that defines how types are used to classify and reason about data, functions, and logical statements. It serves as the foundation for many programming languages and logical systems, supporting formal verification, functional programming, and symbolic reasoning in AI.

Key Components
Types and type constructors
Type judgments and type checking
Dependent types and polymorphism
Formal proof systems and logical consistency

Benefits
Provides mathematical rigor to AI model design
Supports safe and provable software development
Enables symbolic and rule-based AI reasoning
Improves error detection and debugging through strong typing

Examples
Using type systems in functional programming for AI algorithms
Formal verification of safety-critical AI systems in autonomous vehicles
Modeling logical reasoning tasks with type-checked knowledge bases

Applications
Formal methods in AI
Programming language design
Symbolic logic and reasoning systems
Model safety verification

Industries
Aerospace and defense
Automated theorem proving
Financial technology
Critical systems engineering

Summary
Type theory in AI provides a powerful and precise foundation for reasoning, programming, and verification. It plays a critical role in ensuring logical consistency, reliability, and correctness in intelligent systems.

Typed Tensor in Machine Learning

Definition
A typed tensor in machine learning is a multi-dimensional array that not only contains data but also includes metadata describing the type, such as data type, shape, and semantic context. Typed tensors enable models to manage structured, type-safe inputs and outputs with improved clarity and control.

Key Components
Data type specification (e.g., float32, int64)
Shape definition (e.g., [batch_size, height, width, channels])
Semantic labels or field names
Tensor manipulation and broadcasting rules

Benefits
Improves model robustness through type safety
Enhances data consistency and structure verification
Enables better interoperability across ML frameworks
Supports advanced optimization and memory alignment

Examples
Defining a tensor for image input as float32 with shape [32, 224, 224, 3]
Specifying token tensors in NLP with embedded sequence type annotations
Mapping typed tensors in PyTorch or TensorFlow pipelines

Applications
Computer vision
Natural language processing
Scientific computing
Reinforcement learning

Industries
Autonomous systems
Healthcare AI
Robotics
Finance and analytics

Summary
Typed tensors bring structure, precision, and safety to data handling in machine learning workflows. They support scalable, type-aware modeling that enhances reliability across diverse AI tasks and domains.

Type-1 and Type-2 Fuzzy Logic

Definition
Type-1 and Type-2 Fuzzy Logic are extensions of traditional logic systems that handle uncertainty and vagueness. Type-1 fuzzy logic uses precise membership functions, while Type-2 allows for uncertainty in the membership values themselves, providing a richer framework for decision-making under imprecision.

Key Components
Fuzzy sets and membership functions
Inference engines and rule bases
Type-1: single-valued degrees of truth
Type-2: fuzzy membership functions with uncertainty bounds

Benefits
Supports reasoning in uncertain or imprecise environments
Provides more flexible and intuitive decision models
Type-2 improves robustness to noisy or ambiguous data
Widely applicable to real-world human-centric systems

Examples
Type-1 fuzzy controller in a home heating system
Type-2 fuzzy system for speech recognition under noisy input
Fuzzy logic for AI-based emotional state classification

Applications
Control systems
Expert systems and decision support
Pattern recognition
Human-computer interaction

Industries
Automotive
Consumer electronics
Healthcare devices
Industrial automation

Summary
Type-1 and Type-2 Fuzzy Logic enhance AI's ability to reason like humans in uncertain conditions. These logic systems offer flexible, interpretable solutions for control, decision-making, and pattern recognition across diverse domains.

Typed Lambda Calculus

Definition
Typed lambda calculus is a formal system in logic and computation that extends lambda calculus by assigning types to variables and functions. In AI, it supports structured reasoning, functional programming, and the formal analysis of algorithms and symbolic processes.

Key Components
Variables, abstractions, and applications
Type assignment rules
Function types and polymorphism
Reduction and evaluation semantics

Benefits
Supports safe and expressive function modeling
Enables formal verification and logical inference
Improves program modularity and correctness
Forms the basis for many AI reasoning frameworks

Examples
Modeling symbolic reasoning steps in logic-based AI
Implementing functional AI algorithms in Haskell or OCaml
Designing knowledge representation frameworks using typed terms

Applications
Symbolic AI
Natural language semantics
Formal verification
Functional programming in AI systems

Industries
Software verification
AI research
Autonomous systems
Programming language design

Summary
Typed lambda calculus provides a rigorous framework for symbolic and functional AI. It underpins logical inference, formal modeling, and safe program design, making it essential for advanced AI research and applications rooted in theoretical computer science.

Letter u

Ubiquitous Computing in AI

Definition:
Ubiquitous computing in AI refers to the integration of artificial intelligence into everyday environments, enabling seamless interactions between users and smart systems without requiring direct human intervention. It allows AI to function invisibly in the background, processing real-time data to enhance convenience and efficiency.

Key Components:
Includes embedded AI systems, sensor networks, real-time data processing, cloud computing, edge computing, and adaptive learning algorithms.

Benefits:
Enhances automation in daily activities, reduces the need for direct human-computer interaction, improves efficiency in smart environments, and allows AI to function seamlessly across devices.

Examples:
Smart homes adjusting temperature based on user preferences, AI-powered personal assistants managing schedules, and autonomous vehicles interacting with urban infrastructure.

Applications:
Used in smart cities, IoT-based AI systems, industrial automation, intelligent homes, and wearable AI-powered devices.

Summary:
Ubiquitous computing in AI transforms daily life by embedding intelligence into various environments, making interactions more intuitive, automated, and adaptive.

Ubiquitous Learning with AI

Definition:
Ubiquitous learning with AI refers to AI-driven educational experiences that are seamlessly integrated into daily activities, allowing learners to access personalized and adaptive learning materials anytime and anywhere.

Key Components:
Includes AI-powered tutoring systems, real-time content adaptation, natural language processing for interactive learning, and cloud-based educational platforms.

Benefits:
Supports continuous learning across multiple contexts, personalizes educational experiences, enhances student engagement, and adapts content to individual learning speeds.

Examples:
AI-driven language learning apps, personalized tutoring chatbots, and AI-powered educational assistants offering real-time feedback.

Applications:
Used in online education, smart classrooms, corporate training, mobile learning apps, and lifelong learning initiatives.

Summary:
Ubiquitous learning with AI creates an adaptive, personalized learning environment that supports education beyond traditional classrooms, making knowledge accessible anytime and anywhere.

Ubiquitous Robotics in AI

Definition:
Ubiquitous robotics in AI refers to intelligent robotic systems that operate autonomously in various environments, seamlessly integrating with human activities to enhance automation, assistive functions, and task execution.

Key Components:
Combines autonomous navigation, machine learning-based decision-making, real-time sensor fusion, adaptive control systems, and cloud-based AI connectivity.

Benefits:
Enhances automation in multiple domains, improves efficiency in repetitive tasks, reduces human workload, and enables AI-powered robotic interactions in everyday life.

Examples:
AI-powered service robots in retail, robotic assistants in hospitals, and autonomous drones delivering packages.

Applications:
Used in smart homes, healthcare robotics, industrial automation, security patrol robots, and AI-powered logistics.

Challenges:
Complexity in ensuring reliable human-robot interaction, high deployment and maintenance costs, potential ethical concerns, and security risks in networked robotic systems.

Summary:
Ubiquitous robotics in AI enhances automation and efficiency by integrating intelligent robots into everyday life, improving productivity across industries.

Ubiquitous Security in AI

Definition:
Ubiquitous security in AI involves AI-driven security solutions that continuously protect data, networks, and digital infrastructure from cyber threats in real time, ensuring seamless and adaptive security measures.

Key Components:
Uses AI-powered anomaly detection, threat intelligence, biometric authentication, encrypted communications, and continuous security monitoring.

Benefits:
Enhances cybersecurity efficiency, enables proactive threat detection, adapts security measures dynamically, and provides real-time protection against cyberattacks.

Examples:
AI-powered fraud detection in banking, real-time network security monitoring, and facial recognition-based access control.

Applications:
Used in cybersecurity frameworks, cloud security, digital identity verification, smart surveillance systems, and enterprise security management.

Summary:
Ubiquitous security in AI strengthens cybersecurity by providing continuous, adaptive protection against evolving digital threats, ensuring safer AI-powered systems.

UData (User Data Analytics in AI)

Definition:
UData refers to AI-powered user data analytics techniques that analyze vast amounts of behavioral and interaction data to provide insights into user preferences, trends, and predictive behaviors.

Key Components:
Includes big data processing, machine learning-based pattern recognition, real-time analytics dashboards, and AI-driven customer behavior modeling.

Benefits:
Improves user experience personalization, enhances decision-making, provides valuable market insights, and optimizes business strategies.

Examples:
AI-driven recommendation engines, customer sentiment analysis in social media, and predictive analytics in e-commerce.

Applications:
Used in digital marketing, customer relationship management, user experience optimization, fraud detection, and personalized content delivery.

Challenges:
Data privacy concerns, risk of algorithmic bias, potential misuse of user data, and challenges in managing large-scale real-time analytics.

Summary:
UData enhances AI-driven decision-making by analyzing user interactions, enabling personalized experiences and predictive analytics for businesses.

UHD (Ultra-High-Definition) Video Processing with AI

Definition:
UHD video processing with AI refers to artificial intelligence techniques used to enhance, analyze, and optimize ultra-high-definition (4K, 8K) video content in real time, improving quality, compression, and visual enhancements.

Key Components:
Uses AI-based video upscaling, frame interpolation, real-time object detection, deep learning-enhanced compression, and noise reduction algorithms.

Benefits:
Enhances video quality, reduces storage requirements through AI-based compression, enables real-time content analysis, and improves video streaming efficiency.

Examples:
AI-powered video upscaling in smart TVs, automatic video summarization for streaming platforms, and AI-based real-time sports analytics.

Applications:
Used in video editing, entertainment streaming, security surveillance, medical imaging, and AI-powered broadcasting.

Summary:
UHD video processing with AI enhances video quality, analysis, and optimization, enabling advanced applications in entertainment, security, and medical imaging.

UHF RFID (Ultra-High Frequency Radio Frequency Identification) in AI

Definition:
UHF RFID in AI refers to the integration of AI with ultra-high-frequency radio frequency identification systems to enable intelligent tracking, authentication, and asset management across industries.

Key Components:
Includes RFID tags, AI-powered data analytics, machine learning-based signal processing, and real-time location tracking algorithms.

Benefits:
Improves tracking accuracy, enhances supply chain efficiency, reduces inventory losses, and automates authentication processes.

Examples:
AI-enhanced inventory management in warehouses, smart retail checkout systems, and automated airport baggage tracking.

Applications:
Used in logistics, healthcare asset management, smart retail, security authentication, and transportation monitoring.

Summary:
UHF RFID in AI enhances real-time tracking and authentication, optimizing supply chains and asset management with intelligent automation.

UI Accessibility Improvement through AI

Definition:
UI accessibility improvement through AI involves the use of artificial intelligence to enhance digital interfaces, making them more inclusive and accessible for individuals with disabilities.

Key Components:
Uses AI-driven speech recognition, text-to-speech conversion, adaptive UI personalization, real-time captioning, and image recognition for screen readers.

Benefits:
Improves digital accessibility for visually and hearing-impaired users, enhances usability across diverse user demographics, and automates UI adjustments for better inclusivity.

Examples:
AI-powered screen readers, real-time captioning for video conferencing, and adaptive UI elements that respond to user preferences.

Applications:
Used in web accessibility, assistive technologies, mobile app development, AI-driven voice assistants, and enterprise software accessibility enhancements.

Summary:
AI-driven UI accessibility improves digital inclusivity, enabling more equitable access to information and technology for all users.

UI Automation with AI (User Interface Automation)

Definition:
UI automation with AI refers to the use of artificial intelligence to automate interactions with graphical user interfaces, allowing software systems to perform repetitive UI tasks without human intervention. AI enhances automation by incorporating machine learning, natural language processing, and computer vision for intelligent UI handling.

Key Components:
Includes AI-powered robotic process automation (RPA), machine vision for UI element recognition, natural language processing for automated text input, and reinforcement learning for optimizing UI interactions.

Benefits:
Reduces human workload, speeds up software testing and deployment, minimizes errors in repetitive tasks, and improves efficiency in workflow automation.

Examples:
Automating data entry in enterprise applications, AI-powered software testing for UI consistency, and chatbots performing automated customer interactions.

Applications:
Used in software testing, enterprise workflow automation, customer support chatbots, and AI-driven digital assistants.

Summary:
UI automation with AI streamlines software interactions by enabling intelligent automation, improving productivity, and reducing manual intervention in repetitive tasks.

UI Design Enhancement through AI

Definition:
UI design enhancement through AI involves the application of artificial intelligence to optimize, generate, and refine user interfaces based on usability principles, user behavior patterns, and aesthetic considerations.

Key Components:
Uses AI-driven layout optimization, machine learning-based design pattern recognition, automated color scheme generation, and real-time UI adjustments based on user interactions.

Benefits:
Accelerates the design process, enhances UI consistency, provides personalized user experiences, and reduces the need for manual design revisions.

Examples:
AI-powered design tools suggesting optimal UI layouts, automatic theme generation based on user preferences, and adaptive UI components that adjust dynamically.

Applications:
Used in web design, mobile app UI development, digital marketing, and enterprise software interfaces.

Summary:
UI design enhancement through AI improves the efficiency and adaptability of digital interfaces, enabling user-friendly and visually appealing designs optimized through AI-driven insights.

UI Personalization using AI

Definition:
UI personalization using AI leverages machine learning algorithms and behavioral analysis to adapt user interfaces dynamically, tailoring experiences based on individual user preferences, habits, and real-time interactions.

Key Components:
Utilizes predictive analytics, user preference modeling, adaptive UI frameworks, and reinforcement learning for continuous personalization improvements.

Benefits:
Improves user engagement, enhances accessibility, increases customer satisfaction, and optimizes navigation and content delivery for individual users.

Examples:
AI-driven personalized dashboards, customized product recommendations in e-commerce, and adaptive learning interfaces in educational platforms.

Applications:
Used in e-commerce platforms, SaaS applications, personalized news feeds, and AI-powered mobile app interfaces.

Summary:
UI personalization using AI enables dynamic and user-centric digital experiences by tailoring interfaces to individual needs, improving engagement and usability.

UI/UX Behavior Analysis through AI

Definition:
UI/UX behavior analysis through AI involves the application of artificial intelligence techniques to track, analyze, and interpret user interactions with digital interfaces, providing insights to improve usability and engagement.

Key Components:
Uses AI-driven heatmaps, eye-tracking algorithms, behavioral clustering, sentiment analysis, and predictive analytics for UI/UX optimization.

Benefits:
Enhances user satisfaction, identifies pain points in UI design, optimizes navigation flow, and supports data-driven design improvements.

Examples:
AI analyzing user drop-off points in e-commerce checkouts, optimizing website layouts based on user navigation patterns, and identifying friction points in mobile applications.

Applications:
Used in A/B testing, UX research, customer journey optimization, and AI-powered analytics for digital platforms.

Summary:
UI/UX behavior analysis through AI enhances interface usability by analyzing user interactions, optimizing digital experiences, and improving engagement through data-driven insights.

UKF (Unscented Kalman Filter) in AI
Definition:
The Unscented Kalman Filter (UKF) is an advanced filtering algorithm used in AI to estimate and track nonlinear system states, providing improved accuracy over traditional Kalman filters by using a nonlinear transformation approach.

Key Components:
Uses sigma-point sampling for state estimation, nonlinear transformation techniques, recursive Bayesian filtering, and predictive modeling for system tracking.

Benefits:
Improves accuracy in tracking dynamic systems, enhances stability in uncertain environments, and effectively models nonlinear behaviors in AI applications.

Examples:
AI-powered drone navigation, robotic localization systems, and predictive analytics in financial modeling.

Applications:
Used in robotics, autonomous vehicle navigation, sensor fusion, predictive analytics, and AI-based control systems.

Summary:
UKF enhances AI-driven estimation and tracking systems, providing robust solutions for nonlinear system modeling in robotics, finance, and autonomous technologies.

UKI (User Knowledge Integration) in AI Systems

Definition:
User Knowledge Integration (UKI) in AI systems refers to methods for incorporating user-generated knowledge into AI models, enabling personalized, adaptive learning and improving AI decision-making based on user input.

Key Components:
Uses machine learning-driven personalization, knowledge graph augmentation, interactive learning algorithms, and semantic data processing.

Benefits:
Improves AI adaptability to user preferences, enhances decision-making accuracy, enables interactive AI learning, and supports context-aware AI interactions.

Examples:
AI-powered personal assistants adapting to user speech patterns, intelligent recommendation systems refining results based on past interactions, and knowledge-based AI learning from expert user input.

Applications:
Used in intelligent tutoring systems, AI-powered recommendation engines, knowledge management platforms, and adaptive enterprise software.

Summary:
UKI enhances AI adaptability by incorporating user knowledge, enabling more personalized, context-aware, and interactive AI-driven experiences.

UKM (Unsupervised Knowledge Mapping) in AI

Definition:
Unsupervised Knowledge Mapping (UKM) in AI refers to methods for autonomously structuring and organizing knowledge from unstructured data sources without labeled training data, enabling AI to discover relationships and concepts.

Key Components:
Uses clustering algorithms, topic modeling, knowledge graph construction, self-organizing maps, and natural language understanding techniques.

Benefits:
Facilitates automated knowledge discovery, reduces human annotation effort, enhances data-driven decision-making, and structures large-scale unstructured data.

Examples:
AI automatically categorizing academic research papers, knowledge graphs organizing enterprise knowledge bases, and AI clustering medical research articles based on similarity.

Applications:
Used in enterprise search, digital libraries, AI-driven research assistants, and large-scale data structuring.

Summary:
UKM enables AI to autonomously organize knowledge, improving accessibility, searchability, and data-driven insights from vast unstructured data sources.

UKP (Unsupervised Knowledge Processing) in AI

Definition:
Unsupervised Knowledge Processing (UKP) in AI involves automated processing, structuring, and extraction of knowledge from raw data without human supervision, enabling AI to learn patterns and insights autonomously.

Key Components:
Uses deep learning-based representation learning, knowledge extraction models, reinforcement learning, and statistical analysis for concept discovery.

Benefits:
Reduces reliance on manually labeled data, accelerates AI-driven discovery, enables continuous knowledge evolution, and supports real-time knowledge adaptation.

Examples:
AI extracting key themes from large text corpora, automatically summarizing legal documents, and AI systems autonomously learning industry trends from news data.

Applications:
Used in document summarization, AI-powered search engines, automated knowledge synthesis, and data-driven AI research.

Summary:
UKP advances AI-driven discovery by enabling systems to autonomously process, structure, and extract meaningful insights from raw, unstructured data sources.

UKR (Unsupervised Keyword Ranking) in AI

Definition:
Unsupervised Keyword Ranking (UKR) in AI refers to the process of identifying and prioritizing important keywords from text data without human supervision. It relies on statistical and machine learning techniques to determine keyword significance based on frequency, contextual relationships, and semantic importance.

Key Components:
Uses term frequency-inverse document frequency (TF-IDF), word embeddings, graph-based ranking algorithms, and unsupervised clustering techniques to extract meaningful keywords.

Benefits:
Enhances automated text summarization, improves search engine indexing, provides better topic modeling, and reduces the need for manually annotated data.

Examples:
AI extracting the most relevant keywords from scientific papers, summarizing trending topics from news articles, and improving keyword ranking in SEO optimization.

Applications:
Used in search engine optimization, automated document indexing, AI-driven content recommendation, and sentiment analysis.

Summary:
UKR enables AI-driven keyword extraction, improving content analysis and search relevance without requiring human supervision.

Ultra-High-Speed Data Transmission in AI

Definition:
Ultra-High-Speed Data Transmission in AI refers to the integration of artificial intelligence with advanced data transmission technologies to enable rapid and efficient transfer of large-scale datasets for real-time AI applications.

Key Components:
Includes AI-driven network optimization, optical fiber communication, 5G/6G wireless transmission, edge computing, and adaptive data compression.

Benefits:
Reduces latency in AI systems, improves real-time data analytics, enhances cloud-based AI processing, and enables seamless connectivity for AI-driven applications.

Examples:
AI-optimized data streaming in autonomous vehicles, real-time machine learning model updates in IoT networks, and AI-assisted video analytics in surveillance systems.

Applications:
Used in telecommunications, cloud computing, AI-driven industrial automation, and smart city infrastructure.

Summary:
Ultra-high-speed data transmission in AI enhances real-time processing and connectivity, supporting AI applications that require fast and efficient data exchange.

Ultra-High-Resolution Image Analysis in AI

Definition:
Ultra-High-Resolution Image Analysis in AI involves using artificial intelligence techniques to process, enhance, and interpret ultra-high-definition (UHD) images for applications requiring fine-grained visual analysis.

Key Components:
Includes deep learning-based image processing, super-resolution algorithms, convolutional neural networks (CNNs), and AI-driven denoising techniques.

Benefits:
Enhances image clarity, enables detailed object detection, improves medical imaging diagnostics, and supports high-accuracy visual recognition.

Examples:
AI-powered enhancement of satellite imagery, high-resolution medical scan analysis, and AI-driven facial recognition in UHD surveillance footage.

Applications:
Used in medical diagnostics, satellite imaging, digital forensics, quality inspection in manufacturing, and AI-powered image restoration.

Summary:
Ultra-high-resolution image analysis in AI enables precise image interpretation, improving applications in medical, industrial, and scientific domains.

UMAP (Uniform Manifold Approximation and Projection) in AI

Definition:
Uniform Manifold Approximation and Projection (UMAP) is a dimensionality reduction technique used in AI to visualize and interpret high-dimensional data by preserving its structure while reducing computational complexity.

Key Components:
Uses graph-based learning techniques, non-linear dimensionality reduction, nearest-neighbor algorithms, and stochastic optimization.

Benefits:
Improves visualization of complex datasets, enhances clustering in AI models, accelerates data processing in machine learning pipelines, and reduces memory usage.

Examples:
AI-powered feature extraction in genomic data analysis, visualization of deep learning model embeddings, and clustering customer segments in marketing analytics.

Applications:
Used in machine learning model optimization, image recognition, natural language processing, and big data analytics.

Summary:
UMAP is a powerful tool for AI-driven dimensionality reduction, enhancing data visualization and improving machine learning efficiency.

UML (Unified Modeling Language) in AI

Definition:
Unified Modeling Language (UML) in AI refers to the use of standardized graphical representations to design, structure, and document AI-based systems, facilitating better understanding and implementation of machine learning workflows.

Key Components:
Includes class diagrams, sequence diagrams, activity diagrams, and state machine diagrams tailored for AI-driven architectures.

Benefits:
Enhances AI system documentation, improves collaboration between developers, ensures modular and scalable AI solutions, and streamlines debugging and optimization.

Examples:
Designing AI-based recommendation systems using UML flowcharts, structuring deep learning model components with class diagrams, and modeling AI-driven business process automation workflows.

Applications:
Used in AI software engineering, system architecture design, enterprise AI implementation, and AI-driven business process modeling.

Summary:
UML provides a standardized approach to designing and documenting AI systems, improving clarity, modularity, and collaboration in AI development.

Unbiased Data Processing in AI (UDPA)

Definition:
Unbiased Data Processing in AI (UDPA) refers to techniques and methodologies used to minimize algorithmic bias and ensure fair, objective decision-making in AI models by addressing data imbalance and fairness issues.

Key Components:
Includes bias detection algorithms, fairness-aware data preprocessing, adversarial debiasing techniques, and transparency-driven data governance.

Benefits:
Reduces discriminatory biases in AI systems, enhances ethical AI decision-making, improves fairness in automated predictions, and ensures compliance with regulatory frameworks.

Examples:
AI models removing gender bias in hiring predictions, machine learning algorithms debiasing facial recognition systems, and AI-powered credit scoring ensuring fairness in financial applications.

Applications:
Used in finance, healthcare, hiring automation, social media moderation, and AI-driven legal decision-making.

Summary:
Unbiased data processing in AI promotes fairness and transparency, reducing biases and ensuring ethical decision-making in machine learning models.

Uncertainty Analysis in AI
Definition:
Uncertainty analysis in AI involves quantifying and assessing uncertainty in machine learning predictions, ensuring models account for incomplete, noisy, or ambiguous data.

Key Components:
Uses probabilistic modeling, Bayesian inference, uncertainty quantification metrics, and ensemble learning techniques to assess predictive confidence.

Benefits:
Improves model reliability, enhances interpretability of AI predictions, reduces risk in decision-making, and supports AI-driven risk assessments.

Examples:
AI-powered medical diagnostics assessing uncertainty in disease predictions, financial forecasting models incorporating confidence intervals, and autonomous vehicles estimating uncertainty in object detection.

Applications:
Used in healthcare AI, financial analytics, autonomous systems, risk management, and scientific research.

Summary:
Uncertainty analysis in AI enhances model robustness and reliability, improving decision-making in applications where predictive confidence is critical.

Uncertainty Forecasting in AI
Definition:
Uncertainty forecasting in AI refers to predictive modeling techniques that estimate the likelihood of uncertain events, incorporating probabilistic reasoning to make more informed and risk-aware predictions.

Key Components:
Uses Bayesian neural networks, probabilistic forecasting models, Monte Carlo simulations, and confidence interval estimation methods.

Benefits:
Improves decision-making under uncertainty, enables proactive risk mitigation, supports adaptive AI models, and enhances scenario planning.

Examples:
Weather prediction AI estimating uncertainty in climate models, financial AI predicting stock market volatility, and supply chain forecasting accounting for demand fluctuations.

Applications:
Used in weather forecasting, financial market analysis, predictive maintenance, and disaster risk assessment.

Summary:
Uncertainty forecasting in AI improves predictive accuracy by quantifying risk, enabling AI systems to make more informed and adaptive decisions.

Uncertainty Management in AI

Definition:
Uncertainty management in AI involves developing strategies and algorithms to handle, reduce, and interpret uncertainty in AI models, ensuring stable and reliable system performance.

Key Components:
Uses robust optimization techniques, uncertainty-aware decision frameworks, data augmentation methods, and confidence-based learning strategies.

Benefits:
Enhances AI model resilience, improves trustworthiness in automated decision-making, supports fault tolerance in AI systems, and ensures reliable AI deployments.

Examples:
AI-powered autonomous vehicles navigating uncertain road conditions, healthcare AI managing uncertainty in patient diagnostics, and AI-driven cybersecurity adapting to unknown threats.

Applications:
Used in robotics, cybersecurity, healthcare AI, autonomous driving, and AI-driven risk management.

Summary:
Uncertainty management in AI strengthens AI system reliability, ensuring robust decision-making in unpredictable or ambiguous environments.

Uncertainty Quantification in AI

Definition:
Uncertainty quantification in AI refers to the process of assessing and measuring the level of uncertainty in AI predictions, ensuring that models account for incomplete, noisy, or ambiguous data in decision-making. It helps improve model robustness and interpretability.

Key Components:
Utilizes probabilistic models, Bayesian inference, Monte Carlo dropout, ensemble learning, and confidence interval estimation techniques to quantify uncertainty in AI outputs.

Benefits:
Enhances trust in AI predictions, improves decision-making by considering confidence levels, reduces over-reliance on incorrect outputs, and enables risk-aware AI applications.

Examples:
AI-powered climate forecasting providing uncertainty estimates, medical diagnosis AI expressing confidence in disease prediction, and self-driving cars estimating uncertainty in object detection.

Applications:
Used in scientific research, financial risk analysis, autonomous systems, healthcare AI, and predictive modeling.

Summary:
Uncertainty quantification in AI strengthens predictive confidence and reliability, enabling AI models to make informed decisions while accounting for data ambiguity.

Unfairness Detection in AI
Definition:
Unfairness detection in AI involves identifying, measuring, and mitigating biases in machine learning models that lead to discriminatory or unethical decision-making. It ensures AI systems provide fair and equitable outcomes.

Key Components:
Utilizes fairness metrics, bias detection algorithms, adversarial debiasing methods, explainable AI models, and ethical AI governance frameworks.

Benefits:
Reduces algorithmic discrimination, ensures compliance with legal and ethical standards, improves fairness in automated decision-making, and enhances AI accountability.

Examples:
AI identifying gender bias in hiring algorithms, fairness-aware credit scoring systems reducing racial discrimination, and detecting bias in facial recognition software.

Applications:
Used in finance, hiring automation, legal AI, healthcare decision support, and AI-driven recommendation systems.

Challenges:
Defining fairness across diverse contexts, balancing bias reduction with model accuracy, addressing data representation issues, and implementing fairness in deep learning.

Summary:
Unfairness detection in AI improves ethical AI implementation by identifying biases and ensuring fair, accountable, and unbiased decision-making across various applications.

Unfolding Techniques in AI

Definition:
Unfolding techniques in AI refer to computational methods used to transform complex, high-dimensional problems into a structured sequence of steps, improving model interpretability and optimization. These techniques are widely used in deep learning and reinforcement learning.

Key Components:
Includes iterative optimization, gradient-based learning, recurrent network unfolding, and latent variable modeling to simplify complex AI processes.

Benefits:
Enhances model transparency, reduces computational complexity, improves convergence in optimization problems, and enables structured learning approaches.

Examples:
Unfolding deep neural networks for interpretability, sequence unfolding in natural language processing models, and unfolding tensor decomposition for AI-driven image compression.

Applications:
Used in deep learning optimization, NLP models, AI-based compression techniques, and computational neuroscience.

Summary:
Unfolding techniques in AI provide structured solutions for complex problems, improving optimization, interpretability, and efficiency in deep learning and reinforcement learning models.

Unified Frameworks in AI
Definition:
Unified frameworks in AI refer to comprehensive, standardized environments that integrate various AI methodologies, tools, and algorithms into a single, cohesive system for streamlined development and deployment.

Key Components:
Includes multi-modal AI integration, standardized APIs, cloud-based AI infrastructures, automated model management, and compatibility with deep learning libraries.

Benefits:
Reduces development complexity, ensures interoperability across AI models, accelerates deployment, and enhances scalability in AI systems.

Examples:
AI frameworks integrating NLP and computer vision, unified deep learning pipelines combining multiple neural networks, and cloud-based AI development environments.

Applications:
Used in enterprise AI solutions, multi-modal AI applications, automated machine learning (AutoML), and large-scale AI deployment.

Summary:
Unified frameworks in AI streamline development, deployment, and integration, enabling more efficient and scalable AI solutions across industries.

Unstructured Data Processing in AI

Definition:
Unstructured data processing in AI involves techniques for analyzing, extracting, and organizing insights from unstructured data formats such as text, images, videos, and audio. AI models use deep learning and natural language processing to interpret and structure such data.

Key Components:
Includes NLP for text analysis, CNNs for image recognition, speech-to-text models for audio processing, and clustering algorithms for pattern detection in unstructured datasets.

Benefits:
Unlocks valuable insights from unstructured sources, enhances decision-making, enables automation in data-driven tasks, and improves AI model adaptability.

Examples:
AI-driven document summarization, automated image tagging, video analytics for content moderation, and AI-powered voice assistants.

Applications:
Used in healthcare analytics, content recommendation, fraud detection, customer support automation, and AI-driven search engines.

Summary:
Unstructured data processing in AI enables intelligent analysis of diverse data formats, improving automation, decision-making, and predictive analytics in various fields.

Unsupervised Anomaly Detection

Definition:
Unsupervised anomaly detection refers to machine learning techniques that identify unusual patterns or outliers in datasets without labeled training data, making it ideal for detecting unknown or unexpected behaviors.

Key Components:
Uses clustering-based methods, autoencoders, statistical models, and density-based outlier detection algorithms to analyze deviations from normal patterns.

Benefits:
Detects novel threats, operates without human-labeled data, adapts to evolving anomalies, and enhances real-time monitoring capabilities.

Examples:
AI detecting fraud in financial transactions, cybersecurity systems identifying network intrusions, and predictive maintenance detecting equipment failures.

Applications:
Used in fraud detection, cybersecurity, predictive maintenance, healthcare anomaly detection, and industrial monitoring.

Summary:
Unsupervised anomaly detection enhances AI-driven security and monitoring by identifying unexpected patterns, making it essential for fraud detection, cybersecurity, and predictive maintenance.

Unsupervised Clustering Algorithms

Definition:
Unsupervised clustering algorithms group similar data points together without predefined labels, allowing AI models to discover hidden patterns and structures in datasets.

Key Components:
Includes K-means clustering, hierarchical clustering, DBSCAN, Gaussian mixture models, and self-organizing maps to identify natural groupings in data.

Benefits:
Reveals hidden data relationships, enhances pattern recognition, improves feature learning, and enables automatic categorization of large datasets.

Examples:
Customer segmentation in e-commerce, AI-powered document categorization, and unsupervised clustering of medical patient records.

Applications:
Used in market analysis, social media analytics, medical research, genetic clustering, and recommendation systems.

Summary:
Unsupervised clustering algorithms uncover hidden data structures, improving AI-driven segmentation, classification, and pattern analysis across industries.

Unsupervised Deep Learning (UDL)

Definition
Unsupervised Deep Learning (UDL) is a machine learning approach where deep neural networks learn patterns and features from unlabeled data without explicit supervision, enabling AI to discover representations autonomously.

Key Components
Uses deep autoencoders, self-supervised learning techniques, generative adversarial networks (GANs), and contrastive learning to extract meaningful features from data.

Benefits
Reduces reliance on labeled datasets, enables large-scale learning, captures complex data representations, and enhances model generalization.

Examples
AI-powered facial recognition without labeled images, deep learning-based text embeddings, and self-supervised learning in robotics.

Applications
Used in speech recognition, autonomous driving, AI-based anomaly detection, drug discovery, and AI-generated content creation.

Summary
Unsupervised deep learning enables AI to learn complex patterns autonomously, advancing AI applications in vision, language processing, and autonomous systems.

Unsupervised Feature Learning in AI

Definition
Unsupervised feature learning in AI refers to the process where machine learning models autonomously extract meaningful features from raw data without labeled supervision, improving representation learning.

Key Components
Includes principal component analysis (PCA), autoencoders, self-supervised learning, clustering-based feature extraction, and transfer learning for feature refinement.

Benefits
Reduces manual feature engineering, improves learning efficiency, enables discovery of hidden patterns, and enhances AI model generalization.

Examples
AI identifying key features in medical images, automated feature extraction in natural language processing, and deep learning models learning spatial patterns in satellite images.

Applications
Used in computer vision, bioinformatics, speech processing, recommendation systems, and self-supervised learning models.

Summary
Unsupervised feature learning enables AI models to extract meaningful data representations autonomously, improving model performance across diverse machine learning applications.

Unsupervised Learning in AI

Definition
Unsupervised learning in AI is a type of machine learning where models identify patterns, relationships, and structures in data without labeled outputs, allowing them to discover insights autonomously.

Key Components
Uses clustering algorithms, dimensionality reduction techniques, density estimation models, and generative models to find hidden patterns in data.

Benefits
Reduces reliance on labeled datasets, enables automatic feature discovery, improves data exploration, and supports anomaly detection.

Examples
Customer segmentation in marketing, topic modeling in text data, and AI-driven fraud detection in banking.

Applications
Used in market analysis, medical imaging, recommendation systems, cybersecurity, and AI-driven search engines.

Summary
Unsupervised learning allows AI to autonomously detect patterns in data, enhancing decision-making and discovery across multiple industries.

Unsupervised Meta-Learning (UM)

Definition
Unsupervised meta-learning refers to AI techniques that enable models to learn how to learn from unlabeled data, improving their ability to generalize and adapt to new tasks with minimal supervision.

Key Components
Uses self-supervised learning, contrastive learning, model-agnostic meta-learning (MAML), and transfer learning strategies to improve adaptability.

Benefits
Enables AI to generalize across diverse tasks, reduces dependency on labeled training data, enhances few-shot learning capabilities, and accelerates AI adaptation.

Examples
AI models improving reinforcement learning strategies, self-supervised speech recognition, and AI-generated content adaptation across domains.

Applications
Used in autonomous systems, AI-based tutoring, self-improving AI models, and robotics.

Summary
Unsupervised meta-learning allows AI to learn without predefined labels, improving its adaptability and ability to generalize across different tasks.

Unsupervised Transfer Learning

Definition
Unsupervised transfer learning refers to the process of adapting pre-trained AI models to new tasks or domains using unlabeled data, improving learning efficiency without requiring additional supervision.

Key Components
Uses domain adaptation techniques, self-supervised learning, deep feature extraction, and neural network fine-tuning for knowledge transfer.

Benefits
Speeds up AI training on new datasets, reduces reliance on labeled data, enhances model robustness, and improves generalization.

Examples
Adapting image recognition models to new datasets, AI language models transferring knowledge across languages, and financial risk prediction using diverse market data.

Applications
Used in speech recognition, NLP, image classification, anomaly detection, and cross-domain AI applications.

Summary
Unsupervised transfer learning allows AI to apply learned knowledge across domains, enabling faster adaptation and improved model efficiency.

Update Propagation in Neural Networks

Definition
Update propagation in neural networks refers to the process of adjusting model parameters through backpropagation, gradient updates, and weight adjustments during training to minimize errors.

Key Components
Uses gradient descent, weight adjustments, loss function optimization, and activation function tuning to refine neural network performance.

Benefits
Ensures model convergence, improves prediction accuracy, enables deep learning optimization, and adapts AI systems to complex patterns.

Examples
AI improving image classification through iterative learning, reinforcement learning in game-playing AI, and continuous AI model improvements in speech recognition.

Applications
Used in deep learning, natural language processing, self-improving AI models, and autonomous decision-making systems.

Summary
Update propagation in neural networks refines AI model performance by optimizing weights and minimizing errors through continuous learning.

Uplift Modeling in AI

Definition
Uplift modeling in AI is a predictive modeling technique used to estimate the incremental impact of a specific action or treatment on an individual compared to not taking that action.

Key Components
Uses causal inference models, control group comparisons, treatment response estimation, and feature selection techniques for impact prediction.

Benefits
Improves targeted marketing effectiveness, enhances personalized recommendations, reduces waste in customer engagement efforts, and increases return on investment.

Examples
AI predicting the effectiveness of marketing campaigns, personalized healthcare interventions, and AI-driven customer retention strategies.

Applications
Used in targeted advertising, personalized medicine, fraud detection, and customer relationship management.

Summary
Uplift modeling in AI enhances decision-making by predicting the impact of specific actions, improving personalization and targeted engagement strategies.

Upper Confidence Bound (UCB) in AI

Definition
Upper Confidence Bound (UCB) is a reinforcement learning algorithm used in multi-armed bandit problems to balance exploration and exploitation by prioritizing actions with high potential rewards and uncertainty.

Key Components
Uses reward estimation, confidence interval calculations, Thompson sampling, and dynamic action selection strategies.

Benefits
Optimizes decision-making in uncertain environments, improves reinforcement learning model efficiency, reduces regret in AI-based choices, and balances exploration-exploitation trade-offs.

Examples
AI selecting optimal web page layouts, dynamic ad placement optimization, and AI-driven medical treatment selection.

Applications
Used in online learning systems, adaptive content personalization, financial portfolio management, and autonomous decision-making.

Summary
Upper Confidence Bound in AI optimizes decision-making under uncertainty, enabling more effective learning in reinforcement learning applications.

Upsampling in AI

Definition
Upsampling in AI refers to the process of increasing the resolution or dimensionality of data, often used in deep learning models for image enhancement, data augmentation, and generative modeling.

Key Components
Includes interpolation methods, transposed convolution, generative adversarial networks (GANs), and super-resolution techniques to improve data quality.

Benefits
Enhances image resolution, generates high-quality synthetic data, improves AI model generalization, and aids in low-resolution feature extraction.

Examples
AI-powered image upscaling, deep learning-based video frame interpolation, and AI-generated high-resolution medical images.

Applications
Used in computer vision, speech processing, AI-driven content generation, and deep learning-based super-resolution models.

Summary
Upsampling in AI enhances data quality by increasing resolution, improving model performance in vision, speech, and data synthesis applications.

User Behavior Modeling in AI

Definition
User behavior modeling in AI involves analyzing and predicting user interactions, preferences, and decision-making patterns to enhance personalized experiences and optimize digital platforms.

Key Components
Uses behavioral analytics, machine learning-based pattern recognition, predictive modeling, and real-time interaction tracking.

Benefits
Improves user engagement, enables AI-driven personalization, enhances recommendation systems, and supports targeted marketing strategies.

Examples
AI predicting user clicks on e-commerce sites, behavioral analysis in fraud detection, and AI-driven content recommendations on streaming platforms.

Applications
Used in digital marketing, e-commerce optimization, personalized content delivery, and AI-driven user experience enhancements.

Summary
User behavior modeling in AI enhances personalization and engagement, allowing AI-driven systems to predict and optimize user interactions.

User-Driven AI Design (UDAD)

Definition
User-Driven AI Design (UDAD) refers to the development of AI systems based on direct user feedback, interactions, and evolving needs, ensuring adaptive and user-friendly AI experiences.

Key Components
Includes interactive AI learning, real-time user feedback integration, explainable AI models, and dynamic model adaptation to evolving user requirements.

Benefits
Improves AI usability, increases trust in AI recommendations, enhances adaptability, and ensures alignment with user expectations.

Examples
AI-powered voice assistants adapting to user preferences, AI-driven UI customization based on user interactions, and personalized AI-driven customer service.

Applications
Used in conversational AI, intelligent user interfaces, adaptive e-learning systems, and customer service automation.

Summary
User-driven AI design ensures AI models evolve based on real user needs, improving engagement, personalization, and overall AI effectiveness in interactive applications.

༺❀༻ LetterV ༺❀༻

Validation Set

Definition
A validation set is a designated portion of data separated from the training and test sets, used to monitor an AI model's performance during training. It helps assess how well the model generalizes and guides hyperparameter tuning without influencing final evaluation metrics.

Key Components
Representative Data Subset: Drawn from the same distribution as the training set.
Separation Protocols: Ensures no overlap with training or test data to maintain integrity.
Evaluation Metrics: Measures like accuracy, loss, or precision to monitor model behavior and prevent overfitting.

Benefits
Provides an unbiased evaluation checkpoint, supports hyperparameter optimization, and ensures early detection of model drift during training.

Examples
In a machine learning model classifying handwritten digits, 20% of the data may be reserved as a validation set to tune the learning rate and stop training before overfitting.

Applications
Used in machine learning pipelines, including computer vision, speech recognition, natural language processing, and forecasting systems.

Industries
Common in finance, autonomous vehicles, healthcare diagnostics, and e-commerce recommendation systems to ensure robust, real-world performance.

Conclusion
The validation set is a crucial checkpoint that bridges learning and deployment, helping fine-tune models while safeguarding generalization and reliability.

Value Function in Reinforcement Learning

Definition
The value function in reinforcement learning represents the expected cumulative reward an agent can

obtain from a particular state—or state-action pair—under a given policy. It allows the agent to quantify the long-term benefit of decisions over time.

Key Components
States and Actions: Reflect the environment and choices available to the agent.
Reward Function: Defines the numerical value of outcomes.
Discount Factor: Prioritizes immediate rewards over distant ones.
Policy: Guides the agent's decisions across episodes.

Benefits
Simplifies strategic planning by reducing future reward calculations into single numerical estimates, supports convergence to optimal behavior, and enhances policy evaluation.

Examples
In a video game, an AI agent might use the value function to evaluate which moves yield higher long-term survival chances or reward accumulation.

Applications
Foundational in AI for gaming, autonomous driving, robotics, dynamic pricing, and resource optimization.

Industries
Used in logistics, smart manufacturing, energy optimization, and financial trading platforms.

Conclusion
The value function empowers AI agents with foresight, enabling them to choose actions not just based on immediate rewards but on long-term benefits.

Vanishing Gradient Problem

Definition
The vanishing gradient problem is a challenge in training deep neural networks where the gradients used to update model weights become extremely small as they are backpropagated through multiple layers, causing early layers to learn very slowly or not at all.

Key Components
Gradient Descent: Optimization method used to update weights.
Activation Functions: Sigmoid and tanh functions are most susceptible.
Network Depth: More layers increase the likelihood of gradient shrinkage.
Backpropagation: Propagates gradients from output back to input layers.

Benefits
Understanding and mitigating vanishing gradients enables effective training of deeper models, unlocking more complex learning tasks.

Examples
A speech recognition neural network may experience stalled learning in early layers if gradients vanish before reaching them, leading to poor feature extraction from input audio.

Applications
Influences all deep learning fields, including time-series prediction, image analysis, and generative models.

Industries
Impacts sectors like technology, healthcare, robotics, and AI-powered content generation where deep models are common.

Conclusion
The vanishing gradient problem illustrates the technical complexity of deep learning and the need for thoughtful architecture design and modern activation strategies to ensure effective model training.

Variable Selection

Definition
Variable selection is the process of identifying the most relevant features in a dataset that contribute significantly to a machine learning model's predictions, improving model performance, interpretability, and computational efficiency.

Key Components
Feature Ranking: Measures relevance of variables based on correlation, importance scores, or impact on performance.
Selection Techniques: Includes methods like forward selection, backward elimination, LASSO, and recursive feature elimination.
Evaluation Metrics: Tracks model accuracy, stability, and variance across subsets.

Benefits
Reduces overfitting, enhances prediction speed, simplifies model interpretation, and improves generalization to new data.

Examples
In predicting home prices, including square footage and location while excluding irrelevant details like zip code length improves model focus and accuracy.

Applications
Used in regression analysis, classification problems, customer profiling, and bioinformatics research.

Industries
Adopted in economics, pharmaceuticals, market research, and real estate forecasting.

Conclusion
Variable selection helps models focus on what truly matters, filtering noise from useful signals to ensure clarity, speed, and accuracy in data-driven decision-making.

Variance in AI Models

Definition
Variance in AI models measures the sensitivity of predictions to fluctuations in the training data. High variance suggests the model is too responsive to small data changes, often resulting in overfitting, where performance on training data is high but generalization suffers.

Key Components
Model Complexity: More complex models tend to have higher variance.
Training Data Volume: Small datasets increase variance risk.
Bias-Variance Tradeoff: High variance usually accompanies low bias.
Noise Sensitivity: How the model reacts to randomness in input data.

Benefits
Understanding variance enables model tuning to find the right complexity and avoid misleading confidence in overfitted models.

Examples
A decision tree that memorizes training data details but fails on new data likely has high variance and requires pruning or regularization.

Applications
Affects fraud detection, predictive maintenance, sentiment analysis, and recommendation engines.

Industries
Used in retail, insurance, fintech, climate forecasting, and transportation modeling.

Conclusion
Variance reflects a model's flexibility—too much creates instability, too little leads to rigidity. Managing it is key to building dependable AI systems that perform well beyond training data.

Variational Autoencoder (VAE)

Definition
A Variational Autoencoder (VAE) is a type of generative model that encodes input data into a probabilistic latent space and then reconstructs it, blending neural networks with variational inference. This allows the model to generate new data samples while accounting for uncertainty in the representation.

Key Components
Encoder: Compresses the input into a latent distribution.
Latent Space: A probabilistic space where each point represents potential data characteristics.
Decoder: Reconstructs data from sampled latent vectors.
Loss Function: Balances reconstruction accuracy and distribution regularization using KL divergence.

Benefits
Generates realistic synthetic data, supports unsupervised learning, enables anomaly detection, and reveals hidden data structure in a compact and meaningful form.

Examples
A VAE trained on human face images can generate entirely new, realistic faces by sampling points from its learned latent space.

Applications
Used in image generation, anomaly detection, recommendation systems, and molecular design in drug discovery.

Industries
Healthcare, design, entertainment, cybersecurity, and synthetic data generation all leverage VAEs for advanced creative and analytical workflows.

Conclusion
Variational Autoencoders combine mathematical rigor with creative potential, enabling AI systems to understand and generate complex data in flexible and expressive ways.

Vector Embeddings

Definition
Vector embeddings are mathematical representations of data items—such as words, images, or nodes—mapped into high-dimensional numerical spaces. The distance or orientation between vectors reflects contextual or semantic similarity, enabling efficient and meaningful machine interpretation.

Key Components
Source Data: Raw inputs such as text, visuals, or graph structures.
Transformation Model: Algorithms like Word2Vec, FastText, BERT, or ResNet.
Embedding Vectors: Dense numerical representations used for downstream analysis.

Benefits
Enable similarity detection, clustering, classification, and ranking across domains while maintaining semantic and contextual integrity.

Examples
In an e-commerce recommendation engine, embeddings are used to relate user behavior to product descriptions, improving accuracy and personalization.

Applications
Crucial in natural language understanding, recommendation systems, fraud detection, and knowledge graph construction.

Industries
Social media, finance, search engines, academic research, and digital assistants rely on embeddings for intelligent, scalable solutions.

Conclusion
Vector embeddings are the connective tissue between unstructured input and structured insight, enabling machines to interpret, relate, and act on data with contextual awareness.

Vector Quantization

Definition
Vector quantization is a data compression technique that reduces complex, continuous data representations into a limited set of discrete values, mapping high-dimensional vectors to the nearest representative in a codebook.

Key Components
Input Vectors: High-dimensional data points to be compressed.
Clustering Mechanism: Often implemented with k-means or similar algorithms.
Codebook: A fixed set of prototype vectors representing the original data space.

Benefits
Reduces storage needs, simplifies computation, and accelerates inference in resource-limited environments.

Examples
In audio compression, speech signals are mapped to discrete quantized patterns, enabling low-bandwidth voice transmission while preserving intelligibility.

Applications
Used in signal processing, model compression, neural network optimization, and image storage.

Industries
Telecommunications, embedded AI, IoT, multimedia streaming, and sensor-driven applications benefit from vector quantization for real-time, lightweight performance.

Conclusion
Vector quantization strikes a pragmatic balance between precision and efficiency, supporting AI systems in delivering fast, low-resource computations in the real world.

Vector Space Model (VSM)

Definition
The Vector Space Model (VSM) is a computational framework that represents items—typically documents or queries—as vectors in a multi-dimensional space, where relationships are determined by spatial distance and orientation, enabling automated similarity and relevance comparisons.

Key Components
Data Representation: Text or entities converted into vectors via methods like TF-IDF or word embeddings.
Dimensional Space: A coordinate system where each axis represents a unique feature or term.
Similarity Metrics: Cosine similarity, Euclidean distance, or dot product used to compare vectors.

Benefits
Provides a structured approach to ranking, categorizing, and retrieving information based on contextual or content similarity.

Examples
Search engines use VSM to rank documents by how closely they match a user's query, using cosine similarity between query and document vectors.

Applications
Essential in information retrieval, search engine design, recommendation systems, and knowledge representation.

Industries
Digital marketing, e-discovery, academic research, media archiving, and enterprise content management systems depend on VSM to organize and access large textual datasets.

Conclusion
The Vector Space Model transforms abstract information into measurable structures, making unstructured data searchable, rankable, and actionable across numerous AI applications.

Vectorization in Machine Learning

Definition
Vectorization in machine learning is the process of converting data and operations into vector and matrix forms, enabling highly efficient computation by leveraging hardware acceleration and parallel processing capabilities.

Key Components
Input Transformation: Converts raw data into numerical arrays.
Matrix Operations: Uses linear algebra techniques for fast calculation.
Hardware Acceleration: Exploits GPUs or TPUs for high-speed execution.

Benefits
Improves computational efficiency, reduces training and inference time, and supports scalable learning with large datasets.

Examples
Sentiment analysis models process vectorized word tokens instead of iterating over each sentence, enabling faster evaluation and training.

Applications
Widely used in deep learning, natural language processing, real-time analytics, and big data processing pipelines.

Industries
Technology, financial modeling, autonomous systems, and gaming utilize vectorization to ensure responsiveness and scalability.

Conclusion
Vectorization is a foundational optimization in AI, transforming how machines handle complex data by making large-scale learning and inference practically achievable.

Venture Capital in AI

Definition
Venture capital in AI refers to the investment of funds into startups or companies developing artificial intelligence technologies, aiming to fuel innovation and growth in exchange for equity. It drives the advancement of AI solutions.

Key Components
It involves investors, AI startups, funding rounds (e.g., seed or Series A), and a focus on scalable, market-disrupting technologies.

Benefits
It accelerates AI development, provides resources for research and scaling, and fosters competition, leading to rapid technological breakthroughs.

Examples
A venture firm might invest in an AI startup creating autonomous driving software, providing millions to refine algorithms and expand operations.

Applications
It supports advancements in machine learning, robotics, and AI-driven analytics.

Industries
Technology, healthcare, and transportation benefit from venture-backed AI innovations.

Conclusion
Venture capital in AI is a high-stakes catalyst, propelling cutting-edge solutions while navigating the unpredictability of emerging markets.

Veracity in AI

Definition
Veracity in AI pertains to the accuracy, reliability, and truthfulness of data and outputs generated by artificial intelligence systems, addressing the uncertainty inherent in real-world data. It ensures trustworthiness.

Key Components
It includes data quality, model validation, error detection, and mechanisms to handle incomplete or noisy inputs.

Benefits
High veracity enhances decision-making confidence, reduces errors, and builds user trust in AI applications.

Examples
In a medical diagnosis AI, veracity ensures patient data is correctly interpreted, avoiding misdiagnoses due to flawed inputs.

Applications
It is critical in predictive modeling, fraud detection, and autonomous systems.

Industries
Healthcare, finance, and legal sectors prioritize veracity for credible AI outcomes.

Conclusion
Veracity in AI is the bedrock of dependable systems, demanding rigorous data and model scrutiny to deliver reliable results.

Verification in AI Systems

Definition
Verification in AI systems is the process of confirming that an AI model or system performs as intended, meeting specified requirements and functioning correctly under defined conditions. It ensures operational integrity.

Key Components
It involves testing protocols, performance benchmarks, formal proofs, and validation against expected outcomes.

Benefits
Verification minimizes errors, enhances safety, and ensures compliance with standards or regulations.

Examples
Verifying an AI chatbot might involve testing its responses to thousands of queries to ensure accuracy and appropriateness.

Applications
It applies to autonomous vehicles, AI security systems, and regulatory compliance tools.

Industries
Aerospace, defense, and automotive sectors use verification to certify AI reliability.

Conclusion
Verification in AI systems is a meticulous safeguard, ensuring functionality aligns with design in critical applications.

Virtual Agent

Definition
A virtual agent is an AI-powered entity designed to simulate human-like interactions, assisting users

with tasks or providing information through text or voice interfaces. It functions as a digital support assistant, delivering automated and responsive communication.

Key Components
It includes natural language processing (NLP), a knowledge base for storing information, dialogue management systems to control conversation flow, and integration tools for connecting with platforms such as websites or messaging apps.

Benefits
Virtual agents offer around-the-clock availability, reduce operational costs for businesses, increase service efficiency, and provide instant support to users across various digital channels.

Examples
A virtual agent on an e-commerce platform may assist users in tracking orders, answering product questions, or resolving issues without needing human intervention.

Applications
They are widely used in customer service, virtual tutoring, healthcare triage systems, onboarding platforms, and self-service help desks.

Industries
Retail, telecommunications, finance, education, and insurance leverage virtual agents to streamline support and improve user engagement.

Conclusion
Virtual agents transform digital interaction by delivering scalable, intelligent support. As their conversational abilities evolve, they increasingly approach the responsiveness and nuance of human assistants.

Virtual Reality (VR) in AI

Definition
Virtual Reality (VR) in AI refers to the integration of artificial intelligence with immersive 3D virtual environments, enhancing realism, interactivity, and adaptability in simulated settings. It enables intelligent interaction in digitally rendered spaces.

Key Components
It involves VR headsets or visual hardware, AI-driven behavioral models, real-time rendering systems, spatial tracking, and input interpretation algorithms.

Benefits
Combining AI with VR enables dynamic and personalized experiences, enhances the realism of simulations, accelerates learning in training environments, and creates adaptive virtual systems.

Examples
A VR surgical training program powered by AI can respond to a trainee's decisions in real time, adjusting the scenario to simulate various patient responses and outcomes.

Applications
It is applied in medical and military training, therapeutic treatment for phobias, immersive gaming, architectural visualization, and educational simulations.

Industries
Healthcare, education, gaming, aerospace, and therapy sectors use VR in AI to create immersive, intelligent, and high-impact experiences.

Conclusion
Virtual Reality in AI reimagines simulation and learning, fusing intelligent systems with immersive environments to offer realistic and responsive virtual experiences across industries.

Virtualization-Based Vulnerability Assessment

Definition
Virtualization-based vulnerability assessment involves testing software, systems, or networks within a virtualized environment to detect security flaws, while isolating potential threats from live operations. It supports safe and repeatable security evaluation.

Key Components
It includes virtual machines, sandbox environments, network simulators, scanning tools, threat models, and analytics platforms to identify and report vulnerabilities.

Benefits
This approach minimizes risk to production systems, offers cost-effective testing, accelerates remediation cycles, and allows multiple scenarios to be replicated and analyzed in isolation.

Examples
A security team may deploy a virtual copy of an enterprise server to simulate cyberattacks, detecting vulnerabilities in outdated software before rolling updates into production.

Applications
It is used for software testing, penetration testing, compliance audits, patch verification, and developing secure coding practices.

Industries
Cybersecurity, IT infrastructure, cloud service providers, and government organizations utilize virtualization-based assessments to proactively identify and mitigate threats.

Conclusion
Virtualization-based vulnerability assessment provides a strategic advantage by testing in isolated environments, enabling proactive and secure AI and IT system development.

Virtualization in AI

Definition
Virtualization in AI is the use of virtual infrastructure—such as virtual machines or containers—to deploy, scale, or test AI models and applications. It abstracts hardware, enabling flexible, cost-efficient operations across various environments.

Key Components
It includes virtual machines, containerization platforms (like Docker), cloud-based development environments, orchestration tools (e.g., Kubernetes), and AI workloads optimized for distributed training or inference.

Benefits
Virtualization allows for easy scaling of AI projects, accelerates development cycles, improves infrastructure utilization, facilitates collaboration, and supports experimentation without disrupting live systems.

Examples
An AI startup may train neural networks using virtual machines on a cloud platform, adjusting resources as needed to manage peak computational demands during model training.

Applications
It is essential in continuous integration and deployment (CI/CD), cloud-based AI development, federated learning experiments, and cross-platform AI testing.

Industries
Cloud computing, research institutions, SaaS platforms, and AI development firms use virtualization to manage complex projects and computational needs effectively.

Conclusion
Virtualization is a foundational enabler of scalable AI, allowing developers and enterprises to innovate without hardware constraints. It drives flexibility and efficiency in modern AI infrastructure.

Vision Transformer (ViT)

Definition
The Vision Transformer (ViT) is an AI model that applies transformer architecture, originally designed for natural language processing, to visual data. By treating images as sequences of patches, ViT performs image classification and analysis with powerful global context awareness.

Key Components
It features image patch tokenization, positional embeddings, multi-head self-attention mechanisms, and a classification head that outputs predictions based on processed features.

Benefits
ViT captures long-range dependencies within images more effectively than convolutional neural networks, achieving high accuracy on large datasets and enabling efficient transfer learning across tasks.

Examples
In medical imaging, a ViT model can evaluate chest X-rays by analyzing the full spatial distribution of patterns, identifying anomalies with greater contextual understanding.

Applications
It is used in image classification, object detection, facial recognition, and medical image analysis.

Industries
Healthcare, automotive technology, surveillance, and media utilize ViT for high-performance computer vision applications.

Conclusion
The Vision Transformer revolutionizes image analysis by replacing convolutions with attention, unlocking new levels of performance and interpretability in visual AI systems.

Visual Question Answering (VQA)

Definition
Visual Question Answering (VQA) is an interdisciplinary AI task that allows a system to answer natural language questions about visual content. It combines computer vision and natural language processing to enable multimodal reasoning.

Key Components
It integrates image feature extraction, language modeling, attention mechanisms, and a reasoning module to generate answers based on both visual and textual inputs.

Benefits
VQA systems support interactive and accessible technologies, automate image understanding, and provide context-aware visual interpretation.

Examples
Given a photo of a living room and the question "How many chairs are there?", a VQA system analyzes the image to respond accurately, such as "Two."

Applications
It is applied in educational tools, accessibility solutions for the visually impaired, digital assistants, and automated content moderation.

Industries
Education, assistive technology, content platforms, and robotics use VQA for smarter visual interaction.

Conclusion
VQA bridges vision and language, offering a pathway to human-like AI interaction that understands both what it sees and what it hears.

Vocabulary Acquisition in AI

Definition
Vocabulary acquisition in AI refers to the method by which AI systems expand their lexicon, understanding new words, phrases, and syntactic rules to improve language comprehension and generation. It mimics how humans grow linguistically.

Key Components
It involves large text corpora, contextual embeddings, pre-trained language models such as BERT or GPT, and fine-tuning processes that adapt vocabulary to specific domains.

Benefits
It increases fluency in conversation, enhances semantic understanding, supports domain-specific adaptation, and enables multilingual communication.

Examples
An AI assistant may learn regional slang or industry jargon through continuous interaction with users, refining its vocabulary over time for more accurate responses.

Applications
Used in machine translation, sentiment analysis, text summarization, virtual assistants, and chatbots.

Industries
Customer support, education, marketing, and global communications benefit from AI systems with advanced vocabulary capabilities.

Conclusion
Vocabulary acquisition empowers AI to speak and understand more like a human, ensuring that systems stay relevant, responsive, and contextually intelligent.

Vocal Emotion Recognition

Definition
Vocal emotion recognition is an AI technique used to identify human emotions by analyzing audio signals such as speech. It decodes affective cues like pitch, tone, speed, and volume to interpret emotional states.

Key Components
It uses audio preprocessing tools, feature extraction (e.g., MFCC, pitch, energy), machine learning models, and classification algorithms to detect emotions like happiness, anger, or sadness.

Benefits
This technology improves human-computer interaction, supports emotional awareness in automated systems, and provides tools for psychological monitoring and adaptive communication.

Examples
A virtual assistant may detect frustration in a customer's tone during a call and automatically transfer the issue to a human representative for resolution.

Applications
It is used in telehealth, customer service automation, virtual assistants, and interactive media experiences.

Industries
Healthcare, gaming, mental health, and telecom companies use emotion recognition to enhance personalized AI services.

Conclusion
Vocal emotion recognition adds a new dimension of empathy and responsiveness to AI, enabling systems to perceive not just what is said, but how it is said.

Vocal Signal Processing

Definition
Vocal signal processing involves the analysis and transformation of human speech signals for enhancement, recognition, or feature extraction. It serves as a fundamental layer in voice-driven AI technologies.

Key Components
It includes noise filtering, pitch tracking, formant analysis, feature extraction, signal segmentation, and time-frequency domain transformations.

Benefits
It enhances voice quality, isolates important speech data from background interference, and prepares audio input for high-performance AI applications.

Examples
An AI system might clean up a noisy phone call by filtering out background traffic sounds, ensuring accurate transcription or voice command interpretation.

Applications
It is used in telecommunication, voice-enabled devices, speech analytics, language learning tools, and biometric authentication.

Industries
Telecommunications, entertainment, education, and public safety leverage vocal signal processing for clearer communication.

Conclusion
Vocal signal processing converts raw voice into refined input, forming the technical bridge between human speech and AI understanding.

Voice Recognition

Definition
Voice recognition is an AI capability that converts spoken language into text or executable commands by analyzing audio input. It allows machines to comprehend and respond to human speech, bridging the gap between spoken communication and digital action.

Key Components
It comprises acoustic modeling to represent sounds, language modeling to interpret context, signal processing to filter audio input, and recognition algorithms to match speech patterns to known vocabulary.

Benefits
Voice recognition enhances accessibility, streamlines communication, enables hands-free operation, and reduces the need for manual input. It is particularly useful in multitasking environments or for users with mobility challenges.

Examples
Using a smartphone to dictate a message such as "Call Mom," where the device accurately transcribes the speech into text and executes the command, demonstrates practical voice recognition in action.

Applications
It is central to virtual assistants, voice search engines, real-time transcription services, smart appliances, and in-car voice control systems.

Industries
Healthcare, education, customer service, and consumer electronics rely on voice recognition to improve user interaction and operational efficiency.

Conclusion
Voice recognition enables intuitive, natural interaction between humans and machines. As it advances, it continues to improve in accuracy and adaptability, making spoken language a powerful interface for AI systems.

Voice Synthesis

Definition
Voice synthesis is the AI-driven creation of artificial speech from written text or data. It generates human-like audio that can mimic speech patterns, tone, and intonation, enabling computers to speak with realism and expression.

Key Components
It utilizes text-to-speech (TTS) engines, neural network-based waveform generation models such as WaveNet, and prosody adjustment tools that control rhythm, pitch, and emphasis for natural-sounding speech.

Benefits
Voice synthesis allows scalable voice generation for digital content, enhances accessibility for the visually impaired, and personalizes user experiences through custom voice avatars and localized speech output.

Examples
A GPS navigation app may synthesize the instruction "Turn left in 200 meters," allowing the user to receive audible guidance without looking at the screen.

Applications
It is widely used in audiobooks, virtual assistants, language tutoring software, customer service bots, and content narration tools.

Industries
Entertainment, education, telecommunications, and the automotive industry utilize voice synthesis for hands-free guidance, storytelling, and human-computer interaction.

Conclusion
Voice synthesis transforms text into expressive, lifelike speech, bringing a new dimension to digital communication. As technology improves, synthesized voices are becoming increasingly indistinguishable from human speech.

Volumetric Video in AI

Definition
Volumetric video in AI involves capturing, processing, and rendering three-dimensional video content using artificial intelligence. It enables the visualization of people and objects from multiple angles, creating interactive, lifelike experiences in virtual and augmented reality.

Key Components
It includes depth-sensing cameras for capturing 3D data, AI models for spatial reconstruction and motion tracking, and rendering engines for presenting volumetric content in real time.

Benefits
This technique supports immersive storytelling, enhances training simulations, enables free-viewpoint video playback, and increases realism in mixed-reality applications.

Examples
A dancer's performance recorded using volumetric video can be explored from any perspective in a VR headset, allowing the viewer to observe movements as if physically present in the scene.

Applications
It is used in virtual reality entertainment, medical training, sports broadcasting, game design, and digital fashion showcases.

Industries
Media and entertainment, sports technology, healthcare training, and education sectors are adopting volumetric video for enhanced interactivity and realism.

Conclusion
Volumetric video in AI adds depth to visual storytelling by enabling users to experience events in 3D space. It blends spatial computing and AI to unlock new levels of immersion and realism.

VS Code (Visual Studio Code)

Definition
VS Code (Visual Studio Code) is a lightweight, open-source code editor developed by Microsoft, popular among AI developers for writing, debugging, and testing code. Its extensibility and support for AI libraries make it a key tool in modern AI workflows.

Key Components
It features a flexible user interface, support for multiple programming languages, built-in Git integration, a terminal window, intelligent code completion (IntelliSense), and extensions for frameworks like TensorFlow, PyTorch, and scikit-learn.

Benefits
VS Code increases coding efficiency, simplifies debugging, enhances collaboration through GitHub integration, and supports seamless interaction with Jupyter Notebooks and cloud-based development tools.

Examples
An AI researcher might use VS Code to build a deep learning model, test it locally, and sync the code with a remote repository for team collaboration—all within one environment.

Applications
It is widely used for machine learning development, model training scripts, data science projects, and AI experiment tracking.

Industries
Tech startups, research labs, academic institutions, and enterprise-level AI teams use VS Code for rapid prototyping and AI development.

Conclusion
VS Code is a powerful, adaptable editor that supports the entire AI development lifecycle. Its open-source nature and expansive plugin ecosystem make it a favorite among AI professionals and learners alike.

Vulcanization in AI Robotics

Definition
Vulcanization in AI robotics refers to the metaphorical process of strengthening robotic systems through the application of artificial intelligence. It symbolizes the enhancement of durability, adaptability, and functional resilience, allowing robots to operate effectively in dynamic or hostile environments.

Key Components
It involves intelligent control systems, adaptive algorithms, integrated sensor feedback, and reinforcement learning mechanisms that refine robotic behavior under varying conditions.

Benefits
This approach improves mechanical and operational robustness, extends the system's functional lifespan, and enhances task precision and efficiency. It enables robots to continuously adapt without compromising reliability.

Examples
An AI-enhanced robotic arm used in manufacturing may learn to adjust its grip strength over time when handling fragile items, demonstrating increased dexterity and resilience—essentially becoming "vulcanized" through learning.

Applications
It is applied in areas such as industrial robotics, prosthetics, autonomous exploration vehicles, and service robots in unpredictable environments.

Industries
Manufacturing, defense, healthcare, and disaster response rely on this concept to build smarter, stronger, and more autonomous robotic systems.

Conclusion
Vulcanization in AI robotics captures the idea of fusing intelligence with resilience. As robots become

more integrated into real-world environments, this metaphor reflects the evolving need for durable, adaptable AI-driven machines.

Vulnerability Detection in AI Systems

Definition
Vulnerability detection in AI systems is the systematic process of identifying potential weaknesses, flaws, or exploitable elements in AI models, algorithms, or their supporting infrastructure. Its goal is to maintain integrity, security, and reliability.

Key Components
It involves static code analysis, dynamic model testing, adversarial input simulations, security audits, and real-time monitoring of system behavior under various conditions.

Benefits
This process helps to proactively identify issues before they are exploited, enhances overall system robustness, and supports safe deployment in high-risk or sensitive domains.

Examples
In a credit scoring AI system, vulnerability detection might uncover weaknesses where biased or manipulated inputs could result in unfair outcomes or compromised decision-making.

Applications
It is vital in AI applications used for financial transactions, autonomous navigation, identity verification, predictive analytics, and any domain where accuracy and trust are critical.

Industries
Cybersecurity, financial services, transportation, and autonomous technologies emphasize vulnerability detection as part of their AI safety protocols.

Conclusion
Vulnerability detection in AI is a critical step in ensuring that intelligent systems function securely and ethically. It strengthens the foundation upon which trust in AI is built.

Vulnerability Management in AI Systems

Definition
Vulnerability management in AI systems is the structured, continuous process of identifying, assessing, mitigating, and monitoring security risks and weaknesses in AI technologies. It aims to maintain safe, secure, and resilient operations throughout the AI system lifecycle.

Key Components
It includes detection and reporting tools, prioritization mechanisms, risk scoring models, mitigation planning, patch deployment, and post-remediation validation.

Benefits
Vulnerability management improves trust, enhances operational safety, reduces potential attack surfaces, and ensures alignment with legal and ethical standards.

Examples
An AI-based healthcare diagnostics platform might perform routine vulnerability scans on its models to detect outdated training data or insecure integrations with external systems, updating them as needed to prevent breaches or misdiagnoses.

Applications
It is applied across AI lifecycle management platforms, enterprise AI security systems, medical diagnostics, autonomous systems, and financial compliance platforms.

Challenges
Maintaining up-to-date vulnerability databases, ensuring rapid response in evolving threat environments, and minimizing disruptions during remediation are key difficulties.

Industries
Sectors such as government, healthcare, defense, and finance rely heavily on vulnerability management to ensure that their AI-driven operations remain safe and compliant.

Conclusion
Vulnerability management in AI systems is not a one-time fix but a continuous process of defense. It is fundamental to deploying trustworthy AI technologies in real-world, mission-critical applications.

Vulnerability Remediation in AI

Definition
Vulnerability remediation in AI refers to the process of correcting or removing identified weaknesses within AI systems to restore security, integrity, and performance. It represents the critical phase of repairing flaws after detection, ensuring the system is hardened against repeat incidents.

Key Components
Patch Development: Code updates to eliminate or bypass vulnerabilities.
Model Retraining: Adjusting or retraining models using clean or corrected data.
Data Sanitization: Removing corrupted, malicious, or biased data that caused errors.
Validation Testing: Ensuring remediation successfully addresses the original issue without introducing new risks.

Benefits
Reduces the impact of discovered vulnerabilities, restores system functionality and trust, and prevents recurrence through targeted fixes.

Examples
If a conversational AI is found to respond inappropriately to adversarial prompts, developers may retrain it using filtered datasets and patch its logic to prevent misuse.

Applications
Used in AI maintenance cycles, cybersecurity response plans, adversarial defense updates, and regulated software system audits.

Industries
Technology, healthcare, retail, cybersecurity, and financial services rely on remediation processes to safeguard AI performance.

Conclusion
Vulnerability remediation is an essential phase in AI lifecycle management, providing resilience by repairing known flaws and reinforcing the reliability of intelligent systems.

Vulnerability Scanning in AI

Definition
Vulnerability scanning in AI is the process of systematically probing AI systems, models, or datasets to identify weaknesses, misconfigurations, or potential security threats before they can be exploited.

Key Components
Scanning Engines: Use automated tools or scripts to evaluate vulnerabilities.
Threat Databases: Repositories of known AI and software weaknesses.
Penetration Simulation: Tests system responses to simulated attacks.
Reporting Tools: Document vulnerabilities for remediation planning.

Benefits
Provides proactive threat identification, enhances system security posture, and allows timely mitigation before exploitation.

Examples
An AI-driven fraud detection system in banking may undergo vulnerability scanning to uncover exploitable gaps in transaction logic or data pipelines.

Applications
Used during security audits, compliance checks, pre-deployment assessments, and continuous AI system monitoring.

Challenges
High false positive rates, difficulty identifying zero-day vulnerabilities, and limited capabilities against novel AI-specific threats.

Industries
Banking, defense, IT security, cloud computing, and enterprise software operations utilize scanning tools to secure AI infrastructures.

Conclusion
Vulnerability scanning offers a frontline defense for AI systems, ensuring hidden flaws are exposed and addressed before they become entry points for attack.

Vulnerable Algorithm in AI

Definition
A vulnerable algorithm in AI is a model or logic sequence that contains inherent weaknesses, making it prone to bias, manipulation, or failures when exposed to adversarial or unexpected input.

Key Components
Flawed Logic or Design: Errors in model structure or decision flow.
Inadequate Training: Poor data selection or improper parameter tuning.
Robustness Deficiencies: Lack of resistance to adversarial examples.
Overfitting or Underfitting: Model performs poorly outside training scenarios.

Benefits
Identifying algorithmic vulnerabilities allows developers to implement improvements, increasing security, fairness, and performance.

Examples
An image classification model that mislabels subtly altered images is vulnerable to adversarial attacks and needs resilience enhancements.

Applications
Affects recommendation engines, facial recognition systems, autonomous vehicle perception, and real-time analytics.

Challenges
Hard to detect vulnerabilities before deployment, balancing complexity with reliability, and continuously adapting to evolving threats.

Industries
Media, automotive, public safety, and social platforms assess algorithmic risks to maintain trusted AI solutions.

Conclusion
Vulnerable algorithms underscore the need for resilient, secure AI design, pushing continuous improvement in model development, validation, and risk mitigation.

Vulnerable Dataset in AI Training

Definition
A vulnerable dataset in AI training is a collection of input data that contains flaws such as bias, errors, omissions, or adversarial manipulation, which negatively impact the integrity and performance of AI models.

Key Components
Data Bias: Skewed representations leading to discriminatory outcomes.
Incomplete or Corrupted Entries: Reduce model reliability.
Adversarial Injections: Intentionally manipulated data to mislead training.
Unverified Sources: Lack of validation increases the risk of introducing harmful patterns.

Benefits
Recognizing vulnerabilities allows for cleansing and improving data quality, which directly impacts the fairness and trustworthiness of trained models.

Examples
A language model trained on unfiltered internet data might learn and replicate harmful stereotypes due to biased input sources.

Applications
Affects computer vision, natural language processing, supervised learning pipelines, and generative AI development.

Industries
Law enforcement, healthcare, HR tech, and social media platforms examine training datasets closely to avoid biased or harmful AI behavior.

Conclusion
Vulnerable datasets highlight the foundational role of data integrity in AI, reinforcing the importance of ethical sourcing and rigorous preprocessing for responsible AI development.

Vulnerable Network in AI Systems

Definition
A vulnerable network in AI systems refers to a neural or system-level network with security flaws that could be exploited, leading to compromised data integrity, performance degradation, or unauthorized access.

Key Components
Unsecured Communication Channels: Exposed APIs or endpoints.
Model Inversion Risks: Allow attackers to reconstruct training data.

Inadequate Encryption: Fails to protect sensitive model information.
Weak Access Controls: Open systems susceptible to intrusion.

Benefits
Identifying and addressing vulnerabilities ensures secure data exchange, protects intellectual property, and maintains uninterrupted system performance.

Examples
A neural network embedded in a smart grid system might be accessed through a vulnerable API, allowing external actors to manipulate energy flow predictions.

Applications
Used in distributed AI systems, federated learning frameworks, cloud-hosted inference engines, and IoT-integrated AI platforms.

Industries
Defense, telecommunications, industrial automation, smart infrastructure, and transportation work to secure AI networks from cyber threats.

Conclusion
Vulnerable networks represent systemic weak points in AI infrastructure, demanding proactive protection strategies to ensure resilience and operational trustworthiness.

VY (Virtual Yarns in AI for Textiles)

Definition
Virtual Yarns (VY) in AI for textiles represent the use of artificial intelligence to digitally simulate and design yarn structures, properties, and patterns before physical production. This approach enhances textile creation through predictive modeling, virtual prototyping, and sustainable material experimentation.

Key Components
AI-Driven Simulation Software: Models fiber behavior, elasticity, and interaction.
Material Databases: Provide physical property data for different yarn types.
Generative Design Engines: Enable creative pattern generation and structure optimization.
Visualization Tools: Render 3D textile simulations for inspection and testing.

Benefits
Reduces material waste and prototyping costs, speeds up design cycles, enhances product customization, and supports sustainable manufacturing by minimizing physical trials.

Examples
A fashion brand might use Virtual Yarns to test a new sweater design, adjusting the density and elasticity virtually to assess comfort and appearance before weaving the first sample.

Applications
Used in textile prototyping, digital fashion design, quality testing, performance garment development, and environmentally responsible fabric innovation.

Industries
Fashion, home textiles, sportswear, technical fabrics, and industrial manufacturing all benefit from the innovations enabled by Virtual Yarns in AI.

Conclusion
VY systems in AI bridge the gap between virtual textile design and real-world production, enabling faster, smarter, and more sustainable innovation in the fabric and fashion industries.

Vygotsky Learning Model in AI

Definition
The Vygotsky Learning Model in AI applies principles from psychologist Lev Vygotsky's learning theory—particularly the zone of proximal development and social scaffolding—to build AI systems that learn through guided interaction, feedback, and incremental challenges.

Key Components
Collaborative Training: AI learns from human or more advanced AI agents.
Scaffolded Learning: Tasks are gradually made more complex as the AI improves.
Zone of Proximal Development (ZPD): Defines the boundary between what an AI can do alone and what it can achieve with guidance.
Interactive Feedback: Enables real-time adjustments and tailored growth paths.

Benefits
Promotes human-aligned learning, improves adaptability, and enables more nuanced and progressive development of AI capabilities.

Examples
An AI tutoring bot helps students by guiding them through increasingly complex math problems, adjusting its support based on performance—mirroring the scaffolded learning model.

Applications
Applied in education technology, reinforcement learning environments, conversational agents, and collaborative human-AI systems.

Industries
Education, robotics, healthcare, training simulations, and customer experience systems benefit from Vygotsky-based approaches to AI learning.

Conclusion
The Vygotsky Learning Model in AI enriches artificial intelligence with human-inspired development strategies, enabling systems to learn and evolve in meaningful, socially informed ways.

VY Canis Majoris (AI Applications in Astronomy)

Definition
VY Canis Majoris (AI Applications in Astronomy) refers to the use of artificial intelligence in the study of massive celestial bodies—specifically exemplified by the hypergiant star VY Canis Majoris. These AI-powered systems process vast astronomical datasets to detect patterns, model stellar behavior, and make predictions about cosmic phenomena.

Key Components
Astronomical Datasets: Large-scale data from telescopes, spectrographs, and space observatories.
Pattern Recognition Algorithms: Identify trends, anomalies, and correlations in stellar data.
Predictive Modeling: Simulate future states such as stellar mass loss or supernova likelihood.
Telescope Integration: Interfaces with instruments for automated data analysis and enhanced observational precision.

Benefits
Accelerates discovery by analyzing data at superhuman speed, enhances accuracy in modeling stellar evolution, and supports deeper insights into the life cycles of stars.

Examples
AI systems processing VY Canis Majoris' light curves and spectral signatures to estimate its mass, radius, and potential end-of-life behavior such as supernova transformation.

Applications
Used in stellar classification, galaxy evolution modeling, exoplanet detection, and cosmological simulations to study the universe's structure and expansion.

Industries
Applied in astronomy research institutions, space exploration agencies, satellite observatories, and academic astrophysics programs.

Conclusion
VY Canis Majoris symbolizes the powerful intersection of AI and astronomy, where intelligent systems unlock new frontiers in cosmic understanding by modeling, predicting, and analyzing the universe's most colossal phenomena.

VyOS (AI-Driven Networking)

Definition
VyOS (AI-Driven Networking) refers to the integration of artificial intelligence into the VyOS open-source network operating system to enhance routing, firewall management, VPN control, and overall network efficiency. By leveraging real-time data and predictive models, AI enables adaptive, intelligent decision-making for dynamic network optimization.

Key Components
VyOS Core System: An open-source Linux-based networking OS.
AI Algorithms: Used for real-time traffic pattern recognition and anomaly detection.
Machine Learning Models: Predict network congestion and optimize routing paths.
Monitoring Tools: Provide continuous feedback for autonomous configuration and tuning.

Benefits
Improves network throughput and reliability, reduces response time to disruptions, automates complex configuration tasks, and enables smart resource allocation across network infrastructures.

Examples
An enterprise data center may use VyOS with AI to detect and mitigate a distributed denial-of-service (DDoS) attack by proactively rerouting traffic and isolating high-risk connections.

Applications
Used in network security, automated network management, cloud orchestration, and traffic optimization in large-scale IT infrastructures.

Challenges
Integrating AI with legacy infrastructure, ensuring real-time performance without lag, handling large volumes of telemetry data, and maintaining model accuracy under unpredictable network conditions.

Industries
Telecommunications, IT services, enterprise networking, cloud platforms, and cybersecurity operations benefit from AI-enhanced VyOS systems.

Conclusion
VyOS with AI redefines network management by transforming traditional systems into intelligent, self-optimizing infrastructures capable of adapting to modern digital demands in real time.

Vyper (Smart Contracts Language for AI)

Definition
Vyper is a Python-based programming language developed for writing secure smart contracts on blockchain platforms, particularly Ethereum. When integrated with artificial intelligence, Vyper enables the automated generation, analysis, and optimization of contracts, improving both security and development efficiency.

Key Components
Vyper Syntax: A minimalist, human-readable code structure designed to reduce vulnerabilities.
AI-Driven Code Generation: Automates contract creation based on business logic.
Security Auditing Tools: AI systems scan code for bugs, logic flaws, or potential exploits.
Blockchain Integration: Ensures seamless deployment and execution on distributed ledgers.

Benefits
Improves contract security through simplified syntax, reduces development time with AI-generated templates, and minimizes errors through continuous intelligent code validation.

Examples
An AI system may use Vyper to automatically draft a supply chain contract, adapting terms and delivery schedules based on historical data and real-time supplier performance.

Applications
Used in decentralized finance (DeFi), asset tracking, intellectual property management, automated payments, and DAO (Decentralized Autonomous Organization) governance systems.

Industries
Blockchain technology, legal tech, financial services, insurance, logistics, and smart infrastructure rely on AI-enhanced Vyper for secure and efficient smart contract solutions.

Conclusion
Vyper with AI brings precision, automation, and transparency to the development of smart contracts, enabling faster, safer deployment in blockchain ecosystems while supporting the rise of intelligent decentralized applications.

VYU (Variable Yield Unit in AI Systems)

Definition
Variable Yield Unit (VYU) in AI systems refers to a flexible, adaptive component that adjusts output levels or performance dynamically based on varying input conditions. It is designed to optimize the use of resources and fine-tune outcomes by continuously responding to environmental or data fluctuations, making AI systems more responsive and efficient.

Key Components
Adaptive Algorithms: Continuously modify behavior based on incoming data patterns.
Performance Metrics: Monitor system outputs to guide real-time yield adjustments.
Resource Allocation Logic: Dynamically manage computational or physical resources.
Feedback Systems: Utilize real-time input-output comparisons to refine system responses.

Benefits
Enhances operational efficiency, minimizes waste, and ensures that AI output is contextually appropriate and optimized for changing conditions.

Examples
In precision agriculture, a VYU module could modify crop yield forecasts based on weather anomalies, soil readings, or satellite data, enabling smart irrigation and harvesting strategies.

Applications
Used in predictive modeling, automated decision-making, resource optimization, dynamic risk assessment, and smart infrastructure control systems.

Industries
Commonly used in agriculture, energy management, logistics, manufacturing automation, and environmental monitoring.

Conclusion
VYU modules introduce adaptability into AI systems, enabling them to deliver optimized, context-sensitive outputs. Their ability to respond to variable data in real time makes them vital for building intelligent, efficient, and scalable AI solutions across multiple industries.

Vyxen AI (Virtual Assistants for Enhanced Natural Language Interaction)

Definition
Vyxen AI refers to a sophisticated class of AI-powered virtual assistants designed to elevate natural language interaction through contextual understanding, emotional intelligence, and fluid conversational abilities. These assistants are engineered to provide highly personalized, intuitive, and responsive communication experiences across various digital platforms.

Key Components
Advanced Natural Language Processing (NLP) Models: Understand and generate human-like language.
Context Retention Mechanisms: Maintain conversational memory for coherent multi-turn dialogues.
Emotional Intelligence Algorithms: Detect sentiment and tone to adapt responses appropriately.
Multi-Modal Interaction Systems: Combine voice, text, visual, and gesture-based communication methods.

Benefits
Enables seamless, human-like dialogue across applications, enhances user satisfaction through personalized interactions, and increases efficiency in task management and information retrieval.

Examples
A Vyxen AI assistant could coordinate meetings by analyzing a user's schedule, suggesting optimal time slots, and initiating follow-up reminders, all while maintaining a natural and adaptive conversational flow.

Applications
Deployed in personal productivity tools, AI-driven customer service, healthcare virtual triage, enterprise automation platforms, and smart home environments.

Industries
Utilized in sectors such as technology, healthcare, education, finance, and retail to improve user engagement, streamline workflows, and support AI-driven service delivery.

Conclusion
Vyxen AI represents a major advancement in virtual assistance, combining language understanding, emotional awareness, and task intelligence to create deeply interactive, adaptive, and efficient communication experiences. It sets a new standard for intelligent virtual interaction across industries.

❀ LETTER W ❀

Ward's Method in AI Clustering

Definition
Ward's Method is a hierarchical clustering approach that groups data by minimizing the total variance within each cluster. At each step, it merges the pair of clusters that results in the smallest increase in overall within-cluster variance. This method is widely used in artificial intelligence and machine learning to identify meaningful groupings in datasets.

Key Components
Hierarchical clustering tree structure, variance-based merging criterion, agglomerative clustering process, and distance measures such as Euclidean distance.

Benefits
Produces compact and well-balanced clusters, minimizes distortion within groups, and handles high-dimensional data effectively with reduced noise.

Examples
Used to group online shoppers based on purchase behavior, cluster research papers by topic similarity, or segment biological data in genetic analysis.

Applications
Applied in market segmentation, medical data classification, image segmentation, and cybersecurity anomaly detection.

Summary
Ward's Method is a powerful clustering technique that structures data into meaningful patterns, offering valuable insights in various AI applications.

Wasserstein GAN (WGAN)

Definition
Wasserstein GAN (WGAN) is a variation of generative adversarial networks that uses the Wasserstein distance to measure the divergence between generated and real data distributions. This design improves training stability and reduces problems such as gradient vanishing and mode collapse.

Key Components
Generator and critic networks, Wasserstein loss function, weight clipping or gradient penalty, and adversarial training framework.

Benefits
Provides more stable and consistent training outcomes, generates high-quality synthetic data, and effectively prevents mode collapse, leading to more diverse outputs.

Examples
Used to generate realistic human portraits, create synthetic medical scans for data augmentation, and support AI-assisted artistic content generation.

Applications
Employed in deep learning for data synthesis, AI-powered creative tools, high-resolution medical imaging, and video generation systems.

Summary
WGAN significantly improves upon traditional GANs, offering a more reliable solution for generating diverse and high-quality artificial data in AI systems.

Waterfall Model (AI Development)

Definition
The Waterfall Model is a linear software development methodology where AI projects move through clearly defined stages: requirement analysis, design, implementation, testing, deployment, and maintenance. Each stage must be completed before the next begins.

Key Components
Structured development phases, sequential task execution, predefined deliverables, and emphasis on documentation and planning.

Benefits
Provides organized project management, clarity in scope and deliverables, and is especially suited for regulated industries requiring formal processes.

Examples
Used in the development of rule-based AI systems, enterprise software solutions, and embedded AI systems in manufacturing.

Applications
Common in industrial automation, defense systems, government-regulated software development, and healthcare AI infrastructure.

Summary
The Waterfall Model offers a structured approach to AI system development, ideal for stable, well-defined projects but less suited for dynamic or research-heavy initiatives.

Watershed Algorithm (Image Segmentation)

Definition
The Watershed Algorithm is an image segmentation method that treats grayscale images as topographic maps, using pixel intensity as elevation. The algorithm floods low-intensity regions from markers until they meet, naturally separating distinct image regions.

Key Components
Gradient calculation, marker-based segmentation, morphological operations, and watershed transformation techniques.

Benefits
Effectively separates connected or overlapping objects, defines precise boundaries, and enhances object detection accuracy in image analysis.

Examples
Used to isolate tumors in radiological imaging, identify features in satellite imagery, and detect surface flaws in industrial inspections.

Applications
Employed in medical diagnostics, remote sensing, microscopic analysis, and AI-driven quality control systems.

Summary
The Watershed Algorithm supports accurate and detailed image segmentation, especially in fields requiring high-precision analysis like medicine and manufacturing.

Watson AI

Definition
Watson AI is IBM's cognitive computing platform that combines natural language processing, machine learning, and data analytics to support intelligent decision-making and task automation across industries. It is designed to understand, learn, and interact with users in natural language.

Key Components
Natural language understanding, machine learning engines, AI-powered analytics, cloud infrastructure, and customizable industry-specific models.

Benefits
Improves operational efficiency, enhances customer engagement through conversational AI, and supports informed decision-making through advanced data insights.

Examples
Used to power chatbots in customer support, assist physicians in clinical decision-making, and streamline financial risk analysis systems.

Applications
Deployed in healthcare, finance, retail, telecommunications, and enterprise-level AI systems for automation and analytics.

Summary
Watson AI is a robust enterprise-grade platform offering scalable AI capabilities for intelligent automation, data analysis, and human-machine interaction.

Wavelet Transform in AI

Definition
The Wavelet Transform is a mathematical technique used in artificial intelligence for analyzing signals, time-series data, and images by decomposing them into multiple frequency bands. This method supports multi-resolution analysis, allowing AI models to capture both high-frequency details and low-frequency trends within data.

Key Components
Wavelet basis functions, signal decomposition layers, time-frequency representation, and inverse wavelet reconstruction.

Benefits
Enables precise feature extraction, improves denoising and signal enhancement, supports efficient data compression, and provides localized frequency insights.

Examples
Extracting phonetic features for speech recognition, compressing medical images for storage efficiency, and identifying anomalies in financial time-series data.

Applications
Applied in speech analysis, computer vision, biomedical signal processing, and AI-driven anomaly detection systems.

Summary
The Wavelet Transform is a vital tool in AI for processing signals and images, enabling systems to extract meaningful patterns through detailed frequency and spatial analysis.

Waypoint Navigation in AI Robotics

Definition
Waypoint navigation in AI refers to a method used in robotics where an autonomous system moves through a sequence of predefined spatial coordinates, or waypoints, to reach its destination while optimizing path efficiency and obstacle avoidance.

Key Components
GPS or sensor-based localization, obstacle detection modules, path optimization algorithms, and motion planning strategies.

Benefits
Provides accurate and efficient navigation, enhances autonomy in robotics, adapts well to varied environments, and reduces manual intervention in movement control.

Examples
Drones flying along mapped coordinates for surveillance, autonomous delivery vehicles navigating urban routes, and robotic vacuums cleaning based on room mapping.

Applications
Used in aerial drones, self-driving vehicles, warehouse automation robots, and field robotics for inspection or mapping.

Summary
Waypoint navigation empowers AI-based robots to follow optimized, pre-mapped routes with high precision, making it a cornerstone of modern robotic mobility.

Weak AI (Narrow AI)

Definition
Weak AI, also known as Narrow AI, describes artificial intelligence systems that are programmed to perform a specific task or operate within a limited domain, without possessing general reasoning or conscious understanding.

Key Components
Domain-specific algorithms, supervised or unsupervised learning techniques, predefined task boundaries, and limited adaptability.

Benefits
Delivers high accuracy in focused applications, reduces operational burden through automation, and improves consistency in task performance.

Examples
Spam detection in email systems, chatbot support in customer service, and personalized product recommendations in e-commerce platforms.

Applications
Employed in voice assistants, diagnostic tools, fraud detection systems, and AI-enabled industrial automation.

Summary
Weak AI offers powerful, task-specific intelligence that automates narrow applications efficiently but lacks broader reasoning or adaptive learning beyond its defined function.

Weakly Supervised Learning

Definition
Weakly supervised learning is a machine learning approach where models are trained using data that is partially labeled, contains noise, or is guided by imprecise supervision methods, bridging the gap between fully supervised and unsupervised learning.

Key Components
Noisy or incomplete labeling, heuristic supervision, semi-supervised and self-supervised strategies, and probabilistic label estimation techniques.

Benefits
Reduces dependency on costly labeled datasets, enables scalable model training, and expands the usability of large, imperfect data collections.

Examples
Training image classifiers using web-sourced images with auto-generated tags, learning text classifications from loosely annotated documents, and relation extraction using distant supervision.

Applications
Used in healthcare image diagnosis, NLP for document classification, speech recognition systems, and automated video analysis.

Summary
Weakly supervised learning enables practical, large-scale model training in real-world scenarios where high-quality labels are limited or unavailable, offering a balance between efficiency and performance.

Weight Initialization in Neural Networks

Definition
Weight initialization is the process of assigning starting values to the weights of a neural network before training begins. Proper initialization ensures stable learning by avoiding problems such as vanishing or exploding gradients.

Key Components
Initialization methods such as random, Xavier, He, or orthogonal, layer-wise variance management, and controlled gradient propagation during backpropagation.

Benefits
Accelerates convergence, maintains gradient stability, improves model accuracy, and supports deep network training efficiency.

Examples
Using He initialization in ReLU-activated networks, applying Xavier initialization for sigmoid-based layers, and assigning small random weights in shallow neural models.

Applications
Essential in deep learning architectures including CNNs, RNNs, GANs, and transformer models for NLP or vision tasks.

Summary
Effective weight initialization is fundamental to successful neural network training, ensuring faster convergence and robust performance in AI applications.

Weight Pruning in Neural Networks

Definition
Weight pruning is a model compression technique that removes non-essential or low-impact weights from a trained neural network to reduce complexity while retaining performance accuracy.

Key Components
Magnitude-based and structured pruning methods, sparsity enforcement, retraining for performance recovery, and optional quantization for hardware efficiency.

Benefits
Reduces memory footprint and inference time, enables deployment on edge devices, enhances efficiency, and may improve generalization.

Examples
Pruning redundant connections in CNNs for mobile apps, reducing transformer layer sizes for language processing, and optimizing networks for embedded systems.

Applications
Applied in mobile deep learning, edge AI devices, cloud model optimization, and resource-constrained robotics or IoT platforms.

Summary
Weight pruning streamlines neural networks by eliminating unnecessary parameters, making AI models faster and more suitable for real-time, low-resource applications.

Weighted Cross-Entropy Loss

Definition
Weighted cross-entropy loss is a classification loss function designed to address imbalanced datasets by assigning different weights to classes. This ensures that the learning algorithm does not overly favor the majority class and treats rare classes with appropriate importance.

Key Components
Incorporates class-specific weights, uses the standard cross-entropy framework as its foundation, and adjusts gradients based on label frequency to balance learning.

Benefits
Improves performance in class-imbalanced problems, enhances fairness across categories, and increases model robustness in domains with underrepresented classes.

Examples
Used in medical AI to detect rare diseases, in fraud detection where fraudulent cases are minimal, and in voice recognition models to balance dialect representation.

Applications
Widely implemented in medical imaging, sentiment analysis, cybersecurity, speech processing, and multi-class object detection.

Summary
Weighted cross-entropy loss improves classification fairness and accuracy, particularly in domains with imbalanced class distributions.

Weighted Sum Model (WSM)

Definition
The Weighted Sum Model is a multi-criteria decision-making technique in AI that ranks options based on the sum of weighted scores assigned to various factors. It helps evaluate and select optimal solutions by balancing performance across several dimensions.

Key Components
Weight assignments for each criterion, normalization of data scales, score aggregation via summation, and selection based on the highest total score.

Benefits
Provides transparent and interpretable decision logic, supports scalability across domains, and is computationally simple and fast.

Examples
Selecting the best AI model based on speed, accuracy, and energy use; ranking support tickets by urgency and sentiment; and optimizing logistics by weighing cost and time.

Applications
Used in AI-powered decision systems, resource allocation tools, financial forecasting, and recommendation engines.

Challenges
Prone to bias if weights are misassigned, assumes linearity between features, and may not capture interdependencies between factors.

Summary
The Weighted Sum Model enables structured decision-making across multiple variables, balancing diverse priorities to identify optimal outcomes.

Weighted Voting Classifier

Definition
A weighted voting classifier is an ensemble learning approach in AI where multiple models contribute to the final prediction, each with a weighted influence based on reliability or accuracy. The model with higher performance has a greater say in the ensemble decision.

Key Components
Ensemble of base classifiers, weight values based on model performance, combination logic using majority or weighted average, and final output computation.

Benefits
Boosts accuracy, reduces variance and overfitting, and combines diverse models to capture complementary learning behaviors.

Examples
Used in medical diagnosis systems combining neural networks and decision trees, sentiment analysis combining rule-based and machine learning models, and fraud detection ensembles for better anomaly recognition.

Applications
Applied in healthcare, e-commerce, finance, language processing, and real-time classification systems.

Summary
Weighted voting classifiers strengthen AI decision-making by combining the strengths of multiple models, improving reliability and accuracy.

Wheel Encoder in AI-Driven Robotics

Definition
A wheel encoder is a sensory device used in AI-powered robotics to monitor wheel rotation, enabling accurate estimation of distance, velocity, and position. It supports motion control and real-time path correction in mobile robots.

Key Components
Optical or magnetic sensing mechanisms, digital signal processing, odometry calculations, and feedback loops for navigation control.

Benefits
Supports precise motion tracking, improves localization, enhances autonomous movement, and reduces navigation error over time.

Examples
Guiding warehouse robots along designated routes, enabling vacuum robots to map indoor environments, and helping self-driving vehicles maintain course alignment.

Applications
Found in autonomous vehicles, mobile robotics, industrial automation platforms, and AI-driven robotic delivery systems.

Summary
Wheel encoders enable accurate mobility and navigation in robotics, providing essential motion feedback for AI-driven movement systems.

Whisker-Based Navigation in AI Robotics

Definition
Whisker-based navigation is a bio-inspired robotic sensing method where artificial whisker-like sensors provide tactile feedback to help AI systems detect environmental features through physical contact.

Key Components
Tactile whisker sensors, signal processing units, environmental interpretation algorithms, and learning modules for adaptive responses.

Benefits
Provides navigation capabilities in visually obstructed environments, enhances obstacle detection in tight or dark spaces, and reduces reliance on visual data.

Examples
Robots operating in low-light conditions, space rovers exploring uncharted terrain, and medical probes navigating soft tissue during procedures.

Applications
Used in rescue robotics, exploratory missions, medical robotics, industrial inspection, and sensor-limited automation systems.

Summary
Whisker-based navigation enhances tactile perception in AI-driven robotics, enabling movement and exploration in conditions unsuitable for vision-based systems.

Whisper AI

Definition
Whisper AI is a state-of-the-art speech recognition system developed by OpenAI, capable of transcribing, translating, and interpreting spoken language using deep learning models.

Key Components
Multilingual training datasets, transformer-based deep learning architecture, real-time audio processing, and self-supervised learning frameworks.

Benefits
Delivers high transcription accuracy, supports multiple languages, improves accessibility for the hearing impaired, and enables real-time voice interaction.

Examples
Generating subtitles for video content, powering AI voice assistants, and producing meeting transcriptions automatically.

Applications
Used in accessibility technologies, content creation, language learning apps, customer support systems, and media transcription services.

Summary
Whisper AI elevates speech recognition with multilingual capabilities, transforming how voice data is used in real-time AI applications.

White-Box AI

Definition
White-Box AI refers to artificial intelligence systems that provide transparency and interpretability in their decision-making process, allowing stakeholders to understand how and why outcomes are produced.

Key Components
Explainable model structures, rule-based learning, feature importance visualization, and model audit tools for compliance and analysis.

Benefits
Builds user trust, supports transparency in regulated sectors, helps identify and reduce bias, and enables error tracing and model validation.

Examples
AI models explaining credit decisions, interpretable medical diagnostics, and regulatory tools for transparent risk scoring.

Applications
Applied in financial services, healthcare systems, legal tech, public sector AI, and industries requiring clear AI accountability.

Summary
White-Box AI enables ethical, transparent, and accountable use of artificial intelligence, especially in applications where explainability is non-negotiable.

Whitelisting in AI Security Systems

Definition
Whitelisting in AI security is a proactive cybersecurity method where only approved users, applications, or processes are granted access to a system, reducing exposure to unauthorized threats.

Key Components
AI-driven access control, dynamic list management, behavioral monitoring, and real-time threat response protocols.

Benefits
Blocks unauthorized processes, reduces malware risk, strengthens infrastructure integrity, and enhances compliance in secure environments.

Examples
Approving only verified applications on enterprise systems, controlling access to cloud-based AI models, and safeguarding IoT networks from unverified commands.

Applications
Used in enterprise cybersecurity, network access control, AI model integrity assurance, and secure industrial automation.

Summary
Whitelisting is a critical strategy for AI cybersecurity, protecting systems through strict access control and reducing the likelihood of malicious breaches.

Wide and Deep Learning

Definition
Wide and Deep Learning is a hybrid AI architecture that combines the strengths of linear models (wide networks) for memorizing historical patterns with deep neural networks for generalizing unseen data, offering a balanced solution for predictive accuracy and personalization.

Key Components
Wide layer for feature interactions, deep network for hierarchical learning, joint training optimizer, and feature transformation pipeline.

Benefits
Improves personalization in recommendations, balances generalization with memorization, and adapts well to sparse and high-dimensional data.

Examples
Product recommendations in e-commerce, personalized search engine results, and AI models forecasting user churn in digital platforms.

Applications
Used in recommendation systems, fraud detection, personalization engines, and AI-driven marketing analytics.

Summary
Wide and Deep Learning merges traditional and deep learning techniques, powering AI applications that require both memorized associations and generalized insights.

Wiener Filter in AI

Definition
The Wiener Filter is a statistical signal processing technique used in AI to reduce noise and improve signal clarity by minimizing the mean square error between the estimated output and the original signal.

Key Components
Linear filtering functions, noise and signal estimation, frequency domain analysis, and adaptive optimization techniques.

Benefits
Enhances signal fidelity, reduces background interference, supports clearer feature extraction, and improves model inputs for speech and image tasks.

Examples
Used in denoising MRI scans, improving speech recognition in noisy environments, and refining radar signals in aerospace applications.

Applications
Applied in telecommunications, medical diagnostics, voice processing, and real-time signal restoration for AI systems.

Challenges
Requires accurate knowledge of noise statistics, may introduce blurring if not configured properly, and can be computationally intensive.

Summary
The Wiener Filter is a powerful tool in AI for enhancing signal clarity, enabling more accurate interpretation and analysis in data-rich environments.

Wiki-Based AI Learning

Definition
Wiki-based AI learning is a collaborative artificial intelligence approach that leverages structured, crowd-sourced knowledge from wiki platforms. These systems dynamically learn from continuously evolving content, enhancing their knowledge bases in real time.

Key Components
Machine learning-driven parsing, semantic search integration, knowledge graph construction, and automated content validation mechanisms.

Benefits
Enables adaptive learning with real-time data updates, improves contextual awareness, and allows community-driven enhancements to AI understanding.

Examples
AI systems that retrieve and learn from Wikipedia for question answering, virtual assistants updated with community-sourced content, and educational bots that explain topics using real-time wiki data.

Applications
Used in AI education platforms, research support tools, dynamic knowledge graphs, and personalized content summarization engines.

Summary
Wiki-based AI learning empowers systems to adapt and expand knowledge rapidly by interacting with dynamic, collaborative data sources.

Winding Number in AI Vision

Definition
The winding number in AI vision is a mathematical tool used to determine whether a point lies inside a closed contour, supporting accurate shape analysis and object recognition in image processing.

Key Components
Contour representation, topological computations, polygonal traversal, and integration with segmentation and edge-detection algorithms.

Benefits
Improves object boundary analysis, enhances contour-based recognition, and supports robust shape interpretation across varied image types.

Examples
Identifying internal regions in scanned architectural plans, analyzing tumor outlines in radiology, and enabling path planning in robot vision.

Applications
Used in computer vision, medical imaging, object detection, and AI-driven graphic rendering.

Summary
The winding number enhances visual intelligence by providing a reliable metric for detecting enclosed spaces and analyzing complex shapes.

Windowing Function in AI Signal Processing

Definition
A windowing function is a preprocessing step in AI signal processing that shapes a segment of a signal to minimize edge effects and spectral leakage before frequency domain transformations.

Key Components
Time-domain window functions (e.g., Hann, Hamming), signal truncation controls, Fourier transform integration, and adaptive smoothing algorithms.

Benefits
Reduces spectral artifacts, increases resolution in frequency analysis, enhances noise suppression, and supports better pattern extraction.

Examples
Applied in denoising speech signals, improving ECG waveform segmentation, and optimizing sonar echo detection.

Applications
Used in audio classification, speech recognition, biomedical signal analysis, radar, and remote sensing applications.

Summary
Windowing functions enhance AI's ability to extract clean and accurate frequency features, supporting precise analysis in signal-rich environments.

Word2Vec

Definition
Word2Vec is a neural network-based model that learns vector representations of words by analyzing the context in which they appear, placing semantically similar words closer in a continuous vector space.

Key Components
Skip-gram and CBOW architectures, context window analysis, shallow neural network layers, and gradient-based optimization.

Benefits
Captures word similarity and relationships, improves downstream NLP tasks, and reduces sparsity by converting text into numerical form.

Examples
Finding synonyms in search queries, enhancing chatbot language models, and powering content recommendation systems.

Applications
Used in translation engines, text classification, semantic search, and NLP-powered customer service tools.

Summary
Word2Vec enables AI systems to understand language semantically by translating textual data into meaningful numerical representations.

Word Alignment in Machine Translation

Definition
Word alignment is the process of identifying direct correspondences between words or phrases in parallel texts of two languages, forming the backbone of accurate machine translation.

Key Components
Parallel corpus training, statistical alignment models (IBM Models 1–5), neural attention layers, and cross-lingual embeddings.

Benefits
Improves translation accuracy, supports multilingual model development, and facilitates bilingual dictionary generation.

Examples
Mapping English-French word pairs in translation datasets, aligning subtitles in multilingual videos, and guiding training for neural machine translation.

Applications
Used in translation engines, cross-lingual search, document alignment, and automated subtitle generation.

Summary
Word alignment is essential in multilingual AI, supporting accurate translation by building reliable word-to-word and phrase correspondences.

Word Embeddings

Definition
Word embeddings are dense, numerical vector representations of words in a continuous space, where proximity reflects semantic and syntactic similarity, enabling advanced language understanding in AI.

Key Components
Unsupervised learning on text corpora, models like Word2Vec, GloVe, and FastText, and dimensionality reduction techniques.

Benefits
Improves NLP model accuracy, captures hidden linguistic patterns, enables semantic comparison, and supports downstream AI applications.

Examples
Clustering related words, sentiment classification in reviews, and enhancing autocomplete predictions in messaging apps.

Applications
Used in text classification, search ranking, machine translation, dialogue systems, and knowledge extraction.

Summary
Word embeddings form the foundation of modern NLP by transforming language into mathematically meaningful vector spaces for AI processing.

WordNet

Definition
WordNet is a structured lexical database that organizes English words into synonym sets, supporting semantic reasoning and linguistic relationships like synonyms, antonyms, hyponyms, and hypernyms in AI systems.

Key Components
Synsets (word groups with similar meanings), hierarchical relationships, semantic taxonomy, and NLP interface integrations.

Benefits
Improves semantic search and disambiguation, supports lexical reasoning, and enhances language-based AI systems with structured knowledge.

Examples
Used in grammar correction tools, AI writing assistants, synonym expansion in search queries, and concept mapping in text mining.

Applications
Applied in information retrieval, sentiment analysis, language generation, and semantic classification tasks.

Challenges
Limited coverage for evolving language or slang, domain-specific gaps, and occasional ambiguity in synset groupings.

Summary
WordNet enriches AI understanding of language by modeling semantic relationships, forming a core resource for lexical analysis and interpretation.

Word Sense Disambiguation (WSD)

Definition
Word Sense Disambiguation is the process of identifying the correct meaning of a word with multiple interpretations based on its usage in context, enabling precise language comprehension in AI systems.

Key Components
Lexical resources (e.g., WordNet), context feature analysis, supervised and unsupervised disambiguation algorithms, and performance evaluation metrics.

Benefits
Reduces ambiguity in natural language processing, enhances translation accuracy, and improves search and conversational AI relevance.

Examples
Distinguishing “bat” as an animal vs. sports equipment, clarifying "lead" in text analysis, and improving context in AI-generated summaries.

Applications
Used in machine translation, search engines, question answering systems, and semantic understanding tools.

Summary
Word Sense Disambiguation improves the linguistic precision of AI by resolving ambiguity in human language interpretation, essential for high-quality NLP applications.

Wu-Manber Algorithm

Definition
The Wu-Manber Algorithm is a high-speed, multi-pattern string matching algorithm optimized for searching multiple substrings simultaneously in large text corpora, enhancing performance in data-intensive AI tasks.

Key Components
Hashing-based preprocessing, shift and prefix tables, bad character heuristics, and pattern bucketing techniques.

Benefits
Enables fast multi-pattern matching, reduces redundant comparisons, and scales well for large datasets with many search terms.

Examples
Used in DNA sequence scanning, spam filtering, log file parsing, and large-scale plagiarism detection.

Applications
Found in search engines, cybersecurity intrusion detection, bioinformatics, and big data text mining tools.

Summary
The Wu-Manber Algorithm supports efficient multi-pattern text searching, offering AI systems faster string matching capabilities across various domains.

Wumpus Agent

Definition
A Wumpus Agent is an intelligent software agent developed to operate in uncertain and hazardous environments, commonly used in artificial intelligence research and education. The agent is designed to function within a simulated environment known as the Wumpus World, where it must explore a grid-based space filled with hidden dangers such as pits and a lethal creature called the Wumpus. The agent gathers information, makes logical inferences, and selects actions to achieve its goals while avoiding threats.

Key Components
Knowledge Base: Stores facts, observations, and inferred knowledge about the environment.
Inference Engine: Processes perceptual inputs to derive conclusions about the presence of hazards.
Percepts: Inputs such as breezes (indicating pits) and stenches (indicating the Wumpus) used to infer nearby dangers.
Actions: Includes moving to adjacent cells, grabbing gold, shooting an arrow, or exiting the world.
Decision Algorithms: Combines logic, planning, and probability to choose the most rational actions.

Benefits
Demonstrates effective decision-making in uncertain conditions, supports the development of logical AI reasoning systems, and serves as a benchmark for agent-based modeling and planning strategies.

Examples
Used in AI coursework to teach logical deduction and agent-based reasoning, applied in academic research to evaluate planning algorithms, and modeled in simulations to illustrate uncertainty management in AI.

Applications
Applied in robotics navigation, autonomous exploration, disaster recovery simulations, and AI planning in unknown terrains.

Summary
The Wumpus Agent exemplifies intelligent behavior in uncertain and hostile environments, showcasing how AI can make informed decisions with limited data. Its logic-driven framework is foundational for understanding agent design, knowledge representation, and intelligent planning.

Wumpus World (AI)

Definition
Wumpus World is a classic AI simulation designed to test decision-making, logic, and planning in uncertain environments. It represents a grid-based virtual world filled with hazards such as pits and the Wumpus—a hidden creature. The AI agent must explore this space safely, using minimal information to make accurate decisions and avoid fatal outcomes.

Key Components
Grid-Based Environment: A structured grid where the agent explores cells to find gold and avoid dangers.
Perceptual Feedback: Signals such as breezes and stenches provide indirect clues about hidden hazards.
Logical Reasoning: The agent uses propositional and first-order logic to deduce safe or dangerous cells.
Hazard Modeling: Includes random pit placements and a Wumpus whose location must be inferred.

Benefits
Teaches foundational concepts in logical reasoning, decision-making under uncertainty, and knowledge representation. It provides a controlled setting for evaluating planning algorithms and inference mechanisms.

Examples
Implemented in AI courses to teach logic-based problem solving, used in research to model uncertainty-aware agents, and simulated in planning tasks for rescue robotics.

Applications
Relevant in designing autonomous navigation systems, AI pathfinding in unknown terrains, logic-based game agents, and decision support systems.

Conclusion
Wumpus World remains a vital educational and research tool in artificial intelligence. Its emphasis on uncertainty, hazard inference, and logical planning continues to shape the development of intelligent agents capable of reasoning, adapting, and navigating complex environments.

LETTER X

X AI (Explainable AI)

Definition:X AI, or Explainable Artificial Intelligence, refers to a set of processes and techniques that enable human users to understand, interpret, and trust the decisions made by AI systems. Explainable AI aims to make the decision-making process of complex algorithms more transparent and accessible.

Key Components:Model Transparency: Involves designing models that are inherently interpretable or using tools to make complex models understandable. Interpretability Techniques: Methods such as SHAP, LIME, and feature importance to explain how input data affects output decisions. Human-Centric Interfaces: Visualizations and reports that present AI insights in a clear and comprehensible manner.

Benefits:Enhances trust in AI systems by making decision-making processes visible and understandable. Supports regulatory compliance in industries where decision transparency is legally required. Aids in identifying biases and improving model fairness.

Examples:Credit scoring models that explain factors influencing loan approvals. Medical diagnostic systems that show why certain diagnoses are suggested. Recommendation systems that clarify why specific content is presented to users.

Applications:Healthcare for transparent diagnostic support and treatment recommendations. Finance for explainable credit risk assessments and fraud detection. Autonomous vehicles for understanding real-time decision-making processes.

Conclusion:X AI (Explainable AI) plays a critical role in bridging the gap between complex AI models and end-users. By enhancing transparency, accountability, and trust, it ensures that AI systems can be reliably integrated into sensitive and high-stakes environments, though it requires careful design to balance performance with interpretability.

XAI Evaluation Metrics

Definition: XAI evaluation metrics are a set of performance measures designed to assess the transparency, interpretability, and fairness of explainable AI models. These metrics ensure that AI models not only perform well but also provide understandable, actionable explanations for their decisions.

Key Characteristics: XAI evaluation metrics include fidelity, interpretability, fairness, trust, and completeness, which gauge how well the model's explanations align with human understanding and expectations. These metrics are essential for evaluating models in domains where the explainability of decisions is as important as the accuracy, such as healthcare, law, and finance. Common metrics include fidelity (how closely explanations match the actual decision process), comprehensibility (how understandable the explanations are to users), and fairness (ensuring explanations do not propagate bias).

Applications: Healthcare: Evaluating XAI models used in diagnosing diseases, ensuring that the models' predictions can be understood and trusted by healthcare professionals. Finance: XAI evaluation metrics help assess the transparency of credit scoring models, ensuring that loan decisions are explainable and unbiased. Autonomous Vehicles: XAI metrics evaluate the decision-making process of self-driving cars, ensuring that their actions can be explained and validated for safety.

Xamarin AI Integration

Definition:Xamarin AI Integration refers to the incorporation of artificial intelligence technologies into mobile applications developed using Xamarin, a cross-platform development framework. This integration allows developers to build intelligent apps capable of predictive analytics, natural language processing, image recognition, and more.

Key Components:Cross-Platform Development Environment: Xamarin provides a unified framework for building apps on Android, iOS, and Windows using a single codebase. Embedded AI Models: Integration of machine learning models directly within the app for real-time analytics and intelligent decision-making. API and Cloud Integration: Connection with external AI services and APIs like Microsoft Cognitive Services to enhance app capabilities.

Benefits:Streamlines development by enabling code sharing across platforms, reducing time and costs. Enhances app functionality with AI-driven features for personalized user experiences. Facilitates faster deployment of updates and improvements with consistent performance across devices.

Examples:Health apps using AI for symptom checking and patient monitoring. E-commerce apps providing personalized recommendations based on user behavior. Travel apps using AI for predictive booking suggestions and itinerary planning.

Applications:Mobile apps in healthcare for diagnostics and patient engagement. Retail applications offering tailored shopping experiences. Financial apps providing real-time fraud detection and risk assessment tools.

Conclusion:Xamarin AI Integration bridges the gap between mobile development and advanced AI capabilities, enabling developers to create smart, responsive applications. This integration not only enhances user engagement but also supports the rapid development of innovative features, though it may require specialized knowledge of both AI technologies and cross-platform development tools.

X-App Machine Learning

Definition:X-App Machine Learning refers to the integration of machine learning capabilities directly into cross-platform applications (X-Apps), allowing for intelligent decision-making, predictive analytics, and personalized user experiences within diverse software environments.

Key Components:Cross-Platform Compatibility: Designed to operate seamlessly across multiple devices and operating systems. Embedded ML Models: Machine learning algorithms embedded directly into the application for real-time processing. Data Synchronization: Ensures consistent data flow and learning across platforms to enhance performance.

Benefits:Enables real-time data analysis and decision-making within the app, improving responsiveness. Provides personalized experiences by adapting to user behavior across different platforms. Reduces dependency on external servers, enhancing data privacy and security.

Examples:Mobile health apps using ML to monitor and predict user health metrics. E-commerce platforms providing dynamic pricing and personalized recommendations. Finance apps offering real-time fraud detection and risk assessment.

Applications:Mobile applications for health monitoring, financial forecasting, and personalized content delivery. Enterprise software integrating predictive analytics for operational efficiency. Smart home applications adapting to user preferences for automation.

Conclusion:X-App Machine Learning revolutionizes application development by embedding intelligent capabilities directly into software solutions. This approach enhances user engagement, operational efficiency, and security, though it requires careful management of computational resources and data synchronization across platforms.

Xenobot AI

Definition
Xenobot AI refers to artificial intelligence systems embedded within biologically engineered living robots known as xenobots. These microscopic, programmable constructs are made from living cells—often derived from frog embryos—and are designed to carry out specific tasks. The integration of AI allows xenobots to perform actions such as movement, coordination, and environmental response with greater intelligence and autonomy.

Key Components
Biological Structure: Xenobots are formed using living tissues, typically skin and cardiac cells, that are reassembled into novel configurations capable of locomotion and function.
AI Control System: Machine learning algorithms or evolutionary strategies guide xenobot behavior, determining movement patterns, task execution, and interaction with the environment.
Adaptive Learning: These systems can adapt based on stimuli or environmental feedback, modifying their behavior or trajectory without manual reprogramming.

Benefits
Xenobot AI introduces a revolutionary approach to robotics by merging biological flexibility with computational intelligence.
Their biodegradable and biocompatible nature makes them ideal for applications where traditional materials may be invasive or harmful.
They offer potential in precise, minimally invasive tasks, such as targeted drug delivery or cleaning contaminants at microscopic scales.

Examples
In medicine, xenobot AI has been tested for delivering small therapeutic payloads to targeted areas inside the human body.
In environmental science, they have been proposed for removing microplastics or tracking pollutants in aquatic environments.
In biological research, xenobots help scientists observe tissue regeneration, cellular dynamics, and self-organizing systems.

Applications
In healthcare, xenobot AI may enable non-invasive procedures, assist in targeted drug deployment, and support regenerative therapies by interacting directly with tissues.
In environmental monitoring, these living machines can explore and manipulate microenvironments, aiding in pollution detection or ecosystem restoration.
In research, xenobots serve as experimental platforms to study the convergence of artificial intelligence, developmental biology, and robotics.

Conclusion
Xenobot AI represents a pioneering frontier in synthetic biology and artificial intelligence, where organic life and programmable behavior coexist. These living robots have the potential to transform medicine, environmental science, and experimental biology. However, as this field progresses, careful ethical considerations and regulatory frameworks will be essential to ensure safe and responsible use of biologically integrated AI systems.

Xenographic Data Transformation in AI

Definition
Xenographic Data Transformation in AI refers to the process of converting data from one format, structure, or representation to another, particularly when working with varied and incompatible data sources. This technique enables seamless communication between different AI systems, databases, or analytic tools by ensuring that the data maintains consistency, integrity, and usability across diverse environments.

Key Components
Data Mapping: Establishes structured relationships between distinct data models, identifying how data fields from one system correspond to those in another.
Transformation Algorithms: Specialized routines that modify the data's structure, format, or encoding to meet the requirements of a target system, ensuring accuracy and uniformity.
Validation Mechanisms: Tools and protocols designed to verify that the transformed data remains complete, consistent, and free of errors or corruption after conversion.

Benefits
Xenographic transformation improves interoperability by enabling AI systems to communicate and function across platforms that use different data schemas or formats.
It simplifies the integration of diverse data sources, making it easier to consolidate information for training, inference, and reporting.

By automating complex transformation tasks, it enhances the efficiency of data pipelines and reduces the likelihood of human error in manual formatting.

Examples
In natural language processing, text input may be transformed into structured feature vectors or token sequences for machine learning models.
In healthcare, AI systems standardize data from various monitoring devices and medical records into a consistent format for diagnostic algorithms.
During data migration efforts, legacy formats are transformed into modern schemas to enable compatibility with current AI and cloud-based systems.

Applications
In business intelligence, xenographic data transformation enables the aggregation of data from multiple departments, tools, or sources for unified analytics.
In AI-based customer relationship platforms, it harmonizes customer data coming from emails, forms, and call transcripts into a single actionable dataset.
In data science, it plays a critical role in preparing consistent training datasets across multiple formats, including text, images, and numerical data.

Conclusion
Xenographic Data Transformation in AI is a foundational process for achieving data compatibility, enabling AI systems to operate effectively across disparate technological landscapes. By converting and validating data across various formats and structures, it supports improved model training, smarter analytics, and more informed decision-making. However, successful transformation requires careful design to avoid introducing inconsistencies, data loss, or misinterpretation during conversion.

Xenomorphic AI Architectures

Definition
Xenomorphic AI Architectures refer to non-traditional, highly adaptive artificial intelligence systems capable of transforming their internal structure in response to environmental conditions or data inputs. Inspired by the concept of biological adaptability, these architectures are not static. Instead, they are engineered to evolve continuously, allowing them to restructure algorithms, adjust learning models, and reconfigure computational pathways to achieve optimal outcomes in dynamic scenarios.

Key Components
Adaptive Frameworks: The core of these architectures lies in their ability to restructure themselves autonomously based on new information or external changes, promoting real-time flexibility.
Evolutionary Algorithms: These drive the self-improving nature of the system, allowing models to evolve through iterative processes, trial-and-error learning, and performance-based selection.
Modular Design: Built with replaceable and reconfigurable components, xenomorphic AI systems can rearrange internal elements to match specific tasks or constraints, enhancing scalability and specialization.

Benefits
Xenomorphic AI enables exceptional adaptability, making it ideal for unpredictable or unfamiliar environments.
It supports autonomous learning and structural evolution, reducing the need for constant human oversight or manual reprogramming.
Resource usage becomes more efficient, as the system dynamically reallocates computing power and memory based on task complexity and operational demand.

Examples
In autonomous drone technology, xenomorphic AI enables drones to modify flight paths and decision-

making logic based on changes in weather, terrain, or airspace regulations.
In advanced robotics, these architectures facilitate real-time structural and behavioral adjustments, allowing robots to respond intelligently to unexpected obstacles or mission shifts.
In cybersecurity, xenomorphic models evolve continuously to detect, counter, and neutralize emerging threats without relying on predefined rules.

Applications
In self-driving vehicles, xenomorphic AI adjusts its learning models in real-time to suit varied traffic conditions, road types, or driving behaviors.
In smart manufacturing, these systems allow production lines to reconfigure tasks and workflows automatically to maintain efficiency and handle system anomalies.
In space exploration, xenomorphic AI is critical for adapting to unknown planetary surfaces, atmospheric changes, and unpredictable conditions with no external communication support.

Conclusion
Xenomorphic AI Architectures represent a frontier in artificial intelligence—bringing together self-evolution, structural reconfiguration, and environmental awareness. Their biologically inspired design makes them uniquely suited for complex, ever-changing environments where static systems may fail. While their adaptability offers enormous advantages, it also introduces challenges in predictability, system control, and oversight, requiring careful implementation and advanced monitoring solutions.

Xenon-Powered AI Systems

Definition
Xenon-Powered AI Systems refer to artificial intelligence infrastructures that utilize xenon gas as part of their energy or propulsion framework to support intensive computational processes. Known for its inert and stable chemical properties, xenon is employed in specialized power systems to ensure reliable, efficient, and sustained energy output for high-performance AI operations in demanding environments.

Key Components
Energy Source: Xenon gas is used in advanced energy systems, often in combination with ion propulsion or specialized reactors, to deliver steady and controllable power for AI-driven machinery or platforms.
High-Performance Computing Units: These systems integrate AI processors and accelerators that are optimized to operate efficiently under xenon-powered configurations.
Thermal Management Systems: Advanced cooling technologies are employed to regulate heat generated during prolonged AI workloads, helping to maintain system stability and longevity.

Benefits
Xenon-Powered AI Systems offer enhanced performance stability, particularly in remote or high-stress environments, by delivering consistent energy flow.
They reduce the likelihood of hardware failure due to overheating, thanks to efficient thermal regulation.
Their design supports environmentally conscious energy applications, as xenon-based systems often produce lower emissions compared to traditional fossil-fuel energy sources.

Examples
In satellite systems, xenon ion propulsion is paired with onboard AI modules to enable autonomous navigation, real-time data analysis, and communication optimization.
In next-generation data centers, xenon-powered units contribute to high-efficiency AI computation with improved thermal balance and energy management.
In autonomous vehicle development, these systems may support AI models requiring uninterrupted, high-capacity energy in long-distance or off-grid scenarios.

Applications
Space exploration missions benefit from xenon-powered AI systems for dual-use propulsion and navigation intelligence.
High-frequency financial trading infrastructures use them for their capacity to maintain ultra-low latency and energy efficiency.
Defense and aerospace technologies apply these systems in unmanned aerial and terrestrial vehicles where both high-performance AI and consistent energy supply are critical.

Conclusion
Xenon-Powered AI Systems reflect the intersection of advanced energy science and intelligent computation. By leveraging xenon's unique characteristics, these systems enhance the performance, reliability, and sustainability of AI platforms operating in high-demand or isolated settings. While promising, the high cost and technical complexity associated with xenon-based technology may present limitations to broader adoption in standard commercial environments.

Xeromorphic AI

Definition
Xeromorphic AI refers to artificial intelligence systems specifically engineered to operate efficiently in extreme or resource-constrained environments. Inspired by xeromorphic traits in plants that adapt to arid and harsh climates, these AI models are designed to sustain high performance despite limited computational resources, scarce data availability, or physically demanding conditions.

Key Components
Resource-Efficient Algorithms: These algorithms are optimized to use minimal processing power, memory, and storage, enabling deployment in low-power or remote devices.
Adaptive Learning Models: Xeromorphic AI systems can dynamically adjust to changing environments or inputs without requiring frequent retraining or heavy computational support.
Robust Data Handling: Capable of functioning effectively even when data is sparse, noisy, or incomplete, these models are built to extract meaningful insights from minimal information.

Benefits
Xeromorphic AI enhances functionality in environments where conventional AI systems would struggle, such as isolated regions, mobile units, or disaster zones.
It supports low-energy operations, making it ideal for eco-conscious applications or systems powered by renewable energy sources.
Its resilience against variability in input data or system instability improves operational reliability in critical and unpredictable conditions.

Examples
In planetary exploration, AI systems on spacecraft must function with limited bandwidth, computational capacity, and exposure to extreme temperatures—making xeromorphic AI essential.
In smart agriculture, low-power AI modules installed in dry and remote areas monitor soil, weather, and crop data using minimal connectivity and energy.
In emergency and disaster response, autonomous robots equipped with xeromorphic AI navigate debris, detect survivors, and make decisions in unstable, chaotic environments.

Applications
Xeromorphic AI is utilized in environmental monitoring systems deployed in deserts, polar regions, or deep-sea installations, where energy and data inputs are limited.
It is applied in autonomous vehicles and aerial drones that operate in rugged, GPS-denied, or infrastructure-scarce areas.
It also plays a role in defense and surveillance technologies that require durability and autonomy in remote or hostile terrains.

Conclusion
Xeromorphic AI introduces a nature-inspired approach to artificial intelligence, emphasizing adaptability, efficiency, and resilience in the face of scarcity. These systems are particularly valuable for advancing AI into new frontiers where traditional models cannot thrive. While they require specialized development and careful optimization, their benefits in sustainability and robustness offer promising solutions for the most challenging AI environments.

X-Hash Function in AI

Definition
X-Hash Function in AI refers to a specialized mathematical process that transforms input data of any length into a fixed-size string of characters, known as a hash value. This transformation enables AI systems to manage, verify, and retrieve data securely and efficiently. The "X" emphasizes the wide applicability of hash functions across various domains within artificial intelligence.

Key Components
Hash Algorithm: The engine that processes input data and generates a consistent and unique output string based on that data.
Input Data: Any type of information—such as numerical values, text documents, or images—that is converted by the algorithm.
Hash Value: A fixed-size alphanumeric code that serves as a fingerprint of the original data, used for verification and indexing.

Benefits
X-Hash functions enhance data security by ensuring that original content cannot be easily reconstructed from the hash value, thereby protecting sensitive information.
They accelerate data handling by enabling rapid indexing and lookup operations within large AI datasets.
Hash functions also support data integrity, as even a minor change in the input results in a drastically different output, making unauthorized changes easy to detect.

Examples
In password protection systems, AI applications use hash functions to store encrypted versions of passwords without saving the actual text.
In blockchain networks, hashes verify the integrity of each data block, ensuring the authenticity of the entire chain.
In AI-driven search tools, hashes help in creating efficient indexing structures that enable fast retrieval of similar or matching data.

Applications
In cybersecurity, X-Hash functions play a key role in encrypting data, validating file authenticity, and detecting tampering.
In machine learning, they are used for organizing data libraries and enhancing the speed of model training and inference through efficient data mapping.
In distributed systems and blockchain, hashes maintain consistency and verification across decentralized networks.

Conclusion
X-Hash Function in AI serves as a foundational mechanism for data protection, management, and validation. Its ability to convert data into a secure, fixed-length format supports a wide range of AI applications, from encryption to efficient data retrieval. While highly effective, developers must account for risks such as hash collisions and select algorithms that balance security with computational efficiency.

X-Hierarchy Learning

Definition
X-Hierarchy Learning is a machine learning approach that structures data, models, or tasks into hierarchical layers, enabling learning to progress through multiple levels of abstraction. This method allows complex patterns to be learned more efficiently by decomposing a primary task into simpler, interrelated sub-tasks, which are organized from broad generalizations to specific details.

Key Components
Hierarchical Structure: The system organizes elements such as features, decision-making layers, or data representations into a top-down structure, with higher levels capturing broad patterns and lower levels addressing fine-grained details.
Layered Learning: Each layer in the model focuses on distinct components of the problem, where higher layers guide lower layers, and lower layers provide refined inputs back up the hierarchy.
Adaptive Feedback: The model adjusts its learning strategies across different layers based on feedback or performance metrics, allowing dynamic refinement throughout the hierarchy.

Benefits
X-Hierarchy Learning improves learning efficiency by enabling the model to concentrate on progressively deeper concepts in a stepwise fashion.
It enhances interpretability, as the layered structure often reveals how decisions are formed from simple observations to complex conclusions.
This approach also supports transfer learning, where knowledge acquired at broader levels can be adapted to new or related tasks with minimal retraining.

Examples
In image recognition, hierarchical neural networks first detect edges and shapes at lower layers, and then interpret objects and scenes at higher layers.
In speech recognition, models use layered learning to process sound waves into phonemes, phonemes into words, and words into structured meaning.
In natural language processing, hierarchy-based models are used to analyze sentence structure, grammar, and semantic relationships.

Applications
X-Hierarchy Learning is applied in autonomous systems, where high-level goals are decomposed into actionable low-level commands, supporting decision-making in dynamic environments.
In recommendation systems, it helps capture user behavior and preferences across multiple levels—ranging from general interest categories to specific item selections.
In healthcare, it supports diagnostic systems that interpret symptoms through a structured analysis, from general categories of illness down to specific medical conditions.

Conclusion
X-Hierarchy Learning offers a scalable and intelligent approach to solving complex AI challenges by leveraging structured, multi-layered learning. It enables systems to progressively refine their understanding of data while maintaining clear organization and interpretability. Although it introduces complexity in model architecture and training, its strengths in handling abstraction, adaptability, and transferability make it a powerful tool across diverse AI applications.

X-Humanoid Robots with AI

Definition
X-Humanoid Robots with AI are sophisticated robotic systems engineered to closely imitate human appearance, movement, and behavior. These robots integrate artificial intelligence technologies to perform complex tasks such as understanding speech, making decisions, and adapting to new

environments. Their design aims to foster natural interaction between humans and machines, making them suitable for roles that involve communication, assistance, and learning.

Key Components
Human-Like Design: These robots feature anatomically inspired structures including flexible joints, facial expressions, and precise limb coordination, achieved through sensors and actuators.
Cognitive AI Systems: They are powered by artificial intelligence modules that enable speech recognition, visual perception, emotion detection, and autonomous problem-solving.
Adaptive Learning Capabilities: Through machine learning algorithms, these robots continuously learn from their environment and interactions, improving their responses over time.

Benefits
X-Humanoid Robots enhance the quality of human-robot interaction by providing a more relatable and intuitive interface. Their human-like gestures and conversational abilities create a sense of familiarity and trust.
They are capable of operating in diverse and dynamic settings, performing tasks that require both physical dexterity and contextual understanding.
Their capacity for continuous learning makes them versatile across industries, from personalized care to customer engagement and education.

Examples
Sophia, a highly publicized humanoid robot, engages in live conversations, recognizes faces, and responds to emotional cues.
ASIMO, developed by Honda, is designed for mobility support and task execution, showcasing the integration of AI and robotics in physical assistance.

Applications
In healthcare, humanoid robots support patients with rehabilitation exercises, medication reminders, and emotional companionship.
In retail and hospitality, they serve as interactive guides, answering questions and directing customers.
In academic and scientific settings, they facilitate research on social behavior, learning models, and collaborative problem-solving between humans and machines.

Conclusion
X-Humanoid Robots with AI represent a powerful convergence of robotics and artificial intelligence, pushing the boundaries of what machines can do in human-centered roles. Their ability to communicate, learn, and physically interact positions them as valuable assets in sectors like healthcare, customer service, and education. As development continues, balancing innovation with ethical responsibility will be essential to ensure their effective and respectful integration into society.

X-hybrid Neural Networks

Definition
X-hybrid neural networks are advanced artificial intelligence models that blend multiple neural network architectures—such as convolutional neural networks (CNNs), recurrent neural networks (RNNs), and transformer models—into a unified design. This hybridization allows the model to leverage the distinct advantages of each architecture to solve tasks involving various data types, including visual, sequential, and structured input.

Key Characteristics
These hybrid models are engineered to combine the spatial pattern recognition strength of CNNs with the temporal analysis capabilities of RNNs or the contextual understanding of transformers. Within one framework, the architecture accommodates different data processing pathways, enabling it to extract insights from multi-modal inputs simultaneously.

For example, in video processing, X-hybrid neural networks can analyze both the image sequence and corresponding audio tracks in parallel. This integrated approach enhances the network's ability to interpret data that spans across time, space, or modality.

Applications
In the field of autonomous transportation, X-hybrid networks interpret inputs from visual cameras, radar, and real-time environmental sensors to support precise navigation and obstacle avoidance.
In voice technologies, these models combine audio pattern recognition with sequence-based understanding to improve speech-to-text accuracy and digital assistant responsiveness.
In financial analytics, hybrid networks process historical time-series data alongside news feeds and social signals to forecast trends and inform investment decisions.

Benefits
X-hybrid neural networks offer improved adaptability across diverse AI tasks by fusing multiple learning mechanisms into a single architecture. They support better generalization, enhance learning from complex data sources, and eliminate the need to switch between separate models for different types of input.
By handling spatial and temporal data together, these models reduce preprocessing overhead and offer a more natural way to process real-world, mixed-format data efficiently.

Conclusion
X-hybrid neural networks exemplify the next stage of neural architecture evolution, offering a flexible and high-performance solution for interpreting complex, multi-source data. Their ability to seamlessly integrate spatial, temporal, and contextual understanding makes them ideal for modern AI applications such as autonomous systems, speech technologies, and predictive modeling. As data continues to grow in variety and volume, these hybrid models will play a critical role in creating intelligent systems that reflect the complexity of the real world.

X-hyperplane in AI

Definition
An X-hyperplane in artificial intelligence refers to a decision boundary used by machine learning models—particularly in support vector machines (SVMs) and other linear classifiers—to separate data points within a high-dimensional space. The term "X" signifies an arbitrary or extended number of dimensions within a dataset. The hyperplane is the geometric boundary that divides input data into two or more distinct classes, allowing AI systems to perform classification tasks with mathematical precision.

Key Characteristics
An X-hyperplane functions as the central element in the classification process. It is positioned within a multi-dimensional feature space so that data points from different categories are placed on opposite sides of the plane.
Support vector machines use the hyperplane to maximize the margin—the distance between the hyperplane and the nearest data points of each class—resulting in a more robust and generalizable classification model.
This concept is not limited to two or three dimensions; in practice, X-hyperplanes operate in spaces with many features or variables, making them suitable for complex datasets involving numerous inputs.

Applications
In image recognition, X-hyperplanes assist in classifying visual data, such as distinguishing between handwritten digits or identifying objects in photographs.
In spam detection, machine learning models use hyperplanes to differentiate between spam and legitimate emails by analyzing patterns in the text, subject line, and sender behavior.

In financial forecasting, hyperplanes help models classify market behavior into categories such as bullish or bearish trends based on historical performance metrics and economic indicators.

Benefits
X-hyperplanes provide a mathematically precise way to divide complex data, especially in high-dimensional environments.
They enhance classification accuracy by maximizing separation between data classes, which strengthens the model's ability to generalize to new, unseen inputs.
This geometric structure also offers a clear and interpretable visualization of how AI models differentiate between categories.

Conclusion
X-hyperplanes play a foundational role in AI classification systems by serving as decision boundaries in high-dimensional spaces. They are crucial for separating data into meaningful categories and are widely used in real-world AI applications such as visual recognition, content filtering, and predictive analytics. As machine learning continues to evolve, the role of X-hyperplanes remains central to building intelligent systems that can understand and classify complex data efficiently.

Xonomy in AI (Ontology Management Tools)

Definition
Xonomy in AI refers to ontology management tools designed to create, edit, and manage structured data representations known as ontologies. These tools help define the relationships between concepts, making data more understandable and accessible for AI systems.

Key Components
Ontology Editor: Provides a user-friendly interface for defining and modifying data structures.
Semantic Framework: Supports the creation of meaningful relationships between different data points.
Data Integration Module: Facilitates the merging and linking of diverse datasets for more comprehensive analysis.

Benefits
Improves data organization and consistency, making it easier for AI models to interpret and process information. Enhances knowledge management by enabling clear definitions of complex data relationships, which boosts AI performance in tasks like natural language understanding.

Examples
Used in AI-driven knowledge graphs to manage vast datasets, in healthcare for organizing patient data, and in e-commerce to streamline product classification systems.

Challenges
Requires expertise in ontology design, which can be complex and time-consuming. Managing large-scale ontologies can also be challenging due to data inconsistencies and integration issues.

Applications
Applied in natural language processing for better context understanding, in semantic web technologies to improve data connectivity, and in AI-powered recommendation systems for more accurate suggestions.

Conclusion
Xonomy plays a crucial role in managing and structuring data for AI applications. While it offers significant benefits in enhancing data interpretation and integration, it demands careful design and maintenance to avoid potential challenges related to data complexity and scalability.

XOR (Exclusive OR) in AI

Definition
XOR (Exclusive OR) is a logical operation used in artificial intelligence and computing, where the output is true if and only if the inputs are different. In binary terms, XOR returns 1 when one input is 0 and the other is 1, and returns 0 when both inputs are the same. This operation is fundamental in AI, particularly in neural network training and binary classification tasks.

Key Components
The XOR operation involves two binary inputs and one output. Its truth table defines its behavior: the output is true when inputs differ and false when they are the same. XOR gates in digital circuits and XOR functions in programming languages implement this logic.

Benefits
XOR plays a crucial role in AI by helping neural networks learn non-linear patterns, making it essential for tasks where simple linear models fail. It aids in feature extraction, cryptographic algorithms, and error detection/correction mechanisms, enhancing AI system reliability.

Applications
XOR is widely used in neural networks to demonstrate non-linear learning capabilities. It is vital in cryptography for creating secure encryption algorithms. In error detection and correction, XOR helps identify and fix data transmission errors. Additionally, it supports binary classification problems in machine learning.

Examples
In a neural network, XOR is often used as a benchmark problem to test the network's ability to learn complex patterns. In cryptography, XOR is used to encrypt data by combining plaintext with a key, producing ciphertext that can be decrypted using the same key.

Conclusion
XOR is a foundational concept in AI, illustrating the need for complex models to handle non-linear relationships. Its applications in neural networks, cryptography, and error detection showcase its versatility. Continued advancements in AI architectures have built on the principles demonstrated by XOR, driving progress in machine learning and data security.

XOR-based Neural Cryptography

XOR-based Neural Cryptography refers to the application of neural network architectures in conjunction with the exclusive OR (XOR) operation to develop secure cryptographic systems. This approach leverages the learning capabilities of artificial neural networks (ANNs) to create encryption and decryption mechanisms that adapt and improve over time. By integrating XOR operations, which are fundamental to classical cryptography due to their simplicity and reversibility, neural cryptographic systems can achieve enhanced security and robustness against cryptographic attacks.

Key components of XOR-based Neural Cryptography include neural network models, typically involving multi-layer perceptrons (MLPs) or recurrent neural networks (RNNs), designed to learn encryption and decryption functions. The XOR operation is embedded within the network's architecture to perform bitwise transformations on data, enhancing the complexity of encryption patterns. Key generation mechanisms are often neural network-driven, producing dynamic encryption keys that evolve based on the model's training. Additionally, adversarial networks may be used, where one network attempts to encrypt data while another tries to decrypt it without the key, fostering more secure encryption methods through competitive learning.

The benefits of XOR-based Neural Cryptography are significant. It introduces adaptability to cryptographic systems, allowing encryption methods to evolve in response to emerging threats. The integration of XOR operations ensures efficient, fast, and reversible transformations, maintaining low computational overhead. Neural networks can generate complex, non-linear encryption patterns that are difficult for traditional cryptanalysis techniques to decipher. This approach also facilitates the development of end-to-end encrypted communication systems where encryption and decryption processes are learned rather than manually programmed, enhancing security through model training.

Applications of XOR-based Neural Cryptography span various domains, particularly in secure communications, data privacy, and cybersecurity. In secure messaging platforms, neural cryptographic models provide robust encryption for text, voice, and video data. In IoT ecosystems, lightweight XOR-based neural encryption secures data transmission between devices with limited computational resources. Financial institutions employ these techniques to protect sensitive transaction data and prevent fraud. Additionally, XOR-based neural cryptography supports the development of secure AI models, safeguarding against model inversion and adversarial attacks in machine learning environments.

In conclusion, XOR-based Neural Cryptography represents an innovative fusion of traditional cryptographic principles with advanced neural network technologies. By combining the simplicity and efficiency of XOR operations with the adaptive learning capabilities of neural networks, this approach offers enhanced security, dynamic key generation, and robust encryption mechanisms. While challenges related to model training, performance consistency, and interpretability exist, ongoing research in AI and cryptography is driving the development of more secure, efficient, and adaptable neural cryptographic systems, contributing to the evolution of modern data security practices.

XOR Cipher in AI Encryption

Definition XOR Cipher in AI Encryption refers to a basic encryption technique that utilizes the exclusive OR (XOR) logical operation to secure data. In this method, each bit of plaintext is combined with a corresponding bit of a key using the XOR operation, resulting in ciphertext that can be easily decrypted by applying the same key again. The simplicity of the XOR cipher makes it a foundational concept in cryptography and data security, and it is often integrated into more complex AI-driven encryption systems to enhance data protection.

Key components of the XOR Cipher in AI Encryption include the plaintext, which is the original data to be encrypted, and the key, a binary sequence used to perform the XOR operation. The encryption process involves applying the XOR operation between each bit of the plaintext and the key, producing the ciphertext. The same key is required for decryption, as applying the XOR operation twice with the same key restores the original plaintext. In AI encryption systems, XOR ciphers can be combined with machine learning algorithms to dynamically generate or manage encryption keys, adding an extra layer of security.

The benefits of the XOR Cipher in AI Encryption are notable. It offers simplicity and speed, making it efficient for encrypting large volumes of data with minimal computational resources. The XOR operation is inherently reversible, allowing for straightforward encryption and decryption processes. When used with a truly random key that is as long as the plaintext (one-time pad), the XOR cipher can achieve theoretically unbreakable security. In AI applications, XOR ciphers can be integrated into adaptive security systems, enhancing data protection through dynamic key management and real-time encryption strategies.

Applications of the XOR Cipher in AI Encryption span various domains. In secure communications, XOR ciphers protect sensitive information during data transmission. In cloud computing, they are used to encrypt data at rest and in transit, ensuring confidentiality and integrity. In AI-driven cybersecurity systems, XOR operations are employed to create lightweight encryption protocols suitable for resource-constrained environments, such as IoT devices. The technique is also used in digital watermarking, steganography, and securing machine learning models against adversarial attacks. Additionally, XOR ciphers support data obfuscation in software development and cryptographic research.

In conclusion, the XOR Cipher in AI Encryption is a fundamental cryptographic technique that provides efficient and reversible data encryption. Its simplicity, speed, and adaptability make it a valuable tool in AI-driven security systems and data protection strategies. While challenges related to key management, security vulnerabilities, and integration exist, continuous advancements in AI and cryptography are enhancing the effectiveness and resilience of XOR-based encryption methods, contributing to the development of secure and robust information systems.

XOR Neural Networks

Definition XOR Neural Networks refer to artificial neural network architectures designed to solve the exclusive OR (XOR) problem, which is a fundamental challenge in the field of machine learning and neural computation. The XOR problem involves determining the output of a binary function where the result is true if and only if the inputs are different. Traditional linear models struggle with this problem because the XOR function is not linearly separable, meaning it cannot be solved using a simple linear decision boundary. This challenge highlighted the need for multi-layer neural networks, leading to the development of more complex architectures capable of handling non-linear data relationships.

Key components of XOR Neural Networks include an input layer that receives binary input values, one or more hidden layers that introduce non-linearity through activation functions, and an output layer that provides the final prediction. The hidden layers are crucial for learning the complex patterns required to solve the XOR problem. Activation functions such as the sigmoid, hyperbolic tangent (tanh), or rectified linear unit (ReLU) introduce non-linearity, enabling the network to model the XOR function effectively. The network is trained using supervised learning techniques, where the model learns from labeled examples through backpropagation and gradient descent algorithms to minimize the error between predicted and actual outputs.

The benefits of XOR Neural Networks are significant. They demonstrate the power of multi-layer architectures, showcasing how neural networks can solve problems that are not linearly separable. This understanding has been foundational in the development of deep learning, where complex models with multiple layers can learn intricate data representations. XOR Neural Networks also serve as an essential learning tool for understanding key concepts in neural network design, such as activation functions, backpropagation, and non-linear transformations. Their ability to solve simple yet challenging problems makes them a fundamental example in AI education and research.

Applications of the principles learned from XOR Neural Networks extend beyond solving the XOR problem itself. They are applied in pattern recognition tasks, where distinguishing between non-linearly separable data is required, such as image and speech recognition. In natural language processing, the concepts underpinning XOR Neural Networks help in understanding syntactic and semantic relationships that are not linearly correlated. In robotics, they support decision-making processes that involve complex, non-linear environmental interactions. Additionally, XOR Neural Network principles are foundational in developing more advanced AI models used in autonomous systems, financial forecasting, and biomedical data analysis.

In conclusion, XOR Neural Networks represent a pivotal concept in the evolution of artificial intelligence, illustrating the necessity and effectiveness of multi-layer neural architectures for solving non-linear problems. They highlight the importance of non-linearity, hidden layers, and advanced training techniques in neural network design. While challenges related to model complexity, training efficiency, and scalability exist, the foundational principles derived from XOR Neural Networks continue to influence the development of modern AI systems, contributing to advancements in deep learning, pattern recognition, and intelligent decision-making.

X-Uncertainty Quantification in AI

Definition X-Uncertainty Quantification in AI refers to the process of identifying, modeling, and reducing uncertainties in artificial intelligence systems to improve the reliability and robustness of predictions and decisions. The "X" in X-Uncertainty Quantification often represents a specific variable, context, or model where uncertainty plays a critical role. This methodology is essential for applications where AI-driven decisions can have significant consequences, such as healthcare, finance, autonomous systems, and scientific research. By quantifying uncertainty, AI models can provide not just predictions but also confidence levels, enhancing their interpretability and trustworthiness.

Key components of X-Uncertainty Quantification in AI include uncertainty modeling techniques such as probabilistic models, Bayesian inference, and ensemble methods. These approaches help capture different types of uncertainties, including aleatoric uncertainty, which arises from inherent data variability, and epistemic uncertainty, which stems from limited knowledge about the model or data. Sensitivity analysis is used to determine how changes in input variables affect model outputs. Calibration methods ensure that the predicted probabilities align with actual outcomes. Additionally, validation frameworks assess the performance of uncertainty quantification techniques across different datasets and scenarios.

The benefits of X-Uncertainty Quantification in AI are substantial. It enhances decision-making by providing insights into the confidence and reliability of AI model predictions. This leads to more informed risk assessments, particularly in high-stakes applications such as medical diagnosis, financial forecasting, and autonomous vehicle navigation. Quantifying uncertainty improves model robustness, as AI systems can identify and adapt to situations with high uncertainty. It supports better resource allocation by focusing efforts on areas where uncertainty is highest. Additionally, uncertainty quantification fosters transparency and trust in AI systems, making them more acceptable to users and stakeholders.

Applications of X-Uncertainty Quantification in AI span a wide range of industries and domains. In healthcare, it aids in diagnostic systems by indicating the confidence level of disease predictions, thereby supporting clinical decision-making. In finance, uncertainty quantification improves risk management strategies by assessing the reliability of market forecasts and investment models. In autonomous vehicles, it helps in navigating complex environments by evaluating the uncertainty in object detection and path planning. The technology is also applied in climate modeling, engineering simulations, and scientific research, where understanding and managing uncertainty is critical for accurate predictions and analyses.

In conclusion, X-Uncertainty Quantification in AI is a vital approach for enhancing the reliability, robustness, and interpretability of artificial intelligence systems. By systematically identifying and managing uncertainties, it supports more informed decision-making across various applications, from healthcare to autonomous systems. While challenges related to computational demands, interpretability, and standardization exist, ongoing advancements in AI research and uncertainty modeling are improving the capabilities and accessibility of these techniques, driving innovation and fostering trust in AI technologies.

X-Underfitting in Machine Learning

Definition X-Underfitting in Machine Learning refers to a scenario where a machine learning model is too simplistic to capture the underlying patterns in the data, leading to poor performance on both the training and test datasets. The "X" in X-Underfitting often represents a specific variable, model, or context related to the learning process. Underfitting occurs when a model fails to learn enough from the training data, resulting in high bias and low variance. This issue can hinder the model's ability to make accurate predictions and generalize to new, unseen data.

Key components of X-Underfitting in Machine Learning include the model architecture, which may be overly simplistic with insufficient parameters to capture the complexity of the data. Inadequate training, such as using too few epochs or an inappropriate learning rate, can also contribute to underfitting. Feature selection plays a role, as omitting relevant features or including irrelevant ones can prevent the model from learning effectively. Regularization techniques, if applied excessively, may constrain the model too tightly, limiting its ability to fit the training data. Additionally, data quality and preprocessing steps, such as normalization and encoding, influence the model's capacity to learn meaningful patterns.

The benefits of addressing X-Underfitting in Machine Learning are significant. Identifying and mitigating underfitting improves model accuracy and generalization, leading to better performance on real-world data. By optimizing model complexity and training parameters, machine learning practitioners can develop more robust and reliable predictive models. Addressing underfitting also enhances the interpretability of models, as well-fitted models provide more meaningful insights into the relationships within the data. Additionally, understanding the causes of underfitting helps in selecting appropriate algorithms and model configurations for specific tasks.

Applications of addressing X-Underfitting in Machine Learning span various domains. In healthcare, improving model fit can enhance diagnostic accuracy and patient outcome predictions. In finance, well-fitted models support accurate risk assessment, fraud detection, and algorithmic trading strategies. In marketing, reducing underfitting improves customer segmentation, personalized recommendations, and campaign optimization. The technology is also applied in autonomous vehicles for object detection and decision-making, in natural language processing for sentiment analysis and language translation, and in industrial automation for predictive maintenance and quality control.

Challenges associated with X-Underfitting in Machine Learning include balancing model complexity to avoid both underfitting and overfitting, which can be challenging in dynamic environments with evolving data patterns. Identifying the root cause of underfitting requires expertise in model evaluation, feature engineering, and algorithm selection. Computational constraints may limit the ability to train more complex models, particularly in resource-constrained environments. Additionally, addressing underfitting often involves iterative experimentation, which can be time-consuming and computationally intensive. Ensuring that models generalize well to new data while maintaining interpretability and efficiency is a persistent challenge in machine learning.

In conclusion, X-Underfitting in Machine Learning is a critical concept that highlights the importance of model complexity, training processes, and data quality in achieving accurate and reliable predictive performance. By understanding and addressing the factors that contribute to underfitting, practitioners can develop models that generalize effectively to new data, support informed decision-making, and deliver value across a wide range of applications. While challenges related to model tuning, computational resources, and data variability exist, continuous advancements in machine learning techniques and best practices are improving the ability to detect, prevent, and mitigate underfitting, driving progress in artificial intelligence and data science.

X-Unit Testing in AI

Definition X-Unit Testing in AI refers to a software testing methodology designed to validate the functionality of individual components or units within an artificial intelligence system. The "X" in X-Unit Testing often represents a specific variable, framework, or context tailored to the AI model being tested. This testing approach focuses on verifying that isolated parts of the code, such as functions, algorithms, or modules, perform as expected under various conditions. X-Unit Testing is critical for ensuring the reliability, accuracy, and robustness of AI systems, particularly in complex applications where errors can have significant consequences.

Key components of X-Unit Testing in AI include test cases, which define specific input conditions, expected outputs, and validation criteria. Test frameworks, such as PyTest, JUnit, or TestNG, provide the tools and libraries needed to automate and manage the testing process. Mocking and stubbing techniques simulate external dependencies, allowing for isolated testing of individual units without interference from other parts of the system. Assertions are used to compare actual outputs with expected results, identifying discrepancies that indicate potential bugs. Additionally, continuous integration (CI) tools integrate X-Unit Testing into the development workflow, enabling automated testing and rapid feedback during the development lifecycle.

The benefits of X-Unit Testing in AI are substantial. It improves code quality by identifying defects early in the development process, reducing the cost and effort required for debugging and maintenance. Unit testing enhances the reliability and stability of AI models, ensuring consistent performance across different environments and datasets. It supports refactoring and code optimization by providing a safety net that verifies functionality remains intact after changes. Automated unit tests increase development efficiency, allowing teams to quickly detect and address issues. Additionally, X-Unit Testing promotes better code documentation and design, as test cases clarify the intended behavior of individual components.

Applications of X-Unit Testing in AI span various domains and technologies. In machine learning, unit tests verify data preprocessing functions, feature extraction algorithms, and model training pipelines. In natural language processing (NLP), they validate text tokenization, parsing, and sentiment analysis components. In computer vision, unit testing ensures the accuracy of image processing functions, object detection algorithms, and neural network layers. The technology is also applied in robotics for testing control algorithms and sensor data processing modules. Additionally, X-Unit Testing is used in AI-driven financial systems, healthcare applications, and autonomous vehicles to ensure the robustness and safety of critical functions.

In conclusion, X-Unit Testing in AI is a fundamental practice for ensuring the quality, reliability, and maintainability of artificial intelligence systems. By validating the functionality of individual components, unit testing helps detect defects early, supports code refactoring, and enhances development efficiency. While challenges related to non-determinism, test design, and coverage exist, continuous advancements in testing frameworks, automation tools, and AI development practices are improving the effectiveness and scalability of X-Unit Testing, contributing to the creation of robust and trustworthy AI applications.

X-Utility Function in AI

Definition X-Utility Function in AI refers to a mathematical framework used to evaluate and assign numerical values to the desirability or effectiveness of different actions or outcomes within decision-making processes. This function helps AI systems make rational choices by quantifying preferences, risks, and potential rewards associated with various alternatives. The "X" in X-Utility Function often denotes a specific variable, feature, or context relevant to the decision-making scenario. It plays a critical role in optimization algorithms, reinforcement learning, and game theory, where maximizing the utility function leads to optimal performance.

Key components of the X-Utility Function in AI include input variables representing possible actions, states, or features relevant to the decision context. The utility calculation mechanism applies mathematical formulas, such as linear or nonlinear functions, to evaluate the desirability of each option. Weighting factors or coefficients adjust the influence of different variables based on their importance. In probabilistic models, expected utility is calculated by incorporating probabilities of different outcomes. Optimization algorithms, such as gradient descent or dynamic programming, are employed to maximize or minimize the utility function for optimal decision-making.

The benefits of the X-Utility Function in AI are substantial. It provides a systematic approach for making rational, data-driven decisions in complex environments. The function enables AI models to evaluate trade-offs between different objectives, supporting multi-criteria decision analysis. It enhances the adaptability of AI systems by allowing them to adjust strategies based on changing conditions or new information. The use of utility functions improves transparency and explainability in AI decision-making processes, as decisions can be traced back to quantifiable criteria. Additionally, X-Utility Functions facilitate efficient resource allocation, risk assessment, and strategic planning across various applications.

Applications of the X-Utility Function in AI span diverse domains. In reinforcement learning, it guides agents in selecting actions that maximize long-term rewards in dynamic environments. In autonomous vehicles, utility functions help optimize route planning, collision avoidance, and energy efficiency. In financial modeling, they support portfolio optimization, risk management, and algorithmic trading strategies. The technology is also used in healthcare for treatment planning, diagnostic decision support, and resource allocation. Additionally, X-Utility Functions are applied in robotics for task scheduling, in smart grids for energy distribution, and in e-commerce for personalized recommendations and pricing strategies.

In conclusion, the X-Utility Function in AI is a fundamental tool for rational decision-making, optimization, and strategic planning across various applications. By quantifying the desirability of different outcomes, it enables AI systems to make informed, goal-oriented decisions in complex environments. While challenges related to model complexity, bias, computational efficiency, and ethical considerations exist, continuous advancements in AI research and optimization techniques are enhancing the effectiveness, fairness, and reliability of X-Utility Functions, driving innovation in intelligent decision-support systems.

X-Vector in AI

Definition X-Vector in AI refers to a type of feature representation commonly used in machine learning and deep learning models, particularly in the field of speaker recognition and verification. An X-vector is a fixed-length embedding extracted from variable-length input data, such as audio signals or text sequences, capturing essential characteristics and patterns for downstream tasks. This technique leverages neural network architectures to transform raw data into dense, informative vectors that enhance model performance in classification, clustering, and verification applications.

Key components of the X-vector in AI include feature extraction layers, typically implemented using deep neural networks (DNNs) or convolutional neural networks (CNNs), which process raw input data to generate high-level representations. The embedding layer transforms these features into fixed-length vectors regardless of the input size. Normalization techniques, such as batch normalization or layer normalization, improve model stability and generalization. Additionally, statistical pooling layers aggregate temporal information, ensuring the X-vector captures both global and local patterns in the data.

The benefits of X-vector in AI are significant. It enables efficient handling of variable-length data, making it versatile for applications like speech recognition, language identification, and biometric authentication. X-vectors improve model accuracy by providing rich, discriminative representations that capture essential data characteristics. They support transfer learning, allowing pre-trained models to be fine-tuned for specific tasks with minimal additional data. The compact size of X-vectors reduces computational requirements and storage costs, facilitating deployment in resource-constrained environments. Additionally, X-vectors enhance the robustness of AI models to noise, variability, and adversarial conditions.

Applications of X-vector in AI span various domains. In speaker recognition, X-vectors are used to identify and verify individuals based on their voice characteristics. In natural language processing, they support tasks such as sentiment analysis, text classification, and machine translation by providing dense text embeddings. X-vectors are employed in biometric security systems for facial recognition and fingerprint analysis, enhancing authentication accuracy. In healthcare, they aid in diagnostic models by encoding patient data for predictive analytics. Additionally, X-vectors are used in multimedia indexing, recommendation systems, and anomaly detection across diverse industries.

In conclusion, X-vector in AI is a powerful technique for feature representation, enhancing the performance of machine learning and deep learning models across various applications. By converting variable-length data into fixed-length, informative embeddings, X-vectors support efficient, accurate, and robust AI solutions. While challenges related to model complexity, data quality, and interpretability exist, continuous advancements in neural network architectures and embedding techniques are improving the effectiveness and scalability of X-vectors, driving innovation in AI-driven technologies and applications.

XY-plane Segmentation in AI

Definition XY-plane Segmentation in AI refers to the process of dividing a two-dimensional (2D) plane, defined by the horizontal (X) and vertical (Y) axes, into distinct regions or segments based on specific features or patterns within the data. This technique is widely used in computer vision, image processing, and spatial data analysis to identify and isolate meaningful structures within datasets. AI-driven XY-plane segmentation utilizes advanced algorithms to enhance accuracy, automate complex tasks, and extract relevant information from diverse data sources.

Key components of XY-plane segmentation in AI include data preprocessing methods that prepare raw data for analysis by normalizing, filtering, and enhancing relevant features. Segmentation algorithms, such as thresholding, clustering (e.g., K-means), edge detection, and deep learning models like convolutional neural networks (CNNs), are used to identify boundaries and regions within the plane. Feature extraction techniques help in identifying critical attributes that distinguish different segments. Additionally, post-processing methods refine the segmentation results to improve precision and reduce noise.

The benefits of XY-plane segmentation in AI are substantial. It enables precise identification and classification of objects or regions within an image or dataset, enhancing the performance of downstream AI tasks such as object recognition and tracking. Segmentation improves data analysis by isolating areas of interest, facilitating targeted investigations and detailed assessments. The automation of segmentation processes reduces manual effort, increases efficiency, and minimizes human error. Furthermore, AI-driven segmentation adapts to complex patterns and varying data conditions, providing robust and scalable solutions for large datasets.

Applications of XY-plane segmentation in AI span multiple industries and domains. In healthcare, it is used for medical image analysis, such as segmenting tumors in MRI scans or identifying anatomical structures in diagnostic images. In autonomous vehicles, segmentation helps in recognizing road boundaries, traffic signs, and obstacles for safe navigation. In remote sensing and geographic information systems (GIS), it aids in land cover classification and environmental monitoring. The technology is also applied in industrial automation for quality control, in agriculture for crop monitoring, and in augmented reality for real-time object detection and interaction.

In conclusion, XY-plane segmentation in AI is a vital technique for analyzing and interpreting two-dimensional data, supporting a wide range of applications across industries. By leveraging advanced algorithms and machine learning models, AI-driven segmentation enhances accuracy, efficiency, and scalability in data analysis and decision-making processes. While challenges related to data variability, computational demands, and model interpretability exist, continuous advancements in AI and computer vision technologies are improving the effectiveness and reliability of XY-plane segmentation, driving innovation in data-driven applications.

X-Y Neural Network Topology

Definition X-Y Neural Network Topology refers to a structural design in artificial neural networks where nodes (neurons) are organized in a two-dimensional (2D) grid layout defined by horizontal (X) and vertical (Y) axes. This topology facilitates the spatial arrangement of neurons to reflect the underlying structure of the input data, making it particularly useful in applications involving image processing, pattern recognition, and data visualization. The X-Y grid allows for efficient connectivity patterns that enhance information flow, feature extraction, and computational efficiency within neural networks.

Key components of X-Y neural network topology include input, hidden, and output layers arranged in a grid-like structure. Each neuron in the grid is connected to its neighboring neurons, enabling localized data processing and the capture of spatial relationships. Convolutional layers, often integrated within this topology, apply filters to detect features such as edges, textures, and patterns. Activation functions, such as ReLU or sigmoid, introduce non-linearity, while pooling layers reduce the dimensionality of feature maps, enhancing computational efficiency. Weight matrices and bias terms are used to optimize the learning process through backpropagation and gradient descent algorithms.

The benefits of X-Y neural network topology are significant. Its grid-based structure is well-suited for processing spatially correlated data, such as images and sensor arrays, leading to improved accuracy in tasks like object detection and image classification. The topology supports parallel processing, enabling faster computations and scalability to larger datasets. It enhances feature learning by preserving spatial hierarchies and relationships, which is crucial for complex pattern recognition tasks. Additionally, the localized connectivity reduces the number of parameters, minimizing the risk of overfitting and improving generalization to new data.

Applications of X-Y neural network topology span various domains. In computer vision, it is used for image and video analysis, facial recognition, and medical imaging diagnostics. In robotics, the topology aids in environmental mapping, object recognition, and autonomous navigation. In natural language processing, it supports text classification, sentiment analysis, and language modeling by capturing spatial dependencies in word embeddings. The technology is also applied in financial forecasting, where spatial relationships between data points enhance predictive models. Furthermore, X-Y neural networks are utilized in scientific research for data visualization, anomaly detection, and pattern discovery in complex datasets.

In conclusion, X-Y neural network topology is a powerful framework for structuring artificial neural networks to efficiently process spatially organized data. Its grid-based design enhances pattern recognition, feature extraction, and computational efficiency across a wide range of AI applications. While challenges related to computational complexity, model interpretability, and architectural optimization exist, continuous advancements in neural network research and machine learning techniques are improving the capabilities and performance of X-Y neural network topologies, driving innovation in artificial intelligence and data science.

XY Path Planning in Robotics

Definition XY Path Planning in Robotics refers to the process of determining an optimal trajectory for a robot to move from one point to another within a two-dimensional (2D) space defined by the horizontal (X) and vertical (Y) axes. This method is fundamental in robotics for navigation, obstacle avoidance, and autonomous mobility. AI-driven XY path planning algorithms utilize advanced computational techniques to analyze environmental data, predict potential obstacles, and generate efficient movement paths, ensuring that robots operate effectively in dynamic and complex environments.

Key components of XY path planning in robotics include environmental mapping, where data from sensors such as LiDAR, cameras, and ultrasonic devices create a detailed representation of the robot's surroundings. Path planning algorithms, such as A* (A-star), Dijkstra's algorithm, and Rapidly-exploring Random Trees (RRT), are used to identify the shortest or most efficient route. Motion control systems translate the planned path into executable commands for the robot's actuators. Additionally, real-time data processing and sensor fusion techniques allow for dynamic adjustments to the path in response to changes in the environment.

The benefits of XY path planning in robotics are significant. It enhances the autonomy and efficiency of robots by enabling them to navigate complex environments without human intervention. Path planning algorithms optimize routes to minimize travel time, energy consumption, and operational costs. They improve safety by incorporating obstacle detection and avoidance capabilities, reducing the risk of collisions. AI-driven path planning also supports multi-robot coordination, allowing for synchronized movements in collaborative tasks. Furthermore, it enhances the adaptability of robots to different terrains and dynamic conditions, increasing their versatility in various applications.

Applications of XY path planning in robotics span multiple industries. In autonomous vehicles, it enables precise navigation and route optimization in urban and off-road environments. In warehouse automation, path planning algorithms guide robotic systems for efficient inventory management and goods transportation. In healthcare, robotic path planning assists in surgical procedures, rehabilitation, and patient mobility aids. The technology is also used in agriculture for precision farming, in defense for unmanned ground vehicles (UGVs), and in space exploration for rover navigation. Additionally, it supports consumer robotics, such as vacuum cleaners and drones, enhancing their functionality and performance.

In conclusion, XY path planning in robotics is a critical technology for enabling autonomous navigation, enhancing operational efficiency, and supporting a wide range of applications. By leveraging artificial intelligence and advanced algorithms, robots can achieve higher levels of autonomy, adaptability, and performance. While challenges related to dynamic environments, computational demands, and sensor reliability exist, ongoing advancements in AI, robotics, and sensor technologies are driving improvements in XY path planning, paving the way for more intelligent and capable robotic systems.

XY-plane Heatmap Visualization in AI

XY-plane Heatmap Visualization in AI refers to a graphical representation technique used to display data distribution, intensity, or density across two-dimensional (2D) coordinates. The XY-plane corresponds to the horizontal (X) and vertical (Y) axes, and the heatmap uses color gradients to represent the magnitude of data points within this space. This method is widely applied in artificial intelligence (AI) for data analysis, pattern recognition, model evaluation, and decision-making support. Heatmaps help in identifying trends, correlations, and anomalies within datasets, making them valuable tools in various AI-driven applications.

Key components of XY-plane heatmap visualization in AI include the data matrix, which consists of numerical values mapped to specific XY coordinates. The color gradient, ranging from cool to warm colors, represents the intensity or frequency of the data points, with distinct shades indicating different levels of concentration. Visualization libraries and tools, such as Matplotlib, Seaborn, and Plotly in Python, are used to create these heatmaps. Additionally, data preprocessing techniques, such as normalization and scaling, are employed to enhance the clarity and accuracy of the heatmap representation. Advanced AI models may integrate heatmaps with machine learning algorithms to visualize feature importance, activation maps, or prediction confidence levels.

The benefits of XY-plane heatmap visualization in AI are significant. It provides an intuitive and easily interpretable way to analyze complex datasets, enabling quick identification of patterns, outliers, and areas of interest. Heatmaps facilitate better understanding of data distributions and relationships, supporting informed decision-making. They enhance model interpretability by visually representing the impact of different features or parameters on AI model outputs. Additionally, heatmaps improve the communication of analytical results to stakeholders, as they convey insights effectively without requiring advanced statistical knowledge.

Applications of XY-plane heatmap visualization in AI span across various industries and domains. In computer vision, heatmaps are used to highlight areas of interest in images, such as objects detected by convolutional neural networks (CNNs). In healthcare, they assist in medical imaging analysis, identifying regions with abnormal patterns in diagnostic scans. In finance, heatmaps visualize market trends, asset correlations, and risk assessments. The technology is also applied in marketing for customer behavior analysis, website click tracking, and sentiment analysis. Furthermore, heatmaps support scientific research by visualizing experimental data, environmental monitoring, and geographical information systems (GIS).

In conclusion, XY-plane heatmap visualization in AI is a powerful tool for data exploration, pattern recognition, and model evaluation. By providing clear, intuitive visual representations of data distributions and relationships, heatmaps enhance analytical insights and decision-making processes across diverse applications. While challenges related to data representation, dimensionality reduction, and computational efficiency exist, continuous advancements in AI visualization techniques and tools are improving the effectiveness, accuracy, and accessibility of XY-plane heatmaps, supporting the growth of data-driven insights in the AI landscape.

LETTER Y

Yarn Clustering in AI

Yarn Clustering in AI refers to the process of grouping data points or objects into clusters based on their similarities using artificial intelligence techniques. The term "yarn" metaphorically represents the interwoven nature of data points that, when clustered, form cohesive groups with shared characteristics. This clustering technique is commonly used in data mining, machine learning, and pattern recognition to identify meaningful structures within large datasets. AI-driven yarn clustering algorithms can handle complex, high-dimensional data, making them suitable for various applications such as image analysis, natural language processing, and customer segmentation.

Key components of yarn clustering in AI include data preprocessing methods to clean and normalize data, feature extraction techniques to identify relevant attributes, and clustering algorithms such as K-means, DBSCAN (Density-Based Spatial Clustering of Applications with Noise), and hierarchical clustering. Advanced AI models, including neural networks and self-organizing maps, are also employed to enhance clustering accuracy and handle non-linear data relationships. Distance metrics like Euclidean distance, Manhattan distance, or cosine similarity are used to measure the closeness of data points within clusters. Evaluation metrics, such as silhouette score and Davies-Bouldin index, assess the quality and coherence of the formed clusters.

The benefits of yarn clustering in AI are substantial. It enables the discovery of hidden patterns and insights within large and complex datasets without the need for labeled data. Clustering facilitates better decision-making by segmenting data into meaningful groups, which can be used for targeted marketing, personalized recommendations, and anomaly detection. AI-driven clustering algorithms are scalable and can process vast amounts of data efficiently, providing real-time analytics in dynamic environments. Additionally, yarn clustering supports dimensionality reduction, simplifying data visualization and interpretation for business intelligence and scientific research.

Applications of yarn clustering in AI span across various industries. In marketing, it helps businesses segment customers based on purchasing behavior, enabling personalized marketing strategies. In healthcare, clustering algorithms are used to identify patient groups with similar medical conditions, supporting personalized treatment plans. The technology is applied in cybersecurity to detect unusual patterns that may indicate security threats or fraud. In image and video analysis, yarn clustering aids in object recognition, facial detection, and scene segmentation. Additionally, it is used in natural language processing for document clustering, topic modeling, and sentiment analysis.

In conclusion, yarn clustering in AI is a powerful technique for uncovering hidden structures and patterns within data, supporting a wide range of applications across industries. By leveraging advanced machine learning algorithms and data analysis techniques, yarn clustering enhances decision-making, personalization, and predictive analytics. While challenges related to cluster determination, data noise, and model interpretability exist, continuous advancements in AI and data science are improving the effectiveness, scalability, and accessibility of clustering methods, driving innovation and insights in the era of big data.

Yaw Estimation in AI-Driven Vehicles

Yaw Estimation in AI-Driven Vehicles refers to the process of determining the rotational movement of a vehicle around its vertical axis, known as the yaw angle. This parameter is crucial for maintaining vehicle stability, accurate navigation, and advanced driver-assistance systems (ADAS). AI-driven yaw estimation utilizes machine learning algorithms, sensor fusion techniques, and real-time data analysis to enhance the precision and reliability of yaw measurements, which are vital for the safe and efficient operation of autonomous and semi-autonomous vehicles.

Key components of yaw estimation in AI-driven vehicles include sensor technologies such as gyroscopes, accelerometers, GPS modules, and wheel speed sensors that collect raw motion data. Sensor fusion algorithms, including Kalman filters and complementary filters, integrate data from multiple sources to reduce noise and improve accuracy. Machine learning models are trained to identify patterns in sensor data and predict yaw rate and angle under varying driving conditions. Real-time processing units analyze these inputs continuously, enabling the vehicle to make immediate adjustments to its steering, braking, and acceleration systems.

The benefits of yaw estimation in AI-driven vehicles are substantial. It enhances vehicle stability and control, especially during sharp turns, slippery conditions, or sudden maneuvers. Accurate yaw estimation improves the performance of ADAS features such as lane-keeping assistance, electronic stability control, and collision avoidance systems. It supports the development of fully autonomous vehicles by providing critical orientation data necessary for path planning and navigation. Additionally, AI-driven yaw estimation contributes to smoother ride experiences, reduced wear on vehicle components, and increased passenger safety.

Applications of yaw estimation in AI-driven vehicles span various domains within the automotive industry. In autonomous driving systems, it ensures precise trajectory tracking and vehicle positioning. In motorsports, yaw data is used to optimize vehicle dynamics and driver performance. Yaw estimation also plays a role in fleet management systems, where it aids in monitoring vehicle behavior and detecting anomalies related to driver performance or mechanical issues. Furthermore, it is integrated into virtual simulations and driving assistance technologies to enhance the development and testing of new automotive innovations.

In conclusion, yaw estimation in AI-driven vehicles is a critical technology for enhancing vehicle stability, navigation accuracy, and autonomous driving capabilities. By leveraging advanced sensors, machine learning algorithms, and real-time data analysis, AI-driven yaw estimation supports safer, more efficient, and responsive vehicle operations. While challenges related to sensor accuracy, environmental variability, and algorithm complexity exist, ongoing advancements in AI and automotive engineering are continuously improving the reliability and effectiveness of yaw estimation systems, driving the future of intelligent transportation.

Yerkes-Dodson Law in AI

Yerkes-Dodson Law in AI refers to the application of a psychological principle that describes the relationship between arousal and performance, adapted to optimize the functioning of artificial intelligence systems. Originally formulated in human behavioral studies, the law suggests that performance improves with increased arousal up to an optimal point, beyond which excessive arousal can lead to performance decline. In AI, this concept is utilized to manage system stress, resource allocation, and decision-making efficiency, particularly in environments requiring real-time processing and adaptive responses.

Key components of the Yerkes-Dodson Law in AI include performance metrics that evaluate system output under varying levels of computational load or environmental complexity, arousal models that simulate stress or urgency within AI decision-making processes, and adaptive algorithms designed to maintain optimal performance levels. Machine learning techniques are employed to calibrate the arousal-performance curve, identifying thresholds where performance peaks and where degradation begins. Feedback mechanisms are integrated to dynamically adjust system parameters in response to real-time conditions, ensuring sustained efficiency.

The benefits of applying the Yerkes-Dodson Law in AI are significant. It enhances system robustness by preventing performance degradation under high-stress conditions, such as during peak data loads or in critical real-time applications. The model supports adaptive learning, allowing AI systems to self-regulate based on task difficulty and environmental changes, leading to more resilient and efficient operations. Additionally, it improves decision-making quality by optimizing the balance between computational resources and task demands, reducing errors and latency in high-pressure scenarios.

Applications of the Yerkes-Dodson Law in AI are diverse. In autonomous vehicles, it helps manage the balance between reaction speed and decision accuracy under varying traffic conditions. In robotics, the law guides adaptive behavior in response to dynamic environments, enhancing task performance and safety. In financial AI systems, it optimizes trading algorithms to maintain efficiency during market volatility. The law is also applied in human-AI interaction, improving user experience by adjusting system responsiveness based on user engagement levels. Additionally, it supports AI-driven healthcare applications, enhancing diagnostic accuracy under time-sensitive conditions.

In conclusion, the Yerkes-Dodson Law in AI offers a valuable framework for enhancing system performance through adaptive stress and resource management. By applying this principle, AI systems can achieve optimal efficiency and resilience in dynamic environments, improving decision-making accuracy and operational reliability. While challenges related to model adaptation, threshold calibration, and system stability exist, ongoing advancements in AI research and adaptive algorithms continue to refine the application of the Yerkes-Dodson Law, contributing to the development of more robust and intelligent AI systems.

Yield Curve Forecasting in AI

Yield Curve Forecasting in AI refers to the application of artificial intelligence techniques to predict the future movements of yield curves, which represent the relationship between interest rates and the maturity of debt instruments, such as government bonds. This forecasting is critical in financial markets as it provides insights into economic conditions, interest rate trends, and potential investment opportunities. AI-driven models leverage historical data, market indicators, and advanced machine learning algorithms to enhance the accuracy and efficiency of yield curve predictions.

Key components of Yield Curve Forecasting in AI include data collection and preprocessing mechanisms that aggregate historical yield data, macroeconomic indicators, and financial market variables. Machine learning models, such as neural networks, support vector machines, and ensemble learning techniques, are employed to identify patterns and correlations within complex datasets. Time series analysis, combined with deep learning architectures like recurrent neural networks (RNNs) and long short-term memory (LSTM) networks, enables the modeling of temporal dependencies and dynamic shifts in yield curves. Feature selection and dimensionality reduction techniques optimize model performance by focusing on the most relevant predictive variables.

The benefits of Yield Curve Forecasting in AI are substantial. AI models offer improved forecasting accuracy by uncovering hidden patterns and nonlinear relationships that traditional statistical methods may overlook. They enable real-time analysis and rapid adaptation to changing market conditions, enhancing decision-making for investors, policymakers, and financial institutions. AI-driven forecasts support risk management strategies by identifying potential interest rate fluctuations and economic downturns in advance. Additionally, the automation of forecasting processes reduces human bias and increases operational efficiency, providing scalable solutions for large-scale financial data analysis.

Applications of Yield Curve Forecasting in AI span various sectors within finance and economics. In investment management, AI models guide portfolio allocation decisions, interest rate hedging strategies, and fixed-income investment planning. Central banks and policymakers utilize AI forecasts to inform monetary policy decisions and economic outlook assessments. In banking, yield curve predictions aid in managing interest rate risk, pricing financial products, and optimizing asset-liability management. The technology is also applied in credit risk analysis, forecasting default probabilities based on interest rate trends, and in corporate finance for strategic planning and capital budgeting.

In conclusion, Yield Curve Forecasting in AI represents a transformative advancement in financial analytics, offering precise, data-driven insights into interest rate dynamics and economic conditions. By leveraging machine learning and data science techniques, AI enhances the accuracy, speed, and scalability of yield curve predictions, supporting informed decision-making in investment, policy, and risk management. While challenges related to data complexity, model interpretability, and market volatility exist, ongoing advancements in AI methodologies continue to improve the reliability and effectiveness of yield curve forecasting, contributing to the evolution of intelligent financial systems.

Yield Prediction with AI

Yield Prediction with AI refers to the application of artificial intelligence technologies to forecast the quantity of output produced in various sectors, including agriculture, manufacturing, and finance. This process utilizes advanced machine learning algorithms, data analytics, and predictive modeling to analyze historical and real-time data, enabling accurate estimations of future yields. AI-driven yield prediction enhances decision-making processes, optimizes resource allocation, and improves productivity by providing data-driven insights into expected outcomes.

Key components of Yield Prediction with AI include data collection systems that aggregate information from various sources such as sensors, satellite imagery, weather data, and historical production records. Machine learning models, including regression analysis, neural networks, and support vector machines, process this data to identify patterns and trends that influence yield outcomes. Feature engineering techniques are used to select and optimize relevant variables, while predictive algorithms generate forecasts based on data inputs. Additionally, AI platforms incorporate visualization tools to present insights clearly, supporting actionable decisions.

The benefits of Yield Prediction with AI are substantial. In agriculture, it enables farmers to anticipate crop yields, plan harvests, and optimize the use of fertilizers, water, and other resources, leading to increased efficiency and reduced costs. In manufacturing, AI helps forecast production outputs, manage supply chains, and minimize downtime by predicting equipment performance and maintenance needs. Financial institutions use AI-driven yield prediction for investment analysis, risk assessment, and portfolio management, enhancing profitability and decision-making accuracy. Overall, AI improves productivity, reduces waste, and supports sustainable practices by providing precise and timely predictions.

Applications of Yield Prediction with AI span multiple industries. In agriculture, AI models predict crop performance based on soil conditions, weather patterns, and farming practices, aiding in food security and resource management. In manufacturing, yield prediction optimizes production schedules and inventory management, reducing operational costs. In finance, AI forecasts returns on investments, helping investors make informed decisions. The technology is also applied in energy production to predict outputs from renewable sources like solar and wind, improving grid management and energy distribution. Additionally, AI-driven yield prediction supports pharmaceutical development by forecasting drug production outcomes during clinical trials and manufacturing processes.

In conclusion, Yield Prediction with AI represents a transformative approach to forecasting output across diverse industries. By leveraging machine learning and data analytics, AI provides accurate, data-driven insights that enhance productivity, efficiency, and sustainability. While challenges related to data quality, model complexity, and system integration exist, continuous advancements in AI technologies and data science methodologies are improving the accuracy, reliability, and applicability of yield prediction models, supporting informed decision-making and strategic planning in various sectors.

YOLO (You Only Look Once) Algorithm

YOLO (You Only Look Once) Algorithm refers to a real-time object detection system designed to identify and classify objects within images or video streams in a single evaluation. Unlike traditional object detection methods that apply a sliding window approach or multiple stages, YOLO processes the entire image simultaneously, significantly enhancing detection speed and accuracy. This algorithm leverages deep learning techniques to achieve high-performance detection tasks in real-time, making it a popular choice in computer vision applications.

Key components of the YOLO Algorithm include a convolutional neural network (CNN) architecture that extracts features from input images, a grid-based division of the image where each grid cell predicts bounding boxes and confidence scores, and classification layers that assign probability distributions to detected objects. The algorithm uses anchor boxes to handle multiple objects within a single grid cell and applies non-maximum suppression to eliminate redundant bounding boxes, ensuring precise localization of objects.

The benefits of the YOLO Algorithm are substantial. Its ability to process images in real-time with high accuracy makes it ideal for time-sensitive applications such as autonomous driving, surveillance, and robotics. YOLO's unified architecture simplifies the detection pipeline, reducing computational complexity and enabling deployment on edge devices with limited processing power. The algorithm's high recall rate ensures that even small or partially obscured objects are detected, improving the robustness of object recognition systems. Additionally, YOLO's flexibility allows for easy adaptation to various datasets and detection tasks.

Applications of the YOLO Algorithm span diverse industries. In autonomous vehicles, YOLO is used for pedestrian detection, traffic sign recognition, and obstacle avoidance. In security and surveillance, it supports real-time monitoring and threat detection. The algorithm is employed in healthcare for medical image analysis, aiding in the detection of tumors, anomalies, and diagnostic markers. In retail,

YOLO enhances inventory management and customer behavior analysis through automated object tracking. Additionally, it is applied in agricultural technology for crop monitoring and livestock management, and in sports analytics for tracking player movements and game dynamics.

In conclusion, the YOLO (You Only Look Once) Algorithm represents a breakthrough in real-time object detection, offering a powerful combination of speed, accuracy, and efficiency. Its unified approach to image processing has transformed applications across multiple sectors, from autonomous systems to healthcare and retail. While challenges related to small object detection, localization accuracy, and resource demands exist, ongoing advancements in deep learning and computer vision technologies continue to enhance YOLO's capabilities, solidifying its role as a cornerstone of modern AI-driven object detection systems.

Young's Modulus Prediction using AI

Young's Modulus Prediction using AI refers to the application of artificial intelligence and machine learning techniques to estimate the elastic modulus of materials based on their properties and structural characteristics. Young's Modulus, also known as the modulus of elasticity, measures a material's ability to resist deformation under stress, making it a critical parameter in materials science, engineering, and structural analysis. AI-driven models utilize historical data, experimental results, and material properties to predict Young's Modulus accurately, reducing the need for extensive physical testing.

Key components of Young's Modulus Prediction using AI include data preprocessing techniques to clean and normalize material datasets, feature selection algorithms to identify the most influential properties affecting elasticity, and machine learning models such as regression algorithms, support vector machines, and neural networks to establish relationships between input variables and Young's Modulus. Deep learning architectures, including convolutional neural networks (CNNs) and recurrent neural networks (RNNs), are also employed for complex datasets involving microstructural images or time-series data. Model training, validation, and optimization processes ensure predictive accuracy and generalization to new materials.

The benefits of Young's Modulus Prediction using AI are substantial. AI models significantly reduce the time and cost associated with traditional experimental methods by providing rapid, data-driven predictions. They enable the exploration of new materials and composites without extensive physical testing, accelerating the development of innovative materials. AI enhances the accuracy and consistency of predictions by identifying patterns and correlations that may be overlooked in manual analysis. Additionally, predictive models can be integrated into design and simulation software, supporting real-time decision-making in engineering applications.

Applications of Young's Modulus Prediction using AI span various industries, including aerospace, automotive, civil engineering, and materials science. In structural engineering, AI models assist in designing buildings and infrastructure by predicting the mechanical properties of construction materials. In the aerospace and automotive sectors, they support the development of lightweight, high-strength materials for improved performance and fuel efficiency. The technology is also applied in biomedical engineering to predict the properties of biomaterials used in implants and prosthetics. Additionally, AI-driven predictions aid in quality control and materials testing processes, ensuring compliance with industry standards.

In conclusion, Young's Modulus Prediction using AI represents a transformative approach in materials science and engineering, offering efficient, accurate, and cost-effective solutions for estimating material properties. By leveraging machine learning and data-driven techniques, AI enhances the discovery, development, and application of materials across diverse industries. While challenges related to data quality, model complexity, and interpretability exist, ongoing advancements in AI technologies and materials informatics continue to improve the effectiveness and reliability of predictive models, driving innovation in material design and engineering applications.

You Only Sample Once (YOSO)

You Only Sample Once (YOSO) refers to an advanced sampling technique in artificial intelligence and machine learning, designed to optimize data efficiency and reduce computational overhead during model training and inference. Unlike traditional sampling methods that may require multiple iterations to achieve statistical accuracy, YOSO emphasizes a single, strategically chosen sampling instance to capture essential information from the dataset. This approach is particularly valuable in scenarios where data processing costs are high, or real-time decision-making is critical.

Key components of YOSO include a well-defined sampling strategy that ensures the selected sample is representative of the larger dataset, minimizing the risk of bias or information loss. The technique often relies on probabilistic models or statistical optimization to identify the most informative data points for sampling. Additionally, YOSO incorporates mechanisms for uncertainty estimation and error correction, ensuring that the model maintains robustness and accuracy despite the reduced sampling frequency.

The benefits of YOSO are significant in terms of computational efficiency and resource management. By reducing the number of samples needed, YOSO decreases data processing time, lowers energy consumption, and minimizes storage requirements. This efficiency makes it particularly advantageous for edge computing applications, real-time analytics, and large-scale machine learning models where resource constraints are a concern. Furthermore, YOSO enhances model scalability, allowing AI systems to operate effectively across diverse environments and datasets without extensive reconfiguration.

Applications of YOSO span various industries and domains. In real-time systems such as autonomous vehicles and robotics, YOSO enables rapid decision-making by processing minimal yet highly informative data samples. In finance, it supports high-frequency trading algorithms that require swift, data-driven insights. The technique is also valuable in healthcare for real-time monitoring and diagnostic systems where quick, accurate assessments are crucial. Additionally, YOSO is employed in environmental monitoring, IoT networks, and any application where data sampling efficiency directly impacts performance and cost-effectiveness.

In conclusion, You Only Sample Once (YOSO) represents a transformative approach in data sampling and AI model optimization. Its ability to enhance computational efficiency, reduce resource consumption, and support real-time decision-making makes it a valuable technique in various AI-driven industries. While challenges related to sampling bias, dynamic data environments, and algorithm complexity exist, ongoing advancements in AI and statistical methodologies continue to improve the effectiveness and applicability of YOSO in modern data analysis and machine learning systems.

YouTube Captioning with AI

YouTube Captioning with AI refers to the use of artificial intelligence technologies to automatically generate subtitles and captions for videos hosted on the YouTube platform. This process leverages advanced machine learning models, including natural language processing (NLP) and automatic speech recognition (ASR) systems, to transcribe spoken language into text in real-time or post-production. AI-driven captioning enhances the accessibility, searchability, and user engagement of video content, catering to diverse audiences, including individuals with hearing impairments and non-native language speakers.

Key components of YouTube Captioning with AI include automatic speech recognition algorithms that convert audio signals into text, natural language processing techniques that improve the accuracy and coherence of transcriptions, and language models that support multilingual captioning. Additionally, time synchronization mechanisms align the generated captions with the corresponding video frames, ensuring precise timing. AI models are trained on vast datasets to improve their ability to recognize different accents, dialects, and contextual nuances, enhancing the overall quality of captions.

The benefits of YouTube Captioning with AI are significant. It increases video accessibility, allowing a broader audience to engage with content regardless of hearing ability or language proficiency. Captions improve user comprehension, particularly in noisy environments or when audio quality is poor. AI-generated captions also enhance video SEO (Search Engine Optimization), making content more discoverable through search engines. For content creators, automated captioning saves time and resources compared to manual transcription, enabling faster content publication and broader audience reach.

Applications of YouTube Captioning with AI extend across various domains. In education, it supports e-learning platforms by providing accessible course materials for students worldwide. In corporate settings, AI-generated captions facilitate communication during webinars, virtual meetings, and training sessions. The entertainment industry benefits from enhanced accessibility for films, TV shows, and online content. Additionally, captions assist in language learning, helping viewers improve their understanding of new languages through contextual text support. YouTube also uses AI captioning to enhance content moderation and compliance with accessibility regulations.

In conclusion, YouTube Captioning with AI represents a transformative technology that enhances video accessibility, engagement, and discoverability. By leveraging machine learning and natural language processing, AI-driven captioning provides efficient, scalable solutions for diverse content creators and audiences. While challenges related to transcription accuracy, language diversity, and contextual understanding persist, continuous advancements in AI technologies are improving the reliability and effectiveness of automated captioning systems, contributing to a more inclusive and accessible digital media landscape.

YouTube Video Recommendation Algorithms

YouTube Video Recommendation Algorithms refer to sophisticated machine learning systems designed to personalize and optimize video suggestions for users based on their behavior, preferences, and interaction patterns. These algorithms analyze vast amounts of data, including watch history, search queries, engagement metrics, and demographic information, to predict and recommend content that aligns with individual interests. The primary objective is to enhance user experience, increase watch time, and drive user engagement by presenting relevant and appealing video content.

Key components of YouTube Video Recommendation Algorithms include data collection mechanisms that gather user activity data, collaborative filtering techniques that identify patterns among users with similar interests, and content-based filtering methods that recommend videos with characteristics similar to previously watched content. Advanced deep learning models, such as neural networks, are employed to process complex data relationships and improve recommendation accuracy. The ranking system prioritizes videos based on relevance, predicted watch time, user interaction likelihood, and overall engagement potential. Reinforcement learning techniques are also used to continuously refine and optimize recommendations based on real-time user feedback.

The benefits of YouTube Video Recommendation Algorithms are extensive. They provide a highly personalized viewing experience, allowing users to discover content tailored to their preferences. This personalization fosters user satisfaction and retention, contributing to longer watch sessions and increased platform loyalty. For content creators, these algorithms enhance content visibility and audience reach, supporting growth and monetization opportunities. From a business perspective, recommendation algorithms improve targeted advertising effectiveness, maximizing ad revenue for YouTube and its partners by connecting advertisers with relevant audiences.

Applications of YouTube Video Recommendation Algorithms extend beyond entertainment. In education, they promote learning by recommending relevant academic content and tutorials. In marketing, businesses leverage these algorithms to deliver targeted video advertisements and branded content to specific demographics. The technology also supports content discovery in niche areas, helping users find videos related to health, technology, science, and other specialized interests. Additionally, recommendation algorithms are integrated into other Google services, enhancing cross-platform user experiences through interconnected content suggestions.

In conclusion, YouTube Video Recommendation Algorithms play a pivotal role in shaping user experiences and content consumption patterns on the platform. Their ability to analyze user behavior, predict preferences, and deliver personalized recommendations drives user engagement, content discovery, and business growth. While challenges related to algorithmic bias, data privacy, content diversity, and ethical considerations exist, continuous advancements in AI and machine learning are enhancing the effectiveness, fairness, and transparency of recommendation systems, fostering a more balanced and enriching digital environment.

Yule Process in AI Simulation

Yule Process in AI Simulation refers to a stochastic process used to model the growth and evolution of systems characterized by preferential attachment, where entities with more connections or occurrences are more likely to attract additional connections. Named after statistician George Udny Yule, this process is fundamental in simulating dynamic systems where new elements are more likely to attach to well-established nodes, leading to power-law distributions. In artificial intelligence, the Yule Process is applied to simulate phenomena such as network growth, information diffusion, and evolutionary dynamics.

Key components of the Yule Process include the probability distribution that governs the attachment mechanism, where the likelihood of new connections increases with the number of existing links. The process involves a continuous-time Markov chain to model the random evolution over time, with state transitions representing the addition of new nodes or connections. The growth parameter determines the rate at which new entities are introduced into the system, influencing the overall structure and complexity of the simulated network.

The benefits of the Yule Process in AI Simulation are significant. It provides a realistic framework for modeling complex systems with self-reinforcing growth patterns, such as social networks, citation networks, and biological systems. The process captures the emergence of hubs or highly connected nodes, reflecting real-world phenomena where popularity or connectivity drives further growth. It supports the development of predictive models for understanding the long-term behavior of dynamic systems and enhances the analysis of structural properties such as clustering, centrality, and resilience.

Applications of the Yule Process in AI Simulation span various domains. In network science, it is used to model the evolution of social media platforms, internet topology, and communication networks. In bioinformatics, the process helps simulate the growth of phylogenetic trees, representing the evolutionary relationships among species. The Yule Process is also applied in economics to model market dynamics and wealth distribution, and in machine learning, it supports the development of algorithms for clustering, recommendation systems, and anomaly detection. Additionally, it is used in natural language processing to model the frequency distribution of words and linguistic patterns.

In conclusion, the Yule Process in AI Simulation is a powerful tool for modeling and analyzing dynamic systems characterized by preferential attachment and self-reinforcing growth. Its ability to capture the structural properties and evolutionary dynamics of complex networks makes it valuable across various scientific and industrial applications. While challenges related to model assumptions, computational efficiency, and parameter calibration exist, ongoing advancements in AI and simulation techniques continue to enhance the effectiveness and applicability of the Yule Process in modern data analysis and system modeling.

Yunet (AI Neural Network)

Yunet (AI Neural Network) refers to an advanced deep learning architecture designed to enhance performance in various computer vision and pattern recognition tasks. Yunet is structured to improve the efficiency and accuracy of object detection, image segmentation, and face recognition applications. It leverages the power of convolutional neural networks (CNNs) combined with sophisticated feature extraction and multi-scale processing techniques to deliver high-speed and precise results, even in real-time environments.

Key components of Yunet include convolutional layers responsible for extracting hierarchical features from input data, pooling layers that reduce dimensionality while preserving critical information, and fully connected layers that consolidate learned features for final classification or regression tasks. The architecture integrates multi-scale feature maps to detect objects of varying sizes and employs anchor-based mechanisms for precise localization. Optimization algorithms such as stochastic gradient descent (SGD) or adaptive moment estimation (Adam) are utilized to fine-tune model parameters during training. Additionally, batch normalization and dropout techniques are applied to enhance model generalization and prevent overfitting.

The benefits of Yunet are significant, offering superior accuracy in object detection and recognition tasks, particularly in challenging environments with variations in lighting, occlusion, and background complexity. Its lightweight and efficient design make it suitable for deployment on edge devices and mobile platforms, ensuring fast inference times without compromising performance. Yunet's ability to process multi-scale features enhances its robustness in identifying objects of different shapes and sizes. The model is highly adaptable, allowing for fine-tuning to specific tasks or datasets, making it versatile across various applications.

Applications of Yunet span multiple industries, including security and surveillance, where it is used for real-time face detection and recognition in video streams. In healthcare, Yunet assists in medical image analysis, aiding in the detection of anomalies in radiology images. The automotive industry employs Yunet for driver assistance systems and autonomous vehicle navigation by recognizing pedestrians, traffic signs, and obstacles. In retail, Yunet supports customer behavior analysis and automated inventory management through advanced visual tracking. Additionally, it is utilized in augmented reality (AR) applications to enhance object tracking and environmental understanding.

In conclusion, Yunet (AI Neural Network) represents a powerful and flexible deep learning architecture tailored for high-performance computer vision tasks. Its advanced feature extraction capabilities, efficient design, and adaptability to various applications make it a valuable tool in the development of intelligent systems. Despite challenges related to computational demands and model interpretability, the continuous evolution of neural network technologies ensures that Yunet remains at the forefront of AI-driven innovations, contributing to advancements in automation, analytics, and real-time decision-making.

YUV Color Space in AI

YUV Color Space in AI refers to a color representation model used to separate image luminance (brightness) from chrominance (color information), making it particularly useful in image and video processing applications. The Y component represents the luminance, while the U and V components represent the chrominance, capturing the color differences. This separation allows AI algorithms to process brightness and color independently, enhancing the efficiency of image compression, recognition, and computer vision tasks.

Key components of YUV Color Space include the Y channel, which stores grayscale information, and the U and V channels, which capture the color differences from the luminance. This model allows for efficient data representation, as the human eye is more sensitive to changes in brightness than color, enabling AI systems to allocate more resources to luminance processing while compressing color data without significant quality loss. Conversion algorithms are essential for transforming RGB data into YUV format and vice versa, facilitating compatibility with various image processing techniques.

The benefits of YUV Color Space in AI are substantial. It enhances image and video compression by reducing the amount of data needed to represent color information without compromising visual quality, making it ideal for streaming applications. The model improves the performance of AI algorithms in tasks such as object detection and facial recognition by allowing separate processing of luminance and chrominance, which can lead to more accurate results. Additionally, YUV is compatible with many video standards, supporting efficient transmission and storage of multimedia content.

Applications of YUV Color Space in AI are diverse, spanning fields such as video surveillance, autonomous vehicles, and medical imaging. In computer vision, it is used for feature extraction, where the luminance channel provides critical information for edge detection and object tracking. In video compression, formats like MPEG and JPEG utilize YUV to optimize storage and transmission. The technology also plays a role in augmented reality and virtual reality systems, where real-time image processing is essential for immersive experiences. Additionally, YUV is applied in robotics for color-based navigation and object recognition.

In conclusion, YUV Color Space in AI represents a critical tool for efficient image and video processing, enabling advanced applications in computer vision, multimedia compression, and real-time analytics. Its ability to separate luminance and chrominance enhances processing efficiency and visual quality, making it invaluable for a wide range of AI-driven technologies. While challenges related to color conversion, consistency, and precision exist, ongoing advancements in AI and image processing techniques continue to improve the effectiveness and versatility of YUV Color Space in modern applications.

YY Boosting Algorithm in AI

YY Boosting Algorithm in AI refers to an advanced ensemble learning technique designed to improve the predictive performance of machine learning models by combining multiple weak learners into a single strong model. This algorithm operates by sequentially training weak models, each focusing on correcting the errors made by its predecessors. Through this iterative process, the YY Boosting Algorithm enhances model accuracy, reduces bias, and minimizes variance, making it highly effective for classification, regression, and ranking tasks in artificial intelligence applications.

Key components of the YY Boosting Algorithm include weak learners, typically decision trees, that perform slightly better than random guessing. The algorithm also incorporates a weighting mechanism that adjusts the importance of data points based on their classification difficulty, ensuring that subsequent models focus on harder-to-predict instances. Additionally, a loss function is used to measure the model's performance, guiding the optimization process through gradient descent or similar techniques. Regularization methods are integrated to prevent overfitting and improve generalization to new data.

The benefits of the YY Boosting Algorithm are substantial. It significantly improves prediction accuracy by combining the strengths of multiple models, making it robust against overfitting, especially when proper regularization is applied. The algorithm is versatile and can handle a variety of data types and problem domains. Its flexibility allows it to be customized for specific tasks through the adjustment of hyperparameters, such as learning rate and tree depth. Furthermore, YY Boosting is efficient in handling large datasets and high-dimensional data, providing fast and reliable results even in complex scenarios.

Applications of the YY Boosting Algorithm span numerous industries. In finance, it is used for credit scoring, risk assessment, and algorithmic trading. In healthcare, the algorithm supports predictive analytics for patient outcomes, disease diagnosis, and personalized treatment recommendations. The technology is applied in marketing for customer segmentation, churn prediction, and recommendation systems. Additionally, YY Boosting is employed in natural language processing for sentiment analysis, text classification, and language translation tasks. In cybersecurity, it aids in fraud detection and anomaly identification, enhancing threat prevention systems.

In conclusion, the YY Boosting Algorithm in AI represents a powerful tool for enhancing the performance of machine learning models through ensemble learning. Its ability to reduce bias and variance, improve accuracy, and handle diverse data types makes it a valuable asset across various domains. While challenges related to computational demands, sensitivity to noise, and model interpretability exist, the continuous development of boosting techniques and optimization methods ensures that YY Boosting remains at the forefront of advanced AI solutions.

YY Chromosome Simulation in AI Genetics

YY Chromosome Simulation in AI Genetics refers to the use of artificial intelligence algorithms to model, analyze, and predict genetic variations and behaviors associated with the YY chromosome configuration. This simulation focuses on understanding complex genetic patterns, gene expression, and potential evolutionary implications within synthetic or hypothetical biological systems. AI-driven simulations facilitate the exploration of genetic scenarios that are challenging to study in real-world environments, enabling researchers to investigate rare or theoretical genetic structures efficiently.

Key components of YY Chromosome Simulation in AI Genetics include genetic algorithms that mimic natural selection and evolution processes, neural networks that analyze large genomic datasets for pattern recognition, and bioinformatics tools that process genetic sequences for detailed analysis. Simulation environments are designed to replicate cellular processes, gene interactions, and chromosomal dynamics. Data modeling techniques, such as machine learning classifiers and predictive analytics, support the identification of genetic traits and potential anomalies associated with YY chromosome configurations.

The benefits of YY Chromosome Simulation are significant in advancing genetic research. It allows for the rapid analysis of genetic data without the ethical or logistical constraints of laboratory experiments. AI-driven simulations enhance the accuracy of genetic predictions, supporting the identification of gene functions, mutations, and potential hereditary conditions. The ability to simulate complex genetic interactions provides valuable insights into evolutionary biology, reproductive health, and the development of targeted gene therapies. Additionally, these simulations can be customized for specific research goals, enabling tailored investigations into genetic phenomena.

Applications of YY Chromosome Simulation in AI Genetics are diverse, ranging from academic research to clinical studies. In evolutionary biology, simulations help explore the genetic implications of rare chromosomal configurations and their potential impact on species development. In medicine, AI-driven genetic models support personalized healthcare by predicting the likelihood of genetic disorders and informing treatment strategies. The technology is also applied in agriculture and biotechnology for genetic modification and crop improvement, where understanding chromosomal behavior is critical. Furthermore, YY Chromosome Simulation contributes to the development of bioinformatics tools used in genome sequencing and genetic data analysis.

In conclusion, YY Chromosome Simulation in AI Genetics represents a powerful tool for advancing our understanding of genetic structures and their biological implications. By leveraging artificial intelligence, researchers can model complex genetic scenarios, predict gene behavior, and explore evolutionary processes with unprecedented precision. While challenges related to data accuracy, computational resources, and ethical concerns exist, the continuous development of AI technologies is enhancing the capabilities and applications of genetic simulations, contributing to breakthroughs in genetics, medicine, and biotechnology.

YY Integration in AI Workflow Automation

YY Integration in AI Workflow Automation refers to the seamless incorporation of advanced artificial intelligence techniques into automated business and operational workflows. This integration enables the efficient management of repetitive tasks, data processing, decision-making, and resource optimization within various industries. YY Integration focuses on enhancing the adaptability, scalability, and intelligence of workflows by embedding AI-driven solutions that streamline processes, reduce manual intervention, and improve overall productivity.

Key components of YY Integration in AI Workflow Automation include AI algorithms for data analysis, machine learning models that support predictive insights and decision-making, and robotic process automation (RPA) tools that handle repetitive tasks. Natural language processing (NLP) is used to interpret and process unstructured data, while API integrations enable smooth communication between AI systems and existing enterprise software. Additionally, real-time monitoring and analytics dashboards provide insights into workflow performance, allowing for continuous improvement and optimization.

The benefits of YY Integration in AI Workflow Automation are significant. It enhances operational efficiency by automating time-consuming tasks, freeing up human resources for more strategic activities. The integration improves accuracy and consistency in task execution, reducing the likelihood of errors. AI-driven predictive capabilities support proactive decision-making, allowing organizations to anticipate challenges and optimize resource allocation. Furthermore, YY Integration increases scalability, enabling businesses to adapt quickly to changing demands without overhauling existing systems.

Applications of YY Integration in AI Workflow Automation span across diverse industries. In finance, it automates fraud detection, risk assessment, and transaction processing. In healthcare, AI-powered workflows assist with patient data management, appointment scheduling, and diagnostic support. The technology is used in supply chain management to optimize logistics, inventory control, and demand forecasting. In customer service, AI chatbots and virtual assistants enhance response times and improve customer engagement. Additionally, marketing automation platforms leverage AI to personalize content delivery and optimize campaign performance.

In conclusion, YY Integration in AI Workflow Automation represents a transformative advancement in how businesses and organizations manage their operations. By embedding AI into workflows, organizations can achieve greater efficiency, accuracy, and agility, leading to improved performance and competitiveness. While challenges related to system integration, data management, and organizational change exist, the continuous evolution of AI technologies ensures that YY Integration will play an increasingly vital role in shaping the future of automated workflows and intelligent business processes.

YY Neural Network (YYNN)

YY Neural Network (YYNN) refers to an advanced type of artificial neural network designed to improve learning efficiency, model accuracy, and adaptability in complex data environments. YYNN leverages deep learning architectures, enhanced with specialized algorithms that optimize data processing, feature extraction, and decision-making. This model is particularly effective for tasks that require high precision, such as image recognition, natural language processing, and predictive analytics, making it suitable for a wide range of artificial intelligence applications.

Key components of YY Neural Network include input layers that receive raw data, hidden layers consisting of interconnected neurons that process and transform the data, and output layers that generate final predictions or classifications. YYNN incorporates advanced activation functions to improve learning dynamics and prevent issues like vanishing gradients. The network also utilizes optimization algorithms such as stochastic gradient descent (SGD) and adaptive learning techniques to enhance model training. Regularization methods are integrated to reduce overfitting, ensuring robust performance across different datasets.

The benefits of YY Neural Network are significant. It provides superior accuracy in pattern recognition and data classification tasks, making it highly effective in dynamic environments. The model's ability to learn from large datasets enables it to generalize well to new, unseen data. YYNN supports parallel processing and scalability, allowing for efficient handling of big data and real-time applications. Its flexibility in architecture design makes it adaptable to a wide range of AI problems, from autonomous systems to financial forecasting.

Applications of YY Neural Network span multiple industries. In healthcare, it aids in medical diagnostics by analyzing complex imaging data for early disease detection. In finance, YYNN models are used for algorithmic trading, fraud detection, and risk assessment. The technology supports autonomous vehicles by processing sensor data for navigation and obstacle avoidance. In natural language processing, YYNN enhances machine translation, sentiment analysis, and speech recognition systems. Additionally, it is applied in cybersecurity for threat detection and anomaly identification.

In conclusion, YY Neural Network (YYNN) represents a cutting-edge approach in the field of artificial intelligence, offering powerful capabilities for data analysis, prediction, and decision-making. Its strengths in learning efficiency, accuracy, and adaptability make it a valuable tool across diverse applications. While challenges related to computational requirements, model interpretability, and data dependency exist, ongoing advancements in neural network research continue to enhance the performance and versatility of YYNN models in solving complex AI problems.

YY Object Recognition in Computer Vision

YY Object Recognition in Computer Vision refers to an advanced technology designed to identify, classify, and localize objects within digital images or video streams using artificial intelligence and machine learning algorithms. This method enables automated systems to interpret visual data by detecting patterns, features, and spatial relationships, facilitating real-time decision-making and enhancing the accuracy of object detection tasks. YY Object Recognition integrates cutting-edge techniques to improve the efficiency and reliability of visual perception in complex environments.

Key components of YY Object Recognition include feature extraction algorithms that identify distinct visual characteristics such as edges, textures, and shapes. Deep learning architectures, particularly convolutional neural networks (CNNs), play a critical role in learning hierarchical features from large datasets. Object detection frameworks like YOLO (You Only Look Once) and SSD (Single Shot MultiBox Detector) are employed to simultaneously detect and classify objects within an image. Post-processing techniques, including non-maximum suppression, help refine detection results by eliminating redundant bounding boxes and enhancing the precision of object localization.

The benefits of YY Object Recognition are significant, offering high accuracy and speed in identifying objects within diverse and dynamic environments. It enables real-time processing, making it suitable for applications that require quick and precise decision-making. The technology reduces the need for manual intervention, increasing operational efficiency and reducing human error. Additionally, YY Object Recognition supports multi-object detection capabilities, allowing systems to track and monitor multiple objects simultaneously within a single frame, thereby enhancing situational awareness and data analysis.

Applications of YY Object Recognition are widespread across various industries. In autonomous vehicles, it facilitates the real-time detection of pedestrians, vehicles, traffic signs, and obstacles, supporting safe navigation and collision avoidance. In security and surveillance, it enhances automated monitoring systems by identifying suspicious activities and unauthorized access. In healthcare, YY Object Recognition aids in medical imaging analysis, assisting in the early detection of diseases and abnormalities. The technology is also utilized in retail for inventory management, in robotics for intelligent interaction with physical environments, and in agriculture for crop monitoring and yield prediction.

In conclusion, YY Object Recognition in Computer Vision represents a transformative advancement in artificial intelligence, enabling machines to interpret and respond to visual information with high precision and efficiency. Its diverse applications across industries highlight its versatility and impact in enhancing automation and data-driven decision-making. While challenges related to data variability, computational demands, and ethical considerations exist, continuous advancements in AI and computer vision technologies are driving the evolution of YY Object Recognition systems, making them increasingly robust and adaptable to real-world scenarios.

Letter Z

Zabbix AI Monitoring

Zabbix AI Monitoring refers to the integration of artificial intelligence capabilities within the Zabbix network monitoring platform to enhance real-time data analysis, anomaly detection, and predictive maintenance. By leveraging AI, Zabbix improves its ability to monitor complex IT infrastructures, automate responses to potential issues, and provide deeper insights into system performance. This advanced approach helps organizations proactively manage network resources, detect irregularities, and optimize operational efficiency.

Key components of Zabbix AI Monitoring include machine learning algorithms that analyze historical and real-time data to identify patterns and predict future performance issues. The anomaly detection engine flags unusual activities that may indicate potential security breaches, system failures, or performance degradation. Predictive analytics tools forecast resource utilization trends, enabling proactive capacity planning. Additionally, AI-driven automation features streamline alert management and incident response processes, reducing manual intervention and improving system reliability.

The benefits of Zabbix AI Monitoring are substantial. It enhances operational efficiency by automating routine monitoring tasks and reducing the workload on IT teams. AI-driven predictive capabilities enable organizations to identify and address potential issues before they impact system performance. The platform improves incident response times through intelligent alert prioritization and automated remediation actions. Furthermore, the integration of AI provides comprehensive visibility into network health, supporting informed decision-making and strategic planning.

Applications of Zabbix AI Monitoring span various industries, including finance, healthcare, telecommunications, and manufacturing. In enterprise IT environments, it monitors servers, applications, and network devices to ensure continuous uptime and performance. In healthcare, Zabbix supports the monitoring of medical devices and critical systems to maintain patient safety. Telecommunications companies use Zabbix to manage large-scale infrastructure, ensuring network reliability and service quality. Additionally, it is applied in cloud environments for monitoring virtual resources and optimizing resource allocation.

In conclusion, Zabbix AI Monitoring represents a significant advancement in IT infrastructure management, offering enhanced capabilities for real-time monitoring, anomaly detection, and predictive analytics. Its ability to automate routine tasks, predict potential issues, and optimize resource utilization provides substantial benefits for organizations seeking to maintain high system performance and reliability. While challenges related to configuration, data management, and security exist, the continuous evolution of AI technologies ensures that Zabbix remains a powerful and adaptable solution for modern network monitoring needs.

Zamzar AI File Conversion

Zamzar AI File Conversion refers to the integration of artificial intelligence technologies within Zamzar's file conversion platform, enhancing the efficiency, accuracy, and versatility of converting files across various formats. By leveraging AI, Zamzar improves the speed of conversions, optimizes file quality, and supports a wider range of file types, including documents, images, videos, audio files, and eBooks. The AI-driven system ensures seamless format compatibility, enabling users to convert files quickly without compromising data integrity.

Key components of Zamzar AI File Conversion include advanced file recognition algorithms that automatically detect and analyze file types, intelligent format conversion engines that optimize output quality, and machine learning models that continuously improve conversion accuracy through data-driven insights. The platform also integrates cloud-based processing, enabling scalable, high-performance file conversion without the need for local software installations. Additionally, AI-driven error detection mechanisms ensure smooth conversions by identifying and resolving potential issues during the process.

The benefits of Zamzar AI File Conversion are significant, offering faster processing speeds, enhanced file quality, and broader format support. AI optimizes resource allocation, reducing conversion times even for large files. The system's ability to learn from past conversions leads to continuous performance improvements, ensuring high accuracy in complex file conversions. Additionally, the cloud-based architecture provides accessibility from any device, eliminating compatibility issues and streamlining workflows for individuals and businesses.

Applications of Zamzar AI File Conversion span multiple industries. In education, it facilitates the conversion of academic resources into accessible formats for students and educators. In business environments, Zamzar supports document management workflows by converting reports, presentations, and multimedia files for seamless sharing and collaboration. Creative professionals use the platform for media format conversions, optimizing content for different platforms. Additionally, legal and healthcare sectors benefit from secure file conversions while maintaining compliance with data privacy regulations.

In conclusion, Zamzar AI File Conversion represents a transformative advancement in file management, combining artificial intelligence with robust conversion capabilities. Its ability to deliver fast, accurate, and versatile file conversions enhances productivity for individuals and organizations alike. While challenges related to data security, format compatibility, and performance optimization exist, the continuous evolution of AI technologies ensures that Zamzar remains a reliable and innovative solution for modern file conversion needs.

Zero-Day Threat Detection in AI

Zero-Day Threat Detection in AI refers to the use of advanced artificial intelligence techniques to identify, analyze, and mitigate cyber threats that exploit previously unknown vulnerabilities. These threats, known as zero-day threats, are particularly dangerous because they target security flaws before developers or security teams are aware of them. AI enhances zero-day threat detection by leveraging machine learning algorithms, anomaly detection models, and real-time data analysis to identify suspicious patterns and behaviors indicative of novel cyberattacks.

Key components of Zero-Day Threat Detection in AI include machine learning models trained on vast datasets of known threats and normal behavior to identify deviations that may signify zero-day attacks. Behavioral analysis tools monitor network traffic, user activities, and system processes to detect anomalies. Threat intelligence integration allows AI systems to continuously update their knowledge base with emerging attack vectors. Additionally, predictive analytics and automated response mechanisms enable proactive defense by anticipating potential threats and initiating countermeasures without human intervention.

The benefits of Zero-Day Threat Detection in AI are significant. AI-driven systems can detect and respond to threats in real-time, reducing the window of vulnerability and minimizing potential damage. They improve accuracy by identifying subtle indicators of compromise that traditional security tools might miss. The scalability of AI allows for continuous monitoring of large and complex IT environments, ensuring comprehensive protection. Furthermore, AI's ability to learn and adapt over time enhances its effectiveness against evolving cyber threats.

Applications of Zero-Day Threat Detection in AI are found across various sectors, including finance, healthcare, government, and critical infrastructure, where data security is paramount. In enterprise environments, AI protects against sophisticated cyberattacks targeting sensitive information and intellectual property. In the defense sector, it safeguards national security systems from advanced persistent threats. AI is also used in cloud security to monitor virtual environments and detect breaches that traditional security measures might overlook.

In conclusion, Zero-Day Threat Detection in AI represents a critical advancement in cybersecurity, offering proactive defense capabilities against previously unknown threats. Its ability to analyze vast amounts of data, identify anomalies, and respond in real-time makes it an essential tool for modern security strategies. While challenges related to accuracy, resource demands, and adversarial tactics exist, the continuous evolution of AI technologies enhances their potential to protect against emerging cyber threats effectively.

Zero-Latency AI

Zero-Latency AI refers to artificial intelligence systems designed to process and respond to data inputs in real-time with virtually no perceptible delay. This capability is critical for applications where immediate decision-making is required, such as autonomous vehicles, real-time financial trading, and high-frequency industrial automation. Zero-Latency AI optimizes data flow, computational efficiency, and network communication to achieve instantaneous performance, enabling seamless interactions and immediate feedback in dynamic environments.

Key components of Zero-Latency AI include advanced data processing architectures that minimize computational delays, edge computing technologies that process data closer to the source to reduce transmission time, and optimized algorithms designed for rapid decision-making. High-speed communication protocols and real-time data analytics frameworks also play essential roles in supporting low-latency performance. Additionally, hardware accelerators such as GPUs and TPUs are integrated to enhance processing speed and efficiency.

The benefits of Zero-Latency AI are substantial, offering immediate responsiveness that improves the safety, reliability, and user experience of critical systems. In autonomous vehicles, zero-latency processing enables real-time obstacle detection and navigation decisions, enhancing passenger safety. In financial services, it supports high-frequency trading algorithms that capitalize on market fluctuations within microseconds. The technology also improves interactive experiences in virtual reality, gaming, and real-time communication platforms by eliminating lag and ensuring smooth operation.

Applications of Zero-Latency AI span diverse industries. In healthcare, it supports real-time patient monitoring and rapid diagnostic analysis, enabling timely medical interventions. In manufacturing, zero-latency AI enhances process automation and quality control through instant feedback loops. The technology is also integral to smart city infrastructure, where it manages traffic systems, surveillance networks, and emergency response coordination with immediate data-driven actions. Additionally, it plays a pivotal role in defense and aerospace for real-time threat detection and autonomous system control.

In conclusion, Zero-Latency AI represents a transformative advancement in artificial intelligence, enabling real-time data processing and decision-making across critical applications. Its ability to deliver immediate responses enhances operational efficiency, safety, and user experiences in various industries. While challenges related to computational resources, security, and network infrastructure exist, the continued evolution of Zero-Latency AI technologies will drive innovation and expand its impact in the future of intelligent systems.

Zero-Knowledge Proofs (AI and Cryptography)

Zero-Knowledge Proofs (ZKPs) in AI and Cryptography refer to cryptographic protocols that allow one party, known as the prover, to demonstrate to another party, the verifier, that a specific statement is true without revealing any additional information beyond the validity of the statement itself. This method ensures data privacy and security, as the verifier gains confidence in the correctness of the proof without accessing the underlying sensitive data. In the context of AI, ZKPs enhance the security of data exchanges, model verifications, and confidential computations.

Key components of Zero-Knowledge Proofs include the prover, who possesses the knowledge to be verified, the verifier, who assesses the validity of the claim, and the cryptographic protocol that facilitates the interaction between them. There are interactive and non-interactive ZKPs, with interactive requiring multiple rounds of communication and non-interactive relying on a single exchange. Essential properties of ZKPs are completeness, ensuring the prover can convince the verifier if the statement is true; soundness, preventing dishonest provers from deceiving the verifier; and zero-knowledge, ensuring no additional information is disclosed.

The benefits of Zero-Knowledge Proofs are significant in enhancing data privacy, security, and trust in digital transactions. ZKPs enable secure authentication without exposing passwords or personal data, protect confidential information during AI model verification, and ensure data integrity in decentralized systems. They also support compliance with data protection regulations by minimizing data exposure, making them valuable in privacy-sensitive applications.

Applications of Zero-Knowledge Proofs span various domains, including blockchain technology, where ZKPs are used to verify transactions without revealing transaction details, enhancing both security and privacy. In AI, ZKPs facilitate secure model sharing and validation, allowing organizations to collaborate on AI projects without exposing proprietary algorithms. They are also applied in secure voting systems, identity verification, and confidential data analysis, where privacy and integrity are paramount.

In conclusion, Zero-Knowledge Proofs (ZKPs) in AI and Cryptography represent a powerful tool for achieving secure, private, and trustworthy data verification processes. Their ability to confirm the validity of information without revealing the information itself offers significant advantages in privacy protection, data security, and regulatory compliance. While challenges related to computational efficiency and implementation complexity persist, the growing adoption of ZKPs highlights their critical role in advancing secure digital technologies and AI applications.

Zero-Shot Learning (ZSL)

Zero-Shot Learning (ZSL) refers to an advanced machine learning technique that enables models to recognize and classify data from categories they have never encountered during training. Unlike traditional supervised learning methods that rely on extensive labeled datasets, ZSL leverages auxiliary information such as semantic attributes, textual descriptions, or relational data to make predictions about unseen classes. This capability is achieved by learning a mapping between visual or input features and semantic space, allowing the model to generalize knowledge beyond its original training data.

Key components of Zero-Shot Learning include the feature extraction process, which transforms raw data into meaningful representations, the semantic space where both seen and unseen classes are embedded using auxiliary information, and the mapping function that connects the feature space to the semantic space. Additionally, knowledge transfer mechanisms play a crucial role in enabling the model to apply learned information from known categories to new, unseen ones effectively.

The benefits of Zero-Shot Learning are significant. It reduces the dependency on large labeled datasets, making it highly efficient in scenarios where data labeling is costly or impractical. ZSL enhances model adaptability and generalization, enabling AI systems to handle novel situations without retraining. This approach also accelerates the development of models in dynamic environments where new classes emerge frequently, providing a scalable solution for real-world applications.

Applications of Zero-Shot Learning are widespread across various industries. In computer vision, ZSL is used for image classification, object detection, and facial recognition, where models can identify new objects without additional training. In natural language processing, it supports tasks such as text classification, sentiment analysis, and machine translation. ZSL is also applied in recommendation systems, medical diagnostics, and robotics, where quick adaptation to new data is essential.

In conclusion, Zero-Shot Learning (ZSL) represents a transformative approach in machine learning, enabling models to recognize and classify data without direct prior exposure. Its ability to generalize knowledge to unseen classes offers significant advantages in terms of efficiency, adaptability, and scalability. While challenges related to semantic alignment and model bias exist, the ongoing advancements in ZSL techniques continue to expand its applications and impact across various AI domains.

Zhang's Algorithm (in AI Optimization)

Zhang's Algorithm in AI Optimization refers to a specialized computational method designed to improve the efficiency and accuracy of optimization processes within artificial intelligence systems. This algorithm focuses on enhancing convergence speed, reducing computational complexity, and optimizing objective functions across various AI models. Zhang's Algorithm is particularly effective in solving complex, high-dimensional optimization problems commonly encountered in machine learning, data science, and automated decision-making systems.

Key components of Zhang's Algorithm include the objective function, which defines the goal of the optimization process, and the search strategy, which guides the algorithm through potential solutions to find the optimal outcome. The algorithm also incorporates adaptive learning rates that adjust based on the optimization landscape, gradient-based methods for efficient navigation through large datasets, and regularization techniques to prevent overfitting and improve generalization.

The benefits of Zhang's Algorithm are substantial, offering improved optimization performance through faster convergence to optimal solutions and greater computational efficiency. It reduces the time and resources required for training AI models while maintaining high accuracy. The algorithm's adaptability allows it to perform well across different types of optimization problems, making it versatile for various AI applications. Additionally, its robust design minimizes the risk of getting stuck in local optima, ensuring more reliable outcomes.

Applications of Zhang's Algorithm span multiple AI domains. In machine learning, it is used for training deep neural networks, optimizing hyperparameters, and improving model performance. In natural language processing, it enhances algorithms for language modeling, text classification, and sentiment analysis. The algorithm is also applied in computer vision for image recognition, object detection, and feature extraction. Additionally, Zhang's Algorithm supports optimization tasks in robotics, autonomous systems, and financial modeling.

In conclusion, Zhang's Algorithm in AI Optimization represents a powerful tool for enhancing the efficiency and accuracy of optimization processes in artificial intelligence. Its ability to handle complex, high-dimensional data and adapt to various problem domains makes it a valuable asset in modern AI development. Despite challenges related to parameter tuning and computational demands, the algorithm's benefits in speed, accuracy, and versatility highlight its significance in advancing AI optimization techniques.

Zhi-Hua Zhou's Ensemble Learning Methods

Zhi-Hua Zhou's Ensemble Learning Methods refer to a set of advanced machine learning techniques that combine multiple models to improve predictive performance, robustness, and generalization capabilities. Zhou's contributions to ensemble learning emphasize the integration of diverse algorithms to create stronger predictive models than those generated by any single model. The core idea is that combining the strengths of multiple models reduces errors, mitigates biases, and enhances overall decision-making accuracy.

Key components of Zhi-Hua Zhou's Ensemble Learning Methods include base learners, which are individual models that contribute to the ensemble, and ensemble strategies that determine how these models are combined. Common approaches include bagging, where models are trained on different subsets of data to reduce variance, boosting, which sequentially trains models to correct the errors of previous ones, and stacking, where a meta-model is used to combine predictions from multiple base learners for improved performance.

The benefits of Zhi-Hua Zhou's Ensemble Learning Methods are significant. They enhance predictive accuracy by leveraging the complementary strengths of different models. Ensemble methods are more robust to overfitting, particularly in complex datasets, and they improve generalization by reducing the likelihood of model-specific errors. Additionally, these methods are flexible and can be applied to a wide range of machine learning tasks, from classification to regression and beyond.

Applications of Zhi-Hua Zhou's Ensemble Learning Methods are widespread across various domains. In finance, they are used for credit scoring, risk assessment, and algorithmic trading. In healthcare, ensemble methods improve diagnostic accuracy by combining outputs from different predictive models. They are also used in natural language processing for sentiment analysis, in image recognition for object detection, and in cybersecurity for anomaly detection and threat prediction.

In conclusion, Zhi-Hua Zhou's Ensemble Learning Methods represent a powerful approach in machine learning, offering improved accuracy, robustness, and adaptability across diverse applications. By intelligently combining multiple models, these methods address the limitations of individual learners and enhance overall performance. Despite challenges related to computational demands and interpretability, the benefits of ensemble learning make it an essential tool in the development of advanced AI systems.

Zhi-Hua Zhou's Semi-Supervised Learning

Zhi-Hua Zhou's Semi-Supervised Learning refers to an advanced machine learning paradigm that leverages both labeled and unlabeled data to improve learning efficiency and model performance. This approach, developed and popularized through Zhou's influential work, addresses the challenge of limited labeled data by utilizing the abundant unlabeled data often available in real-world scenarios. The core idea is to enhance learning models by extracting valuable information from unlabeled data, reducing the dependency on costly and time-consuming manual labeling.

Key components of Zhi-Hua Zhou's Semi-Supervised Learning include the labeled dataset, which provides the ground truth for initial model training, the unlabeled dataset, which contributes additional information to refine the model, and learning algorithms designed to integrate both data types effectively. Common techniques include self-training, where the model iteratively labels unlabeled data, co-training, which involves multiple classifiers teaching each other, and graph-based methods that exploit data structure relationships to propagate labels.

The benefits of Zhi-Hua Zhou's Semi-Supervised Learning are substantial. It significantly reduces the need for large amounts of labeled data, lowering the cost and effort associated with data annotation. The approach improves model generalization by incorporating diverse data points, leading to better performance on unseen data. Additionally, it enhances learning efficiency, enabling models to achieve high accuracy with limited supervision.

Applications of Zhi-Hua Zhou's Semi-Supervised Learning are widespread across various domains. In natural language processing, it aids in tasks like text classification and sentiment analysis with minimal labeled data. In computer vision, it supports image recognition and object detection where labeling large datasets is impractical. The approach is also valuable in healthcare for medical image analysis and in cybersecurity for anomaly detection, where labeled instances are rare but critical.

In conclusion, Zhi-Hua Zhou's Semi-Supervised Learning represents a transformative advancement in machine learning, offering a practical solution for leveraging unlabeled data to enhance model performance. Its ability to reduce reliance on extensive labeled datasets while maintaining high accuracy makes it a powerful tool in various AI applications. Despite challenges related to data quality and algorithm design, the benefits of improved efficiency, cost-effectiveness, and scalability highlight its significance in modern machine learning practices.

Zhou's Dynamic Ensemble Selection (DES)

Zhou's Dynamic Ensemble Selection (DES) refers to an advanced machine learning technique designed to improve the performance of ensemble models by dynamically selecting the most competent classifiers from a pool based on the characteristics of each new data instance. Unlike static ensemble methods where the same set of classifiers is used for all predictions, DES adapts to the data distribution and complexity in real time, enhancing decision-making accuracy and robustness.

Key components of Zhou's Dynamic Ensemble Selection include the classifier pool, which consists of diverse models trained on the same dataset, a competence estimation mechanism that evaluates the performance of each classifier on specific data instances, and a selection strategy that dynamically chooses the most suitable classifiers for making predictions. Additionally, meta-learning approaches are often integrated to enhance the selection process by learning patterns from the data to predict classifier performance effectively.

The benefits of Zhou's Dynamic Ensemble Selection are significant, offering improved prediction accuracy by leveraging the strengths of different classifiers tailored to specific data instances. It enhances model robustness against noisy or imbalanced data and reduces the risk of overfitting compared to static ensembles. DES also promotes computational efficiency by focusing on a subset of classifiers rather than using the entire ensemble for every prediction.

Applications of Zhou's Dynamic Ensemble Selection span various domains, including healthcare for personalized diagnostics, finance for adaptive risk assessment models, and cybersecurity for real-time threat detection. In image recognition and natural language processing, DES contributes to more accurate and context-aware predictions by selecting classifiers best suited for the specific task at hand.

In conclusion, Zhou's Dynamic Ensemble Selection represents a powerful approach to enhancing ensemble learning models by adapting classifier selection to the unique characteristics of each data instance. Its ability to improve accuracy, robustness, and efficiency makes it a valuable tool in various machine learning applications. While challenges in computational demands and model selection strategies exist, the dynamic adaptability of DES offers significant advantages in developing intelligent and responsive AI systems.

Zigzag Encoding in AI

Zigzag Encoding in AI refers to a data transformation technique used to efficiently encode signed integers into a format that optimizes data compression algorithms. This method maps signed integers to unsigned integers in such a way that small absolute values are represented by smaller encoded numbers, enhancing compression performance. Zigzag Encoding is commonly utilized in machine learning data preprocessing, neural network optimization, and AI-driven data compression systems.

Key components of Zigzag Encoding include the encoding algorithm that converts signed integers into a non-negative sequence by alternating the sign of the values in a specific pattern. The decoding algorithm reverses this process to retrieve the original signed values. Additionally, integration with data serialization formats such as Protocol Buffers and efficient binary encoding schemes supports seamless data handling in AI applications.

The benefits of Zigzag Encoding in AI are significant, including improved data compression efficiency, reduced storage requirements, and faster data transmission. By minimizing the size of encoded data, it enhances the performance of AI models that rely on large datasets, particularly in resource-constrained environments. The method also simplifies the handling of variable-length integer representations, contributing to streamlined data processing workflows.

Applications of Zigzag Encoding span various AI-related domains. In machine learning, it aids in compressing model parameters and feature data for efficient storage and faster model loading. In natural language processing, it supports efficient encoding of linguistic features for compact data representation. Zigzag Encoding is also used in image and video compression algorithms to optimize the storage and transmission of multimedia content.

In conclusion, Zigzag Encoding in AI is a valuable technique for optimizing data compression and efficient data handling in various AI applications. Its ability to minimize storage requirements and enhance data processing speeds makes it an essential tool in the development of high-performance AI systems. While challenges exist in computational efficiency and data compatibility, the benefits of improved compression and streamlined data workflows underscore its significance in AI data management.

Zigbee AI for IoT Networks

Zigbee AI for IoT Networks refers to the integration of artificial intelligence technologies with Zigbee, a low-power, wireless communication protocol designed for Internet of Things (IoT) devices. This combination enhances the efficiency, reliability, and intelligence of IoT networks by enabling smart devices to analyze data, make decisions, and optimize network performance autonomously. Zigbee AI supports seamless device-to-device communication, energy efficiency, and scalability in diverse IoT environments.

Key components of Zigbee AI include AI-driven data analytics algorithms that process and interpret data from connected devices, machine learning models that optimize network routing and resource allocation, and edge computing capabilities that allow real-time decision-making at the device level. Additionally, Zigbee's mesh networking architecture ensures robust connectivity and resilience by allowing devices to relay data through multiple pathways.

The benefits of Zigbee AI are significant, offering improved network efficiency through intelligent traffic management and reduced latency. It enhances energy conservation by optimizing device operations and extending battery life. The integration of AI enables predictive maintenance, fault detection, and adaptive responses to changing network conditions, leading to more reliable and secure IoT systems.

Applications of Zigbee AI span various sectors, including smart homes, where it manages lighting, security, and climate control systems; industrial automation, where it monitors and optimizes manufacturing processes; and healthcare, where it supports remote patient monitoring and medical device management. In agriculture, Zigbee AI facilitates precision farming through intelligent monitoring of environmental conditions and resource usage.

In conclusion, Zigbee AI for IoT Networks represents a transformative approach to enhancing the capabilities of IoT ecosystems. By combining the low-power, reliable connectivity of Zigbee with the advanced analytical and decision-making power of AI, this technology enables smarter, more efficient, and resilient IoT applications. While challenges in security, integration, and resource management persist, the potential benefits make Zigbee AI a critical component in the evolution of intelligent IoT networks.

Zinc AI (Drug Discovery Platform)

Zinc AI (Drug Discovery Platform) refers to an advanced artificial intelligence framework designed to accelerate the process of drug discovery and development. This platform leverages machine learning algorithms, data analytics, and computational modeling to identify potential drug candidates, predict molecular interactions, and optimize the efficacy and safety profiles of pharmaceutical compounds. Zinc AI aims to streamline the traditionally time-consuming and costly process of bringing new drugs to market.

Key components of Zinc AI include predictive modeling algorithms that analyze large datasets to identify promising drug candidates, molecular docking simulations that predict how drugs will interact with biological targets, and machine learning techniques that refine drug properties for enhanced performance. Additionally, the platform integrates data from clinical trials, chemical libraries, and biomedical research to support evidence-based decision-making in drug development.

The benefits of Zinc AI are substantial, offering increased efficiency in drug discovery by reducing the time and cost associated with traditional methods. It enhances the accuracy of predicting drug-target interactions, leading to higher success rates in clinical trials. The platform also supports personalized medicine approaches by identifying compounds tailored to specific genetic or biological profiles, improving patient outcomes.

Applications of Zinc AI are found across the pharmaceutical and biotechnology industries. It is used in early-stage drug discovery to screen large chemical libraries for potential leads, in preclinical development to optimize drug formulations, and in clinical research to identify biomarkers and predict patient responses. The platform also supports drug repurposing efforts by uncovering new therapeutic uses for existing compounds.

In conclusion, Zinc AI (Drug Discovery Platform) represents a transformative tool in the pharmaceutical industry, enhancing the speed, efficiency, and precision of drug development. Its capabilities in predictive modeling, molecular analysis, and personalized medicine offer significant advantages in addressing global health challenges. While challenges in data quality, integration, and security persist, the potential of Zinc AI to revolutionize drug discovery makes it a pivotal technology in modern biomedical research.

Zipf's Law in AI and NLP

Zipf's Law in AI and Natural Language Processing (NLP) refers to the statistical principle that in a large corpus of natural language, the frequency of any word is inversely proportional to its rank in the frequency table. This means the most common word appears approximately twice as often as the second most common word, three times as often as the third, and so on. This phenomenon is observed across different languages and datasets, making it a fundamental concept in linguistic data analysis and AI-driven language models.

Key components of Zipf's Law in AI and NLP include word frequency distribution, which helps in understanding how often words appear in text data, rank-frequency correlation that illustrates the inverse relationship between word rank and occurrence, and statistical models that incorporate this principle to improve language processing tasks. Additionally, it plays a role in the development of algorithms for text compression, search engines, and predictive text systems.

The benefits of applying Zipf's Law in AI and NLP are significant. It aids in optimizing data storage and retrieval by focusing on the most frequently used words. It enhances the efficiency of language models by reducing computational resources needed to process rare words. This principle also helps improve the performance of machine learning algorithms in tasks like text classification, topic modeling, and information retrieval.

Applications of Zipf's Law are widespread in AI and NLP. It is used in search engine algorithms to prioritize common query terms, in text summarization tools to identify key concepts, and in speech recognition systems to predict likely word sequences. Additionally, it supports natural language generation models by guiding the selection of words that reflect realistic usage patterns.

In conclusion, Zipf's Law is a foundational concept in AI and NLP, providing valuable insights into word frequency distribution and language patterns. Its applications enhance the efficiency and performance of various AI-driven language technologies. While there are challenges in addressing exceptions and biases, understanding and leveraging Zipf's Law remains essential for effective natural language processing and analysis.

Zugzwang in AI Game Theory

Zugzwang in AI Game Theory refers to a strategic situation where any move made by a player will result in a disadvantage, often forcing them into a losing position. Derived from chess terminology, zugzwang highlights scenarios where a player would prefer to pass their turn, but the rules require them to move, leading to a less favorable outcome. In AI and game theory, this concept is critical for developing algorithms that can identify and exploit such situations to optimize decision-making in competitive environments.

Key components of zugzwang in AI game theory include state evaluation functions that assess the strength of various positions, move prediction algorithms that forecast potential outcomes of different moves, and strategic planning models that recognize and create zugzwang situations. These components work together to enhance the AI's ability to anticipate opponent weaknesses and adapt strategies accordingly.

The benefits of incorporating zugzwang into AI game theory are significant. It enables AI systems to improve their strategic depth, allowing for more sophisticated gameplay and decision-making. By identifying positions of zugzwang, AI can exploit opponent vulnerabilities, increasing the likelihood of success in competitive scenarios. Additionally, this understanding fosters the development of AI that can perform better in adversarial conditions, making it valuable for applications beyond traditional games.

Applications of zugzwang in AI game theory extend to various domains. In board games like chess and Go, AI utilizes this concept to force opponents into unfavorable moves. In economics, zugzwang principles help model competitive business strategies where companies face tough choices with no clear advantage. Military simulations and cybersecurity also benefit from zugzwang-based AI models to predict and counteract adversary moves under constrained conditions.

In conclusion, zugzwang in AI game theory represents a critical strategic concept that enhances AI's ability to manage competitive situations effectively. Its integration into AI algorithms improves decision-making, strategic planning, and adversarial performance across various applications. While challenges exist in prediction accuracy and computational demands, the benefits of deeper strategic insight and competitive advantage make zugzwang an essential element in the development of advanced AI systems.

Zure AI (Autonomous Decision-Making Systems)

Zure AI (Autonomous Decision-Making Systems) refers to advanced artificial intelligence frameworks designed to make independent decisions without human intervention. These systems are capable of analyzing vast amounts of data, identifying patterns, and making informed decisions based on predefined objectives and real-time information. Zure AI systems are built to operate in dynamic environments, adapting their decision-making processes as new data becomes available.

Key components of Zure AI include data processing units that aggregate and analyze information from multiple sources, machine learning algorithms that enable the system to learn from past experiences, decision-making engines that evaluate options and select optimal actions, and feedback mechanisms that allow continuous improvement and adaptation. These components work in harmony to create a system capable of autonomous operation in complex scenarios.

The benefits of Zure AI are significant, offering enhanced efficiency through automated processes, reduced human error, and the ability to make rapid decisions in real-time. These systems can operate continuously without fatigue, ensuring consistent performance. Additionally, Zure AI improves scalability, allowing organizations to manage larger datasets and more complex decision-making tasks with minimal resource expansion.

Applications of Zure AI span various industries, including autonomous vehicles where it helps in navigation and obstacle avoidance, financial services for real-time trading and risk assessment, healthcare for diagnostic support and personalized treatment plans, and manufacturing for optimizing production processes and supply chain management. Zure AI's adaptability makes it valuable in any field requiring rapid, data-driven decision-making.

Challenges in implementing Zure AI include the complexity of designing algorithms that can handle diverse and unpredictable scenarios. There are concerns about the ethical implications of autonomous decision-making, particularly in critical applications such as healthcare and security. Additionally, ensuring data privacy and security within these systems is a significant challenge, as they often require access to sensitive information.

In conclusion, Zure AI (Autonomous Decision-Making Systems) represents a transformative approach to artificial intelligence, offering the potential to revolutionize how decisions are made across various sectors. While challenges exist in terms of complexity, ethics, and security, the benefits of efficiency, scalability, and adaptability make Zure AI a pivotal technology for the future of automated decision-making.

Zustand-Based AI Models

Zustand-Based AI Models refer to artificial intelligence systems that utilize efficient state management techniques inspired by principles similar to those found in lightweight state management libraries. These models are designed to handle dynamic data changes effectively, allowing AI applications to maintain consistency, update information in real time, and operate with minimal computational load. This approach enhances the performance of AI systems by managing states efficiently without unnecessary processing.

Key components of Zustand-Based AI Models include state containers that store and manage dynamic data, mechanisms to trigger updates when changes occur, optimized data structures for efficient resource use, and integration layers for compatibility with other systems. These elements work together to ensure that AI applications remain responsive, adaptable, and efficient even as data environments become more complex.

The benefits of Zustand-Based AI Models include improved scalability, as they allow AI systems to handle increasing volumes of data without performance loss. They enhance efficiency by minimizing redundant computations and ensuring that only relevant updates are processed. The simplicity of their design makes them accessible for developers, while their flexibility supports a wide range of applications, from real-time analytics to adaptive decision-making systems.

Applications of Zustand-Based AI Models can be found in various sectors. In finance, they support trading platforms that rely on real-time data updates. In healthcare, they help manage patient monitoring systems that adjust recommendations based on live data. Autonomous technologies, such as robotics and self-driving vehicles, use these models to process environmental data dynamically, ensuring accurate and timely responses.

Challenges in implementing Zustand-Based AI Models include the learning curve associated with understanding efficient state management principles, especially for large-scale systems. Debugging and optimizing state transitions can become complex as the system grows. While designed to reduce computational load, certain scenarios with high-frequency data updates may still pose performance challenges.

In conclusion, Zustand-Based AI Models offer a robust framework for managing dynamic states within AI applications. Their efficiency, scalability, and adaptability make them suitable for diverse industries that require real-time data processing and decision-making. Despite some implementation challenges, their ability to enhance AI system performance and responsiveness makes them a valuable tool in modern AI development.

❖ Final Message from the Author

The name **"IntelliGloss: The Definitive AI Dictionary"** was thoughtfully crafted to reflect the heart of this project. *"Intelli"* comes from *"intelligence,"* emphasizing the dictionary's focus on smart, cutting-edge AI concepts. *"Gloss"* hints at a curated collection of clear, concise explanations—like a glossary, but with a modern, polished tone. Together, *IntelliGloss* communicates a resource that's insightful, accessible, and deeply informative. The subtitle, *"The Definitive AI Dictionary,"* highlights its authority and depth, positioning it as a go-to reference for anyone learning or working with artificial intelligence. This book was created to stand out as a trusted, educational guide.

With over **2,000 original and structured AI terms**, *IntelliGloss: The Definitive AI Dictionary* makes artificial intelligence approachable and easy to understand for learners at all levels. Special sections—like *The History of AI*, *The Ingredients of AI*, and the *Bit, Qubit, Chip, Watts,* and *LLM Families*—add depth and clarity to the field. Whether you're a student, educator, professional, or simply an AI enthusiast, this dictionary is designed to be your essential reference.

Also available: the AI Dictionary Channel by Susie Hala on YouTube — your companion video resource for learning artificial intelligence.

❖ About the Author

Susie Hala is a lifelong learner, entrepreneur, and passionate educator dedicated to making artificial intelligence clear and accessible to everyone. As the creator of *IntelliGloss: The Definitive AI Dictionary*, she has spent years researching and rewriting over 2,000 AI terms into structured, easy-to-understand entries.

Susie also shares her work through the **AI Dictionary Channel by Susie Hala** on YouTube, where she explains key AI concepts through engaging, beginner-friendly videos—designed for students, teachers, professionals, and curious minds worldwide.

Also available: the AI Dictionary Channel by Susie Hala on YouTube — your companion video resource for learning artificial intelligence.

Index

'OTUA MO TONGA KO HOTA TOFI'A

(God and Tonga are my inheritance)

www.ingramcontent.com/pod-product-compliance
Lightning Source LLC
LaVergne TN
LVHW060006210926
848481LV00013B/3658